What Makes This Boo

No other Word for Windows book gives you a complete tutorial, valuable hands-on projects, a detailed macros workshop, a handy reference, and a free disk full of useful programs, macros and templates. Whether you're a beginner or an experienced Word user, you'll find what you need in this Super Book. Use this book to learn all about a feature, create special documents, brush up on a procedure, and much more.

Word Features Workshops

Here's where you'll learn to get the most out of Word for Windows. Arranged logically into task-oriented Workshops, these 49 bite-sized chapters teach you the skills you need to maximize Word's powerful features.

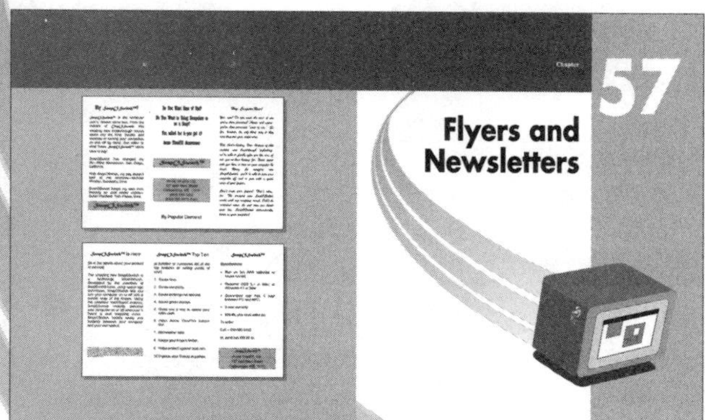

Projects Workshop

Workshop 13 contains eight hands-on projects that walk you through one of the easy-to-use document templates included on the Super Disk. Now you can quickly and easily create papers, business letters, resumes, invoices, proposals, research reports, newsletters, flyers, and even books.

Macros Workshop

Workshop 14 gives you detailed instructions for using the author's included macros, and then tells you how to customize them and write your own new macros from scratch.

Super Disk

The included disk gives you

- Six original document templates—complete with their own customized toolbars
- 40 exclusive macros written by the author expressly for the *Word 6 for Windows Super Book*
- Five decorative **True Type** fonts
- More than 40 pieces of color clip art from the **Masterclips the Art of Business** collection
- And more!

WORD for Windows 6 SUPER BOOK

WORD for Windows 6 SUPER BOOK

Herb Tyson

SAMS PUBLISHING
A Division of Prentice Hall Computer Publishing
201 West 103rd Street, Indianapolis, Indiana 46290

Dedicated…

with unending love to Karen and Katie,
whose love makes everything perfect.

FIRST EDITION
FIRST PRINTING—1994

International Standard Book Number: 0-672-30384-1

Library of Congress Catalog Card Number: 93-86949

97 96 95 94 4 3 2 1

Interpretation of the printing code: the rightmost double-digit number is the year of the book's printing; the rightmost single-digit, the number of the book's printing. For example, a printing code of 94-1 shows that the first printing of the book occurred in 1994.

Trademarks

Composed in Cheltenham and MCPdigital
by Prentice Hall Computer Publishing

Printed in the United States of America

Credits

PUBLISHER
Richard K. Swadley

ASSOCIATE PUBLISHER
Jordan Gold

ACQUISITIONS MANAGER
Stacy Hiquet

ACQUISITIONS EDITOR
Gregg Bushyeager

DEVELOPMENT EDITOR
Mark Taber

PRODUCTION EDITORS
Fran Hatton
David Bradford

COPY EDITOR
Linda Van Hook

EDITORIAL COORDINATOR
Bill Whitmer

EDITORIAL ASSISTANTS
Sharon Cox
Lynette Quinn

TECHNICAL EDITOR
Ned Snell

BOOK AND COVER DESIGNER
Michele Laseau

COVER ILLUSTRATION
Kathy Hanley

DIRECTOR OF PRODUCTION AND MANUFACTURING
Jeff Valler

IMPRINT MANAGER
Kelli Widdifield

PRODUCTION ANALYST
Mary Beth Wakefield

PROOFREADING/INDEXING COORDINATOR
Joelynn Gifford

GRAPHICS IMAGE SPECIALISTS
Dennis Sheehan
Sue VandeWalle

PRODUCTION
Nick Anderson
Angela Bannan
Diana Bigham
Ayrika Bryant
Danielle Byrd
Charlotte Clapp
Lisa Daugherty
Karen Dodson
Rich Evers
Mitzi Foster Gianakos
Dennis Clay Hager
Stephanie McComb
Sean Medlock
Linda Quigley
Ryan Rader
Shelly Palma
Juli Pavey
Angela Pozdol
Michelle Self
Tonya R. Simpson
Suzanne Tully
Dennis Wesner
Alyssa Yesh

INDEXERS
John Sleeva
Suzanne Snyder
Jennifer Eberhardt

Overview

Overview

Workshop XIII Projects

Workshop XIV Macros

Appendices

Contents

Workshop III Files 105

APPENDICES

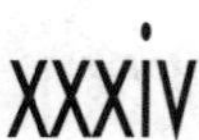

About the Author

Herb Tyson, owner of MVE Consulting, is an internationally respected consultant, developer, and writer. He is the author of the highly acclaimed *Word for Windows Revealed* and *XyWrite Revealed*, as well as *101 Essential Word for Windows Tips*. He also has written the *10 Minute Guide to OS/2* from Alpha Books and *Your OS/2 2.1 Consultant* from Sams Publishing, as well as a number of computer manuals. He is a contributor to *Compute*, *OS/2 Professional*, and a number of other magazines. Tyson frequents a number of electronic bulletin boards and networks, including CompuServe, FidoNet, RIME, RelayNet, and others, where his word processing expertise is widely acknowledged. An econometrician by training, Tyson received his undergraduate degree from Georgetown University in Washington, D.C., and an interdisciplinary doctorate from Michigan State University.

Acknowledgments

Thanks to the folks at Sams for not being too stunned when I presented them with two additional chapters—just when they thought they had it all. Thanks to the understanding editors at Sams who, I hope, recognize the difference between fatigue and grammatical ignorance. Thanks to Mark Taber and Gregg Bushyeager, both of whom knew that I could do it, even though I knew I couldn't. I guess I was wrong. I would also like to thank the members of the Academy... wait a minute... that's the wrong speech! Thanks also to OS/2, without which this book would have taken twice as long to write. Thanks to the folks in Colombia and their magic brown beans, which make lousy chili but which, when roasted and ground into a coarse powder, enable me to remain conscious. Thanks most of all to Karen and Katie who endured my ranting at each GPF, and who, despite many weeks of sacrifice and ill humor, never once threatened me with bodily harm.

Introduction

The *Word for Windows 6 Super Book* is a lofty title, but it's appropriate for this book for several reasons. First, Word for Windows Version 6 is a superb advance in word processing. With a dazzling battery of new features to make using word easier and more productive than ever, it takes a super book to do it justice.

Second, to get to version 6, Word for Windows had to leapfrog versions 3 through 5. Just in case you thought you missed them—you didn't. While the renumbering actually was just to synchronize the numbering of the various versions of Word for different platforms, it's really more than that. Word for Windows 6 represents a kind of super leap in its own right, into the mainstream of object-oriented word processing. To quickly comprehend and expound on a leap this major took nearly superhuman effort. In fact, I wrote this book twice. First, I wrote a book about the old Word for Windows, mistakenly thinking it'd be a quick job to touch it up for Word for Windows version 6. Man, was I ever wrong. When the new version of Word arrived, the number of substantive changes was overwhelming. Moral: Never underestimate the ability of Microsoft to change a product.

Finally, what this book tries to do is to be everyone's book. That's a fairly super goal. The aim is to provide a complete reference that takes on all comers, from near-beginners to experts. That's a pretty super ambition. To do it, we had to find a good starting point, as well as a good ending point. As I'm writing this introduction, I'm inclined to believe we've done a pretty good job. However, you'll have to be the judge. With your comments and encouragement, we hope this book will grow with Word well into the future, providing just the kind of assistance you need to get the most out of Word.

Who Should Buy This Book?

Everyone should buy this book, including people who don't even have computers, or Word for Windows, and even people who can't read. Because of its weight and size, this book makes an excellent doorstop, paperweight, as well as a handy weapon when and if you need to *throw the book at someone*. When David slung the stone at Goliath, it's my understanding that, before resorting to the stone, he was heard to say "Where's Herb's book? Not there... I guess I'll have to use one of these stones, instead."

Who Should Read This Book?

Well, now, that's the right question, isn't it? This book is designed to be a complete companion guide for using and learning Word and its advanced features. If you need to use Word to create documents or to solve word-processing problems, this book is for you. It takes you through every procedure, step by step, pointing out the benefits of one method versus another, the pitfalls, as well as tips learned though years of experience in uncovering the inner workings of Word.

This book is a book you can grow with. If you're a beginner, a seasoned expert and Word connoisseur, this book cuts through the blinding array of features to show you which menus to order from, which buttons to push, and which keys to use to unlock the secrets of Word. As your confidence and abilities with Word grow, so will your awareness of the depth of the book you are now reading. It shows you everything, from the simplest formatting, to the Word philosophy of working with *style*, to customizing the keys, menus, and toolbars, as well as how to customize Word's extensive set of commands, and how to write your own macros.

If you're an expert, well... The average expert uses only 25 percent of Word's capabilities—at most. What happens when you have to delve into one of those areas you've been saving for a rainy day? So, you never had to prepare a Table of Authorities, and now one of your clients wants you to show them how? What about all of Word's brand-spanking-new features? You're not an expert in all of those yet, I'll bet. This book will help you keep your expert image, by quickly bringing you up to speed on the latest and greatest version of Word. You'll know in minutes the kind of in-depth, experience-taught lessons that usually take weeks to master.

What Is the Word for Windows Super Book?

The Word for Windows Super Book is the result of over 10 years of working with every version of Word for DOS, OS/2, and Windows. It is the result of nearly 1,000 hours of working with the new Word 6 release to comprehend, digest, and present all of Word's features in a unique and useful way.

The Word for Windows Super Book is, we believe, the only fully annotated and complete guide to the new Word for Windows. Rather than just describing the procedures or rehashing the contents of the reference that comes with Word, the Super Book goes further. It tells you what commands to use, what alternatives exist, possible stumbling blocks, and it provides dozens and dozens of useful tips, including shortcut keys and seemingly hidden features. It's like having an expert watching over your shoulder as you go through the steps.

How this Book Is Organized

The Word for Windows Super Book is presented logically, from the most-needed features to the most advanced. In a series of 14 Workshops, the Super Book uses carefully-designed skill sessions to show you how to use each of Word's features:

Basic Skills—Quickly brings you up to speed on using the new Word 6. The Basic Skills workshop boils it all down to the essentials, while showing you where to find complete information elsewhere in the Super Book.

Printing—The Printing Workshop tells you everything you need to know about printing and printer setup in Word for Windows, including how to print, how to change printers and other printing options, as well as how to change fonts.

Files—The File workshop covers all the ins and outs of filing, including saving word documents, closing, converting to and from other formats, saving templates and macros, changing options, and setting automatic save and other options.

Formatting—The Formatting workshop takes you through all the major formatting areas and commands, including a concise session on how to choose the correct views for best using Word's formatting commands.

Section Formatting—One of the keys to managing Word documents is in knowing when and how to divide documents into sections. The Section formatting workshop takes you through setting up multicolumn documents, numbering sections, and using headers and footers.

Tables—Tables are one of the areas most enhanced in the new Word. The Tables workshop fully explores all the new features, as well as the old, showing you how to do what, quickly and easily.

Styles, Templates, and Automatic Formatting—Styles are at the core of Word's formatting power. This workshop builds upon all your formatting skills, showing you how to recycle your efforts to keep from having to reinvent the wheel. This workshop also explores Word's new Wizards templates, demystifying them, and showing you how to use them to create perfect documents from the start.

Desktop Publishing and Graphics—With a newly-integrated drawing module, Word joins other sophisticated page composition programs in providing truly-integrated word processing and desktop publishing power. The Desktop Publishing and Graphics workshop expertly guides you through each feature, showing you how to and when to use Word's capabilities.

Writing Tools—Sometimes overlooked, Word comes with a stunning array of writing tools that go beyond the ordinary. The Writing Tools workshop explores each tool, showing you how to use it, as well as how to get the most out of it.

Merging—In the past, working with form documents to perform mail and data merges comprised one of Word's most confusing aspects. Much improved in this release of Word, the sheer number of new capabilities and features is overwhelming. The Merging workshop slices through the window dressing, showing you how to quickly and efficiently get your data merges up and running.

Long Documents—One of the neatest additions to Word's new features is the Master Document. The long documents section shows you how to use Master Documents to manage multifile and multiauthor documents for maximum efficiency and effectiveness. It also shows you how to use Word's much improved features for creating indexes, tables of contents, footnotes, and endnotes.

Customizing Word—Customization is one of the areas where Word truly shines, including the new drag-and-drop customizable toolbars. The customization workshop shows you how to turn Word into a finely-tuned,

well-oiled, document-producing engine. By adding the right personal touches, you can change almost anything you don't like about the defaults.

Projects—The Projects workshop is where it all comes together. In this workshop, we show you how to use a collection of powerful templates included on the Super Disk. The Projects workshop puts all of Word's powerful features to work. In addition, each template comes with its own customized toolbar that lets you quickly and easily put the features to work.

Macros—The Macros workshop shows you how—and why—to create macros to automate your work. It covers the gamut from recording a simple macro through building your own customized dialog boxes using Word's Dialog Editor. The Macros Project chapter puts it all together with a collection of the author's favorite and most useful macros.

New and Improved Features in Word for Windows 6

There's a lot to learn in this new version of Word—ranging from changed default keystrokes to a head-spinning assortment of new features. As you read the Word for Windows Super Book, keep an eye out for important new and changed features in these and other areas:

- Context-sensitive popup menus—activated using the right mouse button.
- Tables—Improved setup, new features, including AutoTableFormat and the Data Form tool for easy table entry.
- Forms—Drop-down form fields, new and improved method for creating forms.
- Toolbars—multiple toolbars, fully-customizable using easy drag-and-drop method.
- AutoCorrect—Automatic correction of common typos as you type, as well as automatic expansion of abbreviations.
- Bullets and Numbering—Completely redesigned, bullets and numbers automatically appear as part of the style.
- Styles—Word now supports character styles.

In addition, there are some annoying changes. For example, the Format menu, which was accessed with Alt+T in Word for Windows 2, is now accessed with Alt+O. Styles, accessed with Ctrl+S in earlier versions, is now Ctrl+Shift+S. The Bullets and Numbering feature, located in Tools in WinWord 2, is now in the formatting menu (where it probably belonged to begin with). **F**ile | **S**ave, which was Shift+F12, is now Ctrl+S. Moreover, some of the tools that were on the default toolbar in WinWord 2 aren't there in version 6—although they're still available. The list goes on and on. If you prefer some things the way they were, then take a look at the customization workshop. When you encounter a key, menu, or toolbar you need to tame, select **T**ools | **C**ustomize and start whipping WinWord into shape.

Conventions Used In this Book

The Word for Windows 6 Super Book employs various conventions to get you up and running with Word for Windows and shorten your learning curve. Understanding these conventions will help you get the most out of the Super Book and Word for Windows from the very beginning.

The Command Reference Card. The tear-out card in the front of this book is designed to give you a convenient reference to many of Word's functions and control key sequences.
Procedures. All of the step-by-step procedures have been numbered by chapter and in numerical order (for example, Procedure 1.1, 1.2, and so on).
Commands. All commands that you must select to do something are stated clearly (for example, "select OK"). This should enable you to quickly scan a procedure and focus on the commands required to accomplish that procedure.
Hot keys. If a command has a hot key equivalent, it appears in bold typeface (for example, "select Save **A**s" and "to access the **F**ile menu").

Several design elements are used throughout the Super Book to draw your attention to important information:

SUPER

NOTE

Notes introduce information related to a topic in the text. Although notes are not required reading, they often provide you with valuable information about why a feature works—or doesn't work—the way it's supposed to.

SUPER

UPGRADE NOTE

This type of note calls your attention to some feature or function of Word for Windows that is new or different in version 6.

SUPER

TIP

Tips are intended to draw your attention to information that will make your work easier. These are valuable insights, direct from the experts to you.

SUPER CAUTION

Don't miss these! Cautions point out potential pitfalls that may cause you big problems. Don't say we didn't warn you!

Basic Skills Workshop

This workshop shows you the basics of using Word for Windows 6. You learn how to start Word, as well as how to create, edit, perform basic formatting on, save, and print a basic document. You also learn about Word's overall approach to document formatting. Learning the basics of templates and styles early will help you achieve full productivity with Word more quickly.

Chapter

1

Getting Started

If you haven't yet installed Word, see Appendix A, "Word for Windows Installation and Setup," for additional information. If you have, then you're all set to go. To start Word from Windows, just double-click the Word icon, as shown in Figure 1.1. To start Word from the DOS command line, change to the Word directory and then give the command to start Windows and Word. Assuming that Word is located on `D:\WINWORD`, for example, you would type:

```
D:
CD \WINWORD
WIN WINWORD
```

FIGURE 1.1.
The Word icon in Windows.

The first time Word starts, you are in a session titled "Microsoft Word - Document1," as shown in Figure 1.2. Plus, until you turn it off (after the novelty wears off), Word also displays the Tip of the Day.

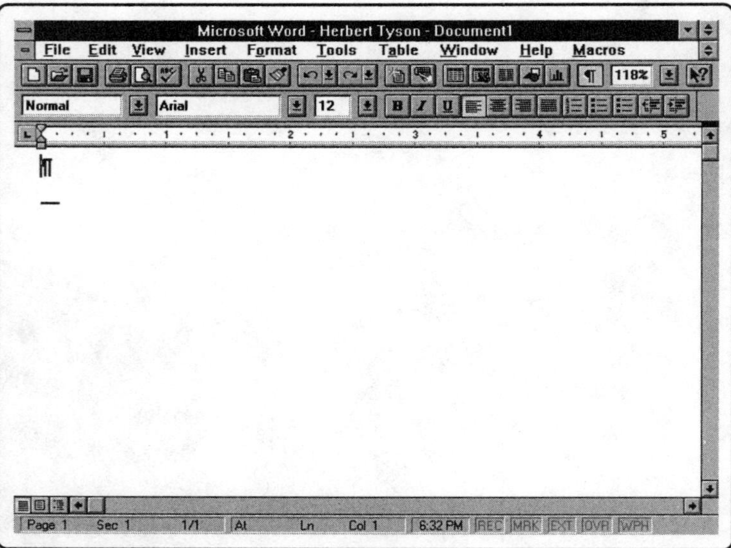

FIGURE 1.2.
Word after it first displays.

Document Strategy

Word's greatest strength is the powerful document control you can achieve by using templates and styles. Many Word users never vary the template they use—they always use the built-in default template called Normal. Many Word users never vary the style they use either. They simply add or subtract formatting from a style called

NORMAL. If you use Word that way, you're missing out on Word's greatest work-saving features. Using Templates and Styles saves time and effort, ensures document consistency, and promotes a professional document appearance. Beginning with Word for Windows 6, there's also a special new class of template called Wizard. Wizards are templates that contain intricate automatic macros for walking you through the creation of special kinds of documents, like award certificates, calendars, meeting agendas, and even one for writing a letter to your mom. Who says Microsoft doesn't have any heart? See Chapter 21, "Templates and Wizards," for additional information.

Templates

What is a template? At its simplest, a template is an already-started document. By using a template, you don't have to write a whole document each time. You just write the parts of the document that are different from what you usually write.

Take a letter, for example. Every letter you write probably has the same return address in the same format and location, so a good letter template would include your return address, already formatted. Letters you write also have the date, so a good letter template would automatically insert today's date in the appropriate place. A letter template would include the word *Dear* (but not the name), a place for the body of the letter, and a closing. It might also include an enclosure line, or at least the formatting for the enclosure line, as well as a conditional page-number header for subsequent pages of multipage letters.

Using templates can save time and effort and eliminate opportunities for typographical errors. A well-proofed template means creating a starting point just once, rather than once every time you create a document.

Why don't people use templates? That's hard to say. One reason is that they're always in a hurry, so they never take the time to think about templates. What's that old saying, "Haste makes waste"? Well, it's true. The little bit of time you save on the first letter by ignoring templates, you waste on every other letter you write. At the very least, most people would use that very first letter as a starting point for the second one they write, the second one as a starting point of the third one, and so on. What's that? You're already doing that? You know what? You're already using a template. Why not go the rest of the way and edit the template *once* so that you don't have to chop it up each time you use it?

Another reason people ignore templates is that, for it to be really useful to you, you need to edit a template so that it conforms to your needs. This takes time. However, it's time you have to spend only once, and it's time you save every time you use that template.

Convinced? Good. If you're in a hurry and are already familiar with the basics, you can jump ahead to Chapter 21, "Templates and Wizards."

Styles

Another key to tapping Word's power is using styles. While templates are starting points for whole documents, styles are starting points for parts of documents. A style can be a combination of text and formatting. Did you ever have a document with some recurring text in it? Consider a chapter title, for example. Every chapter might begin in an identical way:

```
Chapter {seq chapter number}
```

in 24-point Times Roman. Rather than typing and formatting *Chapter* 30 or 40 times, why not use one of Word's Heading styles, in which you define the word *Chapter* as text you want repeated each time the Heading style is inserted? That way, if your editor says, "Oh, by the way, we want all chapters to be in 18-point Century Schoolbook, and we'd really prefer Roman numerals," you can just change the style definition rather than the 30 or 40 occurrences.

Or, consider something like hanging indentation. For example:

1. Combine the flour and water carefully over a low heat, gradually adding enough plutonium to give yourself a slight headache.

Rather than having to stop and think, "Now, how do I do hanging indentation?" each time you want to create hanging indentation, you simply choose a Hanging style from the list of styles.

Styles have much to offer and are changed from earlier versions of Word. As suggested here, you can now designate "starter text" as part of a style's definition. You also can have character styles that vary within a paragraph. If you have a paragraph that always begins with a bold underlined header that is part of the paragraph itself, you can create a special style to handle it rather than formatting each occurrence. If the required formatting changes (for example, to bold italic), you can change just the style.

Formatting Leverage

The key advantage of using templates and styles is the leverage they give you over the documents you create. Leverage, which comes from the word *lever*, refers to your ability to accomplish a lot of work with a little bit of effort. If you do all formatting at the local (document) level, you then have to change each and every document to implement sweeping changes in format or style. If you concentrate formatting decisions into your templates as much as possible, it takes less work anytime you need to make global changes.

Chapter 2

Basic Equipment

This session is a survey of the basic equipment available in Word for Windows 6. In this session, we'll look at the screen, the keyboard, the mouse, windows management, and the help system.

Screen

The Word for Windows 6 screen has changed a bit from earlier versions. Some essentials remain, however. Virtually all of Word's screen elements are optional. Using Word's settings, you can elect to display the menu, the ruler, and the toolbars. Figure 2.1 shows the simplest possible screen.

FIGURE 2.1.
The "clean" look for seeing just text.

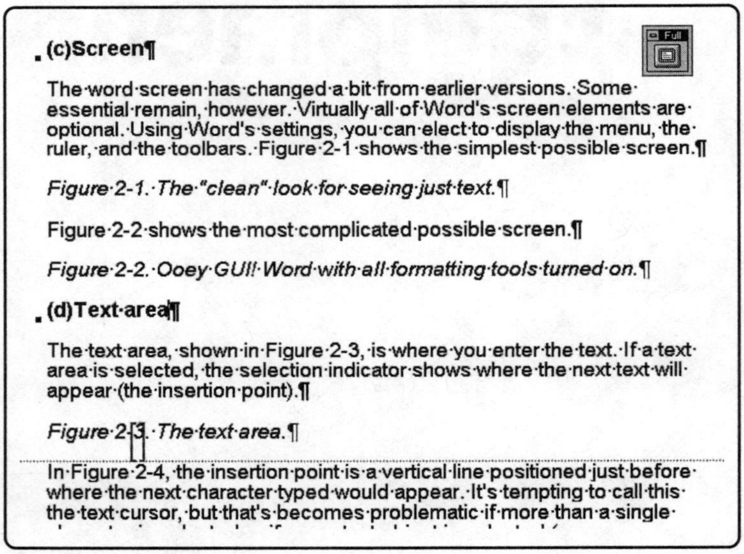

(c)Screen¶

The·word·screen·has·changed·a·bit·from·earlier·versions.·Some·essential·remain,·however.·Virtually·all·of·Word's·screen·elements·are·optional.·Using·Word's·settings,·you·can·elect·to·display·the·menu,·the·ruler,·and·the·toolbars.·Figure·2-1·shows·the·simplest·possible·screen.¶

Figure·2-1.·The·"clean"·look·for·seeing·just·text.¶

Figure·2-2·shows·the·most·complicated·possible·screen.¶

Figure·2-2.·Ooey·GUI!·Word·with·all·formatting·tools·turned·on.¶

(d)Text·area¶

The·text·area,·shown·in·Figure·2-3,·is·where·you·enter·the·text.·If·a·text·area·is·selected,·the·selection·indicator·shows·where·the·next·text·will·appear·(the·insertion·point).¶

Figure·2-3.·The·text·area.¶

In·Figure·2-4,·the·insertion·point·is·a·vertical·line·positioned·just·before·where·the·next·character·typed·would·appear.·It's·tempting·to·call·this·the·text·cursor,·but·that's·becomes·problematic·if·more·than·a·single·

Figure 2.2 shows the most complicated possible screen.

Text Area

The text area, shown in Figure 2.3, is where you enter the text. If a text area is selected, the selection indicator shows the insertion point, or where the next text will appear.

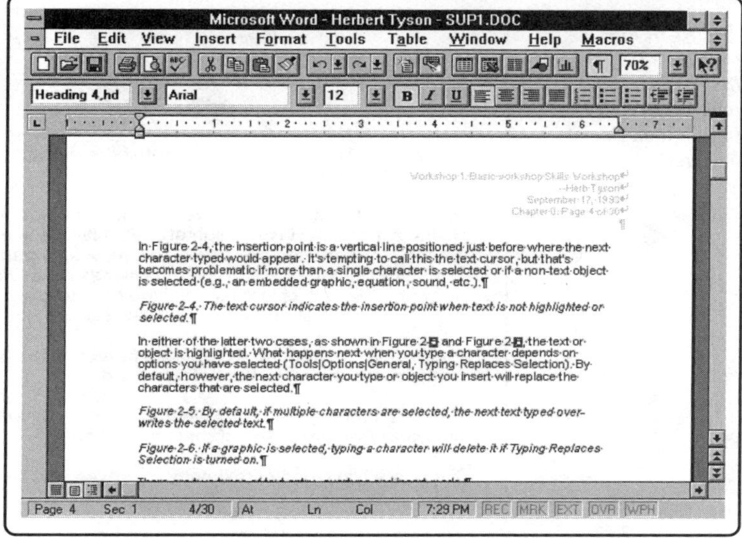

FIGURE 2.2.
Ooey GUI! Word with all formatting tools turned on.

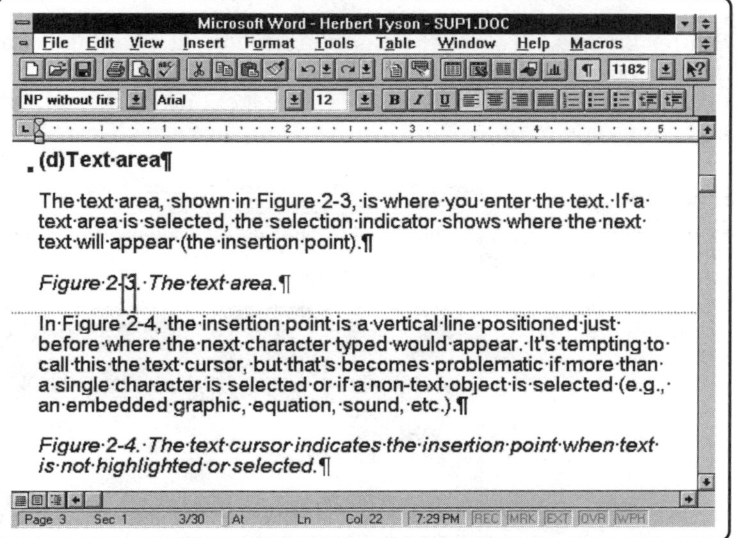

FIGURE 2.3.
The text area.

In Figure 2.4, the insertion point is a vertical line positioned just before the place where the next character typed would appear. It's tempting to call the insertion point the text cursor, but that becomes problematic if more than a single character is selected or if a nontext object is selected (such as an embedded graphic, equation, or sound).

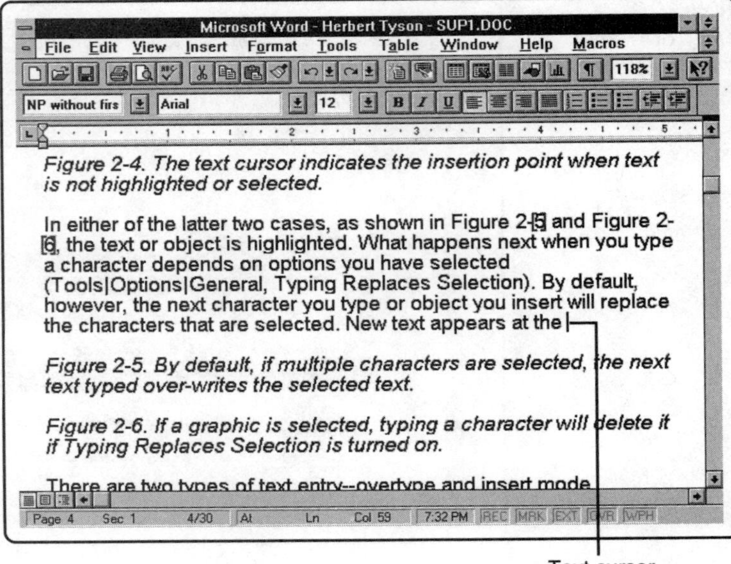

FIGURE 2.4.
A vertical line indicates the insertion point when text is not highlighted or selected.

Figures 2.5 and 2.6 show the cases in which text or an object are highlighted. What happens next when you type a character depends on the options you have selected (Tools | Options | Edit, Typing Replaces Selection). By default, however, the next character you type or object you insert will replace the characters that are selected.

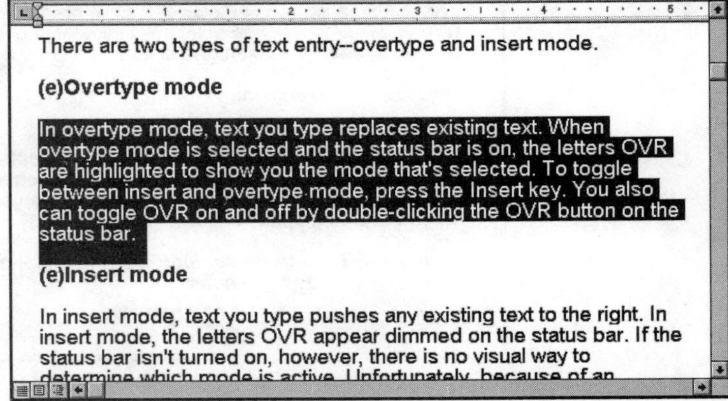

FIGURE 2.5.
By default, if multiple characters are selected, the next text typed overwrites the selected text.

FIGURE 2.6.
If a graphic is selected and Typing Replaces Selection is turned on, typing a character will delete the selected graphic.

Insert and Overtype Modes

Word lets you work in two modes of text entry: Overtype and Insert mode. In Overtype mode, text you type replaces existing text. When Overtype mode is selected and the status bar is on, the letters OVR are highlighted to show you the mode that's selected. To toggle between Insert and Overtype modes, press Insert. You also can toggle OVR on and off by double-clicking the OVR button on the status bar.

Insert Mode

In Insert mode, text you type pushes any existing text to the right. In Insert mode, the letters OVR appear dimmed on the status bar. If the status bar isn't turned on, however, there is no visual way to determine which mode is active. Because of an unfortunate design decision, the selection indicator is identical in Insert and Overtype modes. When the status bar is turned off, your only way to determine what mode you're in is to type and see if something gets pushed or replaced.

SUPER NOTE

Unlike native DOS and OS/2, Windows itself does not have Insert and Overtype modes. If you look for such modes in Notepad or Write, you won't find them.

Types of Text Areas

There are several different types of text areas, and Word behaves differently in each in certain respects.

- *Ordinary text* is sometimes called the body of a document (see Figure 2.3).
- *Headers and footers* are often used for page numbers and section titles and appear at the top or bottom of the page. Headers and footers do not display except in Page Layout view or when you explicitly select **View | Header** and Footer (see Figure 2.7).

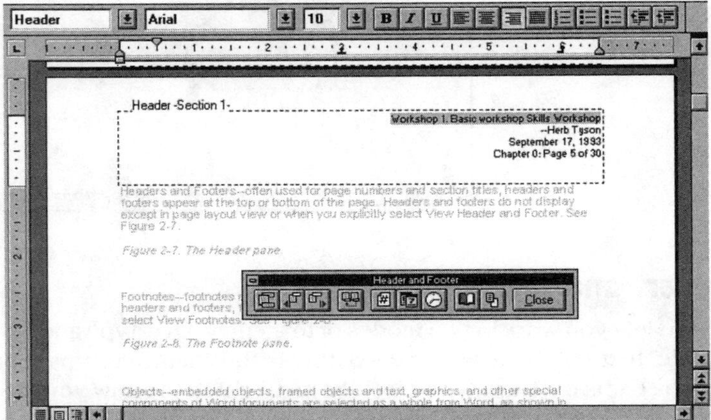

FIGURE 2.7.
The Header pane.

- *Footnotes* appear at the bottom of the page, section, or document. Like headers and footers, footnotes display only when in Page Layout view or when you select **View | Footnotes** (see Figure 2.8).

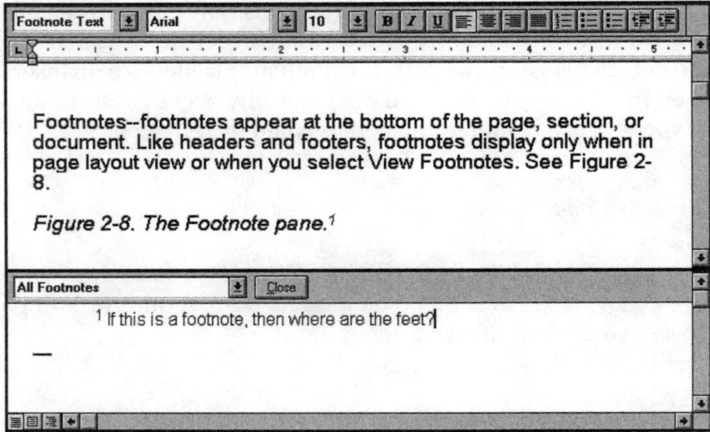

FIGURE 2.8.
The Footnote pane.

- *Objects*—embedded objects, framed objects and text, graphics, and other special components of Word documents—are selected as a whole from Word, as shown in Figure 2.9. You cannot, for example, position the cursor over a graphic and insert text on top of it. You can accomplish that purpose, however, by framing the text and graphic, but special steps are required. See Chapter 24, "Frames," for additional information.

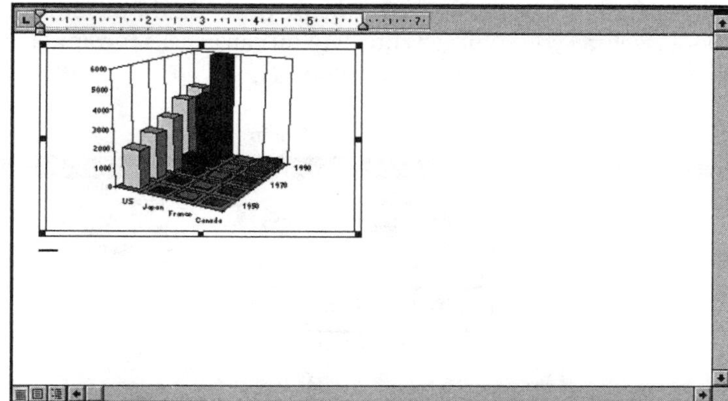

FIGURE 2.9.
Objects and graphics are selected as a whole in Word.

Application Title Bar

The application title bar, as shown in Figure 2.10, identifies the application.

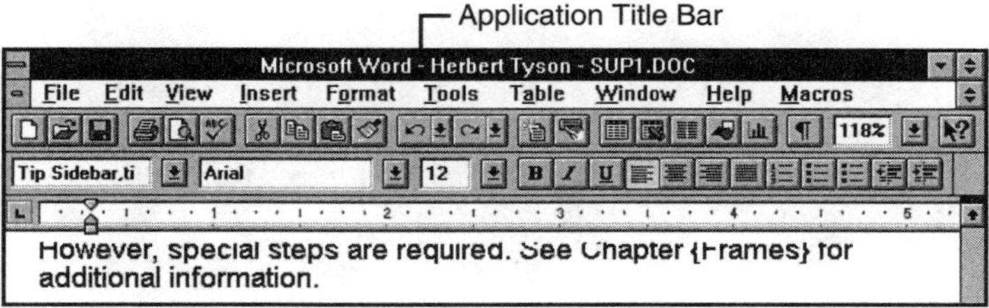

FIGURE 2.10.
The application title bar.

SUPER TIP

You can double-click the application title bar to toggle between maximized and windowed states.

Application Control Box

The application control box, as shown in Figure 2.11, controls Word's behavior as a whole. In Windows and OS/2, the upper-left corner of a window always contains the window control box regardless of whether the window contains an application, a document, a dialog box, or something else.

Generically, the control box for a program is called an application control box. Any time you see a window with a box in the upper-left corner, you can use that box to control the major functions of the corresponding window. You can use Word's application control box to restore, move, resize, or close Word. You also can use it to switch to other running applications. There are other methods for performing most of these tasks as well, as you shall see shortly. You can access the application control box using the mouse, or by pressing Alt+Spacebar.

FIGURE 2.11.
Application control box.

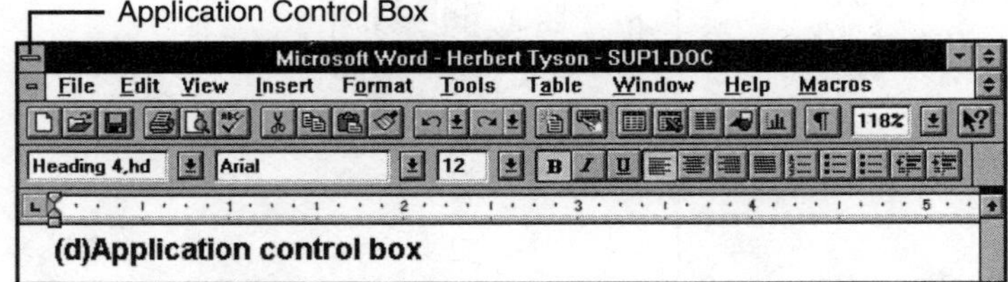

SUPER TIP

Double-click any window control box to close the window.

SUPER NOTE

Word for Windows 2.0 users should also note that the Run choice has been removed from the application control menu. To access the Run command now, select Help | About | System | Info and then click the Run button.

Application Minimize, Maximize, and Restore Buttons

The application minimize and maximize buttons are used to control the whole viewport for viewing Word. When the buttons are as shown in Figure 2.12, the application is maximized. The downward-pointing arrow is the minimize button. Use it to reduce Word to an icon. Reducing Word to an icon doesn't close it. It just gets it out of the way so you can see other things on the screen.

The double-headed arrow button is the *restore* button. Clicking the restore button returns Word to a *windowed* state. When windowed, Word can be resized using the borders and moved using the title bar. When maximized, it cannot.

When the buttons are as shown in Figure 2.13, Word is in a restored or windowed state. The upward-pointing arrow can be used to maximize Word.

FIGURE 2.12.
Word in a maximized state.

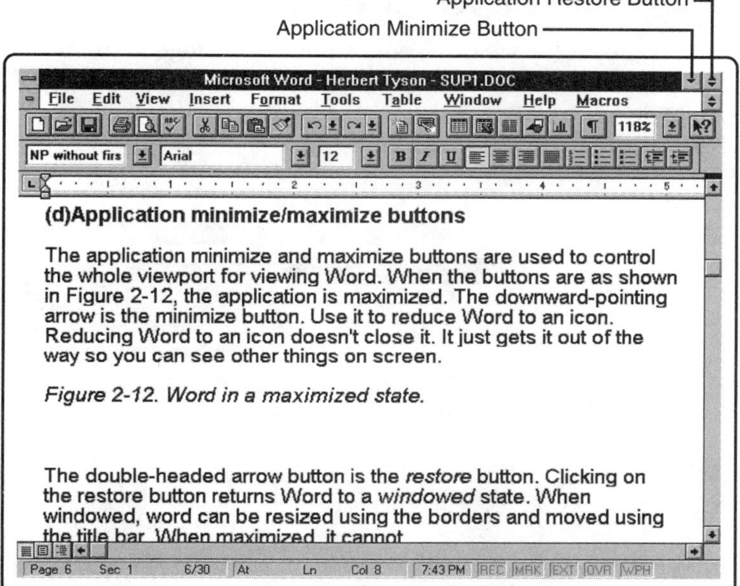

FIGURE 2.13.
Word in a restored state.

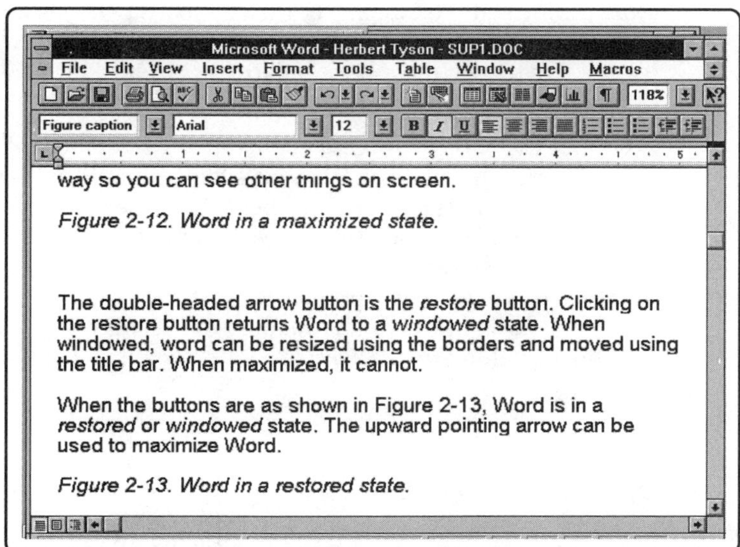

Document (or Window) Control Box

The document (or window) control box is analogous to the application control box. The document control box controls the document window much in the same way that the application control box controls the application window. As shown in Figure 2.14, you can use the document control box to control the window size and position, to close the active window, or to advance to the next logical Word window.

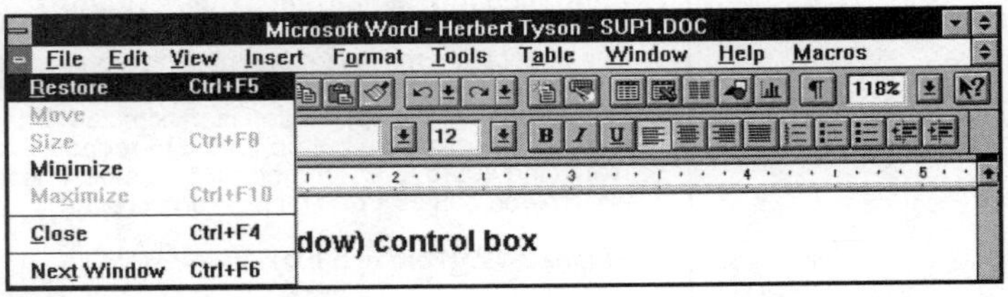

FIGURE 2.14.
The document control box.

SUPER CAUTION

Users often accidentally double-click the application control box instead of the document control box. It's very easy at that point to carelessly answer "No" to the wrong questions, sometimes wiping out work you just performed. You might try the keyboard controls if you're accident prone. Use Ctrl+F4 to close a document window, and Alt+F4 to close Word itself. Even then, the similarity in keystrokes is overwhelming until the difference becomes ingrained.

Another common mistake is confusing the document window control Close command with the File Close command. If you have multiple windows open for a given document (identified for example as SUPEBOOK.DOC:1 and SUPEBOOK.DOC:2), Ctrl+F4 closes just the active window on that document, while File Close (Alt+F followed by C, but there is no single corresponding keystroke) closes the file itself and all open windows in which the document is displayed. If you use multiple windows within Word, exercise caution when closing to avoid closing the wrong thing.

Document Title Bar

The document title bar, as shown in Figure 2.15, identifies the file that's being edited. If the document window is maximized, the document title bar is combined with the application title bar. If the document is windowed, the document title bar appears just above its associated window.

FIGURE 2.15.
The document title bar.

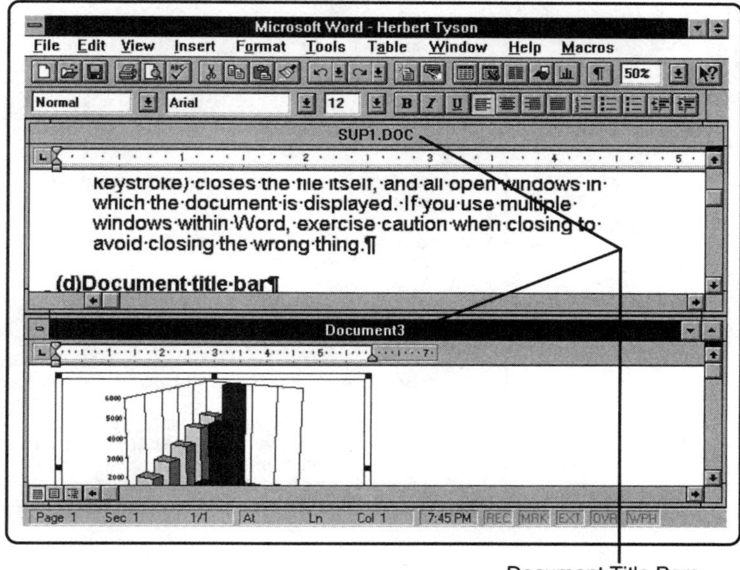

If more than one window is open on a given file, the instance number is identified as well in the document title bar. You open a new window (that is, another view of the same document) with the Window | New Window command. As shown in Figure 2.16, each window for a given document is identified by a colon followed by the instance number (:1, :2, and so on). If the document has not been saved, it will be identified by the name Document#, for which numbers are assigned sequentially as untitled documents are created during a Word session.

SUPER TIP

You can double-click the document title bar to maximize the document window. You can't use this as a toggle, however, since the document title bar is merged with the application title bar when maximized.

Document Minimize, Maximize, and Restore Buttons

The document and application minimize, maximize, and restore buttons are similar in function. The document buttons, however, function wholly within Word's window. Additionally, when the document is maximized, the document restore button is displayed on the same line as the Word menu rather than on a document title bar, as shown in Figure 2.17.

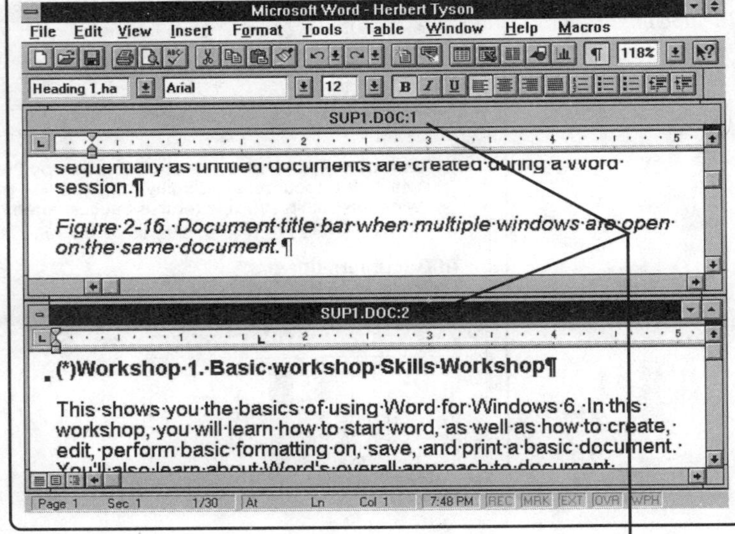

FIIGURE 2.16.
The document title bar when multiple windows are open on the same document.

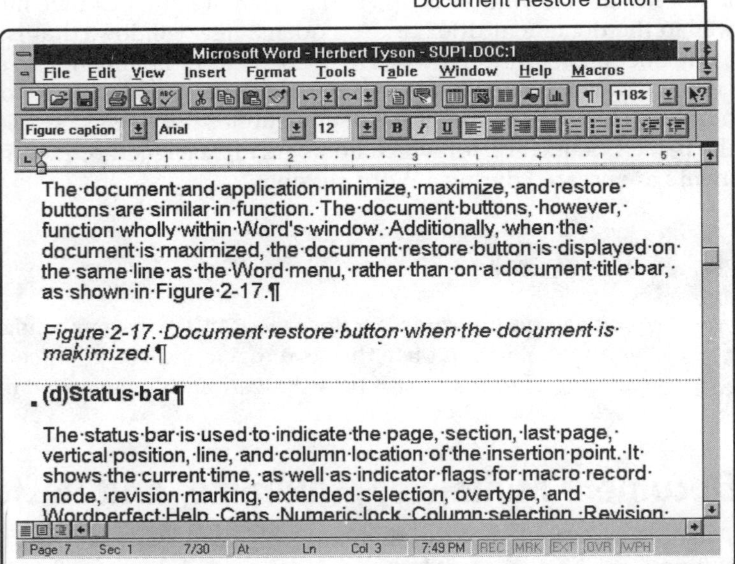

FIGURE 2.17.
The document restore button when the document is maximized.

Status Bar

The status bar indicates the current page (Pg), current section (Sec), current/last page (for example, 2/51), vertical distance from the top of the page (At), number of lines from the top of the page (Ln), number of characters from the left margin (Col), current time, Record mode status (REC), Revision Marking status (MRK), Extend Selection status (EXT), Overtype mode (OVR), and WordPerfect Help (WPH), as shown in Figure 2.18. The status bar can be toggled on and off using **Tools | Options | View** (see Figure 2.19).

> **SUPER UPGRADE NOTE**
>
> Users upgrading from WinWord 2 should take note that the status of NumLock, CapsLock, column selection, and zoom percentage are no longer reported on the status bar.

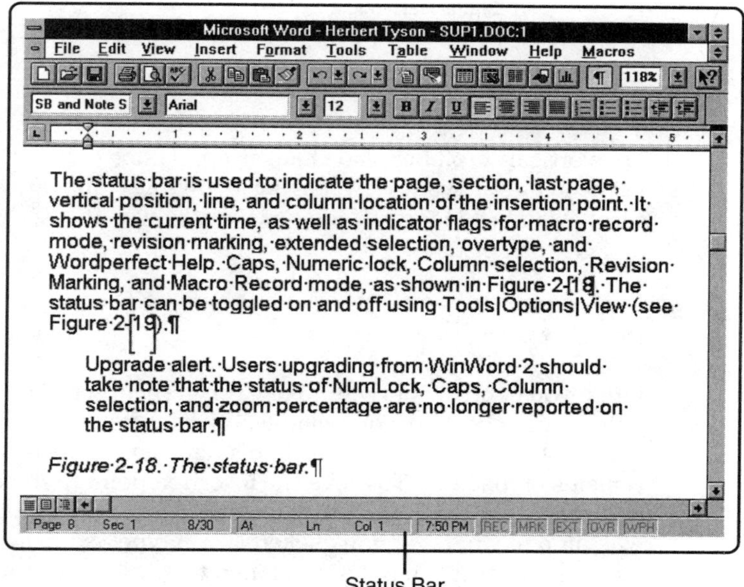

FIGURE 2.18.
The status bar.

Vertical Scroll Bar

The vertical scroll bar is standard Windows equipment (see Figure 2.20). Use it to control your view of the document window. Use the arrows at the top and bottom to scroll one line at a time. Click above or below the scroll box to scroll one screen at a time. You also can drag the scroll box to a position corresponding to the part of the document you want to view.

FIGURE 2.19.
Toggle the status bar using the View option tab.

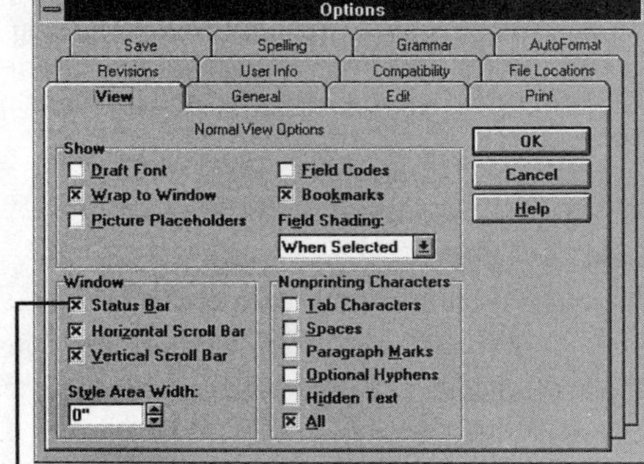

Status Bar Toggle

SUPER NOTE

The vertical scroll bar also changes depending on what view you're using. In Page Layout view, paging arrows also appear, which let you scroll exactly one formatted page up or down.

SUPER CAUTION

When you control your view using the vertical scroll bar, the insertion point is not changed. For example, if you've been typing text on page 17 and use the vertical scroll bar to display page 1, the insertion point remains on page 17. To move the insertion point to the current view, you must click the mouse on the text. At that point, the insertion point will jump to wherever you clicked. If you type text before otherwise moving the insertion point, the typed text will appear at the true insertion point, and your scrolling will have been for naught.

FIGURE 2.20.
The vertical scroll bar.

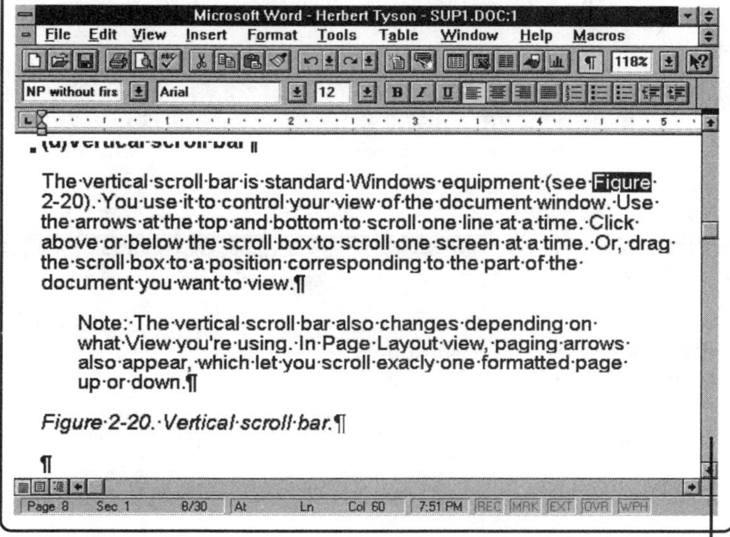

FIGURE 2.21.
Splitsville, man! You can use the split box to split, unsplit, and resize a split.

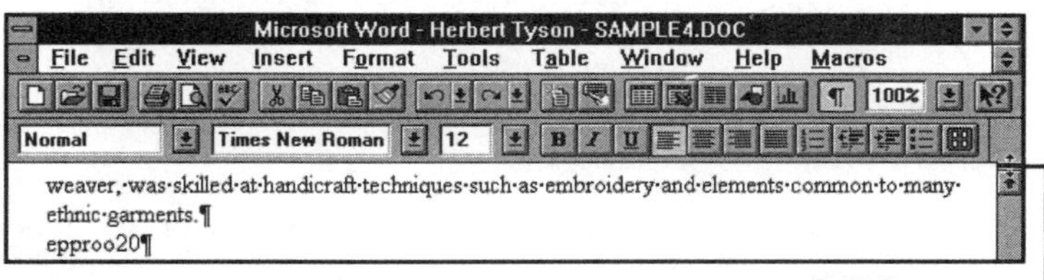

SUPER TIP

Note the area in Figure 2.21 identified as the split box. As shown in Figure 2.22, you can drag the split box to display two views of the current window. This action does not open a new window but merely a new view. The split box is a more efficient use of screen space because it doesn't produce a second document title bar. It's an ideal tool for referring to a different section of a document while typing in another section. You also can use this approach for viewing a document in outline and normal views at the same time. You cannot, however, use this approach to view different outline levels at the same time. Even so, it's a valuable writing tool to know about.

You turn the split box on automatically any time you drag or double-click the split box. To drag the split box, just position the mouse cursor over the split box area until a sizing cursor appears, then press the left mouse button and move the mouse pointer down. You also can split a window by selecting **W**indow | **Sp**lit from the menu.

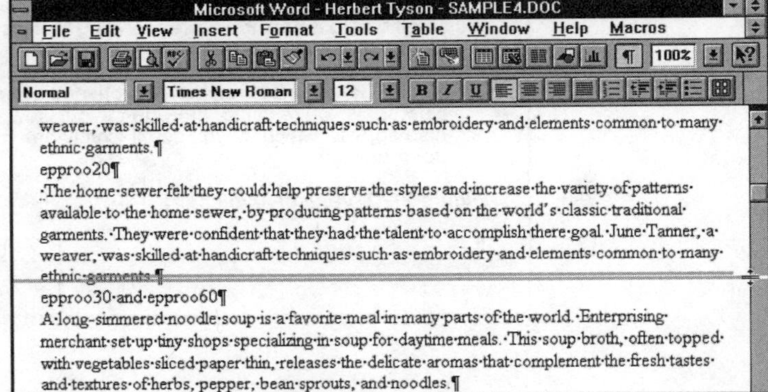

FIGURE 2.22.
Drag the split box to where you want the split. Drag it back to the top or bottom to close the split.

SUPER NOTE

The horizontal and vertical scroll bars are optional and can be toggled on and off using the **T**ools | **O**ptions | **V**iew menu, as described in Chapter 7, "Importing and Exporting."

Horizontal Scroll Bar

The horizontal scroll bar is also standard Windows equipment. Use it in the identical way as the vertical scroll bar (substituting right and left for up and down, respectively) to view parts of the document that are off-screen to the left or right.

Menu

Word's menu, shown in Figure 2.23, is one of several interface approaches for the user.

FIGURE 2.23.
Word's menu.

All standard commands and features can be accessed from the menu. You can activate the menu by clicking any main menu heading (**File**, **Edit**, **View**, and so on), or by tapping the Alt key. You also can access any main menu heading by pressing Alt plus the underlined letter displayed in the menu. Additional menu items have shortcut keys. When you use the menu, any shortcut keys are displayed in the menu, as shown in Figure 2.24.

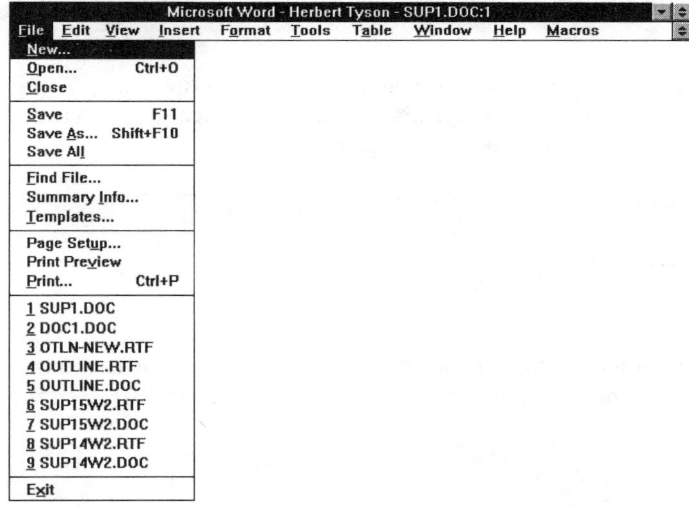

FIGURE 2.24.
The Word menu displays shortcut keys currently defined.

Toolbars

Word's toolbars provide graphical user interface (GUI) access to many of Word's features. Tables, for example, can be created graphically, as shown in Figure 2.25.

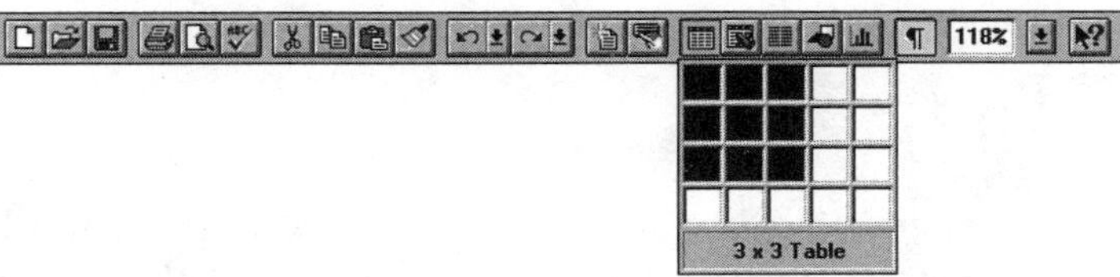

FIGURE 2.25.
The Standard Toolbar makes creating a table inGUItive.

In addition to providing access to built-in features, users can modify toolbars to add their own features (macros) or to make built-in Word features (commands) more accessible. Some Word commands exhibit different behavior when executed from the toolbar. For example, the Table | Insert | Table command, when executed from the menu, displays the dialog box shown in Figure 2.26.

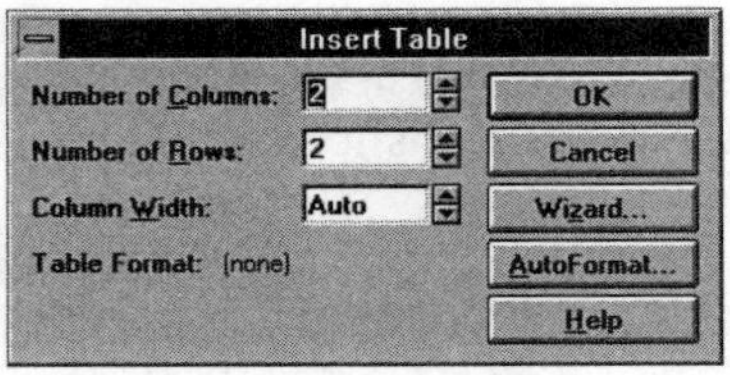

FIGURE 2.26.
The dialog box makes the options explicit, but lacks the intuitive GUI control.

When accessed from the Standard toolbar, however, the graphical aid shown in Figure 2.27 appears. The Format | Columns command exhibits similar behavior for creating a multicolumn document layout.

FIGURE 2.27.
The Column tool on the Standard toolbar.

The toolbars, while useful, can only be accessed with a mouse. I hope you didn't waste a lot of time looking for a keystroke method for activating the toolbar!

SUPER TIP

The icons in the toolbar are supposed to be self-evident. Yeah, right! If you don't find them self-evident, you can use the mouse to determine what action is assigned. Move the mouse over the icon of interest (without clicking any buttons). The description of the assigned macro or command is displayed on the status bar, as shown in Figure 2.28.

SUPER UPGRADE NOTE

Where's the Ribbon? Word for Windows 1 and 2 sported something called a formatting Ribbon. In Word for Windows 6, the Ribbon has been replaced by the Formatting Toolbar. It contains the same basic feature set as Word 2's Ribbon. Better, however, it can be changed to reflect your preferences. Better still, it's mobile! See the following tip.

FIGURE 2.28.
When the cursor is on the toolbar icon, the underlying macro or command description is displayed on the status bar.

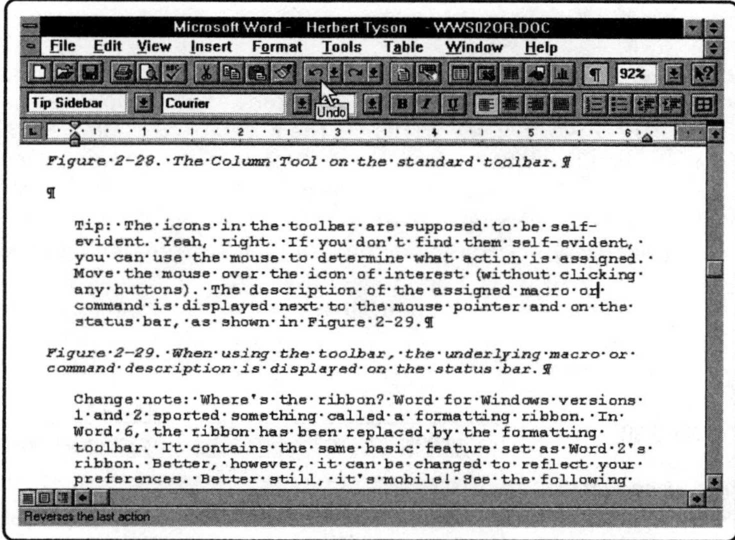

SUPER TIP

Move 'em! If you don't like where the toolbars are, you can move them wherever you want. Just double-click any blank area of a toolbar, and it's transformed instantly into a floating toolbox (see Figure 2.29).

FIGURE 2.29.
You can detach a toolbar and make it float anywhere on screen.

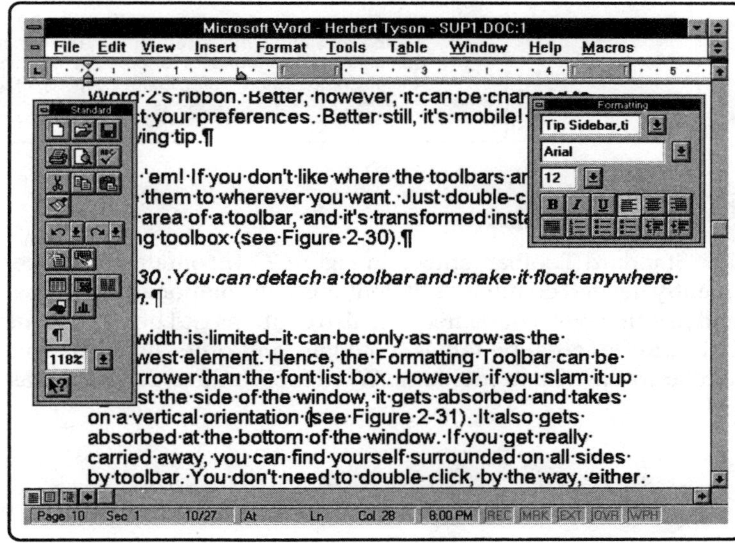

SUPER NOTE

The width of the toolbar is limited—it can be only as narrow as the narrowest element. Hence, the Formatting Toolbar can be no narrower than the font list box. However, if you slam it up against the side of the window, it gets absorbed and takes on a vertical orientation (see Figure 2.30). It also gets absorbed at the bottom of the window. If you get really carried away, you can find yourself surrounded on all sides by toolbar. By the way, you don't need to double-click. Just use any blank area as a handle, and drag the toolbar to a new location using the left mouse button.

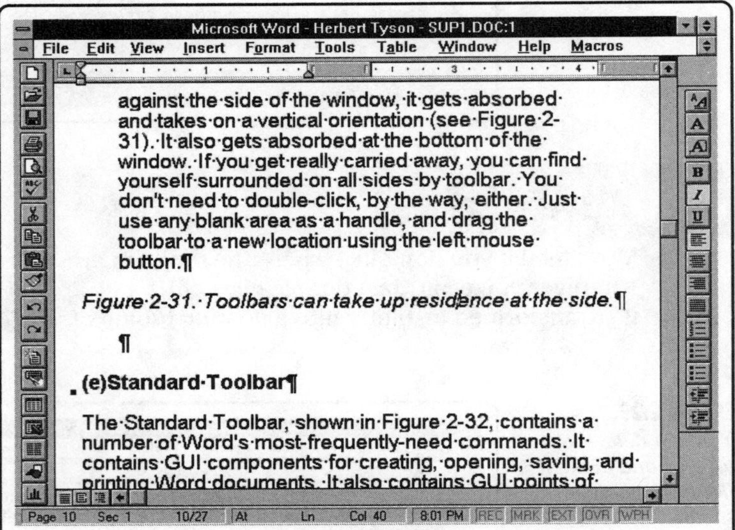

FIGURE 2.30.
Toolbars can take up residence at the side.

Standard Toolbar

The Standard Toolbar, shown in Figure 2.31, contains a number of Word's most frequently needed commands. It contains GUI components for creating, opening, saving, and printing Word documents. It also contains GUI points of control for the clipboard, UnDo, ReDo, creating tables, columns, and other niceties. The Standard Toolbar is similar to the default toolbar in Word for Windows 2.0, but it has been enhanced with color.

FIGURE 2.31.
The default layout of the Standard toolbar.

Formatting Toolbar

The Formatting toolbar, shown in Figure 2.32, was designed to be very similar to the formatting ribbon that came with WinWord 2. It provides access to styles and frequently needed character and paragraph formatting. As you'll see in the Customizing Word Workshop, all of the toolbars provided can be customized easily to create easy access to whatever combinations of commands and macros you need.

FIGURE 2.32.
The default layout of the Formatting toolbar.

Rulers

Word has horizontal and vertical rulers. The horizontal ruler can be displayed at any time, while the vertical ruler is displayed only in Page Layout view. They can be toggled on and off using the View | Ruler menu command.

The horizontal ruler is a GUI tool for accessing Word's most-used paragraph formatting commands. Shown in Figure 2.33, the ruler contains controls for adjusting paragraph indentations, margins, tabs, and table and column boundaries.

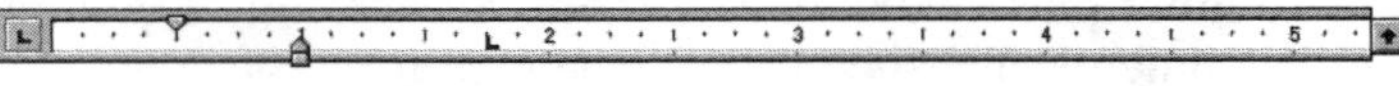

FIGURE 2.33.
The horizontal ruler.

SUPER UPGRADE NOTE

The horizontal ruler in WinWord 2 had three different ruler modes that toggled among paragraph, margin, and table. Some users found the three different modes confusing. In fact, most users didn't even know there were three modes, let alone used them. Word 6 doesn't have these three modes. Instead, the ruler changes dynamically when a table is on screen, and horizontal margins can be viewed and changed at any time without having to enter a special mode.

The vertical ruler is displayed only in Page Layout view (View|Page Layout, also Alt+Ctrl+P), as shown in Figure 2.34. You use the vertical ruler to adjust the top and bottom page margins, the position of headers and footers, and the height of table cells.

FIGURE 2.34.
The vertical ruler.

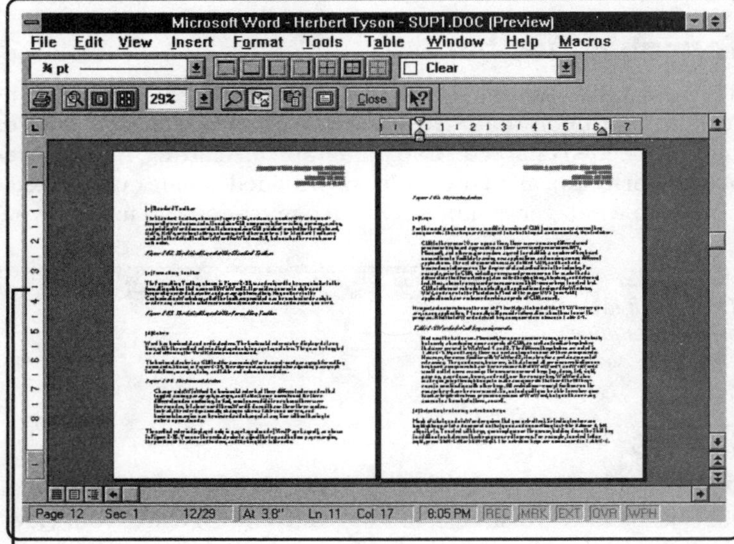

Keys

For the most part, Word uses a modified version of common user access (CUA) key assignments. These keys are designed to be both logical and consistent, if not intuitive.

SUPER

CUA TO THE RESCUE!

Once upon a time, there were as many different word processing keyboard approaches as there were word processing programs. IBM, Microsoft, and other major vendors agreed to establish a number of keyboard conventions to facilitate learning new applications and moving among different applications. The set of conventions was dubbed common user access (CUA) and has had a tremendous influence on the degree of standardization in the industry. For example, prior to CUA, virtually every word processor on the market had a different method for selecting (also called highlighting, blocking, and defining) text.

> Now, almost every word processor uses Shift+cursor keys to select text. CUA's influence extends to virtually all applications designed for Windows, OS/2, and even to the MacIntosh. Most of the major DOS (non-GUI) applications have embraced certain aspects of CUA as well.

An important convention is the use of F1 for Help. It's kind of like dialing 411 for information. Wherever you are, in any application, F1 usually will provide information about how to use the program. A full list of Word's default key assignments is shown in Table 2.1.

Table 2.1. Word 6's default key assignments.

Function	*Key Assignment*
Character Formatting	
All capital letters	Ctrl+Shift+A
Bold	Ctrl+B
Double spacing	Ctrl+2
Double underline	Ctrl+Shift+D
Font	Ctrl+D
Hidden text	Ctrl+Shift+H
Italic	Ctrl+I
Point size	Ctrl+Shift+P
Point size—decrease by 2 points	Ctrl+Shift+<
Point size—increase by 2 points	Ctrl+Shift+>
Point size—decrease by 1 point	Ctrl+]
Point size—increase by 1 point	Ctrl+[
Increase manual kerning	Ctrl+Shift+](?)
Decrease manual kerning	Ctrl+Shift+[(?)
Remove non-style character formatting	Ctrl+Space
Small capital letters	Ctrl+Shift+K
Subscript	Ctrl+=
Superscript	Ctrl+Shift+=
Symbol font	Ctrl+Shift+Q
Toggle case of selected text	Shift+F3

continues

Table 2.1. continued

Function	Key Assignment
Underline	Ctrl+U
Word underline	Ctrl+Shift+W
Styles	
Apply a style name	Ctrl+Shift+S
Apply Normal style	Alt+Shift+N
Apply Heading 1 style	Alt+Ctrl+1
Apply Heading 2 style	Alt+Ctrl+2
Apply Heading 3 style	Alt+Ctrl+3
Apply the List Bullet style	Ctrl+Shift+L
Format Styles dialog box	Ctrl+S twice
Start AutoFormat	Ctrl+K(?)
Reset paragraph formatting	Ctrl+Q
Alignment and Indentation	
Center paragraph	Ctrl+E
Justify paragraph	Ctrl+J
Left-aligned paragraph	Ctrl+L
Right-aligned paragraph	Ctrl+R
Increase left indent by 1 tab	Ctrl+M
Decrease left indent by 1 tab	Ctrl+Shift+M
Increase hanging indent by 1 tab	Ctrl+T
Decrease hanging indent by 1 tab	Ctrl+Shift+T
Spacing	
Single-spacing	Ctrl+1
Double-spacing	Ctrl+2
One and a half spacing	Ctrl+5
Toggle spacing before paragraph between 0 and 1	Ctrl+0 (zero)
Deleting	
Delete character left	Backspace
Delete word left	Ctrl+Backspace

Function	*Key Assignment*
Delete character right	Delete
Delete word right	Ctrl+Del
Delete selected text to the clipboard	Ctrl+X or Shift+Delete
Undo the last action	Ctrl+Z or Alt+Backspace
Delete to the spike	Ctrl+F3
Copy text or graphics	Ctrl+C or Ctrl+Insert
Copy formats	Ctrl+Shift+C
Move text or graphics	F2
Paste text or graphics from the clipboard	Ctrl+V or Shift+Insert
Paste formats	Ctrl+Shift+V
Inserting	
Insert field characters	Ctrl+F9
Insert spike contents	Ctrl+Shift+F3
Insert autotext entry	Autotext Entry Name+Ctrl+Alt+V or F3
Insert line break	Shift+Enter
Insert page break	Ctrl+Enter
Insert column break	Ctrl+Shift+Enter
Insert optional hyphen	Ctrl+Hyphen
Insert nonbreaking hyphen	Ctrl+Shift+Hyphen
Insert nonbreaking space	Ctrl+Shift+Spacebar
Insert copyright symbol	Alt+Ctrl+C
Insert registered trademark symbol	Alt+Ctrl+R
Insert trademark symbol	Alt+Ctrl+T
Insert ellipsis	Alt+Ctrl+Period
Insert single opening quotation mark	Ctrl+‘,‘
Insert single closing quotation mark	Ctrl+’,’
Insert double opening quotation mark	Ctrl+“,”
Insert double closing quotation mark	Ctrl+’,”
Insert page field	Alt+Shift+P
Insert annotation	Alt+Ctrl+A
Insert date and time	Alt+Shift+D

continues

Table 2.1. continued

Function	*Key Assignment*
Insert footnote	Alt+Ctrl+F
Insert endnote	Alt+Ctrl+E
Mark index entry	Alt+Shift+I
Mark citation entry	Alt+Shift+O
Selecting	
Select the nearest character	F8+Character
Extend a selection	F8
Reduce selection	Shift+F8
One character to the right	Shift+Right
One character to the left	Shift+Left
To end of word	Ctrl+Shift+Right
To beginning of word	Ctrl+Shift+Left
To end of line	Shift+End
To beginning of line	Shift+Home
One line down	Shift+Down
One line up	Shift+Up
To end of paragraph	Ctrl+Shift+Down
To beginning of paragraph	Ctrl+Shift+Up
One screen down	Shift+Page Down
One screen up	Shift+Page Up
To end of document (or pane, if in a header, footer, and so forth)	Ctrl+Shift+End
To beginning of document (or pane)	Ctrl+Shift+Home
Entire document	Ctrl+A
Vertical column of text	Ctrl+Shift+F8, then use the arrow keys
Cursor Movement	
Character left	Left
Character right	Right
Word left	Ctrl+Left
Word right	Ctrl+Right

Function	Key Assignment
Paragraph up	Ctrl+Up
Paragraph down	Ctrl+Down
Previous frame or object	Alt+Up
Next frame or object	Alt+Down
One column to the left	Ctrl+Up
One column to the right	Ctrl+Down
Line up	Up
Line down	Down
End of line	End
Beginning of line	Home
Formatted page up	Alt+Ctrl+Page Up
Formatted page down	Alt+Ctrl+Page Down
Window up	Page Up
Window down	Page Down
Bottom of window	Ctrl+Page Down
Top of window	Ctrl+Page Up
End of document	Ctrl+End
Beginning of document	Ctrl+Home
Repeat find or Go To	Shift+F4
Files	
New file	Ctrl+N
Open	Ctrl+O
Close	Ctrl+W
Save	Ctrl+S
Save as	F12
Print preview	Ctrl+F2
Print	Ctrl+P
Exit	Alt+F4
Editing	
Undo	Ctrl+Z or Alt+Backspace
Repeat	Ctrl+Y or F4

continues

Table 2.1. continued

Function	*Key Assignment*
Clear	Delete
Cut (delete to clipboard)	Ctrl+X or Shift+Delete
Copy	Ctrl+C or Ctrl+Insert
Paste	Ctrl+V or Shift+Insert
Select all	Ctrl+A or Ctrl+5 on number pad
Find	Ctrl+F
Replace	Ctrl+H
Go to	Ctrl+G
Bookmark	Ctrl+Shift+F5
Update link	Alt+Ctrl+U
View	
Normal	Alt+Ctrl+N
Outline	Alt+Ctrl+O
Page layout	Alt+Ctrl+P
Header and footer link	Alt+Shift+R
Other Actions	
Spelling	F7
Thesaurus	Shift+F7
Select table	Alt+5 on the numeric keypad
Window split	Alt+Ctrl+S
Help contents	F1
Context-sensitive help	Shift+F1

And now the bad news. Microsoft, for some curious reason, seems to be slowly but surely abandoning some aspects of CUA as well as familiar keystrokes that were present in WinWord 1 and 2. The different keystrokes are noted in Table 2.1. Although there is a certain logic to some of the assignments, this means a certain amount of relearning for users familiar with WinWord 2.

The good news, however, is that almost all previous restrictions on keyboard assignments have been removed. Neither WinWord 1 nor 2 would let users reassign the cursor movement keys (up, down, left, right, page up, page down, home, and end) or the escape key. WinWord also made you jump through hoops to make assignments that used the Alt key—even in combination with other keys. All restrictions—except for those on the escape key—have been removed, so not only will you be able to restore your familiar keystrokes from previous versions of WinWord, but you'll have easy access to a bunch of others as well.

Selecting Text Using Selection Keys

Much of what you do in Word requires that you select text. Selecting text means highlighting part of a document so that you can do something to it: italicize it, left align it, and so on. To select with keys, you simply move the cursor, holding down the Shift key in addition to whatever other keys you need to press. For example, to select left or right, press Shift+Left or Shift+Right. The selection keys are summarized in Table 2.2.

Table 2.2. Text selection key summary.

To select to:	*Press*
End of line	Shift+End
Start of line	Shift+Home
Next line	Shift+Down
Previous line	Shift+Up
End of paragraph	Ctrl+Shift+Down
Start of paragraph	Ctrl+Shift+Up
Bottom of screen	Shift+Page Down
Top of screen	Shift+Page Up
End of document	Ctrl+Shift+End
Start of document	Ctrl+Shift+Home
Entire document	Ctrl+5 (numeric pad)

Selecting Text Using F8

The F8 key is called the ExtendSelection key. You can use the F8 key to select text in a variety of ways. Pressing F8 turns on ExtendSelection, which displays EXT in the status bar (normally dimmed). When EXT is displaying, you can select text in any of the following ways:

Pressing cursor movement keys	Cursor up, cursor down, page up, page down, and so on extend the selection as you move the cursor through the document.

Typing a character	Word extends the selection up to the next occurrence of that character (for example, press F8 followed by a period to select up to the end of the current sentence).
Select Edit|Go To	Word extends the selection to the location you specify.
Select Edit|Find	Word extends the selection to the location of the find.

The F8 key can also be used by itself to select text. Pressing F8 multiple times extends the selection in logical units of text, as shown in Table 2.3.

Table 2.3. Effects of pressing F8 multiple times.

Number of F8 presses	*Effect*
1 press	Begin selection
2 presses	Select word
3 presses	Select sentence
4 presses	Select paragraph
5 presses	Select whole current section
6 presses	Select whole document (if multisection)

SUPER NOTE

With EXT turned on, Shift+F8 reverses the process, shrinking the selection by the indicated units. For example, if a paragraph is selected, Shift+F8 shrinks the selection area to a sentence; another press shrinks it to a word, and another just to a single point.

SUPER NOTE

You can also toggle EXT mode on and off by double-clicking EXT on the status bar (see Figure 2.36). You cannot, however, use the status bar EXT as a substitute for multiple presses of the F8 and Shift+F8 keys to expand and shrink a selection. Note also that you can press Esc to cancel EXT at any time. When you do that, any text already selected remains selected, but EXT special effects are canceled. Once EXT is off, moving the cursor will cancel the selection, and typing a character will replace the selection with that character (assuming that Typing Replaces Selection is turned on).

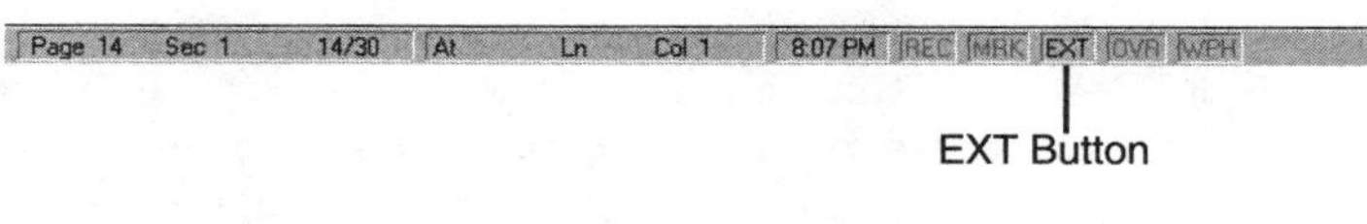

FIGURE 2.35.
You can start and stop EXT mode by double-clicking the EXT button on the status bar.

Undo

One of Word's keys warrants special discussion. It's the Undo key. When you press Alt+Backspace, Word reverses the typing, editing, or formatting you performed most recently. Word also retains an Undo stack and can undo repeated actions performed since the document was opened.

To undo a single action, you just press Alt+Backspace. To step backwards, undoing each distinctive edit or formatting operation in the stack, continue pressing Alt+Backspace (Ctrl+Z is a synonym for Alt+Backspace, just in case you find it an easier combination). Each press of the Undo key undoes the item at the top of the stack.

To view what the next press of the Undo key will do, select Edit and observe the first item on the menu (see Figure 2.36). To see the entire stack, click the Undo tool on the Standard toolbar. The Undo stack is retained per document and holds up to 98 distinct editing and formatting actions. When the stack is full, the top item pushes the bottom out of the stack. Some particularly large edits (for example, deleting a large block of text) can push multiple items off the stack, so at any given moment, you might have up to 98 undo-able actions, but often fewer.

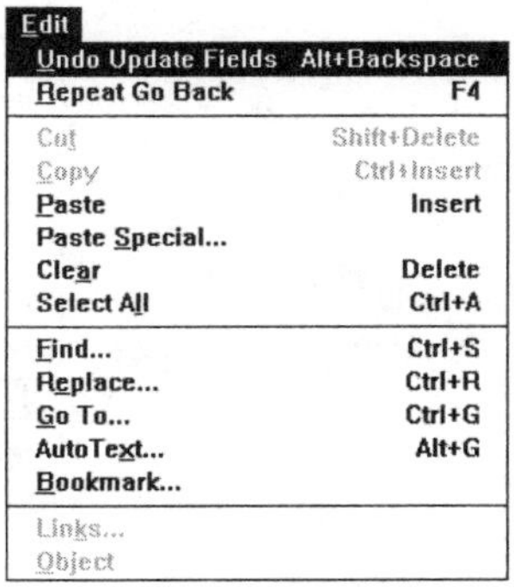

FIGURE 2.36.
The Edit menu shows you what Undo will undo.

Edit
Undo Update Fields Alt+Backspace
Repeat Go Back F4
Cut Shift+Delete
Copy Ctrl+Insert
Paste Insert
Paste Special...
Clear Delete
Select All Ctrl+A
Find... Ctrl+S
Replace... Ctrl+R
Go To... Ctrl+G
AutoText... Alt+G
Bookmark...
Links...
Object

SUPER NOTE

Because some edits (for example, deletions and large insertions) can involve large amounts of text and formatting, the undo feature can require a lot of computer memory. Keep this in mind if Word seems to be using a lot of memory or otherwise appears to be swapping to disk a lot. Note also that the multi-undo feature, unlike the undo features of some other word processing programs, does not wipe out the undo stack each time a document is saved. Thus, it's possible to undo edits that you thought were saved over. This gives you tremendous power to recover from accidental editing mistakes. Once a document has been closed, however, the memory of edits performed during the session are lost.

Repeat/Redo

Another one of Word's key assignments also warrants special discussion. It is F4—the Repeat key. The Repeat key can work alone or in reaction to the Undo key. If the Undo stack has been utilized, the Repeat key steps forward through each undone action, redoing it. In this respect, F4 is the counterpart to Alt+Backspace. If you prefer the main keyboard, Ctrl+Y is a default synonym for the Repeat key.

If nothing has been undone, the Repeat key repeats the most recent distinct editing action you performed. An editing action is something that results in a change to the text or formatting of a document (for example, typing a word, applying bold formatting, and so on). If you press F4, Word repeats the action. To see what Word will do when you press F4, select Edit from the menu. The second item listed on the Edit menu, as shown in Figure 2.37, tells you what F4 will repeat. If editing has been undone, then selecting the Redo tool (see Figure 2.38) will show you what actions can be redone.

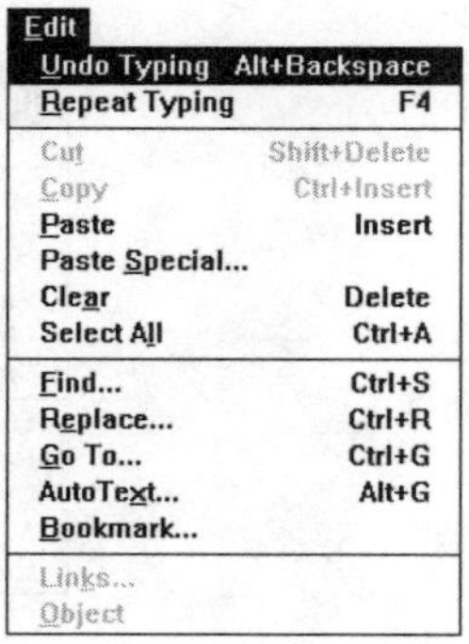

FIGURE 2.37.
The Edit menu shows what the Repeat key will repeat.

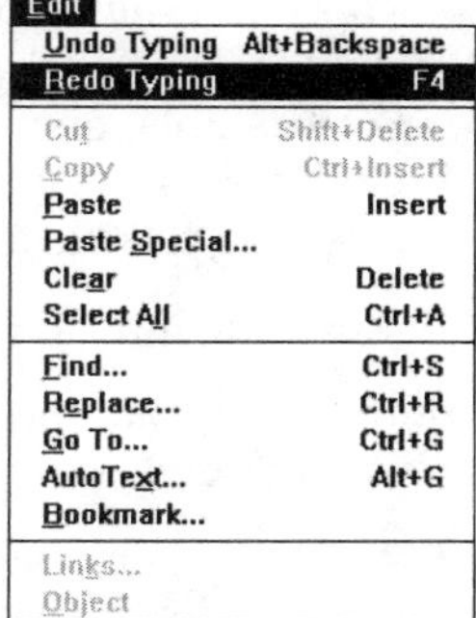

FIGURE 2.38.
The Edit menu shows what the Redo (un-Undo) will reverse.

One of the most productive uses of the Repeat capability is to perform the same formatting or typing in different parts of a document. For example, suppose you are formatting a document and need to apply a style called Hanging to various passages that have already been typed.

PROCEDURE 2.1. USING THE REPEAT (F4) KEY TO REPEAT FORMATTING.

1. Select the area you want to format.
2. Apply the formatting.
3. Select the next area you want to format.
4. Press F4.

For formatting that requires several steps—such as applying a style—using the F4 key can be a big time-saver.

Mouse

The mouse or other pointing device is a graphical method for navigating Word documents and selecting commands.

Basic Mousing

There are four basic things you can do with the mouse:

Point	Aim the mouse somewhere. As indicated in the Mouse Shapes section (below), the mouse pointer sometimes changes, depending upon the context, to indicate what kinds of actions can be performed.
Click	Press and release the mouse button. A single click is used to select text and objects as well as menu, ruler, and toolbar options.

Double-click	Press and release the mouse button twice, of course. Double-clicking is used to carry out an action immediately. For example, clicking a filename in the File | Open dialog box selects the file. Double-clicking is the equivalent of selecting the file and then clicking the OK button.
Drag	Move the mouse while holding down a button.

Depending upon the context and what button you click, each of the possible mouse actions performs different functions.

In Word for Windows 6, the left mouse button is used to make selections and take action, working much the way it did in WinWord 1 and 2 and in other Windows word processing programs. The right button is used to summon a context-sensitive popup. When editing text, the right mouse button summons a context-sensitive editing menu (see Figure 2.39). If the insertion point is in a table, a different context-sensitive menu is presented. Similarly, if a graphic or other object is selected, an appropriate menu of options is displayed.

FIGURE 2.39.
Using the right mouse button to select a column of text.

Figure·2-40.·Using·the·right·mouse·b... ext-sensitive·menu.¶

Cut
Copy
Paste
Insert Rows
Delete Cells...
Table AutoFormat...
Font...
Paragraph...
Bullets and Numbering...

Selecting Text Using the Mouse

PROCEDURE 2.2. SELECTING TEXT WITH THE MOUSE.

1. Move the cursor to where you want the selection to begin.
2. Press and hold the left mouse button.
3. Drag the selection to cover the area you want to select.

PROCEDURE 2.3. SELECTING A WORD WITH THE MOUSE.

1. Double-click the first word you want to select. Keep the mouse button pressed after the second click if you want to extend the selection to cover additional words.
2. To extend the selection, keep the button pressed and drag the selection; it will extend one word at a time. You can drag forward or backwards.

PROCEDURE 2.4. SELECTING A LINE WITH THE MOUSE.

1. Click in the selection area to the left of the text (see Figure 2.40), keeping the button pressed if you want to extend the selection to additional lines.
2. To extend the selection, keep the button pressed and drag the selection; it will extend one line at a time.

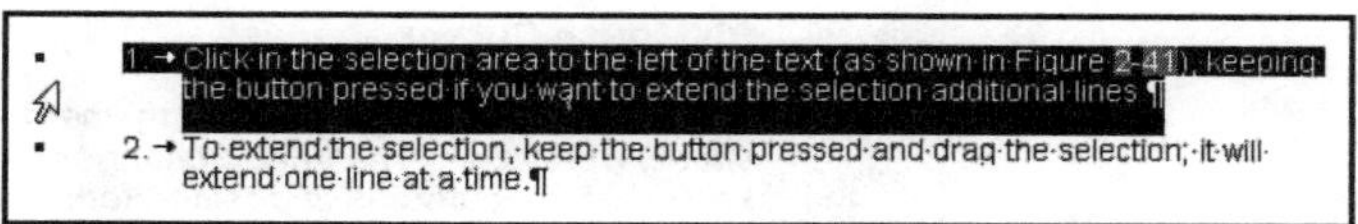

FIGURE 2.40.
The selection bar is the area between the style area (if displayed) and the text.

PROCEDURE 2.5. SELECTING A SENTENCE WITH THE MOUSE.

1. Press Ctrl and click in the sentence you want to select, keeping the button pressed if you want to extend the selection.
2. To extend the selection, keep the button pressed and drag the selection; it will extend sentence by sentence.

PROCEDURE 2.6. SELECTING A PARAGRAPH WITH THE MOUSE.

1. Double-click in the selection area to the left of the text, keeping the button pressed if you want to extend the selection additional lines.
2. To extend the selection, keep the button pressed and drag the selection; it will extend one paragraph at a time.

PROCEDURE 2.7. EXTENDING THE SELECTION WITH THE MOUSE FROM THE INSERTION POINT TO ANY OTHER POINT.

1. Press Shift and click where you want the selection to end; the selection will extend from the previous insertion point to where you Shift-clicked.

PROCEDURE 2.8. SELECTING AN ENTIRE DOCUMENT WITH THE MOUSE.

1. Press Ctrl and click in the selection area to the left of the text.

Mouse Cursor Shapes

Depending on what you are doing, the mouse cursor can take a variety of shapes. The shape changes are designed to let you know that the cursor is in position for a specific type of action. While you're typing text, the mouse cursor disappears and is subsumed (in effect) with the insertion point marker, as shown in Figure 2.41.

FIGURE 2.41.
When you're typing text, there is only one cursor of any kind on-screen.

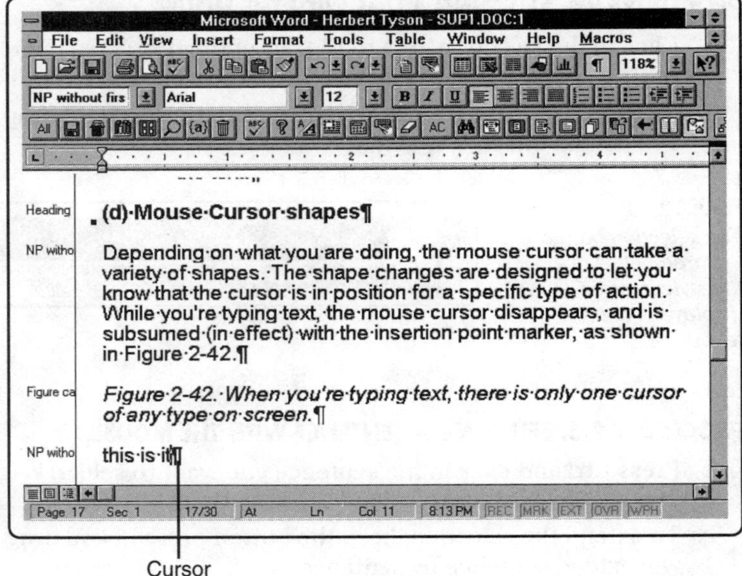

The other mouse cursor shapes are

Text cursor—An I-beam that indicates that a click will move the insertion point to the location of the mouse cursor.

Drag cursor—Indicates that text is being dragged. Releasing the left button moves text to the cursor location (unless the Ctrl key is depressed, in which case text will be copied).

Main Pointer—An arrow pointing to the left that's used to select menus and tools and to manipulate scroll bars and other graphical elements.

Selection Pointer—An arrow pointing to the right that's used at the left edge of text and tables to indicate selection of lines, paragraphs, table rows, and the whole document.

Preview Drag—In Print Preview mode, the plus cursor indicates that the object under it can be dragged.

Wait—An hour glass that indicates Word is unable to process any instructions until the current action is finished.

Help—A question mark indicating that clicking whatever is under the pointer will activate help for that topic.

Horizontal Split—Used to adjust the borders when using a split window via the Split Box.

Vertical Split—Used to adjust the side of the style area name display on the left edge of a document.

Border arrows—Used to adjust the shape and size of window borders.

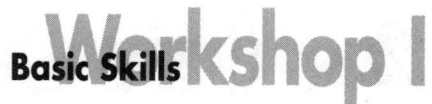

Window Move—A four-headed hollow arrow that appears whenever the Window Move command is selected from the application or document control menu.
Outline—A four-headed solid arrow indicating that the cursor is positioned correctly for moving a framed object. It is also used in Outline view to indicate that the item at the cursor is draggable. Once the drag begins, a horizontal or vertical double-headed arrow shows what kind of drag is occurring. See Chapter 40, "Outlining."
Solid two-headed horizontal arrow—Used as a sizing handle for framed objects. It is also used in Outline view when changing an item's heading level.
Solid two-headed vertical arrow—Used as a sizing handle for framed objects. It is also used in Outline view for dragging a heading up or down.
Solid down arrow—Used in columns to indicate that a click will select the column.
Cloverleaf—Used when making shortcut key assignments. See Chapter 47, "Customizing the Keyboard."
Menu minus—Used when removing menu items. See Chapter 49, "Customizing Menus."
Menu plus—Used when adding menu items. See Chapter 49, "Customizing Menus."

Hidden Shortcuts: Click Everything in Sight!

Word has a number of seemingly hidden double-click shortcuts, as shown in Table 2.4.

Table 2.4. Double-click shortcuts.

Double-Click This	*To Accomplish This*
Title bar	Toggle maximize/restore
Control box	Close window, application, or dialog box
Toolbox title bar	Convert back into a toolbar
Toolbox control icon	Close the toolbox
Status Bar	Edit | GoTo
Blank area on a toolbar	Convert the toolbar into a toolbox
Style area	Format | Style
Blank area in either ruler	File | Page Setup
Tab in the horizontal ruler	Format | Tabs dialog box
Split box	Split or unsplit the current window
Blank area adjacent to toolbar	View | Toolbars

continues

Table 2.4. continued

Double-Click This	*To Accomplish This*
EXT symbol on status bar	Toggle extended selection
MRK symbol on status bar	Toggle redlining (revision marking)
REC symbol on status bar	Toggle Macro Record mode
OVR symbol on status bar	Toggle Overtype/Insert
WPH symbol on status bar	Activate WordPerfect Help
Blank area in the Toolbar	Tools | Options | Toolbar dialog box

Window Management

After all, it's called *Windows*, isn't it? Unfortunately, Word doesn't provide much in the way of automatic windowing utilities. If you have multiple documents open, you cannot instruct Word to just split any two of them horizontally or vertically. Instead, you must manipulate them manually. You can drag or size them however you like, but if you routinely need two documents split vertically or horizontally, Word's built-in options are limited.

Word's Window menu, shown in Figure 2.42, provides the following capabilities:

- Open another window on the current document.
- Arrange (tile) all open document windows on-screen.
- Switch to any open document window.

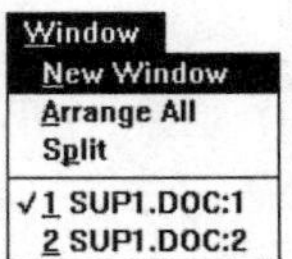

FIGURE 2.42.
The Window menu.

Window | New Window: Opening Another Window on the Current Document

One method of obtaining a second view of a document was shown in Figure 2.42—using the split box. Using the split box opens a second pane in the current window rather than a new window. If you need to see two different parts of the same document—neither in Outline view—this is a good way to do it.

If you need to see two parts of the same document while one of them is in Outline view, however, the split-box approach isn't a good one because, in split view, Word insists on scrolling both panes at the same time. Instead, select Window | New Window to create your second view. Shown in Figure 2.43, opening a second window on the same document allows you to freeze the outline in one window while maintaining completely separate scrolling in another. It also allows you to resize the documents vertically on the same screen or in whole windows (not displayed at the same time). Unless you need some of these capabilities, however, you'll generally find that the split-box approach works better. It's faster and uses fewer resources. You also can display a document in Page Layout view in one split and normal view in another.

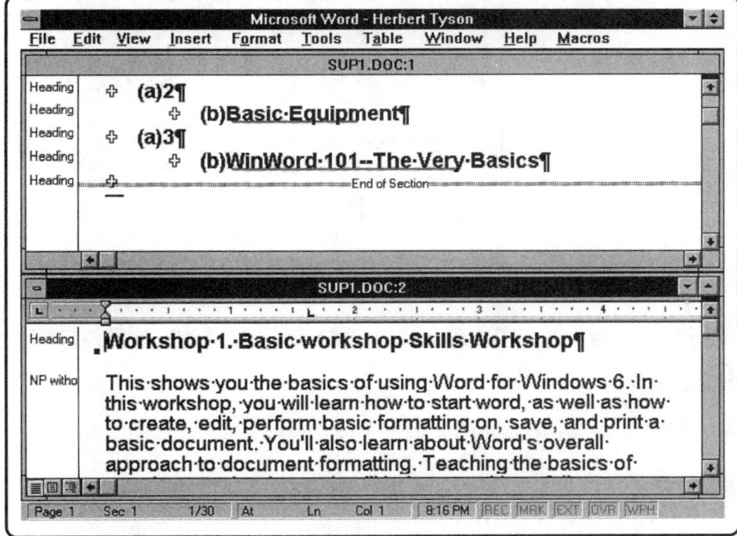

FIGURE 2.43.
Word lets you open multiple windows on the same document.

Window | Arrange All: Tiling All Open Windows

While Word for Windows 6 has a number of exciting new features, one aggravating *old* feature is the inability of Word to selectively window or tile just two windows. When you select Window | Arrange All, Word tiles all open documents. The window pattern you get depends on the number of open windows, as shown in Figure 2.44.

SUPER TIP

The *good* news is that Word is no longer "limited" to just nine windows. In Word 6, the only limit is memory. For example, I opened 20 windows on this document to produce the figure shown in Figure 2.45 before I got bored. Before I finish the book, maybe I'll get time to write a macro to see just where it tops out, in which case, you won't be reading this.

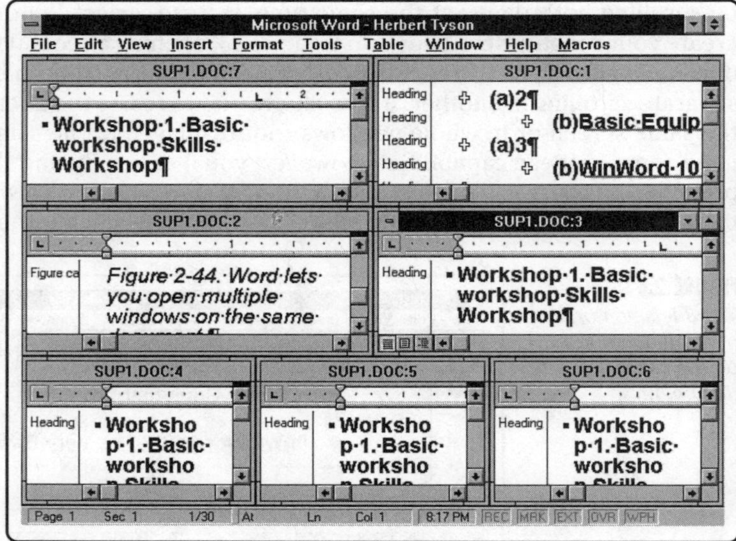

FIGURE 2.44.
The Window | Arrange command's effect depends on how many windows are open.

Window | Split: Dividing a Single Window into Two Panes

The Window | Split command is the menu implementation of the split box.

PROCEDURE 2.9. SPLITTING A WINDOW USING THE MENU.

1. Select Window | Split. A horizontal gray line appears near the middle of the window.
2. Use the mouse or cursor keys to position the split line where you want the split to occur.
3. Press Enter to accept the split (press Esc to cancel).

Help

Word provides context-sensitive help. To use it, press F1 in any situation, and Word will present you with help relevant to whatever is on-screen. For example, if the File | Open dialog box is on-screen, pressing F1 displays the help shown in Figure 2.45. If you are editing a macro, Word displays help for the macro command nearest the cursor.

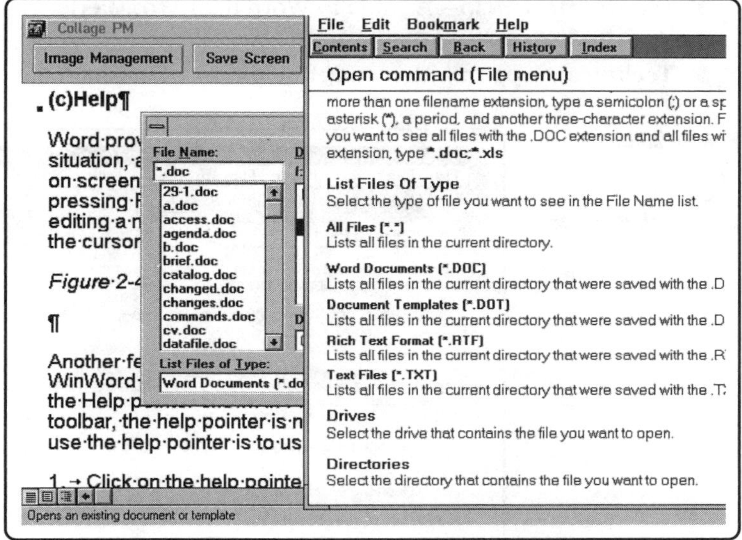

FIGURE 2.45.
Press F1 for context-sensitive help.

A feature that was relatively neglected in previous versions of WinWord is the Help pointer. If you press Shift+F1, Word displays the Help pointer shown in Figure 2.46. Thanks to the Standard Toolbar, the Help pointer is no longer invisible, so an easier way to use the Help pointer is to use the tool.

PROCEDURE 2.10. USING THE HELP POINTER TOOL.

1. Click the Help pointer; the mouse cursor gains a question mark, as shown in Figure 2.46.
2. Click the area of the Word screen, menu, or tool with which you want help.
3. Press Esc to cancel the Help pointer mode.

You can click any area of the screen to display help. For example, clicking the Help pointer on the status bar displays a fairly complete explanation of the information presented in the status bar, as shown in Figure 2.47.

Other Help Features

Other Help-ful features include:

- **Index**—Comprehensive index of Word features (Alt+H I)
- **Quick Preview**—Quick Word 6 tutorial (Alt+H Q)
- **Tips**—Tip of the day, a selection of helpful and silly tips (Alt+H P)

- **WordPerfect Help**—A guide to Word 6 for WordPerfect users (Alt+H W, or double-click on WPH on the status bar)
- **Technical Support**—How to get help from Microsoft (Alt+H T)

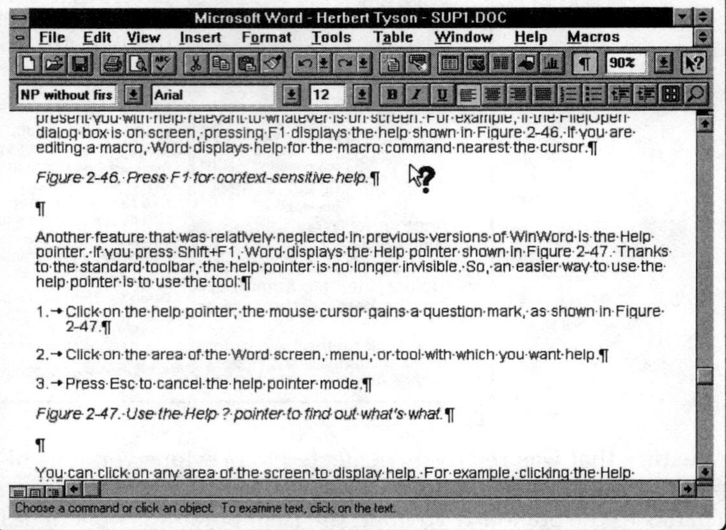

FIGURE 2.46.
Use the Help pointer to find out what's what.

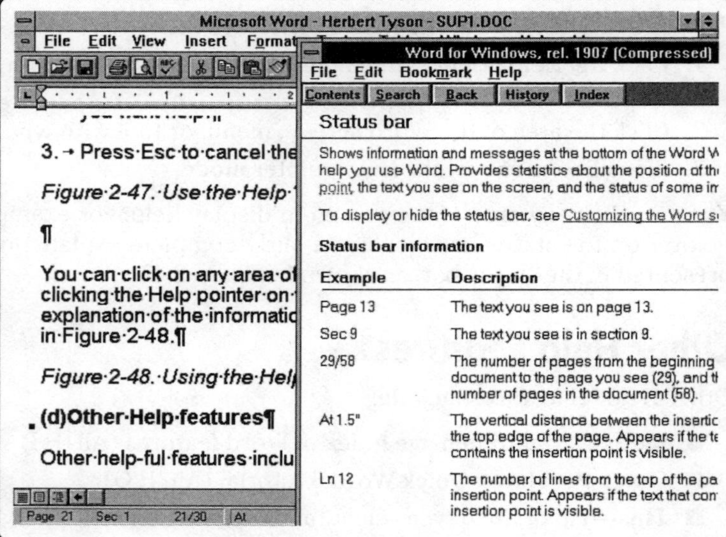

FIGURE 2.47.
Using the Help pointer to check out the status bar.

Chapter

3

WinWord 101: The Very Basics

In this section, I'll take you through the very basics of Word. Don't worry if it looks like methods and topics get short shrift here. That's intentional. The purpose of this lesson is to give beginners just the basics, as a starting point.

Creating a New Document

When you open Word, you should see a screen similar to the one shown in Figure 3.1, depending on what View options are active. It's possible, for example, that the ruler, toolbars, menu, title bar, and status bar are not displayed. The toolbars might also not display or may have different shapes than the defaults shown here. If you're reading this section, however, it's a pretty safe assumption that you haven't yet customized Word to that extent. If you have, then you probably know how to put them back so what you're reading makes sense.

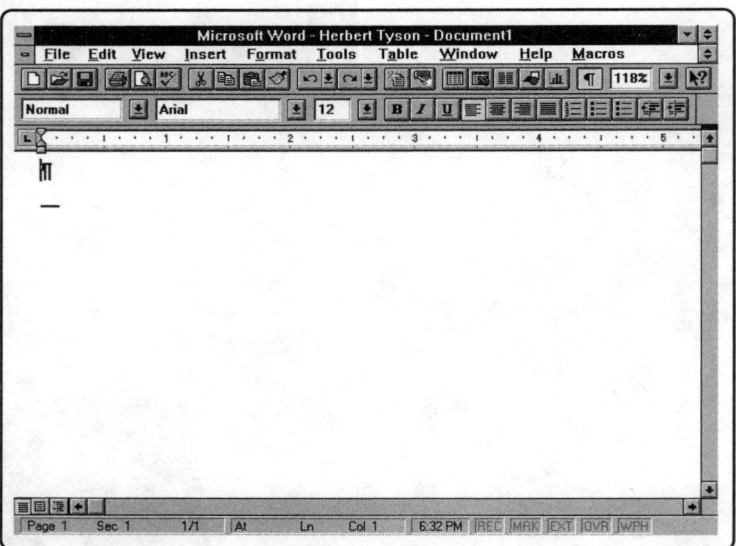

FIGURE 3.1.
Word's opening screen.

Notice the title bar, which says *Microsoft Word - Document1*. This means that anything you type will be inserted into the Document1 window, which has not yet been saved. Once it's saved, the title *Document1* will be replaced by whatever name you give it.

Inserting Text

Word has two insertion modes. The default is Insert mode. When you type in front of existing text, the existing text gets pushed to the right and down. You can change to Overtype mode by pressing Insert or by double-clicking OVR on the status bar. In Overtype mode, text you type replaces existing text, except for paragraph marks. When you're in Overtype mode and come to a paragraph mark, it gets pushed along to the right and down. This prevents you from accidentally destroying text in subsequent paragraphs.

Editing

Editing comprises adding to, changing, and replacing existing text. In addition to editing by simply typing in Insert or Overtype mode, you can also edit by moving, copying, or deleting text.

Moving Text

You can move text by using the Move key (F2), the clipboard, or drag-and-drop.

PROCEDURE 3.1. MOVING TEXT WITH THE MOVE KEY.

1. Select the text you want to move.
2. Press F2.
3. Select the area to which you want to move the selected text (the target selected area, if any, will be dotted, as shown in Figure 3.2).
4. Press Enter.

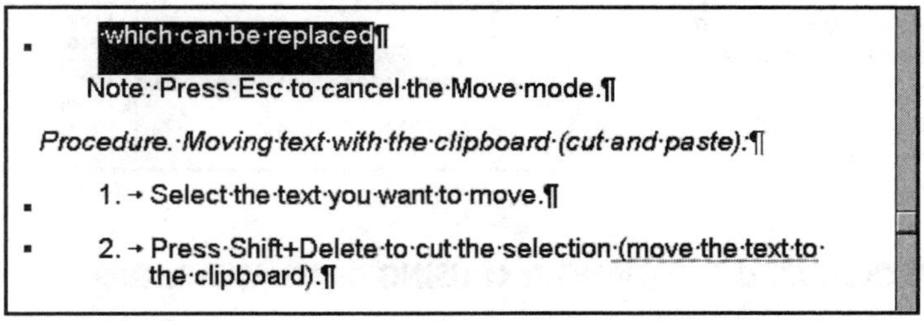

which·can·be·replaced¶

Note:·Press·Esc·to·cancel·the·Move·mode.¶

Procedure.·Moving·text·with·the·clipboard·(cut·and·paste):¶

1.→ Select·the·text·you·want·to·move.¶

2.→ Press·Shift+Delete·to·cut·the·selection·(move·the·text·to·the·clipboard).¶

FIGURE 3.2.
When using the Move key, Word can select a second area of text.

SUPER NOTE

Press Esc to cancel the Move mode.

PROCEDURE 3.2. MOVING TEXT WITH THE CLIPBOARD (CUT AND PASTE).

1. Select the text you want to move.
2. Press Shift+Delete to cut the selection (move the text to the clipboard).
3. Move the insertion point to where you want the text to appear (or, select an area if you're replacing text with the contents of the clipboard).
4. Press Shift+Insert to paste the contents of the clipboard.

SUPER NOTE

You can access the clipboard in any method you prefer: using the keystrokes indicated here, using the alternate keystrokes (Ctrl+C for Copy, Ctrl+X for Cut, and Ctrl+V for Paste), using the Edit menu (Edit | Copy, Edit | Cut, and Edit | Paste), or using the Copy, Cut, and Paste tools on the toolbar.

SUPER TIP

In Word for Windows 6, you can use the right mouse button to display a popup menu for working with the clipboard, as shown in Figure 3.3. This cuts down on the amount of wrist action required. Also, if you like the ergonomic benefits of popup context menus, then consider replacing Windows with OS/2 2. Word 6 works great under OS/2, and you'll have system-wide popup context menus.

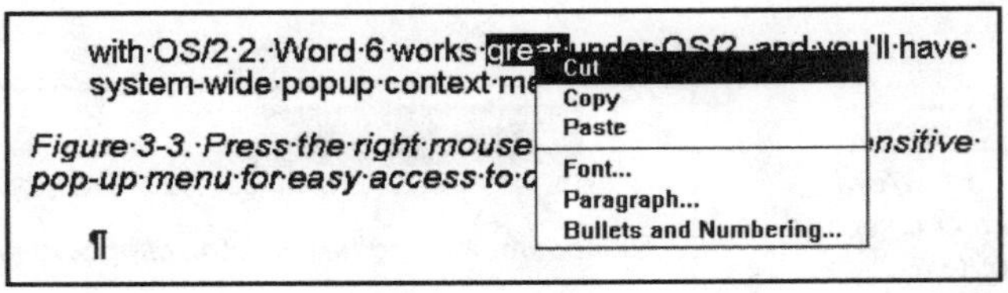

FIGURE 3.3.
Press the right mouse button for a context-sensitive popup menu for easy access to clipboard commands.

PROCEDURE 3.3. MOVING TEXT USING DRAG-AND-DROP.

1. Select the text you want to move.
2. Point the mouse anywhere in the select area and press the left mouse button; the cursor turns into a drag pointer (see Figure 3.4).
3. Move the mouse pointer to where you want the text moved (this is dragging).
4. Release the mouse button to drop the text at the mouse pointer location.

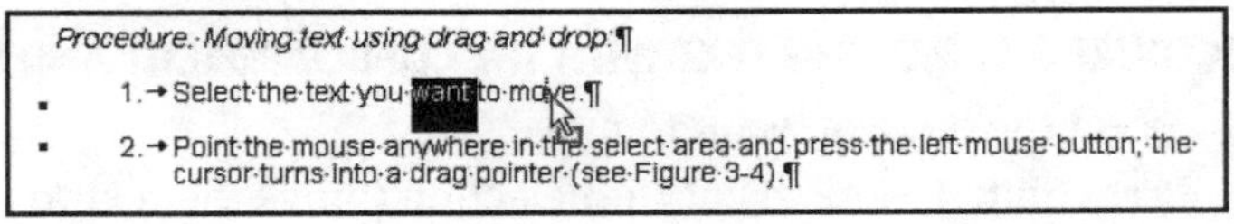

FIGURE 3.4.
The Drag pointer shows that you are dragging text to move it.

What if the selection just goes away in Step 2 rather than turning into a Drag pointer? If so, then perhaps Drag-and-Drop Editing is turned off. Select Tools | Options | View and ensure that Drag-and-Drop Text Editing is enabled.

Copying Text

You can copy text using the Copy key (Shift+F2), the clipboard, or drag-and-drop.

PROCEDURE 3.4. COPYING TEXT USING THE COPY KEY.

1. Select the text you want to copy.
2. Press Shift+F2.
3. Select the area to which you want to copy the selected text (the target selected area, if any, will be dotted, as shown in Figure 3.5).
4. Press Enter.

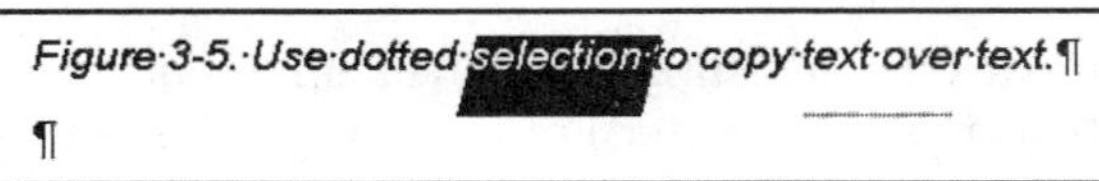
Figure·3-5.·Use·dotted·selection·to·copy·text·over·text.¶
¶

FIGURE 3.5.
Use dotted selection to copy text over text.

NOTE

Press Esc to cancel the Copy mode.

PROCEDURE 3.5. COPYING TEXT USING THE CLIPBOARD (COPY AND PASTE).

1. Select the text you want to copy.
2. Press Ctrl+Insert to copy the selection (copy the text to the clipboard).
3. Move the insertion point to where you want the text copied (or, select an area if you're replacing text with the contents of the clipboard).
4. Press Shift+Insert to paste the contents of the clipboard.

PROCEDURE 3.6. COPYING TEXT USING DRAG-AND-DROP.

1. Select the text you want to copy.
2. Point the mouse anywhere in the select area, press and hold the Ctrl key (see note), and the left mouse button. The + sign on the drag cursor indicates that the text will be copied instead of moved (see Figure 3.6).
3. Move the mouse pointer to where you want the text moved (this is dragging).
4. Release the mouse button to drop the text at the mouse pointer location.

FIGURE 3.6.
When copying, the drag cursor has a + sign to show that text is being copied.

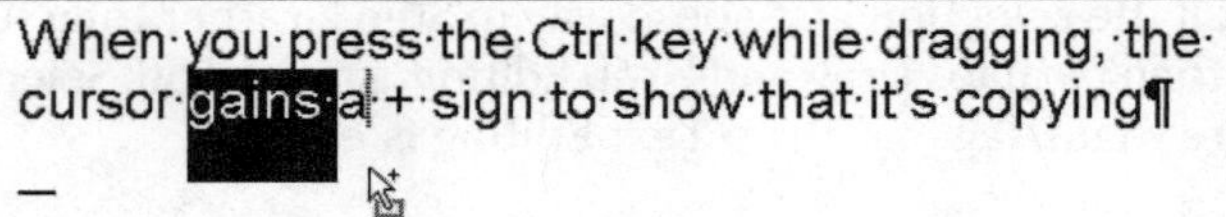

When·you·press·the·Ctrl·key·while·dragging,·the·
cursor·gains·a·+·sign·to·show·that·it's·copying¶

SUPER NOTE

Actually, you can press Ctrl at any point during Steps 2 through 4. The only requirement is you must hold the Ctrl key during Step 4. If you don't hold down the Ctrl key during Step 4, the selection is moved rather than copied.

Deleting Text

You delete text by selecting it and then either cutting it (which, in effect, copies it to the clipboard as it is deleted) or clearing it (which doesn't copy it to the clipboard first). To cut text, use any of the following:

- Select **E**dit | Cu**t** from the menu (the main menu or the right mouse button popup).
- Click the Cut tool (scissors) on the toolbar.
- Press Shift+Delete.

To delete text without first copying it to the clipboard, use either of the following:

- Select **E**dit | Cle**a**r from the menu (note that Edit | Clear isn't available from the right mouse button popup menu).
- Press Delete.

Basic Formatting

Formatting can be applied indirectly, by using styles, or directly, by using individual formatting controls. A style is a set of formats that has a name such as heading 1, footer, Normal (for typing most text), and so on. It's highly recommended that you use styles whenever possible. It makes document format management and subsequent editing much easier.

Using Styles

PROCEDURE 3.7. FORMATTING USING STYLES.

1. Move the insertion point to the paragraph you want to format (or select multiple paragraphs if you want to format more than one).
2. Click the style drop-arrow control in the Formatting toolbar (see Figure 3.7).
3. Click the style you want to apply.
4. If prompted "Do you want to redefine the style *name* based on the selection?," select No.

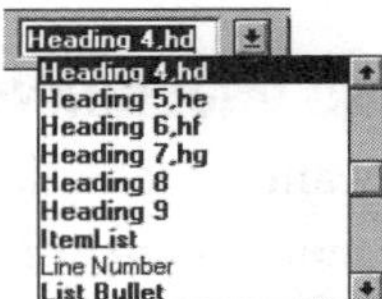

FIGURE 3.7.
The style drop-down arrow shows the list of current styles.

Using Direct Formatting

To apply direct formatting, the easiest way is to use the shortcut keys, the Formatting Toolbar, the ruler, or the text popup menu (click the right mouse button in the text you want to format), depending on what you want to do. These tools offer a combination of frequently used character and paragraph formatting.

PROCEDURE 3.8. APPLYING BOLD FORMATTING.

1. Select the text you want to be bold.
2. Click the bold icon on the Formatting toolbar (see Figure 3.8); alternatively, you can press Ctrl+B.

SUPER TIP

Unlike Word for Windows Version 2, if text is not selected when you choose character formatting, the whole word nearest the insertion point is changed, not just the insertion point. For example, to embolden a single word, move the insertion point to between the first and last letters of the word and press Ctrl+B (or click the Bold button on the Formatting toolbar). This works with other character (font) formatting as well.

FIGURE 3.8.
The bold icon.

PROCEDURE 3.9. APPLYING ITALICS.

1. Select the text you want to be italicized.
2. Click the italic icon on the Formatting toolbar (see Figure 3.9); alternatively, you can press Ctrl+I.

FIGURE 3.9.
The italic icon.

PROCEDURE 3.10. APPLYING UNDERLINING.

1. Select the text you want to be underlined.
2. Click the underline icon on the Formatting toolbar (see Figure 3.10); alternatively, you can press Ctrl+U.

FIGURE 3.10.
The underlining icon.

PROCEDURE 3.11. LEFT-ALIGNING A PARAGRAPH.

1. Select the text you want left-aligned.
2. Click the left alignment icon on the Formatting toolbar (see Figure 3.11); alternatively, you can press Ctrl+L.

FIGURE 3.11.
The left alignment icon.

PROCEDURE 3.12. CENTERING A PARAGRAPH.

1. Select the text you want centered.
2. Click the center alignment icon on the Formatting toolbar (see Figure 3.12); alternatively, you can press Ctrl+E.

FIGURE 3.12.
The center alignment icon.

PROCEDURE 3.13. JUSTIFYING A PARAGRAPH.

1. Select the text you want justified.
2. Click on the justify icon on the Formatting toolbar (see Figure 3.13); alternatively, you can press Ctrl+J.

FIGURE 3.13.
The justify icon.

PROCEDURE 3.14. CHANGING FONTS.

1. Select the text you want to format.
2. Click the down arrow to the right of the font display box (see Figure 3.14).
3. Click the font you want to apply.

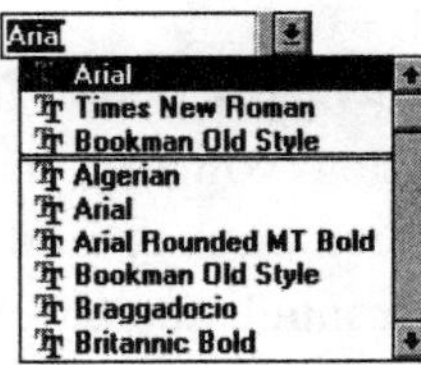

FIGURE 3.14.
The font drop-down arrow displays the list of available fonts. The current font is initially selected.

PROCEDURE 3.15. CHANGING POINT SIZES.

1. Select the text you want to format.
2. Click the down arrow to the right of the point size display box (see Figure 3.15).
3. Click the point size you want to apply.

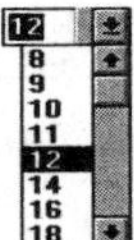

FIGURE 3.15.
The point size drop-down arrow displays available point sizes.

PROCEDURE 3.16. CHANGING MULTIPLE FONT OR PARAGRAPH FORMAT SETTINGS AT ONCE.

1. Select the text you want to format.
2. Click the right mouse button in the selected text to display the Context menu (see Figure 3.16).
3. Click Font or Paragraph, or Bullets and Numbering, depending on what kind of formatting you want to apply.

4. Select your format options.
5. Click OK or press Enter.

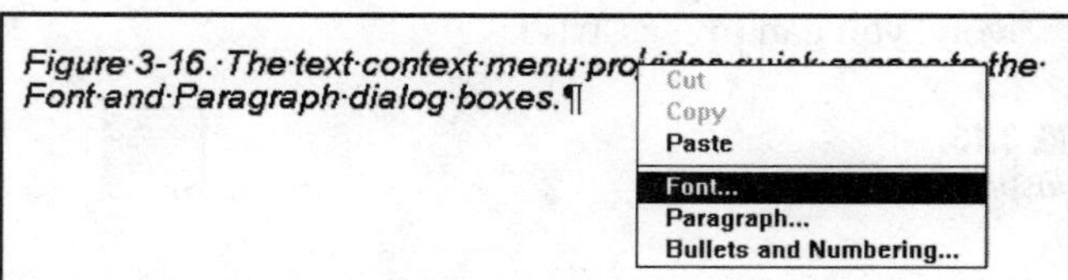

FIGURE 3.16.
The Text context menu provides quick access to the Font and Paragraph dialog boxes.

Printing

Printing is covered in detail in the Printing Workshop. For now, let's just look at the very basics.

PROCEDURE 3.17. PRINTING THE CURRENT DOCUMENT USING THE DEFAULT SETTINGS.

1. Display the document you want to print.
2. Click the Printer icon on the Standard toolbar (see Figure 3.17).
3. If you change your mind, quickly click Cancel.

FIGURE 3.17.
Use the Standard Toolbar's Printer tool to print using the current defaults.

PROCEDURE 3.18. PRINTING THE CURRENT DOCUMENT WITH OPTIONS.

1. Display the document you want to print.
2. Select the portion of the document you want to print, if desired.
3. Select **File**|**Print** from the menu.
4. Select the options you want to use.
5. Click OK.

Saving

Until you save a document, your edits exist only in memory. Saving is the process of making a copy of what's in memory onto your disk.

PROCEDURE 3.19. SAVING CHANGES TO A DOCUMENT.

1. Select **File**|**Save**.

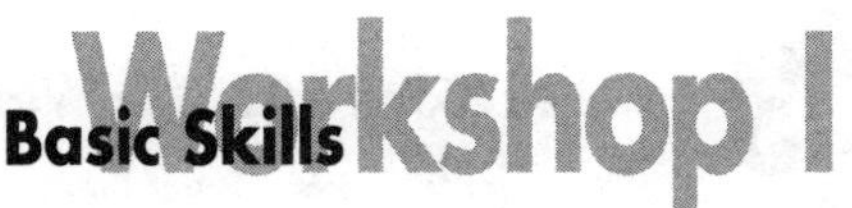

2. If this is the first time a document has been saved, you will be prompted to type a name, as shown in Figure 3.18. Type just a name for the document; Word will automatically add the .DOC extension to the name you give.

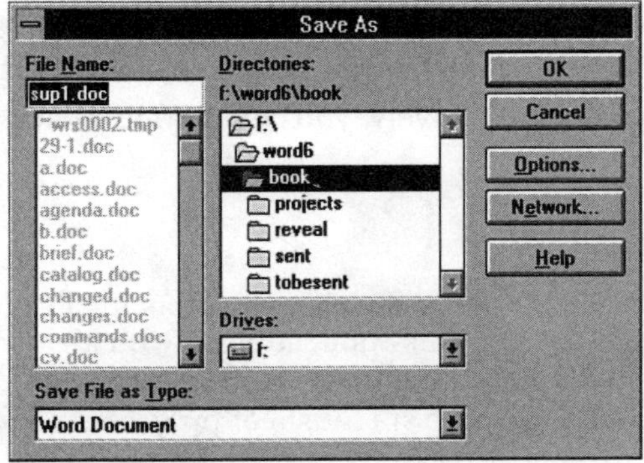

FIGURE 3.18.
The Save As dialog box.

3. If Document Information is turned on, you will be prompted to supply Summary Information (see Figure 3.19). If you make a habit of filling out this information, you can use it later as a basis for searching and organizing your work. You also will have the option of using summary information in your document. Fill out the summary information and click OK. Or, press Esc or select Cancel if you don't want to fill out the summary information at this time.

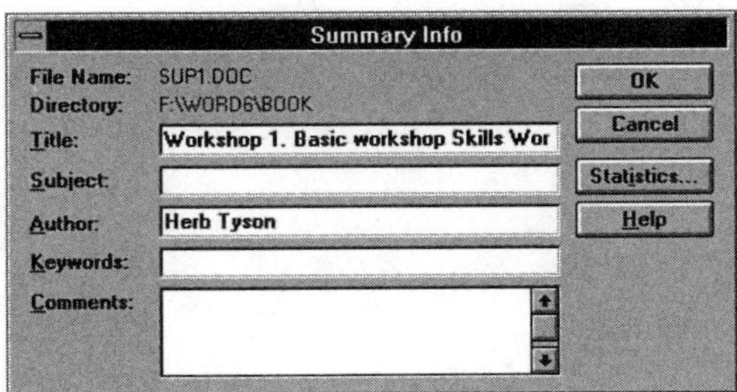

FIGURE 3.19.
The Summary Information dialog box.

Editing an Existing Document

To edit an existing document, you must open it. Some other word processing programs may refer to this as Retrieving, Loading, Calling, Editing, or something else.

PROCEDURE 3.20. OPENING AN EXISTING WORD DOCUMENT.

1. Select **File**|**Open** (or click the Open tool in the Standard toolbar or press Ctrl+O).

2. Click the arrow to the right of Drives to select the drive on which the file is stored.
3. Click the directories listed to navigate, as necessary, to the appropriate subdirectory. Clicking a directory displays all subdirectories for it. All files in the displayed directory are shown in the File Name list box.
4. When you see the file you want to open, click it.
5. Click OK. Alternatively, you could double-click the file to open it.

SUPER NOTE

Word provides the ability to automatically convert a variety of documents from other applications. If you installed the appropriate conversion filters, you can use Word to edit files from other word processing programs, some spreadsheet programs, as well as some database programs. A common mistake for beginners is thinking the conversion will be perfect. It seldom is. However, it's so much better than what word processing program users had to go through in the past that practically nobody complains about the poor quality of conversions.

Printing Workshop

In this workshop, we focus on printing and printer setup. After all, that's the ultimate mission of a word processor for most of us. In Chapter 4, "Printing," you'll learn about printing methods and techniques, as well as how to overcome some basic problems. In Chapter 5, "Printer Setup," you'll learn about installing and setting up printers and fonts.

Chapter

Printing

It may surprise some of you to know that there are some Word users who never print. Consider, for example, some authors who deliver their manuscripts electronically. Many office workers use Word to compose reports and letters and pass them along to a production department that oversees formatting and printing. If you're one of those lucky people, you've probably already skipped this chapter. Right? Right? Hey, where'd you go?

Printing a Document

Word offers several ways to initiate printing. To begin printing immediately, accepting all defaults, just click the Printer icon on the Standard toolbar. By default, this executes the `FilePrintDefault` command. While Word is formatting and spooling (sending the print job to a file for printing), you can cancel the print job by clicking the Cancel button displayed in Figure 4.1.

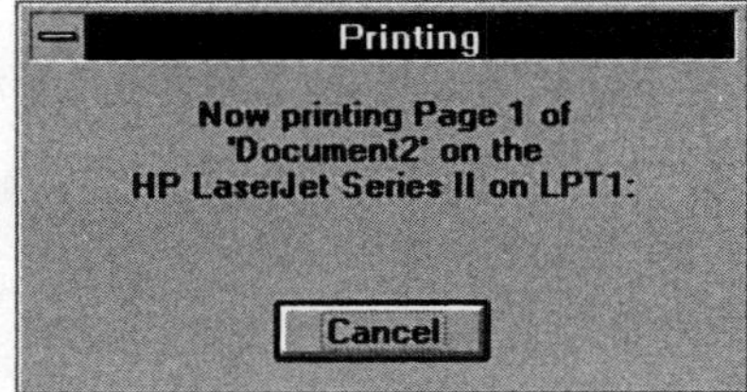

FIGURE 4.1.
Click quick to cancel! When you print using the toolbar, Word assumes all current defaults.

SUPER TIP

If you like using the toolbar for printing but would rather not automatically use the defaults, you can change the command assigned to the Printer icon to FilePrint. See Chapter 48, "Customizing Toolbars," for additional information on changing the toolbar.

The File Print Dialog

To print using the menu, select **File | Print**. Word then displays the dialog box shown in Figure 4.2. To accept the defaults displayed, just click OK. You can also change any of the options shown.

FIGURE 4.2.
*The **File** | **Print** dialog box.*

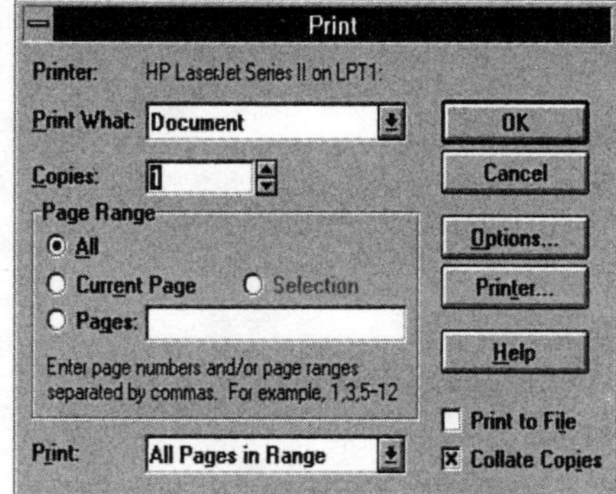

SUPER TIP

You can also select the File | Print dialog by pressing Ctrl+P.

Print and Print Preview may be dimmed as unavailable. You're ready to print something and discover for the first time that Print and Print Preview are not available as options. In Windows, it's not enough to have a printer connected. You have to tell Windows that it's connected. If the Print and Print Preview options are dimmed, it usually means that Windows doesn't "know" that you have a printer. See Chapter 5, "Printer Setup," for information on installing printers and fonts for use under Windows.

PROCEDURE 4.1. PRINTING USING THE FILE | PRINT DIALOG BOX.

1. Preview your document to ensure that the formatting is correct.
2. Select **File** | **Print**.
3. Ensure that the selected printer is the one you want to use (see Figure 4.3). If not, click Printer and select the appropriate printer, clicking OK to return to the Print dialog box.
4. Select any options or settings you need (see the following sections for details).
5. Click OK.

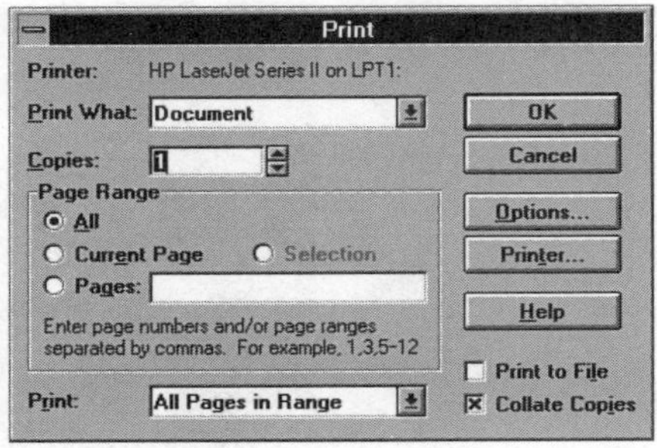

FIGURE 4.3.
The Print dialog box shows the current printer.

Print What

The **P**rint What option lets you select any of the following to be printed, as shown in Figure 4.4:

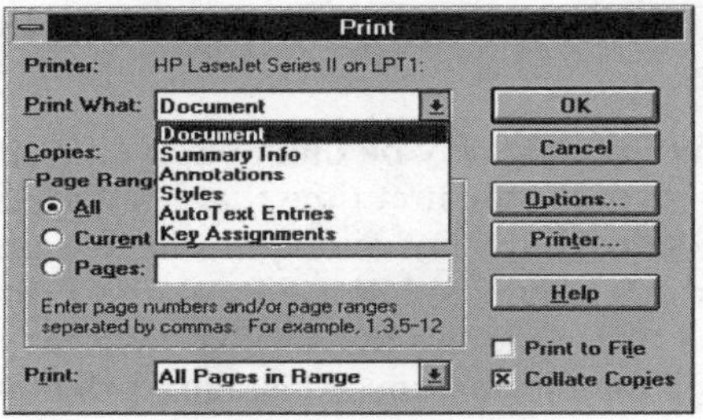

FIGURE 4.4.
*Click the **P**rint What drop-down arrow to display the print options.*

Document	Prints the displayed document (Note: If the document is displayed in Outline view, then just the outline levels showing will be printed.)
Summary Info	Prints the full document information summary, as shown in Figure 4.5
Annotations	Prints just the annotations for a document (Note: To print the annotations at the same time as you print the document, select the Options button from the Print dialog box, and click Annotations. Unfortunately, the annotations will be printed at the end of the document rather than in context.)
Styles	Prints a list of styles contained in the current document along with the formatting specifications for each style, as shown in Figure 4.6
AutoText	Prints a list of AutoText entries along with the text assigned to them
Key Assignments	Prints a list of all user-defined key assignments (key name and the assigned command or macro)

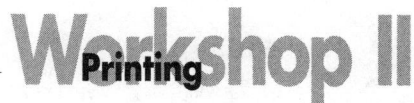

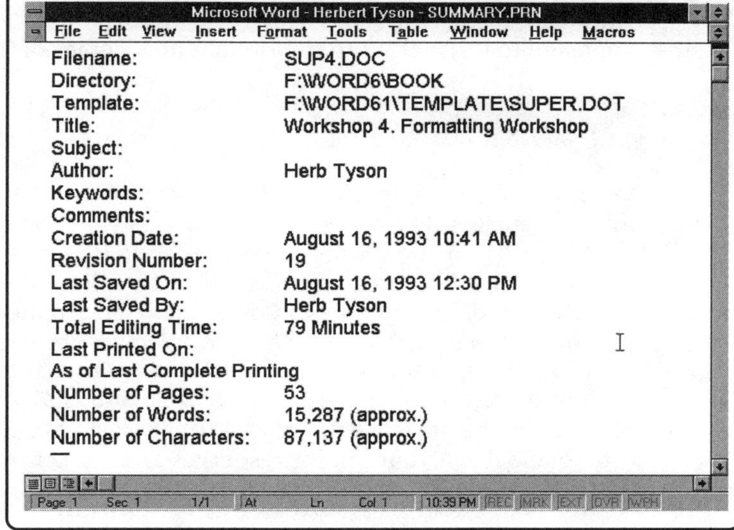

FIGURE 4.5. *Document Summary Information can be printed from the Print dialog box.*

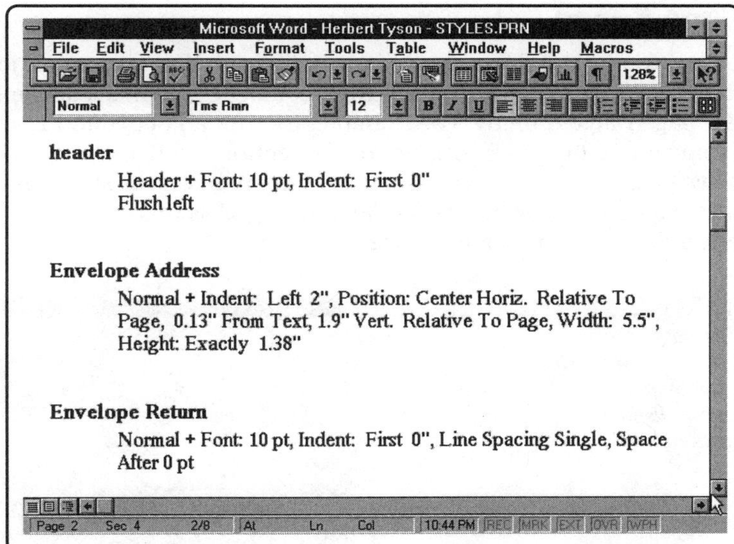

FIGURE 4.6. *Print a list of styles to help with document planning, management, and training.*

Copies

Use this command to instruct Word to print multiple copies of the document.

SUPER TIP

When printing multiple copies on most laser printers, you can speed up printing considerably by turning off collation (the Collate Copies checkbox). If you allow Word to collate, it will have to format and print each page once for each copy. If you turn off collation, Word formats just once, sending a Number of Copies command to the laser printer. This makes the printer mimic a copying machine for each page after the first page. If you're printing three copies of a 100-page document, turning collation off can save as much as 20 or 30 minutes for most laser printers. On the other hand, somebody will then have to collate those pages manually. If your printer resources are scarcer than your human resources, however, this is a handy thing to know.

Page Range

Use the range to tell Word which pages to print. You can specify just pages or a combination of pages and sections. If the document contains a single section, just specify the page range directly. For example, to print all of Section 2, specify *s2* in both the From and To boxes. To print part of a section, such as Pages 3 through 12 in Section 3, use a combination of pages and section numbers, as shown in Figure 4.7. Note that page numbers come before sections—illogical as this may seem. The *p* is optional (for example, *1s2* is the same as *p1s2*).

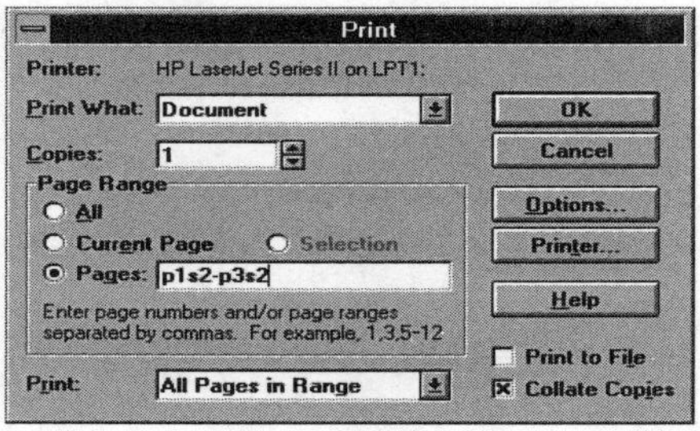

FIGURE 4.7.
The Page Range option lets you print page by page within distinct sections.

SUPER CAUTION

When printing a multisection document, the page range refers to the logical page numbers in the document rather than the actual numbers that appear on the page. For example, when printing a document that contains non-Arabic page numbers (such as *a*, *b*, *c* or *i*, *ii*, *iii*), a range of 1 to 3 means a to c or i to iii. If the document contains a mixture of non-Arabic page numbers (as in a preface or forward) and Arabic page numbers, the numbering encompasses both. If your document has i through v followed by 1 through 50, a range of 1 through 50 would print pages i through 45. Surprise! To avoid surprises, specify pages and section number when printing parts of multisection documents.

SUPER NOTE

To set page numbers for different document sections, select **V**iew | **H**eader and Footer then click the page numbers icon (#). See Chapter 14, "Bullets, Numbered Lists, and Outline Numbering," for additional information.

Print

Use this option (see Figure 4.8) to select among printing all pages in the selected range, just odd, or just even pages. The default is to print all pages (odd and even). You might want to depart from the default if you're printing one side of a two-sided document.

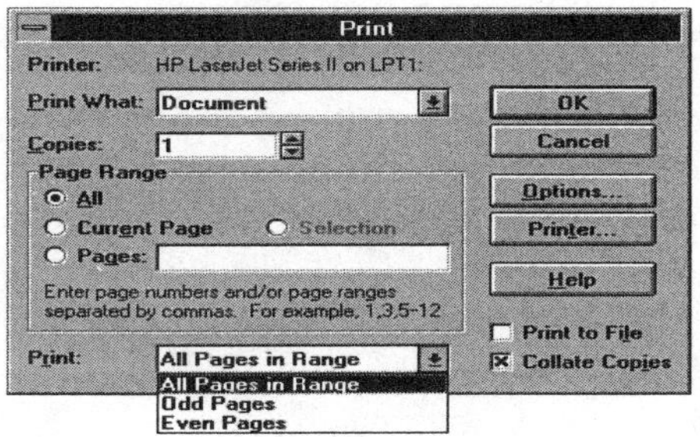

FIGURE 4.8.
Use the Print list to tell Word to print all, just odd, or just even pages.

Print to File

The Print to File option lets you direct printer-formatted text to a file. The file you print will be printer-ready and can be printed elsewhere without using Word or Windows. The primary intended use for this feature is to make Word's printed results portable. The resulting file can be printed on any IBM-compatible (DOS, Windows, or OS/2) equipped with the corresponding printer. This makes it possible for a WinWord user who doesn't have a PostScript printer at home, for example, to take the resulting file to work and print it on the office PostScript printer from any PC.

PROCEDURE 4.2. PRINTING A DOCUMENT TO A FILE PRINTING ELSEWHERE.

1. Select **File | Print**.
2. Select the appropriate print, copies, and range option.
3. Click Printer, and select the printer corresponding to the printer that ultimately will be used to print the document; click the Set as Default Printer option; and then click Close to return to the main Print dialog box.
4. Click the Print to File box.
5. Click OK.
6. When prompted to do so, type a name for the file. Make sure there's room on the disk for the resulting file. Some printer-ready files can be very large.
7. Copy the resulting file to diskette.

SUPER NOTE

Some files will be too large to fit on a single 1.44M diskette. In such cases, it is useful to compress (using PKZIP or another suitable compression/archiver) the file. Some compression programs will compress files directly to multiple floppy diskettes. Another alternative is to use a backup program to copy the file to diskettes. In all instances, however, keep in mind that the system in which you intend to print the file must have the necessary utilities to restore, copy, and decompress the resulting diskettes. A safe but time-consuming strategy is to use DOS's Backup command. It does not compress. However, almost all DOS and OS/2 systems can retrieve files using their respective Restore commands. To use Backup to copy a single file called C:\DOC\PRINT.OUT to the A drive:

Type `BACKUP C:\DOC\PRINT.OUT A:`

You don't need to include the drive and directory specification if you're currently in the correct directory. To use Restore to copy that file at the destination:

Type `RESTORE A: \DOC\PRINT.OUT`

> When restoring a single file by name, you must use the subdirectory name but not the disk. If a corresponding subdirectory doesn't exist, it will be created. You could then change to the directory where the file was copied and use the Print or Copy commands to print the file. For example:
>
> ```
> CD \DOC
>
> PRINT /B PRINT.OUT
> ```

GENERIC/TEXT

When printing to file using the Generic/Text printer drivers, the results often are not what users expect. When using the Generic/Text driver to print to a file, Word prints some lines three times. Why does this happen? The problem is that some users mistakenly believe this to be the correct method for creating an unformatted text file. It's not. To Word, you're simply printing to an ancient impact-type printer. In order to accomplish bolding, it prints some lines three times. If you just want the document as plain text without formatting, use Word's File | Save As command and select whichever flavor of Plain Text best suits your needs.

There are times, however, when File | Save As won't get you where you want to go. For example, if you want a text file that contains just the outline of a document, Save As won't help because it saves either the whole document or just the aspects listed in the Print list box in the Print dialog box.

If you want a text file that contains just the outline, the closest you can come is by using the Generic/Text printer driver. You probably will not like the results very much, however. Not only will you see triple lines where bolding occurs but also underlining characters where underlining was supposed to occur. Moreover, text that spans more than one line will have hard line breaks, and the text will be offset to the right by the amounts of right and hanging margins. All in all, it's not a terribly satisfactory solution. For a better solution, see Chapter 40, "Outlining."

Collate Copies

The Collate option is relevant only when printing multiple copies. If collating is turned on, Word prints Pages 1, 2, 3,... for the first copy and then goes back and prints Pages 1, 2, 3,... for each additional copy of the document. If collating is turned off, then Word prints multiple copies of each page as it comes to it. For example, if you're printing three copies, you would get Pages 1, 1, 1, 2, 2, 2, 3, 3, 3,....

If printing speed is essential, turn collating off when printing multiple copies. If minimizing manual labor (for example, having to collate by hand) is a priority, then turn collating on.

Printer

The Printer button is a link to the Windows Control Panel Printer Setup, discussed more fully in Chapter 5, "Printer Setup." The presence of this button in the Print dialog enables you to change printers and some limited setup options at the last moment (see Figure 4.9). The Print options let you permanently select a number of options that apply to the current and all future printing (until you change them, of course). Note that access to the full printer setup is no longer possible from Word 6 as it was under Word for Windows 2.0. You must now use the Windows Control Panel to access all the printer setup options.

FIGURE 4.9.
The Printer button lets you select the printer and some limited options.

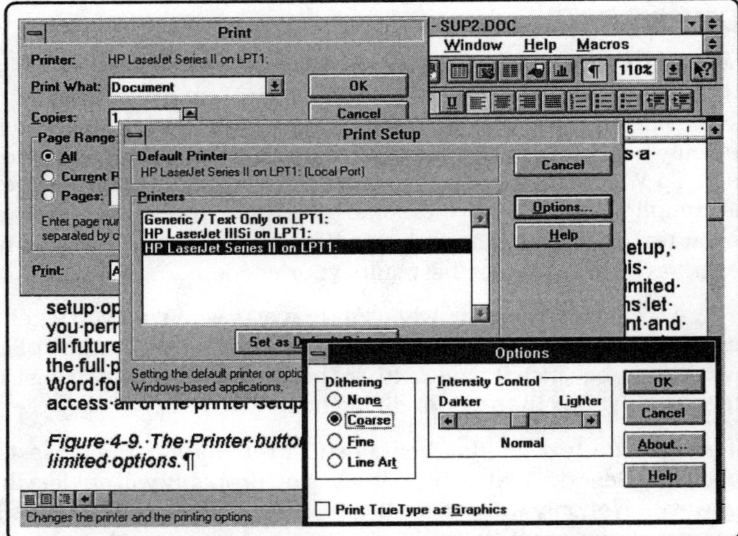

Options

The Options button is a link to **Tools** | **Options** | **Print**, shown in Figure 4.10. The Print Options dialog box lets you set a number of printing options without having to close the Print dialog box.

DRAFT OUTPUT

This option substitutes quick formatting indicators (such as underlining for more complex character formatting and blank frames for pictures) for actual formatting. The result is faster printing that uses less ink or toner.

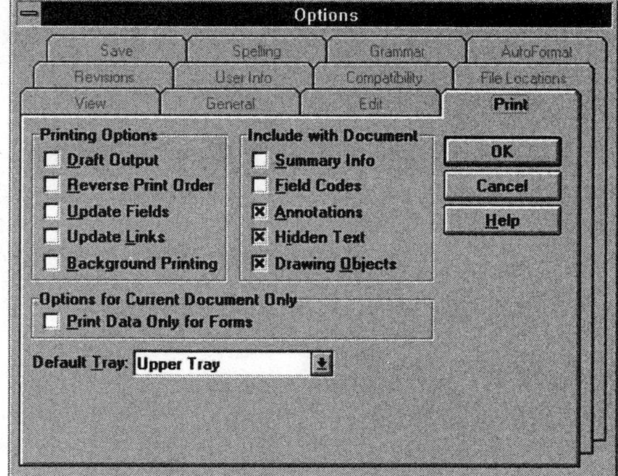

FIGURE 4.10.
The Print Options dialog box.

SUPER NOTE

Unfortunately, Word doesn't suppress all formatting. Consequently, you can't use this option as a method for eliminating triple-printing of bold lines when trying to save an outline to a text file.

REVERSE PRINT ORDER

Select this option to tell Word to print the pages in reverse order, from last to first. On many laser printers, when you leave the rear output tray open (for envelopes and labels, for example), collated print jobs come out backwards. If you select the Reverse Print Order option, you'll get slightly slower printing, but the jobs will be collated correctly.

UPDATE FIELDS

Use this option to force Word to update and resolve all field codes before printing. If the field codes are already updated, this option can slow down printing considerably, depending on how many field codes are contained in the document. On the other hand, having to reprint a long document due to field codes that haven't been updated can waste both time and paper. Ben Franklin clearly had field codes in mind when he said *Haste makes waste.*

UPDATE LINKS

Use this option to tell Word to update any linked information in the document before printing. If linked graphics files or other documents have changed, this tells Word to use the most recent versions available rather than the information that was available

the last time the links were updated. If you want to use the information as it currently displays in the file, however, make sure that the Update Links option is not checked.

BACKGROUND PRINTING

This option tells Word to try to print in the background while you continue to work. This option slows printing down and uses a fair amount of memory. If printing time and memory are not considerations, you may find this setting to your liking. If you have a very long document, however, it really does take a long time and eats up a lot of memory.

SUMMARY INFO

Summary information is the collection of information shown in Figure 4.11. Using the Print list box in the Print dialog, you can selectively print summary information for any given document—but you have to print the summary information and the document itself in separate steps if you go that route. The Print Options dialog enables you to tell Word to include summary information each time you print. The summary information is printed at the end of the document, starting on a new page.

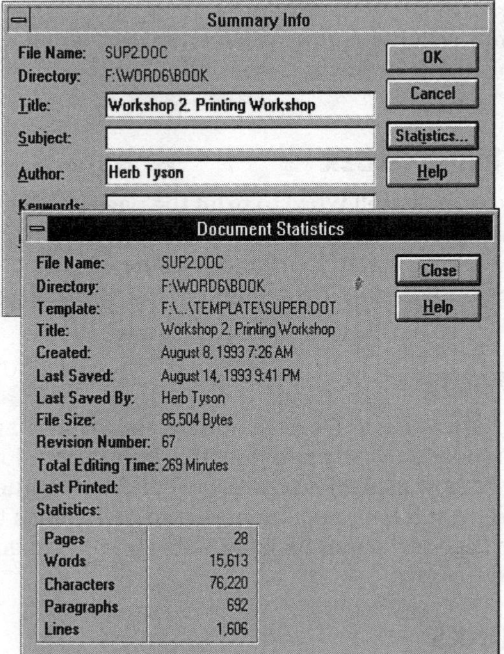

FIGURE 4.11. *Summary information.*

FIELD CODES

The Field Codes option tells Word to print the actual field codes instead of field code results. For example, a sequence number field would print verbatim as *{seq chano}* rather than as the actual sequence number. This is similar to what you see when you toggle field codes on by pressing Shift+F9 while displaying a document in Word. Turning on field codes can be a useful way of checking formulas, index entries, and other field matter that often gets taken for granted after the first insertion. If you have passage insertions from other documents (for example, boilerplate text), this technique can also speed up printing and save paper, letting you review just the parts of the document that aren't already boilerplated.

> **SUPER CAUTION**
>
> When printing with field codes turned on, pagination will usually be different from pagination with field results turned on.

ANNOTATIONS

The Annotations option causes any document annotations to be printed at the end of the document. Unfortunately, there is no way to force Word to print the annotations in context, where most annotation users believe annotations belong. As an alternative, some users find it beneficial to use revision marking, footnotes, or hidden text for annotations during the drafting phase of a document.

HIDDEN TEXT

Use the Hidden Text option to cause Word to include hidden text when printing a document. Unlike Word's poorly thought-out annotation feature, hidden text is printed in context. Some people use hidden text for production and formatting instructions, while others use hidden text for annotations. Hidden text is a character formatting attribute that you can apply by selecting F**o**rmat | **F**ont.

> **SUPER TIP**
>
> If you plan to use hidden text for annotations, you can make it easier to use by creating a special style for it (for example, call it Note). Unlike previous versions of Word for Windows, version 6 lets you create and apply character-based styles within paragraphs.

DRAWING OBJECTS

Use this option to tell Word to print drawing objects created in Word. If you are printing a draft, you can save time by not printing complicated graphics or other artwork that's otherwise not in question. When you're just trying to edit text, it doesn't make sense to spend valuable time and toner printing pictures. On the other hand, when printing the final version, you will need to make sure this option is enabled.

PRINT DATA ONLY FOR FORMS

This option causes Word to print just the data portion of forms. Use this option if you are using preprinted forms for the paper supply and just want Word to fill in the blanks. If you want Word to print the form as well, then deselect this option.

DEFAULT TRAY

This option is available only if it's supported by the printer driver currently in use. Use this option to tell Word where the paper will be coming from, by default.

SUPER TIP

You can set the paper source on a per-document basis (or a per-template basis) using File | Page Setup | Paper Source.

Print Preview

Print Preview lets you get an idea how the document will appear when printed. It's a good way to ensure that headers, footers, headings, footnotes, graphics, and other major document parts appear where they should. It's also a good way to touch up formatting. To display your document as it will appear when printed, select File | Print Preview. Alternatively, you can click the Preview tool in the Standard toolbar, shown in Figure 4.12.

FIGURE 4.12.
Click the Preview tool to see how your document will look when printed.

Using either method changes the view to that shown in Figure 4.13. Print Preview mode is a special editing view that gives you additional tools for viewing and editing your document prior to printing. When you first select Print Preview mode, you are in Zoom mode.

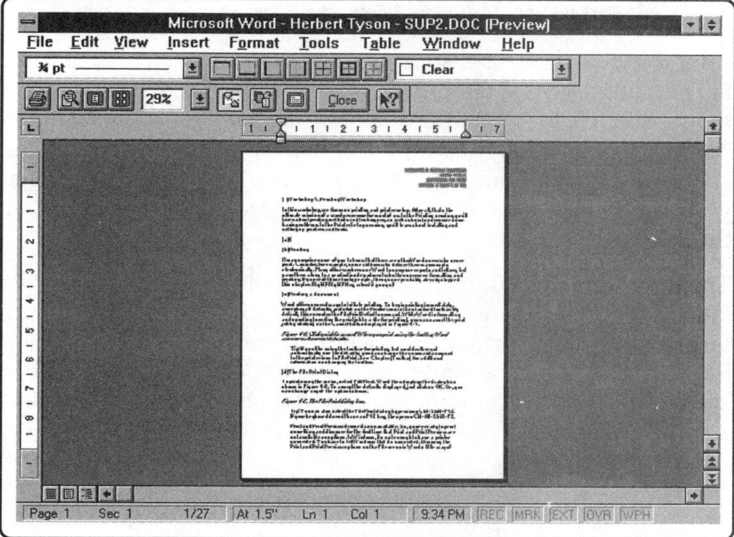

FIGURE 4.13.
Print Preview shows how your document will be printed.

SUPER UPGRADE NOTE

The Print Preview mode is radically different from its counterpart in previous versions of Word for Windows. The most significant change is that the text is fully editable in Print Preview mode. The methods for changing margins are also different, as is the array of available tools, shown in Figure 4.13.

SUPER CAUTION

Be careful about double-clicking window control icons while in Print Preview mode. As shown in Figure 4.13, the preview window omits a document control icon. The control icon shown here is for Word as a whole, not for the document displayed. Note too that, when in Print Preview mode, you cannot switch document windows. Also, as you'll discover, Print Preview mode uses a lot of memory and other system resources. Therefore, use this mode strategically. Once Windows 3.1 system resources fall below 60 percent, you'll often begin to see bizarre behavior in applications, such as incomplete list boxes and an apparent nonresponsiveness to commands. Sometimes this behavior occurs without corresponding error messages about a low memory condition.

The Preview Working Screen

Print Preview mode is a special editing view that gives you additional tools for viewing and editing your document prior to printing. When you first select Print Preview mode, you are in Zoom mode. Note the shape of the mouse pointer in Figure 4.14. In Zoom mode, clicking the cursor on a part of the screen toggles between a view that shows whole pages and a view that shows a 100 percent-sized view of the page on which you click. The pointer shape shows the direction (- for zoom out and + for zoom in) of the next click action.

The alternative to Zoom mode is Edit mode. If you click the Zoom toggle (see the following section) button, Word switches into Edit mode in which you are free to edit, insert, delete, and format the document just as you are in normal (nonpreview) mode. Because Print Preview mode uses so much Windows resources memory, however, you are not free to move among different document windows while Print Preview mode is active.

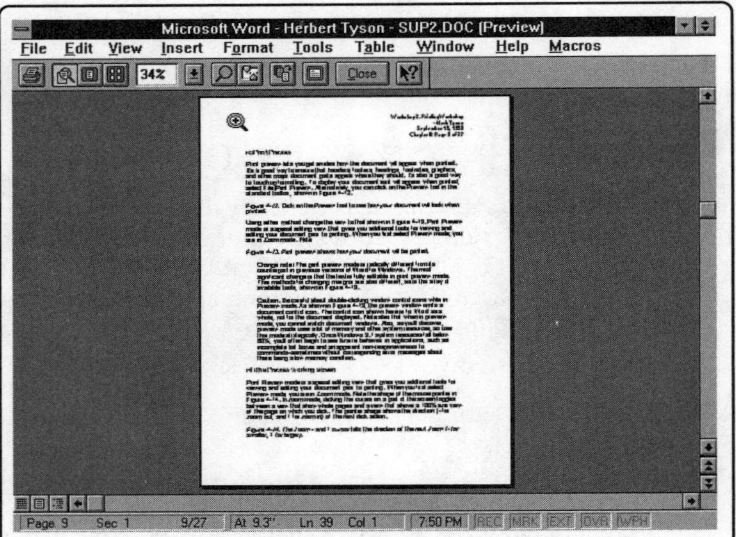

FIGURE 4.14.
The Zoom - and + cursors tells the direction of the next zoom (- for smaller, + for larger).

Print

Click the Print button to print directly from Print Preview mode.

Toggle Zoom In/Out and Edit Modes (Magnifier Tool)

Use the Magnifier button to toggle between Zoom and Edit modes. When Zoom mode is active, the Magnifier toggle button icon has a bright white background. When it is not active, the icon has a plain gray background. Shown with a zoom-in cursor in

Figure 4.14, when Zoom mode is active, the mouse pointer is a magnifying glass with a + (zoom in) or a - (zoom out) sign. Click the plus sign to magnify the area you click to 100 percent. Click the minus sign to zoom out to view whole pages. You can use the zoom percentage tool to set the zoom level at a specific value other than 100 percent if you prefer, even when Zoom mode is not active.

Show Single Whole Page

Use the Single Page button to display a single whole page as it will be printed. This is the default view when you first select Print Preview mode.

Show Multiple Pages

Use the Multi-Page button to display as many as 24 pages at the same time.

PROCEDURE 4.3. DISPLAYING MULTIPLE PAGES IN PRINT PREVIEW MODE.

1. Move the mouse pointer over the Multi-Page button.
2. Press the left mouse button and drag the button down and to the right; the button expands into a graphic that lets you select the number of pages to display.
3. Release the mouse button when the display is correct.

Zoom Control

Use the Zoom Control tool to set the exact zoom level. The Zoom Control tool works even when you're not in Zoom mode.

PROCEDURE 4.4. SETTING THE ZOOM LEVEL.

1. Click the adjustment arrow to the right of the Zoom Control tool; a list of preset percentages appears.
2. Click the percentage you want to display.

SUPER

Alternatively, you can click the zoom percentage field itself and type any value between 10 and 200 percent.

Toggle Both Rulers On and Off (the View Ruler Tool)

Use the View Ruler toggle button to turn the horizontal and vertical rulers on and off. This option provides more display space for the document, especially in Multi-Page view. For even more display space, see the discussion of the Full-Screen button later in this chapter.

Shrink to Fit

Use the Shrink to Fit button to tell Word to reduce the font to fit the text on as few pages as possible. In theory, this is a good idea if you have a letter that barely spills onto the next page and the resulting font reduction is trivial (for example, from 12 to 11 points). However, if you have a multipage document, Word might reduce the font to as low as 7.5 or even 5.5 points. That might be fine if you're trying to produce captions for all those angels that are said to fit on the head of a pin; however, it makes for rather poor reading. If you don't like the result of shrinking to fit, press Alt+Backspace until the font is back to normal.

PROCEDURE 4.5. SHRINKING TO FIT.

1. Display the document you want to shrink.
2. Click the Shrink to Fit button.

SUPER NOTE

If the document still doesn't fit, you have several options. One (and often a better option) is to modify the paragraph formatting to reduce spacing between paragraphs. For example, if you're currently using 12 points between paragraphs, reducing that to 6 or 9 points will still provide adequate paragraph separation while reducing the page count dramatically.

SUPER TIP

The Shrink to Fit button will work from all view modes—not just from Print Preview mode. However, it doesn't show up on any of the default toolbars. To make Shrink to Fit available in other views, add it to one of your existing toolbars. See Chapter 48, "Customizing Toolbars," for additional information.

Full-Screen Toggle

Use the Full-Screen toggle button to hide all menus, scroll bars, rulers, status bar, and the title bar. In Full-Screen view, only the Full-Screen button remains on-screen, as shown in Figure 4.15. Click the Full-Screen button to revert back to your familiar screen.

FIGURE 4.15.
Use the Full-Screen toggle button to start or leave Full-Screen mode.

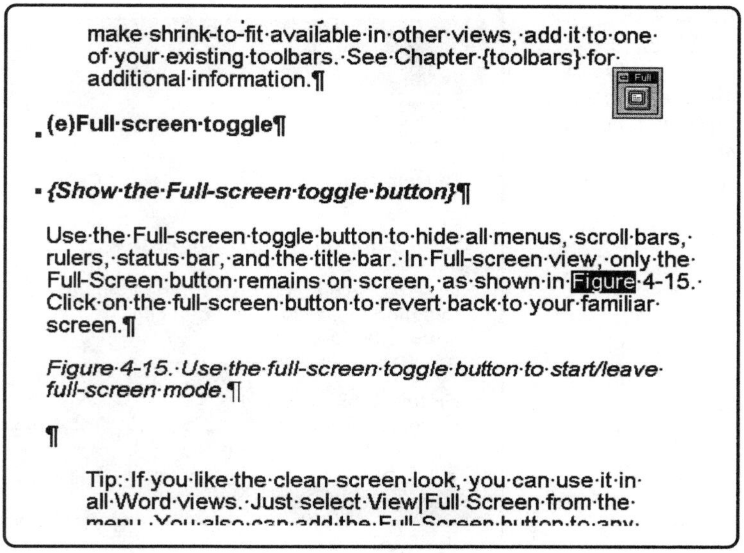

make·shrink-to-fit·available·in·other·views,·add·it·to·one·of·your·existing·toolbars.·See·Chapter·{toolbars}·for·additional·information.¶

(e)Full·screen·toggle¶

{Show·the·Full-screen·toggle·button}¶

Use·the·Full-screen·toggle·button·to·hide·all·menus,·scroll·bars,·rulers,·status·bar,·and·the·title·bar.·In·Full-screen·view,·only·the·Full-Screen·button·remains·on·screen,·as·shown·in·Figure·4-15.·Click·on·the·full-screen·button·to·revert·back·to·your·familiar·screen.¶

Figure·4-15.·Use·the·full-screen·toggle·button·to·start/leave·full-screen·mode.¶

¶

Tip:·If·you·like·the·clean-screen·look,·you·can·use·it·in·all·Word·views.·Just·select·View|Full·Screen·from·the·

SUPER TIP

If you like the clean-screen look, you can use it in all Word views. Just select View | Full Screen from the menu. You may also add the Full-Screen button to any toolbar (see Chapter 51). When in Full-Sreen view, all menus continue to work using keystrokes (for example, Alt+F for File, Alt+V for view, and so on.) The main menu is simply hidden off the top of the screen. A solitary full-screen toolbox floats on-screen to enable you to toggle back out of Full-Screen view. Full-Screen mode affects all of Word, not just the current window.

Close

Use the Close button to exit Print Preview mode. You can also press Esc at any time to go back to the previous view.

Help Pointer

Use the Help pointer button to display the Help pointer. When this mode is active, you can click text to display the underlying formatting details, as shown in Figure 4.16. Press Esc to exit the Help pointer mode.

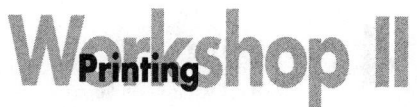

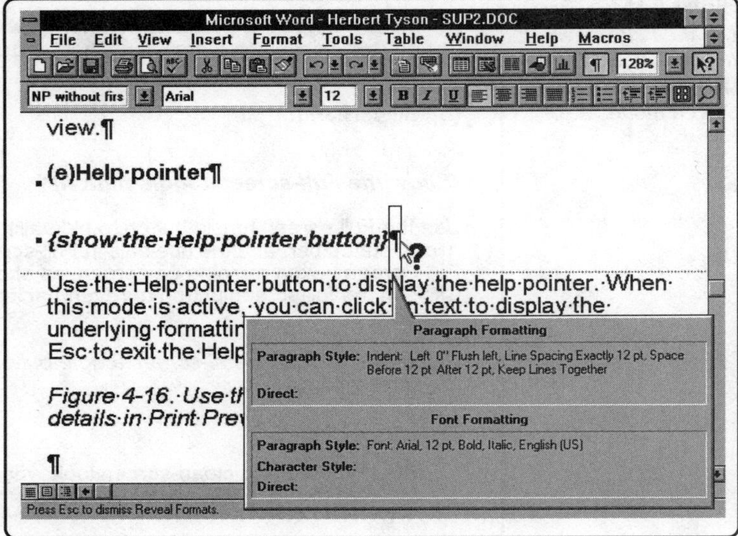

FIGURE 4.16. *Use the Help Pointer to display formatting details in Print Preview mode.*

Formatting and Editing in Print Preview Mode

All formatting controls work in Print Preview mode, as does text entry and editing (the latter does not work in Zoom mode). To adjust the top, bottom, left, and right margins, drag the horizontal or vertical ruler ends to a new measurement. The exposed gray area, shown in Figure 4.17, indicates the amount of white space at the corresponding edge of the paper.

The rulers change depending on the type of text that's selected. If the insertion point is in a header, footnote, frame, table, column text, or other special text area, the appropriate portions of the horizontal and vertical rulers are highlighted. You can expand or shrink the area for the selected text object by dragging the edges of the ruler, as shown in Figure 4.18.

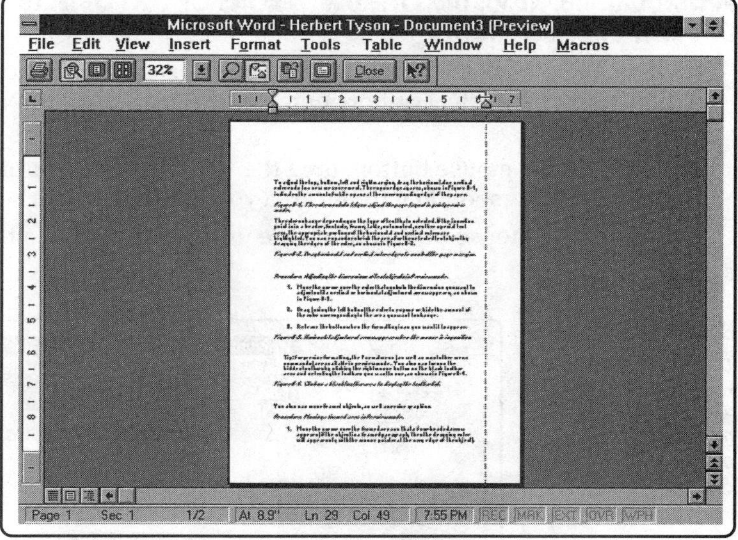

FIGURE 4.17.
The ruler controls let you adjust the page layout in Print Preview mode.

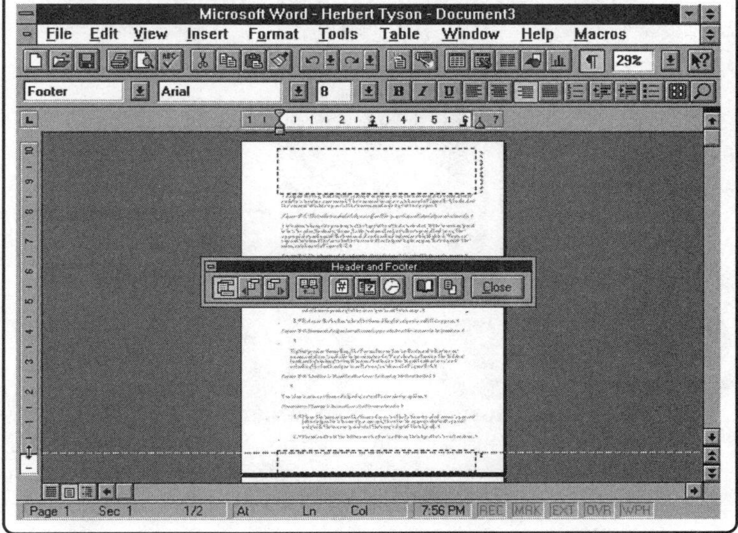

FIGURE 4.18.
Drag horizontal and vertical ruler edges to control the selected text object.

PROCEDURE 4.6. ADJUSTING THE DIMENSIONS OF TEXT OBJECTS IN PRINT PREVIEW MODE.

1. Move the cursor over the ruler that controls the dimension you want to adjust until a vertical or horizontal adjustment arrow appears, as shown in Figure 4.19.
2. Using the left mouse button, drag the ruler to expose or hide the amount of the ruler corresponding to the area you want to change.
3. Release the mouse button when the formatting provides the desired appearance.

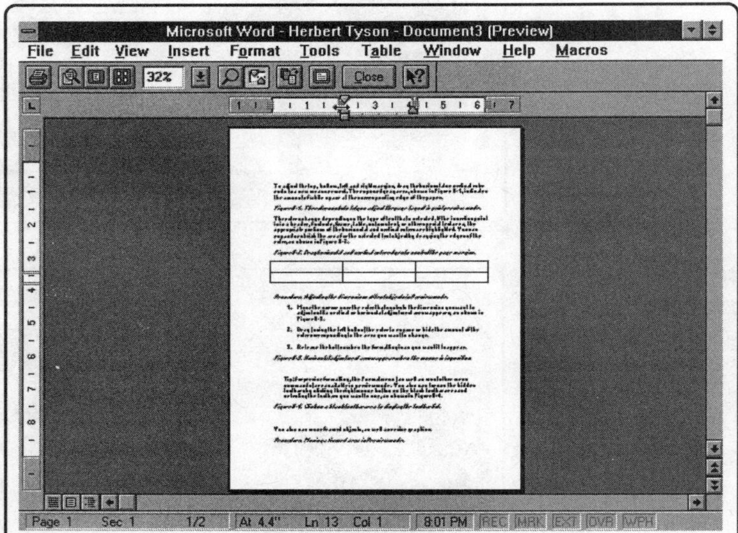

FIGURE 4.19. *The horizontal adjustment arrow appears when the mouse is in position.*

SUPER TIP

For precise formatting, the Format menu (as well as most other menu commands) are available in Print Preview mode. You also can turn on the hidden toolbars by clicking the right mouse button on the blank toolbar area and selecting the toolbars you want to use, as shown in Figure 4.20.

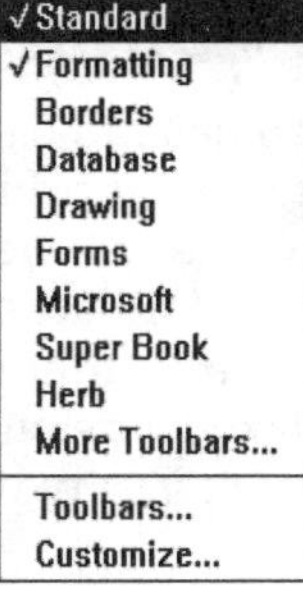

FIGURE 4.20.
Click a blank toolbar area to display the toolbar list.

In Print Preview mode, you also can move framed objects, as well as resize graphics.

PROCEDURE 4.7. MOVING A FRAMED AREA IN PRINT PREVIEW MODE.

1. Move the cursor over the framed area so that a four-headed arrow appears. If the object is a framed paragraph, the dragging ruler will appear only with the mouse pointer at the very edge of the object.
2. Press and hold the left mouse button and drag the object to a new location.
3. Release the mouse button when the object is in the desired location.

PROCEDURE 4.8. RESIZING AND CROPPING A GRAPHIC IN PRINT PREVIEW MODE.

1. Move the cursor over any of the eight sizing handles so that a scaling arrow appears, as shown in Figure 4.21.
2. To scale (size), press the left mouse button and drag the handle to a new location. To crop, press Shift while dragging (note that the cursor shape changes to a cropping cursor when you press the Shift key).
3. Release the mouse button when the object has the desired appearance.

FIGURE 4.21.
A scaling arrow shows that the mouse is positioned correctly to scale or crop the graphic in Print Preview mode.

Using the Print Command to Fax

The advent of the fax board has radically changed the focus of many printing considerations. Rather than routing your print jobs to the local printer, many users are now sending their processed words out the COM port to the telephone. One unfortunate casualty in this innovation is formatting. Because many fax "solutions" often format the page differently than your printer would, you can't tell from looking at a printed draft whether or not your faxed version will be the same. One perfectly formatted page may become a two-page monstrosity when faxed.

Setting the Fax Modem as the Printer

If you use fax software that configures itself as a printer driver, you should assign that printer driver before formatting a document you plan to fax.

PROCEDURE 4.9. SELECTING A FAX PRINTER.

1. Select **F**ile | **P**rint.
2. Click Printer.
3. Click the fax printer driver.
4. Click Set as Default Printer.
5. Click Options; depending on the fax software you're using, you will get different choices. Ensure that any choices that will affect the appearance of your document are selected now.
6. Click OK to close the Setup dialog box.
7. Click Close to close the Printer Selection dialog box.

If you have multiple printer drivers installed for use under Windows, you can perform an interesting experiment. First, select **T**ools | **O**ptions | View and turn off the Draft Font, Wrap to Window, and Picture Placeholders options. Now try the following:

1. Select File | Page Layout; observe the way it looks.
2. Select **F**ile | **P**rint | Prin**t**er and choose a printer that is different from the one that's currently installed (preferably your fax device).
3. After you click Close, then click Close again (so you don't actually print anything) and observe the way the document looks now.

Depending on the printer drivers that are loaded, the appearance of the document may change dramatically. Often the display font changes, along with line and page breaks. A one-page document may suddenly become a two-page document. If you carefully formatted your fax so that it takes up a single page, you might also be in for a surprise.

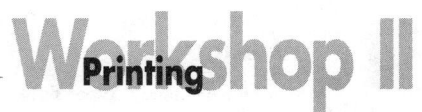

Fax Formatting Considerations

When preparing a document for faxing, there are several considerations that aren't part of your normal document formatting:

- Keep the document as short as possible; don't include unnecessary material in the fax (keep the shrink-to-fit option in mind, but *please* see the note in the next item about minimum point sizes for faxing).
- Select a font and point size that can be read easily when faxed; if you can fax yourself, fax some sample fonts and choose one that is legible. Avoid using fonts smaller than 8 points.
- If your fax software gives a selection of different resolutions, select a medium resolution rather than the highest. Selecting the highest resolution can double or triple the time it takes to transmit a fax. It's not considered polite to tie up a person's fax line by sending too much detail.
- If your fax software doesn't add a header showing your identification and the page numbers of the faxed document, then use headers in Word to add the appropriate header. Many fax machines are shared by a number of different people, and some fax machines can scramble the pages of faxes. You need to make sure that your whole fax can be reassembled easily if it's dropped or shuffled.
- Fax cover sheets are optional only if the receiver knows that only your fax is arriving or if the first page of your fax does a reasonably good job of providing cover information. The cover sheet should include the name and number(s) of both the sender and the receiver, as well as a physical description of the fax (number of pages receiver can expect).
- If you do much faxing, create or customize a fax template (FAX.DOT) to take care of as many details as possible, including setting the printer to the fax device (which you might do using AutoNew and AutoOpen) , setting up a cover page, headers, footers, page numbers, fonts, and point sizes. You might also create an AutoClose macro that resets the printer back to your normal printer when you're done faxing. If you have already sent a fax with which you're satisfied, you might use it as a starting point for creating your own template. You can even use the Fax Wizard (see Chapter 21, "Templates and Wizards") to create the "perfect" fax and then save the result as your own template.
- Preview your fax using Print Preview before sending it to verify that it has the expected number of pages.

Sending a Fax

Sending a fax using computer-based fax software and hardware is not very different from normal printing. However, instead of sending the fax through the LPT port to a printer, you send the fax out the COM port to the fax modem. Fax software varies widely in the options presented and the procedures you use. Carefully check the dialog boxes you see for clues.

PROCEDURE 4.10. SENDING A FAX.

1. Preview your document to ensure that it's what you want.
2. Select **F**ile | **P**rint; observe the Printer field to ensure that the selected printer is your fax device.
3. Select the appropriate options.
4. Click OK.
5. At this point, most fax software provides an opportunity to select the phone number of the fax recipient, as well as the resolution of the fax, whether a cover page is included (independent of your word processor), and header options. Make your selection(s) and click OK.

Chapter

5

Printer Setup

The key to printing is making sure everything is set up correctly. Full printer setup is not part of Word for Windows at all but rather a function of Windows. Being able to print, however, is essential for most Word users. This chapter covers the basics in ensuring that Word is correctly set up to print.

Printer Setup Options

Unlike Word for Windows versions 1 and 2, Word 6 does not enable you to select full printer setup from the Word menu. You can select the printer and some printer options from the **File**|**Print** dialog box, but you'll need to go to the Windows Control Panel|Printer to access the rest of the setup options.

Selecting **File**|**Print**|Printer shows you the Print Setup dialog box shown in Figure 5.1. From this dialog box, you can select the printer and set a few printer options.

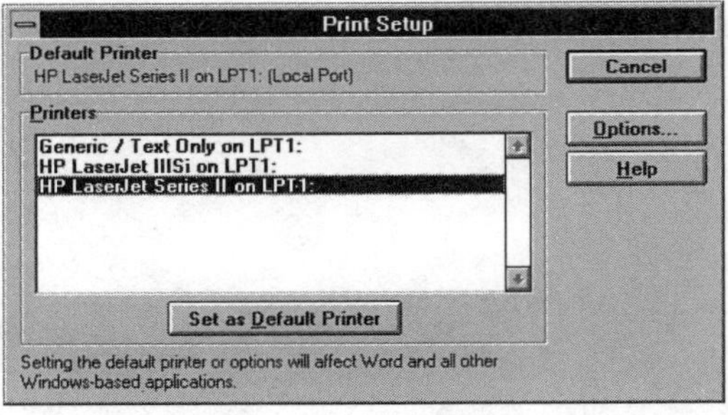

FIGURE 5.1.
Word for Windows 6 has more limited printer setup options than Word for Windows 2.

PROCEDURE 5.1. SELECTING A DIFFERENT PRINTER.

1. Select **File**|**Print**|Printer.
2. Click the printer you want to use.
3. Click Set as **D**efault Printer.
4. Click Close to close the Print Setup dialog box.
5. Click Close to close the Print dialog box (unless you want to print now, in which case you select your printing choices and then click OK).

Although you also can select a limited number of printing options from the Print Setup dialog box, some options—such as paper source, paper size, and orientation—can be set on a per-document basis using the File|Page Setup command, and the Word-wide default paper source (tray) can be set using **T**ools|**O**ptions|**P**rint.

PROCEDURE 5.2. SETTING PRINTER OPTIONS.

1. Select **File**|**Print**|Printer.
2. If necessary, click the printer you want to use, and then click Set as Default Printer.

3. Click Options to display the dialog box shown in Figure 5.2.
4. Set the dithering and darkness as desired or the Print TrueType as Graphics option (don't make this choice unless you are using a matrix printer that doesn't support TrueType directly).
5. Click Close to close the Options dialog box.
6. Click Close to close the Print Setup dialog box.
7. Click Close to close the Print dialog box.

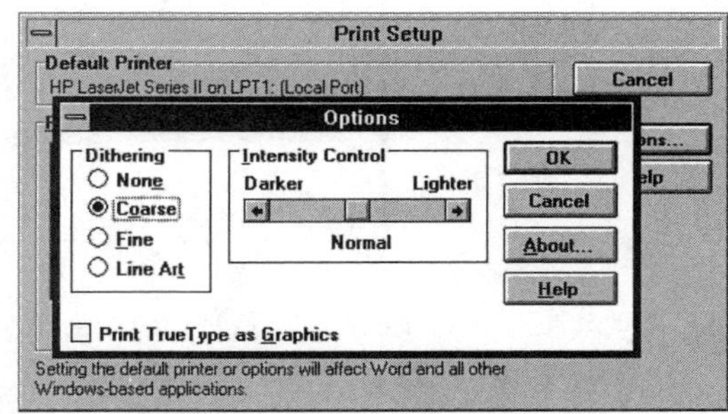

FIGURE 5.2.
The Print Options dialog box.

Accessing Windows Printer Setup

SUPER UPGRADE NOTE

Unlike Word for Windows versions 1 and 2, no longer is there a built-in way to select the full printer setup from Word. This is likely due to Microsoft's desire to maximize compatibility with the Macintosh version of Word. You can, if you like, create a direct access route to the Windows Control Panel by installing the Control Panel macro from the enclosed SuperDisk. See Chapter 60, "Macro Projects," for additional information.

PROCEDURE 5.3. ACCESSING WINDOWS PRINTER SETUP.

1. Switch to the Windows Program Manager.
2. Open the Control panel in the Main group.
3. Open the Printers control.
4. Click the printer you want to change.
5. Click Setup.

The Windows setup dialog for the Hewlett-Packard LaserJet II is shown in Figure 5.3. The dialog box and options offered will vary by printer.

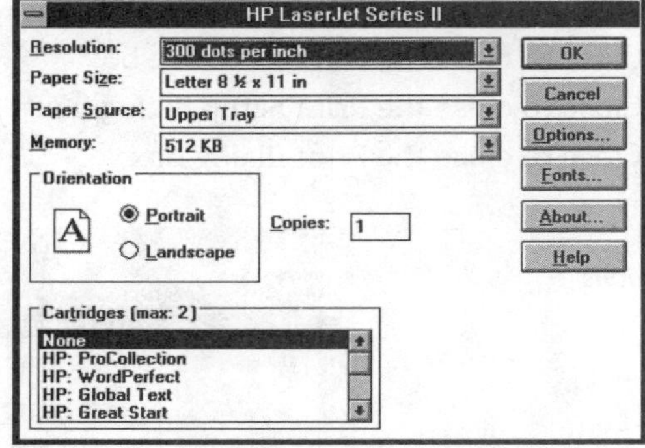

FIGURE 5.3.
The Printer Setup dialog box for the Hewlett-Packard LaserJet II.

For example, if you select Generic/Text, Windows shows you the dialog box in Figure 5.4.

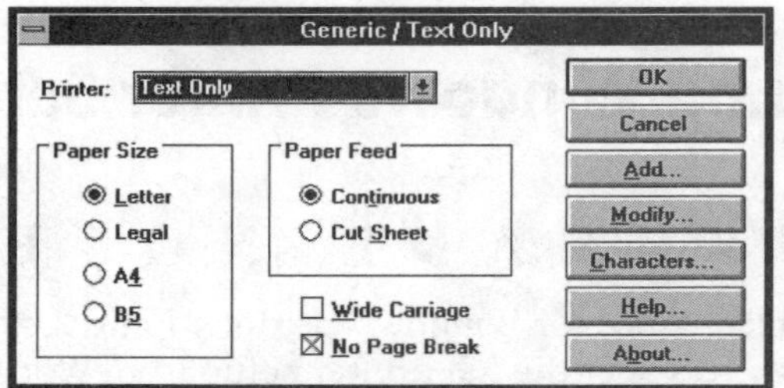

FIGURE 5.4.
The Printer Setup dialog box for the Generic/Text printer.

SUPER HEY, DRIVER!

What's a printer driver? A printer driver is simply a computer program that formats stuff you send to your printer. When Word prints, it sends standard instructions to Windows. Windows gives those instructions to the printer driver, which then creates the appropriate instructions for the printer you're using.

Windows then sends the instructions to whatever device is set up for that printer (COM port, LPT port, fax board, file, and so on). Think of printing as a formula. A Hewlett-Packard LaserJet Series II uses one formula, an Apple LaserWriter II NT uses another, and a Cannon Bubble-Jet BJ-10e uses yet another. When you select a printer driver, you're just telling Word and Windows which formula to use.

Installing and Removing Printers

You can add printers to and remove printers from Windows by using the Windows Control Panel. This affects the availability of printers from within Word as well as other Windows applications.

Installing Printers

If you suddenly discover that you don't have a printer driver installed or that you don't have the correct printer driver installed, you can add one. Before starting, make sure you have your Windows installation diskettes standing by.

PROCEDURE 5.4. INSTALLING A PRINTER.

1. Switch to the Windows Program Manager.
2. Open the Control panel.
3. Double-click Printers.
4. Click Add; this will display the list of printers shown in Figure 5.5.
5. Select the printer you want to add.
6. Click Install.
7. Windows will prompt you to insert the appropriate diskettes. Note that if the drivers are already on your system in a different location, you can use the Browse command to navigate to the appropriate directory.
8. After the hourglass disappears, click Connect and verify your printer connections. Make any changes necessary and click OK to return to the Printers panel.
9. Click Setup; select the options and settings appropriate for your printer (for example, paper source, printer memory, and so on). Click OK to return to the Printers panel.
10. Click Set as Default Printer to select this printer for printing.
11. Click Close to close the Printers panel.
12. Close the Control panel. When you return to Word, the document will be reformatted (possibly repaginated, as well) due to the change in printer resources (assuming you set the added printer as the default, as shown in Step 10).

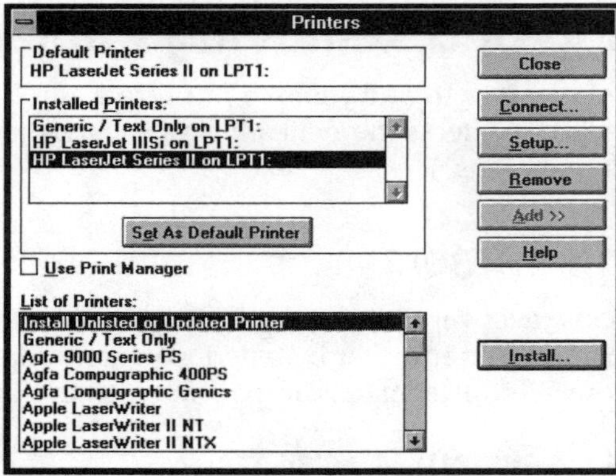

FIGURE 5.5.
Select your default printer from the printer list.

SUPER NOTE

Adding a printer just adds an additional option to the printer selection list (see Figure 5.6). When working in the Control panel, you have the additional option of making any printer listed the default printer for Windows. This may seem a little ceremonious, but, in fact, it's merely the equivalent of selecting a printer to use. When you select a printer from the printer selection list from within Word, you are in fact setting the default printer. You can easily change defaults by selecting **File** | **Print** | **Printer** and choosing a different printer.

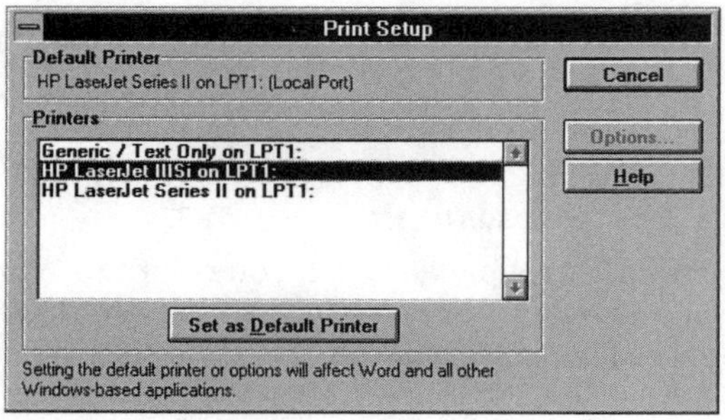

FIGURE 5.6.
The printer list now displays the additional printer.

SUPER TIP

OS/2 CD-ROM users who are running Word from OS/2 can use the Browse button in Step 8 to point the control panel at your OS/2 CD-ROM disk as the source for the printer setup data, as shown in Procedure 5.5.

PROCEDURE 5.5. SELECTING THE OS/2 CD-ROM AS THE SOURCE FOR PRINTER DRIVERS.

1. Insert your OS/2 CD-ROM disk into your drive.
2. Click Browse.
3. Select the drive that contains your OS/2 CD-ROM disk.
4. Click \OS2SE21 (depending on what version you're using, the directory name might be similar but different).
5. Click the directory that corresponds to the diskette you need (that is, PMDD_1 for Printer Diskette 1, PMDD_2 for Diskette 2, and PMDD_3 for Diskette 3).
6. Click OK to close the Browse dialog box; click OK to accept the directory; click OK to begin installation of the selected driver.
7. You may be prompted to insert additional diskettes; simply edit the PMDD_*x* that's shown to insert the corresponding number.
8. Continue with Step 9 of Procedure 5.4.

Removing Printers

Removing a printer from the list of printers is simple.

PROCEDURE 5.6. REMOVING A PRINTER FROM THE PRINTER LIST.

1. Switch to the Windows Program Manager.
2. Open the Control panel.
3. Double-click Printers.
4. Select the printer you want to remove.
5. Click Remove.

SUPER TIP

Removing printers is quite simple. Removing printer driver files from your hard disk, however, seems to be a technology that Microsoft has yet to master. Because Windows doesn't tell you what it added and why, it's sometimes extremely difficult to determine what files you can safely delete when you're removing a printer driver. As a starting point, try looking at the Windows SYSTEM subdirectory for files that are dated the same as the date you added the drive you're trying to remove. You can get some additional clues by looking at CONTROL.INF, also on the SYSTEM subdirectory. As you look through CONTROL.INF, however, note that there are some files—such as UNIDRV.DLL and UNIDRV.HLP—that are shared by different printers. Beyond that, though, you're on

your own. If you accidentally remove the wrong file(s), Windows may no longer work. Unless you're seriously low on disk space, the old saying "Better safe than sorry" might be the best plan.

Windows Screen and Printing Fonts (Including TrueType)

Windows supports several different kinds of fonts and font concepts. Windows itself uses fonts for displaying text on-screen. Some of these fonts also are used for printing. You control these fonts using the Windows Control panel's Font control.

PROCEDURE 5.7. ACCESSING THE FONTS CONTROL PANEL.

1. Switch to the Windows Program Manager.
2. Open the Control Panel.
3. Double-click Fonts (see Figure 5.7).

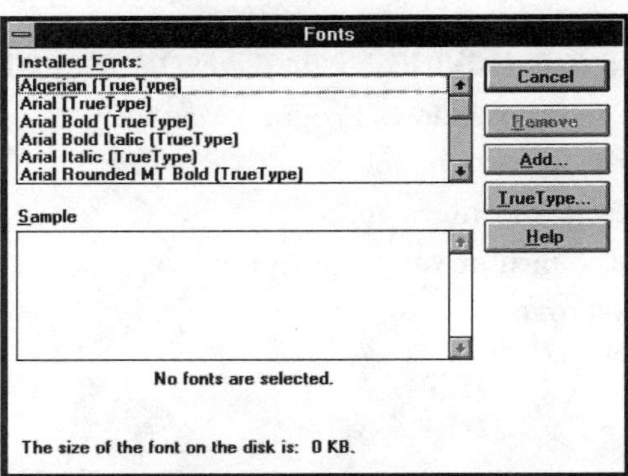

FIGURE 5.7.
The Font panel in the Windows Control panel.

Adding Fonts

You can add fonts to those that Windows uses for display and printing. Fonts you buy often come with their own setup programs. If they do not, you can use the Add button in the Fonts panel to add them.

SUPER NOTE

This procedure adds only screen fonts or TrueType fonts. To add printer fonts, select the Setup button from the Printers panel in the Control Panel, and then click on Fonts.

PROCEDURE 5.8. ADDING FONTS TO WINDOWS.

1. From the Fonts panel, click Add. Windows displays the dialog box shown in Figure 5.8.
2. Use the Drives and Directories list boxes to navigate to the location of the fonts you want to add.
3. Press Ctrl and click to selectively highlight fonts you want to add (press Shift and click the first and last if there is a contiguous block of fonts you want to add).
4. If you just want to make Windows aware of fonts that are on your disk and associated with other applications, you can deselect the Copy Fonts to Windows Directory checkbox to cause Windows to simply point to them where they currently reside. Otherwise, Windows will needlessly duplicate them in the Windows SYSTEM directory.
5. Click OK. Windows now displays the augmented font list with the fonts you just added.
6. Click Close.

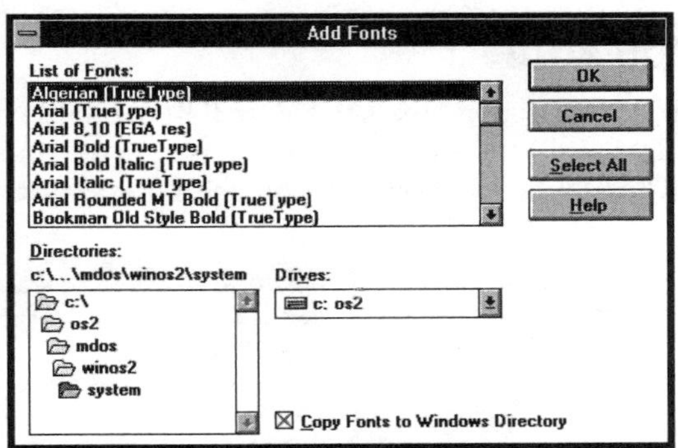

FIGURE 5.8.
Use the Add Fonts dialog box to add fonts to and remove fonts from Windows.

SUPER NOTE

When Windows detects fonts in a selected directory, it displays a list of what it found. If the list of fonts remains empty, then Windows doesn't see any fonts it can use. If fonts are displayed in the list, Windows doesn't tell you which, if any, of the displayed fonts are already installed. It delays giving you that information until you try to add them.

Removing Fonts

Fortunately, removing fonts and their associated files is more straightforward than removing printer driver files.

PROCEDURE 5.9. REMOVING FONTS FROM WINDOWS.

1. From the Fonts panel, select the fonts you want to remove.
2. Click Remove.
3. Windows prompts you to confirm the removal.
4. Click Delete Font File from Disk, if desired, to remove the first selected font.
5. Click Yes to confirm this font and step to the next font you selected.
6. Click Yes to All to remove the remaining selected fonts without further prompts.
7. Click Close.

TrueType Fonts

Use the TrueType dialog box (see Figure 5.9) to enable or disable TrueType fonts and to optionally limit Windows to using just TrueType fonts. If you elect to enable or disable TrueType fonts, Windows prompts you to restart Windows.

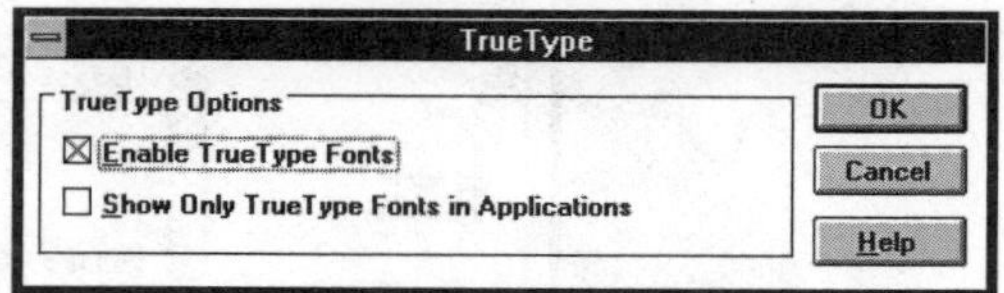

FIGURE 5.9.
Use the TrueType dialog box to control TrueType fonts.

Printer Fonts

Printer fonts are different from the screen and printing fonts installed using the Fonts control panel. When you select the font list in Word, a symbol to the left of each font shows the type of font (see Figure 5.10). Printer fonts and ATM (Adobe Type Manager) fonts have the little printer symbol next to them, while TrueType fonts have a little TT icon.

Some printer fonts are resident in specific printers. For example, only Courier and Lineprinter fonts are resident in the Hewlett-Packard LaserJet II. Hewlett-Packard LaserJet III Si resident fonts include Courier, Lineprinter, CGTimes, ITC Zapf Dingbat, and Univers. Printer fonts also can include downloadable fonts which are sometimes called bit-mapped fonts, as well as outline fonts (similar to TrueType and Adobe Type Manager) geared to specific printers.

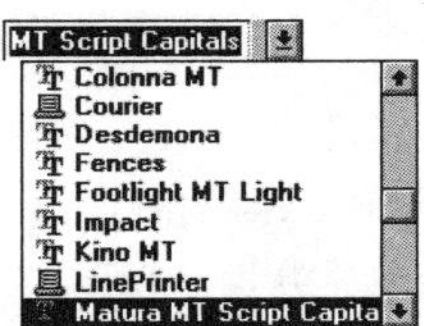

FIGURE 5.10.
Icons identify the different kinds of fonts in the font list.

Downloadable (Soft) Fonts

Downloadable, or soft, fonts are bit-mapped fonts that get sent to your printer. Once they're in your printer's memory, they can be accessed as quickly as your printer's resident fonts. Downloadable fonts make for faster printing than outline and on-the-fly fonts such as ATM, Bitstream Speedo, and TrueType fonts. At the same time, downloadable fonts must be physically sent to your printer, which can be an annoying process (more on this in a moment).

PROCEDURE 5.10. INSTALLING DOWNLOADABLE (SOFT) FONTS FOR THE HEWLETT-PACKARD LASERJET II.

1. Switch to the Windows Program Manager.
2. Open the Control panel.
3. Double-click Printers.
4. Select your printer (if necessary).
5. Click Setup.
6. Click Fonts.
7. Click Add Fonts....
8. Insert the diskette containing the fonts or type the location of the downloadable fonts you want to use.
9. A list of available fonts will appear in the list box on the right (see Figure 5.11). Select the font(s) you want to add.

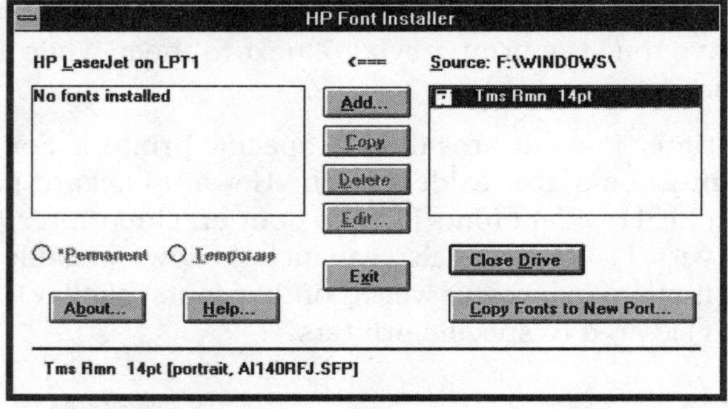

FIGURE 5.11. *Adding downloadable fonts to Windows.*

10. Click Add.
11. Confirm or change the destination location (if you're using fonts already on your hard disk, you can just retype the location you specified in Step 6 to use them where they are).
12. The installed fonts will now appear in the list box on the left. Select any fonts you want to make permanent (see the following section, "Permanent versus Temporary").
13. Click Permanent. If this is the first permanent font installed, Windows displays the message box shown in Figure 5.12. Click OK.

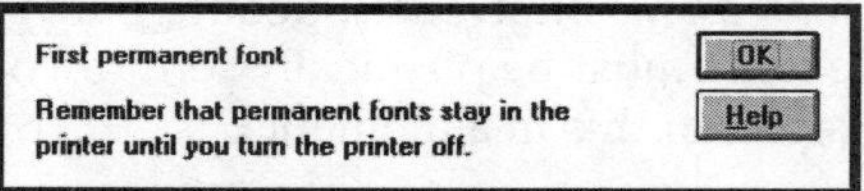

FIGURE 5.12. *The First Permanent Font notice.*

14. Click Exit.
15. Windows now displays the dialog box shown in Figure 5.13. If you plan to use this font all the time, select both options (Download **N**ow and Download at **S**tartup). Click OK to proceed.

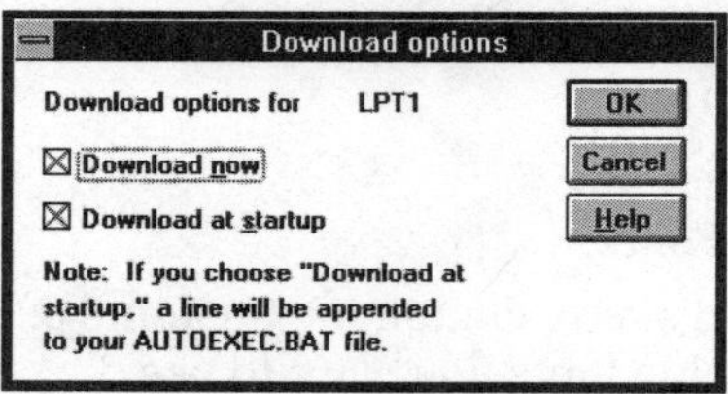

FIGURE 5.13. *The Download Options dialog box.*

16. Click OK to close the Setup dialog box for your printer.
17. Click Close to close the Printers control panel.
18. Close the Control panel.

SUPER NOTE

Procedures vary for different printers.

SUPER TIP

In Step 15, if you want neither option, the temptation is to click Cancel. Windows, however, won't take that kind of "No" for an answer. It will keep displaying the dialog box each time you try to exit until you click OK. Solution: Deselect both options (Download **N**ow and Download at **S**tartup) and then click OK. Aren't Windows dialog boxes fun sometimes?

Permanent Versus Temporary

Most printers that accept downloadable fonts offer a choice of making downloadable fonts permanent or temporary. All things are relative, of course. *Permanent*, in this context, means that the font(s) remain in memory as long as the printer is turned on. *Temporary* means that the fonts are not downloaded to the printer until you actually use them and are then removed from memory after the print job is complete.

The advantage of the Temporary option is that you don't have to think about it. The disadvantage is that you have to wait—sometimes an extraordinarily long time—while the font is downloaded each time you print using that font. On the other hand, using the Permanent option requires that you leave your printer on all the time (or that you selectively run the SFLPT1.BAT file each time you're ready to print; see the next tip).

When you select the Permanent option, Windows offers to add lines similar to the following to your AUTOEXEC.BAT file:

```
rem The Windows HP LaserJet/DeskJet font installer added the next line
F:\WINDOWS\SFLPT1.BAT
```

The SFLPT1.BAT file contains the instructions for downloading the soft font(s) to your printer.

SUPER TIP

Does the idea of leaving your printer turned on all the time bother you? It certainly bothers me—and my electric bill. Moreover, in the summer, my printer generates a fair amount of heat, making my air conditioner have to work a little harder. If you need to use soft fonts and you don't mind a little bit of work, a not-so-bad compromise is to selectively run the SFLPT1.BAT file when you turn your printer on. In this way, you have the advantage of using fonts that stay with you while your printer is on, but you don't have to leave your printer on all the time. For a single print job, the difference between this and Temporary is negligible. However, if you'll be printing several documents using the soft font, this approach can save a lot of time. To run the batch file directly:

1. Open a DOS command line session.
2. Make sure your printer is turned on and is online.
3. Type the batch filename, leaving out the .BAT extension (for example, `F:\WINDOWS\SFLPT1`).

Font Cartridges

A font cartridge is a physical device that plugs into or attaches to your printer. A cartridge contains the instructions your printer needs to print fonts or to print in a certain mode (for example, Postscript). Cartridge fonts are identical to resident fonts in speed.

For example, the only resident fonts my Hewlett-Packard LaserJet II has are Courier and Lineprinter. Using a Pacific Data 25-in-One cartridge, I was able to add a number of additional fonts. Even though—for some inexplicable reason—Windows has never provided explicit support for this popular line of cartridges, I've usually been able to "lie" to Windows and tell it I'm using one of the 25 cartridges this one is supposed to obviate.

Five years ago, using a cartridge to add fast printer fonts was an important capability because the only alternative seemed to be the much slower and more tedious downloadable (soft) fonts. These days, however, I've pretty much abandoned the cartridge in favor of using the ATM fonts that come with OS/2 and the TrueType fonts that come with Windows. While ATM and TrueType are noticeably slower than cartridge fonts, I never have to give a second thought to whether they're going to print correctly in the sizes I've selected. I still wonder why Pacific Data's cartridge isn't on the list of supported cartridges, however.

PROCEDURE 5.11. ADDING AND REMOVING PRINTER FONT CARTRIDGES.

1. Install the cartridge in the printer using the manufacturer's instructions.
2. Switch to the Windows Program Manager.
3. Open the Control panel.
4. Open the Printers panel.
5. Click the printer you want to change.

6. Click Setup.
7. In the cartridge list (see Figure 5.14), click the cartridge(s) you want to add or remove. Select the cartridge to add it; deselect to remove it. Note: If you try to exceed the limit—in this instance, 2—Windows will deselect the one you least-recently selected.
8. Click OK to close the Printer dialog box.
9. Click OK to close the Print Setup dialog box.

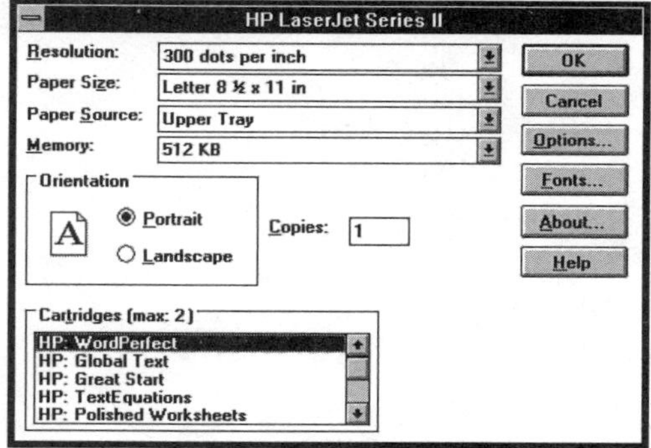

FIGURE 5.14.
The cartridge list shows the available cartridge drivers for the current printer.

SUPER NOTE

Where are my cartridge fonts?!? If you now select the font list (press Ctrl+F or use the mouse) and don't see your cartridge fonts, there may be a simple explanation. In the Font panel, you can tell Windows to display only TrueType fonts in applications. If your fonts don't show up when you press Ctrl+F, invariably the problem is that you've told Windows to use just TrueType fonts. To alleviate the problem:

1. Open the Windows Control panel.
2. Open the Font panel.
3. Click TrueType (see Figure 5.15).
4. Deselect the Show Only Truetype Fonts in Applications option.
5. Click Close.

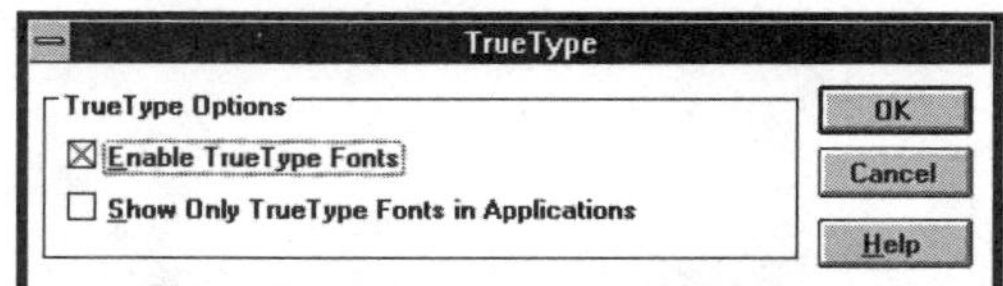

FIGURE 5.15.
The TrueType dialog box.

III

Files Workshop

In this workshop, you look at filing. Filing is a generic name for getting things from and putting things back onto the disk. First, you explore the different kinds of word files as well as how to insert files into documents. Next, you explore the ins and outs of importing and exporting files from and to different formats. Finally, you look at Word's newly enhanced FileFind command. You also see how to use the Windows File Manager when working with Word.

Chapter

Word Files

Word supports two native types of files: documents and templates (the latter of which includes a special type of template called Wizard). In this session, we'll look at the mechanics of creating, editing, merging, and saving files.

SUPER

WIZARDS?

A Wizard is just a particular class of Word template. Users who migrated from Word for Windows 2 and prior might recall that some of the templates that came with prior versions of Word contain automatic macros. Often confusing and stupefying, these macros automatically asked you questions and set up a document. That was fine if that was what you wanted to do, but if you were just curious and opened a template for the heck of it, you were in for quite a shock. In Word for Windows 6, you at least are forewarned: If the document has an extension of .WIZ (or is indicated as a Wizard in the list of templates), then it contains automatic macros that attempt to walk you through the creation of certain kinds of documents. If, however, it's a .DOT from WinWord 6, it should not assault you with automatic macros.

Creating

Creating a file from scratch in Word is a three-step process:

- Use the **F**ile|**N**ew command to open Document or Template window.
- Write your document.
- Use **F**ile|Save **A**s to save the document and give it a name.

The obvious way is to use the **F**ile|**N**ew option, basing the file on an existing template, and to use **F**ile|Save **A**s to name it. Less obvious is that you can use virtually any existing file as a *de facto* template by using **F**ile|**O**pen followed by **F**ile|Save **A**s, and specifying a new name. If you use this approach, you must be very careful not to save it under the original name after making changes to it (at least, if you want to preserve the original as a separate entity).

Documents

A Word document is a file that can retain text, formatting, and styles. A document differs from a template in that a template can also be used to retain macros, toolbar, menu, keystroke, and autotext customizations.

When you create a new document, Word creates a window entitled *Document#*, where # is sequentially the number of such window you have opened during the current session. The first is Document1, the second is Document2, and so forth, as shown in

Figure 6.1. The window retains that name until you save the file (see "Saving" in this chapter). Note that the name *Document1* is not usable as a filename under DOS; Document1 has nine characters, while DOS permits only eight. So, even if you want to keep the temporary name as your own, you can't. Instead, when you save the file, Word offers to save an unnamed file as DOC1.DOC, DOC2.DOC, and so on.

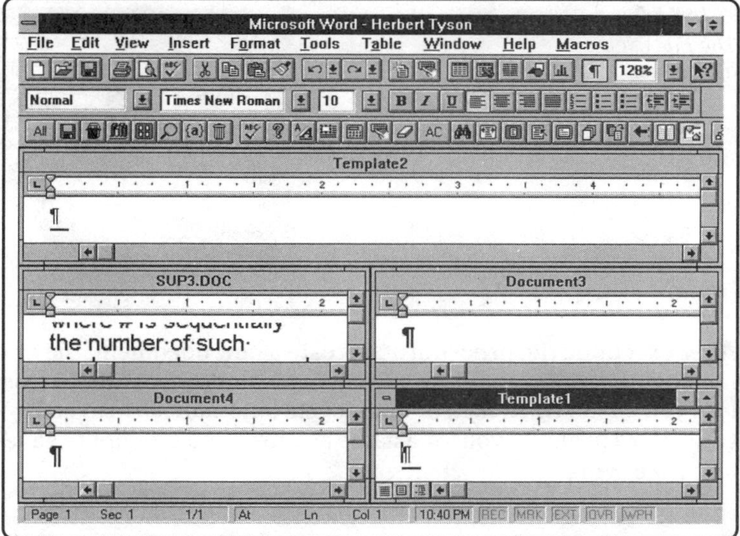

FIGURE 6.1.
Word labels new files as Document# and Template#, until you name them.

SUPER NOTE

While *AutoText* (formerly called the glossary) entries can be stored in templates, *AutoCorrect* entries are stored only in NORMAL.DOT, and not in individual templates. AutoText entries are user shorthands you can create, whose long forms you insert using the F3 key. AutoCorrect entries are automatic shorthands whose long forms are inserted automatically whenever the shorthand is typed.

PROCEDURE 6.1. CREATING A NEW DOCUMENT FROM SCRATCH.

1. Select **F**ile | **N**ew; Word displays the New dialog box shown in Figure 6.2.
2. Select the template you want to use as a starting point (the default is NORMAL).
3. Be sure that the **D**ocument radio button is selected.

4. Click Summary if you want to enter the summary information right now (otherwise, Word prompts you for summary information when you save the document unless the Prompt for Summary Info option is disabled in the **T**ools | **O**ptions | **S**ave dialog box; see "Save Options" later in this chapter).
5. Click OK.

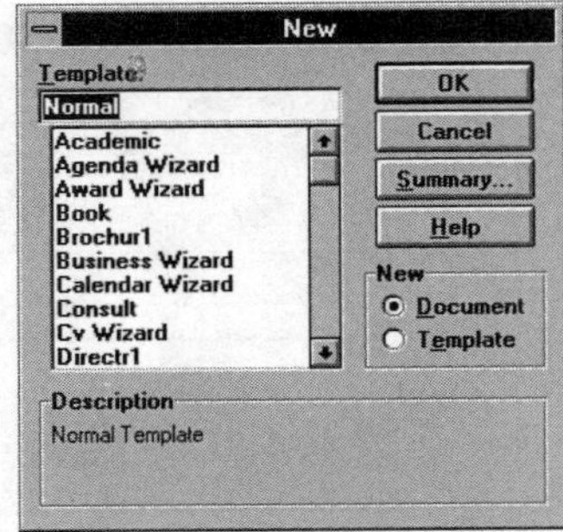

FIGURE 6.2.
The ***F****ile* | ***N****ew dialog box.*

After executing the procedure to create a new document, the document exists only in memory, as represented by a Document window. It will not exist on disk until or unless you explicitly save it, or until it gets automatically saved by Word's AutoSave feature. Word prompts you for a name any time you attempt to save or close the file or to exit from Word.

SUPER TIP

In Step 2, if you want to use another document as your starting point—rather than an actual template—you *can!* Just type the fully specified name of the document you want to use into the template field (for example, F:\WORD6\DOC\LETTER01.DOC). Word uses the document you specify as the template, and opens a *Document#* window. Now you're free to use **F**ile | Save **A**s to give your clone a new name.

Templates

A Word template is a file that can retain text, formatting, and styles as well as customizations to macros, toolbars, menus, keystrokes, and autotext lists.

PROCEDURE 6.2. CREATING A NEW TEMPLATE FROM SCRATCH.

1. Select **F**ile | **N**ew.
2. Select the template you want to use as a starting point (the default is NORMAL).

3. Be sure that the Template radio button is selected.
4. Click Summary if you want to enter the summary information right now.
5. Click OK.

As is the case for documents, the template exists only in memory (as identified by the *Template#* title in the title bar) until you explicitly save it. When you save it, give it the default extension .DOT to save it as an ordinary template. Use the extension .WIZ to tell Word to treat it as a Wizard. Note the distinction between templates and Wizards in Figure 6.3.

SUPER TIP

The first time you save a template, Word offers to name it *DOT#.DOT*, where # matches the # in *Template#*. You should replace the default name with something more informative. Also, you should make sure you fill a description of the template's purpose into the Title field in the Summary Info dialog box ( ). When you create a new file, Word displays each template's title in the Description field in the New dialog box. If you have multiple templates with similar names, the Description can help you quickly locate the correct template.

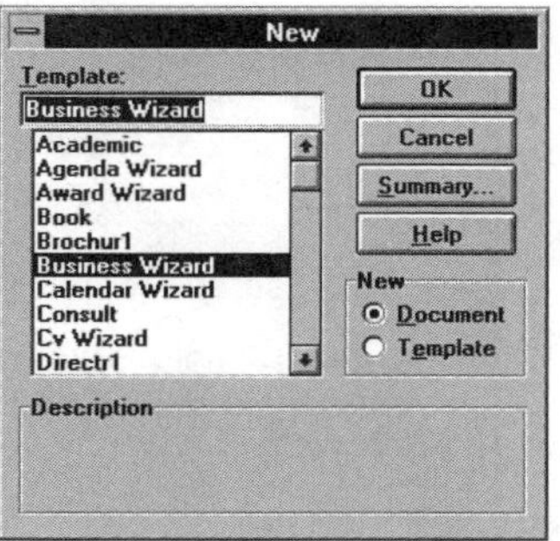

FIGURE 6.3.
Giving templates the .WIZ extension lets users know they contain automatic macros.

SUPER NOTE

In fact, Word itself doesn't treat Wizards any differently from ordinary templates, except insofar as it identifies them as *name* Wizard rather than simply as *name*. The real reason for using the .WIZ extension is to put users on notice that the template contains one or more automatic macros that will be active when you create or open a file based on a Wizard. See the discussion in the next section.

Opening (Editing) an Existing Word File

Word offers a variety of ways to open one or more existing files:

- Select **File** | **Open**
- Press Ctrl+O
- Click the Open button (see Figure 6.4) in the Standard toolbar.

FIGURE 6.4.
*The **File** | **Open** button in the Standard toolbar.*

- Drag one or more files from Windows File Manager and drop it or them onto a nontext area in the Word screen (see Figure 6.5).
- Drag one or more files from Windows File Manager and drop them onto WINWORD.EXE.

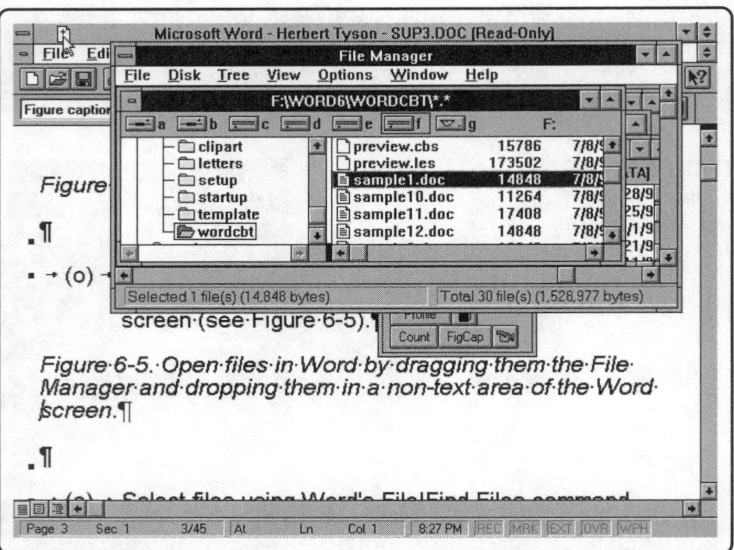

FIGURE 6.5.
Open files in Word by dragging them from File Manager and dropping them in a nontext area of the Word screen.

- Select files using Word's **File** | **Find File** command, and click the Open button.
- Select **File**, and press a number corresponding to a file in Word's list of recently-opened files in the File menu.

Wizards and Other Hazards

Some templates contain automatic macros that execute when files attached to them are created, opened, or closed:

AutoNew	Executed each time a new document is created based on the host template (the Wizards that come with Word contain AutoNew macros, but not AutoOpen macros)
AutoOpen	Executed each time a given document or template is opened at all
AutoClose	Executed each time a given document or template is closed

SUPER

Two additional automatic macros—AutoExec and AutoExit—are executed only when Word opens and closes. See Chapter 59, "Automatic Macros," for additional information about automatic macros.

Most of the time, the behavior inscribed in these automatic macros is exactly what you want. In fact, Wizards' claims to fame are precisely contained in their automatic behaviors. Sometimes, however—like when you're just exploring—you really *don't* want automatic macros surprising you. For those times, you can use the DisableAutoMacros command.

However, the DisableAutoMacros command is not available from any of Word's default menus or toolbars, so you'll have to create a macro to use it (or use the macro on the SuperDisk—called ToggleAutoMacros). This command acts as a toggle to turn off and on Word's responsiveness to automatic macros. It can be very useful when you're exploring, or when an automatic macro keeps you from seeing what's really going on in a file.

SUPER TIP

You can suppress automatic macros by holding down the Shift key when creating, opening, or closing a file. If you use a menu to create, open, or close a file, you can press the Shift key when you press Enter or click to give the command to create, open, or close. To suppress when using the file cache (the numbered list of recently-opened files that's at the bottom of the File menu), then press the Shift key when you click on the file you want to retrieve. Similarly, if you use a File Close button on a toolbar, you can press the Shift key when you click the button to suppress the AutoClose macro.

If you use a keystroke to open a file (Alt+F, followed by a number from the file cache), however, you cannot suppress an AutoOpen by holding down the Shift key when you press the number. Instead, you would need to quickly tap the shift key *after* pressing the appropriate number key. If your computer is very fast, this may not work. Also, when closing a file using Ctrl+F4, you cannot press Shift+Ctrl+F4 to suppress AutoClose. Instead, you would need to very quickly press the Shift key after pressing Ctrl+F4. However, this usually works only if your computer processor is quite slow.

Worse, if a template you receive from someone has a bug in an AutoOpen macro, (often from macros that haven't been sufficiently generalized to work in environments other than the originator's), the operation of the macro may prevent you from seeing what's going wrong. On those occasions, it's useful to be able to turn off automatic macros and, perhaps, execute the offending gem one step at a time to see where it runs amuck. The DisableAutoMacros command enables you to do precisely that.

The Open Dialog

The primary way most users open files is using **F**ile | **O**pen, Ctrl+O, or the Open button to access the Open dialog box, shown in Figure 6.6.

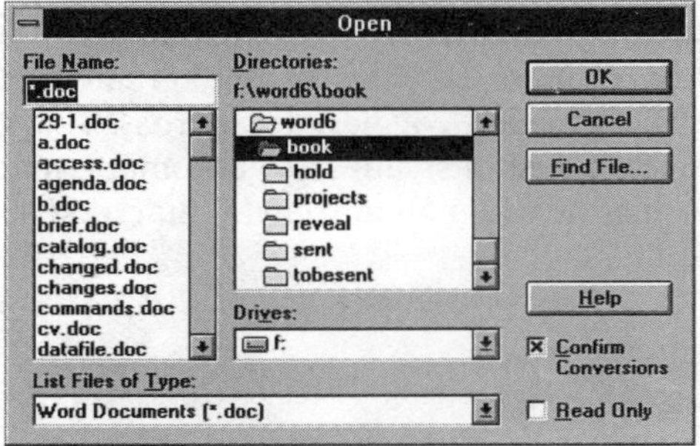

FIGURE 6.6.
*The **File** | **Open** dialog box.*

PROCEDURE 6.3. OPENING A FILE WITH THE OPEN DIALOG.

1. Select **F**ile | **O**pen, press Ctrl+O, or click the Open button in the Standard toolbar.
2. Use the List files of Type, Drives, and Directories controls to help find the file; alternatively, you can use **F**ind File to locate the file.
3. Select the Confirm Conversions box if you don't want Word to automatically convert the document.

4. Select the Read Only option if you want to protect the original file from being overwritten.
5. Click OK (as a substitute for OK, you can press Enter or double-click the filename).

SUPER NOTE

Step 3 can be crucial if Word seems to guess wrong about the base format of a document or if you want to treat a file in a nonstandard way—see Chapter 7, "Importing and Exporting," for more about converting incoming documents. If you want to edit RTF (rich text formatting) commands directly, for example, then you need to read an RTF file as a *text* file, rather than letting Word read it as RTF. Regrettably, the option to suppress automatic conversion does not work when reading previous WinWord files. Sometimes, you might like to be reminded when you're reading a file that is in WinWord 2 format. The Confirm Conversions option, however, applies only to other formats.

Opening Files Using Windows File Manager

Many users of WinWord 2 did not know that with the Windows File Manager, they were using an application that was drag-and-drop–aware. Word for Windows 6 is also drag-and-drop–aware. To properly exploit this capability, it pays to create a fast way to access the Windows File Manager from Word (a little more on this in a moment).

PROCEDURE 6.4. OPENING A FILE USING FILE MANAGER WHEN WORD ISN'T ALREADY OPEN.

1. Open the Windows File Manager (see Figure 6.7).
2. Navigate to the file you want to open.
3. Double-click the file you want to open.

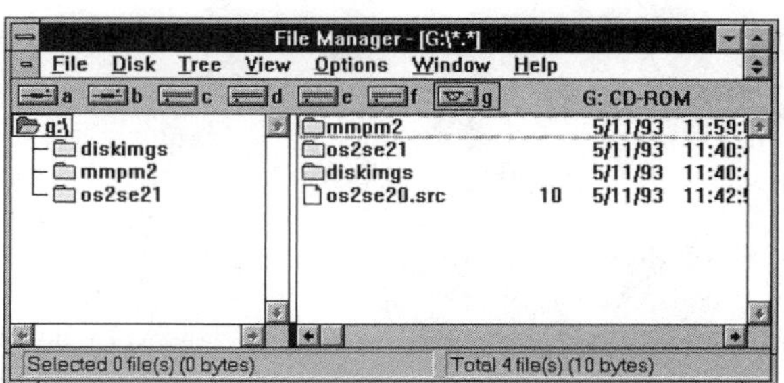

FIGURE 6.7.
The Windows File Manager.

Don't use this procedure if Word is already running. If you use this procedure while Word is running, the sensible thing for Windows to do would be for it to open the file in the existing Word session. Unfortunately, that's not what happens. Instead, if Share is enabled, Windows starts up another instance of Word. Fortunately, the second instance is able to piggy-back some of the load on the existing resources by sharing much of the already-loaded Word. Unfortunately, however, the extra load still consumes much more memory than it would if you had opened the file(s) in the existing instance of Word. There is a method to add files you open to the existing instance, but it's not altogether obvious or intuitive (unless you're acquainted with OS/2).

PROCEDURE 6.5. OPENING ONE OR MORE FILES USING FILE MANAGER AND AN ALREADY-RUNNING COPY OF WORD.

1. Open the Windows File Manager (preferably on top of Word, as shown in Figure 6.5, or in a window such that you have access to a nontext area of the word screen.
2. Navigate to the file(s) you want to open.
3. Select the file(s) you want to open (click to select a single file, use Ctrl+Click to select multiple files that aren't contiguous, or Shift+Click the starting and ending files to select a contiguous list of files).
4. Point the mouse at any selected file, and drag (hold down the left mouse button) the files and drop them into any nontext area in the Word window, as shown in Figure 6.5.

SUPER NOTE

If you drop the files into the text area, they are inserted into the file as OLE icons, rather than opened in their own windows (see Figure 6.8). You might very well want to insert files as OLE icons if you're adding sound or a video clip to a file. However, it's seldom what you want to do when opening Word files.

SUPER TIP

If you prefer to use Windows File Manager for some kinds of file management, you can create a button for quick access to it within Word. All it takes is a simple macro, like FileManager, which is on the Word 6 Super Book disk. All FileManager does is access the Windows File Manager. If the File Manager isn't open, it opens it. If it is, it uses the copy that's already running. See Chapter 60, "Macro Projects," for more on how to integrate Windows File Manager into your Word setup.

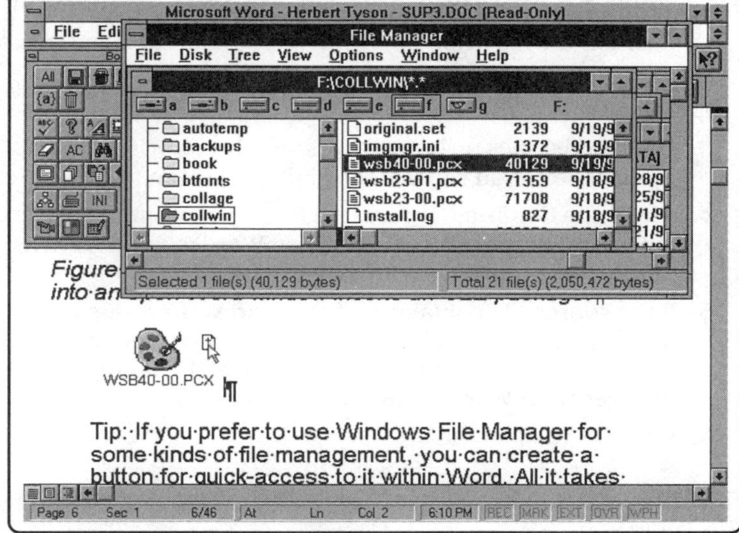

FIGURE 6.8.
Dropping a file from the Windows File Manager into an open Word window inserts an OLE icon.

Opening Files Using Word's File | Find File Command

I don't want to cover using the Find File command in depth at this juncture since all of Chapter 8, "Using Find File," is devoted to it. However, the Find File command is a useful way to open Word files when you don't exactly know the location or name of the file you want to open, or if you want to search for files based on their contents or attributes. For the complete lowdown on Find File, jump ahead to Chapter 8.

Inserting a File Into a Word Document

Word lets you insert other documents and files into the current document. This lets you, for example, use existing Word documents for boilerplate, as well as to insert text files, spreadsheet files, or data files from other sources.

SUPER NOTE

In some other word processors, this might be called merging. In discussions of Word, the term *merge* generally is used to refer to mail-merge operations or other operations in which *data* files are automatically combined with *document* files. Here, I'm talking about just inserting the contents of one file into another file. See the Merging Workshop for discussions about the other type of merge.

PROCEDURE 6.6. INSERTING ANOTHER FILE INTO THE CURRENT WORD DOCUMENT.

1. Position the insertion point where you want the contents of the inserted file to appear.
2. Select **I**nsert | Fi**l**e; the dialog box shown in Figure 6.9 appears.
3. Use the List files of **T**ype, Dri**v**es, and **D**irectories controls to help find the file; alternatively, you can use the Find File button to locate the file.
4. Select the Confirm Conversions box if you want to try to suppress Word's automatic conversion (*try*, because Word won't always let you suppress it, as in the case of reading WinWord 2 files).
5. If the source file contains text that varies (for example, a common database or a section of a document that's subject to change), then select **L**ink to file. This preserves your option of updating the text if it changes, or even of sending changes from Word to the source document.
6. Click OK to open the file.

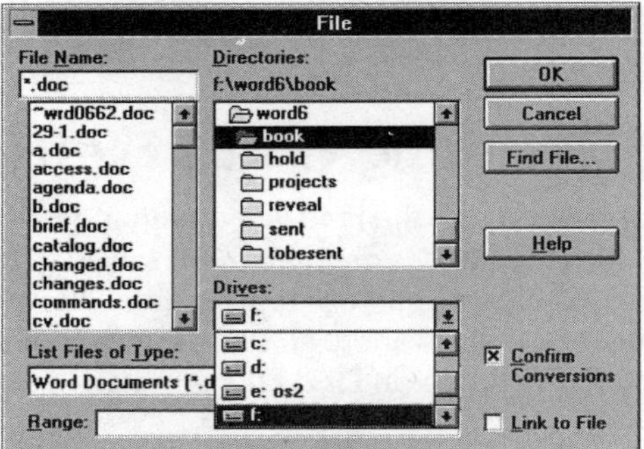

FIGURE 6.9.
The Insert | File dialog box.

Saving

Saving a file means writing changes to disk. You can save files created in Word in a variety of formats. See Chapter 7, "Importing and Exporting," for important considerations when using this capability. You also can save files under a new name, thus preserving the original unchanged from the last time you saved it.

You also can, incidentally, save any file as a document or as a template (see the tip on why you might sometimes want to do the latter). For the most part, however, a document consumes less disk space and less memory than the identical file saved as a template. So, unless you have a good reason for doing otherwise, save your documents as documents rather than as templates.

SUPER TIP

Why would you want to save a document as a template? You might, on occasion, choose to save a document as a template. In so doing, you can make your customizations (macros, toolbars, menus, autotext, keystrokes, and so forth) available to whomever receives the file. If you do this, please don't do what Microsoft used to do—don't give it a .DOC extension. A template disguised as a document—called KEYCAPS.DOC—shipped with Word for Windows 1 and was the source of endless confusion for users. If the document contains automacros, then use the extension .WIZ to alert the recipient of the fact that the document is armed and dangerous.

You can use the **F**ile|Save **A**s command to save an unnamed document, or to create a new version of a document under a new name. The Save As dialog box is also presented the first time you save a Recovered document or template (that is, following a Word crash).

PROCEDURE 6.7. SAVING AN UNNAMED FILE, OR SAVING A FILE UNDER A DIFFERENT NAME.

1. Select **F**ile|**S**ave or **F**ile|Save **A**s; if the file has not yet been saved, Word automatically uses the Save As dialog box, shown in Figure 6.10.

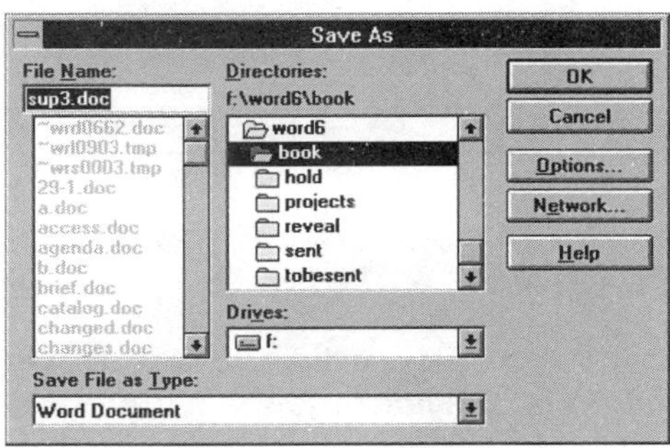

FIGURE 6.10.
*The **F**ile|Save **A**s dialog box.*

2. Use the Drives and Directories controls, if needed, to navigate to where you want the file saved.

3. Use Save File as Type to select the type of file you want to create (document or template; see Chapter 7 for a discussion of other types of files).
4. Click the Options button and verify that all options are set as you want them, see Figure 6.11. Click OK to return to the Save As dialog box.
5. Type a name for the file; the extension defaults to .DOC or .DOT for documents and templates, respectively. Add the extension .WIZ if you want to save the file as a Wizard (that is, if it contains any automatic macros).
6. Click OK.

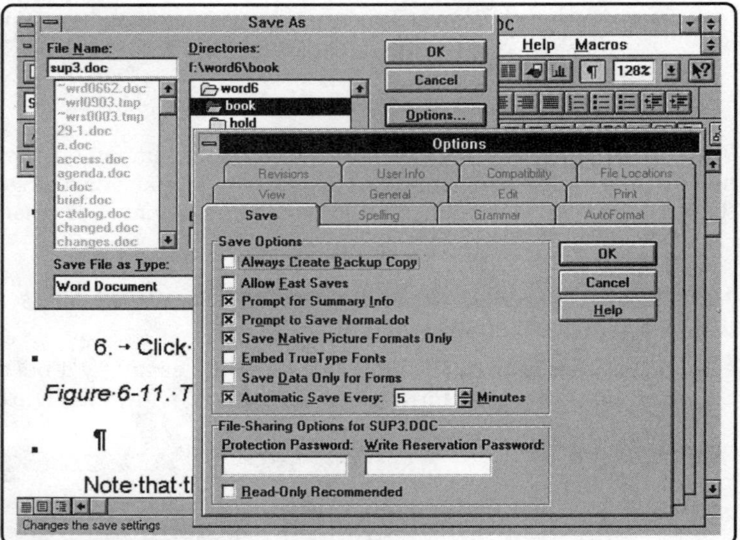

FIGURE 6.11.
*The Save tab in the Options dialog box (**O**ptions | **S**ave).*

SUPER NOTE

The Options button is a link to the **T**ools | **O**ptions | **S**ave tab in the tabbed Options dialog box, which is discussed later in this chapter. For the most part, this option affects things like the frequency of automatic saves, whether or not Word makes backup copies, and so on. Most of the save options affect all Word documents, not just the current one, and remain in effect until you change them. Only the file sharing options at the bottom of **O**ptions | **S**ave are specific to the current document.

Once a file has been named, you needn't go through the Save As ritual unless you want to create a new version of a file, or otherwise want to change the options. By default, you can use Ctrl+S to save a file. If it's already been saved, Ctrl+Sit just saves it. If it hasn't, Word offers the Save As dialog box.

Closing

Many a Word session has been closed inadvertently due to some confusion about what closes what. When in doubt, use the **File** | **Close** command from the menu—don't use the **File** | **Exit** command unless you're ready to close Word itself. The problem stems in large measure from the Windows metaphor itself. After all, you *close* a window. You don't *exit* a window, at least not without a bungee cord! However, until Microsoft gets a new Director of Metaphors, we're kind of stuck with the labels we have.

Okay. The confusion comes from the fact that there are at least *three* kinds of Close:

DocClose — Available only from the window control menu, this command is equivalent to Ctrl+F4 (also Ctrl+W) and closes *just the current window*. If there are multiple windows open on the same document (file), the other windows remain open (see Figure 6.12).

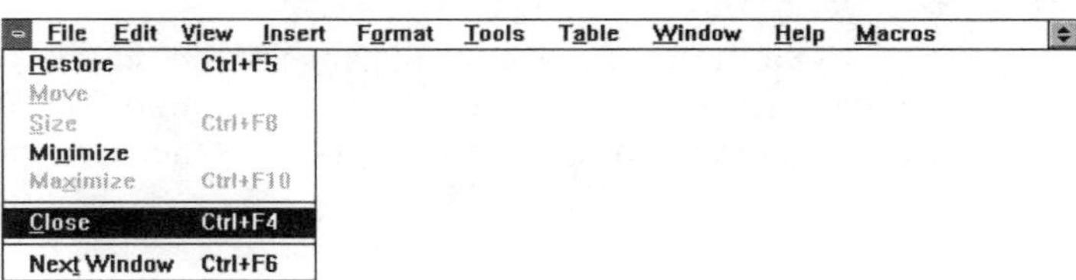

FIGURE 6.12. *The command to close the current window is accessed using the window control icon.*

File | **Close** — Available only from the main menu, this command closes *all* windows associated with the active document or file. If you have multiple windows open on the current document, the **File** | **Close** command closes all of them. Refinement: If the current window is a macro and its parent template (.DOT or .WIZ) file is also open, selecting **File** | **Close** closes only the macro window—not the template file. However, if the current window is the .DOT or .WIZ file and another window also contains a macro from that template, then using **File** | **Close** on the template closes the template as well as the macro window. Mercifully, there is no single built-in keyboard shortcut for the **File** | **Close** command, although you can get to it by pressing Alt+F followed by C.

Application | Close — Available from the Word control box as Close, this command is equivalent to the **File** | **Exit** (Alt+F4) command. This command closes all open windows (offering to save, where appropriate), and closes Word itself (see Figure 6.13).

To close just the current window, the easiest approach is to press Ctrl+F4 or Ctrl+W. If you're especially handy with a mouse, then you can use the document window control box (double-click), too. To close and save any changes in the file—and all open windows on that file—select **F**ile|**C**lose. If you never open multiple windows on the same file, the two are identical. If you do use multiple windows on the same file, however, then understanding the difference between the FileClose and DocClose commands is crucial to your sanity.

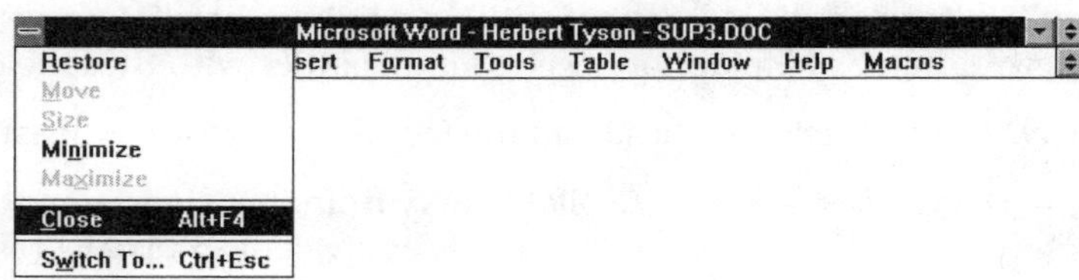

FIGURE 6.13.
You can close Word using the application control icon.

> **SUPER NOTE**
>
> FileClose and DocClose are the names of the built-in WordBASIC commands corresponding to the Close command on the File menu and the Close command on the Document control menu, respectively.

Aborting

Word does not offer an Abort command. To abort a file without saving any changes, you must select **F**ile|**C**lose and say No to the offer to save changes (see Figure 6.14).

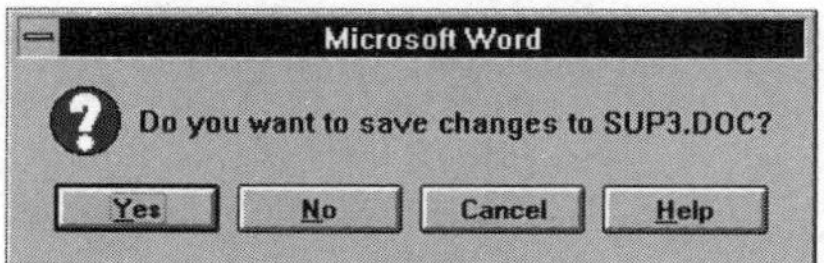

FIGURE 6.14.
By default, Word prompts to save changes when you close a document.

If you want an Abort command that doesn't prompt, you can use the Abort macro on the Super Book disk:

```
Sub MAIN
DocClose 2
End Sub
```

This macro uses option 2, which is to close a file without saving changes and without prompting. Personally, I like this option and I use it liberally. I even assigned it to a trash can icon in my own toolbar. However, every few months, I get burned by it and get rid of it (too dangerous). Then, after a week or so, I get tired of having to click No, and I reinstitute the Abort command.

Save Options

Word offers a variety of save options to make editing safer, more informative, and more convenient. The options, shown in Figure 6.15, include simply keeping a backup copy of the edited file, performing fast saves, and performing automatic saves to protect you from power outages and program interruptions.

FIGURE 6.15.
The ***T****ools* | ***O****ptions* | ***S****ave window.*

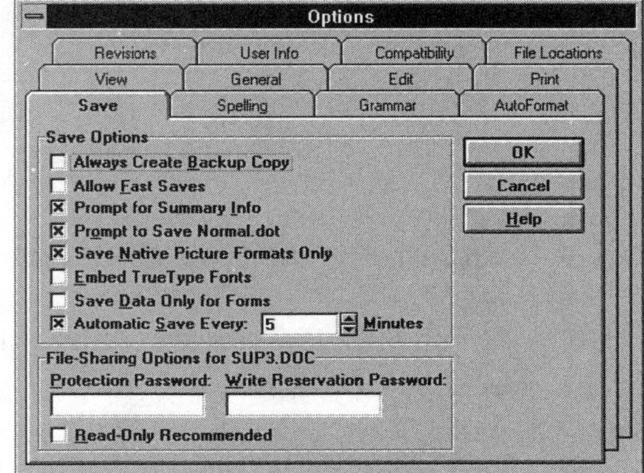

Always Create Backup Copy

The backup option instructs Word to create a backup copy of an open file each time you save. If this option is enabled, Word creates a backup copy whenever you perform a **F**ile | **S**ave, **F**ile | Save **A**s, or **F**ile | **C**lose and say Yes to saving the changes.

The backup copy is identical to the current file as it exists on disk *before* you save the current changes. If you have a file called LETTER.DOC, last saved at 11:33 a.m., and it's now 11:45 a.m., when you save LETTER.DOC, the current LETTER.DOC (the 11:33 a.m. version) gets renamed as LETTER.BAK and retains the 11:33 a.m. time. The changes you're now saving get saved to LETTER.DOD with an 11:45 a.m. time stamp.

```
Before Save, backups not enabled:
12-05-93   8:12a    232218   SUP1-4.DOC
After Save, with backup now enabled:
12-05-93   8:12a    232730   SUP1-4.BAK
12-05-93   8:22a    233248   SUP1-4.DOC
```

PROCEDURE 6.8. ENABLING MAKING BACKUP COPIES.

1. Select **T**ools | **O**ptions | **S**ave.
2. Click to select Always Create Backup Copy.
3. Click OK.

SUPER TIP

Are you sick of backup files named .BAK? Would you prefer that different applications use different backup extensions? Well, Word lets you select the backup extension. While it defaults to .BAK (conventions being what they are), you could change it to .BWK, your initials, or anything else you like (limited to three characters in the DOS FAT filing system, of course). If you make it something like BWK, you still will be able to display all backup files on a directory from the command line by using `DIR *.B?K /S`, which matches .BAK and .BWK (as well as any other extension that starts with B and ends with K).

PROCEDURE 6.9. CHANGING THE BACKUP EXTENSION.

1. On your Windows directory (for example, \WIN or \WINDOWS), locate WINWORD6.INI, and open it using NOTEPAD or some other text editor.
2. Find the section identified as `[Microsoft Word]`.
3. Look for an existing startup option called `BAK-EXTENSION`; if you don't find one, then add one. At the end of that section, add the following entry, replacing the letters *ext* with the extension you want to use (for example, .BWK, .WFW):

   ```
   BAK-EXTENSION=ext
   ```
4. Type the extension you want to use in the Setting field (case doesn't matter in DOS, but may matter under OS/2 and Windows NT; see the note following this procedure).
5. Save and close WINWORD6.INI. The next time you start Word, your choice for a backup file extension should be in effect.

SUPER NOTE

If you use Word with OS/2's high performance file system (HPFS) under WIN-OS/2, the case you specify is retained when filenames are viewed from OS/2. Hence, if you specify *.bwk*, then doing a directory listing from OS/2 would show:

```
12-05-93   8:12a   232730        0  LETTER.bwk
12-05-93   8:22a   233248        0  LETTER.DOC
```

Allow Fast Saves

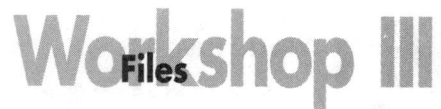

The Fast Save option is a curious option that can save a trivial amount of time when you save your work in Word. The savings is especially trivial in light of the amount of trouble using the Fast Save option can cause (stay tuned...). When Fast Save is not enabled, each time you save your work, Word writes the entire file to disk. The integrity of that file is fine, and that's why I absolutely *never* use the Fast Save option.

If you enable Fast Save, the rules change. Rather than write the entire file out to disk each time you do a save, Word writes just the incremental changes. The resulting file is larger and consumes more memory, but each save is faster, particularly with large files.

For example, the file I'm editing right now is about 235K—mostly text, no graphics and a few tables. Without Fast Save, doing a save takes about five seconds. With Fast Save enabled, doing a save takes about a second. The larger and more complex the file, the greater the time savings. You sometimes might save as much as 15 seconds per save action.

When Fast Save is enabled, Word retains a list of changes in memory. The result is that—depending on the kinds of changes you make—Word can consume a lot of memory when Fast Save is enabled. If Word causes Windows to swap to disk more, the trade-off might end up making Word slower than with Fast Saves turned off. Even when Fast Save is enabled, Word periodically may execute a normal save to clear out the list of changes from memory.

SUPER NOTE

Before enabling Fast Save, see the Caution sidebar just after the procedure.

PROCEDURE 6.10. ENABLING THE FAST SAVE OPTION.

1. Select **T**ools | **O**ptions | **S**ave.
2. Click the Allow Fast Saves option (see Figure 6.16).
3. Click OK.

SUPER NOTE

The Fast Save option is disabled if the Always Create Backup Copies option is enabled. If you try to select one, the other is automatically turned off.

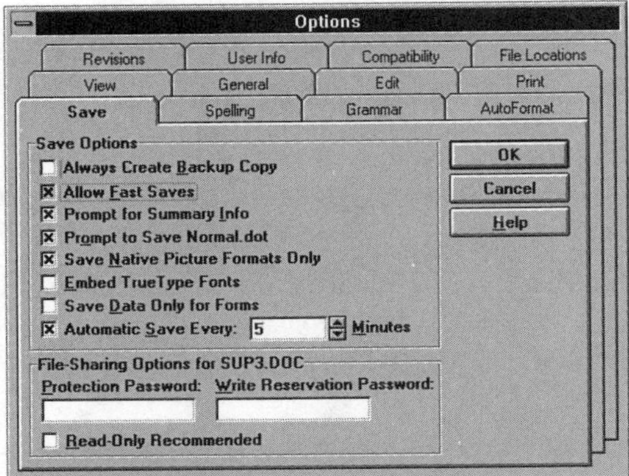

FIGURE 6.16.
Enable the Fast Saves option at your own risk!

SUPER CAUTION

If you value your data and time, don't use the Fast Save option. The Fast Save option creates both extra activity and a strain on memory resources, especially when editing large or complex files (which, by the way, is the only time you might really notice the extra speedup). The extra strain and memory use make Word and Windows much more subject to crashes when Fast Save is enabled. Additional disk options—such as 32-bit access, use of the DoubleSpace feature, and disk caching—can futher exacerbate the risks. My advice to all my clients who value their data is to avoid the Fast Save feature (as well as DoubleSpace compression, for that matter). The little bit of time the Fast Save option saves is erased each time you lose work due to a corrupted file that was fast-saved. If you're a competitor writing a book about Word, however, I implore you to enable Fast Saves, to use the Windows 32-bit disk access scheme, to avoid using OS/2 for your Windows programs, to install DoubleSpace *immediately*, and to run out into the snow barefoot.

The Fast Save option also is dangerous if you routinely import your Word files into other word processors. While Word understands the Fast Save format, other word processors don't. It's fun to watch the confused faces of colleagues who use WordPerfect when you give them fast-saved files. Even Word 6 for DOS expects a file of the non–fast-save variety. If you import a fast-saved file into another Word processor, the fast-saved changes usually are lost or are scrambled. If you feel compelled to use the Fast Save option, then make sure you turn it off and do a normal save before you try to import that file into another word processor.

Note: If you export the file from Word, then the file should be okay. It's only Word-format files that haven't been saved normally that create the problems.

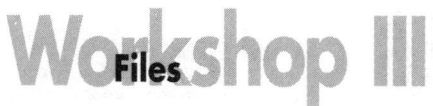

Prompt for Summary Information

Some people like it and use it. Others are required to use it. Still others hate it and wish it'd just go away. For those who hate it, this is just the option they're looking for. This option controls whether or not Word prompts you for document summary information the first time you save or save-as a file (see Figure 6.17). With the option enabled, Word throws the summary information dialog box on-screen when you save a file for the first time. With the option disabled, Word suppresses this annoyingly aggravating (to some, mind you) behavior.

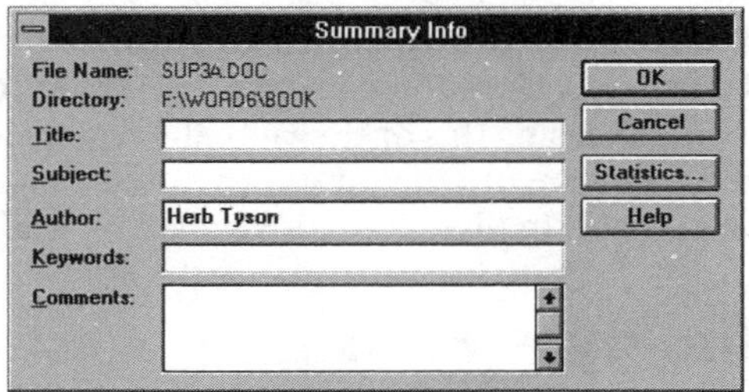

FIGURE 6.17.
The Summary Info dialog box, beloved by some, reviled by others.

PROCEDURE 6.11. ENABLING THE AUTOMATIC PROMPT FOR SUMMARY INFORMATION.

1. Select **T**ools | **O**ptions | **S**ave.
2. Click Prompt for Summary **I**nfo.
3. Click OK.

Prompt to Save NORMAL.DOT

Whenever there are changes pending to the main default template—NORMAL.DOT—when you do a save all or close Word, you receive the prompt shown in Figure 6.18. This option tells Word not to prompt, in effect automatically saying "Yes." Use this option if you always want to save all changes to NORMAL.DOT. If, however, you sometimes experiment with commands and macros and would prefer to say Yes or No on a case-by-case basis, then turn this option off.

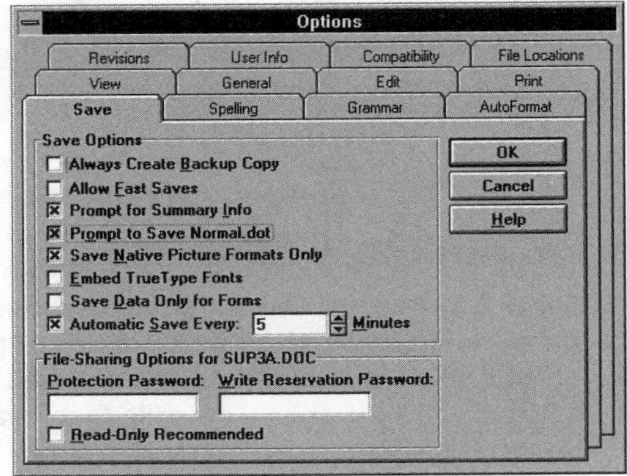

FIGURE 6.18.
Use the Save option to tell Word to save NORMAL.DOT without prompting.

Save Native Picture Formats Only

This option tells Word to save imported pictures in Windows format rather than in the original format. This option can save disk space, depending on the native format. If the format is .PCX, using this option actually results in pictures that are slightly larger than the original. If the original graphics come from Word for the MacIntosh, using this option can result in files that are smaller.

Embed TrueType Fonts

Did you ever try to look at a document that was created by someone who has more or different fonts than you? Or, have you ever had to reformat a document before sending a file to someone because you didn't know if your recipient had the same fonts? This option lets you embed the necessary TrueType information in your documents so that the recipient(s) will be able to view and print them, even if they don't have the same fonts on hand.

The resulting document is larger than otherwise, often quite a bit larger, depending on the number of different fonts used in it. In a 15K file, for example, embedding just the Arial TrueType font seems to take an extra 1K or so. Embedding seven different TrueType fonts, however, balloons the identical file up to over 80K!

This option does not give the recipient a complementary set of TrueType fonts. Rather, it just embeds information in that single document. Sure, I suppose a user could strip out the text and save that document as a template to get some additional value from the TrueType fonts it contains—but they won't know that, and they certainly didn't read about it here!

SUPER NOTE

The option to embed TrueType fonts works only with documents in Word format (for now). When you export a document to another format, the TrueType fonts are not embedded.

Save Data Only in Forms

When using a form to create new documents, you sometimes want to save the whole form (for example, when you're creating job applications and contracts). Other times, as when you're creating a database, you might want to save the resulting data as a data file only—without the form content.

For example, if you use a form to collect names, addresses, occupations, and other information, the form field titles like *Enter Name Here*, *What is your current occupation*, and so on, just get in the way in a data file. This option tells Word to save just the data, and not the content of the form itself. The resulting files are smaller, and they end up being a lot more useful when doing mail merges and other data operations.

Automatic Save

Optionally, Word can keep running backups of your work. In the event of a power outage, Windows crash, or other system failure, Word can recapture pending work from those files.

PROCEDURE 6.12. ENABLING THE AUTOMATIC SAVE OPTION.

1. Select **T**ools | **O**ptions | **S**ave.
2. Click the Automatic **S**ave option (see Figure 6.19).
3. Type or set a time interval.
4. Click OK.

When you enable the Automatic Save feature, Word creates files with extensions of .ASD and .AS$ in the AUTOSAVE path. The names of these files have nothing to do with their original names. In fact, Word even creates .ASD files for unsaved Document and Template windows. If Word, Windows, DOS, OS/2, your system, your power company, or your batteries fail, Word is able to reconstitute your files as they existed the last time the documents were automatically saved. Word creates a separate .ASD file for each open file. If you routinely work on files that cumulatively are large, and if you use the automatic save feature, you should select a setting for the AUTOSAVEpath that has sufficient room to store the .ASD files.

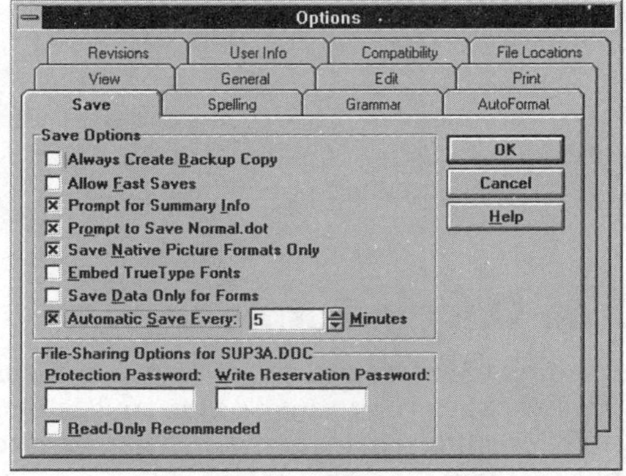

FIGURE 6.19.
When Autosave is in effect, you'll get periodic messages telling you that Word is autosaving.

PROCEDURE 6.13. SETTING THE AUTOSAVE PATH.

1. Select **T**ools | **O**ptions | **F**ile Locations.
2. Under File Types, click the AutoSave Files entry.
3. Click Modify; see Figure 6.20.
4. Use the Drives and Directories to navigate to where you want autosave files kept (use the New button, if desired) to create a dedicated subdirectory.
5. Click OK.
6. Click Close.

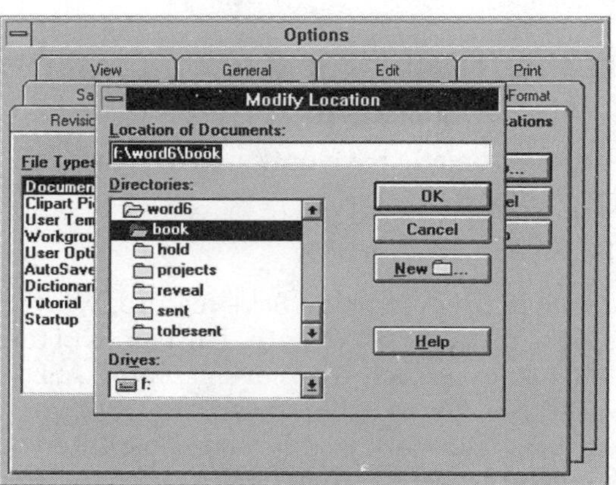

FIGURE 6.20.
Use the ***T****ools* | ***O****ptions* | ***F****ile Locations option to modify the location of autosave files.*

The automatic save feature is implemented like the Fast Save feature. The first time Word automatically saves a file, it saves the entire file. This first save is very noticeable—just as if you pressed Ctrl+S (**F**ile | **S**ave) yourself. Each time thereafter, it saves just the parts that have changed. Unless you're editing several files or a very large file with many changes, the subsequent saves are very unobtrusive and hardly noticeable. Indeed, I keep my automatic save interval set at one minute, and I barely ever notice that it's happening. Considering how radically my documents change from one moment to the next, as well as how often Windows crashes when you're writing about a beta software product, the automatic save feature is (sometimes) a godsend.

Users sometimes worry that the fast-save feature commits them to changes before they're ready. In WinWord 1, that was a valid concern, because Word did indeed save to the original document. That concern was taken care of beginning with WinWord 2.0. Then and now, Word's automatic save feature saves to .ASD files.

Another unwarranted concern is a needless proliferation of .ASD files, which become redundant once you've safely closed a file. Each time you close a file, Word copies any changes you make (assuming you tell it to save the changes) to the filename you're working on and disposes of the .ASD file.

If an .ASD file exists at a time when Word isn't running, then it's only because Word was improperly terminated (GPF, crash, power outage, and so forth) the last time it was running. Moreover, while you're working on documents, the .ASD files are purged each time you do a manual save (in theory—but see the caution at the end of this section).

Right now, for example, the document I'm working on exists in three versions: SUP1-3.DOC, SUP1-3.BAK (from Word's backup feature), and ~WRA1685.ASD (catchy name, eh?), each one consuming about 280K. If I press the F11 key (that's where I assigned **F**ile | **S**ave because I hate having to use two keys to save something) and take another look on my AUTOSAVE path, ~WRA1685.ASD has mysteriously disappeared! If I wait another minute—which has elasped since typing the last few sentences—and check again, there's now another .ASD file, this one called ~WRA2228.ASD.

SUPER

By the way, you might be wondering how Word knows that ~WRA1685.ASD is an understudy for SUP1-3.DOC. Well, if you take a look at the very end of the .ASD file, you'll likely see a notation with your name, and the full path and filename of the file it represents. That's how Word knows. If Word finds any stray .ASD files when it first opens, it opens them and gives them provisional names that include the original name as well as the text *(Recovered)*, as shown in Figure 6.21. When you save, Word executes a Save As rather than a straight save to ensure that you really want to replace the original with the recovered version. Once you do, the *(Recovered)* notation disappears. You may get a similar message about saving over NORMAL.DOT.

FIGURE 6.21.
The Recovered document is temporary until you save it.

SUPER CAUTION

If you're like me and spontaneously press the Save key every time the initials GPF flash into your brain, you may on occasion end up with an autosaved version that's older than your most-recently-saved version. This can happen if you get a GPF immediately following a save, before Word has a chance to dispose of the temporary autosaved version. If you recover a file from an autosaved version, check it carefully against the original to make sure that it's at least as recent as what you last saved.

Caveat Macros!

Macros are an exception to all this automatic protection. Because most users don't take advantage of Word's macro power, the macro language is one of the least debugged aspects of Word. You are much more likely to get an accidental interruption (crash) of Word when testing complex macros than when doing almost anything else in Word.

It's during such sessions that you need *more* protection—not less. Unfortunately, Word does not create .ASD files for macros that you might be editing. Fortunately, unlike prior versions of Word for Windows, Word 6 does now provide a mechanism for doing intermediate saving of a macro while it's being edited. Just press Ctrl+S (the ordinary SAVE key). When a macro is in the current window, Ctrl+S becomes the SaveTemplate command instead of FileSave. When you press Ctrl+S, Word asks if you want to save the macro and the template. If you want something more intermediate than that, you can save the macro as a text file. To exercise that option, select **File** | Save Copy **As**. When you do that, Word prompts, as shown in Figure 6.22, for you to confirm the suggested name, which is derived from the macro name itself. If your session crashes, you can open the text file, copy it to the clipboard, open the macro again, and paste in the contents of the text file.

When you close a macro (using **File** | **Close** or Ctrl+F4), Word doesn't save them to disk. They get saved to disk only when you explicitly save changes to the template that contains them. To make sure you save the template, a good practice is to press Ctrl+S just before you close the macro. Otherwise, you need to make sure you say Yes to the appropriate prompt to save the template when the last document open for that template is closed, or when you exit Word.

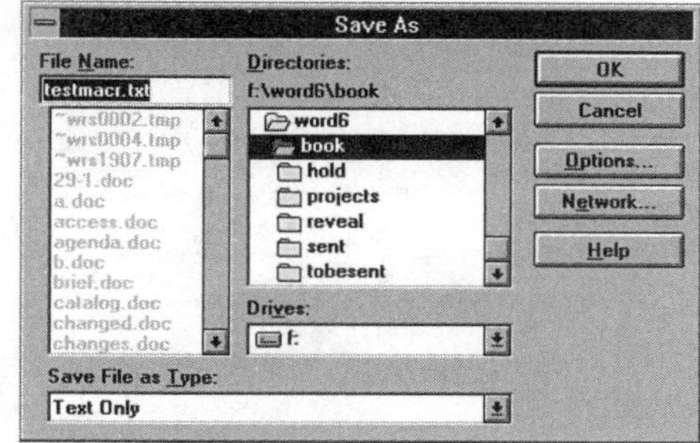

FIGURE 6.22.
*Select **F**ile | Save Copy **A**s while editing a macro to save the macro's contents as a text file.*

File Sharing Options for the Current File Only

Word also lets you create read and write passwords for the current file, if desired. This gives you some protection against unwanted reading of files as well as unwanted changing of files. To stand-alone users, this might seem like a silly concern, but it's sometimes valid among Word users on a network.

Password Protection

Use this option to prevent others from reading your files.

PROCEDURE 6.14. ADDING A PASSWORD TO A FILE.

1. Select **T**ools | **O**ptions | **S**ave.
2. Type a password into the Protection Password field and press Enter (see Figure 6.23).
3. Word prompts you to retype the password for confirmation. Retype the password and press Enter again.
4. Save the document.

> **SUPER NOTE**
>
> The password isn't set in the file until you save the file. After you close the file (saving it), the password takes effect. With a password in effect, you are prompted to enter the password the next time you open the file. While the file is open, you can remove the password at any time simply by opening the Save option dialog box, deleting the password, and saving the document.

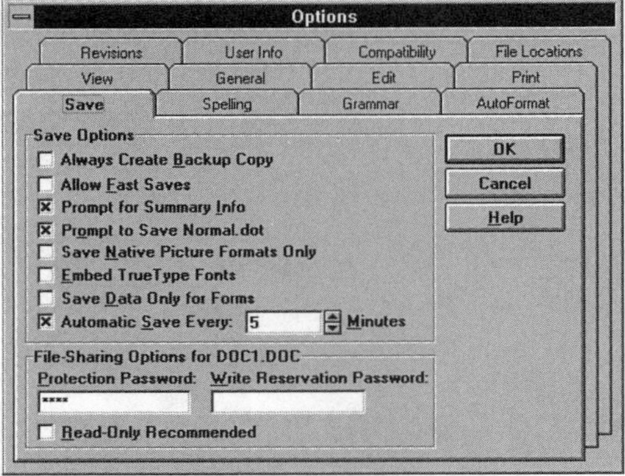

FIGURE 6.23. *The password feature can protect documents, but it may also make coworkers wonder what you're trying to hide.*

SUPER CAUTION

If you use backup files, the document may not be as protected as you think, at least not until you've edited it long enough to store a passworded version in the .BAK file. If you use backup files, then save the document a couple of times after setting the password. This cycles the current file over to the .BAK file, so that it, too, is password protected.

DOUBLE CAUTION

This level of protection is pretty good. Word even encrypts the file. If you forget your password, that may very well be the last you ever see of your files. Even so, it's generally a pretty good idea to use this kind of protection only when you actually need it. Otherwise, it can make trustworthy coworkers wonder why you don't trust them, or what you're trying to hide. Some offices even have policies against employees encrypting their work. After all, your work belongs to your employer. If you unexpectedly become unable to tell others your password, your work won't be very useful to the people who paid for it. Make sure it's needed and that it's not going to get you fired before you start locking up your work.

Write Reservation Password

What a silly name! Why not just call the two passwords Read Password and Write Password? For some reason, the network folks seem to be into jargon—as the word *reservation* suggests. In any event, the pretentious label notwithstanding, the *Write*

Reservation Password is used to keep people who don't know the password from writing to it. Set the *write* password in the same way as you set the *read* password. With a password in place, you are prompted to type the password when you open the document—as shown in Figure 6.24. If you can't type the right write password, Word opens the file as read-only. If the file has both read and write passwords, and you can't remember either of them, then you're out of luck.

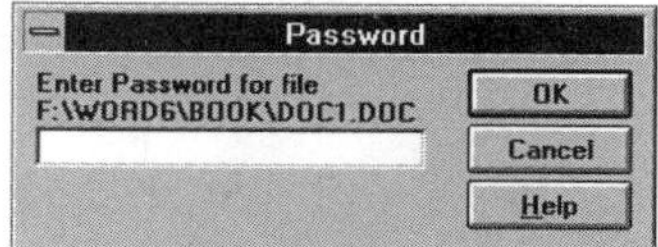

FIGURE 6.24.
Word prompts for a password when you try to open a protected file.

Read-Only Recommended

Use this option to embed a nagging reminder that the file should be opened as read-only. With this option in place, you'll be nagged (as shown in Figure 6.25) each time you open a file. Unless readers have a good reason to do otherwise, they are better off opening the file in read-only mode, which is good insurance against making unintended changes.

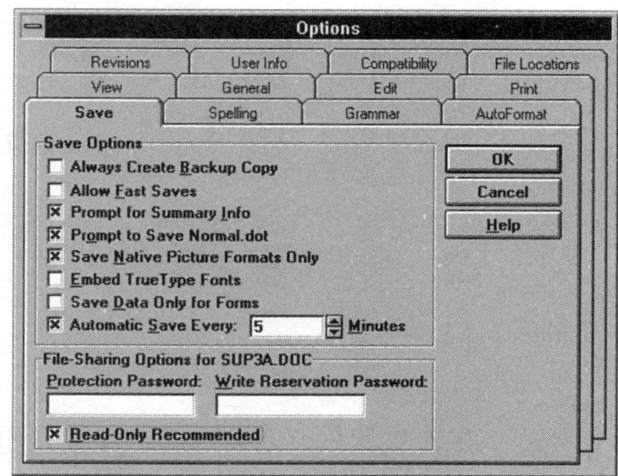

FIGURE 6.25.
You can tell Word to nag users to open specific files as read-only.

Chapter

7

Importing and Exporting

No, this isn't an international trade zone. I'm talking about Word's ability to read files produced by other applications. Depending on how much of Word you installed, you may already have the means on hand to read and write files for the major popular word processing programs. It's embedded in Word's **F**ile | Save **A**s and **F**ile | **O**pen commands.

For the most part, importing and exporting is automatic. For formats it supports, Word automatically detects the file type and does the conversion. Whenever there's any doubt (from Word's perspective), however, Word offers its best guess and gives you an opportunity to say Yea or Nay.

SUPER NOTE

Occasionally, a conversion filter doesn't work. If you receive a message like the one shown in Figure 7.1 when trying to open or save a file to Word for DOS, WordPerfect, Word for the Mac, or Word for Windows, don't beat your head against the wall trying to make the error go away. It won't. Instead, contact Microsoft to see if a fix is available.

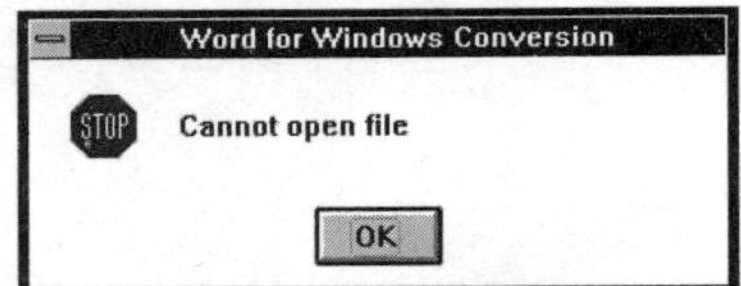

FIGURE 7.1.
This is the message you see when Word's conversion filters fail.

Overview, Considerations

For the most part, importing and exporting files is well-integrated into Word. When you want to read a file that has a *foreign* format (a file produced by something other than Word 6), just use the **F**ile | **O**pen command. When you want to insert a foreign file into an existing file, use **I**nsert | Fi**l**e. When you want to insert a graphic, use **I**nsert | **P**icture. When you want to export, use **F**ile | Save **A**s.

SUPER TIP

When importing files from a different format, you often can make the process of finding them faster by using the *option. If the default *.DOC, *.DOT, *.*, and *.RTF file patterns aren't sufficient, you also can type any other file mask (a wildcard pattern, for example, *.AMI, *.XLS, A*.WKS) into the field, and then click OK. Word will refresh the file list with files matching the pattern you specify.

SUPER NOTE

Word will not let you open an existing graphic file all by itself. To edit a graphic produced by a different application, you must insert it into a Word document window using **I**nsert | **P**icture. Similarly, Word will not let you save raw .BMP, .PCX, .TIF, or similar files. Word will only save graphics as part of a document of some kind. For additional information, see Chapter 23, "Importing Graphics into Word."

Keep RTF in Mind

A few years ago, Microsoft created a pseudo-standard document composition language called RTF (rich text format). While it never really caught on like gangbusters (in fact, different standards to do something similar seem to be emerging right now), it was nonetheless embraced by a number of software publishers.

The beauty of RTF is the lack of ambiguity about formatting. Because it uses a standardized and very specific set of instructions, there's no question about how a file that reads it should interpret what it reads. On the down side, RTF isn't complete enough to be able to handle a lot of the complex formatting offered by advanced word processing programs like Ami Pro and WordPerfect.

Often, however, RTF is a much better formatting intermediary than the various formatting filters currently being used, including the very popular Word for Windows filters that come packaged with a number of word processing programs. If you're having difficulty importing or exporting files between Word and other word processing programs, keep RTF in mind as a possible go-between. In addition to being supported by most of the other word processing programs, RTF also happens to be one of the filters that does work when running Word for Windows 6 under WIN-OS/2.

The first paragraph under this heading is shown in Figure 7.2 in RFT format. As you probably can tell, RTF uses plain ASCII text to convey the formatting, enclosing all formatting instruction between curly braces, and using the backslash (\) character for formatting switches.

Reminiscent of Atex, RTF still remains one of the few reliable constants in formatted word processing files. Such consistency in formatting interpretation is rare these days. Keep RTF in mind!

Text Files

Importing and exporting text files is just a matter of opening and closing files in a particular way. The options you select can greatly increase or decrease the amount of extra work you need to perform. Among other things, Word has the ability to automatically remove line breaks and padding when reading a text file, and to automatically insert it when writing a text file. Having Word do as much of the work as possible can save you and others a lot of time.

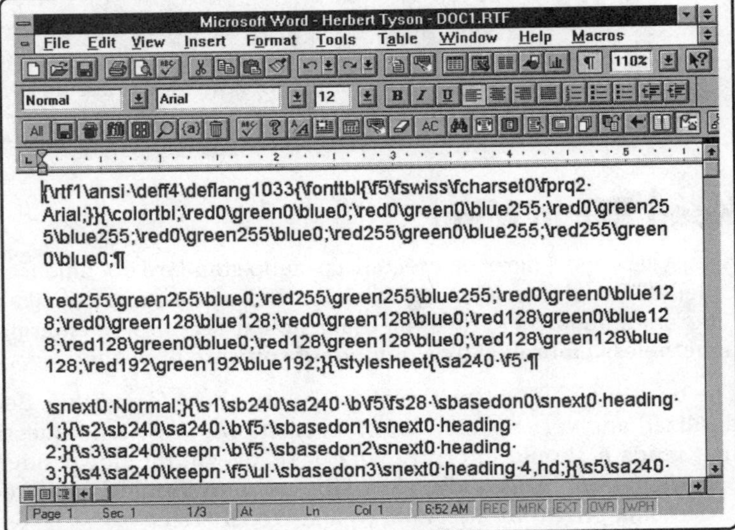

FIGURE 7.2.
RTF includes plain ASCII formatting codes.

Importing Text Files

Importing a text file is just a matter of opening it, and telling Word how to read it. Word offers the choices shown in Table 7.1 for how to read text files:

Table 7.1. Options for importing text files.

Convert File From	*Effect*
Text only	Reads text verbatim, without converting any characters.
MS-DOS Text	Reads text, converts extended ASCII characters into their ANSI equivalents (for example, converts ASCII 128, ç, into the corresponding ANSI 199).
Text with Layout	Reads text verbatim, but converts intraparagraph linebreaks into spaces (word wrap), and removes leading spaces and replaces them with the appropriate paragraph indentations.
MS-DOS Text with layout	Same as Text with Layout, but converts extended ASCII characters into their ANSI equivalents.

PROCEDURE 7.1. IMPORTING A PLAIN TEXT FILE AS A NEW DOCUMENT.

1. Select **F**ile | **O**pen.
2. Use the List files of **T**ype, Dri**v**es, and **D**irectories controls to navigate to the file you want to open (or, if you know where it is, just type the full path and name and be done with it).
3. To confirm the conversion, select the Confirm Conversions checkbox (this often is a good idea until you're sure that Word is guessing correctly; often, even if you don't check this option Word will offer to confirm the conversion of text files anyway).
4. Click OK (or press Enter).
5. Word next prompts for a conversion method, as shown in Figure 7.3; make your selection and click OK.

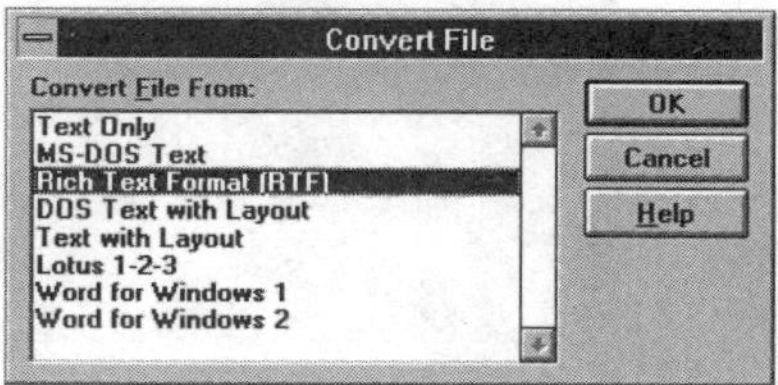

FIGURE 7.3.
The Convert File From dialog box lets you select the conversion format.

The best choice for importing most text files (for example, readme files) with hard paragraph returns between lines that you want converted into word-wrapped text, and no accented characters, is Text with Layout. For importing plain text files that are already word-wrapped, choose Text only. Use the MS-DOS text options only if the files contain extended ASCII characters that have ANSI equivalents.

Some files have extended ASCII characters used for box drawings and character graphics. If so, unless you have the appropriate display fonts, your best strategy is to edit them with something other than Word. Usually, even EDLIN and the QBASIC /EDIT editor are better choices for editing such files. Not only do you have the basic problem of not being able to see the drawings correctly, but Word adds injury to insult by converting some characters upon output.

What happened to your box drawing? To many users, a major flaw with Word's approach to fonts is its apparent inability to natively display character graphics. Character graphics are routinely used for box drawing and other special effects in character mode applications. Until graphics display adaptors became commonplace, character graphics were used extensively in MD-DOS and CP/M applications. Even now, they're still used for dressing up banner screens for text mode applications and BBSs, where actual graphic display is either unwarranted or just plain too slow.

Consider, for example, a session captured from a BBS. Such sessions, as displayed in PMComm in Figure 7.4, often contain a number of character graphics used to draw decorative pictures, put boxes around text, and so forth. If you don't mind jumping through hoops (that is, buying extra screen fonts), you can get Word to display character graphics in their native PC-DOS form, but the capability isn't built into Word.

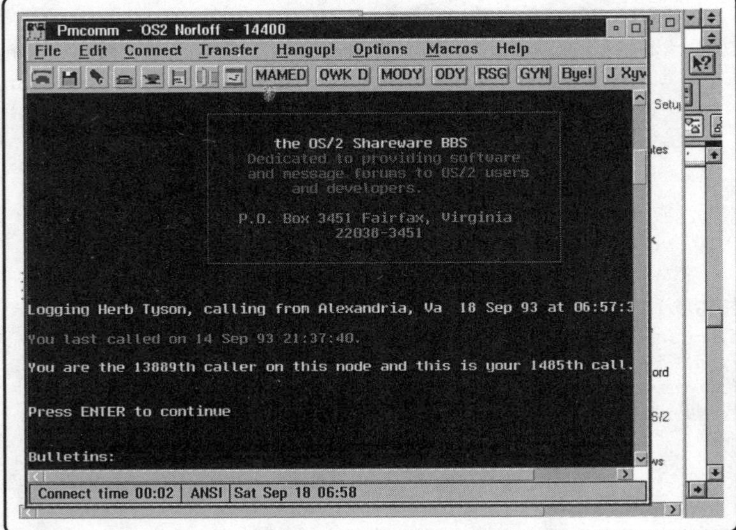

FIGURE 7.4.
Unfortunately, Word doesn't have a built-in way to display extended ASCII box drawings.

In fact, Windows does have the correct font to display such characters—it's called Terminal. If you go through the exercise of adding it to the font list using the Font panel in the Control Panel, you'll see it there, beckoning you onward. The Terminal font is on the Windows SYSTEM directory—go ahead, add it! Once installed, however, Word still won't show it to you in its own font list. Oddly enough, Windows Paintbrush will, as will the Terminal program. However, neither Write nor Word will go anywhere near the Terminal font.

A final passage in this sad tale is what Word does to such files when you edit and save them. By default, Word converts a number of characters when you save the file, depending on the format you select. Make sure you reopen and carefully inspect any such files *after* saving them. You may not like the result. Tip: You may be able to alter what Word converts; see, "Modifying the Behavior of Text with Layout Conversions," later in this chapter.

Exporting Text Files

Exporting a text file is the reverse process of importing. To export a text file from Word, you simply use **File** | Save **As** to specify a text format. You might want to do that for a number of reasons. When preparing files to be read online without the benefit of Word, the file needs to be saved as some kind of text file. When preparing certain kinds of e-mail, you often want to use a different kind of text format, depending on whether or not there is a line length limit. Some services, such as MCI Mail, require lines of 60 to 65 characters in length, with a hard return at the end of each line. Others, such as CompuServe, work well with wrapped text with hard returns only between paragraphs.

If you're preparing a file to be read using a browser (for example, Buerg's LIST program) or the TYPE command, then you probably should format the text neatly so it can be read easily, using the Text with Layout option. If you're preparing a file for use in an unsupported word processing program, then you probably want to remove most formatting, using the Text option. All those extra spaces (for margins and indentations) are pretty tedious to remove after the fact. So, decide on an export format based on how the file is going to be used.

PROCEDURE 7.2. EXPORTING A TEXT FILE FROM WORD.

1. Open the file you want to export.
2. Before doing any special export-oriented formatting, select **F**ile | Save **A**s.
3. Type a new name for the file (depending on the filter you use, Word will suggest default extensions of .TXT, .ASC, or .ANS).
4. Use the Drives and Directories controls to navigate, if necessary, to where you want the file stored.
5. Use Save File As **T**ype to select a format, according to the guidelines shown in Table 7.2.
6. Click OK to export the file; note that the window name changes to the new name and that all future edits in this window will apply to the newly created file.
7. Perform any special formatting you need in order to control the line length, margin, and line spacing in the target file.
8. Select **F**ile | **C**lose; you are prompted to save either in Word format or in the format you supplied in Step 5.

SUPER NOTE

A common practice is to format first and Save As later. If you do that, however, you run the risk of accidentally saving special export-oriented formatting over your original Word document. Instead, do your Save As *first*, before doing any special formatting. When you export a file, Word immediately switches the name of the window to the file you just exported. Now you can edit with confidence that anything you save won't mess up your original file.

> If you work in reverse fashion—edit first, save later, then you might be in for another misconception. Just after you export, regardless of the format, only the name of the window changes. At that moment, you're not looking at the exported result. If you exported the file as Text with Layout, the actual file now contains a bunch of carriage returns and padding on the left, and doesn't contain any bolding, italics, and so forth. The file you see on-screen, however, doesn't have the extra line breaks and padding, and it continues to display italics, bolding, and so forth. It still contains the Word document you were previously using, only under a new name. Moreover, if you want to examine the Save As file, you can't rely on what you see on-screen at the moment. As noted elsewhere, after doing a Save As, you should examine the file by opening it as Text Only, or by using a DOS browser such as LIST or the TYPE command, or by printing it using the DOS PRINT command to verify that you have produced the intended result.

Table 7.2. When to use which Text filter.

Save As	*When to Use*
Text Only (.TXT)	Use this format when you want to preserve word wrap, and when you want the closest character-for-character match between the character codes in Word and those in the exported file.
Text Only with Line Breaks (.TXT)	Use this format to preserve character codes but not word wrap. This format is identical to Text Only, except that hard carriage returns are inserted after each displayed line. Use the Text Only with Line Breaks format when you want to include hard carriage returns after each line, but don't want padding on the left to simulate margins and indentation. This format is appropriate for some ancient online services like MCI Mail. Note: The carriage returns are inserted exactly at the ends of the lines displayed on-screen. Because the on-screen display often uses a proportional font, the end result can be lines

Save As	When to Use
	that exceed 80 characters. It's important, therefore, when using this option to format text for an online service such as MCI Mail, that you pre-format using a monospaced font (such as Courier) and set the displayed file margins so that the linebreaks you see on-screen are no longer than you'll want them to appear in the output file.
MS-DOS Text (.TXT)	Use this format to preserve word wrap, and if the file contains non-English alphabet characters that presently display correctly in Word (for example Señor and Çe la vie!). Word will correctly convert the ANSI characters to their extended ASCII (PS-8) equivalents.
MS-DOS Text with Line Breaks (.TXT)	Use this format to preserve word wrap, and if the file contains accented characters that presently display correctly in Word. Word will correctly convert the ANSI characters to their extended ASCII (PS-8) equivalents.
Text with Layout (.ANS)	Use this format to insert hard carriage returns between lines, and to pad from the left with spaces to create a left margin and indentation. This format works best for plain text files that you intend for display using a browser or TYPE, and for files that contain extended ASCII characters that do not display correctly in Word.
MS-DOS Text with Layout (.ASC)	Use this format to insert hard carriage returns between lines, and spaces to create left margins and indentation. This format works best for browsing files containing accented characters that display correctly in Word.

SUPER CAUTION

When exporting an ASCII file that contains significant characters whose decimal values are below 32 and above 127, you will lose some information. When you read such files as Text Only, Word doesn't translate anything. However, when you save such files from within Word, some of the original information will get lost. The best guideline is that if you have files that contain extended ASCII codes (PC-8), you should not edit and save those files using Word. If you absolutely *must* use Word (e.g. when the file is too large for NOTEPAD), reading and writing the file as Text Only is your best bet. Even then, at least 11 distinct ASCII characters will get wiped out (7, 11, 12, 14, 30, 31, 145 through 148, and 160). So, avoid using Word for such files.

Formatting Considerations

When using the text Save As options, you can use Word formatting to control the appearance of your output file. It pays to keep in mind the following points:

- Text formatted for printing by the DOS PRINT command needs to be generic enough to work on the least capable printers. Line length generally should not exceed 65 monospaced characters, and it should have a left margin of at least one inch.
- Text formatted for display on a monitor generally should not exceed 79 characters (some monitors automatically wrap on the 80th character); some monitors may even require a maximum width of 40 characters.
- Characters displayed in Word for Windows conform to ANSI; characters displayed in straight DOS conform to ASCII. Accented character codes for ANSI and ASCII are different.

When preparing to save a text file for a specific purpose, you generally should use a monospaced font so that Word doesn't think there is more than one character per display unit of width on the monitor and printer. The margins displayed on-screen also control the width of the output line, as well as the width of the simulated margins you get (the latter, when using Text with Layout). Thus, if you want a next block of text, 60 characters wide, with a 1.25-inch left margin, then set your text up on-screen so that it displays that way before exporting to a text file.

If you want to use Word to verify the formatting of text files you create, you do *not* necessarily want to use the same conversion format for reading as you did for writing. Keep in mind that if you use a Text with Layout filter, Word will convert any paragraph marks and left-margin padding into word-wrapped text with the appropriate margin and indentation settings. When opening a text file you've created to verify the formatting, use the Text Only filter option. If you need to verify that accented characters appear correctly, then you should use a DOS character-mode editor or browser, like TYPE, LIST, EDLIN, or EDIT, instead of Word (unless you have a PC-8 font available for use with Word).

Modifying the Behavior of Text with Layout Conversions

When using the Text with Layout filters, you can modify some of the character translations using the CharMaps setting in the `[TextLytConv]` section of WIN.INI. For this to work, you must have the following setting in WINWORD6.INI:

```
[MSWord Editable Sections]
TextLytConv=yes
```

In WIN.INI, you would have the following (it's probably already there, so you'll just need to modify it rather than create it):

```
[TextLytConv]
CharMaps=from1,to1:from2,to2...from3,to3
Width=length
PointSize=size
```

To modify Word's translation of characters when saving text files with layout, you must change the CharMaps settings. To cause Word to capitalize everything, for example, you could have:

```
CharMaps=a,A:b,B,c,C: and so on through z,Z
```

Extending the Maximum Line Length When Using Text with Layout

NOTE

Ignore this section unless you have some really mundane printing chores that need to be performed outside Word using ancient equipment.

How many characters per line you get depends on the formatting you apply in your document, as well as the defaults set in the `[TextLytConv]` section of WIN.INI. No matter what you set in your document, however, when using the Text with Layout filter, Word will output lines of no more than 80 characters—unless you change the defaults. You can use the `Width` and `PointSize` settings in the `[TextLytConv]` section of WIN.INI to tell Word how many characters per line to use. The default `[TextLytConv]` settings are

```
[TextLytConv]
CharMaps=a,a
Width=80
PointSize=12
```

The default and maximum `Width` setting of 80 tells Word to consider the width of the line as 8 inches. The default `PointSize` of 12 instructs Word to use pica spacing of 10 characters per inch. At these settings, you can fit only 80 characters on an 8-inch line. What if, however, you're going to print on a line printer that can go a full 132 or 136 characters? Or, what if you can use a compressed font that can print more than 80 characters wide? Despite the capabilities of your printer, the default settings won't give you more than 80 characters per line, regardless of how you set the paper size option in the Word document. The maximum width *setting* is 80.

Although the maximum width *setting* is 80, the maximum *width* is *not* 80. You can vary the effective width by changing the pointsize setting. Characters per inch is inversely proportional to pointsize. At a pointsize of 12, the width is 80. If you set the pointsize to 10, Word will now allow 12 characters per inch, or 96 characters in the theoretical 8-inch width. At a point size of 7, you'll get approximately 15 characters per inch, or 120 characters per line. A setting of 10 yields 12 characters per inch (how's that for a paradox: pica 12 gets you 10 and elite 10 gets you 12), and 7 yields approximately 15 characters per inch.

This stuff doesn't actually change how close the characters are together in the output file, of course. And you don't have to concern yourself with it if you don't want more than 80 characters on a line. Rather, it's a way to trick Word into putting more than the maximum 80 characters on a line while using the Text with Layout option. You also don't have to worry about it if you can get away with using the Text with Line Breaks options. Under that option, Word will make the lines exactly as long as they are on-screen, since the `[TextLytConv]` settings apply only to the Text with Layout and DOS Text with Layout conversions.

Files from Other Applications

Word supports exporting and importing documents from a variety of other popular word processing programs, as well as importing from Lotus, Excel, Multiplan, and dBase. The supported formats are summarized in Table 7.3. Note that some formats are supported for import only, despite the curious fact that they show up on the *Save File as Type* list.

Table 7.3. Formats supported by Word 6.

File format	*Comments*	*Word Version*
dBase	II, III, III+, and IV (Import only)	Windows

File format	*Comments*	*Word Version*
DisplayWrite	Versions 4, 4.2, 5, and 5.2 (Import only)	Windows
Lotus 1-2-3	Versions 2.x and 3.x (Import only)	Windows
MacWrite		Mac
MacWrite II	Version 1.1	Mac
Microsoft Excel	Versions 2.x, 3.0, and 4.0 (Import only)	Both
Microsoft Publisher for Windows	Version 1.x	Windows
Microsoft Word for DOS	Versions 3.0, 4.0, 5.0, 5.5, and 6.0	Both
Microsoft Word for the Macintosh	All versions	Both
Microsoft Word for Windows	All versions	Both
Microsoft Works for DOS	Versions 1.0, 2.0, and 3.0	Windows
Microsoft Works for Macintosh	Version 2.0	Mac
Microsoft Works for Windows	Versions 1.0 and 2.0	Windows
Microsoft Write For Windows	All versions	Windows
MultiMate	Versions 3.3, Advantage, Advantage II, and 4.0	Windows
Multiplan	Versions 3.x and 4.2 (Import only)	Windows
PM Word for OS/2	All versions	Windows
RFT-DCA		Both
RTF (Rich Text Format)		Both
WordPerfect for DOS	Versions 4.1, 4.2, 5.0, and 5.1	Both
WordPerfect for Windows	Version 5.1 and 5.2	Both
WordStar	All versions starting with 3.3	Windows

Importing Files from Other Applications

Importing is translating a file from its native format into Word's format. Technically, even importing Word for Windows 2.0's files—Word 6's closest ancestor—involves the use of an import filter, although Word doesn't give you an option to do otherwise.

PROCEDURE 7.3. IMPORTING A FILE CREATED BY ANOTHER APPLICATION.

1. Select File | Open.
2. Navigate to the file you want to open, using List files of Type, Drives, and Directories controls.
3. If you have any doubt about Word's ability to correctly recognize the format of your document, click Confirm Conversions (note: in particular, Word has difficulty distinguishing between Wordperfect 5.1 and 5.2).
4. To avoid accidentally overwriting the original file, select Read Only (note: you will still be able to Save As the file under a new name).
5. Click OK to open the file.

You also can use virtually the same procedure to insert a file with a non-Word format into an existing document. Replace Step 1 with Insert | File, and then follow the remaining steps.

> **SUPER NOTE**
>
> If you don't see the format you need, it's possible that you didn't install the necessary conversion modules (*.CNV) files when you installed Word. You may need to run the Word Setup program to add the needed filters. Note also that the Confirm Conversions is not effective when importing Word for Windows 2 files.

Exporting Files to Other Applications

Exporting is the flip side of the coin. To export a file, use Save As and specify the format you want to use. As noted previously, if you don't get the result you want, then it sometimes pays to use RTF (rich text format) as an intermediary instead of the native format.

However, filters, for the most part, are getting better. So, give the native filter a try before resorting to RTF. Or, because the computer can do what it does so much more quickly than you can reformat manually, try several different ways and use the one that requires the least amount of touch-up editing. I once determined that the best intermediary between DeScribe 3 and Word for Windows 2 was Word for DOS 5 format. That no longer may be the case, but you never can tell when an unintuitive choice is the best choice. When it comes to file conversion filters, it pays to experiment.

PROCEDURE 7.4. EXPORTING A FILE FROM WORD TO ANOTHER WORD PROCESSING PROGRAM.

1. Select **F**ile | Save **A**s.
2. Type a new name for the file; if the filter automatically provides a default extension, you're generally better off to accept it.
3. Use the Drives and Directories controls to navigate, if necessary, to where you want the file stored.
4. Use Save File As **T**ype to select a format.
5. Click OK to export the file; note that the window name changes to the name you supplied in Step 2.
6. Perform any formatting you need to ensure that the final form will be as compatible as possible with the target format.
7. Select **F**ile | **C**lose; you will be prompted to save either in Word format or in the format you supplied in Step 4.

As previously noted, one potentially confusing thing about Word's exporting is that it renames the current window as the "exported" file for editing in the current window. So, don't imagine that you can just continue working on the *original* file. Note also that the results you see on-screen now may be different from what you would see if you physically close the current window and read from the file you just created. One presumes that the programmers think that you Save As first, and *then* edit, rather than edit first and then Save As. It probably doesn't really matter what comes first. The main thing, however, is to avoid accidentally saving any special compatibility-oriented formatted into your original file.

Compatibility

Word provides a group of settings that can affect how Word works when dealing with documents for other applications. Specific settings are provided for Word for Windows (versions 1 and 2), Word for Macintosh, Word for DOS, and Wordperfect.

PROCEDURE 7.5. SETTING COMPATIBILITY OPTIONS FOR THE CURRENT DOCUMENT.

1. Select **T**ools | **O**ptions and click the Compatibility tab, as shown in Figure 7.5.
2. Click the drop-down arrow for the Recommended Options For list box.
3. Click the application for which you want to maximize compatibility with the current document.
4. Adjust the Options, if necessary.
5. Click OK.

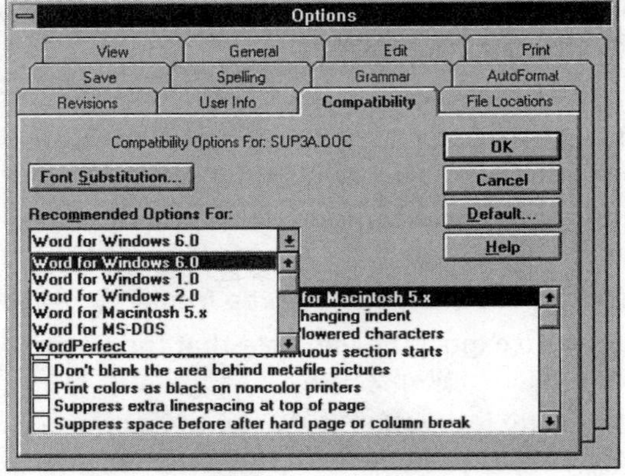

FIGURE 7.5.
The Compatibility screen lets you set options for the current document.

PROCEDURE 7.6. SETTING COMPATIBILITY OPTIONS FOR THE CURRENT DOCUMENT.

1. Select **T**ools | **O**ptions and click the Compatibility tab.
2. Click the drop-down arrow for the Recommended Options list box.
3. Click the application you want to use as the default for your compatibility settings (if you just use Word 6, set it to Word 6; if you work in a group with users of Word for Windows 2 or Wordperfect, then select one of those). Or, if you select Custom, proceed to Step 4 and customize the settings.
4. Adjust the Options, if necessary.
5. Click OK.

Honing the Exports

Some filters have limitations as well as extra user-settable options. Consult the online README.HLP for additional information. To open this file:

1. Press F1.
2. Select **F**ile | **O**pen.
3. Navigate (if necessary) to your main Word 6 program directory.
4. Select README.HLP

Note that there is a special section on file conversions. Because this information changes from time to time, I won't try to cover it in detail here, but alert you to its existence and how it can possibly help you. In particular, this file contains an outline of instructions for modifying converter options contained in the WIN.INI file. If you see something you don't like happening in your conversion results, there's a fairly good chance that you can change it!

Chapter

Using Find File

In some ways, the **Find** File command is one of Word's strongest features. In other ways, however, it's one of the more infuriating features. In this session, we'll explore the various uses for **F**ind File and show ways it can help improve your productivity in Word.

Changed from Word for Windows 2.0, the **F**ind File command now has features to make its use a bit more convenient. One in particular is the ability to save specific sets of search criteria for later use. Another is the inclusion of multithreading in the search engine. In Word for Windows 2, when you select the **F**ind File command you're forced to endure the dreaded hourglass until the search completes—even if it's an old left-over search that no longer interests you. In Word for Windows 6, however, you get just a brief flash of the hourglass as the search starts up, followed by the search dialog box shown in Figure 8.1.

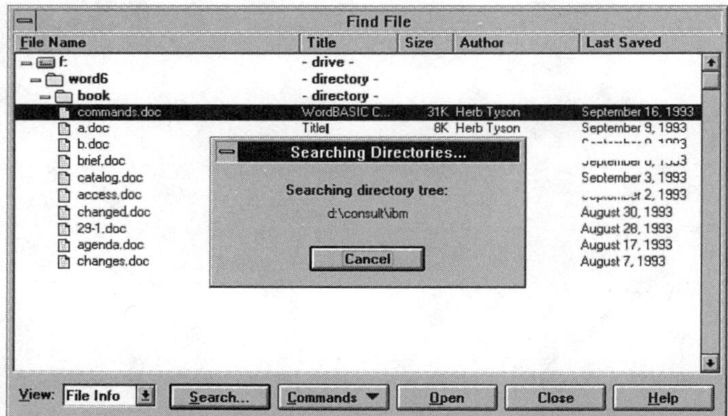

FIGURE 8.1.
The Word 6 Search window.

SUPER

MULTITHREADING IN WORD?

Really? Yes! Note the little spinning indicator in the upper-right corner of the window search window in Figure 8.1. When that icon is present, it means that Word is performing a search in the background. You can interrupt the background searching at any time by clicking the Search button. After a moment, the background activity ceases. Meanwhile, you can now specify the search you *really* wanted in the first place. When you return to the main **F**ind File window, if you didn't specify new search criteria, the old search is resumed. If you did specify new search criteria, then the new one is launched in the background. In either case, there might now be a Building File List message box on-screen, as shown in Figure 8.2. If you cancel it, the search continues in the background, enabling you to begin examining files already found, or to proceed with whatever task you need to perform. If you close the **F**ind

File dialog box, unfortunately, the search stops. Too bad there isn't an option to have it search while you continue editing your document. Now, that would be *real* multithreading. Maybe it'll be there in a future version.

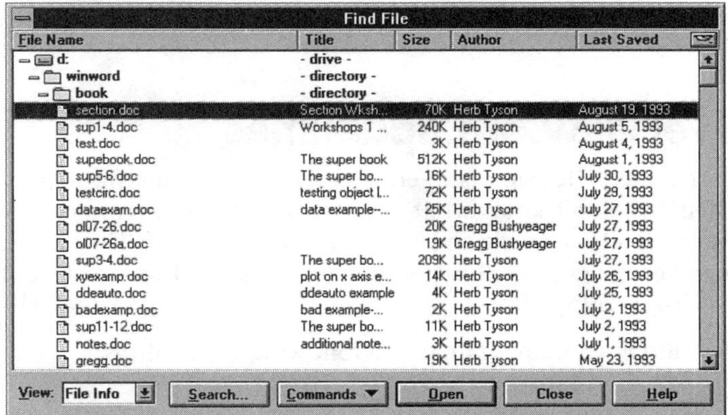

FIGURE 8.2.
If you cancel the Building File List message box, it continues building in the background.

SUPER

NOW THE BAD NEWS...

Find File is terribly slow at just finding files. Using File Manager, it took approximately eight seconds to do a first search (unaided by caching) for 274 files matching *.DOC on my 150MB D: drive (the drive has a 12ms access time and the processor is a 486-33). It took Find File a full minute to come up with the same list. If you're just looking for files by name and aren't concerned about being able to view their Summary Info or contents, then File Manager is a much faster choice. As noted in Chapter 6, "Word Files," you can use the File Manager to open multiple Word files at the same time using drag-and-drop. Moreover, File Manager is much more flexible and much faster at sorting files by date or other normal DOS attributes. Keep the File Manager alternative in mind if you don't need the other capabilities of Word's **F**ind File command.

If you're using Word in the OS/2 environment, you also could use PMSeek (Seek and Scan Files) in the Productivity folder. Like File Manager, PMSeek is also much faster than the **F**ind File command. Moreover, PMSeek enables you to search for text in files, search multiple disks at the same time (as does **F**ind File), as well as to specify a default editor (for example, Word). Using **F**ind File, it took over a minute to locate eight files containing a client's name. Using PMSeek, it took exactly half as long to come up with the same list. Moreover, PMSeek is multithreaded and can perform its searches completely in the background while you continue word processing. When you don't like waiting for your computer, the choice of tools can make an enormous difference.

Overview of Capabilities

Word's **F**ind File command enables you to search for and preview files on your disks. When you don't know what's where, and the contents of the files can help you find out, the **F**ind File command is a great way to explore. The only major limitation is speed. However, given that the **F**ind File command often is your only alternative to the tedium of opening files one-at-a-time, the speed issue usually is moot.

The **F**ind File command has the following capabilities:

Searching

- Based on filename (for example, using wildcards and filenames)
- Based on any Summary Info fields (for example, search for words contained in the title, author, keywords, and subject field)
- Based on text in the file itself
- Based on file dates (creation and last-saved)
- Based on the last person who edited the file
- On multiple drives at the same time, including across a network
- Lets you name and save search criteria (for example, "Word 6 Super Book Directories") so you can easily recall past searches

Viewing Options

- Summary Info for displayed files
- Preview of files (shows the contents of the file in a window)
- File statistics (size, date, and so forth)

Management Options

- Open files in Word
- Open as read-only
- Print
- Show summary information box

- Delete
- Copy
- Sort file list

Starting Find File

What happens when you start Find File depends on whether or not you've used it before. Find File is in the File menu.

PROCEDURE 8.1. USING FIND FILE TO SEARCH FOR FILES.

1. Select **File | Find File**; if this is the first time you've used Find File, the Search window appears, as shown in Figure 8.3. Otherwise, the Find File window appears. If you get the Find File window, then click the Search button to display the Search window.
2. In the File Name field (under Search For), type as much of the filename as you want to specify. Alternatively, for common patterns (*.DOC, *.DOT, *.BMP, *.WMF, and *.*), click the drop-down arrow and select any pattern showing.
3. In the Location field, type the directory you want to search (including disk), or use the drop-down list box to specify a location.
4. If desired, select the Include Subdirectories option.
5. Click OK.

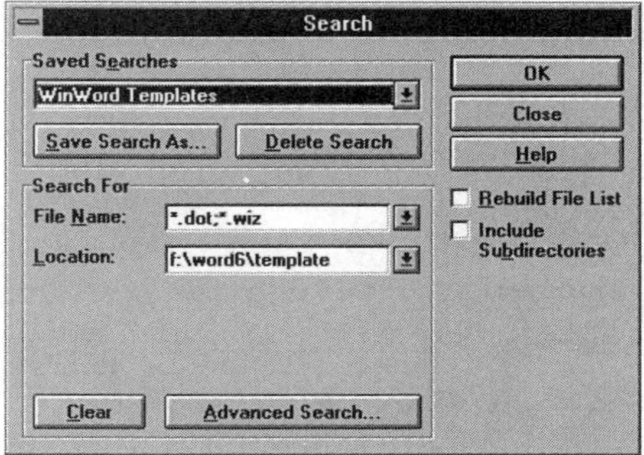

FIGURE 8.3.
The Find File search window.

Searching

The procedure outlined in the preceding heading just barely touches the tip of Find File's searching capabilities. Not only can you save search criteria for future use, but you can use complex criteria to check for multiple conditions.

Saved Searches

Word's Find File command provides the ability to store the searches you perform. This enables you, for example, to set up project-specific file lists, maintenance file lists, workgroup file lists, and so on. To save your seach list, type a name in the Saved Searches box and click Save Search As, as shown in Figure 8.4. To delete a named search you no longer want to retain, select the name from the list and click Delete Search.

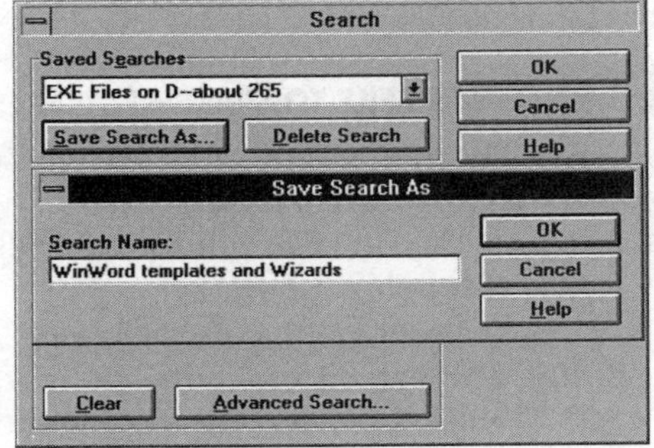

FIGURE 8.4.
The Saved Searches feature lets you save search criteria for specific projects.

Search For

The Search For options let you specify what you're looking for and where to look.

File Name

The File Name field most often is used for typing a wildcard file specification. In this field, you should type only *names*, and *not* directories. Acceptable names include standard DOS-type wildcards only. Use * to accept any group of characters up to the longest DOS name. Use ? to substitute for any single character. For example, the following are all valid specifications:

*.DOC	Matches all files ending in .DOC as well as files without extensions at all.
.	Matches all files.
*	Matches all files (same as *.*).
B*.DOC	Matches all .DOC files that start with B.
B*.*	Matches all files that start with B.
*.B?K	Matches all files with extensions of BcharacterK (e.g., BAK, BWK, B1K, BOK, and so forth).
????.DOC	Matches all four-letter file names ending in .DOC.

SUPER TIP

You also can include multiple file specifications by separating them with semicolons. For example, *.TMP;*.BAK;~*.* searches for all files matching *.TMP, *.BAK, and ~*.*.

Location

Use the location field to specify the disk and/or directory where you want Word to search. You must specify at least a drive location to search (for example, C:, D:, E:, A:, B:, and so forth). If you specify a directory without a drive reference, the search will fail. As in the case of filenames, you can specify multiple locations separated with semicolons. The following are valid search locations specification:

```
E:\WORD6;F:\DOC\DATA;C:\OS2\MDOS\WINOS2
F:
A:
G:\DATA\DIR\DOCS;H:\LETTERS
```

Clear

Use the Clear command to clear all current file, search, and location criteria, including items in the Advanced Search screen.

SUPER TIP

If seeing **F**ind File launch into a search each time you start upsets you—even knowing you can interrupt at any time by clicking Search—then you can use the Clear button to clean the slate for a fresh start next time. After you use the Clear button, the next time you start **F**ind File, you will immediately get the Search dialog box instead of the **F**ind File screen.

Advanced Search

The Advanced Search options let you refine the search based on file characterstics. It also provides a good point-and-click mechanism for building the search path (location).

LOCATION

The Location tab of the Advanced Search setup folder enables you to build your location search path without having to type the information. This prevents you from making typing errors that might otherwise make you think your files aren't there ("Arrrrggggg! My files are gone!" you scream, just before you notice that you typed WINWORF instead of WINWORD).

PROCEDURE 8.2. BUILDING A SEARCH PATH LOCATION STRING.

1. From the Find File screen, click Search.
2. Click Advanced Search.
3. Click the Location tab (see Figure 8.5).
4. If desired, you can enter file specifications to search, either in the Advanced Search dialog box or in the main Search dialog box. Keep in mind that you can specify multiple files by separating them with semicolons.
5. To remove paths you don't want searched, alternately click the path you want to remove and the Remove button until the list contains only paths you want searched. You can click Remove All to clear the list completely.
6. Use the Drives and Directories controls to navigate to each drive and directory you want to include.
7. To add locations to the Search In list, alternately click the directory you want to include and the Add button.
8. Click the Network button to connect to a network drive. Select the drive, type the resource specification and the password, and click OK to return to the Location tab.
9. If desired, click Include Subdirectories to tell Word to search each directory you specified and all their subdirectories.
10. Click OK to return to the Search screen.
11. Click OK to begin the search.

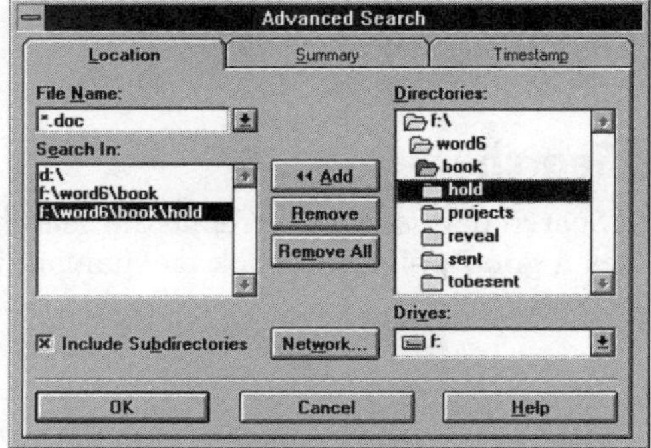

FIGURE 8.5.
Use the Location screen to build your search path.

SUMMARY

Use the Summary tab to specify search criteria based on the file's attributes and contents (see Figure 8.6). The summary fields (Title, Author, Keywords, and Subject), Containing text, and any other criteria you select, are logically ANDed for the purposes of the search. Consider, for example, what happens if you specify the search criteria shown in Table 8.4.

FIGURE 8.6.
The Summary screen lets you set up search criteria for the ***F****ind File command.*

Table 8.1. Sample search specification for Find File.

Criterion	*Entry*	*Effect*
Title	Green	Any Title containing *Green*
Author	David	Any Author containing *David*
Keywords	soup,doughnuts	Any Keywords matching *soup* OR *doughnuts*
Subject	cost	Any Subject that contains the word *cost*
Text	dogs&cats	Any file that mentions *dogs* AND *cats*

Given these search criteria, you will match *only* files that meet all conditions. Even though the Keywords specification here will match *soup* OR *doughnuts*, Word will match just files that meet all other conditions (for example, have *Green* in the title, *David* in the author's name, *cost* in the subject, and both *dogs* AND *cats* in the text).

SUPER IT'S LOGICAL, CAPTAIN!

A logical AND means that *all* conditions stated must be true in order to find a match. A logical OR means that *any* one must be true to find a match. A logical NOT means that the stated condition must not be true to qualify as a match. If you want to find Spock and no one else, for example, you would search for pointed ears, AND a weird haircut, AND someone who's incessantly logical. If you used OR logic, instead, you might find Satan, David Letterman, and William F. Buckley. That's an odd trio, by any standards, and certainly *not* the Kingston Trio. In any event, I'll leave it to you to figure out who matches what!

SPECIFYING THE SUMMARY AND TEXT

The search text for the summary fields and for the Containing Text fields all follow the same rules. Keep in mind that different rules apply when specifying text for **F**ind File than when doing a normal **E**dit | **F**ind. For the **F**ind File search fields, for example, a comma (,) is used as a logical OR, meaning that Word matches text on either side of the comma. Thus, if you want to find files in which Microsoft, Borland, WordPerfect, or Lotus were mentioned, you would specify the Containing Text as

```
Microsoft,Borland,WordPerfect,Lotus
```

If you want to locate files in which *all four* were mentioned, you would use the logical *and* operator, &:

```
Microsoft&Borland&WordPerfect&Lotus
```

If you combine them as

```
Microsoft,Borland&WordPerfect&Lotus
```

then the & groups are combined as a single condition and interpreted as an OR condition (i.e., match documents that either mention all of Borland, WordPerfect and Lotus, or that mention just Microsoft).

The search operators are shown in Table 8.5.

Table 8.2. Search operators used in the summary and text fields.

?	Replace any single character; **T?n** to match tin, ton, tan, ten, and so forth.
*	Replace any group of characters; **T*n** to match Teen, Ton, Tarpaulin, and so forth.

""	Treat the enclosed character as a normal character; use **"?"** to search for ?, rather than treating ? as a special character.
~	Not. Match items that do not contain this text. For example, set the author field to ~**Mike** to find documents not created by Mike.

PATTERN MATCHING: ADDITIONAL SEARCH OPTIONS FOR THE CONTAINING TEXT FIELD

In addition to using the operators shown in Table 8.5, you can use the same special characters for the Containing Text field that you can in regular **Edit | Find** searches by selecting the Pattern Matching option. The pattern options are shown in Table 8.6. See Chapter 28, "Search and Replace," for complete information and examples. In addition, you can use the Special button to aid in entering the pattern searches.

Table 8.3. Pattern matching characters.

?	Any single character
*	Any group of characters
[]	Any character in the set
[*x*-*y*]	Any character in the range from *x* to *y*.
[!]	Any characters except the ones in the brackets
[!*x*-*y*]	Any characters not in the range of *x* through *y*.
{*n*}	Exactly *n* occurrences of the preceding character or expression (for example, [aeiou] is an expression; **[aeiou]{2}** looks for any double vowel).
{*n*,}	At least *n* occurrences of the preceding character or set (for example, **[a-c]{2,}** matches two or more a, b, and c permutations, like ab, ac, abc, acb, bac, cab, and so forth).
{*n*,*m*}	From *n* to *m* occurrences of the preceding character (for example, **0{3,6}** would match strings containing 3, 4, 5, or 6 zeros).
@	Same as {1}.
<	Beginning of a word (for example, **<dog** matches dogma, dogmatic, and doggie, but not hounddog, hotdog, and corndog).
>	End of a word (for example, **ing>** matches matching, petting, and betting, but not ringer, singer, or Ingersoll).

MATCH CASE

Use the Match Case option to tell Word that the case specified in the Containing Text box must match the exact capitalization you type. The Match Case option applies only to the Containing Text field, and not to the summary search items.

TIMESTAMP

Select the Timestamp tab to base your search on the file dates for creation and last-saved (see Figure 8.7). You can specify the date pretty much any way you want. Microsoft really outdid itself this time; the following formats (and probably others) are recognized and converted to 02/01/93 format for the date February 1, 1993:

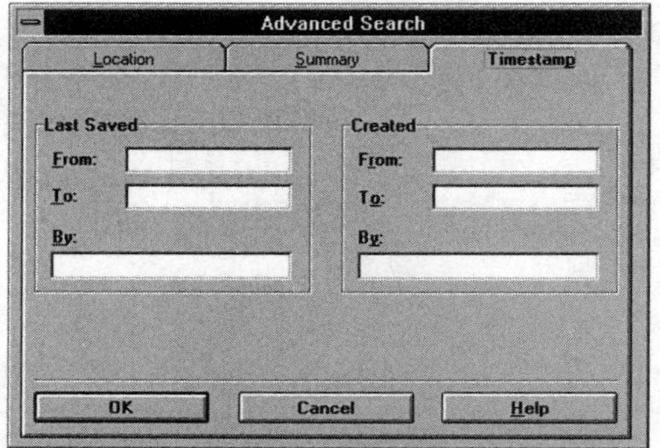

FIGURE 8.7.
Use the Timestamp tab to zero in on a specific range of dates.

```
01 02 93
1 Feb 93
2/1/93
February 1, 1993
93 02 01
1 February 93
```

LAST SAVED AND CREATED

The Last Saved date (also called the last *revision* date) refers to the last date the file was written to on the disk. The Created date is the date the file was created. You use the From and To fields to specify a range of dates. If you specify both last-saved and created dates, then both conditions must be satisfied simultaneously. Be especially careful about typos, since Word doesn't check for logical consistency. If you specify revision dates that precede creation dates, or ranges where the *to* occurs before the *from*, Word will not alert you to the logical error. You also can use the By field to specify who created or last saved a file.

Rebuild

Word doesn't always automatically update the list of files after you change the search criteria. Use this option to force Word to build a new list.

Include Subdirectories

Use this option to tell Word to search in the subdirectories of the directories you specify. This option duplicates the Include Subdirectories option in the Location search dialog.

View

When viewing a list of files, Word provides three viewing options:

```
Preview
File Info
Summary
```

Each option is appropriate at different times, depending on what you're trying to find or find out.

PROCEDURE 8.3. SETTING THE VIEW.

1. From the **F**ind File screen, click the drop-down arrow to the right of the View box (see Figure 8.8).
2. Click the View you want to use.

FIGURE 8.8.
Word provides three different choices of view.

Preview

The Preview option attempts to show you the file. As shown in Figure 8.9, this option imports the selected file into a small window so you can see what it looks like. This is one of **F**ind File's strongest features. Rather than guessing about a file, you can actually see its contents. The Preview option works on all of the graphics, spreadsheet, database, and word processing formats supported by the conversion filters.

One potential problem with the Preview mode is that it can be extremely slow. You might want to keep the view set at File Info until you hone in on the file you want to view. Just a few 30-second file conversions will convince you of that fact when you're trying to find a file in a hurry.

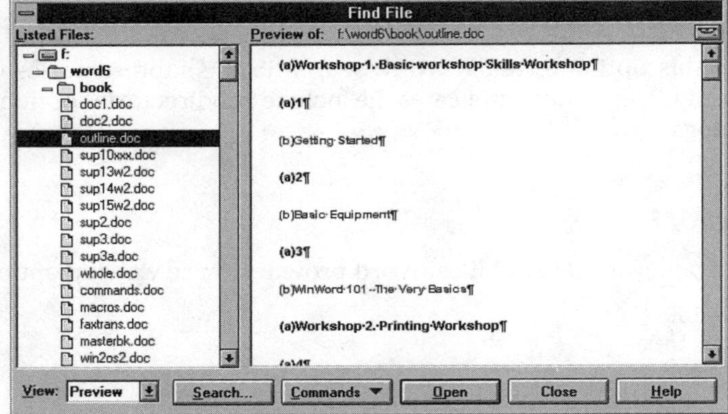

FIGURE 8.9.
Find File's Preview view.

File Info

The File Info display is similar to a typical DOS directory. It displays the file size and the last-saved date for different files at the same time, as shown in Figure 8.10. Unfortunately, it does not display the last-saved file time, which often is crucial in determining the differences among different versions of a file. If you need this type of listing to make your decision, it usually is better to use the Windows File Manager, which shows the size, date, time, and file attributes.

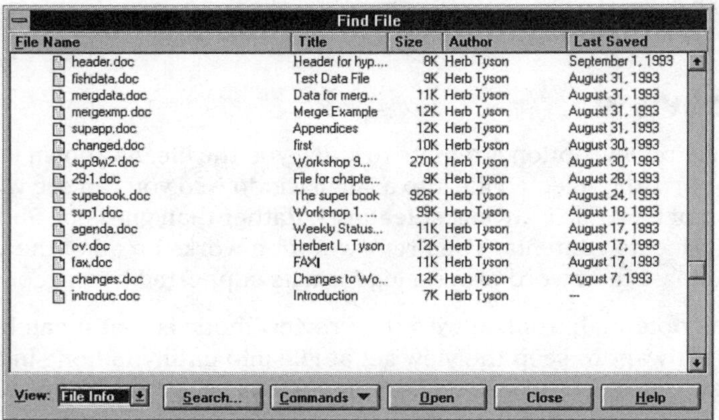

FIGURE 8.10.
Find File's File Info view.

Summary

The Summary display is an amalgam of information from the Summary Info display that you get when you select **F**ile|Summary **I**nfo and when you press the Statistics button from within the Summary Info window. In fact, it would be nice if Word would show the same comprehensive view for **File** | **Summary Info** that it does in the **Find File** Summary window. As shown in Figure 8.11, the Summary view shows the following:

```
Title
Subject
Keywords
Template
Comments
Created By
Created Date
Last Saved By
Last Saved Date
Last Printed Date
Revision number
Total Editing Time
Document Size (bytes, pages, words, and characters)
```

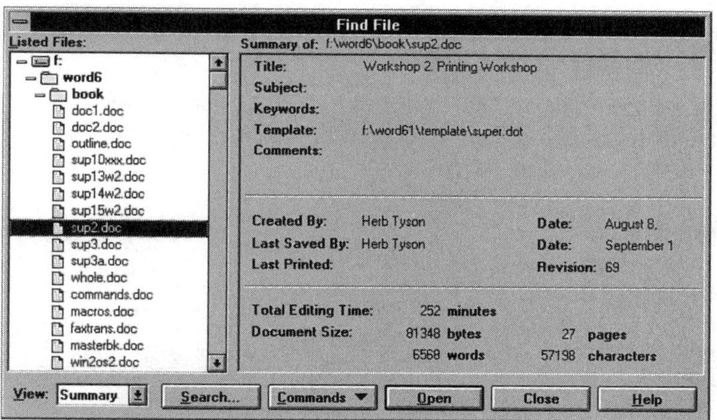

FIGURE 8.11.
The Find File Summary view.

SUPER NOTE

The last item has the number of bytes and the number of characters. You might be used to those two items being the same thing. Well, in popular computer jargon, they usually are. However, in this instance, the byte count is the actual size of the file on disk, while the character count is the number of text characters. The byte count includes all of the graphics, formatting instructions, summary information, style list, and so on, that are included in the file. The character count includes just the number of characters. For example, if I select **File** | **New**, create a new file, type the word "Hello," and save it, the character count would be just 6 (5 for Hello and 1 for the automatic paragraph mark that Word inscribes at the end of each file). As shown in Figure 8.12, the byte count (file size), however, is quite a bit larger. How much room the file takes up on disk depends on a number of factors, including how many styles were in the template, whether or not you have the Save options set to embed TrueType fonts, and so forth. Keep the size difference in mind if you're trying to figure out how many files you can fit onto a floppy disk.

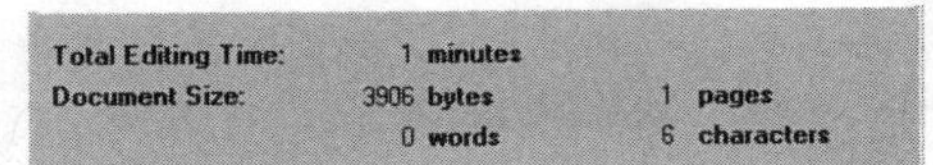

FIGURE 8.12.
Byte counts give the file's physical size, while the character count tells the number of text characters.

Managing Files

The **F**ind File window includes the Commands button, as shown in Figure 8.13. Use this button to access commands for opening files as read-only, deleting, printing, copying, and sorting.

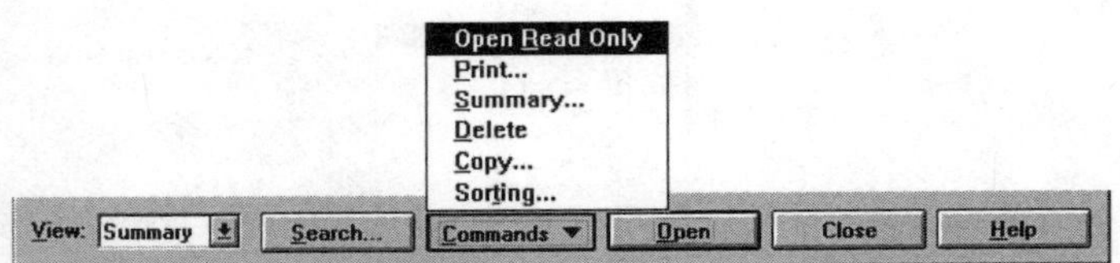

FIGURE 8.13.
*The **F**ind File Commands button displays options for opening, deleting, printing, copying, and sorting.*

Opening

The **F**ind File window provides several ways to open files in Word:

- Double-click the filename in the list.
- Select the file(s) and click the Open button.
- Select the file(s) and then select **C**ommands | Open **R**ead Only.

PROCEDURE 8.4. OPENING MULTIPLE FILES FOR READ/WRITE ACCESS.

1. Select the file(s) you want to open (three methods: click the first file you want, then use Ctrl+Click on each additional file; drag, by pressing the left mouse button, over the range you want to select; or press Shift+Click on the first and last files you want to select).
2. Click the Open button or press Enter.

SUPER NOTE

When selecting multiple files, you can't open the list by double-clicking. A plain double-click has the effect of deselecting all files except for the one to which you're pointing. If you really want to open them using a double-click method, do this: select the files, then Ctrl+Double-Click any one of the selected files.

PROCEDURE 8.5. OPENING MULTIPLE FILES FOR READ-ONLY ACCESS.

1. Select the file(s) you want to open, using a method described in the previous procedure.
2. Select Commands | Open **R**ead Only.

SUPER TIP

When opening files just to examine their contents, it's always a good idea to open them as read-only. If you're like me, you might spontaneously press Ctrl+S (Save) several times a minute—or every time the lights flicker. Even if you haven't actually changed anything, Word writes the file to disk anyway (even when fast save is enabled). Worse, there might be automatic macros that update key fields, like dates and times. Perhaps you (or the original author, if that's not you) don't want them updated. Often, however, the times and dates associated with a file are important too, as well as the name of the last person who saved it. If you incidentally change that information—especially in a work group setting—you might suddenly find yourself beseiged by questions: *What did you change? Why were you editing my files?* If you like to avoid needless hassles, then use read-only unless you really plan to change the file.

Deleting

Word also lets you use **F**ind File for file management. It's a good idea to periodically clear out duplicates and backup files you no longer need, as well as files that you might have created accidentally (you might notice a number of DOC1.DOC, DOC2.DOC, or similar files lying around, which is Word's default naming scheme when you save a document and don't supply a name of your own choosing).

PROCEDURE 8.6. USING FIND FILE TO DELETE FILES.

1. From the Find File screen, select the file(s) you want to delete.
2. Select Commands | Delete (note: if you select a directory instead of a file, the Delete command does not work).

SUPER CAUTION

Beware of deleting .TMP files. Word makes an effort to prevent you from accidentally deleting .TMP files it's still using. It may or may not be able to prevent you from deleting .TMP files being used by other programs that are still running—it depends on how those other programs opened the files, as well as what environment you're using (you'll find more protection under OS/2 and Windows NT than under actual Windows). What may look like left-over garbage to you might be the essence of a running program's existence. When in doubt—leave it alone. Otherwise, Windows may come crashing down around you. This advice applies especially when using Windows File Manager while other programs are running.

Printing

One of the nicest features of the Find File command is its ability to print a Word file or even multiple files without your having to open them. If you have complete documents, a series of chapter files, or what-have-you, you can print them as a group using the Find File print feature.

PROCEDURE 8.7. USING FIND FILE TO PRINT FILES.

1. From the Find File screen, select the file(s) you want to print.
2. Select Commands | Print.

SUPER NOTE

This procedure is roughly equivalent to opening each file and printing it. Word makes no attempt to coordinate the updating of fields, indices, or other items apart from the linkages already set up in the files. Thus, if you have a set of table numbers in file #2 that pick up where file #1 leaves off, you yourself have to set that up when you create files #1 and #2. As convenient as Commands | Print is, it can't read your mind.

Copying

The Find File command can be used to copy files to a new location. It also can be used to copy a single file to a new name.

PROCEDURE 8.8. USING FIND FILE TO COPY FILES.

1. From the Find File screen, select the file(s) you want to copy.
2. Select Commands | Copy.
3. Use the Drives and Directories lists to navigate to where you want the copy to appear.
4. If necessary, you can use the New button to create a new subdirectory.
5. Click OK.

SUPER NOTE

You cannot use the Copy command to copy multiple files to a new set of names (for example, *.DOC to *.BK2). You can, however, use the Copy command to copy a single new file to a new name.

PROCEDURE 8.9. USING FIND FILE TO CREATE A COPY OF A SINGLE FILE UNDER A NEW NAME.

1. From the Find File screen, select the file you want to copy.
2. If desired, use the Drives and Directories to navigate to a new location, or use the New button to create a new directory.
3. In the Path field, add a \ plus the whole name for the file, as shown in Figure 8.14. If you omit the .DOC when copying a word file, the Find File Copy command will *not* add it for you.

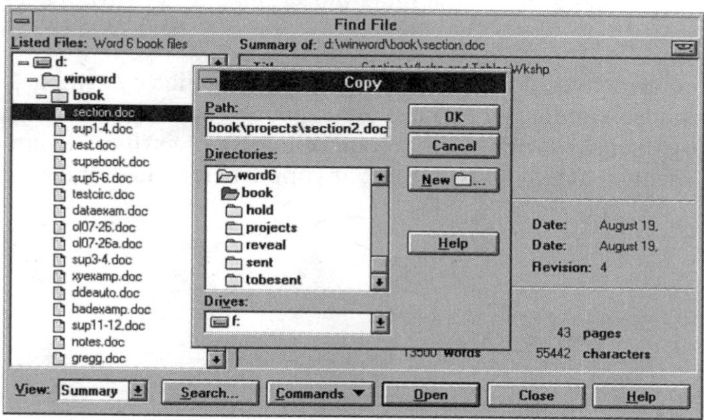

FIGURE 8.14.
Using Find File's Copy command to copy a single file to a new name.

Sorting

Use the Sorting option to tell the **F**ind File command how to sort the files on the list. As shown in Figure 8.15, Word gives you the option of sorting by

- **Author**—The original creator (of the document, not the universe)
- **Creation Date**—The date the file came into existence
- **Last Saved By**—The name of the person at the helm the last time the file was written to
- **Last Saved Date**—The last date on which the file was written to on disk
- **Name**—The filename, as it appears on disk
- **Size**—The file size (which can differ from the document's character count, and can produce different results; files that contain graphics often have a much larger file size to character count ratio than files that contain just text and formatting).

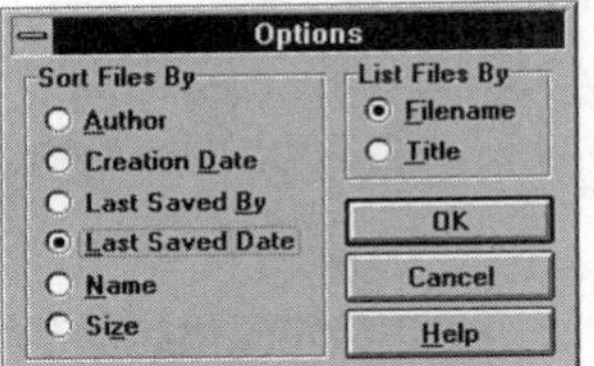

FIGURE 8.15.
Find File lets you sort the file list by author, date, name, or size, and lets you display either the file title or the filename.

SUPER

Don't you just love this evangelical jargon? Creation Date, Last Saved By, and so forth. It's almost enough to make you want to change your online names, just to see others' reactions to documents that were created by God and last saved by Billy Graham. I can hardly wait for next April 1st.

Word also gives you the option of displaying files by Title or by File Name. If you use document summary information religiously (so to speak), you might very well find that using document titles is much more informative than filenames. It's almost as good as having a native file system that supports long filenames.

Formatting Workshop

In this workshop, you learn the ins and outs of formatting a Word document. This creates a strategic dilemma, however. The most important leverage you have in formatting documents is the appropriate use of templates and styles, yet many Word users completely ignore these powerful tools. So, what do you do? Do you jump immediately to a discussion of templates and styles, which many people don't use, but should? Or, do you present information in the order in which most users would want to find it?

Well, the customer is always right, as they say. However, it would be a shame to hand you a street map of Paris without first telling you how to get to France. So, while I postpone a full discussion of Templates and Styles, I want to emphasize their importance in developing an overall document strategy in Word.

In this workshop, I begin by describing the roles of templates, styles, and document formatting. Then, I go into the specifics of different kinds of formatting, hoping you remember that you'll save time by not trying to reinvent the wheel each time you reach for your formatting keys. That is, any time you format a section of a document in Word and want to reuse those formatting ideas for something else, you should think about immortalizing it as a style.

Similarly, a document that you think would be a good model for creating similar documents in the future is an excellent candidate for a document template. It's easy, it's fun, and it saves a lot of work in the long run.

Chapter

9

Formatting Overview

The single most important concept in mastering Word is formatting. The most important habit a Word user can form is to learn to take advantage of Word's powerful formatting tools—and the most important formatting tools in Word are templates and styles. In this chapter you'll get just an overview of what templates and styles are, and how they relate to formatting individual documents. For a more complete discussion of templates and styles, see Chapter 21, "Templates and Wizards," and Chapter 22, "Styles and AutoFormat." For now, just keep in mind that you have the option of immortalizing your formatting specifics as styles, and your document layouts as templates.

Templates

Formatting in Word documents is managed using a hierarchy of controls. The master control is the document *template*. At its simplest, a template is a document that's already been started. Things that are common to a given type of document are preserved in document templates. This might include text as well as preset types of formatting called *styles*. Each time you start a new document of that type, you save time by using the template as your starting point rather than having to reinvent the wheel each time.

At its most complex, a template is an environment for creating and maintaining documents. Templates can contain automatic macros that swing into action each time you create, edit, or close a document. That kind of template is called a Wizard. Templates can house special toolbars, commands, and menus for working on particular kinds of documents. In the Formatting Workshop, however, we're most interested in looking at a template's role in formatting documents. Let's just put that macro, menu, and toolbar stuff aside for now.

SUPER

SECRETS OF THE TEMPLATE WIZARDS

Beginning with Word 6, Microsoft has now decided to call templates that contain automatic macros *Wizards*. Wizards are wizards at walking you through the creation of documents without any special knowledge on your part. The first day I received Word 6, I used the Award Wizard to create an impressive reading award certificate for my five-year-old daughter—in about 2 minutes. Try it! I think you'll be as impressed as she was, although you might not ask "Can I color it?" when it's finished.

A template is a collection of document-wide formatting, section formatting, styles, and text, organized in a particular way. Templates are a kind of DNA for your Word documents. They control the way a document looks. For example, you might use a letter template as a starting point for your letters, a memo template for memos, and a report template for reports.

Templates save you time, because they keep you from having to start at ground zero each time you create a new document. They also help to ensure consistency in formatting. This is especially important in a workgroup setting. Using templates can ensure not only that a given document has formatting that is internally consistent, but that all documents of a given type have a uniform quality and appearance. Templates also promote habits that speed up production of your documents. Rather than puzzling over formatting decisions, you simply choose from the array of existing formatting options, relying on decisions you've already made.

Styles

A template can be thought of as a *boilerplate document*. Among other things, templates contain a collection of ready-made styles. A *style* is a collection of formatting instructions. You use different styles for different parts of a document.

For example, in a letter, one style can be used to control the formatting of the letterhead, another for the inside address, and others for the salutation, date, body of the letter, closing, signature, enclosure, post-script message, and page numbers. Unlike a typewriter, where you must count the number of times you tab over for placement of a signature, date, or other information, you simply choose the appropriate style, and Word handles the formatting automatically.

Consider the LETTER1.DOT template that comes with Word (in the WINWORD6\TEMPLATE subdirectory). More than just consider it, open it and take a look, as shown in Figure 9.1.

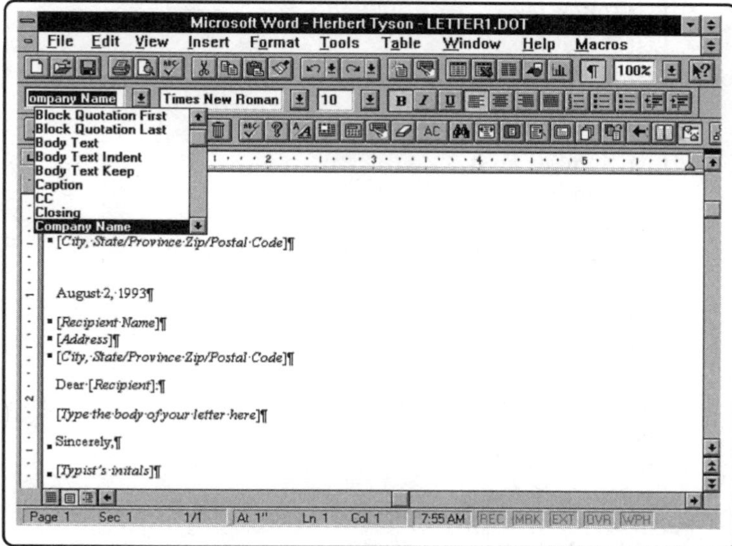

FIGURE 9.1.
The LETTER1.DOT template that comes with Word.

The LETTER1.DOT template has more than 30 *user-defined* styles (the exact number can vary depending on which release of Word 6 you received), including:

Address
Attention Line
Block Quotation
Block Quotation First
Block Quotation Last
Body Text Indent
Body Text Keep
Company Name
Date
Element Heading
Emphasis
Footer Even
Footer First
Footer Odd
Footnote Base
Header Base
Header Even
Header First
Header Odd
Heading Base
Index Base
Inside Address
Lead-in Emphasis
List Bullet First
List Bullet Last
List First
List Last
List Number Cont
List Number First
List Number Last
Message Header
Picture
Return Address
Salutation
Signature CC
Signature Closing
Signature Company Name
Signature Enclosure
Signature Job Title
Signature Name
Signature Reference Initials
Subject Line
Superscript

> **SUPER NOTE**
>
> The style list contains three styles that are in a different typeface: Emphasis, Lead-in Emphasis, and Superscript. When you display the style list in Word 6 (Ctrl+Shift+S), *Paragraph* styles are displayed in bold, and *Character* styles are displayed in normal text.

Each style pretty much indicates what it's used for. Making it even easier, a good letter template would not only contain a list of relevant styles, but would have already formatted certain paragraphs in the document using those styles. So, all you would need to do is put your cursor in the correct place and start typing.

For example, if you want to write a salutation, just position your cursor into a section styled as Salutation, and type *Dear John*. If you want to type the body of the letter, just put your cursor between *Dear* and *Sincerely* and start typing. A good template can go beyond this, by the way, automatically inserting the current date, prompting for the inside address, and even typing Dear and taking a stab at *who*—which is what Wizard templates do. The point, however, is that you don't have to decide how far to indent the date, the Dear, or the Sincerely. The styles for Date, Salutation, and Signature Closing have already taken care of the details. Just choose the style for what you want to include and start typing.

Styles Versus Direct (Variant) Formatting

Every once in a while, someone will send me a document on disk, in Word format. One time, I looked at the document and it was very elaborately formatted, with a number of intricate recurring patterns of formatting. I glanced up to the Formatting toolbar and noticed that the styles were all called Normal. In fact, this individual didn't know about styles. Instead, he applied different formatting twists and turns to Normal to sculpt the document into the form he desired. I sure hope he knew how to copy formatting from one paragraph to another. Otherwise, it must have been a pretty tedious exercise.

All this points up the difference between using styles to format and using direct formatting. If you want a paragraph to have a hanging indentation, you can carefully drag the margin marks on the Formatting toolbar to achieve a hanging indentation. Or, you can select a style called Hanging (assuming Hanging already exists). Either way, you get the identical effect. If you apply the hanging indentation by dragging the margin marks, or by selecting Format Paragraph, you're using direct formatting. Many users use only direct formatting, and seemingly do just fine. They're not using Word's full potential, but perhaps they don't need to.

It's no crime, by the way, to use direct formatting. I do it all the time and have never been arrested for it. However, once I get a paragraph or other section of text looking just the way I want it, I usually save the formatting as a style—particularly if it's a look I'll want to use later in the same document. You might call this style-by-example. Use direct formatting to make the paragraph look the way you want it, and then give that look a name. For me, this beats the heck out of selecting Format Style New and punching the Format | Font or Format | Paragraph buttons. Direct formatting definitely has valid uses in Word. Just remember to save anything you'll have to do again as a new style.

Document Subdivisions

Different kinds of formatting can be applied to different subdivisions of a document. Conceptually, a Word document can contain the following divisions and subdivisions:

Document
Sections
Pages
Paragraphs
Tables
Sentences
Lines
Words
Characters

Some kinds of formatting—like page layout—usually apply to an entire document. At the very least, by definition, page layout controls the way text appears on any given page. This includes aspects such as orientation (portrait versus landscape), top, bottom, and side margins, paper size (legal, letter, envelope, and so forth), and paper source (sheet feeder, top tray, envelope tray, and so forth).

Other kinds of formatting—like section formatting—apply within user-defined sections. Section formatting includes things like line numbering, page layout, headers and footers, vertical alignment, and footnote printing. Sections are created by inserting section breaks in a document. You might use a section break, for example, to separate a preface (with small Roman numerals) from the main portion (with Arabic numerals).

The document subdivision with which most people are familiar is the paragraph. In Word, a paragraph is all of the text between two paragraph breaks. In previous versions of Word for Windows, the paragraph was the most important formatting consideration when talking about styles. That's because styles were assigned only at the paragraph level. In Word 6, however, Word for Windows joins other versions of Word in letting the user have different *character* styles within a given paragraph. This opens up powerful new formatting opportunities, as well as the potential for confusion in users accustomed to the old limitation.

In the next skill session, we'll take a look at an important formatting tool—the View. How you look at a document determines what you see. Sometimes you need a microscope, and sometimes you need a telescope. In the next skill session, you'll learn *when* to use *which*.

Chapter

10

Document Views: Use the Right View When Formatting

It all depends on how you look at it. Word provides a variety of ways to look at one or more documents. Your satisfaction with Word, as well as how efficiently you work, depends in large part upon creating the right work environment. In this section, you learn about the different views, when they're appropriate, and how they affect your ability to format a document.

Normal

When you first open Word—before you've customized or changed anything—you're in Normal view. There's that awful word Normal again; it sure seems like Microsoft could've used a thesaurus that day. In this *context*, Normal has nothing to do with NORMAL.DOT, the style named Normal, nor even with Normal, Illinois. Instead, it describes a compromise view that shows some, but not all, formatting. To select Normal view, select **V**iew | **N**ormal (Alt+V N).

SUPER TIP

If the horizontal scroll bar is displayed, you can use the Normal View button to switch to Normal view, as shown in Figure 10.1.

FIGURE 10.1. *Normal, Page Preview, and Outline views are available from the view tools on the Horizontal scroll bar.*

Notice the dot beside the word Normal, as shown in Figure 10.2. The dot indicates that Normal view is selected. Notice also that the alternatives to Normal are Outline, Page Layout, and Master Document. Another alternative to these three is called Page Preview. However, Page Preview has a number of restrictions and limitations—as well as a number of special powers—so it's logically distinct. In fact, it's not even on the View menu at all (it's on the File menu, and you can't see the Page Preview unless you have a printer installed).

Normal is a good view to use for general document composition when you want to see the effects of character and paragraph formatting immediately, but you don't really care about seeing headers, footers, footnotes, exact page information, and other items that don't appear on the page.

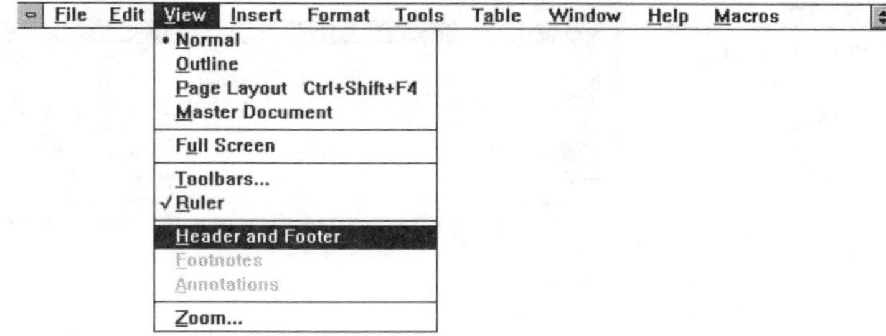

FIGURE 10.2.
Follow the moving dot. The dot shows the current display view.

Outline

Outline view is a way to get an overview of your document. You do not have to actually insert an outline into Word to use Outline view. All you have to do is use the built-in heading levels (heading 1 through heading 9) for formatting your heading. You can, if you like, call your headings HA, HB, HC, HD, and so forth. However, if you do, you give up the ability to use outline view. To enter Outline view, select **V**iew | **O**utline (Alt+V O, or click the Outline tool on the Horizontal scroll bar, shown in Figure 10.1).

Notice that the active view dot now points to Outline view. In Outline view, the Formatting toolbar is replaced by the Outline bar, as shown in Figure 10.3. The Outline bar provides a variety of tools to help you display your document at different levels, as well as reformat by changing levels. See Chapter 40, "Outlining," for additional information about outlining.

FIGURE 10.3.
The Outline bar. A great place for outliners to meet and share a cold brew after a long, hot day of outlining.

Draft

Draft view is an alternative way to display the screen in Normal and Outline view. Draft view is not available in Page Layout view.

PROCEDURE 10.1. DISPLAYING WORD IN A DRAFT FONT.

1. Select **T**ools | **O**ptions | View.
2. Click Show **D**raft Font.
3. Click **P**icture Placeholders (not essential, but aids in speeding up the display).

Contrast the views shown in Figures 10.4 and 10.5, which show the same view in draft and nondraft modes.

FIGURE 10.4.
Draft view, using picture placeholders.

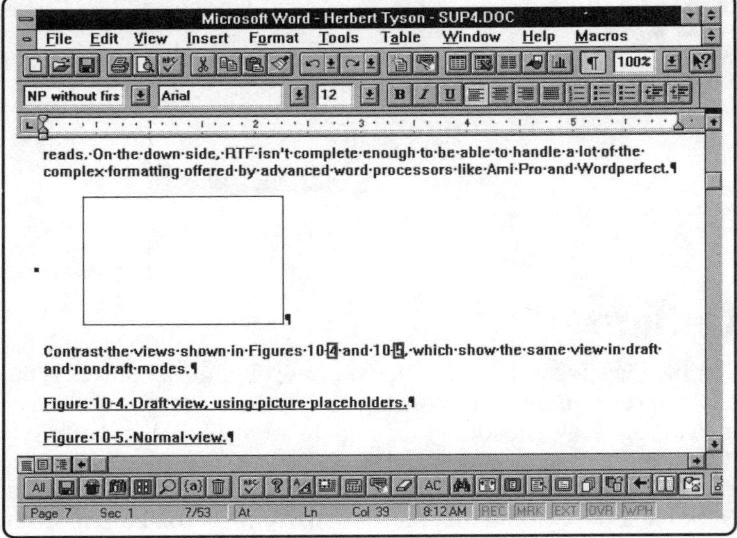

FIGURE 10.5.
Normal view.

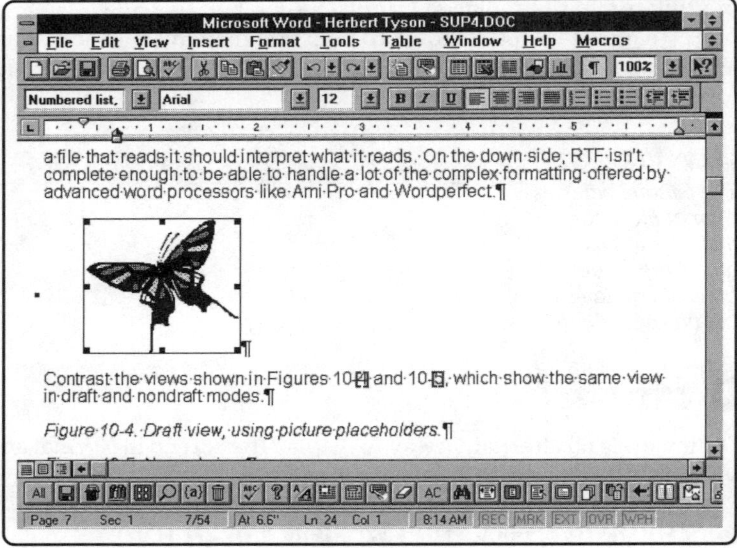

In draft view, all character formatting is displayed as underlined. Hence, bold, hidden, strikethrough, italics, and even underlining itself display as underlined. Font and point size changes aren't displayed at all (20=point and 4=point look identical, for example), while small caps and all caps are displayed simply as all caps. Colors, subscript, and superscript are displayed, but the latter two don't display the actual character sizes.

Also, if you select **P**icture Placeholders (as was done in Step 3 of the procedure), graphics are displayed in empty frames.

The advantage of draft view is that it's fast and usually much easier to read than nondraft because of the increased contrast. It's also easier to read when working with small fonts, since draft view always uses the same size font. When composing a document, it's appropriate that at times you're more interested in the words than in how they look. If your interaction with Word is primarily composing rather than formatting text, then you might never leave draft view. On the other hand, if you do care about formatting, you probably should switch out of draft mode before printing. Otherwise, you might be in for some unpleasant surprises.

SUPER CHANGE

Word for Windows 2 had a Draft option in the View menu. Unfortunately, Word 6 makes you work a little harder. You can add Draft view back to the View menu, if you like. C'mon, it'll only take a second.

PROCEDURE 10.2. ADDING DRAFT TO THE VIEW MENU.

1. Select **T**ools | **C**ustomize, and click the **M**enus tab.
2. Under Sa**v**e Changes In, select NORMAL.DOT.
3. Click the View category.
4. Under Commands, click ViewDraft.
5. Click Add.
6. Click Close.

SUPER

Now, to select draft view, just type Alt+V D. Or, if you're really feeling adventurous, jump ahead to the Customization Workshop to see all the other neat ways you can make Word work in your style. (P.S. If you like the change, make sure you save your changes to NORMAL.DOT. Otherwise, it won't be there the next time you open Word.)

Page Layout

Page Layout view is at the opposite extreme from draft view. Page Layout view, as shown in Figure 10.6, shows headers, footers, footnotes, and graphics, all as they will appear when printed and in their actual relative sizes. Like Normal view, Page Layout view is editable and zoomable. It's a handy view for doing touch-up formatting for a document you're close to printing. It's also quite a bit slower than Normal view, since Word needs to calculate actual pages and to resolve any references contained on each page.

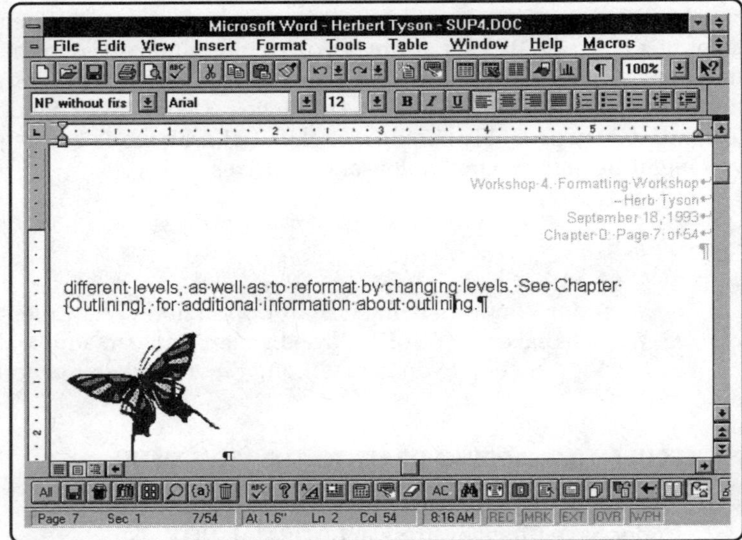

FIGURE 10.6.
Page Layout view.

To enter Page Layout view, select **V**iew | **P**age Layout (Alt+V P).

In Page Layout view, two additional controls are available on the Vertical scroll bar, as shown in Figure 10.7. The double scroll arrows are used to scroll up and down one full page at a time, maintaining the same relative position on each page. If you position the view so that the page bottom displays, then using the double arrows shows you the same view of every page. Note also that Page Layout view also displays a vertical ruler for formatting top and bottom margins, as well as formatting the height of various page elements (headers, table rows, and so forth).

Print Preview

Print Preview is designed to show you the major document parts, letting you adjust the top and bottom margins, headers, footers, and footnote sizes, as well as the location of hard page breaks. To activate Print Preview, select **V**iew | **P**age Layout (Alt+V P).

Print Preview mode is especially useful for troubleshooting printing problems. For example, if you find that the top of the page is printing too far down on the page, Print Preview mode can be a useful way to see the relative position of the header on the page, and to adjust it if necessary. For additional information on using Print Preview mode, see the discussion in Chapter 4, "Printing."

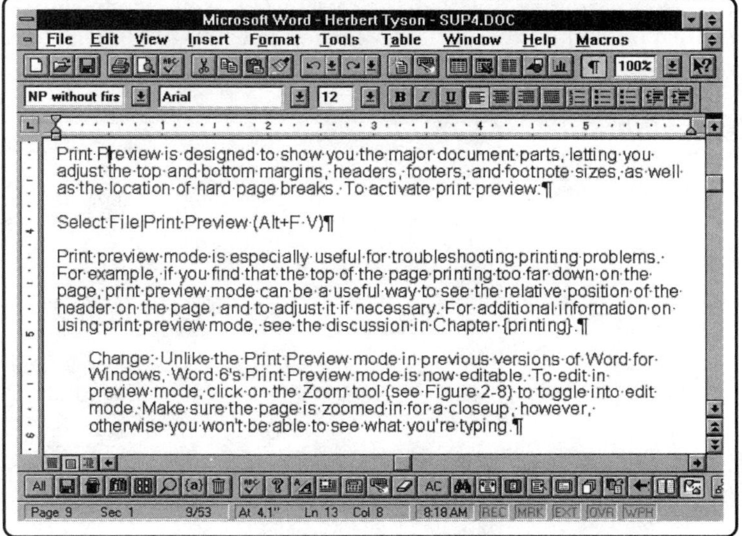

FIGURE 10.7.
Page layout view sports two additional GUI scroll controls and a vertical ruler.

> **SUPER UPDATE NOTE**
>
> Unlike the Print Preview mode in previous versions of Word for Windows, Word 6's Print Preview mode is now editable. To edit in Print Preview mode, click the Zoom tool (see Figure 10.8) to toggle into edit mode. Make sure the page is zoomed in for a close-up, however, or you won't be able to see what you're typing.

FIGURE 10.8.
Click the Zoom/Edit toggle button to switch between Zoom and Edit modes when previewing a document.

Toolbars

One of Word's newest and most flexible features is the toolbar. Word lets you display as many toolbars as you like at the same time, and you can put them wherever you like. However, it's possible to go overboard, as shown in Figure 10.9. They're so easy to turn off and on that it hardly makes sense to clutter the screen with tools you're not using.

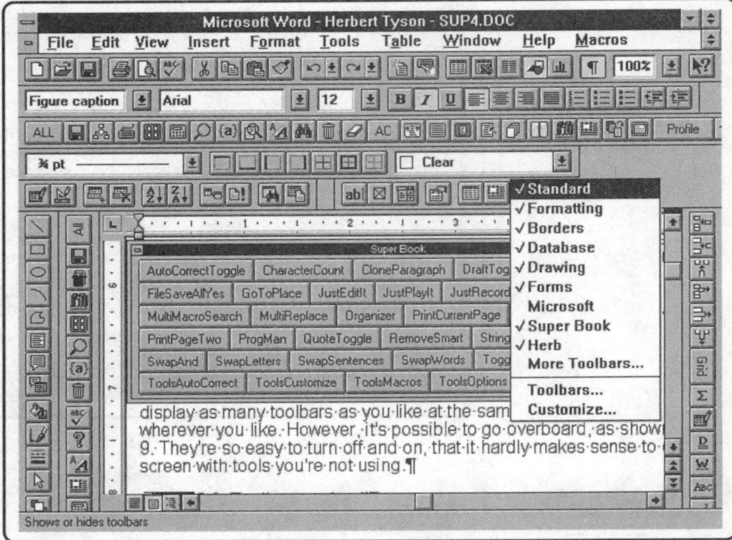

FIGURE 10.9.
Toolbar overload!

PROCEDURE 10.3. TOGGLING THE DISPLAYING OF TOOLS.

1. Select **V**iew | **T**oolbars.
2. Click so that an **X** appears in the box next to each toolbar you want to display (see Figure 10.10). Deselect any you want to hide.
3. Click OK.

SUPER TIP

To toggle the display of a single toolbar at a time, you can click the right mouse button in any toolbar area to display a popup tool selection list, as shown in Figure 10.11. Click the toolbar you want to toggle. Alternatively, click Toolbars for the same menu you get from selecting **V**iew | **T**oolbars. If a toolbar is displayed as a floating toolbox, you can hide it instantly by clicking its control icon in the upper-left corner. You don't even have to double-click.

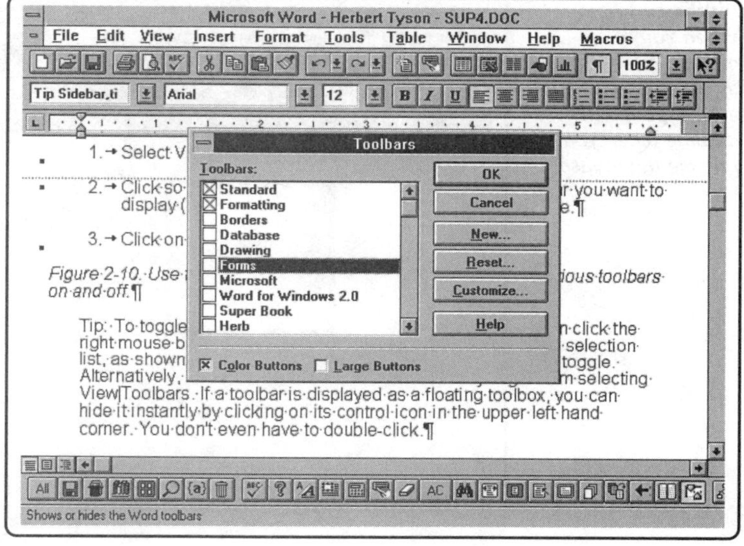

FIGURE 10.10.
Use the Toolbars dialog box to turn the display of various toolbars on and off.

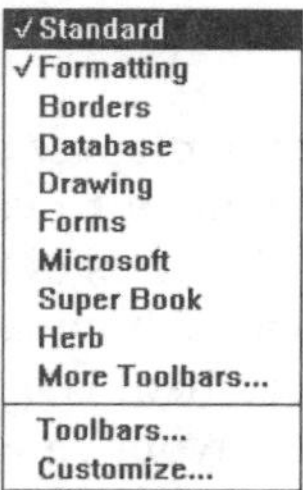

FIGURE 10.11.
The popup toolbar selection list.

PROCEDURE 10.4. CHANGING A TOOLBAR INTO A FLOATING TOOLBOX.

1. Aim the mouse at any blank area in the toolbar.
2. Drag the toolbar to wherever you want it to appear, by pressing the left mouse button and moving the mouse at the same time.
3. An outline of the toolbar appears while it's being moved. Note that the toolbar changes shape depending on where it is on-screen (see Figure 10.12).
4. Release the mouse button to set the toolbar in the new location.

TIP

You can toggle a toolbar or toolbox between its toolbar location and its last floating position by double-clicking any blank area of the toolbar.

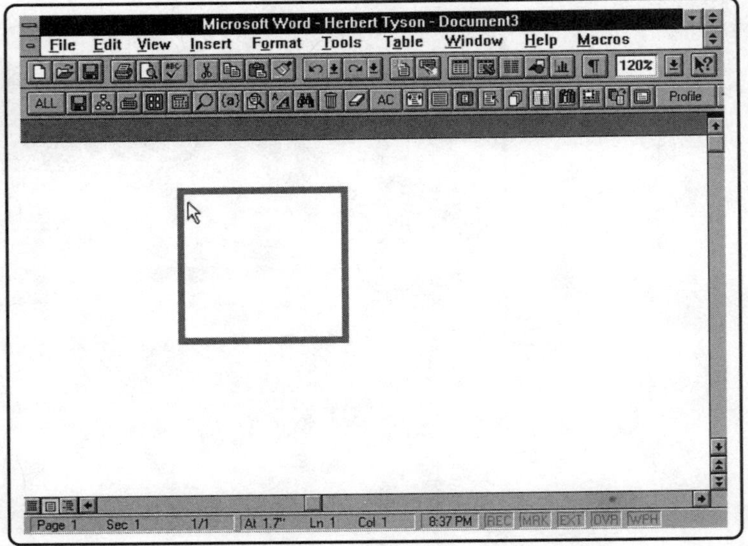

FIGURE 10.12.
When you're moving a toolbar, its outline tells you the shape it will assume when you release the mouse button.

Zooming

Zooming refers to scaling the display up and down in size. You might think of zooming as subjecting your document to various levels of magnification. At 100 percent, Word attempts to display the sizes of text and objects roughly as they would appear on paper. At 200 percent (maximum zoom), the document appears twice the normal size. At 25 percent, the document is one-quarter normal size. Zooming is available in Normal, Outline, and Page Layout views, both draft and nondraft. In draft view, however, the text size is not scaled. To select the zoom control, select **View | Zoom** (Alt+V Z).

When you select the zoom dialog box, Word offers you six preset options as well as the ability to adjust the zoom from 10 percent to 200 percent. In addition to the obvious options, shown in Figure 10.13, the Zoom dialog offers three additional options:

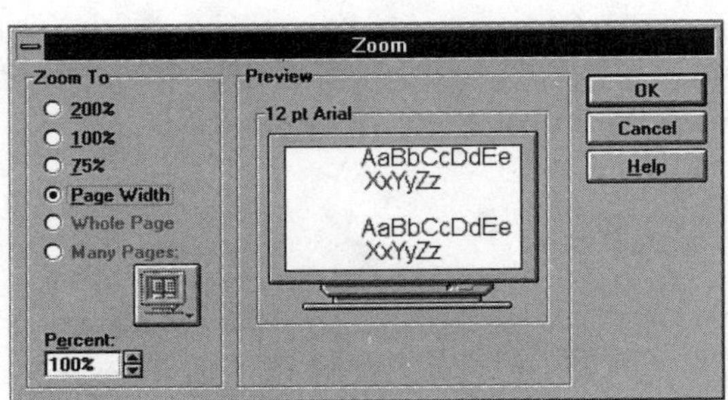

FIGURE 10.13.
Who's zooming who? The Zoom dialog box lets you zoom it.

Page Width — This option scales the view to show all text on the page horizontally, allowing for a side style area display as well as the Vertical scroll bar. This option corresponds to the Page Width tool (see Figure 10.14).

SUPER UPGRADE NOTE

The Zoom Page Width tool, which was in the Word for Windows 2 toolbar, is not in the default Standard toolbar in Word 6. It is in the Word for Windows 2 toolbar (choose **View | Toolbars** and select Word for Windows 2). You also can use the techniques shown in Chapter 48 "Customizing Toolbars" to put the Zoom Page Width tool wherever is convenient for you.

FIGURE 10.14.
The Page Width tool zooms just wide enough to show the width of the text.

Whole Page — This option, available only in Preview and Page Layout views, scales the view to show all text on the page vertically, allowing for rulers, toolbars, Horizontal scroll bar, and status bar, as shown in Figure 10.15.

Many Pages — This option, also available only in Preview and Page Layout View, can show as many as *forty-five* pages at once at 1024 × 768 resolution, as shown in Figure 10.16.

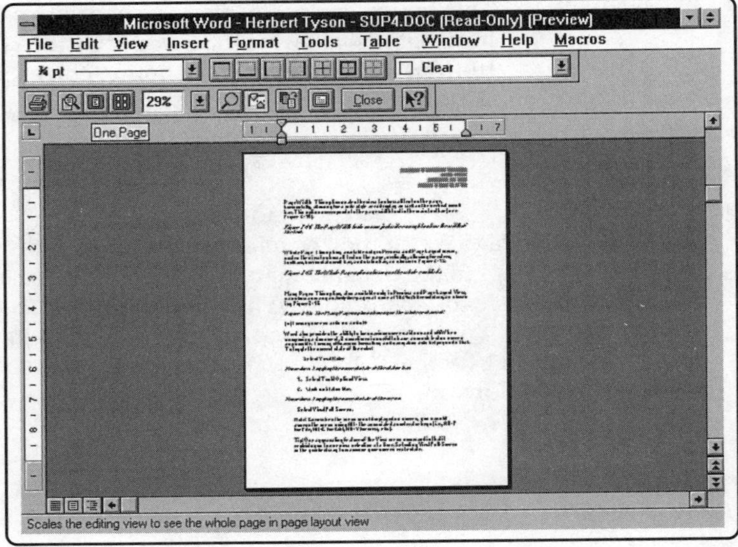

FIGURE 10.15.
The Whole Page option shows you the whole enchilada.

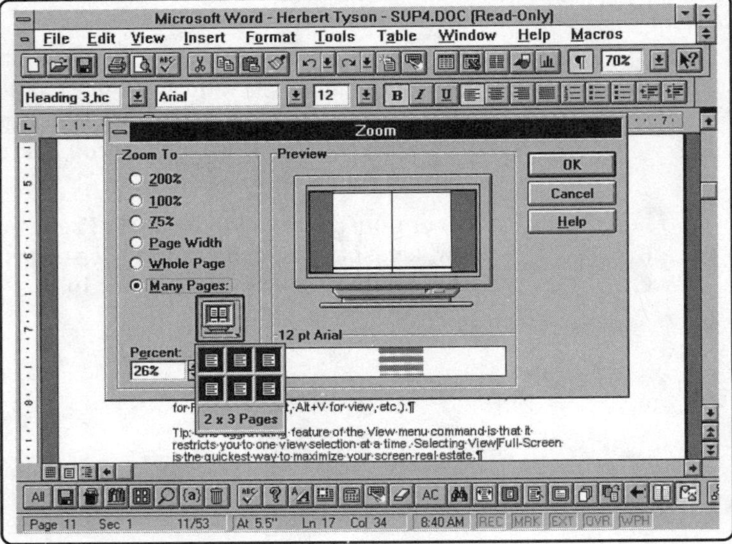

FIGURE 10.16.
The Many Pages option shows you the whole restaurant!

Turning Screen Aids On and Off

Word also provides the ability to turn various screen aids on and off. When composing a document, it sometimes is useful to have as much text on-screen as possible.

Turning off various formatting and navigation aids helps you do that. To toggle the current state of the ruler, select View | Ruler.

PROCEDURE 10.5. TOGGLING THE CURRENT STATE OF THE STATUS BAR.

1. Select Tools | Options | View.
2. Click Status Bar.

PROCEDURE 10.6. TOGGLING THE CURRENT STATE OF THE MENU.

1. Select View | Full Screen to turn off the menu and all GUI aids except for the single-button Full toolbar.
2. Click the Full Screen toggle button in the floating toolbar to turn menus and other GUI aids back on.

SUPER TIP

Even when the menu is not displayed on-screen, you can still access the menu using Alt+ the associated accelerator keys (that is, Alt+F for File, Alt+E for Edit, Alt+V for View, and so forth).

SUPER TIP

One aggravating feature of the View menu command is that it restricts you to one view selection at a time. Selecting View | Full Screen is the quickest way to maximize your screen real estate.

Style Area

The style area is one of Word's most frequently overlooked features. Shown in Figure 10.17, the style area is a convenient way to see what styles are in effect in various passages in a document.

The style area is especially useful with unfamiliar templates. As shown in Figure 10.18, you would have to move the cursor through the document, one paragraph at a time, to see what the various parts of the template are designed to format. With the style area turned on, you can tell at a glance.

Tip Sidebar,ti — Tip: One aggravating feature of the View menu command is that restricts you to one view selection at a time. Selecting View|Full is the quickest way to maximize your screen real estate.¶

Heading 3,hc — (c)Style area¶

NP without first lin,np — The style area is one of Word's most-frequently-overlooked features Figure 2-17, the style area is a convenient way to see what styles a various passages in a document.¶

Figure caption — *Figure 2-17. The style area can be made wider or narrower using th*

NP without first lin,np — ¶

NP without first lin,np — The style area is especially useful when using unfamiliar templates. Figure 2-18, you would have to move the cursor through the docum paragraph at a time, to see what the various parts of the template a to format. With the style area turned on, you can tell at a glance. To

FIGURE 10.17.
The style area can be made wider or narrower using the mouse.

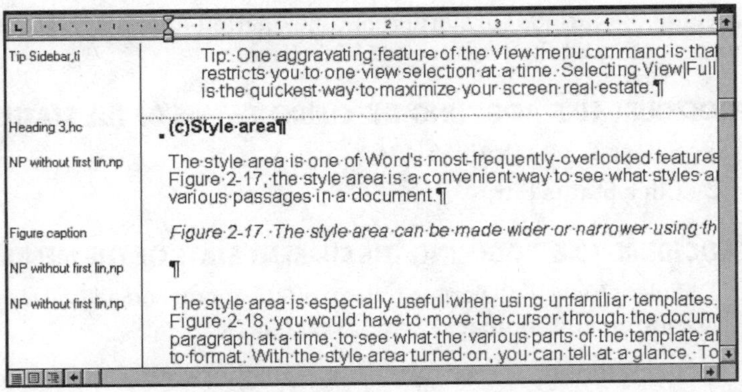

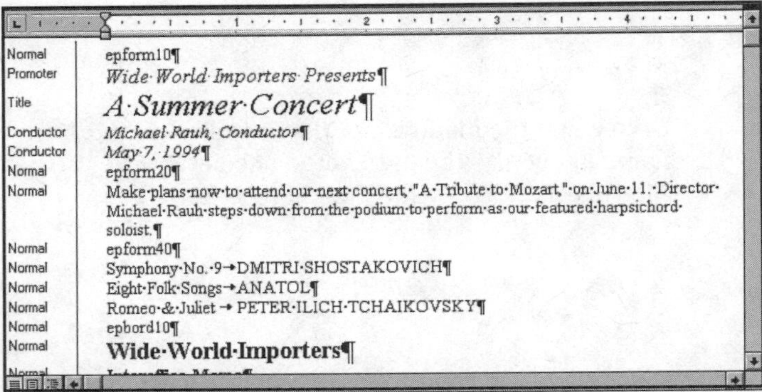

FIGURE 10.18.
The style area lets you see at a glance what styles are in fashion.

PROCEDURE 10.7. DISPLAYING THE STYLE AREA.

1. Select **T**ools | **O**ptions | **V**iew.
2. Click the Style Area Width box.
3. Use the graphical up and down arrow to drag the style area to a width wide enough to accommodate your styles.
4. Click OK.

NOTE

The style area width option is not available when working in Page Layout or Print Preview views.

SUPER TIP

In a text box with scroll arrows, you also can use the up and down arrows on the keyboard to increase or decrease the value in the box. Once the style area is turned on, you also can use the mouse to drag the style area to the left or right, or to hide it altogether. Once hidden, however, you have to go back to the menu to turn it on.

SUPER TIP

Use a macro to toggle the style area on and off. Adopt this macro as your own and assign it to a key. I use Ctrl+Alt+Shift+S.

STYLEBARTOGGLE (ON THE WORD 6 SUPER BOOK DISKETTE):

```
Sub MAIN
Dim TOV As ToolsOptionsView
GetCurValues TOV
Widthn = Val(TOV.StyleAreaWidth)
Print Widthn
If Widthn = 0 Then WidthC$ = "0.5" Else WidthC$ = "0"
ToolsOptionsView .StyleAreaWidth = WidthC$
End Sub
```

Other Viewing Aids

Word includes a variety of additional viewing aids that can be turned on or off, all of which are accessible from the **T**ools | **O**ptions | View menu, as shown in Figure 10.19.

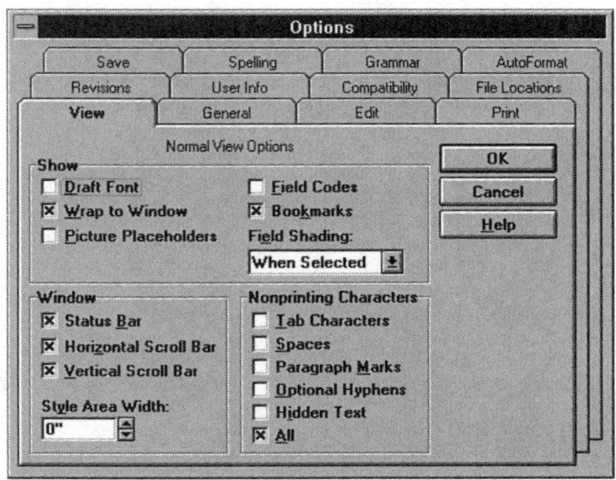

FIGURE 10.19.
Tools | Options | View dialog provides the same options in Normal, Outline, and Master Document view.

The options you see on the View screen change depending on your view. When editing a macro, you get the same view as shown in Figure 10.19, but with irrelevant options dimmed out. Shown in Figure 10.20 are the options you get in Page Layout view. The View options are not available at all in Print Preview mode.

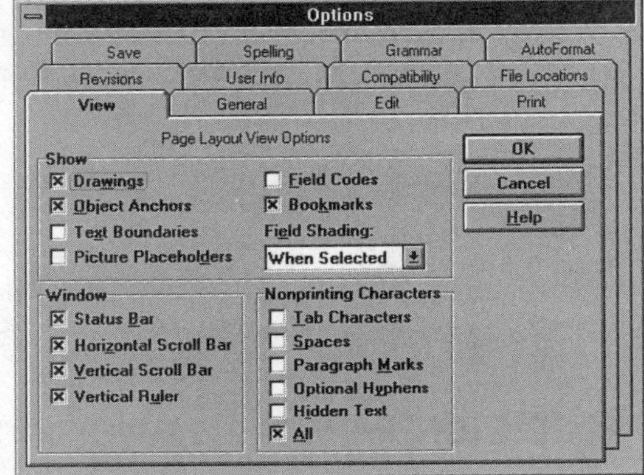

FIGURE 10.20.
Page Layout options.

Scroll Bars

Both Horizontal and Vertical scroll bars can be turned off.

PROCEDURE 10.8. TOGGLING THE HORIZONTAL SCROLL BAR.

1. Select **T**ools | **O**ptions | **V**iew.
2. Click Hori**z**ontal Scroll Bar.

PROCEDURE 10.9. TOGGLING THE VERTICAL SCROLL BAR.

1. Select **T**ools | **O**ptions | **V**iew.
2. Click **V**ertical Scroll Bar.

Table Gridlines

Table gridlines, shown in Figure 10.21, are useful when preparing tables without borders, as they help you get a better picture of the cell divisions. To toggle the display of table gridlines, select T**a**ble | Grid**l**ines.

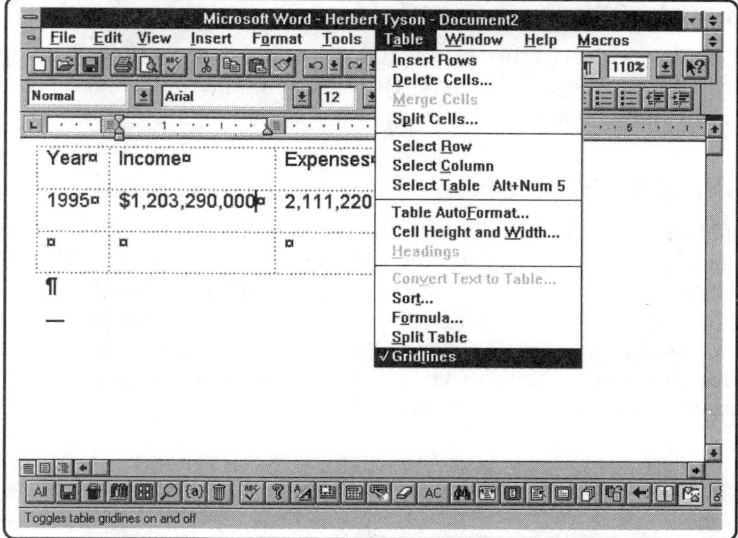

FIGURE 10.21.
Table gridlines help you get GUI control of a table.

> **SUPER CHANGE**
>
> Under Word for Windows 2, table gridlines were selectable from the View options dialog box. They're now available only from the Table menu.

Formatting Aids

Word has a number of optional aids it can display to help you edit and compose documents. To select or deselect any of the following, select **Tools | Options | View**, and click the appropriate box(es) to turn the display of the respective features on or off.

> **SUPER CHANGE**
>
> Note that the View options are now very different from what they were in prior versions of Word for Windows.

Draft Font

Use this option to turn off the display of most formatting. This option corresponds to Word for Windows 2's **View | Draft** option. This option is unavailable in Page Layout and Print Preview modes.

Wrap to Window

This option tells Word to wrap the text so that it fits in the current window rather than displaying line breaks as they will appear when printed. This option requires considerably less time and memory on the part of Word, and it results in a faster display. It corresponds in part to Word for Windows 2's Line Breaks and Fonts as Printed view option. The fact that it now wraps to fit the window means that you can have comfortable fonts regardless of your display resolution. This option is unavailable in Page Layout and Print Preview modes.

SUPER

By default, when you select the Wrap to Window option, Word automatically scales to zoom to 100 percent. At higher resolutions, this can give text a faded on-screen appearance, making it hard to see, as shown in Figure 10.22. If you zoom the scale up (to 125 percent, for example), the text *still* wraps to fit, and the display darkens, as shown in Figure 10.23. At higher resolutions, this makes Word much easier on the eyes.

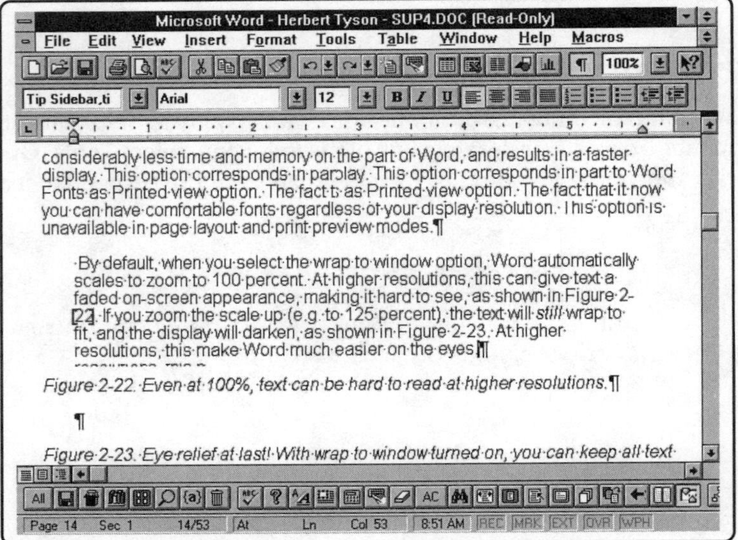

FIGURE 10.22.
Even at 100 percent, text can be hard to read at higher resolutions.

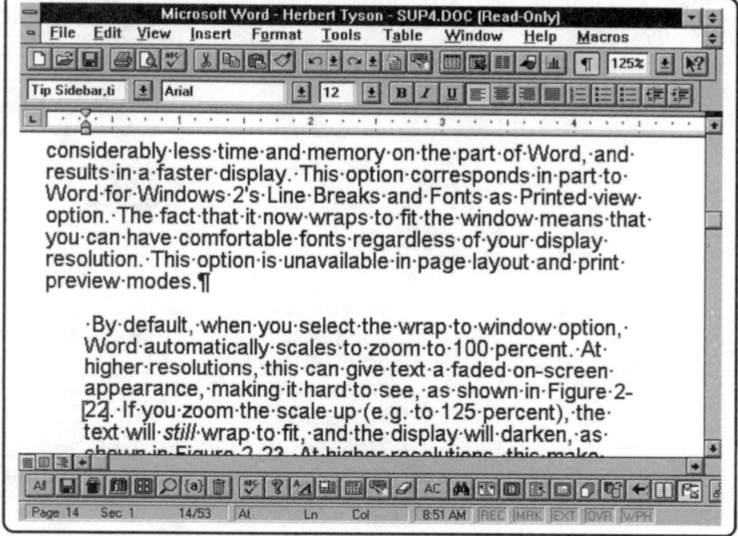

FIGURE 10.23.
Eye relief at last! With Wrap to Window turned on, you can keep all text on-screen at any zoom.

Picture Placeholders

The **P**icture Placeholders option is used to replace the display of graphics with a blank frame. If your document contains graphics, the display update will be quite slow and tedious. There's simply no reason to make your display work that hard all the time. You can speed up the display by showing graphics only when absolutely necessary.

Field Codes

Use this option to toggle the display of field codes and field code results, as shown in Figure 10.24. This can be a useful diagnostic tool when a field displays either as an error result or as a result you didn't expect. Displaying field codes also is useful both for direct editing, as well as to speed up the display of graphics or other fields whose results are long passages of text.

SUPER TIP

You can use Ctrl+F9 as a shortcut for **T**ools | **O**ptions | **V**iew | **F**ield Codes. If the document is very long, it's often faster and just as revealing to use Shift+F9 to toggle the display of just a single field code. In order for the latter to work, the cursor must be on the field code (use F11 to advance to the nearest field code, or Shift+F11 to go back to the nearest previous field code).

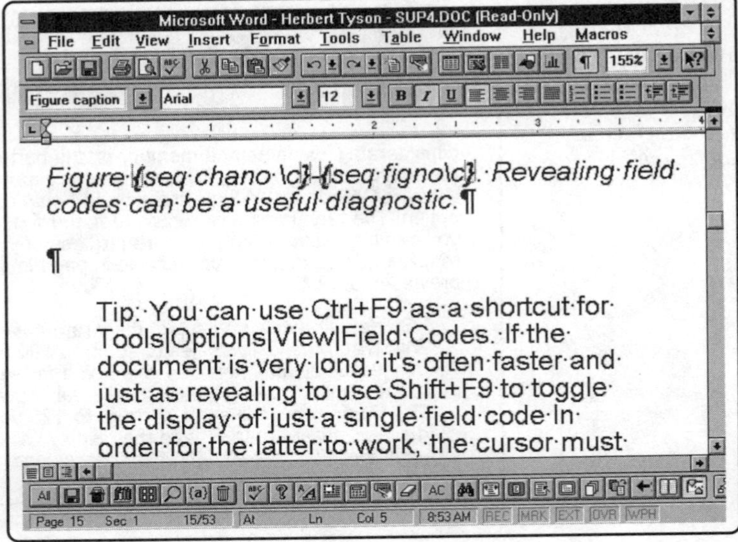

FIGURE 10.24.
Revealing field codes can be a useful diagnostic.

Bookmarks

When enabled, this option encloses bookmarks with brackets, as shown in Figure 10.25. If you use bookmarks extensively, this can be a valuable aid in seeing what's going on. Be careful about overlapping bookmarks, however; it may sometimes appear that you're looking at a single bookmark when in fact you're looking at a point where two overlap.

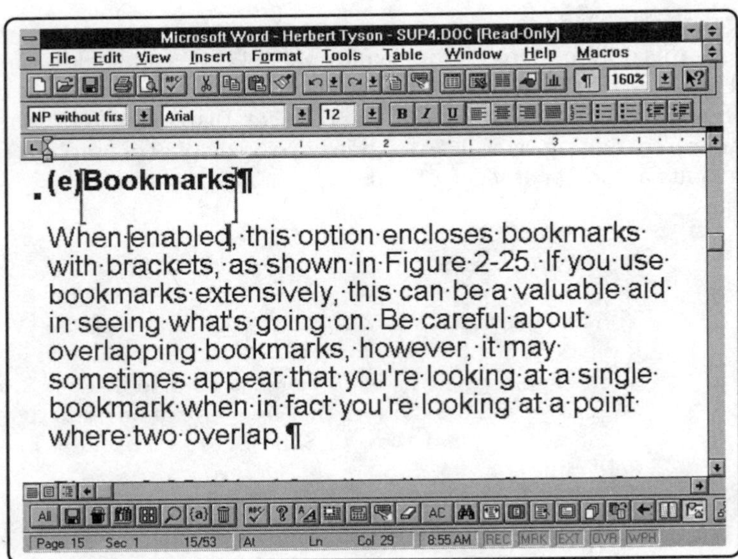

FIGURE 10.25.
Word 6 optionally uses [brackets] to display the locations, but not the names, of bookmarks.

Field Shading

Another handy formatting aid is the ability to shade field codes. Have you ever forgotten that something was a field? Use this feature to shade it. That way, you can tell at a glance that something is a field code rather than normal text.

PROCEDURE 10.10. SETTING THE DISPLAY OF FIELD CODES.

1. Select **T**ools | **O**ptions | **V**iew.
2. Click the drop-down arrow under Field Shading.
3. Select Never, Always, or When Selected.
4. Click OK.

SUPER

The When Selected option is a nice compromise between the obtrusive Always and the working-blindly Never.

Drawings

Use this option (available only in Page Layout view) to toggle the display of drawings. With drawings turned off, you can't tell where they are. However, unless you need to see them, suppressing their display can speed up screen refreshing.

Object Anchors

Every drawing object is anchored to a paragraph in a document. If you move the drawing over a different paragraph, the anchor changes. In some documents, particularly those with close spacing and columnar layout, it can be difficult to see where a drawing is anchored. Use the Object Anchors option to display an anchor symbol. When a drawing is selected, as shown in Figure 10.26, Word uses a real anchor as the icon.

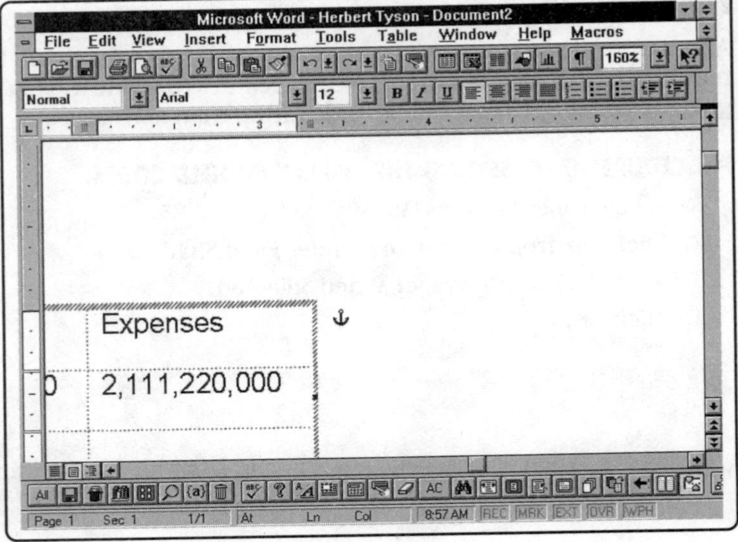

FIGURE 10.26.
Object anchors show which paragraph an object is anchored to.

Nonprinting Characters

Word lets you selectively turn on or off the display of various nonprinting characters:

- Tabs
- Spaces
- Paragraph Marks and End-of-Line Marks
- Optional Hyphens
- Hidden Text

As shown in Figure 10.27, displaying these characters can be quite useful in determining why text behaves as it does.

Note that the difference between tabs and spaces (or even the difference between a single and a double space) is instantly obvious when nonprinting characters are displayed. Similarly, the difference between end-of-line markers and paragraph markers is clarified by turning on the display of paragraph marks.

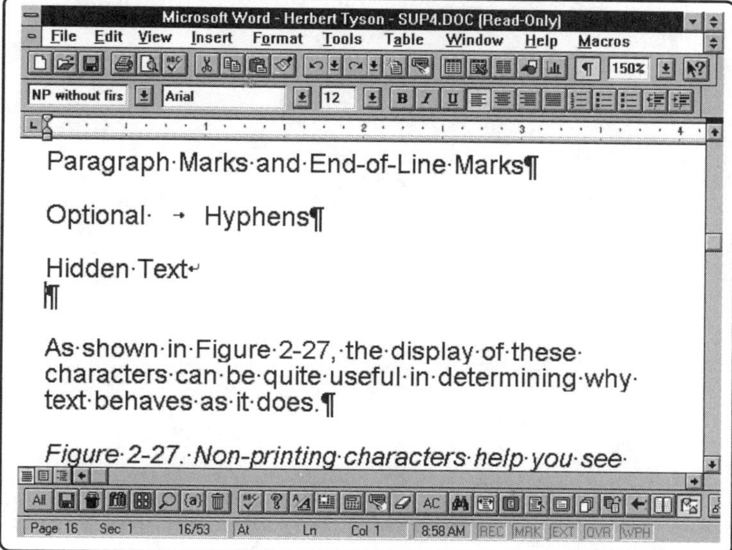

FIGURE 10.27.
Nonprinting characters help you see where paragraphs end as well as the difference between tabs and spaces.

SUPER NOTE

The options in the Nonprinting Characters section are sometimes a source of confusion, due to the availability of the All option in the same section. In fact, the All option is a different aspect, and it can be toggled on and off by clicking the paragraph symbol in the Standard toolbar or by pressing Ctrl+* (on the number pad, or Ctrl+Shift+8 on the main keyboard). If paragraph marks are checked in the Options | View dialog box, then pressing Ctrl+* has no effect on the display of paragraph marks—they are displayed all the time. Similarly, you can force Word to display spaces as a small dot all the time. The confusion sometimes comes when users wonder why turning All on and off has no effect. If the display of a nonprinting character is turned on individually, then the All option (or clicking the paragraph symbol or pressing Ctrl+*) has no effect.

Chapter

11

Font Formatting

For some bizarre reason, Microsoft likes to shift its terminology from time to time. Rather than change the several uses of the word *normal*, about which many people were confused (NORMAL.DOT, Normal Style, Normal font style—meaning not bold or italic—and View Normal), they chose instead to change F**o**rmat|**C**haracter to F**o**rmat|**F**ont.

At the same time, their Help and manuals still talk about *character* formatting. So much for having mastered the learning curve...If I accidentally slip and call it *character* formatting (which I plan to do since it seems to be the only way to establish a common language among past, present, and future users, as well as to be consistent with Word's own documentation), then you'll have to forgive me and my editors. You see, we all have something like ten years of habit to overcome.

Oh, why did they do this? Perhaps they did it because Word for Windows 6 now supports *character* styles. And, pray tell, what kind of formatting do you apply to a character style? Why, *character* formatting, of course (language formatting, too)! The one place where the dual terminology *might* conceivably have served to prevent confusion rather than cause it, and they blew the opportunity. Oh, well...

By definition, character formatting (whoops, *font* formatting) is all formatting that can vary within a paragraph. This includes font, font style (formerly called character style—normal, bold, italic, and bold italic), point size, underlining, and effects (strikethrough, superscripts, subscripts, hidden, small caps, and all caps), color, and character spacing. Oh, and language, too. This chapter shows you how to apply and vary character (font) formatting, as well as how to copy character (font) formatting.

Considering the great variety of character formatting Word offers, try to avoid RNS—ransom note syndrome. The stereotypical ransom note has a series of words cut from various magazine and newspaper sections, such that the fonts and sizes vary wildly, as shown in Figure 11.1, `{badexamp.doc}`. In general, the only time you'd want to see this much variety on a page is when you're trying to compose a bad example!

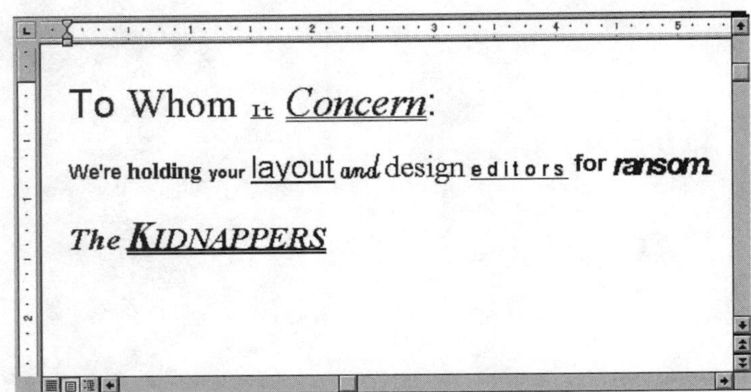

FIGURE 11.1.
Help! I'm being held hostage by a crazed word processor!

Another thing to try is to use styles for formatting whenever you can, especially when there's a chance that the underlying format for a certain type of text may change. If you have a formatting requirement that calls for book and magazine titles to always appear italicized and in a certain font, then create a style for it (for example, booktitle). Later, if your formatting requirements change, you can change the book titles all at once by changing the style rather than having to meticulously search for each title. The latter can be especially difficult if text other than book titles shares similar formatting characteristics.

SUPER NOTE

Character (font) formatting is essentially the same process whether you're applying formatting directly to a text passage or defining the characteristics for a style. The material presented in this session applies equally when setting up a style format, per the discussion in Chapter 22, "Styles and AutoFormat."

Changing Character Formats

There are a number of ways to change character (font) formats. The primary method is to use the Format Font dialog box, shown in Figure 11.2, which you can activate in any of the following ways:

- Click **F**ormat and then **F**ont using the menu.
- Press Alt+O, followed by F.
- Click the right mouse button in the text and then click Font.
- Press Ctrl+D (yeah, it seemed stupid to us, too).
- Select **M**odify | F**o**rmat | **F**ont from the Style dialog box.

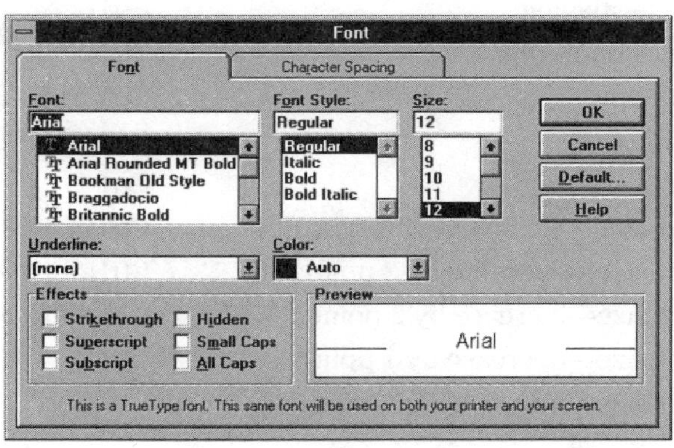

FIGURE 11.2.
Use the Format | Font dialog box to change character formats.

Very often, however, it's inconvenient to use the Format Font dialog box to change the formatting of a single word, especially when applying bold, italic, or underlining. If you're mouse-oriented, you can use the Formatting Toolbar to apply some character formatting. Once you select text in a document, clicking the Bold (**B**), Italic (*I*), or Underline (u) icons will toggle that formatting on or off for the selected text. You can combine formatting in this way, too. For example, to apply bold italic formatting to a word, click the Bold and Italic icons. To convert bold italic to just italic, click the Bold icon to toggle it off.

SUPER TIP

When you use the Font tool on the toolbar, Word "caches" the most recently used fonts at the top of the list. Hence, if you've been using Times New Roman and Playbill, you don't have to wade through Algerian, Arial, Bookman, and so on, to get to the fonts you've been using. You also can jump to fonts beginning with a particular letter by pressing that letter. For example, press T to jump to the first font that begins with a T.

If you're keyboard-oriented, you can use built-in shortcuts, as shown in Table 11.1. I'm sure that Word for Windows version 2 users will be delighted to know that Ctrl+A, Ctrl+D, Ctrl+F, Ctrl+H, Ctrl+P, and a few others have changed! If you were looking for a reason to learn how to customize Word, well, here's your motivation.

Table 11.1. Shortcut character formatting keys.

Formatting Effect	*Keystrokes*
All capital letters	Ctrl+Shift+A
Bold	Ctrl+B
Double spacing	Ctrl+2
Double underline	Ctrl+Shift+D
Font name	Ctrl+Shift+F or Ctrl+Shift+P
Hidden text	Ctrl+Shift+H
Italic	Ctrl+I
Point size	Ctrl+Shift+P or Ctrl+Shift+F
Point size—decrease by 2 points	Ctrl+Shift+<
Point size—increase by 2 points	Ctrl+Shift+>
Point size—decrease by 1 point	Ctrl+]
Point size—increase by 1 point	Ctrl+[

Formatting Effect	Keystrokes
Increase manual kerning	Ctrl+Shift+]
Decrease manual kerning	Ctrl+Shift+[
Remove nonstyle character formatting	Ctrl+Space
Small capital letters	Ctrl+Shift+K
Subscript	Ctrl+=
Superscript	Ctrl+Shift+=
Symbol font	Ctrl+Shift+Q
Toggle case of selected text	Shift+F3
Underline	Ctrl+U
Word underline	Ctrl+Shift+W

Changing Character Formats While Composing

There are two approaches to changing character formats: while composing and after the text is typed. The usual way is to assign character formats as you compose a document. For example, when you come to a section you want to appear as bold, press Ctrl+B (or select Format | Font and click Bold) to make new text you type bold. Press Ctrl+B again when you want to turn bold formatting off. You can use any of the keyboard shortcuts shown in Table 11.1 to change character formats while typing.

SUPER UPGRADE NOTE

In Word for Windows 6, when inserting text inside a word (that is, no word separator follows the insertion point), Word is in word formatting mode. That means that any character formatting you apply when no text is selected is applied to the entire word (all contiguous characters) rather than just to the characters that you are about to type. This is different from what happened in previous versions of Word for Windows. For the most part, it's probably good. It means that you can now embolden or italicize a word without first having to select it. If you were used to inserting new text *after* an existing space instead of *before*, however, you'll have to change your habits. The new rules do not apply to the ResetChar command (Ctrl+Space or Ctrl+Shift+Z), however. You still must select text before pressing Ctrl+Space to remove direct character formatting from text.

Reset Character Formatting

Throughout this book, I will emphasize and reemphasize the virtues of using style-based formatting whenever possible. Several of Word's formatting commands are geared to this concept. In Table 11.1, note the effect of Ctrl+Spacebar: Remove non-style character formatting. This keystroke corresponds to the ResetChar command. When executed, this command removes any variant (direct) formatting from the selected text and sets the character format of the selected text to that of the underlying style. The purpose of the ResetChar command is to return formatting leverage to the style command. Once you remove all character formatting that doesn't come from the style, you can control the formatting for the whole styled area by adjusting the style definition.

A common misunderstanding is that pressing Ctrl+Spacebar will render the selected text devoid of any special formatting at all. That's not what Ctrl+Spacebar does, although it may appear to be the effect, depending on the underlying style's character format. For example, if the character formatting of the current style is Arial, 12 point, bold, pressing Ctrl+Spacebar will remove all formatting except for Arial, 12 point, bold. If the selected text is underlined or italicized—not part of the style's character format—pressing Ctrl+Spacebar will remove the underlining and italics.

Even though Ctrl+Spacebar is not designed to be a command that clears italics, bolding, underlining, and so on wherever they occur, it can be used that way if the underlying style has those attributes turned off. For example, if you need to press Ctrl+B and Ctrl+I to turn bold italics on as you are entering text, you can press Ctrl+B and Ctrl+I again to turn them off. You can also press Ctrl+Spacebar to turn them both off at the same time. Ctrl+Spacebar doesn't turn them off because they're on. It turns them off because bold and italic are off in the underlying style's character formatting.

I once saw a Word for Windows user go crazy trying to remove bold from a heading by pressing Ctrl+Spacebar. Why didn't it work? The heading's character formatting included bold as an attribute. The poor fellow should be getting out of the mental facility in another few months. I wonder what he'll think when he discovers that Word for Windows jumped from version 2 to version 6 and that **Format** | **Character** (Alt+T C) has now become **Format** | **Font** (Alt+O F). Uh oh! Better get the tranquilizer darts ready!

Format Font Dialog Box

The Format Font dialog box enables you to change the following character attributes:

- Font
- Point size
- Style (bold, italic, strikethrough, hidden, small caps, all caps, underlining)
- Color
- Super/subscripts (Vertical alignment)
- Horizontal spacing
- Underlining

PROCEDURE 11.1. CHANGING THE CHARACTER FORMAT OF EXISTING TEXT.

1. Select the text you want to format.
2. Select Format | Font (my favorite method is to press Ctrl+D).
3. Click the Font or Character spacing tab, depending on what you want to change.
4. Select the attribute(s) you want to change.
5. Click OK.

SUPER NOTE

For check boxes, X is on, blank is off, and gray (where it occurs) means ambiguous or multiple settings (that is, the selection contains more than one setting for the formatting attribute whose setting is grayed out). For list boxes, you can select from the list or directly type what you want. Be careful, however, about inventing new fonts that don't exist—they may not print terribly well! For "spin" controls, you can enter the number directly or use the up/down controls (or the up/down cursor keys) to raise or lower the value shown.

Using Format Font to "Read" Character Formats

The Format Font dialog box enables you not only to set character formats but also to determine character formats. When the dialog box appears, Word determines which settings are in effect in the text that is selected (or, at the insertion point if no text is selected). In Figure 11.3, for example, note that the font is Arial and underlining (single) is turned on. However, neither a point size nor font style is selected, and small caps is gray rather than checked. Why?

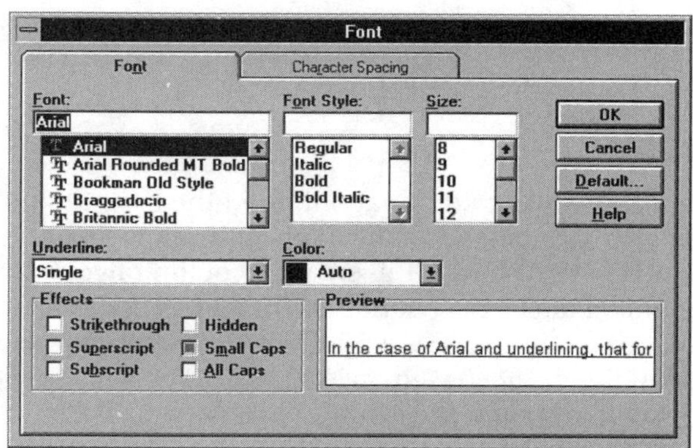

FIGURE 11.3.
Use the Format | Font dialog box to read your formatting.

In the case of Arial and underlining, that formatting is unambiguously turned on in the selected section of text. However, notice that part of the text is larger than another part, and part of the text is italic and small caps while another part is not. When a selection of text is not uniformly formatted for any given attribute, Word will display nothing at all (in the case of point size and font style) or will gray a check box (for small caps) to tell you that those attributes vary within the selection. If you now fill in a point size or click the check box so that italic is definitely on or off, Word will homogenize the selection for those attributes. If you want them left varied, then leave those attribute settings alone when selecting character formatting. That's similar to saying "Stet" or "Leave As-Is" for those attributes.

If you click the gray check box next to small caps, it will toggle among X, blank, and gray. You have the option of toggling gray only if a check box is gray when the Format Font dialog box first appears. In this example, hidden will toggle only between X and blank. If you think about it, that makes perfect sense. If you were to take a bold selection and instruct Word to format it as mixed bold and nonbold in one fell swoop, I don't think you'd like the result (unless you're composing a random [ransom] note).

SUPER CAUTION

Don't jump to conclusions! When more than 50 page elements (paragraphs, table cells, section breaks, column breaks, and page breaks) are selected, Word loses its ability to read a selection's formatting. If a table has more than 50 cells, for example, you will not be able to use the Format Font dialog box to read the font and point size of the table even though it may be consistent throughout. Keep this limitation in mind before you call out a search party to find the hidden variation in a selection. You can still use the Format Font dialog box to format large selections, though. It'll work just fine. However, you won't be able to use the Format Font dialog box after the fact to verify that the selection is uniformly formatted. Instead, you will need to look at the selection piecemeal. Fortunately, you don't need to format it piecemeal.

Default

You can exercise an additional option in the Format Font dialog box by clicking the the pushbutton labeled Default. This curious inclusion was Microsoft's reaction to complaints by WinWord 1.1 users who couldn't figure out how to change the default font. Default changes the character format of a style called Normal in the current template. Whether this option would affect your work depends on how you work. If you're currently editing a file based on NORMAL.DOT, selecting Default changes the Normal style's character format in that template. If you're currently editing a file based on LETBLOCK.DOT, Default changes the Normal style's character format in that template. Word changes only the Normal style, even if your cursor is currently in a section based on a different style and even if you never use the Normal style.

PROCEDURE 11.2. CHANGING THE DEFAULT FORMATTING FOR THE NORMAL STYLE.

1. Select Format | Font.
2. Select any formatting you want to use as your Normal model.
3. Click Default; note the dialog box similar to the one shown in Figure 11.4.
4. Click Yes to change the default format of the Normal style in the indicated template; click No to change your mind.

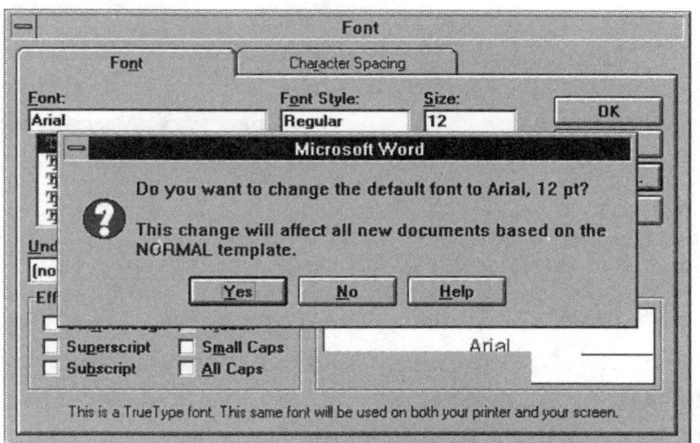

FIGURE 11.4.
The Use as Default option affects only the Normal style in the current template.

Depending on how your template and styles are set up, selecting Yes may very well change the default font. If all of the styles in your template are based on Normal, the change will trickle down to them. If not all of your styles are based on Normal, then only some will be changed (possibly just Normal itself, at the extreme). Furthermore, if you don't use Normal at all in your documents but instead use something called Body, Indented, or some other nonstandard style, selecting Default won't have any effect. In order to really change your default character format in such cases, you need to edit the underlying template itself or modify your styles and select Add to Template in each instance.

How to Really Change the Default Character Format

You can change the default character format in NORMAL.DOT as well as any other template.

PROCEDURE 11.3. CHANGING THE DEFAULT FORMAT BY EDITING NORMAL.DOT.

1. Select **F**ile | **O**pen.
2. Under List Files of Type, select Document Templates (*.DOT), as shown in Figure 11.5.

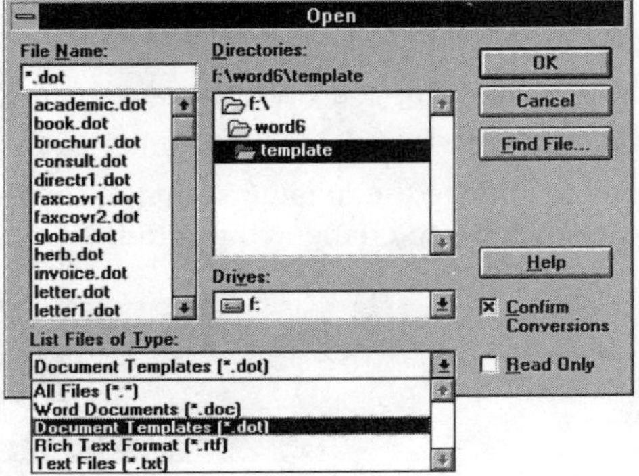

FIGURE 11.5.
Use the file types to zero in on the type of file you want to open.

3. Use the Directories control to navigate to the location of NORMAL.DOT (usually \WINWORD or \WINWORD\TEMPLATE).
4. Select NORMAL.DOT.
5. Press Ctrl+* (numeric pad), if necessary, to turn on the display of paragraph marks.
6. Press Ctrl+A to select the entire document (which should be just a single paragraph mark).
7. Press Ctrl+Shift+S twice.
8. Click Modify.
9. Click Format.
10. Click Font.
11. Select the character formatting you want.
12. Click OK to go back to the previous dialog.
13. Click OK.
14. Click Close.
15. Select **F**ile | **C**lose.
16. Click Yes to confirm the prompt `Do you want to save changes to NORMAL.DOT?`"

Now, whenever you start a new document based on NORMAL.DOT, the paragraph marker you just edited will be where you start inserting text. Thus, the text you type will have the formatting you just assigned.

To set the default format for other templates, you apply the same process to the template you want to change—except for Step 6. Note that, in many templates, there is not just a single insertion point where text could appear. There may be preexisting text. If you use Normal as your base style (see Chapter 22, "Styles and AutoFormat"), you can often change the default format just by changing the Normal style. If you use something else as your base, you may have to study your styles carefully to effect a change. Rather than going into all of the considerations here, however, complete Chapter 22. After that, how it all works should be crystal clear.

SUPER NOTE

You can modify a template's styles by editing any file based on it and selecting the Add to Template option each time you make a change. Depending on how much you have to do, that can get downright tedious. That's why I suggest modifying the template directly.

Language: Also a Character Format?

Missing from the Format Font dialog box is an option to select the Language. In fact, it's on the Tools menu (Tools | Language). So why am I insisting that it's a character format? Even though Language is on a different menu stem, it looks, acts, and feels like character formatting. Language can vary within a paragraph—or even within a word, if you want to get silly about it. Also, when you press Ctrl+Spacebar, the Language gets reset to the default for the current style along with all of the other character formatting. Still not convinced? Okay, then. How about the fact that when you format a character style, there's Language sitting there as big as day? See Figure 11.6 for the smoking menu.

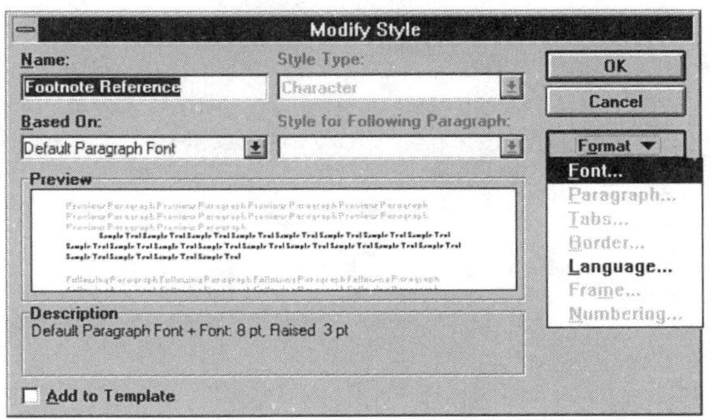

FIGURE 11.6.
Tool | Language, despite being on a different menu, is a character format.

Setting the Language format for a document or parts of a document doesn't suddenly translate your document into another tongue. Instead, this feature is used only when you have multiple dictionaries and other proofing tools available and installed for Word. For example, if I go back and format *For example* as Brazilian Portuguese and then try to run the spell checker on it, I get the warning box shown in Figure 11.7, telling me that Word cannot find the MSSP2_PT.LEX spelling file for Brazilian Portuguese.

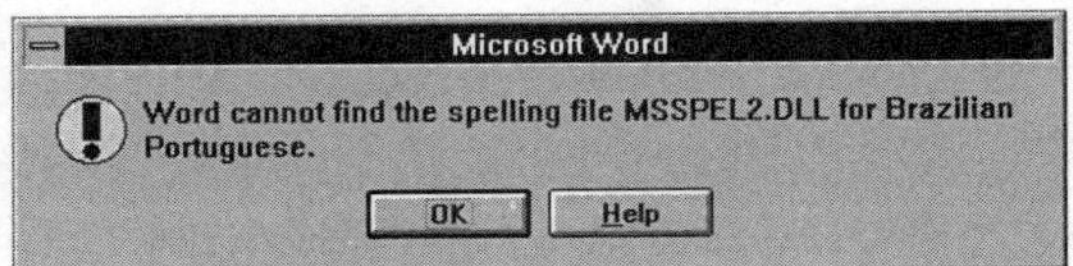

FIGURE 11.7.
Some of Word's features might inspire the practical joker in you.

Copying Character Formatting

Word enables you to copy character formatting from already-formatted text to text you select. This can be useful if formatting is complex, as it keeps you from having to repeat something you've already done.

PROCEDURE 11.4. COPYING CHARACTER FORMATTING WITH THE MOUSE.

1. Select or click some text having the format you want to copy.
2. Click the Format Painting tool on the Standard toolbar as shown in Figure 11.8.
3. Use the mouse .

SUPER UPGRADE NOTE

Note that this technique is different from the mouse technique used in Word for Windows version 2. In version 2, you could select a section of text, press Ctrl+Shift, and click the section having the format you wanted to copy. This method does not work in Word 6. It was eliminated in Word for Windows version 3.5, just in case you missed it (a little Microsoft version humor, just to see if you're paying attention).

FIGURE 11.8.
Use the Format Painting tool to clone character formatting.

PROCEDURE 11.5. COPYING SECTION FORMATTING.

1. Select or click the text having the format you want to copy.
2. Double-click the Format Painting tool on the Standard Toolbar.
3. Use the mouse to select the section you want to format. When you release the mouse button, the formatting is applied.
4. Repeat Step 3 for each section you want to format.
5. Press Esc when you're done.

PROCEDURE 11.6. COPYING CHARACTER FORMATTING USING THE KEYBOARD.

1. Select the text having the format you want to copy.
2. Press Ctrl+Shift+C to copy just the format to the clipboard.
3. Select the text to which you want to apply the format.
4. Press Ctrl+Shift+V.
5. Repeat Steps 3 and 4 in as many locations as you want.

Repeat Formatting

Another formatting time-saver is the Repeat key (F4), which repeats the last edit you performed. If the last distinct edit was entering text, the Repeat key provides an instant encore at the insertion point. If the last distinct edit applied both bold and italics to a selection (using F**o**rmat | **F**ont, but not using Ctrl+B and Ctrl+I in succession; see the Upgrade Note below), Repeat applies the same formatting to the current selection. Repeat is very handy when applying formatting to already-entered text.

PROCEDURE 11.7. USING REPEAT (F4) TO REPEAT FORMATTING.

1. Format a section of text using standard formatting techniques such as shortcut formatting keys, menu, or toolbars (see note following procedure).
2. Select another section of text for which you need the same formatting.
3. Press F4.

SUPER UPGRADE NOTE

Repeat will not accumulate individually-applied formatting. If you select a section of text and press Ctrl+B and Ctrl+I to make it bold italic, F4 will repeat just the Ctrl+I step, not both. However, if you select text and use F**o**rmat | **F**ont to apply bold and italics, F4 repeat it and apply *both* bold and italics. This is different from the behavior of Word for Windows version 2, which did accumulate individually-applied formatting.

Chapter

12

Paragraph Formatting

Paragraph formatting is formatting that applies to an entire paragraph and which cannot vary within a paragraph. This includes alignment (left, right, centered, justified), indentation, line spacing, unbreakable blocks (a setting that forces a paragraph to occur on a new page, on the same page as the paragraph that follows, or altogether on the same page), line numbering, tabs, and borders (lines and boxes drawn around, between, or beside paragraphs).

Changing Paragraph Formats

Word offers a variety of tools for changing paragraph formats. As with character formatting, paragraph formatting is available from the menu, shortcut keys, and the toolbar. Some paragraph formatting can also be accomplished using the ruler. Paragraph formatting shortcut keys are shown in Table 12.1.

Table 12.1. Shortcut paragraph formatting keys.

Formatting Effect	*Keystrokes*
Styles	
Apply a style name	Ctrl+Shift+S
Apply Normal style	Alt+Shift+N
Apply Heading 1 style	Alt+Ctrl+1
Apply Heading 2 style	Alt+Ctrl+2
Apply Heading 3 style	Alt+Ctrl+3
Apply the List style	Ctrl+Shift+L
Format Styles dialog box	Ctrl+Shift+S twice
Start AutoFormat	Ctrl+K
Reset paragraph formatting	Ctrl+Q
Alignment and Indentation	
Center paragraph	Ctrl+E
Justify paragraph	Ctrl+J
Left align paragraph	Ctrl+L
Right align paragraph	Ctrl+R
Increase left indent by 1 tab	Ctrl+M
Decrease left indent by 1 tab	Ctrl+Shift+M
Increase hanging indent by 1 tab	Ctrl+T
Decrease hanging indent by 1 tab	Ctrl+Shift+T

Formatting Effect	*Keystrokes*
Spacing	
Single space	Ctrl+1
Double space	Ctrl+2
One and a half space	Ctrl+5
Toggle space before paragraph between 0 and 1	Ctrl+0 (zero)

Reset Paragraph

The Reset Paragraph command (ResetPara, Ctrl+Q) removes from the current paragraph all direct paragraph formatting that is different from the current style (called *variant* formatting in Word for DOS). If you receive a document from someone who has applied additional formatting to paragraphs, you can remove all formatting that is different from the current style by pressing Ctrl+Q. Strictly speaking, there is no built-in GUI method for doing this. However, if you abhor using the keyboard, you can achieve the same effect using the following procedure.

PROCEDURE 12.1. PERFORMING RESET PARAGRAPH USING THE RIBBON.

1. Click the style list-expansion arrow on the ribbon.
2. Click the highlighted style (this is the style for the current paragraph).
3. Word prompts, as shown in Figure 12.1, whether you want to redefine the style according to the current selection or reformat the selection according to the style.
4. Choose the first option to redefine the style (style by example) or the second option to reapply the style.

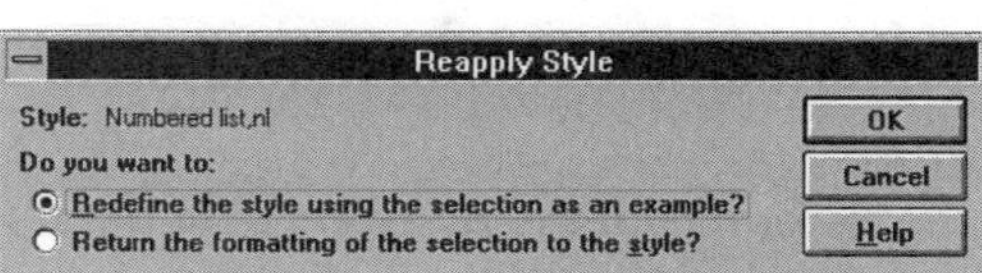

FIGURE 12.1.
Word prompts to see what to change: the formatting of the style or the formatting of the selection.

The Reset Paragraph command only removes extraneous paragraph formatting. The Reset Paragraph command does not affect extraneous character formatting. You can, however, remove all extraneous formatting—both character and paragraph—by selecting it and pressing Ctrl+Q (ResetPara) and Ctrl+Spacebar (ResetChar).

SUPER NOTE

As with other paragraph formatting, you do not need to select a paragraph when using ResetPara on a single paragraph. Because paragraph formatting—by definition—cannot vary within a paragraph, all you need to do is put the insertion point into the target paragraph. If you want ResetPara to apply to multiple paragraphs, however, you need to select at least part of all paragraphs you want to change.

Paragraph Formatting Using the Toolbars and Ruler

The ruler and Formatting toolbar provide GUI access to paragraph alignment, indentation, margins, and tabs. To set the alignment for the current paragraph, click the left, center, right, or justify icons on the Formatting Toolbar shown in Figure 12.2.

FIGURE 12.2.
Use the Formatting Toolbar alignment icons to set paragraph, object, and cell alignment.

PROCEDURE 12.2. SETTING TABS USING THE RULER.

1. Click the tab type button at the left end of the ruler to toggle among the four types of tabs (Left, Center, Right, or Decimal) as shown in Figure 12.3.

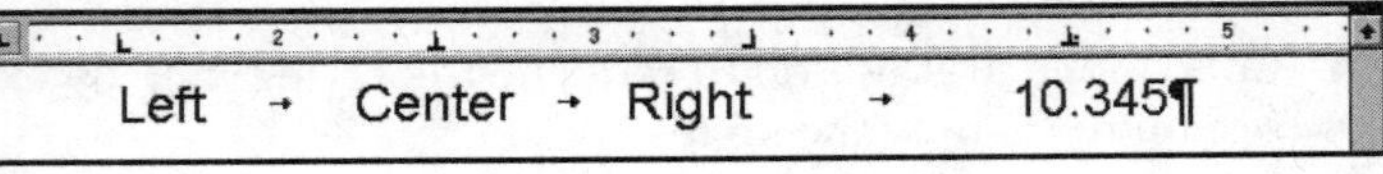

FIGURE 12.3.
The Formatting Toolbar graphically indicates the different types of tab.

2. Click the lower half of the ruler where you want to set the tab (when a decimal tab is set, the decimal points of all numerical entries will be aligned at the tab).
3. Drag the tab, if necessary, to position it where you want it (drag by pointing the mouse at it and holding down the left mouse button while moving).

To move both indents (first and following) at the same time, drag the bottom (square) indent tool, as shown in Figure 12.4.

FIGURE 12.4.
The left indent tool components can be dragged together or separately.

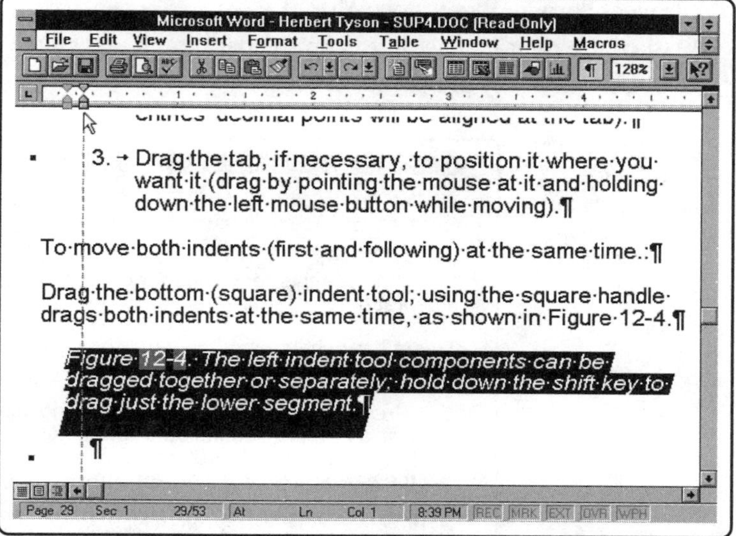

To set the left indentation of the first line of a paragraph, drag just the first indent tool (the top triangle) to the desired location.

To change the paragraph body indentation without changing the first indent, drag just the body indent tool (the bottom triangle). Use this technique for creating or changing hanging indentation.

To set the right indentation, drag the right indent tool to the desired location.

TIP

Press Alt while formatting with the ruler to display a precise indicator of the distance between the two ends of the ruler and the point of impact for the part you're dragging, as shown in Figure 12.5.

Format Paragraph Dialog Box

You can use the Format Paragraph dialog box to perform all paragraph formatting except for Borders. To activate the Paragraph dialog box, shown in Figure 12.6:

1. Select Format | Paragraph (Alt+O P).
2. Click the right mouse button on the paragraph and click Paragraph.
3. Double-click any of the indent tools.

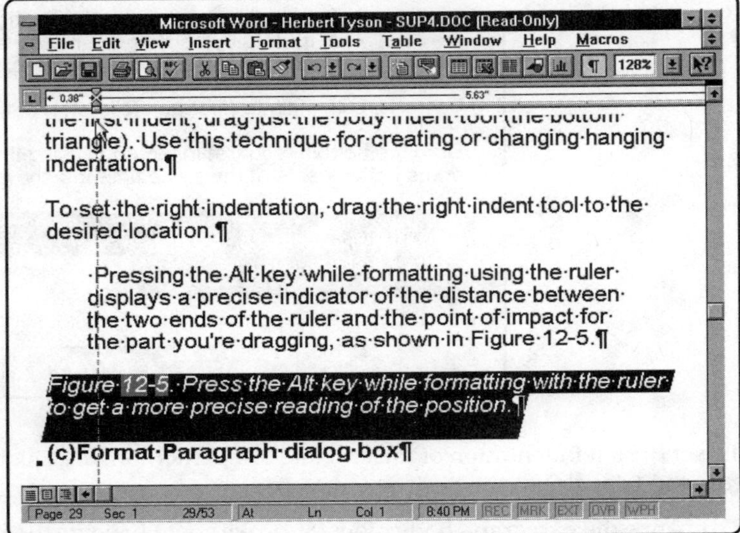

FIGURE 12.5.
Press Alt while formatting with the ruler to get a more precise reading of the position.

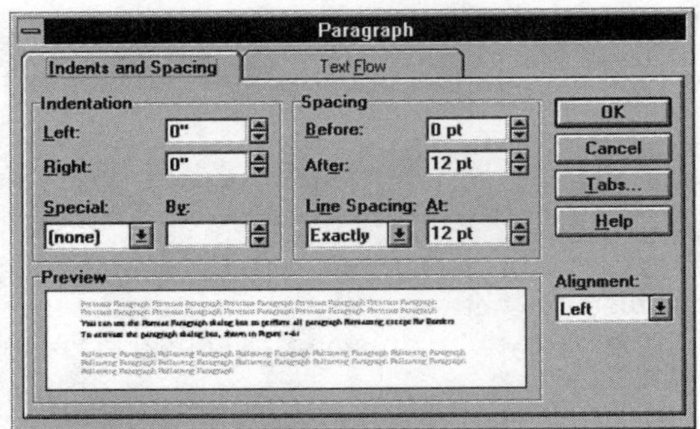

FIGURE 12.6.
Use the Format Paragraph dialog box to perform paragraph formatting.

Alignment

To set paragraph alignment:

To	*Dialog Box*	*Mouse*	*Keyboard*
Align Left	Alignment: Left	Left Icon	Press Ctrl+L
Align Right	Alignment: Right	Right Icon	Press Ctrl+R

To	Dialog Box	Mouse	Keyboard
Center	Alignment: Center	Center Icon	Press Ctrl+E
Justify	Alignment: Justified	Justify Icon	Press Ctrl+J

Indentation

To change paragraph indentation:

Setting	Dialog Box	Mouse
Left	Type or use spin controls to set From Left.	Drag both left indent markers using square handle.
Right	Type or use spin controls to set From Right.	Drag right indent marker.
First Left	Click Special, select First Line, then type or use spin controls.	Drag top left indent marker using triangular handle.
Hanging	Click Special, select Hanging, then type or use spin controls.	Drag bottom left indent marker using triangular handle.

SUPER TIP

You can use keyboard-only shortcuts if you want indentation set at any of the default half-inch increments. Press Ctrl+M and Ctrl+Shift+M, respectively, to move the left indent one half inch to the right or left. Press Ctrl+T and Ctrl+Shift+T, respectively, to move the hanging indent one half inch to the right or left.

Spacing

Using the spacing controls, you can set the spacing before, after, and within a paragraph.

Before

Use Before spacing to control the amount of leading space before a paragraph. This setting is most useful for heading paragraphs and the first lines of tables to provide a logical separation from the preceding text.

PROCEDURE 12.3. CHANGING SPACING BEFORE A PARAGRAPH.

1. Select Format | Paragraph and click the Indents and Spacing tab.
2. Click Before.
3. Type a value or use the spin control (mouse or cursor up/down arrows) to select the desired spacing.
4. Click OK.

You can use the OpenOrCloseUpPara toggle, Ctrl+0 (zero), to toggle the Before spacing between 0 and 1 line (12 points).

After

Use After spacing to control the amount of trailing space after a paragraph. This setting is useful to set headings from the paragraph that follows. It's also commonly used to create automatic double-spacing between paragraphs without having to press Enter twice.

PROCEDURE 12.4. CHANGING THE SPACING AFTER A PARAGRAPH.

1. Select Format | Paragraph and click the Indents and Spacing tab.
2. Click Before.
3. Type a value or use the spin control (mouse or cursor up/down arrows) to select the desired spacing.
4. Click OK.

SUPER NOTE

There is no equivalent to Ctrl+0 for spacing after, so you'll have to use the dialog box.

Line Spacing Within a Paragraph

Use Line Spacing to set line spacing within a paragraph. This setting is often used for squeezing a letter onto a single page (a slightly different approach from the Shrink to Fit tool on the Print Preview Toolbar). Optimally, it would be used to create a pattern of text that is a compromise between efficiency and legibility.

SINGLE SPACING

Single (Auto in Word for Windows 2) tells Word to use its own built-in formula for setting line spacing. When using proportional fonts, Single usually results in line spacing two points larger than the character point size. For example, if the character point size is 12, Single sets the line spacing at 14 points. If the line spacing is set to the point size, it usually results in crowding of text. At very large point sizes, the "inflation" factor increases. For monospaced fonts, Word does not inflate line spacing.

> **SUPER TIP**
>
> You can set single spacing within a paragraph by pressing Ctrl+1 (top row).

1.5 SPACING

The 1.5 spacing option results in spacing that is 50 percent greater than the font point size. 1.5 spacing is frequently used for reports and proposals. It results in easier reading and some additional room for margin notes—helpful when reviewing proposals and reports—while not wasting as much paper as double spacing.

> **SUPER TIP**
>
> You can set 1.5 spacing in a paragraph by pressing Ctrl+5 (top row).

DOUBLE SPACING

Double spacing results in line space that is twice the font point size. Double spacing is often used for drafts and school reports, as well as some proposals.

> **SUPER TIP**
>
> You can set double spacing in a paragraph by pressing Ctrl+2 (top row).

AT LEAST

The At Least option is similar to Single but enables you to set a minimum line spacing for the paragraph. In some instances with spacing set at Single, lines that contain very small point sizes don't provide enough room. Using the At Least option, you automatically adjust for lines that contain large point sizes, but you keep the spacing from dropping below a desired spacing for lines that contain very small point sizes. The At Least option is often used in scientific reports, in which additional spacing is needed to accommodate subscripts and superscripts.

EXACTLY

The Exactly option is used to obtain consistent line spacing that accommodates a variety of point sizes and special effects. The Exactly option is frequently used in formatting dropped capitals to achieve uniform spacing, as shown in Figure 12.7. If you used Single, spacing for the first line would be greater than for subsequent lines, resulting in very uneven text.

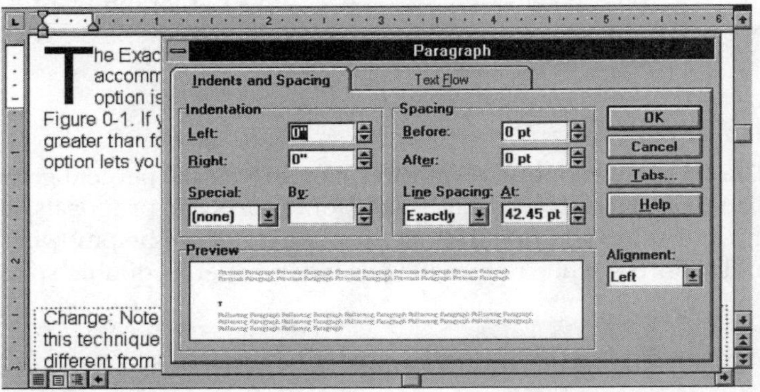

FIGURE 12.7.
Dropped capitals are used to create dramatic chapter openings.

MULTIPLE

The Multiple option is used to create higher-order versions of 1.5 and double spacing. The default is 3. Type the number you want to use into the At box.

Pagination

The Text Flow tab in the Format Paragraph dialog box offers four pagination options for paragraphs. Without any of the special pagination options turned on, paragraphs would print as they occur, with no special effort to keep all or part of a paragraph on the same page. Widow and Orphan Control should almost always be used. The other options should be used in various situations, as described in this section.

Widow and Orphan Control

Widow and Orphan Control is used to prevent the first or last line of a multiline paragraph from appearing on the top or bottom of a page without any other paragraph lines.

SUPER NOTE

Widow/Orphan Control doesn't help single-line paragraphs such as headings and captions. To keep them with their logical partners, use the Keep with Next option.

Page Break Before

This option forces a paragraph always to start on a new page. A typical use is for titles of chapters or sections that logically begin on a new page.

Keep with Next

This option forces a paragraph to print on the same page as the first lines of the paragraph that follows. A typical use is for one-line headings that otherwise don't look like widows or orphans. This option, in effect, forces Word to treat two consecutive paragraphs as a unit. Without this option, you might have to manually ensure that no heading falls at the bottom of a page.

Keep Lines Together

This option forces all of a paragraph to print on the same page. A typical use is for multiline items that lose continuity if broken across two pages. Warnings and cautions frequently use this option to avoid losing their impact.

Suppress Line Numbers

The Format Section Layout dialog box has an option that enables you to print line numbers along the left margin of a document. In some states, briefs, depositions, contracts, and other legal documents have margin numbers. The Suppress Line Numbers option enables you to turn off line numbers for some paragraphs, such as heading sections, for which they might not be appropriate.

Don't Hyphenate

Gee, that about sums it up, and it sounds like pretty good advice for most of us, considering how inappropriately hyphenation seems to be used these days. Obviously, this option is used to suppress hyphenation.

Tabs

By default (unless you explicitly change it), Word defines preset tabs every half inch. You can use the tab button in the Format Paragraph dialog box to define additional tabs, as well as to specify the format for tabs.

PROCEDURE 12.5. ACCESSING TAB OPTIONS.

1. Select Format | **P**aragraph.
2. Click **T**abs to display the dialog box shown in Figure 12.8.

As a shortcut, double-click any existing tab or the bottom edge of the ruler to display the Tabs dialog box.

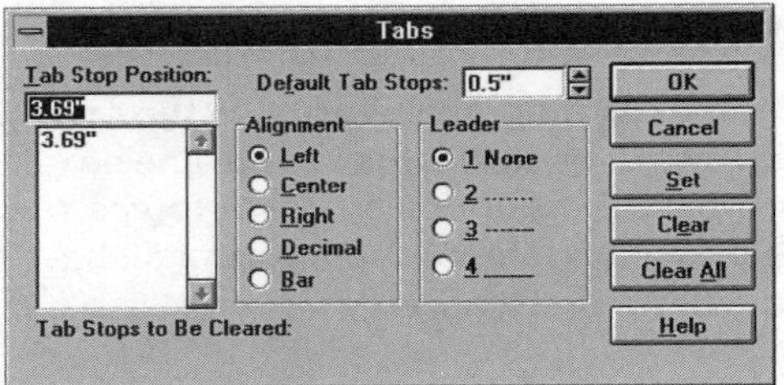

FIGURE 12.8.
Use the Tabs dialog box to set tab options.

Default Tab Stops

Use this option to define the distance between the default tabs for the entire document, not just for the current paragraph. By default, Word sets tabs every half inch (36 points). If you need them set every quarter inch, every inch, and so on, use the spin control to set the interval accordingly. When using very small fonts (that is, less than 8 points), you might consider reducing the default below one-half inch to make better use of vertical space.

Tab Stop Position

Use this option to set individual tabs one at a time. If you use the ruler to set tabs, each individually set tab will be displayed here, but the default tabs will not. You can use this control to set new tabs, modify existing tabs, or delete existing tabs.

PROCEDURE 12.6. SETTING A TAB USING THE TAB DIALOG BOX.

1. Type the location for the tab on the ruler (using the default measurement units).
2. Select the alignment type (Left, Right, Center, Decimal, or Bar) by toggling the tab type button at the left edge of the ruler.
3. Select any leader (see the "Leaders" heading later in this chapter).
4. Click Set.

SUPER

BAR? SAY WHAT???

Yes, this is a new option with Word 6, an option inherited from Word for Mac. The Bar tab creates a vertical bar through the paragraph. As shown in Figure 12.9, the bar tab works pretty much as advertised. Note, however, that there is no way to select the Bar tab from the ruler.

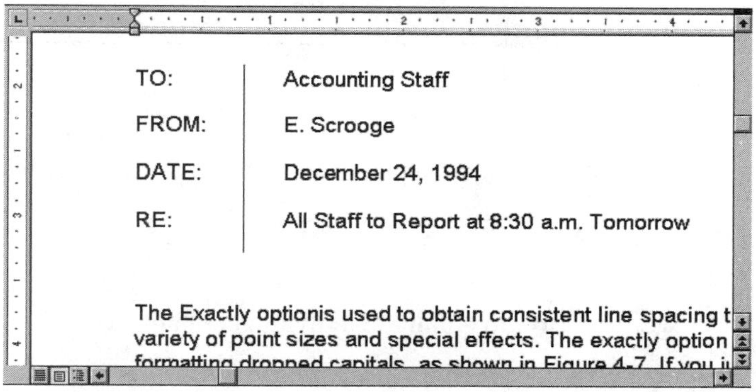

TO: Accounting Staff
FROM: E. Scrooge
DATE: December 24, 1994
RE: All Staff to Report at 8:30 a.m. Tomorrow

The Exactly optionis used to obtain consistent line spacing t variety of point sizes and special effects. The exactly option

FIGURE 12.9.
Katie, bar the, er, paragraph? Microsoft salutes Norm, of Cheers, by creating the Bar tab that nobody ever has to pay.

Alignment

Alignment specifies where tabbed text aligns. Use Left to cause text to begin at the tab. Use Right to cause text to end at the tab. Use Center to cause text to be centered under the tab. Use Bar when you want to confuse your readers or when you want to convince your office manager that you need a new printer. Use Decimal when aligning numbers that have different numbers of significant digits. If any of your numbers do not contain decimal points, Word aligns them at an imaginary decimal point after the ones column. The five types of alignment are shown in Figure 12.10.

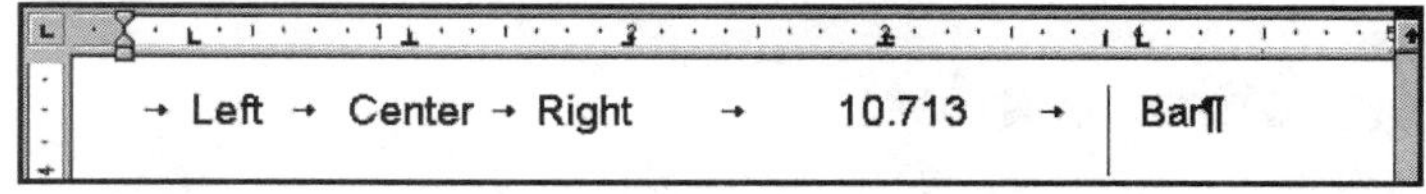

FIGURE 12.10.
Word offers five alignment options: Left, Center, Right, Decimal, and Bar tabs.

Leaders

Tab leaders are characters that fill the space between the tab and the tabbed text, as shown in Figure 12.11. Leaders are often used in tightly spaced tables where it's crucial to link items together visually. For example, in a budget listing or other financial document, its crucial that the names of items be correctly associated with the corresponding number. Leaders also are often used in indexes, lists of tables and figures, and tables of contents.

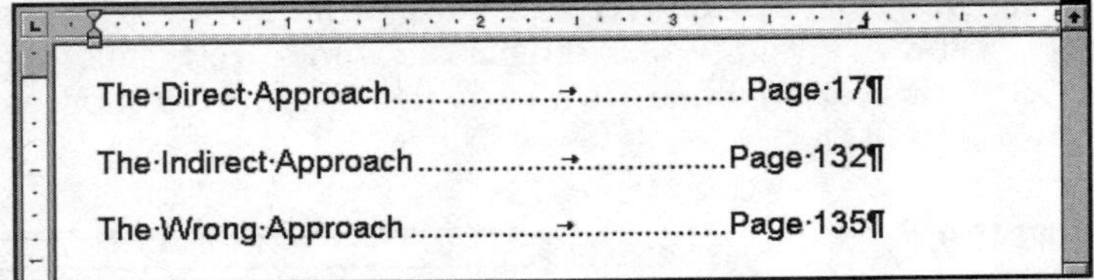

FIGURE 12.11.
Use tab leaders as a visual aid in presenting tabular data.

Set

Use the Set button to set changes in alignment, position, or leader for individual tab stops.

Clear

Use the Clear button to eliminate individual tab stops.

Clear All

Use Clear All to eliminate all individually set tab stops.

Borders and Shading

Although not set using the Format Paragraph dialog box, Borders and Shading are paragraph-level format controls. Borders determine whether or not lines or boxes are drawn beside, between, and around paragraphs. Borders are used most frequently in tables but are especially useful in setting up sidebars, tips, and warnings, as well as setting off graphics. Shading determines whether or not the background area behind the text is clear or shaded.

Formatting Borders

Borders can be turned on or off for selected paragraphs. To format multiple paragraphs with the same borders, they must have identical margin settings.

PROCEDURE 12.7. SELECTING A BORDER.

1. Select the text you want to format. Because bordering is a paragraph format, you don't need to select the whole paragraph if you're just bordering a single paragraph.

2. Select Format | **B**orders and Shading (Alt+O B); see Figure 12.12.
3. Click the **B**orders tab.
4. Click the preset Border option that most closely matches the effect you want.
5. Click the line style you want to use.
6. If desired, use the Border template to add or remove interior or exterior lines; click to toggle individual segments on or off.
7. Alternate Steps 5 and 6, if desired, to assign different line styles to different border segments.
8. Use the From Text option to set the spacing between the borders and the interior text.
9. Use the Color option to set the colors of the borders; you can set different colors for different segments.
10. Click OK.

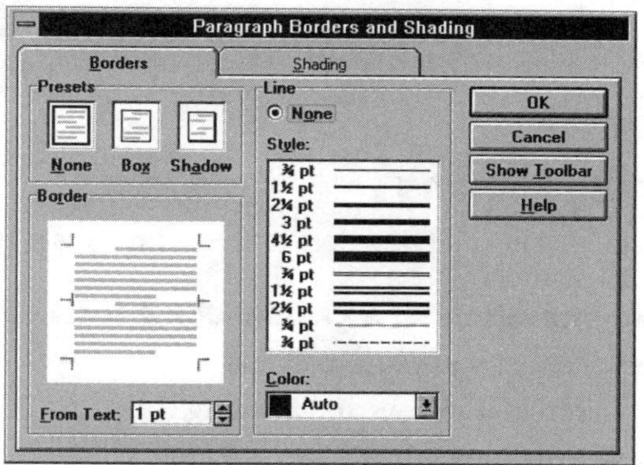

FIGURE 12.12.
Use the Format Borders dialog box to select a border.

Optionally, you can click the Show **T**oolbar button to display the Borders tools instead of the Paragraph Borders and Shading dialog box. As shown in Figure 12.13, you actually can turn on the borders toolbar any time you want using **V**iew | **T**oolbars or by using the toolbar pop-up list (by clicking the right mouse button in any toolbar area). Once it's displayed, you can substitute using it for the dialog box. It substitutes specific buttons for each segment and for interior and exterior lines. Use the Line Style pull-down to select the border line styles and the Shading pull-down to select a shading type. The only border option missing is Shadow, and that can be accomplished by selecting thicker line types for the right and bottom segments than for the top and left.

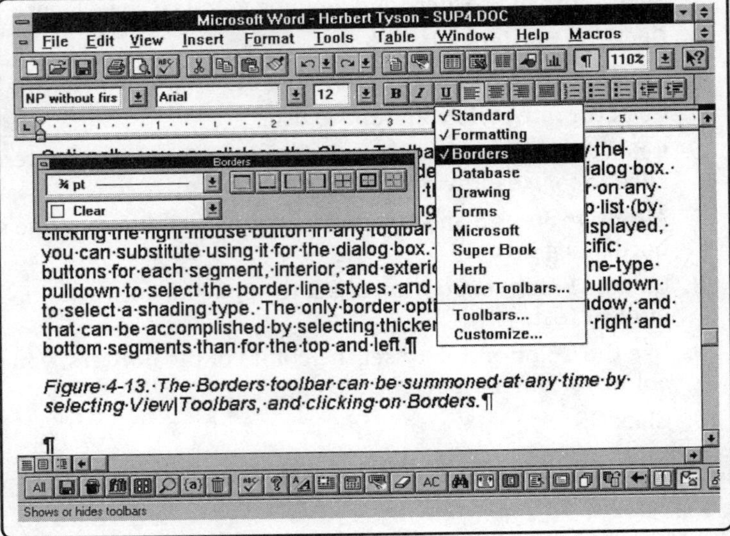

FIGURE 12.13.
The Borders toolbar can be summoned at any time by selecting View | Toolbars and clicking Borders.

Formatting Shading

You also can use Format | **B**orders and Shading to set paragraph shading.

PROCEDURE 12.8. SHADING A PARAGRAPH, A TABLE, OR A TABLE CELL.

1. Select the text you want to shade.
2. Select Format | **B**orders and Shading.
3. Click the **S**hading tab.
4. Click Sha**d**ing to select the type of fill you want.
5. Click Foreground to select the color of lines or dots.
6. Click Background to select the background color.
7. Click OK to close the Borders and Shading dialog box.

PROCEDURE 12.9. REMOVING SHADING.

1. Select the text you want to unshade.
2. Select Format | **B**orders and Shading.
3. Click the **S**hading tab.
4. Click the **N**one radio button.
5. Click OK to close the Borders dialog box.

SUPER TIP

If shading was applied as a style variant (that is, if shading is not part of the underlying style's definition), you can press Ctrl+Q to remove shading. Ctrl+Q resets all paragraph formatting to conform to that of the underlying style.

Copying Paragraph Formatting

All of a paragraph's formatting is contained in the paragraph marker. You can copy paragraph formatting by copying another paragraph's marker.

PROCEDURE 12.10. USING THE CLIPBOARD TO COPY FORMATTING FROM ONE PARAGRAPH TO ANOTHER.

1. Press Ctrl+* (on numeric pad), if necessary, to toggle the display of paragraph markers on.
2. Select just the paragraph marker in the paragraph whose format you want to clone.
3. Press Ctrl+Insert to copy the paragraph marker to the clipboard.
4. Select the paragraph marker in the paragraph you want to reformat.
5. Press Shift+Insert to replace the selected marker with the one in the clipboard.

You also can use the Shift+F2 Copy key to copy paragraph formatting without using the clipboard.

PROCEDURE 12.11. COPYING FORMATTING WITHOUT USING THE CLIPBOARD.

1. Press Ctrl+* (on numeric pad), if necessary, to toggle the display of paragraph markers on.
2. Select just the paragraph marker in the paragraph whose format you want to clone.
3. Press Shift+F2; note the `Copy to where` prompt on the status bar.
4. Select the paragraph marker in the paragraph you want to reformat.
5. Press Enter to complete the copy.

You also can use the format painter tool to copy paragraph formatting.

PROCEDURE 12.12. COPYING FORMATTING USING THE FORMAT PAINTER.

1. Press Ctrl+* (on numeric pad), if necessary, to toggle the display of paragraph markers on.

2. Select just the paragraph marker in the paragraph whose format you want to clone.
3. Click the format painter tool.
4. Select (paint) the paragraph marker(s) of the paragraph(s) you want to format.

PROCEDURE 12.13. COPYING FORMATTING TO MORE THAN ONE LOCATION USING THE FORMAT PAINTER.

1. Press Ctrl+* (on numeric pad), if necessary, to toggle the display of paragraph markers on.
2. Select just the paragraph marker in the paragraph whose format you want to clone.
3. Double-click the format painter tool.
4. Select (paint) the paragraph marker(s) of the paragraph(s) you want to format.
5. Repeat Steps 3 and 4 to format as many paragraphs or sets of contiguous paragraphs as you like.
6. Press Esc to turn the format painter off.

Repeat

As with character formatting, the Repeat key (F4) also works with paragraph formatting. It can be especially handy for going back and assigning heading styles to lines that you created on the fly. Using the Repeat key with paragraph formatting is actually easier than with character formatting. Because paragraph formatting can't vary within a paragraph, if you're formatting just a single paragraph, you don't have to select the whole paragraph. All you need to do is place the cursor into the paragraph you want to reformat and press F4 to repeat the most recent formatting you performed.

Chapter 13

Envelopes and Labels

Word maintains an internal template for use in formatting and printing envelopes and labels on the fly.

Envelopes

The envelope printing tool is most useful when you are editing a letter that already contains the delivery address. You can use envelope printing as is, but entering the appropriate addresses may require a bit of work. With a letter open, printing an envelope requires minimum effort. It only takes a little preparation to turn envelope printing into a one- or two-step operation, with both delivery and return addresses automatically inserted for you.

SUPER UPGRADE NOTE

Word for Windows 2 had the envelope button on the default toolbar. For some reason, Word 6 does not. If you display the Word for Windows 2 toolbar (**V**iew|Toolbars, click Word for Windows 2), the envelope button will be available. However, you'll have a number of redundant functions. If you replace the Standard toolbar with the Word for Windows 2 toolbar, you'll be missing some new functions. Clearly, if you plan to do a lot of enveloping, the thing to do is to select **T**ools|**C**ustomize and add the envelope button to one of your main toolbars.

PROCEDURE 13.1. ADDING THE ENVELOPE BUTTON TO THE STANDARD TOOLBAR.

1. If you want the envelope available in a particular template only, then open that template now.
2. Select **T**ools|**C**ustomize.
3. Click **T**oolbars.
4. Under Save Changes In, select the template you want to receive the envelope tool.
5. Under Categories, click Tools.
6. Find the envelope button (second from the top left) and drag it to the toolbar where you want it (press the mouse button while the pointer is on the envelope and then move the mouse; the envelope button's outline will follow the cursor as you move the mouse).
7. Release the mouse when the envelope is in the toolbar.
8. Click Close.
9. Select **F**ile|**C**lose and verify saving the template you just modified.

PROCEDURE 13.2. PRINTING AN ENVELOPE USING THE ENVELOPE BUTTON OR TOOLS | ENVELOPES AND LABELS COMMAND.

1. If a document containing the recipient's address is on-screen, select the recipient's address.
2. Select **T**ools | **E**nvelopes and Labels or click the envelope button.
3. Click the Envelope tab.
4. If necessary, type or correct the **D**elivery Address of the recipient in the Address To: box (see Figure 13.1).
5. If the return address is not filled in, type the **R**eturn Address or click Omit Return Address, whichever is appropriate.
6. Click **O**ptions.
7. Select the correct envelope size.
8. Word can automatically include the POSTNET (Postal Numeric Encoding Technique) bar code with the ZIP (Zone Improvement Plan) code, as well as a FIM (Facing Identification Mark) for use with presorted mail (consult your post office to see what kinds of discounts this will give you). Select these options if desired.
9. Using the preview window, adjust the positions of the return and delivery addresses (note: the delivery address invariably is too low on a Hewlett-Packard LaserJet II printer; try setting it at 1.9" from the top).
10. If desired, click the Font button(s) and adjust the fonts (the default is to use the font of the Normal style: 12 points for delivery, 10 points for return).
11. Click OK.
12. Click Feed and select the feed options appropriate for your printer; click OK when you're done.
13. Verify that your printer is turned on and is set up to print an envelope.
14. Click Print.

SUPER NOTE

Unfortunately, Word doesn't remember your adjustments to the address fonts and positions from session to session (surprise!). This means that you'll have to go through this nonsense with the first envelope you print during each session. If you'd rather turn this into a one- or two-step process, instead of 14 steps, see "Reformatting the Envelope," later in this chapter.

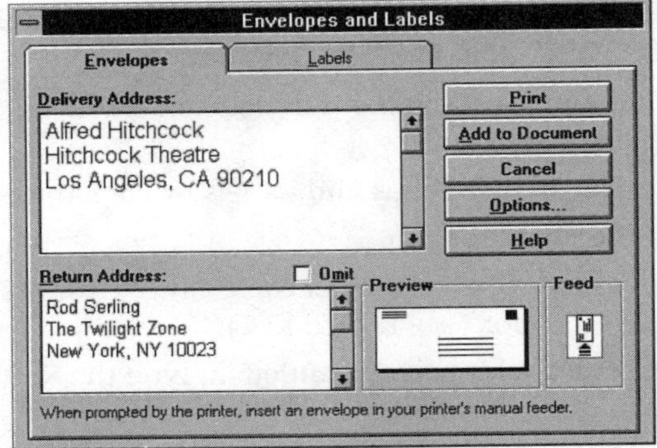

FIGURE 13.1.
You can fill in the address manually or automatically.

SUPER TIP

Rather than retyping the delivery address (now in your document), you can save some time by copying it to the clipboard before clicking the envelope tool. Then press Shift+Insert in the Address To: box to insert the address.

Adding an Envelope to a Document

If the format of the envelope isn't quite right and if the options provided in the envelope routine aren't flexible enough, you may need to add the envelope to your document so you can modify the format. To add the envelope to your document, follow the steps outlined in the previous section, but click Add to Document instead of Print in Step 14. Word will insert a new section at the top of the current document, as shown in Figure 13.2. Now you can modify the envelope format as needed so that it prints correctly.

Reformatting the Envelope

Once an envelope has been added to your document, you can reformat it, as necessary. You can even make your formatting changes permanent. Remember how I've harped on styles elsewhere in this book? Well, if you don't like Word's built-in envelope format, you'd be up the creek without styles.

Using the Envelope Return and Envelope Address styles, you can change the default envelope format. Furthermore, you can make these changes apply to all envelopes you create from here on out. One option is to change the position of the delivery address on the envelope. First, open the template you want to use for writing letters (that is, the one that would be active when you print envelopes). Run the envelope routine and select the option to add the envelope to the current document. With the envelope on-screen, follow Procedures 13.3 through 13.5 to modify the envelope formatting.

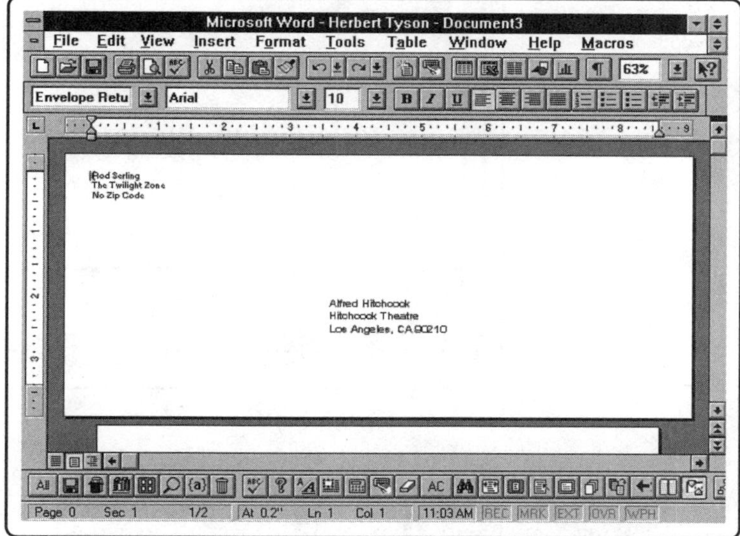

FIGURE 13.2.
Envelope added to a letter using the envelope feature.

PROCEDURE 13.3. MODIFYING THE DELIVERY ADDRESS POSITION.

1. Select **V**iew | **P**age Layout to switch into Page Layout view.
2. Note that the Delivery Address is framed; click outside the To Address area, so that the frame is not selected.
3. Move the mouse pointer over the edge of the frame until you see a four-headed arrow (see Figure 13.3).
4. Press the left mouse button and drag the Address To frame to the position you want to use.
5. When you're satisfied with the new position, press Ctrl+Shift+S.
6. Select Envelope Address and press Enter.
7. Select Redefine the style, using the selection as an example, and click OK.

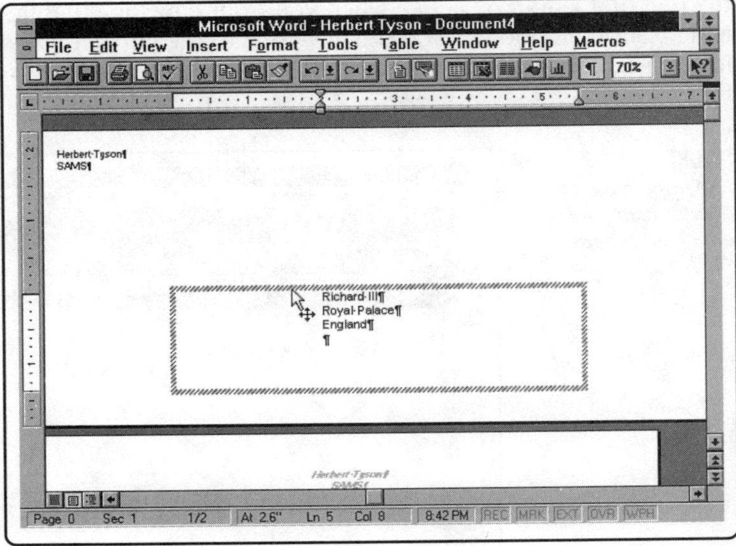

FIGURE 13.3.
The four-headed arrow shows when the cursor is positioned for a drag.

SUPER TIP

When you change a paragraph's format and redefine the style based on that change, as we're doing here, it's called *style-by-example*. It's a speedy way to add formatting information to a style's definition. Ordinarily, if you want to add the changed style to the underlying template, you have to make sure you select Add to Template in the full Styles dialog box. However, since you're editing the actual letter template (for example, LETTER.DOT or something like that), you don't need to do that. If you are editing a document based on the template rather than the template itself, you'll have to press Ctrl+Shift+S twice; click Modify, Add to Template, OK, and Close; and then make sure you save the template. Otherwise, your change won't take.

You also can change other aspects of the envelope formatting to get it looking just the way you want. Except for the position of the delivery address frame, all other formatting is best handled at the style level. Press Ctrl+Shift+S twice (or select Format | Style from the menu), click Modify and Add to Template, and then click the Format button to change whatever aspects need to be changed.

PROCEDURE 13.4. CHANGING THE DELIVERY ADDRESS FORMAT.

1. Move the cursor into one of the delivery address lines.
2. Press Ctrl+Shift+S twice to summon the Styles dialog box; verify that the style Envelope Address is selected.

3. Click Modify.
4. Click Add to Template. This is very important if you want your envelope changes to be permanent. The Add to Template option affects only styles that are changed while the Add to Template option is selected (see Chapter 22, "Styles and AutoFormat," for additional information).
5. Click Format.
6. Click Font, Paragraph, or another formatting option to adjust any aspect of the format you want to change.
7. Modify the format and click OK to return to the Styles dialog box.
8. Repeat Steps 5 through 7 until you've adjusted all of the formats you want to change.
9. Click OK when you're satisfied with the format of the style.

PROCEDURE 13.5. CHANGING THE RETURN ADDRESS FORMAT.

1. Move the cursor into one of the return address lines.
2. Press Ctrl+Shift+S twice to summon the Styles dialog box; verify that the style Envelope Return is selected.
3. Click Modify.
4. If you're not editing the actual template, then click the Add to Template option. This is very important if you want your envelope changes to be permanent. The Add to Template option affects only styles that are changed while the Add to Template option is selected (see Chapter 22 for additional information).
5. Click Format.
6. Click Font, Paragraph, or another formatting option to adjust any aspect of the format you want to change.
7. Modify the format and click OK to return to the Styles dialog box.
8. Repeat Steps 5 through 7 until you've adjusted all of the formats you want to change.
9. Click OK when you're satisfied with the format of the style.

SUPER NOTE

The return address is not enclosed in a frame. However, if it would be more manageable, you can frame the return address and then add that aspect to the envelope return style definition. As above, working with frames is best handled graphically. Then use the style-by-example approach to add the frame information to the envelope return style definition.

Once you have finished changing the envelope style formats, print a sample envelope to ensure that the formats are what you want. Once you're satisfied, select File | Save All from the menu and make sure you say Yes to the prompt to save changes to the template (assuming you aren't editing the template). By the way, you can also delete the envelope section of your document. Now that the envelope styles have been made a permanent part of the document template, you can modify them at any time in the future without having to first add an envelope to your document.

When all this is done, all envelopes created using this template will use your modified envelope styles. Later, if you want to add the changed envelope formats to other templates, you can do so using the templates Organizer feature. See Chapter 21, "Templates and Wizards," for additional information.

SUPER TIP

When modifying the envelope styles, try to restrict changes to those that can be accomplished using style formatting options. Any nonstyle changes you make (such as adding or deleting paragraph markers) cannot be made part of the envelope's permanent format.

Automating the Return Address

For the return address, Word checks to see if the current document contains a bookmark called `envelopereturn` (no space). If it does, it uses the bookmarked text as the return address. If not, it uses the mailing address specified in the User Info dialog box. Fill in this information to get the most from the envelope feature.

PROCEDURE 13.6. ADDING YOUR RETURN ADDRESS TO WORD.

1. Select **T**ools | **O**ptions | **U**ser Info.
2. Click in the Mailing Address box.
3. Type your return address.
4. Click OK when you're satisfied.

Sometimes, especially when more than one user share the same computer, the User Info option is unsatisfactory. While this isn't often a problem in offices that use preprinted envelopes, it can be a problem for home users of Word. That's when Word's other return address option comes in handy: include in each user's letter templates the user's return address. For example, my wife, daughter, and I print from the same computer system. We each have our own letter templates that we use when writing letters. Thanks to the `envelopereturn` bookmark feature, envelopes are completely automatic.

PROCEDURE 13.7. BOOKMARKING A RETURN ADDRESS.

1. Open the letter template you want to modify (for example, LETTER.DOT).
2. Select the return address.
3. Select **E**dit | **B**ookmark (Ctrl+Shift+F5).
4. Type `envelopereturn` and click Add.

SUPER TIP

In cases where you create your own letterhead, this procedure probably wouldn't produce an acceptable return address for envelopes. You're probably thinking, "Shucks—I'm outta luck." Think again—think *hidden*! Insert your return address, bookmark it as `envelopereturn`, and then format it as hidden text. When you print your letter, make sure the hidden text option is turned off (**T**ools | **O**ptions | **P**rint, deselect Hidden). Even though the return address is hidden in the document, the envelope tool will still see it and use it!

Automating the Delivery Address Field

When you select the envelope tool, Word will automatically suggest text for the Delivery Address field. If there is a bookmark called `envelopeaddress` (no space), word will use the bookmarked text for the delivery address field. If there is no envelope address bookmark but text is selected, Word will use the selected text—up to the first paragraph mark—as the Address To text. This means that, to use the text-selection technique, you must use line breaks (Shift+Enter) instead of paragraph breaks between different lines of the address (see Figure 13.4). The most automatic solution, therefore, is to permanently bookmark the inside address section of your letter templates as `envelopeaddress`, assuming it's not already marked. The delivery address space in the letter templates on the Word 6 Super Book disk is already bookmarked `envelopeaddress` for your convenience.

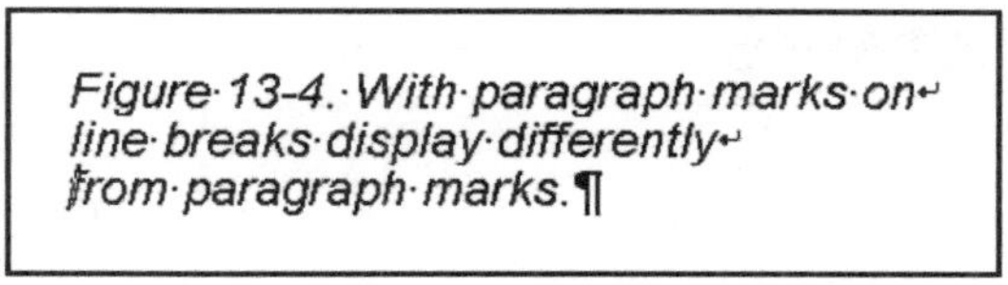

FIGURE 13.4.
With paragraph marks on, line breaks display differently than paragraph marks.

Figure·13-4.·With·paragraph·marks·on↵
line·breaks·display·differently↵
from·paragraph·marks.¶

Printing an Attached Envelope

If you choose to attach your envelope to a document, Word inserts it as Page 0.

PROCEDURE 13.8. PRINTING AN ATTACHED ENVELOPE.

1. Move the insertion point into the envelope.
2. Select **File|Print**.
3. Click Current Page.
4. Verify that your printer is online and set up for printing envelopes.
5. Click OK.

Labels

Word 6 also has a feature to print labels. Some of the label printing is fine; other aspects leave a lot to be desired. The printing of Avery 5164, in particular, is not terribly satisfactory. In any event, if you lack other label solutions, I suppose the built-in solution is better than nothing.

Printing Labels

Unfortunately, Word isn't quite as smart with labels as it is with envelopes. With a little bit of effort, though, you might be able to make the label printing feature work for you. Before you get too excited, however, let me quickly tell you that this feature will not perform a data merge; see Workshop 10, "Merging Workshop," for that capability. The label printing feature will print just a single address on a single label or on a whole sheet of labels. If this is what you want, you've come to the right place.

By default, if you have addresses on-screen, Word looks for them to be set up with a single hard paragraph mark between each line of the address and two paragraph marks between each address, as shown in Figure 13.5. When the insertion point or selection is anywhere inside an address block, Word will print everything bounded by two carriage returns at the top and bottom (if you're at the top or bottom of the document, Word will accept the top or bottom in lieu of two carriage returns). If you don't have your addresses on-screen, you can always type them into the label dialog box window.

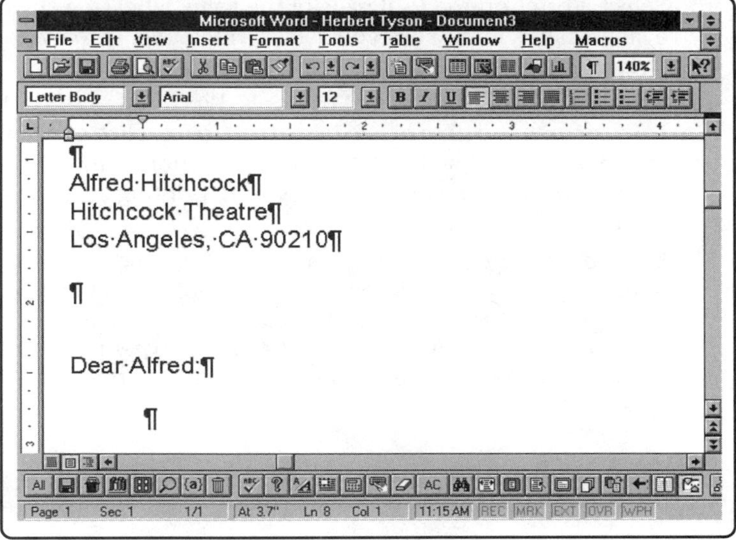

FIGURE 13.5.
To save a little work, preformat your addresses as shown here.

PROCEDURE 13.9. PRINTING LABELS USING TOOLS|ENVELOPES AND LABELS.

1. If you have addresses on-screen, move the insertion point to the address you want to print.
2. Select **T**ools|**E**nvelopes and Labels (or click the Envelope button if you have one set up).
3. Click the Labels tab.
4. Note the address in the address field; you can accept it, click Use Return Address to substitute the User Info address, or type an address from scratch.
5. Click in the Label block or the Options button to select the type of label.
6. Select the appropriate printer information.
7. Select the label product type.
8. Select the type of label; if you don't have Avery labels or corresponding codes, then use the size guides.
9. Click in the Label Information block or the Details button to adjust the label format.
10. Using the preview picture as a guide, adjust the format until the label looks as you want it to print.
11. Click OK to return to the Label Options dialog box.
12. Click OK to return to the main Label dialog box.

13. Select a print option (full page of the same label or a single label). If you select a single label, make sure you select which one. Often you can reinsert a partial page of labels into your printer, but check your warranty first.
14. If you're printing a full sheet of labels, Word offers the option of creating a new document with just the label table on it; click Create New Document to exercise this option. Do not select this option until all other options and settings have been completed. If you're printing a single label, the Create New Document option is unavailable.
15. If you didn't or couldn't exercise the option to create a new document, insert a blank sheet of paper into the printer (unless you have lots of labels you want to waste) and click Print. If you did create a new document, you can either continue trying to format the labels to get them to look the way you want, or you can go ahead and print them as if they were a normal document.

Chapter

14

Bullets, Numbered Lists, and Outline Numbering

Word has a number of internal macros that save you work. The paragraph numbering feature, for example, can automatically add numbers and hanging indentation to a list of items. The book you are reading contains zillions of Procedures. Each and every one of them was numbered using this feature. The bulleted lists were created using Word's automatic bullet feature.

SUPER **UPGRADE NOTE**

The bullets and numbering tool in Word for Windows 2 inserted actual bullets and numbers. The default tools in Word for Windows 6, however, do not. If you require actual numbers or bullets in your documents, you can use the older-style commands:

ToolsBulletsNumbers	The dialog box from Word for Windows 2
ToolsBulletListDefault	The bullet tool from Word for Windows 2
ToolsNumberListDefault	The number tool from Word for Windows 2

Before you decide to revert, however, you should note that there is an enormous advantage to using the new tools. In WinWord 2, you had to reformat a section each time you added a new bulleted or numbered item. In Word 6, the bullets and numbers actually are part of the formatting. When you insert or remove an item that has the bulleting or numbering format applied, the numbers and bullets are added automatically, and the numbering automatically adjusts. This is a terrific time-saver.

Numbered Lists

Word can automatically number or renumber a numbered list.

PROCEDURE 14.1. CREATING A NUMBERED LIST USING THE DEFAULT FORMAT.

1. Select the items you want to be numbered (see Figure 14.1).
2. Click the Numbering tool (see Figure 14.2).

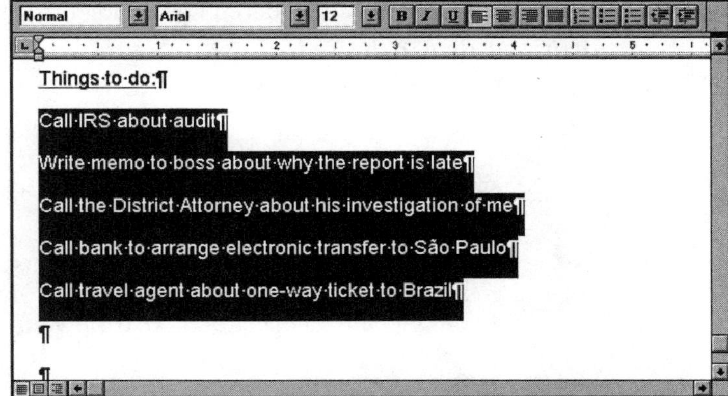

FIGURE 14.1.
Select the list you want to number.

PROCEDURE 14.2. MODIFYING AN ALREADY-NUMBERED LIST.

1. Make any additions to or deletions from the list of items.
2. Select the list; ensure that the first item in the selection is numbered correctly.
3. Click the Numbered List tool.

FIGURE 14.2.
Click the Numbered List button to apply the Numbered format to a selection.

Using the Numbered List Dialog Box

If you need to select options different from the default, use the Format Bullets and Numbering dialog box. This dialog box lets you select the format (numbering style—numbers, letters, and so on), before and after text, font, position, and starting point, as well as specify a hanging indentation.

PROCEDURE 14.3. CREATING A NUMBERED LIST USING THE BULLETS AND NUMBERING DIALOG BOX.

1. Select the items you want to be numbered.
2. Select Format | Bullets and **N**umbering.
3. Click **N**umbered.
4. Click the pattern that matches the numbering style you want to use.
5. Click **M**odify to select any options you want (see the items described below).

6. Click OK to close the Modify Numbered List dialog box.
7. Select Hanging Indent, if desired.
8. Click OK.

SUPER NOTE

The separator option you select in Step 4 becomes the default for the balance of the current session, including when you use the toolbar. However, if you ever use the Numbered List feature to renumber an already-numbered list whose format differs from your current setting, Word will attempt to "learn" the format by reading the separator you applied in the first item. In doing so, Word will conveniently forget the default you set.

Text Before

Use this option to set text you want inserted ahead of the numbers. Popular options include using (or - to create numbers enclosed in parentheses or dashes, such as (1) or -1-.

Number

Use this option to specify the type of numbers to use: Arabic (1, 2, 3...), Roman, alphabetic, and so on.

Text After

Use this option to specify the text following the number, such as .,), -, and so on. (Note: A tab will be inserted following the *text after* text if you select the Hanging Indent option.)

Font

Use this option to specify the font to use for the text before, the number, and the text after.

Start At

Type the number or letter that Word should assign to the first item in the selected list.

Alignment of List Text

Specify the alignment for the list: left, centered, or right.

Distance from Indent to Text

Specify the total distance from the left margin to the text; in effect, this is where you would set a tab if you were formatting the list manually. For a hanging indent, this value generally is .25" greater than the distance from the number to the text.

Distance from Number to Text

Specify the distance from the number to the text. By default, the number is flush left. If you want the number indented, change this distance to move the number. Watch the preview picture carefully to determine when you have the correct setting. If hanging indentation is set, this number can be used to modify the amount of the hanging indentation.

Hanging Indent

Click this option to cause lines after the first line to align under the text rather than flush left.

Bulleted Lists

To create a bulleted list using the built-in defaults, you can use the Bullet button on the Formatting toolbar.

PROCEDURE 14.4. CREATING A BULLETED LIST USING THE DEFAULTS.

1. Select the text you want to bullet.
2. Click the Bullet button in the Formatting toolbar (see Figure 14.3).

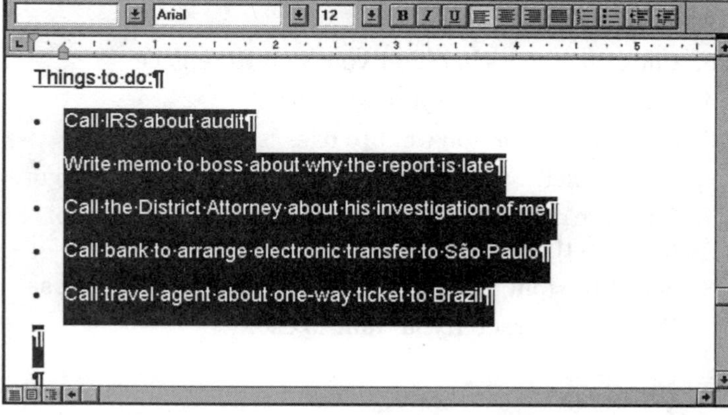

FIGURE 14.3.
The Bullet button automatically creates bulleted lists.

Using the Bulleted List Dialog Box

The toolbar version of the bullet routine applies the default bullet. If you require other options, then you must access the bullet command from the menu.

PROCEDURE 14.5. ACCESSING THE BULLETS AND NUMBERING DIALOG BOX.

1. Select the text you want to format.
2. Select Format | Bullets and **N**umbering.
3. Click Bulleted (or press B) to display the dialog box shown in Figure 14.4.

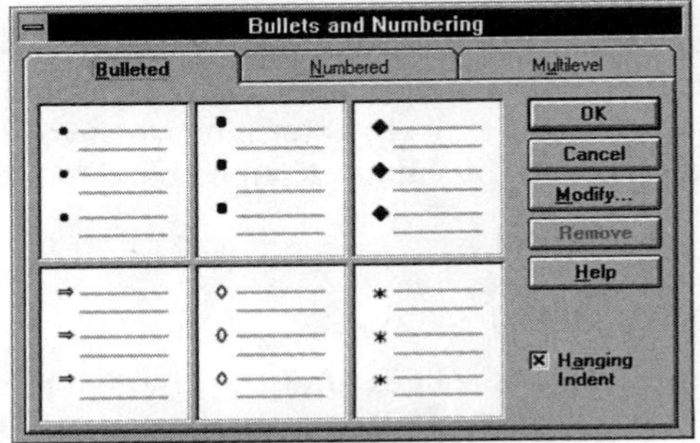

FIGURE 14.4.
Bulleted can be selected in the Bullets and Numbering dialog box.

Bullet Character

Use this option to select the default bullet character. Once you select a new default, Word will use it until you change it. You are not limited to just the list of six bullets shown. In fact, you might consider the list of six as a kind of bullet palette. You can replace any bullet that's on the palette with any character you prefer, using any font that's available on your system.

PROCEDURE 14.6. REPLACING AN EXISTING BULLET WITH A NEW ONE.

1. Select Format | Bullets and **N**umbering.
2. Click **B**ulleted.
3. Click the bullet character you want to replace.
4. Select the point size you want to use.
5. Select the color you want to use.
6. Click **B**ullet… for the Symbol dialog box shown in Figure 14.5.
7. Click the drop-down arrow to the right of the Symbols From list box, which displays the available fonts.
8. Select the font that contains the bullet you want to use.
9. Click the character you want to use.

10. Click OK.
11. Click OK to apply the bullet to the current selection (which also sets the default to the new bullet), or click Close to accept the choice as the new default.

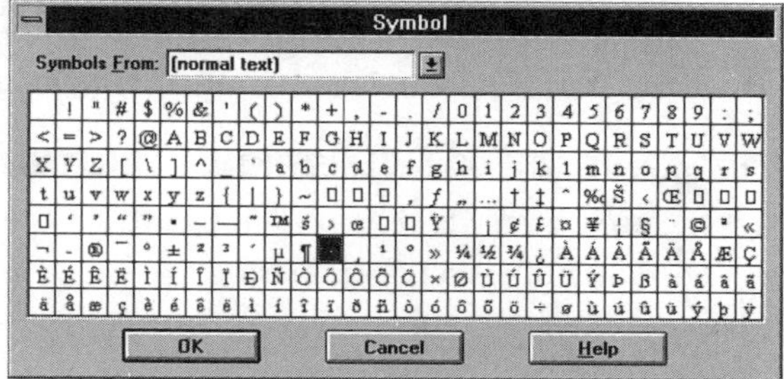

FIGURE 14.5.
Use the Symbol dialog box to replace an existing bullet.

SUPER TIP

In Step 7, the Symbols From list box shows you just the special symbols fonts, along with something called `normal text`. You can, in fact, use any font installed in Windows. Click in the Symbols From box and type the exact name of the font you want to use (even though it's not listed). Then click in the symbols area itself. Word will now display the characters that are available in the font you specified. When you click OK, the font and character you select will replace the bullet you are editing. You won't be able to see the underlying font, however, until you actually insert a bullet and display the field code for the symbol that is inserted.

Distance from Indent to Text

Specify the total distance from the left margin to the text; in effect, this is where you would set a tab if you were formatting the list manually. For a hanging indent, this value generally is .25" greater than the distance from the bullet to the text.

Distance from Bullet to Text

Specify the distance from the bullet to the text. By default, the bullet is flush left. If you want the bullet indented, change this distance to move the bullet. Watch the preview picture carefully to determine when you have the correct setting. If hanging indentation is set, this number can be used to modify the amount of the hanging indentation.

Hanging Indent

Select this option if you want lines after the first to wrap under the preceding text, rather than be flush against the left margin.

Removing Bullets and Numbering

You can use Format | Bullets and Numbering to remove bullets and numbering.

PROCEDURE 14.7. REMOVING BULLETS FROM A BULLETED LIST.

1. Select the area from which you want to extract the bullets.
2. Select Format | Bullets and Numbering.
3. Click on the **B**ulleted tab.
4. Click Remove.

PROCEDURE 14.8. REMOVING NUMBERING FROM A NUMERED LIST.

1. Select the area from which you want to extract the numbers.
2. Select Format | Bullets and Numbering.
3. Click on the **N**umbered tab.
4. Click Remove.

SUPER NOTE

You cannot use the Word 6 command to remove bullets and numbers created using Word for Windows 2.

Multilevel Numbering of Non-Heading Text

The Multilevel numbering tab in the Bullets and Numbering dialog box is used to create patterns of numbering—outline style, technical numbering, legal numbering, and so forth—for the select paragraph(s), regardless of the style(s) that are in effect. Multilevel numbering can be a trifle confusing, however, because of some unwritten rules and assumptions (see "Unwritten Rules for Using Multilevel Numbering"). Those rules and assumptions won't make sense until you've been through the basic procedure a couple of times. Just let me begin by saying that using the multilevel numbering scheme is usually incompatible with a consistent and proper use of styles, and should not be relied upon very heavily. You would be well-advised to avoid using the multilevel numbering features, and to use Heading Numbering instead. Reserve using the multilevel numbering feature only for those times when your Heading 1 through Heading 9 styles are already otherwise engaged.

SUPER NOTE

You can actually apply these procedures to heading level text (text that uses Heading 1 through Heading 9 styles), but the results are not what you'd want or expect. For multilevel heading numberings, use Format | Heading Numbering, instead.

PROCEDURE 14.9. CREATING MULTILEVEL NUMBERING FOR NON-HEADING LEVEL TEXT.

1. Insert a paragraph marker, and apply whatever non-heading style you want to use (for example, Normal, Hanging, and so on). **Important**: Whatever style you use must have the Next Style set to be the same as the style you're using; for example, if you're using Normal, the Next Style setting must be Normal.
2. Select Format | Bullets and Numbering, and click on the Multilevel tab.
3. Select the numbering style you want to apply.
4. Click OK; and note that the item now has a number in front of it. Note also that you cannot select the number. It is part of the underlying formatting and can only be removed or applied using the Format | Bullets and Numbering dialog box.
5. Type the text of your first item, and press Enter. Note that the next number in the sequence is inserted at the beginning of the new line.
6. To demote the current item down to the next level in the numbering scheme, click the Increase Indent button on the Standard toolbar, or press Alt+Shift+Right. As you do this, note that the numbering style changes automatically depending on the level selected. Word supports nine levels (despite the fact that Word's Help says that it supports only eight).
7. To promote the current item up to the previous level, click the Decrease Indent button on the Standard toolbar, or press Alt+Shift+Left.

As long as you add items by duplicating paragraph marks already in the list, items will continue to be numbered automatically, and will continue to be adjustable using Alt+Shift+Right and Left, and the Indent buttons on the toolbar. If you change styles, however, items with the new style you apply will not be numbered. If you reapply the current paragraph format, Word will ask if you want to reformat the style according to the underlying formatting or if you want to reapply that style. If you select the former option, Word will incorporate multilevel numbering formatting into the current style definition. If you select the latter option, Word will reapply the named style and, most likely, will remove the multilevel numbering formatting.

SUPER TIP

For better results, you should create a style, perhaps called Multilevel, into which you incorporate the numbering scheme you want to use. That way, you will be able to apply numbering without having to worry so much about changing the underlying style, or forever being prompted about what you want to do when you apply styles to an already-numbered area. If you reapply the style you use, however, any indented items will be returned to the same level and indentation of the style. This wipes out the indentation and lower-level numbering of everything in the selection. You can, of course, reestablish the lower-level numbering by using Alt+Shift+Left and Right, or by using the Indent buttons on the Standard toolbar. If your list is extensive, however, this process can be quite annoying. For the most part, you're much much better off using Heading level styles to accomplish complex multilevel numbering. See Chapter 22, "Styles and AutoFormat," for additional information on creating and using styles.

You can also apply multilevel numbering to text that already exists.

PROCEDURE 14.10. APPLYING MULTILEVEL NUMBERING TO TEXT THAT ALREADY EXISTS.

1. Select the text you want to number.
2. Select Format | Bullets and Numbering, and click the Multilevel tab.
3. Select the numbering style you want to apply.
4. Click OK.
5. You can adjust the level using the Increase and Decrease Indent buttons on the Standard toolbar, or by pressing Alt+Shift+Right or Left, respectively.

Unwritten Rules for Using Multilevel Numbering

Multilevel numbering can be quite useful if you just want to create a brief outline without resorting to using Heading 1 through Heading 9. You might want to do this, for example, if you're writing a larger document for which you're not using heading numbering, but in which you need to present an outline. For those occasions, the multilevel numbering tool is *perfect*, provided you know and follow the rules:

- To apply multilevel numbering to multiple paragraphs, only those paragraphs that contain text will be numbered.
- When applying multilevel numbering to existing text, text that is indented at least .5 inch will automatically be promoted to the next level; however, the

numbering command does not distinguish gradations below one-half inch. Thus, indentations below .5 inches will all be assigned level 1, from .5 up to (but not including) 1 inch become level 2, from 1 up to (but not including) 1.5 get level 3, and so forth. Even if you modify the numbering style to set the indentations to a lower value, Word will still not discriminate with half-inch gradations for existing indentations.

- If you reapply the style to numbered text, the numbering will be removed *unless* it is part of the underlying style.
- You cannot make multilevel numbering part of a nonheading style's definition using the Modify Styles dialog box. When you click Modify | Format | Numbering from the Style dialog box, only the bullets and numbering tabs are available. The only way to incorporate multilevel numbering into a nonheading style definition is to apply multilevel numbering, then try to reapply the style, and select the option to redefine the style according to the selection.
- If you reapply a style to already-numbered text—even if multilevel numbering is part of the style definition—all lower-level indentation and numbering will be replaced with the top level numbering. You would then need to reindent to reestablish the lower level numbering.

Modifying Multilevel Numbering

You can modify multilevel numbering to create special effects. Suppose, for example, that you wanted to have a style that would automatically be numbered but that had a lower-level counterpart with just bullets. In fact, you already have that option—it's the right-top choice when you select Format | Bullets and Numbering and click the Multilevel tab. But, what if you prefer 1. instead of 1)? In that case, use the Modify button.

PROCEDURE 14.11. MODIFYING MULTILEVEL NUMBERING.

1. From the Multilevel numbering dialog box, click Modify.
2. Using the Level scrollbar, select the level you want to change.
3. In the Text Before and Text After boxes, type the text you want to enclose the number (note: Text Before and Text After aren't available for bullets).
4. In the Bullet or Number list, select the numbering or bullet style.
5. If desired, select the font by clicking the font button. The font is applied to the number (or bullet) as well as the before and after text.
6. Select the desired Start At value.
7. Select the desired Number Position options.

8. Note that Include from Previous Level is not available if the level is set at Level 1; otherwise, you can select Nothing, Numbers, or Numbers and Position. If you select Nothing, then a scheme of I A 1 would should show just A or 1 in levels 2 and 3, respectively. If you select Numbers, then an A item (level 2) would include the I (for example, I.A), and a 1 item (level 3) would include I.A.1. If you select Number and Position, then the indentations of the previous items would be inherited as well, and added to the beginning of the indentation for selected level.
9. Repeat Steps 2 through 8 for each level you want to modify. Note that the Preview window shows the effects of your choices. Click OK when the Preview window shows the view you want.

Multilevel Versus Heading Numbering

Users sometimes get a little confused when using the Multilevel tab in the Bullets and Numbering dialog box, and when using the Heading Numbering dialog box. That's because the two contain a number of features and controls that are quite similar. The two, however, work differently. Knowing which to use, and when, can save you quite a bit of confusion.

You should use the Multilevel numbering feature when you want to accomplish multilevel numbering only for part of a document, rather than for its entire structure. If you want to include an outline in part of a document, but don't want to outline the entire document itself, then the Multilevel numbering is what you want. If you want a pattern of numbering applied to the headings of a document, then use Heading Numbering, instead. The latter is flexible enough—especially if you use the Modify button and change the settings for various levels—to fit most purposes.

Heading Numbering

The heading numbering feature is the ideal tool for automatically numbering headings in a document. The feature is quite flexible, allowing you to turn numbering off or on for any level(s) you choose. For example, if you want Heading 1 not to be numbered, but all other levels to be numbered, Word can do it. Just select the basic format that looks closest to what you want, and modify the levels to achieve the effect you desire.

SUPER NOTE

When using heading numbering, all heading level text throughout the document is changed. The underlying styles in the document are automatically changed as well. You cannot apply heading numbering to part of a document without applying it to the entire document.

SUPER CAUTION

Applying Heading Numbering will remove any other number or bullet formatting that is in effect for any single heading level, including bullets or numbers created using Word 2's ToolsBulletsNumbers command. Generally, this is exactly what you want to do. Just be aware of the sweeping nature of this command before applying it. You should also explicitly save your document before applying Heading Numbering. Very often, the effects are so sweeping and far-reaching that you cannot completely reverse them using Undo. That being the case, your only fall-back position might be the most-recently-saved version of the document.

PROCEDURE 14.12. ENABLING HEADING NUMBERING.

1. Select Format | Heading Numbering from the menu.
2. Click the type of numbering you want to use (if what you want isn't shown exactly, then click Modify and proceed as shown under "Modifying Heading Numbering").
3. Click OK.

Modifying Heading Numbering

Modifying Heading Numbering is similar to modifying Multilevel Numbering. A key difference, however, is the meaning of *level*. When modifying Multilevel Numbering, *level* refers to indentation levels. When modifying Heading Numbering, level corresponds to Heading 1 through Heading 9. Modifying Heading Numbering is especially useful when you need numbering or special numbering for only some, but not all heading levels, or when you need to combine numbering and bullets.

PROCEDURE 14.13. MODIFYING HEADING NUMBERING.

1. From the Heading Numbering dialog box, click Modify.
2. Using the Level scrollbar, select the level you want to change.
3. In the Text Before and Text After boxes, type the text you want to enclose the number.
4. In the Bullet or Number list, select the numbering or bullet style.
5. If desired, select the font by clicking the font button. The font is applied to the number (or bullet) as well as the before and after text.
6. Select the desired Start At value.

7. Select the desired Number Position options.
8. Select the desired Include from Previous Level setting.
9. If you want numbering to start anew in each section, click the indicated checkbox.
10. Repeat Steps 2 through 7 for each level you want to change.
11. Click OK when the Preview window shows the view you want.

V

Section Formatting Workshop

One of the most important and useful features of Word is the capability to divide a document into distinctly formatted sections. If you work only on correspondence, memos, and short reports, you may never have a need to create multisection documents. When you need distinctly and differently numbered parts (for example, a preface versus the body, versus the appendix), different header and footer styles, or different numbers of columns, then you need to divide your document into different sections. The Section Formatting Workshop takes you into section formatting, showing when you need it, as well as how to use it to accomplish specific effects.

Chapter

15

Section Formatting

Word uses section breaks to separate distinctly formatted parts of a document. Most documents, in fact, have just a single section. Only when you need to apply different section formats within the same document do you need to create a multisection document. Different sections are necessary for variations in the following kinds of formatting:

- Headers and footers, including changes in page numbering style.
- Footnotes, which are turned on or off for an entire section at a time.
- Changes in line numbering style, except for suppression on a paragraph by paragraph basis.
- Margins. You can vary indentation within a section but not margins.
- Orientation—landscape versus portrait.
- Paper size—8.5 x 11, 8.5 x 14, and so on.
- Paper source—upper tray, envelope feed, manual feed, and so on.
- Columns—snaking newspaper-style columns, the number of which can't change within a section.

For example, if you want part of a document to have three columns and another part to have a single column, the two parts must be in separate *sections*. Similarly, if one part of a document has a 1-inch margin and another has a 2-inch margin, they must be separated by a *section break*.

Section Breaks

Section breaks can occur within a page or between pages. You also can use a section break to force Word to skip to the next odd or even page. Some procedures will automatically insert a section break. For example, if you select Format | Columns and choose This Point Forward from the Apply To drop-down list, Word will automatically insert a section break. If you apply column formatting using the column tool on the toolbar, however, you must insert your own section break(s) to set off the differently columned text.

PROCEDURE 15.1. INSERTING A SECTION BREAK.

1. Position the cursor where you want the section break to occur.
2. Select Insert | Break.
3. Select the Section Breaks option:

Next Page	Causes the new section to begin on the next page
Continuous	Enables both sections to coexist on the same page
Even Page	Causes the new section to begin on the next even page
Odd Page	Causes the new section to begin on the next odd page

4. Click OK.

SUPER NOTE

The Even and Odd Page options typically are used when formatting books in which a chapter must begin on an odd or an even page.

Pagination

A typical use for section breaks is to enable the use of different kinds of numbering within a document. For example, a preface might have lowercase Roman numerals (i, ii, iii,...), while the body of the document might have Arabic numerals, beginning with 1.

PROCEDURE 15.2. FORMATTING TWO PARTS OF A DOCUMENT WITH DIFFERENT PAGE NUMBERING STYLES.

1. Insert a section break (**N**ext Page) between the two distinct sections (for example, between a preface and the main text).
2. Move the cursor into the first section (**E**dit | **G**o To, Section, 1).
3. Select **V**iew | **H**eader and Footer; Word switches to the view shown in Figure 15.1.

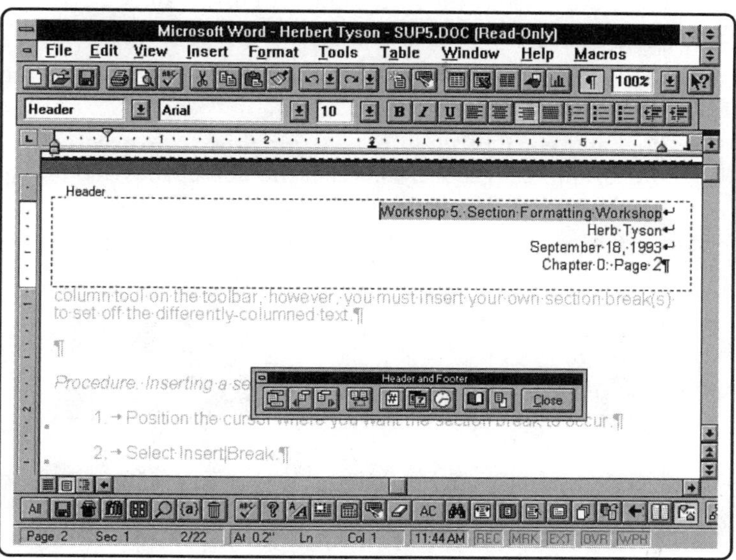

FIGURE 15.1.
Header and Footer view is Page Layout view.

4. If necessary, click the Jump Between Header and Footer button (the first one on the Header and Footer Toolbar, as shown in Figure 15.1) to jump to the appropriate part of the page, depending on whether you want to have page numbers in the header or in the footer.
5. Click the Page Number button to insert a page field.
6. Select **I**nsert | Page N**u**mbers for the dialog box shown in Figure 15.2.

FIGURE 15.2.
Use the Page Numbers dialog box to set page numbering options.

7. Ignore the **P**osition and **A**lignment options and select or deselect **S**how Number on First Page, depending on whether you want a page number to be displayed on the first page.
8. Click the Format button to display the Page Number Format dialog box.
9. Click the list expansion arrow beside the Number Format box and select the desired format (for example, i, ii, iii,…); ignore all other options in the dialog box for now.
10. Click OK to close the Page Number Format dialog box.
11. Click Close.
12. Click the Show Next Section Header and Footer button on the Header and Footer Toolbar.
13. Repeat Steps 6 through 11, selecting the appropriate Number Format in Step 8 (for example, 1, 2, 3,…), and set the numbering to Start At 1 so your pages go: i, ii, iii, iv, 1, 2, 3,… instead of i, ii, iii, iv, 5, 6, 7,….
14. Click Close to return to the normal text area (or just double-click in the text area).

SUPER TIP

In extreme cases such as when formatting a complicated booklet, you may have to set page numbering in as many as six different headers or footers to accomplish the desired effect. You can save a lot of time by making sure you click the Show Next Header and Footer button (Step 12 and shown in Figure 15.3) rather than closing and opening the header and footer area separately for each section.

FIGURE 15.3.
Use the Show Next Header and Footer button to jump to the next section.

SUPER NOTE

The role of the Insert | Page Numbers command may be confusing. That command actually has several purposes. It can be used to insert a framed page number field that you can drag anywhere in the header area. It also can be used to tell Word what kind of page numbering to perform in each section. In this example, it was used only for the latter purpose because the page number field (unframed) had already been inserted using the Page button in the Header and Footer Toolbar. Another use for the Insert | Page Numbers command is discussed in the next chapter.

Chapter

16

Numbering

Word provides several field codes for automatically numbering different aspects of a document. A field code is a special combination of characters that Word interprets dynamically. This makes it possible for the identical code to mean different things in different parts of the same document. We saw an example of a *page* field code at the end of the preceding section.

Page Numbering

Page numbering usually is accomplished by including PAGE field codes in document headers or footers. A PAGE field code is simply `PAGE` inserted between two field characters.

PROCEDURE 16.1. CREATING A HEADER WITH A PAGE NUMBER.

1. Select **V**iew | **H**eader and Footer from the menu.
2. Word switches into Page Layout view and opens the Header and Footer area, as shown in Figure 16.1. Note the Header and Footer Toolbar. Type the header text you want to use such as the document title, your name, and so on.
3. Click any or all of the Page Number, Date, or Time buttons to insert fields for page, date, and time where you want them to appear.
4. If necessary or if desired, you can click the Link to Previous button, as shown in Figure 16.1, to make the current section use the same header and footer as the previous section. Word will prompt before overwriting the current header and footer.
5. Click Close when you're done.

SUPER NOTE

The Link to Previous button on the Header and Footer Toolbar controls whether the header and footer in the current section is the same as or different from the header and footer in the previous section. If it appears depressed (a whitish face on the button instead of gray), the words `Same as Previous` will appear just above the header outline. If the current header or footer is not the same as in the previous section, the Link to Previous button will be gray (unpushed), and the `Same as Previous` message will not appear.

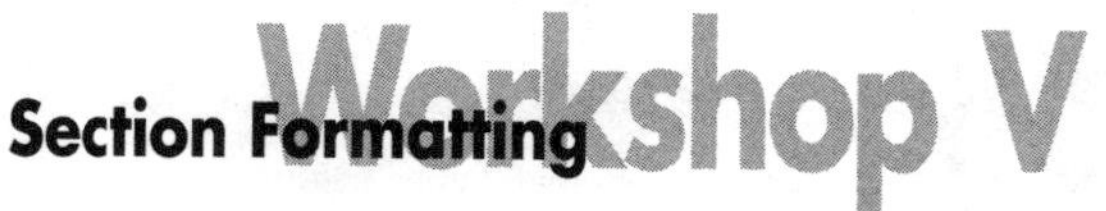

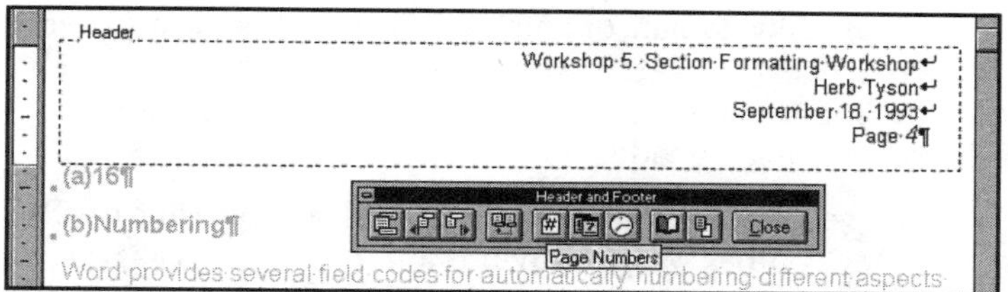

FIGURE 16.1.
The Header area with the Header and Footer Toolbar displayed.

SUPER TIP

Create all the headers you'll ever need—just once. If you include a header like the one shown in Figure 16.2 in your templates, you may not have to worry much about headers in the future. Here, field codes are displayed so you can see just how automatic this header is. Note the extensive use of field codes. The NUMPAGES field is used to provide the total number of pages in the document. The title, subject, and author fields from the document summary are also used. If you systematically supply the Title and Subject document summary information for each document you create, your headers will be both consistent and automatic.

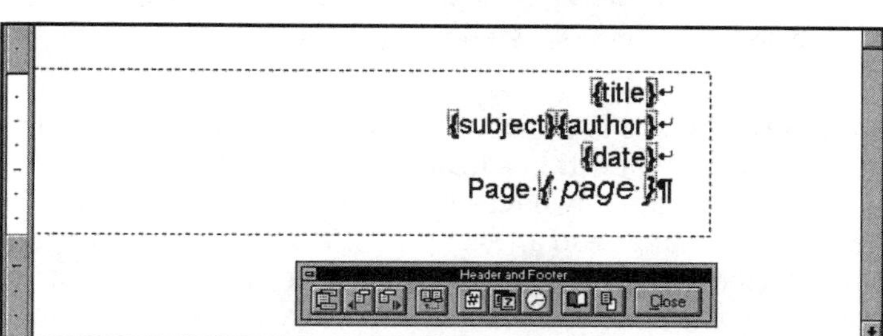

FIGURE 16.2.
Using document information field codes can save time and create consistency across your documents.

The Insert|Page Numbers Command

The **I**nsert|Page **Nu**mbers command is sure to cause some confusion. That's because it's used not only for inserting page numbers, as the name implies, but also for formatting them for different document sections. In fact, it would have been a *lot* clearer if there had been a separate Format|Page Numbers command. But, hey! If it was clear and straightforward, there wouldn't be a market for third-party books, right? So, what am I complaining about? Keep up the good work, Microsoft!

In the example at the end of the previous chapter, you saw how to use the Format button in the **I**nsert|Page **Nu**mbers command to control the numbering style (for example, Arabic, Roman, or alphabetic) as well as the number with which to start (continue from previous versus start at some other number, such as 1). You have not yet seen the other use for the **I**nsert | Page **Nu**mbers command: inserting a framed page field for creating a header or footer.

So far, we've looked at inserting a page field only by using the Page button on the Header and Footer Toolbar. Word provides another method as well, albeit somewhat confusing until you understand the underlying rationale and strategy. In the examples of inserting a page field shown so far, you had to rely on ordinary placement of things like carriage returns and alignment to determine where the page number prints. An alternative is to put the page number (and possibly the entire header or footer text) into a frame. You can then drag the frame wherever you like, which gives you more direct control on where and how the text prints. To frame header or footer text or a page number, you have several practical choices. One obvious choice is to create the header or footer text or page number, select it, and then frame it. Another choice is to insert a text frame into a header or footer and then compose your header or footer text within it.

SUPER NOTE

You cannot frame a header or footer *per se* because a header or footer is really just a reserved area in the top or bottom margin. Therefore, you'll see references to framing the header or footer *text* instead of framing the header or footer itself.

Yet another choice is to use the **I**nsert | Page **Nu**mbers command to insert a framed `{PAGE}` field for you within a header or footer. What's unintuitive about this choice is that a user may already have an *un*framed header or footer already started, to which they simply want to add a `{PAGE}` field. When you use the **I**nsert | Page **Nu**mbers command, instead of getting a `{PAGE}` field that's part of your already-established header or footer, you get a floating `{PAGE}` field in a frame that you can't quite seem to line up with the rest of the header.

The secret is that the **I**nsert | Page **Nu**mbers command assumes two things. First, it assumes that you don't have any idea of what you're doing and, therefore, haven't yet created header or footer text. Second, it assumes that people who don't have any idea of what they're doing will now somehow make the quantum leap and intuitively understand that the header and footer text could be added *to* the already-framed `{PAGE}` field instead of inserted independently and unframed. If you're not particularly fond of leaps, let alone quantum leaps of logic, the following procedure should help *frame* the issue a little better.

SUPER NOTE

The following procedure assumes that the header or footer area is empty. It inserts a {PAGE} field in a text frame that can be used for additional header information.

PROCEDURE 16.2. USING THE INSERT|PAGE NUMBERS COMMAND AS A BASIS FOR A HEADER OR FOOTER.

1. Select **V**iew|**H**eader and Footer; your view will switch to Page Layout, and the focus will be on a header. If you want to work on the footer instead of on the header, click the Jump to Footer button. (If header or footer text already exists, ignore it for the moment. After all, this procedure *assumes* that the header or footer area is empty, right?)
2. Select **I**nsert|Page N**u**mbers.
3. Select a **P**osition (header or footer) and **A**lignment for the frame; note the preview screen.
4. Click **S**how Number on First Page, if desired.
5. Click the **F**ormat button.
6. Select your Number **F**ormat, Include Chapter **N**umber, and Page Numbering options (as needed).
7. Click OK to close the Format Page Numbers dialog.
8. Click OK to close the Page Numbers dialog. Note that a framed page field appears on-screen in the header or footer area.
9. If you previously had a header or footer, you have three choices:
   - Select it and move it into the frame.
   - Delete it and add any additional information you want to the page number *inside the frame*.
   - Leave the existing header or footer text as is and have a devil of a time trying to decide where to drag the page number field so that the header or footer doesn't confuse the reader.

   If you take the first or second option, you've probably chosen an easier path. If you opted for the third choice, *good luck!* If you do move the balance of the header or footer text into the framed area, you now may experience a problem of the framed text exceeding the top or bottom margin and overwriting the main page. To fix this problem, you have three choices:

   - Change the header text (by reformatting, reducing the number of lines, and so on) so that it isn't so darned big.

- Drag the frame up far enough on the page so that it doesn't conflict with the text area (but you'll have to be careful not to spill into the nonprintable region, especially on laser printers).
- Turn on the vertical ruler (View | **R**uler) and widen the top or bottom margin so that there's more room for the header or footer.
- Or (I really meant that you have *four* choices), leave the framed area and insert enough paragraph marks to cause the header or footer to expand to where the frame fits comfortably.
- Or (okay, so I really mean that you have *five* choices), select Format | Fra**m**e, click Remove Frame, and go back to using an ordinary, easy to understand, *un*framed header or footer arrangement.

  Personally, I'm fond of the last option. It has a nice feel to it. Framing page numbers and headers generally makes sense only for special purposes, such as to create watermarks or decorative page numbers that transcend the rest of the header or footer.

Section and Chapter Numbering

You can use `Seq` fields to provide automatic counters for virtually anything you want numbered in a document. They're especially ideal for numbering document sections or chapters. An `Seq` field is an automatic numbering or counter field that you create. It takes the form:

```
Seq name [switches]
```

The *name* can be anything you choose, but choose something logical. You can have as many distinctly defined `Seq` fields as you like.

PROCEDURE 16.3. CREATING AN AUTOMATIC SECTION OR CHAPTER NUMBER.

1. Put the insertion point where you want the section title to occur (that is, at the beginning of the section).
2. Type the section or chapter leader (for example, `Chapter`, `Section`, or `Part`).
3. Select **I**nsert | Fi**e**ld.
4. From the Field **N**ames list, click Seq (note that the corresponding field code appears in the Field Code text box as you scroll through the list of field types).
5. Click in the **F**ield Code text box.
6. After the field code Seq, type a name you want to give the counter (for example, `Chapter`). Make sure there is a space between `Seq` and the name you type.
7. Click **O**ptions and the **G**eneral Switches tab (see Figure 16.3).

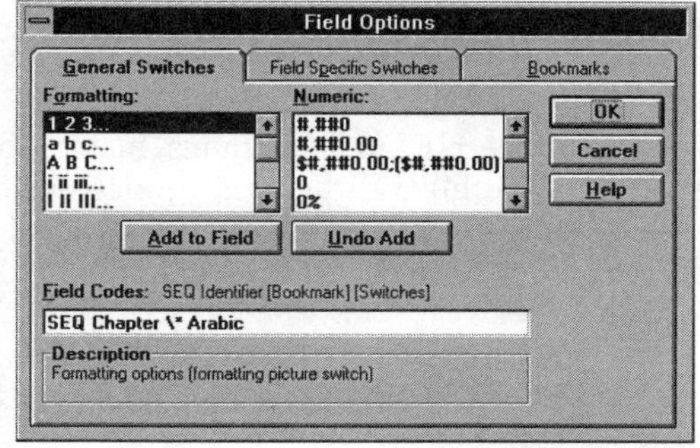

FIGURE 16.3.
The Field Options dialog box lets you build your fields without needing to know field code syntax.

8. Select a **Formatting** option (such as 1, I, A, and so on) and click the **Add to Field** button so that the field now looks as shown in Figure 16.4.
9. Click OK to close the Field Options dialog box.
10. Click OK to insert the field into your document.

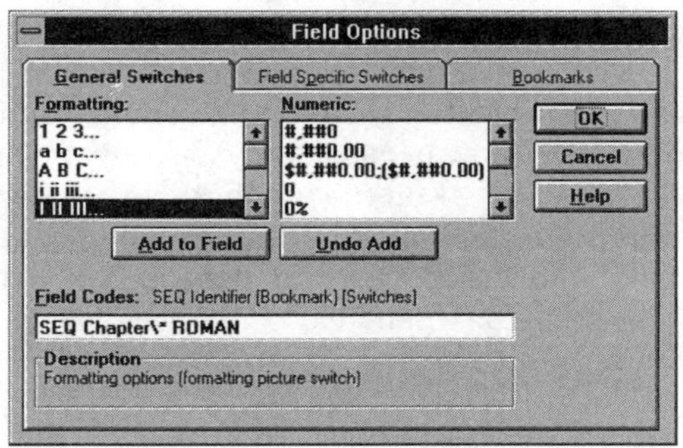

FIGURE 16.4.
*Use the **Add to Field** button to add the formatting options.*

Each time a `{seq name}` field is inserted in your document, it will be displayed as the next number in the sequence. For example, if you insert six `{seq chapter}` fields in your document, they will display as 1, 2, 3, 4, 5, and 6:

Chapter `{seq chapter}`	Chapter 1
Chapter `{seq chapter}`	Chapter 2
Chapter `{seq chapter}`	Chapter 3
Chapter `{seq chapter}`	Chapter 4
Chapter `{seq chapter}`	Chapter 5
Chapter `{seq chapter}`	Chapter 6

SUPER TIP

After using Insert | Field a few times, many Word users yearn for a more direct entry method. It's generally much easier to insert simple field codes directly. Press Ctrl+F9 to insert the field code braces, type `seq chapter`, and then press F9 to update the field.

SUPER NOTE

The field code characters {} are not actual braces. They are in fact ASCII characters 19 and 21, respectively. However, in Word, the only ways to create them are by using a command that inserts a field (such as Insert | Field and Insert | Page Numbers) or by pressing Ctrl+F9. Note also that neither { nor } can be selected individually. When selecting text, once you cross { or }, the entire field is selected. That helps remind you that these are *not* your father's curly braces and keeps you from being able to delete either field brace without deleting the other (no doubt, this would result in some odd disequilibrium in your document, but we'll never know because they can only be inserted or deleted as a pair). Alt+19 and Alt+21 on the number pad creates some things, but they're not useful as field braces. Knowing they're really ^19 and ^21 isn't wasted information, though, because you can use ^19 and ^21 to search for field codes (when field codes are displayed).

Using Chapter Numbers in Headers or Footers

Sometimes it's convenient to use a chapter or section number in a header or footer. A common page style, for example, is Page I-3, where I is the section number and 3 is a page within that section. The easiest way to accomplish this is to use a `\c` switch in the `Seq` field that contains the counter you want to use. For example:

```
Page {seq chapter \c\*Roman}-{page}
```

Here the `\c` switch tells Word to use the current number in the Seq CHAPTER series. `\*Roman` is the instruction to use capital Roman numerals. `\*roman` would yield i, ii, iii,… instead.

PROCEDURE 16.4. CREATING COMBINED CHAPTER-PAGE NUMBERS.

1. Ensure that each distinct chapter is separated from the previous chapter with a section break.

2. Select **I**nsert | Page **Nu**mbers and click Format.
3. Click Start **A**t and set to 1 (this tells Word to number each section beginning with page 1).
4. Click OK to close the Page Number Format dialog box.

   Click Close (don't click OK!) to close the Page Numbers dialog box.
5. Select **V**iew | **H**eader and Footer.
6. Type the header or footer as you want it to appear.
7. Move the insertion point to where you want the chapter-page number to occur.
8. Press Ctrl+F9 and type `seq chapter \c\*Roman`.
9. Press F9.
10. Click the # icon (for Page Number) to insert the page number.
11. Click Close.

SUPER NOTE

Don't use the `{numpages}` field when doing this kind of numbering. Unfortunately, `{numpages}` refers to the total number of pages in the document rather than the number of pages in the section. Word has no built-in way to get the number of pages per section. See Chapter 31, "Bookmarks and Cross-References," for a laborious but workable method of doing this.

Numbering Tables, Figures, and Illustrations

Numbering tables, figures, illustrations, and so on is similar to numbering chapters and sections: use a sequence field with an appropriate name to create a unique counter for each series you want to enumerate. You also can use sequence fields for numbering lists, but it's generally easier to use the Format | Bullets and **N**umbering feature described in Chapter 14, "Bullets, Numbered Lists, and Outline Numbering."

PROCEDURE 16.5. CREATING FIGURE, TABLE, AND ILLUSTRATION NUMBERS.

1. Position the insertion point where you want the number to appear (for example, just after the word *Figure*).
2. Press Ctrl+F9 to insert the field characters.
3. Type `Seq`, a space, and the name you want to give the series (for example, `figure`, `table`, or `illustration`).
4. Press F9 to display or update the field.

SUPER TIP

If you have many such fields to insert, it is sometimes faster to create an autotext entry to do most of the work for you. You would still have to press F9 to update the field, however.

Numbering Figures in Distinct Chapters or Sections

In some documents, figures and tables are numbered consecutively within each section or chapter as **&&**`Figure 1-1, 2-3, 4-15`**&&**, and so on. To include the current section or chapter as part of the numbering scheme, include the field **&&**`{seq` *`chapter`* `\c}`**&&**, where *chapter* is the name of the section or chapter seq series you're using for chapter or section numbering. Again, the \c switch tells Word to use the most recent value in the series.

This procedure creates the problem of having to restart each figure or table series within each section. To do this, you have several choices. The easiest choice is to include a hidden reset field at the beginning of each section, for example: **&&**`{seq figure \r\h}`**&&**. The word *figure* is the series name, `\r` means **reset** to 0, and `\h` means **hide this field**. This way, the first *un*hidden occurrence of a **&&**`{Seq FIGURE}`**&&** field will begin numbering at 1.

This approach is easy because you can simply copy the **&&**`{seq figure \r\h}`**&&** field (along with series-restart fields for any other Seq series you have, such as tables or charts) at the beginning of each chapter. For example, I'm writing this near a chapter boundary right now. At the moment, all I see is **&&**`Chapter 17`**&&**, marking the beginning of the next chapter. When I select that line and press Shift+F9 (to display field codes rather than field code results), I suddenly see:

&&`Chapter {seq chapter}{seq figurenumber \r\h}{seq tablenumber \r\h}`**&&**

&&`Chapter {seq chapter}`**&&** resolves as **&&**`Chapter 14`**&&**, while the remainder of the line gets hidden (due to the `\h` switches).

Another, less easy, approach is to use a `\r1` (restart at 1) switch in the first sequence field in each chapter. While seemingly more direct, this approach is problematic because it makes the Seq field with the `\r1` switch location-sensitive. If the figure gets moved or deleted or another figure gets inserted ahead of it, the `\r1` switch will then be attached to the wrong field and would need to be moved to whichever seq counter is now first in the chapter. Instead, it's much easier to always include a hidden reset-to-zero counter at the beginning of each chapter. That way figures and tables can be moved around with wild abandon.

Referring to a Figure Nnumber

When using figure and table numbers, you invariably need to refer to them. Once a figure or table number as been inserted using a sequence field, you can refer to it by repeating the sequence field and using the `\c` (current) switch. For example, to refer to the most recent figure, I would type **&&**`See Figure {seq chapter \c}-{seq figurenumber \c}`**.&&.**

This technique works almost all the time. It doesn't work when two figures are inserted together. For example, if I insert **&&**`Figures 4 and 5`**&&**, one right after another, I can use **&&**`{seq figurenumber \c}`**&&** to refer only to **&&**`figure 5`**&&**. What about **&&** `figure 4?`**&&** Fortunately, such insertions are rare. When they occur, however, I give each sequence field a unique bookmark name, and then refer to it by its bookmark. For example:

```
&&Figure {seq figurenumber}. John climbing a tree.&&
&&Figure {seq figurenumber}. John falling from a tree.&&
```

I would select the first figure number field, press Ctrl+Shift+F5, and type some descriptive text like *climb* to [book]mark that figure as climb. This lets me refer to it as **&&{**`seq figurenumber climb`**}&&**. Fortunately for John, who's now in a hurry to get to the hospital, I don't have to waste time bookmarking the "falling" figure. I can refer to it using the \c switch.

Chapter

17

Headers and Footers

Headers and footers are one of the most misunderstood concepts in word processing. Microsoft Word continues in that fine tradition. In this session, you'll learn about headers and footers—what they are, how to create them, and how to avoid the usual problems that plague so many users.

Understanding Headers and Footers

To understand what a header or a footer is, you have to understand a little about the printable area of a page, the text area of a page, and the margin area of a page. As shown in Figure 17.1, the printable area of a page is defined by your printer. Some matrix printers can print anywhere on the page. Most—if not all—laser printers, however, are physically unable to print within roughly 1/4 inch of the edge of the paper. If you set the margins too close to the edge of paper, you'll sometimes get a message like the one shown in Figure 17.2.

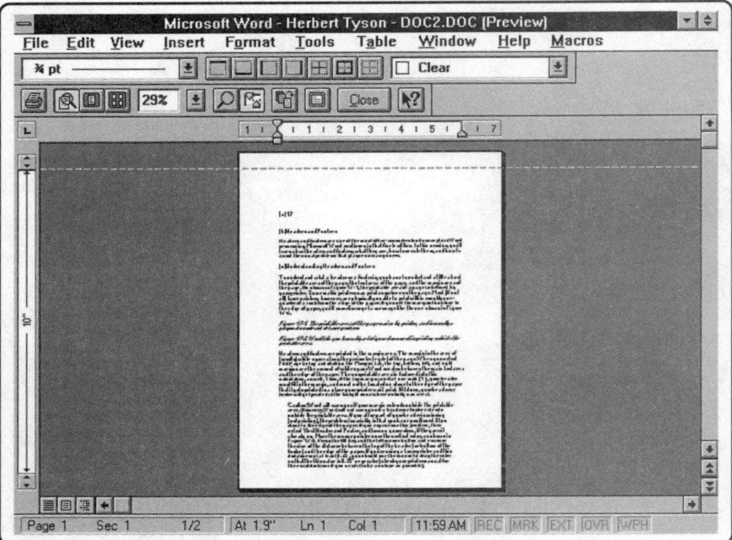

FIGURE 17.1.
The printable area of a page varies by printer and is mostly a physical constraint of laser printers.

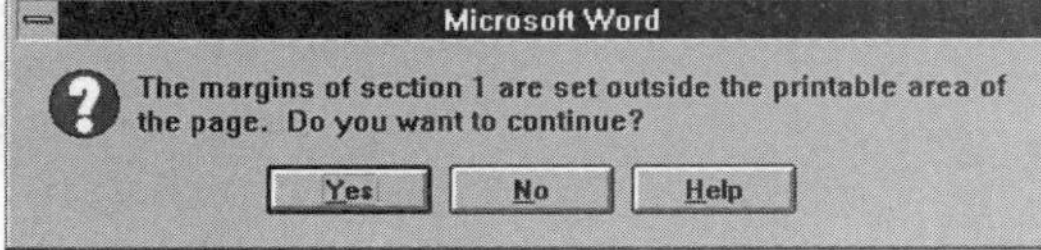

FIGURE 17.2.
Word tells you if part of your document is printing outside the printable area.

Headers and footers are printed in the margin area. The margin is the area of [mostly] white space along the perimeter (edge) of the page. When you select **File | Page Setup** and click the Margins tab, the top, bottom, left, and right margins are the amounts of white space Word creates between the main text area and the edge of the paper. The nonprintable area is factored into this calculation, as well. Thus, if the top margin is set at 1 inch (1"), your header must fit in the margin and must not be located so close to the edge of the paper that it would print in a place your printer can't print. If it is too close to the edge, your header or footer will get printed in the twilight zone where nobody can see it.

SUPER CAUTION

Word warns you if your margin extends outside the printable area. However, Word does not warn you if a header or footer extends outside the printable area. If all or part of your header is missing (not printing), the problem invariably is that you have positioned it too close to the edge of the paper. If you experience this problem, select **View | Header** and Footer and turn on your rulers, if they aren't already on. Move the mouse pointer over the vertical ruler, as shown in Figure 17.3. Press Alt and the left mouse button and examine the distance between the top of the header (or bottom of the footer) and the edge of the paper. If you're using a laser printer and this distance isn't at least 0.25", use the mouse to drag the ruler so that this value is 0.25" or greater (check your printer manual for the exact distance if you need it to be as close as possible).

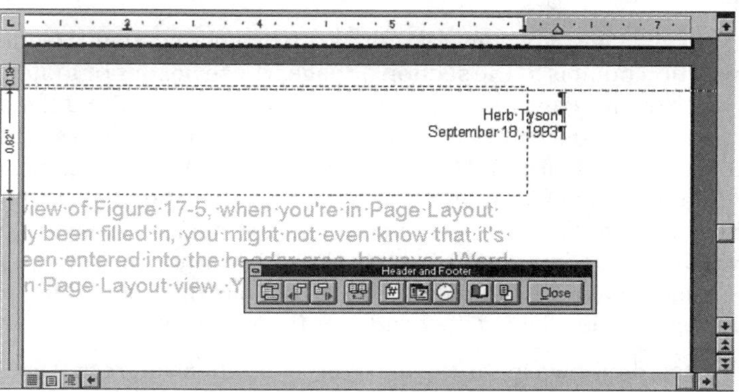

FIGURE 17.3.
Make sure your margins aren't too small for your printer. Press Alt and click here to see the exact measurement.

Word enables you to create a variety of headers and footers for your documents, supporting up to three distinct headers or footers for each document section: first page, even (left) pages, and odd (right) pages. Word enables you to create different headers and footers on a per section basis as well. Depending on the options you choose, you may select:

- Identical header and footer for each page (most often used in drafts)
- One header and footer for the first page and a different header and footer for all subsequent pages (most often used in reports that have a blank header and footer on page 1 and a page-number header and footer on subsequent pages)
- Distinct header and footer for left and right pages (most often used in book-type formats in which left page headers are flush left and right page headers are flush right)
- Distinct header and footer for left and right pages and a different header and footer for the first page (similar to previous, but with an option to treat the first page differently—usually a blank header and footer on that page)

From Word's point of view, headers and footers are the same concept. While they produce different printed results, the tools and techniques are identical. The only difference is where they appear on the page. For simplicity, I'll use "header" to refer to headers, footers, either, or both. I hope the footer fetishists in the audience won't feel slighted.

Creating Headers (or Footers)

Conceptually, users generally think of having to create or insert headers. Notice, however, that there is no Insert Header command. Instead, there's a View Header command. In Word, every document already has a header. It's built-in; you don't have to insert it. But why don't you see it? It's blank until you actually add text to it.

In normal view, you can edit headers by selecting **V**iew | **H**eader and Footer while the insertion point is in the section or page whose header or footer you want to edit. Word switches into Page Layout view (just while you're editing the header or footer), highlights the header or footer, and dims the normal text area so that it's clear what you're editing (see Figure 17.4). When you're already in Page Layout view, Word also highlights the header or footer and dims the normal text area, making it unambiguously clear that that's what you're editing. That makes it easy to avoid getting mixed up, which was a common problem in Word for Windows Version 2. Note also that when editing in Page Layout view, you can bypass the **V**iew | **H**eader and Footer command by just double-clicking the header or footer you want to edit—assuming it's not blank.

Even so, as shown in the top of Figure 17.5, when you're in Page Layout view, if a header hasn't already been filled in, you might not even know that it's there. No header is visible in Figure 17.5, even though, technically, a header is present. Once information has been entered into the header area, however, Word displays it automatically in Page Layout view. You can then edit the header simply by double-clicking it. While the header is blank, however, the only way to access the header area in Page Layout view is by selecting **View** | **Header and Footer**.

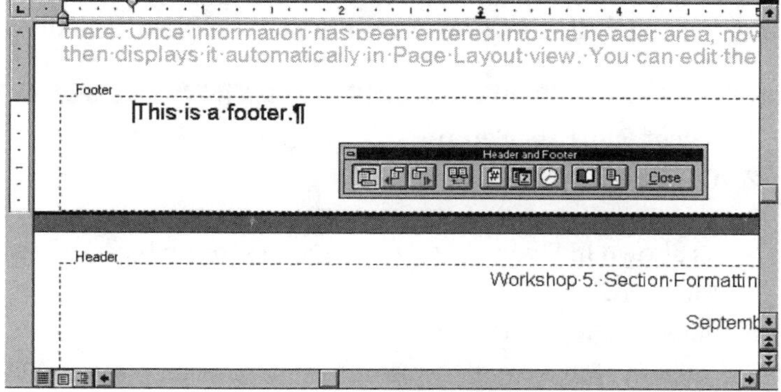

FIGURE 17.4.
Unlike Word for Windows Version 2, WinWord 6 makes it clear that you're editing a header or footer when you're in Page Layout view.

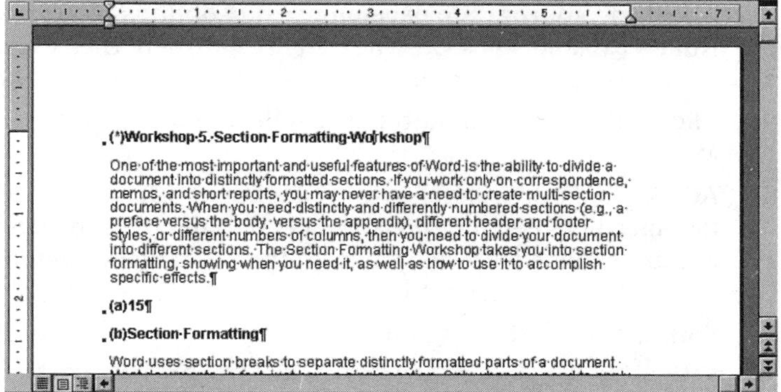

FIGURE 17.5.
Searching for headers and footers in Page Layout view can be tricky until you've explictly added text to them.

SUPER UPGRADE NOTE

Unlike Word for Windows Version 2, **View** | **Header and Footer** no longer provides a dialog box for selecting whichever header or footer you want to edit. Instead, it automatically switches to Page Layout view, ending the ambiguity users faced in prior versions of Word for Windows. Instead, **View** | **Header or Footer** selects the header or footer pertaining to the current page. You can then use the Jump Between Header and Footer, Next Header or Footer, and Previous Header or Footer buttons to move to whichever header or footer you want to edit. To edit the first header, move to the first page; to edit an even header, move to an even page; and so on.

Single Header

Use a single header when you want all pages of a document to have the same header. This kind of header often is appropriate for drafts, as well as information with a company logo ("Confidential" or "Proprietary") on the top of all pages.

PROCEDURE 17.1. CREATING A SINGLE HEADER FOR ALL DOCUMENT PAGES.

1. Select **F**ile | Page Set**u**p.
2. Click the **L**ayout tab.
3. Ensure that Different **O**dd and Even and Different **F**irst Page are not selected, as shown in Figure 17.6 (an X appears in the box when they're selected).
4. Click OK.
5. Select **V**iew | **H**eader and Footer.
6. Click the Page Number button (#) to insert a page number field (if desired).
7. Click **I**nsert | Page N**u**mbers and the Format button.
8. Select the appropriate page numbering options. To close the Format Page Number dialog, click OK when you're satisfied; then click Close (don't click OK unless you want to insert a framed page number field).
9. Click the Page Setup button in the Header and Footer toolbar; then click the Margins tab.
10. Adjust the Header and Footer From Edge settings, if necessary, to set the distance between the top of the header and the top edge of the page (higher numbers move a header down on the page; higher numbers move a footer up on the page). Click OK to close the Page Setup dialog.
11. Format the header; use the header style whenever possible (see the following tip).
12. Type the header text, inserting page, date, time, or other information, as needed.
13. Click Close when you're done.

SUPER TIP

You can press Alt+Shift+C instead of having to click on the Close button. This works with any of the various special-purpose toolbars that contain the word Close with an underlined C (Close).

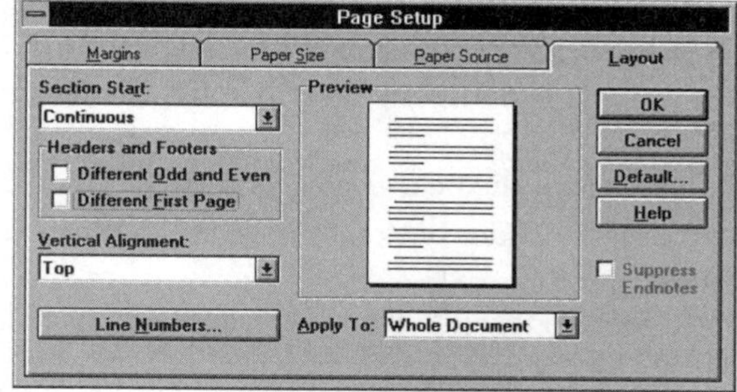

FIGURE 17.6.
*For a single header, make sure that Different **O**dd and Even and Different **F**irst Page are not checked.*

SUPER TIP

Do it with style. In the long run, you'll save yourself some formatting work if you take the time to modify the header and footer styles. Users often want the header and footer to be smaller than the body text and centered or right-aligned with single spacing between paragraphs. Therefore, it makes sense to modify the style definition in the underlying template so you don't have to spend time formatting headers each time you create a new document. To save even more time, you could open the template itself and create standard headers that use field codes for document title, author, date, and page number. Done right, it need be done only once for each template you use.

Varying Headers

If necessary, you can create different headers for different parts of a document by inserting a section break and formatting the header in the new section differently.

PROCEDURE 17.2. CREATING MULTIPLE HEADERS WITHIN A DOCUMENT.

1. Move the insertion point to the beginning of the first section where you want a new header to take effect.
2. If no section break exists, select **I**nsert | **B**reak and a section break option (**N**ext Page, usually).
3. Repeat Steps 1 and 2 to break the document into as many separate sections as you need.
4. Select **V**iew | **H**eader and Footer.
5. Use the Previous Header button or the Next Header button to move to the first header you want to format (this is very important because of the action of the Unlink button in the following step; you must work from front to back,

not vice versa). Note that the document section number is identified on the dotted header area outline, as shown in Figure 17.7.

6. Click the Unlink button to break the link between this header and the previous header.
7. Edit and format the header as needed.
8. Use the Next Header button to navigate to the next header you want to change.
9. Repeat Steps 6 through 8 to unlink and modify all the section headers you want to change.

SUPER NOTE

The preceding procedure applies equally to footers and headers. Just substitute the word "footers" when you're working with footers.

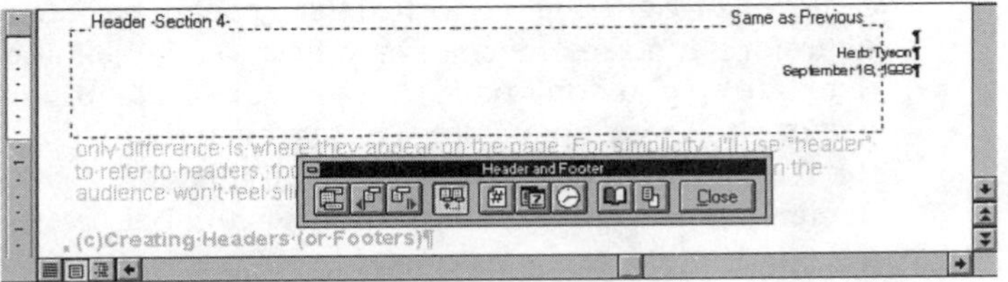

FIGURE 17.7.
The header outline tells you which section you're in.

SUPER NOTE

Word has only one built-in header style per document. The formatting associated with the style called header is document-wide. You can either use that style as a common denominator for all headers or create new styles for each distinctly formatted header. If you add header styles, base them all on the original header style (using the Based On option in the Define section of the Style dialog box). That way you maintain leverage over the base format (font, point size, line space, and so on, assuming they don't vary).

Different First Page

The Different First Page option is most often used to create a blank header or footer for the first page in a document or section. First pages of letters, reports, books, and other documents generally are handled differently from subsequent pages.

PROCEDURE 17.3. SETTING A DIFFERENT HEADER FOR THE FIRST PAGE OF A SECTION OR DOCUMENT.

1. Select **File**|Page Set**u**p.
2. Click the **L**ayout tab, if desired.
3. Click Different **F**irst Page to check it.
4. Click OK to close the Page Setup dialog box.
5. Use the procedure described under "Single Header" to create and format headers for the first and subsequent pages.

Different Left and Right Pages

The Different **O**dd and Even option is most often used for books, booklets, and other strictly-formatted documents.

PROCEDURE 17.4. CREATING DIFFERENT HEADERS FOR ODD AND EVEN PAGES.

1. Select **File**|Page Set**u**p.
2. Click the **L**ayout tab, if desired.
3. Click Different **O**dd and Even.
4. Click on OK to close the Page Setup dialog box.
5. Use the procedure described under Single Header to create and format odd and even page headers.

SUPER SIDEBAR

What happened to my header? If you select the Different Even and Odd Pages option in an established document with an existing header, the existing header becomes the odd page header and the even page header is blank. If you want to use the odd page header as a starting point, just copy the odd page header to the clipboard and paste it into the even page header.

PROCEDURE 17.5. COPYING AN ODD (OR EVEN) PAGE HEADER TO AN EVEN (OR ODD) PAGE WITHOUT LINKING.

1. Press PageDown to move to the next page's header (if you're editing a header, PageUp and PageDown scroll you to the next page's header, respectively).
2. Press Ctrl+A to select the whole header.
3. Press Ctrl+Insert to copy the header to the clipboard.
4. Press PageUp to move back to the previous page's header.
5. Press Ctrl+A to select the whole header.

6. Press Shift+Insert to paste the copy from the clipboard into place.
7. Adjust the format as necessary, add salt to taste, and *voilà*!

Header and Footer Toolbar

The Header and Footer Toolbar contains several tools for working in headers and footers, as shown in Figure 17.8. Each tool is described in Table 17.1.

FIGURE 17.8.
The Header and Footer Toolbar.

Table 17.1. Header and Footer Toolbar.

Tool	*Purpose*
Jump	Jumps between Header and Footer on the current page
Previous Section	Advances to the previous section's header or footer (if any)
Next Section	Advances to the next section's header or footer (if any)
Link/Unlink	Links or unlinks the current header or footer with the previous section
Page#	Inserts a {page} field
Date	Inserts a {date} field
Time	Inserts a {time} field
Page Setup	Displays the File Page Setup dialog box
Toggle Text Display	Toggles the display of the text area between dimmed (the default) and hidden
Close	Closes the header and footer area and restores the previous view

Chapter 18

Columns

Word enables you to print all or part of your document in multicolumn format. This format is sometimes called *newspaper columns* or *snaking columns*.

A multicolumn layout is often used for newsletters, academic journals, and magazines. Anyone who's ever taken an Evelyn Wood Reading Dynamics class knows why, too. Narrow columns can be read more quickly and with greater comprehension than the identical text presented in wider columns. When and if you're presenting difficult or complex materials or materials that must be read quickly (for example, written instructions handed out at a conference), bear this in mind.

In this chapter, I do not talk about *inserting* columns. That's because every document already has at least one column. Instead, the purpose of column formatting is to *change* the column formatting: adding a line between columns, changing the number of columns, or changing the spacing between columns.

Creating Multisection Documents

Column formatting is a section-formatting attribute. Each part of a document that has a different number of columns must be sectioned off using a section break.

PROCEDURE 18.1. INSERTING A SECTION BREAK.

1. Move the insertion point to where you want a column change.
2. Select **I**nsert | **B**reak.
3. Select one of the following types of section breaks and click OK:

   - Continuous—Inserts a section break only. Use this option when you want to use different numbers of columns on the same page. This option is frequently used to put a one-column title over a multicolumn article, as shown in Figure 18.1.

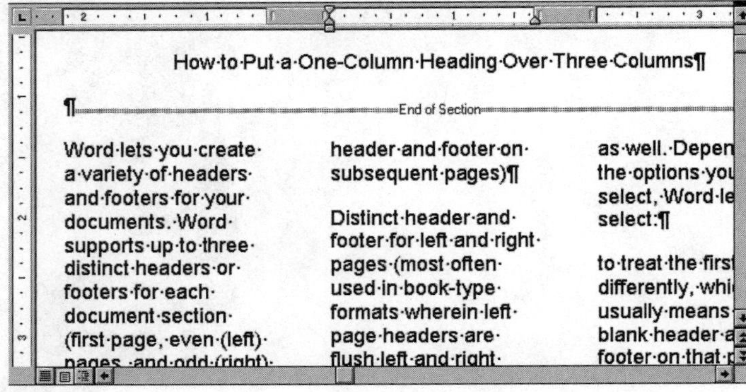

FIGURE 18.1.
Use a continuous section break to have different numbers of columns on the same page.

- **N**ext Page—Inserts a combination page and section break. Use this option when the columnar text must appear on a separate page.
- **E**ven Page—Inserts a combination page and section break, forcing the next page to be even. This option is often used in formatting journals and multipage newsletters.
- **O**dd Page—Inserts a combination page and section break, forcing the next page to be odd. This option is used in similar circumstances as the Even Page option.

SUPER NOTE

Once inserted, the four types of section breaks are visually indistinguishable. The resulting section breaks all appear to be the identical ASCII 12 character. If you need a particular type of section break, don't hesitate to delete the existing one and insert the type you need. It's easier than guessing.

SUPER TIP

The current section is displayed on the status bar, as shown in Figure 18.2. Use this information as a guide for knowing where you are in a multisection document.

FIGURE 18.2.
The status bar indicates the current page and section.

Page 2 Sec 4 2/4 At 4.3" Ln 9 Col 9 12:21 PM REC MRK EXT OVR WPH

Creating Multicolumn Sections

Once your document has been divided into distinct sections, you can format the different sections for different column layouts. You can set the number of columns using the toolbar or the menu. Use the toolbar if you want to set just the number of columns. Use the menu if you need to change other column formatting options as well.

PROCEDURE 18.2. CHANGING COLUMN LAYOUT USING THE TOOLBAR.

1. Position the insertion point anywhere inside the section you want to change; note the section number on the status bar.

2. Move the mouse cursor over the column tool, as shown in Figure 18.3, and press and hold the left mouse button.
3. Drag the column tool to highlight the number of columns you want to create (a maximum of 12 columns).
4. Release the mouse button when the number of columns highlighted is correct.

> **SUPER NOTE**
>
> For some odd reason, the column tool sometimes stops at six columns. If you need more than six columns and the tool lets you down, use the **F**ormat | **C**olumns approach described in the next section.

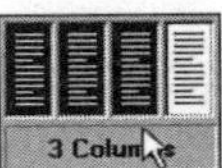

FIGURE 18.3.
The column tool.

If you're in Page Preview or Page Layout view, the text is immediately reformatted into the number of columns you selected, as shown in Figure 18.4. If you're in normal view, however, the width of the text changes to reflect the column width, but the columns aren't displayed side-by-side. As shown in Figure 18.5, the horizontal ruler changes to reflect the new formatting. If you're in normal view with Wrap to Window selected (**T**ools | **O**ptions | **V**iew), the text does not narrow, but the horizontal ruler does reflect the new formatting.

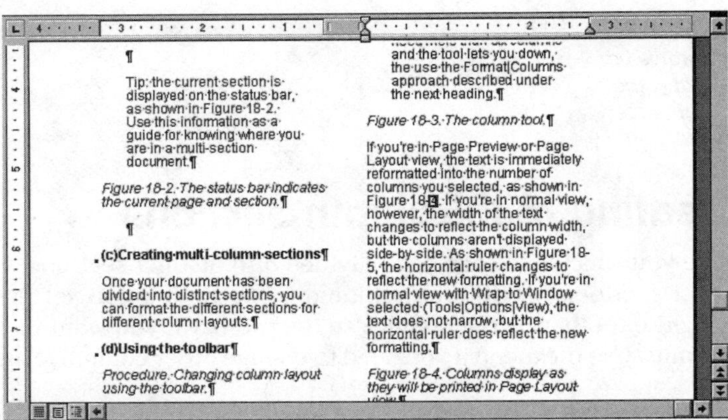

FIGURE 18.4.
In Page Layout view, columns display as they will be printed.

FIGURE 18.5.
In Normal view, the text narrows to show that you're editing a column narrower than the page.

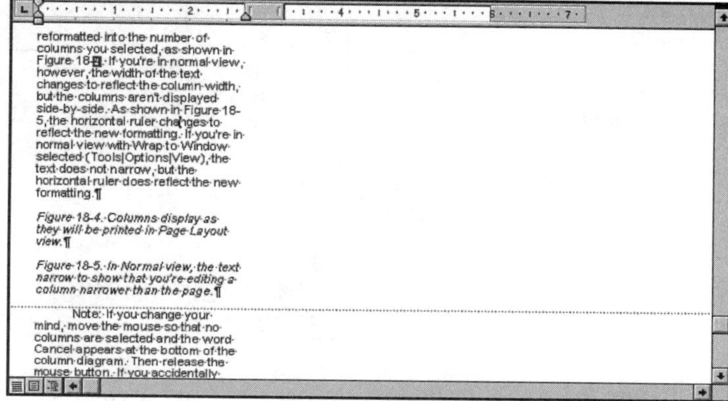

SUPER NOTE

If you change your mind, move the mouse so that no columns are selected and the word Cancel appears at the bottom of the column diagram. Then release the mouse button. If you accidentally change the formatting, you can also press Alt+Backspace to undo it.

You also can use the Format | Columns menu command to change the number of columns, as well as to vary the spacing between columns, to put lines between columns, to begin a column with a column break, or to insert a section break as you're creating the column structure.

PROCEDURE 18.3. CHANGING COLUMNS USING THE MENU.

1. Move the insertion point to the column where you want the change to take effect.
2. Select Format | Columns.
3. Type or spin the Number of Columns, or select a Preset if one of them matches what you want to do.
4. Using the Preview window as a guide, type or spin the column widths and distance between columns; this option has no effect on a one-column document. If necessary, deselect Equal Column Width to enable the width and spacing controls.
5. Select Line Between if you want a dividing line between columns (see Figure 18.6).

FIGURE 18.6.
The Line Between option draws a vertical line between columns.

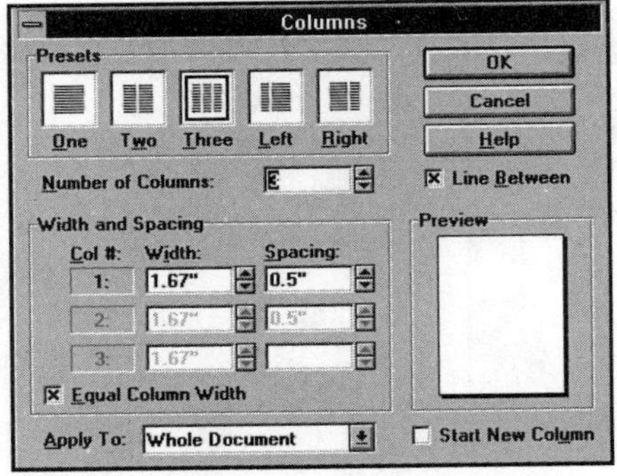

6. Select Start New Column to insert a column break (see note).
7. Select an Apply To option and click OK.

The Apply To options are

- This Section—If the document contains multiple sections, the change affects only the current section.
- This Point Forward—Word inserts a section break and applies the change to the new section.
- Whole Document—If the document contains multiple sections, the change is applied to all sections (the section breaks remain intact, however).

SUPER NOTE

Column breaks and section breaks are not the same thing. A section break marks the boundary between sections and is often used to separate sections that have different column layouts. A column break is analogous to a page break. It is used to force text to the top of the next available column. You might use a column break to force a heading into the next column to keep it from being stranded at the bottom of a column without the text it heads.

Balancing Columns

When you come to the end of a columnar document, you often are faced with the situation pictured in Figure 18.7. Ideally, you'd like all of the columns on the last page to be of equal lengths (usually). If so, there's an easy solution.

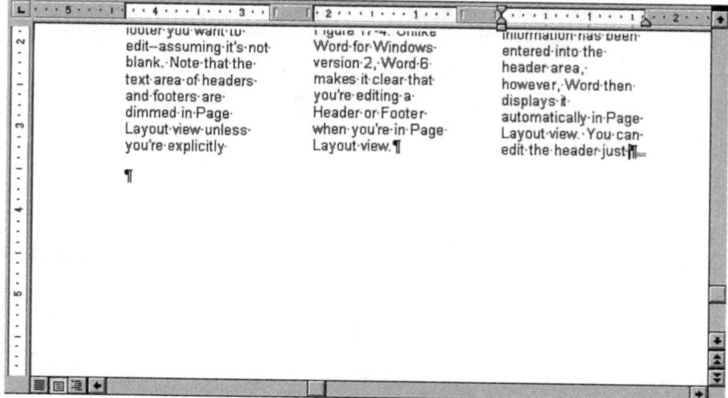

FIGURE 18.7.
Word makes it easy to balance columnar text on the last page.

PROCEDURE 18.4. BALANCING COLUMNS ON THE FINAL PAGE OF A MULTICOLUMN DOCUMENT.

1. Press Ctrl+End to go to the bottom of the document.
2. If there are any unneeded trailing paragraph breaks at the end of the text, delete them. The document should end with a single paragraph mark, as shown in Figure 18.7 (click the Show/Hide nonprinting characters tool in the Standard Toolbar, if necessary, to display paragraph marks).
3. **Select** View | **P**age Layout so you can see the effect of Step 3 instantly.
4. Select **I**nsert | **B**reak and double-click Con**t**inuous for an instant balancing act.

SUPER NOTE

Continuous is a *section* break, not a column break. So, what's going on? The trick is that you've ended the section, and Word now tidies up loose ends to make the rest of the page available for whatever else you have in store. Because it wouldn't do to have this little text effectively eating up the whole page (consuming the first column down to the bottom of the page), Word neatly divides the text among the columns.

Break It Up!

When working with columnar text, there are times when you want the text to do something other than just go with the flow, so to speak. You'll undoubtedly need not only the Continuous Section Break trick shown in the preceding section but a few other breaks as well. Keep the keystrokes in Table 18.1 in mind.

Table 18.1. Keys for inserting breaks.

Command	*Keys*	*Purpose*
Insert Section Break	Alt+I B, then	
	N	**N**ext Page
	T	Con**t**inuous
	E	**E**ven
	O	**O**dd—Separates sections of a document that have different numbers of columns (among other things)
Insert Page Break	Ctrl+Enter	Forces the following text to the next physical page
Insert Column Break	Ctrl+Shift+Enter	Forces the following text to the top of the next column

VI

Tables Workshop

One of the Word's most powerful features is its prowess with tables. Tables can also be one of Word's most frustrating features until you understand a few basics about why it works the way it does.

Tables have been strengthened considerably in this release of Word. In this workshop, you learn the ins and outs of tables, how to bring tables in from other applications (like spreadsheets), and how to use tables as minispreadsheets, complete with math formulae.

Chapter

19

Tables and AutoTable

Tables are one of Word's most powerful and useful tools. They're extremely flexible and easy to create and manipulate, both graphically and by using the menu. Best of all—for Word for Windows 2 upgraders—longstanding problems with tables that span multiple pages have been solved. For the tablephobe, a couple of new features can create tables and table formats automatically.

Automating Tables

As easy as it is to create tables in Word, Microsoft wanted to make it a little easier. Users upgrading from previous versions of Windows should take note of two additions to the Insert Table command: Wizard and AutoFormat. Both new offerings can automatically insert a formatted table for you, and Table AutoFormat can format a table you've already inserted. While neither is necessarily going to give you exactly what you want, both provide good starting points for users unfamiliar with the intricacies of creating and formatting Word tables.

SUPER TIP

Another new feature that simplifies working with tables is a tool called the Data Form. Available from the Database toolbar, this wonderful dialog box presents a data-entry form for entering data into a table. It uses the column headings from the first row to create a mini-database entry window. There, you just type the data and press Enter. See Chapter 38, "Data Files," in the Merging Workshop for additional information. Or, just activate the Database toolbar and click on the first tool (Data Form) to learn first-hand!

Table Wizard

The Table Wizard is a detailed Word macro written by Microsoft. The Table Wizard takes you through up to seven setup screens to create a table. You don't have to go through any of the normal table setup to use the Table Wizard. Just answer the questions and you emerge at the end with a neatly formatted table.

The Table Wizard can be used only to create a table, not to format a table you've already created, and not to create a table when converting text to a table. Despite the presence of the Wizard button in the Convert Text to Table dialog, the Table Wizard is unavailable from that dialog. Instead, to automatically format an existing table, use Table | Table AutoFormat.

PROCEDURE 19.1. USING THE TABLE WIZARD TO CREATE A TABLE.

1. Move the insertion point to where you want the table to appear, and make sure no text is selected.
2. Select Table | Insert Table.
3. Click Wizard. (Note: Word does not use the numbers of columns and rows you specify in the Insert Table dialog; instead, you provide that information directly to the Wizard.)
4. The Table Wizard dialog appears (see Figure 19.1); note that in the background your current window title bar has changed to an unnamed document window. Don't worry. Your document is safe. The Table Wizard has simply opened a new window to use as a workspace.

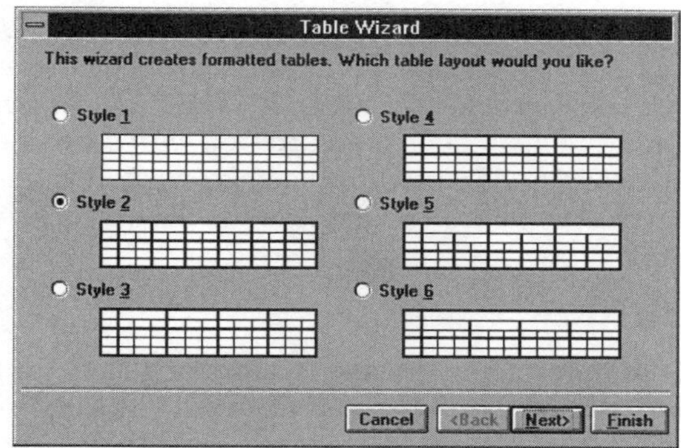

FIGURE 19.1.
The Table Wizard automatically creates and formats tables.

5. Select a table layout style. From this point forward, the Table Wizard offers slightly different choices depending on which layout style you select.
6. Click the Next button to proceed to the next setup dialog. You can click Back to go back and change a choice, Finish to accelerate to the end, or Cancel to cancel. If you select Cancel, the whole Insert Table command is canceled, not just the Wizard routine.
7. When you click Finish, Word completes the table and automatically runs the Table AutoFormat command (see Figure 19.2). Make any selections you want, and click OK.

SUPER NOTE

Even if you click Cancel, Word has already finished creating a basic table, and it will be copied to your document after you click Cancel. To remove a just-inserted table, press Ctrl+Z or Alt+Backspace (Undo).

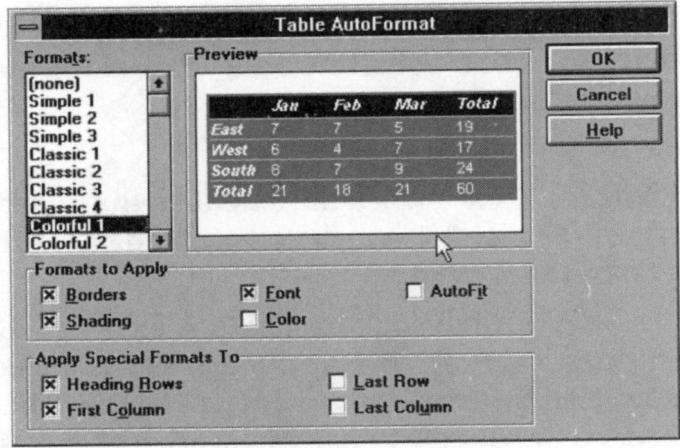

FIGURE 19.2.
Table AutoFormat offers 34 different table formats.

Depending on which style layout you select, the Table Wizard proceeds along slightly different paths. One possible point of confusion is the number of columns. Each time the Table Wizard asks for the number of columns, it's asking for the total number of columns, not the main columns bordered with dark lines. This is potentially confusing because the preview pictures seem to suggest otherwise. Some experimentation may be necessary before you achieve the desired results.

AutoFormat

The Table AutoFormat command is a format gallery for tables. The AutoFormat command offers a choice of 34 named formats. You can use the settings to create additional formats, but you cannot save the formats you create as named formats (wouldn't *that* have been nice?). When you select **T**able | **I**nsert Table, note the Table Format: item in the Insert Table dialog box. Initially, this changes to match the AutoFormat format you select, as shown in Figure 19.3.

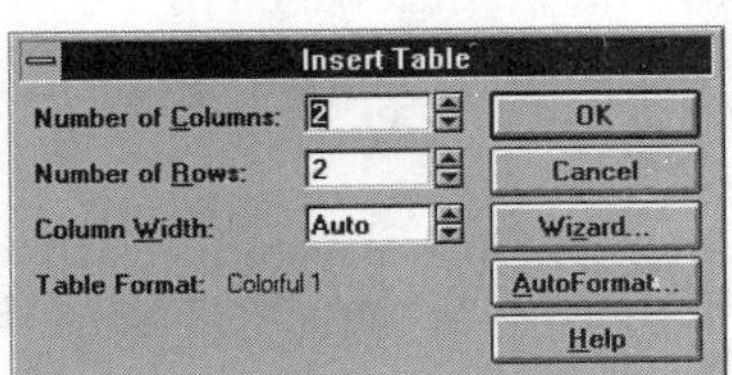

FIGURE 19.3.
The Insert Table dialog box shows if an automatic table format has been applied to the current table.

The Table AutoFormat command is somewhat more flexible and more useful than the Table Wizard. For one thing, you don't have to navigate a maze of setup dialogs. For another thing, the Table AutoFormat format can be changed at will, as well as applied to existing tables or when converting text to a table.

PROCEDURE 19.2. USING TABLE AUTOFORMAT TO FORMAT AS YOU CREATE A TABLE.

1. Select Table | Insert Table.
2. Select the number of columns, rows, and column width from the dialog box shown in Figure 19.3.
3. Click AutoFormat, for the dialog box shown in Figure 19.4.

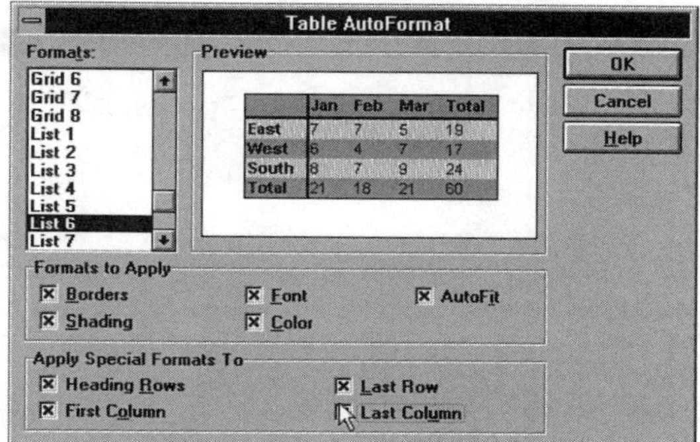

FIGURE 19.4.
The Table AutoFormat dialog is available from the Insert Table dialog.

4. Scroll through the Format list, observing changes in the preview screen as you go along. You can selectively choose the Formats to Apply and Apply Special Formats To options as you go along to see different effects.
5. When you find the format you want (remember, you can always change your mind or manually adjust the format), click OK to insert the table.

SUPER NOTE

If you deselect all of the Formats to Apply and Apply Special Formats To options, all 34 table formats are identical. The different formats are achieved by applying different types of fonts, borders, and shading.

When the table is finished, you can now go into it and start filling in the details. If you already have a table and want to experiment with different formats, you also can use the Table AutoFormat command to format it.

PROCEDURE 19.3. USING TABLE AUTOFORMAT TO FORMAT AN EXISTING TABLE.

1. Move the insertion point to anywhere inside the table; the Table AutoFormat formatting is applied to the entire table, even if only part of the table is selected.
2. Select Table | Table AutoFormat (or, click the right mouse button anywhere in the table and click Table AutoFormat, as shown in Figure 19.5).

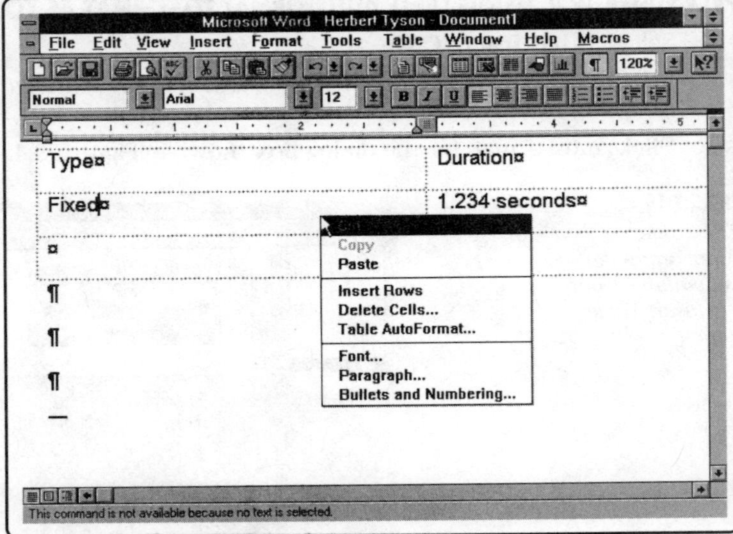

FIGURE 19.5. *Table AutoFormat is available from the table popup menu.*

3. Scroll through the Format list and make your selection.
4. To make the table automatically expand or shrink to fit the columns, click AutoFit. This is a very handy remedy to Word's tendency to create tables that span the entire margin from left to right.
5. Click OK.

Figure 19.6 shows a table created using the Table button on the toolbar, and the resulting formatting from a variety of formats on the list. Even if Table AutoFormat doesn't produce *exactly* the format you want, it's often much easier to modify an already-formatted table than to format a table from scratch.

Creating a New Table

If you decide to forego the Wizard and Table AutoFormat, Word lets you create tables the old-fashioned way using the standard toolbar or using the menu. Using the menu, you have more control over the column dimensions. However, it's often easier to use the toolbar to create the table, and then use the mouse to resize the columns as needed.

Creating a New Table Using the Toolbar

The standard toolbar provides a GUI way to create tables. Unless you have very precise specifications for your table, you will probably find the toolbar method much more intuitive and direct than using the menu.

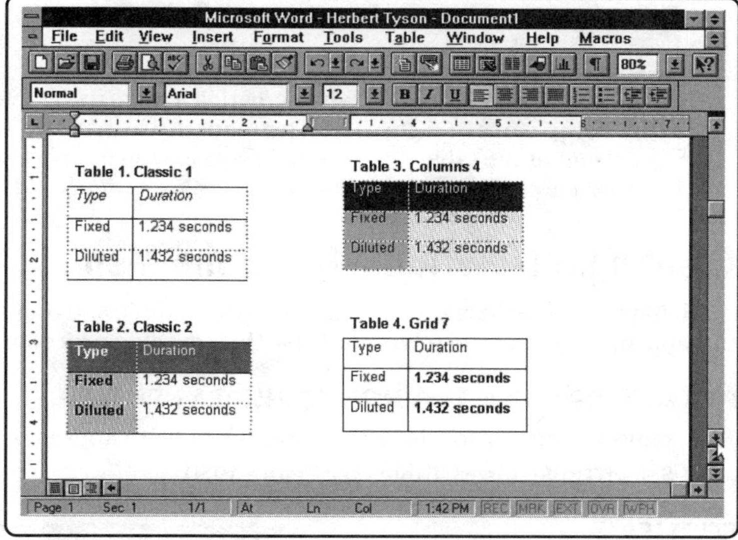

FIGURE 19.6.
Table AutoFormat formatting applied in a variety of ways to the same table.

PROCEDURE 19.4. USING THE TOOLBAR TO CREATE A NEW TABLE.

1. Move the cursor to where you want the table to appear.
2. Move the mouse to the table button (see Figure 19.7).

FIGURE 19.7.
Use the Table button to automatically insert a table.

3. Press the left mouse button; drag down and to the right.
4. A grid appears, as shown in Figure 19.8; drag the grid until the diagram matches the table you want to create. The darkened area indicates the number of rows and columns that will be created in the resulting table.

FIGURE 19.8.
The table grid makes creating a table visually intuitive.

5. Release the mouse button to create the table.

SUPER NOTE

If you change your mind while creating a table using the table button, drag the mouse up and to the left until the word Cancel appears in the bottom of the table diagram; then release the mouse button.

Creating a New Table Using the Menu

If you have exact dimensions for a uniform-width table and don't particularly like the GUI approach, you can use Word's Table | Insert Table procedure to create a table.

PROCEDURE 19.5. USING THE MENU TO INSERT A NEW TABLE.

1. Move the cursor to where you want the table to appear.
2. Select Table | Insert Table (see Figure 19.9).

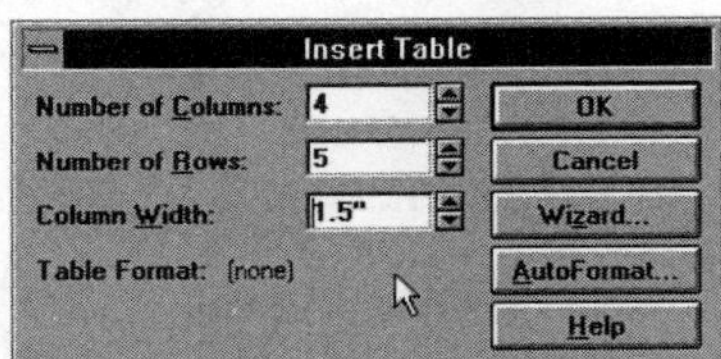

FIGURE 19.9.
The Insert Table dialog box.

3. Select the number of columns and rows.
4. Select the Column Width. (Note: Word lets you set the width only for all columns; if you want columns of different widths you can adjust them after the table has been created, or use the tip below.)
5. Click OK.

Creating a New Table with Different Column Widths

When using the Table button on the toolbar, or using the Insert Table command, Word's Insert Table command creates a table *seemingly* only with uniform column widths. You can specify that width using the Table | Insert Table command, but there is no obvious way to specify different widths for different columns while creating. You instead must edit the table after it's created to establish different column widths. You *could*, as described in the tip under "Converting Text to Tables," insert tabs in an otherwise empty paragraph (one for each column—not one for each column boundary) and define tab stops where you want each column to end. However, it may not be worth the trouble. Then again, maybe it would be.

PROCEDURE 19.6. CREATING A TABLE WITH DIFFERENT COLUMN WIDTHS.

1. Insert a paragraph mark where you want the table to be.
2. Tap the Tab key once for each column boundary you want in the table (four tabs for a five-column table, five tabs for a six-column table, and so forth).
3. Use the mouse to insert tab stops on the ruler line where you want the right side of each column to appear, as shown in Figure 19.10 (for example, one tab stop for each column, despite the fact that you end up with one fewer tabs).
4. Select the paragraph.
5. Click the Table button on the Standard toolbar (or select Table|Insert Table).

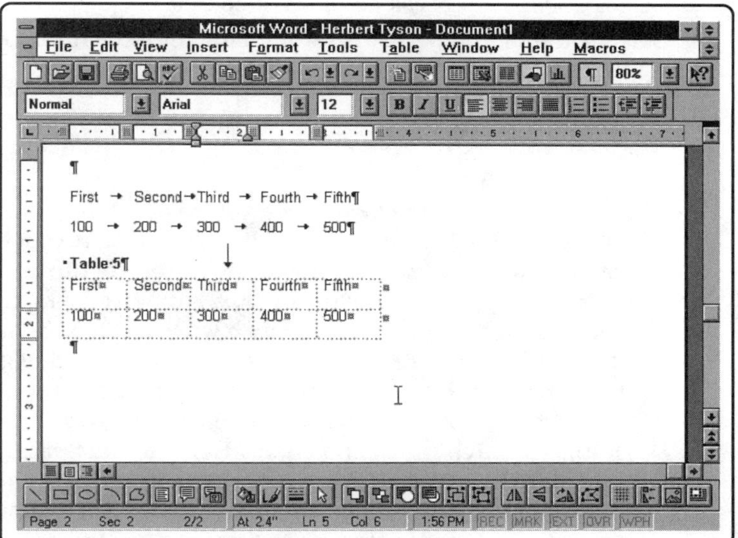

FIGURE 19.10.
Use five tabs and six tabstops to trick Word into automatically formatting a six-column table correctly.

Converting Text to Tables

Word lets you convert text to tables. Word creates columns where you currently have commas or tabs, and it will create rows where you currently have paragraph marks. If Word detects commas and tabs, it prompts you to say how it should create the table.

PROCEDURE 19.7. CONVERTING TEXT TO A TABLE.

1. Select the text you want to convert.
2. Click the Table button in the toolbar.
3. If necessary, Word displays the dialog box shown in Figure 19.11:

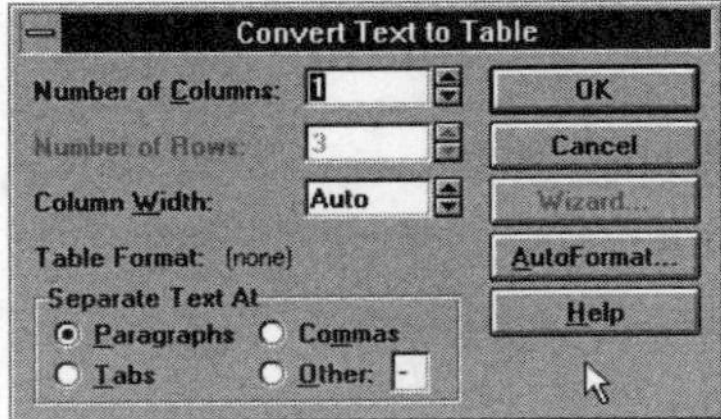

FIGURE 19.11.
When Word can't deduce the format, it prompts you to decide.

- Select Paragraph Marks to create a one-column table with one cell per row.
- Select Tabs to break columns at tabs.
- Select Commas to break columns at commas.
- Select Other and type a separator character if the other options aren't appropriate.

SUPER TIP

A common problem when converting text to tables is the sometimes-odd column widths that are created. If the selected text does not contain any explicit tab settings, Word bases the column widths on the default tab stops in the Format Tabs dialog box. For most users, this results in columns that are only one-half inch wide—which is unacceptably narrow. You can minimize the amount of column-dragging you have to perform by setting tabs for the text selection before you click the table button. Once you've explicitly set some tabs, Word sets the column widths to match the tab positions. Hint: Set the tabs at what will become the right edges of each column—not the left edges—including a tab for the end of the last column. Otherwise, the final column probably will be too wide. Yes, this is counterintuitive and contrary to how tabs are normally used. If it were logical and intuitive, however, you wouldn't need this book to find out about it!

SUPER TIP

If you convert text to a table and discover you don't like the result, or if it was done improperly, select Edit | Undo Insert Table. While converting table-to-text is an alternative, you frequently cannot use table-to-text to restore the text to its exact original format.

SUPER UPGRADE NOTE

In previous versions of Word for Windows, if the text to be converted contained any field codes, Word created only single-column tables. That limitation has been removed in Word 6.

Converting Tables to Text

Word lets you convert selected rows or a whole table to text. This can be handy when preparing data for other applications that don't support Word's tables. When you import data from Excel, Word automatically converts it into a table, whether you want it that way or not. This feature is handy for converting it back into text so you can format it as you need.

PROCEDURE 19.8. CONVERTING A TABLE TO TEXT.

1. Select the whole table or just the rows you want to convert.
2. Select Table | Convert Table to Text.
3. Word offers to separate the entries in the dialog box shown in Figure 19.12:

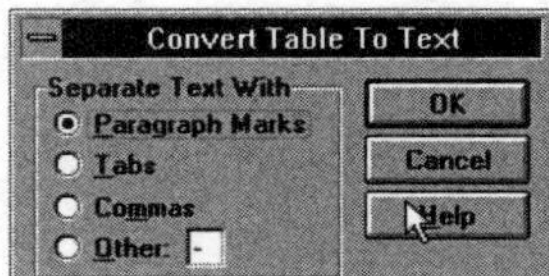

FIGURE 19.12.
Word offers to separate columns with paragraph marks, tabs, or commas.

- Select Paragraph Marks to convert each table cell into a separate paragraph.
- Select Tabs to create one paragraph per row, with each item separated by tabs.
- Select Commas to create one paragraph per row, with each item separated by commas.
- Select Other, and type a different separator to create one paragraph per row, with each item separated by that character.

Modifying Table Columns and Rows

Once a table has been inserted, you can edit the format of a table directly using the mouse, the rulers, or indirectly using the menu.

Changing Column Widths Using the Mouse

You can use the mouse to change column widths and row (cell) heights, the latter only in Page Layout or Print Preview mode.

SUPER NOTE

If you change your mind *while* dragging a column, press Esc to cancel the operation. If you change your mind *after* dragging, or discover that you don't like the result, press Alt+Backspace (Edit|Undo) to undo it.

PROCEDURE 19.9. USING THE MOUSE TO CHANGE COLUMN WIDTH.

1. To change the column widths of some rows, but not all, select just the rows you want to change; if you want to change the whole table, ensure that nothing is selected or that the whole table is selected.
2. Move the mouse pointer over a column boundary until the pointer assumes a column-adjust shape, as shown in Figure 19.13.

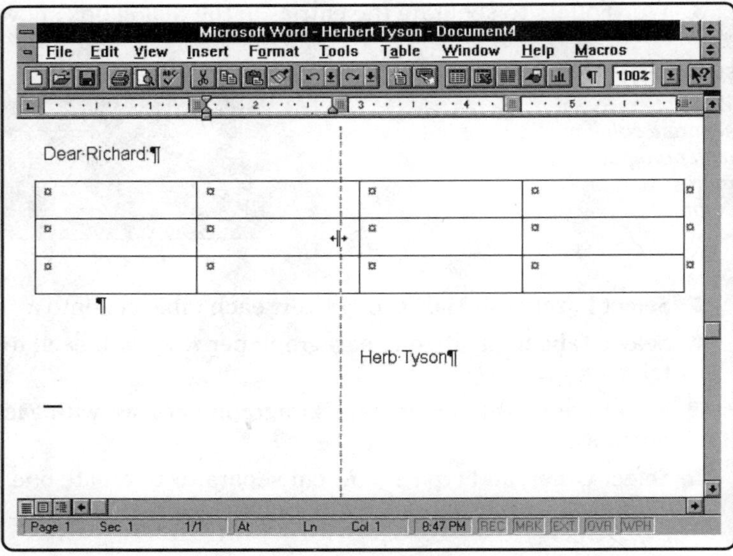

FIGURE 19.13. *The mouse pointer in column-adjust position.*

3. To adjust the current column while leaving other column widths alone, press the left mouse button and drag the column boundary where you want it to go (see Figure 19.14).

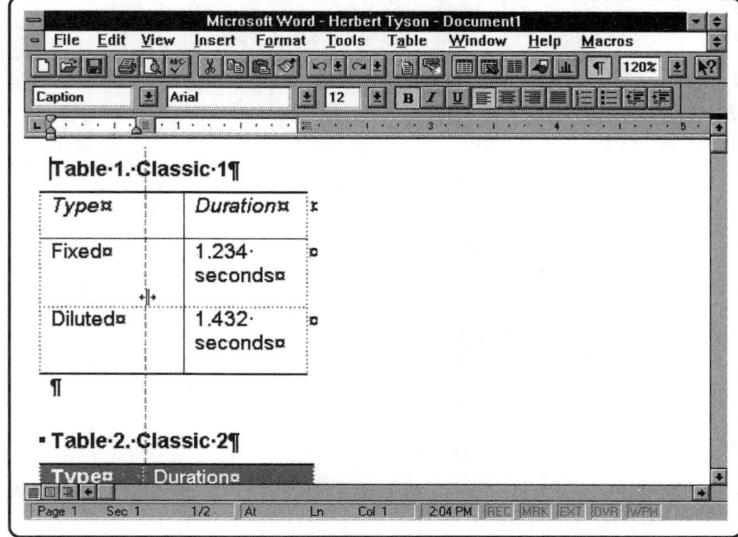

FIGURE 19.14.
Dragging a column with no keys pressed leaves the other column dimensions untouched.

You can drag columns using either the column division lines in the table, or using the column markers on the ruler line. Both methods have the following effects:

- As you drag one column boundary, all other columns to the right are shifted as you drag, and compressed or expanded (keeping their relative sizes, if different) in the remaining space to the right; the right edge of the table remains fixed.
- Just One Variation. To change just a single *column*, leaving all other column widths unchanged, press Ctrl+Shift and the left mouse button to drag. The right edge of the table is adjusted by the amount you widen or narrow the single column.
- Just Two Variation. To drag just a single *boundary*, locking the rest of the table in place, press Shift and the left mouse button to drag. This operation changes the relative widths of just the two columns adjacent to the boundary you are dragging. The other columns remain fixed, as does the overall table width.
- Row Heading Variation. To cause all columns to the right to be equally divided in the remaining space (even if they're different to begin with), press Ctrl and the left mouse button to drag. Columns to the right are resized so that they become and remain equal in width to each other. The overall table width does not change. This feature is handy when you need to size the first column differently for row headings, but want the rest of the columns to be equal in width.
- Show Measurement. Hold down the Alt key while using any of these methods to make Word display the column dimensions on the horizontal ruler while you're dragging (see Figure 19.15).

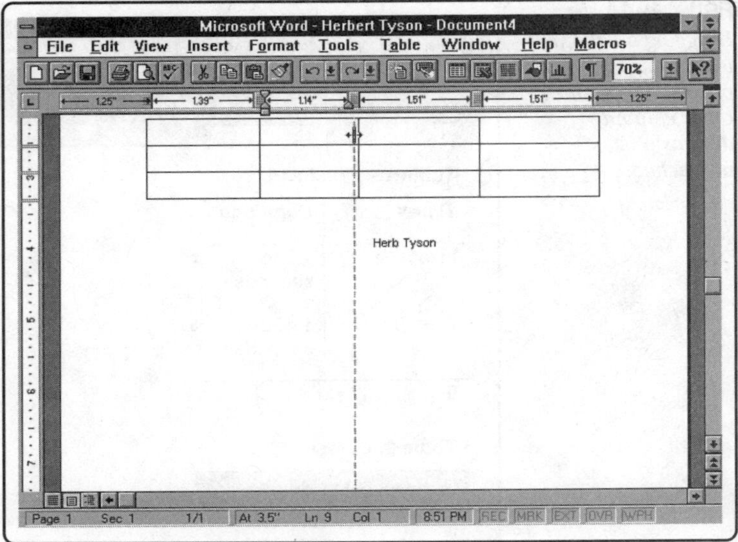

FIGURE 19.15.
Hold down the Alt key while adjusting column widths to display the exact measurements.

SUPER TIP

If you have difficulty getting the column-adjust mouse pointer to display, you can drag the column markers on the ruler, instead of dragging the column boundaries. Everything works exactly the same regardless of which method you use.

Modifying Column Width Using the Menu

While not as cute, you can use the menu to modify table columns. Some users find this method easier, some harder. You decide.

PROCEDURE 19.10. MODIFYING COLUMNS WITH THE MENU.

1. Select the rows you want to modify.
2. Select T**a**ble|Cell Height and **W**idth, as shown in Figure 19.16.
3. Click the **C**olumn tab.
4. To adjust all columns simultaneously, observe that the dialog box first shows that you are adjusting the widths of all columns.
5. To adjust a single column, click the Next Column or Previous Column button until the column you want to adjust is highlighted.
6. Type or spin the **W**idth you want to use.

7. Select the Space Between Columns (you are allowed just one value for the entire row).
8. Repeat Steps 5 and 6 to adjust each column width, as needed.
9. Click OK.

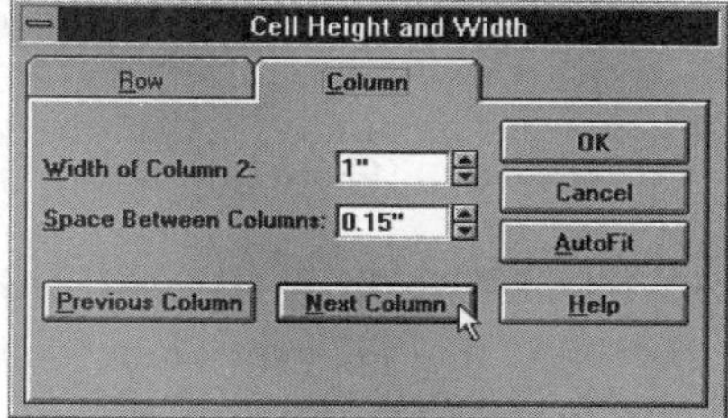

FIGURE 19.16.
The Cell Height and Width dialog box.

SUPER TIP

You can click the right mouse button in the table in lieu of going up to the menu. The Cell Height and Width option is available from the popup menu, as shown in Figure 19.17.

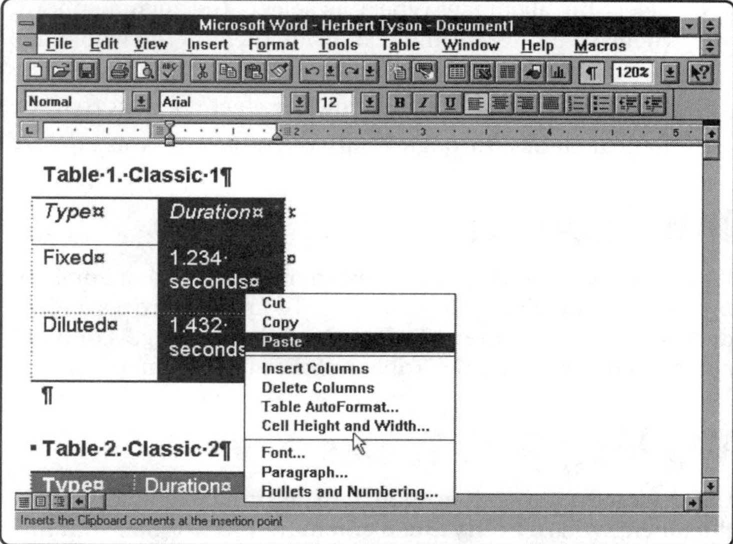

FIGURE 19.17.
Select the Cell Height and Width dialog box from the table popup menu.

Modifying Row Format

One of Word's most overlooked features is the menu command for changing row format. One reason it's often overlooked is that the command name is a misnomer. It's in the Row tab in the Cell Height and Width dialog box. Row height—something that seemingly takes care of itself in tables—is something that users seldom have need to change. What about centering a whole table, however? When you use the paragraph center alignment, the items within each cell get centered, but not the table as a whole. Well, care to guess where the ability to center a table has been hiding all this time? That's right, in the Table | Cell Height and Width dialog box, in the Row tab!

PROCEDURE 19.11. MODIFYING ROW FORMATTING.

1. Select the part(s) of the table you want to modify.
2. Select Table | Cell Height and Width dialog box and click the Row tab.
3. Type or spin a value for Indent from Left; this value offsets the entire table or selected rows (not the text in the cells) to the right. Use a negative value to offset to the left. Note: This value is ignored if the table is right-aligned.
4. Select a row height option (Auto: automatically adjust row height for font height and line spacing of text inside; At Least: similar to automatic, but the row height is never below the height you specify; Exact: height always exactly the height you specify).
5. Type or spin the height you want (not available for Auto).
6. Select the alignment type; this selects the alignment for the table rows themselves, not for the text inside them (if the whole table is selected, you can use the alignment type to center the entire table between the margins).
7. Use Previous Row or Next Row to select the next row you want to modify.
8. Repeat Steps 3 through 7 until the table format is correct.

Table Borders

Word lets you use the Format | Borders and Shading command to shade and draw borders around all or part of a table. To create borders and/or shading, see the Borders heading in Chapter 12, "Paragraph Formatting." For a quick start with borders and shading, try using the Table AutoFormat command.

Working with Tables

Unfortunately, it's seldom enough to just create a table. Once the dang things are in a document, you're pretty much committed to working with them to make them work for you. This section discusses a variety of techniques for working with and manipulating tables.

Using Gridlines

When working with tables, it is highly recommended that you use gridlines. Gridlines show you where the table cells are. When editing a table without borders, gridlines are essential, showing you where to place the mouse cursor to drag parts of the table. They also alert you to potential formatting problems, possibly saving a little on wasted paper.

PROCEDURE 19.12. DISPLAYING TABLE GRIDLINES.

1. Select Table | Gridlines.

Inserting Tabs into a Table

Users quickly discover that pressing the Tab key while in a table advances to the next cell. Pressing Shift+Tab moves to the previous cell. Okay, so what if you really want to enter a tab into a cell? What then?

To insert an actual tab into a table cell, press Ctrl+Tab.

Splitting Tables

Occasionally you may need to break a table into multiple tables. Word lets you split a table between rows, but not between columns (see Figure 19.18).

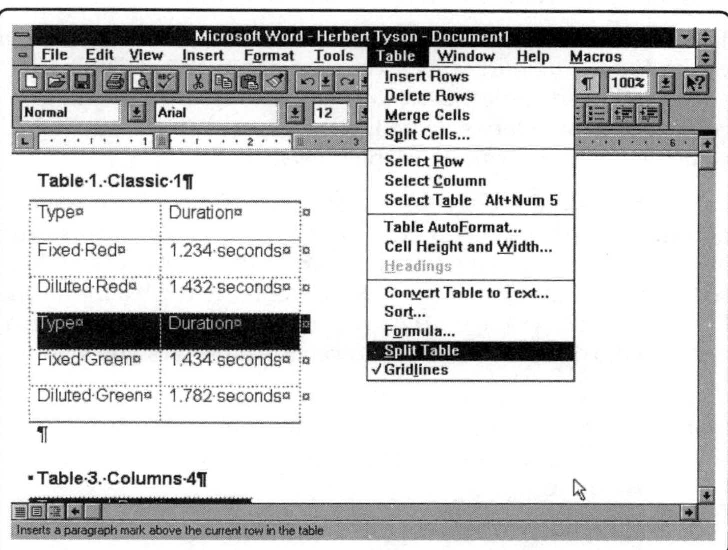

FIGURE 19.18.
Breaking a table between columns.

PROCEDURE 19.13. SPLITTING A TABLE INTO TWO TABLES.

1. Move the insertion point into any cell in the row that you want to be the top of the bottom table.
2. Select Table | Split Table.
3. Word breaks the table, sends rows above the cursor to a top table, and rows at or below the cursor into a bottom table. Word adds a paragraph break between the two new tables.

Inserting Text Before a Table at the Top of a Document

Using Word for Windows 2, if you inserted a table at the very beginning of a document—with no paragraph marker before the table—you were unable to insert nontable text before the table without using the Table | Split Table command, or inserting a break of some kind while in the first cell. Using Word 6, however, you can now insert a carriage return before the table simply by pressing Enter at the beginning of the first cell.

So, what if you really wanted to insert a paragraph mark at the beginning of the first cell, instead of creating space before the table? Simple. Press Enter; then move the cursor down into the first cell and press Enter again. Pressing Enter in the first cell inserts a paragraph marker ahead of the table *only* when the table is at the very top of the document. Otherwise, it has the expected effect of inserting a paragraph marker.

Selecting Tables and Table Parts

To select an entire table, the easiest method is to press Alt+5 on the numeric pad. If you're fond of menus, you can choose Table | Select Table from the menu. Similarly, you can choose Table | Select Row or Table | Select Column from the menu to select a column or a row. Once selected, you can press Shift+Left, Right, Down, or Up to select adjacent columns or rows, respectively.

If you're rodent-driven, you also can use the mouse. To select the entire table, position the mouse in the first cell (upper left) and drag (press and hold the left mouse button) diagonally to the last cell (lower right). To select a table row, move the mouse so that the pointer is just outside the table (to the left), with the pointer shown as in Figure 19.19. Click to select the row. To select multiple rows, press the left mouse button and drag up or down to select however many rows you want.

To select a column table, position the mouse over the column you want to select, so that the pointer changes to the column selection pointer shown in Figure 19.20. To select multiple columns, drag the selection to the left or right while holding down the left mouse button.

FIGURE 19.19.
Click in the selection bar to select a row.

Table·1.·Classic·1¶

Type¤	Duration¤
Fixed·Red¤	1.234·seconds¤
Diluted·Red¤	1.432·seconds¤
Type¤	Duration¤
Fixed·Green¤	1.434·seconds¤
Diluted·Green¤	1.782·seconds¤

¶

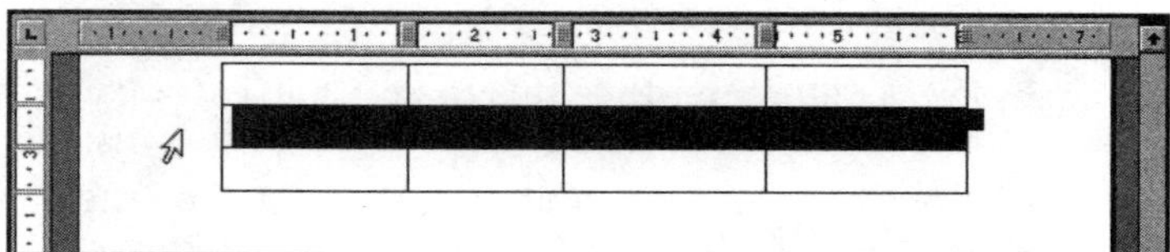

FIGURE 19.20.
Click when the column selector pointer displays to select a column.

To select a single cell, you need to distinguish between selecting the cell and the cell contents. To select the cell's contents, double-click. To select the cell as well as its contents, then triple-click. Once a cell is selected, you can extend the selection in the same row or column by dragging the selection where you want it to go, or by pressing Shift+Click where you want the selection to end.

Deleting Tables and Table Parts

Word lets you selectively delete any part or all of a table.

Deleting a Whole Table

If you select a whole table and press the Delete key, the table's contents get zapped, but the table structure remains in place. That turns out to be a good way to empty out a table so you can set it for the next course. Deleting a whole table—lock, stock, and borders—can be done in several ways, none of them perfectly obvious or intuitive.

PROCEDURE 19.14. CUTTING A TABLE TO THE CLIPBOARD (CUTTING).

1. Select the whole table.
2. Press Shift+Delete, or click the scissors icon.

If you don't want to disturb what's in the clipboard, then you can use the **D**elete Rows command from the menu. For some inexplicable reason, however, Microsoft omitted the **D**elete Rows command from the table popup (right mouse button) menu when the whole table is selected. It's there when you select a single row, or multiple rows, but not when you select all of the rows. So you'll have to do the carpal tunnel twist if you're using a mouse.

PROCEDURE 19.15. DELETING A TABLE USING THE MENU.

1. Select the whole table.
2. Select Table | Delete Rows.

SUPER TIP

If you're not fond of having to use the clipboard, mouse, and menu to delete a table, you can delete a table by selecting all of the table and a single paragraph mark before or after the table and then pressing the Delete key. For example:

1. Press Enter after the table to insert an extra paragraph marker (if you already have an extra one there, then use it instead).
2. Move back into the table and press Alt+5 on the number pad.
3. Press Shift and cursor down to additionally select the empty paragraph marker that follows the table.
4. Press the Delete key.

SUPER

While seemingly more steps, I find that this technique ends up being faster since I don't have to deal with the table menu nor disturb my usually-occupied clipboard. For me, the table menu is so cluttered and the placement of items on it is so unintuitive that it's faster to just use this brute-force technique than it is to have to scan the table menu for the **D**elete Rows command. Too bad Microsoft didn't put it on the popup menu, where it would be convenient.

Deleting Cells

You can delete the contents of cells as well as cells. For the most part, using the Delete key deletes the contents, while using Cut (Shift+Delete) deletes the whole structure (the row or column and its contents). An exception to this is with cells. If only part of a row or column is selected (one or more cells, but not the entire row or column), Delete and Cut both delete just the contents.

PROCEDURE 19.16. DELETING TABLE CELLS.

1. Select the cell(s) you want to delete.
2. Select Table | Delete Cells.

3. If cells are below and to the right of the selected cell(s), Word prompts for how they are to be treated, as shown in Figure 19.21:

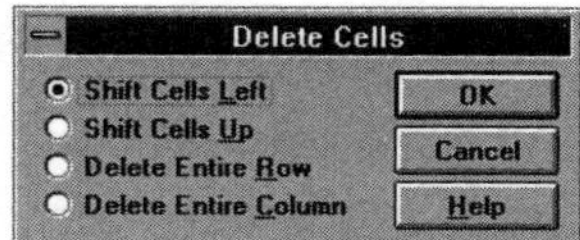

FIGURE 19.21.
When deleting cells, Word prompts you to indicate how you want the remaining cells to be handled.

- Select Shift Cells **L**eft to cause cells to the right to move leftward.
- Select Shift Cells **U**p to cause cells below to move up.
- Select Delete Entire **R**ow to delete the whole row.
- Select Delete Entire **C**olumn to delete the whole column.

Deleting Columns

To delete the contents of a column, select the column and press Delete. To delete a whole column (or columns), select the column(s) and press Shift+Delete. The latter moves the deleted columns into the clipboard. You can leave your clipboard's contents alone by using the menu or popup Delete **C**olumns command.

PROCEDURE 19.17. DELETING TABLE COLUMNS.

1. Select the column(s) you want to delete.
2. Select T**a**ble | **D**elete Columns (from the menu or from the right mouse button popup).

Deleting Rows

To delete the contents of a row, select the row and press Delete. To delete a whole row (or rows), select the row(s) and press Shift+Delete. As is the case with columns and the whole table, the latter moves the deleted rows into the clipboard. To remove columns without using the clipboard, use the **D**elete Rows command in the table menu or on the table popup menu.

PROCEDURE 19.18. DELETING TABLE ROWS.

1. Select the row(s) you want to delete.
2. Select T**a**ble | **D**elete Rows.

Inserting Table Parts

Word also lets you insert parts of tables into an existing table—additional rows, columns, or cells.

Inserting Cells

PROCEDURE 19.19. INSERTING CELLS.

1. Select a cell in the row or column where you want to insert a new cell.
2. Click the Table (Insert Cells) button.

> **SUPER NOTE**
>
> When ToolTips are turned on (see Chapter 48, "Customizing Toolbars"), the exact action to be performed by the Table button is displayed when you move the mouse button over the button on the toolbar. In this instance, the ToolTip displays the text `Insert Cells`.

3. If there is ambiguity about what to do with existing cells, Word prompts you for additional instructions, as shown in Figure 19.22.

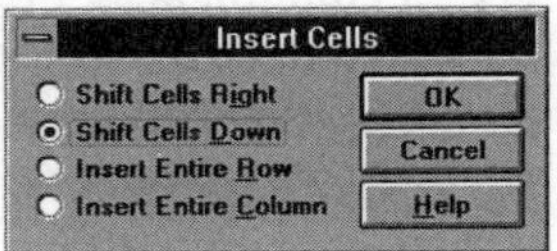

FIGURE 19.22. *Word prompts to see how you want adjacent cells adjusted.*

> **SUPER TIP**
>
> If you need more than one cell inserted, select the number of cells you want created, assuming enough cells exist. For example, to create three new cells, select three existing cells.

Inserting Rows

PROCEDURE 19.20. INSERTING ROWS.

1. Select one or more rows to create the same number of new rows.
2. Click the Table (Insert Rows) button.

> **SUPER TIP**
>
> To add an additional row to the end of a table (for example, when you're entering data into a table), just press the Tab key. When you press the

Tab key in the last cell of a table, Word doesn't have a next cell to go to, so it creates a new row!

Inserting Columns

PROCEDURE 19.21. INSERTING COLUMNS.

1. Select one or more columns to create the same number of new columns.
2. Click the Table (Insert Columns) button.

Moving and Copying Table Parts

Cells, rows, and columns can be moved around and copied just as in ordinary editing.

Moving Columns

PROCEDURE 19.22. MOVING COLUMNS.

1. Select the column or columns you want to move.
2. Drag the selection into the destination column.

SUPER RESULT

The column being moved "pushes" the destination column to the right, with no net change in the number of columns.

SUPER NOTE

Always drag the column into the column you want pushed to the right. If you want to move a column to the right end, then drag it to the right edge of the table rather than into the far right column.

Moving and Copying Columns

PROCEDURE 19.23. MOVING COLUMNS.

1. Select the column or columns you want to move.
2. Drag the selection into the destination column.

SUPER RESULT

The column being moved "pushes" the destination column to the right, with no net change in the number of columns.

To copy a column, press the Ctrl key while dragging. The column(s) is inserted, as before, but the original column remains where it was.

SUPER NOTE

Always drag the column into the column you want pushed to the right. If you want to move a column to the right end, the drag it to the right edge of the table rather than into the far right column.

Moving and Copying Rows

PROCEDURE 19.24. MOVING ROWS.

1. Select the row or rows you want to move.
2. Drag the selection into the destination row.

SUPER RESULT

The row being moved "pushes" the destination row down, with no net change in the number of rows.

To copy a row, press the Ctrl key while dragging. The row(s) are inserted, as before, but the original row remains where it was.

SUPER NOTE

Always drag the row into the row you want pushed down. If you want to move a row to the bottom, drag it to the bottom edge of the table rather than into the bottom row.

Moving and Copying Cells

PROCEDURE 19.25. MOVING CELLS.

1. Select the cell or cells you want to move.
2. Drag the selection into the destination cell.

SUPER RESULT

The cell(s) being moved will overwrite the destination cell(s).

To copy a cell or cells, press the Ctrl key while dragging. The cell(s) overwrite the destination cell, as before, and the original cell that was copied remains where it was.

Merging Cells

Sometimes it's useful to turn multiple cells within a row into a single cell. I do this when I've created a table and want to use the top few rows as headers for what follows. I might merge the top row into one big cell for an overall title, and then merge the second row into subheads. It's also useful to create borders of varying thicknesses to accentuate the table divisions, as shown in Table 19.1.

Table 19.1. Merging table cells for heading and subheading.

Grain Sources for the Acme Grain Company				
	United States		*Canada*	
	Corn	Barley	Corn	Barley
1990	100	70	80	65
1995	105	75	87	83

In Table 19.1, the top row was merged into a single cell. The *Corn* and *Barley* column components were merged for each country, providing a convenient country heading.

If a group of cells already contains text, the contents of each cell is placed into a separate paragraph within the merged cell. If no text exists, Word still inserts a paragraph marker for each original cell.

Splitting Cells

You might never notice the capability, but Word also lets you split a cell to match cells in the adjoining row. As shown in Figure 19.23, the Split Cells option is available from the Table menu. The Split Cells option splits the selected cell into the original cell divisions over the column area covered. Effectively, the Split Cells option undoes the merge for the selected cells. If the cell has no adjoining rows to guide the split, Word divides the cell exactly in half.

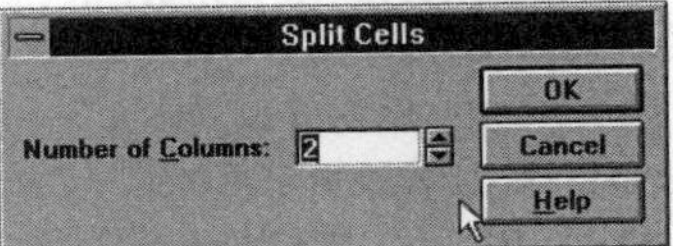

FIGURE 19.23.
The Split Cells dialog box.

When you split a cell into multiple cells, Word tries to allocate existing text to the new cells from end to start. If you have *n* paragraph marks, Word creates *n+1* cell entries. Word "carves" text between the end of the cell and the previous paragraph marker into new cell entries. Word then counts the number of entries and fills only that number of cells from right to left. If Word detects more data entries than available cells, all text to the left of what was used for the second entry becomes the entry for the first cell. If all this sounds a bit confusing, you're not alone. You really need to experience it to understand it. If it's an experience you'd rather forego—nobody blames you one little bit. If you're splitting to undo a merge and haven't done any interim editing, splitting usually restores your table as it was prior to the merge. If you've done some editing, the results may be pretty bizarre. If you're just a curiosity-seeker, you've come to the right place!

Working with Multipage Tables

Word 6 offers several enhancements over previous versions for tables that span multiple pages. In particular, Word gives you the option to break rows at page breaks. This is especially useful in technical documents, many of which use extended amounts of text in tables. Word also provides the ability to designate certain rows as headings that repeat at the top of each page.

Controlling How Tables and Rows Break Across Different Pages

Word provides the option to selectively allow rows to break (or not) across different pages. In text-based tables, this ability is crucial. Some table rows, in fact, span multiple pages. In technical and statistical tables, on the other hand, you often don't want the table to break at all.

PROCEDURE 19.26. PREVENTING A TABLE FROM BREAKING ACROSS DIFFERENT PAGES.

1. Select the table (press Alt+5 on the number pad, or choose **Table | Select Table** from the menu).

2. Choose Format | Paragraph.
3. Click Text Flow.
4. Select the Keep with Next option.
5. Click OK.

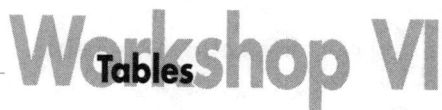

SUPER NOTE

Intuitively, you might select the Keep Together option. Nice try, as they say. The problem is that different table cells qualify as different paragraphs. Thus, all the Keep Together option does is keep a single cell on the same page. Instead, giving all of the "paragraphs" (cells) in a table the Keep with Next attribute effectively keeps the table from breaking across a page.

You also can tell Word to allow or disallow breaking table rows (all or some) across a page. Consider, for example, a multipage text table. Tables are a very handy format for organizing certain kinds of information. Often, however, a single cell can contain many lines of text. If, as was the case in previous versions of Word for Windows, you can't break a row across different pages, tables cease being a handy format for text tables. Fortunately, Word 6 enables you to selectively (or all at once) allow or prevent rows from breaking across different pages.

PROCEDURE 19.27. CONTROLLING WHETHER ROWS BREAK ACROSS DIFFERENT PAGES.

1. Move the insertion point into the table you want to format.
2. To change the breaking behavior for the entire table, select the whole table or none of it. Or, select just the rows you want to affect.
3. Select Table | Cell Height and Width (or click the right mouse button on the table and select Cell Height and Width from the popup menu).
4. Click the Row tab.
5. Click Allow Row to Break Across Pages, as shown in Figure 19.24; check the box to enable breaking across pages, or deselect to disable the behavior.

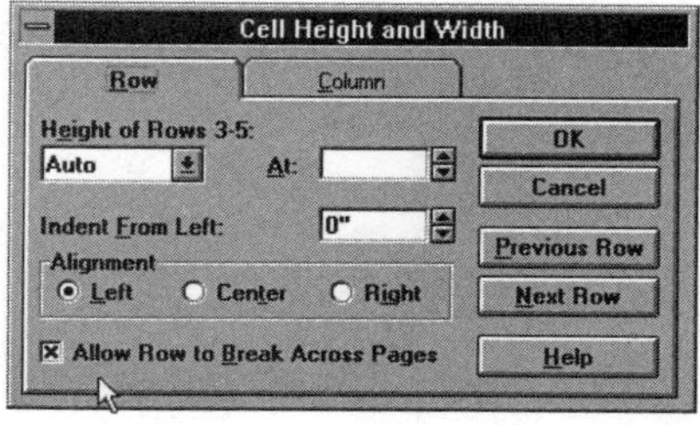

FIGURE 19.24.
The Allow Row to Break Across Pages option lets you decide whether or not you want to break it up.

6. If desired, click **N**ext Row or **P**revious Row to change rows.
7. Repeat Steps 5 and 6 for all rows you want to change.
8. Click OK.

SUPER NOTE

Actually, Allow Row to **B**reak Across Pages is the default behavior. A more common use of this command feature is to *dis*allow any part of a table from breaking across pages, or to disallow a particular row.

Trouble spot. If you make the change to allow a row to break, but it doesn't, then check the paragraph format to ensure that the Keep with Ne**x**t option isn't turned on. If it is, it prevents a row from breaking across pages. Deselect the Keep with Ne**x**t option for that row to enable breaking across pages.

Repeating Row Headings Across Pages

Word 6 lets you designate one or more rows as headings. Those rows, which must include the top row, are then repeated at the top of each new page.

PROCEDURE 19.28. CREATING A ROW HEADING.

1. Format and select the row(s) you want to use for a heading.
2. Select T**a**ble | **H**eadings from the menu.

SUPER NOTE

The Heading command is used to toggle the heading attribute on and off. When you choose the Table menu, Heading is checked or unchecked for any given row. To remove a row as a heading row, select T**a**ble | **H**eadings, and the check disappears.

Chapter 20

Table Math

Word provides the capability to manipulate and aggregate data in tables and to display mathematical results from tables elsewhere in the text of a document. If you have Quattro for Windows, Lotus 1-2-3 for Windows, Excel, or some other Windows-based spreadsheet program (or OS/2-based, if that's your environment), however, you'd be well-advised not to spend a lot of time trying to get Word's tables to act like spreadsheets. While it can be done, it can be horribly tedious—not a pleasant way to while away the hours.

Limitations

The following limitations may dissuade you from using Word's table math any more than you have to:

- All cell addresses are absolute.
- You cannot use selected text as a basis for calculations.
- All cell addresses must be determined by you.
- When you move items in a table, formula references are not updated.
- When you copy a formula, it's copied verbatim and must be edited to be used in parallel rows and columns.
- When you add data to a table that contains formulas specifying ranges, the ranges are not updated. Hence, if you insert a column after column 2, a range specified previously as `B2:E2` remains that way. You'd need to manually change the latter address to `F2`.

Referring to Cell References in Table Math Formulas

Cell references can be used only inside one of the following reduction functions:

```
AVERAGE
COUNT
MAX
MIN
PRODUCT
SUM
```

For example, consider the product of two sums, which logically might be

```
(A2+A3) * (B2+B3)
```

Intuitively, you might write the formula that way. Then you see the `PRODUCT` function and figure "Hmm, maybe `*` doesn't work," so you try

```
=PRODUCT(A2+A3,B2+B3)
```

and you discover that *that* doesn't work either. Then you suddenly remember the `SUM` function and discover that in order to calculate the product of two sums, you might have to use something ridiculous like:

```
=PRODUCT(SUM(C2,C3),SUM(B2,B3))
```

Eventually, you probably would even discover that a simpler form:

```
=SUM(C2,C3)*SUM(B2,B3)
```

works just fine. The real trick is discovering that you can't refer to B2 and B3 as if they were variable names. After you've enclosed them inside a reduction function, you're free to combine functions and other noncell operators just as you would in performing ordinary (well, almost ordinary) calculations.

Tables as Mini-Spreadsheets

Word provides the ability to perform simple calculations on tables. Each cell in a Word table has a spreadsheet-like address, with the numbered rows and lettered columns, as shown in Table 20.1.

Table 20.1. When used for math, table cells have spreadsheet-like addresses.

A1	B1	C1	D1	E1
A2	B2	C2	D2	E2
A3	B3	C3	D3	E3
A4	B4	C4	D4	E4

SUPER

WHAT'S YOUR ADDRESS?

When specifying cell, column, and row addresses, you refer to the contents of each cell by its address: B1, C5, and so forth. To specify two cells in a function reference, separate them with a comma. To specify a range, separate the starting and ending cell with a colon: B1:B3. To specify a whole row or a whole column, use the respective number or letter. Or, you could specify the range (for example, A2:E2 for row 2, B1:B4 for column B). Note that B1,B2,B3,B4 is identical to B1:B4.

Totaling Over Rows and Columns

To a certain extent, Word can recognize the difference between cells that contain just numbers and cells that contain text. Consider Table 20.2. The numerical cells are preceded by dollar signs. If you use Word's Table|Formula command to tally the totals, Word kindly adds a $ to the totals (as well as .00, even when it's not specified above, unfortunately, but it's easy enough to prevent).

Table 20.2. Word displays dollars and cents—even when it doesn't make sense.

Japan	$200,000	$300,000
Canada	$40,000	$45,000
United States	$300,000	$500,000
Total Expenditures	$540,000.00	$845,000.00

PROCEDURE 20.1. TOTALING NUMBERS IN A ROW OR A COLUMN.

1. Position the cursor in the cell where you want a total to appear.
2. Select Table|Formula.
3. Word displays the dialog box shown in Figure 20.1. Word attempts to guess what you want to do. If the selection has numbers above it, Word suggests the formula `SUM(ABOVE)`. If the selection has numbers to the left, Word suggests `SUM(LEFT)`. If the situation is ambiguous, Word offers the = for the beginning of the formula.

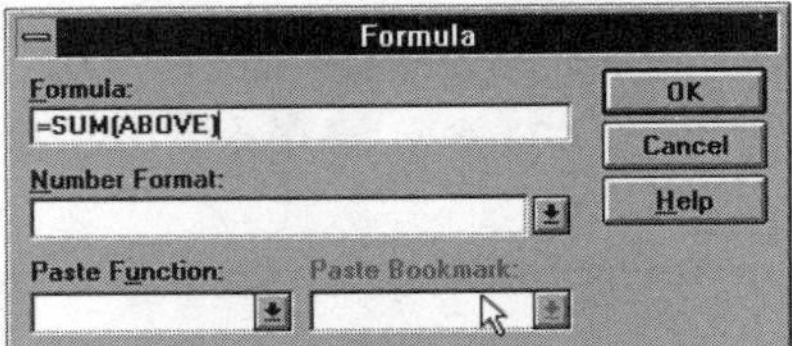

FIGURE 20.1.
The Formula dialog box helps you set up table math.

4. If desired, click the arrow next to Number Format and select a format. Word inserts the necessary format switch into the result.
5. Click OK.

If you're successful, Word enters a field code for a formula. The field code default formula for summing everything above looks like `{=SUM(ABOVE)}`.

SUPER TIP

You can prevent Word from adding cents (.00) to your dollar totals when you don't want it to. In Step 4, select the $#,##0.00;($#,##0.00) number format. Then delete the 0.00 part(s). In the 0.00 part, the first 0 tells Word to use a leading 0 before the decimal point if the total is less than one dollar. The two trailing zeros tell Word to show numbers out to hundredths (cents). The parenthetical format tells Word to enclose negative numbers (if any) in parentheses, per standard accounting practices. If you'd rather have a negative sign, delete the parentheses and everything between them.

The *above* and *left* method works fine if you don't have ambiguous numbers or labels. Consider, however, the situation shown in Table 20.3, where the years were obviously included in the totals. In this kind of situation, the *above* route doesn't quite work.

Table 20.3. Wait 'til you see our revenue for the year 2000!

Bake Sale Items	*1985*	*1995*
Brownies	$200	$300
Cookies	$300	$500
Total Sales	$2,485	$2,795

One possibility would be to arbitrarily put some text in front of the years, like `FY` (fiscal year) or just plain `Y`. Done that way, the totals would then show the correct numbers because `Y1985` and `Y1995` aren't numbers.

If that's not to your liking, another possibility is to limit the formula to adding up just the two cells above, rather than everything above.

PROCEDURE 20.2. SUMMING OVER A SPECIFIC RANGE OF CELLS.

1. Position the cursor in the cell where you want a total to appear.
2. Select T**a**ble | F**o**rmula.
3. Replace the word *above* with the range you want to total (for example, `C2:C3` for summing 1995 sales in Table 20.4).
4. Select a number format, if desired.
5. Click OK.

The Formula dialog box provides some limited capacity for help you build your formulas. Unfortunately, it won't tell you the cell references, and it won't correct your syntax if you screw it up. Those little items you pretty much have to figure out for yourself.

PROCEDURE 20.3. USING THE FORMULA DIALOG BOX TO BUILD FORMULAS.

1. Position the insertion point where you want the formula field to appear.
2. Select T**a**ble | F**o**rmula.
3. Select the drop-down arrow by Paste Function (see Figure 20.2).
4. Click a function; Word adds the function plus `()` to the insertion point within the Formula field. Note that you can reposition the cursor within the Formula fill-in area to paste functions wherever you need them.
5. Add whatever references you need within the parentheses, including a comma or a colon between *arguments* if necessary.

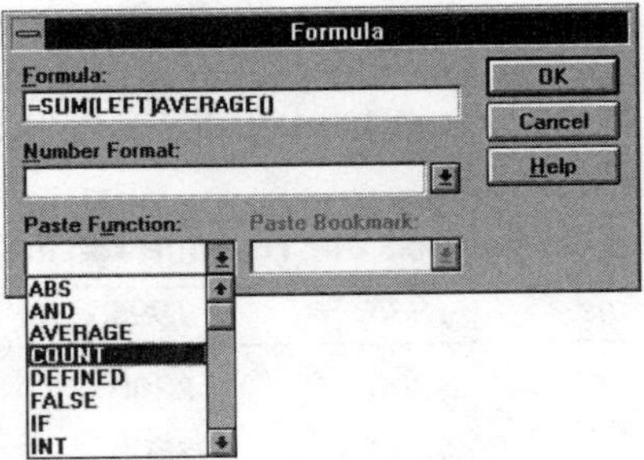

FIGURE 20.2. *The Paste Function option inserts a function into the Formula field.*

6. Add any operators needed to combine the function with any other functions you might add.
7. Repeat Steps 3 through 6 to add whatever functions you want.
8. Select a Number Format, if desired.
9. Click OK to insert the field.

Using Bookmarks in Formulas

Well, maybe by now you've noticed the Paste Bookmark field option in the **Table** | **Formula** dialog box, which I've ignored until now. The Paste Bookmark item gives you some additional ways to address cells, tables, and numbers that aren't in cells. So far, we've looked only at math *within* a single table. However, what about references to a number in a table from *outside* the table? Or, what about references from within a table to another table? Or, references to numbers that aren't in a table at all?

Consider any of the table examples in this chapter. You could, if you wished, select a table and give it a bookmark name. Once you do, you can refer to any of the cells in that table by preceding the cell references with *bookmark* and enclosing the bookmark name in square brackets `[]`.

PROCEDURE 20.4. BOOKMARKING A TABLE.

1. Select the table (press Alt+5 on the number pad).
2. Select **Edit** | **Bookmark** (Ctrl+Shift+F5).
3. Type a bookmark name (for your sanity, something that describes the table—for example, `Sales`).
4. Click Add.

Once you've bookmarked a table, you can then refer to any cell in it using the bookmark name as part of the address. When using a reference to a cell in a bookmarked table, keep in mind it is still a cell reference and still must be enclosed in a function. For example, to refer to the total sales for 1995 in Table 20.4, you might bookmark the table as *Bakesale* and then refer to 1995 sales as

```
{ =sum(bakesale[b4])}
```

Why would you want to do that? Well, perhaps you've included the table in a report about anticipated activities in 1995, saying something like "…and we hope to achieve at least `{ =sum(bakesale[b4])}` in sales in 1995." Of course, by then you will have fixed the fact that the total in that table seems to have been included the year as part of the total.

While we're at it, you can just go ahead and bookmark a table cell itself, rather than bookmarking the whole table. Once you do that, you can then use the bookmark field itself as an operator in a formula. For example, if you bookmark 1985 sales and 1995 sales as `sales1985` and `sales1995`, respectively, you could display their sum anywhere in the document with just

```
{={sales1985}+{sales1995}}
```

Now that we're not dealing with cell addresses anymore, you can use the bookmark fields directly in formulas. To insert a bookmark field, by the way, all you need to do is to enclose it in a field.

PROCEDURE 20.5. INSERTING A BOOKMARK FIELD.

1. Press Ctrl+F9 to insert the field characters.
2. Type the bookmark.
3. Press F9 to update the bookmark.

Back to how this discussion got started. Recall that we had ignored the Paste Bookmark (a librarian's nightmare!) option in the Formula dialog box. You can use it to summon up bookmark names when building a formula. The advantage of using the Paste Bookmark option, by the way, is that it knows the names of all of your bookmarks in the current document. Thus, using the Paste Bookmark option ensures that you don't get an `!Undefined Bookmark` error message when you try to update your formula field.

PROCEDURE 20.6. USING THE FORMULA DIALOG BOX TO INSERT A BOOKMARK INTO A FORMULA.

1. Select T**a**ble | F**o**rmula.
2. Build your formula according to the procedure shown previously.
3. To add a reference to a bookmark for purposes of cell references, click the drop-down arrow beside Paste Bookmark.
4. Click the bookmark you want to use.
5. Type square brackets `[]` to enclose any cell references you want to use.
6. Finish building your formula.
7. Select a Number Format, if desired.
8. Click OK.

Note that in this procedure, you are not using a bookmark field, but rather are simply using the bookmark as part of a field.

> **SUPER TRICKY TIP**
>
> If you bookmark a single number or cell, you can use that bookmark in the text by enclosing the name of the bookmark in field characters (inserted by pressing Ctrl+F9). If you want the added security of being able to select the bookmark from a list, rather than risking typing it wrong, you can use the Table|Formula command.

PROCEDURE 20.7. USING FORMULA DIALOG BOX TO INSERT A BOOKMARK FIELD.

1. Select Table|Formula.
2. Delete the = in the Formula field.
3. Click the drop-down arrow beside the Paste Bookmark box, and select the bookmark.
4. Click OK (or press Enter).

Other Calculations and Functions

Word can perform a variety of calculations using 18 built-in field math functions. If you need these, then you probably need a real spreadsheet program even more. However, because this is a super book, I suppose we're obligated to show you how to do it. In the following functions, the ones with empty parentheses can contain any number of arguments. Keep in mind that only the following functions can accept table cell addresses as arguments (as well as `ABOVE`, `BELOW`, `LEFT`, and `RIGHT`):

```
AVERAGE
COUNT
MAX
MIN
PRODUCT
SUM
```

> **SUPER CAUTION**
>
> Math fields are extremely syntax-sensitive. Some logical errors aren't interpreted as syntax errors, either. Be sure to verify field results before relying on them.

ABS(*mathematical expression*)

The ABS function calculates the absolute value of an expression (positive distance from 0). For example, the field formula `=ABS(Sum(A2)-Sum(A3))` calculates the difference between the values contained in cells A2 and A3 in a table.

AND(*a,b*)

The AND function calculates the logical combination of two expressions. Use a logical AND when you need to test the simultaneous truth of two statements. For example, suppose a table contains population and average income. You might be interested in determining whether population and average income both exceed some threshold:

```
=AND(POPULATION>=1,000,000,AVEINCOME>=10000)
```

This field formula would be 1 (true) if population is at least one million and average income is at least $10,000. If both conditions aren't met, then the value of the field is 0 (false).

AVERAGE(*list of arguments or a range*)

Use the AVERAGE function to calculate the simple arithmetic mean of the items enclosed. For example:

```
AVERAGE(A1:A5)
```

adds up A1 through A5 and divides by 5.

COUNT(*list of arguments or a range*)

You can use COUNT to determine how many items are in a list or a range. Suppose you needed to calculate the *unbiased* estimate of the mean (a statistical term) rather than the simple arithmetic mean. You could use the Sum field and the Count field together to devise your own formula:

```
{=Sum(ABOVE)/(Count(ABOVE)-1))}
```

DEFINED(*expression*)

Use the DEFINED function to determine if the *expression* is a valid mathematical expression or a defined bookmark. Hence, `DEFINED(18/sales)` equals `1 (true)` if sales is a nonzero expression, and it returns `0 (false)` if sales either isn't defined or is `0 (0 divide error)`.

FALSE

FALSE is used to negate otherwise tedious expressions. If you have a complex expression of inequality already formed, and you're interested in the converse condition, you can use FALSE rather than having to reverse all of your logic. For example, the following statement is true (1):

```
{=17<4=FALSE}
```

IF(*a*,*b*,*c*)

The IF function evaluates *a*, and returns a value of *b* if *a* is false, and returns a value of *c* if *a* is true. For example, the expression {=IF(netsales>0,40,400)} would return a value of 40 if netsales is not greater than 0, and it would return a value of 400 if netsales is greater than 0.

INT(*expression*)

INT is used to determine the integer portion of a real number. For example, {=INT(3.64)} returns 3. Contrast this with ROUND.

MAX(*list or range*)

MAX is used to determine the largest number in a list or a range. For example, {=MAX(A1:A10)} equals the larger number in column A, from row 1 through row 10.

MIN

MIN is used to determine the smallest number in a list or a range.

MOD(*a*,*b*)

MOD is used to return the remainder from the division of *a* by *b*. For example {=MOD(7/5)} returns 2, because 7 divided by 5 equals 1 2/7.

NOT(*expression*)

The NOT function returns the negation of an expression.

OR(*a*,*b*)

The OR function is used to test either/or logic. It evaluates as true (1) if *a*, *b*, or both are true. It evaluates as false (0) only if neither *a* nor *b* is true (nonzero). For example, the field expression {=OR(netsales>=100000000,netlosses>=100000} would be false only if netsales are below 100,000,000 *and* netlosses are below 100,000.

PRODUCT(*list or range*)

The PRODUCT function is used to multiply a list of arguments or everything in a range. For example, the field {=PRODUCT(9,8,7,6,5,4,3,2,1)} is equivalent to 9! (9 factorial, which is 9 × 8 × 7 × 6 × 5 × 4 × 3 × 2 × 1).

ROUND(*a,b*)

The ROUND function is used to round *a* up to the nearest *b*th place, where *a* is a floating point real number, and *b* is a negative or positive integer. If *b* is positive, rounding is to the nearest 1/10*b*. If *b* is negative, then rounding is to the nearest 10*b*. For example, {=ROUND(45345,-3)} equals 45,000.

SIGN(*expression*)

The SIGN function is used to determine if an expression is below, equal to, or above zero. If the expression equals 0, SIGN returns 0. If the expression is negative, SIGN returns -1. If the expression is positive, then SIGN returns 1.

SUM(*list or range*)

Use the SUM function to add up a list or a range of numbers. For example {=SUM(A2:F6)} sums all cells from A2 through F6 (that is, A2, A3, A4, A5, A6, B2, B3, B4, B5, B6,...F2, F3, F4, F5, F6).

TRUE(*expression*)

TRUE is similar to FALSE but always equals 1. Since X>Y equals X>Y=TRUE, TRUE is really unnecessary as an operator. Some users might like it, however, simply because it makes the logic clearer.

ToolsCalculate: Out of Sight, But Not out of Mind

Word's ToolsCalculate command can be used to perform calculations in tables. This can be especially handy, not only in adding up numbers in tables, but also in checking calculations. This provides a good double-check when you've entered all of the numbers from another source. It also can be a lot less hassle than using field code math. Unfortunately, ToolsCalculate is not provided as a tool on any default toolbar, is not available as a default keystroke, and is not on any of the default menus. So, if you used it in Word for Windows 2 and want to use it here, you can either run it from the macro menu or assign it to a toolbar or keystroke.

PROCEDURE 20.8. ASSIGNING TOOLSCALCULATE TO A KEYSTROKE.

1. Select Tools | Customize.
2. Click the Keyboard tab.
3. Under Categories, click All Commands.
4. Under Commands, click ToolsCalculate.
5. Click the Press New Shortcut Key field, and press the combination you want to assign (hint: Alt+= on the top row and number pad don't have built-in assignments, so I assigned both to it).
6. Click Assign.
7. Under Save Changes In, select `NORMAL.DOT`.
8. Click OK.

SUPER NOTE

Don't forget to save your changes to NORMAL.DOT if you want this shortcut to be available in the future.

Now that ToolsCalculate is a keystroke away (assuming you followed the preceding procedure), you can use it to perform calculations. One of the neat things about it is that it displays the result of the calculation on the status bar and copies the result of the calculation to the clipboard. That way, if you need the result to paste into a table cell, you've got it.

PROCEDURE 20.9. ADDING NUMBERS IN A TABLE.

1. Select the row, column, or combination of cells you want to add.
2. Press Alt+= on the top row or number pad (depending on where you assigned it).
3. Word displays the result on the status bar and copies it to the clipboard as well.
4. Move the insertion point to where you want the result to appear.
5. Press Shift+Insert to paste the result into the text.

In performing calculations, Word uses the following rules:

- Word ignores non-numeric components (this lets you include descriptive text as well as numbers with $, £, %, commas, or other characters).
- Word recognizes the operators % (divides number by 100), ^, *, /, +, and -.
- Operations are performed from left to right, using the normal mathematical order of precedence for operators: % first, then ^, then * and /, and finally + and -.

- Operations enclosed in parentheses are performed first; use parentheses to modify the order of calculation, just as in normal math.
- Word treats numbers in parentheses as subtractions.

You also can use ToolsCalculate to evaluate any expression you type, even if it's not in a table. For example, if you have a sudden urge to find out the cube root of 1,331, type:

```
1331^(1/3)
```

then select it and press your ToolsCalculate key. Hey, it's 11!

Workshop

VII

Styles, Templates, and Automatic Formatting Workshop

In this workshop, you learn about Word's major formatting time savers—Style, Templates, and AutoFormat. It's possible to use Word without ever touching the style commands, and without ever even stopping to think, "What is a template, anyway?" If you do use Word that way, however, you're missing out on the strongest feature. Styles cut down dramatically on the amount of time you have to spend formatting a document. They enable you to format consistently, and to achieve professional results with minimal effort. Similarly, Templates are collections of styles that enable you to create documents in a fraction of the time they would take if you were to start from scratch each time. For those of you who have resisted using styles, Word also sports the AutoFormat command. The AutoFormat command can take an unstyled document (one that was created using manual formatting rather than by applying distinct styles) and apply styles automatically—after the fact.

Chapter

21

Templates and Wizards

One dictionary definition of a template is a pattern or a mold. You trace over the template to try to make a new *something* that looks exactly like the template. Another definition comes from genetics. A template is a single strand of DNA or RNA used to make an identical new strand. The template contains all of the genetic information (genes) necessary to make a complete duplicate. Included are genes for how something will look and act, as well as its native potential.

When talking about Word's templates, I like both definitions. I'm especially fond of the genetics definition because it goes beyond the standard "look" definition into dimensions of potential and behavior. With this definition, we begin to take stock of the fact that a template is a multifaceted starting point for creating a Word document.

Overview

A template can be something as simple as an already-started letter—with your return address and the word *Dear* already in place—or it can be a collection of document-specific macros, styles, autotext shorthands, a customized toolbar and menus, and a specially tailored set of key assignments. That's the *multifaceted* part. A template's pattern for your document can include not only what goes into the document and how it looks, but what tools are available as well. In short, a template is a specialized work environment for creating documents.

Imagine an artist's studio. This particular artist has stacks of already-started canvasses. She has one stack of canvasses with an ocean and beach scene started, another stack with snowy-peaked mountains, another with a living room, and yet another with a busy urban skyline. Now imagine that this artist has a kit for each type of painting she's going to do. The beach kit has lots of bright colors, some sand for special effects, and a special set of brushes. The mountain kit has extra white and green for snow and mountain evergreens, some pine scent to add another dimension to her paintings, and some large brushes for building up the terrain where necessary. Another kit handles the living room and urban scenes.

Consider each kit and already-started canvas a kind of working environment for doing particular kinds of paintings. In much the same way, templates are working environments for doing particular kinds of documents. A fax template might include two already-started pages—one for the cover sheet and another for a memo. A fax template might also include a macro for actually "printing" the fax to your fax software (assuming that's the way you send faxes). It might have a print hot key that is assigned to that macro, or a tool on the toolbar for doing the same thing. The fax template might include an Addressee item on the Insert menu, for extracting fax numbers. All these things make up the work environment for creating and sending faxes.

Two Major Components

One problem some users have in understanding Word's use of documents and templates is the fact that two major components don't always get treated as separate. They are the *work environment* component and the *document* component:

Work environment	menus, toolbars, macros, autotext, and keyboard
Document	text, formatting, and styles

Here's the tricky part. A Word template file (.DOT) can contain both types of components—work environment as well as text, formatting, and styles. Thus, a .DOT file actually is a special kind of document that contains not only the already-started document (if applicable) and a list of styles, but any special macros, autotext, menu items, keyboard assignments, and toolbar changes you may have made.

A Word document file (.DOC) contains only the text and formatting (including the styles). You cannot store menus, macros, autotext, key assignments, or tools in a regular Word document. Instead, each Word document contains a notation that indicates what template is *attached* to the document. When editing a document that is attached to a particular template, the work environment defined in that template is made available to you. When you edit a document attached to a different template, then a different work environment is presented.

Even when they realize that the document and work environment are two separable components, many users mistakenly think that the style list is part of the work environment rather than the document. That's wrong. When you create a document, the existing styles and text are copied into the new document. Thereafter, however, the styles and text in that new document take on a life of their own. If you change the Heading 1 style to 16-point Century Schoolbook, then it's changed only in that document (unless you take special action). Similarly, other documents based on the same template can either keep the original Heading 1 definition or change it. Not only can different documents based on the same template define styles differently, but they can have different style lists as well.

You can change the styles in the underlying template, but it takes special effort. It is by no means automatic, and for a good reason. Think about it for a moment. Have you ever changed the formatting of a letter or a report to make it all fit onto fewer pages? If you're like most Word users, you've done it plenty of times. What would happen if each style change trickled back to the template and in turn affected documents created from that template? It'd be a formatting nightmare. Instead, Word makes it a bit more difficult and explicit to change templates. You either have to edit the .DOT file itself or explicitly select the Add to Template check box when editing styles. In the latter case, you must do it for each style change. It's not a one-time-does-it solution.

Just remember all this the next time you wonder why a style change didn't trickle back to the underlying template. Autotext, menus, key changes, toolbar changes, and macro changes are all stored in the template file (.DOT). Anytime you get a prompt similar to the one shown in Figure 21.1, it's either because one of the work environment features changed, or because you explicitly told Word to add a changed style to the underlying template. However, it's usually because the work environment changed.

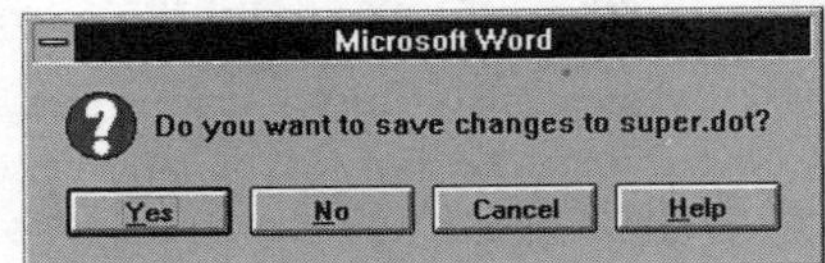

FIGURE 21.1.
Word prompts to confirm changes to template files whenever the underlying template has changed.

The Chain of Command

How Word's documents and templates interact can be difficult to grasp. Once you get it, however, it's like taking the case off a complicated mechanical clock to see how everything works. The purpose of this section is to try to strip away the case so you can see what's really going on.

Everything starts in Word itself. Word uses its built-in defaults to create NORMAL.DOT, which then becomes a master work environment for everything you do in Word. It also is the default template for newly-created documents, unless you specify something different when you use the **F**ile | **N**ew command.

You can modify NORMAL.DOT and save it under a different name (for example, REPORT.DOT, LETTER.DOT, or CONTRACT.DOT). In fact, that's how the templates that come with Word were created. Somebody started with Word's built-in defaults and modified them to create working tools for creating specific kinds of documents.

If you create a new document based on one of the new templates, Word uses that template as a starting point for each new document. When you're working on that document, the commands, macros, menus, key assignments, and autotext in that template control how Word behaves. Moreover, everything from NORMAL.DOT (except for the parts that are different from the other template) is available to you as well.

Consider, for example, the key chain of command shown in Table 21.1, which traces five key assignments. I'll talk in detail about key assignments in Chapter 47, "Customizing the Keyboard." For now, however, key assignments is a useful example.

By default, Word assigns specific behaviors to Ctrl *plus* E, F, L, O, R, and S. Here, the user has redefined Ctrl+F, Ctrl+O, and Ctrl+R, storing them as global changes in NORMAL.DOT. The starting environment for this user customizes Ctrl+F, Ctrl+O, and Ctrl+R, leaving Ctrl+E, Ctrl+L, and Ctrl+S set as the factory defaults. When editing or creating a document based on NORMAL.DOT, this user sees the key assignment shown in the Normal Document column, which consists of Word's built-in defaults with three modifications.

When editing or creating a document based on LETTER.DOT, however, this user gets a combination of the built-in defaults, plus the NORMAL.DOT modifications, plus the LETTER.DOT modifications. When editing a document based on LETTER.DOT, the customizations in that template take precedence. After that, NORMAL.DOT takes precedence. Any Word defaults that LETTER.DOT and NORMAL.DOT don't change remain in effect.

Table 21.1. The chain of command.

Key		*Key Defined In:*		*Key's Effect In:*	
	Word Default	NORMAL.DOT	LETTER.DOT	Normal Document	Letter Document
Ctrl+L	LeftPara	n/a	n/a	LeftPara	LeftPara
Ctrl+R	RightPara	EditReplace	n/a	EditReplace	EditReplace
Ctrl+E	CenterPara	n/a	Envelope	CenterPara	Envelope
Ctrl+0	OpenUpPara	FileOpen	Overtype	**F**ile | **O**pen	Overtype

Word's Defaults

Let's imagine that you deleted all of your .DOT files from your hard disk (heaven forbid). Word still has the following basics, which are hard-coded into Word itself:

- Menus
- Commands
- Keyboard
- Toolbars
- Styles (73 built-in styles, 6 of which are displayed by default)

If you change the menus, autotext, keys, styles (with Add to Template turned on), toolbar, or if you create a macro, and then exit, Word prompts `Changes have been made that affect the global template NORMAL.DOT. Do you want to save those changes?`, as shown in Figure 21.1. Let's assume that you had previously deleted NORMAL.DOT. If you say yes at the `Save global` prompt, Word creates a file called NORMAL.DOT and puts your modifications and additions there.

Are styles saved in NORMAL.DOT? Not automatically. You must explicitly tell Word to do it. If you never click the Add to Template check box in the main style dialog box, then Word saves just the list of built-in styles to the re-created NORMAL.DOT file, and not any changes or additions you may have made.

When a document is created (Document1, Document2, and so on), you can add to, delete, or change any of the text and formatting. You can change and add to the styles.

You also can delete any nonstandard styles that aren't in use. *Standard* styles are 73 built-in styles that are native to Word. You can reformat standard styles as you wish. You cannot, however, delete standard styles; they are part of Word's genetic makeup. Nonstandard styles are those other than the 73 built-in styles whose names are chiseled into Word. You can add any number of styles to a document, and you can delete them at will.

SUPER CAUTION

You can even delete user-created (nonstandard) styles that are *in use*. Word does not warn you about the deletion, and it reformats any text using those styles as Normal.

When you save the document, the text, formatting, and styles (as defined in that document) are saved to the file name you specify. The styles are saved with the document. Styles do not automatically get copied to the underlying template unless you instruct Word to do so. If you create a new style called Hangbullet, for example, the Hangbullet style exists only in that document. It will not get copied to the underlying template unless you explicitly tell Word to add it.

Templates—They're Everywhere!

A user who prides himself on using as few of Word's capabilities as possible once proudly declared, "I never use templates." He was wrong. If you start Word for Windows, you're using a template. If you don't select a specific template for creating a document, then Word uses a built-in template called NORMAL.DOT. The Document1 you see when Word first starts is based on NORMAL.DOT.

SUPER NOTE

Even if you were to delete NORMAL.DOT, Word would still offer NORMAL as a template choice when creating documents. That's because the blueprint for NORMAL.DOT, and the ability to re-create it, are programmed into Word.

The NORMAL.DOT template is Word's default starting point for every document for which you do not select a template. NORMAL.DOT is also the starting point for all other templates that get created. It is a repository for properties that trickle down to all other templates. Until you actually change those properties (key assignments, menu, toolbar, autotext, macros, or standard styles), the built-in template remains unchanged. Once you change a property (for example, modify or add a key assignment, or add to or change a toolbar), Word saves those changes into NORMAL.DOT.

Making the changes *global* means they are available throughout Word, regardless of what template you're using (unless specifically modified by that template). NORMAL.DOT is a kind of umbrella template always in effect, even when another template is controlling most of the action for a given document. Anything not explicitly set in the current template is controlled by NORMAL.DOT. NORMAL.DOT conveys virtually thousands of settings—most of which you'll never change. If you do make a change in NORMAL.DOT, however, that change becomes the new global default, which is in effect regardless of which template you're using (unless it explicitly says otherwise).

As indicated, you can override global defaults and customizations while editing documents based on a particular template. For example, perhaps you want the default font to be 12-point Arial (Helvetica) when creating a fax (for maximum readability), but you prefer 4-point Times New Roman when creating a contract. You can do that by including 12-point Arial as your default FAX.DOT font, and 4-point Times New Roman as your default CONTRACT.DOT font. Thus, while global features (NORMAL.DOT) are a kind of common denominator for your work, you can easily modify specific templates to create exceptions for specific types of documents.

SUPER NOTE

All customizations to macros, toolbars, autotext, keys, and menus must reside either in NORMAL.DOT or in a specific template. Style and format customizations, however, can reside in NORMAL.DOT, a specific template, or in a specific document. If you change the Heading 1 style in a document so that it's centered and 72-point Arial, that change does not automatically get stored in the underlying template. Users have to modify individual document formats often—sometimes to make a business letter fit onto a single page, or to perform other one-time tasks. It would be a nightmare for consistency if each one-time formatting change were saved into the underlying template. Instead, Word keeps a separate list of style definitions for each document. When a document is created, it gets a starting list of styles from the underlying template. If you change a style's formatting in that document and want to change the style in the underlying template, you must explicitly instruct Word to save the changes to the template by selecting the Add to Template check box in the Modify Style dialog box. We'll get to this shortly.

Normal Confusion (NORMAL.DOT Versus Normal Style)

An unfortunate ambiguity exists in Word with respect to the word Normal. The word Normal is used as a name for the default style in Word documents, as well as the name of the default document template. There's even a normal view and something else called `(normal text)` that you see when you select Insert | Symbol. It would have been much clearer if Microsoft had elected to call the default document template GLOBAL.DOT. Had they done that, I might not have needed to write this section. Most users eventually understand the ambiguity. However, the ambiguity delays their mastering this most fundamental of Word's powerful tools.

SUPER

Sometimes, just knowing right up front that all these uses of Normal are referring to different things can help. It puts users on alert status. It's like when you're teaching English to someone from Spain and have to explain homonyms: *write*, *right*, *Wright*, and *rite* may sound alike, but they're different. There's a story in there somewhere about having two Wright weddings on the same day, and having to write how to get to the right Wright rite.

When you create a new document (**F**ile | **N**ew), Word offers something called NORMAL as the template, as shown in Figure 21.2. If you have never saved a file called NORMAL.DOT (either deliberately or implicitly), Word uses a built-in version. This built-in version has five styles that show up by default:

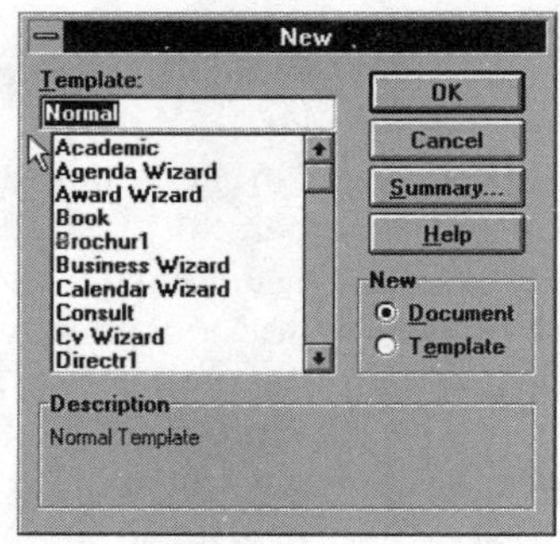

FIGURE 21.2.
When you create a new document, Word offers Normal as a choice, even if no NORMAL.DOT exists yet.

Default Paragraph Font (character style)
Heading 1 (paragraph style)
Heading 2 (paragraph style)
Heading 3 (paragraph style)
Normal (paragraph style)

This last Normal sometimes causes confusion, because it is a style called Normal and does not refer to the name of the template at all. Every template has a style called Normal. This stems from the fact that all templates are ultimately based on Word's default built-in template (you know, the one I wish they'd called GLOBAL.DOT).

The part of Word many users find hardest to understand is the fact that you don't have to use NORMAL.DOT to use the Normal style. In fact, if you do nothing to change it, Word defaults to using the Normal style in any template you designate. Consider the templates NORMAL.DOT and WEEKTIME.DOT:

NORMAL.DOT
Heading 1
Heading 2
Heading 3
Normal

WEEKTIME.DOT
Address/Phone
ColumnHead
Company Name
Dates/Notes
Default Paragraph Font
Form
Heading 1
Heading 2
Heading 3
NonDecimalTableData
Normal
Normal Indent
Slogan
TableData
Title

Notice that both of these templates have the styles Default Paragraph Font, Heading 1, Heading 2, Heading 3, and Normal. That's because all templates are based on Word's built-in template, and the built-in style names cannot be deleted. So, whatever else you might do with a template you create and modify, you are stuck with a set of style names that you cannot erase (although you can control the display of them in the dialog box style list).

Even so, the Normal style (as well as the three built-in heading levels) is not necessarily the same in each template. Even though you're stuck with the names, you're not stuck with how they are formatted. The Normal style in NORMAL.DOT might be 10-point Times New Roman, while the Normal style in WEEKTIME.DOT might be 12-point Arial.

Remember these two points:

1. Just because you're using a style called Normal, that doesn't mean that you are using (or have to use) NORMAL.DOT; and

2. The Normal style in one template can be and often is radically different from the Normal style in other templates.

> **SUPER NOTE**
>
> By the way, the default style for any given template—including NORMAL.DOT—doesn't have to be Normal. You can edit a template and restyle the insert point's paragraph marker to any style you prefer.

Okay, so Normal isn't the same thing as NORMAL.DOT. It's kind of like New York, New York. There's New York the city, and there's New York the state. NORMAL.DOT is like the state, and Normal the style is like the city. They're not the same thing, although one is located in the other. Moreover, there might be New York cities in other states as well. New York, New York would look and feel nothing at all like New York, Montana. And they'd both be different from New York, California. New Yorkers would shudder at the very thought!

Template: Customization Warehouse

Templates are a repository for user-customizations. Templates are used to store changes to

Keyboard	Defines the actions (commands and user-defined macros) keys perform.
Menus	Defines what items display on the menu, as well as what actions they perform.
Toolbars	Defines the tools that display on the toolbar and the actions they perform.
Autotext	A list of shorthands (*dc* for Washington, D.C., *ms* for Microsoft, and so forth).
Macros	User-created commands and programs (written in Word's macro language).
Commands	Built-in commands, which can be changed by substituting user-created macros under the same name(s).
Styles	Styles can be saved in the template, but aren't unless you explicitly tell Word to do it.

SUPER NOTE

Word also has something called AutoCorrect, a feature similar to Autotext, but which automatically expands shorthands as you type them. AutoCorrect shorthands are stored *only* in NORMAL.DOT.

Automatic Macros

Another interesting, sometimes-wonderful, and often-aggravating aspect of templates are automatic macros. Word lets you create up to five types of automatic macros:

AutoExec — If present, a global macro (stored in NORMAL.DOT) named AutoExec runs each time Word is started. AutoExec is relevant only at the global level—a template-specific AutoExec never runs, due to the way Word is engineered. AutoExec macros typically set up Word however you want. This might include setting up the display, setting up the printer, or making sure that the Word window is maximized (or minimized). You might also use AutoExec to automatically open a series of working documents.

AutoExit — Like AutoExec, AutoExit is relevant only at the global level (for example, NORMAL.DOT). AutoExit is run each time you exit Word. If you have any AutoClose macros, they are run before AutoExit (in relevant contexts, of course). AutoExit, like AutoExit, is a good way to make sure that everything is closed the way you want. For example, perhaps you need to copy your working documents to a floppy drive each time you exit Word. Or perhaps you need to make sure you return the printer to a more genial setup for your other Windows applications.

AutoNew — If a document template contains a macro called AutoNew, it is run each time you use that template to create a document. AutoNew macros are especially handy in the Wizard templates. In fact, by convention, templates that have AutoNew or AutoOpen macros are called Wizards. For example, when you create a letter based on the Letter Wizard, an AutoNew macro prompts you for all information you need to create a letter. It even has pieces of canned (prewritten) letter you can use as starting points. Using the other Wizard templates, AutoNew macros can walk you through the creation of a variety of documents.

SUPER NOTE

AutoNew, AutoOpen, and AutoClose macros stored in NORMAL.DOT are run when creating a document based on NORMAL.DOT. If template-specific versions do not exist in other templates, the AutoNew, AutoOpen and AutoClose macros stored in NORMAL.DOT also are run when documents based on other templates are created, edited, or closed, respectively.

AutoOpen AutoNew macros control what happens when a document is created. AutoOpen macros control what happens thereafter. If a template contains an AutoOpen macro, it is run each time an existing document based on that template is opened. If you're editing an existing letter, you wouldn't want the AutoNew macro to automatically change the date and reinsert the date. An AutoOpen macro is a useful way to set up the editing environment—turning on any GUI elements (rulers, toolbars, scroll bars) you might want to have on, as well as setting up the view in a specific way. AutoOpen macros can be global- or template-specific.

AutoClose AutoClose macros are run when you close a document. Technically, AutoClose is triggered each time you run the FileClose command. However, Word executes the context-relevant AutoClose macro(s) whenever you issue any command to exit Word. Also, when you create a document based on something other than NORMAL.DOT (Document 1), AutoClose (NORMAL.DOT's or the AutoClose in the template) runs when you close the document, even if the document has not been named yet. If the document is based on NORMAL.DOT, however, AutoClose does not run until the document has been saved at least once.

Suppressing Automatic Macros

SUPER TIP

You can suppress AutoOpen and AutoNew by pressing and holding the Shift key just *after* giving the instruction to open a file or create a new file. You can suppress AutoExec by holding down the Shift key just *after* issuing the command to start Word. If you hold down the Shift key *while* double-clicking, Word starts in the background instead.

SUPER TIP

You also can suppress AutoExec by including a /m switch as a parameter for Word in the Properties box—not a terribly efficient approach for occasional suppression, but you might consider setting up a separate program item for a *don't-do-it* version of Word. There's no law that says you can have only one program item per application. The /m switch typically is used to provide an alternative startup macro to Word. Another approach to suppressing automatic macros in general is discussed in Chapter 60, "Macro Projects."

PROCEDURE 21.1. SUPPRESSING EXECUTION OF AUTONEW.

1. Select **F**ile|**N**ew.
2. Click the template you want to use.
3. Click OK.
4. Immediately press a Shift key and keep it pressed until the document is open.

PROCEDURE 21.2. SUPPRESSING EXECUTION OF AUTOOPEN.

1. Select **F**ile|**O**pen.
2. Navigate to the file you want to open, and then click it.
3. Click OK.
4. Immediately press a Shift key and keep it pressed until the document is onscreen.

PROCEDURE 21.3. SUPPRESSING EXECUTION OF AUTOEXEC.

1. Open the Windows group that contains Word, and select the Word icon.
2. Double-click or press Enter.
3. Immediately *after* double-clicking or pressing Enter, press and hold the Shift key, and keep it pressed until Word appears.

Other Global Templates

With prior versions of Word for Windows, users expressed a desire to have macros and other customizations available from different templates without having to explicitly copy them from one template to another. With Word 6, you can now do that. Word offers two ways:

- In addition to NORMAL.DOT, templates you copy to the STARTUP subdirectory are automatically loaded each time you start Word.
- You can, during a session, designate specific templates as *global*.

Suppose you (as I do) share your computer among different users. When I'm using it, I want my own keyboard setup, my own macros, my own toolbars, and so forth. When my wife uses it, she wants it without any customizations so she can rely on the internal and printed documentation for help. Previously, we had to shuffle HERB.DOT and KAREN.DOT back and forth each time a different user sat down to use the system. Now, we just keep the common customizations in NORMAL.DOT. I load HERB.DOT when I'm using it, and she loads KAREN.DOT when she's using it. It works out pretty well.

PROCEDURE 21.4. MAKING TEMPLATE CUSTOMIZATIONS GLOBALLY AVAILABLE.

1. Select **F**ile | **T**emplates, for the dialog box shown in Figure 21.3.
2. Under **G**lobal Templates and Add-ins, click Add; this gives you a file selection screen for picking templates.
3. Navigate to a template you want to make globally available, and select it.
4. Click OK; note that the template you selected was added to the list of **G**lobal Templates and Add-ins.
5. Repeat Steps 2 through 4 to add any number of templates to your template palette.
6. Select by clicking each template you want to make globally available (an X appears in the box beside selected templates).
7. Click OK to close the Templates and Add-ins dialog box.

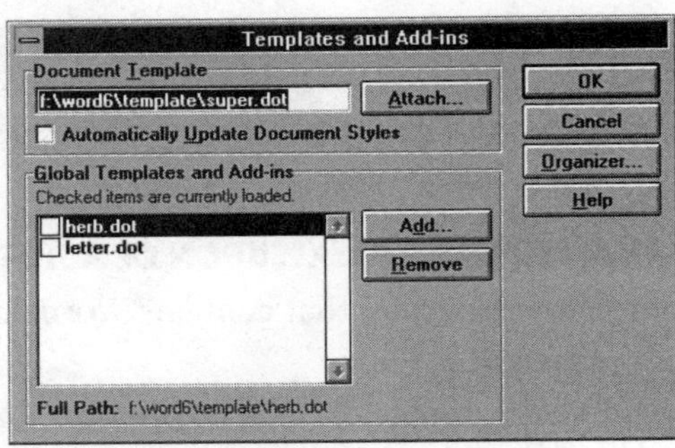

FIGURE 21.3.
The Templates and Add-Ins dialog box lets you attach a template as well as designate templates as global.

PROCEDURE 21.5. DEACTIVATING A GLOBAL TEMPLATE.

1. Select **F**ile | **T**emplates.
2. Click each template you want to deactivate, removing the X from the check box.
3. Click OK.

PROCEDURE 21.6. REMOVING A GLOBAL TEMPLATE FROM THE LIST.

1. Select File | Templates.
2. Select the template you want to remove.
3. Click Remove.
4. Repeat Steps 2 and 3 to remove all templates you don't want on the list.
5. Click OK.

SUPER

And now for the bad news. When you make a template globally available, only its macros, menus, toolbars, autotext (not autocorrect), and keyboard customizations are made globally available. Any styles contained therein are not made available. The first thing I noticed when I decided to rename my well-honed NORMAL.DOT as HERB.DOT, and load the latter globally, was that my autocorrect shortcuts stopped working. Even though they were still located in HERB.DOT, Word uses them only if they're in NORMAL.DOT. So, unless I can convince my wife that having abbreviations she doesn't know about suddenly explode into words is a good thing, I guess we're back to having to copy HERB.DOT or KAREN.DOT over to NORMAL.DOT depending on who's using the system. Besides, she prefers Times New Roman as a default font, and I prefer Arial.

Another problem with making templates globally available is memory. Having multiple templates loaded at the same time eats into system resource memory—you know, the kind that has nothing to do with the amount of installed RAM. So, after discovering and lauding the "make 'em global," I'm now back to not using it. I might eventually find some comfortable uses for it, but probably not until you can explicitly designate any given template as the only global source for all customizations (turning off NORMAL.DOT), including autocorrect entries and styles.

The Startup Directory

Word also uses a startup directory. Any templates you copy to it are automatically added to and checked in the Global Templates and Add-ins list in the File | Templates dialog box. When you remove the files from the startup directory, they automatically disappear from the list. You also can designate which directory, if not the one called STARTUP, Word looks to when it decides which templates to make global when you start Word.

PROCEDURE 21.7. CHANGING THE STARTUP DIRECTORY.

1. Select **T**ools | **O**ptions | File Locations.
2. Click Startup.
3. Click Modify.
4. Select a new directory (for example, TEMPLATES).
5. Click OK to close the Modify dialog.
6. Click Close.

If you like, you can suppress Word from automatically loading the startup items. You might want to do this if there are some projects for which you want an especially clean setup. To do this, you add a `/a` switch after WINWORD.EXE in the command line when setting Word's properties. You also can use the `/m`*macroname* switch to designate a specific macro or command to start when you start Word, or leave off the *macroname* part to suppress any AutoExec macro that might be active (equivalent to holding down the Shift key while Word is loading). The `/a` switch does not suppress the AutoExec macro and doesn't suppress Word's automatic use of NORMAL.DOT.

Using Word's Templates

Word comes with a variety of already-built templates. In this section, we'll survey each of them.

Wizards

Wizard is the name designated for templates that contain AutoNew or AutoOpen macros that swing into action when a document is created or opened. Word comes with eleven Wizards, ready to write your resume, your letters, your faxes, and your newsletters and memos. Heck, you can even use the Award Wizard to create yourself an award for being such a wonderful writer!

Using Wizards

Different Wizards are set up in different ways. Nearly all of them, however, have a combination of boilerplate text and placeholders. In the case of boilerplate text (words like MEMO, Subject, and so forth), you can leave it as-is, or replace it with your own. In the case of placeholders (things like `[Insert your message here]`), you should replace the placeholder with the appropriate text, unless you want to look like a dunce to the recipient.

Some of the Wizards put the placeholder text in a special color so you can readily see it. It would have been a little bit better, perhaps, if all of the Wizards had done that or had placed bookmarks at the appropriate locations. In any event, make sure you locate and change each of the sections with the appropriate text.

One interesting aspect of Wizards is that the ones that come with Word do not associate themselves as templates with the documents they create. They explicitly reset the template for the resulting documents to NORMAL.DOT. Because of that, you don't have to worry about automatic macros taking over your computer each time you open documents created using Wizards.

Using Wizards to Create Your Own Templates

After you use a Wizard to create a document, and after you've edited it to your satisfaction, you can use the resulting document as a template. You might sometimes want to create a new template rather than go through using the Wizard each time. You can. As noted, Microsoft's Wizards don't associate themselves with documents they're used to create. Therefore, you don't have to worry about disabling automatic macros. However, depending on the type of document, you might want to create your own AutoNew or AutoOpen macros to facilitate filling in the appropriate pieces of information.

PROCEDURE 21.8. CONVERTING A WIZARD-PRODUCED DOCUMENT INTO A NON-WIZARD TEMPLATE.

1. Select **F**ile | **N**ew.
2. Click T**e**mplate.
3. In the **T**emplate field, type the fully-qualified name of the document you want to convert into a template (for example, C:\WINWORD\DOC\AGENDA1.DOC).
4. Select **F**ile | Save **A**s.
5. Type a name for the new template (for example, AGENDA.DOT).
6. Click OK.

WORDWIZ.INI

When you use the Wizards that come with Word 6, they use the macro commands `SetPrivateProfileString` and `GetPrivateProfileString` to create, write to, and read from a file called WORDWIZ.INI in your Windows directory (not your Word directory). Each time you run a Wizard, the automatic macros inscribe your preferences into the WORDWIZ.INI file. That's why the Wizards seem to be so smart about what you've done in the past. If you want the Wizards to remain smart, make sure you make occasional backup copies of any .INI files that Word 6 creates in your directories. Unfortunately, the days when applications confined their shenanigans to their own directories are gone. So, it's no longer sufficient to look at an application's own directory to see what you need to safeguard. If you reinstall Windows at some point, you'll also need to try to backup WINWORD6.INI as well as MSTXTCNV.INI, EQNEDIT.INI, ODBCINST.INI, and others (that is, all of them).

AGENDA.WIZ

This Wizard automatically walks you through the creation of a meeting agenda, as shown in Figure 21.4. It even creates a form for taking meeting notes for you. Unfortunately, Wizards won't attend dull meetings for you, or make dull meetings otherwise. If you have coworkers who might be tempted to call even more needless meetings because of the Agenda Wizard, you could volunteer to install Word 6 for them. Check in the documentation for your operating system under the heading `Removing unwanted files` for a nifty way to neutralize the threat posed by AGENDA.WIZ.

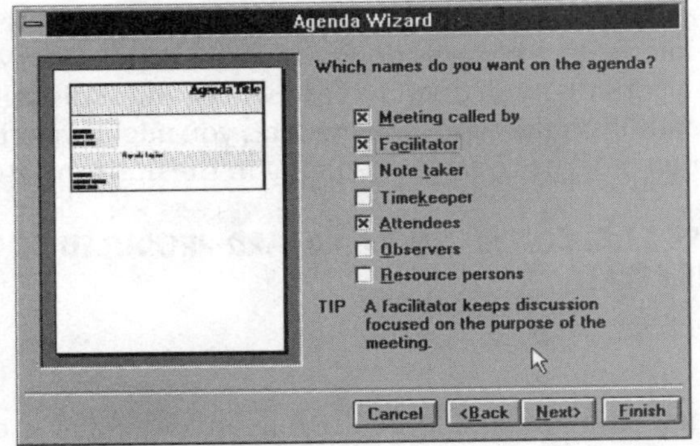

FIGURE 21.4.
The Agenda Wizard makes it easier than ever to plan bothersome meetings to annoy your coworkers!

AWARD.WIZ

Use the Award Wizard to create awards and certificates, as shown if Figure 21.5.

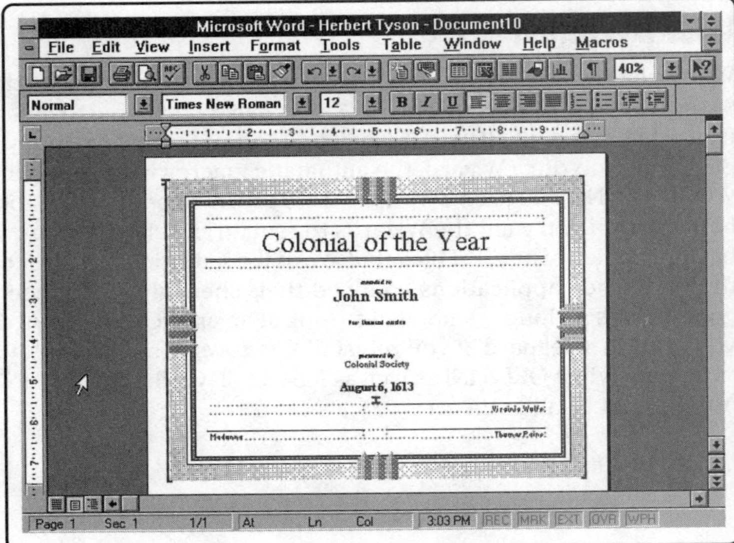

FIGURE 21.5.
Use the Award Wizard to certify yourself as a Word Wizard.

CALENDAR.WIZ

Use the Calendar Wizard to create a calendar for a week (shows seven days in a planning-style calendar), a month, or a whole year.

CV.WIZ

Use the CV (curriculum vitae, a pretentious name for a resume) Wizard to write lofty resumes that will add class to the recipient's otherwise-mundane *round file*.

SUPER HINT

If you use the CV Wizard to write a professional resume, *don't* include your marital status, nationality, age, place of birth, or parents. They don't belong in a professional resume.

SUPER NOTE

Both CV.WIZ and RESUME.WIZ are included at the moment; it's likely that only CV will ship with the finished Word, due to a problem Microsoft appears to be having with the word *resume*. The two .WIZzes appear to be substantially identical in most respects.

FAX.WIZ

Use the Fax Wizard to create a fax cover sheet, but don't send a cover sheet unless you really need one. It wastes paper and time.

LEGAL.WIZ

Use the legal Wizard to create legal pleading papers, a format required by the courts in some jurisdictions.

LETTER.WIZ

Use the letter Wizard to create a variety of prewritten business letter, or to create your own business or personal letters.

MEMO.WIZ

Use the memo Wizard to create a variety of differently-formatted memos.

NEWSLTTR.WIZ

Use the newsletter memo—you guessed it—to create interesting-looking newsletters.

RESUME.WIZ

Use this Wizard to create resumes.

TABLE.WIZ

Use the table Wizard to set up tables. The Wizard lets you select from among six table formats, as well as other options. The Wizard doesn't guide you through data entry, but it can save you a little time if you're nervous about creating tables from scratch.

The Non-Wizard Templates

Word also comes with a variety of non-Wizard templates. For the most part, they are a collection of already-started and already-completed documents that you can edit for your own needs. Unlike the Wizards, these templates do not contain any automatic macros. In fact, most of them contain no macros at all. Some are designed to work with the Wizards. For example, the Memo Wizard uses MEMO1.DOT, MEMO2.DOT, and MEMO3.DOT for its classic, contemporary, and typewriter style memos. Despite their intended purpose, you're free to use them as standalone templates without using the respective Wizards.

BROCHUR1.DOT
DIRECTR1.DOT
FAXCOVR1.DOT
FAXCOVR2.DOT
INVOICE.DOT
LETTER1.DOT
LETTER2.DOT
LETTER3.DOT
MANUAL1.DOT
MANUSCR1.DOT
MANUSCR3.DOT
MEMO1.DOT
MEMO2.DOT
MEMO3.DOT
PRESENT1.DOT
PRESREL1.DOT
PRESREL2.DOT
PRESREL3.DOT
PURCHORD.DOT
REPORT1.DOT
REPORT2.DOT

REPORT3.DOT
RESUME1.DOT
RESUME2.DOT
RESUME4.DOT
THESIS1.DOT
WEEKTIME.DOT

Switching Templates

Word lets you change templates at any time. When you change the template that is attached to a document, you change the work environment and can optionally change the styles as well. The work environment consists of your customizations to the keyboard, menus, toolbar, macros, and autotext. The work environment does not include styles or text. Recall that a template's styles and text are copied to a document when it is first created. After that, however, the text and styles in a document assume a life of their own.

When you switch templates, you can optionally replace or supplement the styles in the current document with those in the template you attach. You also have the option of selectively replacing styles using the style organizer.

Attaching

Attaching is a misnomer. The word *attached* creates the impression that the .DOT file is physically attached to your document. Not only is that not what happens, but it would be very inconvenient and wasteful of disk space if it did. Consider, for example, that NORMAL.DOT files for some users approach or exceed 100K. If you have 1,000 documents based on NORMAL.DOT, it's easy to see that you do not want each one to be 100K before you even start writing. For 1,000 files, that would add 100 megabytes to your storage needs!

Instead of attached, a word like *associated* or *linked* might be more descriptive. When you attach a different template to a document, you're simply plugging it into a different set of resources.

PROCEDURE 21.9. ATTACHING A DIFFERENT TEMPLATE TO A DOCUMENT.

1. Select **F**ile | **T**emplates, for the Templates and Add-ins dialog box.
2. Click Attach to open the Attach Template dialog.
3. Navigate to the template you want to attach.
4. Click OK to return to the Templates and Add-ins dialog.
5. To update styles in the current document with those in the template, click Automatically Update Document Styles (see note).
6. Click OK.

SUPER NOTE

When you click Automatically Update Document Styles, Word combines the styles in the template you're attaching with the styles already in the current document:

- Styles in the current document that aren't defined in the template are left alone.
- Styles in the template that aren't defined in the current document are added.
- Styles in the current that are also in the template are redefined (updated) using the style definitions in the template.

Organizing

Using the Automatically Update Document Styles option adds in the template styles wholesale, and doesn't get rid of any deadwood styles that are not in use in the current document. It also adds in autotext, toolbars, macros, as well as keyboard and menu customizations from the template you attach. If you want more control—to selectively add just some elements, for example—you can use the template organizer. The template organizer is a convenient tool for copying styles, autotext, toolbars, and macros between different templates. Using this powerful tool, you can assemble templates that are comprehensive and concise, offering just what you need for working on a particular kind of document.

The organizer is available both from the **F**ile | **T**emplates (Templates and Add-ins) dialog box and from the style dialog box.

Using the Organizer to Manage Styles

You can use the Organizer to transfer styles between documents and templates. The files you select from the organization needn't be just the types you see when you first open the Organizer window. When changing styles from the style menu, it's very easy to forget to click the Add to Template button. The organizer is a much more efficient and convenient method for adding styles to the template.

PROCEDURE 21.10. COPYING STYLES FROM THE CURRENT DOCUMENT TO NORMAL.DOT.

1. Select **F**ile | **T**emplates, and click the **O**rganizer button, for the dialog box shown in Figure 21.6.
2. Click the **S**tyles tab; note that if a document is open, the current document is listed in the left list box and NORMAL.DOT is listed at the right.

3. In the left list, select the style(s) you want to copy to NORMAL.DOT. Note that the direction of the Copy button now points toward NORMAL.DOT; you can copy only in one direction at a time.
4. Click the Copy button.
5. Click the Close button (not the Close File buttons) when you're finished.

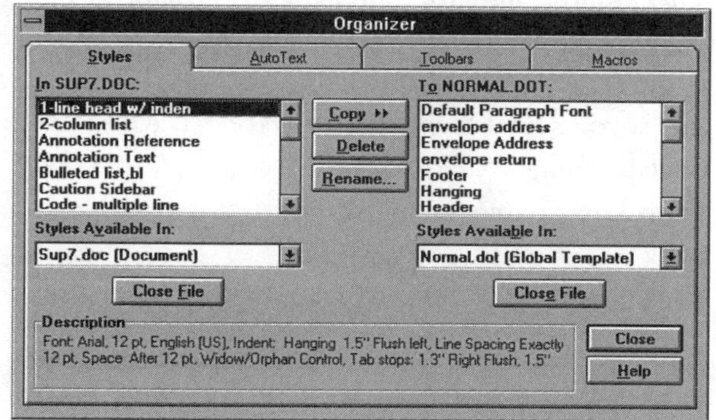

FIGURE 21.6.
Use the Organizer to copy styles to where you need them.

You also can use this procedure to selectively update (redefine) styles in the current document with those in NORMAL.DOT. Just repeat the procedure, this time clicking selectively in the NORMAL.DOT list on those styles you want to update. For example, perhaps you redefined (accidentally or intentionally) a Heading 2 style in the current document and want to reinstate the definition contained in the current NORMAL.DOT. You can do that by copying the Heading 2 style from NORMAL.DOT to the current document.

> **SUPER NOTE**
>
> The changes you make when copying styles to an open document are not saved until the document is saved.

You also can use the Organizer to selectively delete from the current document. Since you can select multiple styles at the same time, this can be considerably more efficient than the one-at-a-time approach you must use in the Styles dialog.

PROCEDURE 21.11. DELETING STYLES FROM THE CURRENT DOCUMENT.

1. Select **F**ile | **T**emplates, and click the **O**rganizer button.
2. Click the **S**tyles tab.
3. In the style list for the current document, select the styles you want to delete.

4. Click the Delete button.
5. Click Close.

You can use the organizer to rename styles, but only one at a time.

PROCEDURE 21.12. RENAMING STYLES.

1. Select **F**ile|**T**emplates, and click the **O**rganizer button.
2. Click the **S**tyles tab.
3. In the style list you want to change, select the style you want to rename; note that if you select more than one style, the **R**ename button dims.
4. Click **R**ename.
5. Type a new name for the style.
6. Click OK.
7. Click Close.

SUPER TIP

In Step 5, you can create an alias or alternate name for the style name without losing the original name. This is covered more thoroughly in Chapter 22, "Styles and Autoformat." For now, however, if you want to be able to access a style by an alternate name, just type a comma followed by the alternate name. When you press Ctrl+Shift+S to change styles, just type the alternate name (for example, H1 for Heading 1) and press Enter to apply the style to the current paragraph or selection.

Changing the Files Used by the Organizer

In addition to changing aspects of just the current document and NORMAL.DOT, you can change aspects of the associated template, as well as files that aren't currently loaded.

PROCEDURE 21.13. SWITCHING THE ORGANIZER TO A DIFFERENT ACTIVE FILE OR TEMPLATE.

1. With the organizer already on-screen, click the drop-down arrow in the Available In list (see Figure 21.7).
2. Click the document or template whose styles, macros, tools, or autotext list you want to display.

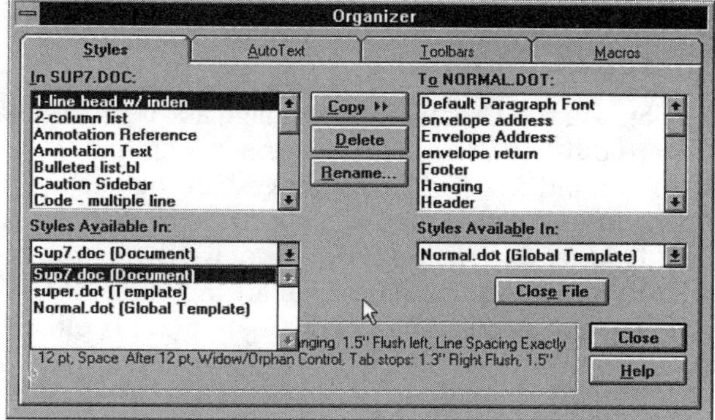

FIGURE 21.7.
Use the Available In list to select a file or template.

If the file you want to use is not already active, you can still access it by closing one of the current files listed in the organizer window and opening an alternative file.

PROCEDURE 21.14. SWITCHING THE ORGANIZER TO A FILE OR TEMPLATE THAT'S NOT CLOSED.

1. With the organizer already on-screen, click the drop-down arrow in the Styles Available In list.
2. Click the Close File button under the list with which you are now finished; note that the list disappears and the Close button changes into Open.
3. Click Open.
4. Navigate to the file you want to use, and click OK.

SUPER TIP

For more flexibility, in Step 4 you can select a document associated with a template instead of a template. That gives you access to the document, its template, and to NORMAL.DOT from the Available In list.

When you open a template or document from the organizer, you are prompted to confirm and save changes when you select the Close or Close File buttons from within the Organizer. When you make changes to a template or document that's open in the current window, however, you won't be prompted to confirm changes until you close the document or template from the current window.

Using the Organizer to Manage Autotext, Toolbars, and Macros

You also can use the Organizer to manage autotext, toolbars, and macros. While the elements are different, the procedures are identical. To avoid getting confused, you must keep in mind what's being changed. In the case of autotext, you can copy, delete, and rename individual autotext entries. For macros, you can copy, delete, and rename individual macros. In the case of toolbars, you can copy, delete, or rename whole toolbars, but you cannot manipulate individual tools on the bars. To do the latter, you would need to access the **T**ools|**C**ustomize|**T**oolbars command from within the template you want to change.

SUPER NOTE

When organizing styles, the files can be documents or templates. When organizing autotext, toolbars, and macros, however, you can only use templates. That's because autotext, toolbars, and macros are stored only in templates, and not in documents.

PROCEDURE 21.15. COPYING AUTOTEXT, WHOLE TOOLBARS, OR MACROS USING THE ORGANIZER.

1. Select **F**ile|**T**emplates, and click the **O**rganizer button.
2. Click the tab for the element you want to change (see Figure 21.8, Figure 21.9, Figure 21.10, and Figure 21.11).
3. Use the Available In drop-down or the Close File/Open File procedures to select the templates you want to use.
4. Working from either side of the Organizer window, select the elements you want to copy, delete, or rename, and click the appropriate button(s).
5. Repeat Steps 3 and 4 as needed to modify the templates you want to change. If you made changes, you are prompted to confirm saving them in files that are not open in the current window before opening other files.
6. Click Close when you're done.

Modifying Templates

There are several strategies for modifying templates. How to proceed depends on what you want to modify.

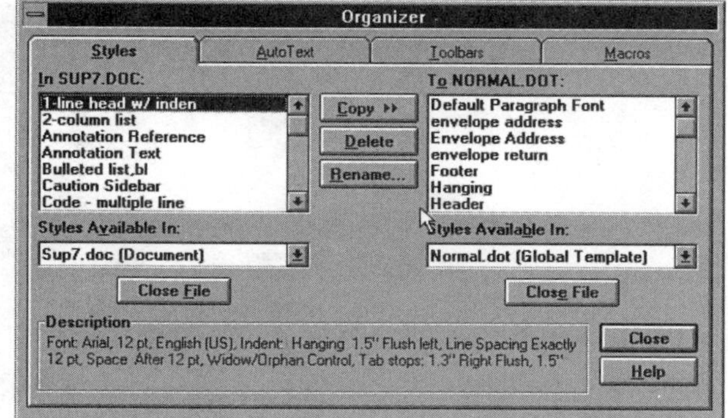

FIGURE 21.8.
The Styles organizer tab.

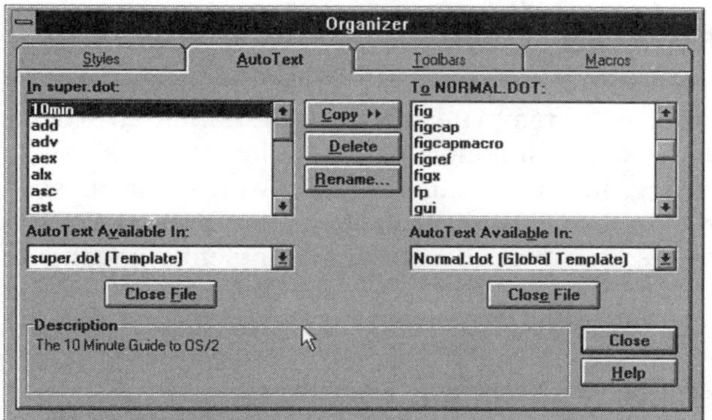

FIGURE 21.9.
The AutoText organizer tab.

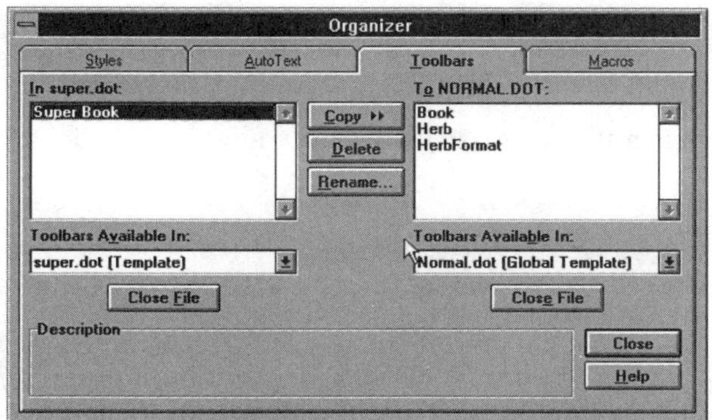

FIGURE 21.10.
The Toolbars organizer tab.

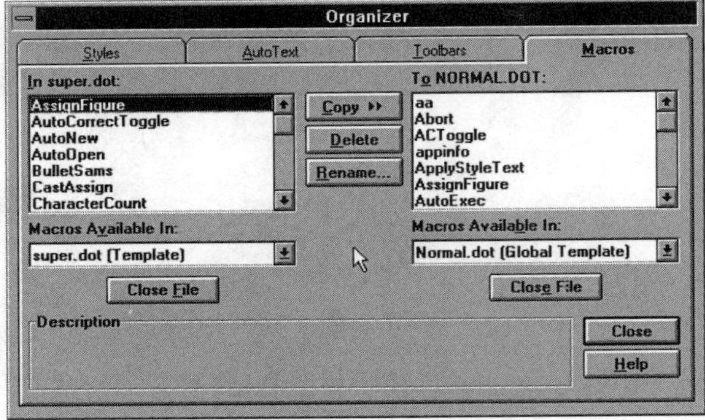

FIGURE 21.11.
The Macros organizer tab.

Modifying the Text and Formatting

For modifying the text in a template, the only method is to edit the template itself. When you edit a template, it's much like editing an ordinary document. The difference, of course, is that a template, in addition to containing document components (text, formatting, and styles), also contains work environment components (toolbar, menu, macros, keyboard, and autotext customizations). For modifying just the text, format, and styles, however, the work environment components present themselves just as they would when editing a document based on the template, except that you don't have to click the Add to Template option when modifying styles.

PROCEDURE 21.16. EDITING A TEMPLATE.

1. Select **F**ile | **O**pen.
2. Under List Files of Type, select *.DOT, Document Templates.
3. Using the Drives and Directories list boxes, navigate to the directory that contains the template you want to modify.
4. Select the template you want to modify and click OK.

SUPER **CAUTION**

Wizard templates, as well as templates imported from earlier versions of Word for Windows, often contain automatic macros—AutoOpen and AutoClose—that presume you're editing a document based on the template rather than the template itself. If you have an AutoOpen macro that you don't want to run, make sure you press the Shift key after giving the **F**ile | **O**pen command to make sure that the AutoOpen macro doesn't do something you don't want done. If the document contains an AutoClose macro you don't want to run, you can't just press Ctrl+F4 and then press the Shift key. Ctrl+F4 works too quickly for that to work.

PROCEDURE 21.17. SUPPRESSING AN AUTOCLOSE MACRO WHEN CLOSING A TEMPLATE.

1. When you're done editing the template, press Alt+F (File).
2. Either: use the cursor down arrow to move to the Close command and press Shift+Enter; or press the Shift key and click the Close command.

This suppresses the AutoClose macro. Incidentally, you can use this trick any time you want to suppress an AutoClose macro, including when you edit a document based on a template rather than a template itself.

Modifying the Styles in a Template

For modifying the styles in a template, you have several options:

- Edit a document based on the template, and remember to click the Add to Template box in the Styles dialog box each time you modify a style you want preserved in the underlying template.
- Edit the template directly and modify the styles (in this scenario, you don't need to fidget with the Add to Template box because you're already in the template).
- Edit any document based on the template, and run the Organizer to copy styles where you want them.

Modifying the Work Environment in a Template

If you want to modify a template's work environment (toolbar, menus, macros, autotext, and keyboard), you can do it by editing any document based on the template or by editing the template itself. You also can selectively copy macros and other features from one template to another using the organizer, as described earlier in this chapter. The latter feature is new to Word 6.

PROCEDURE 21.18. MODIFYING TOOLBAR, MENUS, MACROS, AUTOTEXT, OR KEYBOARD FOR A SPECIFIC TEMPLATE.

1. Open the template or a document based on it.
2. Make any changes you want to make, ensuring each time that the Available In template matches the template you want to change.
3. When you're done, select **File|Close**, and click **Yes** to confirm saving the changes.

SUPER NOTE

Use the procedures described in the previous section to suppress the AutoOpen and/or AutoClose macros if needed.

Creating Templates

New templates can be created in a variety of ways, depending on what you want to accomplish.

Creating a New Template from Scratch

You can use File | New to create a new template from scratch.

PROCEDURE 21.19. CREATING A NEW TEMPLATE FROM SCRATCH.

1. Select File | New.
2. Click Template under New.
3. Click the template you want to use as a starting point (if you truly want to start from scratch, then click NORMAL).
4. Click Summary and fill in at least a descriptive title—you'll thank yourself later on (this creates a Template# window and opens the summary information dialog box).
5. Click OK.
6. Enter any text or formatting you want to include in the base template, customize your work environment and styles as you want.
7. When done, select File | Save As (Save File as Type should already say Document Template).
8. Replace Word's suggested name (DOT#.DOT) with a more meaningful name (up until now, it's been called something like *Template 4*, but Word suggests a numerical DOT name), and click OK.

SUPER NOTE

In Step 4, you could just click OK. That's what I used to do. However, I recently decided that having titles on my documents and templates is a real time-saver. So I spent a couple of hours retrospectively adding titles to hundreds of untitled templates and documents. Not only are they now victims of my inability to remember why I created them (over a ten-year period), but it would've taken so little time if I'd just taken five seconds each time I created a document. So, do yourself a favor and get into the title habit early. Who knows, at some point in the near future, you might be able to use those titles as actual filenames—you can come darned close right now when you tell Find File to list files by title instead of name, in fact. The title "Template for Letters asking clients for more money" is so much more informative than MONEYLT.DOC.

Hey! That's not my NORMAL! In Step 3, if you select NORMAL as the template for creating your new template, you might be in for a little surprise. Ordinarily, when you use NORMAL as a template for creating documents, your own NORMAL.DOT—with its styles, macros, and so forth—is used. If you specify NORMAL when creating a new template, however, Word uses its own built-in formula for NORMAL. Among the surprises are the fact that none of your global macros, autotext, keyboard assignment, toolbar assignments, or menu assignments are included in the new template. If you want them, you'll have to use the cloning method described next.

Cloning an Existing Template NORMAL.DOT

As discussed above, creating a new template based on NORMAL clones Word's built-in NORMAL rather than your own. So, how do you clone your own NORMAL.DOT? Paradoxically, the easiest way to clone an existing NORMAL.DOT from Word is to create a new *document* (not a template) based on it, and then save the new document as a *template* rather than as a document. Another way would be to use File Manager to copy the template you want to clone to a different filename in your template directory. For this to work, the *path* field must contain the whole filename, including the disk and path. Otherwise it won't work. For my money, however, the **F**ile | **N**ew (document) and Save As (template) option seems to be the least work.

PROCEDURE 21.20. CLONING NORMAL.DOT.

1. Select **F**ile | **N**ew and create a new document based on Normal.
2. Select **F**ile | Save **A**s, and select Document Template in the Save File as Type box, as shown in Figure 21.12.
3. Type the new name for the template you want to create (for example, NEWNORM.DOT).
4. Click OK.

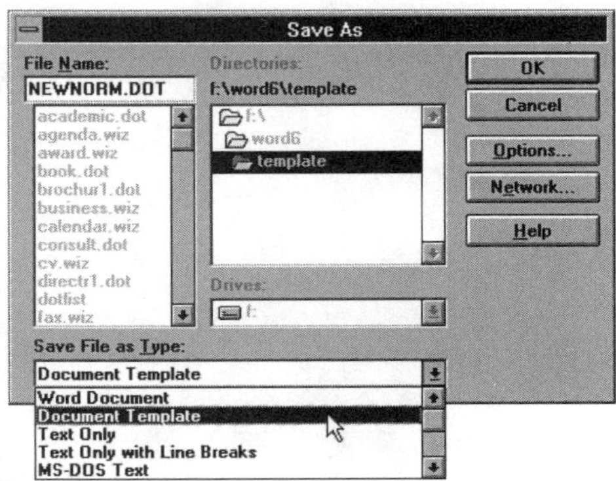

FIGURE 21.12.
Cloning NORMAL.DOT.

This procedure clones the entire NORMAL.DOT, including any text, styles, and work environment (macros, menus, keyboard, toolbar, and autotext). You are now free to modify it as needed.

Chapter

22

Styles and AutoFormat

One succinct way to think of styles is as formatting recipes. If you're a computer jock, however, you may prefer to think of styles as formatting macros—shortcuts for formatting sections of text.

When you apply a style to a section of text, all of that style's formatting is applied to the target text—all at once. Consider the section of text shown in Figure 22.1. To format the heading shown, you could apply bold, underlining, and a 14-point font. You could also set the paragraph spacing before and after to set the heading off from the surrounding text. You could also set the paragraph paging so that this heading won't ever appear at the bottom of a page without at least a few lines from the first paragraph that goes under that heading.

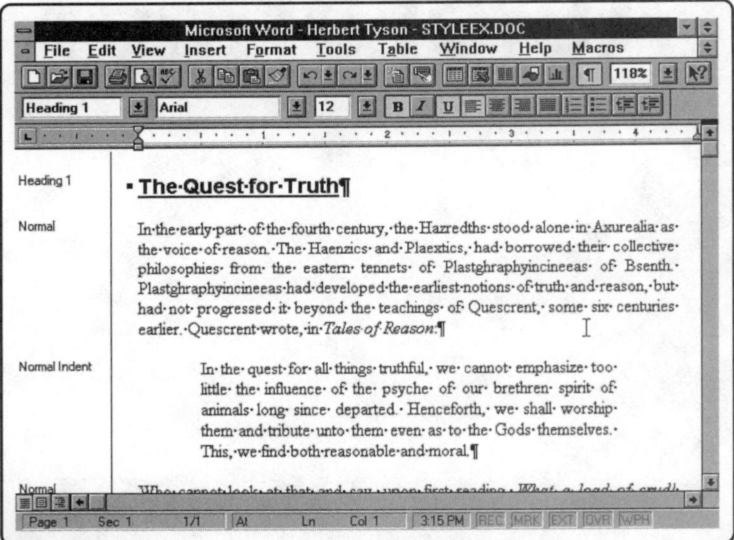

FIGURE 22.1.
Using styles simplifies formatting complex combinations of formatting.

But then, to format the paragraph that follows the heading, you'd have to turn off the bolding and underlining as well as revert to a 10-point font. You must also change the before-spacing back to some lower value, and you no longer need to set the paragraph paging to keep this paragraph with the one that follows. For the indented paragraph, you have to go through additional formatting to set the indents and reduce the font. When you switch back to nonindented, you have to undo the indents and increase the fonts.

Somewhere, somebody said, "Enough!" They must have decided to take all of the formatting for the heading and create a macro to apply all of the formatting at once. They named that macro Heading 1. Similarly, for most paragraphs, they wrote a macro to turn off a whole lot of special formatting and called it Normal. Then, they did a variation of Normal, with the paragraph indented from the left and right, and called it Normal Indent.

Now, instead of meticulously applying the font, paragraph spacing, paging, and other formatting, you simply choose the collection of formatting for any given section of text. If you come to a section that needs to be formatted differently from anything in your existing bag of style trick, you format it manually. Once done, you give that formatting a name.

Used intelligently, styles often are all the formatting you need. They can keep you from having to insert multiple carriage returns between different kinds of text, from inserting multiple tabs or spaces to try to force a particular type of horizontal formatting, or even from ever having to manually insert page breaks to prevent headings from appearing at the bottom of a page without any following text.

Word 6 has two types of styles: character styles and paragraph styles. When you select the Format | Style dialog, paragraph styles are displayed in bold, and character styles are displayed in normal text, as shown in Figure 22.2. For most Word for Windows users, this feature is both welcome and long-overdue. Previous versions of Word for Windows had paragraph styles only, while Word for DOS has offered character styles all along. The availability of character styles not only improves the compatibility between Word for DOS and Word for Windows but also expands the power for users of the latter.

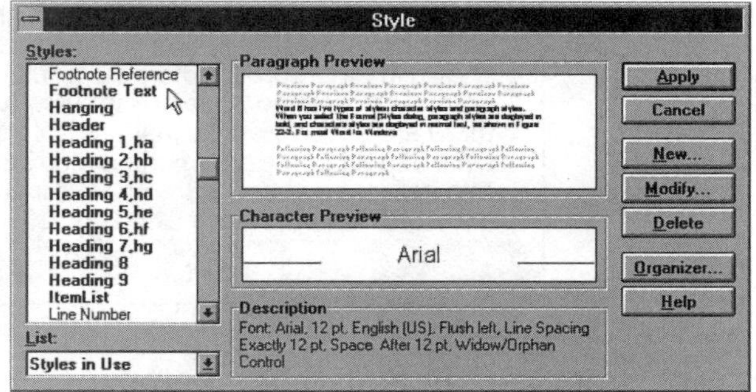

FIGURE 22.2.
The style list shows paragraph styles in bold and character styles in normal text. Styles in effect at the cursor are checked.

Paragraph Styles

By definition, a paragraph style is one that affects the entire paragraph. When you apply a paragraph style to a section of text, all *paragraph level* formatting is replaced by the formatting of the applied style. Paragraph level formatting includes

- Line spacing
- Spacing before and after a paragraph
- Paragraph pagination rules
- Tabs
- Borders and shading
- Framing

You can have only one kind of paragraph style within any given paragraph or table cell. Paragraph styles also contain character formatting (font, pointsize, bolding, and so forth). However, when you apply a new paragraph style to a selection, all manually-applied (direct) character formatting, as well as formatting applied though characters styles, is preserved. For example, consider the paragraph shown in Figure 22.3. The paragraph is formatted as 12-point Arial, with no special attributes turned on. However, several words are bold and italic. The 12-point Arial aspect comes from the underlying style. The bolding and italics, however, were applied individually by selecting the words and pressing Ctrl+B or Ctrl+I, respectively.

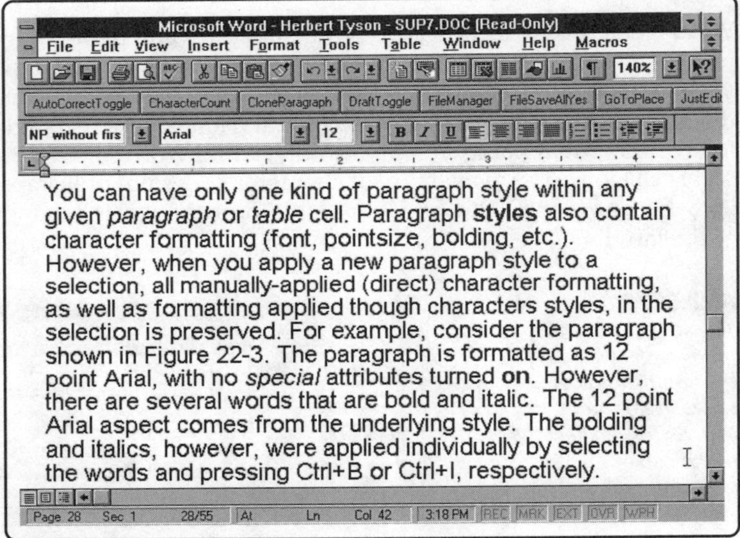

FIGURE 22.3.
Direct character formatting applied to part of a paragraph is preserved when you apply a new paragraph style to a paragraph.

If you apply a new paragraph style to this paragraph—one whose underlying font is 10-point Times New Roman—the base font of the paragraph changes, even though it is character-level formatting. The bolding and italics, however, remain unchanged. Character formatting applied only through the paragraph style changes each time you apply a new style. Character formatting that is not part of the paragraph style, however, is preserved when you apply a new style to an already-formatted paragraph. As you have seen, the ResetChar command can remove all nonstyle character formatting from the paragraph, but merely applying a style does not disturb the bolding and italics in your carefully crafted passages.

SUPER NOTE

If a paragraph has a character style, perhaps called *Emphasized*, then applying the ResetChar (Ctrl+Space) command to it resets the character formatting to that of the underlying paragraph style. ResetChar does not reset a selection to the underlying character style. To do that, you must reapply the character style.

Character Styles

Word for Windows 6 also lets you have *character styles* in your documents. Missing from previous versions of Word for Windows, character styles enable you to apply several character formats at once within a paragraph. By default, a paragraph style has a single character style. However, you can have as many character styles within a paragraph as you like. By doing this, you can use the paragraph's character formatting as a kind of baseline or common denominator formatting, and use individual character formatting or character styles to handle variation from the baseline.

Character formatting includes

- Font
- Point size
- Language
- Distance from baseline (superscript and subscript)
- Style (bold, italic, hidden, underlining, and so forth)
- Character spacing (condensed, expanded, and so forth; see Figure 22.4)
- Color

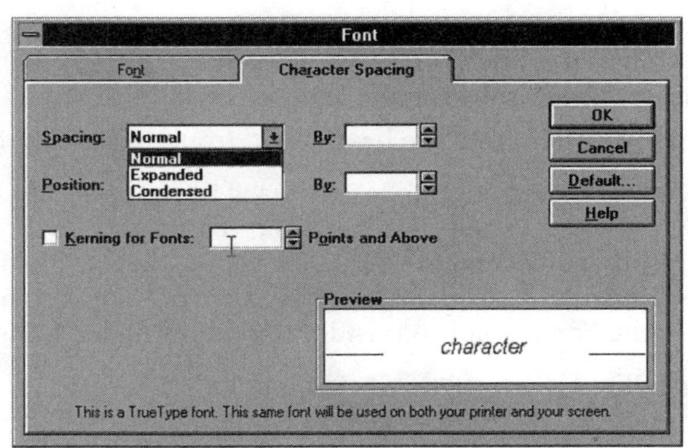

FIGURE 22.4. *The character spacing option lets you condense and expand text for special effects.*

If you never used Word for DOS, you might be wondering why you would want to use character styles. Consider something as seemingly innocent as formatting references to books, articles, and magazine titles. Depending on the publication standards being asserted, book and magazine titles might have to be formatted as underlined, italic, bold, bold-italic, or bold-underline. What if, in a long journal article, you meticulously apply italics to hundreds of journal titles, and then discover that the journal to which you're submitting the article wants you to use bold italics instead?

You could try your hand at doing character formatting search and replace. However, the same publisher previously told you to use italics for unfamiliar terms. So, you'd have to examine each occurrence of italics, one-by-one, and make a decision about whether or not it needs to be changed. Ouch!

What if, however, you had wisely decided to format each title with a special character style called *title reference*. Now, all you have to do is redefine the formatting of the *title reference* style, and all titles automatically change to the new format. While you're at it, I also hope that you used a special style for those unfamiliar terms as well. A publisher who changes the formatting requirements *after* you've written something might just as easily do it again.

Style Hierarchies

Before you start formatting willy-nilly, it might help to have some overall formatting strategies in mind. Word has several tools that can make using styles very automatic. It helps to have an overall strategy in mind as you go about setting up your styles.

Based on

When you create a style, Word lets you base it on an existing style. By doing that, you can link styles together to give your formatting a head start. Consider a heading style, for example. All heading styles usually have several features in common:

- Keep with next (forces a paragraph to print on the same page as the paragraph that follows; prevents a heading from appearing on the bottom of a page without the first few lines of the following paragraph)
- Spacing after (sets the heading off from the section it heads)

If all heading styles have those features in common, then why not format the first heading (*Heading 1*) and base all other heading styles on *Heading 1*. For some documents, *Heading 1* becomes the foundation for all other heading styles. If you have other aspects that cumulate, you might base *Heading 2* on *Heading 1*, *Heading 3* on *Heading 2*, and so on. For example, consider the following list of heading styles:

Heading 1	18-point, Arial, bold, 1.5 before, 1.0 after, keep with next, based on Normal

Heading 2 — 16-point, Arial, bold, 1.0 before, 1.0 after, keep with next, based on Heading 1

Heading 3 — 14-point, Arial, bold, .5 before, 1.0 after, keep with next, based on Heading 2

Heading 4 — 12-point, Arial, bold, 0 before, 1.0 after, keep with next, based on Heading 3

Heading 5 — 12-point, Arial, 0 before, 1.0 after, keep with next, based on Heading 4

If you base 2 on 1, 3, on 2, 4 on 3, and 5 on 4, much of your style setup work can be done automatically. In this case, all heading styles use the Arial font, keep with next (meaning a heading won't appear at the bottom of a page without some text from the section it heads), and 1.0 spacing after. You need to define those attributes only once. When you set up Headings 2 through 5, they automatically inherit those attributes from the styles upon which they are based. The next savings comes with Heading 5. Here, it inherits the point size and the 0 lines before spacing from Heading 4.

Consider the document that requires the same font throughout (Century Schoolbook, for example). If you create a heading hierarchy, as shown here, with all styles ultimately linked to *Normal*, then the font definition in the style called *Normal* controls the typeface throughout the document. Variations in pointsize would be handled by the different styles, but the typeface itself would be set in just one place. If you wanted to work on your document in Arial (because you find it easier on your eyes), you could leave Normal's font set at Arial while you're composing. Then, when you're ready to print, just change it to Century Schoolbook. One change takes care of everything.

PROCEDURE 22.1. BASING A STYLE ON ANOTHER STYLE.

1. Select **F**ormat | **S**tyle (shortcut: press Ctrl+Shift+S twice), to select the Style dialog box, shown in Figure 22.5.

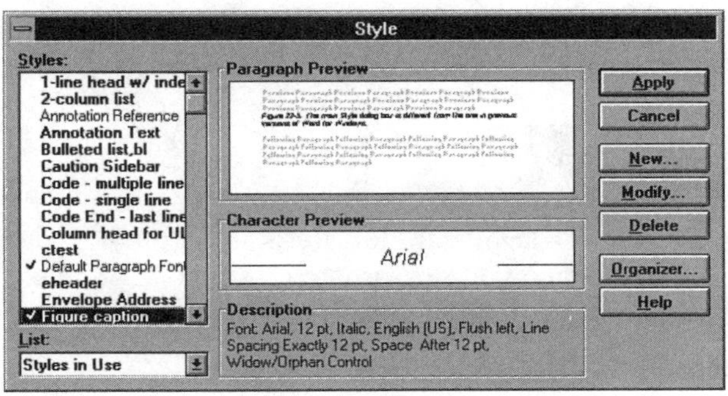

FIGURE 22.5. *The main Style dialog box is different from the one in previous versions of Word for Windows.*

2. Select the style you want to change.
3. Click **M**odify to display the Modify Style dialog box, as shown in Figure 22.6.
4. Click the **L**ist expansion arrow for Based on.
5. Select the style upon which you want to base the style you're changing.
6. Click OK.
7. Click Close.

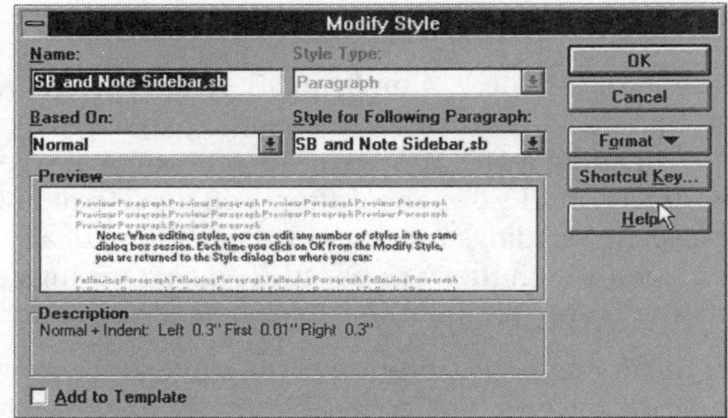

FIGURE 22.6.
Changes to styles begin in the Modify Style dialog box.

SUPER NOTE

When editing styles, you can edit any number of styles in the same dialog box session. Each time you click OK from the Modify Style, you are returned to the Style dialog box where you can:

- Select another style to edit
- Apply the style you've been editing to the selection
- Click Close to close the Style dialog without applying the style to the current selection

SUPER SIDEBAR

If you're editing multiple styles, remember to click Close rather than Apply when you're ready to close the dialog box.

SUPER NOTE

When modifying styles that you'll want to add to the template, you can meticulously select the **A**dd to Template box each time. Unfortunately, Word unchecks the **A**dd to Template option each time you select the **M**odify button. To some Word users, this is infuriating. A more palatable alternative is to go with the flow and copy the files you've changed to the template using the Organizer when you're done. See Chapter 21, "Templates and Wizards," for more on how to use the organizer.

Style for Following Paragraph

Another formatting convenience is Word's ability to automatically switch to a new style when you press Enter after editing a particular style. For example, each time I finish typing the text in a heading style, I invariably want the next paragraph to use the style called *Normal*. If I set the Style for Following Paragraph to *Normal*, Word automatically switches to *Normal* when I press the Enter key at the end of a heading.

PROCEDURE 22.2. SETTING THE STYLE FOR FOLLOWING PARAGRAPH.

1. Select **F**ormat | **S**tyle.
2. Select the style you want to change.
3. Click **M**odify.
4. Click the **L**ist expansion arrow for Style for Following Paragraph.
5. Select the style you want to always follow the style you're modifying.
6. Click OK.
7. Click Close.

Outlining and Aliases

Another major consideration in setting up styles is their use in outlining. When I first started using Word, I was tempted to name my major headings *1head*, *2head*, *3head*, and so forth. That way, when I pressed Ctrl+S, I could just type a number (1 for 1head, 2 for 2head, and so forth) to immediately hone in on the heading I wanted to use. I quickly discovered, however, that Word's outlining works only with the nine headings named *Heading 1* through *Heading 9*. If you want to use Word's outlining, you must use those heading names. You can redefine the heading formats in any way you like. However, Word uses those nine names as a basis for collapsing, expanding, and organizing text in outlining mode.

Enter Word for Windows 6! Somebody at Microsoft finally saw the light and decided to let us use *aliases* (alternative names) for styles—including heading styles. This means that you can now do exactly what I wanted to do. Even better, you can now give your Word for Windows styles the same succinct two-character names you could in Word for DOS. This also means that I can satisfy my publisher's need to have styles identified as HA, HB, HC, and so forth, instead of Heading 1, Heading 2, and Heading 3. Previously, acquiescing to that requirement meant foregoing the delights of outlining. Now we can have it both ways.

PROCEDURE 22.3. CREATING A STYLE NAME ALIAS FOR THE CURRENT STYLE.

1. Click the Style box in the formatting toolbar, and add a comma, plus the alias (alternative name) after the current style name (`N` for Normal, `H1` for Heading 1, and so forth).
2. Press Enter.

PROCEDURE 22.4. APPLYING A STYLE USING ITS ALIAS.

1. Click the Style name box (or press Ctrl+Shift+S).
2. Type the alias and press Enter.

PROCEDURE 22.5. ADDING ALIASES USING THE STYLE DIALOG BOX.

1. Select **F**ormat | **S**tyle (or press Ctrl+Shift+S twice).
2. Select the style you want to modify (change the list using the list options, if necessary, to display the style you want to modify).
3. Click **M**odify.
4. In the name field, add a comma, plus the alias after the current style name.
5. Click OK.
6. Repeat Steps 2 through 5 as needed, adding aliases for any number of styles.
7. Click Close.

PROCEDURE 22.6. REMOVING ALIASES.

1. Select **F**ormat | **S**tyle.
2. Select the style you want to modify (change the list using the list options, if necessary, to display the style you want to modify).
3. Click **M**odify.
4. Edit the name field, and remove the alias and the comma.
5. Click OK.

Why Use Aliases Instead of Keyboard Shortcut Assignments?

Well, that's a perfectly valid question. Some styles (like Normal, Heading 1, Heading 2, Heading 3, and the List style) have built-in shortcuts, as shown in Table 22.1. The L, 1,

2, 3, and N choices are, by and large, pretty intuitive. However, notice that one is Alt+Shift, another is Ctrl+Shift, and the other three are Alt+Ctrl. Which shift key to press is not intuitive—not by a long shot. Add to this the fact that many keyboards may already be chock-full of keyboard assignments their owners can't or simply won't remember. Nevertheless, a simple, consistent, easy-to-remember alias or abbreviation for a style name might be a welcome time-saver. Moreover, users migrating from Word for DOS might need this final nudge to take the Word for Windows plunge.

Table 22.1. Built-in style keyboard shortcuts.

Style	*Shortcut*
Normal	Alt+Shift+N
Heading 1	Alt+Ctrl+1
Heading 2	Alt+Ctrl+2
Heading 3	Alt+Ctrl+3
List	Ctrl+Shift+L

Built-in Styles

Every Word document has 73 built-in (standard) styles. When you first acquired Word, you may have noticed that documents based on NORMAL (the template) have only five styles, as shown in Figure 22.7.

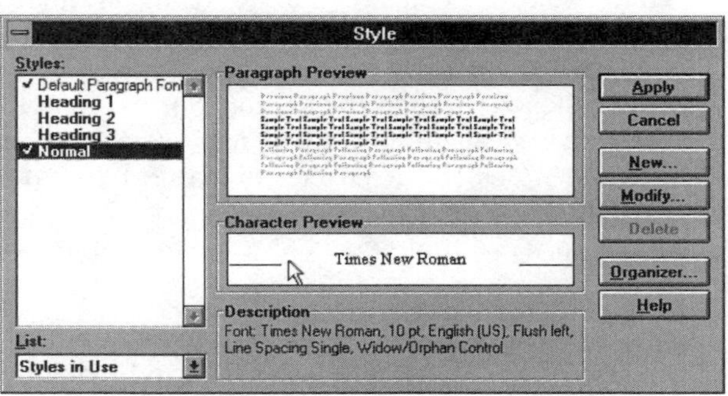

FIGURE 22.7.
The basic style list before any user customization.

However, with the Style dialog box on-screen, you can display just this limited list, the nonstandard (user-created) styles, or all styles, as shown in Figure 22.8. Whenever you select a feature that automatically uses one of the built-in styles (for example, annotation text and annotation reference), Word automatically starts displaying that style in the Styles in Use list that accompanies that template. Once a built-in style gets onto that list and is saved to a template, you're pretty much stuck with seeing it, unless you use the Organizer to rebuild the template from scratch, carefully omitting that style from what you want to copy.

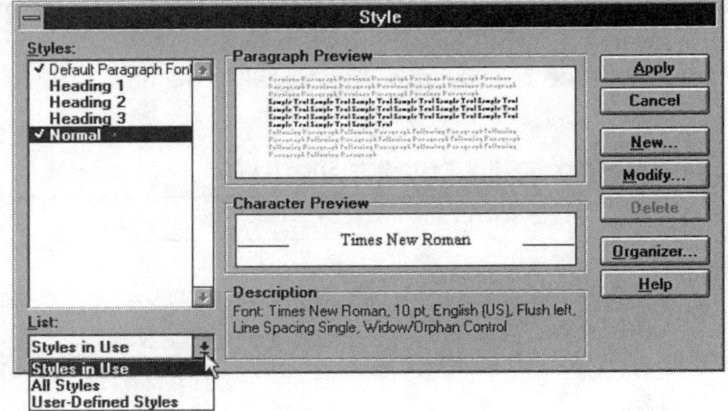

FIGURE 22.8.
Select a List option to display all styles, the user-defined styles, or just those in use.

PROCEDURE 22.7. CHANGING THE STYLE LIST.

1. Select `Format¦Style`.
2. Click the List expansion arrow next to the List options.
3. Select Styles in Use, All Styles, or User-Defined Styles.

SUPER

"Wait a minute!" you say. "I'm not using all those styles!" Yeah, well, if you get technical about it, the styles you see if you select the Styles in Use list aren't exactly just the styles in use. It's a combination of the five basic styles you see in the default Normal template, as well as any standard styles actually in use, any user-created styles, and any user-modified styles. In the case of the latter two types, it doesn't matter if they're actually in use. The fact that you created or modified them signals to Word that you want them available, so they go on the Styles in Use list.

None of the styles on the starting list of 73 can be deleted. As shown in Figure 22.9, whenever a built-in style name is displayed, the Delete option is unavailable. You can, however, change any of the built-in styles as much as you please, even adding aliases to them for easier access. In fact, I don't think I've ever encountered any Word user who's been content to leave the Normal and Header styles alone.

FIGURE 22.9.
You can change, but not delete, the 73 built-in style names.

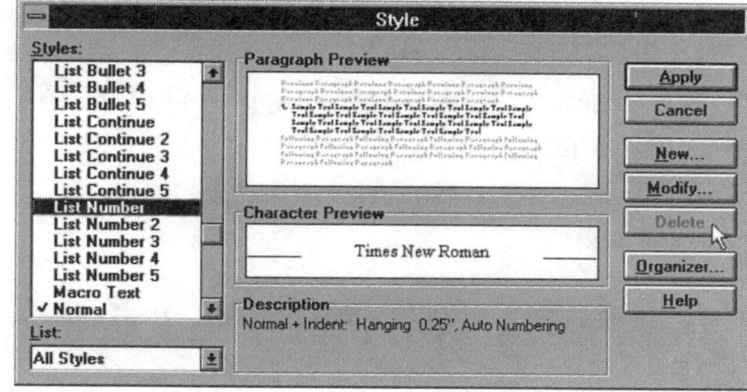

Using Styles

Styles can be applied in several ways. To apply a paragraph style to a single paragraph, all you have to do is have the insertion point anywhere in that paragraph and then select that style. To apply paragraph styles to multiple paragraphs or a character style to text, you must first select the text to which you want the style to apply.

Applying Styles to Text you are About to Type

To apply a style to text you are about to type, simply select the style and begin typing. If you want to apply a different paragraph style to a new paragraph you are about to type, you must press Enter to end the current paragraph before selecting the new style. If you select the new style at the end of a paragraph that already contains text, the style of the whole paragraph changes to the new style. Make sure that the insertion point is in the new paragraph before applying the style.

PROCEDURE 22.8. SETTING THE STYLE FOR TEXT YOU ARE ABOUT TO TYPE.

1. If you're creating a new paragraph, press Enter.
2. Press Ctrl+Shift+S.
3. Either type the name of the style you want to apply and press Enter, or use the cursor keys to select the style you want to use and press Enter.
4. Type the text.

SUPER TIP

In Step 3, type the first one or two letters of the style name to accelerate the cursor to it. The next press of the down-arrow selects the first style that begins with those letters. Or, add an alias to the style so you don't need to press the down arrow.

PROCEDURE 22.9. SETTING THE STYLE FOR TEXT YOU ARE ABOUT TO TYPE USING AN ALIAS.

1. If you're creating a new paragraph, press Enter.
2. Press Ctrl+Shift+S.
3. Type the alias and press Enter.
4. Type the text.

Applying Paragraph Styles to Existing Text

PROCEDURE 22.10. APPLYING A PARAGRAPH STYLE USING THE MOUSE.

1. Click in the paragraph you want to format, or select the paragraphs you want to format if you're formatting more than one.
2. Click the **List** expansion arrow beside the style name on the formatting toolbar (see Figure 22.10).
3. Scroll to the style you want to apply.
4. Click the style to apply it.

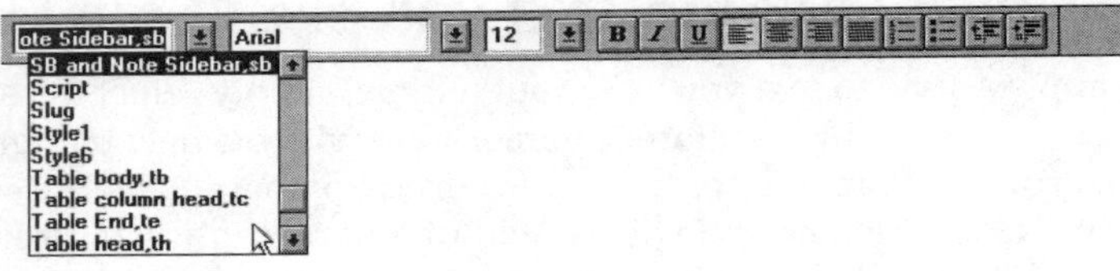

FIGURE 22.10.
Use the style drop-down list from the formatting toolbar to apply styles with the mouse.

SUPER NOTE

If you click the same style as the one currently in effect, and if the current formatting contains any paragraph formatting different from the style you're applying, Word issues the prompt shown in Figure 22.11. If you select the first option, Word redefines the style to match the current selection. All other paragraphs with the same style name (even those that aren't selected) also are changed. If you select the second option, Word applies the style to the current selection, removing the deviation from the applied style (the equivalent of having pressed Ctrl+Q, Reset Paragraph).

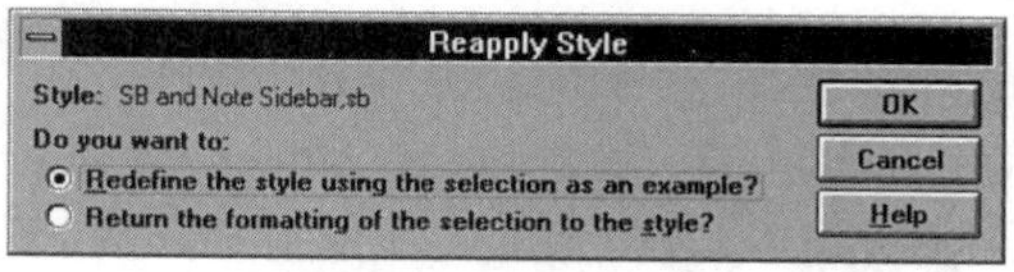

FIGURE 22.11.
Word offers to redefine the style or reformat the text when the defined style differs from the current formatting.

PROCEDURE 22.11. APPLYING A PARAGRAPH STYLE USING THE KEYBOARD.

1. Press Ctrl+S.
2. Type the first letter or letters of the style you want to apply.
3. Press the Down arrow (unless you typed the whole style name or alias in Step 2).
4. Verify that the style is selected, and press Enter.

SUPER CAUTION

Using the shortcut technique of typing the first few letters of the style name can sometimes result in accidentally creating a new style rather than applying an existing one. For example, if you type `Nor` for *Normal* and press Enter without first pressing the Down arrow, Word creates a style called *Nor* instead of applying *Normal*. You must press the Down arrow after typing the first few letters of a style name in order to get Word to select the style whose name you started. Otherwise, you'll end up with a new style. If you use this technique for applying styles (instead of creating keyboard shortcuts), you would be wise to assign aliases to frequently-used style names.

Applying Character Styles to Existing Text

To apply a character style to existing text, use the same technique and rules that you use when applying any other character formatting to text. To apply character formatting to a word, either the cursor must be between the first and last character of the word, or the word must be selected. To apply character formatting to any unit of text other than a word, you must first select it.

PROCEDURE 22.12. APPLYING A CHARACTER STYLE TO A SINGLE WORD.

1. Click anywhere on the interior of the word (that is, after the first character or before the last character).
2. Press Ctrl+Shift+S.
3. Type the first letter or letters of the style you want to apply.

4. Press the Down arrow (unless you typed the whole style name or alias in Step 3).
5. Verify that the style is selected, and press Enter.

To apply a character style to a select, select the text you want to format, and then follow the procedure beginning at Step 2.

Using Style by Example

Styles can be modified and created in several ways. The most natural method is probably *style by example*. Using style by example, you perform whatever formatting you want, and then you give it a name.

Using Style by Example to Modify a Style

You first use individual formatting techniques—ruler, toolbars, keystrokes, and so forth—to format a passage of text as you want it to appear. Then select the style and tell Word to redefine it according to the selected text.

PROCEDURE 22.13. USING STYLE BY EXAMPLE TO MODIFY A STYLE.

1. Select the text whose style you want to change. Use the formatting toolbar to confirm that the section contains just that style (if the selection contains multiple styles or more than 50 paragraphs, the style name in the toolbar is blank).
2. Use whatever technique you want to reformat the text (for example, Ctrl+O to set before paragraph spacing to one line, Ctrl+B for bold, Ctrl+E for center, the formatting toolbar to change the font and point size, and so forth).
3. Press Ctrl+Shift+S (the style of the current selection should automatically be highlighted; if not, then select it).
4. Press Enter.
5. Word offers you the two choices shown in Figure 22.11. Select the first choice to redefine the style according to the current formatting. (If you select the second choice, the formatting is reset to the current style).

Using Style by Example to Create a Style

Creating a new style is similar to modifying an existing style. In fact, some users accidentally create new styles while trying to modify an existing one.

PROCEDURE 22.14. USING STYLE BY EXAMPLE TO CREATE A PARAGRAPH STYLE.

1. Select the text whose style for which you want to create a new style. Disregard the style name that is currently showing.

2. Use whatever technique you want to reformat the text (for example, Ctrl+O to set before paragraph spacing to one line, Ctrl+B for bold, Ctrl+E for center, use the formatting toolbar to change the font and point size, and so forth).
3. Press Ctrl+S.
4. Type a name for the new style, and press Enter.

PROCEDURE 22.15. USING STYLE BY EXAMPLE TO CREATE A CHARACTER STYLE.

1. Select the text whose style for which you want to create a new style. Disregard the style name that is currently showing.
2. Use whatever technique you want to reformat the text (for example, Ctrl+B for bold, Ctrl+I for italic, or the formatting toolbar to change the font and point size).
3. Press Ctrl+Shift+S, twice.
4. Click **N**ew.
5. In the **N**ame field, type a name for the character style.
6. Under Style **T**ype, select Character.
7. If desired, click Add to Template.
8. If desired, select a different **B**ased On style.
9. Click OK.
10. Click Close.

Using the Style Dialog Box

You can use the Style dialog box to make explicit changes to styles, make shortcut key assignments, as well as to access the Organizer to copy styles to and from different templates. You also can use the Styles dialog box to "read" the makeup of a style. To display the Style dialog box, select **F**ormat | **S**tyle, or press Ctrl+Shift+S twice.

Selecting a Style

You can use the Style dialog box to set a style for the current paragraph or to create a new style.

PROCEDURE 22.16. APPLYING A STYLE USING THE STYLE DIALOG BOX.

1. Select the text you want to format.
2. Press Ctrl+Shift+S; note that as you scroll the list of styles, a description is shown in the bottom window, a character preview is shown in the middle window, and a paragraph preview is shown in the top window. Note also that character styles are shown in normal font, while paragraph styles are bold. The current character and paragraph styles are shown as checked, as shown in Figure 22.12.

3. Use the Up or Down arrow or mouse to select the style you want to apply.
4. Press Enter or click Apply (or double-click the desired style in Step 3).

SUPER NOTE

You can use the List feature to change the styles that are displayed.

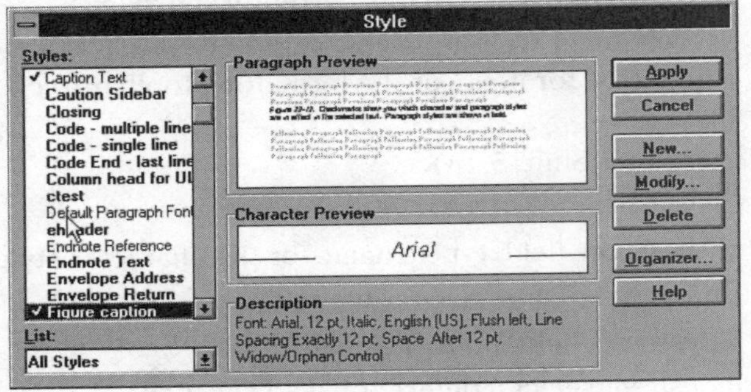

FIGURE 22.12. *Checkmarks show you which character and paragraph styles are in effect in the selected text. Paragraph styles are shown in bold.*

Formatting Toolbar Versus Style Dialog Box

One interesting thing to note is the different behavior of the style list box on the formatting toolbar. If the current paragraph contains variations from the underlying style (the current paragraph was explicitly left-aligned, for example, instead of the default, centered style), if you try to apply the style using the formatting toolbar, Word asks if you want to redefine the style based on the selection (style by example). If you use the Style dialog box, however, Word applies the style you select without prompting, automatically reformatting the current selection. This turns out to be a convenient way to override the prompt when you want to reset the formatting of the current paragraph to the underlying style. To remove all selection-wide formatting that is different from the underlying style, follow the procedure shown here.

PROCEDURE 22.17. REMOVING NONSTYLE FORMATTING FROM A PARAGRAPH.

1. Select the text you want to format (if applying a paragraph style, you need only have the insertion point in the paragraph; the whole paragraph does not need to be highlighted).
2. Press Ctrl+Shift+S; note that the current style is already selected.
3. Press Enter or click Apply.

SUPER NOTE

Reapplying the current style this way bypasses the `Do you want to...?` prompt. This procedure replaces all formatting in the selection with that of the style you apply.

Reapplying a Style Versus Reset Paragraph

You can reset the paragraph-level formatting of a paragraph to the current style by pressing Ctrl+Q (Reset Paragraph). This is similar but not identical to applying a style using the style dialog box. When you use Ctrl+Q, only the paragraph-level formatting is set to the current style. The character formatting is left untouched. When you use the style dialog box, however (which is equivalent to using the style list box on the formatting toolbar and then answering No to the `What do you want to do...` prompt), the character formatting of the selection may be reset to the current style as well.

If the whole paragraph or selection has identical character formatting that is different from the style's character formatting (that is, the selection is all italic, but the style is not), the italics are removed (see Figure 22.13) when you reapply a style, but not when you use Ctrl+Q. If part of the selection is italic, however, that character formatting is preserved using either technique. To remove all character variations from the underlying style—including individual words—you would need to use the ResetChar command (Ctrl+Space).

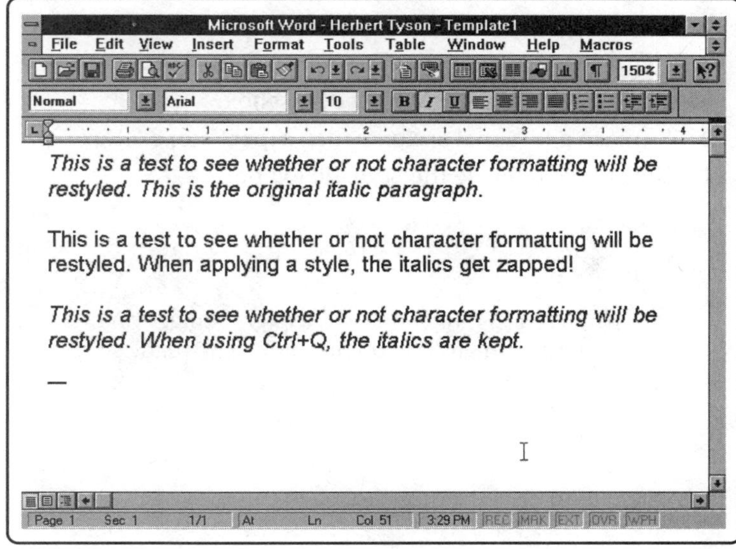

FIGURE 22.13.
Applying a style using the Style dialog box resets variant character formatting if it is uniform throughout the style's domain. Using Ctrl+Q (Reset Paragraph) would preserve the variation.

Keyboard Shortcuts

You can use the Style dialog box to create keyboard shortcuts for styles. For example, the book I'm writing right now uses a number of styles, some of which I use repeatedly. I'm able to speed up my work by assigning keyboard shortcuts to the styles I use most often. For the sake of logic, I assigned Ctrl+Shift+1 through Ctrl+Shift+7 to *Heading 1* through *Heading 7* (the built-in Alt+Shift+1 through +3 assignments for *Heading 1* through *3* notwithstanding). I also assigned Ctrl+Shift+0 to a style called *NP without first lin*, which appears to be the style my publisher wants me to use for most paragraph formatting (like this one).

If you want to make multiple keyboard assignments to styles, don't use the Style dialog box to do it. It's entirely too cumbersome, as you can see in the procedure shown. Instead, use the **T**ools | **C**ustomize procedure, shown just after the Style method.

PROCEDURE 22.18. ASSIGNING SHORTCUT KEYS TO STYLES USING THE STYLE DIALOG BOX.

1. Select F**o**rmat | **S**tyle (or press Ctrl+Shift+S).
2. Select the style you want to change.
3. Click **M**odify.
4. Click Shortcut **K**ey; a partially-enabled version of the Customize screen appears, as shown in Figure 22.14.
5. Press the key combination you want to assign.
6. Use the Sa**v**e Changes In box to tell Word where to store the key assignment (for example, the current template or NORMAL.DOT).
7. Click **A**ssign.
8. Click Close, to close the Customize dialog box.
9. Click OK to close the Modify dialog box.
10. To make additional assignments, repeat steps 2 through 9.
11. Click Close to close the Style dialog box.

> **SUPER TIP**
>
> If you need to make multiple assignments, don't use the procedure just shown. Use the following procedure instead.

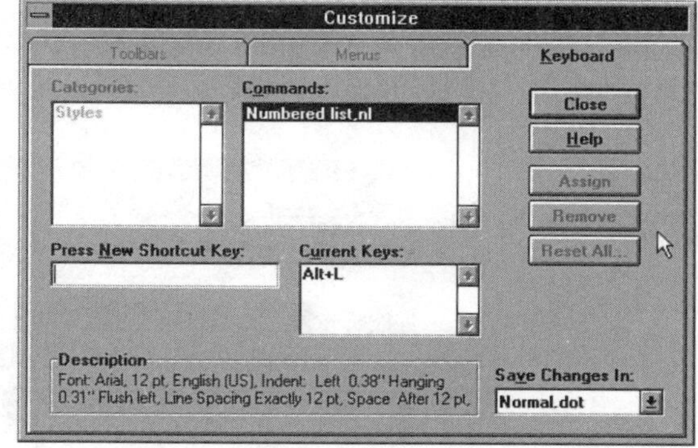

FIGURE 22.14.
When assigning shortcut keys from the Style dialog box, you're limited to a tedious one-at-a-time process.

PROCEDURE 22.19. ASSIGNING SHORTCUT KEYS TO STYLES THE EASY WAY USING CUSTOMIZE DIALOG BOX.

1. Select **T**ools | **C**ustomize.
2. Click the **K**eyboard tab.
3. Under Categories, select Styles, as shown in Figure 22.15.
4. Click the Style you want to assign.
5. Click in the Press **N**ew Shortcut Key field.
6. Press the shortcut key you want to use.
7. Click **A**ssign.
8. Repeat Steps 4 through 7 for each style you want to assign.
9. Click Close.

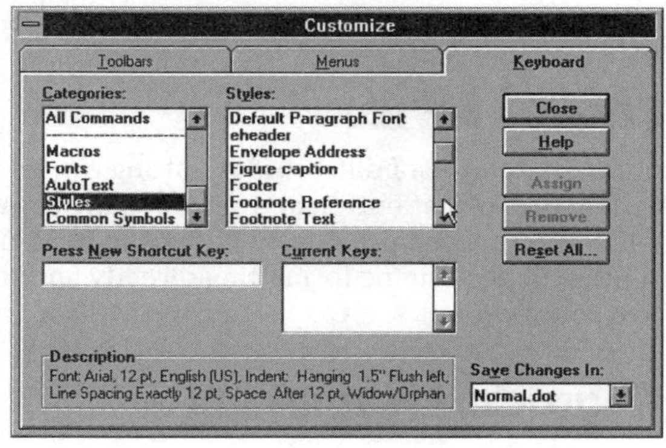

FIGURE 22.15.
When making style key assignments using ***T****ools |* ***C****ustomize, you can easily make multiple assignments in one pass.*

Description

When the Style dialog box is displayed on-screen, Word shows you a description of the style. Note the description shown in Figure 22.16. The notation **Heading 1 + Font:**

12 pt means that the *Heading 2* style shown here is the same as *Heading 1*, but has one difference: the font is 12 points, instead of whatever the font for *Heading 1* is. Note that the **Heading 1 +** also tells you that *Heading 2* is based on *Heading 1*.

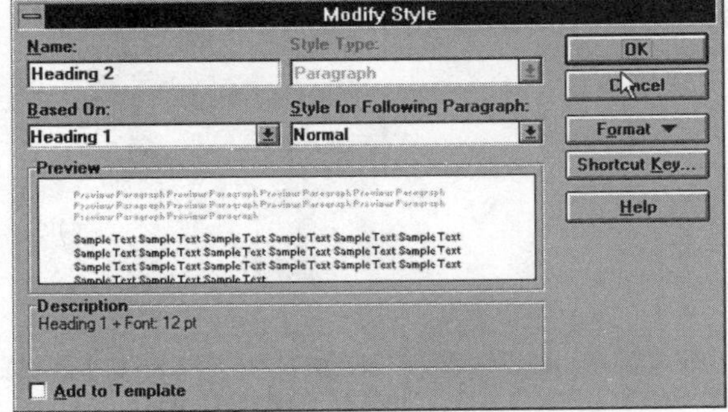

FIGURE 22.16. *The description tells you what the style is based on, and how it differs.*

SUPER UPGRADE NOTE

In Word for Windows 2, when the Style dialog box was on-screen, you could use shortcut formatting keys to manipulate the style definition (for example, pressing Ctrl+L to set the alignment to left, or pressing Ctrl+F to change the font). Under Word 6, unfortunately, those helpful shortcuts are gone. You now must suffer the tedium of clicking the F**o**rmat button and selecting from among the formatting options. This setback makes style-by-example (format first, then give it a style name) all the more attractive.

Elements of Style

Styles embrace a number of different formatting elements. You can access these elements by using the F**o**rmat button and selecting the appropriate options, as shown in Figure 22.17. As discussed previously under the heading *Style by example,* you also have the option of performing formatting directly and then redefining the format according to a selection.

Font (Character) Formatting

The character formatting section is identical to the Format | Font dialog box discussed in Chapter 11, "Font Formatting."

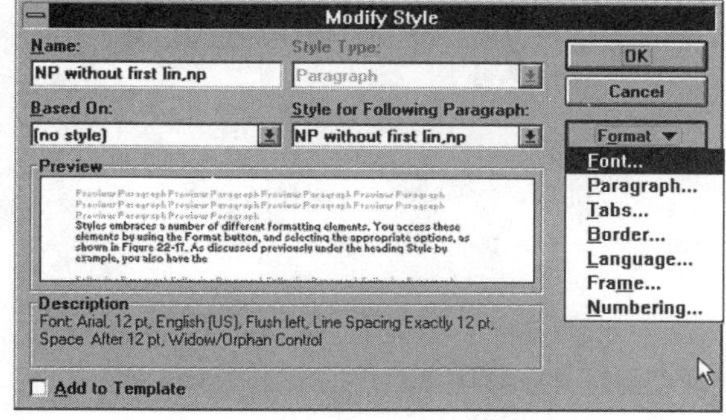

FIGURE 22.17.
*The F**o**rmat button has a drop-down list of formatting choices.*

PROCEDURE 22.20. SETTING CHARACTER FORMATTING USING THE FONT OPTION.

1. Select F**o**rmat | **S**tyle.
2. Select the style you want to change (if different from the current style).
3. Click **M**odify.
4. Click the **A**dd to Template option, if desired.
5. Click the F**o**rmat button.
6. Click the **F**ont option (for the dialog box shown in Figure 22.18).
7. Select the Fo**n**t or Cha**r**acter Spacing tab.
8. Select the formatting you want.
9. Click OK to close the Font dialog.
10. Click OK to close the Modify dialog.
11. Click Close to change the style; click Apply to change the styles and to apply the style to the current selection.

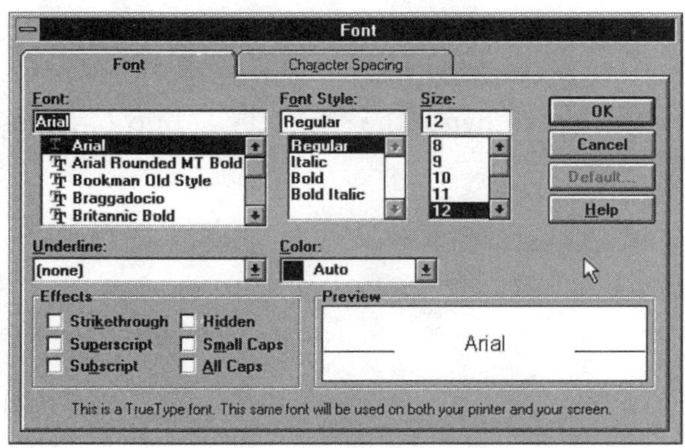

FIGURE 22.18.
Selecting Font characteristics from the Modify Styles dialog.

SUPER NOTE

Do not select Apply if the style name of the current selection is different from one you are changing unless you want to apply a different style. After selecting Close, all text matching the style you change is automatically reformatted according to the changes you made.

Paragraph Formatting

The paragraph formatting dialog box is identical to the Format | Paragraph dialog box discussed in Chapter 12, "Paragraph Formatting." The difference is that formatting you change here is not applied to the selection unless you select the Apply button. If you select Close, the changed style is applied only to text already formatted with that style.

PROCEDURE 22.21. SETTING PARAGRAPH FORMATTING USING THE PARAGRAPH BUTTON.

1. Select **F**ormat | **S**tyle.
2. Select the style you want to change (if different from the current style).
3. Click **M**odify.
4. Click the **A**dd to Template option if desired.
5. Click the F**o**rmat button.
6. Click the Paragraph option (for the dialog box shown in Figure 22.19).
7. Click the **I**ndents and Spacing or Text **F**low tab, depending on what you want to change.
8. Select the formatting you want.
9. Click OK to close the Paragraph dialog.
10. Click OK to close the Modify dialog.
11. Click Close to change the style; click Apply to apply the style to the current selection.

Tabs

The tabs formatting dialog box is identical to the Format | Tabs dialog box discussed in Chapter 12. It is also the same as the Tabs buttons you get in the Format | Paragraph dialog box.

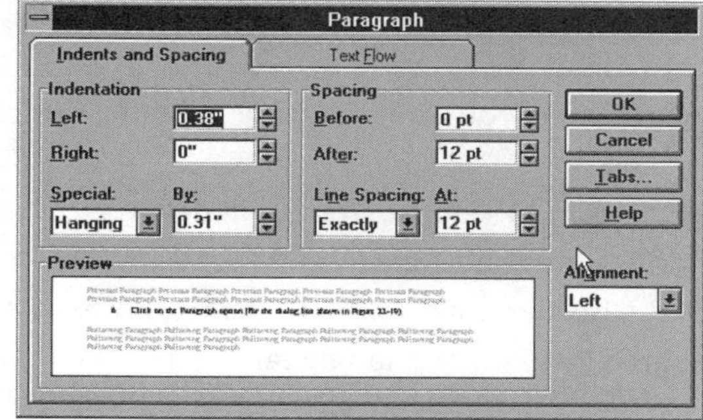

FIGURE 22.19.
Selecting Paragraph formatting from the Modify Styles dialog.

PROCEDURE 22.22. SETTING TAB FORMATTING USING THE TABS BUTTON.

1. Select **F**ormat | **S**tyle.
2. Select the style you want to change (if different from the current style).
3. Click **M**odify.
4. Click the **A**dd to Template option if desired.
5. Click the F**o**rmat button.
6. Click the **T**abs option (for the dialog box shown in Figure 22.20).
7. Select the formatting you want.
8. Click OK to close the Tabs dialog.
9. Click OK to close the Modify dialog.
10. Click Close to change the style; click Apply to apply the style to the current selection.

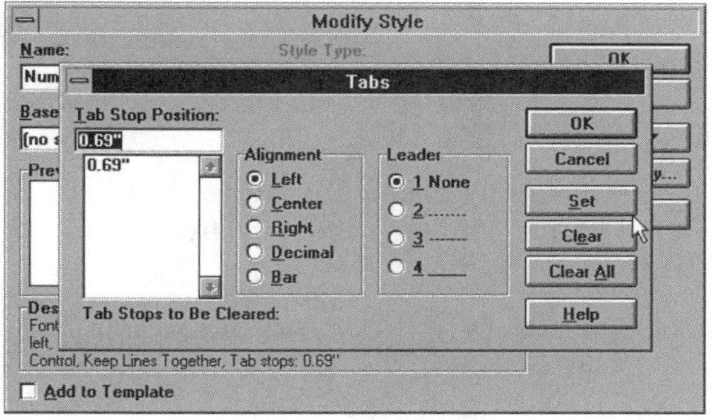

FIGURE 22.20.
Selecting Tab formatting from the Modify Styles dialog.

Borders

The borders formatting dialog box is identical to the Format | Borders dialog box discussed in Chapter 12. Borders are a paragraph-level formatting characteristic, although treated separately by Word.

PROCEDURE 22.23. SETTING BORDER FORMATTING USING THE BORDERS BUTTON.

1. Select **F**ormat | **S**tyle.
2. Select the style you want to change (if different from the current style).
3. Click **M**odify.
4. Click the **A**dd to Template option if desired.
5. Click the F**o**rmat button.
6. Click the Border option (for the dialog box shown in Figure 22.21).
7. Select the **B**orders or **S**hading tab.
8. Select the formatting you want.
9. Click OK to close the Borders dialog.
10. Click OK to close the Modify dialog.
11. Click Close to change the style; click Apply to apply the style to the current selection.

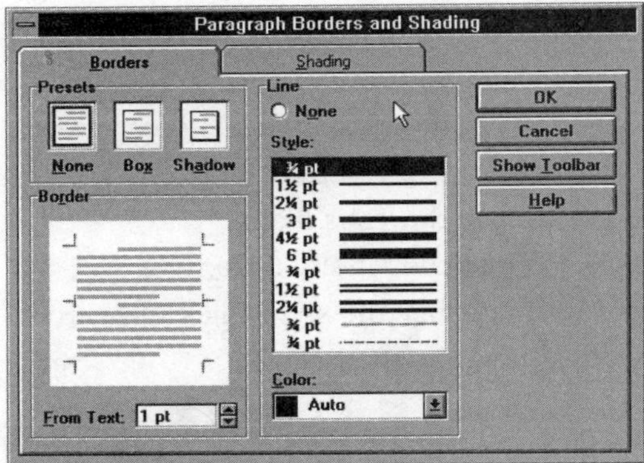

FIGURE 22.21.
Selecting Border formatting from the Modify Styles dialog.

Language Formatting

The language formatting dialog box is identical to the Format | Language dialog box discussed in Chapter 11. Language is really a character (font) format, but for some reason it is treated separately by Word.

PROCEDURE 22.24. SETTING LANGUAGE FORMATTING USING THE LANGUAGE BUTTON.

1. Select **F**ormat | **S**tyle.
2. Select the style you want to change (if different from the current style).
3. Click **M**odify.
4. Click the **A**dd to Template option if desired.

5. Click the Format button.
6. Click the Language option (for the dialog box shown in Figure 22.22).
7. Select the formatting you want.
8. Click OK to close the Language dialog.
9. Click OK to close the Modify dialog.
10. Click Close to change the style; click Apply to apply the style to the current selection.

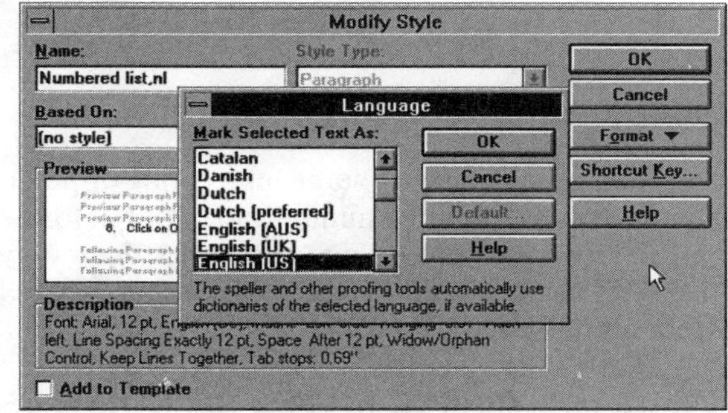

FIGURE 22.22.
Selecting Language formatting from the Modify Styles dialog.

Frames

The Frames formatting dialog box is identical to the Format|Frame dialog box discussed in Chapter 24, "Frames."

PROCEDURE 22.25. SETTING FRAME FORMATTING USING THE PARAGRAPH BUTTON.

1. Select Format|Style.
2. Select the style you want to change (if different from the current style).
3. Click Modify.
4. Click the Add to Template option if desired.
5. Click the Format button.
6. Click the Frame option (for the dialog box shown in Figure 22.23).
7. Select the formatting you want.
8. Click OK to close the Frame dialog.
9. Click OK to close the Modify dialog.
10. Click Close to change the style; click Apply to apply the style to the current selection.

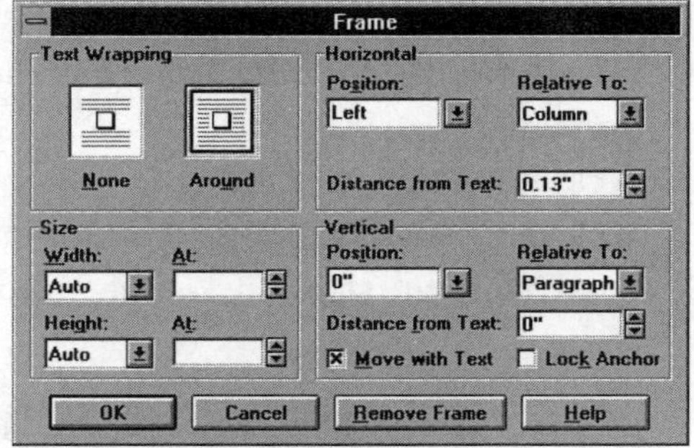

FIGURE 22.23.
Selecting Frame formatting from the Modify Styles dialog.

Numbering

The numbering option presents some interesting opportunities in Word 6. In addition to the obvious uses for creating numbering patterns for heading level paragraphs, you can also trick Word into providing leading text for every occurrence of a particular style, regardless of whether you want numbering, *per se*. First, the obligatory how-to for adjusting numbering formatting.

PROCEDURE 22.26. SETTING NUMBERING FORMATTING USING THE PARAGRAPH BUTTON.

1. Select **F**ormat | **S**tyle.
2. Select the style you want to change (if different from the current style).
3. Click **M**odify.
4. Click the **A**dd to Template option if desired.
5. Click the F**o**rmat button.
6. Click the **N**umbering option (for the dialog box shown in Figure 22.24).
7. Click the Bulleted or Numbered tab, depending on what you want to format.
8. Select the formatting you want.
9. Click OK to close the Bullets and Numbering dialog.
10. Click OK to close the Modify dialog.
11. Click Close to change the style; click Apply to apply the style to the current selection.

Now for the interesting option. Have you ever had a certain type of paragraph or heading that simply *must* begin with the identical text—always? If so, you can use the numbering option to supply the text. Suppose, for example, that you have a paragraph that always starts with the word *Caution:*. You can make Word display the word *Caution* every time a particular style is inserted. Let's call this style Caution Note.

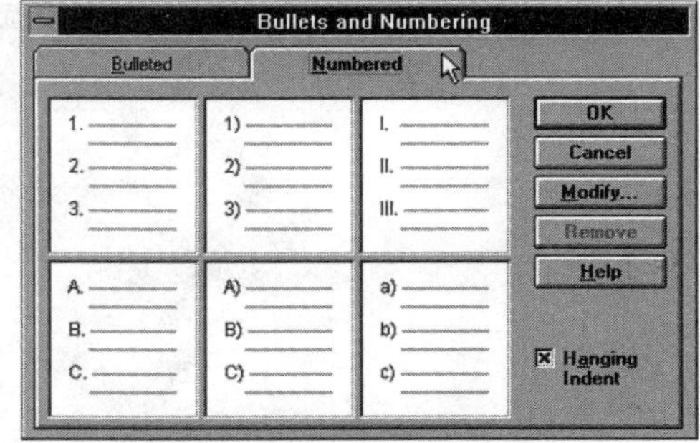

FIGURE 22.24.
Selecting Numbering formatting from the Modify Styles dialog.

PROCEDURE 22.27. ADDING LEADING TEXT TO THE BEGINNING OF A STYLE.

1. Select **F**ormat | **S**tyle.
2. Click **N**ew.
3. In the **B**ased On field, select the name of a style which, except for the text you want to add (for example, `Caution`), is already identically formatted as you need it.
4. In the **S**tyle for Following Paragraph field, type the same style as you did in Step 3 (if the caution note needs multiple paragraphs, this ensures that the word `Caution` shows up only at the beginning).
5. Select Format, and then click the **N**umbering option.
6. Click the **N**umbering tab.
7. Deselect the H**a**nging Indent option, to ensure that your style provides all of the formatting.
8. Click **M**odify.
9. In the Text **B**efore box, type your text (for example, `Caution:`); see Figure 22.25.
10. In the **N**umber box, select (none).
11. In the Text **A**fter box, delete the period.
12. Click OK to close the Modify Numbered List dialog.
13. Click OK to close the New Style dialog.
14. Click Close.

Now, each time you insert the newly-created style, it begins with the text you set in Step 11. You can change that text any time you like as well, simply by changing the style. However, the text doesn't really exist in your file. Go ahead and try to select it. See? It's not really there. It shows up, however, when you print. It also shows up if you save the file to a text with layout file, but not if you save to a plain text file. Keep this in mind if you need to export your cautions to text files.

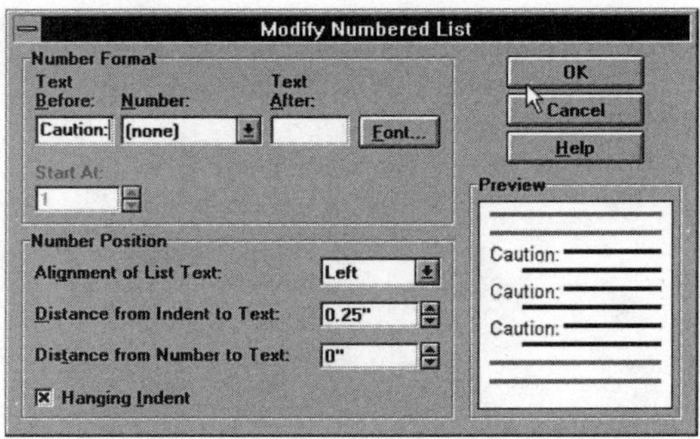

FIGURE 22.25.
Shhhh. Don't tell anyone, but you don't have to use numbering when selecting the numbering option!

The Style Gallery

An interesting and highly useful feature in Word 6 is the style gallery. It's part of Microsoft's stepped-up campaign to get users to learn about and use styles whenever possible, by making it easy to use styles. The style gallery lets you preview how your document looks with various sets of styles applied to it. For the templates that come with Word, it also shows you a sample document using the styles available in the template as well as examples of each of the styles. Once you find a set of styles you like, the style gallery applies those styles to your current document.

PROCEDURE 22.28. USING THE STYLE GALLERY TO PREVIEW STYLES.

1. With a document open in the current window, select **F**ormat | Style Gallery; Word displays the view shown in Figure 22.26, which is a preview of the current document formatted in the current styles.
2. In the Template list, select a template to see how your document would look if its styles were applied to your document; note that the preview window can change dramatically.
3. Use the vertical scrollbar in the preview window to see different parts of the preview document.
4. Use the **P**review options to select **D**ocument (the document in the current window), **E**xample (an example stored as an Autotext entry in the document as Gallery Example), or **S**tyle Sample (examples of each of the available styles).
5. To select other templates not shown, you can use the Browse button to navigate to different directories; note that the template list in the Style Gallery doesn't get updated until you click the OK button in the Select Template Directory (browse) dialog.
6. When and if you see a template whose styles you want to use, click OK; Word applies the styles in the previewed template to the document in the current window.

7. To dismiss the Style Gallery without applying a new set of styles to the current document, select Cancel or press Esc.

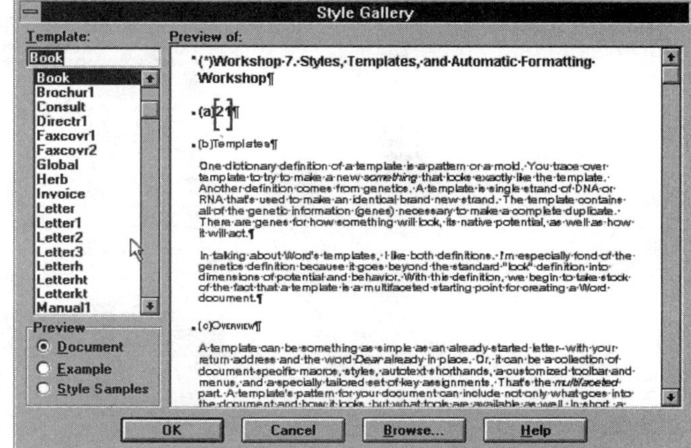

FIGURE 22.26.
*The **F**ormat | **S**tyle Gallery command lets you test a variety of formatting scenarios.*

When you apply styles using the style gallery, Word does not attach the template to your document. Macros, autotext, toolbars, keyboard, and menu assignments from the template are not made available in the current document. Rather, it copies the styles *en masse*. It is equivalent to using the Organizer (**F**ormat | **S**tyle | **O**rganizer) to select all styles in the displayed template and copy them to the current document. It has the following effects:

- Replaces all styles common to both files with the styles in the previewed template.
- Styles in the template but not in the current document are added to the current style list.
- Styles in the current document but not in the template are left as is.

SUPER TIP

It's not obvious, and certainly not easy, but you can use the style gallery to test-drive styles from a nontemplate document, as well. Rather than using the template list, type the fully-qualified document name (for example, `F:\WORD6\BOOK\SUP3.DOC`) into the template name field over the list, as shown in Figure 22.27; but *do not press Enter* just yet. Now, click any preview option, and note that the preview screen changes. If you like what you see, press Enter to apply the displayed styles to your current document.

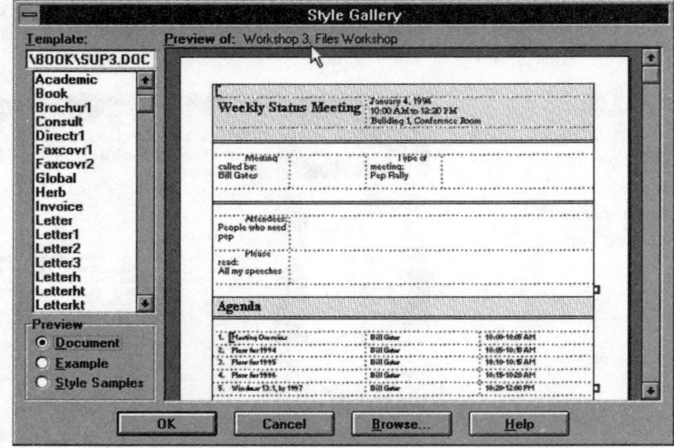

FIGURE 22.27. *Type the fully-qualified filename to use a document instead of a template in the gallery.*

SUPER

Having to type the whole name, and not being able to select from a list, makes this process a bit tedious. However, if you want to apply the styles from another document, wholesale, this can be faster than using the organizer to have to select styles you want to copy. Try it once and see if it can be useful to you. If so, good. If not, then at least you now know that Word's features aren't always as limited as they appear. Or, if you have a group of *.DOC files you'd like to use, then make copies of them (being careful not to overwrite any existing *.DOT files) onto your template directory, naming the copies as *.DOT (for example, `COPY DATA001.DOC \WORD6\TEMPLATE\DATA001.DOT`). Edit the .DOT files to remove any extraneous text (all you need is the styles, right?), and save them as templates.

SUPER TIP

Create your own Gallery Examples. For the Example preview option, Word uses a hidden autotext entry. Take a look at the DIRECTR1.DOT file that comes with Word. You will not see any autotext entries listed. If you select Edit|Autotext, and type a `G`, the words `Gallery Example` suddenly appear, as if by magic! To create your own Gallery Examples:

1. Open a representative document that's based on the template you want to use.
2. Select the text you want to use for the example.

3. Select **E**dit | Auto**T**ext.
4. Set the **M**ake AutoText Entry Available To option to the template to which you want to add the Gallery Example.
5. In the **N**ame field, type `Gallery Example`.
6. Click Add.
7. Select **F**ile | Save A**l**l and confirm saving changes to the template.

This exercise can be a bit tedious. If, however, you manage a number of users who use Word, it can be worth the time and trouble to ensure that Word users have useful examples in the Gallery.

Automatic Formatting

As part of the campaign to get people to use styles—by hook or by crook—Word 6 now sports an automatic formatting feature. Word can now take a document that has no style formatting and add "appropriate" styles to it. For users accustomed to using styles, this might seem a little silly. For users who don't use styles, however, it might be just the jump start they need.

Here's how automatic formatting works. Word searches through your document for formatting patterns and changes. By default, Word applies automatic formatting only to text styled as Normal, leaving styles applied by you intact. So, to get a true test of this feature, the document you submit for automatic formatting should all be styled as Normal, using direct formatting to accomplish all effects.

If the AutoFormat command detects a single, largish, bold, one-line piece of text that might be a heading, then Word formats the text as Heading 1. If AutoFormat finds a bunch of one-line text entries all together, then it's assumed to be a list. If AutoFormat finds smaller, single, bold or otherwise differently-formatted one-liners, then the text is formatted as Heading 2, Heading 3, and so forth, depending on the order of appearance and the kind of formatting they contain.

All in all, the end result isn't terribly bad. As an experiment, I reformatted part of this chapter as Normal and used direct formatting to make the headings and other parts look the way I wanted them to look. I then selected F**o**rmat | **A**utoFormat, and accepted all of the changes. While the resulting document is not what my publisher wants to see, it wasn't unattractive. With a few refinements, a previously unstyled document can become a first-rate example of how formatting should be applied.

SUPER TIP

Even if you already use styles, the **A**utoFormat command is a great way to strip out extraneous tabs, paragraph marks, and other useless formatting you might have acquired when you imported a document from another application. It also can replace straight quotes with typographic quotes, `(c)` with the copyright symbol, and `(o)` with bullets, depending on the options you have selected. So, while, as a refined Stylist, you might rightly sneer at the idea of Style Helper (a la Hamburger Helper), the **A**utoFormat command can save you a lot of manual toil if you use it selectively.

PROCEDURE 22.29. USING AUTOFORMAT TO FORMAT A DOCUMENT THAT HAS NO STYLES.

1. Use direct formatting to make the document look roughly the way you want it to look.
2. Don't select any text unless you want to limit AutoFormat to a specific section of the document.
3. From the menu, choose F**o**rmat | **A**utoFormat (see Figure 22.28).

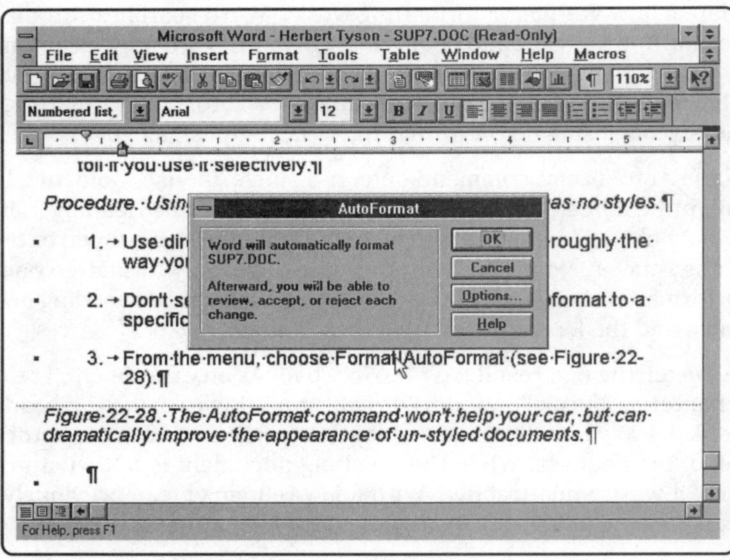

FIGURE 22.28. *The* **A***utoFormat command won't help your car, but it can dramatically improve the appearance of unstyled documents.*

4. Click the **O**ptions button and select any options you want (see Procedure 22.31, Setting AutoFormat Options), and click OK to return to the AutoFormat message box.

5. Click OK to begin autoformatting.
6. When it's done, Word displays a revised AutoFormat message box, as shown in Figure 22.29.
7. AutoFormat applies styles as defined in the current template; click Gallery to see how the AutoFormat changes would look if you were using a different template. If you click OK while the Gallery is displayed, Word incorporates the new styles into the AutoFormatted revisions.
8. Select Review Changes to step through the changes one-by-one (see Procedure 22.30, Reviewing AutoFormat Changes). Select Accept Changes to accept what AutoFormat did. Select Reject All to forget the whole thing.

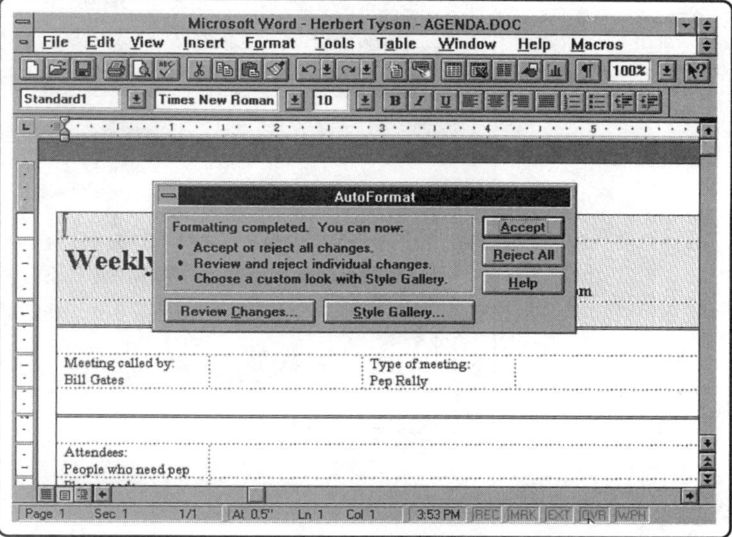

FIGURE 22.29.
AutoFormat offers to take you on a tour of the formatting changes.

SUPER TIP

While the AutoFormat message box (Step 6) is displayed, you can scroll the document window to see how the formatting looks. The message box dims as the document window becomes active. You can even select **V**iew | **P**age Layout to take a more structured look at the autoformatted document, as well as enter and delete text, and select styles and other formatting commands using any active toolbars (even though the Format menu is disabled). Any formatting or text changes you make while in this view are preserved if you accept the revisions, but are scrapped if you cancel the AutoFormat. Once you've had a look around, you can then either go on a structure review (see Reviewing AutoFormat Changes), Accept, or Reject the changes. Keep in mind that if you reject the changes, the ones you made manually while perusing are lost.

PROCEDURE 22.30. REVIEWING AUTOFORMAT CHANGES.

1. From the AutoFormat message box, select Review **C**hanges, for the view shown in Figure 22.30.

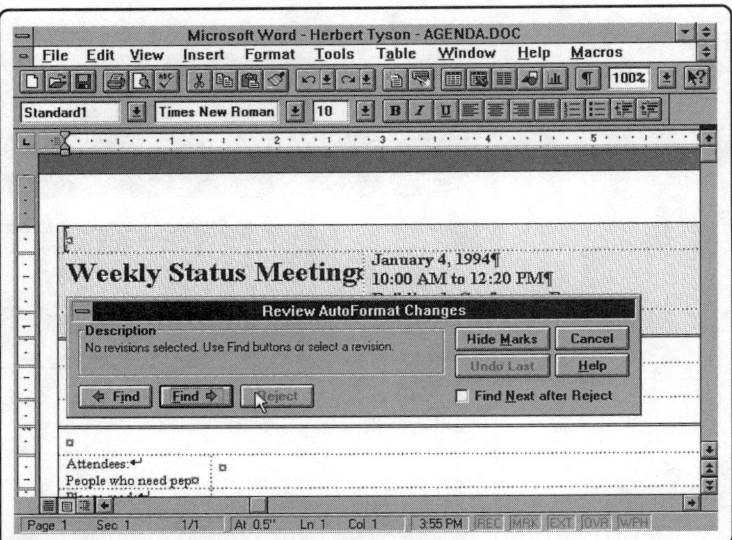

FIGURE 22.30.
Use the Review box to selectively reject changes.

2. Use the Hide **M**arks/Show **M**arks button to toggle the revision marks on or off.
3. To move around, use the **F**ind Previous or F**i**nd Next buttons to move from revision to revision; or, click in the document window and use the mouse and/or keys to scroll around, as desired.
4. Use the **R**eject button to selectively reject the AutoFormat changes. Note that there is no explicit one-by-one Accept button. All remaining nonrejected formatting is accepted (or rejected) all at once from the main AutoFormat message box once the review is done.
5. Click the Find **N**ext after Reject button to automatically advance to the next change after each rejection.
6. Click Close (or Cancel—it becomes Close only if you actively reject some changes) when you've finished the review session.

7. Click **S**tyle Gallery, if desired, to test-drive the fomatting under different style scenarios.
8. Click **A**ccept or **R**eject.

PROCEDURE 22.31. SETTING AUTOFORMAT OPTIONS.

1. From the AutoFormat message box, choose Options, or select Tools | Options | AutoFormat.
2. Select the options you want to use for all AutoFormatting sessions; these options affect the behavior of AutoFormat for this and all future uses until you come back to the options screen and make more changes. See Table 22.2 for a summary of the options.
3. Click OK.

Table 22.2. Summary of AutoFormat Options.

Name of Option	*Effect or Purpose*
Preserve	
Previously Applied **S**tyles	Doesn't disturb nonnormal styles already applied in the document.
Apply Styles To	
Hea**d**ings	Automatically tries to detect and apply Heading 1 through Heading 9 styles.
Lists	Automatically tries to detect and apply list and bullet styles to numbered, bulleted, and multilevel lists. In so doing, Word removes manually-inserted numbers or bullets, or numbers and bullets applied by previous versions of Word.
Other **P**aragraphs	Automatically tries to detect and apply paragraph styles other than headings and list to things like addresses and salutation.
Adjust	
Paragraph **M**arks	Substitutes spacing before and after formatting for extra paragraph marks.

continues

Table 22.2. continued

Name of Option	*Effect or Purpose*
Adjust	
Tabs and Spaces	Replaces spaces with tab characters and removes unnecessary tab characters and spaces.
Empty Paragraphs	Removes extraneous paragraph marks.
Replace	
Straight **Q**uotes With Smart Quotes	Changes ditto marks and apostrophes into directional single and double-quotes.
Symbol Characters With Symbols	Replaces characters commonly used in place of symbols with symbols (for example, *(TM)* and *(C)* with the trademark and copyright symbols).
Bullet Characters With Bullets	Replaces common bullet substitutes (+, *(o)*, and so forth) with bullets per the **F**ormat | Bullets and **N**umbering command.

VIII

Desktop Publishing and Graphics Workshop

Word provides a number of tools for working with graphics. In Chapter 23, “Importing Graphics into Word,” you take a look at moving existing graphics into Word. Chapter 24, “Frames,” shows how to frame and border graphics to achieve desired effects, such text wrapping around pictures. Chapter 25, “Modifying Graphics,” shows how to modify graphics using cropping, scaling, and shading. The last two graphics sessions show how to use Word’s drawing module and Microsoft Graph to create and edit graphics. By combining the tools and procedures shown in these chapters, you can create an exciting variety of compound documents that contain text and graphics. If you’re so inclined, you can use Word, in fact, to produce camera-ready copy, ready for the printshop.

Chapter

23

Importing Graphics into Word

Word provides import "filters" for importing a variety of different graphics formats into Word documents, as shown in Table 23.1.

Table 23.1. Word 6's graphic import filters.

Windows Bitmaps	.BMP
Computer Graphics Metafile	.CGM
AutoCAD Format 2-D	.DXF
Micrografx Designer/Draw	.DRW
Encapsulated Postscript	.EPS
HP Graphic Language	.HGL
Zenographics Mirage	.IMA
Paintbrush	.PCX
Lotus 1-2-3 Graphics	.PIC
Video Show Import	.PIC
AutoCAD Plot File	.PLT
Tagged Image Format	.TIF
Windows PICT	.PCT
Windows Metafile	.WMF
Wordperfect graphics	.WPG

SUPER CAUTION

Import filters are nice, but they're not perfect. The filters for .DRW in particular, have a number of limitations. If you have problems importing into Word in one format, open the files from their original application(s) and try saving them in a different format, and then try again.

Insert Picture

You can use the **Insert|Picture** dialog box to import graphic files in any of the supported formats. If you did not install the necessary filter(s) when you installed Word, you must install them before you can use Insert Picture. See the last section in this Workshop for instructions for adding filters after installation.

SUPER

Actually, the word *picture* is a bit of a misnomer. Word doesn't mean just pictures, *per se*. To Word, graphs, drawings, line art—virtually anything that's not text—is a picture. So, if you're looking for a special flavor of Insert for inserting graphs you created in Lotus 1-2-3 or Excel, **I**nsert | **P**icture is probably what you want. Of course, you may also have DDE and/or OLE options (see later sections). However, **I**nsert | **P**icture can do the job, too.

PROCEDURE 23.1. INSERTING A GRAPHIC INTO A WORD FILE.

1. Move the cursor where you want the graphic to appear.
2. Select **I**nsert | **P**icture.
3. Set List Files of **T**ype to the desired type.
4. Use the **D**irectories and Dri**v**es controls to navigate to the location of the file you want to insert.
5. Click Preview to verify that the graphic is what you want as well as to verify that Word can properly import the file.
6. Click **L**ink to File to reserve the ability to update the picture if it is later modified (see Figure 23.1).

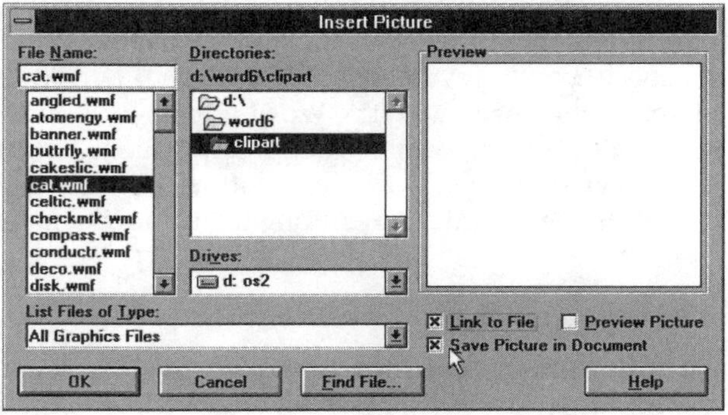

FIGURE 23.1.
Link to File lets you use a picture that might be changed by other applications.

7. If you select the Link option, you can optionally deselect the default Save Picture in Document.
8. Click OK.

SUPER NOTE

It's a good idea to use Preview. Word uses the same filters for previewing as it does for displaying the graphic in a Word document. If you have several different versions of a graphic from which to choose, using Preview lets you select the one that looks best.

SUPER NOTE

The option shown in Step 7 is new with Word 6. If you opt not to save the picture in the document, Word files are much smaller. If you usually work with graphics turned on (**T**ools | **O**ptions | **V**iew, **P**icture Placeholders not enabled), not saving the picture with the file can result in even slower screen updates due to the constant need to reimport the picture each time it's saved.

Here's what happens. When you select the **I**nsert | **P**icture command, Word inserts one of several different fields into the current document:

- Link to File turned off. Word inserts an EMBED field, (for example, `EMBED Word.Picture.6`), with no reference to the file. The picture is stored in the Word file using Word's internal format.
- Link to File turned on. Word inserts an INSERTPICTURE field, (for example, `INCLUDEPICTURE F:\\WORD6\\CLIPART\\BUTTRFLY.WMF \* MERGEFORMAT`). The picture gets stored with the Word document in the original format as well as in Word's internal format. The resulting file is bigger than with Link turned off. If the Save Picture in Document option is disabled, a `\D` switch is added at the end of the field, and the resulting file is much smaller.

Updating Links

The Link option is often misunderstood. When you select the Link option when inserting a graphic into a file, Word does not create a link to the application that created the graphic. Instead, the link is to the graphic file itself, regardless of source. Word inserts an INCLUDEPICTURE field into the current document. You can later update the link by selecting the graphic or field and pressing F9.

SUPER CAUTION

The temptation in Word is to double-click a graphic to edit it. In the case of linked graphics inserted using the Insert Picture command—don't do it unless you're sure it's what you want to do. You may not like the result! When you double-click a linked graphic, Word automatically converts the INCLUDEPICTURE field—which is an application-neutral link to the file—into an EMBED field that defaults to Word's own drawing tools (formerly Microsoft Draw, which is now integrated into Word). The problem is that Word's drawing module may or may not be the appropriate environment for editing and maintaining the graphic. Something created with Windows Paintbrush might very well be maintainable using Word's drawing tools. Something created with Corel Draw or Micrografx Designer, however, is not.

Clipboard

Another method for inserting graphics into Word is to simply paste them in from the clipboard. In general, this method is more appropriate when you are unable to use one of Word's filters to properly import the graphic. For example, some Micrografx Draw drawings don't import well into Word. When you encounter difficulties using an import filter, you sometimes can achieve acceptable results by instead using the clipboard.

When the import filter fails, or doesn't otherwise result in the picture you want, you can start the application that created the graphic, copy the picture to the clipboard, and then paste it into Word.

PROCEDURE 23.2. INSERTING GRAPHICS USING THE CLIPBOARD.

1. Open the application used to create the picture (see note following the procedure).
2. Open the file that contains the picture.
3. Select the graphic (usually **E**dit | Select **A**ll).
4. Copy the graphic to the clipboard (usually Ctrl+Insert or **E**dit | **C**opy).
5. Switch to Word (depending on how much memory you have, you may want to close the graphic application as well; if it asks if you want to retain the data in the clipboard, then say *Yes*).
6. Position the insertion point where you want the graphic to appear.
7. Press Shift+Insert to paste the graphic into position.

When you paste an object from the clipboard that does not have an OLE link to a specific server, Word creates an EMBED field with Word 6 itself as the server:

```
{EMBED Word.Picture.6}
```

SUPER NOTE

The application must be capable of copying an image to the host clipboard. If you're using Windows, then any Windows application should be able to do the job. If you're using OS/2, then almost any Windows or PM application should be able as well, expanding your options somewhat. In the latter case, you would need to make sure that the clipboard is public in Word as well as in the graphics application (this is the default). Note also that some OLE servers automatically create their own OLE object when you copy to the clipboard. So, even if you prefer to use the clipboard and bypass an OLE link to the original application, you may not be able to.

Using OLE (Object Linking and Embedding) to Insert a Graphic

OLE (object linking and embedding) is a concept that tries to hide the details of files and applications from the user. When you use OLE, all of the information pertaining to the graphic is included in the Word file. If you display field codes rather than field results, all you see is an embed field, which contains a reference to the OLE server. For example, when you paste after you convert a picture into a Word picture (for example, when you double-click a linked graphic), its field code displays:

```
{EMBED Word.Picture.6}
```

SUPER NOTE

A *server* is an application that creates an OLE object; a *client* is an application that uses an OLE object created by a server. When Word uses a Windows Paintbrush drawing, Word is the client, and Paintbrush is the server. When you embed a Word document into an Excel spreadsheet, Word is the server and Excel is the client.

Windows Paintbrush, Excel, and a number of other Windows programs automatically create an embedded object when you use the clipboard. So, one way to embed an object into Word is to proceed as shown in the previous section, and the resulting graphic is an EMBED field rather than a clipboard image. You also can launch a number of OLE servers directly from Word.

PROCEDURE 23.3. USING OLE TO CREATE A GRAPHIC IN WORD.

1. Position the insertion point where you want the graphic to appear.
2. Select **I**nsert | **O**bject.
3. Select the OLE server (object type—for example, Microsoft Word Picture (formerly MS Draw), Windows Paintbrush, Micrografx Draw).
4. Click OK.
5. Perform the action(s) necessary to create or display the graphic.
6. Close the OLE server (Alt+F4).
7. Confirm the Update prompt (see Figure 23.2).

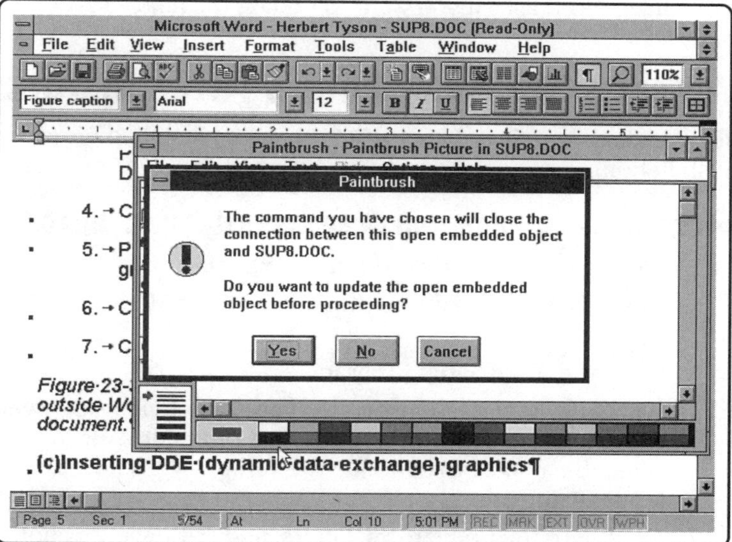

FIGURE 23.2.
When inserting or editing OLE objects using OLE servers outside Word, you are prompted to confirm updating the Word document.

Inserting DDE (Dynamic Data Exchange) Graphics

OLE is a process that hides the details of the file from you. DDE, on the other hand, makes the linkage clear, and can (where necessary) automatically update the object for you. DDE is sometimes confusing because users don't really understand what it is. Moreover, DDE never became as popular as Microsoft first anticipated. As a result, there really aren't very many DDE servers (again, a DDE server is an application that makes its services available to a DDE client for creating and updating files). Naturally, Microsoft Excel 3.0 for OS/2 is a DDE server (indeed, one of the few I could find).

PROCEDURE 23.4. USING DDE TO CREATE A GRAPHIC IN WORD.

1. Open the DDE server (for example, Microsoft Excel 3.0 for OS/2).
2. Do what's necessary to display the graphic you want to use.
3. Select the graphic and copy it to the clipboard.
4. Switch to Word.
5. From the menu, select **E**dit | Paste **S**pecial.

The first D in DDE stands for dynamic. That means that data in the client (Word, in this instance) is updated automatically. If you have graphs created in Excel, based on data that are changing, you should use a DDE link or a link to a spreadsheet (static data exchange inserted using **I**nsert | Fi**l**e). Any time you edit a document that contains DDE links, Word asks if you want to update the link.

Adding Graphics Filters After Installation

If you did not install graphics filters when you installed Word, you can add them after installation.

PROCEDURE 23.5. INSTALLING GRAPHICS FILTERS INTO WORD.

1. Close any copies of Word that are running.
2. Open the program group that contains the Microsoft Word Setup program item.
3. Open the Word Setup program.
4. Click Add/Remove (if programs you cannot close are open, you may see a different prompt before the one that offers the Add/Remove choice; if so, select the choice to continue the setup). Word now displays the Maintenance Mode dialog box.
5. Make sure the Convertors, Filters, and Data Access choice is selected. Do not change other selections. If you remove an X from a checkbox, Word interprets that action as your desire to uninstall the feature. So, don't remove any existing X unless you really want to uninstall the corresponding feature.
6. To select or deselect individual filters, click Change Options. Click OK to return to the Maintenance Mode dialog box.
7. Click **C**ontinue.
8. Follow the remaining instructions to insert the required diskettes.

Chapter 24

Frames

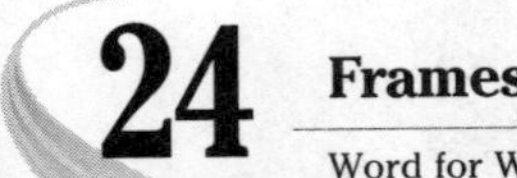

A frame is a way of marking text and graphics so that they appear on the same place on the page, either fixed absolutely or relative to text. Using frames is key when trying to wrap text around graphics, as often is done in newsletters.

Inserting a Frame

Working with frames is much more straightforward in Page Layout view than in Normal or Draft view. If your Word screen isn't already in Page Layout view when you select the Frame command, Word offers to switch to that view before inserting the frame (see Figure 24.1).

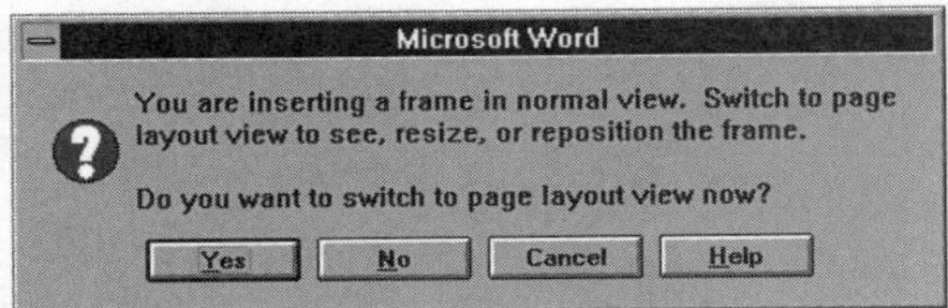

FIGURE 24.1.
Word prompts you to change to Page Layout view when inserting a frame.

Inserting an Empty Frame

In planning a newsletter, article, or other document, you might sometimes want to reserve room for a picture or other graphic that isn't ready yet. You can do that by inserting an empty frame.

PROCEDURE 24.1. INSERTING AN EMPTY FRAME.

1. Move the cursor approximately where you want the frame to appear (don't worry about exact positioning right now).
2. Select **Insert | Frame** or click the Frame tool if the Drawing toolbar is active (see Figure 24.2).

FIGURE 24.2.
The Frame tool is available on the Drawing toolbar.

3. If Word asks if you want to go into Page Layout view, say yes (see Figure 24.1).
4. Note the message on the status bar (see Figure 24.3); you must now click and drag to insert the frame. Use the + cursor as a guide.

Note: You can press the Esc key at any point before step 6 to cancel the
Click and drag to insert a frame.

FIGURE 24.3.
Word prompts you to use the mouse to draw your frame.

5. Hold down the left mouse button and move the mouse to form a box the size and shape you want. Don't worry about exact dimensions—the frame can be more easily sized later.
6. Release the mouse button when the frame is as you want it to appear.

SUPER NOTE

You can press the Esc key at any point before Step 6 to cancel the frame.

SUPER BORDER PATROL!

When you insert an empty frame, you're actually framing a paragraph marker, which is essentially the same as framing text—although the text you're framing might simply be a paragraph marker at the moment. Any time you frame text, Word automatically formats a border around the paragraph. If you want the area framed but not bordered, select Format | Borders and Shading, click None, and then click OK. Hint: Until you have actually filled the frame, leave the border turned on. It makes it easier to find. Moreover, if you later fill the frame with a graphic, Word automatically turns the border off. See Chapter 25, "Modifying Graphics," and Chapter 19, "Tables and AutoTable," for more about border formatting.

Framing Existing Graphics or Text

When you insert a picture or other graphic, Word does not automatically insert a frame. You can insert a picture directly into an existing frame, or frame a picture after the fact. When you frame existing text, Word automatically formats the framed paragraph with a border attribute; when you frame existing graphics, Word does not.

PROCEDURE 24.2. FRAMING EXISTING GRAPHICS.

1. Select the graphic you want to frame.
2. Select Insert | Frame or click the Frame tool (see Figure 24.4).

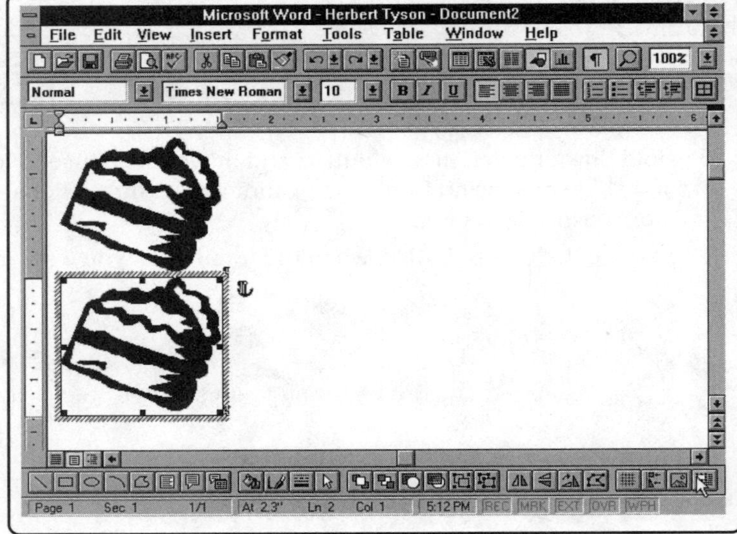

FIGURE 24.4.
Use the Frame tool to frame a graphic for dragging and text-wrapping.

PROCEDURE 24.3. FRAMING EXISTING TEXT.

1. Select the text you want to frame.
2. Select **I**nsert | **F**rame or click the Frame tool.

SUPER CAUTION

If you select part of a paragraph, Word inserts a paragraph break at the end of the selection and frames just the selected text. Make sure you select all the text you want to frame.

Inserting a Graphic into a Frame

When you insert graphics into an existing frame, several things happen:

- Word removes any border format that was automatically applied when the frame was created.
- If you haven't manually applied any border formatting to the frame, the frame size is reset to Auto when you insert the graphic.
- If you manually applied border formatting, the frame sizing is adjusted for "best fit" but is not reset to Auto.

- Word attempts a *best fit* of the graphic into the frame. Best fit means providing the largest possible picture in the frame you set without resorting to distortion (that is, the horizontal and vertical scaling factors are kept identical). If both frame dimensions can be reset to Auto, best fit means that horizontal and vertical sizes of the graphic are scaled up or down to produce the largest possible picture in the existing frame. If the frame sizes cannot be reset to Auto (due to manually-applied border formatting), one of the dimensions remains at exactly the size you set and the other dimension is reset to at least the size you set.

SUPER TIP

If you insert a graphic without a frame, the graphic's native size prevails. As a strategy, therefore, if you want true-sized graphics, insert the graphic first, and then frame it. If you want to limit the graphic to a predetermined amount of space, insert the frame and then the graphic. In either case, you can resize and rescale. However, it's easier if you don't have to.

PROCEDURE 24.4. INSERTING A GRAPHIC FILE INTO AN EXISTING FRAME.

1. Select the frame (click the frame so that the sizing handles appear, as shown in Figure 24.5).

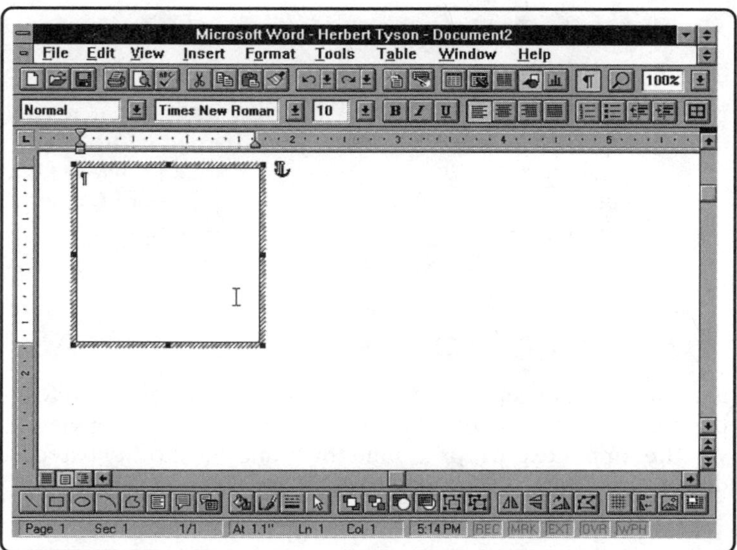

FIGURE 24.5.
Sizing handles show where to pull.

2. Select Insert | Picture.
3. Using the Directories and Drives list boxes, navigate to the graphic you want to use.
4. Preview the graphic to verify that it's the one you want and that Word's import filter will work correctly.
5. Click Link to File, if desired (if you do, that also opens up the option not to save the picture in the Word file).
6. Click OK.

Sometimes the graphic you want cannot be imported directly by Word. If you're using Windows or Win-OS/2 and you can display the graphic using a Windows or OS/2 PM application, you can use the clipboard to transfer the graphic into Word.

PROCEDURE 24.5. INSERTING A GRAPHIC FROM THE CLIPBOARD INTO AN EXISTING FRAME.

1. Open a Windows or OS/2-PM application that can display the graphic, and copy it to the clipboard.
2. Switch to Word.
3. Select the frame (click the frame so that the sizing handles appear, as shown in Figure 24.5).
4. If you don't need a link to the original file and application, press Shift+Insert to paste the graphic into the frame.

> **SUPER NOTE**
>
> If you want to try to retain a link to the original file and application, select Edit and see if the Paste Special option is available (see Figure 24.6). If Paste Special is available, then you often can use Paste Link to retain a link to the original application and file. Depending on the application, Word might insert an OLE (EMBED) field or a DDE field into your document.

Formatting Frames

If a frame isn't exactly as you want it to appear, you can reformat it. Size, shape, and position can be adjusted using the mouse in Page Layout view. Other aspects, such as whether or not text wraps around the frame, must be adjusted from the Format | Frame dialog box.

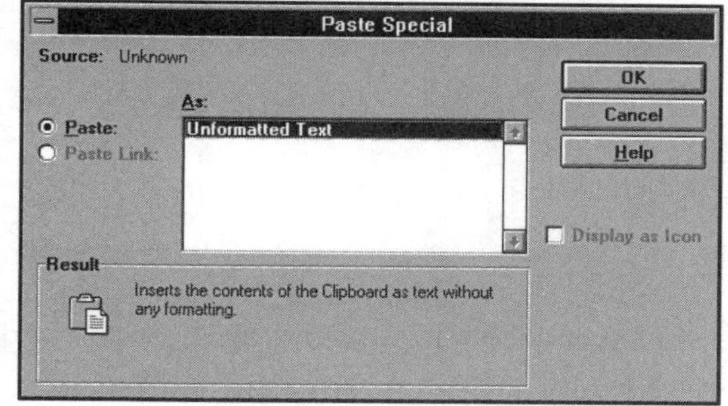

FIGURE 24.6.
Use Paste Special to access OLE and DDE links from the clipboard.

PROCEDURE 24.6. MOVING A FRAME WITH THE MOUSE (DRAG AND DROP).

1. Switch to Page Layout view (you must be in Page Layout view to move a frame with a mouse).
2. Move the mouse over the hashed area of the frame edge until a double-arrow pointer appears (see Figure 24.7).

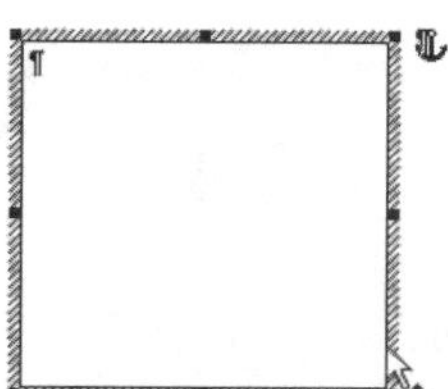

FIGURE 24.7.
The mouse pointer changes shape to show when dragging can occur.

3. Press and hold the left mouse button and drag the frame to a new location.
4. Release the mouse button to drop the frame in the new location.

PROCEDURE 24.7. RESIZING A FRAME WITH THE MOUSE.

1. Switch to Page Layout view (you must be in Page Layout view to resize a frame with a mouse).
2. Click the outside edge of the frame with the left mouse button once; this causes sizing handles to appear around the frame (see Figure 24.8).

FIGURE 24.8.
Click the edge of the frame—not the interior—to expose the sizing handles.

3. Move the mouse to the side or corner you want to adjust until the correct sizing cursor appears (see Figure 24.9).

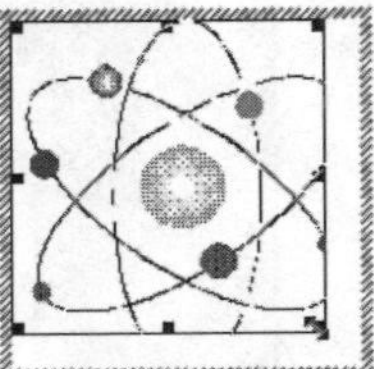

FIGURE 24.9.
When the mouse is positioned correctly, the pointer changes to a sizing shape.

4. Hold the left mouse button and drag the side or corner to a new position.
5. Release the mouse button to set the new position.

Frame Dialog Box

If you don't have a mouse, or if you need to adjust frame attributes other than position and size, you need to use the Frame dialog box, shown in Figure 24.10. Display the Frame dialog box by selecting Format | Frame from the main menu or from the right mouse button popup menu (click the right mouse button in the frame).

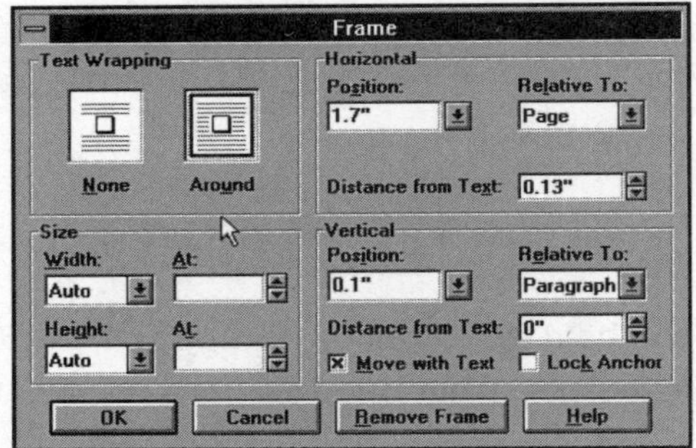

FIGURE 24.10.
The Frame dialog box.

Text Wrapping

Select this setting to cause text to flow around the frame. This is common practice when framing pictures in newsletters and magazines. You could also frame a bit of text with a quote to pique the reader's interest, as shown in Figure 24.11.

Size

Set the Height and Width to Auto to tell Word to make the frame automatically adjust to the size of the graphic or text. This is crucial if you plan to crop or scale the graphic. Set the height and width to Exactly if you're following a rigid format with dimensions you cannot exceed. In this case, you would need to adjust the text or graphic itself to ensure that it's not clipped by the frame.

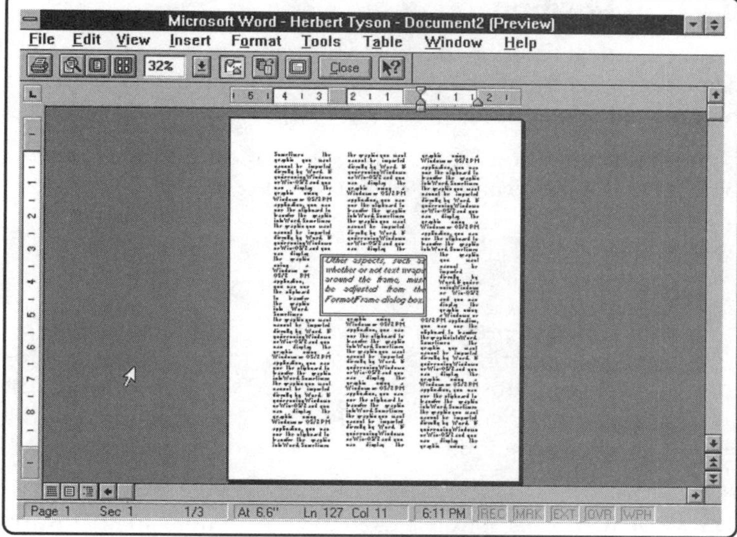

FIGURE 24.11.
Quote framing is a common practice in popular periodicals.

Horizontal Position

Set the horizontal position to where you want the frame to appear. You can select a preset position, or type the exact position. The preset positions are

Left	Relative to Margin, Page, or Column
Right	Relative to Margin, Page or Column
Center	Relative to Margin, Page or Column
Inside	In the margin area between the text edge and the binding
Outside	In the margin area between the text and the edge of the page

The Distance from Text setting is used to create a blank area between the frame and the surrounding text.

SUPER NOTE

A common problem is pictures and text that seem to be offset from the left. Graphics are subject to the current paragraph formatting. If you find that the Distance from Text setting doesn't alleviate an offset problem, the problem may be that an indent is set. Check the F**o**rmat | **P**aragraph settings to ensure that indentation is not turned on.

Vertical Position

Set the Vertical Position to where you want the frame to appear. The vertical position can be set exactly by replacing preset position names with an actual measurement, relative to the margin, page, or paragraph.

Use the Distance from Text setting to create a gutter or buffer between the top and bottom of the frame and the object within.

SUPER

A common problem with vertical positioning is incorrect line spacing for the paragraph format. If the graphic is cut off or has too much spacing at the top or bottom, select F**o**rmat | **P**aragraph and ensure that line spacing is set to Auto, and that Before and After spacing are set to 0. Once that's done, the Distance from Text setting has the expected effect.

The Move with Text option is used to allow a frame to float with the text. If Move with Text is not selected, the frame is "anchored" in place. This option is used sometimes for watermark effects, as well as for imposing logos in areas outside the header.

The Lock Anchor option is use to weld the frame to the current paragraph. Framed objects are always anchored to a paragraph. When you move a framed object around in a document, it gets reanchored to the nearest paragraph. You can ensure that an object does not move relative to a particular paragraph by selecting the Lock Anchor option.

Remove Frame

The Remove Frame option is used to remove a frame from graphics or text. When a frame contains graphics or text, you cannot use editing keys to remove the frame without deleting its contents. If you need to access the graphic without the frame, use this option to remove just the frame.

PROCEDURE 24.8. REMOVING A FRAME FROM GRAPHICS OR TEXT.

1. Click the right mouse button inside the frame.
2. Select F**o**rmat | Fra**m**e.
3. Click **R**emove Frame.

Chapter

25

Modifying Graphics

Word makes it fairly easy to modify and enhance graphics. You can scale and crop using a mouse or the menu and make other adjustments using the menu.

Different kinds of graphics exhibit different kinds of behavior when cropping and scaling. Embedded and framed graphics can be cropped and scaled. Plain Microsoft Word pictures, however, can be changed using the drawing tools but are not subject to normal cropping and scaling. In fact, cropping and scaling can be performed in normal view, but Microsoft Word pictures can be seen only in Page Layout or Print Preview mode. If you come across a picture that seems to resist the techniques described in this session, it's probably a Microsoft Word picture rather than an embedded graphic.

Converting a Microsoft Word Picture into an Embedded Graphic

You can create Word pictures at any time. However, they are not represented by an EMBED field and cannot be displayed in Normal view. If you prefer being able to work with a picture as an embedded object, you can convert it by framing it.

PROCEDURE 25.1. CONVERTING A WORD PICTURE INTO AN EMBEDDED PICTURE OBJECT.

1. Select the picture you want to convert.
2. Select **I**nsert | **F**rame.

> **SUPER TIP**
>
> If the Drawing toolbar is active, you can select the picture and click the Frame button (see Figure 25.1).

3. If you want to leave the picture as a framed object, the procedure is finished. If you'd prefer that it be unframed, select **I**nsert | **F**rame and click Remove. The picture will remain as an embedded Word picture rather than a Word picture.

Scaling with a Mouse

Scaling means changing the displayed size of a graphic relative to its actual original size. If you insert an unframed graphic, the scaling is 100 percent, both vertically and horizontally. If you insert a graphic into an existing frame, the picture is scaled accordingly to fit without distortion. When you scale an embedded picture in Word, the original picture isn't actually changed. Only your view of it is changed. Thus, if a picture is linked to a file, the actual file isn't changed. Changing the scale is like looking at something through a magnifying glass. You can make the picture look smaller or larger or distort its appearance. When you remove the magnifying glass, however, the original picture has not been changed.

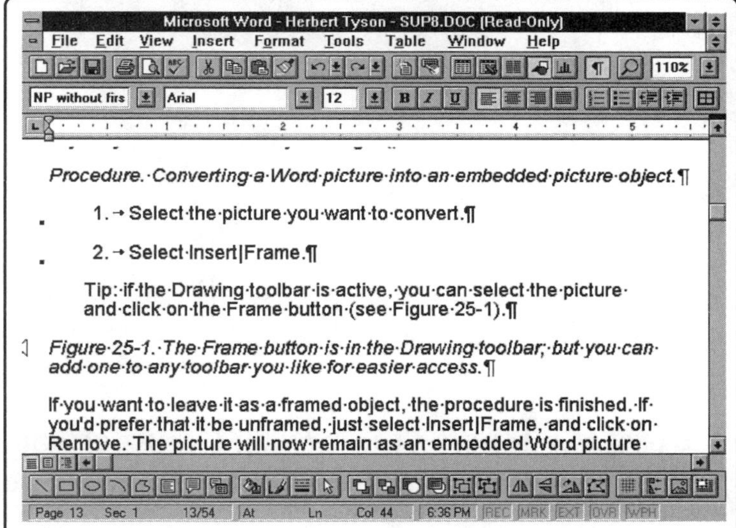

FIGURE 25.1.
The Frame button is in the Drawing toolbar, but you can add one to any toolbar you like for easier access.

SUPER CAUTION

If your document contains Microsoft Word pictures or embedded picture objects that are not linked to files, editing or scaling *will* actually change the picture. In the case of embedded objects that begin life as a file, you retain the option of using **Insert | Picture** to reinsert the original if you screw up. If you screw up a picture or an object that exists only in the Word file, then your only retreat might be Word's Undo stack. Before doing any editing on the original of any picture, it pays to make a good solid backup so you can recover from editing mistakes and other catastrophes.

SUPER NOTE

Distortion occurs when horizontal and vertical scaling are not equal. As shown in Figure 25.2, as long as vertical and horizontal scaling are equal, the object retains its normal shape. When vertical and horizontal scaling differ, the object becomes distorted—sometimes deliberately in order to produce more visual information.

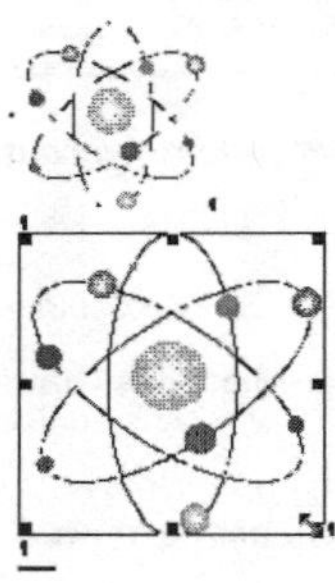

FIGURE 25.2.
To avoid distortion, adjust horizontal and vertical scaling at the same rate.

PROCEDURE 25.2. SCALING A GRAPHIC WITH A MOUSE, WITHOUT DISTORTION.

1. Switch into Page Layout view (not essential, but advisable if you're concerned about the actual appearance on the page).
2. Click the picture to turn on the sizing handles (see Figure 25.3).

FIGURE 25.3.
Sizing handles show you where to drag.

3. To scale the picture up or down without distorting it, move the mouse pointer over any of the four corners until a diagonal two-headed arrow appears (see Figure 25.4).
4. Press and hold the left mouse button; drag the corner closer to the opposite corner of the picture to scale smaller or farther away to scale larger. As you drag the corner sizing handles, the status bar reports the scale factors for both width and height.
5. Release the mouse button when the picture is the desired size.

FIGURE 25.4.
The mouse pointer shows you when to drag.

PROCEDURE 25.3. SCALING A GRAPHIC WITH A MOUSE, WITH DISTORTION.

1. Switch into Page Layout view.
2. Click the picture to turn on the sizing handles.
3. To distort the picture, move the mouse pointer over any of the four sides until a vertical or horizontal two-headed arrow appears (see Figure 25.5).

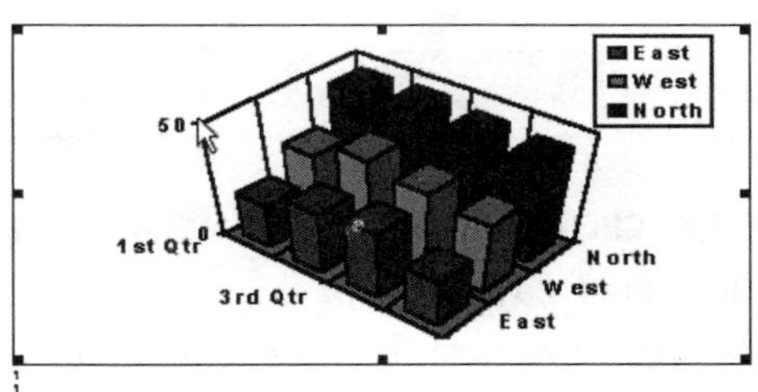

FIGURE 25.5.
Here, a picture was deliberately stretched horizontally to show more crucial detail.

4. Press and hold the left mouse button and drag the side to produce the desired effect. As you drag, the status bar reports the scale factors for the dimension being changed.
5. Release the mouse button when the picture is the desired size.

Cropping with a Mouse

Cropping refers to limiting the view of a picture. Some pictures show too much. Consider, for example, a screen shot. If I want to include a picture of a dialog box, I capture the entire screen, as shown in Figure 25.6. Showing the whole screen, however, is not only irrelevant and confusing, but it uses up much needed space as well. Thus, when I do a screen shot, I indicate the relevant portion, and the publisher crops out everything that shouldn't be there.

Word gives you the same ability. You are not actually cropping the picture when you use Word's cropping procedures. Instead, you are just changing your view. Cropping with Word is like cutting a hole into your document so that a picture underneath can show through or constructing a cardboard overlay for a picture. You want to make the hole a size and shape so that only the relevant part of the picture shows through.

FIGURE 25.6.
Sams asks for the whole screen: "Leave the cropping to us!"

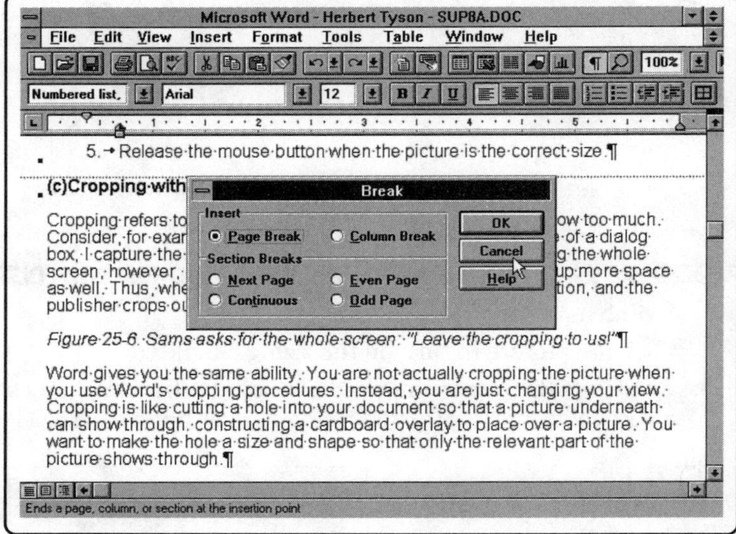

PROCEDURE 25.4. CROPPING A GRAPHIC WITH A MOUSE.

1. Switch into Page Layout view.
2. Click the picture to turn on the sizing/cropping handles.
3. Move the mouse over any of the eight sizing handles until a two-headed arrow appears. The arrow indicates the direction(s) for cropping.
4. Press Shift and then press and hold the left mouse button; drag the handle to hide or expose the portion of the picture you want (see Figure 25.7). As you drag, the status bar reports the amount of cropping and the dimension(s) being cropped.
5. Release the mouse button when the picture has the appearance you want.

FIGURE 25.7.
When you press Shift, the mouse pointer turns into a cropping pointer.

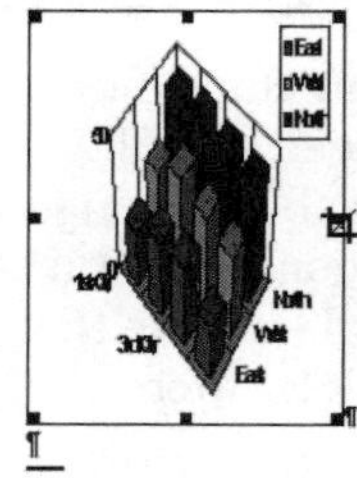

SUPER TIP

Feeling a little finger fatigued? In Step 4, once your finger is on the mouse button and the pointer has changed into a cropping pointer (and the status bar registers the fact that you're cropping instead of scaling), you can take your finger off the Shift key.

Borders

Framed graphics do not have borders by default in Word. You can easily create a border around a framed graphic, however. You also can create a border around a picture, without using a frame.

SUPER NOTE

By default, when you frame text, Word does create a border around it. If you want to remove the border, select F**o**rmat | **B**orders and Shading; then click **N**one and OK.

PROCEDURE 25.5. CREATING A BORDER AROUND A FRAME.

1. Click the right mouse button inside the framed area.
2. Select Borders and Shading from the popup menu and click the **B**orders tab if necessary.
3. Click the **P**resets border that most closely matches the effect you want.
4. Click the **L**ine style you want to use.
5. To alter any single border, click the border segment you want to modify; then click the Line Style.
6. Use the **F**rom Text option to create white space between the framed area and the border.
7. Click OK.

SUPER TIP

If you prefer working interactively, click the Toolbar button to display the Borders and Shading toolbar. When the toolbar is displayed, you can see each change as you apply it. In fact, you can bypass the Borders and Shading dialog box completely by clicking the right mouse on any displayed toolbar and then clicking Borders. You can drag the Borders toolbar anywhere on-screen to make it more convenient. The only things you give up by using the Borders tool is access to the From Text setting (which you don't care about when formatting a picture) and the ability to set the line and shading colors (which you might care about). When applying borders and shading from the toolbar, the current color settings are used (the last ones you set from the dialog box).

PROCEDURE 25.6. USING THE BORDERS TOOLBAR TO APPLY BORDERS TO A GRAPHIC.

1. Click the right mouse button on any toolbar and click **B**orders to display the Borders toolbar.
2. Click the Line Style drop-down arrow and select the thickness and type of line you want.
3. Click the Outside Border tool to display a border around the graphic.

SUPER NOTE

When using the Borders toolbox, selecting a line style does not change the line style of the border on the frame. Instead, it changes the line style of the border tools. First you assign the characteristics to the border tools, and then you use a border tool to apply a border to the object in your document. When you change shading, on the other hand, shading is applied to the selection rather than to tools on the toolbar.

Shading

You can apply shading to a frame. If the frame contains text, the shading will display and print. If the frame contains a graphic, the shading will display only around the edge of the graphic. If the frame contains both text and a graphic, the shading will display only over the text.

PROCEDURE 25.7. SHADING A FRAMED AREA.

1. Select the area you want to shade; shading will apply to the entire graphic or paragraph. If the frame contains multiple paragraphs or a combination of graphics and paragraphs, only the graphics or paragraphs included in the selection will be shaded.
2. Select F**o**rmat | **B**orders and Shading.
3. Click the **S**hading tab.

4. Select the Shading pattern and the Foreground and Background colors you want to apply; observe the Preview window that shows the effect.
5. Click OK to close the dialog box.

SUPER

As was the case with borders, you also have the option of selecting shading from the Borders toolbox. Shading will be applied in whatever colors are currently set. You must select the Borders and Shading dialog box to adjust the colors.

Modifying Graphics with the Format|Picture Command

If you don't have a mouse, want utter precision, or otherwise just don't feel terribly gooey (GUI), you can modify graphics using the menu.

SUPER NOTE

Don't confuse the Format|Picture and Format|Drawing Object commands. The Format|Picture dialog box is used for cropping and scaling and is available for any graphic. The Format|Drawing Object dialog box is for changing the fill (color and shading), line, size, and position of Microsoft Word pictures (a dialog box presentation of some of the Drawing toolbar features). The latter is available only when editing Microsoft Word drawings.

PROCEDURE 25.8. MODIFYING GRAPHICS USING FORMAT|PICTURE.

1. Click the picture you want to modify; sizing handles signal that the picture is selected.
2. Select Format|Picture.
3. Select the desired options (see Crop From, Scaling, Size, and so on below).
4. Click OK.

All of the dimension controls are adjusted using the same techniques.

PROCEDURE 25.9. ADJUSTING A DIMENSION IN THE FORMAT|PICTURE DIALOG BOX.

1. Click the dimension you want to adjust.
2. Click the up or down icon to adjust the dimension up or down in the units shown. Alternatively, you can use the up and down arrows or type the exact dimension directly.

Crop From

Use the Left, Right, Top, and Bottom controls to expose or hide as much of the picture as you want. Negative cropping is possible and will result in a wider blank area between the graphic and any border or surrounding text. Unfortunately, the cropping does not display until you click OK. Use a mouse (see Procedure 25.4) if you need immediate visual feedback while you're cropping.

Scaling

You can adjust the size of a picture by changing the scaling or the size. As you change the scaling, note that the size changes too.

SUPER NOTE

The Format | Picture dialog box does not have a way of adjusting the width and height scaling at the same time. If you want the picture not to be distorted, adjust the scaling so that the width and height percentages are equal to one another.

Size

If you need to have your picture an exact size, use the size controls. As you adjust the size, the scaling adjusts at the same time. One technique is to use the size controls to make the graphics approximately as large as you want; then use the scaling to reduce distortion to an acceptable level (that is, try to make the width and height scaling percentages match).

Original Size

The Original Size section of the dialog box displays the original dimensions of the graphic in its native format.

Reset

The Reset button can be used to reset the width and height scaling to 100 percent.

Frame

Use the Frame button to access the Format | Frame dialog box from within the Format | Picture dialog box. Once you access the Frame dialog box, by the way, selecting Cancel from it will *not* return you to the Format | Picture dialog box.

Troubleshooting Graphics

When working with graphics, everything does not always go as planned. From time to time, you run into a head-scratcher of a problem that seems to defy solution. In this section, you'll learn about the most common problems users have in trying to get graphics to do what they want.

Picture Cut Off

If the picture appears to be cut off, scaling will not help. It will make the picture bigger, but it won't reveal the part that's cut off. Instead, try removing all cropping. If the picture is still cut off, then the problem is probably with the paragraph formatting. Select F**o**rmat | **P**aragraph and verify that Line Spacing is set to Auto. If Line Spacing is set otherwise, the graphic will be cut off.

Picture Offset from the Left or Right

The usual cause of offset from the left or right is an indent in the paragraph formatting. Select F**o**rmat | **P**aragraph and verify that all unwanted indents are set to 0. Another possibility is that Crop From Left and Right are set unevenly. Select the graphic; then select F**o**rmat | Pictu**r**e to verify that left and right cropping are balanced.

Picture Offset from the Top or Bottom

The most common causes of offset from the top or bottom include too much cropping in one dimension or the Before or After paragraph spacing set unevenly. Select the picture; then select F**o**rmat | Pictu**r**e. Verify that Crop From Bottom and Top values are set the same. If they are, select F**o**rmat | **P**aragraph and ensure that Spacing Before and After are set to the same value (generally 0).

Chapter 26

Word as a Drawing Program

To someone who has always used a painting program like Windows Paintbrush or PC Paintbrush, a drawing program such as the one contained in Microsoft Word (called Microsoft Draw in previous versions of Word for Windows) or Micrografx Draw can come as quite a shock. After you get used to it, however, the extra flexibility starts to grow on you.

In fact, you might consider graduating to a fuller-featured drawing program such as Micrografx Draw or even Micrografx Designer. These programs have the same approach as Word's drawing module, but they add the ability to convert lines and text into curves for further manipulation.

Overview

Word's drawing module can be used in two modes. One mode creates Microsoft Word Picture objects. This is analogous to the way Microsoft Draw worked in Word for Windows 2. The other mode creates nonobject pictures in Word documents. In the first way, you must select **I**nsert | **O**bject and interact with the drawing module pretty much as you would with any other OLE server application—the only exception being that Word does not prompt you to confirm updates when you close the object after creating or editing.

Where it makes a difference, using the Microsoft Word drawing module as an OLE server is referred to in this chapter as *embedding* a Word drawing into a document. Using Microsoft Word just to create drawings (without embedding them as objects) is called simply *drawing*. Aside from the different characteristics of the two uses (see Table 26.1), the mechanics of using the drawing tools under either approach is virtually identical.

Table 26.1. Differences between an embedded and nonembedded Word drawing.

Embedded	*Nonembedded*
Displays in Normal view.	Displays only in preview and page layout view.
Embeds an EMBED field.	No field code.
Can be cropped, scaled, and edited.	Can be edited, but can't be cropped and scaled.
Can't be displayed under the text in the main page area except when included in a header or a footer.	Can be displayed underneath text (for example, as a background or "watermark").
Text can wrap around automatically.	Text does not wrap around.

Creating a Word Drawing

Creating a Word drawing (nonembedded) is as easy as inserting text. Just turn on the drawing toolbar and draw wherever you like.

PROCEDURE 26.1. CREATING A WORD DRAWING.

1. Click the Drawing button on the Standard toolbar (see Figure 26.1).
2. Select a drawing tool.
3. Point the mouse wherever you like—including over text—and draw, as described in Using Word's Drawing Tools.

SUPER NOTE

You also can activate the Drawing toolbar using **V**iew | **T**oolbars or by clicking the right mouse button on any toolbar and selecting Drawing. If you use either of these two methods, however, Word prompts to confirm switching to Page Layout view the first time you actually try to draw something.

FIGURE 26.1.
Activate the Drawing toolbar from the Drawing button.

When you're done, there's no special wrap-up. Just click in the text area and type. You can jump between the text and drawing at will, since the drawing is literally part of the document. The only catch is that you can't see the drawing in Normal view.

Embedding a Microsoft Word Picture Object

After you learn how to use the Word drawing module, it's easy enough to embed a drawing (into a Word file).

PROCEDURE 26.2. EMBEDDING A WORD DRAWING OBJECT INTO A WORD FILE.

1. Move the insertion point to where you want the drawing to appear.
2. Select **I**nsert | **O**bject, and click Microsoft Word 6.0 Picture (see Figure 26.2).

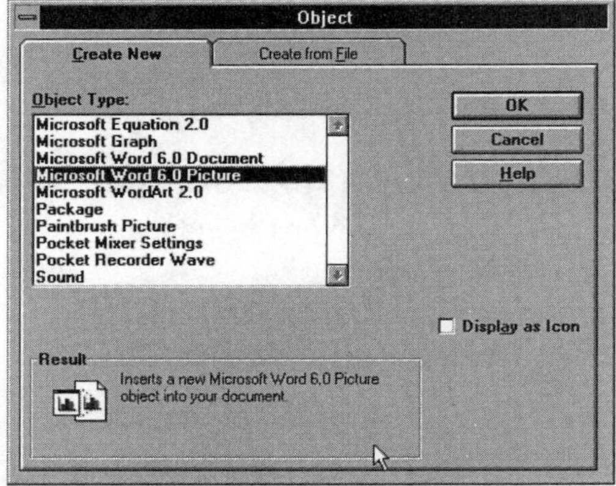

FIGURE 26.2. *Select Microsoft Word 6.0 Picture to embed a Word drawing as an OLE object.*

3. The drawing toolbar and the picture control tool appear (see Figure 26.3). Draw the drawing you want to use.

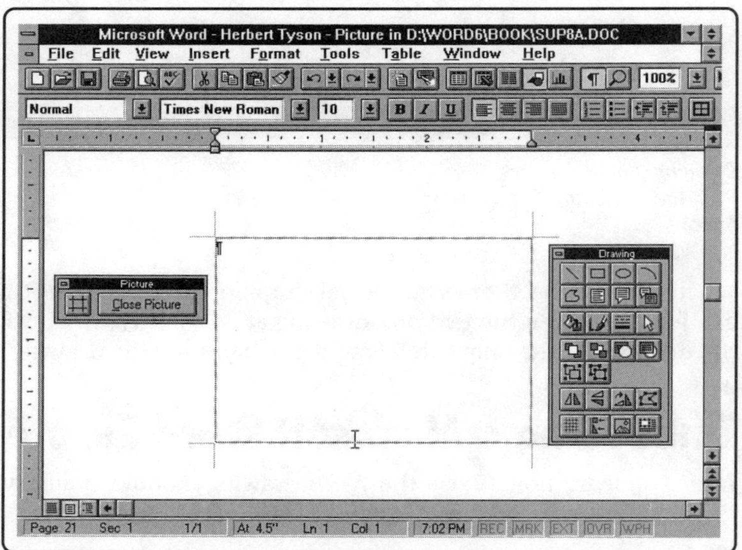

FIGURE 26.3. *The drawing screen features the drawing toolbar and the picture control tool.*

4. Click the Close Picture button on the Picture toolbar when you're done.

SUPER NOTE

You can reactivate drawing mode at any time just by double-clicking the picture.

When you insert a picture in this way, Word creates an embed field into your document—`{EMBED Word.Picture.6}`. In fact, all such drawing fields look identical when you show field codes instead of the picture. Word retains the information about each drawing behind the scenes. For better or worse, the only *file* associated with the drawing is the Word document itself. If your Word documents suddenly become much larger than you expected, you should be aware that even simple drawings can consume enormous amounts of disk space.

The Picture Toolbar

When you're editing a picture container rather than a plain picture, the Picture toolbox floats nearby for easy access. Use the Close Picture button to close the drawing editing session. Unlike when you're using other OLE applications, Word doesn't prompt you for permission to save; it does it automatically. You can always press Alt+Backspace to undo if you change your mind.

Note also that Word opens another window rather than your document window for doing the editing. The other tool, shown in Figure 26.4, is used to close all of the margins around the object you're editing. This ensures that the finished drawing consumes only the space necessary for display when it's embedded into the actual Word document.

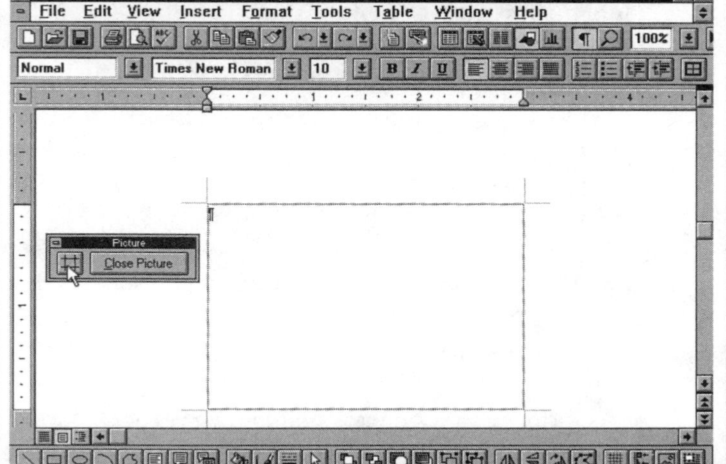

FIGURE 26.4.
Use the # tool to limit a graphic to the size of the picture.

Using Word's Drawing Module

Word's Drawing module is very different from Windows Paintbrush, which is more familiar to most Windows users. Windows Paintbrush is a *painting* program. In a painting program, you have a canvas, and you add paint until the painting looks the way you want it to look. You have tools such as color erasers and a pixel editor to help you deal with details. However, the image you draw is all in one piece. If you draw a circle that's too big, you must carefully delete it and draw another one. If the circle is mixed together with something else, you'll have considerable difficulty replacing it with a circle of a different size.

In a *drawing* program, you create elements and assemble them. Each circle, square, freehand, text, or other element you draw is a separate piece. If a circle component is too big or too small, you select just that component and resize it. The strategy in a drawing program is to assemble and layer pieces so that they form the picture you want. You maintain considerably more flexibility than you have in a painting program. On the other hand, you'll find no erasers in a drawing program. Instead of erasing a section, you can delete elements. If you want to erase just part of an element, you must reshape that element (if possible) so that the part you want erased no longer exists.

Drawing Toolbar

Use Word's Drawing toolbar to select and create picture elements (also called objects). The individual parts of the drawing tool, and how to use them, are shown below.

SUPER TIP

When using the drawing tools, you usually can modify the action of a tool by pressing the Shift, Ctrl, or Ctrl+Shift keys before holding down a mouse button. Pressing the Shift key causes the element (circles, squares, arcs, lines, and freehand tool) to do the following:

Line	Draws only horizontal, vertical, or diagonal lines
Rectangle	Draws a square
Arrow	Selects or deselects the object without deselecting other objects
Zoom	Unzoom (negative magnification)
Ellipse	Draws a perfect circle
Arc	Draws circular arcs only
Freeform	Connects points with vertical, horizontal, and diagonal line segments only

When you hold down the Ctrl key while using the Line, Ellipse, Rectangle, or Arc tools, the objects are drawn from the center out, rather than from an end, corner, or edge. When you hold down the Ctrl+Shift keys at the same time, the center-out effect is added to the Shift effect (for example, Ctrl+Shift draws a perfect circle from the center out). Use the Shift key when you need to draw perfectly shaped objects. Use the Ctrl key when objects must be centered at the same point.

Word's drawing module lets you draw a variety of types of objects—lines, ellipses, rectangles, freeform objects, and text. The details for creating and editing these objects are similar, but not identical; it pays to note the differences. The procedure for moving objects, however, is always the same.

Line Tool

Use the line tool to draw straight lines.

PROCEDURE 26.3. DRAWING LINES.

1. Click the line tool.
2. Point the mouse where you want the line to start.
3. Press and hold the left mouse button (press the Shift key first to limit the lines to 45-, 90-, 135-, or 180-degree lines; press the Ctrl key to draw the line from the center outward; press both keys for both effects).
4. Drag the line end to the length and direction you want; see Figure 26.5.
5. Release the mouse button to complete the line.

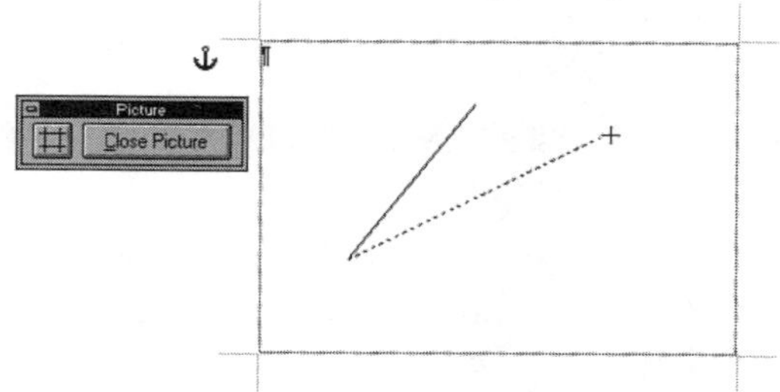

FIGURE 26.5.
Word lets you drag lines to move and stretch them.

PROCEDURE 26.4. EDITING A LINE.

1. Click the line to select it; selection handles appear at each end of the line.
2. Point the mouse at either handle, and drag it to rotate or stretch the line to a new shape or position.
3. Release the mouse button to fix the object in the new location.

SUPER TIP

Press the Shift key while dragging to adjust just the length without disturbing the angle. Press Ctrl+Shift while dragging to adjust the length from the center outward without affecting the angle. Press the Ctrl key while dragging to change the angle and length without affecting the center.

PROCEDURE 26.5. MOVING A LINE.

1. Click the line to select it; selection handles appear at each end of the line.
2. Point the mouse at the line but not on a handle, and drag it to a new location.
3. Release the mouse button to fix the object in the new location.

SUPER TIP

Press the Shift key while dragging to limit the angle of movement to a multiple of 45 degrees. When you press the Shift key, the line can move straight up, down, left, or right, or at 45 degree angle multiples. Use this capability when you need to place a line exactly, relative to another object.

Ellipse and Circle Tool

Use the ellipse and circle tool to draw ellipses and circles.

PROCEDURE 26.6. DRAWING AN ELLIPSE OR CIRCLE.

1. Click the ellipse/circle tool.
2. Point the mouse where you want the ellipse to start.
3. Press the left mouse button and drag the mouse pointer until the ellipse is the size and shape you want.
4. Release the mouse button to fix the ellipse at the displayed size and shape.

SUPER TIP

Press the Shift key before you press the mouse button to draw a perfect circle. Press the Ctrl key before pressing the mouse button to draw from the center out. Press both keys to combine the effects. After you've begun drawing, you can release the key(s).

PROCEDURE 26.7. EDITING AN ELLIPSE OR CIRCLE.

1. Click the ellipse or circle; four selection handles appear around it.
2. Drag any handle in the direction you want to shape the circle or ellipse (see Figure 26.6).
3. Release the mouse button when the ellipse or circle achieves the desired shape.

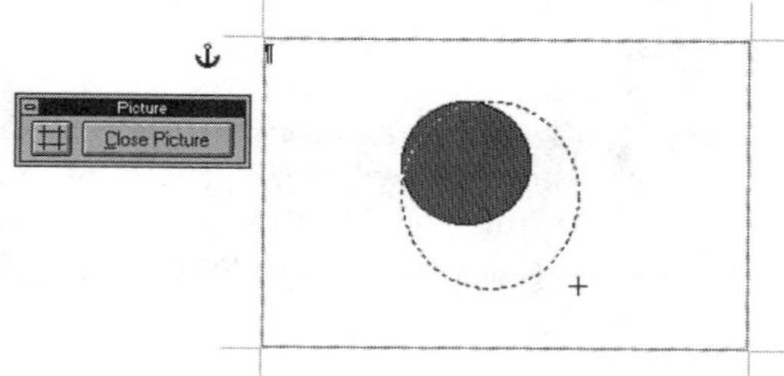

FIGURE 26.6.
Drag to reshape an ellipse or circle.

SUPER TIP

Pressing the Shift key before you press the mouse button enables you to keep the height or width constant while varying the opposite dimension, or to vary both dimensions uniformly. If you drag diagonally, height and width change at the same time in the same proportions. This lets you grow or shrink the ellipse or circle without changing its aspect ratio. If you drag horizontally, the object expands in width while remaining the exact same height. If you drag vertically, the width is frozen while the height is allowed to vary. Pressing the Ctrl key causes the ellipse or circle's center to remain unchanged. Press the Ctrl+Shift keys to combine both effects.

PROCEDURE 26.8. MOVING AN ELLIPSE OR CIRCLE.

1. Click the circle or ellipse so that the selection handles appear.
2. Hold down the left mouse button and drag the object to a new location.
3. Release the mouse button to drop the object in the new location.

Rectangle and Square Tool

Use the rectangle tool to draw rectangles or squares. Word for Windows 2 had another tool for drawing rounded rectangles; you can turn on the rounded attribute by using **F**ormat | Drawing **O**bject.

PROCEDURE 26.9. DRAWING A RECTANGLE OR SQUARE.

1. Click the rectangle tool.
2. Point the mouse where you want the object to start.
3. Press the left mouse button and drag the mouse pointer until the object is the size and shape you want.
4. Release the mouse button to fix the object at the displayed size and shape.

SUPER TIP

Press the Shift key before you press the mouse button to draw a perfect square. Press the Ctrl key before pressing the mouse button to draw from the center out. Press both keys to combine the effects. After you've begun drawing, you can release the key(s).

PROCEDURE 26.10. ROUNDING THE CORNERS IN A RECTANGLE.

1. Click the rectangle to select it.
2. Choose F**o**rmat | Drawing **O**bject.
3. Click the **L**ine tab.
4. Click **R**ound Corners.
5. Click OK.

SUPER NOTE

Round Corners remains turned on until you turn it off. It affects rectangles, text boxes, and callouts.

PROCEDURE 26.11. EDITING A RECTANGLE OR SQUARE.

1. Click the object; four selection handles appear at the four corners.
2. Drag any handle in the direction you want to shape the rectangle (see Figure 26.7).
3. Release the mouse button when the rectangle achieves the desired shape.

FIGURE 26.7.
Drag to change the size and shape of rectangles.

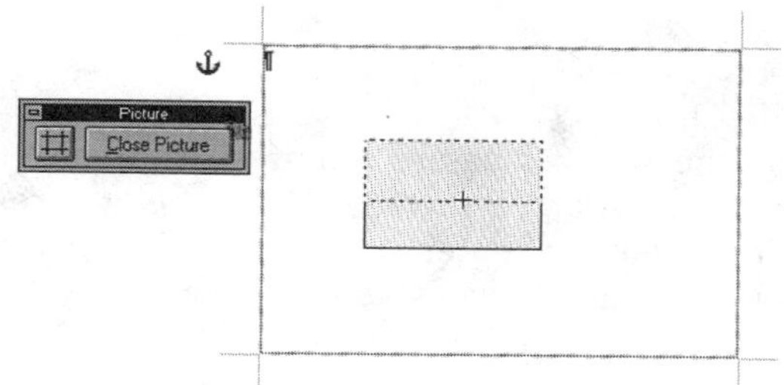

SUPER TIP

Pressing the Shift key before you press the mouse button enables you to keep the height or width constant while varying the opposite dimension, or to vary both dimensions uniformly. If you drag diagonally, height and width change at the same time in the same proportions. This lets you grow or shrink the rectangle or square without changing the relative proportions. If you drag horizontally, the object expands in width while remaining the exact same height. If you drag vertically, the width is frozen while the height is allowed to vary. Pressing the Ctrl key causes the object's center to remain unchanged. Press the Ctrl+Shift keys to combine both effects.

PROCEDURE 26.12. MOVING A RECTANGLE OR SQUARE.

1. Click the rectangle so that the selection handles appear.
2. Hold down the left mouse button and drag the object to a new location.
3. Release the mouse button to drop the object in the new location.

Arc Tool

The arc tool lets you draw circle and ellipse segments. The arc tool draws only one quadrant of a circle or an ellipse. The ability to edit the drawn arc to any part of a circle you want, which was present in Word for Windows 2, seems to be missing in Word 6.

PROCEDURE 26.13. DRAWING AN ARC.

1. Click the arc tool.
2. Point the mouse where you want the arc to start.
3. Press the left mouse button and drag the mouse pointer until the arc is the size and shape you want.
4. Release the mouse button to fix the arc at the displayed size and shape.

SUPER TIP

Press the Shift key before you press the mouse button to draw a perfectly circular arc. Press the Ctrl key before pressing the mouse button to draw from the center out. Press both keys to combine the effects. After you begin drawing, you can release the key(s).

PROCEDURE 26.14. EDITING THE SIZE AND SHAPE OF AN ARC.

1. Click the arc; four selection handles appear around it.
2. Drag any handle to reshape the arc in the direction you want (see Figure 26.8).
3. Release the mouse button when the arc achieves the desired shape.

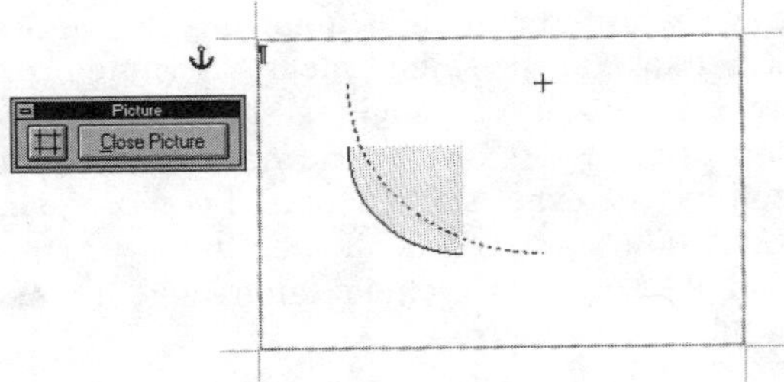

FIGURE 26.8.
Drag the arc to the size and shape you want.

SUPER TIP

Pressing the Shift key before you press the mouse button enables you to keep the height or width constant while varying the opposite dimension, or to vary both dimensions uniformly. If you drag diagonally, height and width change at the same time in the same proportions. This lets you grow or shrink the arc without changing its aspect ratio. If you drag horizontally, the object expands in width while remaining the exact same height. If you drag vertically, the width is frozen while the height is allowed to vary. Pressing the Ctrl key causes the arc's center to remain unchanged. The center of the arc is the point where the two radii meet, not the geometric center of the mass of an arc. Press the Ctrl+Shift keys to combine both effects.

PROCEDURE 26.15. MOVING AN ARC.

1. Click the arc so that the selection handles appear.
2. Hold down the left mouse button and drag the object to a new location.
3. Release the mouse button to drop the object in the new location.

Freeform Drawing Tool

Use the freeform tool to draw any shape you like. The freeform tool works by creating a selection handle each time you change directions while drawing. While the freeform tool does not draw actual curves, you can achieve a curved look by creating a sufficiently large number of selection handles. After the object is drawn, you can reshape it as well as add and delete selection handles.

PROCEDURE 26.16. DRAWING A FREEFORM OBJECT.

1. Click the freeform tool.
2. Point the mouse where you want the object to start.
3. Press the left mouse button and draw the object mouse pointer until the arc is the size and shape you want. While drawing, release the left mouse button between segments you want to be straight; hold the mouse button to draw freehand. Both effects can be combined while drawing.
4. Release the mouse button when you're ready to finish.
5. To close the object (that is, join the two endpoints), click the point where you want the object closed. Any gap between the last point and there is joined with a straight line.
6. To finish the object without closing it (for example, to create an open polygon or freeform shape), press Enter or Esc, or double-click the final position, or click outside the drawing area.

SUPER NOTE

With the default colors, it might not be immediately obvious just what is considered part of the object you draw. To see it more clearly, select a fill color that is different from the default background (white). Even if you leave the object open, Word's drawing module fills in any fillable areas with color or shading.

PROCEDURE 26.17. EDITING THE SIZE OF A FREEFORM OBJECT.

1. Click the freeform object; four selection handles appear around it.
2. Drag any handle to stretch or shrink in the direction you want (see Figure 26.9).

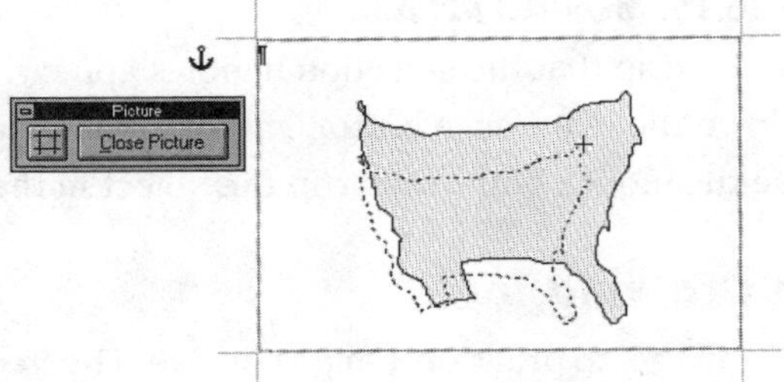

FIGURE 26.9.
They don't call it freeform for nothin'!

3. Release the mouse button when the freeform object is the desired size.

SUPER TIP

Press the Shift key before dragging to limit the freeform object to expanding and shrinking at right or 45-degree angles from the origin. Press the Ctrl key to cause the object to expand and shrink relative to the center rather than a corner. Press both keys to combine the effects.

Text Tool

Use the text tool to add text to your drawing. While you can use this feature to caption your drawing, it's generally better to use Word for that so that the captions can be edited directly in Word. Instead, use the text tool to annotate or enhance your drawing.

PROCEDURE 26.18. ADDING TEXT TO A DRAWING.

1. Click the text tool.
2. Click the mouse pointer where you want the text box to appear and drag to create a rectangular area (see Figure 26.10). Any size box will do for starters; you can always resize it as you go along.

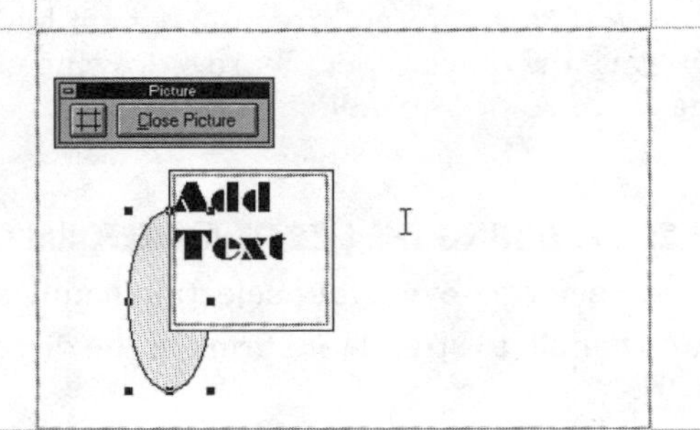

FIGURE 26.10.
Add a text box for titles or notes.

3. Type your text.
4. If desired, select Format | Drawing Object to add additional effects.
5. Click away from the text area to close the edit.

SUPER NOTE

To change text formatting, you can select normal font and paragraph formatting from the menu or using the right mouse button popup menu. Unlike the text boxes in Word for Windows 2, you can mix various types of formatting within the same text box.

Callout Tool

The callout box works very much like the text box, but also has an arrow to show where you're pointing.

PROCEDURE 26.19. INSERTING A CALLOUT BOX.

1. Click the callout tool.
2. Click the mouse pointer where you want the callout box to appear and drag to create a rectangular area (see Figure 26.11).

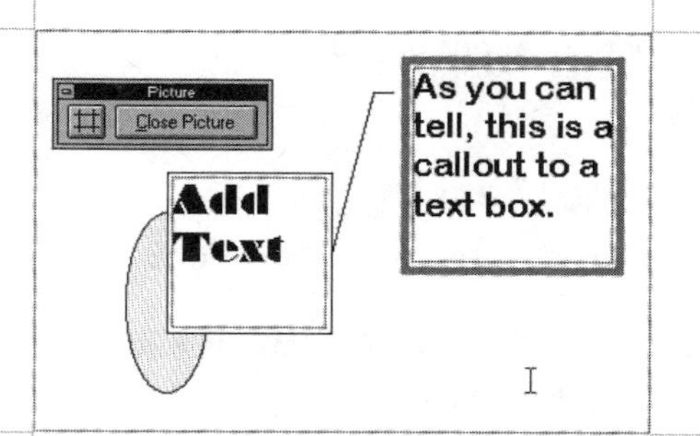

FIGURE 26.11.
Add a callout box to call attention to part of the drawing.

3. Type your text.
4. If desired, select Format | Drawing Object to add additional effects.
5. Click the end of the arrow and drag it to point wherever you want.
6. Click away from the text area to close the edit.

After you insert it, the callout box can be dragged wherever you like (for the most part). You also can drag and stretch the line, or even add one or two pointers (arrow heads).

PROCEDURE 26.20. ADDING AN ARROW TO THE CALLOUT TOOL POINTER LINE.

1. Move the mouse over the pointer line so that a four-headed arrow is displayed, and double-click (see Figure 26.12).

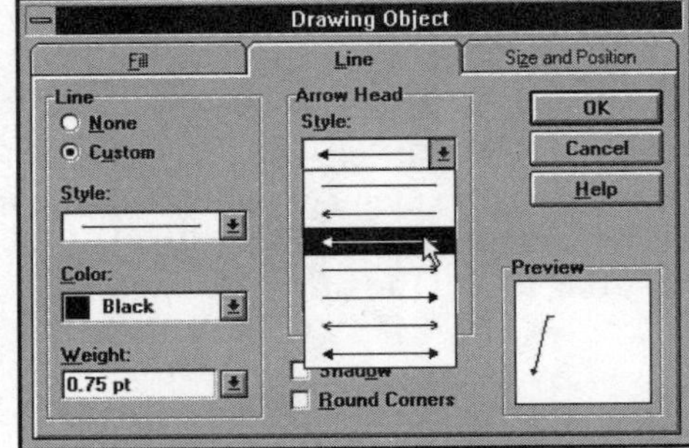

FIGURE 26.12.
Double-click the callout pointer line to select a line format.

2. The Drawing Object (format) dialog box appears, with the **L**ine tab folder showing.
3. Select a Line format (**S**tyle, **C**olor, and **W**eight).
4. Select an arrow head format (S**t**yle, Wi**d**th, and Len**g**th).
5. Select special effects, if desired (**R**ound Corners for the callout text box and Shad**o**w for the line and box).
6. Click OK.

If the format of the callout box is too rigid, then click the Format Callout tool to try a different format.

Format Callout Tool

The Callout Format button is used to choose different formats for the callout box.

PROCEDURE 26.21. APPLYING A CALLOUT FORMAT TO A CALLOUT BOX.

1. Select the callout box.
2. Click the Format Callout tool, which displays the dialog box shown in Figure 26.13.
3. Select a callout Type (straight down, angled, two-segment, or three-segment).
4. Select a Gap (distance between the end of the callout line and the box), **A**ngle, Dro**p** direction, and **L**ength.
5. Select Text **B**order, A**u**to Attach (prevents the pointer line from crossing the text box), and Ac**c**ent Bar (a line calling attention to the callout box), shown in Figure 26.14.
6. Click OK.

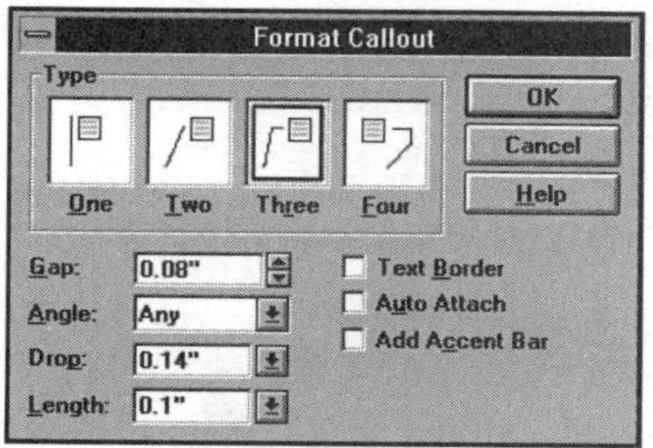

FIGURE 26.13.
Use the Format Callout dialog box to select a callout format.

SUPER NOTE

If you click the Format Callout tool with no callout box selected, Word displays the Callout Defaults dialog box. Use the Callout Defaults dialog box to set the default formatting for subsequent callouts you insert.

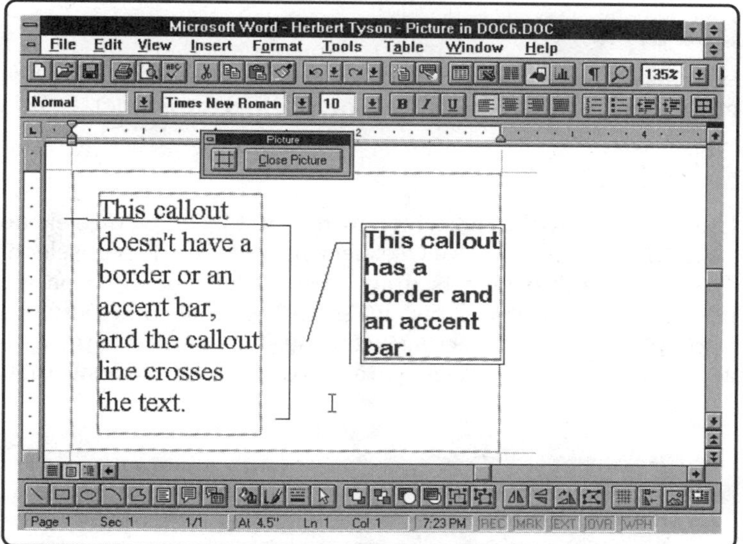

FIGURE 26.14.
You can add a text border and accent bar; the Auto Attach option prevents the line from crossing the callout text box.

Fill Color

Use the Fill Color tool to select a fill type and color for an object. The fill color you select remains in effect for the select object and all new objects you draw until you change it.

PROCEDURE 26.22. CHANGING THE FILL COLOR OF AN EXISTING OBJECT.

1. Select the object you want to change.
2. Click the Fill Color tool.
3. Click the color you want.

> **SUPER TIP**
>
> Additional color options (including shading, foreground, and background) can be set using the Format | Drawing Object dialog box. Select the object you want to change, then select Format | Drawing Object from the menu.

Line Color

Use the Line Color tool to select the outside color for object edges and for lines.

Line Style

Use the Line Style tool to select a line thickness and type. You also can double-click any line segment to display the Line folder in the Format | Drawing Object dialog box.

Selection Tool

Use the arrow tool to select a new object. Click a picture element to select it. Press Shift while clicking to select/deselect an object without deselecting any other objects. To select a group of objects, drag (press the left mouse button while moving the mouse pointer) the mouse. As shown in Figure 26.15, this draws a selection rectangle around a group of elements, selecting just those elements within the rectangle. Press the Shift key before you begin dragging to avoid deselecting elements that are already selected.

> **SUPER TIP**
>
> If the text area is selected and drawing objects are behind it, you can't select them using the text cursor. Click the drawing pointer and suddenly you can select your drawing objects. To deselect all objects, click any blank area in the drawing area. To select the text area, double-click the text.

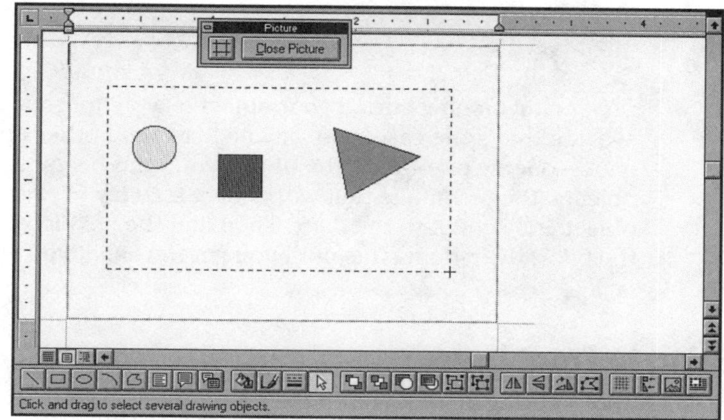

FIGURE 26.15.
Use the marquee technique to select a group of objects.

Bring to Front

A drawing consists of a number of objects. Use this command to bring an object to the front.

PROCEDURE 26.23. BRINGING AN OBJECT TO THE FRONT.

1. Click the object you want to move to the front.
2. Click the Bring to Front tool.

SUPER

MS Draw, which came with Word for Windows 2, had shortcut keystrokes for Bring to Front, Send to Back, and other drawing operations. Word 6 no longer has those shortcuts.

Send to Back

Sometimes you need to send an object to the back to get at elements that are covered up.

PROCEDURE 26.24. SENDING AN OBJECT TO THE BACK.

1. Click the object you want to send to the back.
2. Click the Send to Back tool.

SUPER TIP

Depending on how buried your object is, you may not even be able to see it. If that's the case, you may need to send other objects to the back—one by one—until the object you want becomes visible. To layer objects, the technique that works best is to try to reveal the lowest object and send it to the back. Then find the next lowest and send it to the back. Keep doing this until you get the effect you want.

Bring to Front Layer

Use this tool to bring an object into the foreground, in front of the text, as shown in Figure 26.16. If the text cursor is showing, then click the Arrow tool before trying to select the background object.

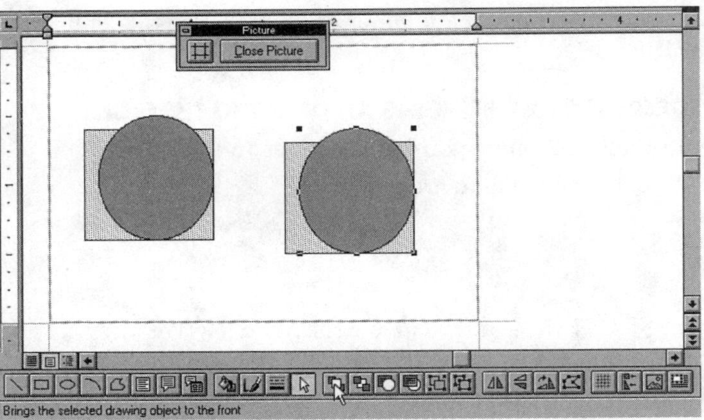

FIGURE 26.16.
Drawing objects can be out front…

PROCEDURE 26.25. BRINGING BACKGROUND DRAWING OBJECT IN FRONT OF TEXT.

1. If the text cursor (I-beam) is showing, click the Arrow tool in the drawing toolbar.
2. Click the object you want to bring out.
3. Click the Front Layer tool.

Send to Back Layer

Use this tool to send an object into the background, behind the text, as shown in Figure 26.17.

FIGURE 26.17.
...and out back. Use the Send to Back tool to place graphics, such as logos and watermarks, behind the text.

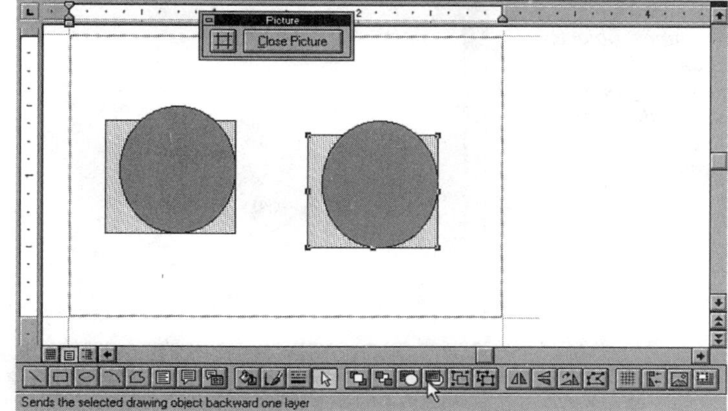

PROCEDURE 26.26. SENDING A DRAWING OBJECT BEHIND THE TEXT.

1. Click the object you want to send back.
2. Click the Back Layer tool.

Group Selected Objects

Use the Group command to bind different picture parts together as a compound object for manipulation. If you try to move parts around the screen that have not been grouped, you have to move them one at a time. If you group them, they all move as a collection, their relative positions remaining unchanged. At the same time they retain their separate identities for editing. They can be ungrouped at any time if you need to edit any of the parts.

PROCEDURE 26.27. GROUPING SEPARATE OBJECTS FOR GROUP MANIPULATION.

1. Select the objects you want to group.
2. Select the Group tool.

NOTE

You can use the marquee method to mark by dragging a selection rectangle around the objects you want to select. Or, you can use Shift+Click to select multiple objects, one at a time. Use the latter approach to remove several parts from a collection of objects that are too closely spaced for the marquee approach to work (see Figure 26.18).

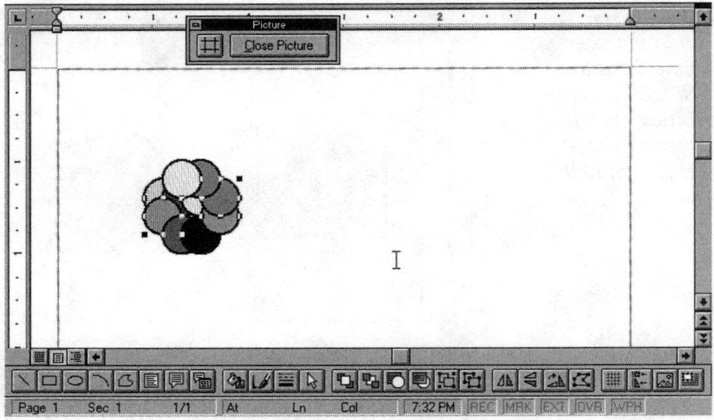

FIGURE 26.18.
Sometimes, objects are too closely spaced for you to pick out the ones you want using marquee selection.

Ungroup Select Objects

You can ungroup grouped objects if you need to edit the individual components.

PROCEDURE 26.28. UNGROUPING OBJECTS.

1. Select the compound object you want to ungroup.
2. Click the Ungroup tool.

Flip Horizontally

Use the Horizontal Flip tool to turn an object over, from left to right. You sometimes might use this technique when designing objects with lateral symmetry. Draw one side, copy it, and flip it. Then assemble the two sides to form a complete object. Most butterflies are drawn this way!

PROCEDURE 26.29. FLIPPING AN OBJECT HORIZONTALLY.

1. Select the object you want to flip; if you want to flip multiple objects at the same time, you must select and group them first.
2. Click the Horizontal Flip tool.

SUPER NOTE

You can flip drawing objects, but text in text boxes won't flip. If you need special text effects, try the Word Art application instead.

Flip Vertically

Use the Vertical Flip tool to turn an object upside down.

PROCEDURE 26.30. FLIPPING AN OBJECT VERTICALLY.

1. Select the object you want to flip; if you want to flip multiple objects at the same time, you must select and group them first.
2. Click the Vertical Flip tool.

Rotate 90°

Use the Rotate tool to turn an object 90 degrees at a time.

1. Select the object you want to rotate; if you want to rotate multiple objects at the same time, you must select and group them first.
2. Click the Rotate tool.

SUPER NOTE

You can rotate drawing objects, but not text in text boxes. Try the Word Art application instead.

Edit Freeform Object

You can manipulate the shape of a freeform object by moving the individual control handles, adding new handles, and deleting handles.

PROCEDURE 26.31. EDITING THE SHAPE OF A FREEFORM OBJECT.

1. Click to select the freeform object.
2. Click the Edit Freeform object tool; all of the control handles appear, as shown in Figure 26.19.
3. Move the mouse pointer over the handle you want to move (it takes on a + shape when it's in position).
4. Using the left mouse button, drag the handle to a new position.
5. Release the mouse button to fix the position.
6. Repeat Steps 3 through 5 to mold the object into shape.
7. Click outside the freeform object to close the edit.

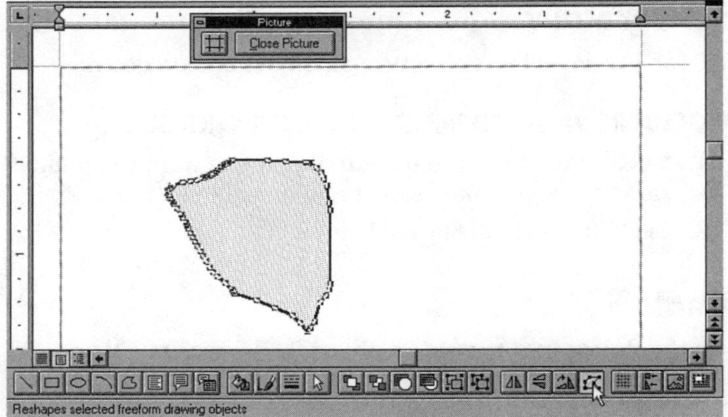

FIGURE 26.19. *Control handles show you where to drag to change the shape of a freeform object.*

PROCEDURE 26.32. ADDING OR DELETING CONTROL HANDLES TO A FREEFORM OBJECT.

1. Click to select the freeform object.
2. Click the Edit Freeform object tool.
3. To add control handles, press the Ctrl key and note that the shape of the mouse changes from an arrow to a circled plus sign with crosshairs, as shown in Figure 26.20. To delete handles, also hold down the Ctrl key, and move the mouse over an existing handle. Note that the mouse pointer shape turns to an X (see Figure 26.21).

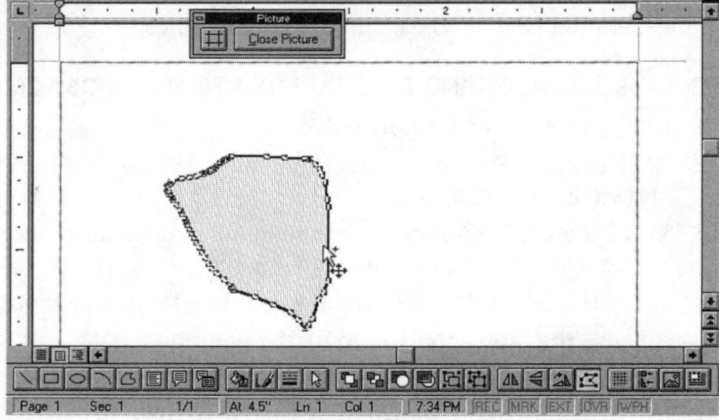

FIGURE 26.20. *With the Ctrl key depressed, the mouse pointer turns into a + to show that clicking adds new handles.*

4. Using the left mouse button, click the mouse where you want to add or delete control handles.
5. Click outside the freeform object to close the edit.

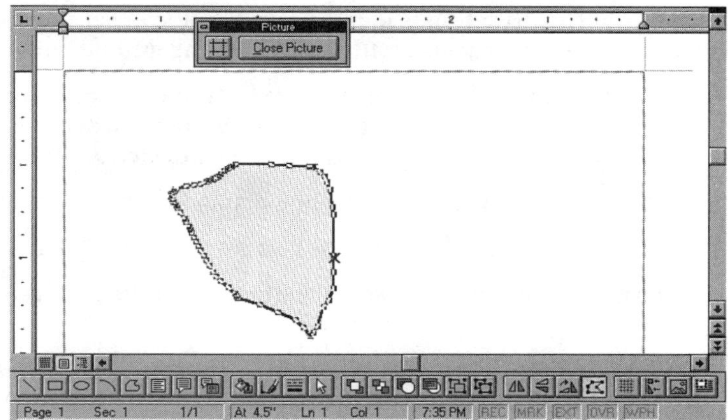

FIGURE 26.21.
Press Ctrl and click the left mouse button to delete existing handles; the X shows what action the click performs (delete).

SUPER NOTE

If you're editing a closed object, you can add control handles only between existing handles by clicking on line segments. If you're editing an open object, you can click an existing line to add a control handle between the adjacent handles. Alternatively, you can click off a line to add control handles to the logical end (where you ended the object) of the freeform object.

PROCEDURE 26.33. MOVING A CLOSED OR FILLED OPEN FREEFORM OBJECT.

1. Click the object.
2. Press and hold the left mouse button and drag the object to a new location.
3. Release the mouse button to drop the object in the new location.

PROCEDURE 26.34. MOVING AN UNFILLED OPEN FREEFORM OBJECT.

1. Point the mouse at the freeform object edge.
2. Press and hold the left mouse button and drag the object to a new location.
3. Release the mouse button to drop the object in the new location.

Set Up Snapping Grid

Word has an invisible grid system. The horizontal and vertical gridlines are 7.2 points (one-tenth of an inch) apart by default. If **S**nap to Grid is enabled, any objects you create or move automatically snap to the closest imaginary gridline. This feature facilitates aligning graphic elements. The **S**nap to Grid setting applies to future actions and does not affect objects already in position.

Use the Grid tool to set up a snapping grid. You can set the spacing and gradations down to .05 points, or you can turn the snapping grid off altogether.

Snap to Grid	Turns **S**nap to **G**rid on or off. When **S**nap to **G**rid is off, you can place graphics wherever you want. When the grid is on, you can place graphics only on the grid.
Hori**z**ontal Spacing	Horizontal distance between imaginary vertical lines.
Vertical Spacing	Vertical distance between imaginary horizontal lines.
Horizontal **O**rigin	Distance from the left-hand edge of the page where the grid originates.
Vertical O**r**igin	Distance from the top edge of the page where the grid originates.

Align Objects

Use the Align tool to align different objects with each other.

PROCEDURE 26.35. ALIGNING OBJECTS.

1. Select the objects you want to align (use the marquee method of dragging a rectangle around them (after clicking on the arrow tool), or press Shift and click each drawing object you want to select.
2. Click the Align tool to display the Align dialog box.
3. Select the alignment types desired, as well as whether the types are relative to each other or relative to the page.

Insert Picture Container

Use this command to create a blank embedded picture object (`{ EMBED Word.Picture.6}`) into a Word document. This is equivalent to selecting **I**nsert | **O**bject and clicking Microsoft Word 6.0 Picture.

Frame

Use the Frame tool to frame a drawing. By the way, you also can use the frame tool to frame anything that needs framing—including text.

PROCEDURE 26.36. FRAMING A PICTURE.

1. Select the drawing or picture objects you want to frame (you don't have to group objects together, but you can if you like). Word frames just those objects that are selected.
2. Click the Frame tool.

SUPER NOTE

When you frame a drawing, it gets converted into an EMBED field. Thereafter, when you edit it, it is edited as an object rather than a plain picture.

Format Drawing Object

In addition to creating and editing tools using the Drawing toolbar, you also can format drawing elements using the Format | Drawing Object dialog box (shown in Figure 26.22).

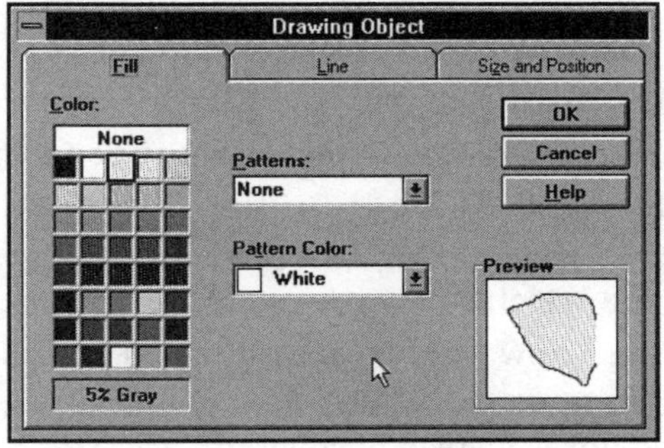

FIGURE 26.22.
The Drawing Object and Drawing Defaults dialog boxes are one in the same.

The Drawing Object folder has three tabbed divisions:

Fill	Used to format the interior of an object
Line	Used to format the edge of an object as well as lines
Size and Position	Used to format the size and position of the object

You can select the Format Drawing folder at any time. If a picture is not selected, the folder is displayed as Drawing Defaults, and settings specific to a single drawing are dimmed as unavailable. If a picture or part of a picture is selected, then the Drawing Object title bar is used and all relevant options are available.

Fill

Use the Fill tab to set the interior coloring and shading for a drawing object.

PROCEDURE 26.37. SETTING THE FILL.

1. Click the right mouse button on the item you want to format.
2. Select Format Drawing Object from the popup menu.

3. Click the **F**ill tab.
4. Using the Preview as a guide, select the **C**olor, **P**atterns, and Pa**t**tern color.
5. Click OK.

The pattern, if selected, consists of dots, lines, or other patterns. The main Color option is the background. The pattern color is the color of the dots, lines, or other patterns on the background. If no object is selected when you activate the fill settings, the selections you make are used as the default color and pattern for the next object you edit or create.

Line

Use the Line tab to set the line **S**tyle, thickness (**W**eight), coloring (**C**olor), Arrow Head type, and other line formats for a drawing object.

PROCEDURE 26.38. SETTING THE LINE FORMATTING.

1. Click the right mouse button on the item you want to format.
2. Select **F**ormat Drawing Object from the popup menu.
3. Click the **L**ine tab.
4. Using the Preview as a guide, select the line **S**tyle (solid, dashed, and so on), **C**olor, and **W**eight.
5. Select the Arrow Head S**t**yle, Wi**d**th, and Len**g**th.
6. Select Shad**o**w if you want a shadow effect, and **R**ound Corners if you want rounded boxes instead of squared boxes (for rectangles, callouts, and text boxes).
7. Click OK.

Size and Position

Use the Size and Position tab to set the location and size of the drawing object on the page. You also can use the Callouts button to access Callouts defaults and formatting (as described earlier in this chapter).

If the drawing is embedded, the size and position settings affect only the size and position of the object within its cropping area. If the drawing isn't embedded, then the size and position settings affect the absolute size and position on the page.

Ordinarily, you might not need this control because it's much easier and much more direct to format using the mouse. If you need to place an object exactly, however, you might prefer the certainty a dialog box guarantees. Before using this command, however, you should move and size the object as nearly as you can using the mouse, and then use this command for the finishing touches.

PROCEDURE 26.39. SETTING THE SIZE AND POSITION OF A GRAPHIC.

1. Select the object you want to format (Note: It's not enough to select the cropping or framed area of an embedded graphic; you must actually open the object for direct editing by double-clicking).
2. Click the right mouse button, then select **F**ormat Drawing Object and Si**z**e and Position.
3. Select the position settings you want; if the object is embedded, this determines only the object's location within the frame or cropping area, not its location on the page.
4. Select Lock **A**nchor if you want the object married to the current paragraph.
5. To set the picture off from the frame or border, increase the size of the **I**nternal margin.
6. Click OK.

Chapter

27

Microsoft Graph, WordArt, and Equation Editor

Microsoft Graph provides basic graphing capabilities for use in Word. While the capabilities are well below those provided by full-featured spreadsheets and graphics programs, they are sufficient for doing some basic and attractive data presentations. However, please, make sure you understand your data and how to present it before inflicting graphs and charts on your readers. While a picture may be worth a thousand words, an incomprehensible graph often evokes words you'd rather not hear!

SUPER NOTE

Before you read this chapter, here's a little piece of advice. If you have and know how to use Quattro Pro for Windows, Lotus 1-2-3 for Windows, or Excel, use one of them instead of MS Graph. You won't be sorry. While useful, MS Graph lacks the power to do truly useful graphic presentations of data. Thanks to MS Graph, however, many people who don't understand data are wasting others' time with useless and inappropriate presentations of it. The next time you get a letter with a bar chart, line graph, scattergraph, or other data presentation that makes no sense, keep in mind how easy MS Graph makes it to clutter documents with meaningless graphs.

Embedding a Graph

Embedding a graph or chart is easy. It's especially easy if your data is already organized in the form of a table, or otherwise available in a spreadsheet.

PROCEDURE 27.1. EMBEDDING A GRAPH BASED ON A WORD TABLE.

1. Select the table that contains the data you want to use—including labels.
2. Click the MS Graph tool in the toolbar (see Figure 27.1).

FIGURE 27.1.
The Microsoft Graph tool.

3. This opens the MS Graph applet, as shown in Figure 27.2.
4. Select **G**allery, then click an appropriate graph type.
5. Select **F**ile | **U**pdate to send the graph to your Word document while keeping MS Graph open; if you're utterly satisfied with the graph, then by all means select **F**ile | **E**xit and return.

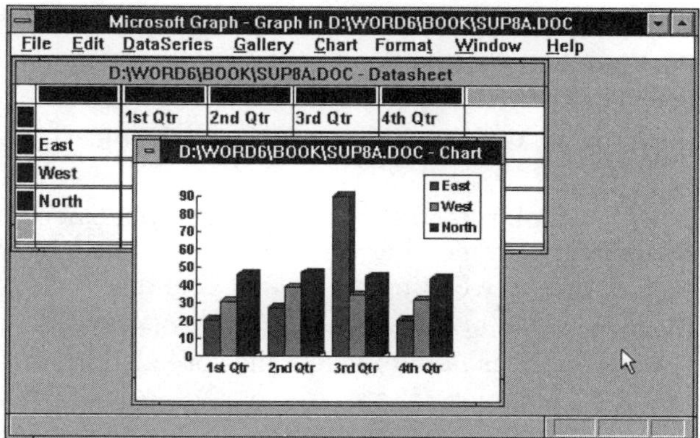

FIGURE 27.2.
The Microsoft Graph screen.

SUPER NOTE

Printed quality of MS Graph results (especially the 3-D versions) is often very bad. Do some test prints of your graphs early on before committing to MS Graph as a solution, or even before settling on a specific type of graph.

Data Sources

MS Graph can use data from a variety of sources:

- MS Graph datasheet
- Clipboard
- Word table
- Tabbed text files (data separated by tabs)
- CSV files (comma-separated values, but must have the extension .CSV)
- Spreadsheets in the formats .WKS, .WK1, .WR1, .XLS, or .SLK
- Excel charts (.XLC files; when you import an Excel chart, MS Graph imports the underlying data as well)

Graph Datasheet

To use an MS Graph datasheet, type your data into the minispreadsheet that comes with MS Graph. If you enter column and row labels, MS Graph automatically uses them as data labels.

PROCEDURE 27.2. ENTERING YOUR OWN DATA IN MS GRAPH.

1. Position the insertion point in your Word document where you want the graph or chart to appear.
2. Click the MS Graph tool, or select **I**nsert | **O**bject | **C**reate New | Microsoft Graph.
3. The MS Graph screen shows a default spreadsheet and graph (you can reset the default to something you prefer, including a blank spreadsheet and graph, by the way—see Setting the Default Graph later in this session).
4. Clear the existing data; press Ctrl+A (to select all) and then press the Delete key; select Clear **B**oth to delete the spreadsheet and graph.
5. Along the left edge, in the first column, beginning in the second row, type your row labels. To complete each entry, press Enter, or simply press a cursor key in the direction you want to move.
6. Along the top edge, in the first row, beginning in the second column, type your column labels (see Figure 27.3).

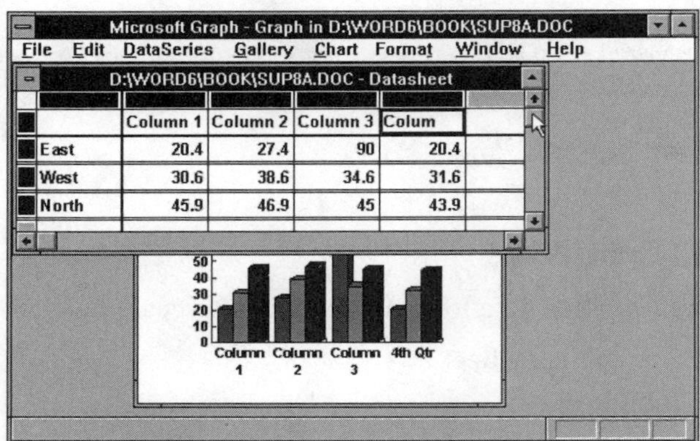

FIGURE 27.3.
Column labels go across the top.

7. Type your data into the cells.
8. Edit the chart, if needed.
9. Select **F**ile | **U**pdate to send the graph to Word.

SUPER NOTE

The chart or graph gets created as you go along. You can go back and select the type of graphic once the data is entered.

Word Table

If you have data in a Word table, you can select the table. When you start MS Graph, the table data is automatically used by MS Graph.

PROCEDURE 27.3. USING A WORD TABLE FOR MS GRAPH.

1. Select the entire table (Alt+5 on numeric pad, with Num Lock off), or the portion of the table you want to use; be sure to include any labels you want to use.
2. Click the MS Graph tool.
3. Edit the chart, if needed.
4. Select **F**ile | **U**pdate to send the graph to Word.

Spreadsheet or Data File

You can import all or part of an existing spreadsheet or data file into MS Graph. If the file is a data file without a .CSV extension, items must be separated by tabs and paragraph marks. If the data is separated by commas, items in the data that contain commas must be enclosed in quotes, and the file must have a .CSV extension.

PROCEDURE 27.4. IMPORTING A SPREADSHEET INTO MS GRAPH.

1. Click the MS Graph tool.
2. Select **F**ile | **I**mport Data.
3. Use the **D**irectories and **F**iles lists to navigate to the file you want to use.
4. Click the file you want to import.
5. Click **A**ll or **R**ange, and type the range, if appropriate (*top left*:*bottom right*; for example, `A1:F5`).
6. Click OK.
7. Edit the chart, if needed.
8. Select File | Update to send the graph to Word.

Importing an Excel Chart

MS Graph can read Excel charts. You are not able to save changes back into an Excel chart, however. Word itself also can use Excel charts, using Excel itself as a DDE server. If you have Excel, then by all means use it. It's capable of much more powerful graphics than MS Graph. Use Excel charts in MS Graph only if you don't have Excel or if you're otherwise a glutton for punishment.

PROCEDURE 27.5. USING AN EXCEL CHART.

In Word, move the insertion point to where you want the chart to appear.

`Select File¦Open Microsoft Excel Chart.`

Word warns you that opening the Excel chart overwrites the current data and chart; ensure that it's nothing you need to save and click OK to proceed.

1. Use the **D**irectories and **F**iles list boxes to locate the file.
2. Click the file.
3. Click OK.
4. Edit the chart, if needed.
5. Click **U**pdate to send the chart to Word.

Using Graph

MS Graph has two windows: the Datasheet and the Chart. When you open MS Graph, a default datasheet and chart are already displayed. You can switch between the datasheet and chart by clicking or by selecting the one you want from the Window menu. When you expand the chart window by dragging the borders, the chart is automatically expanded as well. When you send the chart into Word, it will be the size currently set in MS Graph.

SUPER CAUTION

Multiple copies of MS Graph can be running at any time, so when you switch to MS Graph from Word, make sure you go to the correct one by taking a look at your data and chart. Many a chart has been screwed up by not paying attention to the street signs.

File

Use the **F**ile menu (shown in Figure 27.4) to import data or charts, send results back to Word, and set the default chart and datasheet.

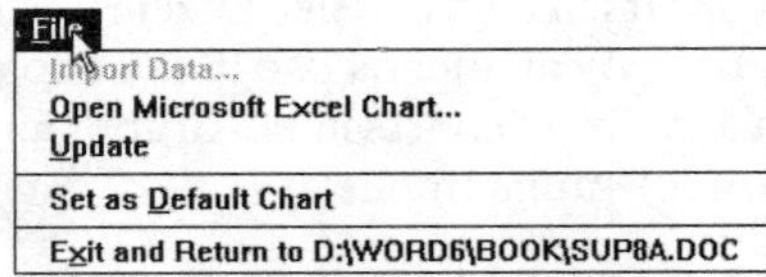

FIGURE 27.4.
The File menu.

Import Data

Use the Import Data option to read plain data files and spreadsheets in supported formats.

Open Microsoft Excel Chart

Use this command to open Excel charts. The data and chart information are both used by MS Graph.

Update

Use the Update command to send the current chart results to Word without closing MS Graph. When you use this option, MS Graph does not prompt before replacing the current image stored in Word. The image isn't saved permanently in Word, however, until you do a File|Save in Word itself.

Set as Default Chart

Use this option to set current chart as the default chart (the one you first see when you start MS Graph).

Exit and Return to (*document name*)

Use this option to send the current chart to Word and to close MS Graph. Unlike the Update command, MS Graph prompts before sending the chart to Word.

Edit

The Edit menu provides basic clipboard functions for people who don't like to learn keyboard shortcuts, as well as commands for inserting and deleting columns and rows from the datasheet.

Undo

Reverses the effect of the most recent edit.

Keyboard shortcuts:

Alt+Backspace
Ctrl+Z

Cut

Deletes the selection to the clipboard.

Keyboard shortcuts:

Shift+Delete
Ctrl+X

Copy

Copies the selection to the clipboard.

Keyboard shortcuts:

Ctrl+Insert
Ctrl+C

Paste

Copies (pastes) the contents of the clipboard. When pasting the contents of the clipboard, you cannot control where the paste occurs. The best you can do is to paste the selection and then move it where you want it.

Keyboard shortcuts:

Shift+Insert
Ctrl+V

Clear

Deletes the selection without putting it into the clipboard.

Keyboard shortcut:

Delete

Select All

Selects the entire drawing.

Keyboard shortcut:

Ctrl+A

Mouse shortcut:

Click joint row/column selection cell (see Figure 27.5).

Delete Row/Column

Use this command to delete whole rows or columns. It offers the popup shown in Figure 27.6. If one or more whole rows or columns are already selected, the popup is bypassed and the selection is deleted immediately. If only part of a row or column is selected, the popup menu appears.

Keyboard shortcut:

Ctrl+-

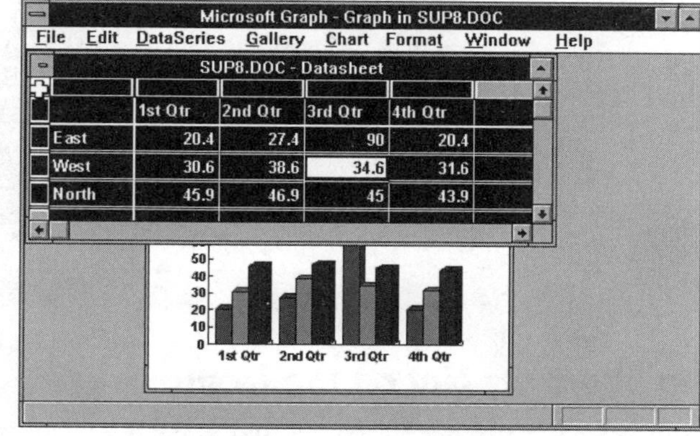

FIGURE 27.5.
Joint row/column selection cell.

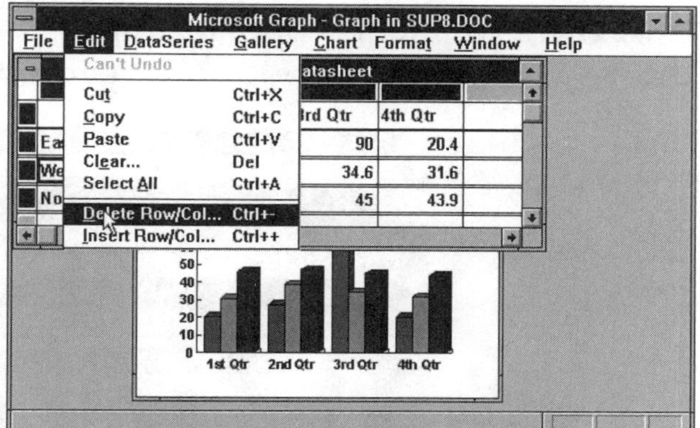

FIGURE 27.6.
Delete Row/Column.

Insert Row/Column

Use this command to insert whole rows or columns. It offers the popup shown in Figure 27.7. If one or more whole rows or columns are already selected, the popup is bypassed and the MS Graph inserts the same number of columns or rows above or to the left of the ones that are selected.

Keyboard shortcut:

Ctrl++ (Ctrl+Shift+= on the top row, or just Ctrl++ on the numeric pad)

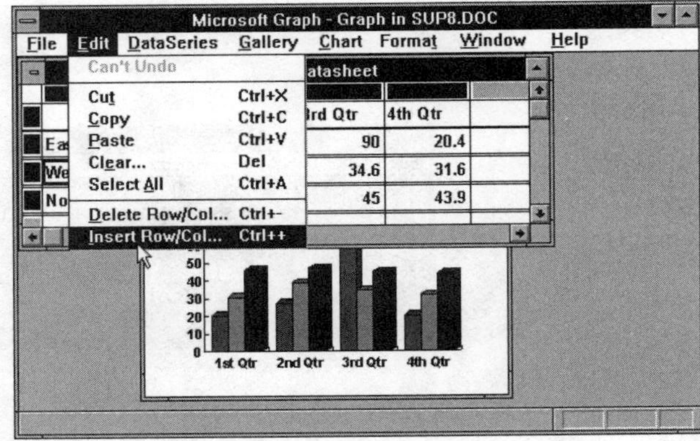

FIGURE 27.7.
Insert Row/Column.

Editing Shortcuts Not on the Menu

MS Graph has a few editing shortcuts that make it a little easier to use.

PROCEDURE 27.6. SPEED SELECTION OF WHOLE ROWS.

1. Click the selection cell at the beginning of the row (shown in Figure 27.8).

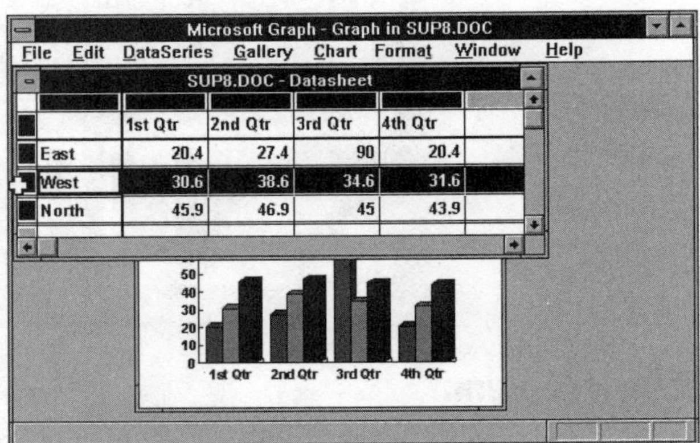

FIGURE 27.8.
Click a row selection cell to select the entire row.

2. Drag the mouse to select multiple rows; alternatively, you can press Shift and click the first and last rows to select a group of rows.

SUPER NOTE

You cannot select multiple nonadjacent rows.

PROCEDURE 27.7. SPEED SELECTION OF WHOLE COLUMNS.

1. Click the selection cell at the top of the column (shown in Figure 27.9).

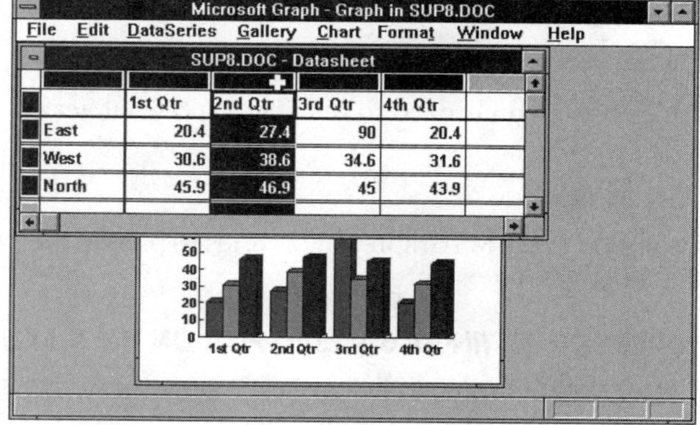

FIGURE 27.9. *Click a column selection cell to select the entire column.*

2. Drag the mouse to select multiple columns; alternatively, you can press Shift and click the first and last columns to select a group of columns.

SUPER NOTE

You cannot select multiple nonadjacent columns.

PROCEDURE 27.8. CHANGING COLUMN WIDTH WITH THE MOUSE.

1. Move the mouse pointer so it's between two column selection cells (see Figure 27.10); the mouse cursor changes to indicate that the column boundary is selected.

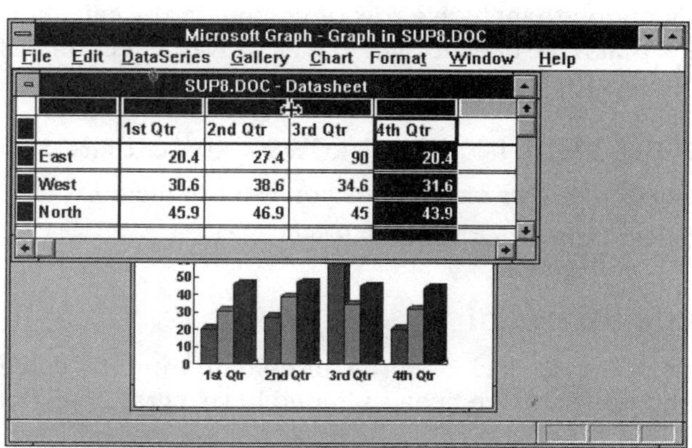

FIGURE 27.10. *The pointer changes to show that a column boundary is selected.*

2. Hold down the left mouse button and drag the column boundary to a new position.
3. Release the mouse button to end the operation.

DataSeries

The **D**ataSeries menu is used to tell MS Graph what series get graphed where.

Plot on X Axis

Use this option to tell MS Graph which series to plot on the X axis (vertical). This option is available only for XY scattergraphs.

PROCEDURE 27.9. SETTING A SERIES TO PLOT ON THE X AXIS.

1. Select **D**ataSeries and click Series in **R**ows or Series in **C**olumns to orient MS Graph to the series you want to use.
2. Select a cell in the target series.
3. Select **D**ataSeries | **P**lot on X Axis to set the current row or column to plot on the X axis. An X appears over or beside the column or row, respectively (see Figure 27.11).

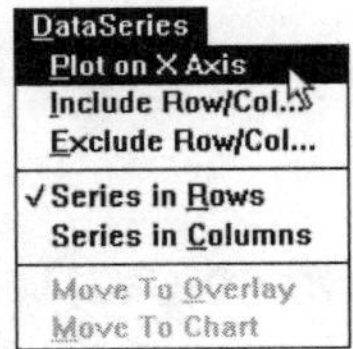

FIGURE 27.11.
*The **Plot** on X Axis menu.*

Include Row/Col

Use this option to include a row or column in the calculation of the chart. Rows and columns that have been excluded have a gray selection cell (see Figure 27.12). Rows and columns that are included have a black selection cell.

PROCEDURE 27.10. INCLUDING ROWS AND COLUMNS.

1. Select the rows or columns you want to include.
2. Select **D**ataSeries | **I**nclude Row/Col.

Exclude Row/Col

Use this option to exclude a row or column from the calculation of the chart. Rows and columns that have been excluded have a gray selection cell. Rows and columns that are included have a black selection cell. When importing data, you may sometimes find that empty rows or columns were erroneously included. Use this procedure to exclude them from the chart.

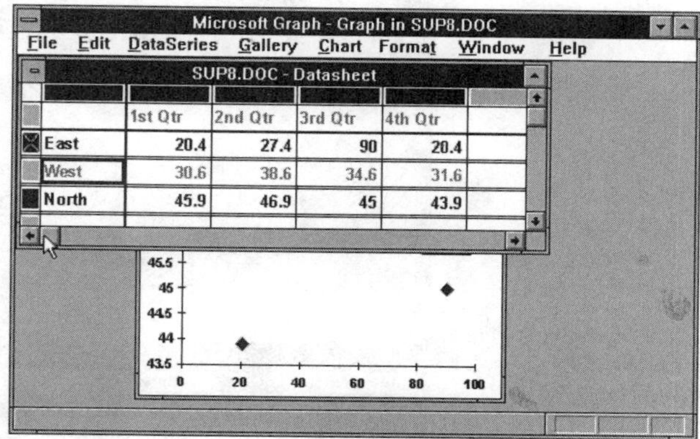

FIGURE 27.12.
Excluded rows are grayed out.

PROCEDURE 27.11. INCLUDING ROWS AND COLUMNS.

1. Select the rows or columns you want to include.
2. Select **D**ataSeries | **E**xclude.

Series in Rows/Series in Columns

Use this command to tell MS Graph where to find the data series.

SUPER NOTE

When series are in rows, double lines separate the rows. When series are in columns, double lines separate the columns (see Figure 27.13).

Move to Overlay

When using a combination chart, some series are presented in the main chart and others are presented in the overlay (a second graph superimposed over the first). Use this command to select which series will be used in the overlay. When a column or row is selected for **O**verlay, a large dot appears in the selection cell (see Figure 27.14).

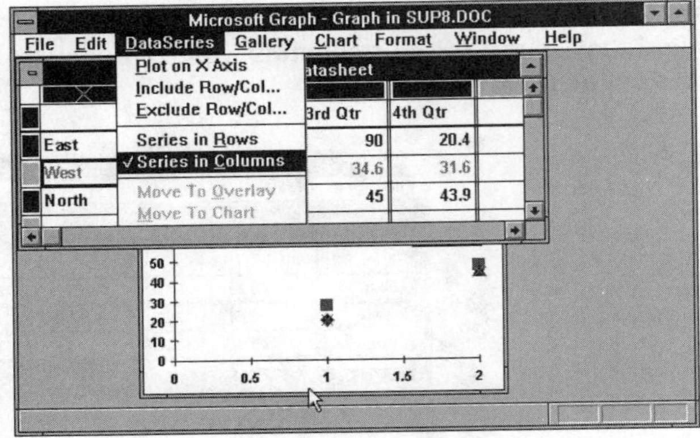

FIGURE 27.13.
Double lines show that the series are in the columns.

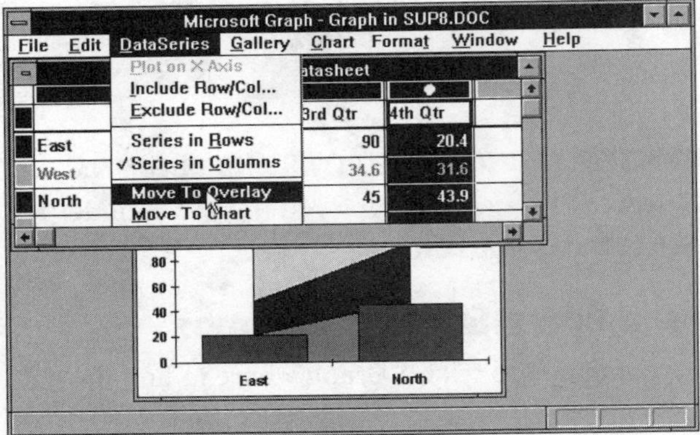

FIGURE 27.14.
Dot's nice! The large dot shows which columns or rows are selected for Overlay.

PROCEDURE 27.12. SELECTING SERIES FOR OVERLAY.

1. Select any cell in the series row or column.
2. Select **D**ataSeries | Move to **O**verlay.

Move to Chart

Use this command to select which series in a combination chart will be used in the chart.

PROCEDURE 27.13. SELECTING SERIES FOR THE CHART (AS OPPOSED TO OVERLAY).

1. Select any cell in the series row or column.
2. Select **D**ataSeries | **M**ove to Chart.

Gallery

The Gallery is a collection of graph and chart types that you can select as starting points for your graphs and charts. Use the gallery to make an initial selection. Note that each graph type includes an additional button called Custom. The Custom options vary by graph type. Use the Custom options to modify the graph or chart. Once you've gone as far as you can there, use the Chart and Format menus to refine the graph, editing and adding labels, legends, and so forth.

Area

Shows relative change in magnitude over time. It's similar to a line graph, but it emphasizes the changes in proportions over time. See Figure 27.15.

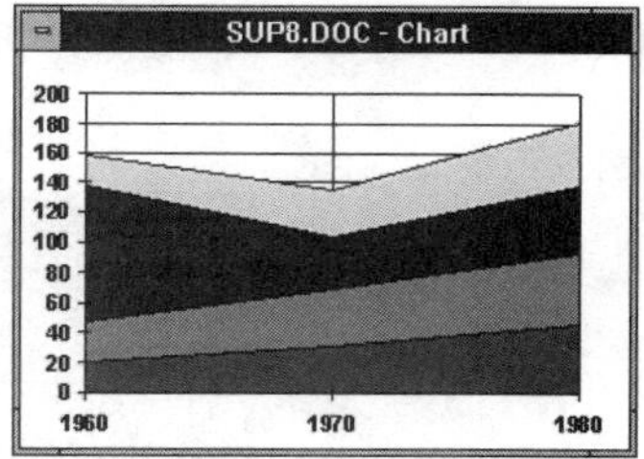

FIGURE 27.15.
Area graphs are useful for showing changes in proportions over time.

Bar

Horizontal bar chart that compares different factors at a specific time or shows the progression of a single factor over time. See Figure 27.16.

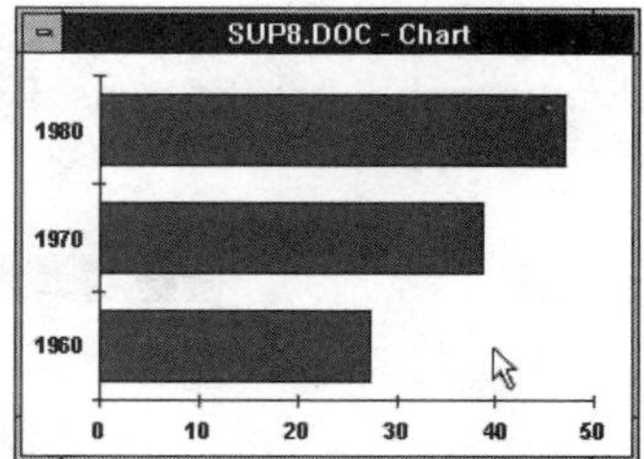

FIGURE 27.16.
A horizontal bar chart showing the progression of a factor over time.

Column

Vertical bar chart. Commonly used to compare sales volume of different products or companies, or of a single factor over time. The vertical dimension emphasizes the magnitude of differences. See Figure 27.17.

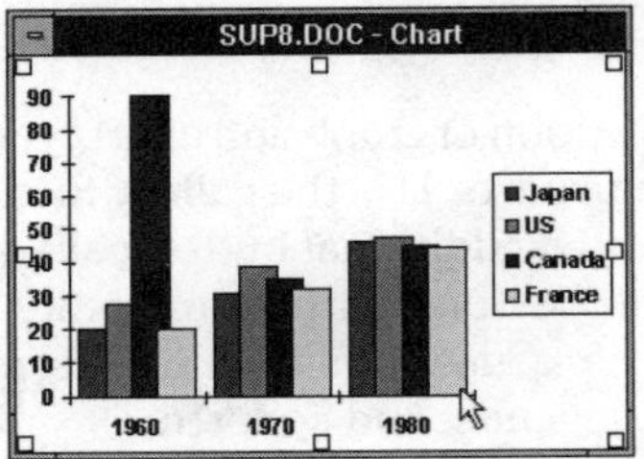

FIGURE 27.17.
A vertical bar chart showing the progression of a factor over time.

Line

Line graph is used to show trends and fluctuations over time. Technically, line graphs are especially suitable for continuous data because they let you interpolate between the plotted points. Line graphs are often used in presenting economic data such as GDP (gross domestic product), unemployment, stock prices, and housing starts. See Figure 27.18.

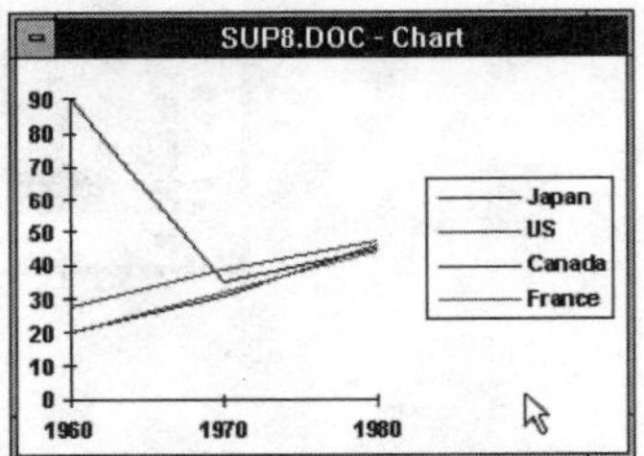

FIGURE 27.18.
Line graphs make for good economics presentations—just ask Ross!

Pie

Shows the relative shares or breakdown of parts of a whole. Often used to show market share and demographic breakdowns. By design, a pie chart shows only one concept at a time, for a single point in time. See Figure 27.19.

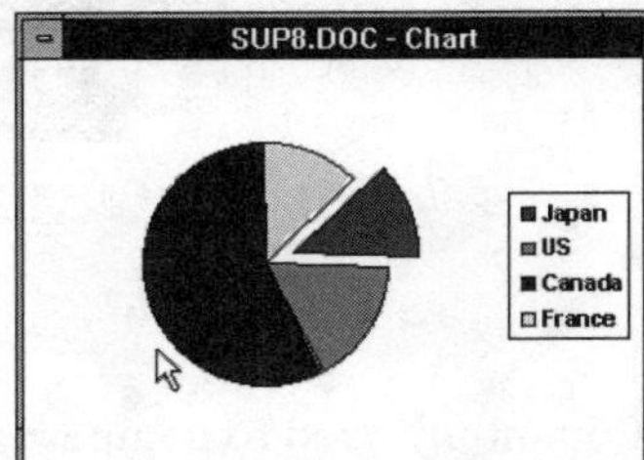

FIGURE 27.19.
Pie charts don't work for everything, but they do work well for some things.

XY (Scatter)

Plots data series over time. A scatter plot is appropriate when data vary wildly. Scatter plots are one of the few graphical forms that accurately portray much economic data. Scatter plots are especially useful in econometric analyses when looking for data problems such as heteroskedasticity (nonrandom variance). See Figure 27.20.

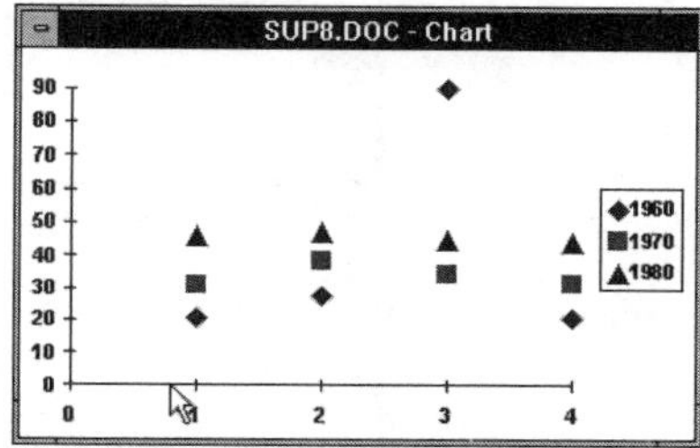

FIGURE 27.20.
Scatter plots can show patterns of change over time.

Combination

Used to show different kinds of data on the same graph. Especially useful when different data use vastly different scales, but are nonetheless related, such as unemployment, inflation, and GDP. See Figure 27.21.

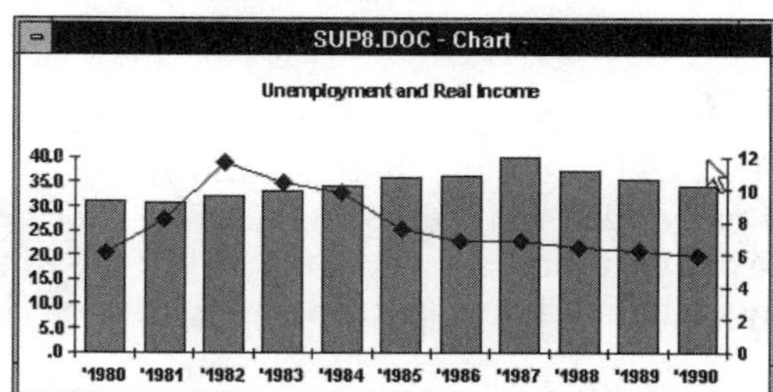

FIGURE 27.21.
Use a combination graph to show related but incompatible graphics.

3-D Area

Potentially useful, 3-D area charts can enhance the presentation of data—even though no variation is actually displayed in the third dimension, as shown in Figure 27.22.

3-D Bar

The 3-D view often is used only to make an otherwise-boring chart look more important than it is. Unfortunately, MS Graph doesn't display anything in the third dimension (that is, the thickness of the bars is purely aesthetic, and doesn't measure any data). See Figure 27.23.

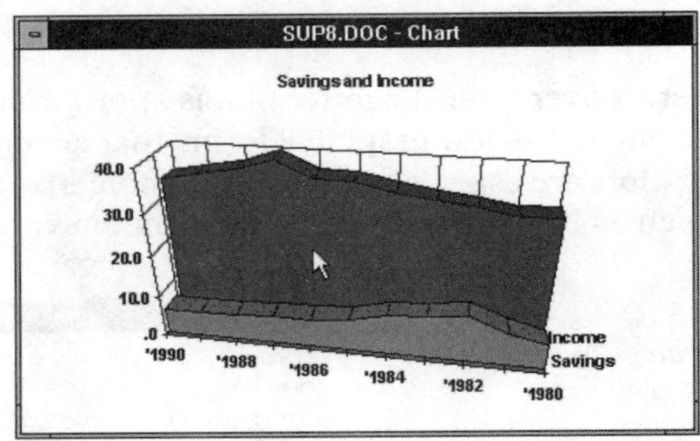

FIGURE 27.22.
3-D area charts can help emphasize data comparisons.

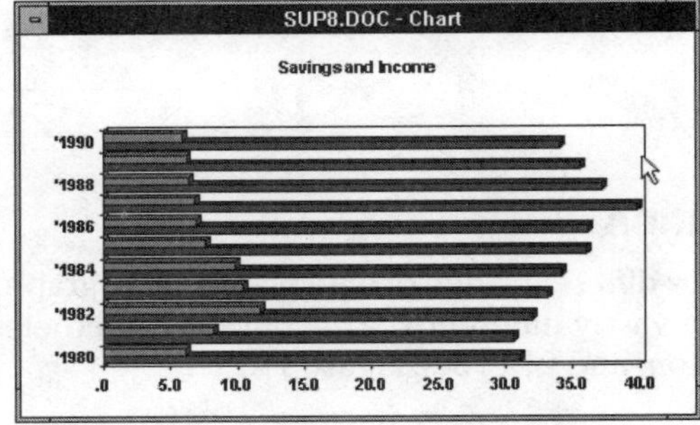

FIGURE 27.23.
3-D bar chart.

3-D Column

Shows a 3-D view of a column chart. As shown in Figure 27.24, the 3-D aspect can be used to emphasize different series in the same chart. Too bad MS Graph didn't allow the same flexibility in the 3-D bar graph. Even so, the thickness of the bars doesn't measure any data, but it does serve to give a better visual impression of the data.

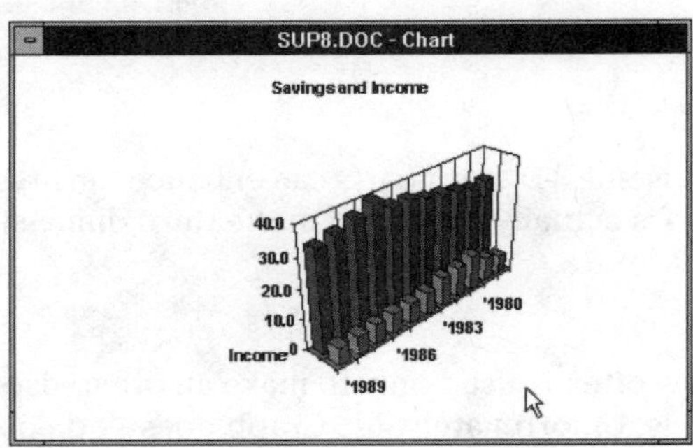

FIGURE 27.24.
Rotating a 3-D column chart to the right angle can help emphasize differences among series in the same chart.

3-D Line

Sometimes called a ribbon graph, lines are shown as strips rather than lines, sometimes helping to compare data, but other times distorting the relationship among data series. As with other MS Graph 3-D graph implementations, the width of the ribbons is purely aesthetic and doesn't actually measure any data. See Figure 27.25.

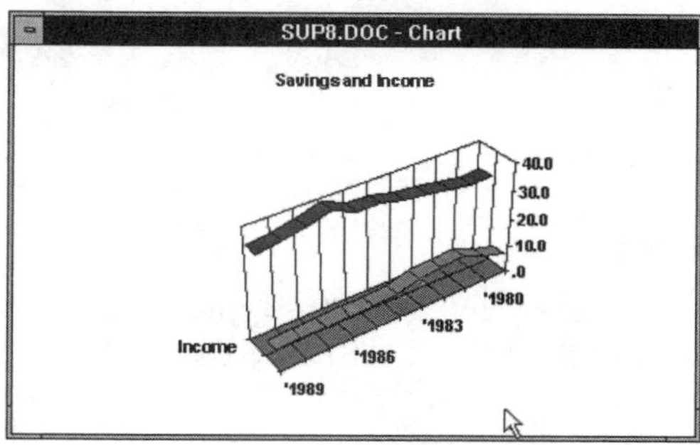

FIGURE 27.25.
A 3-D ribbon chart.

3-D Pie

Shows a pie chart with height to the slices. While 3-D pie charts look heftier, they actually convey no additional information as implemented in MS Graph. See Figure 27.26.

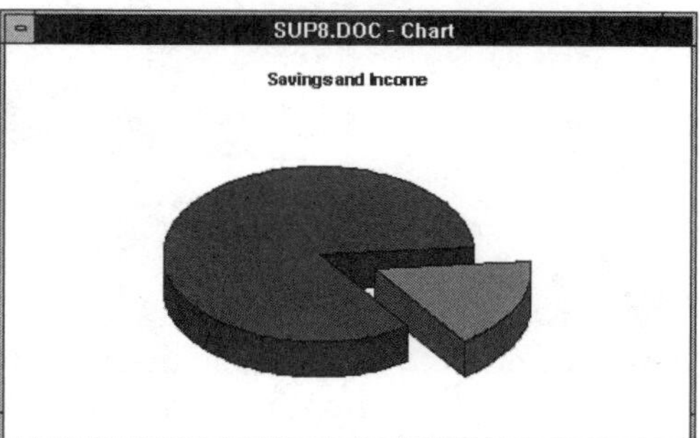

FIGURE 27.26.
3-D pie chart.

Chart

Use the Chart menu to manage the overall appearance of the chart and what it includes—titles, labels, legend, and so forth.

Titles

Use the Titles options to select independent titles placed in up to five different areas in a chart (see Figure 27.27). The Titles option is available for selection only when the Chart is the active window.

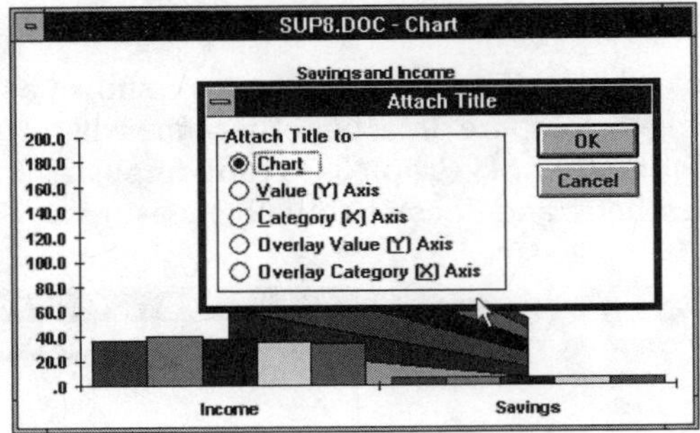

FIGURE 27.27.
The Titles option is available only when the Chart is the active window.

Data Labels

Use the Data Labels option to set the types of data labels you want to use (none is the default, as shown in Figure 27.28). The Data Labels option is available only when the Chart is the active window.

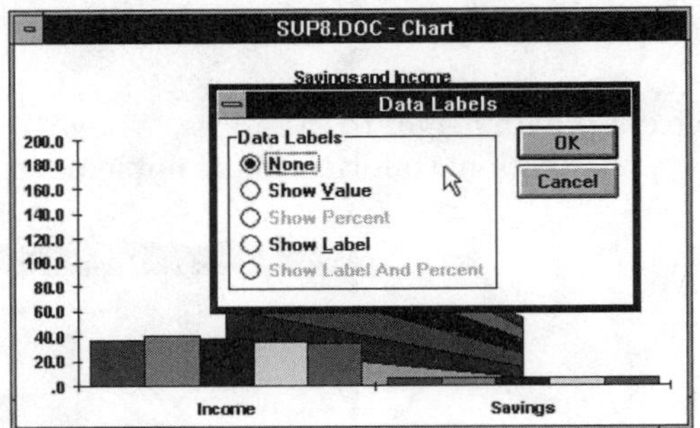

FIGURE 27.28.
The Data Labels option is available only when the Chart is the active window.

Add Arrow

Use the Add Arrow option to toggle an arrow on and off. You can move the arrow by dragging the line to a new location. You can resize and change the arrow's direction by dragging the handle at either end to a new location. As you drag, the opposite end remains anchored in place (see Figure 27.29).

Add Legend

Use the Add Legend/Delete Legend option to toggle the legend on and off (see Figure 27.30). You can reformat the legend (fonts, attributes, and so forth) by clicking the legend and then selecting options from the Format menu.

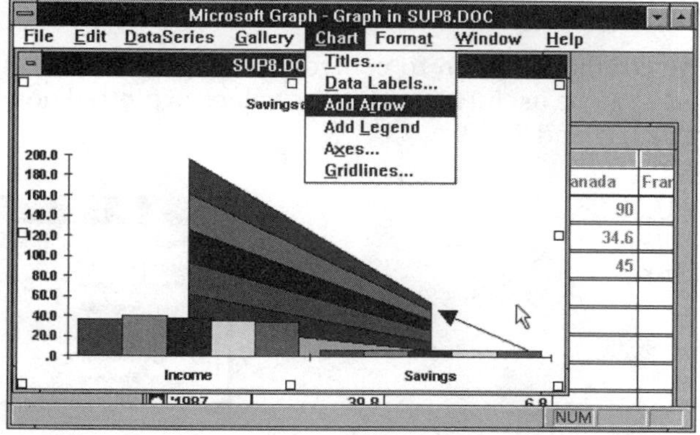

FIGURE 27.29.
Use the Add Arrow option to toggle an arrow.

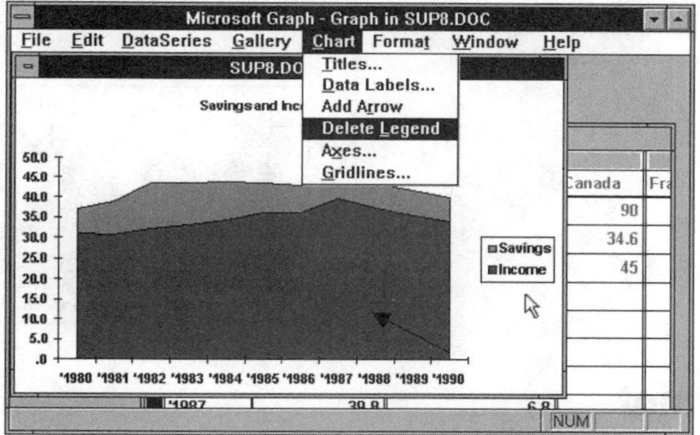

FIGURE 27.30.
Add Legend/Delete Legend controls the display of the legend.

Axes

Use the Axes options to control whether or not axes are visible. Figure 27.31 shows two charts with Axes turned off (left) and on (right).

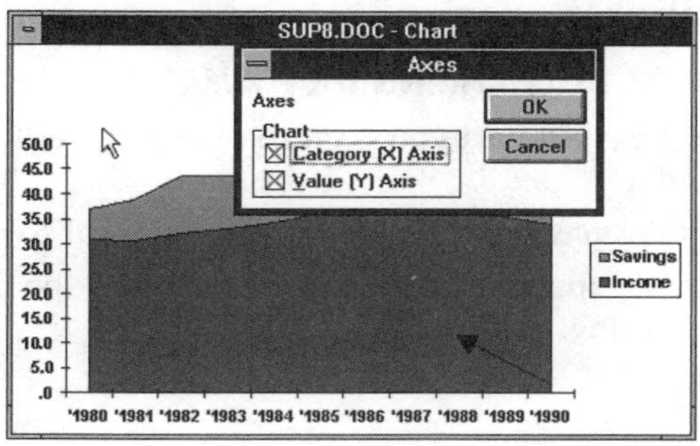

FIGURE 27.31.
Axes can aid in reading values from a chart.

Gridlines

Use the **Gridlines** option to control the display of vertical and horizontal gridlines. Gridlines can be useful for seeing the values of plotted points and graphs, as shown in Figures 27.32 and 27.33.

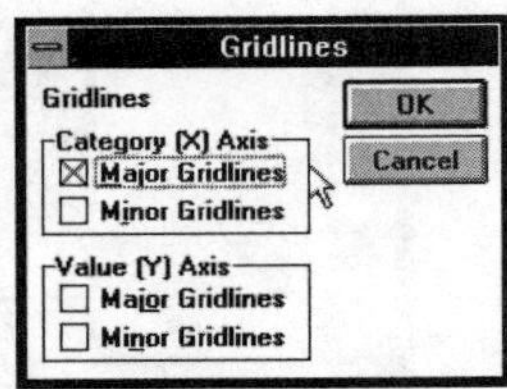

FIGURE 27.32. *The Gridlines dialog box.*

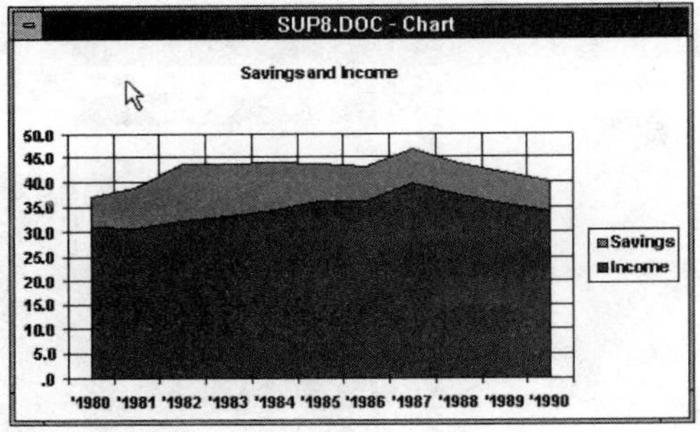

FIGURE 27.33. *Gridlines aid the eye in a busy chart.*

Format

The Forma**t** menu is used to control the format of chart parts. You also can use the format options to format the font used for the datasheet as a whole (all cells must have the same display format), column width, and numerical format (commas, dollar signs, significant digits, and so forth).

The procedure for changing formats is the same for all formats, although the individual options may vary.

PROCEDURE 27.14. CHANGING THE FORMAT OF CHART PARTS.

1. Click the chart part you want to reformat; verify that selection handles appear around it.
2. Select Forma**t** and then the option you want to change.
3. Select the specific formatting you want for the chart part you are reformatting.
4. Click OK.

SUPER NOTE

Select Edit | Undo immediately after an action if you don't like the result (also Alt+Backspace). It's sometimes hard to remember what you did even a few moments later.

Patterns

Use the **P**atterns option to change the interior of fill areas in pie charts, bar graphs, and so forth, as well as the line colors and backgrounds of other chart parts (see Figure 27.34). The **P**atterns options can be applied to virtually every element of the chart. The **P**atterns options apply just to the chart, and not to the datasheet.

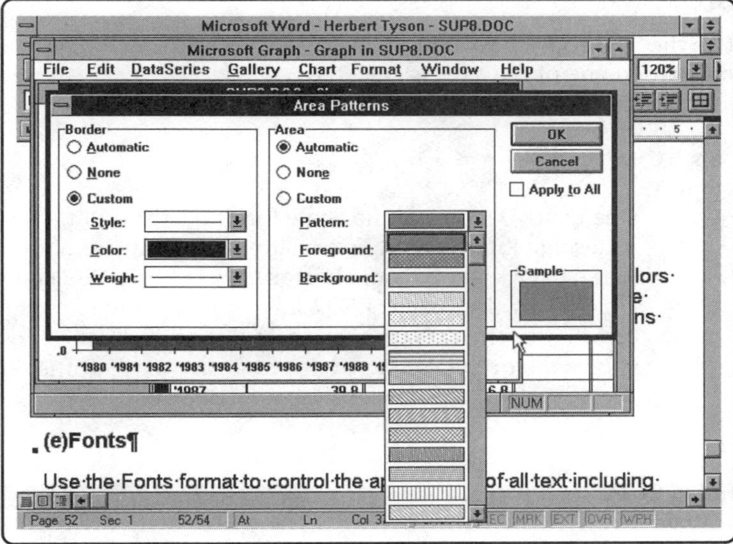

FIGURE 27.34.
*The **Patterns** option affects fill and line colors of virtually every part of a chart.*

Font

Use the **F**ont format to control the appearance of all text including the datasheet.

Text

Use the **T**ext options to change the alignment and orientation of text. Text options change depending on the type of text that is selected. When data labels are selected, for example, you have the additional option of displaying the legend key color/pattern as well as changing the display of labels versus values for individual points (see Figure 27.35).

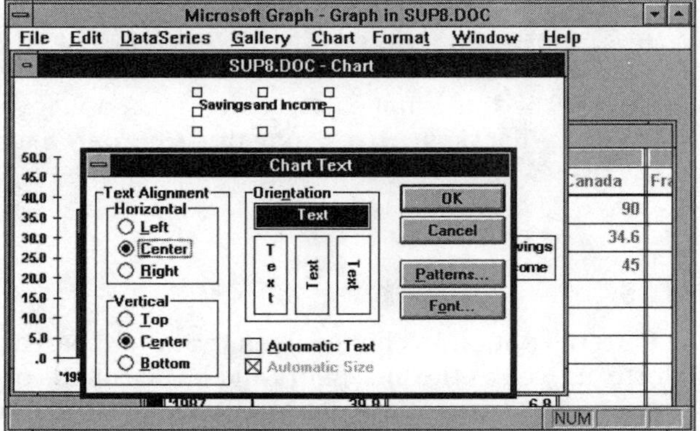

FIGURE 27.35.
Text options are context-sensitive.

Scale

Use the **S**cale option to adjust the way scales are drawn. The Scale option is available only when one of the axes is selected.

> **SUPER TIP**
>
> One handy feature of the **S**cale format is the ability to reverse the ordering along an axis. For example, in using 3-D bar columns, taller bars in the front can obscure shorter bars in back. You can rotate the whole chart using the Format | 3-D View, or you could simply reverse the ordering of the axis categories. In Figure 27.36, the view on the left shows the original view. In the view on the right, the countries and years were reversed to show as much detail as possible.

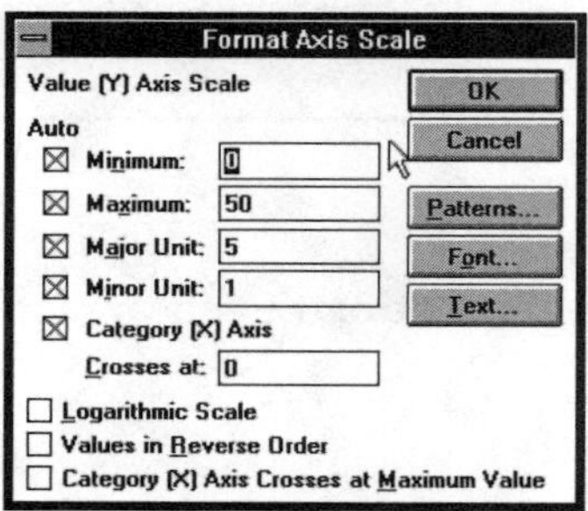

FIGURE 27.36.
You can use the Scale to reverse the order of data to keep data from hiding.

Legend

Use the Legend format options to control the placement of the legend. The legend, unlike other chart parts, can also be dragged wherever you like it. As shown in Figure 27.37, the selection handles for the legend are black, while the selection handles for other text areas are open. MS Graph uses the different handle types to indicate that objects on the chart are fixed (open) or movable (solid).

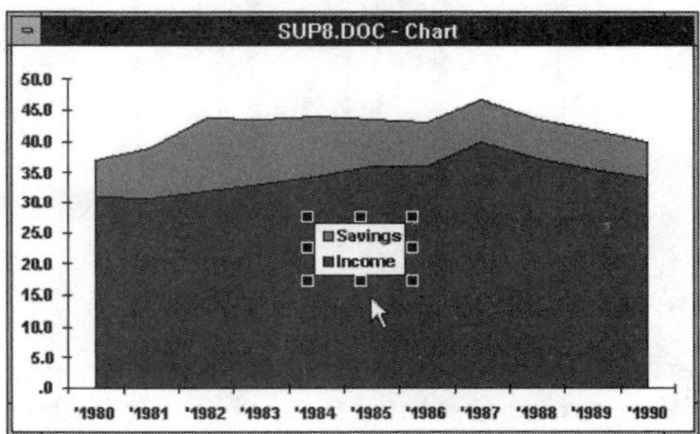

FIGURE 27.37.
MS Graph uses different handles for the legend.

Number

Use the Number format options to control the display of numbers. This option is available only when the datasheet is selected. This option can be exercised on a cell-by-cell basis, if desired. The formatting is applied only to the cells that are selected. You can add dollar signs, commas, as well as control the display of cents. You also can format numbers as dates and times.

Column Width

Use the Column Width option to set the width of one or more columns. To set the width of a single column, just select any cell in that column. To set the width of multiple adjacent columns, select any cells in those columns. You also can change column widths by dragging the column walls in the selection cells at the top of each column (see Figure 27.38).

Chart

Use the Chart format options to control the formatting of the chart (as opposed to the overlay in a combination graph). Some options are partially redundant with those found in the gallery. However, finding those options under Format | Chart may be a little more direct. Among other things, you can select the type of chart for the gallery type, the width, depth, and spacing of bars. The Chart formatting options vary by type of chart.

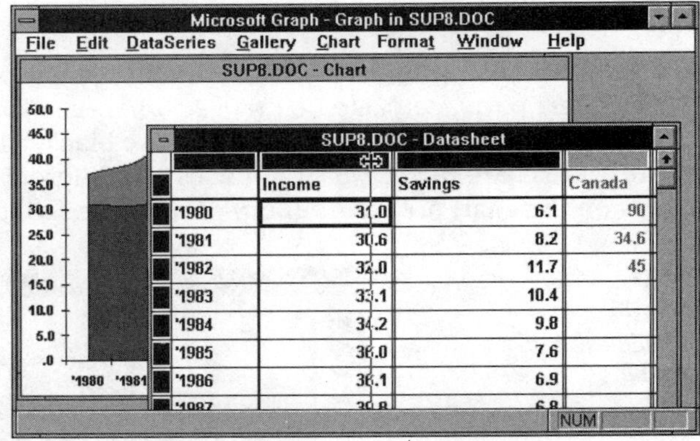

FIGURE 27.38.
You can adjust column width by dragging column walls.

Overlay

Use the **O**verlay format options to control the format of the overlay part of a combination graph. You can control the type of graph for the overlay (line, bar, column, pie, area), as well as how the overlay and main chart are shown together.

3-D View

Use the **3**-D View options to control the appearance of 3-D charts. A primary use of this option is to rotate the chart to optimize the view. As shown in Figure 27.39, the angle of view makes the difference between a 3-D chart showing everything or nothing. It helps to think of a 3-D view as a cube. Using the controls provided, you can rotate the cube to any angle to optimize the display of data.

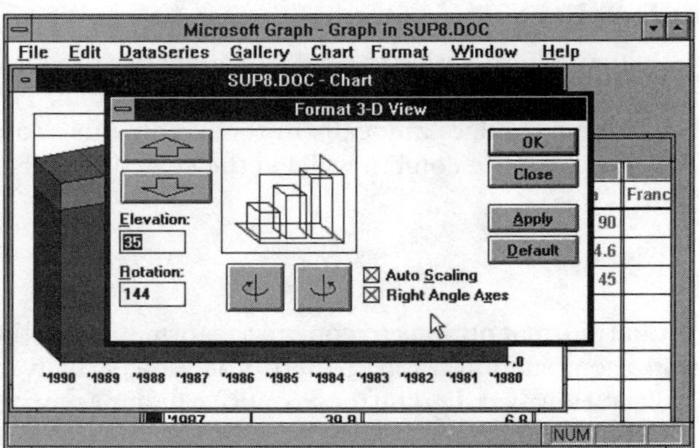

FIGURE 27.39.
The angle of view makes 3-D charts more useful.

Color Palette

Use the Color Palette to control the colors on the palette. The colors in the chart are linked to the colors on the palette. If you edit yellow on the palette, for example, all yellow items in the chart are reset. This can be a blessing or a curse, depending on how soon you discover that fact.

Window

Use the **W**indow menu to select between the **C**hart and **D**atasheet windows. You also can use it to select from among six different chart magnifications (views). The different levels of magnification are available only if the chart is the active window. Alternatively, you can use the mouse or other standard window sizing controls (in the application control box) to resize the window. The chart is redrawn and scaled accordingly.

WordArt

WordArt is a special OLE module for creating stylized titles and banners, such as those shown in Figure 27.40. It's easy to use and is a good way to create special effects in a way that you can't do in Word itself. This session surveys the workings of WordArt, showing the variety of things you can do and how to do them.

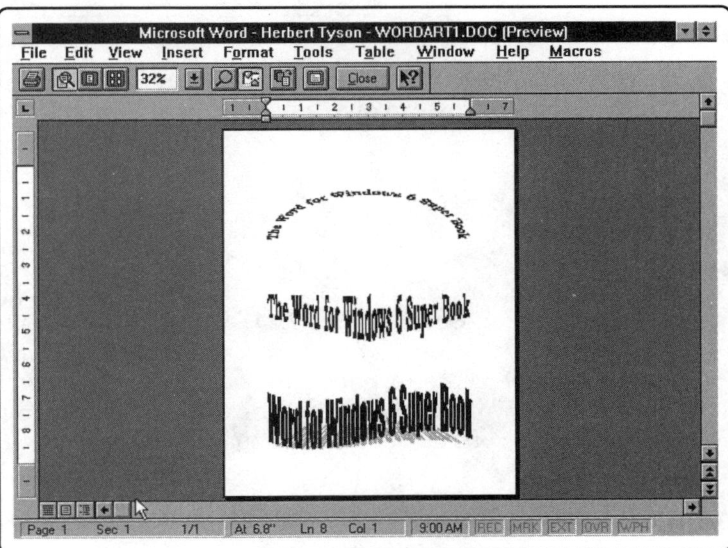

FIGURE 27.40.
WordArt can create a variety of banner-type effects.

Creating WordArt

In the default Word setup, WordArt can be started from the menu or by double-clicking an existing WordArt object. However, if you use WordArt frequently, you can easily add a tool for it to a Word toolbar.

PROCEDURE 27.15. STARTING WORDART.

1. Select **I**nsert | **O**bject.
2. Click to select MS WordArt, as shown in Figure 27.41.

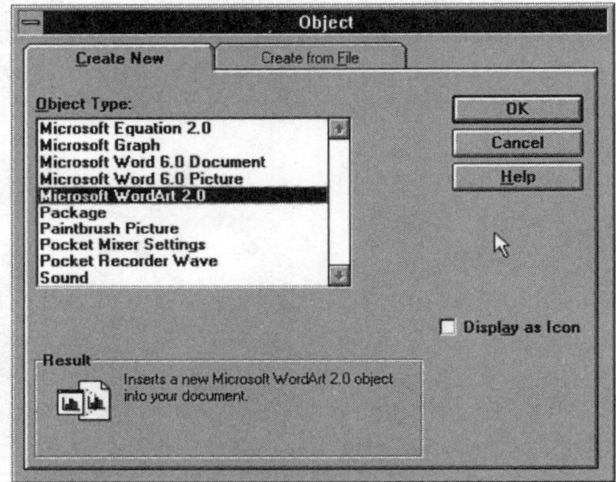

FIGURE 27.41.
*Start WordArt from the **I**nsert | **O**bject menu.*

3. Select Displ**a**y as Icon, if desired (this causes Word to display the resulting object as an icon instead of as a picture, as shown in Figure 27.42).
4. Click OK.

SUPER NOTE

If you select the Display as Icon option, Word displays the WordArt dialog box (shown in Figure 27.44) instead of a WordArt editing window. Even though the dialog box has a Cancel button, however, the moment you click OK in Step 4, above, the object is created instantly. If you cancel the WordArt dialog box, the object still exists and must be deleted, or you can use Alt+Backspace to undo its insertion.

When you start WordArt, a view like that shown in Figure 27.43 is displayed.

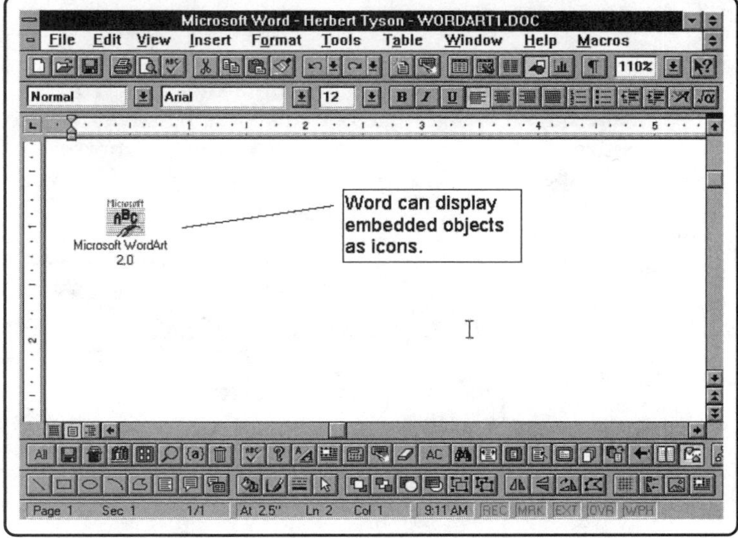

FIGURE 27.42.
WordArt objects can be displayed as icons for quicker document response.

FIGURE 27.43.
The main WordArt editing view.

SUPER NOTE

When you start WordArt by double-clicking a WordArt object icon, the view shown in Figure 27.44 is displayed instead. While you're working entirely in a dialog box, the tools and other controls work the same as described in Table 27.1.

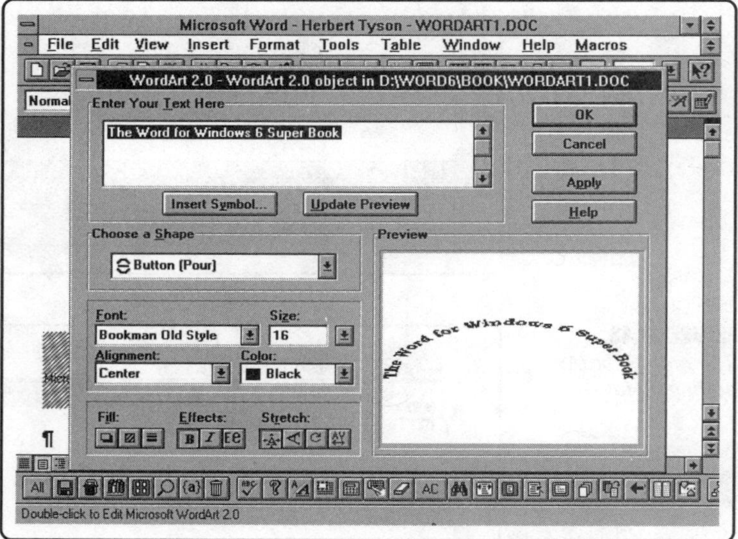

FIGURE 27.44. *When WordArt is displayed as an object, you create and edit the object using the WordArt dialog box.*

Once WordArt is started, creating WordArt is an intuitive process. You simply type the text you want to use into the framed area or into the Your Text Here box, and use WordArt's formatting controls to make it look the way you want. You can access the formatting controls using either the WordArt toolbar, the WordArt menu (for the most part) or both.

The Enter Your Text Here Box

The Enter Your Text Here box is provided not so much for Word as for other applications that might not support the display of the frame. Even so, the Enter Your Text Here box mode is the default mode when using WordArt. Each time you switch to a window that contains a WordArt object that's being edited, the Enter Your Text Here box is activated. When using WordArt from the Enter Your Text Here box, you need to click the Update button each time you make a change.

You also can access a limited Symbols dialog box from within the Enter Your Text Here box, as shown in Figure 27.45. Note that you cannot change the font. When you click the Insert Symbol button, whatever font is in effect is the one displayed in the symbol box.

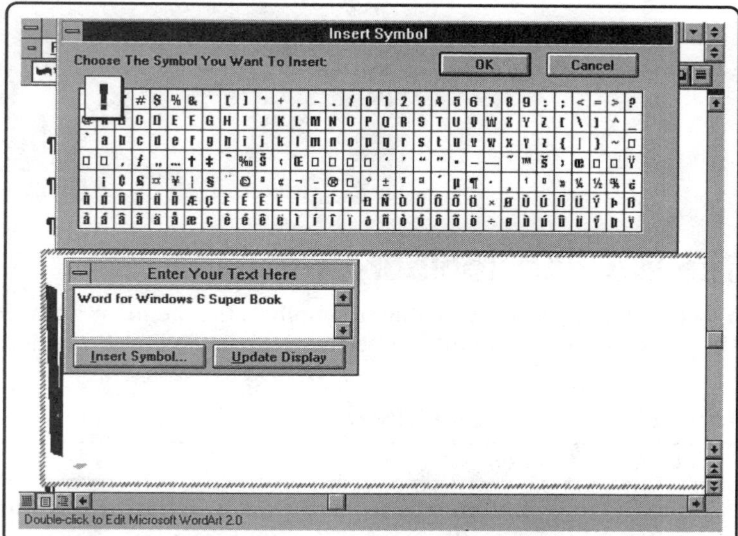

FIGURE 27.45.
The Symbols dialog lets you select characters only from the current font.

Adding WordArt to a Toolbar

If you use WordArt a lot, then accessing from a toolbar might be more convenient for you. You can add it to any existing toolbar, or create your own customized toolbar, as shown in Chapter 48, "Customizing Toolbars."

PROCEDURE 27.16. ADDING WORDART TO A TOOLBAR.

1. Select Tools | Customize.
2. Click the Toolbars tab.
3. Click Insert in Categories to display the Insert tool buttons.
4. In the Save Changes In box, select the template you want to customize.
5. Drag the WordArt button to the desired toolbar, as shown in Figure 27.46.
6. Click Close.

Don't forget to save your changes to the template if you want the WordArt button to continue to be available the next time you start Word.

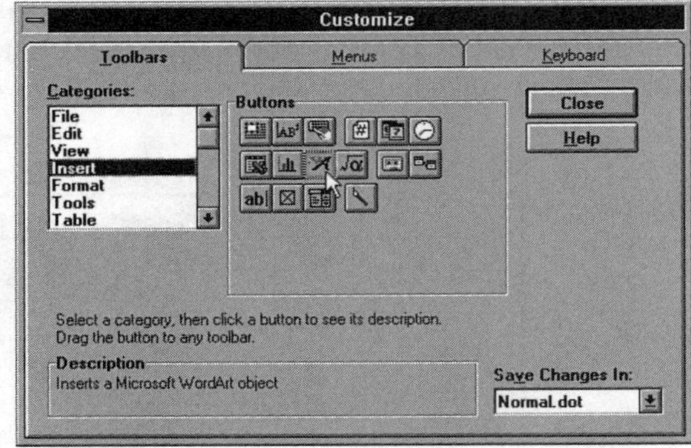

FIGURE 27.46.
For easier access, you can add a WordArt button to a toolbar.

The WordArt Toolbar

You can control WordArt using the toolbar, the menu, or both. For most Word users, the more intuitive method is with the toolbar. The tools are described in Table 27.1.

Table 27.1. The WordArt toolbar.

Button	*Purpose*
Shape	Determines the basic shape of the text, as shown in Figure 27.47
Font	Selects the font to display the text (note: you cannot vary the font within a WordArt object—it must all be the same font)
Size	Selects the relative size of the object, approximately in points
Bold	Applies bold formatting to the text
Italic	Applies italic formatting
Even	Makes all characters the same height, despite case
Flip	Turns the text on its side
Stretch	Stretches the text to fit the size of the frame
Alignment	Sets the alignment of the text in the frame: center, left, right, stretch justify, letter justify, or word justify
Spacing	Sets the spacing between characters
Rotate	Specifies the exact rotatation and slant
Shading	Changes the shading of the text
Shadow	Adds shadow effects to the text
Text border	Turns on and changes the type of border

The WordArt toolbar is different from other Word toolbars, because it's part of WordArt itself rather than part of Word. The WordArt toolbar cannot be moved, floated, or customized.

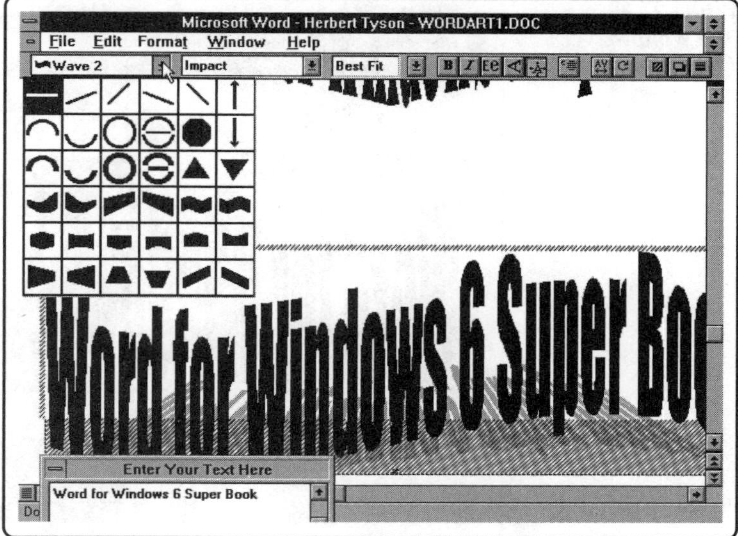

FIGURE 27.47.
Use the Shape button to change the basic shape of the text.

The WordArt Menu

The WordArt menu is actually a combination of Word's own menu and WordArt's menu. Unlike some other Word procedures, you can readily switch between a window that contains a WordArt object that's being edited and a normal Word window. To change to a different window, just select Window from the menu and switch to the window you want.

SUPER NOTE

You can't use Alt+W for the Window menu when the Enter WordArt Text dialog box's title bar is active. You can use the mouse and, if the text frame is active instead of the title bar, Alt+W and other menu hot keys.

WordArt's File menu is the same as Word's own regular file menu. The Edit menu contains just an Edit WordArt Text command, which moves the cursor into the Enter Your Text Here box. The Window and Help menus are just what you'd expect—control for windows and help.

The real action, menu-wise, for WordArt is in the Format menu, shown in Figure 27.48. The menu options correspond to the toolbar buttons with the same names. Note that the text Shape, Font, and Size cannot be accessed using the WordArt menu.

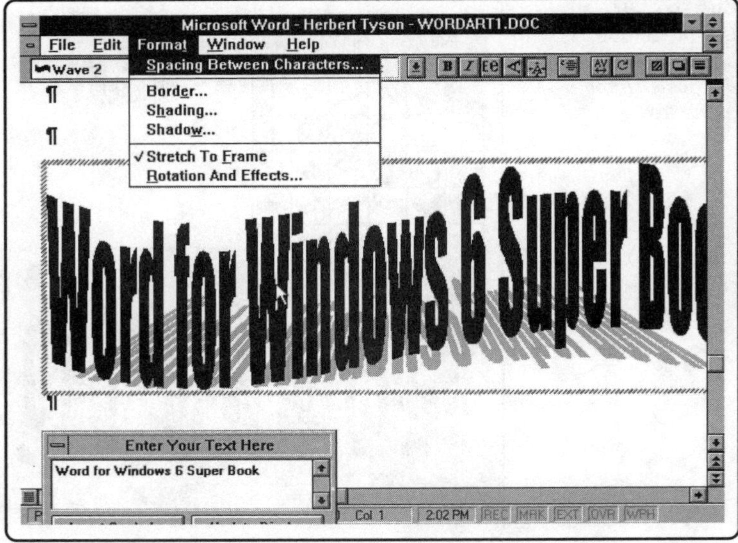

FIGURE 27.48.
The WordArt Format menu.

Editing a WordArt Object

You can edit an existing WordArt object in several ways. The easiest way by far is to double-click the WordArt object. If the object is displayed as a picture, Word reopens the same view. If the object is displayed as an object, the WordArt dialog box opens. You also can edit an existing WordArt object using the menu.

PROCEDURE 27.17. EDITING OR OPENING A WORDART OBJECT.

1. Select the WordArt object (click it or move the cursor onto it with the keyboard).
2. Select **E**dit | MS WordArt **O**bject, and then click Edit or Open, as shown in Figure 27.49.

SUPER NOTE

Word has two ways to edit an existing WordArt object, one called Edit and another called Open. For WordArt objects displayed as object icons, Edit and Open both open the WordArt dialog box. For WordArt objects displayed as pictures, however, Edit opens the full-screen editing view, while Open displays the WordArt dialog box.

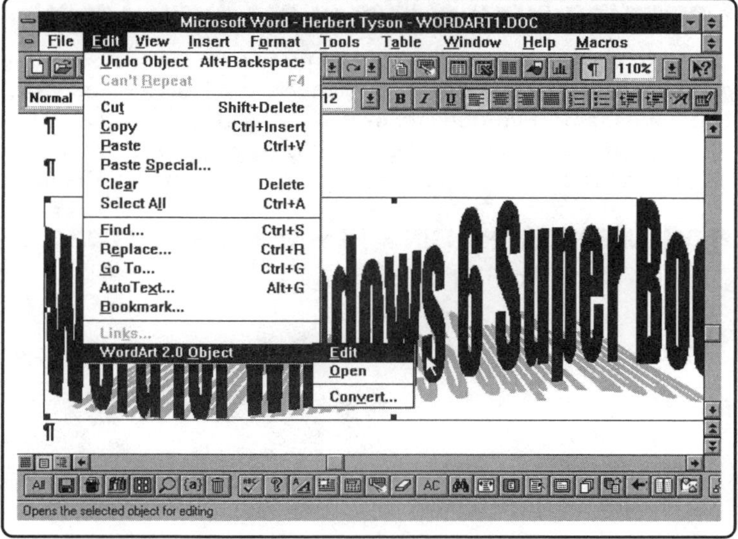

FIGURE 27.49.
You can edit or open a WordArt option from Word's Edit menu.

SUPER TIP

You also can open or edit a WordArt object using a right-mouse-button popup menu, as shown in Figure 27.50.

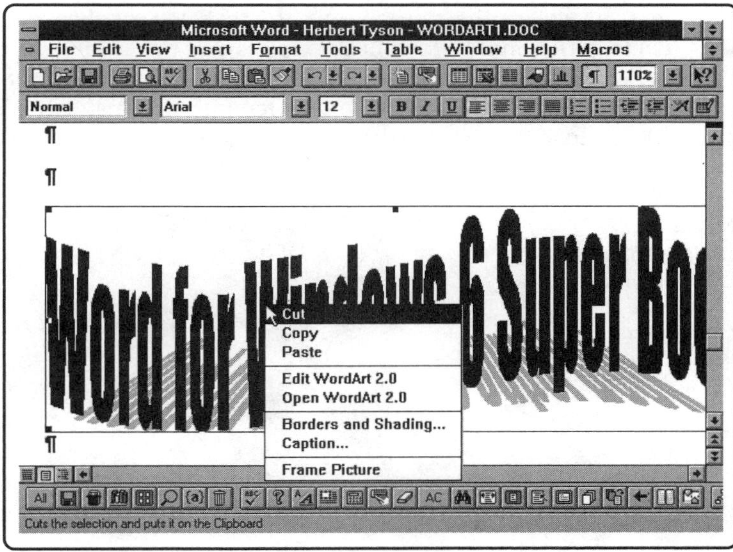

FIGURE 27.50.
WordArt objects can be edited or opened using the right-mouse-button popup menu.

Changing How a WordArt Object Displays

You can display WordArt objects as pictures or as icons. When WordArt objects are displayed as icons, document scrolling is much faster, and Word uses less memory. If you have many such objects, or if you just prefer quicker document response time, you can turn off the display of WordArt as pictures. If you need to adjust the way the picture looks, or when you need to print, you can turn them back on.

PROCEDURE 27.18. CHANGING THE WAY A WORDART OBJECT DISPLAYS.

1. Select the WordArt object.
2. Select Edit | MS WordArt **O**bject.
3. Click Con**v**ert to display the Convert dialog box, shown in Figure 27.51.

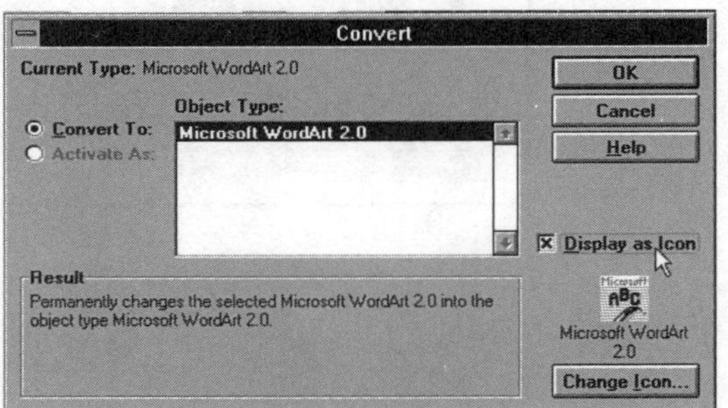

FIGURE 27.51.
The Convert dialog box lets you change the way a WordArt object is displayed.

4. Select or deselect the **D**isplay as Icon option.
5. If you're changing the object to display as an icon, you also can change the icon, as well as the caption text (the text that displays under the icon) by clicking the Change Icon button to display the Change Icon dialog box shown in Figure 27.52. From there, you can display any of the Shape icons, or select a file (*.EXE or *.DLL) that contains icon images (using the Browse button, click OK to close the Browse dialog box). Click OK to close the Change Icon dialog box.

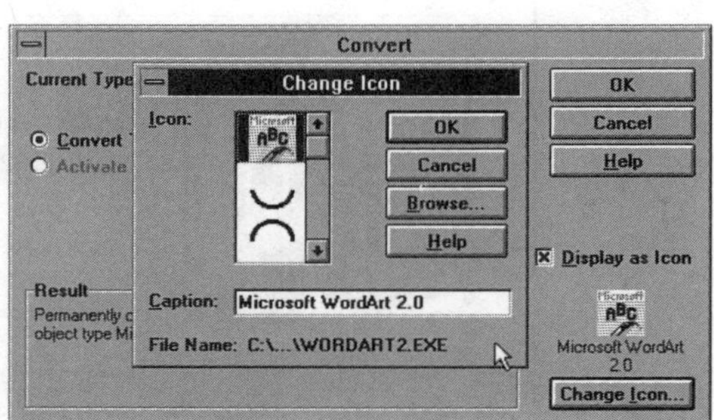

FIGURE 27.52.
Use the Change Icon button to change the icon and icon caption text used to identify a WordArt object.

6. Click OK to close the Convert dialog box.

If necessary, you can always repeat the procedure and make a different selection in Step 4.

SUPER CAUTION

When a WordArt object is displayed as an icon, that's the way it prints too! If you display WorldArt objects as icons to save time while editing, that's fine. However, it's unlikely that the WordArt icon will work terribly well as a banner headline for your newsletter, so don't forget to convert the object back when you're ready to print.

Captions

Using the **I**nsert | Capt**i**on | AutoCaption feature, you can instruct Word to automatically insert captions when you insert WordArt objects. Given that most WordArt objects usually are used to create banner text for titles, buttons, badges, and other special effects, you may seldom have a need to include a caption with a WordArt object. However, if you do need to use Word to present a graphic, rather than special effects for text, it's nice to know that captioning can be done automatically.

PROCEDURE 27.19. TURNING ON AUTOMATIC CAPTIONS FOR WORDART OBJECTS.

1. Select **I**nsert | Capt**i**on, and click AutoCaption.
2. In the **A**dd Caption When Inserting list, click to select Microsoft WordArt.
3. Select the Use **L**abel and **P**osition appropriate for your document.
4. If an acceptable label doesn't already exist (Figure, Table, and so forth), click the **N**ew Label button to create a new label.
5. If desired, click N**u**mbering to set up the numbering for the caption.
6. Click OK to close the Caption dialog box.

To turn automatic captioning off, just reverse the procedure: deselect WordArt in Step 2, then click OK to close.

The Equation Editor

Anyone unfortunate enough to try to use field codes to present equations using Word for Windows 1 most certainly came to appreciate the inclusion of the Design Science equation editor in version 2. Word 6 provides version 2.0 of Design Science's equation editor. This session surveys the equation editor's capabilities and operation.

Inserting an Equation

Equations are created and edited using the Equation Editor that comes with Word. The Equation Editor is an OLE server that works with Word. As with other OLE servers, you use the Insert menu to insert a blank equation, and then use the Equation Editor to add some substance to it.

PROCEDURE 27.20. INSERTING AN EQUATION OBJECT.

1. Move the insertion point to the place in your document where you need to confuse your reader.
2. Select **I**nsert | **O**bject, and click Microsoft Equation 2.0.
3. Click OK.

SUPER

CAUTION

Word can have multiple instances of the Equation Editor open at the same time. You can switch to different instances by using the Windows Task List (Ctrl+Esc). However, if multiple instances are open on the same document, the task list does not differentiate them. You must do that yourself by sight. If equations in different parts of the document are similar or identical, it's very easy to accidentally edit the wrong one. For this reason, when you return to the Equation Editor, it's usually better to do it by double-clicking the equation rather than selecting the Equation Editor from the task list. If necessary, you can use **E**dit | **G**o To to move from equation to equation. Watch carefully, however, because many users get confused.

PROCEDURE 27.21. USING EDIT|GO TO TO FIND EQUATIONS.

1. Select **E**dit | **G**o To.
2. Under Go to **W**hat, click Object.
3. Under **E**nter Object Name, select Equation.
4. Click Nex**t** or **P**revious to move to an equation; the Go To dialog box, like the Find dialog box, can remain suspended on-screen as you work in the document.

SUPER

TIP

In Step 2, many users mistakenly click Equation, which is wrong for locating an equation object. The Equation entry in the Go to What list refers to equation *fields* (EQ), not equation objects.

Adding the Equation Editor to a Toolbar

You can add the Equation Editor to any existing toolbar or create your own customized toolbar, as shown in Chapter 48.

PROCEDURE 27.22. ADDING THE EQUATION EDITOR TO A TOOLBAR.

1. Select **T**ools | **C**ustomize.
2. Click the **T**oolbars tab.
3. Click Insert under Categories to display the Insert tool buttons.
4. In the Sa**v**e Changes In box, select the template you want to customize.
5. Drag the Equation Editor button to the desired toolbar, as shown in Figure 27.53.
6. Click Close.

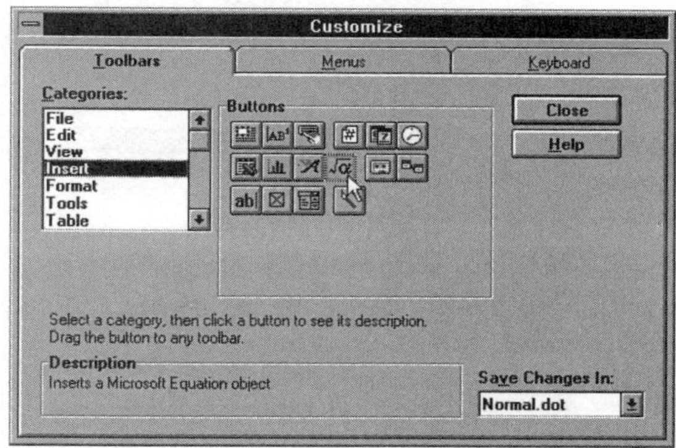

FIGURE 27.53.
For easier access, you can add the Equation Editor button to a toolbar.

Don't forget to save your changes to the template if you want the Equation Editor button to continue to be available the next time you start Word.

Editing an Equation

The Equation Editor inserts an `{EMBED MSEquation.2}` field into your document, which displays as an equation. To edit the equation, you use the Equation Editor, which opens automatically when you double-click an existing equation. Alternatively, you can select **E**dit | Equation **O**bject from the Word menu or from a right-mouse-button popup menu (that is, click the right mouse button on an existing equation), and click Edit Equation.

Using the Equation Editor

When you open the Equation Editor, the view shown in Figure 27.54 appears. You create equations by selecting elements from the toolbar, typing text, and selecting options from the menu.

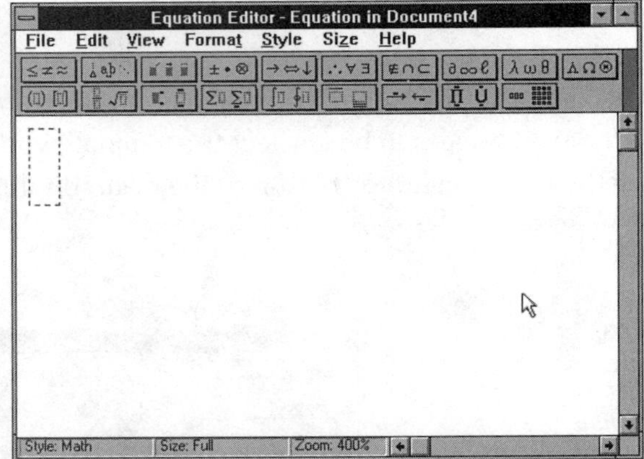

FIGURE 27.54.
The opening view of the Equation Editor.

To type text, a variable name, or a letter, for example, just type the letter or name corresponding to what you want to enter. If you need a special symbol or special effect (like subscripting, superscripting, enclosure in a radical, and so forth), then select the appropriate element from the toolbar.

There are two kinds of elements on the toolbar: a symbols palette and a templates palette. The top row consists of symbols, and the bottom row consists of templates. Symbols are single characters you can insert. Actually, by using the Insert | Symbol command, or by typing the appropriate characters and fonts, you could enter the symbols directly into the text of a Word file. However, assembling them into a coherent equation might take a bit of work.

Templates are compound elements that comprise reserved locations for symbols and other characters you type. Some templates, such as the sigma and pi templates, include symbols that form part of the expression (radical, capital sigma, capital pi, and so forth). Templates have four kinds of contents indicated by symbols, black rectangles, dark-shaded rectangles, and white-dotted fill-in areas. The symbols are produced verbatim in the equation. The black areas are used to apply the indicated position formatting to a selected character or expression already in the equation, or to the next character(s) you type. The dark-shaded rectangles indicate elements that are not affected by the template. The white-dotted fill-in slots are where you can enter symbols, characters or other expressions.

A key to working with the Equation Editor is to understand the location of the insertion point. For example, to create the expression $E=mc^2$, you could do the following procedure.

PROCEDURE 27.23. INSERTING AN EQUATION USING A ONE-SLOT TEMPLATE.

1. Activate the Equation Editor (select **I**nsert | **O**bject, then Microsoft Equation 2.0 from the **O**bject Type list; or, use the Equation Editor tool button).
2. Type `E=mc`.
3. Select the subscript/superscript palette and click the superscript template, shown in Figure 27.55.
4. Type `2`.

FIGURE 27.55.
The superscript template.

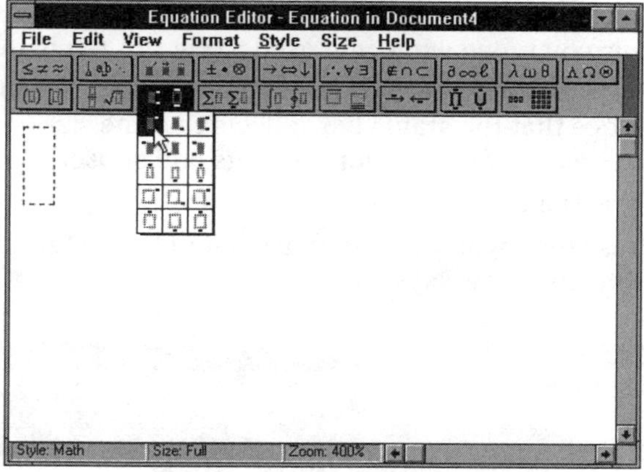

Next is where the confusion begins for some users. At this point, if you were to continue typing after typing the `2`, anything you type would continue to be superscripted. That's because you're actually typing into a *slot* that makes all text typed superscripted. That's fine if you want:

$E=mc^{2+i}$

But, what if you wanted:

$E=mc^{2}+i$

To cause `+i` to not be superscripted, you need to move the insertion point out of the superscript slot before typing. Do that simply by pressing the right cursor key. In fact, if you press the right key, and then press the left arrow key several times, you'll see the position and size of the cursor change. It becomes evident, in fact, that you could insert additional superscripted matter before or after the `2` you already typed. You also could move the insertion point back before the slot and insert additional nonsubscripted characters. Notice that as you move the cursor, the status bar at the bottom of the Equation Editor window indicates the size of the slot the insertion point is in: full, subscript, sub-subscript, symbol, subsymbol, and so forth.

Another approach to doing the identical equation is to use a two-slot template.

PROCEDURE 27.24. INSERTING AN EQUATION USING A TWO-SLOT TEMPLATE.

1. Select the subscript/superscript palette and click the symbol and superscript template, shown in Figure 27.56, to insert the template.
2. Note that the status bar indicates that the cursor is in the Full position, which means that it's not in the symbol slot that you just inserted. Press the Down cursor key to move the cursor into the Symbol slot. The status bar changes to indicate Symbol.
3. Type `E=mc`. Notice that the characters you type appear larger than the symbols you typed when you used a one-slot template.
4. Press the Up arrow key to move the insertion point into the superscript slot. Notice that the status bar reflects that the size is now Subscript. It doesn't say Superscript because superscripts and subscripts are both the same size.
5. Type the `2`.
6. Press the Right arrow to move out of the superscript slot, and notice that the status bar now says Full.

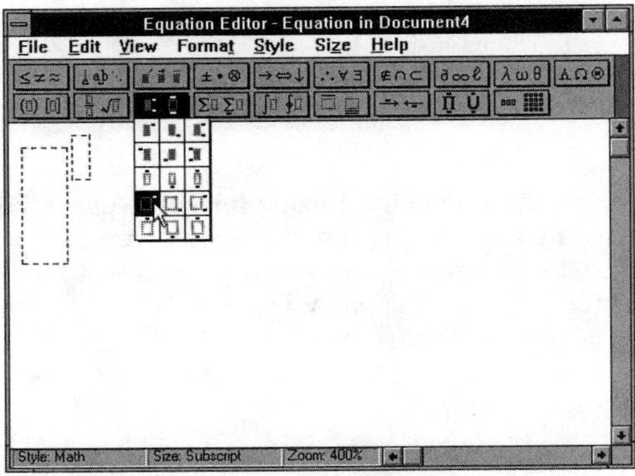

FIGURE 27.56.
The symbol and superscript template.

The same procedures and logic hold true for creating equations using any of the other templates. Just for practice, let's create the equation shown in Figure 27.57, which is the formula for *sample variance*.

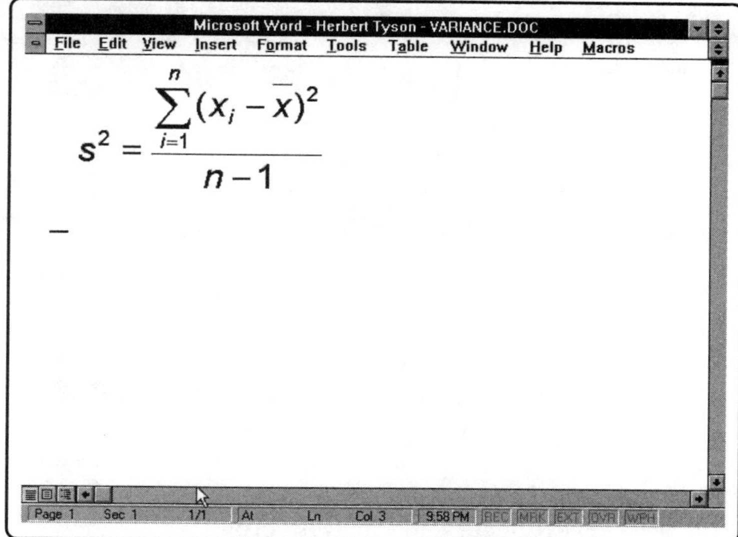

FIGURE 27.57.
The formula for sample variance.

PROCEDURE 27.25. ENTERING THE FORMULA FOR SAMPLE VARIANCE.

1. Type a lowercase `s`.
2. Select the superscript template by using the palette or by typing Ctrl+H.
3. Type a `2`.
4. Press the Right arrow key to move the insertion point past the superscript slot.
5. Type `=`.
6. Select the fraction bar template (Ctrl+F) to insert a fraction bar, with slots for the numerator and denominator.
7. Select the two-slot summation template shown in Figure 27.58 (Ctrl+T, S).
8. Press the Up arrow to move above the summation (sigma) sign, and type a lowercase `n`.
9. Press the Down arrow twice to move below the summation sign, and type **`i=1`**.
10. Press the Up arrow once and type `(Xi-X)2`.
11. Press Shift and the Left arrow once, then type Ctrl+H. This raises the `2` to a superscript (actually, it inserts a superscript slot and puts the `2` into it).
12. Press the Left arrow twice, then press Shift+Left again, followed by Ctrl+-. This adds the mean bar over the `x`.
13. Press the Left arrow three times, then press Shift+Left, followed by Ctrl+L. This lowers the `i` to a subscript.

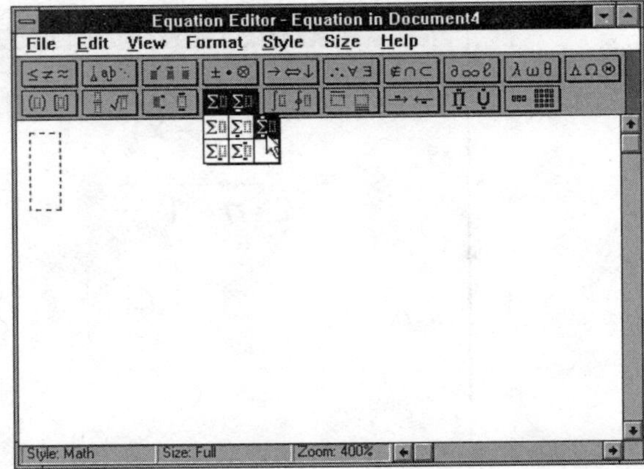

FIGURE 27.58.
A two-slot summation.

14. Press the Down arrow six times (or click in the slow below the fraction line), and type **n-1**.
15. Select **F**ile | **U**pdate, and wipe your brow.

While this procedure may seem a little laborious, it grows on you, especially if you commit the shortcut keys (shown in Table 27.2) to memory. For the most part, they can become intuitive.

Table 27.2. Summary of Equation Editor shortcut keys.

Key	*Action*
Ctrl+1	Zoom 100 percent
Ctrl+2	Zoom 200 percent
Ctrl+4	Zoom 400 percent
Ctrl+D	Redraw Equation
Ctrl+Y	Show All
Ctrl+Shift+L	Align Left
Ctrl+Shift+C	Align Center
Ctrl+Shift+R	Align Right
Ctrl+Shift+=	Math Style
Ctrl+Shift+E	Text Style
Ctrl+Shift+F	Function Style
Ctrl+Shift+I	Variable Style
Ctrl+Shift+G	Greek Style
Ctrl+Shift+B	Matrix-Vector Style
Ctrl+F Or Ctrl+T, F	Fraction

Key	Action
Ctrl+/ Or Ctrl+T, /	Slash Fraction
Ctrl+H Or Ctrl+T, H	Superscript (High)
Ctrl+L Or Ctrl+T, L	Subscript (Low)
Ctrl+J Or Ctrl+T, J	Joint Sub/Superscript
Ctrl+I Or Ctrl+T, I	Integral
Ctrl+T, |	Absolute Value
Ctrl+R Or Ctrl+T, R	Root
Ctrl+T, N	Nth Root
Ctrl+T, S	Summation
Ctrl+T, P	Product
Ctrl+T, M	Matrix Template (3¥3)
Ctrl+T, U	Underscript (Limit)
Ctrl+Shift+-	Overbar
Ctrl+~	Tilde
Ctrl+Alt+-	Arrow (Vector)
Ctrl+Alt+'	Single Prime
Ctrl+"	Double Prime
Ctrl+Alt+Period	Single Dot
Ctrl+Left	Nudge Left By 1 Pixel
Ctrl+Right	Nudge Right By 1 Pixel
Ctrl+Down	Nudge Down By 1 Pixel
Ctrl+Up	Nudge Up By 1 Pixel
Tab-Or Enter	End of the slot or next slot if already at the end
Shift+Tab	Previous Slot
Right	Right one unit within the current slot or template
Left	Left one unit within the current slot or template
Up	Up one line
Down	Down one line
Home	Beginning of the current slot
End	End of the current slot
Ctrl+Tab	Insert a tab
Backspace	Delete character left
Del	Delete character right

continues

Table 27.2. continued

Key	*Action*
Ctrl+Alt+Space	1-point space
Ctrl+Space	Thin space (one-sixth of the letter m)
Ctrl+Shift+Space	Thick space (one-third of the letter m)

One thing to note in these procedures is that many (if not most) effects can be applied to slots that already have special formatting. For example, you can superscript a superscript, and subscript a subscript, for special effects. Another thing to note is that the positioning performed with keys also can be performed with the mouse. As someone who's created my fair share of equations, however, I can attest to the frustration of moving from mouse to keyboard and back again repeatedly; it gets *old* in a hurry. You might want to collect your actions together so you can use the keyboard or mouse in two passes rather than going back and forth multiple times. For example, you could have written the preceding equation by first typing all of the parts that get typed:

```
s2=ni=1(xi-x)2n-1
```

That done, you could now go to the mouse and apply the appropriate formatting to the parts of the equation and watch it take shape. Or, you could apply the formatting using the keyboard. After you get the hang of it, it all becomes much more fluid.

The Equation Editor Toolbar

The Equation Editor toolbar is designed to be intuitive; for the most part, it speaks for itself. One thing that might go overlooked is the fact that the Equation Editor toolbar is detachable and movable. It cannot be reshaped, however. You also can turn the toolbar off. If you haven't memorized the keys, you might wonder why. However, once you know the keyboard equivalents for your most-used templates and symbols, you might not need the toolbar anymore, and you might prefer to use the space to display equations instead. If the toolbar is detached and has a control icon, you can turn it off by double-clicking the upper-left corner. Otherwise, you can turn it off and on by selecting **View** | Toolbars from the menu.

The Equation Editor Menus

The Equation Editor menus are used to further control the equation-editing process, as well as to specify and define default behavior.

File Menu

Use the File menu choices as follows:

Update:	Sends the current equation to the Word document without closing the Equation Editor
Exit	Sends the equation to Word and closes the Equation Editor

Edit Menu

Use the Edit menu to access Undo and the clipboard. Keep in mind that the Equation Editor has only one level of Undo.

View

Use the View menu to control the zoom level as well as the display of the toolbar. The zoom levels control only the size of the display, not the size of the printed result. Use the Redraw command to "clean up" the display of the equation (that must be Microsoft-ese for "the screen redraw APIs are buggy, so you'll have to do manual redraws until we can get it right"). The Show All option is used to toggle the display of special characters in the equation, including tabs and spaces. You'll do yourself and your sanity a favor by selecting this option!

Format

Use the Format menu, shown in Figure 27.59, to set the alignment of symbols, characters, and expressions typed into template slots. You also use the Format command to customize matrix and spacing formatting.

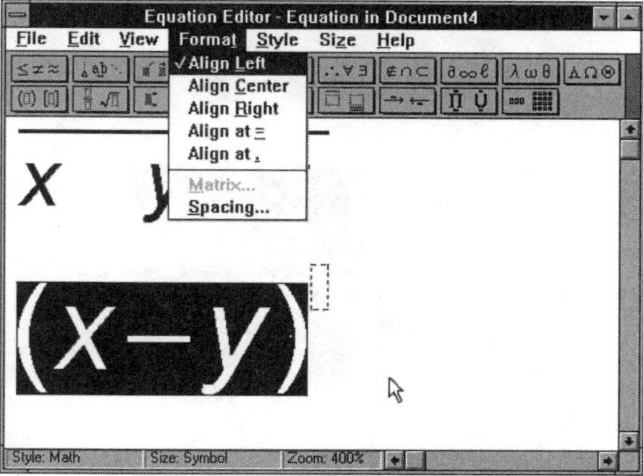

FIGURE 27.59.
The Format menu.

Style

Anything you type in the Equation Editor is inserted in a particular style. Use the Style menu, shown in Figure 27.60, to select the style for the next character you type (or for selected text), as well as to customize and define the styles.

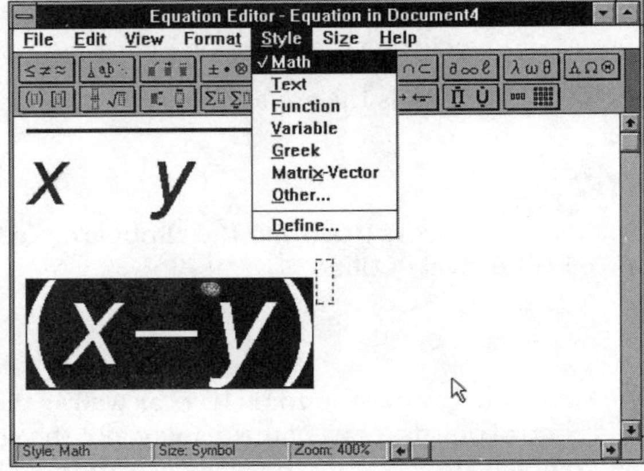

FIGURE 27.60.
The Style menu.

Size

Sizes are set by type rather than explicit point size, for the most part. The Size menu, shown in Figure 27.61, lets you select from among five preset size types. You also can select the Other option to specify the size (in points) exactly, or select Define to specify the sizes associated with each of the preset size types.

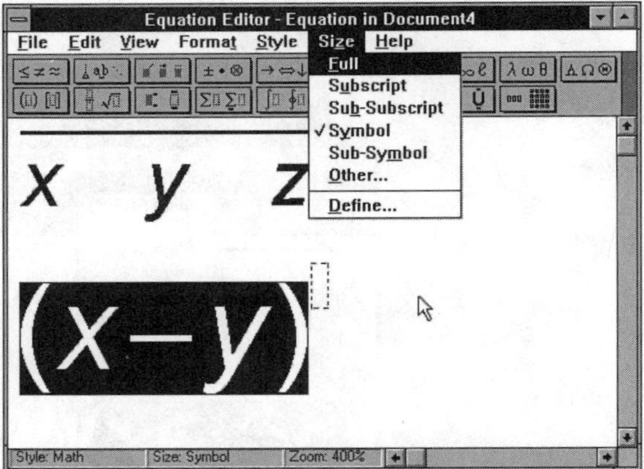

FIGURE 27.61.
The Size menu.

Help

Oddly enough, you can use the Help part of the menu for help. Anyone serious about using the Equation Editor should spend a half hour perusing the Help for the Equation Editor. It is extensive and informative.

IX

Writing Tools Workshop

The Writing Tools Workshop is the most eclectic workshop in the Word for Windows 6 Super Book. That's because it deals with a number of time-saving features in Word. These features are designed to save writers time and effort when using Word. In this workshop, we'll look at Search and Replace, Fields, Summary Information, Bookmarks and Cross-References, AutoCorrect, AutoText, Annotation, Symbols, Proofing, and Revision Marking. Seemingly disjoint, these features all have in common the fact that they enable you to use Word more efficiently, letting your computer automatically do the work writers used to have to do by hand.

Chapter

28

Search and Replace

Word provides a collection of powerful search and replace facilities, especially when it comes to searching for and replacing formatting. For example, if you need to change all instances of a style called HA to Heading 1, you can do it. If you need to locate just the occurrence of bold italics, you can do that too. Unlike earlier versions of Word for Windows, Word for Windows 6 also has facilities for locating text patterns, as well as the ability to distinguish numbers, letters, and word boundaries. These new capabilities provide more flexible editing and macro facilities than were previously available.

Searching for Text

PROCEDURE 28.1. FINDING TEXT.

1. Press Ctrl+F (**Edit** | **Find**); the Find dialog box is displayed (see Figure 28.1).

FIGURE 28.1.
Begin your search in the Find dialog box.

2. Type the text you want to find.
3. Select any options you want, as described below.
4. Press Enter or click **Find** Next; the Find dialog box remains on-screen.
5. If Word finds the text, it highlights the found text, as shown in Figure 28.2. Click **Find** Next to go to the next instance, or press Cancel to clear the Find dialog box from the screen.
6. If Word doesn't find a match, it displays a dialog box saying that the text was not found. If the search excluded part of the document, Word prompts you to continue the search through the remaining portion, as shown in Figure 28.3.

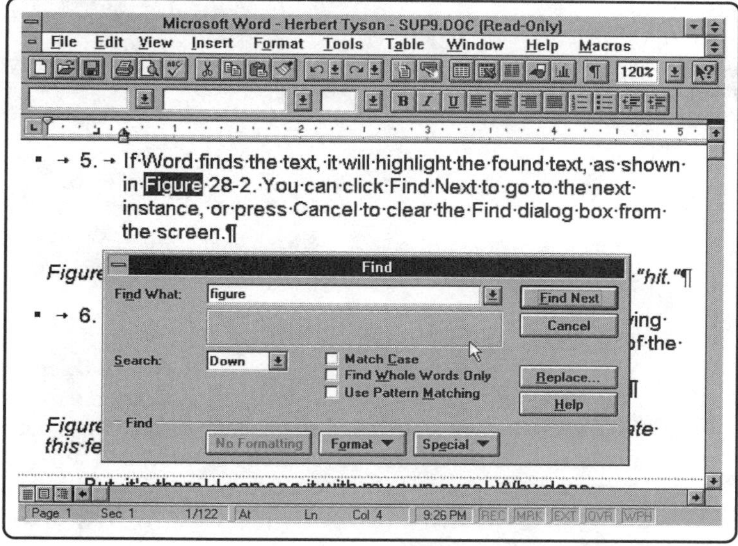

FIGURE 28.2.
Word selects the matching text when Find gets a "hit."

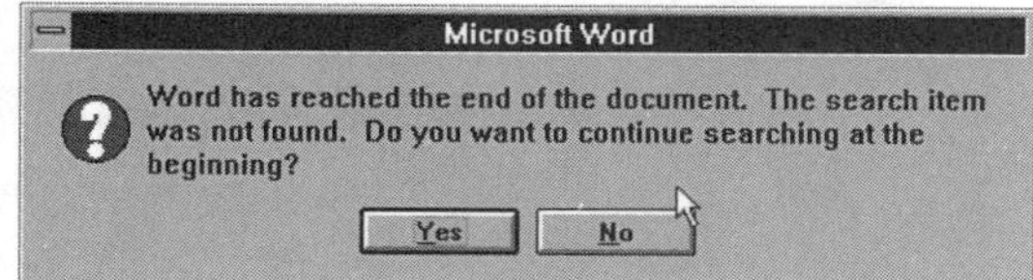

FIGURE 28.3.
Word nags you to continue. Some users really hate this feature!

SUPER

BUT, IT'S THERE!

I can see it with my own eyes! Why does Word say `The search item was not found`? One new feature in Word 6 is the ability to search *just the selection*, or to widen the search to include text outside the selection. Note carefully the message in Figure 28.4. It says `Word has finished searching the selection`. If any text is selected when you begin a search, Word searches just the selection and then offers to continue to search the remainder of the document. Former Word for Windows users especially get caught by this one because it's an unexpected change. If Word can't find something you know is there, check to make sure that no text is selected and that Word is searching in the correct direction. Sometimes, a leftover Up from an earlier search gets ignored when you start searching for something else.

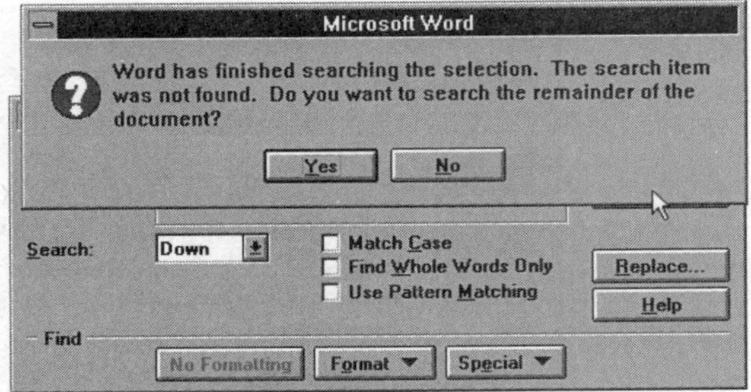

FIGURE 28.4.
Word can search just the selection, but it's easy to not notice that text was selected.

Yet another possibility is that the Use Pattern Matching option is turned on. While pattern matching is a terrific enhancement when you need it, be aware that all searches are case-sensitive when pattern matching is turned on. Even though `Match Case` is dimmed (see Figure 28.5) when pattern matching is turned on, it may be dimmed because you have no choice. If your searches are coming up empty, make sure you have the right options selected.

FIGURE 28.5.
All pattern match searches are case-sensitive.

SUPER TIP

You can scroll and work in your document, even while the Find dialog box is still on-screen! This is very handy when you're looking for problem areas. Just click in the text area; the Find dialog box's title bar dims. Fix the problem and then click the Find dialog box to go back to searching.

SUPER TIP

Depending on your preferences, you may find it handy to assign Find to a toolbar icon. Word has a built-in icon standing by—just drag it to a toolbar and you're all set.

PROCEDURE 28.2. ASSIGN FIND TO A TOOLBAR.

1. Select Tools | Customize.
2. Click the Toolbars tab.
3. Under Save Changes In, select the template where you want the customization to reside (select NORMAL.DOT if you want this tool to be available by default when editing any document; it won't be available in templates that specify otherwise).
4. In the Categories list, click Edit.
5. Move your cursor over the Find icon (binoculars, shown in Figure 28.6) and drag it to a toolbar. Notice that the Description box provides a description of the item you're dragging.
6. Click Close.

Don't forget to save the changes to the template(s) you customize. That way, any tools or key assignments continue to be available the next time you use Word.

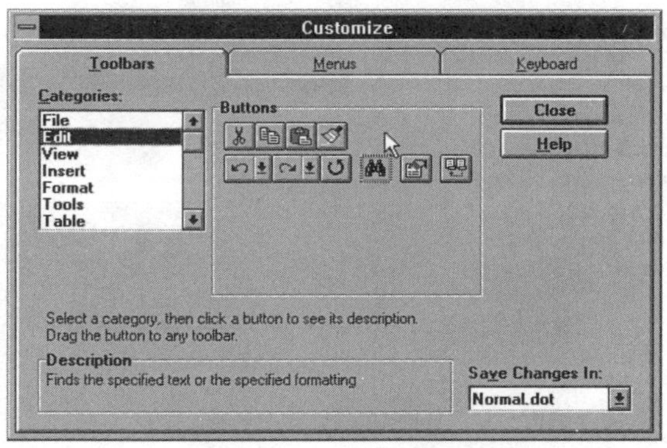

FIGURE 28.6.
Use Tools | Customize | Toolbars to assign Edit | Find to a toolbar.

See Chapter 48, "Customizing Toolbars," for additional information.

Find What

The Find What field can contain a search string of up to 255 characters, including text and special characters. To find text, just type the text you're looking for. If your search text contains a ^ character combined with any of the special characters, however, you must precede it with a ^ to keep Word from treating it as a special character. For example, to search for an occurrence of ^?, type ^^?. Otherwise, Word treats ^? as a request to search for any single character.

SUPER TIP

Did you ever accidentally overtype an entry in a text fill-in area and wish you could undo it? Well, you can! Alt+Backspace or Ctrl+Z toggles between the current and previous entry in a dialog box text field. This trick works in the Find and Replace fields when searching and replacing text. It also works in any other dialog box text fill-in area.

SUPER

A significant enhancement over prior versions of Word for Windows is that the Find What field now remembers the last four search strings. To select any of the last four, click the drop-down arrow to the right of the fill-in area, as shown in Figure 28.7. If you're clever, you can get Word to remember the last *five* search strings, but the fifth is only remembered during the current instance of having the Find or Replace dialog box onscreen.

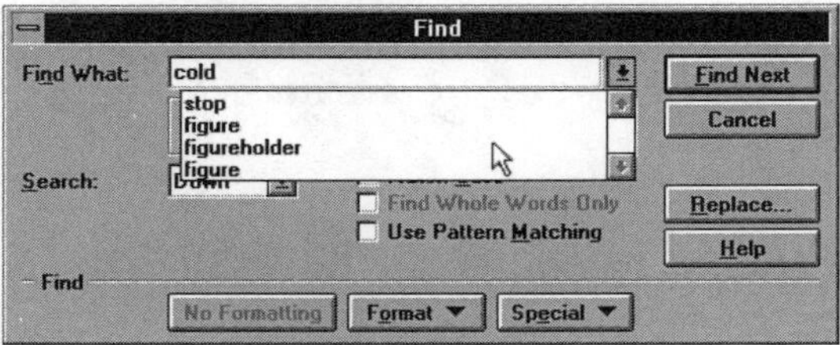

FIGURE 28.7. *Word's Find and Replace fields now remember the last four Find What and Replace With items.*

SUPER TIP

Are you ever confronted with the need to search for the next occurrence of a tedious word or phrase that you see? Instead of retyping it in the Find What box, copy and paste it as follows:

1. Select the text whose next occurrence you wish to find.
2. Press Ctrl+Insert (or Ctrl+C) to copy it to the clipboard.

3. Select **Edit | Find**.
4. Press Shift+Insert (or Ctrl+V) to paste it into the Fi**n**d What box.
5. Select your search options.
6. Click **F**ind Next.

Special

Use the Sp**e**cial button to insert special characters into the Fi**n**d What box. As shown in Figure 28.8, with Pattern Matching enabled, the Special list is context-sensitive. You get different special lists depending upon whether Pattern Matching is enabled and whether you're in the Fi**n**d What or Re**p**lace With field.

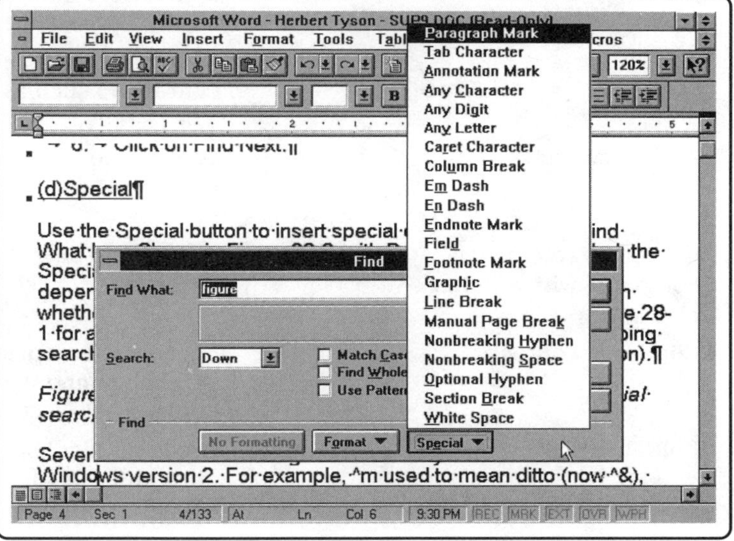

FIGURE 28.8.
Use the Special button to pull down a list of special search characters.

See Table 28.1 for a list of all special characters recognized by Word when doing searches. Most of these can be inserted using the Special button. Note that several special characters have changed substantially since Word for Windows Version 2. For example, `^m` used to mean ditto (now `^&`) but now searches for a manual page break. Also note that all special search characters that use `[^]` must be typed in lowercase. `^w` searches for white space, while `^W` generates the error message shown in Figure 28.9. To search for `^w`, you must type `^^w`. The comments in Table 28.1 indicate whether the special characters work with search, replace, or both.

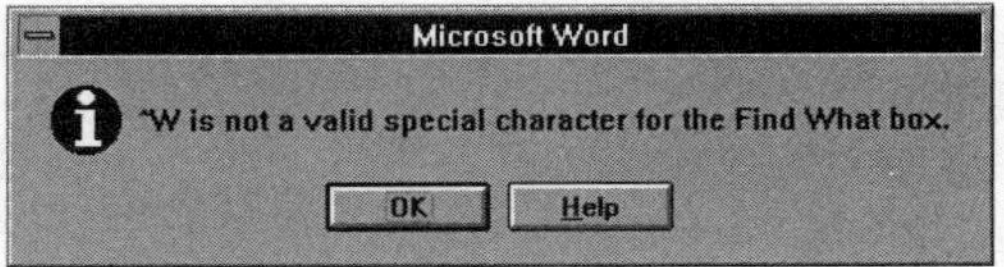

FIGURE 28.9. *All alphabetic ^ special characters must be lowercase (*`^w`*, not* `^W`*).*

Table 28.1. Special characters for Find and Replace.

To Match	*Use*	*Explanation or Comment*
Any single character	`^?`	`m?t` matches *mat*, *mit*, *mot*, *mut*, *mnt*, *m1t*, and so on. Search only.
Annotation	`^5` or `^a`	Search only.
ANSI character	`^0nnn`	Use `^0226` to search for *^a* by its ANSI code. Search or Replace.
Any digit	`^#`	Match any number from 0 to 9. Search only.
Any letter	`^$`	Match any letter, including accented characters such as *á*, *é*, *í*, *ö*, and *ù*. Search only.
ASCII character	`^nnn`	Use `^131` to search for *^a* by its extended ASCII code. Search or Replace.
Caret character when combined with another character	`^^`	Use `2^^3` to search for *2^3*. Search or Replace.
Clipboard contents	`^c`	Specify `^c` to replace the found text with the contents of the clipboard. Replace only.
Column break	`^n` or `^14`	Use in multicolumn text to force following text to the top of the next column. Search or Replace.
Ditto	`^&`	To change *Alexandrina* to *Alexandrina Rogmanonov*, use `Alexandrina` as the search text and `^& Rogmanonov` as the replace text. Replace only.
Em dash	`^+` or `^0151`	The long dash used as a substitute for the typewriter's double dash (—) is called an em dash because it's supposed to be the width of the letter m (em). Search or Replace.

To Match	Use	Explanation or Comment
En dash	`^=` or `^=150`	Shorter than an em dash, it's so named because it's the width of an n (–). Search or Replace.
End-of-line character (Break line without breaking paragraph, Shift+Enter)	`^l` or `^11`	Shift+Enter is often used in addresses and lists. Searching for *^l* may be a handy shortcut to locate an address or list. Search or Replace.
Endnote mark	`^e` or `^2`	This is similar to a footnote mark. Use `^e` and `^f` to look only for endnotes or footnotes, respectively. Use `^2` to look for either. Search only.
Field	`^d`, `^19`, or `^21`	These work only when field codes are displayed. Use `^19` to locate a SEQ field. Search only.
Footnote reference mark	`^2` or `^f`	Search only.
Footnote separator	`^3`	Search only.
Graphic	`^1` or `^g`	Used to search for pictures as well as embedded objects (including sound), these work only when field codes are displayed as results. Search only.
Linefeed	`^10`	This may be needed when dealing with imported text. Search or Replace.
Manual page break (Ctrl+Shift+Enter)	`^m`	In most standard ASCII files, *^12* (ASCII 12) is a form feed (page break). In Word, *^12* is used for both page and section breaks. Use `^12` when searching for either; use `^b` or `^m` when you're being particular. Search or Replace.
Manual page break or section break	`^12`	When used on the replace side, it changes section breaks into page breaks. For more precise handling, use `^b` (section break) or `^m` (manual page break). Search or Replace.

continues

Table 28.1. continued

To Match	*Use*	*Explanation or Comment*
Nonbreaking hyphen	`^~` or `^30`	Use to prevent a hyphenated word from being split across two lines. Search or Replace.
Nonbreaking space	`^s` or `^0160`	Use when you don't want Word to break up certain text. For example, to create an effect, you might use `H E L P`. To search for *H E L P*, typing `H^s` only would probably be suffficient. Search or Replace.
Optional hyphen	`^-` or `^31`	This is most often used when using search and replace to eliminate optional hyphens. Search or Replace.
Paragraph mark or carriage return (Enter)	`^p` or `^13`	`^p^p` searches for two carriage returns. Search or Replace.
Section break	`^b`	This searches for any of the four different types of section break you can insert with Insert|Break. Search or Replace.
Tab	`^t` or `^9`	`.^t` searches for a period followed by a tab, a common pattern in numbered lists. Search or Replace.
White space	`^w`	Any number or combination of nonprinting characters (space, tab, page breaks, section breaks, column breaks, paragraph marks, end of line marks, and end of cell marks). Search only.

Pattern Matching

Word provides the ability to perform pattern match searching. This is similar in some ways to a facility called GREP (GeneRal ExPressions), often found in advanced programming editors.

You can, in effect, use this feature to create your own wildcards. Let's say, for example, that you want to search for vowels only. You would enable pattern matching and specify `[aeiouy]` as the search text. In addition to the operators described below, you can also use parentheses to group search text and expressions.

SUPER NOTE

You should note that pattern matching itself works only in the Find What field. If you specify `[aeiouy]` for the search and `[AEIOUY]` as the replace, each instance of `a`, `e`, `i`, `o`, `u`, or `y` gets replaced with `[AEIOUY]` rather than a capitalized version of the letter. To force Word to deal only with the matching string, use `^&` in the Replace With field. Word then uses the actual found text for the replace operation. One application for this trick is to do something special with each occurrence of any letter in a set. For example, you could use `[AaEeIiOoUuYy]` as the search text and `^&` with bold formatting turned on as the replace text to embolden every vowel in a document (or in a selection). Th**i**s m**i**ght b**e** **a** h**a**ndy tr**i**ck **i**f **you'r**e **a** t**ea**ch**e**r tr**y**ing t**o** d**e**m**o**nstr**a**t**e** th**e** pr**e**v**a**l**e**nc**e** **o**f v**o**w**e**ls.

SUPER

Keep in mind that all pattern matching strings are case-sensitive. If you need case-tolerance in your searches, you must design case-tolerance into your search pattern strings. For example, to match for *any* occurrence of a word with a second letter *a* (upper or lowercase), you would have to construct a search string that takes both `A` and `a` into account:

```
<?[aA]*>
```

in which

< is the beginning of a word
`?` is any single character
`[aA]` is a or `A`
`*` is any string (that is, the balance of the word)
> is the end of a word

Any Character: ?

When pattern matching is enabled, use the `?` character all by itself (without the caret) to search for any single character.

Any String: *

The `*` character serves as a wildcard for any string of any length in a document. For example, to match this sentence, you could specify the search text `For example*.`. The sentence appears to end with two periods because `For example*.` is meant to include both the asterisk and the period. This is a handy way to select whole declarative sentences that begin with `For example`.

In Set: []

Use the `[` and `]` delimiters to create your own character sets for performing searches. For example, `^#` is the built-in search shortcut for `[0123456789]`, and `^$` is the built-in search shortcut for any alphabetic character. If these aren't sufficient, you can create your own. For example, the set `[01234567890abcdefghijklmnopqrstuvwxyzABCDEFGHIJKLMNOPQRSTUVWXYZ]` can be used to specify any alphanumeric character. `[^$^#]` cannot be used because you can't do special searches within a pattern search. Also, note that the pattern text is *case-specific*. Word gives you a total of 255 characters to build your search string, which is usually sufficient.

SUPER TIP

Use `[“”]` when you need to convert “smart quotes” back into straight typewriter quotes ("). As nice as “” might look, they're sometimes inappropriate. This is especially true when preparing text for publishers who wish that word processing programs like Word *didn't* have the capability to do things like hyphenation and smart quotes. In any event, if you use `[“”]` as the search string and `"` as the replace string, Word's pattern matching feature can convert both left and right curved quotes into ditto marks in one fell swoop.

Range: [*x*-*y*]

Use `[` and `]` with the `-` separator to specify a range of characters. For example, to search for any lowercase letter in the alphabet, specify `[a-z]`. The range must be specified from lower character code to higher. Thus, a range of `[z-a]` produces the error message shown in Figure 28.10.

SUPER

You can also specify ANSI codes as a range for searching for higher-order character groups or characters above 127. You can use ASCII codes, but the resulting series may not be in ANSI order and you might get the same invalid range message shown in Figure 28.10. Characters above Chr$(127) (standard BASIC notation for the 128th character position in an IBM-PC video ROM) sort differently when using ASCII versus ANSI codes. Because Windows is ANSI-oriented, you must use ANSI ordering when specifying a range. Consider `[^128-^255]`. If you enter these as ASCII codes by typing

Alt+128 followed by Alt+255 on the number pad, Word converts them into the characters Ç and _, which are the same as ANSI 199 (^0199) and ANSI 95 (^095). Since 95 is lower than 199, the effective range is invalid. The range `[^0128-^0255]`, however, is valid.

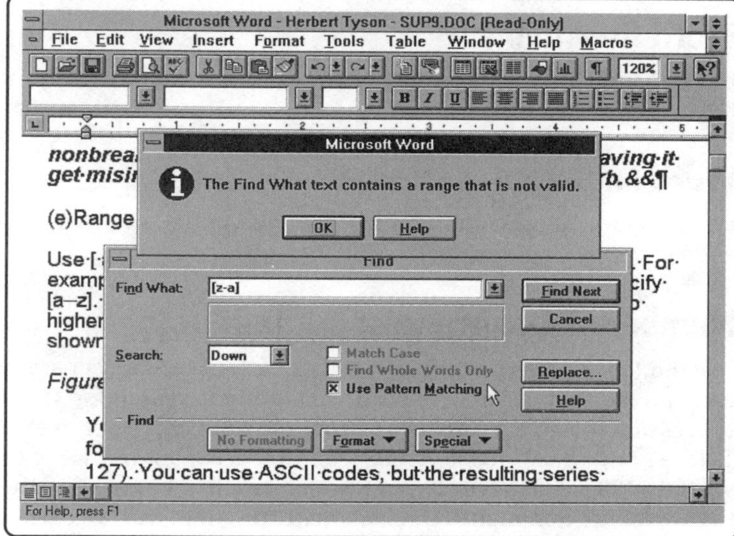

FIGURE 28.10.
Word tells you if you specify an invalid range.

Have you ever wondered if there are any accented characters lingering in a document? To find out, use `[^0128-^0255]` as the range in a pattern matching search. Do you want to look for any kind of section breaks or other special characters represented by characters below ASCII 32 (space)? Just specify `[^01-^031]` as the range.

Not In Set or Range: [!]

Precede a set or a range with `!` to tell Word to skip characters in the range or set. For example:

`<[!a-g]@>`	Match whole words that don't contain any lowercase letters from `a` through `g`.
`d[!u]g`	Match any `dog` and `dig` but not `dug`.
`<[!ABCD]@>`	Match any word that doesn't contain a capital `A`, `B`, `C`, or `D`.

Any Number: @

Use @ to indicate any number of the preceding character or expression. For example, e@ matches any number of occurrences of the letter *e*. The string o@d matches one or more occurrences of *o* followed by a lowercase *d* (*good*, *god*, *God*, *mod*, *mood*, *oddity*, *modern*, *moodring*, and so on). The string <[0-9]@> matches whole numbers not embedded as part of a word.

Word Beginning: <

Use < to indicate the beginning of a word. For example, <[Ii] matches all words that begin with the letter *i*.

Word Ending: >

Use > to indicate the end of a word. For example, ent> would match any word that ends in *ent*.

Number of Occurrences: {x}, {x,}, {x,y}

Use the {x} expression to find exactly x of the preceding character or expression. For example, to search for 4 consecutive numbers, search for <[0-9]{4}>. Use the {x,y} expression to find occurrences of from x to y of a character or expression. For example, 13{3,6} finds 1333, 13333, 133333, and 1333333, but not 13 or 133. However, it would still find 13333333 (seven 3s) but would match only the 1 and the first six 3s. Use {x,} to set just the minimum. For example, 1.{2,} finds any occurrence of a 1 followed by two or more periods.

Treat as Literal: \

Use the \ character to tell Word to treat the next character as a literal character rather than as a pattern matching character. For example, to search for any bracketed character group that doesn't start with a lowercase letter, use \[[!a-z].

Rearrange: \n2 \m1

Use \\$n$\\$m$ to rearrange words in the matching text, where n and m indicate the relative positions of the matching text that gets found. For example, suppose you need to swap the items in the following list (<item><tab><item><tab>):

```
Daly<tab>Chicago<tab>Mayor
Moscone<tab>San Francisco<tab>Mayor
Hart<tab>Colorado<tab>U.S. Senator
```

You could do it with the following specifications:

```
Find What: (^013)(*)(^t)(*)(^t)
Replace With: \1\4\3\2\5
```

The parentheses divide the Find What expression into five logical pieces:

1. Leading paragraph mark
2. Everything up to the next tab
3. Tab
4. Everything after the tab and up to the next tab
5. Tab

You use the Replace With string to tell Word to reorder the five pieces, swapping Pieces 4 and 2.

Match Whole Word Only

Select this option to force Word to match only words with white space at both sides. To find the beginning or end of a word, precede or follow the text with `^w`. Selecting the whole word option is equivalent to bracketing the word with `^w` at both ends. For example, `^wprint^w` matches *print* but not *printing*, while `^wprint` would match *printing* but not *sprinting*. If the situation permits pattern matching, you also have the option of using < and > to bracket the beginning and ending of a word.

Match Case

Select this option to force Word to match the exact case of a word. Otherwise, Word ignores case.

Search Direction

Word searches **D**own (from the insertion point toward the end of the document) by default. Select **U**p to search backwards toward the beginning of the document. Lest you worry about missing something, Word issues a prompt offering to continue searching at the other end of the document. Select All to force Word to search the whole document and not to nag you with the prompt shown in Figure 28.11.

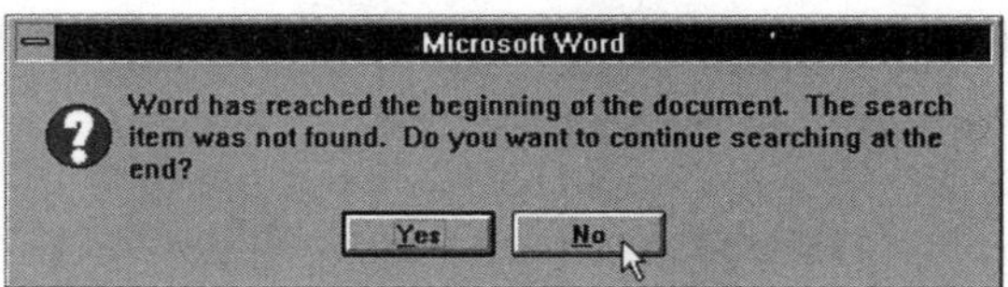

FIGURE 28.11.
*When searching **U**p or **D**own from the interior of a document, Word prompts to search the balance of the document.*

SUPER NOTE

The Edit|Find macro command has an additional direction option that tells Word not to issue the sometimes annoying `Continue at beginning` prompt.

Sounds Like

An additional new option with Word 6 is to search for homonyms of a particular pattern of text. For example, suppose you need to search for the name McCoy, but you don't know if it's McCoi, McKoy, McKoi or something similar in the text. If you enable the Sounds Like option, Word stops at words it thinks sound like McCoy.

SUPER NOTE

Unfortunately, this feature still needs a few more minutes in the oven. At this writing, searching for *McCoy* matched Make, McKoy and McKoi, but failed to match on either McCoy or McCoi. Don't take a Not Found result as proof-positive that the item you seek isn't there in some other form.

Searching for Formatting

Word enables you to search for text, formatting, or both. You can search for character formatting (font), paragraph formatting, language, or instances of style use, individually or in combination with other types of formatting.

PROCEDURE 28.3. SEARCHING FOR TEXT, IF DESIRED, AND FORMATTING.

1. Press Ctrl+F (Edit|Find).
2. Type the text you want to find, if any.
3. Select any special options, as desired (Match Case, Find Whole Words Only, and Down).
4. Click Format.
5. Select the kind of formatting you want to find (Font, Paragraph, Language, or Style).
6. Select the formatting attributes you want to search.

7. Click OK.
8. Repeat Steps 5 and 6 until all formatting preferences have been made.
9. Click Find Next.

SUPER

You can search for formatting occurrences only, regardless of the text, by leaving the text area blank. This is useful in instances where you've used a particular kind of formatting—such as Red—for certain kinds of passages.

SUPER TIP

When selecting formatting in the Find dialog box, the toolbars and shortcut formatting keys can be used to access formatting attributes. Depending on the formatting you want to find, it's often more convenient than selecting the Format and the Font or Paragraph options. For example, to specify bold, press Ctrl+B. Press Ctrl+B three times to cycle through three different search states: Bold, Not Bold, and Don't Care. The default is Don't Care and is indicated by Bold not being mentioned at all. When either Bold or Not Bold is selected, however, the selected formatting appears just under the search text, as shown in Figure 28.12. You can achieve the identical effect by clicking the Bold button on the Formatting toolbar.

FIGURE 28.12.
The search formatting appears under the search text.

SUPER NOTE

If you reassign keys to something other than their built-in assignments, they do not work within the Find dialog. Moreover, if you have assigned different keys to perform the same functions, your substitutes won't work in the Find dialog box either. For example, if you reassign Ctrl+B, neither these keystrokes nor any substitutes select Bold within the Find dialog box. Keep this in mind if some of the keystrokes shown in Table 28.2 fail to work for you.

Formatting shortcut keys can be used when specifying formatting in the Find and Replace dialog boxes. As long as they haven't been reassigned, you can use the keys shown in Table 28.2.

Table 28.2. Formatting shortcut keys that work in the Find dialog box.

Formatting Effect	*Keystrokes*
Clear all character formatting	Ctrl+Spacebar
Subscript	Ctrl+=
Superscript	Ctrl+Shift+=
Single space	Ctrl+1
Double space	Ctrl+2
One and a half line space	Ctrl+5
Bold	Ctrl+B
Double underline	Ctrl+Shift+D
Centered	Ctrl+E
Font	Ctrl+Shift+F
Hidden text	Ctrl+Shift+H
Italic	Ctrl+I
Justified	Ctrl+J
Small capital letters	Ctrl+Shift+K
Left align	Ctrl+L
Revision insertions	Ctrl+N
Point size	Ctrl+P
Clear paragraph formatting	Ctrl+Q
Right align	Ctrl+R
Underline	Ctrl+U
Word underline	Ctrl+Shift+W

Searching for Style Formatting

Word lets you search for occurrences of text that have a particular style applied or to search just for the style itself. For example, a useful way to jump among headings without having to enter Outline view is to search for the heading styles.

PROCEDURE 28.4. SEARCHING FOR STYLE FORMATTING.

1. Press Ctrl+F (**E**dit | **F**ind).
2. Type the search text in the Fi**n**d What field, if any.
3. Click Format and select Style from the drop-down list.
4. Locate the style you want to search for on the list, as shown in Figure 28.13.
5. Double-click the style name (or, click the style name and then OK or, if you're using the keyboard, just press Enter).
6. Click Find Next.

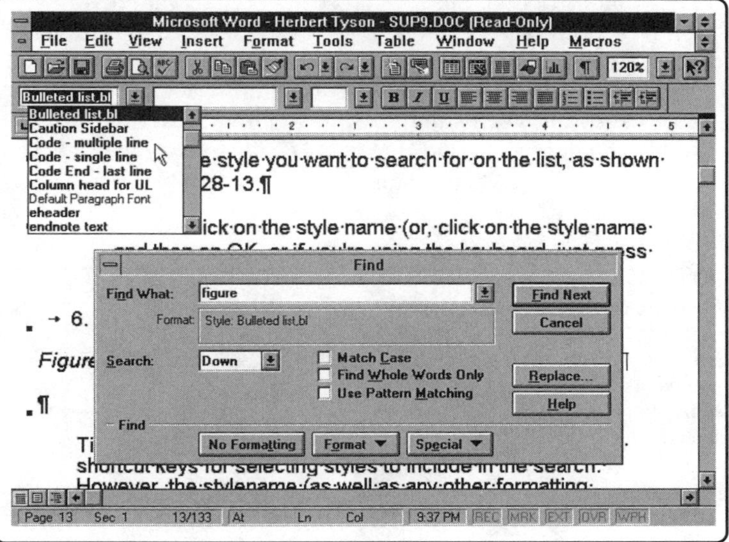

FIGURE 28.13.
Select the search style from the drop-down list.

SUPER TIP

Unlike character and paragraph formatting, there are no shortcut keys for selecting styles to include in the search. However, the stylename (as well as any other formatting that's there) can be selected using the toolbar. In lieu of Steps 3 and 4, just click the drop-down arrow beside the style list box in the Formatting toolbar and select the style you want to search for.

Replacing Text

Word lets you replace text occurrences. This is useful if you discover a misspelling in a proper name or otherwise change your mind about how you want something to appear in a document.

SUPER TIP

Word 6 enables you to limit Find and Replace operations to a selected block of text. Simply select the area to which you want to confine the search before you begin. When Word finishes in the selected block, it issues the prompt shown in Figure 28.14. If you are done, click No and Close. Keep the capability of limiting search operations to a selected block if Word suddenly doesn't find something you know is there. Chances are good that text is selected in the document. Just deselect the text and try again.

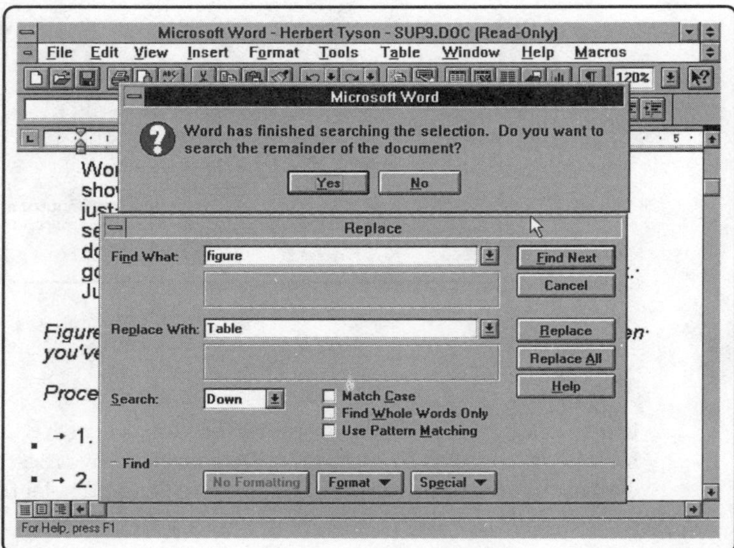

FIGURE 28.14.
Read the fine print carefully—Word tells you when you've been searching in a selected block.

PROCEDURE 28.5. REPLACING TEXT WITH TEXT.

1. Press Ctrl+H (**E**dit | R**e**place).
2. Type the text to be replaced in the Fi**n**d What field (for example, `clock`).
3. Type the new text in the Re**p**lace With field (for example, `timepiece`).
4. Turn on Find **W**hole Words Only, if applicable.
5. Turn off Match **C**ase, if applicable.
6. Select a **S**earch direction (Up, Down, or All).
7. Click **F**ind Next.
8. If Word finds a match, it displays the portion of the document that contains the match. Study the occurrence and decide if you want to make the replacement. If so, click Replace. Word makes the replacement and moves to the next match. If you don't want to make the replacement, click **F**ind Next to skip to the next match. If you're satisfied that you'll want all occurrences replaced, click Replace All and cross your fingers.

SUPER TIP

You can switch between the document and the Replace dialog box during a replace operation, just as you can during a Find or a Spelling check. If you encounter an instance you didn't anticipate, simply click in the text and fix it. When you're ready to resume, click Find Next back in the Replace dialog box.

SUPER NOTE

When Replace and Match Case are selected, Word searches for an exact match and replaces what it finds with exactly what you place in the Re**p**lace With field. When Match Case is turned off, Word disregards case in looking for a match. However, in doing the replacement, Word scans the case of the matching text. If it is capitalized, then Word capitalizes the replacement. If you want `clock` replaced with `Timepiece` (always capitalized), enable Match **C**ase. If you want the replacement case to vary according to the case of the match, turn off Match **C**ase. If you're replacing `clock` with `timepiece`, the replacements have the same case as the matching text; `Clock` is replaced with `Timepiece` and `clock` is replaced with `timepiece` (and `old junk` is replaced with `priceless antique`).

Replacing Formatting

Replacing formatting is straightforward. You can replace text and formatting or formatting only.

PROCEDURE 28.6. REPLACING FORMATTING.

1. Press Ctrl+H (Edit | Replace).
2. Click in the Find What field and type the search text (if any).
3. Use the Format button, formatting keys, or toolbars to select the formatting you want to find.
4. Click in the Replace With field; type the replacement text (if any) or `^&` to "ditto" whatever you entered in the Find What field.
5. Select the replacement formatting.
6. Click Find Next.
7. If you're sure you want to change all occurrences, click Replace All.

Replacing Special Characters and Wildcards

Using special characters in the Replace With field is similar to using them in the Find What field. Some, however, work only for one or the other rather than both. The status of the various wildcards and special search characters is indicated in Table 28.1 (Search only, Replace only, or Search and Replace).

You must be careful about some wildcards and special characters in the Replace With field. For example, when pattern matching is enabled, a `?` in the Find What field matches any single character (and `??` matches two characters, and so on). A `?` in the Replace With field, however, really means `?`. It changes each character to a `?`.

If you need to change your numbering format, you might be tempted to use the following:

```
Find What: [0-9]@.^t
Replace With: ^t[0-9]@.^t
```

Here, the Replace field is identical to the Find field except for the addition of `^t` (tab) at the beginning of the replacement text. Unfortunately, the before and after of your text would look like this:

```
Before: 1.<tab>
```

```
After: <tab>[0-9]@.<tab>
```

To perform nondestructive wildcard replacements, you are limited to using `^&` and `\num`. As described earlier, when doing pattern matching searches, you can use parentheses to group your search text into distinct pieces and then use `\n` to rearrange the pieces.

You also can use ^& as a kind of ditto mark. ^& in the replace field tells Word to use whatever it actually matched based on the Find specification. If it matches 1.<tab>This is the way to do nondestructive wildcard searches, then Word uses the match text verbatim instead of the characters ^&. Thus, while changing the replacement shown above doesn't work, the following works just fine:

```
Find What: [0-9]@.^t
Replace With: ^t^&
```

Clipboard

If you have text that's too long or too complex, you can use the special characters ^c to tell Word to insert the contents of the clipboard as the replace field. For example, suppose you want to replace multiple occurrences of an explicit graphic with a field linked to a file. Rather than searching for the graphic and executing the **I**nsert | **P**icture command for each occurrence, simply do it once. Then copy the picture (which is actually a field code) to the clipboard and perform search and replace to replace the graphic with the field.

PROCEDURE 28.7. REPLACING TEXT WITH THE CONTENTS OF THE CLIPBOARD.

1. Press Ctrl+H (**E**dit | R**e**place).
2. Type ^g into the Fi**n**d What field (recalling from Table 28.1 that ^g matches any graphic).
3. Click **F**ind Next.
4. Delete the graphic (the Replace dialog box remains suspended but available).
5. Select **I**nsert | **P**icture.
6. Click **L**ink to File (after all, that is what this example's about).
7. Select the graphic file you want to use.
8. Click OK to complete the **I**nsert | **P**icture command.
9. Select the resulting import field (for example, {IMPORT 2DARROW2.WMF * mergeformat}); press Ctrl+Insert to copy it to the clipboard.
10. Click the Replace dialog box.
11. Leave the Fi**n**d What text as ^1.
12. Type ^c into the Re**p**lace With field (important: c must be lowercase).
13. Click **F**ind Next.
14. If the matching graphic is one you want replaced, click Replace; otherwise, click **F**ind Next. If you're sure all of the graphics in the document need to be replaced with the identical field, then click Replace **A**ll.

Chapter

29

Fields

The **Insert | Field** command is one of Word's most powerful tools. Fields provide information about a document, control the execution and flow of mail and data merges, perform calculations, display statistical equations and formulas (if you prefer that to using the equation editor), and control the setup of indexes and tables (of contents and authorities).

Fields enable you to represent variable and complex information in a variety of ways. Used effectively, fields transform static documents into dynamic information tools.

There are 68 distinct field types, but when combined with the various option switches, there are literally tens of thousands of things you can do with fields—all of them legal in most states! In this chapter, you'll get a solid feel for fields, what you can do with them, and some things you need to watch out for.

Inserting Fields Using the Insert | Field Command

Fields can be created in a number of ways. The methods you use should be determined by how often you use fields in a particular way and by whether you need to understand the underlying syntax and options.

All field types can be created with the **Insert | Field** dialog box command. The **Insert | Field** approach is similar to the Macro Record method of creating macros. FIrst, choose the options you want. When you're done, Word creates a field that you can look at to see how it's done. You can also use **Insert | Field** each time, assuming it gives you all that you need.

An advantage of using the **Insert | Field** command is that it lists all of the different types of fields. It also shows the major options and is especially useful for learning how picture format syntax is supposed to look. Another advantage is that the dialog box shows you a rough syntax model for most field types. Furthermore, the **Insert | Field** command performs an automatic UpdateFields command when the field is first inserted.

A disadvantage of using the **Insert | Field** command is that it doesn't necessarily guarantee a syntactically correct field statement. Word doesn't intervene or otherwise inform you when you make syntax errors using the **Insert | Field** command. For example, Word uses \ (backslash) for switches (an ill-advised choice, considering the prevalent use already reserved for \ in specifying paths). In order to use a backslash for filenames, you must use two (for example, `F:\\WORD6\\CLIPART\\BANNER.WMF` instead of `F:\WORD6\CLIPART\BANNER.WMF`). If you type the specification yourself (as opposed to selecting from Word's **Insert | Picture** dialog box), Word doesn't even tell you that you've committed a syntax sin. Instead, if you use \ instead of \\ to refer to a file's directory location in an INCLUDEPICTURE field, the field displays as a large framed X (see Figure 29.1).

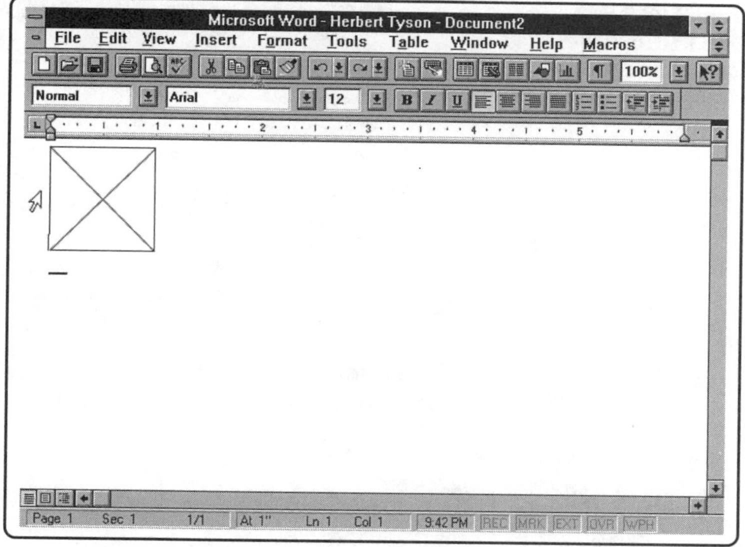

FIGURE 29.1.
X marks the spot—the missing graphic spot, that is. If you type your own file names, make sure you use double-strength \\ for paths.

When trying to include a text file (the INCLUDETEXT field), the same *faux pas* nets you `Error! Cannot open file`. This is the same message Word gives when the file you specify doesn't exist. It would help if Word had a different error message for such occasions—such as `Invalid switch`—but such is not the case.

If you're unfortunate enough to discover the **Insert | Field** command before you discover the **Insert | File** command, it may take you close to forever to figure out what you did wrong. The **Insert | File** command correctly uses \ instead of \\ and, in fact, doesn't give you a chance to do it wrong. When using the **Insert | Field** command, keep the high syntax error potential in mind. Field commands are extremely syntax-sensitive and not terribly forgiving or informative when your specification is "a little wrong." Don't get me wrong. Using **Insert | Field** often is the best or only clean way to insert a field. Just don't expect a lot of intelligence from it, because it's simply not there.

PROCEDURE 29.1. USING INSERT | FIELD TO INSERT A FIELD CODE.

1. Select **Insert | Field**.
2. Click a category in the **C**ategories list, based on the kind of field you want to insert (if you already know the field name, select `[All]` and use the Field Name list to find the field you want).
3. Click the field name you want from the Field Name list. Note that the Description area changes to provide a rough idea of each field's purpose or effect. The `Field Codes:` area shows you a syntax model for the command (see Figure 29.2).

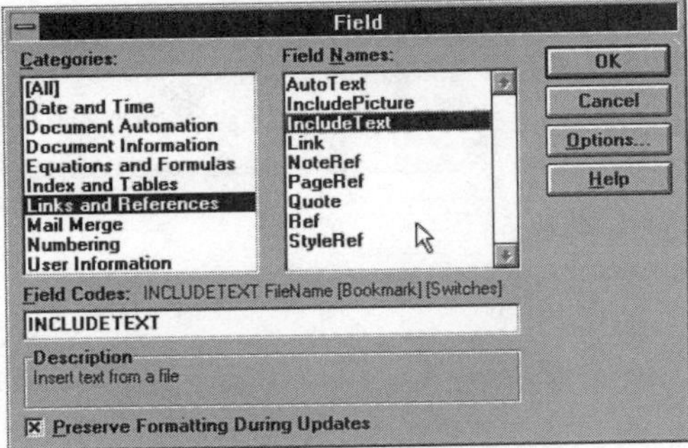

FIGURE 29.2. *The* `Field Codes:` *area shows you the syntax.*

4. When you click the field name, Word updates the Field Codes text box. Word uses the `Field Codes:` area to enable you to build your field code.

> **SUPER NOTE**
>
> You can press F1 at this stage to display excellent context-sensitive information about each field, including that you must use two \s in file specifications rather than just one.

5. If the **O**ptions button is available, click it to display either a dialog or set of tabbed options, as shown in Figure 29.3. Note that the current dialog continues to show the Field Codes: syntax model, the Field Codes text area where the code is being built, and the Description.

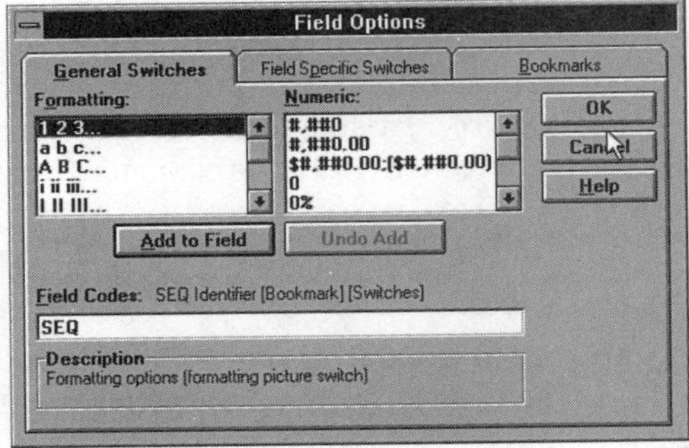

FIGURE 29.3. *The Options button shows different options for different fields.*

6. Observe the syntax model to see what the field needs next. If it needs text, then type the text. If it calls for a different entry, then click the tabbed area (if more than one is shown) corresponding to the option you need to enter. Depending upon the field type, the Field Options dialog box offers tabbed areas of formatting, switches, bookmarks, autotext, or other options.

7. Make your selection from the list of displayed choices, as shown in Figure 29.4. Click the Add to Field button to add the displayed item to the field you're building.

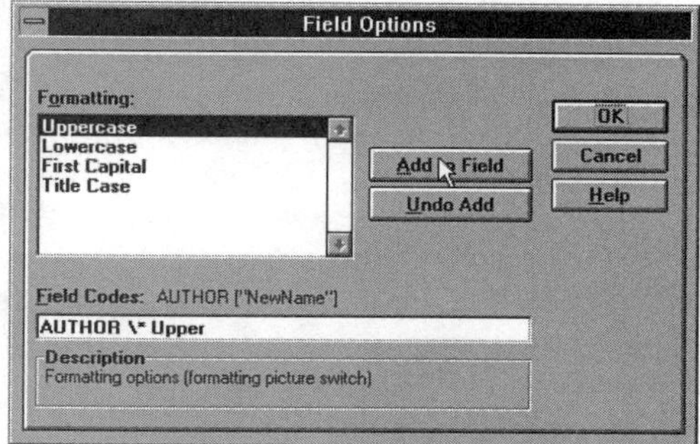

FIGURE 29.4.
Use Add to Field to build your field code.

8. Repeat Steps 5 through 7, as needed, to build your field.
9. Click OK to close the Field Options dialog box.
10. Click OK to insert and update (cause the field to display a result) the field.

A second and more direct method for creating fields is the keystroke that performs the InsertFieldChars command. This command (executed using Ctrl+F9 by default) inserts a pair of field characters. If text is selected, the selected text is placed inside the field. You can then type the rest of the field command directly, without the menu. One disadvantage of this method is that there's no automatic first update when the field is inserted manually. Another disadvantage is that you have to know the syntax. Once you know the syntax, however, this method is a lot faster and more direct for a knowledgeable Word user. Knowing how to insert a field manually also invites shortcuts, like writing macros that enable you to clone existing text for inclusion in fields, where appropriate. This is especially useful and almost essential when preparing index and manual table of contents entries.

PROCEDURE 29.2. MANUALLY INSERTING A FIELD CODE.

1. Press Ctrl+F9 to insert the field characters ({}); note that the cursor is positioned inside the field to begin typing the code.
2. Type the field name, options, and switches.
3. Press F9 to update the field.

For some fields, the Ctrl+F9 method may be the quickest and easiest way to insert a field. For others, the syntax assistance you get is worth the extra time. Keep the manual method in mind, however, if you get tired of having to go through the menu.

SUPER

Let's take a brief look at the field code characters for a moment. Press Ctrl+F9 to insert them. Now try selecting either { or }. You cannot do it. Actually, when you use another application to look at a Word field code in a document or if you use the StringValue macro included on the Word Super Book disk, you see that { and } are characters with underlying decimal codes of `19` and `21`. When Word inserts the characters into a file as a field code, however, they take on a life of their own. If you use Alt+019 and Alt+021 to insert characters `19` and `21`, they display as little boxes and aren't useful as field code characters at all. The only way to get these characters recognized as a field code is to use a Word command that inserts them.

A third and less direct approach for creating fields doesn't work for all fields, but it is preferable when you're experiencing syntax problems. Some fields—such as INCLUDEPICTURE, INCLUDETEXT, TOC (table of contents), INDEX, and XE (index entry)—can be inserted with various options from the Edit and Insert menus. **I**nsert | Fi**l**e, for example, creates an INCLUDETEXT field when you select the **L**ink to File option. Insert | Page Numbers inserts a PAGE field. **I**nsert | **P**icture inserts an INCLUDEPICTURE field when you select the **L**ink to File option. The **E**dit | Paste **S**pecial menu command can insert a DDE field, depending on the options you select and the applications involved. The **I**nsert | Inde**x** and Tables commands also insert a variety of field types.

When you use options from the Edit and Insert menus to insert fields, the results are much more syntax-certain than when using the **I**nsert | Fi**e**ld dialog box. Although they don't inform you that they're going to create fields, the **I**nsert | Fi**l**e and **I**nsert | **P**icture commands do correctly insert double backslashes for path statements. In fact, **I**nsert | Fi**l**e and **I**nsert | **P**icture even work correctly if you type your filename directly (for example, `C:\WKS\PROFIT.WK1`, not using `\\` instead of `\`) rather than using the Directories and Drives controls to navigate to your file. Thus, this method for inserting fields is relatively error-proof.

The method you use to insert fields should be determined by how you work and think, as well as by how often you use fields. If you work a lot with mail merge documents, you might quickly resort to the manual method. If you seldom need fields, you'll likely use the **I**nsert | Fi**e**ld method when you know that a field is what you want, but you might use the indirect **I**nsert | Fi**l**e method to avoid the `Error! Cannot open file.` syndrome. If you ever have to index a large document, you'll almost certainly develop a macro to do most of the work for you by automating the manual creation technique.

Beware of Editing Field Code Results and Deleting Fields

A potential problem exists when you don't realize something *is* a field and you edit the displayed result of a field code. The next time you update the field, it will revert to the original. For example, suppose you have a date field that prints as `August 26, 1994`. If you manually edit this to say `AUG 26 1994`, it may appear that you've succeeded. However, the moment you press F9 to update this field, it will revert to `August 26, 1994`. For a date, this is perfectly obvious. But what if you perform extensive editing on a long passage inserted by using an INCLUDETEXT field? If you have somehow forgotten (or didn't know, as might be the case if you're editing someone else's document) that it's a field result and not actual text, all your work may be for naught.

SUPER

Don't edit the displayed results of field codes directly. If you want to change a field code's displayed result, you can use UnlinkFields (Ctrl+Shift+F9) to convert the field result into actual text, which you can then edit with gay abandon. Or, if it's a date or some other number whose display is controlled by field format switches, you can edit the date format of the field code itself. To do this, select **T**ools | **O**ptions | **V**iew, and select **F**ield Codes so you can see the field code rather than the displayed result. If the field is an INCLUDETEXT field reference to a Word file, and if your modifications supersede the original, you might also consider using UpdateSource to actually change the text in the original file.

One way to avoid accidentally mistaking field code results for actual text is to enable the option to display field codes as shaded text. Using this option, you can cause fields to have a shaded appearance:

- Never
- When the insertion point or selection is within the field
- Always

Most users find the first option too much like working in the dark; they'd much prefer to know that a field is a field when they encounter it. On the other hand, the Always option may be a little too obtrusive for many users. In a document that uses many fields, all those little pockets of shading can be pretty distracting. Try the latter two ways and see which *you* prefer.

PROCEDURE 29.3. ENABLING THE SHADING OF FIELDS.

1. Select Tools | Options.
2. Click View.
3. Click the drop-down arrow next to Field Shading.
4. Select Never, When Selected (actually means when the cursor is anywhere inside the field, not just when the field is selected), or Always.
5. Click OK.

Turning on the shading *definitely* helps when you delete fields. You cannot delete a field using the Delete or Backspace keys unless you select the whole field. If you try, Word won't beep or otherwise let you know that it failed to do what you wanted. Instead, it just refuses. So, if you're a very self-assured touch typist, it's possible that Word can get you out of synch (especially if you think something is deleted that wasn't).

PROCEDURE 29.4. DELETING A FIELD.

1. Enable field shading as a visual aid, if desired. Then move the cursor to the beginning of the field.
2. Press Shift+Right to select the whole field.
3. Press Delete or Backspace (or Shift+Delete if you want to cut it to the clipboard).

SUPER NOTE

You can also start at the end of the field and press Shift+Left to select. You must start the selection at the beginning or end, or only the ostensible interior gets selected. The moment you extend the selection over either end, however, the whole field suddenly gets selected. You must use the same procedure whether or not field codes or field code results are displayed. If field code results are displayed, you cannot select one field delimiter ({ or }) without selecting the other and everything in between.

SUPER

Another note from the field, so to speak, concerns how Word behaves when changing a selection that includes a field. When selecting text, you can press Shift+cursor left/right keys to select text that includes a field. However, if you discover that you went too far and need to deselect, you will find that Shift+cursor left/right movements in the reverse direction will stop cold when you reach the field. This little annoyance has been part of Word for Windows since Version 1. To extend or shrink a selection, you can use Shift+cursor up/down or the mouse, but Shift+cursor left/right can't be used to shrink a selection past a field. To work around this, hold down Shift and click the mouse where you want the selection to end.

Displaying Field Codes

Sometimes, like it or not, it's necessary to look inside field codes to see what's going on. Perhaps you suddenly see an `Error! Bookmark not defined.` message in your file, or maybe a graphic that displayed fine yesterday was replaced by a large X when you updated the field this morning. In any case, you have two goals:

- Fix the problem.
- Find out what went wrong so it doesn't happen again.

It's often much quicker and easier to delete the errant field code and reissue the command(s) you previously gave to create it. However, if there's a problem with your technique that resulted in the error message, this approach may get you the same error message later on.

Some very common problems that users encounter with fields include accidentally deleted bookmarks, linked files that have been moved or deleted, and fields that have been improperly edited. Formatting switches are especially easy to mess up. If, after editing a field, you fail to immediately update it, it continues to display its old result. It may be days or weeks later when you finally do update it and discover the error. By then, you may have forgotten having edited the field, what you did, or even why you did it.

In any case, the solution is to display the field code to try to track the problem down. One way to try to prevent a recurrence is to leave the errant field code in place, insert a new one that works (using the appropriate command), and then display and compare the two field codes. If the problem is a missing bookmark or files, for example, you'll quickly get to the root of the problem when the corresponding commands don't display the bookmarks or files you thought were there.

There are two approaches to displaying field codes. You can display all of them or just a few. In large documents with many field codes, the latter approach is generally preferable. It takes much less time, and there is less chance of your breaking other codes while you're trying to fix one.

SUPER

Troubleshooting: When a previously correct field code suddenly displays as `Error! Bookmark not defined.`, the reason invariably is that bookmarked text was deleted, taking the bookmark with it. The solution is to find out if the equivalent location still exists and, if so, rebookmark the area (see Chapter 31, "Bookmarks and Cross-References"). An ideal solution would be for Word to incorporate a feature that lets you protect an area of a document against deletion. You can do that in a limited way when working with forms, but that doesn't help you with other kinds of files. You also can protect a whole document by making it read-only or assigning a password to it. The capability to mark a block of text as undeletable would be a great boon to Word users, perhaps applied as a character format. You could then unprotect as needed to make a change and reapply protection when you're done.

SUPER CAUTION

When you display field codes, be especially alert to unintended Replace operations, especially with the Replace All option. Field codes often contain switches or other unusual combinations of text that are usually invisible to you. For example, if you see that you've incorrectly used \ instead of / in various text passages, you might be tempted to run Replace to change \ to /, figuring that, because you never use \, any occurrence must be wrong. If field codes are displayed, however, you'd be changing field switches from \ to /—and that's a good way to make your fields stop working! So, always beware of global Replace operations, but be especially vigilant when field codes are displayed.

PROCEDURE 29.5. DISPLAYING SELECTED FIELD CODES.

1. Select the field code(s) you want to display.
2. Press Shift+F9 (the ToggleFieldDisplay command).

SUPER NOTE

For Shift+F9 to work when no text is selected, the cursor must be immediately in front of or on the field. If the cursor is just past the field, Shift+F9 will not have any effect. Also note that the effect of Shift+F9 is different in Normal view than it is in Page Layout view. In Normal view, only the selected field gets toggled. In Page Layout view, unfortunately, all fields get toggled *and* the document gets repaginated. As a general rule, avoid toggling field codes in Page Layout view, especially in long documents.

SUPER TIP

If you work a lot with field codes, you might quickly discover that pressing Shift+F9 is unduly tedious. If so, you might consider assigning the F10 key to the ToggleFieldDisplay command. It's right next to the F9 (UpdateFields) command, making for a handy edit-update one-two punch combination. Moreover, the F10 key is redundantly assigned to the Alt key. Press F10 and observe the left end of the menu bar. Now tap Alt and make the same observations. See? You don't need the F10 key, do you?

PROCEDURE 29.6. ASSIGNING F10 TO TOGGLEFIELDDISPLAY.

1. Select **T**ools | **C**ustomize and click the **K**eyboard tab.
2. Under **C**ategories, select All Commands.
3. Under C**o**mmands, select ToggleFieldDisplay (hint: click in the Commands list, tap T, and press PageDown five times to get to commands that start with *tog*).
4. Click in the Press **N**ew Shortcut Key field and press F10.
5. Check the Sa**v**e Changes In field and ensure it's set to NORMAL.DOT (assuming that's where you want it).
6. Click **A**ssign and Close.

Don't forget to save your changes to NORMAL.DOT if you want the new shortcut preserved for posterity.

PROCEDURE 29.7. DISPLAYING ALL FIELD CODES.

1. Select **T**ools | **O**ptions.
2. Click the **V**iew tab.
3. Click **F**ield Codes.
4. Click OK.

SUPER TIP

Forget this procedure and just press Alt+F9 anytime you want to toggle all field codes on or off.

Updating Fields

Updating fields means to refresh the display according to the contents of the field. If you press Shift+F9 to toggle a field code display ON, then edit the field, and immediately press Shift+F9 again to toggle the field code display OFF, it usually does not immediately display the editing results. You must update it first.

PROCEDURE 29.8. UPDATING FIELDS.

1. Select the text that contains the field you want to update.
2. Press F9.

It might seem at first glance that you always want your fields updated. That's not always true, however. Consider, for example, what would happen if you used a date field in a letter and wanted to use that date to track when the letter was sent. If the date field gets updated, you lose track of the original date. Another time you wouldn't want to update a field is when it's a link to a file that's not currently available. Access to that file may be blocked by another user on a network, or the file might have been deleted. In either case, if you need to see the results in the current document, then you certainly don't want to update—at least not when the file is unavailable.

SUPER TIP

If you update a field linked to a file and lose the information (for example, a graphic is replaced by a large X or you see the `Error! Cannot open file.` message), you should immediately press Alt+Backspace or Ctrl+Z to undo the update. Then do some troubleshooting to see what file the field is looking for and what happened to it. If the original file is completely gone but you need the displayed result anyway (even in the absence of the file), press Ctrl+Shift+F9 to unlink the field (see "Unlinking a Field" later in this chapter). This converts the field either to Word text or to a Word picture. Depending upon the original format, you might be able to re-create the original file by copying what you have in Word to the clipboard and pasting it to the original application.

Most fields can be updated in one of three ways:

- Mail Merge
- File Print, with the Update Fields option turned on
- F9 (Update Fields)

Exceptions to this are fields that are explicitly locked using the `/!` switch or the LockFields command. In addition, there are some additional fields for which updating is either automatic or not applicable:

```
AUTONUM
AUTONUMLGL
AUTONUMOUT
EQ
GOTOBUTTON
MACROBUTTON
TOC
XE
```

In addition, if you manually create an EQ field with field codes turned off, you'll find that it's impossible to make it display the result by using F9 or toggling ShowAll. Instead, use Shift+F9 (ToggleFieldDisplay) or ViewFieldCodes from the menu to toggle field codes on and then off. This forces the field result to display. EQ fields entered with the **Insert | Field** command or while field codes are visible are displayed correctly the next time either ShowAll or ToggleFieldDisplay is executed. EQ fields are updated immediately when they're created. The F9 (UpdateFields) key isn't applicable to EQ fields and has no effect.

Locking Fields

One approach to protecting a field from ill-considered updating is to lock it. If you try to update a locked field, Word responds with the message shown in Figure 29.5. If a selection contains one or more locked fields, Word honors an update attempt only for the unlocked fields. It then advises you that the selection contained some locked fields.

FIGURE 29.5.
When you try to update a locked field, Word just says "No."

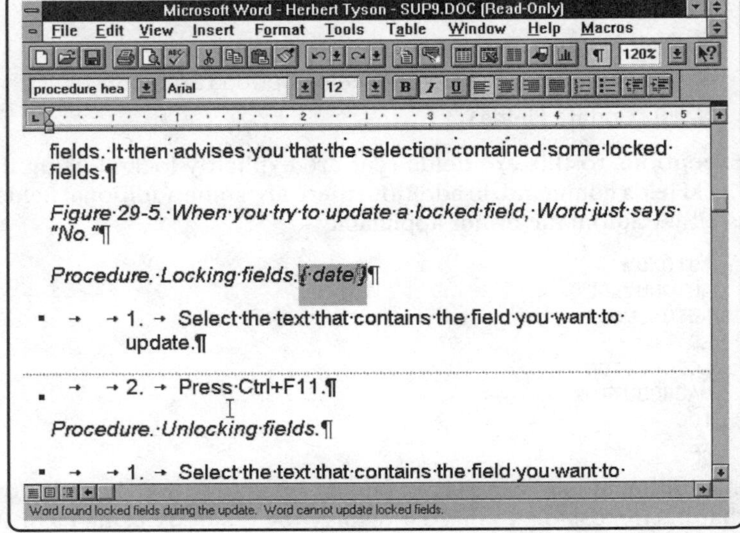

PROCEDURE 29.9. LOCKING FIELDS.

1. Select the text that contains the field you want to update.
2. Press Ctrl+F11.

PROCEDURE 29.10. UNLOCKING FIELDS.

1. Select the text that contains the field you want to update.
2. Press Ctrl+Shift+F11.

Another approach to locking *some* fields is to use the \! switch. This switch prevents updating some linked fields unless the original text has also changed since the last update. The \! switch works with the following fields:

```
INCLUDETEXT
[REF] BOOKMARK
```

SUPER NOTE

At this writing, the \! switch seems not to be necessary anymore. Under Word for Windows 2, if you had a bookmarked reference to a section of a Word document, any fields displayed in the reference were updated when you updated the bookmarked reference, even though the source had not changed. In effect, the bookmarked field was acting as if it contained the actual fields rather than a reference to their presence elsewhere. The `\!` switch prevented the reference from treating the fields they contained as if they were independent. In the present version of Word 6, this problem seems to have been overcome, and correct field behavior can be obtained without `\!`.

Converting Fields to Text (Unlinking)

Sometimes you might want to convert a field into its result. This is called unlinking, since the field is no longer contingent upon any external conditions being met. This is similar to replacing a variable with a constant in math.

PROCEDURE 29.11. UNLINKING A FIELD.

1. Select the text that contains the field you want to unlink.
2. Press Ctrl+Shift+F9.

The UnlinkFields command is used to convert a field's displayed result into the value displayed. For example, if a field displays as `November 9, 1994` with field codes turned off and `{DATE}` when field codes are displayed, pressing Ctrl+Shift+F9 permanently converts that field into the text `November 9, 1994`. Once done (unless undone with Edit | Undo—Alt+Backspace), the field is permanently converted into text. Similarly, if a field is `{INCLUDETEXT "more.doc"}`, the field is linked to the file MORE.DOC. When field codes are turned off, you see the text of MORE.DOC at that point in your file. If you press the UnLinkFields key, however, the field is replaced by the text of MORE.DOC. Once done, if you update MORE.DOC, you no longer are able to update the copy of the file in your document because the link has now been broken. The Update Source command also ceases to work once the field has been unlinked.

Now that you've had a chance to absorb the potential usefulness of the UnlinkFields command, you should know that it doesn't work on some fields. Notably, it does not have any effect at all on the following:

```
AUTONUM
AUTONUMLGL
AUTONUMOUT
EQ
RD
TC
TOC
XE
```

It would be nice to have something like the AUTONUM fields converted into text, as well as the EQ (equation) fields. Still, having no effect is better than the effect UnlinkFields has on field codes which themselves do not display a result. It deletes them! If your document contains the following, you should be prepared to kiss them good-bye if you subject them to the UnlinkFields command:

```
ASK
FILLIN
NEXT
NEXTIF
PRINT
SET
SKIPIF
```

Unlinking also has undesirable effects on a few others, too, such as MacroButton and GotoButton. Unlinking these fields results in them being replaced by their display text setting (actually, if the display text isn't enclosed in quotes, they'll get reduced to just the first word of the display text).

In addition, unlinking deletes any otherwise displayable field (such as a bookmark, expression, and so on) that was never initially updated or displayed as text. For example, if you manually create the field `{ =5280/3 }` by pressing Ctrl+F9 and typing `=5280/3` but never press F9 to calculate the expression, UnLinkFields simply deletes the field. For all Word knows, you might be trying to unlink an existing field result because you want to preserve the displayed result—precisely because the underlying value has changed, as in a date. Therefore, it's up to you to make sure that manually created fields have been properly displayed or updated at least once before using UnLinkFields. Fields inserted with the Insert | Field dialog box are automatically updated at creation time. However, manually inserted or modified fields are not.

Furthermore, if any fields are presently in error, unlinking causes the error message itself to be converted into text. For example, you might have a file referenced in an INCLUDETEXT field that you expect to have available but don't presently have. In many offices, this isn't an uncommon situation. If you try to unlink, the field will be replaced with the text `Error! Cannot open file.` Later, you might want to determine which file it was that Word couldn't open. You'll be out of luck! Usually this won't happen if you unlink fields on a one-by-one basis—you'll see the error message as it happens. However, if you just select an entire document and press Ctrl+Shift+F9, you probably won't like the results.

All this points to one important fact: *Use the Unlink Fields command only when absolutely appropriate*. Otherwise, it's likely you will not like the results.

Update Source

Another kind of update can occur when a document contains a reference to another Word document. Perhaps you use a pool of boilerplate files that contain contract clauses. If you make a significant but desirable modification to the version of the boilerplate in one document, you might say "Hmmm; that's better than what we've been using," and decide to change the source. Ordinarily, you might think you'd have to copy the new version to the clipboard, open the source document, and paste the clipboard over the old version. If you use a link to the original file to access the boilerplate text, however, you can use the Update Source command. Update Source sends changes from the current document back to the original. It's kind of a reverse of the Update Fields command. Rather than change the current text, you change the original—even if the file is closed and is located on a network drive.

PROCEDURE 29.12. UPDATING THE SOURCE.

1. Edit a displayed field result that is the result of an included Word document (for example, an INCLUDETEXT field).
2. Select the edited field.
3. Press Ctrl+Shift+F7.

SUPER NOTE

When you press Ctrl+Shift+F7, you should see some disk activity as the source file is updated, unless the source file is already loaded in a Word window. If you don't see some kind of activity, then it's possible the link isn't specified correctly. You should open the source file and make sure that it was indeed changed. If the source file is already open in another Word window, the change is reflected in that window. However, the change to the source has *not* yet been made permanent. If you close the source file without saving, the update will be lost. If the source file is open, you must save it after doing an Update Source command if you want the change to be permanent.

Field Syntax

Some fields are very simple. Their only syntax is the keyword by which they're identified. The field `{AUTONUM}`, for example, uses no parameters whatsoever. Other fields can be rather complex, requiring both parameters and switches to achieve the desired effect. Furthermore, for some reason known only to Microsoft, some fields require quotes around literal arguments, while others do not.

While syntax can vary substantially for various field types, a number of general rules apply. The general form for any field statement is

```
{keyword arguments] switches]}
```

The keyword can be any one of 68 field types. The field character pair (which you can insert by pressing Ctrl+F9) can also be used to enclose just a bookmark reference, such as `{duedate}`. In such cases, the `REF` keyword is implied, and the reference is equivalent to {REF duedate}. Any time the first word in a field statement isn't one of the 68 recognized keywords, Word tries to interpret the field as a bookmark. If you made a mistake (or if the bookmark name isn't otherwise defined), when you update the resulting field, Word informs you that something is wrong with an Error! Bookmark not defined. message. If you see this message, it almost always means that you've mistyped a keyword. Of course, it could also mean that you mistyped a bookmark, so take your choice!

The actual ordering of arguments and switches matters at some times and not at others. As a general rule, switches that affect the entire field come before any arguments. Switches that affect a particular parameter usually appear immediately after the parameter they affect.

There are four types of general switches that you can use with a number of different fields and that affect how the results of fields are displayed:

- Text format
- Numeric format
- Date format
- Field lock

The field lock switch was discussed under "Locking Fields" earlier in this chapter. The others are discussed in the sections that follow.

Text Format Switches

Text format switches have the following syntax:

```
\* format
```

and are used to affect how certain text will appear. The format options can be any of the 14 keywords that follow.

Alphabetic

This switch converts the numerical result of an expression into lowercase letters, producing an alphabetical numbering result. For uppercase letters, capitalize the first letter of the alphabetic switch: Alphabetic.

The numbers 1 through 26 are a through z, 27 through 52 produce aa through zz, 53 through 78 produce aaa through zzz, and so on. For example, {= * alphabetic 2} displays as a single lowercase b. If you add 26 to it (28), it displays as two bs. If you add 26 again (54), you get three bs, and so on. The maximum number you can display this way is 780, which displays as 30 zs. The field {=* alphabetic 780 } yields zzzzzzzzzzzzzzzzzzzzzzzzzzzzzz. This is known as the *Rip Van Winkle effect.*

Arabic

This switch is the default and results in normal Arabic numbers. For example, `{=2^16 \* Arabic}` displays as `65536`.

Caps

Any text in the resulting expression is displayed in initial caps. For example, with the SET bookmark field `{SET greeting "dear senator"}`, the corresponding bookmark reference `{greeting \* caps}` would result in `Dear Senator`.

Cardtext

This switch displays a numeric expression in cardinal form. For example, `{=999999 \* cardtext}` displays as `Nine Hundred Ninety-Nine Thousand Nine Hundred Ninety-Nine`. The benefits of this should be obvious to anyone who hates writing out numbers (see `Dollartext`, below, for a special version of this).

Charformat and Mergeformat

The `charformat` switch affects the character format of text that's displayed. If neither `charformat` nor `mergeformat` are specified, the text is displayed exactly as it appears in its original form.

If `\*charformat` is specified, the displayed result has the same character formatting as the first character in the field keyword or bookmark name. This lets you permanently fix the formatting of the displayed result.

If `\*mergeformat` is specified, the displayed result takes on the character format of the current result the next time the field is updated. When no format switch is used, note that a reformatted field always reverts to the original format when updated. If you change the text contained in the bookmark when `\*mergeformat` is specified, any new formatting done to the displayed field result will be applied to the field when it gets updated. Without `\*mergeformat`, the displayed formatting of the field will revert to that of the text it references. Use these guidelines when you have to decide which switch to use:

- Use no switch at all when you want to preserve original formatting. An example might be such things as logos whose original appearance must not vary by context.
- Use `\*charformat` when you want to make certain that the displayed result matches what you're typing right now, such as boilerplate text, an address, or the signature line in a letter. The first letter of the bookmark will be in your current font and size (unless you explicitly change it), pretty well guaranteeing that the displayed text will blend in.

- Use `\* mergeformat` when you plan to reformat the displayed text and want that formatting retained. You might use this approach for special text—such as a book title or product name—for which the font might vary markedly (depending on where you're using it, or for when you crop or scale an imported graphic).

Dollartext

The `dollartext` argument is a variation of `cardtext`, producing the kind of result you might want when writing the amount in long form on checks. For example, `{= 1017.95 \* Dollartext}` produces `one thousand seventeen and 95/100`.

Firstcap

The `firstcap` argument capitalizes the first word only. For example, `{QUOTE \* firstcap "now is the time for all good folks"}` results in `Now is the time for all good folks`, as does: `{QUOTE \* firstcap "NOW IS THE TIME FOR ALL GOOD FOLKS"}`.

Hex

The `hex` specification displays a number in hexadecimal notation. For example, `{= 5280 \* hex}` displays as `14A0`.

Lower

The `lower` format argument displays text as all lowercase. For example, `{QUOTE \* lower "FOURSCORE AND SEVEN YEARS AGO"}` is displayed as `fourscore and seven years ago`.

Ordinal

`Ordinal` displays in street form. For example, `{QUOTE \* ordinal "53"}` results in `53rd`.

Ordtext

`Ordtext` is similar to `ordinal` but displays in text. `{=66322 \* ordtext}` displays as `sixty-six thousand three hundred twenty-second`.

Roman

`Roman` displays a number as a Roman numeral. For example, `{=1991 \* roman}` produces `mcmxci`, while `{=1991 \* Roman}` produces `MCMXCI`.

Upper

The `upper` parameter causes the field's text to display in all caps. For example, `{QUOTE \* upper "This is uppercase"}` quite honestly proclaims `THIS IS UPPERCASE`.

Switch Combinations

Some of the switches can be combined. For example, `charformat` or `mergeformat` can be combined with any other format. `{quote \* charformat \* ordtext "9"}` produce *`ninth`* (in italics, because the *`q`* in `quote` is in italics). However, none of the numeric arguments can be combined with case arguments, except for alphabetic. You can combine `alphabetic` with `upper` to produce uppercase alphabetic counters (but don't—specify `ALPHABETIC` instead).

Numeric Format Switches

Numeric format switches (sometimes referred to as *numeric picture switches*) have the following syntax:

```
\# format
```

and are quite versatile, enabling you to format numbers in almost any way imaginable.

(Number)

There's sometimes confusion about the number picture switch because the switch itself, `\#`, can also use `#` as an argument. For example, the field `{=5 \#}` generates the message `Error! Switch argument not specified.` That's because `\#` is the switch itself, but as shown, there's no switch argument. The field `{=5 \#$#.00}`, on the other hand, prints out as `$5.00`. As a field argument, `#` is used as a number spaceholder, so the field `{=5 \#$###.00}` prints out with two spaces between the `$` and the `5` (`$  5.00`). This kind of switch might be suitable for aligning a column of numbers that vary in order of magnitude at a time when a decimal tab is not an option. Each `#` guarantees at least that much space between the dollar sign and the decimal point.

0 (Zero)

Zero is used as a placeholder to guarantee the same order of precision in numbers. This is useful if you have multiple formula fields that ordinarily might yield different precisions. For example, it's generally considered unacceptable to list the same statistic for different individuals using different precisions, such as:

Bob	6.5
Katie	6.4444
Karen	6.501
Mike	6.61111
Jan	6.49996

Suppose these numbers were all coming from calculations, and you didn't know *a priori* how much precision Word would generate. You could guarantee identical precision by using the same numeric switch in all of the calculation fields: something like {=58/9 \#0.000}. This ensures that the result is always shown out to thousandths with a leading zero, if necessary (for example, 0.223 instead of .223).

x

When x is used at the left edge of any other arguments, Word truncates additional digits that don't fit in the reserved space. For example, {=98765 \#x#.00} displays as 65.00 because x# reserves only two places to the left of the decimal point. When used to the right of the decimal point, x is identical to #.

. (Decimal)

The decimal point is used in conjunction with # and 0 (zero) placeholders to specify the precision of the displayed result.

, (Commas for Multiples of 1,000)

The comma is used to insert commas to separate three-digit series (thousands) to the left of the decimal point. If you only want commas and numbers, the comma and any other number placeholder (except x) will work. You don't need {=45000 \###,###} to get 45,000. The field {=45000 \#,#} or {=45000 \#,0} works just fine.

+ (Force the Sign to Display)

The addition sign forces the positive or negative display of the number; it uses + if the number is positive and - if it's negative. No sign is displayed for zero. For example:

```
The temperature in downtown Fairbanks was {=sum(temptable[A1])\#+#}.
```

If the A1 cell says -34, it displays as -34. If it's 26, it displays as +26.

; (Semicolon)

The semicolon is used to specify different formats for positive, negative, and zero. If a single semicolon is used, the picture format to the left controls the display of positive and zero values, and the picture format to the right of the semicolon is used to display the format of negative numbers:

```
{keyword  \#positive or zero format;negative format}
```

If two semicolons are used, the first argument specifies just the positive format, the second argument specifies the negative format, and the third argument specifies the zero format:

```
{ \#positive format;negative format;zero format}
```

For example, the switch `\#*+###*;^+###^;=0.#=` would yield

Number	*Displays As*
45	*+45*
-3	^- 3^
0	=0.0=

' (Quote)

Single quotes are used to insert literal text. For the most part, text is inserted verbatim with the quotes to prevent Word from interpreting verbatim text as a numeric switch argument. For example:

```
{=6.5 \#"Please add #.0% '9sales tax'9"}
```

When you use single quotes, double quotes must surround the entire picture clause (everything to the right of `\#`).

SEQ Identifier

You can use the current value of a sequence number (SEQ field) in your field by enclosing it between grave accents (usually the lowercase complement to the tilde key; press Alt+96 on the number pad if you're not sure). This switch can be used to refer to a table or figure number. For example, if you already have a field `{seq tabno}` used to number a table, you can use the name `serial` as part of another field when referencing that table number: `{= Sum(Sales[E5]) \# "$#,# 'total sales, shown in Table' tabno"}` displays as `$345,000 total sales, shown in Table 2`. Using `tabno` in the field guarantees that the table number reference will be correct.

Date Format (Date-Time Picture Switches)

Date-time picture switches have the following syntax:

```
\@ format
```

and enable you to format dates in a variety of ways. You can specify a desired default format in your WINWORD6.INI file by adding the line

```
DATEFORMAT=MMMM d, YYYY
```

to the `[Microsoft Word]` section. That way, the `{DATE}` field will display as the more traditional `October 25, 1991` instead of the default `10-25-91`. Often this is preferable to using `{ TIME \@ "MMMM d, yyyy" }` each time you want to insert today's date. (Note: The `TIME` and `DATE` keywords can both be used to display time, dates, or both.)

SUPER TIP

Date-time picture switches can work with any dates—not just with date fields. If you have a date contained in a bookmark, such as `{SET duedate "11/25/94"}`, you can print that date out in long format by using the field `{duedate \@ "MMMM D, YYYY"}`. This works even though `duedate` isn't a Word keyword or a date field. Unfortunately, this works for only one date at a time. If you have a whole file filled with long dates that you want converted to short, you can't just bookmark the whole document and then add a date picture format to convert them all. In fact, if you do that, the REF field displays just the first date contained in the bookmarked field (in the correct format, of course) and nothing else.

Date Format Components

Date formats use key letters to represent parts of dates and times, as shown in Table 29.1. These key letters affect only the component that gets displayed, not the capitalization. You must add the appropriate `\*` switch to effect different forms of capitalization. The field `{ date \@ "MMM" }` produces `Aug (uppercase M produces months, while a lowercase m produces minutes)`. You would need to add `\*upper` to get `AUG`: `{ date \@ "MMM" \*upper }`. Other formatting attributes can be added as well: `sequence` to refer to a SEQ identifier, `\*Roman` to really confuse your colleagues, and so on.

Table 29.1. Time and Date Picture Switch Format Specifiers.

Format	*Effect*
`AM/PM`	`AM` and `PM`
`am/pm`	`am` and `pm`
`A/P`	`A` and `P` (groceries, anyone?)
`a/p`	`a` and `p`
`d`	Date, with no leading zero
`dd`	Date, with a leading zero
`ddd`	Abbreviated name of the day of the week (`SUN`, `MON`, and so on)
`dddd`	Full name of the day of the week (`Sunday`, `Monday`, and so on)
`h`	Hour, 12-hour format, no leading zero
`hh`	Hour, 12-hour format, leading zero
`H`	Hour, 24-hour format, no leading zero
`HH`	Hour, 24-hour format, leading zero

Format	Effect
M	Numeric month, no leading zero
MM	Numeric month, leading zero
MMM	First three letters of month (Aug, Sep, and so on)
MMMM	Full month name (August, September, and so on)
m	Minutes, no leading zero
mm	Minutes, no leading zero
s	Seconds, no leading zero
ss	Seconds, leading zero
y or yy	Year, 2-digit format (93, 94, and so on)
yyyy	Year in 4-digit format (1994, 1995, and so on)
'string'	You can supplement date and time text by adding additional text in single quotes, such as `{ date \@d \*ordinal}{ date \@"' of 'MMMM}` to produce the 28th of August.

Chapter

30

Summary Information

Word, like most word processing programs, provides a summary information feature for keeping track of documents. In addition to document management, the summary information feature, if used, provides a useful source of header and footer information.

Accessing Summary Information

Summary information can be accessed in several ways:

- The Summary Info command on the File menu
- The Summary button on the File | New dialog box
- Automatic prompt when you first save a file (if the option is enabled)
- The Summary View from the File | Find File dialog box
- Summary Info fields

Using the File | Summary Info Command

The most direct method of accessing summary information is from Word's File menu. You can use this method both to change as well as to examine the editable summary information fields. You can also use this method to examine the statistics for the document.

PROCEDURE 30.1. ENTERING AND EXAMINING SUMMARY INFORMATION.

1. Select File | Summary Info.
2. Word displays the user-settable information dialog box shown in Figure 30.1. Fill in a document Title, Subject, Author, Keywords, and Comments, as desired.

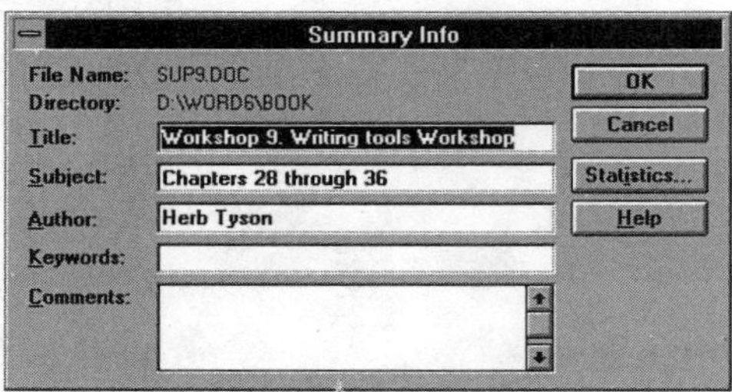

FIGURE 30.1.
Fill in the user-settable information fields, as desired.

3. To see information about the document, click Statistics; click Close to return to the main dialog box.
4. Click OK to close.

SUPER NOTE

Each of the five fill-in areas can hold up to 255 characters apiece.

SUPER TIP

The first time you save a document (assuming you didn't fill in summary information from the New dialog box), Word initially uses the first paragraph of your document (up to 255 characters) as the title. This is a change from previous versions of Word for Windows, in which you actively had to enter a title. Now, you get a default title (the first paragraph in the document), which you are free to change at any time.

In practice, this turns out to be a pretty good default for reports, articles, and other documents that begin with an actual title. It's often not a very good default for correspondence, however, since the first actual line of many letters is the first line of the letterhead. However, if you put your letterhead into a first-page header or use preprinted letterhead, then the title usually ends up being the date. While that's probably better than nothing, it's redundant with other file information and not as useful as the recipient's name or something having to do with the contents of the letter.

Statistics

The Statistics dialog box, shown in Figure 30.2, is not subject to direct user entry. (So, I guess it's really a monologue box.) If you only want to check the upper information and don't want to recalculate the word count, you can press Esc to stop the count. A second press of Esc, or clicking Close, returns you to the main Summary Info dialog box.

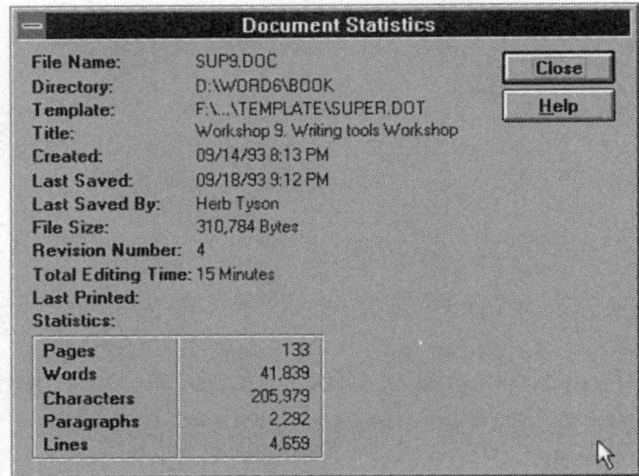

FIGURE 30.2.
The Statistics dialog box gives you the document's vital statistics.

Accessing Summary Info from the File|New Dialog Box

If you're an inveterate self-starter, you probably appreciate the fact that you can access the Summary Info box right from the get-go when you create a document.

PROCEDURE 30.2. ACCESSING SUMMARY INFO WHEN YOU CREATE A FILE.

1. Select **F**ile|**N**ew.
2. Select a **T**emplate from the list of those available.
3. Select the type of file you're creating (**D**ocument or T**e**mplate).
4. Click the **S**ummary button; at this point, Word opens a new window for your document or template and activates the summary information dialog.
5. Fill in the summary information fields.
6. Click OK to begin work.
7. If you change your mind about creating a document, press Ctrl+F4 (select **F**ile|**C**lose).

SUPER NOTE

In Step 4, Word has already created a document or template window for your work. Once you enter any summary information and click OK (Step 6), Word sets the IsDocumentDirty flag to true. (IsDocumentDirty is a function that Word uses, and which you can use from within WordBASIC). When this flag is set to true, Word prompts you to save changes, even if you haven't actually typed anything into the text area yet.

Enabling Automatic Prompt for Summary Info

Many users routinely fill in summary information and never miss a beat. Others among us cringe at the very thought and ignore the heck out of it. Still others of us—most, in fact—use one or two fields, ignoring the rest. The fact that Word 6 creates an automatic title is certainly going to help. You can automate even further, if you like, so that Word reminds you to fill in summary information the first time you save an unnamed document.

PROCEDURE 30.3. ENABLING THE AUTOMATIC PROMPT FOR SUMMARY INFORMATION.

1. Select **T**ools | **O**ptions and click the **S**ave tab.
2. Select Prompt for Summary Info, as shown in Figure 30.3.
3. Click OK.

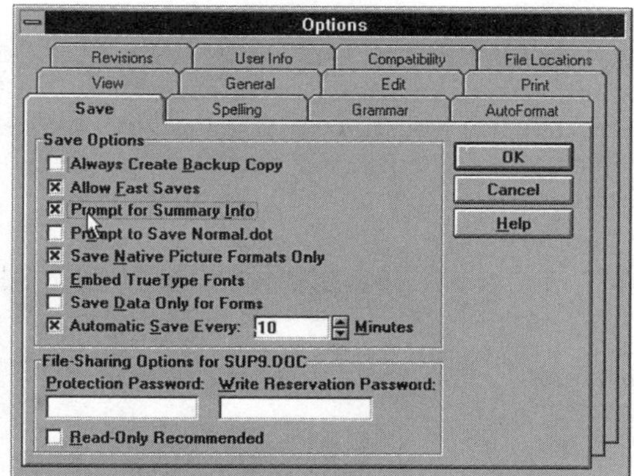

FIGURE 30.3.
If you select the Prompt for Summary Info option, Word won't let you forget!

Viewing Summary Information from the File | Find File Dialog Box

If you're diligent about filling in summary information, all that hard work *finally* begins to pay off for you at the File | Find File dialog box. Using the Find File dialog, you can select summary information as the default view when looking at lists of files. You also can search for files based on summary information. You can even instruct the File | Find File command to list files by title instead of file name.

PROCEDURE 30.4. VIEWING SUMMARY INFORMATION USING FILE | FIND FILE.

1. Select **F**ile | F**i**nd File (Alt+F, F).
2. Click the drop-down arrow to the right of the **V**iew list box (see Figure 30.4).
3. Click Summary.

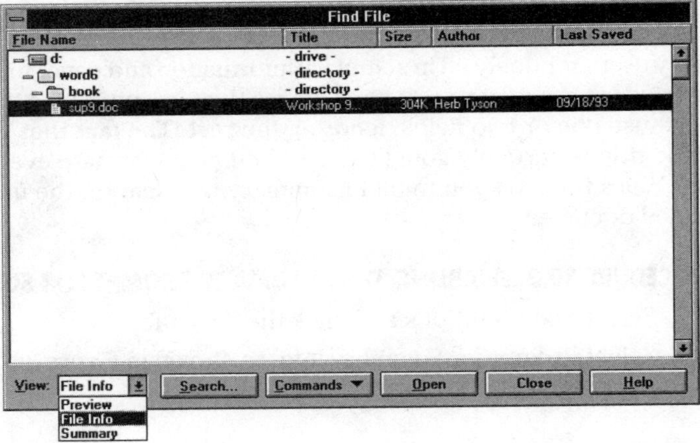

FIGURE 30.4. *Use the View list to tell Find File to show summary information.*

Word now displays the view shown in Figure 30.5. As you scroll through the list of files, the summary information box for each file is displayed. Note also that this summary sheet is different from the one you see when you select **File | Summary Info**. Rather than make you press yet another button to see the statistics, Word displays a compound summary sheet that shows all of it at once.

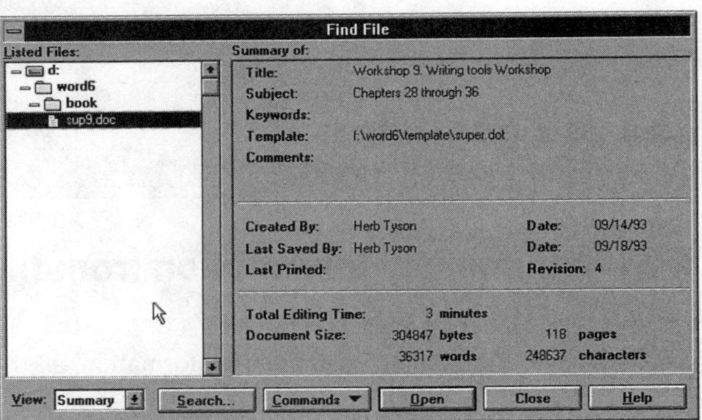

FIGURE 30.5. *With Summary view, you can quickly examine all of the summary information in one fell swoop.*

If a file is open as you're viewing summary information from the Find File dialog box, the statistics you see are those that were stored the last time the document was saved. They often don't agree with the current statistics. However, you can update them without leaving the Find File dialog box, as well as make other adjustments to summary information. However, Word does not update the information displayed in the main Find File view window until you actually save the file that is open.

PROCEDURE 30.5. CHANGING SUMMARY INFORMATION FROM WITHIN FILE|FIND FILE.

1. From the main Find File window, click the **C**ommands button.
2. Choose **S**ummary.
3. Word now displays the same Summary Info dialog it does when you select **F**ile|Summary **I**nfo while editing a document.
4. Make any changes you need to make.
5. If desired, click Stat**i**stics. If a file is open, Word recalculates the word count and other statistics (because the Find File window shows only saved changes already on disk, this information is not passed back to the main Find File view window until the document is actually saved). Click Close to return to the Summary Info dialog.
6. Click OK when finished.

You also can perform searches on the basis of information in the summary fields.

PROCEDURE 30.6. SEARCHING BASED ON SUMMARY INFORMATION.

1. Select **F**ile|**F**ind File.
2. Click the **S**earch button.
3. Click **A**dvanced Search, for the view shown in Figure 30.6.

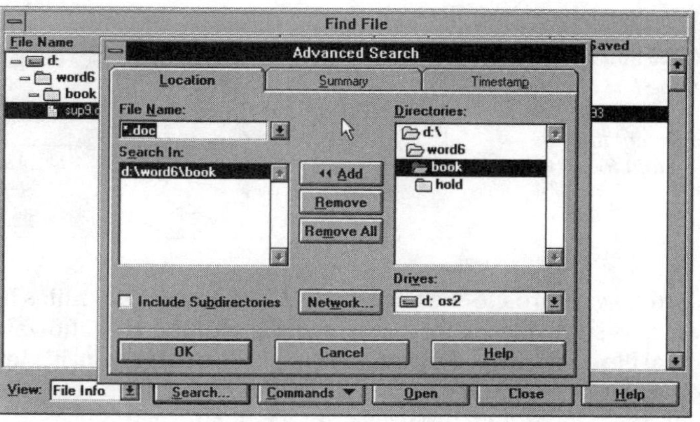

FIGURE 30.6.
Use Advanced Search to set Location, Summary, and Timestamp search criteria.

4. Click the **S**ummary tab to specify search criteria based on summary fields or to search based on document contents.
5. Click the Timestam**p** tab to specify search criteria based on save and creation information.
6. Click the **L**ocation tab to specify the subdirectories and disks to search.
7. Click OK.

8. If desired, click **S**ave Search As to save the search criteria with a name.
9. Click **R**ebuild file list and any other desired options.
10. Click OK to return to the main Find File screen; Word builds a new list based on the new criteria.

SUPER NOTE

See Chapter 8, "Using Find File," for complete details on specifying search criteria for the various Summary and Timestamp fields.

If you've been really diligent about entering useful file titles, you can effectively use those titles as if they were expanded file names. The Find File command gives you the option of displaying files by their titles instead of by their actual file names.

PROCEDURE 30.7. DISPLAYING FILES BY TITLE INSTEAD OF FILE NAME.

1. From the main Find File dialog box, click **C**ommands.
2. Choose Sor**t**ing.
3. Click List Files by **T**itle under List Files By, as shown in Figure 30.7.
4. Click OK.

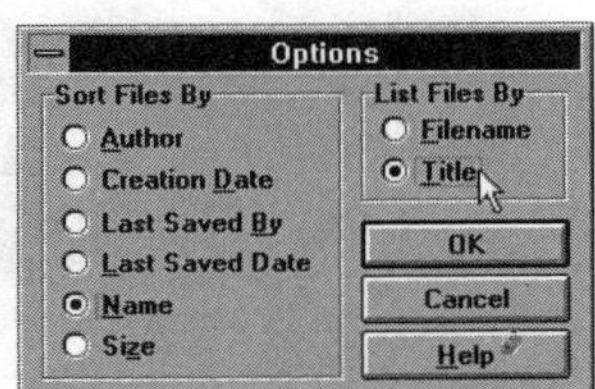

FIGURE 30.7.
Set the List Files by Title option to use document titles as the main focus.

Word now returns to the File Find window and displays files by title rather than by file name, as shown in Figure 30.8. Regardless of the view, however, Word still shows the actual file name. That information isn't hidden from you; it's just that you get the added convenience of seeing file titles all the time, with titles being the focus rather than being a kind of "Oh, and by the way…" piece of information.

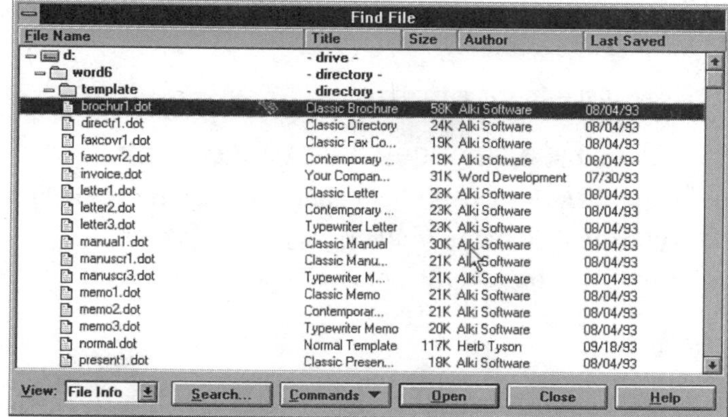

FIGURE 30.8.
When listed by title, Word still shows the file name, but it's no longer the center of attention.

Using and Changing Summary Information with Fields

One of the best uses of summary information is to create useful headers for documents. Headers for reports, letters, and other documents can be entirely self-creating if you use document summary information in a consistent manner. Consider, for example, a header that consists of the following (appropriately formatted, of course):

```
{Title}
{Author}
{Date}
Page {Page} of {NumPages}
```

For documents that use a true title as the first paragraph, this header is completely automatic (assuming that your document titles aren't unmanageably long).

As discussed in Chapter 29, "Fields," you can use summary information fields not only to display information in a document but to change it as well. Creating a field just to change the document title or subject is hardly ever more efficient than selecting **F**ile | Summary **I**nfo from the menu. However, in automating some documents, the fact that you can do so gives you additional flexibility. The following summary information fields can be used to update and display document information:

```
Author ["new"]
Comments ["new"]
Keywords ["new"]
Subject ["new"]
Title ["new"]
```

You can display information for any of the preceding simply by enclosing the keyword (`Author`, `Comments`, and so on) in field delimiters. You can change the information by including optional new text (enclosed in quotes if it's more than one word) after the field name. For example:

```
{info keywords "data automation"}
```

PROCEDURE 30.8. INSERTING AN INFORMATION FIELD.

1. Press Ctrl+F9 to insert field characters, as shown in Figure 30.9.
2. Type the field name (*Author*, *Subject*, *Keywords*, and so on).
3. Press F9 to update the field and display the result.

FIGURE 30.9.
Field characters look like curly braces.

SUPER NOTE

Unfortunately, the `\h` (hide result) switch does not work with information fields. So, if you only want to use this procedure to update information fields, you also will need to select and delete the field you just inserted. If you're looking for an ergonomic replacement for File|Summary Info, you haven't found it. If, however, you hate dialog boxes, this is one way to produce the information without ever having to look at a dialog box.

In the case of the Keywords field, instead of replacing the existing set of keywords, you might often wish to add to the list of existing keywords. The preceding procedure won't do that. It just replaces any existing keywords. If you want to add to the list of keywords, a field-oriented procedure then becomes hopelessly complicated, and not worth the effort. Just bite the bullet, select **F**ile|Summary **I**nfo, and add to the end of the current list.

You also can display the noneditable document information fields. *Noneditable* means that their contents cannot be edited by you directly. Instead, they are updated as the document changes. The noneditable document information fields are

```
CreateDate
EditTime
FileName
FileSize
LastSavedBy
NumChars
```

```
NumPages
NumWords
PrintDate
SaveDate
RevNum
Template
```

See Chapter 29, “Fields,” and Appendix B, “Field Types,” for additional information on these fields.

Chapter

31

Bookmarks and Cross-References

A bookmark is a way of naming a point or an area in a Word document so that it can be easily located or referenced. Bookmarks can be used for something as simple as a place marker. They are essential when you want to refer to parts of a document elsewhere (for example, when using table results outside a table). They can also be cornerstones in setting up boilerplate creation of documents, as well as reference points for automatic macros and envelope addressing.

Understanding and Displaying Bookmarks

You can have any number of bookmarks in a document. However, any given bookmark in a document you create is unique. If you create a bookmark called `here` and later create a bookmark somewhere else called `here`, the new one replaces the old one. If you paste or insert material from another file into the current document, its bookmarks come with it. If the current document already has bookmarks by the same name, however, the bookmarks in the current document are preserved, and the bookmarks in the text you add are erased (the bookmarks—not the text itself).

Bookmarks can be a single point or a range of text. The same section of text can have multiple bookmarks. Bookmarks can also overlap. A useful option when working with bookmarks is to turn on their display. This often can alleviate confusion about them. Unfortunately, while you can display the presence of bookmarks on-screen, there is no way to examine a selection of text to determine which bookmarks are in that selection.

PROCEDURE 31.1. CONTROLLING THE DISPLAY OF BOOKMARKS.

1. Select Tools | Options.
2. Click the View tab.
3. In the Show section, click Bookmarks; an `X` beside it causes bookmarks to display, as shown in Figure 31.1.
4. Click OK.

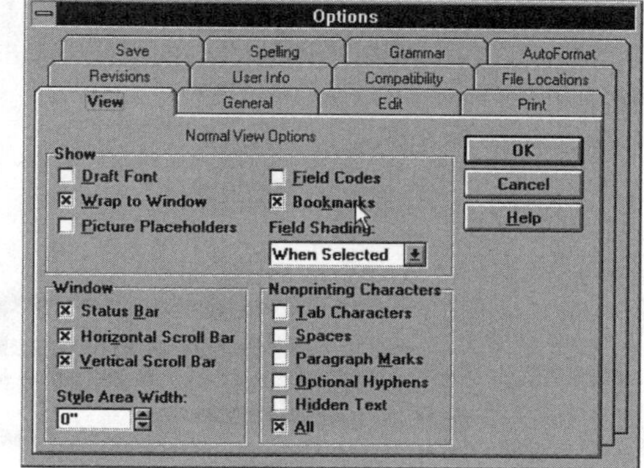

FIGURE 31.1.
Use the View to make bookmarks stand out.

Inserting Bookmarks

Bookmarks can be inserted by using a keystroke or the menu. When creating a bookmark name, unless it is just a temporary placeholder, it pays to give at least a little careful thought to the names so that you can remember them later on.

PROCEDURE 31.2. INSERTING A BOOKMARK.

1. Select the text you want to name (if you're bookmarking a table, make sure Num Lock is off and press Alt+5 on the number pad).
2. Select **E**dit | **B**ookmark (Ctrl+Shift+F5).
3. Type a **B**ookmark Name.
4. Select the **A**dd button.

SUPER NOTE

If a bookmark by the same name already exists, pressing Enter in Step 4 selects the Go To button instead of the Add button.

Going to a Bookmark

To go to a bookmark, use **E**dit | **G**o To. If the bookmark is a single point, the insertion point is moved to it. If the bookmark is a block of text, the text is selected. Be careful, therefore, in what you do immediately after going to a bookmark. If the Typing Replaces Selection option is enabled, pressing a key could delete the bookmarked text.

PROCEDURE 31.3. GOING TO A BOOKMARK.

1. Select Edit | Go To (press Ctrl+G), to display the dialog box shown in Figure 31.2.
2. Click Bookmark in the Go to What list.
3. Type the name of the bookmark into the Enter Bookmark Name field.
4. Press Enter.

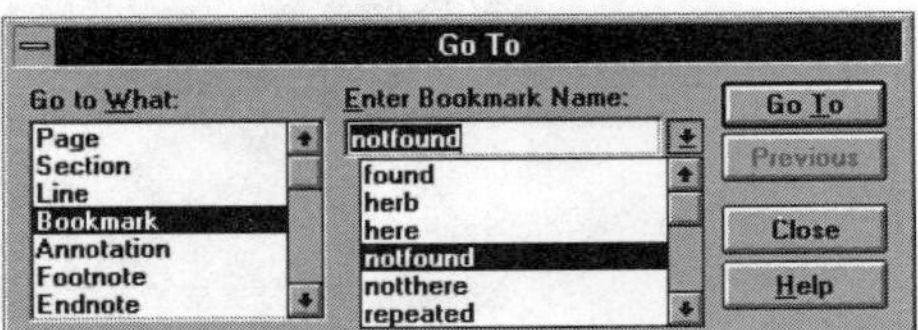

FIGURE 31.2.
Use Edit | Go To to find bookmarks.

SUPER TIP

Skip Step 2 and just type the bookmark name into the Enter field, regardless of what's displaying in the Go to What list. The Go to What categories are designed to facilitate using the bookmark feature for people who don't already know how. Once you know how, however, having to make a detour in the Go to What list is a needless encumbrance. If you have a bookmark by the name you type, Go To takes you there. Otherwise, if there's a built-in bookmark that matches what you typed, Word takes you there (see the following section for more about built-in bookmarks). For example, `p1` generally means "page 1." If you create a bookmark by that name, however, then typing `p1` into the Enter field takes you to your bookmark, even if Page is selected in the Go to What field.

Built-in Bookmarks

Word has a number of built-in bookmarks you can use. They are especially useful in macros, but you may find them convenient in other types of navigation as well. To use them, just type the bookmark as you would any other. For example, type `\CELL` to select the current cell in a table, `\HEADINGLEVEL` to select everything in the current heading level, or `\SECTION` to select the whole current section.

The built-in bookmarks are shown in Table 31.1. Some of them, like `\ENDOFSEL`, `\STARTOFSEL`, and `\STARTOFDOC`, are really only useful in macros because their keyboard equivalents are much easier to manage. Others, like `\d` (for field) are gems in that they give you a means to go to specific types of fields without having to display field codes.

Table 31.1. Built-in bookmarks for use with the Go To command.

Bookmark Name	*Result*
`\CELL`	Selects the current cell in a table.
`\CHAR`	Selects the current character.
`\DOC`	Selects the entire document.
`\ENDOFSEL`	Cancels selection and moves cursor to the end of the selection.
`\HEADINGLEVEL`	Selects the entire current heading level.
`\LINE`	Selects the current line.
`\PARA`	Selects the current paragraph.
`\PREVSEL1`	Moves the cursor to the site of the most recent edit.
`\PREVSEL2`	Moves the cursor to the site of the second most recent edit.
`\SECTION`	Selects the current section.
`\SEL`	The current selection (use with the CmpBookmarks macro function).
`\STARTOFDOC`	Moves to the beginning of the document.
`\STARTOFSEL`	Cancels selection and moves cursor to the start of the selection.
`\TABLE`	Selects the current table.
`a[+/-]`*n*	Moves to the next/previous annotation or to annotation *n*.
`s[+/-]`*n*	Moves to the beginning of section *n* (can be `+` or `-` relative to current).
`[p][+/-]`*n*	Moves to the beginning of page *n*.
`[blank]`	Moves to the start of the next page.
`l[+/-]`*n*	Moves to line *n*.
`d[-]'`*field*`'`	Moves to the next (`-` previous) *field*; for example, `-d'seq'` moves to the previous `{seq label}` field (omitting *field* takes you to the next/previous field, regardless of type). Note: This wonderful command works even when field codes are not displayed!
`e[+/-]`*n*	Moves to endnote *n* (`e-` moves to the previous endnote).
`f[+/-]`*n*	Moves to footnote *n* (`f+` moves to the next footnote; `f1` moves you to the first footnote).
`g[+/-]`	Moves to next or previous graphic.
`q[+/-]`	Moves you to the next or previous equation object.

continues

Table 31.1. continued

Bookmark Name	*Result*
`o[+/]`*object*	Moves you to the next or previous *object* type; for example `o'word art'`.
`t[+/-]`	Moves to the next or previous table.
`%`*n*	Moves absolutely to *n* percentage of the document.

SUPER NOTE

For bookmarks indicated with `+/-`, `+` without a number means "next", and `-` without a number mean "previous." When you use `+` or `-` with a number, *n*, it means to move forward or backward from the current location by the number of items (footnotes, fields, and so forth) specified by *n*. For example, `f+4` means to move ahead to the fourth footnote from the current location. If you omit `+` or `-` and include a number, *n*, then Word goes to *n*th item. Specifying `f4`, for example, tells Word to move to the fourth footnote, counting from the beginning of the document, not the fourth relative to the current insertion point. If you omit a sign (`+/-`) and also don't specify a number, then Word just moves to the next item of that type (for example, `g` tells Word to move to the next graphic).

Go Back

In addition to bookmarks you create and built-in bookmarks, Word also has a *de facto* built-in bookmark of the insertion point and the last three locations where editing occurred in your document. The GoBack (Shift+F5) key toggles the selection among the current and previous three locations where editing occurred. Just press Shift+F5.

SUPER TIP

When you first open a document, pressing Shift+F5 moves the insertion point to where it was when the document was last closed. If you already have other documents open, however, the GoBack command may take you back to the previous location in the other document instead. The GoBack command remembers for all documents open, not just the current window. This lessens GoBack's utility and predictability when working with multiple documents. However, if you generally work with one document at a time, it's a handy thing to know.

Modifying Bookmarks

You can modify a bookmark at any time simply by selecting the text you want bookmarked and reapplying the name. The intention of Word's designers is that bookmarks be as accessible and movable as real bookmarks made out of paper or leather. Because a real book doesn't prompt `"Are you sure?"` when you move a bookmark, neither does Word. One just wishes that other Word commands would give the user as much credit for native intelligence (or at least provide the option to suppress all of the `"Are you sure?"` prompts).

Deleting Bookmarks

Deleting bookmarks is easy. It's not generally necessary, because bookmarks don't really take up much room. However, when preparing documents and templates for others to use, it's not a bad idea to tidy up to avoid confusing others.

PROCEDURE 31.4. DELETING BOOKMARKS.

1. Select **E**dit | **B**ookmark.
2. Select the bookmark you want to remove.
3. Click Delete.

Bookmark Applications

Aside from being handy ways to remember where you are and where you were, bookmarks have a number of essential uses in Word. They are used in quoting (including) sections of other Word documents, in performing table math (as shown in Chapter 20, "Table Math"), as well as in setting up cross references. See Chapter 43, "Indexing," and Chapter 44, "Cross References," for additional information and specific procedures.

Chapter

32

AutoCorrect, AutoText, and the Spike

Two of the best features for writers in Word for Windows are AutoCorrect and AutoText. Both are ways to create shorthands for frequently needed text and graphics. AutoCorrect is new in Word 6. AutoText, the manual counterpart, is Word's new name for Glossary, a long misnamed feature that's been a part of Word for years.

AutoCorrect

At long last, Word for Windows finally has a long yearned-for enhancement for writers. It's called AutoCorrect. While not as powerful as the fabled "writer's dream" program, XyWrite, Word's implementation adds new dimensions in utility.

AutoCorrect is the capability of Word to automatically expand user-created shorthands into longer forms. For example, wouldn't it be convenient if, each time you typed a set of initials, the name of your organization suddenly appeared; or if anytime you accidentally typed `teh` instead of `the`, Word automatically corrected it? Perhaps you'd like for Word to automatically fix those annoying typos that occur when you accidentally capitalize the first two letters of CHicago. Well, now you have it. In fact, I had to work overtime to get `the` and `CHicago` to stay put. Each time I typed them, Word automatically corrected them!

Enabling AutoCorrect

The AutoCorrect feature is enabled from the Tools menu. The AutoCorrect dialog box controls not only user-defined AutoCorrect features but also independent features controlled by Word that can operate even when the automatic replacement feature is not turned on.

PROCEDURE 32.1. ENABLING AUTOCORRECT.

1. Select Tools | Auto Correct to display the dialog box shown in Figure 32.1.
2. Enable or disable the independent AutoCorrect options (described following this procedure).
3. To enable automatic replacement as you type, click the Replace Text as You Type checkbox.
4. Click OK.

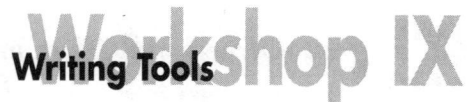

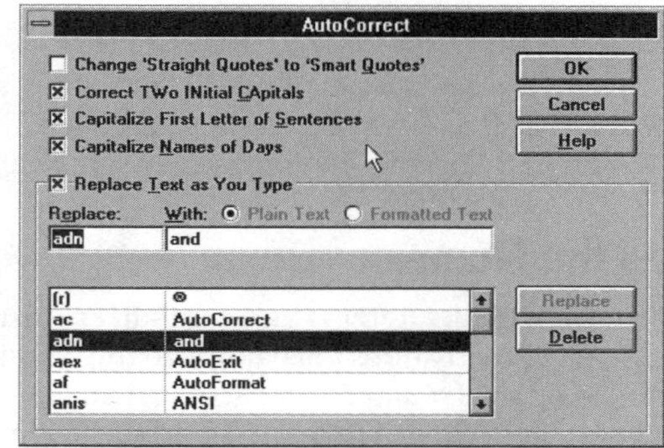

FIGURE 32.1.
The AutoCorrect options can be set independently.

Change 'Straight Quotes' to 'Smart Quotes'

When you press the ' or " keys on your computer keyboard, most computer programs obligingly respond by putting a ' or a " on the screen and embedding an ASCII 39 or 34 character into your file. The advent of the ANSI character set, however, brought additional options sometimes known as typographic quotes. The left and right versions curve to enclose the text, producing ‘this’ or “that” rather than "this".

Word optionally can convert ' and " to the correct left or right single or double quotes as you type. To determine which of the two characters to insert, Word has to quickly examine the context. It has to be “smart”—hence, “smart quotes.” Whether or not using them is smart, however, depends on your work. Right now, for example, I don’t know if I should be using them or not. I suppose the editors will tell me later, after they’ve read this section.

In any case, if you select this option, Word automatically replaces ' (ASCII 39) with ‘ or ’ (ANSI 0145 and 0146, respectively), depending on the context. All apostrophes used in contractions are changed to '. Word also changes " into “ and ” (ANSI 0147 and 0148, respectively), which may or may not be what you want when you type 30°36’43”. Then again, 30°36'43"may not be what you want, either. You also and most definitely don’t want the typographic quotes when writing WordBASIC programs. For better or worse, Word disables the AutoCorrect feature when you’re writing in a macro window, so it’s not a problem. It is, however, if you’re writing a book that aims to produce correct syntax for macros! Fortunately, Word converts the curved quotes into straight quotes when you export a Word document to a text file.

Correct TWo INitial CApitals

Some features require no additional explanation. This one speaks for itself. The only time you might want to be careful is in typing stylized names that might actually be correct that way.

Capitalize the First Letter of Sentences

This feature can automatically capitalize the first letter of sentences, and it's smart enough to know that `i.e.` isn't the end of a sentence. If your sentence ends like `this.` however, Word won't know to capitalize the word that follows.

Capitalize the Names of Days

This feature automatically detects and capitalizes the names of the days of the week. Oddly enough, it correctly does *not* capitalize the names of the days of the week when you're writing in Spanish (that is, with **T**ools | **L**anguage set to Spanish). When you're writing in Spanish, however, Word does continue to capitalize the English days. Therefore, it's impossible to tell if the lack of capitalization in Spanish is because Word knows the correct thing to do or because it doesn't know about Spanish days.

Replace Text as You Type

Enable this option to have shorthands and frequently mistyped words automatically change to the desired text as you type. AutoCorrect entries you create, along with some preinstalled corrections that come with Word, automatically change to their respective replacement text as you type.

The replacement occurs immediately if you type a space following the replace item. If you type a nonalphabetic character other than a space, however, the replacement doesn't occur until you type a space, press Enter, or press Shift+Enter after it.

For example, if you have an AutoCorrect entry ac with replacement text of `AutoCorrect` and type `ac<space>` or `ac<enter>`, the replacement occurs immediately. However, if you type ac<s followed by any other nonalphabetic character(s)—ac<s, for example—the shorthand doesn't get replaced until you type a space, press Enter or Shift+Enter.

SUPER NOTE

The AutoCorrect entry you type must not have any alphabetic characters between it and the nearest space, carriage return, line return, or cell division to the left and right. Thus, something like `Tools¦ac` does not cause the ac to be replaced. If you fail to type a space after the end of a sentence (for example, `this is the end.ac`), the entry also does not expand. However, the entry does expand, even if you have a wall of separators to the left and right, as long as they are not alphabetic. For example, if for some ungodly reason, you type

```
1234567 890)(*& ^%#@!ac!@#$%^&*()1234567890
```

the deeply buried ac is replaced with the replacement text just as soon as you type a space or press Enter.

Creating AutoCorrect Entries

You can create AutoCorrect entries either by using the menu or by selecting replacement text you've already typed.

PROCEDURE 32.2. CREATING AUTOCORRECT ENTRIES USING THE MENU.

1. Select **T**ools | **A**uto Correct.
2. Ensure that Replace **T**ext as You Type is selected.
3. Type what you want replaced into the Re**p**lace field (for example, `nyc`). The replace text can be up to 31 characters long, but that's hardly a shorthand.
4. Type the replacement text into the **W**ith field (for example, `New York City`). When creating AutoCorrect entries this way, you are allowed up to 255 characters.
5. Click **A**dd.
6. Repeat Steps 3 through 5 to create additional AutoCorrect entries, if desired.
7. Click OK.

NOTE

When AutoCorrect entries are created this way, the **P**lain Text option is preselected because Word can't read formatting in the dialog box.

PROCEDURE 32.3. CREATING AUTOCORRECT ENTRIES WITH SELECTED TEXT.

1. Select the text you want to be the replacement text. It can be any size and can include objects and graphics.
2. Select **T**ools | **A**uto Correct.
3. Select the **F**ormatted Text option.
4. Click **A**dd.
5. Click OK.

Modifying AutoCorrect

Plain text AutoCorrect entries can be edited directly from the AutoCorrect dialog box. Formatted text entries, however, cannot be edited directly.

PROCEDURE 32.4. MODIFYING A PLAIN TEXT AUTOCORRECT ENTRY.

1. Select **T**ools | **A**uto Correct.
2. Select the Re**p**lace entry in the replace list. Do not type the entry; it must be selected from the list.

3. Click in the **W**ith text box and make any changes.
4. Click the Repl**a**ce button to overwrite the previous definition; click **Y**es when Word prompts to confirm the change.
5. Click OK or Close.

Modifying a formatted text AutoCorrect entry requires a little more work. You must first insert the entry, make the change(s), and then re-create the entry using the modified section.

PROCEDURE 32.5. MODIFYING A FORMATTED TEXT AUTOCORRECT ENTRY.

1. Using an empty new document window as a workspace, type the AutoCorrect shorthand and type a space or press Enter to expand it into the replacement text.
2. Modify the expanded text.
3. Select the portion of the text that you want to redefine.
4. Select **T**ools | **A**uto Correct.
5. Type the shorthand entry in the Re**p**lace field.
6. Select **F**ormatted Text.
7. Click Repl**a**ce.
8. Click **Y**es to confirm the replacement.
9. Click OK or Close.

Deleting AutoCorrect Entries

Given that AutoCorrect entries take up space in NORMAL.DOT, you may periodically want to clear out large entries you no longer need.

PROCEDURE 32.6. DELETING UNWANTED AUTOCORRECT ENTRIES.

1. Select **T**ools | **A**uto Correct.
2. Type the shorthand entry in the Re**p**lace field.
3. Click **D**elete.
4. Repeat Steps 2 and 3 to remove any additional entries you no longer need.
5. Click OK or Close.

NORMAL.DOT

AutoCorrect entries are stored in NORMAL.DOT. You cannot store different AutoCorrect entries in different templates, nor can you specify different AutoCorrect behavior for different templates. The only way to create different sets of AutoCorrect entries is by systematically creating and renaming your NORMAL.DOT file. Even if you rename your NORMAL.DOT file to something else and make it global using the Templates and Add-ins dialog box, however, the embedded AutoCorrect entries are not accessible until you rename the file as NORMAL.DOT and replace any other NORMAL.DOT file that might be in your template directory.

Formatted AutoCorrect entries can be any size and can include graphics. For this reason, if you include a number of large entries, don't be surprised if your NORMAL.DOT file suddenly starts getting huge. The AutoCorrect feature hasn't been tested long enough yet to determine if huge NORMAL.DOT files create a problem. However, you might want to exercise some caution nonetheless. A better strategy for associating large blocks of text with AutoCorrect entries might be to enclose such passages in bookmarked areas of document files and then refer to them using bookmark fields. You could assign the bookmark field as the replacement text instead of assigning large blocks of text.

AutoText

AutoText is Word's new name for what used to be Glossary. AutoText entries are nearly identical to AutoCorrect entries in performance, except that you must press a key combination or select Edit | AutoText to cause the AutoText shorthand to expand into full form.

Creating AutoText Entries

Unlike AutoCorrect entries, AutoText entries can be created using only selected text. Also unlike AutoCorrect entries, AutoText entries can be stored in different templates for use in different kinds of documents.

PROCEDURE 32.7. CREATING AN AUTOTEXT ENTRY.

1. Select the text for which you want to create an AutoText entry.
2. Choose Edit | AutoText from the menu.
3. In the Name field, type a name for the AutoText entry. The name can be up to 32 characters.
4. Under Make AutoText Entry Available To, select the appropriate template.
5. Click Add.

Like formatted AutoCorrect entries, AutoText entries can be as large as you like. Keep in mind, however, that they get stored in templates and can increase the memory resources required to use specific templates. A much better strategy for long boilerplate text is to use bookmarked sections of boilerplate documents.

Inserting (Expanding) AutoText Entries

There are three ways to insert (or expand) AutoText entries:

- Keyboard (F3)
- The AutoText button on the toolbar (see Figure 32.2)
- Edit | AutoText from the menu

FIGURE 32.2.
It's hard to imagine someone using it instead of F3, but the AutoText button expands AutoText entries.

Use either the keyboard or the toolbar if you want to insert the AutoText as formatted text, using any original paragraph and direct formatting that was copied to the AutoText definition. Use the menu if you need to suppress the original formatting.

PROCEDURE 32.8. EXPANDING AN AUTOTEXT ENTRY USING THE TOOLBAR OR THE KEYBOARD.

1. Type the name of the AutoText entry.
2. Click the AutoText tool in the Standard toolbar or press F3.

SUPER TIP

You don't have to type the whole name. Word requires at least the first two letters of each AutoText entry name containing two or more characters. If the first few letters are enough to uniquely identify the AutoText entry, you can type just that much and then press F3 (or Alt+Ctrl+V). To see how much you have to type, select Edit | AutoText and type the first few letters of the entry name. Word zeros in on the entry as you narrow it down by typing more letters. When the entry you want moves into the Preview box, you will know how much of the name you'll need to type in the text to get it to expand. In effect, the first entry under each letter in the alphabet can be expanded using just the first two letters in the name.

PROCEDURE 32.9. EXPANDING AN AUTOTEXT ENTRY USING THE MENU.

1. Select **E**dit | AutoTe**x**t.
2. Type enough of the entry name for the expanded form to display in the Preview box.
3. Select **F**ormatted or **P**lain Text (the degree of difference, if any, depends on the state of the text when the AutoText definition was created).
4. Click **I**nsert.

SUPER NOTE

AutoText text is formatted when it is created, taking on the formatting of the selected text. What this means later on, however, depends on how much formatting is applied using styles versus direct formatting, as well as whether the selection encompasses a paragraph mark. If the selection does not cross any paragraph or table cell boundaries, the no-style information is conveyed with the formatting. Additionally, if all formatting was applied using a style instead of direct formatting, then that too does not go into the AutoText definition. In most instances, no differences exist among the three different methods for expanding an AutoText entry. If, on the other hand, direct formatting was applied (for example, a different point size), that formatting is included in the definition, and selecting Plain versus Formatted does make a difference.

For example, if the current style is Heading 1 and the selection is a phrase in a heading but does not contain any direct (variant) formatting and no paragraph marks, then there is no difference between inserting it as formatted or plain text. The expanded AutoText takes on whatever formatting is in effect at the time it is inserted.

If the current style is Heading 1 and the selection is a phrase that is formatted differently and does not contain any paragraph marks, then only the differential aspects are copied to the AutoText entry formatting. If the underlying style is 12-point Arial and the selected text is 14-point Arial, only the 14-point aspect goes with the style; the fact that it's Arial does not. When you insert the entry, selecting the Formatted Text option inserts text that is 14-point, but all other formatting is identical to that in the passage in which it's inserted.

If the selection contains paragraph marks, then the style associated with the text in those paragraphs, along with any variant formatting, is copied to the AutoText entry. Any partial paragraphs that do not have paragraph marks in the selection do not take any of the original

formatting with them. When you insert such an entry into a document, selecting the Formatted Text option results in part of the text blending in and the part with paragraph marks retaining the original style name from the selection in effect when it was defined.

Modifying AutoText Entries

AutoText entries must be modified in the same manner as AutoCorrect entries.

PROCEDURE 32.10. MODIFYING AN AUTOTEXT ENTRY.

1. Using an empty new document window as a workspace, type the AutoText name and press F3 to insert the long form into the document (alternatively, if you have a section of text you want to use as the replacement for the existing text, just select it and proceed to Step 4).
2. Modify the text.
3. Select the text that you want to use for the modified entry.
4. Select **E**dit | AutoTe**x**t.
5. Type the shorthand entry in the Re**p**lace field.
6. Select **F**ormatted Text.
7. Click **R**eplace.
8. Click **Y**es to confirm the replacement.
9. Click OK or Close.

Deleting AutoText Entries

AutoText entries are stored with templates and are loaded when the template is in use. Keeping many long entries (especially ones that contain graphics) can have an impact on performance and memory. So, it's advisable to periodically cull out the unneeded entries.

PROCEDURE 32.11. DELETING UNWANTED AUTOTEXT ENTRIES.

1. Select **E**dit | AutoTe**x**t.
2. Type the shorthand entry in the **N**ame field or select it from the list.
3. Click **D**elete.
4. Repeat Steps 2 and 3 to remove any additional entries you no longer need.
5. Click Close.

The Spike

The Spike is a special AutoText entry that Word creates for you. In addition to **Edit | Clear** and **Edit | Cut**, there is a third kind of deletion that has not been discussed yet. It's called Spiking. Named for those bureaucratic weapons that decorate the desks of receipt-collectors, the Spike is used to collect text you delete, with an odd little twist. Rather than collecting just the pieces, Word adds to each piece the paragraph mark from the paragraph in which text resided at the time it was spiked.

Like the desk version, Word's Spike collects deletions to it in LIFO (last in, first out) order, with the oldest deletions at the bottom and the most recent deletions at the top. Unlike the desk version, however, Word's Spike can't regurgitate its contents piece by piece. Instead, it can only dump the whole pile all at once, including the paragraph marks.

The Spike is useful for collecting bits and pieces that you want to use elsewhere. While its habit of collecting paragraph marks may seem a little annoying, it actually serves a purpose. Because it collects paragraph marks, you have the option of retaining the native formatting of each inhabitant of the Spike. With such cultural diversity, each little bit of the Spike is capable of seeding other paragraphs, each with the original style of its founding father, so to speak. Unfortunately, the Spike insists on deleting the original each time it's used, making the built-in feature not as useful as it would be if you had the option of adding to the Spike without gutting the original document. However, stay tuned....

PROCEDURE 32.12. DELETING TO THE SPIKE (OR, LET'S GO SPIKING!).

1. Select the text you want to Spike.
2. Press Ctrl+F3.

SUPER TIP

If you immediately press Alt+Backspace or Ctrl+Z to undo the deletion, the addition to the Spike is not undone. Thus, you can use the Ctrl+F3, Ctrl+Z combination to add stuff to the Spike without ruining the original document. Clever, eh?

PROCEDURE 32.13. INSERTING AND CLEARING THE SPIKE.

1. Position the cursor where you want the Spike spewed.
2. Press Ctrl+Shift+F3 (InsertSpike).

SUPER NOTE

The InsertSpike command inserts the contents of the Spike and deletes the AutoText entry at the same time.

PROCEDURE 32.14. INSERTING THE SPIKE WITHOUT CLEARING IT.

1. Position the cursor where you want the Spike spewed.
2. Type `Spike`.
3. Press F3 (ta da!).

The Spike can be inserted as often as you like in this manner without clearing the contents. Just use it as an ordinary AutoText entry. One imagines that the reason for the default behavior is that Microsoft figures that the Spike can get pretty big and you won't want it hanging around cluttering up your templates once you've inserted it elsewhere. That's generally not a bad assumption. However, for those times that it is not a correct assumption for *you*, just use the Spike as an AutoText entry.

Printing AutoText Entries

Word provides a method for printing your AutoText entries. You might want to do that from time to time to see what's there, because Word's performance can be improved dramatically by clearing out the deadwood. Printing the AutoText entries lets you examine the wood to determine if, in fact, it's dead.

PROCEDURE 32.15. PRINTING AUTOTEXT ENTRIES.

1. Open a document based on the template whose AutoText entries you want to print (for NORMAL.DOT, just selecting **F**ile | **N**ew with the defaults is sufficient).
2. Select **F**ile | **P**rint.
3. Using the drop-down arrow beside **P**rint What, select AutoText entries.
4. Select any additional options you might want.
5. Click OK.

Chapter 33

Annotations

Annotation is the process of adding notes to a document. Depending on what you do, you may sometimes need to have your work reviewed or commented upon by other Word users. When you do, annotation is often the best way to solicit those comments.

Annotations are a special type of endnote. They are distinct from the text and are marked by the initials set in the User Info area (**T**ools | **O**ptions | **U**ser Info). Word enables you to add both written and voice annotations.

SUPER CAUTION

Voice annotations sound niftier than they are. First, given license to talk, people are seldom as concise as you'd like them to be. Second, if the reviewer does manage to say something profound, you're stuck transcribing it to make use of it. Third, voice annotations take up an incredible amount of disk space. Unless you have gobs and gobs of disk space, as well as a convenient method for transferring the annotated file among users, voice annotations are not nearly as good an idea as they might seem at first.

Annotation is a bit friendlier than revision because the annotations are distinct from the text and don't clutter it up so much. It's also easier to cut and slice the added notes in your own way rather than in a way that might be incompatible with your style. All in all, annotations are a good idea and vastly underutilized. They're not perfect, mind you. Ideally, when you're reading a document, it would be nice to see the annotations on the same pages to which they apply. Unfortunately, Word doesn't enable you to do that. When you print annotations, they're printed at the end.

Locking a Document for Annotations

Before you give a document to someone for annotation, it's often a good idea to lock the document so that that's the only kind of editing that can be performed. After all, the person reviewing your work may not be as expert in using Word as you are. They may not know the difference between annotations and revisions. Heck, they may think that annotate means for them to edit it like crazy.

PROCEDURE 33.1. LOCKING A DOCUMENT FOR ANNOTATIONS.

1. Select **T**ools | **P**rotect Document.
2. Click **A**nnotations (see Figure 33.1).
3. If you think the reviewer won't get the message, type a password. Word prompts you to retype the same password to protect you against accidentally typing something you didn't notice.
4. Click OK.

FIGURE 33.1.
Word enables you to protect your documents so they can be annotated but not edited.

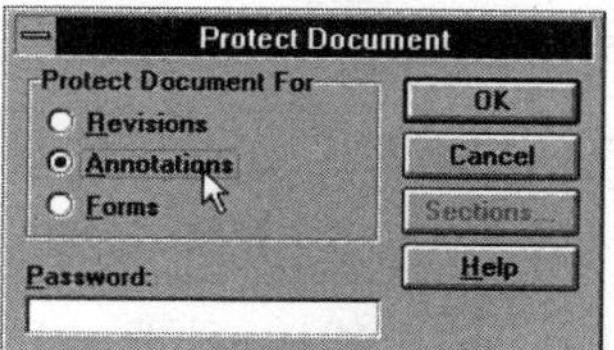

To unlock a document, reverse the procedure.

PROCEDURE 33.2. UNLOCKING A DOCUMENT FOR ANNOTATIONS.

1. Select **T**ools | Un**p**rotect Document.
2. Word prompts for the password; type the password and press Enter.

Inserting Annotations

Annotations are inserted very much the same way as endnotes and footnotes. Annotations are numbered sequentially in a document. The initials of the reviewer appear in color and in brackets at the point where each annotation is inserted along with the number of the annotation, as shown in Figure 33.2.

FIGURE 33.2.
The reviewers' initials identify who said what.

shown·in·Figure·33-2.[HT1]¶

Figure·33-2.·The·reviewers'·initials·identify·who·said·what.¶

PROCEDURE 33.3. INSERTING AN ANNOTATION.

1. Select **I**nsert | **A**nnotation.
2. An annotation pane opens, as shown in Figure 33.3. Type your annotation, including graphics and sound if you like. Note: You do not need to press Enter in your annotation unless it spans multiple paragraphs. Word automatically separates different annotations for you.
3. If you insist on recording a sound annotation, click the Record icon and keep it short and to the point.
4. Click Close to close the annotation pane. Note: You can keep the annotation pane open if you like and use the F6 key to toggle between the document and annotation pane.

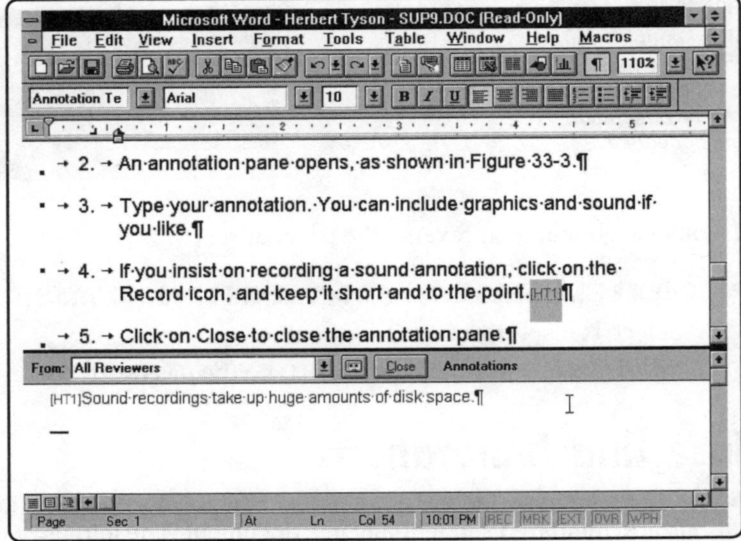

FIGURE 33.3.
Annotations are inserted in an annotation pane. Use F6 to switch between the annotation and the document windows.

When working with annotations, keep the following tips and pointers in mind:

- You can make the annotation window as large or small as you like by dragging the split box on the vertical scroll bar, as shown in Figure 33.4.
- To insert additional annotations while leaving the annotation pane open, select **I**nsert | **A**nnotation again. Word creates a new `[initials]#` mark for each distinct annotation you insert.
- When you select an annotation in the annotation pane, Word automatically moves the document pane to the location of the annotation mark.
- You can create an AutoCorrect or AutoText entry for an empty annotation mark and use it to insert subsequent annotations.

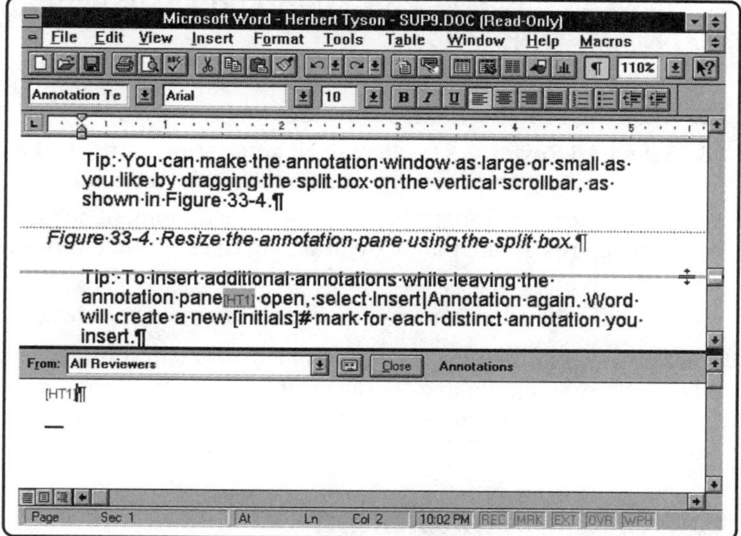

FIGURE 33.4.
Resize the annotation pane using the split box.

Displaying, Editing, and Viewing Annotations

Annotation markers are created as hidden text. This gives you the option of ignoring even their markers when you want. While you are creating annotation, annotation marks are visible in your document. When you close the annotation pane, annotation marks cease being visible unless you have hidden text turned on for display.

PROCEDURE 33.4. SETTING HIDDEN TEXT TO DISPLAY.

1. Select **T**ools | **O**ptions and click the **V**iew tab.
2. In Nonprinting Characters, click H**i**dden Text or **A**ll (all will display tabs, spaces as dots, paragraph markers, and hidden text).
3. Click OK.

If you usually have the **A**ll option turned on, hidden text is already displayed. If you do not have H**i**dden Text checked in the View tab, you can toggle hidden text display by pressing Ctrl+* (this also toggles any other nonprinting characters that are not checked).

The other way to view annotations is to open the annotation pane. This opens the annotation pane without inserting a new annotation.

PROCEDURE 33.5. OPENING THE ANNOTATION PANE WITHOUT CREATING AN ANNOTATION.

1. Select View | Annotations.
2. Click the drop-down arrow beside the From box.
3. Select All Reviewers to display all annotations, or select a single reviewer's name to limit the display to that reviewer's notes only.
4. As you scroll through the revisions, the document scrolls in the other pane; you can resize the panes by dragging the split box in the vertical scroll bar area.
5. Select Close when you no longer want to view annotations (Alt+Shift+C).

While the annotation pane is open, you can edit annotations as desired. You can cut, paste, and copy, as needed, between the annotation pane and the main document window. You can click in the window you want or press F6 to move between the two panes.

Aborting an Annotation

The moment you select Insert | Annotation, an annotation mark is created in your document, so technically, there is no way to abort an annotation. However, you can easily remove the annotation mark using the Undo command (Alt+Backspace or Ctrl+Z).

Searching for Annotations

There are several ways to search for annotations, depending on whether or not hidden text is displaying. If hidden text is showing, you can use either the Edit | Find or Edit | Go To commands to move among annotation marks. If hidden text is, er, hidden; Edit | Find can't see it, but Edit | Go To can.

PROCEDURE 33.6. FINDING ANNOTATION MARKS WITH EDIT | FIND.

1. Select Edit | Find (Ctrl+F).
2. Click Special and select Annotation Mark (or type `[af]a`); pattern matching need not be selected.
3. Click Find Next.

Many users find the Edit | Go To command a bit more convenient for locating annotations. Not only does it locate them even when hidden text is not displayed, but it has Next and Previous buttons for easily moving in either direction (contrast this with Edit | Find, which makes you select Up or Down, weak substitutes for Previous and Next). The Edit | Go To command also enables you to hone in on a single reviewer.

PROCEDURE 33.7. FINDING ANNOTATION MARKS WITH EDIT|GO TO.

1. Select Edit|Go To (Ctrl+G).
2. In Go To What, click Annotation.
3. In Enter Reviewer's Name, select Any Reviewer or just the one you want to see.
4. Click Next or Previous (see Figure 33.5).

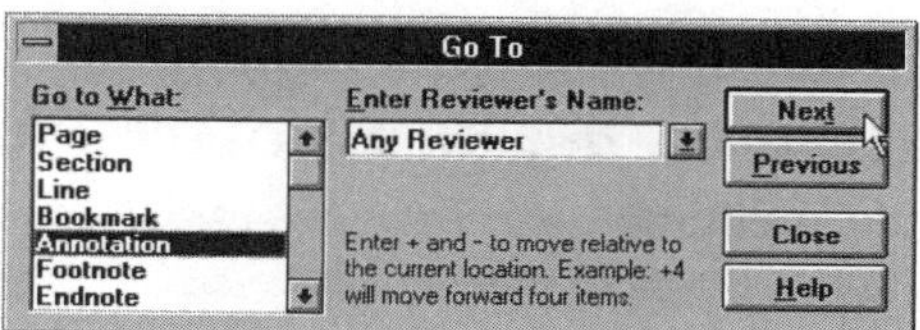

FIGURE 33.5.
Use Next or Previous to move to another annotation.

SUPER TIP

The Go To dialog box works the same way the Find, Replace, and Spelling dialog boxes do. While the Go To dialog box is on-screen, you can click in the text area without dismissing the dialog box. The title bar on the Go To dialog dims and the focus is switched to the document. When you want to resume Go To-ing, just click the Go To title bar.

Printing Annotations

Word enables you to print annotations. Unfortunately, if you print them at the same time you print a document, Word prints them only at the end.

PROCEDURE 33.8. PRINTING ANNOTATIONS ONLY.

1. Select File|Print.
2. Use the drop-down arrow beside the Print What box to select Annotations.
3. Click OK.

You also can instruct Word to print annotations with the document.

PROCEDURE 33.9. SETTING THE PRINT OPTIONS TO INCLUDE ANNOTATIONS.

1. Select Tools|Options and click the Print tab.
2. In Include with Document, click Annotations.
3. Click OK.

Now, when you print your document (Print What set to Document), the annotations are printed also, at the end of the document.

Converting an Annotation into a Footnote

Sometimes an annotation is so good or appropriate that you want to turn it into a footnote or an endnote. You can do this by copying the annotation to the clipboard, creating a footnote (or endnote), and pasting the annotation into the footnote pane. Unfortunately, you cannot display annotation and footnote panes at the same time.

PROCEDURE 33.10. COPYING AN ANNOTATION TO A FOOTNOTE OR ENDNOTE.

1. Open the annotation pane and select the text you want to copy; avoid copying any paragraph marks, if possible.
2. Press Ctrl+Insert to copy the selected text to the clipboard.
3. Click in the document pane and select **I**nsert | Foot**n**ote (or Endnote) from the menu. Note that the annotation pane automatically closes and the footnote pane opens.
4. Press Shift+Insert to paste the contents of the clipboard into the appropriate footnote.
5. If the pasted text includes paragraph markers, the Annotation Text style is copied into the footnote pane. Select the footnote, press Ctrl+Shift+S, and reset the style to Footnote Text (see "Annotation Text" in the next section).
6. Click Close or press Alt+Shift+C to close the footnote pane.

Reformatting Annotations

You can control the appearance of annotations and annotation reference marks by editing their respective styles. Annotation text is controlled by a *paragraph* style called, oddly enough, Annotation Text. The annotation reference marks are controlled by a *character* style called—are you ready for this?—Annotation Reference. If you want to permanently change the way annotations or their reference marks appear in future documents, you should modify the styles, saving the changes to the appropriate template. See Chapter 22, "Styles and AutoFormat," for additional information, if needed.

Removing Annotations

There are several approaches to removing annotations. Annotation marks (the `[initial]` marks that show up in the body of the document) can be removed only by deleting the `[initial]` marks. When you delete a mark, the entire note associated with that mark is also deleted in the annotation area. Users sometimes delete the annotation itself from the annotation pane. Who could blame them? After all, that's where most of the stuff you want to delete is hiding, so it's the intuitive thing to try. However, that method removes only the annotation text, not the mark in the document.

PROCEDURE 33.11. REMOVING AN ANNOTATION.

1. Select **V**iew | **A**nnotations so you can see the annotations you're about to delete.
2. Look through the annotation pane or use **E**dit | **G**o To, **E**dit | **F**ind, or any other method you might choose to locate the annotation you want to remove.
3. Click in the text area (not the annotation pane).
4. Select just the annotation mark (that is, `[initials]`).
5. Press Delete or Backspace.

If you have many annotations you want to remove, this method can get a little tiring. A more efficient method for removing multiple annotations is to use the Replace command, replacing the annotations you find with nothing.

PROCEDURE 33.12. REMOVING MULTIPLE ANNOTATIONS.

1. Select **V**iew | **A**nnotations and scroll to the top of the annotation pane. This moves the document and annotation window to before the first annotation.
2. Click in the document pane.
3. Select **E**dit | R**e**place (Ctrl+H).
4. In the Fi**n**d What field, type `[af]a`.
5. Delete anything that might be in the Re**p**lace With field.
6. Click **F**ind Next.
7. Examine the annotation that appears. Click **R**eplace to delete it (replace it with nothing) or click **F**ind Next to move to the next annotation.
8. Repeat Step 7 to remove all unwanted annotations, or click Replace **A**ll to wipe them all out in one stroke.

Chapter

34

Symbols

Word provides the **Insert | Symbol** command to insert a variety of special characters. In a departure from Word for Windows 2, Word 6 no longer inserts a symbol field when you use the **Insert | Symbol** command to insert characters. Instead, Word inserts symbols in a special format that cannot be changed or reformatted.

Inserting Symbols

The Symbol dialog box is one of Word's new persistent dialog boxes that can stay on-screen while you're editing a document. This provides much greater flexibility in inserting and editing special characters. Unlike Word for Windows 2's **Insert | Symbol** command, you are not limited to a single symbol at a time. This takes better account of the ways in which symbols are actually used.

Unfortunately, the **Insert | Symbol** dialog box inserts actual formattable characters only for regular text fonts (Arial, Times New Roman, Courier, and so on) and not for the special decorative and symbol fonts (Algerian, Braggadocio, Symbol, Wingding, and so on). While you can use decorative and symbol fonts for character formatting, you won't be able to use the Symbol map as a guide for which characters get inserted (except by using a special trick, described later in this chapter).

NOTE

If you want to insert accented foreign characters, don't use the following procedure. Instead, see Procedure 34.6.

PROCEDURE 34.1. INSERTING SYMBOLS USING THE SYMBOL DIALOG BOX.

1. Move the cursor to where you want the symbol to appear.
2. Select **Insert | Symbol** and click the **Symbols** tab (see Figure 34.1).

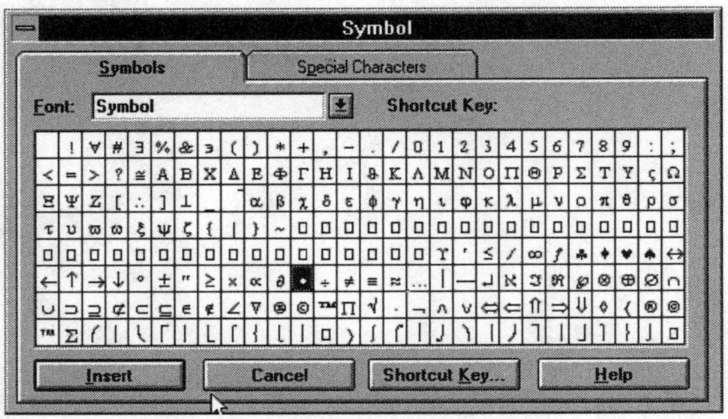

FIGURE 34.1.
*The **Symbols** tab enables you to insert symbols.*

3. Use the drop-down arrow next to **F**ont to select the desired font. Select `(normal text)` to insert a character in the default font for the current style (the special symbol format is not applied). Note that the displayed symbols change to show the symbols or characters available.
4. Click the character you want to insert and then click **I**nsert. Alternatively, you can double-click the desired character to insert it. Note that the Symbol dialog box remains on-screen until you select Cancel or Close.
5. Repeat Step 4 for any characters you want to insert.

SUPER TIP

After inserting a character, you can, if desired, click in the text area of your document, move the insertion point to a new location, and then click back in the Symbol dialog box to select another character.

If you insert characters in (normal text), they are inserted in the default font for the current style, even if a different font is in effect at the current insertion point. For example, if the current style is Normal and the defined font for Normal is 10-point Arial, then (normal text) inserted characters are in 10-point Arial, even if the font assigned at the insertion point is Symbol, Times New Roman, or something else. However, you can use normal font formatting to change the font of the inserted character(s) at will.

If you insert characters using any of the other fonts displayed in Symbol's pull-down menu, however, Word does not insert ordinary characters. Instead, it inserts special package fonts that cannot be reformatted using Word's font formatting. If you want to change such a symbol, you have to delete it and insert a new one.

When you insert symbols in anything other than `(normal text)`, the characters are not recognizable by their original ANSI or ASCII codes (in Step 4 of the procedure, take note that Word uses the status bar to display the underlying character codes of characters you select). If you use **I**nsert | **S**ymbol to insert a Braggadocio letter `A`, you will not be able to use **E**dit | **F**ind to find an `A` nor to find Braggadocio font formatting. This could make it exceedingly difficult to locate symbols inserted using the Symbol dialog box, especially in long documents. However, you can find special symbols by searching for a left parentheses character: `(`. Of course, the `(` search also matches actual left parentheses, but that's probably not as bad as being unable to hone in on the symbols at all.

In Step 3 of Procedure 34.1, instead of selecting a font from the drop-down list, you also have the option of typing the name of a font that does not appear, such as Arial, Courier, Courier New, and so on. Since the (normal text) option forces the default font of the underlying style, you can force the actual or desired font by typing its name directly. Be careful about your typing, however—past versions of Word for Windows have shown incredible memories for accidental font names, dredging them up in all sorts of odd situations.

After one of the specially formatted symbols has been inserted, you can search for it using (. But what if you'd really rather have the actual character in your document with the appropriate font applied rather than the specially formatted (nonreformattable) symbol? Well, you can do it, but it takes a little work, especially if you don't know the corresponding character.

PROCEDURE 34.2. CONVERTING A SPECIAL SYMBOL INTO A NORMAL WORD CHARACTER WITH THE CORRESPONDING FONT APPLIED.

1. Select Insert | Symbol and click the Symbols tab.
2. Use the drop-down **F**ont arrow to select the font you want.
3. Click the character you want to assign.
4. Use the drop-down **F**ont arrow to select (normal text).
5. Click **I**nsert (don't change the character, even though it now looks very different from how it appeared in Step 3).
6. Click Close to close the Symbol dialog box.
7. Select the character you just inserted.
8. Click the drop-down font arrow on the Formatting toolbar and select the same font you previously selected in Step 2.

Once a symbol has been inserted, it sometimes can be difficult to determine the underlying character code. There is a trick you can use, however. This trick uses the fact that a dialog text box cannot digest formatting. When you paste the symbol into the text box in Step 3, Word converts it into its original character minus any special formatting.

PROCEDURE 34.3. USING A DIALOG BOX TO DISCOVER A SYMBOL'S UNDERLYING CHARACTER.

1. Select the symbol and press Ctrl+Insert to copy it to the clipboard.
2. Select any dialog box that has a fill-in text box (for example, **E**dit | **F**ind, Ctrl+F).
3. Press Shift+Insert to paste the character from the clipboard into a dialog box text box.
4. Use Shift+Left arrow to select the character in the dialog box text box; then press Ctrl+Insert to copy it to the clipboard.
5. Press Esc to cancel the dialog box.
6. You can now press Shift+Insert to paste the character wherever you like; or, you can use the StringValue macro on the Word 6 Super Book diskette to "read" its underlying character code.

Assigning Symbols to Keystrokes

If you use some symbols frequently, you can use the Symbol dialog box to assign them to keystrokes.

PROCEDURE 34.4. ASSIGNING SYMBOLS TO KEYSTROKES.

1. Select **I**nsert | **S**ymbol and click the **S**ymbols tab.
2. Use the drop-down **F**ont arrow to select the font you want.
3. Click the character you want to assign.
4. Click Shortcut **K**ey; a partially-enabled keyboard customization dialog box appears, as shown in Figure 34.2.

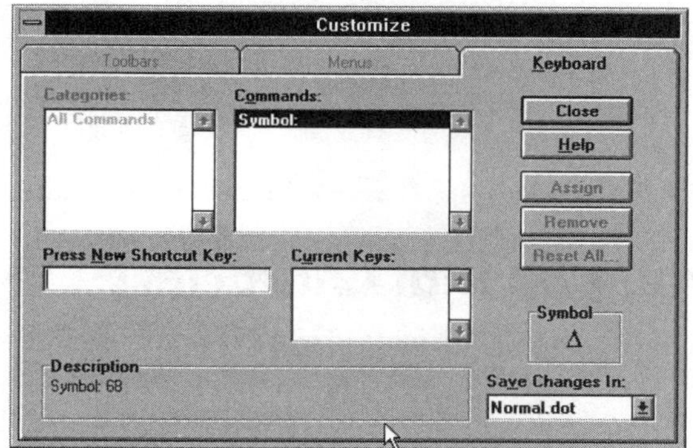

FIGURE 34.2.
*The Shortcut **K**ey button provides limited access to the keyboard customization dialog.*

5. Click in the Press **N**ew Shortcut Key area.
6. Press the key you want to assign.
7. Click Close to return to the Symbol dialog box.

SUPER TIP

If you have a number of symbols to assign, you might consider using two-key combination assignments instead of dedicating one key per symbol. To do this, press the trigger key in Step 6 and then an extra key. For example, you might consider using an unused Alt key, like Alt+Q. Then, for a Symbol bullet, add a `b` to it, as shown in Figure 34.3; for a Symbol capital pi, add a `p` to it; and so on. Once the assignments are done, you would be able to enter a bullet by typing Alt+Q followed by a `b`; to enter a capital pi, type Alt+Q p; and so on. Such assignments may be easier to remember than using Alt+Shift for one, Alt+Ctrl for another, and so on. You can make multiple assignments while the Symbol dialog box remains on-screen.

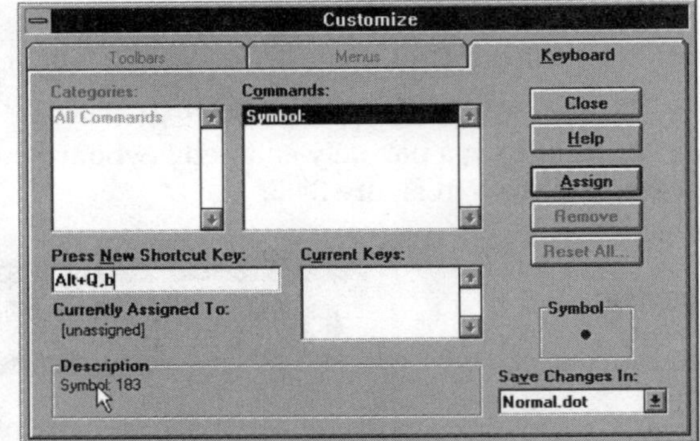

FIGURE 34.3.
With two-keystroke combinations, you get more mileage out of your key assignments.

Inserting Special Characters

In addition to specially formatted symbols, you can also use the Symbol dialog box's Special Characters tab to insert other kinds of special characters, such as em dashes, en dashes, copyright, and so on. You should note that most of these characters also have dedicated built-in key assignments.

PROCEDURE 34.5. INSERTING SPECIAL CHARACTERS USING THE INSERT | SYMBOL COMMAND.

1. Set the insertion point where you want the special character to appear.
2. Select **I**nsert | **S**ymbol.
3. Click the Special Characters tab.
4. Double-click the character you want to insert (or click it and then click Insert).
5. Click in the text area where you want the next character to appear.
6. Repeat Steps 4 and 5 to insert however many characters you need.
7. Click Close to end the procedure.

Inserting Accented Characters

If you need to insert accented foreign characters, you'll be delighted to know that you don't have to go through the **I**nsert | **S**ymbol dialog box at all. Word 6 now sports an intuitive, easy-to-use way to insert such characters. For most such characters, in fact, you won't need any aids at all, because the procedure—once learned—is so intuitive. From time to time, you probably have noticed the presence of a grave (`), acute (´), tilde (~), and other marks on your keyboard. Well, taking a cue from other internationally oriented word processing programs, Word 6 now uses those keys to produce accented characters. For example, to type é, you type Ctrl+' followed by e. To type ö, type Ctrl+: (Ctrl+Shift+;) followed by o. To type û, just type Ctrl+^ (Ctrl+Shift+6) followed by u.

PROCEDURE 34.6. INSERTING ACCENTED CHARACTERS.

1. Type Ctrl+ the accent you want to use. Add the shift key if the accent is on the shifted portion of the key, such as for , ~, and :.
2. Type the letter you want accented.

Word uses the key combinations shown in Table 34.1 to produce accented and other international characters.

Table 34.1. Key combinations to produce international characters.

Key Combination	*Plus*	*To Produce*
Ctrl+'	adeiouyADEIOUY	ád́éíóúý ÁD́ÉÍÓÚ
Ctrl+`	aeiouAEIOU	àèìòùÀÈÌÒÙ
Ctrl+^ (Ctrl+Shift+6)	aeiouAEIOU	âêîôûÂÊÎÔÛ
Ctrl+: (Ctrl+Shift+;)	aeiouyAEIOUY	äëïöüÿÄËÏÖÜŸ
Ctrl+~ (Ctrl+Shift+')	anoANO	ãñõÃÑÕ
Ctrl+@ (Ctrl+Shift+2)	aA	åÅ
Ctrl+& (Ctrl+Shift+7)	aoAOS	æ_Æ_ß
Ctrl+,	cC	çÇ
Ctrl+/	oO (letter *o*, not zero)	õÕ
Ctrl+Alt+? (Ctrl+Alt+Shift++)		¿
Ctrl+Alt+! (Ctrl+Alt+Shift+1)		¡

Chapter

35

Proofing

Word provides a variety of proofing tools, including a spelling checker, a thesaurus, and a grammar checker. Another tool included here is hyphenation. Although technically it's not really proofing, the hyphenation feature lets you ensure that hyphens are where they're supposed to be and that you don't accidentally hyphenate proper names. Proofing—short for proofreading—ultimately is still in the hands of humans. However, careful selection and use of the tools that come with Word can make the job quicker and easier.

Spelling

Word can check the spelling of a word, a selection, or a whole document. Word can include not only the main built-in word list but also word lists you create. In addition, other word lists for other languages are available from Microsoft. Language is also a character formatting attribute that you can use to mark all or part of your documents to tell Word which word list to use.

SUPER NOTE

The documentation for Word refers to the word list as a dictionary. The terms *main dictionary* and *custom dictionary* are misleading. Instead of dictionaries, they're essentially lists of acceptable spellings. Actually, Word's thesaurus is more like a dictionary, because it does provide meanings for words. If you want word meanings, try the thesaurus (Shift+F7) instead.

Checking Spelling

You can activate Word's main spelling checker in any of the following ways:

- Click the spelling tool on the Standard toolbar.
- Select **T**ools|**S**pelling from the menu.
- Press F7.

If text is not selected when you activate the speller, Word starts checking at the insertion point. Word checks for words that aren't in the main dictionary as well as words that aren't in the custom .DIC file and repeated words (two or more occurrences of the same word without an intervening paragraph mark or sentence separator). Word checks toward the end of the document. When it reaches the end, it then wraps back to the top to check the portion between there and where you began. If you want Word to start checking from the beginning of the document, you must go to the top of the document before starting the speller. If you do not want Word to automatically jump to the top of the document when it reaches the end, you must select text from the insertion point to the end of the document. Even then, Word prompts to see if you want to continue checking the balance of the document.

PROCEDURE 35.1. CHECKING SPELLING.

1. Move the cursor to where you want the checking to begin.
2. Press F7.

Word checks the spelling. If it encounters a word not in the main or custom dictionaries, it displays the dialog box shown in Figure 35.1. The questionable word is shown in the Not in Dictionary field and is highlighted in the text area on-screen. If Word encounters a repeated word or unusual capitalization, it displays the dialog boxes shown in Figure 35.2 and Figure 35.3, respectively. Select one of the actions discussed in Table 35.1.

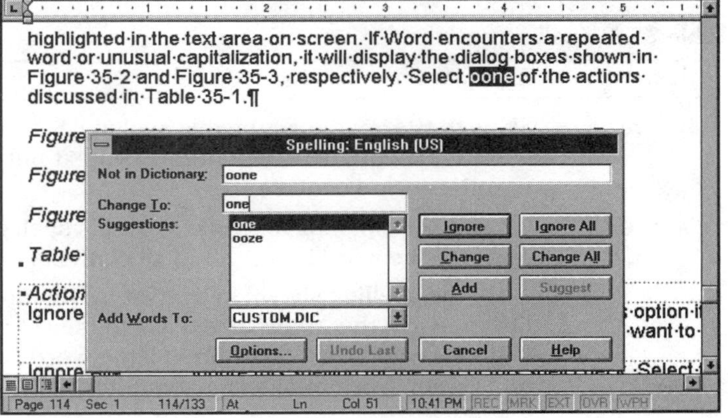

FIGURE 35.1. *Word displays the kind of error—Not in Dictionary.*

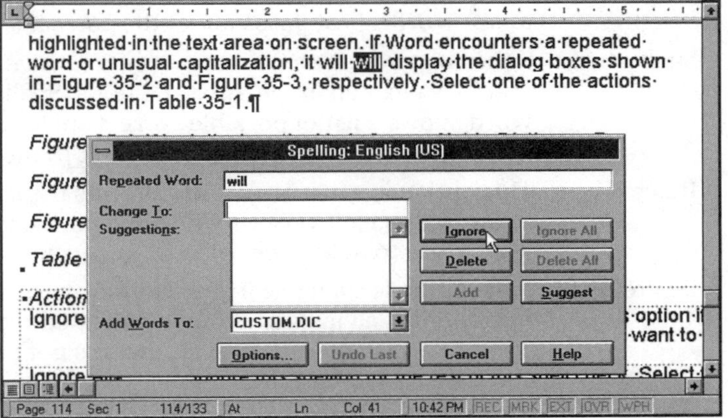

FIGURE 35.2. *Word displays the kind of error—Repeated Word.*

FIGURE 35.3.
Word displays the kind of error—Capitalization.

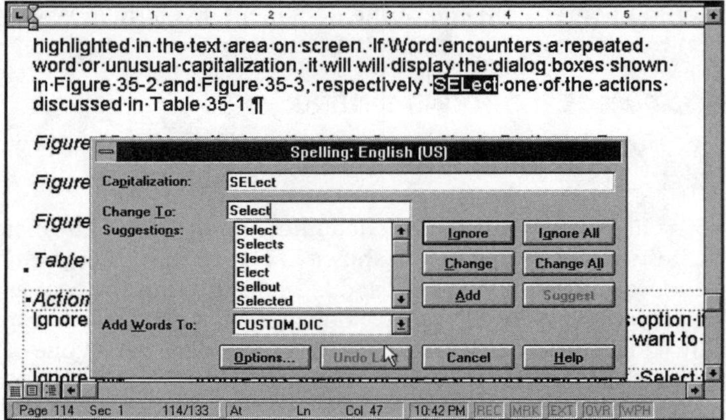

Table 35.1. Spelling options.

Action	*Explanation*
Ignore	Skips to the next questionable spelling. Select this option if the word is acceptable to you in this context but you want to examine future occurrences.
I**g**nore All	Ignores this spelling for the rest of this spell check. Select this option if the word is correct in all contexts in this document.
Add	Adds the spelling shown in the Not in Dictionary field to the .DIC file shown in the Add Words To field (select a different .DIC file, if necessary). Select this option if the word is correct and you don't want Word to nag you about it when the .DIC file shown is loaded.
Suggest	If the suggestions are not shown automatically, click this button to see Word's best guess about the correct spelling.
Suggestio**n**s	If the Suggest option was selected (or if the Always Suggest option is enabled in the **T**ools | **O**ptions | **S**pelling dialog box), Word shows a list of possible correct spellings. If the correct spelling is displayed, click it to move it to the Change To field.
Delete	This option is available if Word detects the same word twice in a row, which isn't very very uncommon. Select this option if you want Word to delete the selected occurrence.
Delete **A**ll	This option is available if Word found a repeated word. Select this option if all instances of the indicated repeated word are wrong. Keep in mind, however, that it's not unusual for a header and the first word of the sentence that follows to be the same.
Cancel	Select this option if you need to dismiss the dialog box.

Action	Explanation
Change	Changes the spelling of this word to the spelling indicated in the Change To box. Select this option if the spelling is correct this time but may not be correct for other occurrences.
Change All	Changes the spelling of this word now and any other time it's encountered to the spelling shown in the Change To box. Select this option if you always want the indicated spelling changed.
Undo Last	Select this option if you have sudden second thoughts about the last change you made. Word undoes the change and returns the focus of the spell check to that word so you can make a new decision.
Options	Select this option to change the main spelling preferences in the Tools | Options menu.
Change To	Type the correct spelling into the Change To text box, and then click Change or Change All. Select this option if the suggestions are wrong or if Suggest is not enabled and you prefer to type the correct spelling.

If the spelling and context are so hopelessly fouled up that you can't take care of it using the dialog box options, you can click in the text to suspend the speller. The Spell dialog box remains on-screen with the title bar dimmed out. The first Ignore button is replaced with the Start button, as shown in Figure 35.4. Fix the problem and then click Start to resume.

FIGURE 35.4.
Word enables you to suspend the spelling dialog; just click Start to resume.

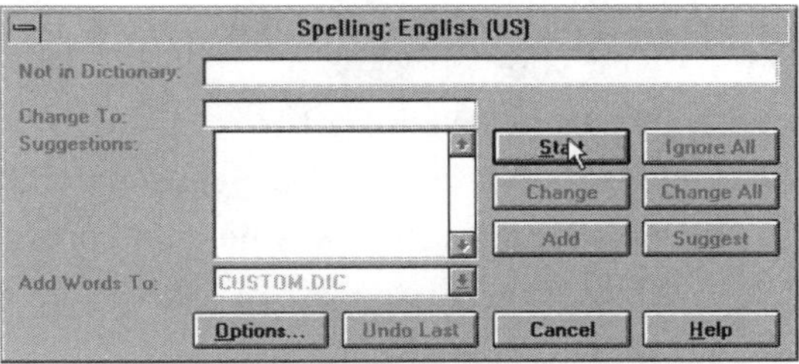

A variation of this is to click in the text below the problem to cause Word to just skip the problem area. If, for example, you have a section of a computer program with variable and keyword names that defy any speller, you can just click or otherwise scroll the document past that section of text and then click Start to resume checking spelling from the new location.

SUPER TIP

In addition to the Undo Last option, Word's multiple Undo feature reverses not only the last correction but the last hundred or so, one at a time. Just keep pressing Alt+Backspace (or Ctrl+Z) until you get back to where you want.

Checking a Single Word

When you press F7, you are running Word's ToolsSpelling command. Word has another built-in command as well: ToolsSpellSelection, which unfortunately is not assigned to any key, menu, or toolbar. If you prefer to do an occasional check on words that look questionable to you, you might benefit by assigning the ToolsSpellSelection command to a dedicated keystroke. In many ways, this command is much better than the default. If no text is selected, the ToolsSpellSelection command selects the word nearest the cursor and checks its spelling. If it's okay, Word offers to continue the spell check for the rest of the document.

If you'd like the convenience of having ToolsSpellSelection assigned to a key, a likely candidate for assignment is Alt+F7 because F7 is already assigned to ToolsSpelling. Given that ToolsSpellSelection ultimately feeds into the same dialog box as ToolsSpelling, you might also consider assigning F7 to ToolsSpellSelection.

PROCEDURE 35.2. MAKING TOOLSSPELLSELECTION AVAILABLE FROM A KEY.

1. Select **T**ools | **C**ustomize.
2. Click the **K**eyboard tab.
3. In the Sa**v**e Changes In drop-down list, select NORMAL.DOT (or wherever is appropriate for your work style).
4. In the **C**ategories list, click **T**ools.
5. In the C**o**mmands list, click ToolsSpellSelection.
6. Click the Press **N**ew Shortcut Key field and press the key you want to assign (Alt+F7, F7, and so on).
7. Click **A**ssign.
8. Click Close.

Creating Custom Dictionaries

Word can create custom dictionaries, or lists of acceptable spelling, for use when running the spell checker. You also can create these yourself, either using Word's Add button or through editing. If you are moving from another word processing program, you can also easily transfer words into the .DIC files used by Word.

PROCEDURE 35.3. CREATING A NEW CUSTOM DICTIONARY.

1. Select Tools | Options and click the Spelling tab.
2. Click New.
3. Select a location and new Name for the .DIC file, using a descriptive name such as MEDICAL.DIC or LEGAL.DIC.
4. Click OK. Word automatically adds the new file to the list of custom dictionaries, as shown in Figure 35.5.
5. Click OK to close the Options dialog box.

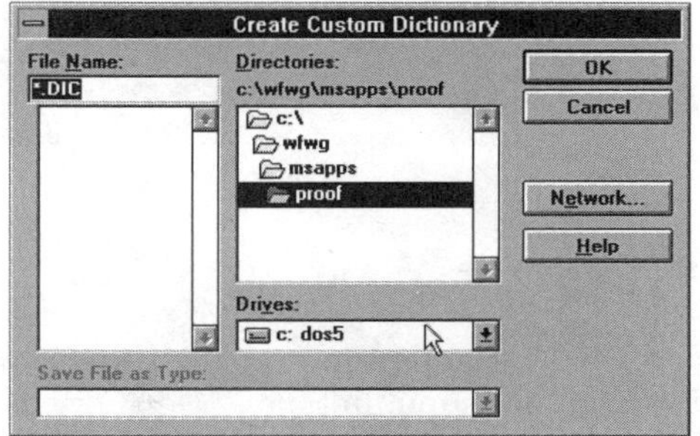

FIGURE 35.5.
When you create a new dictionary, Word adds it to the list.

A new custom dictionary is empty until you add words to it. You can do this in two ways. You can edit the dictionary from Word, adding the words yourself and saving it as a text file, or you can gradually build your word list as Word encounters spellings it can't find in the main dictionary. Unless you have a list already standing by (for example, a programmer might have a list of programming commands, variables, and keywords they don't want questioned), the most efficient method usually is to create the list gradually.

PROCEDURE 35.4. ADDING WORDS TO A CUSTOM SPELLING LIST (DICTIONARY).

1. Press F7 to start the speller.
2. When Word questions the spelling, it displays the dialog box shown in Figure 35.6.
3. Click the arrow beside Add Words To and select the .DIC file into which you want to add words.
4. Click Add if the word is correct for your purposes.
5. Optionally, you can change the target custom dictionary as often as you like while checking spelling. Word continues to use that dictionary until you change it again.

FIGURE 35.6.
When Word can't find the word, you can add it to a custom dictionary (word list).

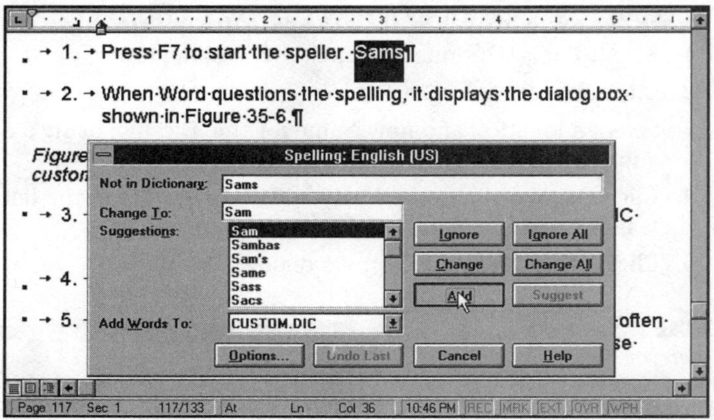

SUPER CAUTION

It's very easy when performing long spell checks to accidentally add something that shouldn't have been added. You might consider periodically checking your custom dictionaries to ensure that you haven't accidentally added something you didn't really want or have long since stopped needing.

Creating an Exception Dictionary

There might be some words about which you and Word disagree. For example, in the human resources arena, a widely preferred spelling for *employee* is *employe*. You might prefer not to accept the other spelling. You might also object to *color* for *colour*. Perhaps you find that you often misuse *it's*, *its*, *there*, *their*, and *they're* and might like to flag each occurrence so you can make sure you didn't screw up.

For such occasions, Word enables you create an exception list. The exception list must reside on the same directory as the .LEX file and must have the same name but with the extension .EXC (for EXCeption). If you're using `C:\WIN\MSAPPS\PROOFING\MSSP2_EN.LEX`, the exception file must be called `C:\WIN\MSAPPS\PROOFING\MSSP2_EN.EXC`. `MSSP2_EN.LEX` is, by the way, the standard American English word list used by Word for Windows 6.

PROCEDURE 35.5. CREATING AN EXCEPTION LIST.

1. Select File | New.
2. Type the words you want Word to question (for example, `employee`, `their`, `there`, `they're`, and so on), pressing Enter after each one.

3. Select File | Save As.
4. Under Save File as Type, select Text Only.
5. Use the Drives and Directories lists to navigate to the location of MSSP2_EN.LEX (or whatever your .LEX file happens to be called).
6. Type the name `MSSP2_EN.EXC` (or the appropriate name, if different).
7. Click OK.

From here on out, Word uses the .EXC file automatically when using the .LEX file by the same name. If you have multiple .LEX files used by Word's speller, you can create different .EXC files for each.

Setting Spelling Options

Word provides several spelling options to make spelling more tolerable. If you write technical reports, for example, you might prefer that Word *not* bother checking spelling of terms that include numbers. If you work for IBM, you might also prefer that the constant barrage of uppercase acronyms not be checked either. Word enables you to set these and other options by selecting Tools | Options | Spelling. The options are explained in the headings that follow.

Always Suggest

Depending on the kind of writing you do, Word's suggestion may be right on target or irrelevant. You can tell Word to cease and desist in the suggestions department by deselecting the Always Suggest option. Even with this option turned off, you still are able to click the Suggest button from the Spell dialog box.

From Main Dictionary Only

Word uses a pattern-matching algorithm to determine what to suggest. By default, Word uses only words from the main dictionary. Deselect this option to instruct Word to use selected custom dictionaries as well.

Ignore Words in UPPERCASE

If you use a lot of acronyms (IBM, ASPCA, CIA, MADD, and so on), you might prefer that Word not question them. If you select the Ignore Words in Uppercase option, Word ignores words that are entirely in uppercase. However, if words are mixed case, as in `THis`, Word suggests that your capitalization is wrong, as shown in Figure 35.3.

Ignore Words with Numbers

Select this option to have Word ignore items such as WW2_Data, 3M, M1, B-52, I-95, Item1, and so on. This is a handy option for many kinds of technical reports.

Custom Dictionaries

You can elect to load as many as 10 custom dictionaries at the same time. However, spelling will be slower the more you have loaded and the larger they are. If you use Word's spell checker mostly for checking the spelling of unfamiliar words as you encounter them, you should probably leave most (if not all) custom dictionaries turned off when just writing. Then when you are checking the spelling of a long document all at once, wherein you're not controlling which words are being checked, turn on the relevant custom dictionaries to avoid unnecessary queries.

Thesaurus

Are you ever at a loss for words? If so, then try the thesaurus. The thesaurus is capable of providing synonyms and antonyms for a variety of words and phrases. Yes—phrases, too! That comes as a surprise to most users. However, Word's thesaurus can look up individual words and phrases that consist of several words. Of course, the longer the phrase, the less likely you are to get a hit. When the word you seek is right on the tip of your tongue, you sometimes can shake it loose using the thesaurus.

Using the Thesaurus

To look up a word in the thesaurus, just move the insertion point into the word. To look up a phrase, select the phrase. Then press Shift+F7 (or select **T**ools | **T**hesaurus from the menu). If Word finds the word or phrase, it displays the dialog box shown in Figure 35.7. If Word doesn't find the word or phrase, it displays the dialog box shown in Figure 35.8

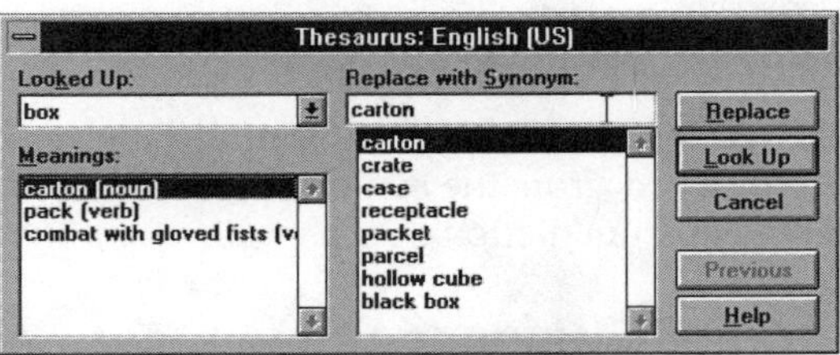

FIGURE 35.7. *When Word finds the word, it displays a list of meanings and synonyms.*

FIGURE 35.8. *If Word can't find the word, it displays an alphabetical list of possibilities.*

Word displays the word it looked up in the Looked Up field. You cannot type into this field. If you get lost, however, and can't remember exactly which word Word looked up, this is it. If Word cannot find the word in the thesaurus, then Looked Up is replaced with Not Found.

Word uses the Meanings list to display the different ways the word or phrase can be used. Of course, this list is by no means exhaustive, but it's often pretty good. If the word has logical opposites (as many action verbs, adjectives, and adverbs do), Word also displays antonyms. If Word doesn't find the word in the thesaurus, the Looked Up box turns into a Not Found box, and Word displays an Alphabetical List of words similar in spelling instead of a Meanings list.

To use the Meanings list, click a meaning or a word. As you do, note that the list of synonyms on the right changes. The word *do*, for example, displays seven different meanings and an antonym category. Among the seven different meanings for *do*, a total of 38 synonyms and four different antonyms are offered.

Depending on the word, the thesaurus sometimes can't come up with a synonym. Instead, Word sometimes displays Related Words in the Meanings list to indicate that the corresponding words in the list at the right are related rather than synonyms of the word shown in the Looked Up box. One instance in which this occurs is when the word you look up is a form of a word that's in the thesaurus rather than a separate entry (for example, *likes* is a form of *like*, which is listed).

If Word can't find the word at all, it displays a list of near matches for the spelling of the word you looked up. Note that, as shown in Figure 35.9, the list of synonyms is empty because the word in the Not Found box remains the same. To change the word in the Not Found box, click the Look Up button (or double-click the word you want to look up). If you want to look up a word not on the list, you can type a new word in the Replace with Synonym box and then click Look Up.

FIGURE 35.9.
Word can't show you what's not there.

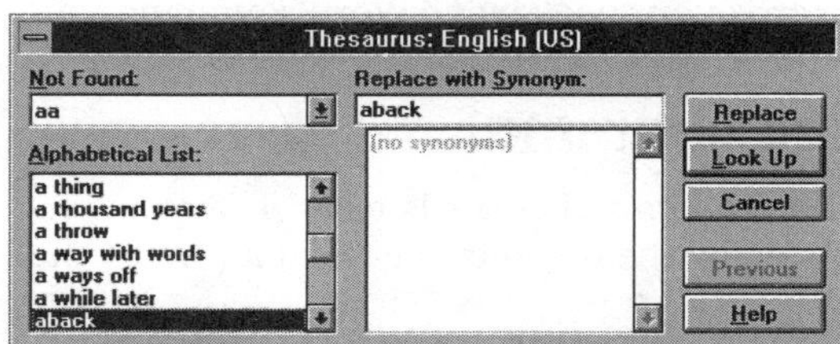

PROCEDURE 35.6. LOOKING UP A WORD OR PHRASE IN THE THESAURUS.

1. Select the word or phrase you want to look up.
2. In the Meanings or Alphabetical list, click the meaning or word closest to what you mean.
3. In the Synonyms list, click the word you want to use.

4. Click **L**ook Up to go deeper; click Previous to step backwards through words you've already seen; click Replace to replace the selected word or phrase with the word in the Replace With **S**ynonym box; or click Cancel to give up.

SUPER FUN TIP

You can use the thesaurus as a game. The object is to take two seemingly unrelated terms and see how many lookups you have to do to get from one term to the other. For example, as far as I can tell, there's no relationship between the words *carrot* and *cow*. Try to get from *carrot* to *cow*, and see how many lookups it takes. It took me five!

Grammar

Word provides a grammar checker to help you make sure your writing is as clear and precise as possible. The grammar checker isn't always right, but it's wrong seldom enough to be useful. Moreover, the grammar checker is flexible enough that you can focus on specific areas if you want. For example, one of the favorite areas for computer book publishers to harp on is the use of active versus passive voice.

Word's grammar checker comes in handy here. A writer can now write in passive voice and then use the grammar checker to find it after the fact. After a while, you get so darn tired of seeing the grammar checker harp on this passive voice phobia that you start to change your writing style to avoid it. Like mice subjected to electric shocks, writers minimize deviations from active voice to minimize the amount of rewriting needed before passing their words onto their publishers. I'm not saying that this passive voice bugaboo is a good thing; rather I'm only saying that, assuming minimizing passive voice is your goal, using Word's grammar checker can help you reach it.

Checking Grammar

Running the grammar checker is easy. Tolerating its defaults is difficult. However, because changing the defaults is easy, it all works out in the end.

PROCEDURE 35.7. CHECKING GRAMMAR.

1. Position the cursor where you want the grammar checking to begin or select the passage you want to check.
2. Select **T**ools | **G**rammar. Word checks your grammar. If you haven't changed the defaults, Word may very well stop on every sentence and display the dialog box shown in Figure 35.10.

FIGURE 35.10.
Left to its own devices, Word can find something wrong with almost every sentence you type.

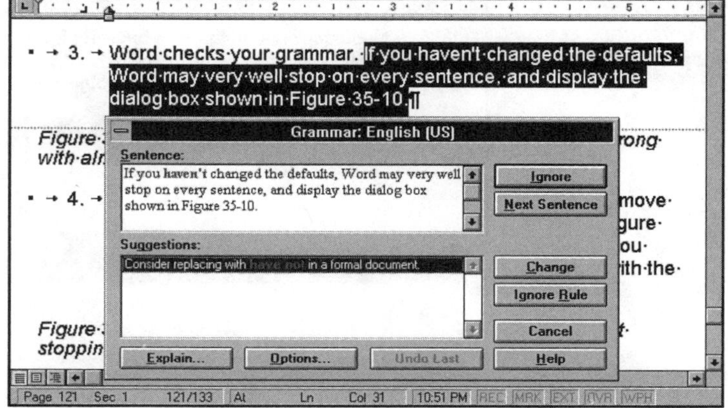

3. Like the spell checker, the Grammar dialog permits you to move freely between the text and the dialog box, as shown in Figure 35.11. When the grammar checker makes a suggestion with which you agree, you can click in the text area to revise your text.

FIGURE 35.11.
The Grammar dialog box can be suspended without stopping the grammar check.

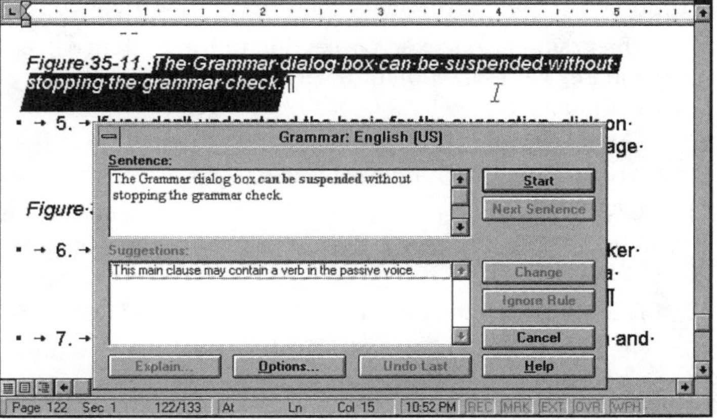

4. If you don't understand the basis for the suggestion, click **E**xplain. As shown in Figure 35.12, Word displays a message box indicating the reason for its objection.
5. If the Check Spelling option is enabled, the grammar checker automatically links with the spell checker. If it encounters a problematic spelling, it displays the spelling dialog box.
6. Select the **I**gnore option to ignore the current rule violation and move on to the next.

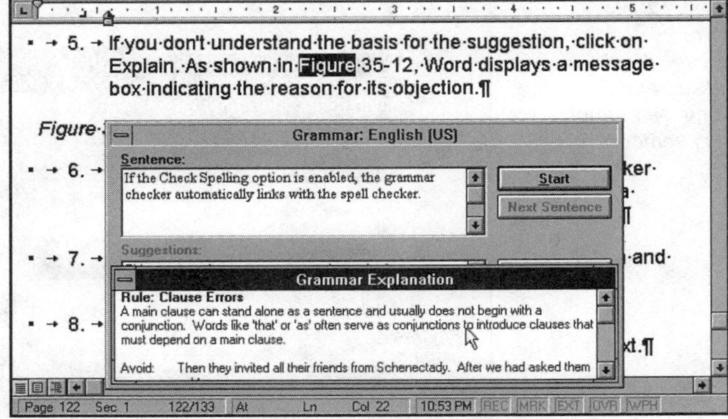

FIGURE 35.12.
The grammar checker cites the rule.

7. Select the **N**ext Sentence option to ignore all remaining problems with the current sentence and move on to the next.
8. Select Ignore **R**ule to turn off the rule for the remainder of the grammar check (the rule is turned back on the next time you start the grammar checker). Because of this, it's important not to cancel the grammar checker until you're done with the current check.
9. If the grammar checker's objection to the sentence is easy to fix (for example, changing capitalization or a verb's person), it suggests a specific change. Click the **C**hange button to accept the change.
10. Click the **O**ptions button to change the options (see the following section, "Customizing the Grammar Checker").
11. Click Cancel to quit the grammar check. Remember, when you do this, Word loses track of any Ignore Rule instructions you selected during the current check.
12. Click Undo **L**ast to reverse the last change you agreed to.
13. When the check is finished, Word displays the readability statistics, unless you turned that option off.

Customizing the Grammar Checker

Word provides for complete customization of the grammar checker. This enables you to be as strict or as liberal as you like when running grammar checks. To change the grammar options, select **T**ools | **O**ptions and click the **G**rammar tab. During grammar checking, you can reach the same dialog by clicking **O**ptions on the Grammar dialog box.

Use Grammar and Style Rules

Word offers three built-in sets of grammar rules:

- Strictly (all rules)
- Business (a lot of rules)
- Casual (fewer rules)

Word also provides three Custom choices you can use to create your own sets of rules. This gives you the option of leaving the built-in named sets alone and creating three new sets.

Customize

If you choose to change the settings of the built-in sets as well, click the Customize Settings button. You can call the same dialog by choosing **T**ools | **O**ptions | Grammar | Cus**t**omize Settings.

GRAMMAR RULES

Click the **G**rammar button to enable or disable specific rules. Grammar rules are strict interpretations of grammar such as subject-verb agreement, double negatives, and the like. Word has 19 grammar rule categories you can modify according to your needs.

STYLE

Click the **S**tyle button to enable or disable specific style checks. Style rules are often subjective considerations that some organizations like and others don't. Style considerations include such things as clichés, contractions, jargon, and pretentious words. Word has 25 style options.

SPLIT INFINITIVES

The infinitive form of a verb is the word *to* followed by the verb. For example, *To be or not to be* is perhaps the most famous infinitive verbal expression in the English language. If Shakespeare had written *To contentedly be or not to contentedly be*…, he might have gotten in trouble with Word's grammar checker.

When you separate the word *to* from the verb, it's called a split infinitive. To carelessly and needlessly split (ha!) a verb from its *to* is a no-no in some circles. If splitting an infinitive is a no-no in your world, you can tell Word to keep an eye out for it and set the sensitivity of the checking to always; split by one, two, or three words; or never.

CONSECUTIVE NOUNS

Using too many nouns in a row without modification by verbs, adjectives, or other words can make for difficult reading. Use this option to tell Word to be on the lookout for instances of two, three, or four consecutive nouns or not to check for consecutive nouns at all. An example? Sure! *The circus tent builder dance was canceled.*

PREPOSITIONAL PHRASES

A prepositional phrase is a group of words that begins with a preposition, er, like *with a preposition*. One or two prepositional phrases can add a little vitality and variety to an otherwise drab piece of writing. More than two, however, can start to muddle the meaning: *On the way to the store at the corner of Broadway and First streets, Simple Simon met a pieman*. With Word, you can opt not to check at all or to catch instances of two, three, or four prepositional phrases in a row.

SENTENCES CONTAINING MORE WORDS THAN

Word's grammar checker also enables you to check for long sentences. The default is 35 words, which is a pretty long sentence. If you're writing hard computer books, the readability can be improved dramatically by keeping them short. You might consider setting the check down to something in the range of 20 or so, lest you incur the wrath of those otherwise peaceful people who object strenuously to reading sentences that approach the length of the one you're reading now. See what I mean?

EXPLAIN

If you can't figure out what a rule is used for, click the **E**xplain button. Word provides a detailed explanation of the rule, as well as examples. For example, under the grammar rule Mass vs. Count, **E**xplain explains about the difference between *less* and *fewer*.

Check Spelling

By default, Word checks both spelling and grammar at the same time when you engage the grammar checker. If you prefer to focus entirely on grammar, deselect the Check **S**pelling option. Unlike the options set through the Customize button, the Check Spelling option applies to all Grammar and Style Rule sets.

Show Readability Statistics

Some types of writing must keep text simple so that most of the population can understand what they're reading. This is important especially when writing warnings and tax instructions. Alternatively, if you're trying to upgrade the reading skills of a target audience, readability statistics can help you see if you're on target.

As shown in Figure 35.13, the readability statistics counts words, characters, sentences, and paragraphs and calculates the average word length, words per sentence, and sentences per paragraph. It also counts the number of passive sentences and calculates the Flesch reading ease index as well as three grade-level indicators.

With the Flesch reading ease index, the higher the number (maximum is 100), the easier the work is to read. With the grade level indicators, the higher the number, the more difficult the work. The index and grade levels are based on factors such as syllables per word and sentence length.

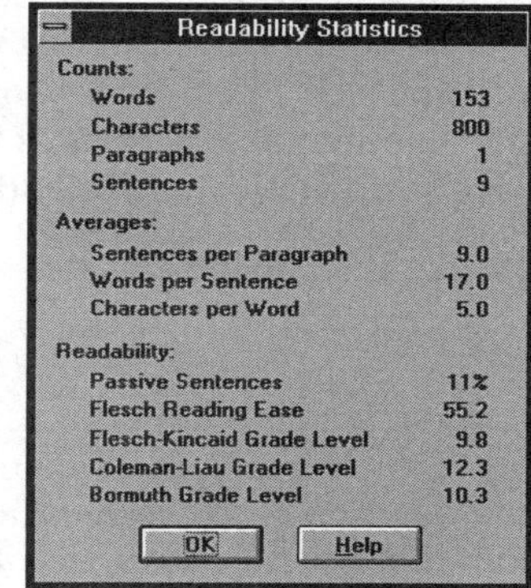

FIGURE 35.13.
Word displays readability statistics after finishing the grammar check.

Hyphenation

Word can hyphenate your documents for you. You have the option of instructing Word to do the work automatically or instructing it to take you through the document with you making the decision about *optional* hyphens and inserting them manually where desired.

PROCEDURE 35.8. ENABLING AUTOMATIC HYPHENATION.

1. Select Tools | **H**yphenation; Word displays the dialog box shown in Figure 35.14.

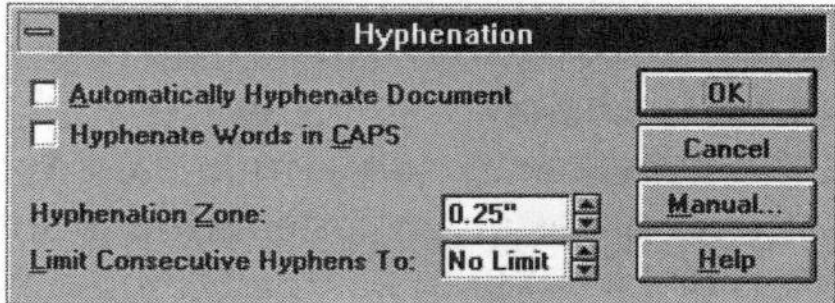

FIGURE 35.14.
Set hyphenation preferences in the Hyphenation dialog box.

2. Select **A**utomatically Hyphenate Document.
3. If desired, select Hyphenate Words in **C**APS.
4. Set the Hyphenation **Z**one, or the amount of allowable space between the edge of the text and the right margin.

5. Set the number of consecutive hyphens, if desired (Limit Consecutive Hyphens To). Some style manuals or other document specifications limit the number of consecutive lines that can end with hyphens.
6. Click OK.

If the current view is Normal, Word does not do anything special when you click OK. As you scroll through the document, however, you should notice hyphenation where none existed before. If you're in Print Preview or Page Layout view, Word repaginates each time you change hyphenation options. If the document is very long, therefore, it's a good idea to save hyphenation until all other text revision has been completed.

SUPER NOTE

The hyphenation zone is a key setting for optimal hyphenation. The larger the zone, the more unused space there can be at the right side of the document and the more ragged the appearance of the right margin. For maximum readability, use higher numbers. To minimize the amount of paper you're using, use lower numbers. If you use justified margins, setting higher numbers spaces out your text. Some spacing helps improve readability. Too much spacing, however, can make justified text look weird. Use Word's Print Preview or Page Layout views to optimize the settings for your documents.

Word also enables you to perform manual hyphenation.

PROCEDURE 35.9. HYPHENATING MANUALLY.

1. Select the passage you want to hyphenate or move the insertion point to where you want to start.
2. Select Tools | Hyphenation.
3. Click Manual. Word switches into Page Layout view and begins hyphenation at the current insertion point or at the beginning of the selection. If text is not selected, Word automatically wraps back to the beginning of the document if it does not encounter any hyphenation points. When Word encounters a hyphenation point, it displays the dialog box shown in Figure 35.15.

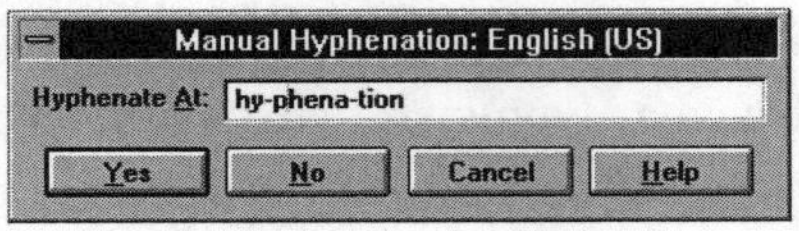

Manual Hyphenation: English (US)
Hyphenate At: hy-phena-tion
Yes | No | Cancel | Help

FIGURE 35.15.
The Manual Hyphenation dialog box.

4. To accept the suggested break, click **Y**es or press Enter. To accept a different break, move the cursor to a new position in the word (using keys or mouse) and then click **Y**es or press Enter.
5. To *not* hyphenate the displayed word and to move on to the next word, select **N**o.
6. To stop hyphenating, select Cancel.

Removing Hyphenation

Word uses four kinds of hyphens. The least problematic are automatic hyphens that appear and disappear when you select or deselect automatic hyphenation. The second least problematic are nonbreaking hyphens, which tell Word to treat them the same as letters in a word (for example, as in hyphenated proper names that you don't want broken across two lines, or hyphenated expressions that are difficult to read if broken across two lines—for example, A-OK and B-52).

The more potentially problematic kinds of hyphens are dashes and optional hyphens. Dashes are problematic because people just use them without thinking about what Word does with them. In the previous paragraph, for example, even though hyphenation is turned off in this document, Word chose to break B-52 across two lines when I first typed it. After I replaced the ordinary dash with a nonbreaking hyphen (Ctrl+Shift+- on the top row), however, B-52 became welded at the hyphen.

Optional hyphens, inserted during manual hyphenation and by pressing Ctrl+- (top row), are potential troublemakers because they don't automatically go away when you turn off automatic hyphenation and because they don't display on-screen by default (they display as ordinary hyphens in Page Layout view, which masks the fact that they are optional hyphens). If you leave them in your document and don't want any hyphenation, you may later be surprised to discover that your document is hyphenated anyway.

PROCEDURE 35.10. REMOVING UNWANTED OPTIONAL HYPHENS.

1. Select the text for which you want to remove optional hyphens.
2. Press Ctrl+H (**E**dit | R**e**place).
3. In the Fi**n**d What field, type ^-.
4. Blank the Replace With field.
5. Click Re**p**lace All.

When optional hyphens are displayed on-screen, they display as shown in Figure 35.16.

FIGURE 35.16.
Optional hyphens are a little bent.

When·optional·hy¬phens·are·displayed·on·screen,·
they·display·as·shown·in·Figure·35-16.¶

PROCEDURE 35.11. DISPLAYING OPTIONAL HYPHENS.

1. Select Tools | Options and click the View tab.
2. Under Nonprinting characters, select Optional Hyphens.
3. Click OK.

Chapter 36

Revision Marks (Redlining)

Revision marking is one of Word's most useful features for people who must share documents for review and revision. When revision marking is turned on, Word displays both insertions and deletions on-screen, using a different color for each reviewer (based on reviewer name, not initials). Word also displays a revision bar on the left side of each paragraph that contains revisions. The revision dialog box can take you through the document, letting you easily move among revisions to decide what to do (accept, reject, modify, and so forth).

Turning On/Off Revision Marks

You can access the revisions control dialog box either by using the menu or by double-clicking the MRK button on the status bar.

PROCEDURE 36.1. TURNING ON REVISION MARKING.

1. Select **T**ools | Revisions (Alt+T, V), or double-click the MRK button, to display the dialog box shown in Figure 36.1.

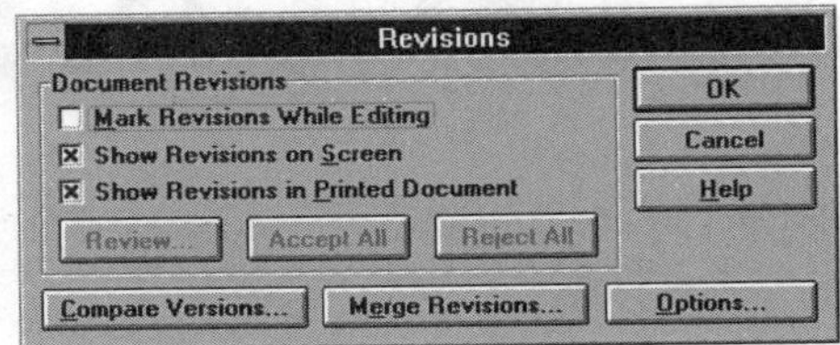

FIGURE 36.1. *The Revisions dialog box.*

2. Select **M**ark Revisions While Editing.

While revision marking is on, text you add is displayed in color (depending on what options you have set) and underlined. Text you delete is displayed as strikethrough, as shown in Figure 36.2. Optionally, you can instruct Word to display revisions as it would ordinary text. This means that text you add is not displayed in a special way, and text you delete is hidden from view as you delete it.

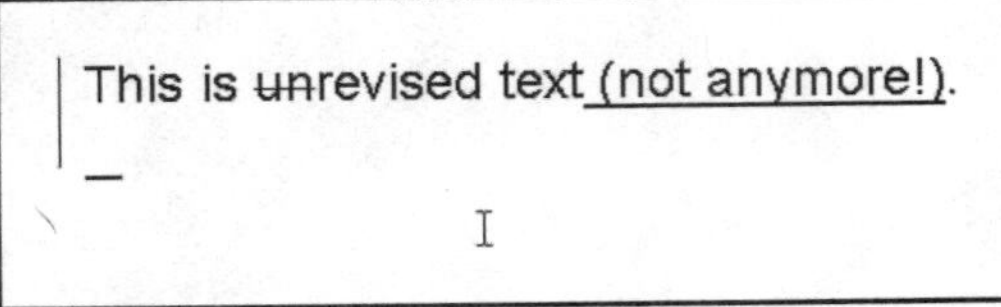

FIGURE 36.2. *Word displays added text as underlined and deleted text as strikethrough.*

PROCEDURE 36.2. TURNING OFF THE DISPLAY OF REVISIONS.

1. Select **T**ools | Revisions, or double-click MRK.
2. Click Show Revisions on **S**creen.
3. Click OK.

Working in this mode, you get a clearer idea of the impact of your revisions. When you want to see your revisions, you can turn the display of revisions back on, and text you have added or deleted is again displayed in color and with underlining and strikethrough attributes.

SUPER NOTE

The underlining and strikethrough attributes are for display only. If you select revised text, you will notice that the character formatting attributes for color, underlining, strikethrough, and so forth are not actually turned on. Word simply displays the text that way for your convenience. How Word displays revised text is controlled by settings in the **T**ools | **O**ptions | **R**evisions dialog box.

Setting Revision Options

Revision options can be set either through the Revisions dialog by clicking the Options button, or from Word's main Options dialog.

PROCEDURE 36.3. SETTING REVISION MARKING DISPLAY.

1. Select **T**ools | **O**ptions and click Revisions to display the dialog box shown in Figure 36.3.

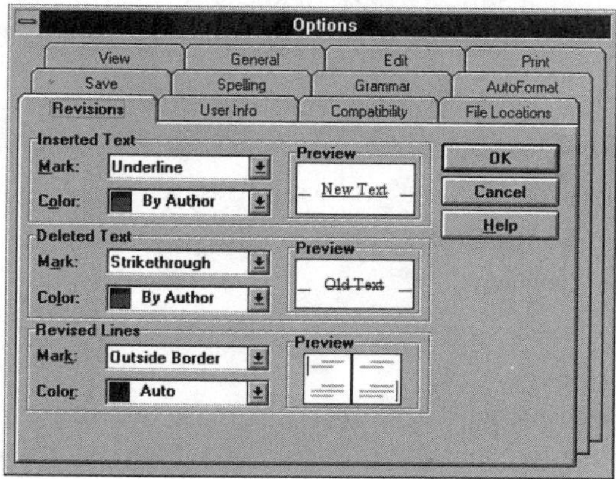

FIGURE 36.3.
Revision options.

2. Select an attribute display preference (**M**ark) for Inserted text; the default is underlined. Note that Word displays a preview of this and all other effects as you change them.

3. Select a Color display preference for inserted text; the default is to display a different color for each author.
4. Select a display preference (Mark) for Deleted text; the default is Strikethrough, and the only other option is Hidden.
5. Select a Color display preference for Deleted text; the default is to display a different color for each author.
6. Select Revised Lines options; the default for Mark is to display a vertical bar beside the paragraph along the Outside border. You can also choose a Color for the Revised Lines mark.
7. Click OK.

SUPER CAUTION

Selecting (none) for Inserted and Hidden for Deleted give the same effect as turning off the display of revisions in the Revisions dialog box, but it does not change the X in that dialog box. Be careful, therefore, about selecting those as display options, because it might subsequently appear that the Show Revisions on Screen setting is broken.

Locking for Revisions

Have you ever given a document to someone, requesting that they edit it in revision mode, and then it comes back to you—very much changed, but with no revision marks? Well, there's an easy solution. Lock the document so that all edits are performed in revision mode.

PROCEDURE 36.4. LOCKING A DOCUMENT FOR REVISIONS.

1. Open the document you want to lock.
2. Select Tools | Protect Document.
3. Click Revisions.
4. To be really tough about it, click in the Password field and type a password.
5. Click OK.
6. Word prompts you to retype the password, to ensure that you don't accidentally get locked out yourself. Type it and click OK.

When you protect a document for revisions, the MRK button on the status bar turns on, and revision marking is automatically turned on. As shown in Figure 36.4, the option to turn it off is disabled from the Revisions dialog box. All future edits of this document are protected from unmarked revisions until the document is unprotected by someone who knows the password.

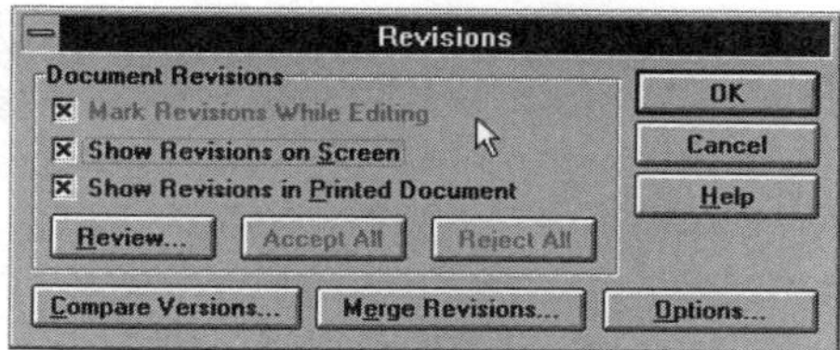

FIGURE 36.4.
When locked for revisions, revision marking can't be turned off.

PROCEDURE 36.5. TURNING PROTECTION OFF.

1. Open the document you want to unlock.
2. Select Tools | Unprotect Document.
3. Word prompts for the password; type it and click OK.

Searching for Revision Marks

You can search for revision marks in several ways. The systematic way is to select the Revisions dialog box and use the Review feature. However, you can also just look through the document for revision bars and colored text. You also can use Edit | Find to search for revision insertions, but not for deletions.

Managing Revisions from the Revision Dialog

Word gives you the option of accepting or rejecting revisions all at once, or reviewing and making a decision about each one.

PROCEDURE 36.6. HANDLING REVISIONS.

1. Select Tools | Revisions, or double-click MRK.
2. To accept all revisions, click Accept All and confirm the prompt.
3. To reject all revisions, click Reject All and confirm the prompt.
4. To review revisions, click Review (see procedure Reviewing Revisions).
5. Click Close or Cancel to end, depending on which button is displayed (Cancel is displayed if you haven't done anything; otherwise, Close is displayed).

The revision feature has a very flexible review feature. It can step you forward or backward from revision to revision. You can systematically accept, reject, or modify revisions, one by one.

PROCEDURE 36.7. REVIEWING REVISIONS.

From the Revisions dialog box, click the Review button to display the dialog box shown in Figure 36.5. Like the spelling and grammar dialog boxes, the Review Revisions dialog box can remain on-screen while you edit the document. This gives you the ability to modify revisions as you go along.

FIGURE 36.5.
The Review dialog box.

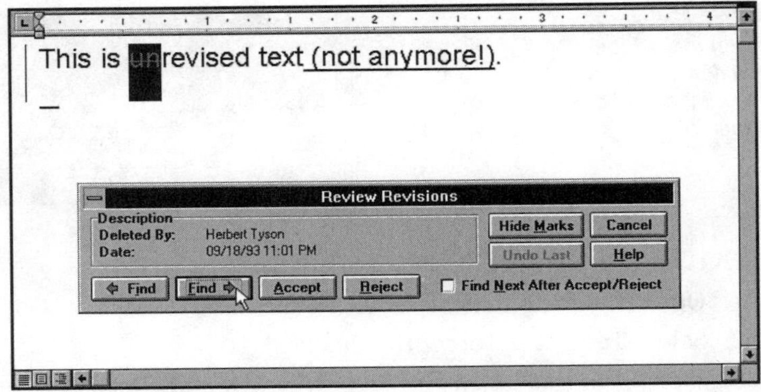

1. Click ← Find to move to a previous revision, or Find → to move to the next revision.
2. Select the Find **N**ext After Accept/Reject option to cause Word to move forward to the next revision after each Accept or Reject action.
3. Click **A**ccept to accept the revision; the text is updated immediately.
4. Click **R**eject to reject the revision; the text is restored to the original.
5. Click **U**ndo Last to restore the previous revision; you can now make a fresh decision regarding that revision.
6. Click in the text area and make direct modifications, if desired.
7. Click Cancel to end the Review Revisions session without taking any actions, or click Close if actions have been taken but you're ready to stop.

SUPER TIP

You can work in Review Revisions mode with revision marking enabled or not. Most users prefer to have additional revision marking disabled at this point. It's your choice, however. To enable/disable revision marking while in Review Revision mode, simply click in the text area or in the menu and select Tools | Revisions. Note that if you select Review from that menu, it simply reactivates the dimmed review box and does not start a new one. If the document was edited by someone else, incremental revisions you make now are in a different color. If you want to distinguish your own revisions, you can also select Tools | Options | User Info and make a slight modification to your name to force Word to record revisions you make while reviewing in a different color.

Comparing Documents That Don't Have Revision Marks

Sometimes, despite your best efforts, a document comes back to you without revision marks. Or, perhaps you merely want to compare a file with an old backup version. Or, perhaps the document was converted to a different word processor and has been returned. Regardless, you can use Word's document comparison feature to locate the additions and deletions.

Compare Versions

Activated from the Compare Versions button in the Revisions dialog box, the comparison feature automatically compares two documents, adding insertion and deletion revision marks.

PROCEDURE 36.8. COMPARING A DOCUMENT AGAINST A VERSION WITH UNMARKED REVISIONS.

1. Open the original document.
2. Select **T**ools | Revisions.
3. Click **C**ompare Versions.
4. Navigate to the file that contains the changes, and click OK.
5. Word now automatically "redlines" the document opened in Step 1. The result is how the document selected in Step 4 would have looked if it had been edited with revision marking turned on. You might want to quickly save that document under a new name to preserve your original.

You can now proceed as previously shown to review the changes made to your document.

Merging Several Revisions

Sometimes you send your document out to multiple people for review and revision. You then get back several different versions. It can be a real nightmare to try to integrate changes contained in many different files. Word has a terrific solution—Merge Revisions. The Merge Revisions feature takes documents based on the same starting point and merges them into a single document, incorporating all of the different revisions. Revisions from different reviewers are marked in different colors.

PROCEDURE 36.9. MERGING REVISIONS.

1. Open a file that contains revisions you want merged with other revisions.
2. Select **T**ools | Revisions.

3. Click Merge Revisions.
4. Select the file that contains additional revisions and click OK.
5. Repeat Steps 2 through 4 until all revised documents have been merged.

For the Merge Revisions command to work, all documents must be based on the same starting point. If reviewers 1, 2, and 3, all began working with the identical document, it's fine. If they had slightly different documents at the outset, then the Merge Revisions command won't work correctly. All is not lost, however. You can restore parity to the different revisions by running the Compare Versions command on each of them. Or, open your "best" version and run the Compare Versions command on each to incorporate the different revisions.

Merging Workshop

Merging is the combination of data and documents to produce a finished product. By combining data and a document in a certain way, it's possible to use a single document for many recipients. Applications include form letters, invoices, mailing labels, and contracts.

In this workshop, you learn about mailmerges, data files, mailing labels, and forms. The focus is on how to use Word to create well-structured documents and data files, and how to combine them to produce printed results that vary according to what's in the data file.

Chapter

37

Mail Merge

Mail merge is the ideal solution when you have a well-structured document that's going to vary just a little for each recipient. In fact, if you're enterprising enough, you can use reference fields to make even the contents of the document vary by recipient. Using Word's resources exclusively or in combination with other Windows applications, you can easily create letters and other documents that use information from data files to create distinct results for each recipient.

Mail Merge Overview

Mail merge is the process of combining a main document (a Word document) and a data source. The main document is the letter, invoice, or other document whose basic structure is identical for every individual (record) in the data file. Instead of including individual data in each copy of the letter, invoice, or other document, you include references (MERGEFIELD fields) to data in a data file. The data source can be a Word file, but also can come from other applications as well, including Microsoft Excel and Access, Lotus 1-2-3, Quattro Pro, Paradox, and other applications.

According to the Mail Merge Helper screen shown in Figure 37.1, mail merge is a three-step process:

- Create and format the main document.
- Set up or create a data file.
- Merge the document and data to produce a new document (or printed result) for each individual in the data base.

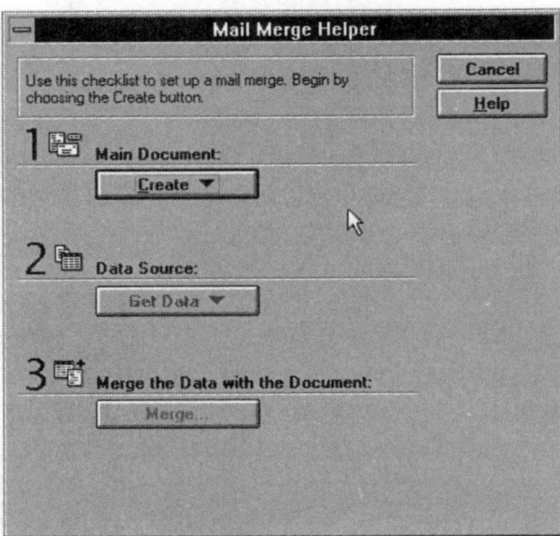

FIGURE 37.1.
Mail merge is a three-step process.

However, that's correct only if your main document and data files already exist. If they don't already exist, you face a little chicken-and-egg problem in trying to set things up. In order to set up your main document file using the Mail Merge toolbar, You already must have a data file set up. And, in order to get to the point where Word offers you an Edit Data button, you already must have specified a main document file. Alas, the logic is a bit difficult to follow, even after you understand it.

So, here are the *real* steps needed:

1. Create your database; it can come from another application (Microsoft Access, Excel, and so forth).
2. Create the basics for your main document. If you already have a letter, invoice, or other document you'd like to use as a template, then make a copy and use it.
3. Run the **T**ools | Mail Me**r**ge routine to open your main document and associate a data file with it.
4. Edit the main document using the Mail Merge toolbar, so you can insert data fields into it.
5. Use the Mail Merge toolbar to merge and print.

SUPER DO IT YOURSELF

Word's mail merge procedures are suitable for setting up a variety of data and document merges, including invoices, contracts, inventory lists, personnel rosters, and membership lists. Just because the Mail Merge Helper dialog box doesn't mention any of these doesn't mean that you can't do them. Moreover, just because the Mail Merge Helper dialog box *does* mention form letters, mailing labels, envelopes, and catalogs, doesn't mean that you *have* to use the Mail Merge Helper dialog box to create your own form letters, mailing labels, envelopes, and catalogs. Any time the built-in procedures seem too rigid, just break loose and set up your own procedures. You still need to use the Mail Merge Helper dialog box, but just to designate the document you set up as a mail merge document and to associate a data file. The rest of the design and control can be set up entirely by you.

Data File

Microsoft has gone to lengths to try to simplify the mail merge process. Unfortunately, a few pieces are still missing. The biggest missing piece is making sure that you have your data file standing by when you create your main document. Because we have to worry about chickens and eggs, this chapter assumes that your data file is ready, willing, and able. If that assumption is wrong, see Chapter 40, "Data Files," for additional information on getting your data into shape.

Main Document

There are several types of Word documents, and some have special properties. These types include templates, regular documents, forms, and mail merge files. What sets a mail merge file apart from a regular file is the fact that you designate it as a mail merge file using the Tools | Mail Merge command (the Mail Merge Helper dialog box). Once you designate a file as a mail merge document file, it suddenly has some different properties. For example, each time you open it, the Mail Merge toolbar appears. A mail merge document also has associations with data and possibly a data header file.

Creating a main document for mail merge is easy. Word's Tools | Mail Merge command, the Mail Merge Helper, takes you through the process, step by step. You can create a main document from scratch. Alternatively, if you have a letter, invoice, or other document you want to use as a basis for the main document, you can use that as well.

PROCEDURE 37.1. ASSOCIATING A MAIN DOCUMENT AND DATA FILE FOR MAIL MERGE.

1. If you have a document you want to use as a basis for the main document (a letter, invoice, envelope, and so forth), open it.
2. Select Tools | Mail Merge.
3. Click the Create button under Main Document to display the options shown in Figure 37.2.

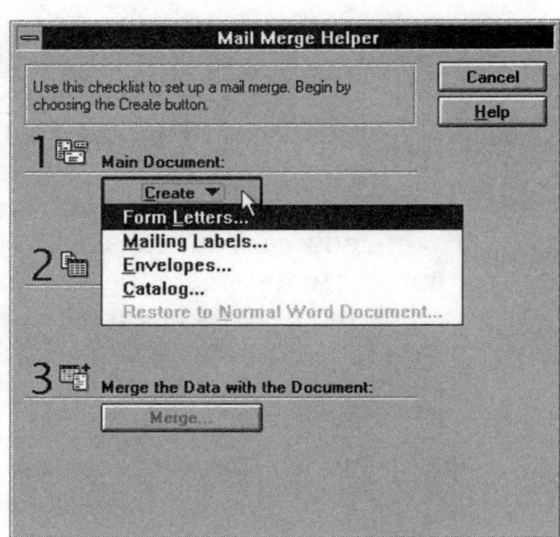

FIGURE 37.2.
The Create button gives you a choice of types of mail merge documents.

4. Word displays the options shown in Figure 37.3, to use the current document or to start a new main document. Click to select your preference.

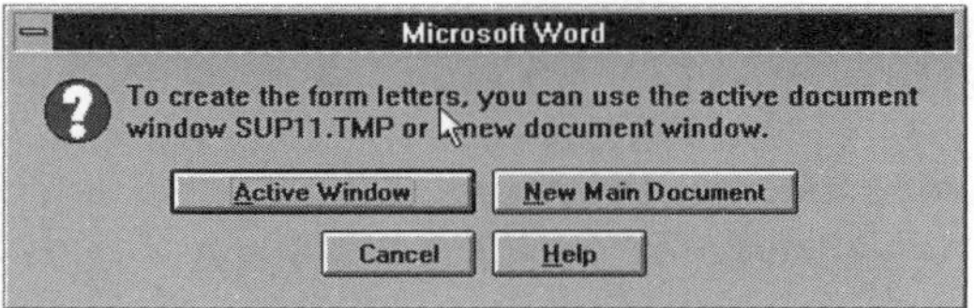

FIGURE 37.3.
Word creates a mail merge document from scratch, or uses the document that's already open.

5. Word adjusts the Mail Merge Helper text to reflect the source of the main document.
6. Click **G**et Data. Select **C**reate Data Source to create a new data file, this very minute (see Chapter 40). Select **O**pen Data Source to use an existing data file. Select **H**eader Options if your data and header information are in different files. For the sake of simplicity, we'll assume that you click Open.
7. Use the **O**pen Data Source dialog box, shown in Figure 37.4, to navigate to your data file and click .

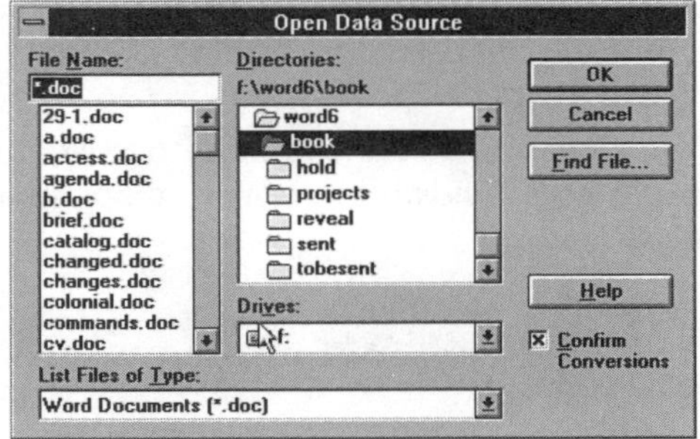

FIGURE 37.4.
*Use the **O**pen Data Source options to open your data file.*

8. Confirm the data source, as shown in Figure 37.5, and click OK.

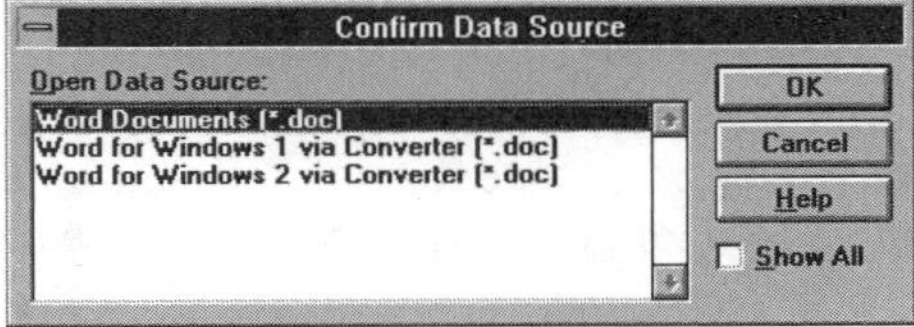

FIGURE 37.5.
Confirm the data source.

9. What happens next varies widely, depending on the data source. If the file is in an unacceptable format, the Header Records Delimiters dialog box appears; see the procedure Setting Header Records Delimiters.
10. If the file is a Microsoft Access database, you must first prepare the data using **I**nsert | **D**atabase, as described in Chapter 40.

11. If the data file is in an acceptable format (assuming that you have not yet inserted any merge fields into your main document file), Word displays the dialog box shown in Figure 37.6, telling you that you now need to edit the main document to insert merge fields. Click Edit to adjust the text and to insert mail merge fields. If the document already has merge fields, then you're set to start printing (or whatever).

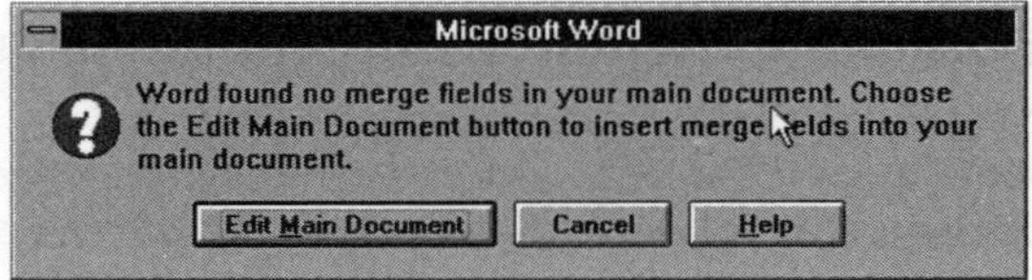

FIGURE 37.6.
If Word doesn't find any mail merge fields, you need to edit the document to insert them.

12. At this point, Word displays the Mail Merge toolbar, shown in Figure 37.7. Each button's action is discussed in Table 37.1.
13. If you're creating a new document, then type and format the text that will be identical in each merged document. If it helps, use dummy names (for example, type `Dear` *name*, or something like that) as placeholders where you expect to insert data.
14. Go to each location where you want to use data from the data file, and click the Insert Merge Fields button; Word displays a list of available fields from the data file.

FIGURE 37.7.
The Mail Merge toolbar.

Creating or Opening a Header File

In step 6 of procedure 37.1, it was assumed that you would select Open as the option. Another likely possibility is that the data file you want to use does not already have a header, and that you don't really want a header added to it. Such would be the case if your data are in an acceptable format and you have other applications that use that data and that will no longer work correctly if the data file suddenly adds a header at the front.

Word lets you specify a separate header file. This file should be a one-row Word table with one column for each field in the data file it describes. Word guides you through the creation of the header file if you select the Header option in Step 6 of the Associating a main document and data file for mail merge procedure.

PROCEDURE 37.2. CREATING OR ASSIGNING A HEADER FILE FOR A MAIL MERGE DATA FILE.

1. Click **G**et Data in the Mail Merge Helper dialog box, and select Header Options.
2. Word displays the Header Options dialog box shown in Figure 37.8; click **O**pen to associate an existing header file with the mail merge operation; click **C**reate to create a new one.

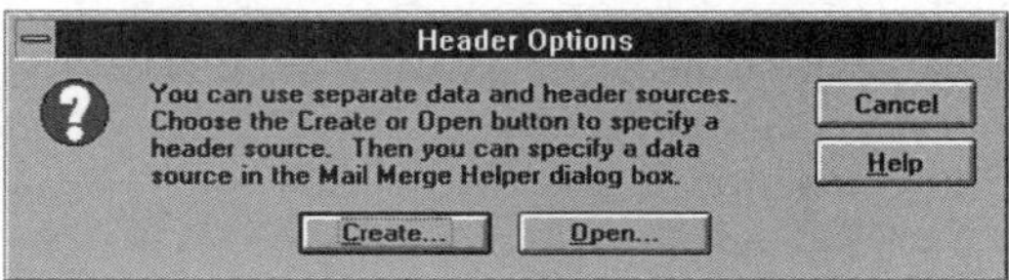

FIGURE 37.8.
The Header Options dialog box.

3. Assuming you click **C**reate, Word displays the Create Header Source dialog box shown in Figure 37.9. This dialog box has preassigned a structure consisting of 13 common data fields.

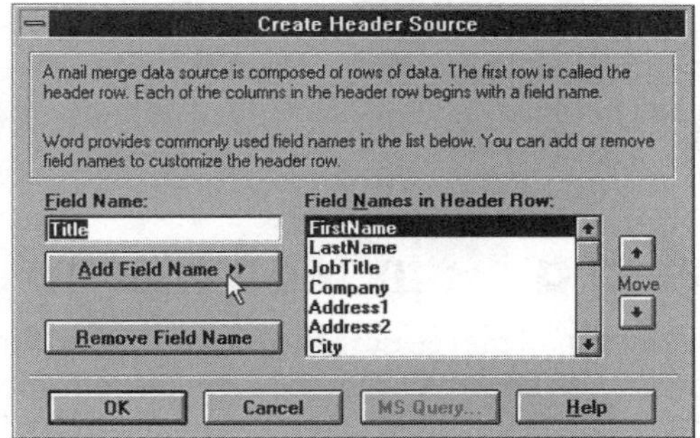

FIGURE 37.9.
The Create Header Source dialog box.

4. To add a new field to the structure, type a new field name in the **F**ield Name text box and click **A**dd Field Name. Note that the field name must begin with a letter, can contain letters, numbers, and the _ character, and can contain up to 40 characters.
5. To remove preassigned fields that don't fit your data, select the field in the Field **N**ames in Header Row list and click Remove.
6. To move a field, select the field you want to move in the Field **N**ames in Header Row list; then click the Move Up or Move Down button(s) until the Field is in the proper position.
7. Click OK when the header correctly describes the data in the data file.

SUPER NOTE

It usually is easier to create a data file header if you're looking at the data file at the same time. If you have the option, open the data file so you can verify the structure. Note also that once you associate a header with a mail merge document, you cannot get rid of it. Instead, you'll have to first restore the mail merge document to a normal document, then convert it back into a mail merge document, reestablishing the data file association, this time omitting the header file option. See procedure 37.4 on restoring or converting a mail merge document into a normal Word document later in this session.

SUPER CAUTION

If you apply the incorrect header file to a mail merge document that already contains merge fields, only the merge fields that are defined in the current header are displayed. If merge fields suddenly disappear from the screen, you may need to press Alt+F9 to toggle the display of merge fields on to see exactly what happened.

Preparing a Main Mail Merge Document

When you open a mail merge data file for editing, a window opens with the mail merge toolbar at the top, as shown in Figure 37.10. The mail merge toolbar's buttons are shown in Table 37.1.

FIGURE 37.10.
The Mail Merge dialog box.

Table 37.1. Merge toolbar buttons.

<table>
<tr><th>Button</th><th>Action</th></tr>
<tr><td>Insert Merge Field</td><td>Inserts a <code>MERGEFIELD</code> field (for example, {<code>MERGEFIELD</code> <code>Address</code>}) at the cursor's location</td></tr>
<tr><td>Insert Word Field</td><td>Inserts one of nine Word Mail Merge control fields, used to conditionally control the mail merge, to prompt for information during the merge, and to insert text using bookmarks (see Figure 37.11; refer to Chapter 29, "Fields," for additional information).</td></tr>
<tr><td>«» (3rd button)</td><td>The View Merged Data button toggles <code>MERGEFIELD</code> fields between display as <code>«Address»</code> and the actual data.</td></tr>
<tr><td><code>|<</code></td><td>Goes to the first record in the data file.</td></tr>
<tr><td><code><</code></td><td>Goes to the previous record in the data file.</td></tr>
<tr><td>Go To Record</td><td>Specifies which record to use, by number.</td></tr>
<tr><td><code>></code></td><td>Goes to the next record in the data file.</td></tr>
<tr><td><code>>|</code></td><td>Goes to the last record in the data file.</td></tr>
<tr><td>Mail Merge Helper</td><td>Displays the Mail Merge Helper dialog box, which lets you specify the main file, data file, and initiate merges and queries.</td></tr>
<tr><td>Check for Errors Error (<code>Check for Errors</code>)</td><td>Checks the merge for errors.</td></tr>
<tr><td>Merge to New Document</td><td>Sends the results of the currently defined merge to a Document window.</td></tr>
</table>

continues

Table 37.1. continued

Button	*Action*
Merge to Printer	Sends the results of the currently defined merge to the printer.
Merge Dialog box	Displays the Merge Dialog box, which lets you set additional options, and then send the merge to a document or to the printer.
Find Record	Lets you search a field in the currently defined data file; this is useful when you're using a mail merge for a specific record (handy for managing address lists for addressing correspondence and envelopes).
Edit Data Source (`EditOpen Data SourceFile`)	Opens the data file for editing/browsing using a form-type dialog box.

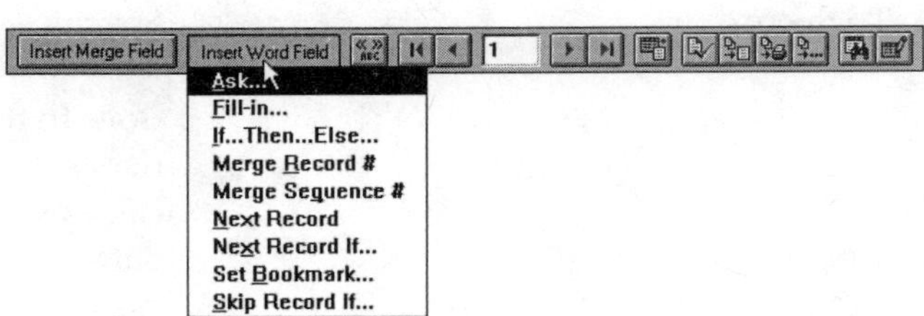

FIGURE 37.11.
The Insert Word Field dialog box provides access to nine common mail merge fields.

When a data file has been associated with the mail merge document, the main document and data file are, in effect, connected at all times. If you have inserted any merge fields (for example, using the Insert Merge Field button), you probably have some data tokens displaying on-screen, such as

```
«Contact_Name»
«Company_Name»
«Address»
«City», «Region»  «Postal_Code»
«Country»
```

At any given moment, each set of tokens is associated with data in the data file. If you click the `MailMergeViewData` toggle, the tokens now display the current data record:

```
Melissa Adams
77 Overpass Ave.
Provo, UT  84604
USA
```

You can display any record at any time, simply by clicking the record number field in the Mail Merge toolbar and filling in a record number. Or, if you prefer, you can use the ¦<, <, >, or >¦ buttons to position the record at the first, previous, next, or last record in a data file.

At this point, however, you have seen only two of the three possible ways to display the merge field. If you press Alt+F9, you'll see yet another view—the real view—which tells you what's really happening on the other side of the curtain:

```
{MERGEFIELD Contact_Name }{IF {MERGEFIELD Title}<> "" ", " ""}{MERGEFIELD
Title}
{MERGEFIELD Company_Name }
{MERGEFIELD Address }
{MERGEFIELD City }, { MERGEFIELD Region }  { MERGEFIELD Postal_Code }
{MERGEFIELD Country}
```

Note the `IF` field in the first line. There is no hint of it in the displayed data. There also is no hint of Melissa's title, nor of a company name in the data. By default, in Word 6, if a field is empty, Word does not try to print it out. This means that if a field is empty, Word does not insert a blank line into the merged data. Note that you do not need an `IF` field to keep the `Company_Name` from printing a blank line (more on this in a moment).

The `IF` field tells Word to *conditionally* insert a comma followed by a space whenever the Title field is not blank (<> `""`). If the Title field is blank, the comma and space are not inserted. This means that if Melissa had a title in the data file, it would be separated from her name with a comma and a space:

```
Melissa Adams, CEO
```

When the title field is blank, however, the IF field prevents the merged record from displaying a now useless comma:

```
Melissa Adams,
```

It is often useful to toggle the display of tokens and data while editing and creating a main document for mail merges. However, you should keep in mind Word's defaults when displaying the data. Otherwise, you might forget that empty fields do not display and inadvertently prepare the document in a way that is not consistent with them. When you think you have the document formatted correctly, try a number of different records to make sure that Word looks correctly for more than just the current one.

SUPER NOTE

When moving among records in a mail merge document window, it's much faster to go forward than backwards. If you're on record 7 and want to go to record 6, it takes much longer than if you want to go to record 8. That's because Word isn't able to directly address data records. It has to count from the beginning. So, if you're on record 100 and want to go to record 99, you see a message on the status bar as Word goes back to 1 and counts up to 99. It's not a very efficient mechanism, and the larger the data file, the more inefficient it becomes. Keep this in mind when sampling records in a mail merge window, and always go forward, if possible.

Show the actual buttons in the first column, if possible.

Changing Data Files

When editing a mail merge document, you can change data files at any time.

PROCEDURE 37.3. CHANGE DATA FILES.

1. Click the Mail Merge Helper tool in the Mail Merge tool (**T**ools | Mail Mer**g**e).
2. Click **G**et Data.
3. Click Create or **O**pen, and follow the prompts (see "Using Mail Merge Helper to Create a Dialog Box" in Chapter 40).

SUPER NOTE

When you change data files after inserting merge fields in the mail merge document, the only merge field tokens that display are those defined in the current data file or header. Field names are exact, and any variation in spelling causes the tokens or data not to display. Word alerts you to the mismatch when you attempt to merge, but it's useful to know *now* rather than when you're trying to complete an actual merge. Keep this in mind when changing data files. Press Alt+F9 to reveal the underlying field codes, if necessary.

Restoring a Mail Merge Document as a Normal Word Document

At times you might want to convert a mail merge document back into a regular document. One time it's necessary is when you want to remove a header file from a mail merge association.

PROCEDURE 37.4. RESTORING OR CONVERTING A MAIL MERGE DOCUMENT INTO A NORMAL WORD DOCUMENT.

1. Click the Mail Merge Helper tool (or select **T**ools | Mail Me**r**ge).
2. Click **C**reate.
3. Select the last option, Restore to **N**ormal Word Document (see Figure 37.12).

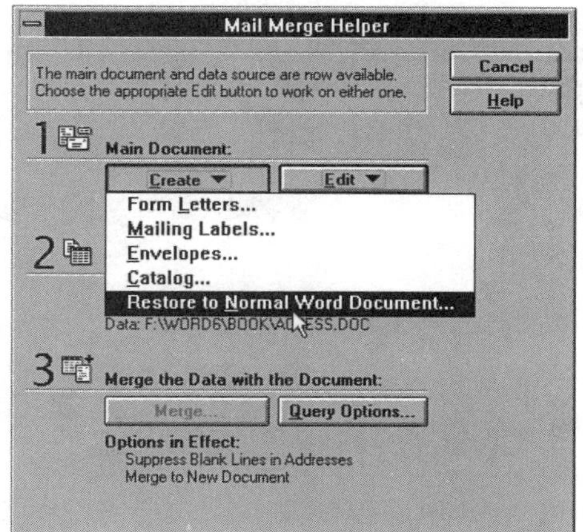

FIGURE 37.12.
To convert a document back into a normal Word document, select the Restore to Normal Word Document option.

SUPER NOTE

If you associate a header file with a mail merge document and later decide that you don't want it (for example, perhaps you decided to attach a header to the data file or were just experimenting with the commands, like I was when writing this book), you won't find any commands in the Mail Merge Helper dialog box or anywhere else for removing a header association. You can change it or create a new one, but you can't tell Word that you changed your mind about wanting one at all. In order to shake the connection, you'll have to convert the mail merge document back into a normal Word document, and then back into a mail merge document again. When you reassociate your data file, simply ignore the Header options this time around.

Merging, Checking, and Printing

Merging is the act of filling in the MERGEFIELD data field in a main document with data from a data file. When a mail merge document is on-screen, it is filled in with data from a single record at a time. If you click the MailMergeViewData toggle button («» ABC), Word toggles between the display of the merge tokens and actual data for the current record. If you select File | Print or click the Print icon on the standard toolbar, in fact, Word prints the mail merge document using information from the current data record. If you just want to print a single envelope, label, letter, or what-have-you, using the current data record, you can. Just print as you would from an ordinary document.

If you want to print more than one document, then you need to select one of the merge features. It generally is a good idea to merge first to a document window to verify that the data and document mesh correctly. When merging, Word provides several options. If you click the Merge to Document or Merge to Printer buttons, in fact, you might never discover those options. If you click the Merge button, however, you then get to see the Merge dialog box, as shown in Figure 37.13. When first starting out, use the Merge dialog box to learn what features are available. Later on, after everything is Fully specified, you can use the Merge to Document or Merge to Printer buttons to save time.

FIGURE 37.13.
The Merge dialog box.

PROCEDURE 37.5. MERGING USING THE MAIN MERGE DIALOG BOX.

1. Click the Merge button, as shown in Figure 37.14 (or select **T**ools | Mail Mer**g**e and click the **M**erge button, or click the Mail Merge Helper button and then the **M**erge button).

FIGURE 37.14.
*The **M**erge button activates the Merge dialog box, oddly enough.*

2. Using the Mer**g**e To drop-down list, select the destination for the merge: document or printer. It's always a good idea when you've been editing a mail merge setup to merge first to a document to verify that everything is set up correctly.

3. In the Records to be Merged section, select **All** or specify a range (**From**/**To**).
4. If the range and All options are too broad, click the **Q**uery Options button to further specify the merged data. See the procedure Using Query Options.
5. Click the Check Errors button to set the error reporting options. Word can simulate the merge and report errors now (this is equivalent to selecting the Error Check button on the toolbar), can report errors interactively while performing the merge, or can report errors in a separate window while doing the merge.
6. Select an option for how you want Word to treat blank fields. If a line contains just one or more blank fields, Word can suppress printing it. Select the Don't print blank lines option for most mail merge printing. However, if you have a need to know that fields are blank (for example, when printing out a copy of your data for auditing), make sure you select the option to print blank lines.
7. Click OK when you're ready to print.

SUPER CAUTION

When merging to a document, Word gives you the option to press Esc at any time to stop the merge. For some stupid reason, you don't have an equivalent option when merging to the printer. Instead, the Cancel option just cancels the document for the current record. I guess they figured that they need to protect the environment from all those wasted document windows, whereas wasted paper is of no particular concern. Keep this in mind, and be absolutely sure you're ready to print before you give Word the green light. Otherwise, you could end up with a pile of useless paper. Scratch pads, anyone?

Using Query Options to Sort or Limit a Merge

If you want to limit a merge to specific records, you have a variety of options. One option, of course, is to limit your data file to just the records you want to use. It's a good idea when setting up your data file to omit records for which you have absolutely no use. As mentioned elsewhere, displaying data records in a mail merge window is faster when you have fewer records.

Sometimes, however, you want to limit the data further, just for a particular document or merge run. Another option—for example, when setting up a limited-mailing document such as a delinquency notice—is to use Word fields (like IF) to limit the merge just to deadbeats. If you have a specialized document that would never be sent to anyone outside of a well-identified subset of your data, then use IF fields in your mail merge document to limit that document to the specific group.

Other times, you might have a document that could go to any part of the database at any time but which varies for different merge runs. For that kind of document, it doesn't make sense to embed IF fields. Instead, use Query Options to limit the data for just this run. You also can sort records.

SUPER TIP

Query Options can be selected and changed at any time from the Merge dialog box, not just when you're ready to print. After you sort or limit your data, the Cancel button in the Merge dialog box is replaced by a Close button. You can dismiss the Merge dialog box and examine your document using the new data selection or ordering before proceeding with the merge.

SUPER TIP

Use the Sort Order option to save on mailing costs. Depending on your mail volume, you often can save money by presorting your mail by zip code.

PROCEDURE 37.6. USING QUERY OPTIONS.

1. From the Merge dialog box, click **Q**uery Options; the Query Options dialog box appears.
2. To select records based on data values for specific fields, click **F**ilter Records, shown in Figure 37.15. Starting at the top, use the drop-down arrow to select a field, comparison operator (equal, less than, and so forth), and a comparison value (for example, `ZIP Less than 20000` to select northeastern U.S. locations, or `STATE EQUAL VA` to select just Virginia records). Work your way down, combining different conditions with `AND` (means both) or `OR` (means either), as needed.
3. To sort records by up to three fields, select the S**o**rt Records tab, shown in Figure 37.16. Use the drop-down arrow to select the field to sort by, then click Ascending or Descending. Set up to three sort fields, as needed.
4. If you want to clear previously assigned criteria, click **C**lear All.
5. Click OK when you're done.

Word immediately refreshes the current window with the changed data, even while the Merge dialog box is still on-screen. If, after the shuffle, you see a `0` in the current record of the Mail Merge toolbar, then Word did not find any matching records. You need to select the **Q**uery Options button again to respecify your criteria.

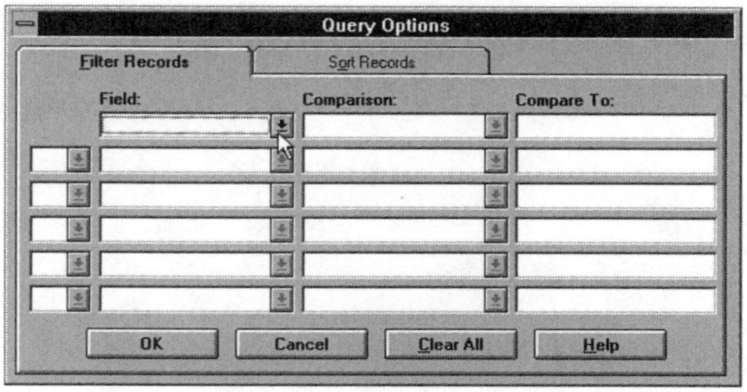

FIGURE 37.15.
The Filter Records option lets you hone in on just the records you want.

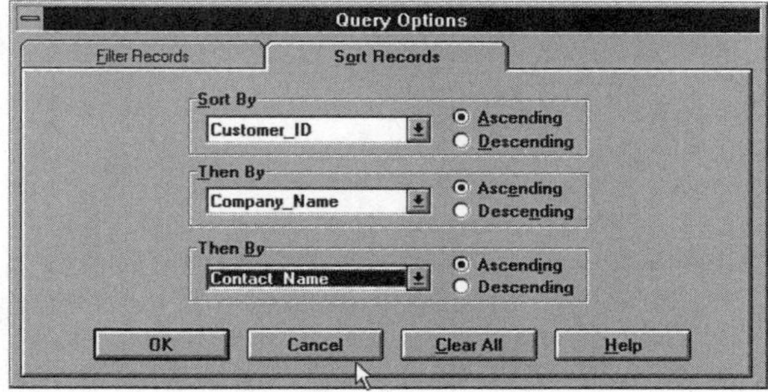

FIGURE 37.16.
Use the Sort Records tab to put your data in order.

Chapter 38

Data Files

Word gives you a number of options for creating and using data files. It's important to realize up front that you have a lot of flexibility in what you can do, and probably no single correct way to do it. Understanding this can help you avoid confusion later on.

There are basically two approaches to doing data with Word:

- Use data directly from a compatible file format (including plain text files)
- Create a data file using a Word document, manually or using the Mail Merge Helper

Using Data from a File in a Compatible Format

If you have a compatible data file already set up, you can use it directly. At the very least, you can use the Mail Merge Helper dialog box to determine whether or not Word can use the existing file.

PROCEDURE 38.1. USING AN EXISTING DATA FILE.

1. From the Mail Merge Helper dialog box (Tools | Mail Merge), click Get Data, then select Open Data Source, as shown in Figure 38.1.

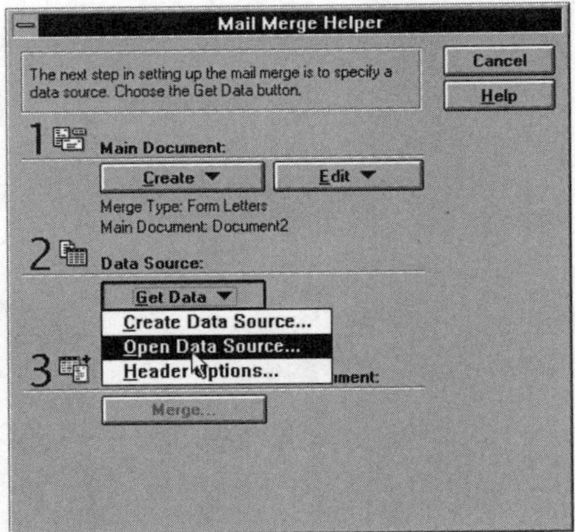

FIGURE 38.1.
Select Open Data Source to associate a data file with a main mail merge document.

2. If the file is not in a compatible format, Word displays the dialog box shown in Figure 38.2. If Word displays this kind of message, use the procedures described under the heading, "Converting a Data File into a Compatible Word Data File," to adjust the data file so that it fits.

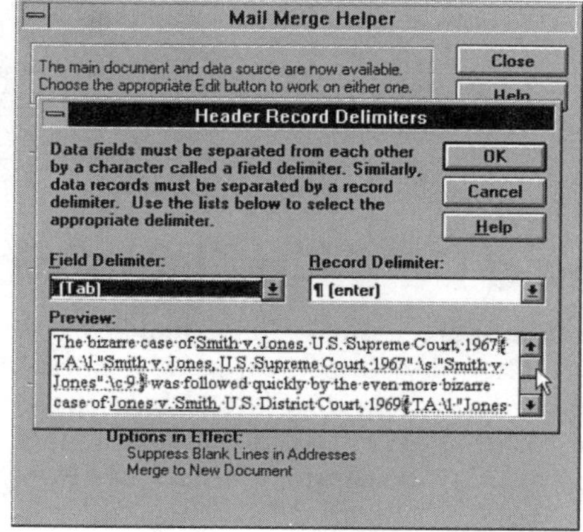

FIGURE 38.2.
Word lets you know if it doesn't recognize your data format.

3. If you're sure that the file doesn't have an unequal number of fields per record, then use the Field and Record delimiter pulldown lists to select the Field and Record delimiters that are used in the data file. If the list doesn't contain the ones that are in use, then you need to change them into something Word can use. If you are successful in identifying the correct delimiters, click OK to associate the data file with the main mail merge document file.
4. If the document contains merge fields already, then you can proceed as shown under the heading, "Merging, Checking, and Printing," in Chapter 37, "Mail Merge." If the document doesn't contain merge fields, then click Edit Main Document and follow the procedures shown under the heading, "Preparing a Main Mail Merge Document."

Often, it's possible that the format *is* compatible but has some other kind of problem, like an uneven number of fields per record. For example, the following kind of data file would produce the dialog box shown in Figure 38.2:

```
Title\Name\City\State
President\John Adams\Quincy\MA
President\Bill Clinton\AR
President\George Bush\MEaine
```

If you tell Word that the \ character is the field delimiter, you are able to get past the dialog box shown in Figure 38.2. However, when you try to use any record other than the first, Word displays the message shown in Figure 38.3. Notice that the fields and data don't align correctly due to the missing city data in records two and three. Because of the persistent and annoying error messages, it's usually too troublesome to try to go ahead and use the data anyway (even for simple addresses). The easiest solution is simply to insert \ characters into the data file where you are missing data. Only when the data file has the same number of field delimiters (even with missing data) are you *finally* able to get Word to move ahead to a successful merge.

FIGURE 38.3.
Word alerts you to the fact that your records don't contain the same number of fields.

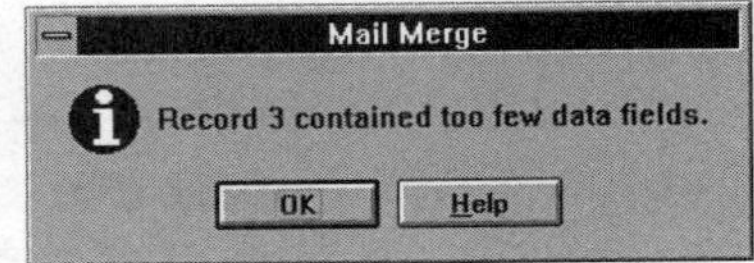

Creating a Data File Using Word

You can create a Word data file (a normal Word document that you set up as a data file) from scratch, or by converting data from another source. The most manageable format for a Word-based data file is a table, with the first row reserved for field names, as shown in Table 38.1. However, the identical data, with fields separated by tabs and records separated by paragraph markers, also works just fine.

Table 38.1. Typical Word-based data file.

Last	*First*	*Address*	*City*	*State*	*Zip*
Suddell	Wyatt	11 Elm Street	Anytown	VA	22542
Gates	William	One Microsoft Way	Redmond	WA	98052
Smith	John	1 Smithway	Williamsburg	VA	23333
Jones	Davy	1 Locker Circle	New Billings	SC	44444

You have a variety of choices in how you create a Word-based data file. There are at least four general approaches:

- Use Mail Merge Helper to step you through it
- Import the data you want to use (from Access, Excel, Lotus, a text file, and so forth), converting the format, as needed
- Convert an existing Word document that contains data (assuming conversion is needed)
- Manually enter and create the data file without using Mail Merge Helper

Using Mail Merge Helper to Create a Data File

The Mail Merge Helper dialog box provides an entry to the Create Data Source data design dialog box. A nifty utility, this dialog box first prompts you to set up the structure of your data (list of variables or fields), and then provides an entry form for filling in the data. The end-result is a Word table, the first row of which is column headers, and each subsequent row are the data records (sometimes called observations).

PROCEDURE 38.2. USING THE CREATE DATA SOURCE DIALOG BOX TO CREATE A DATA FILE.

1. From the Mail Merge Helper dialog box (Tools | Mail Merge), click **G**et Data, and select **C**reate Data Source from the drop-down menu. Word displays the dialog box shown in Figure 38.4.

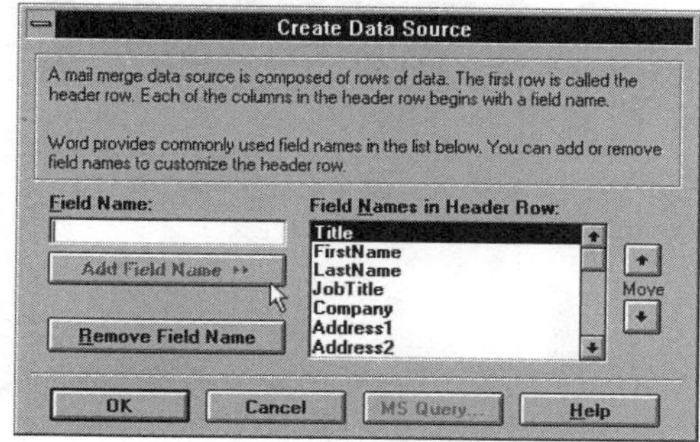

FIGURE 38.4.
The Create Data Source dialog box.

2. The **C**reate Data Source dialog box prompts you to first create a data header. Follow the procedure to create a header for the data file, and then click OK to continue.
3. Word now prompts you for a filename into which to save the newly-created data header, and which also will be used for the data file you create. Type a name and click OK. Depending on your save options, Word may also prompt for summary information.
4. Because you're creating a data file, Word next sends you a message that your data source doesn't contain any records (big surprise there, huh?); click the Edit **D**ata Source option, shown in Figure 38.5.

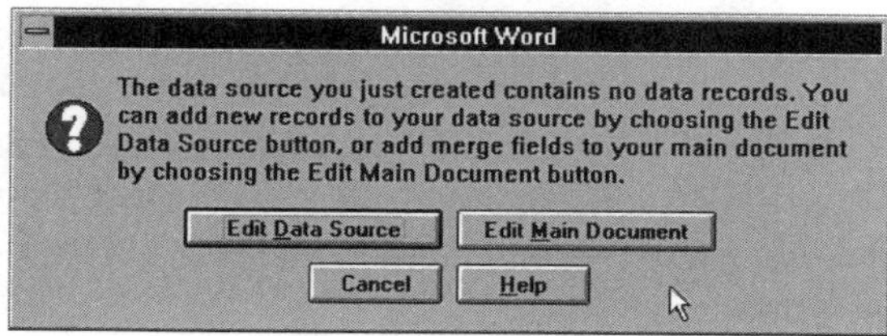

Microsoft Word
The data source you just created contains no data records. You can add new records to your data source by choosing the Edit Data Source button, or add merge fields to your main document by choosing the Edit Main Document button.
Edit Data Source
Edit Main Document
Cancel
Help

FIGURE 38.5.
Select the Edit Data Source option to access the Data Form dialog box.

5. Word now displays the Data Form dialog box. It displays fill-in areas for each field specified in the header you created in Step 2. Click **V**iew Source to display the file as well as the Database toolbar.

6. Word now displays the Database toolbar, as shown in Figure 38.6 and described in Table 38.2. At this point, you can click the first tool to display the Data Form dialog box (for guided data entry) or fill in the data without using the dialog box by just adding data in the table.

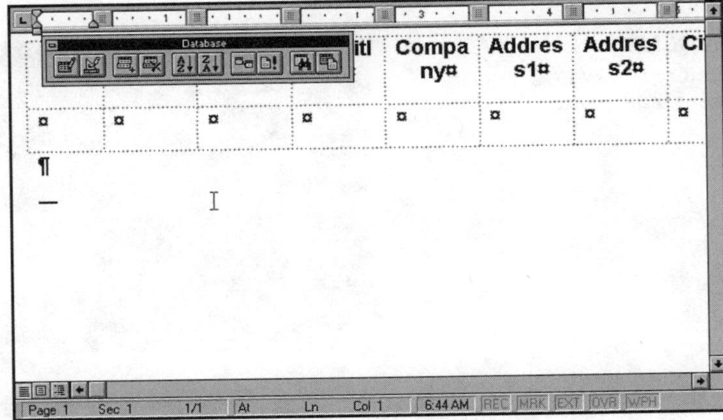

FIGURE 38.6.
The Database dialog box.

7. If entering data using the Data Form dialog box, click OK when you're done. Additional options are

Add New	Create a new record at the end of the data file.
Delete	Delete the current record
Restore	Undo all changes to the current record
Find	Displays the Find in Field dialog box, with which you search for data by field—in other words, to locate a specific record.
View Source	If the source isn't already displayed on-screen, this option displays it and the database toolbar.
Record	Use the Record options to display the first, previous, exact (by number), next, or last record in the data file.

8. When done entering data using the form, click OK to close the Data Form dialog box.
9. Press Ctrl+S to save the data file.

Table 38.2. The Database toolbar.

Button	*Description*
Data Form	Displays the Data Form dialog box for entering data into a Word table

Button	*Description*
Manage Fields	Adds or deletes a field (column) to or from a Word data table
Add Record	Adds a record (row) to a Word data table
Remove Record	Deletes a record (row) from a Word data table
Sort Ascending	Sorts the table in ascending order based on column 1 (the top row is assumed to be a header and is ignored)
Sort Descending	Sorts the table in descending order based on column 1 (the top row is assumed to be a header and is ignored)
Insert Database	Activates the Insert | Database dialog box
Update Fields	Runs the Update Fields command (same as pressing F9)
Search Field	Searches any field you specify for matching text
Main Document	If you're editing a database that's associated with a main mail merge document, this button switches to the main document window

The resulting data file should be usable by Word for mail merge purposes. Furthermore, just in case you've forgotten by now, this data file is already associated with the main document file that's open. You can now proceed to that window to finish setting up the mail merge.

Converting a Data File into a Compatible Word Data File

Data files can be converted into Word files in a number of ways. If you can easily convert your data into a Word table, as shown, you're home free. Your data can be used instantly by the Mail Merge Helper. If your data can't be readily converted, however, you have to do a little bit of work. The minimal requirements:

- The first record in the data file should be a header that says what is in each field (for example, last name, first name, address, and so on, as shown in Table 38.2).
- Each field must be separated from the next by an unambiguous field separator that doesn't occur in the fields themselves (for example, Tab, colon, semicolon, >, <, and so on).
- Each record must be separated from the previous record with a separator that is different from the field separator (in Table 38.2, information about Wyatt Suddell is record 1, William Gates is record 2, John Smith is record 3, and Davy Jones is record 4).

If you're unlucky enough to have a format that isn't supported directly by Word, you have to work a little to convert it. A single-field-per-record strategy is shown under the heading "Converting an Incompatible Data File Format into One-Field Records." A more tedious strategy is shown under the heading "Converting an Incompatible Data File Format into Multifield Records."

Converting an Incompatible Data File Format into One-Field Records

Unfortunately, the minimal requirements do not allow for one popular data layout format used by a substantial number of people, which is a single paragraph marker between each field, and two between each record. For example:

```
Wyatt Suddell
11 Elm Street
Anytown, VA 22542

William Gates
The Microsoft Corporation
One Microsoft Way
Redmond, WA 98052

John Smith
1 Smithway
Williamsburg, VA 23333
```

This popular format is widely used by many as a format for correspondence addresses. While seemingly inflexible for many purposes, it serves very well for addressing letters and envelopes. Alas, it's not a format that works as a Word data file, for two reasons. The first problem is that Word does not provide a mechanism for recognizing two paragraph marks as a record separator. The second problem is that there are different numbers of fields for the different records. The second record has four fields (name, company, address, and location), while the other records omit a company name.

A solution that requires the least amount of work is to convert this kind of data base into single-field data files, as shown in Table 38.3. This does not give you access to the name or other elements as separate fields. Because you didn't have that type of access to begin with, however, you're not losing anything.

Table 38.3. For some address files, a single-field record is the easiest solution.

Address
Wyatt Suddell<Shift+Enter> 11 Elm Street<Shift+Enter> Anytown, VA 22542

Address
William Gates<Shift+Enter> The Microsoft Corporation<Shift+Enter> One Microsoft Way<Shift+Enter> Redmond, WA 98052 John Smith<Shift+Enter> 1 Smithway<Shift+Enter> Williamsburg, VA 23333

The procedure can look a little confusing unless you understand the strategy, which is to convert this kind of data file into a format that causes Word's Convert Text to Table command to put each whole address into a single table cell, rather than one cell per address line. To do that, the easiest strategy is to convert the present line endings into line breaks instead of paragraph breaks and to convert the double paragraph returns between addresses into a single paragraph break. The procedure shown here does those two things, then converts the resulting data into a Word table.

PROCEDURE 38.3. CONVERTING A SIMPLE ADDRESS FILE INTO AN ACCEPTABLE WORD DATA FILE FORMAT.

1. Select **F**ile|**N**ew to create a new file (use Normal as the template).
2. Select **I**nsert|Fi**l**e, and navigate to the file you want to use, selecting the appropriate type of file (text, for example).
3. Press Ctrl+H (**E**dit|R**e**place), and type `^p^p` into the Find What field.
4. Type `<CR>` in the Re**p**lace With field.
5. Click Replace **A**ll; Word performs the replacement and might display a message box about continuing at the top. Click No to remove the message box, if necessary.
6. Type `^p` into the Fi**n**d What field.
7. Type `^l` (lowercase L) into the Re**p**lace With field.
8. Click Replace **A**ll; Word performs the replacement and displays a message box. Click No to remove the box, if necessary.
9. Type **`<CR>`** in the Fi**n**d What field.
10. Type **`^p`** in the Re**p**lace With field.
11. Click Replace **A**ll; Word performs the replacement and displays a message box. Press Esc twice to remove the message box and the Replace dialog box.
12. Move to the top of the file and type **`Address`**, then press the Enter key.

13. Press Ctrl+End to go to the end of the data file, and remove any extra paragraph marks or other extraneous punctuation (press Ctrl+Shift+8, if necessary, to display paragraph marks).
14. Press Ctrl+A to select the entire file.
15. Click the table button in the standard toolbar (or select Table | Convert Text to Table).

You should now save this file under a suitable name (for example, ADDRESS.DOC). You can now use this file directly with mail merge, using just the single field called Address as the whole address, name and all.

Converting an Incompatible Data File Format into Multifield Records

The main reason for going with a single-field-per-record in the preceding discussion was simplicity. If you don't take that approach, and if your data file looks like the example shown in the previous heading, you instead would have to convert the file into a multifield-per-record data file. This task can be tedious because much of it must be performed manually and by sight. The longer the data file, the more tedious it is. Here's the general strategy:

1. Convert the double paragraph breaks between records into a temporary but unambiguous record separator (`<REC>`).
2. Convert the single paragraph breaks between address lines into unambiguous field separators (Tab, `^t`).
3. Convert the `<REC>` separator back into a normal paragraph break.
4. Insert blank fields for missing data (for example, Company Name).
5. If desired, divide the name field into First and Last (perhaps allowing for a middle initial as well).
6. If desired, divide the location field into City, Region (a generic name for State or Province), and Postal Code (a generic name for zip code).
7. If desired or appropriate, add a Country field.

Unfortunately, automation can go only so far in this exercise. You could begin by employing the Replace command to convert the double-paragraph breaks between records into something like `<REC>`. The next step is to convert the known field separators into something other than a paragraph break (like tabs). Unfortunately, the further you go with this, the more difficult it becomes to see your data clearly. The clear separation that exists at the outset quickly gets lost once the paragraph breaks get converted into something else.

So, while seemingly backwards, the best strategy usually is to keep the original format until you have a uniform number of fields per records (sometimes called *padding* with blank fields), and only then perform the paragraph break conversions. You must make sure, however, that you don't add purely empty paragraph fields to the file. Consider, for example, what happens if you just insert a blank line in an address:

```
Wyatt Suddell
<blank line>
11 Elm Street
Anytown, VA 22542
```

Unfortunately, it now looks like Wyatt Suddell is a one-line address and everything from 11 Elm Street to 22542 is another one-line address. So, instead of inserting a blank line, it's better to put something *on* that line:

```
Wyatt Suddell
<company>
11 Elm Street
Anytown, VA 22542
```

You can later use the Replace command to delete the meaningless field placeholders.

If you want to separate the last line of the address into three separate fields, you have a little more work. If you aren't plagued with a number of company names that include commas (such as AAAAcme Industries, Ltd.) and if your addresses are all uniform:

```
<City><Comma Space><Two Character State><Space><5-digit Zip>
```

you could use Word's Replace command to try to sort it out for you.

PROCEDURE 38.4. BREAKING AN ADDRESS LINE INTO CITY, STATE, AND ZIP FIELDS.

1. Press Ctrl+H (**E**dit | **Re**place).
2. Set Find What to: **`([ A-z]@)(, )([A-Z][A-Z])( )([0-9][0-9][0-9][0-9][0-9])`**.
3. Set Replace with: **`\1^t\3^t\5`**.
4. Set Pattern **M**atching to On.
5. Click **F**ind Next and verify that you've typed things correctly for Word to find the address line. Then click **R**eplace and verify that tabs now separate the city, state, and zip.
6. When satisfied, click Replace **A**ll.
7. Set Fi**n**d What to: `([ A-z]@)(, )([A-Z][A-Z])( )([0-9][0-9][0-9][0-9][0-9])`.
8. Set Re**p**lace With to: **`\1^t\3^t\5`**
9. Select Pattern **M**atching.

> **SUPER NOTE**
>
> In Step 1, there is a *space* before the initial `A-z`, to allow for multiword cities such as New Orleans. The specification is deliberately `A-z`, not `A-Z`, because cities might include any letter from *capital* A through *lowercase* z. Keep in mind that all pattern-match searches are case-exact. Note also the space in the expression `(, ): (,<space>);` and in the seemingly empty `( ): (<space>)`.

If the City, State, and Zip are perfectly structured, this **R**eplace command replaces the comma and space between City and State with a tab (`^t`) and the space between the State and Zip with a tab. Complexities such as Canadian postal codes (six digits, letters and numbers) make the specification more difficult, but it can be done with a bit of experimentation. It's sometimes quicker and easier, however, to do the exceptions *by hand* than to invest tons of time trying to find a single elegant, fits-all solution.

Separating the names is a little more difficult because it's often hard for a search routine to distinguish between names that are part of an address and names that are those of a person. You can use the fact that each address starts with a person's name, however, to do the legwork for you. What you can't do easily, however, is accommodate names that range from Cher to William H. Remmington, III, Esq. If you decide that you absolutely *must* have separate fields for last and first names, *good luck!*

Just kidding. One strategy is to go with the general case and manually take care of the exceptions. Here, let's just assume there are only two names per field.

PROCEDURE 38.5. BREAKING A NAME LINE INTO NAME FIELDS.

1. Insert two paragraph marks at the top of your file so that the following search string won't skip the first record, and put the cursor at the top of the file.
2. Press Ctrl+H (**E**dit|**Re**place).
3. Set Fi**n**d What to: **`([^013][^013])([A-z]@)( )([ .,A-z]@)([^013])`**.
4. Set Re**p**lace With to: **`\1\2^t\4\5`**.
5. Select Pattern **M**atching.
6. Click **F**ind Next and verify that you've typed things sufficiently correctly for Word to find the name fields; then click **R**eplace and verify that a tab was inserted between the first and subsequent names on the Name line.
7. When satisfied, click Replace **A**ll.

SUPER NOTE

You cannot use `^p` in a pattern matching search. Instead, use `[^013]` for each paragraph mark character. Note also that `[ .,A-z]` includes a space, period, and comma before the `A-z`, to allow for middle initials, *Jr*, *III*, and so forth. If your data has things like *3rd* instead of *III*, you also need to include a `3` in there, as well as any other odd characters.

This search strategy separates the first whole word of the name from the rest of the name with a tab. This lets you write Dear John letters, but not Dear Mr. Smith letters, assuming that your data base doesn't (luckily) have just first/last combinations. If you want further definition of the fields, you'll have to not only figure out a strategy (manual), but you'll have to pad nonconforming fields with dummy placeholders as well. If you use `<Dummy>` as a placeholder, by the way, make sure you don't inadvertently leave `<Dummy>` in your data file. Otherwise, you might not get many people attending that important presentation you're planning!

After you've done as much field separating as you can, your next step is to convert the rest of the field separators (single paragraph breaks) into tabs and the record separators (double-paragraph breaks) into single paragraph breaks. The best strategy is to follow Steps 3 through 15 in Procedure 38.3, with the following modification: change `^l` to `^t` in Step 7. After doing this, your data should now look roughly as shown in Table 38.4. If your data is misaligned—some zips are in the wrong place, for example—then it's likely that you didn't pad correctly. You can press Alt+Backspace to undo the table, fix things, and then create the table again. However, unless alignment problems are extensive, it's usually easier to just fix them manually by dragging and copying items to the correct cells.

Table 38.4. Data converted to a table, before field labels are applied.

Wyatt	Suddell		11 Elm Street	New Anytown	VA	22542
William	Gates	The Microsoft Corporation	One Microsoft Way	Redmond	WA	98052
John	Smith		1 Smithway	Williamsburg	VA	23333

The final step is to add a header (field labels) to the top of the data file:

PROCEDURE 38.6. INSERTING A HEADER LINE AT THE TOP OF A DATA TABLE.

1. Select the first row of the table.
2. Click the right mouse button on the selection, and click Insert Rows.
3. Type a logical field name at the top of each column (for example, `First`, `Last`, `Company`, `Address`, `City`, `State`, and `Zip`).

Chapter

39

Form Letters, Mailing Labels, Envelopes, and Catalogs

As shown in Figure 39.1, when you use Tools | Mail Merge to initiate a mail merge setup, Word prompts you to indicate which type of mail merge you want to perform:

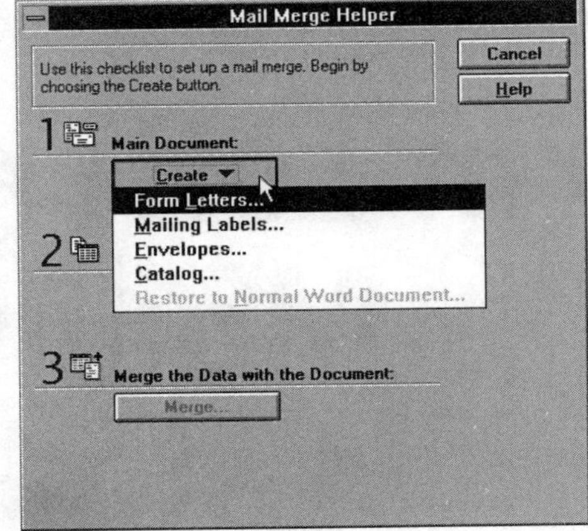

FIGURE 39.1.
Word gives you a choice of types of mail merge operations to set up.

- Form Letters
- Mailing Labels
- Envelopes
- Catalog

Depending on your selection, Word can automatically supply the correct document layout for a form letter, a sheet of mailing labels, an envelope, or a catalog. If you select Form letter, Word doesn't do anything special except supply a normal 8.5 × 11-inch document for creating the letter. Use the procedures described in Chapter 37, "Mail Merge," if you're setting up a form letter. It's frequently better, however, to start with an existing letter or template, then replace existing name, address, and other information with the respective merge fields.

Mail Merge to Mailing Labels

When you specify Mailing Labels as the type of merge, Word ultimately asks you to specify the type of labels and prompts you to set up the label format. Word then creates a document that looks like a sheet of labels, multicolumn formatting (depending on the type of label), using NEXT fields to print multiple data records on any given page.

PROCEDURE 39.1. SETTING UP A MERGE TO MAILING LABELS.

1. Select Tools | Mail Merge.
2. Click Create under Main Document, and select Mailing Labels.

3. Click **N**ew Main Window.
4. Under Data Source, click **G**et Data. Follow the procedures shown in Chapter 37 or Chapter 38, "Data Files," to specify a data file.
5. Word next displays the message box shown in Figure 39.2. Click **S**et Up Main Document.

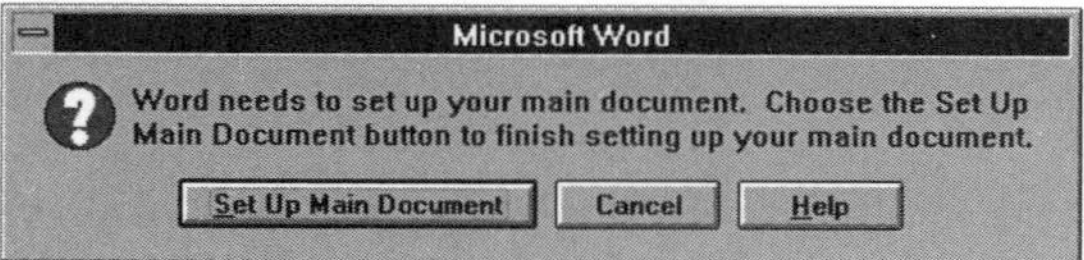

FIGURE 39.2.
Click Setup to activate the Label Options dialog box.

6. Word displays the Label Options dialog box shown in Figure 39.3.

FIGURE 39.3.
The Label Options dialog box.

7. Select the appropriate printer options and label type.
8. Click **D**etails to customize the label setup (positioning, size, and so forth), as shown in Figure 39.4.

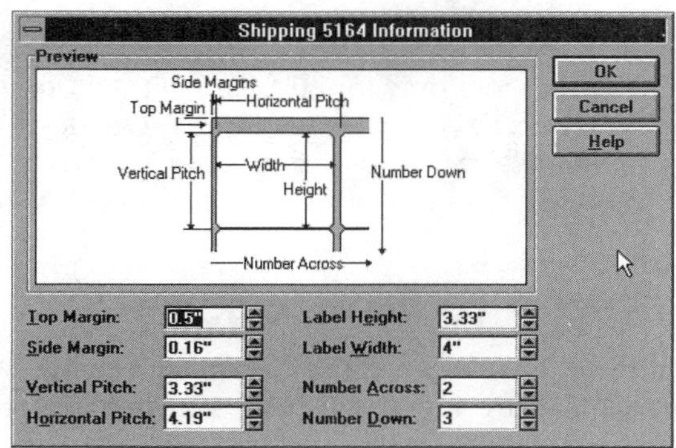

FIGURE 39.4.
*Use the **Details** button to customize the label format.*

9. Click OK when you're satisfied with the setup.

10. Word now displays the Create Labels dialog box, shown in Figure 39.5; you have the choice of inserting merge fields here or pressing Esc and working directly in the label document window.

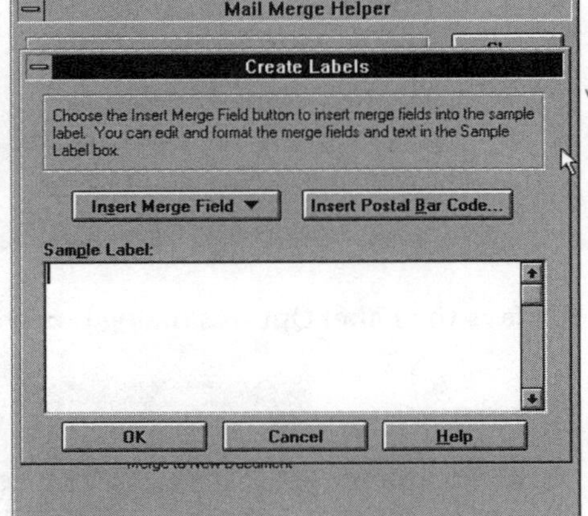

FIGURE 39.5.
The Create Labels dialog box.

11. If you elect to work in the Create Labels dialog box, click In**s**ert Merge Fields and/or Insert **B**arcode to set up the label with the appropriate format; click OK when you're satisfied.
12. At this point, Word lands you back at the Mail Merge Helper dialog box. You can click **E**dit under Main Document or click **M**erge to proceed. The first few times you set up mailing labels, it's a good idea to take a look before merging, just to make sure everything is as you think it should be.

SUPER NOTE

Barcodes work only for addresses in the United States. If you have addressees in your data file for non-U.S. destinations, you should set up two mailing label documents—one for the U.S. and another for non-U.S.

Mail Merge to Envelopes

When you select **E**nvelopes as the type of mail merge, Word asks you to specify information about the envelope (size, feed, and so forth), then provides a dialog box for setting up the envelope.

PROCEDURE 39.2. SETTING UP A MERGE TO ENVELOPES.

1. Select Tools | Mail Merge.
2. Under Main Document, click Create and select Envelopes.
3. Click New Main Document.
4. Under Data Source, click Get Data. Follow the procedures shown in Chapter 37 or Chapter 38 to specify a data file.
5. Word next displays the prompt shown in Figure 39.6. Click Set Up Main Document.

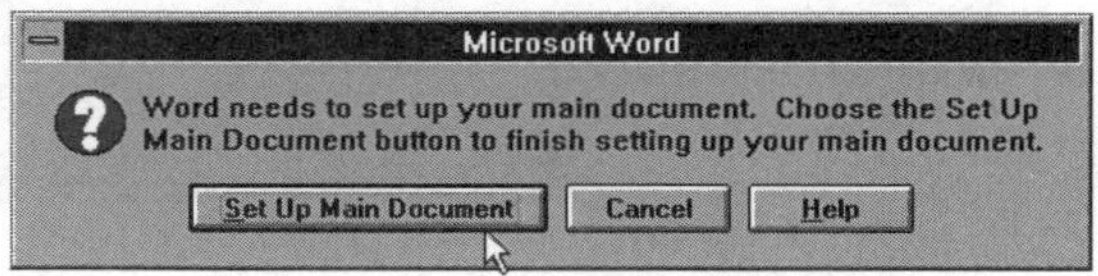

FIGURE 39.6.
Click Set Up Main Document to display the Envelope Options dialog box.

6. Word displays the Envelope Options, a tabbed dialog box shown in Figure 39.7.

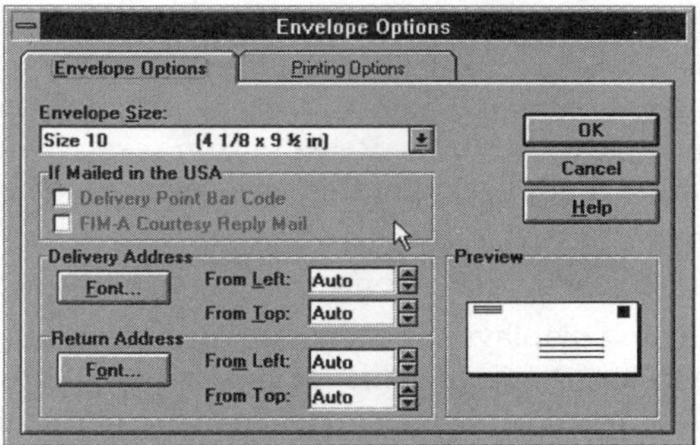

FIGURE 39.7.
The Envelope Options dialog box.

7. In the Envelope Options section, select the appropriate Envelope Size, Bar Code, and facing identification marker (if appropriate—U.S. addresses only).
8. Specify the format for the Delivery Address, setting the Font and the position from the Left and Top. The position settings are crucial for the envelope; Word uses the position information to set the location of the Delivery Address frame on the envelope.
9. Specify the position for the Return Address, setting the font and distance From Left and From Top. Note that because the Delivery Address is framed, you can delete the return address without affecting the position of the Delivery Address on the envelope. If you have preprinted envelopes, make sure you delete the Return Address.

10. Click the **P**rinting Options tab to display the Printing Options dialog box shown in Figure 39.8.

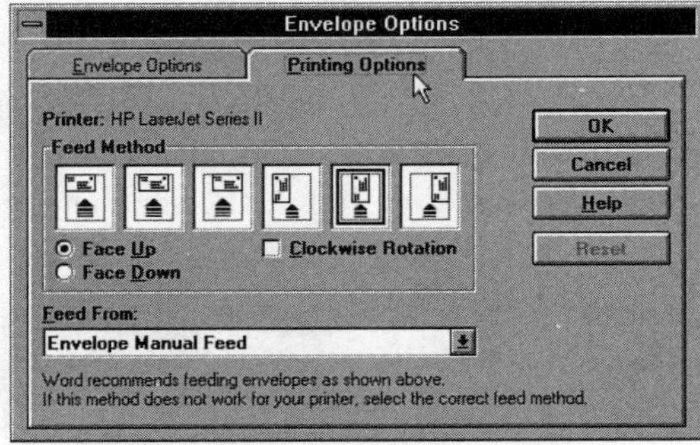

FIGURE 39.8.
The Printing Options dialog box.

11. Note the Printer: installed information, making sure it's correct.
12. Select a Feed Method—portrait or landscape.
13. Select a **F**eed From option.
14. If you get a persistent message at the bottom of the dialog box saying `You have changed Word's default envelope handling method for this printer. These changes could be incorrect. Choose Reset to return to Word defaults`, you could have the wrong printer set as the default (for example, Generic/Text Only).The **R**eset button resets Word's envelope defaults, but it usually will not get rid of this message. You usually can safely ignore the message.
15. Click OK when you're done, to close the Envelope Options dialog box.
16. Word next displays the Envelope Address form shown in Figure 39.9. Use this form to insert merge fields for the Delivery Address. Unlike the Mailing Labels routine, Word sets up a single envelope per page.
17. Use the In**s**ert Merge fields to compose the address (include name, company name, address, city, state or region, zip or postal code, and country, where appropriate).
18. Select the Insert Postal **B**ar Code, if necessary for your mailing class (you might set up U.S. and non-U.S. versions of the envelope form).
19. Click OK when ready.

Word returns to the Mail Merge Helper. Click **E**dit under main Document, and select the document. Word next displays an envelope in page layout view. Choose Edit or Close (or just press Escape) if you need to adjust or view the format. When setting up an envelpoe format for the first time, make sure you do this, and try test-printing a few different kinds of addresses on the back side of scrap paper before wasting a stack of envelopes (different numbers of lines, different line lengths in the address). Choose

Query to select/sort records. Choose Merge to set up the merge. Try a few addresses to make sure the layout is correct.

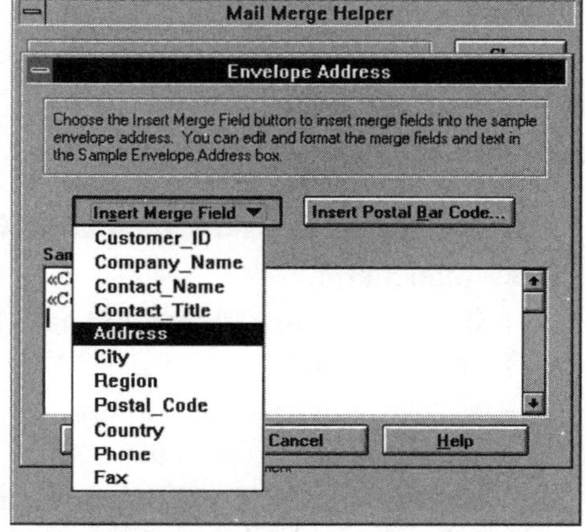

FIGURE 39.9.
You can use the Envelope Address form to insert merge fields for the delivery address.

If the formatting isn't correct, you have several options. However, if you're going to change the format, change it now and not after you've merged. To change the address positions, drag the frame(s) to a new location. To change paragraph spacing or fonts, you're better off changing the Envelope Address style. Make sure you select the Add to Template option if you want all future envelope formats based on the current template to use the changed Envelope Address style.

When you're finished formatting, you can use the Mail Merge toolbar to check your formatting with some different addresses and to print. While the Mail Merge Helper dialog box makes setting up envelopes relatively straightforward, it's nice to avoid reinventing the wheel once you have one that rolls. So, make sure you save the envelope mail merge form for future use, especially if you had to experiment with the positioning to get the addresses to look correct.

Mail Merge to a Catalog

Catalogs are excellent candidates for merging. Product information, pricing, availability, and similar types of information are generally kept in a data base, and they change regularly. By using a merge to generate your catalogs, you are sure to have the latest products and pricing.

When setting up a merge to a catalog, Word doesn't provide the same level of assistance as it does when setting up envelopes and mailing labels. In fact, the setup for a catalog is identical to the setup for a form letter. It's up to you, therefore, to determine how you want the catalog to appear. Some of the major considerations are

- Layout of each item: product name, descriptions, size, shipping weight, price, any hyperbole you care to lace in, and perhaps a graphic with a picture or drawing of the product.
- Use of color, if color printing and copying will be used.
- Number of products per page.
- Header or footer for page numbers.
- Columnar format (single, double, triple, and so forth).

PROCEDURE 39.3. SETTING UP A MERGE TO A CATALOG.

1. Select Tools | Mail Merge.
2. Under Main Document, click Create and select Catalog.
3. Click New Main Document.
4. Under Data Source, click Get Data. Follow the procedures shown in Chapter 37 or Chapter 38 to specify a data file.
5. Word next displays the prompt shown in Figure 39.10. Note that this is different from the prompt offered at this stage in the setup for envelopes and mailing labels. Click Edit Main Document.

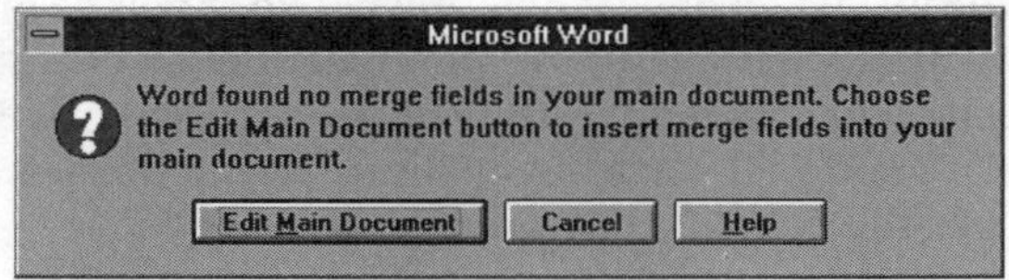

FIGURE 39.10.
Unlike Labels and Envelopes, the Catalog routine doesn't offer any special setup options.

At this point, the procedure is largely manual. Follow these general steps:

1. Set up a Word table for the catalog format, as shown in Figure 39.11.

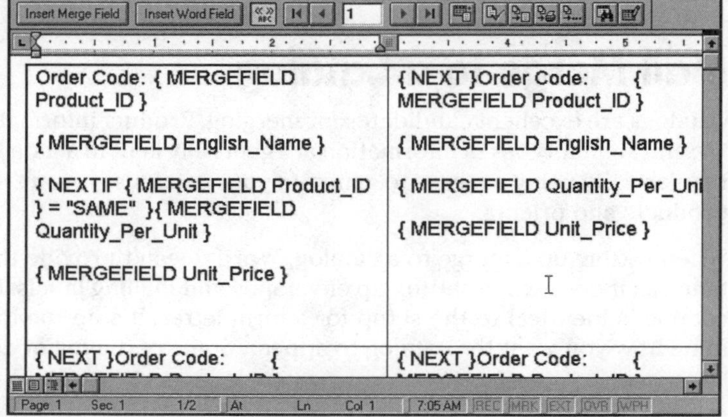

FIGURE 39.11.
Catalogs come in a variety of different formats.

2. Applying whatever formatting you need, use the Insert Merge Fields button to create a prototype for a single catalog entry (name, product number, description, price, and so forth); turn on the display of data (click the « _» button) to ensure proper formatting.
3. Copy the prototype catalog entry into each table cell.
4. Use the Insert Word Field command to insert a Next Record field at the beginning of every cell except for the first one (otherwise, each catalog page would have a number of entries for the identical item).

When you're ready to perform the merge, Word will not let you merge the catalog results directly to the printer. Instead, you must first merge to a new document. After verifying the formatting there (and preferably saving the catalog so you don't have to do it again—at least not until the data changes), you can then print the catalog as you would an ordinary document.

Workshop

XI

Long Documents Workshop

Don't get thrown by the title of this workshop. Although the title indicates that it's about creating long documents, that's not necessarily true. It's simply that the tools and techniques featured in this workshop typically get used most in long documents. In this workshop, you learn how to use Word's tightly integrated outlining to get a better handle on your documents. You also see how to integrate footnotes, end notes, tables of contents, indexes, and cross-references into your Word documents. For really long documents, especially those being created in a work group setting, you learn about Word's new Master Document feature, which lets you maintain control over multiple files maintained by many different users.

Chapter

40

Outlining

The beauty of Word's outlining is that it's really just a different way of working with styles. You're not inserting new information into the file, you're using heading style names to get a better handle on the document for organizing material. When you promote or demote a heading level (change its relative position in the outline—that is, moving from I or 1 to an A level), you're really just changing the style being applied to the current selection. All in all, outlining is a great bargain power tool for Word. You get all this extra power without having to add any complexity to a document (assuming you're already using the heading styles).

Overview

Word's outlining is linked directly to the use of the styles Heading 1 through Heading 9, along with Normal. When you use Heading 1 through Heading 9 as styles for your main headings, you have the option of viewing your document headings by selecting View | Outline from the menu. If you have used your headings in outline fashion, as is common, then switching to Outline view in fact shows you an outline of your document.

In Word's Outline view, whether you use outline numbering or not (most often, you don't), it may help to think in terms of a traditional outline to see the relationship between heading styles and outline structure:

I. Heading 1

II. Heading 1

    A. Heading 2

        1. Heading 3

            a) Heading 4

            b) Heading 4

        2. Heading 3

            a) Heading 4

                (1) Heading 5

                    (a) Heading 6

                    (b) Heading 6

                (2) Heading 5

                    (a) Heading 6

            b) Heading 4

        3. Heading 3

            a) Heading 4

B. Heading 2

1. Heading 3

III. Heading 1

A. Heading 2

B. Heading 2

Word is set up in such a way that you could *intuitively* type an outline for a document, and then use the resulting outline as the structure for a document. The word intuitive is emphasized because, as they say, "Different strokes for different folks." If you were to sit down at a keyboard or typewriter and start writing an outline, you might begin in the following way:

```
I. Main heading text 1st item (Heading 1)
<tab>A. Secondary heading text 1st item (Heading 2)
<tab><tab>1. Tertiary heading text 1st item (Heading 3)
<tab><tab><tab>a). Subheading text (Heading 4)
<tab><tab><tab>b). More subheading text (Heading 4)
<tab><tab>2. Tertiary heading text 2nd item (Heading 3)
<tab><tab><tab>a). Subheading text (Heading 4)
<tab>B. Secondary heading text 2nd item (Heading 2)
II. Main heading text 2nd item (Heading 1)
```

Every place you see `<tab>` is where you're likely to want to press Tab, to indent the next heading level. In Word's outlining, however, Tab doesn't work quite the same way. Once a heading is at a given level, it stays there without your having to press Tab again. In fact, pressing Tab again sends you deeper, to the next level, and pressing Shift+Tab takes you back out, to the previous level. Once you get accustomed to the differences, however, you can easily use Word's outlining view to create a structure for your document.

Aside from just getting a different view of your document, Word's outlining also gives you enormous flexibility. You can, for example, display your document at any level of detail. If you display at level 3, for example, you might display just the main headings in a book chapter. For example:

Aquatic Treasures (Heading 1)

Chapter 1 Understanding Fish (Heading 2)

Redfish (Heading 3)

Eels (Heading 3)

Bluefish (Heading 3)

Flatfish (Heading 3)

Catfish (Heading 3)

In an ordinary outline, what would happen if you decided that you wanted your fish to be in alphabetical order? You would simply reorder the listing. But in a document, text might be associated with each level—perhaps a deeply-layered structure. If you wanted to reorganize, you might need to select all of the text under the Bluefish level and carefully move it to the top of the list. Then you'd move Catfish, then Eels, and so on.

Well, in Word's outlining view, you don't need to select all the text under a given heading. Here, the view is set at Heading 3. When you select the line Bluefish, all subordinate text (all text from Bluefish up to Flatfish) is automatically selected. If you move the Bluefish heading up or down, all text that belongs with that heading automatically goes with it. Similarly, if you decide that Bluefish instead belongs under another heading, and perhaps should itself be a Heading 4 level instead of Heading 3, you can *demote* it. When you demote it, the Heading 3 gets turned into Heading 4, and all other headings under Bluefish are similarly demoted. If you decide that another kind of fish should be changed from Heading 4 to Heading 3, just *promote* it. All subordinate text under it is promoted as well, to the next higher logical level.

All text that is not a heading level (Heading 1 through Heading 9) is treated as *body text*. By default, Word wants to assume that body text has the style Normal. Even so, you can call it something else if you prefer. When viewing in outline mode, all text that does not have a heading level style is presented equally (as shown in Figure 40.1) or is hidden from view. The reason for showing text in this way is to emphasize the outline itself. When you're ready to pay attention to formatting rather than overall document structure, then outline view is not the view of choice.

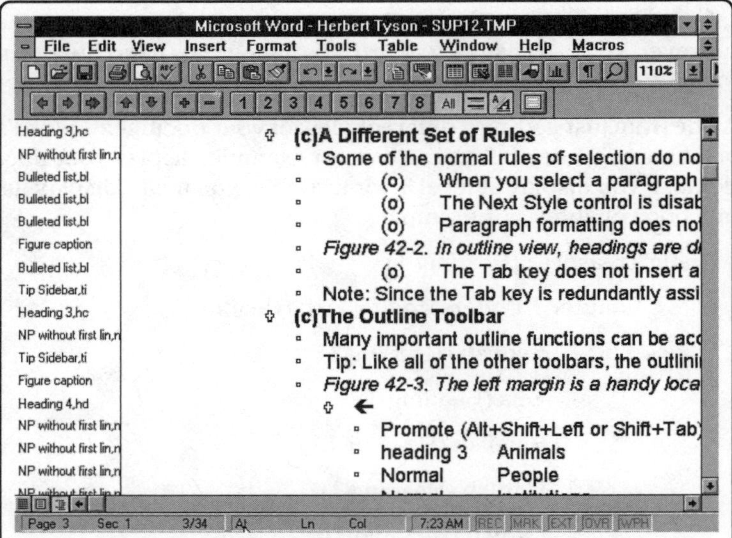

FIGURE 40.1.
In Outline view, all nonheading text looks the same.

A Different Set of Rules

Some of the normal rules of selection do not apply when working in Outline view. For the most part, the different rules (potentially) provide more leverage in working in outline view. If you fail to notice the differences, however, you can end up with unexpected results. Even though you can't change these basic behaviors, it pays to know about them, if only because it can help you understand what's happening. A few key differences:

- When you select a paragraph mark, the entire paragraph and all subordinate text is selected. This makes it more difficult to move or delete part of a paragraph or section. Keep in mind when working in Outline view that a lot of text can be hidden at any moment. Thus, selecting and moving a paragraph moves more than just what you see.
- The Next Style control is disabled. When you aren't in Outline or Master Document view, pressing Enter at the end of a paragraph causes the Next Style setting to be applied to the new paragraph. In Outline or Master Document view, pressing Enter at the end of a heading level causes another heading level of the same type to be inserted. If you compose text other than headings in Outline view, keep this in mind.
- Paragraph formatting does not display the same as in Normal view. As shown in Figure 40.2, in Outline view Word changes the display of paragraph formatting to maximize the resemblance to the outline paradigm. If you work in Outline view, however, make sure that you don't start reformatting your document trying to change the way it looks. When you return to Normal view, the effects likely are very different from what you intended.

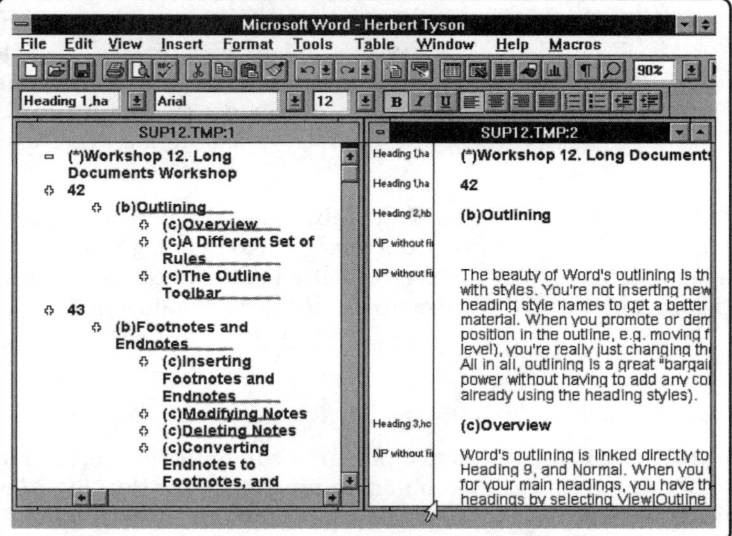

FIGURE 40.2.
In Outline view, headings are displayed as an outline, rather than in their actual formatting.

- The Tab key does not insert a tab. Instead, it Demotes the current level to the next level. To insert a tab in Outline view, press Ctrl+Tab. Note that Shift+Tab is a synonym for Promote.

SUPER NOTE

Since the Tab key is redundantly assigned with Alt+Shift+Left and Alt+Shift+Right, it might occur to you that you could reassign the Tab key so that it always means Tab. No dice. The geniuses at Microsoft seem to think that a Tab key that acts differently in different contexts is intuitive. So don't waste a lot of time trying to get consistent behavior from the Tab key.

The Outline Toolbar

Many important outline functions can be accessed either through the keyboard or by using the Outline toolbar. If you use outlining infrequently, you will find the Outline toolbar a handy way to navigate. However, if you use it a lot, you'll soon discover the value of knowing the keyboard shortcuts. Let's look at the Outline bar, the tools on it, and keyboard shortcuts.

SUPER TIP

Like all of the other toolbars, the Outline toolbar can be made into a floating toolbox, or it can be made to cling to any of the four sides of the Word window, as shown in Figure 40.3. Given that the left margin is naturally wide in Outline view, the left side of the window seems a naturally-accommodating location for the Outline toolbar. Once positioned there, it continues to reappear in that location until you move it.

Promote (Alt+Shift+Left or Shift+Tab). This tool increases a heading level to the next higher level (for example, from Heading 3 to Heading 2). If the current selection is not a heading level, then it gets reformatted to the most recent heading level that occurs before it in the text. For example, consider the following:

Heading 3	Animals
Normal	People
Normal	Institutions

If you are in Outline view and place the cursor in the People or Institution line, selecting Promote causes that line to be promoted to a Heading 3 level. If you select Promote again while in the same line, it is promoted to Heading 2. If a line is at Heading 1 level, then selecting Promote has no effect.

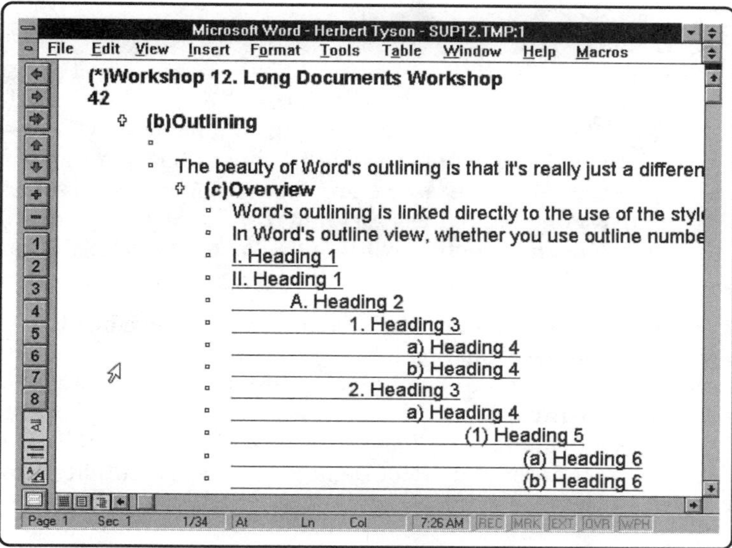

FIGURE 40.3.
The left margin is a handy location for the Outline toolbar.

SUPER NOTE

Promote has differing effects depending on what's showing in Outline view. If all levels are displayed, then selecting Promote promotes only the current paragraph. If all sublevels are collapsed below the current paragraph (that is, if you're promoting a Heading 3 paragraph while levels below are hidden), then everything below the promoted paragraph is promoted as well. Also, if more than one heading level is selected, then all heading levels in the selection are promoted; however, nonheading levels in the selection are not promoted at all. This differs from how nonheading levels are treated if only a single paragraph is selected. When you hit the wall (Heading 1) for any included heading level while promoting a selection that contains multiple heading levels, the headings that haven't yet reached Heading 1 continue to be promoted until all are Heading 1. Once that happens, however, the relative nesting of heading levels is lost. If you do inadvertently reformat a section, use Edit | Undo (press Alt+Backspace) to recover. Otherwise, you may end up having to reapply your formatting manually.

SUPER TIP

You can promote a heading level without being in Outline view by using Alt+Shift+Left. Demote, move up, and move down also work without having to be in outline view. Suppose you want to insert a new heading at the same level as the previous heading. Just press Enter to start a new paragraph, and press Alt+Shift+Left. This is a fast way to expand your document structure without having to reach for the mouse.

Demote (Alt+Shift+Right or Tab). Demote decreases a heading level to the next lower level (for example, from Heading 5 to Heading 6). If the selected paragraph is already at level 9, then Demote has no effect. If you select Demote while in a nonheading paragraph, Word assigns the next lower heading level. For example, if the previous heading is a Heading 3 level called Birds and you want to begin a subheading called Parrots, press Enter and select Demote (or press Alt+Shift+Right), and the new paragraph is at Heading 4.

>>

Demote to Body Text (Ctrl+Shift+N). Demote to Body Text applies the Normal style to the current selection, effectively demoting it to body text. This command is equivalent to applying the Normal style from the formatting ruler or pressing the Normal shortcut key.

Move Up (Alt+Shift+Up). The Move Up button swaps the current selection with the previous paragraph. This command is similar to dragging a selection. If you hold Alt+Shift and repeatedly press Up, you can move the current selection to any earlier location in the document.

Move Down (Alt+Shift+Down). The Move Down button swaps the current selection with the next paragraph. This command is similar to dragging a selection to a later point in the document. If you hold Alt+Shift and repeatedly press Down, you can move the current selection to any later location in the document. With the Alt+Shift keys pressed, using Up and Down lets you move the current selection anywhere else in the document. If no text is selected, Move Down moves the current paragraph.

+

Outline Expand (Alt+Shift+= or Alt+Shift++ on the number pad). Outline Expand reveals all of the body text under the current heading (or selected headings if multiple headings are selected). This command works only when the first paragraph in the selection is a heading level, even if a later part of the selection includes a heading level. This command is equivalent to double-clicking the plus sign at the left edge of a heading in Outline view, when the current level is collapsed.

-

Outline Collapse (Alt+Shift +- or Alt+Shift+- on number pad). Outline Collapse hides all of the body text under the current heading (or selected headings if multiple headings are selected). Like Outline Expand, this command works only when the first paragraph in the selection is a heading level, even if a later part of the selection includes a heading level. This command is equivalent to double-clicking the plus sign at the left edge of a heading in Outline view, when the current level is expanded.

`through 8`

ShowHeading1 through ShowHeading8. These buttons control which level of the outline is displayed. Use the ShowHeading buttons to view just the outline for a document, and to control how much of the outline is displayed. If you click ShowHeading1, only Heading 1 text is displayed. If you click ShowHeading2, only Heading 2 and above (Heading 1) are displayed. If you click ShowHeading8, then Headings 1 through 8 are displayed, but no body text.

SUPER TIP

In Word for Windows 2.0, Outline view also showed level 9 on the Outline toolbar. If you use that level and want it back, use **T**ools|**C**ustomize|**T**oolbars to put it back.

PROCEDURE 40.1. REINSTATING LEVEL 9 TO THE OUTLINING TOOLBAR.

1. Select **V**iew|**O**utline to display the Outline toolbar.
2. Select **T**ools|**C**ustomize and click the **T**oolbars tab.
3. Under **C**ategories, click View; the Outline toolbar components, among others, are displayed, as shown in Figure 40.4.
4. Using the left mouse button, drag the `[9]` icon from the dialog box to the Outline toolbar, just to the right of the `[8]`, and release the mouse button.
5. Under Sa**v**e Changes In, ensure that the correct context is selected (for example, NORMAL.DOT—unless you want to use a different template).
6. Click Close.

`All`

All (Alt+Shift+A) toggles the display between showing the current level and showing all levels and body text. When used to show all, this command is equivalent to selecting the entire document and clicking the Expand button.

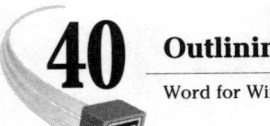

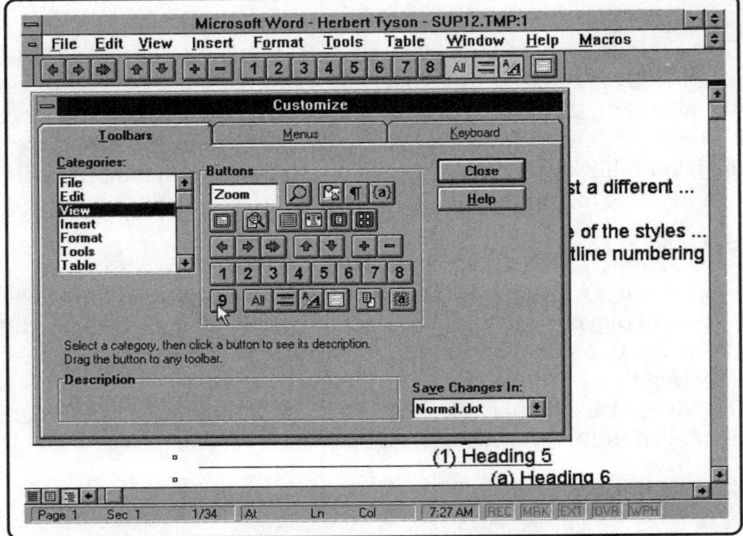

FIGURE 40.4.
The Outline toolbar components are kept with the View buttons.

=

OutlineShowFirstLine (Alt+Shift+L). OutlineShowFirstLine toggles between showing all of the body text and just the first line in the current displayed level. For example, if the Heading 3 level is displayed, Alt+Shift+L toggles just the first line of level 3 headings.

AA

Outline Show Format. Use this command to toggle the display of character formatting in Outline view. Depending on the number of levels and the relative size of the fonts used, it can sometimes be distracting to see character formatting. When you just want to concentrate on the outline structure, use the Outline Show Format button to toggle the display of character formatting off. The next click restores the display of character formatting.

Master Toggle

Master View Toggle. The Master View Toggle button toggles the display between master and normal Outline view. The two views are similar, except that Master Document view provides an additional group of buttons for manipulating the components of a master document. See Chapter 45, "Master Documents," for additional information.

Chapter

41

Footnotes and Endnotes

By design, footnotes and endnotes contain material that, if presented in the text, would disrupt the flow. In some kinds of documents—legal, academic, and journal materials—footnotes or endnotes, as well as a particular style of presentation, are mandatory. In other kinds of documents—reports and proposals—footnotes or endnotes are less common, but not unheard of. In normal correspondence, however, you rarely if ever see anything resembling a footnote.

Footnotes are presented in the text, beginning on the page where they are first referenced. In some complicated legal and technical documents, it's not unusual for several footnotes to begin on one page and extend well into the document. While clumsy, it does enable you to begin reading the note without having to find the end of the article.

Endnotes are deferred until the end of the document. In a book, endnotes usually occur at the end of a chapter. In a magazine or journal, they usually occur at the end of the article to which they pertain.

With Word you can have footnotes or endnotes, or both. Word also lets you determine, for the most part, how they are presented. Word even provides a mechanism for setting the footnote and endnote separator, continuation separator, and the continuation notice. Given that many publications are quite specific about how to present each, Word's flexibility enables you to readily conform to a variety of different requirements.

Inserting Footnotes and Endnotes

To create footnotes or endnotes, or to access footnote and endnote options, use the Insert | Footnote command from the menu. When you select the Insert | Footnote command, the Footnote and Endnote dialog box appears, as shown in Figure 41.1.

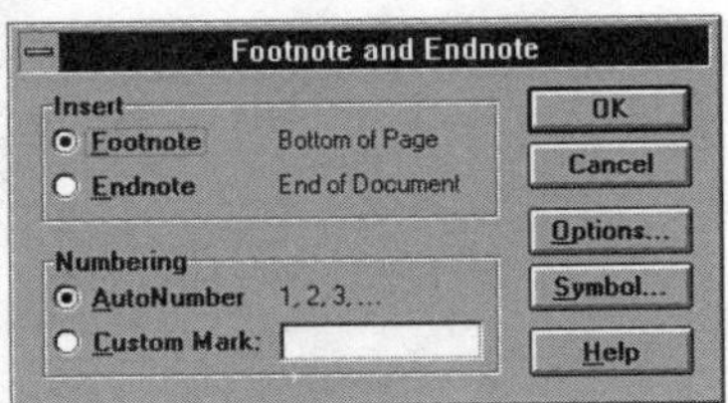

FIGURE 41.1.
The Footnote and Endnote dialog box.

SUPER TIP

If you have already taken care of options and simply want to insert a footnote or endnote, then use the InsertFootnoteNow or InsertEndnoteNow shortcut keys:

Alt+Ctrl+F	Insert Footnote without using the dialog box
Alt+Ctrl+E	Insert Endnote without using the dialog box

When you use Alt+Ctrl+F or Alt+Ctrl+E, a footnote or endnote reference mark is inserted into the text at the cursor's location and the corresponding footnote or endnote pane opens for inserting the footnote or endnote. In page layout view, a pane doesn't open. Instead, the cursor is moved to the footnote or endnote area, as shown in Figure 41.2.

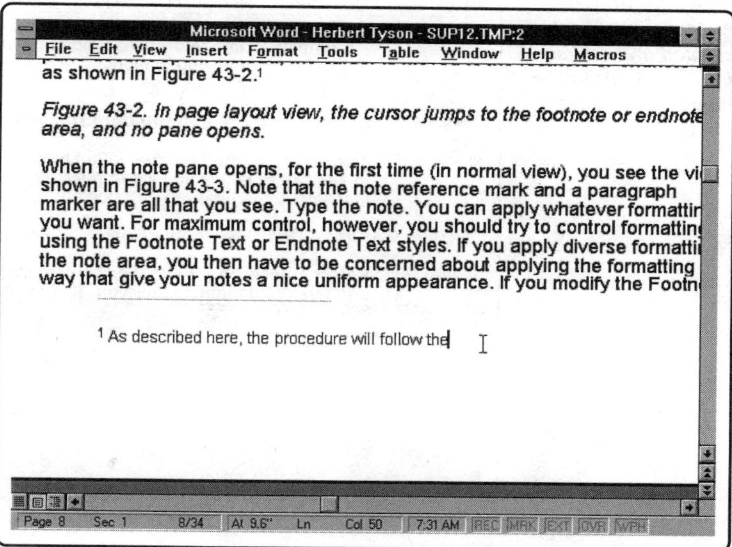

FIGURE 41.2.
In page layout view, the cursor jumps to the footnote or endnote area, and no pane opens.

When the note pane opens for the first time (in normal view), you see the view shown in Figure 41.3. Note that the note reference mark and a paragraph marker are all that you see. Type the note. You can apply whatever formatting you want. For maximum control, however, you should try to control formatting using the Footnote Text or Endnote Text styles. If you apply diverse formatting in the note area, you then have to be concerned about applying the formatting in a way that gives your notes a nice uniform appearance. If you instead modify the Footnote Text or Endnote Text styles, you can simply type your footnotes without worry.

When you're done typing your note, you have several choices. If you want to continue to look at the footnote while composing the body text, just click in the main text pane and continue working. The note pane remains open. You also can use F6 to toggle between the note and main pane. To close the note pane, click Close on the note toolbar, or press Alt+Shift+C.

By default (that is, unless you modify the Footnote Text or Endnote Text styles), Word uses the same note text style for additional paragraphs you create (the Next Style setting for the note text styles is set to be the same as the note style itself). You do not need to apply styles for each new paragraph you type. If your note consumes just a single paragraph, *do not press Enter at the end of it.* Word automatically inserts the necessary paragraph mark when you insert a note. If your note spans several paragraphs, just press Enter between each paragraph, but not at the end of the last one.

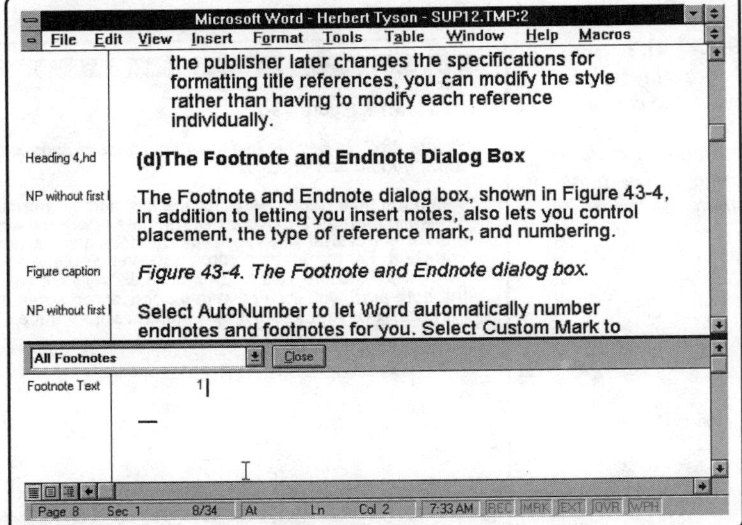

FIGURE 41.3.
Footnotes and endnotes are created and edited in panes in normal view.

SUPER TIP

If you must format journal titles or other publication titles in a specific way, especially if the format is subject to change, create a character style to handle the formatting. For example, you might create a character style called Journal, Magazine, or Book. If the publisher later changes the specifications for formatting title references, you can modify the style rather than having to modify each reference individually.

The Footnote and Endnote Dialog Box

In addition to letting you insert notes, the Footnote and Endnote dialog box (shown in Figure 41.4) also lets you control placement, the type of reference mark, and numbering.

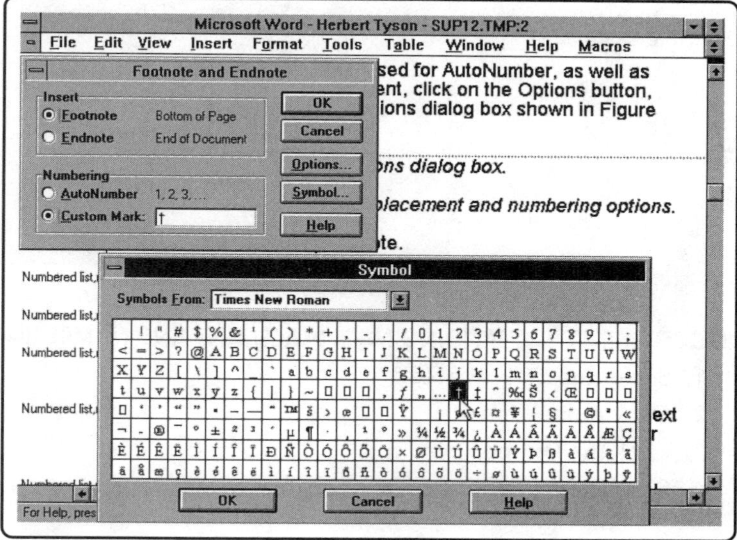

FIGURE 41.4.
The Footnote and Endnote dialog box.

Select AutoNumber to let Word automatically number endnotes and footnotes for you. Select Custom Mark to designate a particular character for Word to use instead. Use the Symbol button to insert the character if you don't know how to insert the character you want to use.

SUPER TIP

If you want to use legal-style reference marks, *don't* use the Custom Mark feature. Instead, select AutoNumber, and select the appropriate format in the Note Options dialog box. The number format options include a set of legal style reference marks: *, _, _, **, __, __, ***, ___, ___, and so forth.

To change the numbering used for AutoNumber (as well as footnote or endnote placement), click the Options button, which displays the Note Options dialog box shown in Figure 41.5.

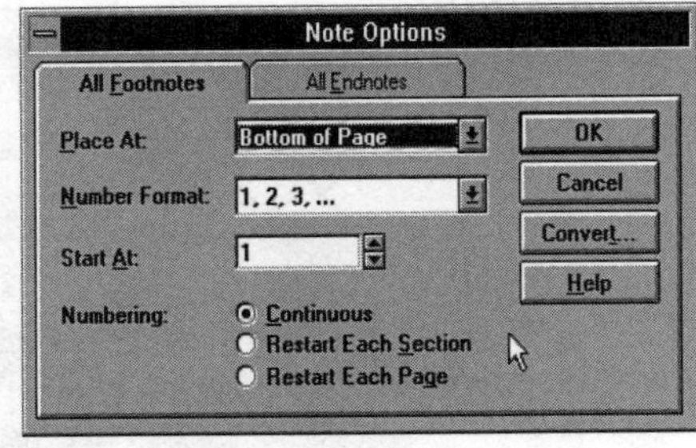

FIGURE 41.5.
The Note Options dialog box.

PROCEDURE 41.1. CHANGING NOTE PLACEMENT AND NUMBERING OPTIONS.

1. Select Insert | Footnote.
2. Click AutoNumber.
3. Click the Options button.
4. Click the All Footnotes or All Endnotes tab, depending on which you want to change.
5. Under Place At, select Bottom of Page or Beneath Text for footnotes; and End of Document or End of Section for endnotes.
6. Use the Number Format pull-down to select 1, 2, 3, I, II, III, i, ii, iii, a, b, c, and so forth.
7. Select a Numbering option (Continuous, Restart Each Section, Restart Each Page), depending on whether you're setting options for footnotes or endnotes.
8. Click OK to return to the Footnotes and Endnotes dialog box.
9. Click Close to close the dialog box without inserting a footnote or endnote.

Modifying Notes

To modify footnotes, you must either click in the note area when in Page Layout view, or select View | Footnotes. Note that the View | Footnotes command places you in the Footnote area and that no View | Endnotes command exists. Instead, you must select Endnotes from the drop-down menu on the Footnote toolbar. When in Page Layout view, you must instead scroll to the end of the document to view Endnotes.

PROCEDURE 41.2. MODIFYING FOOTNOTES IN NORMAL VIEW.

1. Select View | Footnotes.
2. Locate the note you want to change; note that the top pane scrolls as you select different footnotes.
3. Make your changes, being careful not to insert stray paragraph marks or to delete any reference marks.

4. Press Alt+Shift+C (or click Close) to close the note pane.

PROCEDURE 41.3. MODIFYING ENDNOTES IN NORMAL VIEW.

1. Select **V**iew | **F**ootnotes.
2. Use the drop-down arrow to display the options shown in Figure 41.6.

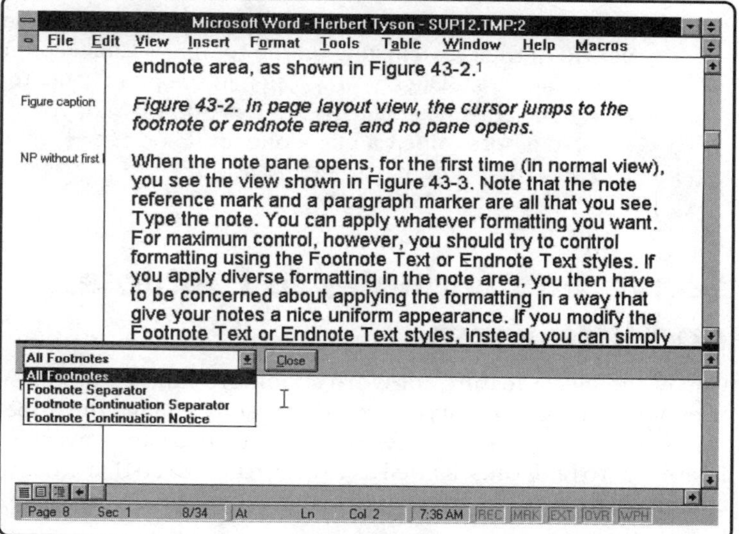

FIGURE 41.6.
The drop-down arrow provides access to footnotes, endnotes, separators, and continuation notices.

3. Click All Endnotes.
4. Locate the note you want to change; note that the top pane scrolls as you select different footnotes.
5. Make your changes, being careful not to insert stray paragraph marks or to delete any reference marks.
6. Press Alt+Shift+C (or click Close) to close the note pane.

Deleting Notes

Deleting notes is an area that sometimes causes confusion for users. The temptation is to open the footnote or endnote area and delete the note at the source. Except… that's not really the source. The source is the note reference itself in your document. That's where you have to do your deleting.

PROCEDURE 41.4. DELETING A FOOTNOTE OR ENDNOTE.

1. Locate the note reference mark in your document; if necessary, you can select **V**iew | **F**ootnotes or **E**dit | **G**o to Footnote to help you pinpoint the note exactly.

2. In the body text (*not* in the note area), select just the note reference mark.
3. Press the Delete key.

SUPER

HOW DO I CANCEL A FOOTNOTE?

One irritation about footnotes and endnotes is that, unlike dialog boxes, you cannot simply cancel them by pressing the Escape key. Nor can you get rid of them by clicking on the toolbar's Close command without typing any text. Once you've opened the pane using the Insert | Footnote command (or by using Alt+Ctrl+E or Alt+Ctrl+F), you have in fact already created a note (albeit a blank one until you type something). The only way to cancel a note is to delete it.

Converting Endnotes to Footnotes, and Vice Versa

One of the nicest features of Word's footnotes and endnotes suite is that it's editor-friendly. Using various styles, you can readily change the appearance of your notes. Another feature is a sometimes-overlooked ability to convert Endnotes to Footnotes, Footnotes to Endnotes, as well as to swap the two so that what was End becomes Foot and vice versa.

PROCEDURE 41.5. CONVERTING ENDNOTES TO FOOTNOTES, AND VICE VERSA.

1. Select **I**nsert | Foot**n**otes.
2. Click **O**ptions.
3. Click Conver**t**, to display the dialog box shown in Figure 41.7.

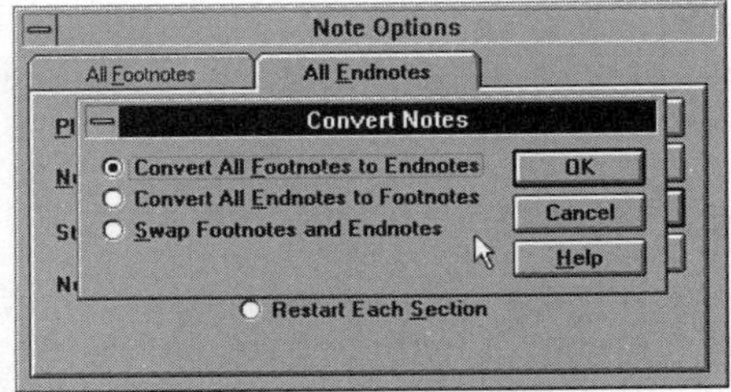

FIGURE 41.7.
Converting endnotes to footnotes, and vice versa.

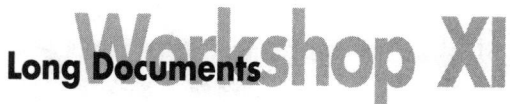

4. Choose Convert All **F**ootnotes to Endnotes, Convert All **E**ndnotes to Footnotes, or **S**wap Endnotes and Footnotes.
5. Click OK to close the Convert Notes dialog box.
6. Click OK to close the Notes Options dialog box.
7. Click Close to close the Footnotes and Endnotes dialog box.

SUPER NOTE

Word only lets you convert *all* footnotes or endnotes. If you want to convert just one, you'll have to resort to the clipboard. Don't forget to make sure that the appropriate style (Footnote Text or Endnote Text) is applied.

Converting Body Text into a Footnote or Endnote

When you think about it, many of the footnotes you create in reports and other documents (except in circles where footnotes and endnotes are endemic) began life as part of the body text. Then, some right-thinking editor decides that a sentence (or two, or three...) interrupts the flow, and is too large to just enclose with parentheses. "Just turn it into a footnote," they say.

Using the clipboard, that's a pretty simple and straightforward task—potentially. Just cut the text to the clipboard, press Alt+Ctrl+F (or Alt+Ctrl+E), Shift+Insert, and presto! However, what if the text you want to convert contains paragraph markers? Chances are the underlying style is *not* Footnote Text or Endnote Text. When converting body text into a note, you must take stock of whether or not the text includes any paragraph markers. If it does, then you need to reapply the Footnote Text or Endnote Text style after you paste the text into the footnote area.

Note Reference Marks

It's easy to miss unless you watch carefully, but Word uses character styles called Footnote Reference and Endnote Reference for reference marks in the notes and text. If you need to modify the way the notes are presented, you can do so by modifying the style.

If you require different kinds of footnote reference marks in the text and in the footnote or endnote list itself, Word does not provide a built-in mechanism. Instead, you must create a dedicated character style (most likely for the reference notes in the endnote area, rather than in the text). A common style is to prefer numbering endnotes as a numbered list. The simplest option is to wait until your document is finished, then reformat the entire endnote area, applying the Numbered List style, and then use the ResetChar (Ctrl+Space) command to remove the extraneous formatting. Unfortunately, that leaves you with the unpleasant chore of manually inserting the period and tab after each note number.

Separators

Word lets you select the separator to separate notes from the text, as well as from the continuation notice (a notice to indicate that the note is continued on the next page). Don't look on the menu for these, however; access them from the footnote or endnote pane itself.

PROCEDURE 41.6. CHANGING THE NOTE SEPARATOR, CONTINUATION SEPARATOR, OR CONTINUATION NOTICE.

1. Select **V**iew | **N**ormal to ensure that you are in Normal view.
2. Select **V**iew | **F**ootnotes.
3. Click the drop-down list arrow in the note toolbar, as shown in Figure 41.8.

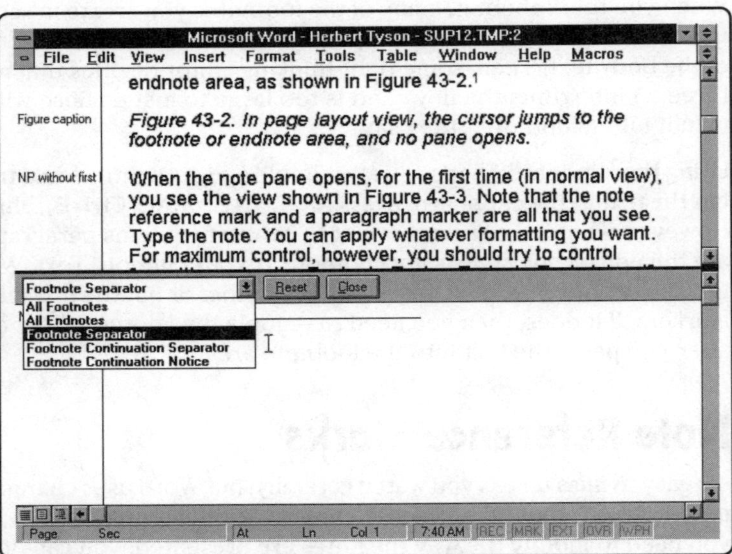

FIGURE 41.8.
Use the drop-down list to select the component you want to edit.

4. Click the type of separator or continuation notice you want to modify.
5. Reformat or change the text of the separator.
6. Press Alt+Shift+C to close the pane.

Chapter

42

Tables of Contents, Figures, and Authorities

Tables of contents, figures, and authorities are each created with distinct operations. For the most part, tables of contents and figures can be created in a fairly automatic way. Tables of contents can be created from heading-level text. Tables of figures (or other tables) can be created based on sequence (SEQ field) identifiers and styles. Tables also can be created manually, by inserting TC fields for the headings you want to use. Word also provides a flexible method for creating tables of authorities for composing legal briefs.

Table of Contents

A table of contents, quite simply, is a heading-oriented list of what's in a book and on what page it occurs. If you use Word's built-in heading styles religiously, you may never have to worry about some of the finer points of Word's Table of Contents commands. If, on the other hand, you need additional flexibility, you can use other styles as well as direct TC entries to create a table of contents.

Using Heading Styles

By far, the easiest way to create a table of contents is to use Word's built-in Heading 1 through Heading 9 styles to organize your documents. Not only does this afford you easy access to Word's outlining capabilities, but it also gives you an easy way to create concise tables of contents.

PROCEDURE 42.1. CREATING A TABLE OF CONTENTS BASED ON HEADING LEVELS.

1. Create a document, using Heading 1 through Heading 9 styles for the document heading and subheadings.
2. Position the insertion point where you want the table of contents to appear.
3. Select **I**nsert | Inde**x** and Tables from the menu.
4. Click Table of Contents (see Figure 42.1, the Table of **C**ontents tab in the Index and Tables dialog box).

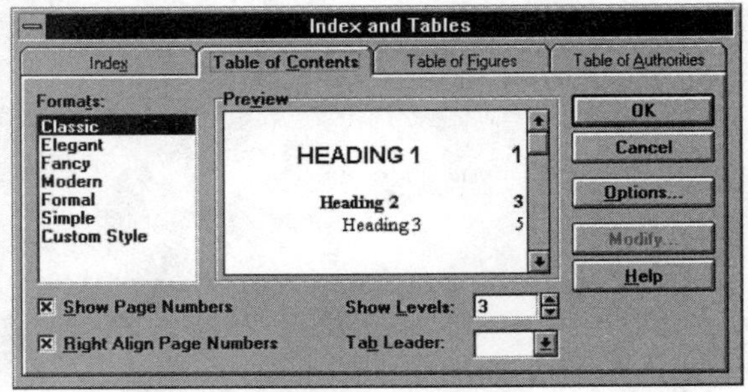

FIGURE 42.1.
The Table of Contents tab.

5. Select one of the Formats (Word shows you the results of the selected format in the Preview window).
6. Select Show Page Numbers to display page numbers in the table of contents.
7. To cause page numbers to appear exactly at the end of the table heading rather than right-aligned, deselect **R**ight Align Page Numbers.
8. If the **R**ight Align option is selected, choose a Ta**b** Leader option (the character between the text of the table of contents entry and the page number.
9. Select a level of detail for the table of contents using Show **L**evels. Select 3 to list only down to Heading 3 level (the default). Many documents go quite deep in heading levels. Providing too much detail in the table of contents can make a table of contents difficult to read.
10. Click OK to insert the table of contents.

Here's how it works. When you perform the procedure shown, Word uses the information to build a TOC field—for example, `{ TOC \o "1-3" }`. The `\o "1-3"` switch tells Word to build the table of contents using the built-in Heading styles, levels 1 through 3. If you had specified a different level of detail in Step 9, then `"1-3"` would be different. You need not begin with 1, either. If you want a limited range of headings included in the table of contents—for example, Headings 3, 4, and 5—then specify `\o "3-5"`.

Table of Contents Formatting

When Word creates a table of contents, it uses nine built-in styles: TOC1 through TOC9. The default formatting is hardly ever exactly what you want. However, the instinctive tendency is to try to reformat the displayed table of contents directly. Unfortunately, if you later update the TOC field, Word replaces any manually-applied formatting with the TOC styles. The best way to adjust the formatting of a Word table of contents is to modify the TOC styles, using the procedures discussed in Chapter 22, "Styles and AutoFormat."

SUPER NOTE

An additional option exercised by some users is unlinking the TOC field by selecting it and pressing Ctrl+Shift+F9. Once unlinked, any manual formatting you apply cannot be undone if you attempt to update the table of contents. That's because unlinking converts the field into actual text. However, once unlinked, you won't be able to update the table of contents using the Update Fields key (F9). Instead, you likely would need to reinsert the table of contents using the **I**nsert | Inde**x** and Tables dialog box, which would result in your losing any manually-applied formatting. The only sure way to avoid the hassles of constantly having to reformat a table of contents is to modify the TOC styles.

Using Nonheading Styles to Create a Table of Contents

What if you didn't use the built-in Heading 1 through Heading 9 styles? What if you have additional styles you'd also like to include in the table of contents? Word lets you use additional styles to identify table of contents entries, either in combination with the built-in heading styles or instead of them.

PROCEDURE 42.2. USING NONHEADING STYLES TO BUILD A TABLE OF CONTENTS.

1. Open the document and identify the styles you want to use.
2. Move the insertion point to where you want the table of contents to appear.
3. Select **I**nsert | Inde**x** and Tables from the menu.
4. Click Table of **C**ontents.
5. Select one of the **F**ormats.
6. Select **S**how Page Numbers to display page numbers in the table of contents.
7. To cause page numbers to appear exactly at the end of the table heading (rather than right-aligned), deselect **R**ight Align Page Numbers.
8. If the **R**ight Align option is selected, choose a tab leader option (the character between the text of the table of contents entry and the page number).
9. Using Show **L**evels, select a level of detail for the table of contents. Select 3 to list only down to the 3 level (the default). You will associate levels with specific styles in the next step.
10. Click the **O**ptions button to display the Table of Contents Options dialog box, shown in Figure 42.2.

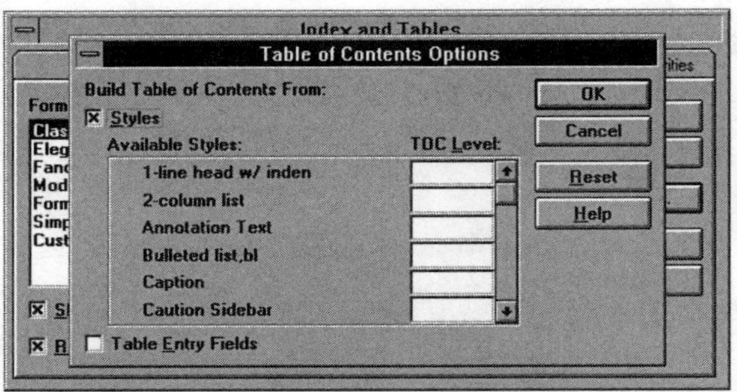

FIGURE 42.2.
The Table of Contents Options dialog box.

11. Ensure that **S**tyles is selected.
12. Using the mouse, scroll through the list of styles displayed. Depending on the level specified in Step 9, Word shows Heading 1 through Heading 3 (the default) already associated with table of contents levels 1 through 3, respectively. You can keep them and supplement by associating additional styles

with TOC levels, or you can remove the heading associations and just create your own associations. To remove the displayed headings from the table of contents, delete the numbers displayed under TOC Levels. To add additional styles to the table of contents, type the desired TOC Level number (1 through 9) under TOC Levels.

13. Click OK to accept your selection.
14. Click OK to insert the table of contents.

SUPER NOTE

In Step 12, you can select from available *paragraph* styles only. Character styles aren't an option.

SUPER TIP

In Step 12, all you're doing is telling Word which styles to use and how to format them. Word uses the entire text associated with each instance of the styles you designate. If they're heading-type text (for example, a single succinct descriptive line as opposed to entire paragraphs), Word uses the text associated with them as table of contents entries. If they're not heading-type text (that is, if they are complete paragraphs), Word also uses them.

SUPER

If you accidentally use *Normal* as a table of contents style, you probably won't like the results. However, you can use this behavior to advantage if you like. As it turns out, this is an excellent way to get Word to list identically-styled excerpts from a document. For example, if you want to excerpt every bulleted item in a document, you could do a table of contents for the document, using just the style you have for your bulleted lists. Tell Word *not* to include a tab leader and page numbers, and *presto*! Instant list! You can also do this for any captions, figure headings, or table headings that you have used to identify any special text for which you wish to create a list. In fact, Word uses exactly this technique when you select the Table of Figures tab in the main Index and Tables dialog box.

Using TC Entries

Another approach to creating or supplementing tables of contents is to use TC fields to create or add entries to a table of contents. Described more fully in Chapter 29, "Fields," the TC field is used to create table of contents entries. For example, to create an entry called `"Appendices"` and formatted as TOC3, use the following field:

```
{tc \l3 "Appendices"}
```

SUPER NOTE

Are weird items showing up in your table of contents? Perhaps some hidden TC fields are hanging around. TC fields do not collapse into displayed field code results. If you have enabled the display of hidden text (**T**ools | **O**ptions, **V**iew), TC fields are displayed as field codes. If hidden text does not display, the TC fields are hidden from view. Because so many users *don't* display hidden text and seldom turn on the display of all field codes, it's easy for leftover TC fields to remain undetected in your documents. TC fields were used much more extensively in prior versions of Word for Windows, so be especially vigilant when working with documents you're converting for use in Word 6.

You can also use the TC field to create different lists. When you supply an identifier with the `\f` switch (`\fA`, `\fB` and so on), Word creates a separate table for TC `\fA` items, another table for TC `\fB`, and so on. If you used the style *Caption* in a ubiquitous way that improperly lumps different kinds of items together, you can use TC with a `\f` grouping to create separate tables. Unfortunately, you must include the text for the table in the TC field itself. For example, the following creates a level 3 entry for a series we'll call `"repro"`:

```
{tc \f"repro"\l3 "Reprint 131. Monet's cathedral paintings used color to
create impressions of shape."}
```

Often, in fact, the easiest way to create TC entry fields is to copy an existing caption to the clipboard, create the TC field, and then paste the caption text between the quotes.

PROCEDURE 42.3. INSERTING A TC ENTRY FIELD.

1. Select **I**nsert | Fi**e**ld from the menu (note: TC fields can be inserted anywhere).
2. Under **C**ategories, click Index and Tables.
3. Under Field **N**ames, click TC.
4. Click **O**ptions.

5. Click `\f` to specify a series, `\l` to specify the level, or `\n` to tell Word to suppress the page number for this item (to create table of contents grouping categories, for example). If you specify `\f`, include an identifier. If you specify `\l`, then include the level (1 through 9) you want to use for this TC item.
6. In the Field Codes field, type the text in quotes ("*text*") you want included in the resulting table.
7. Click OK to insert the field.

SUPER TIP

Word's internal documentation seems to suggest that the letters A through Z are the identifiers you should use for the `\f` switch. However, many users could benefit by choosing some kind of descriptive plain language label instead. In the preceding example, we used `"repro"`. Choose something simple, and make a mental note of the first letter. When you use the Insert | Index and Tables command to compile the table, under the Table Identifier, choose the first letter of the label you used. For the `"repro"` label, for example, choose R. If you have labels `"repro"` and `"reprint"` in the same document, Word will, unfortunately, collect both types of TC fields in the TOC `\fR` table of contents. Even modifying the TOC field itself to exactly specify `"repro"` or `"reprint"` does not change this behavior. So, regardless of the utility of your labels, each must begin with a unique letter of the alphabet.

Lists of Items (Figures, Tables, Pictures, Equations, and So Forth)

Using the same kinds of operations you use to create a table of contents, you can also create lists of Figures, Tables, Drawing, Sounds, and so on. Word lets you use the occurrence of specific styles, sequence labels (for example, `{seq` *label*`}`), and TC entries to compose your list.

Using Caption Labels (and Sequence Numbers) to Create a List of Items

If you use Word's Insert | Caption command to create captions for the tables, figures, or graphs you insert into your documents, Word can automatically use those captions to produce lists (tables) of items.

PROCEDURE 42.4. CREATING A LIST (OR TABLE) BASED ON CAPTIONS.

1. Position the insertion point where you want the list to appear.
2. Select Insert | Index and Tables.
3. Click the Table of Figures tab, as shown in Figure 42.3.

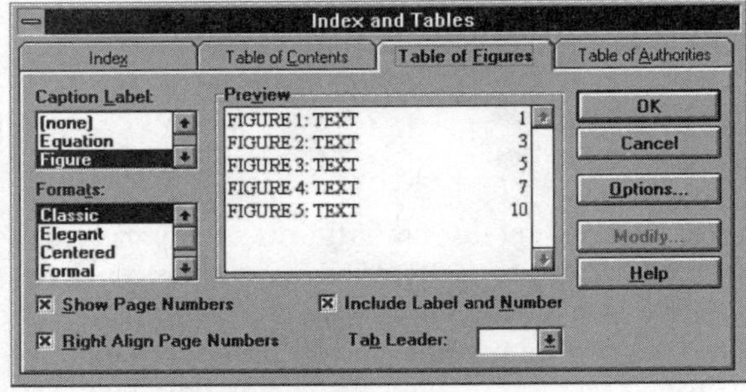

FIGURE 42.3.
The Table of Figures tabbed dialog box.

4. Under Caption Label, click the label you want to use.
5. Under Formats, select a format you can live with.
6. Select the appropriate options to include Show Page Numbers, Right Align Page Numbers, the Include Label and Number, and Tab Leaders between the items and the respective page numbers.
7. Click OK to insert the list (or table).

SUPER NOTE

When creating a list of items in this way, you do not need to have the *Caption* style associated with each item. Instead, all that's necessary is that the indicated sequence identifier (for example, `{seq` *identifier*`}` be present. Word includes every original occurrence of each `{seq` *identifier*`}` item in the resulting list. If you do what I do, however, and use `{seq Figure}` for each original mention, and then use `{seq Figure \c}` in the actual caption, you're out of luck. Word grabs the paragraph that contains `{seq Figure}` *without* the `\c` switch. Unfortunately, this probably means that you have to bookmark every `{seq Figure}` field in your document to refer to it, because captions for items invariably occur *after* the first mention, rather than before.

What if you have captioned items with sequence numbers, but you didn't insert them using the Insert | Caption command? Well, all is not lost. You have several choices. If all of the items have the identical and exclusive use of a style (*FigureLabel*, for example), you could use the procedure shown in the section "Using Styles to Create Lists of Figures." If the style you used is not identical for each caption, or if the captions don't have exclusive ownership of the style, you could register your sequence number with the Insert|Caption command. This can be tricky, however, because Word *insists* on using the caption label as the sequence identifier. If you use the `{seq Figure}` for figures, you're all set. If you use `{seq figno}` for figures, however, you need to either *not* include the label in the list you create, or you have to change all of your `{seq figno}` fields into `{seq Figure}` fields.

PROCEDURE 42.5. REGISTERING A SEQUENCE IDENTIFIER AS A CAPTION LABEL.

1. Select **I**nsert|Capt**i**on to display the Caption dialog box.
2. Click **N**ew Label to display the New Label dialog box, and in **L**abel type the name of the sequence identifier (as it appears in the `{seq` *identifier*`}` field.
3. Click OK to close the New Label dialog box.
4. Click Close to close the Caption dialog box.

After the label has been registered as a caption, you can follow procedure 42.4, Creating a list (or table) based on captions.

Using Styles to Create Lists of Figures

Another option for creating a list of items (figures, graphs, pictures, and so forth) is to base the entries on the occurrences of a specific style. The procedure is similar to that of creating a table of contents based on nonheading styles. It differs, however, in that you use just a single style when creating a list of figures, graphs, or what-have-you.

PROCEDURE 42.6. USING A STYLE TO CREATE A LIST OF ITEMS.

1. Position the insertion point where you want the list to appear.
2. Select **I**nsert|Inde**x** and Tables.
3. Click the Table of **F**igures tab.
4. Under Caption Label, click (none).
5. Click the **O**ptions button to display the Table of Figures Options dialog box, shown in Figure 42.4.

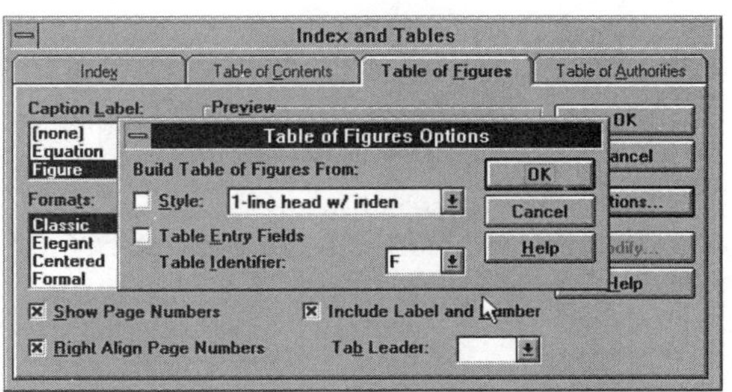

FIGURE 42.4.
The Table of Figures Options dialog box.

6. Click to select the **S**tyle check box, and choose the style you want to use.
7. Click OK to close the Options dialog box.
8. Select the appropriate options to include page numbers, right-align page numbers, the label and sequence number (usually deselected when using a style), and tab leaders between the items and the respective page numbers.
9. Click OK to insert the list.

For example, while writing this book, I've been using a style called *Procedure head* for the titles of the procedures. I could create a list of all of the procedures in this workshop by following the procedure just shown, and selecting *Procedure head* in Step 6.

Using TC Entries

Another option in compiling a list is to use TC field to explicitly define entries. The procedure is identical to using TC Entries for a table of contents.

Tables of Authorities

For preparing citations in legal briefs and other legal writings, Word also provides a tables of authorities feature. In a brief, lawyers must cite a source for each point of law, making reference to a specific law, court case, rule, constitutional provision, and so on. Setting up a table of authorities manually is pure tedium. Word takes much of the tedium out of it, but not all. What's worse, some poor soul is probably going to have to read all those citations.

Creating a tables of authorities essentially is a three-step process, although Word's documentation seems to suggest just the latter two steps:

- Define the categories of authorities (if different from the defaults)
- Mark the citations in the text
- Insert the tables of authorities

Word leaves out the first step most likely because it gets incorporated into the second. When you cite an authority in the text, Word presents you with the option to define or refine categories.

PROCEDURE 42.7. MARKING A FIRST CITATION FOR A TABLES OF AUTHORITIES.

1. Find the first occurrence of a long citation that you want to mark, and select the entire citation (for example, *Smith vs. Jones,* U.S. Supreme Court, 1974).
2. Press Alt+Shift+I (or select **I**nsert | Inde**x** and Tables, then click the Table of **A**uthorities tab and Mark Citation); the Mark Citation dialog box appears, as shown in Figure 42.5.

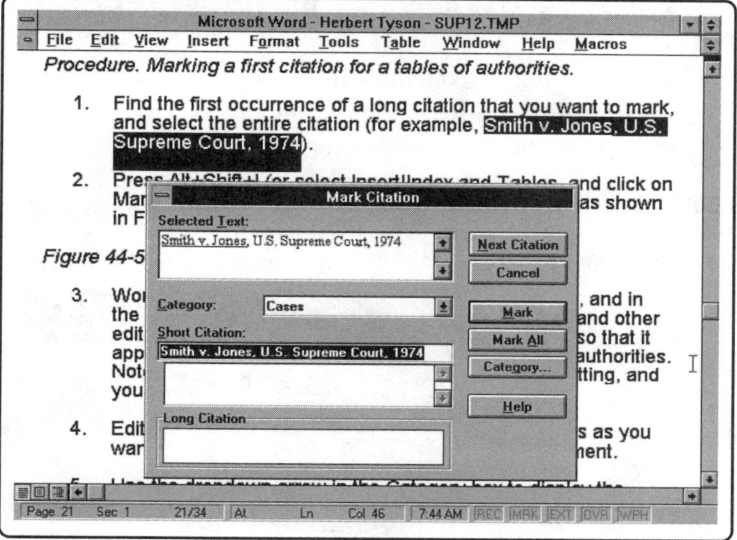

FIGURE 42.5.
The Mark Citation dialog box.

3. Word displays the selection in the Selected **T**ext area and in the **S**hort Citation area. Use shortcut formatting keys and other editing keys to edit the text in the Selected **T**ext area so that it appears just as you want it to appear in the tables of authorities. Note that you can use keys only for editing and formatting, and you cannot apply styles.
4. Edit the text in the **S**hort Citation box so that it appears as you want short citations of this authority cited in the document.
5. Use the drop-down arrow in the **C**ategory box to display the categories; click the category you want to use (see the procedure Adding or modifying a category) if the category you want isn't there.
6. Click **M**ark to mark just the current citation, or click Mark **A**ll to mark all matching citations in the current document.

SUPER TIP

You can leave the Mark Citation dialog box open while scrolling through the document. Like the Spelling, Find, Replace, and some other dialog boxes, the Mark Citation dialog box can be suspended (dimmed) without closing it. In fact, you can have *both* the Find and the Mark Citation dialog boxes on-screen at the same time. This makes it possible to search for citation-like strings, moving freely among the text area, Find dialog box, and Mark Citation dialog boxes.

PROCEDURE 42.8. MARKING A SECOND OCCURRENCE OF AN EXISTING AUTHORITY.

1. Press Alt+Shift+I to display the Mark Citation dialog box.
2. Select the authority from the scrollable list (between the short and long citation areas, as shown in Figure 42.6).

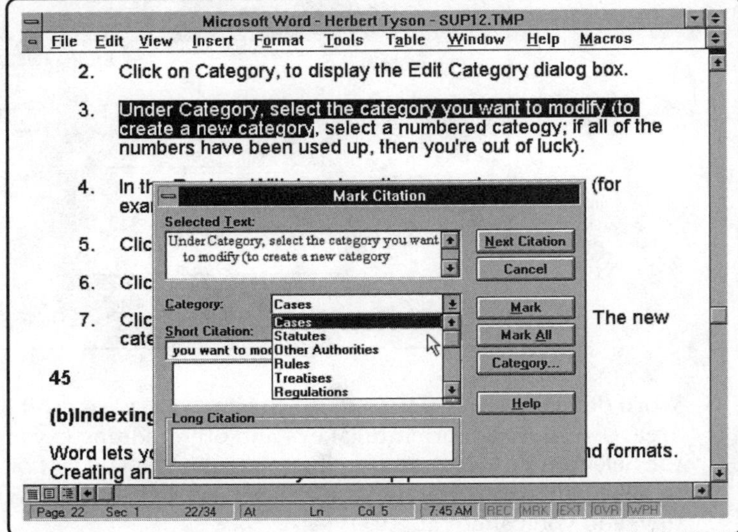

FIGURE 42.6. *Select the authority from the scrollable list.*

3. Click **M**ark.

With Word, you also can modify or add categories. For example, you might need to add a category for state supreme courts, the U.S. Supreme Court, or other specific sets of regulations or codes.

PROCEDURE 42.9. ADDING OR MODIFYING A CATEGORY.

1. Press Alt+Shift+I to display the Mark Citation dialog box.
2. Click the Cate**g**ory button to display the Edit Category dialog box.
3. Under **C**ategory, select the category you want to modify (to create a new category, select a numbered category; if all of the numbers have been used up, then you're out of luck).
4. In the Replace **W**ith box, type the new category name (for example, `U.S. Court of Appeals`).
5. Click **R**eplace.
6. Click OK to close the Edit Category dialog box.
7. Click Cancel to close the Mark Citation dialog box. The new category is remembered.

Chapter

43

Indexing

Word lets you create indexes in a variety of styles and formats. Creating an index is basically a two-step process:

- Create index entries (locations and text you want indexed, as well as categories and subentries)
- Format and Compile the index

Creating Index Entries

Index entries are the items you want to appear in the index. For example, if you were indexing this text, you might want to include an item about creating an index entry. You might simply include the word `Index` in the index. Alternatively, if indexes are mentioned extensively, you might have a main entry of index and subentries about creating entries and compiling indexes.

PROCEDURE 43.1. CREATING AN INDEX ENTRY.

1. Select the text you want to index.
2. Press Alt+Shift+X (or select Insert | Inde**x** and Tables, click the Inde**x** tab, then click Mar**k** Entry… or, as I said, just press Alt+Shift+X). The Mark Index Entry dialog box appears.
3. The selected text is displayed in the Main Entry area; use editing keys and shortcut formatting keys to make the text appear as you want it to in the index.
4. If desired, include a **S**ubentry; this is a category within the main entry. For example, if the main entry is *`index`*, a subentry might be *`marking entries`*. Use editing keys and shortcut formatting keys to adjust the formatting and text as necessary.
5. Select **B**old or **I**talic for the page number, if desired (in some publications, it's common to include definitional entries in bold or italic so that key items can be identified more readily).
6. To make this entry a cross-reference to another index entry, click **C**ross-reference and type the text corresponding to the Main **E**ntry of the other index entry.
7. To refer to a range of pages rather than a single page, select Page **R**ange and use the drop-down arrow to select a bookmark that comprises the pages you want included. You might do this to refer to a whole chapter or heading, for example.
8. Click **M**ark to insert an index entry field (`{ XE "`*text*`" }`). Alternatively, click Mark **A**ll to insert XE fields for all text matching the Main Entry text.

SUPER NOTE

XE entries are displayed only as field codes, not results, and are not displayed at all unless your view is set to display hidden text.

SUPER TIP

The Mark Index Entry dialog box is persistent; it can remain on-screen while you work in your document, similar to the Find and Replace dialog boxes. This enables you to display both the Mark Index Entry and Find dialog boxes at the same time, so that you can search for items to index and move freely between the text and the two dialog boxes.

Automatically Marking Index Entries Using a List of Entries

One of the nicest features about Word's indexing is that it enables you to create a list of words you want indexed, and then use the AutoMark feature to cause Word to insert `XE` entries for all of the words on the list. For example, consider the list shown in Table 43.1:

Table 43.1. A concordance table for automatic indexing.

fish	`{XE "fish"}`
hamster	`{XE "hamster"}`
camels	`{XE "camel"}`
oyster	`{XE "oyster"}`

If you create a concordance file as shown, you could instruct Word to read that file and automatically mark all occurrences of fish, hamsters, camels, and oysters for the index. A concordance file is a Word table with two columns. The first column contains the *exact* text you want matched in the file—including capitalization. If you want Fish, Fishes, fishes, fishery, fisheries, Fishery, Fisheries, and fish, you would need to include each separately. The second column contains the `XE` field you want inserted. Each row is a separate word or phrase you want indexed. When you use the AutoMark command, Word locates each occurrence of each word or phrase in the first column and inserts the `XE` field from the second column into the text.

PROCEDURE 43.2. AUTOMATICALLY INSERTING INDEX ENTRIES USING A LIST OF WORDS AND TERMS.

1. Create a concordance file that contains the words or phrases you want indexed; save the file as a normal Word document.
2. In the document you want indexed, select **I**nsert | Inde**x** and Tables and click the Inde**x** tab.
3. Click A**u**toMark to display the Open Index AutoMark File dialog box.
4. Select the concordance file and click OK; Word responds by automatically inserting the XE entries from column two of the concordance file for each item matching column one.

Compiling Indexes

Compiling an index is the act of collecting all of the XE entries and putting them into index form.

PROCEDURE 43.3. COMPILING (INSERTING) AN INDEX.

1. Insert XE entries for each item you want indexed.
2. Select **I**nsert | Inde**x** and Tables.
3. Click the Inde**x** tab.
4. Select the type of Index, **I**ndented or Ru**n**-in; observe the effects of your selections in the Preview window, as shown in Figure 43.1.

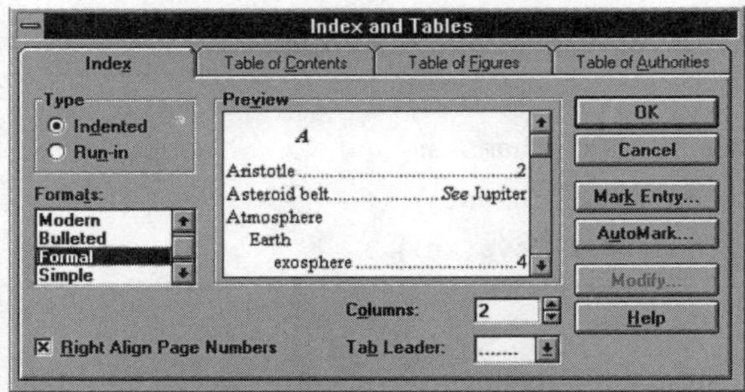

FIGURE 43.1.
The Preview window shows the effects of your choices.

5. Select one of the index Forma**t**s. To create your own format, select Custom Style and click the **M**odify button.
6. Select **R**ight **A**lign Page Numbers, the number of index C**o**lumns, and a Ta**b** Leader, if desired.
7. Click OK to compile and insert the index.

Creating Multiple Indexes

Word lets you create up to 26 separate indexes for a document. Unfortunately, no automatic support is provided. To create separate indexes, you must include a `\f`*index* switch in the `XE` and `INDEX` fields. For example, consider the entries:

```
{ XE \fa "ice cream" }
{ XE \fa "peach pie" }
{ XE \fb "broccoli" }
{ XE \fb "cauliflower" }
```

The `\fa` switch makes the ice cream and peach pie items go into an index that includes the `\fa` switch, and broccoli and cauliflower will go into the `\fb` index:

`{index \fa}`	Indexes just the deserts
`{index \fb}`	Indexes just the vegetables

Chapter

44

Cross-References

Cross-references are instances where you tell the reader to look elsewhere in a document for additional information—for example, "see **Referring to Page Numbers**, on page 542." Word lets you refer to page numbers, footnotes, endnotes, headings, chapter numbers, paragraph numbers, section numbers, and so on. Creating a cross-reference conceptually is a two-step process, although Word often eliminates the first step for you:

1. Insert a bookmark at the point where you want to refer the reader.
2. Insert a reference field that acts as a page number variable, depending on what page the bookmark is printed.

When inserting a reference to most standard items in a Word document (headings, footnotes, captions, sequence number fields, and so on), Word automatically inserts a bookmark around the referenced item. If you set bookmarks to display (as [brackets] by selecting **T**ools | **O**ptions | View and clicking Bookmarks), you see the telltale bookmark brackets. However, you do not see this bookmark displayed when you select **E**dit | **G**o To. The Go To dialog box lists only user-created bookmarks, and these special bookmarks don't show up on the list of user-created bookmarks. Instead, they are internal utility bookmarks that Word creates for you. After you know the internal name, you can refer to it, if you like. However, often the only way to know what it is is to insert a cross-reference, which usually is what you wanted to do in the first place. So, it's all a wash.

Using Bookmarks

If you use Word's built-in features to create captions, headings, and other elements of your documents, you seldom need to manually insert your own bookmarks for creating cross-references. However, if you use SEQ fields in an atypical way, if you don't use the built-in heading styles, or if you want to refer to a range of pages, then you need to insert bookmarks. For example, if you use SEQ fields in an atypical way, you need to bookmark the field that produces the number for use in a cross-reference. When you select the **I**nsert | Cross-**r**eference command, any bookmarks you have created are listed.

> **SUPER TIP**
>
> Bookmarks are easy to insert, but once inserted, it's impossible to determine just by looking at bookmark brackets what the bookmark is. If you want to know what bookmark is represented by the telltale brackets, the only method is trial and error using Word's Go To command, Ctrl+G. Even then, however, there's no guarantee that you'll discover what bookmark is hiding there. That's because bookmarks that Word inserts when compiling tables of contents, authorities, and figures, or when creating cross-references, don't show up on the Go To list.

PROCEDURE 44.1. INSERTING A BOOKMARK.

1. Select the text you want to bookmark; to bookmark a point, don't select any text at all.
2. Select **E**dit | **B**ookmark.
3. Type a name for the bookmark.
4. Click the **A**dd button.

> **SUPER NOTE**
>
> Many of Word's commands prompt if you attempt to reuse a name that already exists. For example, if you try to use an autotext entry name that already exists, Word prompts you to confirm replacing the existing one. When you create a bookmark, however, Word does *not* prompt to confirm the replacement. On the one hand, this makes creating bookmarks very easy, since you aren't interrupted by the extra prompt. On the other hand, it makes it very easy to unintentionally overwrite an existing bookmark. Therefore, you should take care in assigning bookmarks, lest you overwrite one that's already being used and about which you've forgotten.

Inserting a Cross-Reference

Cross-references can be to text, pages, or numbered items (figures, headings, footnotes, and so on). Word's **I**nsert | Cross-**r**eference command makes it much easier than in prior versions of Word. The advantages of using Word's cross-referencing rather than hard-coding page and item numbers and text references are obvious. Not only do the references to page and item numbers get updated when a referenced item moves, but so do reference headings. If I were to refer to the title of this section elsewhere, I might write, "See the section titled **Inserting a Cross-Reference**." If that section title later gets changed to **Inserting Cross-References**, then I would have to locate all references to it and manually change them to reflect the change in title. If, instead, I insert one of Word's cross-reference fields, the references can be updated just by updating the respective fields.

PROCEDURE 44.2. INSERTING A CROSS-REFERENCE.

1. Move the insertion point to where you want the cross-reference to appear, and type any preparatory text (for example, `see page`).
2. Select **I**nsert | Cross-**r**eference to display the Cross-reference dialog box, as shown in Figure 44.1.

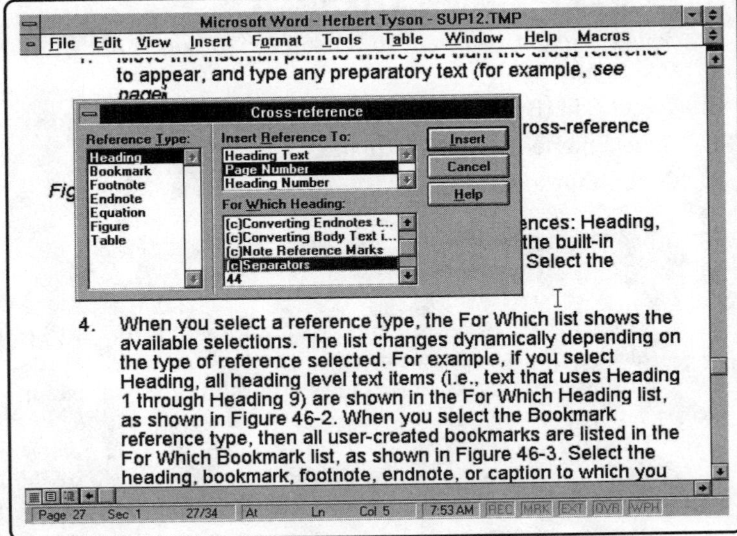

FIGURE 44.1.
The Cross-reference dialog box.

3. The Reference **T**ype list lists the types of references: Heading, Bookmark, Footnote, and Endnote, as well as the built-in caption types for Equation, Figure, and Table. Select the Reference Type you want to use.
4. When you select a **R**eference **T**ype, the For **W**hich list shows the available selections. The list changes dynamically depending on the type of reference selected. For example, if you select Heading, all heading level text items (for example, text that uses Heading 1 through Heading 9) are shown in the For Which Heading list, as shown in Figure 44.2. When you select the Bookmark reference type, then all user-created bookmarks are listed in the For Which Bookmark list, as shown in Figure 44.3. Select the heading, bookmark, footnote, endnote, or caption to which you want to refer.
5. In the Insert **R**eference To list, select the reference form: text, page number, caption, and so forth. The list changes dynamically depending on the Reference Type that's selected. For example, if Heading is selected, the reference forms are Heading Text, Page Number, and Heading Number. If Bookmark is selected, the references are to the bookmarked text itself, to a page number, or to a paragraph number (assuming you've numbered your paragraphs).
6. Click **I**nsert to insert the appropriate cross-reference field.

Like some of the other marking features (for example, Index and Tables of Authorities), the Cross-reference dialog box can remain on-screen while you're working in your document. Setting up cross-references can be a very tedious process, and you often must go back and forth between the text and the dialog box. By having it remain on-screen, Word lets you go back and forth easily. This also permits you to keep the Find dialog box on-screen at the same time—a powerful combination for ensuring that your cross-references are correct.

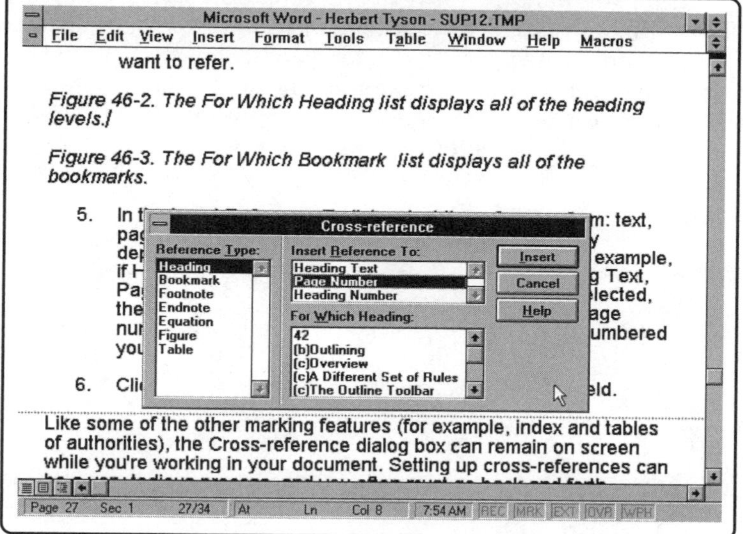

FIGURE 44.2.
The For Which Heading list displays all of the heading levels.

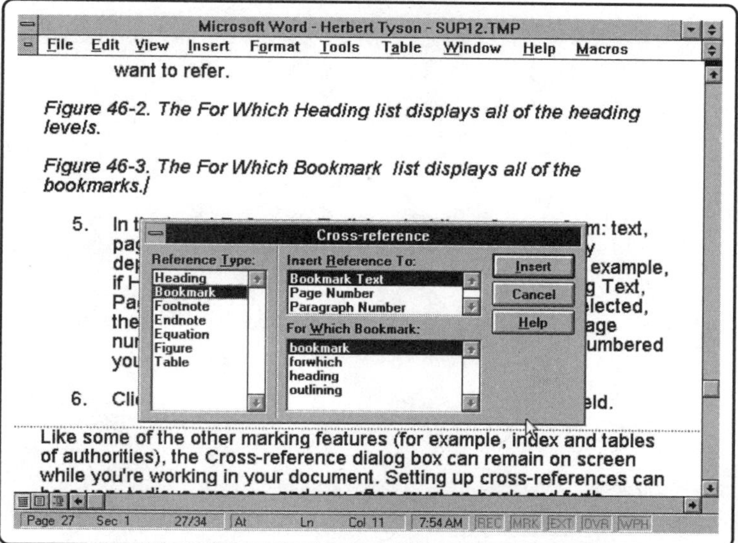

FIGURE 44.3.
The For Which Bookmark list displays all of the bookmarks.

SUPER TIP

If you want to cross-reference material from other Word documents, you should assemble your different components using a master document and create your cross-references from within it. When you insert cross-references from a master document, the cross-reference dialog box lists items from all of the subdocuments. See Chapter 45, "Master Documents," for additional information.

Chapter 45

Master Documents

Anyone who's ever struggled with a multifile Word document will appreciate Word 6's new Master Document feature. Briefly, a master document lets you create a single small file from which you can access and control a number of component documents, called *subdocuments*.

Using a master document solves a variety of problems, not least of which is managing a complex maze of cross-references in a multifile document, as well as creating wholly-inclusive tables of contents, indexes, and other lists. Perhaps the biggest benefit is one of the simplest: the perfect coordination of headers, footers, and page numbering.

SUPER

THE LIMITS OF PROGRESS

Make no mistake—a master document uses just as much memory as if all of the subdocuments were contained in the same file. Depending on the size of the assembled components, using a master document can feel a bit like trying to maneuver an aircraft carrier through a village pond. Also, a master document can't exceed 32M, nor can it contain more than 80 subdocuments. While those limitations might not seem important to some users, others undoubtedly will bemoan them.

Overview

It helps to understand exactly what a master document is. A master document, in essence, is a framework for a collection of related Word files. The master document itself contains very little native text. It might contain a main title, some header and footer definitions, a table of contents, lists of figures and tables, and an index. It might also contain an introduction. Beyond that, a master document contains references to subdocuments.

SUPER

TIP

Like many of Word's powerful organization features, master documents work best if you use Word's Heading 1 through Heading 9 styles to organize your documents. Keep this in mind if you're just reading a little now and plan to read more later. While it's not essential, you might also consider reserving the Heading 1 style for use in the master document itself, and using Heading 2 or 3 as the top level for any document you plan to integrate using a master document.

SUPER TIP

Have you ever needed to perform Replace operations across multiple files? If you assemble those files into a master document, you can reduce a multistep Replace into a single replace operation. Even if you never plan to use the master document for anything else, this single use can net you tremendous gains in productivity.

Creating a Master Document

Creating a master document is pretty simple. There are essentially three approaches, which (to a certain extent) can be mixed and matched, once you understand the basic principles involved:

- Creating from scratch—create a new document, write an outline, and then use Master Document view to subdivide the document into separate subdocuments.
- Organizing existing files—create a master document, from which you assemble and coordinate Word files that already exist.
- Converting an existing file—convert an existing (unwieldy) file into a master document, consigning major sections as subdocuments.

The Master Document Toolbar

When you select **V**iew | **M**aster Document, Word displays the Master Document toolbar, shown in Figure 45.1. Use the tools provided for easy access to master document features. The Master Document toolbar's tools are described in Table 45.1.

Table 45.1. The Master Document toolbar.

Toolbar Button	*Action or Purpose*
Create Subdocument	Transforms selected outline items into subdocuments. Each major outline division becomes a separate file.
Remove Subdocument	Merges the contents of the selected subdocument(s) into the master document. If you perform this operation across all subdocuments, the resulting document is no longer a master document.

continues

Table 45.1. continued

Toolbar Button	*Action or Purpose*
Insert Subdocument	Inserts an independent file into the master document as a subdocument. Use this approach to assemble existing files into a master document.
Merge Subdocument	Combines two adjacent subdocuments into a single subdocument. The newly-combined subdocument inherits the name of the first subdocument.
Split Subdocument	Splits the selected subdocument into new subdocuments at the next level of organization.
Lock Document	Toggles the write state of subdocuments in the selection on and off.

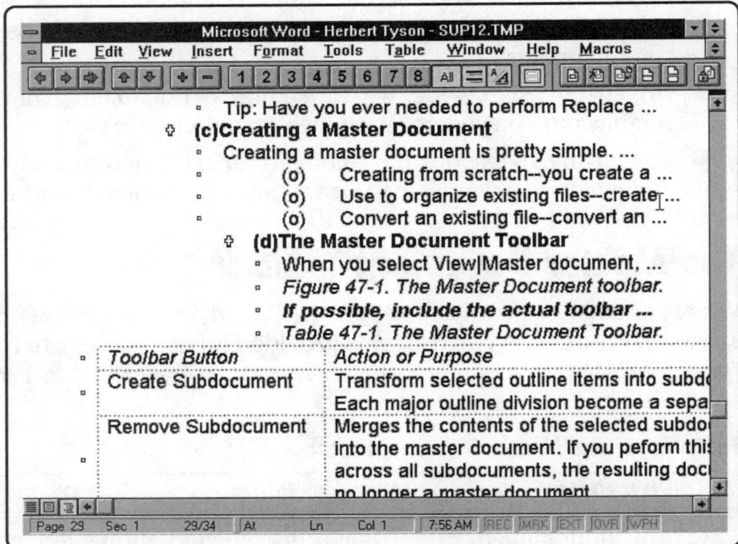

FIGURE 45.1.
The Master Document toolbar.

Creating a Master Document from Scratch

Often, beginning from ground zero helps you better understand the basic principles involved. That's certainly the case with master documents. Any document you create in Word has the potential for becoming a master document. It's all controlled by what you do with it.

A document becomes a master document the moment you use Master Document view to consign different sections into different physical files on your disk. This gives you a flexible tool for working with features that logically must use all of the document components, as well as for working on one component at a time.

If you plan to create large documents that must be indexed, have a table of contents, and use cross-references, using a master document to create and control all of the pieces can save you enormous amounts of time and work. In particular, if you work with others in a work group, you can even use files that reside at different locations on a network to put the whole works together.

PROCEDURE 45.1. CREATING A MASTER DOCUMENT FROM SCRATCH.

1. Select **F**ile | **N**ew from the menu.
2. Select **V**iew | **M**aster Document. Word puts the document into a modified outline view, with the Master Document toolbar appended to the end of the Outline toolbar, as shown in Figure 45.1 (see "The Master Document Toolbar").
3. Create an outline for your document, using Word's Heading 1 through 9 styles, as shown in Figure 45.2. It's usually best to reserve Heading 1 (and possibly Heading 2) for use in the master document itself, and to make Heading 2 or 3 the top level in each subdocument.

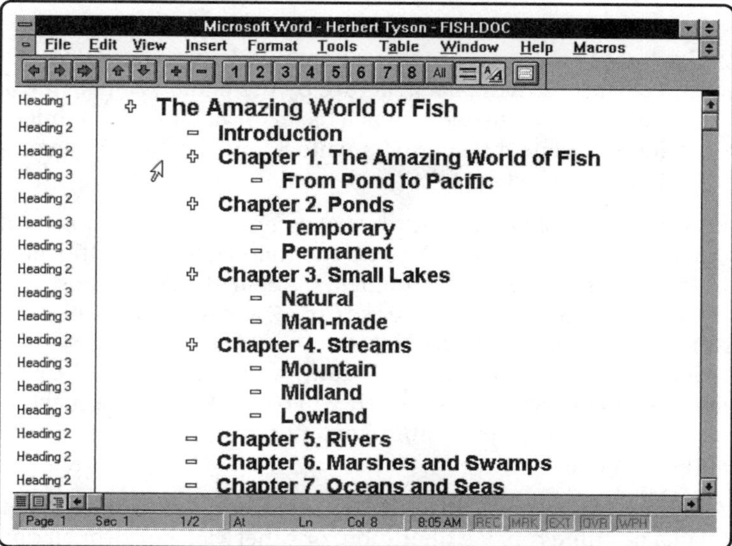

FIGURE 45.2.
Use headings to create your subdocument structure.

4. Select the lower headings that you want to become subdocuments, and click the Create Subdocument tool in the Master Document toolbar (see Figure 45.3).

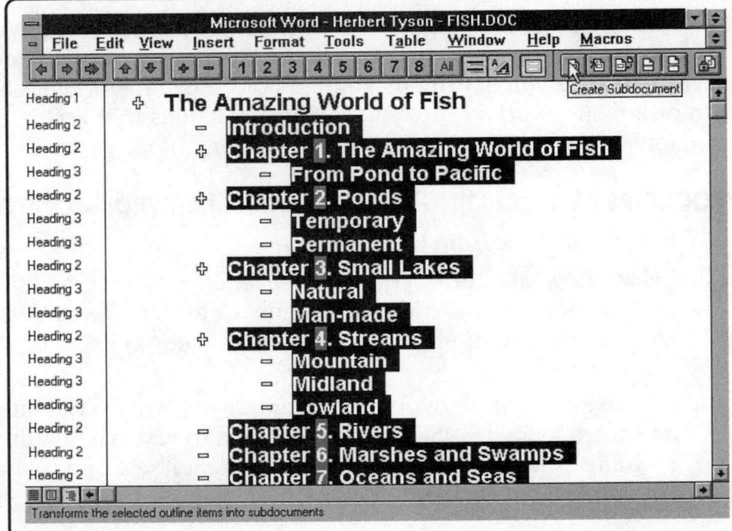

FIGURE 45.3.
Click the Create Subdocument tool to split the document into subdocuments.

5. Press Ctrl+S, and provide a name for your master document. Word automatically saves the main structure by the name you provide and uses the beginning of each subsection as a basis for naming the subdocuments. You can later rename the subdocuments if you like (see "Renaming Subdocuments" later in this chapter).

Congratulations! You're now the proud new owner of a master document. From here, you have several choices. You can continue working in the master document, adding to the outlines of the subdocuments. Any material you add is automatically saved in the subdocument when you press Ctrl+S, and all subdocuments are individually saved at the same time. You can switch into normal view and work on the subdocuments from the master document. Again, any text you add or change occurs at the subdocument level, even though you're working at the master document level. You also can double-click a subdocument icon (see Figure 45.4) and work just on the subdocument.

Any time you want to create cross-references, a document-wide table or index, perform a multifile replace operation, or otherwise perform an option that applies to all of the subdocuments, use the master document. A master document can be viewed in **N**ormal, **P**age Layout, Print Preview, **O**utline, or **M**aster Document views—just like an ordinary document. Anything you can do to a document, you can do to a master document.

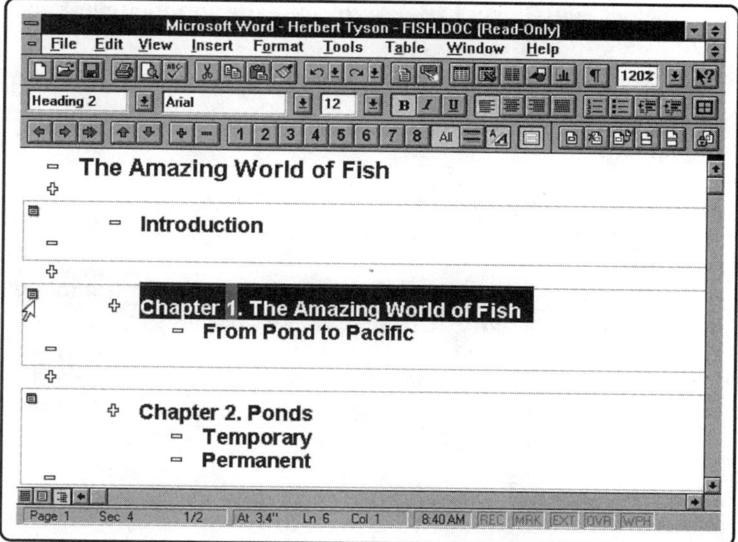

FIGURE 45.4.
Double-click a subdocument icon to open the subdocument in its own window.

When working on the text of subdocuments, you'll often find that the response time of Word is much better if you work on the subdocument itself, rather than on the master document. When you save, for example, just the subdocument gets saved. Scrolling, revealing, or updating fields that pertain just to the subdocument can be handled much more quickly if you don't have all of the other components in memory at the same time.

Renaming Subdocuments

When you use the Create Subdocuments tool to create subdocuments, Word automatically supplies the names. Sometimes Word's naming is fine, but other times it isn't. You can change the name of a subdocument, but you must be careful how you do it. The master document *must* also be open, and you must have opened the subdocument from the master document itself.

PROCEDURE 45.2. RENAMING A SUBDOCUMENT.

1. Open the master document.
2. Double-click the subdocument icon for the subdocument you want to rename, in order to open the subdocument.
3. Select **F**ile | Save **A**s, type a new name for the subdocument, and click OK (you can even save the components to other locations along a network—for example, when routing subdocuments for annotation, review, or writing).

4. Select **File** | **Close** (Ctrl+F4) to close the subdocument and then return to the master document.
5. Repeat Steps 2 through 4 to rename any components you like.
6. Press Ctrl+S to save the changes to the master document (or press Ctrl+F4 to close).

SUPER CAUTION

Unfortunately, Word doesn't support a pure renaming function. Instead, when you perform a Save As, you're creating a second copy of the file under a new name. Unless you have tons of disk space or otherwise want to preserve the originals, you should use Word's Find File command, the Windows File Manager, or some other means to prune out the files you no longer need.

SUPER CAUTION

Do not rename subdocuments using Find File, File Manager, or any other means other than the procedure shown. If you do, the master document has no way of tracking what happened to the subdocuments. If you do accidentally rename a file, you can always merge it back into the master document. However, by then you may already have suffered a coronary upon thinking that your document was destroyed.

Using a Master Document to Organize Existing Files

If you just acquired Word 6 in the middle of a big project, it's not too late to take advantage of the Master Document feature. You can use it to get a better organizational handle on your own documents, as well as documents being written by a number of different authors.

PROCEDURE 45.3. INTEGRATING EXISTING FILES INTO A MASTER DOCUMENT.

1. Select **File** | **New** to create a new file to serve as the master document.
2. Select **View** | **Master** Document to switch to master document view.
3. Click the Insert Subdocument icon on the toolbar to display the Insert Subdocument dialog box shown in Figure 45.5.

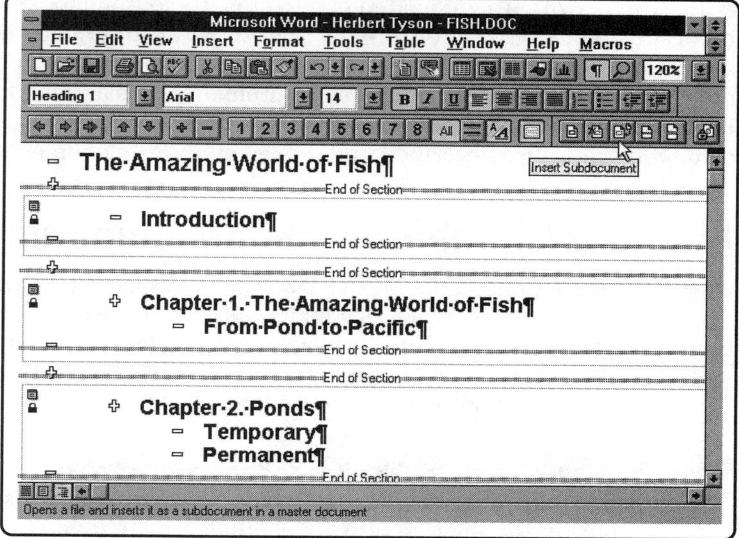

FIGURE 45.5.
The Insert Subdocument tool.

4. Select the file you want to insert, and click OK.
5. Repeat Steps 3 and 4 for each document you want to include.

Converting a Single File into a Master Document

If you have a large file that's getting unwieldy, it may be a logical candidate for conversion into a master document. This lets you work on the subdocument components using less memory, resulting in faster system response time. At the same time, using the master document framework ensures that all internal references are consistent across the parts of the master document.

PROCEDURE 45.4. CONVERTING A FILE INTO A MASTER DOCUMENT.

1. Open the file you want to convert.
2. Select **V**iew | **M**aster Document.
3. Use the Outline toolbar to set the view of the document so that heading levels correspond to the way you want to subdivide the document. If you want to subdivide each Heading 2 level into a subdocument, then click [2] in the Outline toolbar to view level 2 and above.
4. Select just the heading levels you want to convert.
5. Click the Create Subdocument button.

When you perform the indicated conversion, the outline looks very much like it did before, except that section breaks now separate the major heading levels and a subdocument icon appears beside each subdocument. When you save the master document, each of the subdocuments automatically is assigned a name based on the beginning text of each subdocument. If you don't like the names, you can change them using the procedure described under "Renaming Subdocuments."

Merging (Combining) Subdocuments

One of the limitations of the Master Document feature is that you cannot have more than 80 subdocuments. While this limit might seem meaningless, someday you may bump up against it. One solution is to combine smaller subdocuments into larger ones, using the Merge Subdocuments command. You might also want to use this command if you discover that you're having to flit from file to file more often than you'd like.

PROCEDURE 45.5. MERGING MULTIPLE SUBDOCUMENTS.

1. While in master document view, select the subdocuments you want to combine into a single subdocument, ensuring that you include the whole of each subdocument.
2. Click the Merge Subdocument button.

SUPER NOTE

Immediately upon merging the selected subdocuments, the several subdocument icons are replaced by a single one. All of the merged subdocuments are combined into a single file that keeps the name of the first subdocument in the selection.

Locking Subdocuments

When managing a complex project, you may sometimes not want parts of a master document changed. Using the Lock Document button on the Master Document toolbar, you can turn off write access to all or part of a master document. When locked, a lock appears next to the subdocument icon, as shown in Figure 45.6; others can read the subdocuments, but they cannot change them. When unlocked, the lock disappears, and write access is restored.

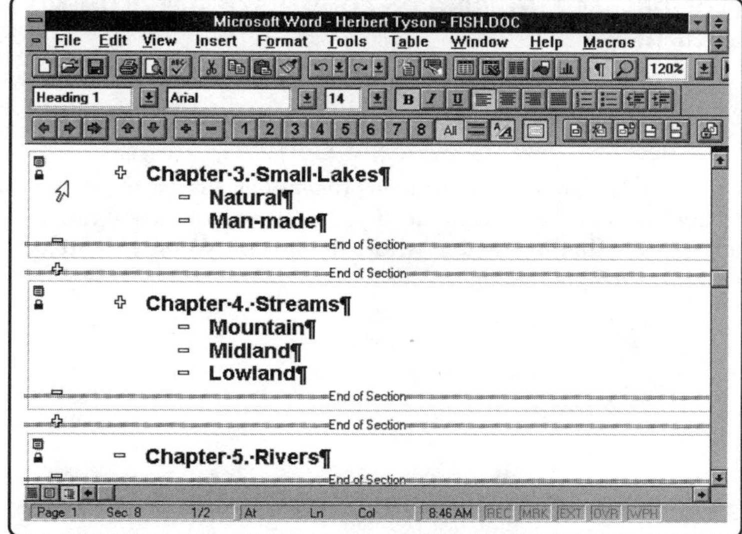

FIGURE 45.6.
The lock symbol tells you that a subdocument is write-protected.

PROCEDURE 45.6. LOCKING SUBDOCUMENTS FROM WRITE ACCESS.

1. Select the subdocument(s) you want to lock.
2. Click the Lock Document button.

SUPER NOTE

The Lock Document button is a toggle. Repeat the procedure to unlock the subdocument(s).

Converting a Master Document into a Single Document

Once a master document's components have been finished, the utility of their remaining separate entities may fade. In fact, once you've endured a few 20-file-save sessions when you press Ctrl+S, you may be more than ready to reduce that overhead a bit. When that time arrives, you can convert part or all of a master document into a single document by merging the subdocuments into the master file.

PROCEDURE 45.7. MERGING THE CONTENTS OF SUBDOCUMENTS INTO A MASTER DOCUMENT.

1. Select the subdocuments whose contents you want merged into the master document.
2. Click the Remove Subdocument button.

Note that the subdocument icons disappear, indicating that what you see is now actually a part of the current file. If you merge all of the subdocuments, you are left with a single file that is now the whole document. When you press Ctrl+S, you'll now see just the single file being saved.

Workshop

XII

Customizing Word Workshop

Word provides a number of ways to hone your word processing environment for maximum utility and productivity. In this section, you learn about controlling Word's option, keyboard, toolbars, and menus.

Chapter

46

Options Menu

The Options tabbed dialog box is a kind of customization grand central station. Similar in concept to the Options menu in WinWord 2, Word 6's Options include a few extras, but exclude a few as well. The Keyboard, Toolbar, and Menu sections have been moved to their own tabbed Customize dialog box, and are discussed in Chapters 47, "Customizing the Keyboard," 48, "Customizing Toolbars," and 49, "Customizing Menus." Another element that appears to be missing in action is the option to control settings in WIN.INI. Some Word settings are still maintained in WIN.INI, but others are now maintained in WINWORD6.INI. Settings for both are now controlled using the ToolsAdvancedSettings command, which is not on any of Word's built-in menus. You'll see how to put it onto a toolbar, shortly.

To display the tabbed Options dialog box, select **T**ools | **O**ptions, which displays the dialog box shown in Figure 46.1. From here, you can access any of the twelve different tabs, which are described below.

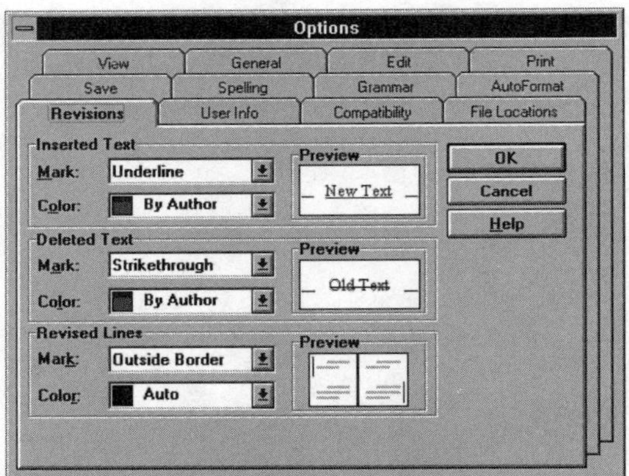

FIGURE 46.1.
The tabbed Options dialog box.

View

The **V**iew tab, shown in Figure 46.2, is used to control the way information is presented on-screen. The View options vary depending on whether Word is displayed in Normal, Page Layout, or Outline view. View options are not available at all in Print Preview mode. See Chapter 10, "Document Views," for the complete picture.

General

The **G**eneral settings, shown in Figure 46.3, are really just a hodgepodge of options that were left over. Some, like **B**ackground Repagination, might technically be a print option, while others, like setting the color to white on blue or 3-D dialog effects, really seem like leftover View options. Whatever the logic, the general settings control a number of options that can affect your satisfaction with Word.

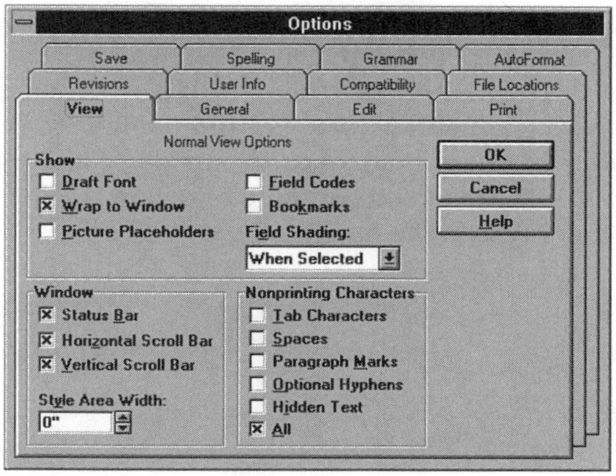

FIGURE 46.2.
The View tab in the Options dialog box.

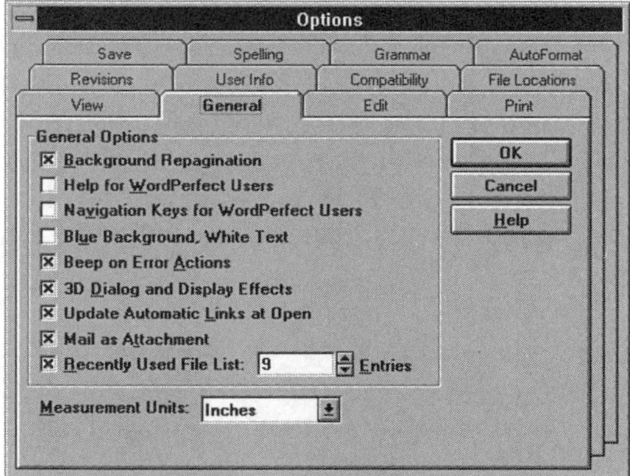

FIGURE 46.3.
The General tab in the Options dialog box.

Background Repagination

By default when working in Normal view, Word repaginates documents when you pause between editing and typing. Ordinarily, most users don't notice the activity. However, with larger documents, this activity may become more noticeable. It can slow down Word's performance a bit, as well as use up more memory resources. Disabling this option can improve performance when working in Normal view. You cannot disable **B**ackground Repagination when working in Print Preview or Page Layout view.

Help for WordPerfect Users

Word has a special help module geared especially to WordPerfect users. When you enable this option, Word provides help when you press WordPerfect function keys. For example, in Word the F2 key is used for moving selected text. In WordPerfect, the

F2 key is used to begin a search. When WordPerfect Help is enabled, pressing F2 displays the dialog box shown in Figure 46.4, which provides information on how to perform a search (Edit | Find) in Word. WordPerfect Help also provides the Demo button, which shows an animated demonstration of how to perform the command in Word. The WordPerfect Help dialog box is persistent and can remain on-screen while you work in Word. This lets you continue to review the help text or the demo while trying to perform the Word command.

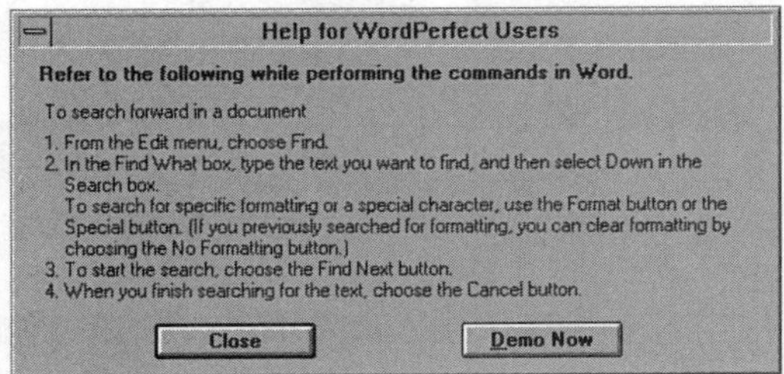

FIGURE 46.4.
WordPerfect Help shows you how to do it in Word.

You can also control WordPerfect Help options from the main Word Help menu. Select Help | WordPerfect Help, and click Options to display the dialog box shown in Figure 46.5. From this dialog box, you can control the Help for WordPerfect Users setting, WordPerfect Navigation keys, as well as the type and speed of the demonstrations.

FIGURE 46.5.
WordPerfect Help Options.

Navigation Keys for WordPerfect Users

Select this option if you're hopelessly addicted to WordPerfect's use of the cursor pad keys—Up, Down, Left, Right, PageUp, PageDown, Home, End, and Esc. With this option selected, Word emulates WordPerfect's use of those keys.

Blue Background, White Text

Another WordPerfect-related option, this feature displays the text area as bright white on a blue background. Word's other colors—toolbar, rulers, and so forth—remain unchanged.

Beep on Error Actions

This setting can be used to silence Word. By default, Word beeps when you make an error. Deselect the check for this option to have Word quietly inform you when an error has occurred.

SUPER NOTE

If you don't seem to get beeps and you actually want them, two additional settings may be interfering. First, you must enable system sounds in the sound module in the Windows Control Panel. Second, the BEEP setting for Microsoft Word in WIN.INI must not be set to NO.

3D Dialog and Display Effects

Purely aesthetic, this control determines whether Word has a Windows 4 or a Windows 3.1 look. By default, Word displays the newer look.

Update Automatic Links at Open

By default, Word automatically tries to update any existing DDE or OLE links when a file is opened. Usually, this is what you want to do. Sometimes, however, you might prefer to look at the older version of the data, or not at the data at all. In the latter cases, suppressing automatic updating of links speeds up opening a file, consumes less memory, and results in faster performance.

Mail as Attachment

When you send a Word document as mail via Microsoft Mail, you have the option of converting the document into Mail format or attaching the Word document, which retains the original Word format. If, for some reason, you do not want the Word document sent, but instead want to use Microsoft Mail format, deselect the Mail as Attachment option.

Recently Used File List

By default, Word keeps track of the last four files you opened. These files, also known as the File Cache, are displayed at the bottom of the file menu. Optionally, Word can remember up to nine files.

Measurement Units

In the U.S. version of Word, the default unit of measurement is inches. Use this setting to specify inches, points, centimeters, or picas.

Edit

Use the **E**dit options to affect a variety of editing behaviors.

Typing Replaces Selection

By default in Windows and OS/2, when text is selected, the next text you type causes the selection to be deleted and replaced by the new text you type—or, if you paste, the pasted text replaces the selection. For some users, this is a difficult adjustment. You can disable this option in Word's text area. When you turn off the **T**yping Replaces Selection option, Word deselects text when you type a new character or perform a paste in the text area. The new text is inserted just before whatever was selected. Word continues to exercise the **T**yping Replaces Selection behavior in dialog boxes.

SUPER NOTE

Think twice before disabling the Typing Replaces Selection option. While you might find it hard to get used to at first, it's system-wide behavior for Windows and OS/2. In fact, you can disable **T**yping Replaces Selection only in the text in Word. You will not be able to disable it in dialog boxes. This leaves you with inconsistency not only across Windows, but within Word as well. Disabling it in Word means that you'll have to get accustomed to Word behaving differently in the text area than it behaves in dialog boxes and in every other Windows or OS/2 application. Sooner or later, you'll have to get used to it. Most users find that it's easier to get used to if it's the unanimous behavior.

Drag-and-Drop Editing

By default, Word lets you drag-and-drop a selection. When text is selected, you can press and hold the left mouse button to drag or copy text to a new location. The alternative is to have the identical action cancel the previous selection and begin a new selection. Unlike the Typing Replaces Selection option, drag-and-drop is not a Windows-wide phenomenon. If you find drag-and-drop editing too tedious to manage and would prefer that Windows behave consistently across all applications, you can disable this option.

Automatic Word Selection

By default, most Windows applications select from the insertion point when you drag to select text. Optionally, you can force Word to select the entire first word, even if the insertion point began inside that word. Think about how you edit text. If you usually want the whole word selected but often miss, then select this option. On the other hand, if you often select just part of a word—deliberately—then turn this option off. This option affects only mouse selection, and does not affect selections using Shift and the left and right arrow buttons.

Use the INS Key for Paste

In Word for DOS, many users became accustomed to using the Insert key to insert the contents of "scrap" (a rough equivalent to paste). In Word for Windows, the Insert key is used to toggle Overtype mode on and off. If you seldom use the Insert key for overtype, or if you come from Word for DOS, selecting this option causes Word to assign the Paste function to the Insert key. Note that Shift+Insert also continues to paste.

TIP

When this option is enabled, you can toggle Overtype mode on and off by double-clicking the OVR button on the status bar.

Overtype Mode

This option simply selects Overtype mode. If you don't have a mouse and if you have the Insert key set to paste, you can use this option to control Overtype mode. Otherwise, use the Insert key or just double-click the Overtype button on the status bar.

Use Smart Cut and Paste

When Smart Cut and Paste is enabled, Word attempts to correctly adjust spaces and punctuation when you cut and paste text. It's an acquired taste. Sometimes, using this feature results in the placement of unwanted spaces. Try it and see if it works for you.

Allow Accented Uppercase

Use this option to allow Word to suggest accented uppercase characters when working in French or other languages that allow uppercase accented characters.

Picture Editor

Use this option to specify the default picture editor for Word. By default, Word itself is the default. If you have Micrografx Draw, Designer, Corel Draw, or some other drawing program you prefer to Word's default drawing module, then use this option to specify your preference.

Print

Use the **P**rint options to control a variety of printing behaviors and defaults. See Chapter 4, "Printing," for full details.

Revisions

Use the **R**evisions options to set the display of text in Revision mode. See Chapter 36, "Revision Marks (Redlining)," for information.

User Info

Use the **U**ser Info options, shown in Figure 46.6, to specify your name, initials, and address. The **N**ame and **I**nitials items are used in tracking revisions and annotations, as well as in determining the authorship of documents. The **M**ailing Address setting is used with Word's envelope and mailing labels commands.

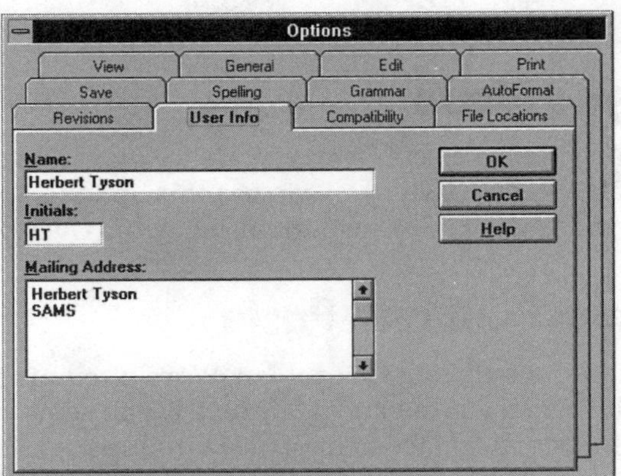

FIGURE 46.6.
The User Info tab in the Options dialog box.

Compatibility

Use the Compatibility settings to set a variety of default behaviors for Word, shown in Figure 46.7. Word sets compatibility with itself, Word for Windows 1 and 2, Word for Macintosh, Word for DOS, and WordPerfect. Each compatibilility choice corresponds to a different combination of options. You can also select Custom in the Recommended Options For list, and mix and match the options to your liking. Most users coming from Word for Windows 2 will probably find the Word 6 defaults fairly livable. The default for Word 6 is all options turned off.

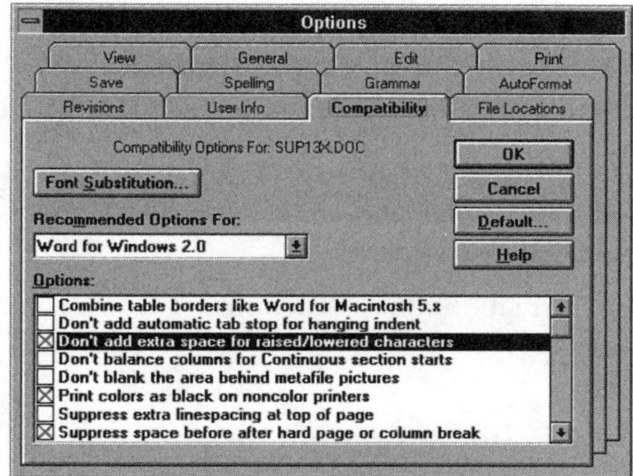

FIGURE 46.7.
*The **Compatibility** tab in the Options dialog box.*

File Locations

Use the File Locations dialog box, shown in Figure 46.8, to set the locations where Word looks for documents, templates, and other files. To change the default location, click Modify, and navigate to the desired location.

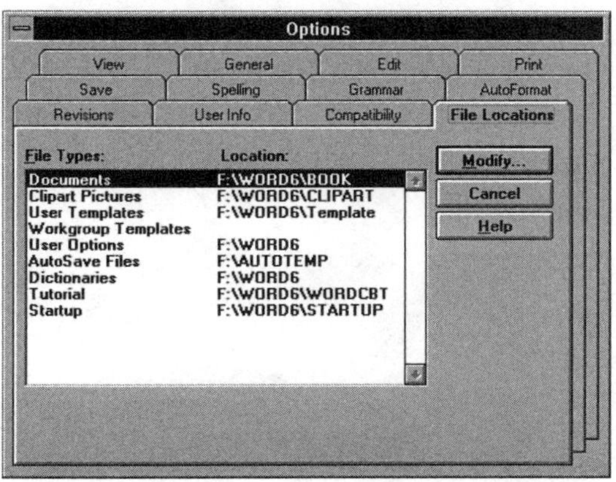

FIGURE 46.8.
*The **File Locations** tab in the Options dialog box.*

Save

Use the Save dialog box to set a variety of file-related options. See "Save Options" in Chapter 6, "Word Files," for additional information.

Spelling

Use the **S**pelling options to set defaults related to spelling. See Chapter 35, "Proofing," for additional information.

Grammar

Use the **G**rammar options to customize the grammar checker. See Chapter 35 for details.

AutoFormat

Use the **A**utoFormat options to customize how Word performs automatic formatting. See Table 22.2 in Chapter 22, "Styles and AutoFormat," for additional information.

Chapter

47

Customizing the Keyboard

In Word, you can map most keys however you like. A few keys—like F1, Esc, and Tab—resist reassignment, but most are fair game. Unlike Word for Windows versions 1 and 2, the cursor keys and keys using Alt are now accessible through the keyboard assignment dialog box.

Overview

Word's basic repertoire of keystrokes is defined in Word itself. When you make changes, those changes are stored either in NORMAL.DOT or in any other template you designate.

> **SUPER TIP**
>
> It's usually confusing for Word's keys to behave differently in different templates. Unlike menus and toolbars, where you get immedidate visual clues about what does what, you don't know what a key does until you press it.

To understand how keyboard shortcuts work, you must first understand how Word works. Every menu item, every toolbar item, and every assigned keystroke (except for those that type text, like A, B, c, d, 1, 2, ", ;, [, and so on), in effect executes some kind of Word command or macro. For example, when you press the left arrow key, you're actually executing a Word command called `CharLeft`. When you press the right arrow key, you're actually running the `CharRight` command. When you press the F7 key, you're running a command called `ToolsSpelling`.

> **SUPER**
>
> Don't waste your time trying to assign the following keys using the menu: Tab, Esc, F1, Backspace, character keys (keys that type text), shifting keys (that is, you can assign Shift+*something*, but you can't assign Shift all by itself), Print Screen, Scroll Lock, Pause, or NumLock. On the other hand, the editing keys—up, down, left, right, Home, End, Page Up, and Page Down—were not valid targets for reassignment in Word for Windows 2, but they are in Word 6.

In order to assign an action to a keystroke in Word, it usually helps to know the name of the command you want to assign. For example, if you use the Bullet tool a lot, you might want to assign a keystroke to it. To do so, it might help to know that the name of the command is `FormatBulletDefault`. If, as in this example, the command you want to assign is already available as a menu or toolbar item, then you can use the Ctrl+Alt++

(number pad) approach (see Procedure 47.1). Using the Customize menu directly, however, it's not always obvious what Word command is associated with any given menu or tool.

Other commands, however, might be available as push buttons from within some dialog boxes, and thus aren't as availing. One way to learn what command is assigned to a given menu or tool is to record a macro during which you execute the menu or tool feature. Then, examine the macro to determine what commands were actually recorded. Another way, although not as definitive, is to open the Customize dialog box, select the Category that matches the feature (for example, Format for bullets), then click Keyboard and scroll through the list of commands to look for likely candidates.

Sometimes, in performing this last exercise, you might even discover that an assigned keystroke already exists. In that case, you can either just use the built-in keystroke or assign one of your own.

Assigning Keystrokes

There are two approaches to assigning keystrokes in Word. The first and easiest approach is to use the `ToolsCustomizeKeyboardShortcut` key (Ctrl+Alt++ on the numeric pad). The second, more general, approach is using the keyboard section of the Tools | Customize tabbed dialog box. The second approach requires a bit more knowledge about Word commands, and it may take some trial and error (or even a little detective work) to discover the correct command.

PROCEDURE 47.1. ASSIGNING A KEY TO A WORD COMMAND USING *TOOLSCUSTOMIZEKEYBOARDSHORTCUT*.

1. Press Ctrl+Alt++ (the gray + sign on the numeric pad); note that a cloverleaf mouse cursor appears, as shown in Figure 47.1.

FIGURE 47.1.
Press Ctrl+Alt++ (numeric pad) to customize a single key.

⌘

2. Select the menu or toolbar feature you want to assign (for example, to assign Window | Arrange All, click Window and then Arrange All; to assign the drawing module, click the Draw tool).
3. Word responds by displaying a limited version of the Customize dialog box, as shown in Figure 47.2. Note that the Word command corresponding to the feature you selected in Step 2 is shown in the Commands area (for example, if you clicked the Draw tool in Step 2, Word would display the `ViewDrawingToolbar` command; if you selected Arrange All from the menu, then Word would display the `WindowArrangeAll` command).

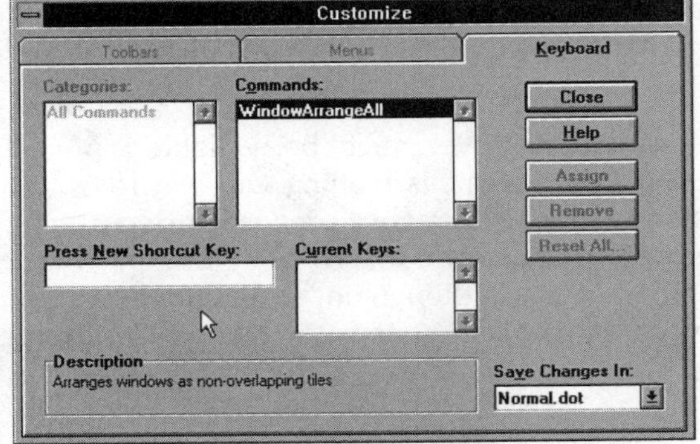

FIGURE 47.2.
The Keyboard tab shows just a single command when the cloverleaf pointer is active.

4. Ensure that the cursor is in the Press **N**ew Shortcut Key area, and press the key combination you want to assign.
5. Word responds by displaying, under `Currently Assigned To:`, the current assignment, or `(unassigned)` if the key is not already assigned.
6. Ensure that Sa**v**e Changes In is set to NORMAL.DOT (you can save assignments in another template if you prefer, but assigning different keystrokes in different templates for the same user is seldom a good idea).
7. Click **A**ssign, and then click Close.

Test the keystroke to make sure that it works correctly. Make sure that you save changes to NORMAL.DOT. Otherwise, the assignment disappears after the current session.

Sometime, when trying to assign a feature, you end up getting the Customize dialog box before you want it. For example, suppose you want to assign a keystroke to the Strikethrough formatting command. When you press Ctrl+Alt++ (number pad) and then select Format Font, the menu, the Customize dialog box appears before you get a chance to select the Strikethough checkbox. Note also that on the default formatting toolbar, Strikethrough is not an option. If you need to assign a Word command that's not readily available through a menu or a toolbar, then you need to access the Customize dialog box directly. It also helps to know the name of the command you want to assign—and it's not always intuitive or obvious.

PROCEDURE 47.2. ASSIGNING A KEY TO A WORD COMMAND USING THE CUSTOMIZE MENU.

1. Select **T**ools | **C**ustomize, and click the Keyboard tab, to display the dialog box shown in Figure 47.3.

FIGURE 47.3.
The Keyboard Tab in the Customize dialog box.

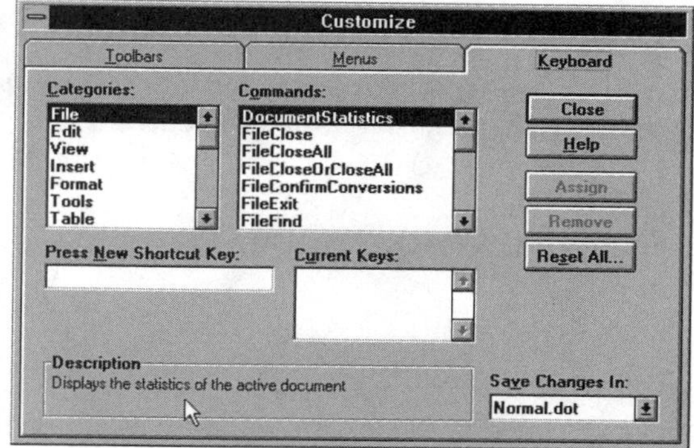

2. In Save Changes In, ensure that NORMAL.DOT is selected (this isn't mandatory but helps prevent confusion later on).
3. In Categories, choose the type of command to which you want to assign a keystroke (or, if you know the name of the command, you can click the All Commands category and go directly to the command you want).
4. Look through the Commands list for the command you want to assign, and select it.
5. Note the Current Keys list. Often, a command you want to assign to a key already is assigned. If the current assignment is acceptable, you can just press Esc and use the built-in assignment.
6. Click in the Press New Shortcut Key area, and press the key combination you want to assign (for example, Alt+Z). Note that the key combination you pressed, along with its current assignment status, is displayed just under the Shortcut Key text box.
7. Click Assign to add the keystroke to the Current Keys list.
8. You can now make additional assignments, if desired, or click Close to close the Customize dialog box.

SUPER NOTE

When you make new key assignments, existing assignments for the same command are not erased. For example, if you add the assignment Ctrl+C to be another way of changing the case of selected text, the default Shift+F3 is not destroyed. Both combinations now work for the same command.

Assigning Keystrokes to User-Created Macros

Word also lets you assign keystrokes to macros you create. For example, suppose you have a macro, SwapWords, that swaps the current and previous words:

```
Sub MAIN
WordLeft 1
WordLeft 1, 1
MoveText
WordRight 2
OK
End Sub
```

For this macro to be very useful, it should be assigned to a keystroke—for example, Alt+Shift+W. That way, when editing text, if you see words that are misplaced, just put the cursor in the second word and press the assigned key combination.

PROCEDURE 47.3. ASSIGNING A KEY COMBINATION TO A USER-CREATED MACRO.

1. Select **T**ools | **C**ustomize and click the **K**eyboard tab to display the Customize dialog box.
2. In Sa**v**e Changes In, ensure that NORMAL.DOT is selected.
3. In **C**ategories, choose Macros.
4. In the Macr**o**s list, click your macro (for example, SwapWords).
5. Click in the Press **N**ew Shortcut Key area and press the key combination you want to assign (for example, Alt+Shift+W). Note that the key combination you pressed, along with its current assignment status, is displayed just under the Shortcut Key text box.
6. Click **A**ssign to add the keystroke to the C**u**rrent Keys list.
7. Click Close to close the Customize dialog box.

Two-Part Key Assignments

New with Word 6 is the ability to make two-part key assignments, rather than just single key assignments. For example, consider the way the accented keys work in Word. To type the letter é, you type Ctrl+' followed by the letter e. You could assign Ctrl+E to insert an é—but what about è and ë ? The system used by Word is a clear pattern that provides a definitive way to get accented characters.

If you have a series of related macros, it might make sense to use a two-part key combination, rather than dedicating a one-part assignment to each one. For example, consider the previous SwapWord example. What if you have a series of swapping macros:

SwapLetters	Swaps the two letters that adjoin the insertion point (that is, to change *teher* to *there*, put the cursor between the two letters you want to swap).

```
Sub MAIN
CharLeft 1, 1
MoveText
CharRight 2
OK
End Sub
```

SwapWords	Swaps two words

```
Sub MAIN
WordLeft 1
WordLeft 1, 1
MoveText
WordRight 2
OK
End Sub
```

SwapSentences	Swaps the current and previous sentences

```
Sub MAIN
ExtendSelection
ExtendSelection
ExtendSelection
MoveText
SentLeft 2
OK
End Sub
```

SwapAnd	Swaps two words surrounding a middle word (that is, change *span and spic* to *spic and span*; put the cursor in the middle word, and then run the macro).

```
Sub MAIN
WordLeft 1
WordLeft 1, 1
MoveText
WordRight 2
OK
WordRight 1, 1
MoveText
WordLeft 3
OK
End Sub
```

SUPER NOTE

These macros are not the most intelligent macros in the world. Depending on where the cursor is, they may sometimes leave a space in the wrong place, or otherwise do something unexpected. For best results, use them only on the interior of a paragraph. They're on the Super Book diskette.

You could assign Alt+Shift+W to one, Alt+Shift+L to another, and so on, but that uses a separate Alt+Shift assignment up for each one. Instead, it might make sense to assign Alt+Shift+S to the concept of swapping, and adding an L to swap letters, W to swap words, S to swap sentences, and A to swap two words surrounding *and*.

PROCEDURE 47.4. MAKING TWO-PART KEY ASSIGNMENTS TO A GROUP OF RELATED MACROS.

1. Select **T**ools | **C**ustomize and click the **K**eyboard tab to display the Customize dialog box.
2. In Sa**v**e Changes In, ensure that NORMAL.DOT is selected.
3. In **C**ategories, choose Macros.
4. In the Macr**o**s list, click your macro (for example, SwapLetters).
5. Click in the Press **N**ew Shortcut Key area and press the key combination you want to assign (for example, Alt+S). Note that the key combination you pressed, along with its current assignment status is displayed just under the Shortcut Key text box. Now press a second key (for example, L). As shown in Figure 47.4, Word displays the first and second keys as a sequence.

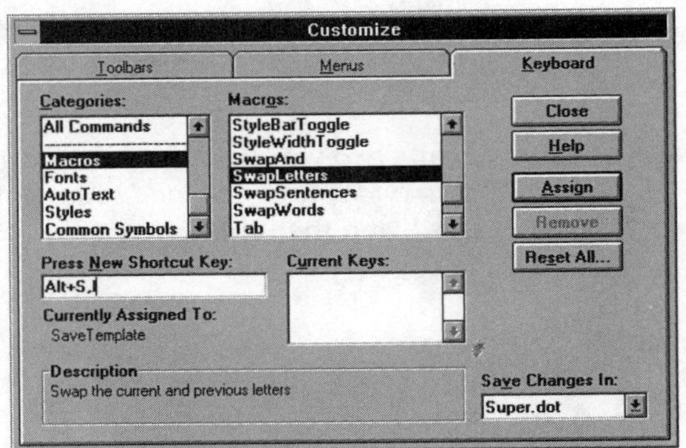

FIGURE 47.4.
Use a two-key sequence to economize on Ctrl and Alt keys.

SUPER CAUTION

When pressing Alt+*key* combinations in the keyboard dialog box, make sure that the cursor is in the Press **N**ew Shortcut Key area. Otherwise, you might inadvertently select a button (like Re**s**et All) instead. Word is aware of this possibility and prompts for a confirmation before carrying out a Reset. If you accidentally do perform a reset, make sure you don't save your template, because UnDo will not undo a reset.

6. Click Assign to add the keystroke to the Current Keys list.
7. Repeat Steps 4 through 6 to assign other keys and macros.
8. Click Close to close the Customize dialog box.

Assigning Keys to Other Word Features

Word also lets you assign keys to styles, autotext, fonts, and symbols. Symbols can also be assigned to keys from the Symbol dialog box, just as Styles can also be assigned to keys from the Modify Styles dialog box, as shown in Chapter 22, "Styles and AutoFormat." However, in both cases, it's much more efficient to make assignments directly from the Customize dialog box, especially if you're making multiple assignments.

PROCEDURE 47.5. ASSIGNING KEYS TO STYLES, AUTOTEXT, FONTS, AND SYMBOLS.

1. Select Tools | Customize, and click the Keyboard tab.
2. In the Categories list, click the kind of assignment you want to make (styles, autotext, fonts, or symbols). The Commands list changes to a Styles, AutoText, Common Symbols, or Fonts list, depending on your selection.
3. In the corresponding list of styles, autotext, fonts, or symbols, select the specific value you want to assign to a key.
4. Click in the Press New Shortcut Key area and press the key or keys to which you wish to make the assignment (note: assignments to styles, autotext, fonts, or symbols are excellent candidates for two-key assignments, since they share clear common bonds).
5. Ensure that the Save Changes In setting is correct.
6. Click Assign.
7. Repeat Steps 2 through 6 to make any additional assignments, and click Close when you're done.

Restoring Default Assignments

It is not generally necessary to remove a key assignment before assigning a key to something else. If you want to assign Ctrl+S to Edit | Find (search), for example, you likely will discover that Ctrl+S already means File | Save. You do not need to track down the File | Save command and remove the Ctrl+S before assigning it to Edit | Find. Because a key can be assigned to only one thing at a time, Word automatically removes a key's previous assignment when you give it a new one.

The only time when you might want to explicitly remove a key assignment is to prevent a key from having a certain effect. For example, perhaps your old word processor used F7 to save a document. Each time you press F7, however, you're greeted with the spelling dialog box. If you never use the spelling dialog box or don't care to do so using a keystroke, you might prefer to just disable the F7 key altogether. You could go ahead and make F7 mean File | Save, by the way—but there are instances in which users want to learn Word's built-in keystrokes (Ctrl+S for Save), and having F7 work as Save does would prevent them from learning Word's built-in keystrokes.

PROCEDURE 47.6. REMOVING A KEY'S ASSIGNMENT.

1. Select **T**ools | **C**ustomize, and click the **K**eyboard tab.
2. Ensure that the Sa**v**e Changes In box reflects your choice of templates.
3. Click in the Press **N**ew Shortcut Key area, and then press the key assignment you want to remove.
4. Observe the description under the key to see the key's exact current assignment.
5. Use the **C**ategories list to select the correct category, and then scroll the commands (or whatever) list to display the key's current assignment.
6. In the C**u**rrent Keys box, click to select the key assignment you want to remove.
7. Click **R**emove.
8. Click Close to close the dialog box.

SUPER TIP

After removing a built-in key assignment, its status is `unassigned`. There are two ways to restore an unassigned key to its original definition. One way is to reassign it to the corresponding Word command, using the procedure Assigning a key to a Word command using the Customize menu. If you don't know the key's original assignment, here's a trick you can use. First, assign the key to anything—but make it something easy to get to. Second, use the procedure shown just above to remove that assignment. Presto! In removing the assignment, Word restores the built-in assignment and doesn't take it all the way back to `unassigned`.

After assigning a built-in key to something of your own choosing, you also can restore that key to its original state. Just use the Removing a key's assignment procedure. When a key has a user-assignment, the procedure restores the individual key to its built-in definition.

Chapter

48

Customizing Toolbars

Word comes with a number of built-in special-purpose toolbars. In addition to the default standard toolbar, and the formatting toolbar you see when you first start Word, Word has eight toolbars that you can display at any time. As if that weren't enough, Word controls additional special-purpose toolbars such as the Macro toolbar, the Macro Record toolbar, the Mail Merge toolbar, and others. Plus, you can add to and take away from the toolbars to your heart's content, as well as create your own. Not only that, as pointed out early in this book, you can display toolbars either as floating dialog boxes, or glued to the sides, top, or bottom of the Word screen.

Overview

Word's tools for manipulating toolbars are an excellent example of drag-and-drop technology. Rather than having to work (entirely) with a cumbersome set of menus, Word lets you work directly on the toolbars themselves, dragging here, dropping there. Anyone who spent any time trying to work with the inflexible toolbar in Word for Windows 2 will appreciate the newfound flexibility and ease of use in Word 6.

There is one nagging deficiency in Word's implementation of toolbar customization, however. It's often difficult to determine which Word command is assigned to a tool. For example, consider the numbering tool on the formatting toolbar. If I wanted to use the corresponding command in a macro, I could easily spend half the day perusing the Customize dialog box trying to determine exactly which command the numbering tool uses. It's pretty easy to find the button in the Format category, as shown in Figure 48.1. Unfortunately, when you click the numbering button, all you learn is that it "Creates a numbered list based on the current defaults." But that doesn't tell you what command it uses.

FIGURE 48.1.
The numbering button is easy to find on the toolbar, but it's not so easy to figure out the exact name of the corresponding Word command.

You could select **T**ools | **M**acro, select Word Commands under Macros **A**vailable In, and start scrolling through the list until you see a description that matches "Creates a numbered list..."—but that would take forever. Or, you could go through the list of formatting commands displayed in the **T**ools | **C**ustomize, **K**eyboard tab, looking for a match. That would take only half of forever. Or, you could simply make an educated guess. But none of this is nearly as simple as it would have been if Word had included the command name as part of the toolbar customization dialog box.

SUPER TIP

Oh well, enough of this. If you see a button on the toolbar and want to know what command it runs, here's a quick and dirty trick to find out:

1. Press **Ctrl+Alt++** (number pad) to display the cloverleaf key-assignment pointer.
2. Click the tool button that interests you.
3. Word now displays the Keyboard tab of the Customize menu, with the corresponding command highlighted, as shown in Figure 48.2. Press Esc to close the dialog box.

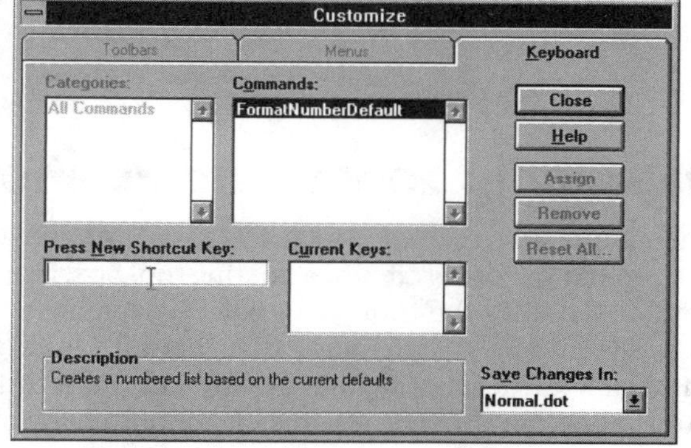

FIGURE 48.2. *The corresponding command is highlighted in the Keyboard tab of the Customize dialog box.*

SUPER

If the button of interest is in one of the groupings in the Toolbar tab of the Customize menu, you have to first drag it to an existing toolbar before using this trick. Once you've learned its secret identity, you can then remove it from the toolbar. Stay tuned for details.

Templates and Tools

Toolbars are stored in templates. You can store them in NORMAL.DOT or in specific templates. If you create document-specific sets of tools, it's probably not a bad idea to store them in a dedicated template. That way, if you give the document to someone else, they'll be able to use your tools by using the same template, rather than having to modify their own NORMAL.DOT file. If you're creating a ubiquitous set of tools that you want available everywhere, then it generally works out best to save your tools in your own NORMAL.DOT file. You specify where your toolbar customizations are stored using the Save Changes In section of the Customize dialog box, as shown in Figure 48.3.

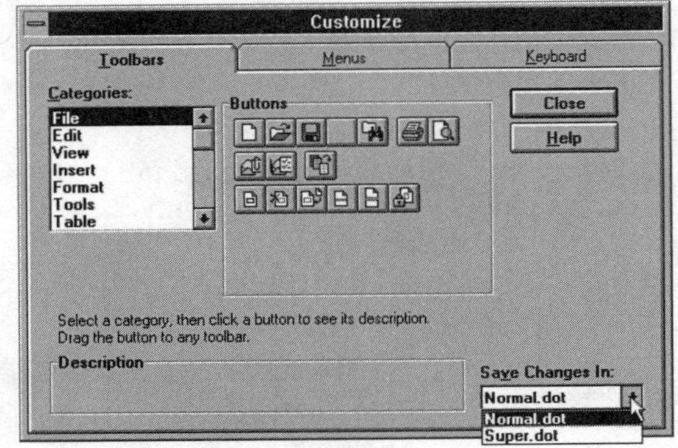

FIGURE 48.3.
Use the Save Changes In option to make sure you save your changes in the right place!

Changing the Shape and Position

You can manipulate the shape and location of toolbars at will. Double-click any blank area on a toolbar to convert it into a floating tool box. Use any blank area on the toolbar as a handle, and drag the toolbar to wherever you want it, as shown in Figure 48.4. While it's being dragged, it displays as a frame. The shape of the frame changes if you bump up against the top, bottom, or sides of the Word window. When it's floating, just double-click the title bar to cause it to jump back to its last fixed position. Even when it's in a fixed position on one of the four sides of the Word window, you can move it to the left or right.

SUPER TIP

When you run Word in a "seamless" window under OS/2, you can even move a toolbar completely off the Word window, as shown in Figure 48.5. Seamless toolbars! Who would have imagined it?

FIGURE 48.4.
You can drag the toolbar anywhere on the Windows screen.

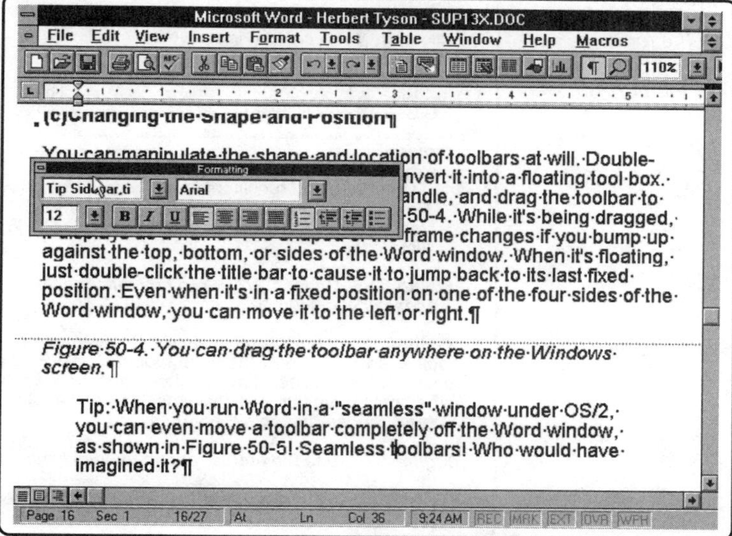

FIGURE 48.5.
Under OS/2, Word toolbars can float in their own "seamless" windows.

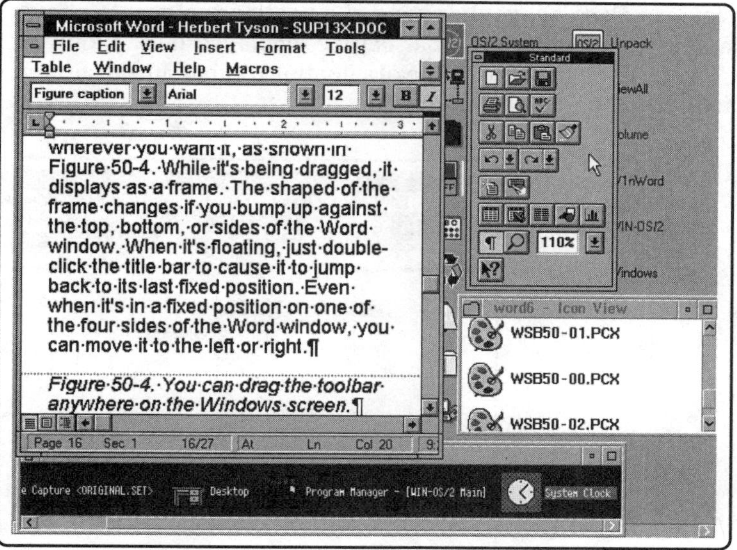

To turn a fixed toolbar off, just click the right mouse button on any blank toolbar area to display the toolbar popup (see Figure 48.6), and deselect the check box next to the toolbar you want to dismiss. To turn off a floating toolbar, just click its control icon (the upper-left corner), or use the toolbar popup.

FIGURE 48.6.
Use the toolbar popup to quickly turn toolbars on or off.

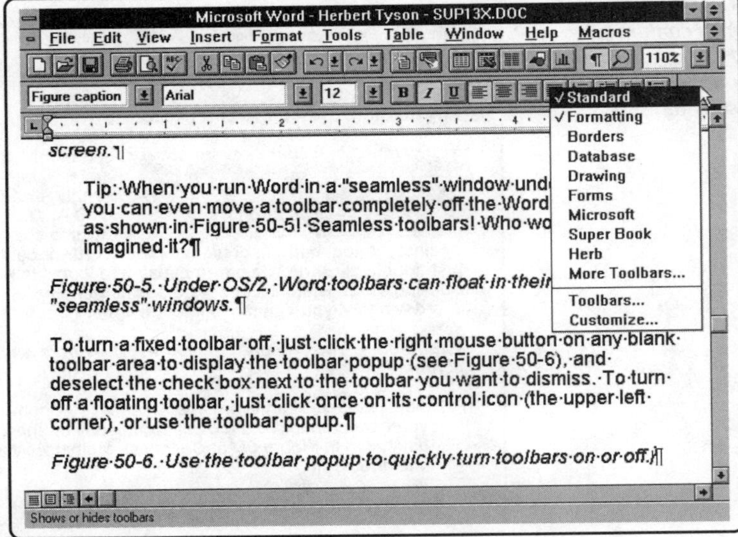

You can also change the shape of a floating toolbar. As shown in Figure 48.7, for example, the standard toolbar can be displayed horizontally, vertically, or even as a square. To change the shape of a floating toolbar, just drag any of the corners or sides until the shape is what you want.

FIGURE 48.7.
Toolbars can be virtually any rectangular shape. Sorry, no triangles!

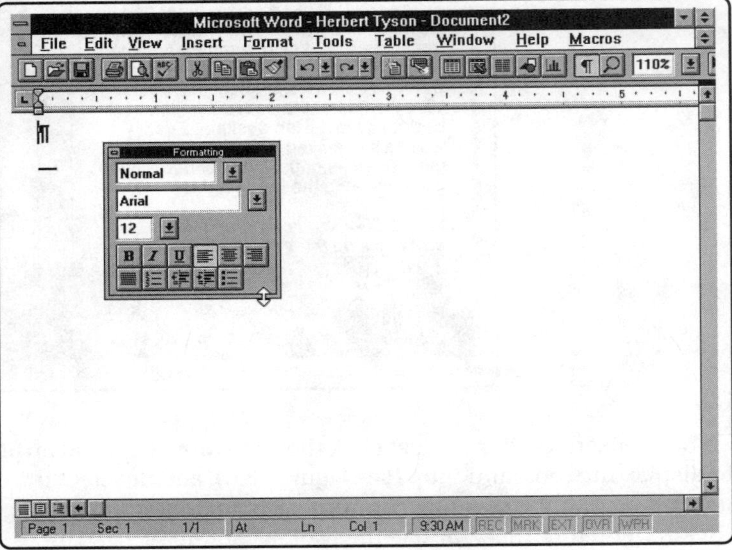

Controlling Toolbars: Creating, Deleting, and Resetting

Another way to turn toolbars on and off is using the Toolbars dialog box. To display the Toolbars dialog box, shown in Figure 48.8, select View|Toolbars. The Toolbars dialog box is used to turn on and off the display of toolbars, as well as to manage the creation, modification, resetting, and deleting of toolbars.

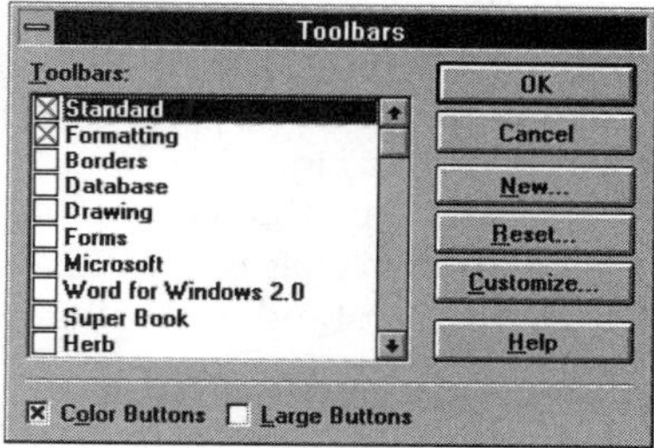

FIGURE 48.8.
Use View|Toolbars to create and delete toolbars.

PROCEDURE 48.1. CREATING A NEW TOOLBAR.

1. Select View|Toolbars.
2. Click New.
3. Type a new name for the toolbar, and select the template where you want the new toolbar stored.
4. Click OK.

> **SUPER TIP**
>
> You also can create a new toolbar on the fly by dropping a tool button on an unassigned toolbar area when working in the Toolbar tab of the Customize dialog box. New toolbars created that way are named Toolbar 1, Toolbar 2, and so on. To give them more meaningful names, see the next section, "Renaming Toolbars."

Before you discover that you can *deliberately* create toolbars, you might accidentally create a few, as well. You also might have a need to delete other toolbars as you build Word into a word processing powerhouse.

PROCEDURE 48.2. DELETING USER-CREATED TOOLBARS.

1. Select View|Toolbars.
2. Click the toolbar you want to wipe out.
3. Click Delete.

SUPER NOTE

You cannot delete built-in toolbars. At most, you can hide them or reset them.

Sometimes you might go overboard in customizing Word's built-in toolbars, or simply decide to reorganize your approach to Word. For example, my immediate impulse is to change everything in sight so that it reflects my preferences. Unfortanately, that then created a dilemma when it came to doing screenshots for this book. While my customizations might be very functional for me, a picture of *my* standard toolbar (the way it looked a few hours after I installed Word 6) wouldn't help you at all, because it bore no resemblance to the one that comes with Word. An alternative, I quickly discovered, was to create my own customized toolbars under different names. That then left me with my overmodified standard toolbar, which I wanted to restore to the factor default.

PROCEDURE 48.3. RESETTING A BUILT-IN TOOLBAR TO THE DEFAULT.

1. Select **V**iew | **T**oolbars.
2. Click the toolbar you want to reset.
3. Click **R**eset.

SUPER NOTE

The Reset command is available only for Word's own toolbars. If you select a user-created toolbar, the Reset command is replaced with the Delete command.

Renaming Toolbars

Have you spent a few minutes now looking at the Toolbars dialog box, trying to figure out how to rename a toolbar? It's not there! Instead, Microsoft decided that this significant feature belongs in the Template Organizer. Yeah, I can't quite grasp the logic of that, either, but at least you now know where to find it.

PROCEDURE 48.4. RENAMING A TOOLBAR.

1. Select **F**ile | **T**emplates, and click the **O**rganizer button (see Figure 48.9).
2. Select the Toolbars tab.
3. Using the Toolbars A**v**ailable In control, select the template whose toolbar(s) you want to rename.

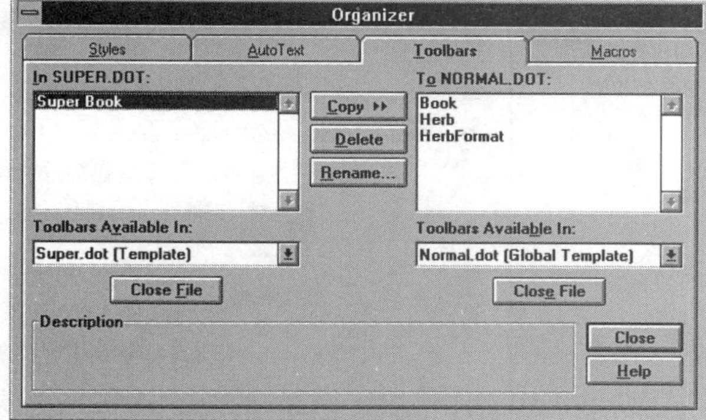

FIGURE 48.9.
*Click the **O**rganizer button for more toolbar controls.*

4. Word displays all user-created toolbars in the list. Click the toolbar you want to rename.
5. Click **R**ename.
6. Type the New **N**ame, and then click OK.
7. Repeat Steps 4 through 6 to rename any others, and then click Close to close the Organizer.

Changing Existing Tools

Word also lets you change existing toolbars by adding and removing buttons.

Adding Buttons

Word lets you add built-in buttons as well as buttons you create yourself. You can assign those buttons to built-in Word commands as well as to user-created macros.

PROCEDURE 48.5. ADDING A BUTTON TO A TOOLBAR.

1. Make sure that the toolbar you want to change is displayed on-screen (select View | Toolbars, if necessary, and turn on the toolbar you want to modify).
2. Select **T**ools | **C**ustomize, and click **T**oolbars.
3. Observing the Buttons list, browse through the Categories to find the button you want to add; when you click a button, a description of it is displayed in the Description area.
4. Using the mouse left button, drag the button to the target toolbar. Make sure that it is within the borders of the toolbar, and drop it when it's in place (as shown in Figure 48.10).

FIGURE 48.10.
Pardon me, but did you drop a button on this toolbar?

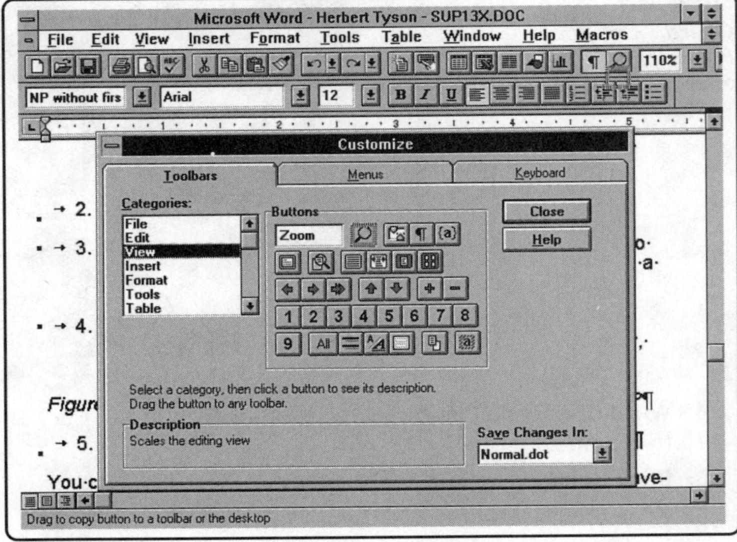

5. Repeat Steps 3 and 4 to add as many buttons as you want.

You can also add buttons for commands, macros, styles, or what-have-you, that don't have built-in buttons. Word gives you the option of either using a text button, or of drawing your own icon for the button.

PROCEDURE 48.6. ADDING A BUTTON WHEN THERE IS NO BUILT-IN BUTTON.

1. Make sure that the toolbar you want to change is displayed on-screen (select View | Toolbars, if necessary, and turn on the toolbar you want to modify).
2. Select Tools | Customize, and click Toolbars.
3. Using the Categories list, select the category for the type of action you want to add to the toolbar. Note that commands only are listed for the categories All Commands, Macros, AutoText, Fonts, and Styles; the button list is replaced by a corresponding list of commands, macros, and so forth.
4. Click the item you want, drag it to the target toolbar, and drop it where you want it (see Figure 48.11).
5. Word now displays the Custom Button dialog box, shown in Figure 48.12. You can modify the Text Button Name and then click Assign to use a text button; select a prefabricated button and then click Assign to use a prefab button; or click Edit to create your own.

FIGURE 48.11.
When you drag a text command to a toolbar, it turns into a button.

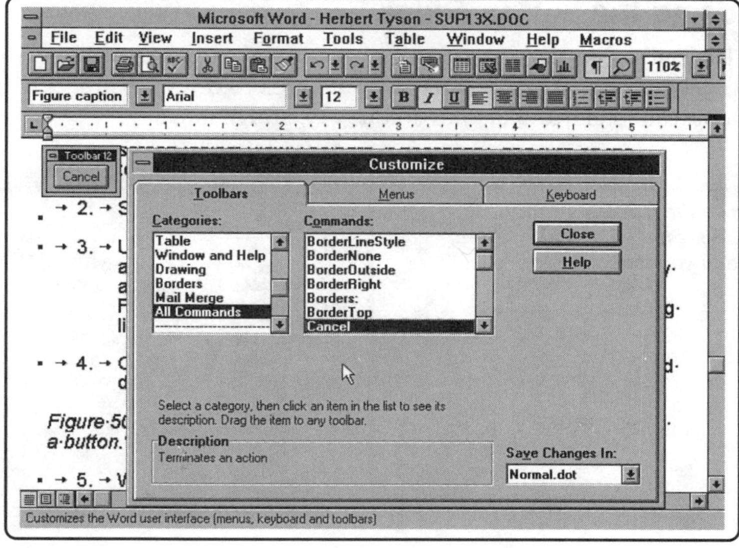

FIGURE 48.12.
The Custom Button dialog box.

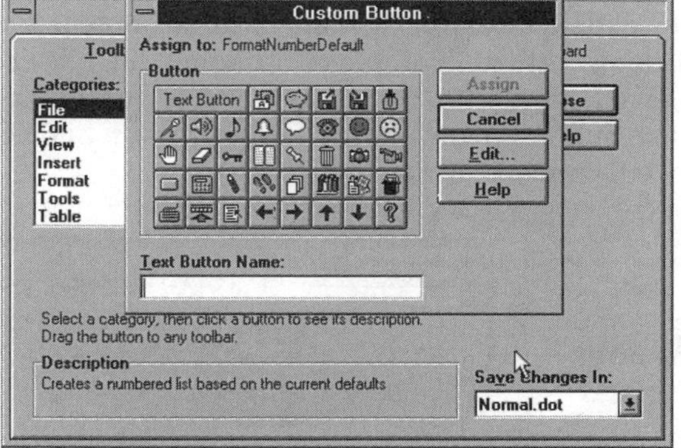

6. Click Close to close the Customize dialog box.

SUPER TIP

In Step 5, if you want to create your own, but want to use an existing prefab button as a starting point, select the button closest to what you want before clicking on Edit. Word uses it as a starting point.

Using the Button Editor

The button editor, shown in Figure 48.13, is intuitive, although fairly primitive. It is a pixel editor that lets you use tiny squares to draw a picture. You can use it to create a button image and also to edit any existing image.

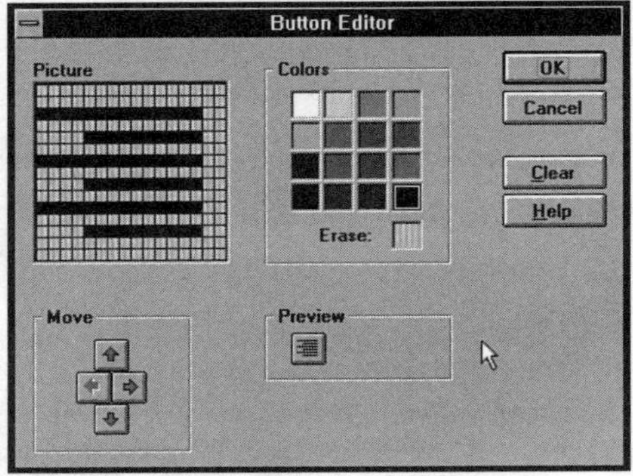

FIGURE 48.13.
Use the Button Editor to create and edit your buttons.

The Button Editor can be activated only while the Toolbars Customize dialog box is displayed. With the Customize dialog box on-screen, you can activate the Button Editor by clicking Edit (as in Step 5 of the preceding procedure) when adding a button. You can also activate the Button Editor from a button popup menu by clicking the right mouse button on any button in a button bar, and selecting the Edit Button Image option (see Figure 48.14).

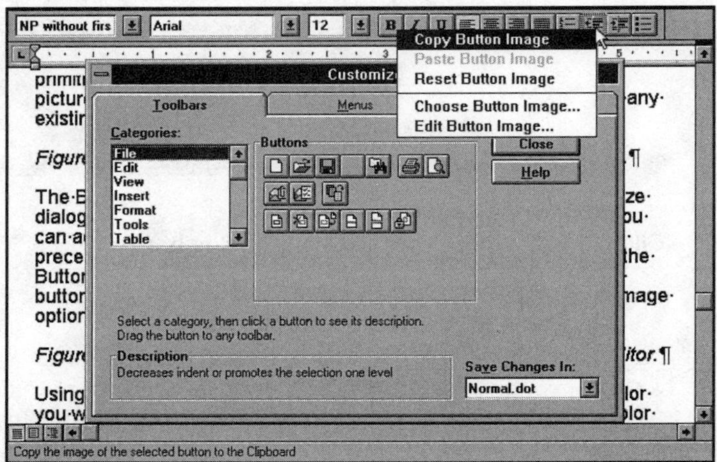

FIGURE 48.14.
Use the button popup menu to activate the Button Editor.

Using the Button Editor is fairly straightforward. You click the color you want to use, and the use the right mouse button to apply that color to the image. To erase a color from a block, just click again. To erase period (regardless of color), choose Erase instead of a color. To clear the whole image, click (you guessed it) Clear.

You can use the Move buttons to move the image around in the drawing area. When the image reaches the edge, it stops. The Preview diagram shows what the image will look like on the button bar.

Working with Button Images

You also can display the Custom Button dialog by selecting the Choose Button Image from the button popup menu. If you're not satisfied with a button's appearance, you can use any of the prefab buttons as a new image or as a starting point for one you want to create. While the Toolbar tab of the Customize dialog box is active, you also can copy, paste, and reset button images.

PROCEDURE 48.7. COPYING AN IMAGE FROM ONE BUTTON TO ANOTHER.

1. Select **T**ools | **C**ustomize, and click the **T**oolbars tab.
2. Click the right mouse button on the button you want to copy (you can copy only button images from actual toolbars, not from the buttons in the dialog box), and click Copy Button Image.
3. Move the mouse pointer to the target button, and click the right mouse button. Click Paste Button Image.

Moving and Copying Buttons

You can easily move or copy a button from one toolbar to another, or to a new location on the same toolbar.

PROCEDURE 48.8. MOVING A BUTTON BETWEEN TOOLBARS.

1. Display the source and target toolbar(s).
2. Select **T**ools | **C**ustomize, and click the **T**oolbars tab.
3. Move the mouse pointer over the button you want to move.
4. Press the left mouse button and drag the button to the new location; drop it into place by releasing the mouse button.

To copy a button instead of moving it, press and hold the Ctrl key in Step 4. As shown in Figure 48.15, a + sign appears next to the button outline to show that you are copying instead of moving. Using this technique makes it easy to mix and match from existing toolbars to build custom toolbars for special projects or tasks.

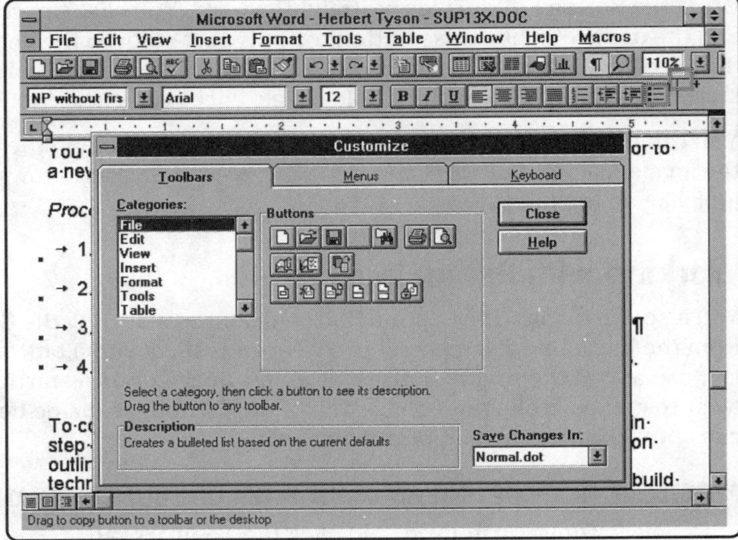

FIGURE 48.15. *When you hold down the Ctrl key when dragging buttons between toolbars, the button is copied instead of moved.*

Removing Buttons

Removing buttons from a tooolbar is not exactly intuitive, but it's easy once you know how. It's just a matter of dragging the button away from the toolbar and dropping it someplace where it doesn't belong.

PROCEDURE 48.9. REMOVING A BUTTON FROM A TOOLBAR.

1. Display the toolbar.
2. Select **T**ools | **C**ustomize, and click the **T**oolbars tab.
3. Move the mouse pointer over the button you want to remove.
4. Press the left mouse button and drag the button anywhere on-screen except to a toolbar. Just to be on the safe side, you can drag it to the Customize dialog box and release the mouse button.

Replacing the Action Assigned to a Button

Sometimes you customize a command and want to replace the built-in command with your version. Or, you just want an existing button to perform a different action entirely. Unfortunately, intuition doesn't win this time. Intuitively, it'd be nice to just drop a new command onto an existing button, but it doesn't work that way. Instead, doing that just adds the command to one side of the existing button. Even so, this is a good start.

PROCEDURE 48.10. REPLACING THE ACTION ASSIGNED TO A BUTTON WITH A DIFFERENT ACTION.

1. Display the toolbar.
2. Select **T**ools | **C**ustomize, and click the **T**oolbars tab.
3. In the **C**ategories list, select the category that contains the action you want to assign.
4. In the action list (commands, styles, macros, and so forth), select the new action.
5. Drag the action to either side of the button you want to use and drop it there. Let Word assign the default text button for now.
6. Click the right mouse button on the button whose image you want to use, and click Copy.
7. Click the right mouse button on the text button you just installed in Step 5, and click Paste.
8. Move the mouse to the old button, drag it to the Customize dialog box, and drop it there.

Chapter

Customizing Menus

Word lets you add to and take away from menus. You can add to, remove from, rename, and change *almost* any menu items you like. If you, like some others, think that Microsoft's annoying practice of having unintuitive letters assigned to menu items is stupid, you can fix it. Consider, for example, a main menu in which the first letter of each main item could be used to activate that item. Wouldn't it be wonderful if Format could be accessed with Alt+F and Table with Alt+T? Well, you can do it. What about File and Tools? Just rename each to something with first letters that isn't already taken, like Disk and Utility. After all, aren't those names just as potentially meaningful as File and Tools? Of course, nobody else would be able to use your setup—but maybe that's an advantage, especially if you're plagued with coworkers who insist on taking over your work station.

Of Word's various customization tools, menus seem to be the most confusing. Part of the confusion sometimes results because you might be looking at a compound menu that includes customizations from a specific or global template, as well as from NORMAL.DOT. As long as you're sure about what you're modifying, the confusion can be kept to a minimum.

Overview

Word lets you change the existing main menu bar (File, Edit, View, Insert, Format, Tools, Table, Window, and Help) and any of the pull-down menus. You can add to the main menu bar, remove items from it, or rename the ones that are there. You can add, remove, and rename items on the pull-down menus as well.

Templates and Menus

Like toolbars, autotext, and keys, menu customizations are stored in templates. When customizing menus, you can save a lot of grief by making sure that you save your changes where you intend. When using global templates and document-specific templates at the same time, it's often difficult to know what's coming from where. For better overall results, you'd be well advised to turn off global templates when modifying menus. That way, you won't be fighting with yourself.

Adding, Removing, and Changing Items on a Menu

Word lets you add, remove, or change any menu using the Menus tab of the Customize dialog box, shown in Figure 49.1. You need to be careful when doing so, however, for two reasons. First, unlike some dialog boxes, the Menus dialog box doesn't have a Cancel button. The moment you click the Add or Remove button, the command has been added to the menu. Second, the Menus dialog box doesn't have a single-item reset feature. If you inadvertently remove a built-in item and can't remember what it was, you might have to use Reset All to get it back.

FIGURE 49.1.
The Menus tab of the Customize dialog box.

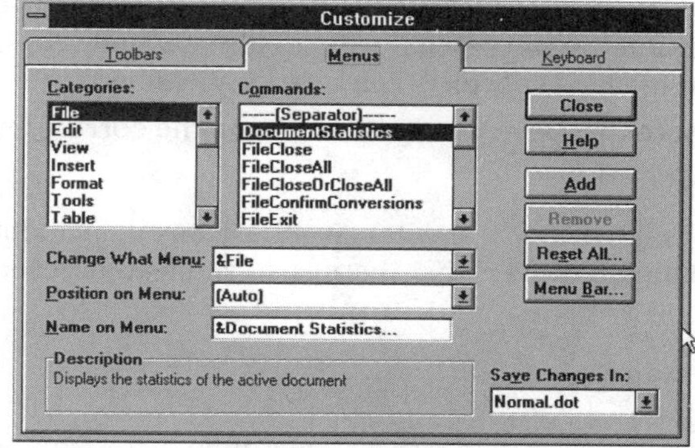

SUPER TIP

You can sometimes recover by quitting Word without saving the current changes to NORMAL.DOT (or whatever template has the problem). If you accidentally removed or changed a built-in feature—one you can't seem to remember how to re-create—you have another option. You can quit Word, saving the current changes to NORMAL.DOT. Then, use File Manager or some other means to temporarily rename NORMAL.DOT as something else (for example, NORMTEMP.DOT). Then restart Word. Select **T**ools | **C**ustomize | **M**enus and take a good look at the feature you mucked up—take notes if necessary. Then, open NORMTEMP.DOT directly and put the original command or feature back the way it was, and save NORMTEMP.DOT. Quit Word again (don't save NORMAL.DOT), and rename NORMTEMP.DOT as NORMAL.DOT.

PROCEDURE 49.1. ADDING A MENU ITEM TO WORD.

1. Select **T**ools | **C**ustomize and click **M**enus to display the Menus portion of the Customize dialog box, shown in Figure 49.1.
2. Use the **C**ategories and **C**ommands list to locate the command, macro, or other item you want to add to the menu (remember: the middle list starts out as Commands, but changes dynamically when the category is macros, styles, fonts, or autotext).
3. In Change What Men**u**, select the menu you want to change.
4. In **P**osition on Menu, select (Auto), unless you have a specific location where you want the item to go.

5. In **N**ame on Menu, edit the item so that it appears the way you want it to appear on the menu. Precede the speedkey character with a `&` (the speedkey character appears with an underline in the menu, and you can speed to that item by tapping that key when the menu is displayed; choose a unique character in the name that's not already underlined in the current menu, so that the new speedkey can be unambiguous).
6. Ensure that Sa**v**e Changes In reflects the correct template file.
7. Click **A**dd.

You can remove *almost* any item from any menu, including most of the built-in items. Keep in mind, however, that there is no single-item reset feature.

SUPER NOTE

Word will not let you remove some items from the menus. In the Tools menu, for example, all of the proofing items are clumped together as `(List of Proofing Tools)`, as shown in Figure 49.2. Note that the Remove button is dimmed as unavailable. None of the parenthetical groupings can be removed—not even with a chisel.

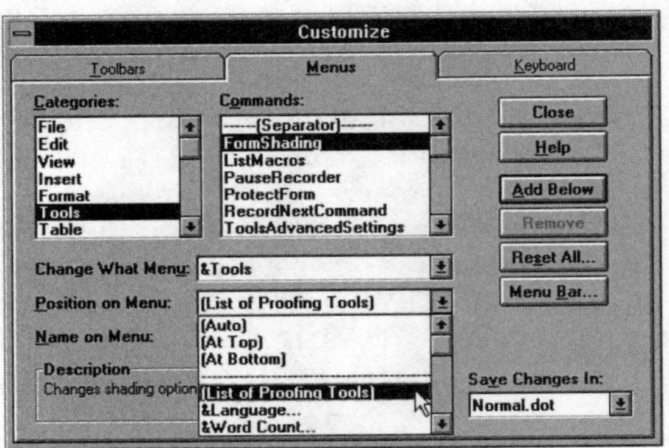

FIGURE 49.2.
You cannot remove some items, like `(List of Proofing Tools)`.

PROCEDURE 49.2. REMOVING AN ITEM FROM A MENU.

1. Select **T**ools | **C**ustomize and click **M**enus to display the Menus portion of the Customize dialog box.
2. In Change What Men**u**, select the menu you want to change.
3. In **P**osition on Menu, select the item you want to remove.
4. Click **R**emove.

While it isn't intuitively obvious, you also can change an item on a menu, kind of, by trying to assign an item a different command or feature. Word won't let you overwrite in this way, but it does let you add the item immediately below the existing item. Once you have, you can then remove the original item, effectively replacing it.

PROCEDURE 49.3. ASSIGNING A DIFFERENT FEATURE TO AN EXISTING MENU ITEM (KIND OF).

1. Select Tools | Customize and click Menus to display the Menus portion of the Customize dialog box.
2. Use the Categories and Commands list to locate the command, macro, or other item you want to substitute.
3. In Change What Menu, select the menu you want to change.
4. In Position on Menu, select the command you want to change. For example, if you want to replace Word 6's infuriating FormatBulletsAndNumbering command with Word for Windows 2's ToolsBulletsNumbers command, then select ToolsBulletsNumbers in Step 2 and Bullets and Numbering in Step 4.
5. In Name on Menu, edit the item so that it appears the way you want it to appear on the menu.
6. Ensure that Save Changes In reflects the correct template file.
7. Note that the Add button is now Add Below. Click it.
8. Select the original command—now just above the one you added—and click Remove.

Using the Shortcut Method for Removing Items from a Menu

You also can remove an item from a menu using a keyboard shortcut. Just as with the Customize dialog box, however, you cannot remove parenthetical groups (proofing tools, mail tools, object verbs, and so on) from a menu. The only exception is that you can remove individual file cache items from the bottom of the File menu. This can be useful if the cache now contains files that have been renamed or deleted or that are on inaccessible drives.

PROCEDURE 49.4. REMOVING AN ITEM FROM A MENU—THE QUICK WAY.

1. Press Ctrl+Alt+- (top row); note that a big minus sign cursor appears, as shown in Figure 49.3.

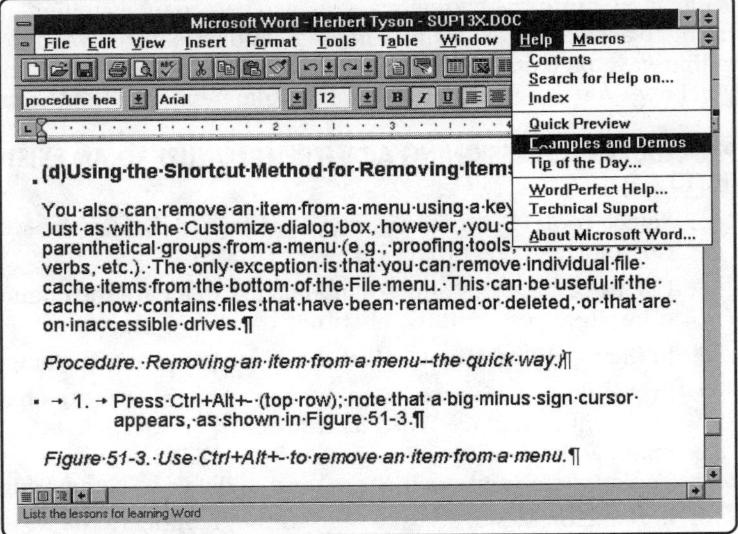

FIGURE 49.3. *Use Ctrl+Alt+- to remove an item from a menu.*

2. Select the menu item you want to remove (for example, select **T**ools | **L**anguage to remove Language from the tools menu).

So, why would you want to remove an item from a menu? Well, maybe you put it there and no longer want it. Or, perhaps you're customizing a pared-down version of Word for a temporary employee who doesn't need to be overwhelmed by Word. Or, maybe you're just a minimalist by nature.

Changing the Main Menu Bar

Word also lets you add to, remove from, or change the Main Menu bar. This is a great boon to people who don't particularly share Microsoft's fondness for menu items whose speedkeys aren't intuitively connected to the underlying menu command. For example, in Word for Windows 2, Format was accessed with Alt+T; in Word 6, it's Alt+O. That's closer to the F than before, but still way off base. How about instead calling the whole menu Style instead of Format? After all, both are fairly arbitrary terms—right? And, what about the fact that Table is Alt+A? Why not give it the T back, and rename Tools as Utility?

In addition, you can add your own items to the menu. Do you have a lot of macros? Maybe you'd care to add a Macro item to the main toolbar, and make often-needed macros accessible from their own menu stem.

PROCEDURE 49.5. ADDING A MENU TO THE MENU BAR.

1. Select Tools | Customize and click the Menus tab.
2. Click the Menu Bar button.
3. In Name on Menu Bar, type the name for the menu you want to create, using the `&` to precede the speedkey character you want to assign.
4. Click Add, and then click Close to return to the main Menus dialog box.
5. Follow the procedures shown earlier to populate the new menu with the commands or other items of your choosing.

As mentioned previously, you also can change the name of existing menus. Fortunately, you don't have to add the new one and then remove the old one, as you do when replacing items in the menus themselves.

PROCEDURE 49.6. RENAMING AN EXISTING MENU.

1. Select Tools | Customize, and click the Menus tab.
2. Click the Menu Bar button.
3. In Position on Menu Bar, select the item you want to rename (for example, `F&ormat`).
4. In Name on Menu Bar, type the new name—for example, `&Style` (note: until you perform this step, the Rename button is dimmed).
5. Click Rename.

If you're reorganizing a menu, you sometimes need to remove a menu from the main menu bar. Word lets you remove any items you don't want.

PROCEDURE 49.7. REMOVING A MENU FROM THE MAIN MENU BAR.

1. Select Tools | Customize, and click the Menus tab.
2. Click the Menu Bar button.
3. In Position on Menu Bar, select the item you want to remove.
4. Click Remove.

Changing the Menu Indirectly by Modifying Commands

In addition to the methods noted, you also can change menus indirectly by modifying the commands themselves. You do this by creating a macro with the same name. For example, the File | Open command, by default, always starts off by showing you just the *.DOC files. What if you'd really rather *always* see a list of all files on the directory? Well, you can do it. Just create a special version of the `FileOpen` macro that initializes the file specification as `*.*` instead of `*.DOC`. Even though you haven't really touched the menu itself, its native assignment is the `FileOpen` command. Any macros you have that have the same name as built-in commands take precedence over the built-in commands themselves. Thus, when you select **File | Open** or press Ctrl+O, you get your modified version of `FileOpen` instead of the original. All in all, it's a lot easier than having to create a macro *and* modify the menu. It also makes it easier to revert later on, should the need to do so arise.

Oh yeah, here's the macro to always get `*.*` instead of `*.DOC`. I don't always practice what I preach, so instead of calling the macro `FileOpen`, it instead is called *`FileOpenAll`* on the Super Book diskette. Note that in line 4, we're plugging in the value `*.*` for the name. If you want, instead, to force `FileOpen` to always start with `*.DOC`—especially after you've been working with a different extension—you can substitute `*.DOC` instead of `*.*`. Or, if you don't like futzing with the List Files of Type drop-down menu, you could even create some specialized `FileOpen` commands and put them into your File menu (or, create a new menu, perhaps called Open). You might have macros called `FileOpenRTF`, `FileOpenDOC`, `FileOpenAll`, and so on.

FileOpenAll

```
Sub MAIN
On Error Goto Endit
Dim dlg As FileOpen
GetCurValues dlg
dlg.Name = "*.*"
Dialog dlg
FileOpen dlg
EndIt:
Select Case Err
Case 0, 102
Case Else : Error Err
End Select
End Sub
```

XIII

Projects Workshop

The Projects Workshop is a demonstration of Word for Windows 6 in action. In this workshop, we take you through the creation of seven of the major kinds of documents used by businesses and individuals. The projects are complemented by template files on the Word for Windows 6 Super Book diskette. Each of the templates comes with its own customized toolbar to facilitate using the special styles and features appropriate for each type of document.

Econometrics: Science or Sham?

by

Herbert Tyson

October 29, 1993

Page 1

Preface

This is the preface. Replace this text with the preface you really want. Otherwise, your paper will end up looking kind of odd right off the bat. Preface paragraphs in this paper are not indented. The preface title is 14 point, bold, Times New Roman, and the preface text is 12 points, with automatic 12 point spacing after each preface paragraphs. Preface page numbers are in small roman numerals, centered at the bottom of the page.

Page i

ABSTRACT

This is how many academic papers begin, particularly those presented at symposia. They begin with an abstract (sometime's called an Idiot's Summary). Often, one look at the abstract tells you whether or not the rest of the article is relevant to your work.

INTRODUCTION

This is the text of your paper, using a style called Body Text. Body Text here is 12 point Times New Roman, with automatic 12 point spacing (Spacing After, in the paragraph formatting) between paragraphs.

One of the more common inclusions in academic papers is extensive indented quotes. I've forgotten who said it, but someone once wrote that academic writing is the process of moving bones from one cemetery to another. For some reason, nobody seems to respect your work unless you can demonstrate evidence that you've endured reading through reams of long-forgotten journal articles and obscure dissetations, buried under inches of high quality dust. What's that old joke? When someone asked the old professor what the notation on his business card meant, B.S., M.S., Ph.D., he replied "Well, everybody knows what B.S. is. M.S. means *More of the Same* and Ph.D. means *Piled hip Deep*.

SECTION TITLE

Rules vary, but the general rule is that if you're quoting enough to make the reader nervious, you just use italics or "quotes." If you're quoting enough to induce nausea, then indent the quote. If you're quoting enough to cause a nosebleed, then you're probably bordering on plagerism, and well on the way to a successful career in academic writing:

> This is an indented quotation. Don't use quotation marks for this kind of quote. Check with your publisher to see if "smart quotes" are tolerated or are instead anathema. When quoting, always follow up with a reference (usually a footnote) to let your readers know where the real blame lies.[1]

CONCLUSION

In the final analysis, we're all extinct. Seaonally adjusted, there is no Christmas. Further research is needed, since there are still next year's journals that will need stuff to fill them up.

---

[1] This footnote is 10 points, with automatic 5 point spacing between footnote paragraphs, and a quarter inch first-line indent. If this were a real footnote, it'd say something like:

See M.N. Intguy, "Straightening snake bites," *The Siberian Journal of Herpetological Prosthodontics*, January 1935, pp. 1078-2096.

Page 1

To create a bibliography, just type the entries. Because of the underlying style, they will be numbered automatically. Don't worry about alphabetizing them right now. Once the list is complete, click on the Sort tool to sort them.

BIBLIOGRAPHY

(1) Einstein, Elmo, *The Theory of Relatives*, 1987, R.U. Smart Publishing Inc., ISBN 0-000-00000-0.[2]

(2) Smith, John, "On not being believed," *Journal of Plausible Deniability*.

(3) U.S. Department of Cranial Agripuncture, pamphlet, How to tell the difference between your head and a hole in the ground, 1983.

---

[2] A nonbreaking space was inserted between ISBN and the beginning of the number. Nonbreaking hyphens were inserted between the number groups. To nonbreaking spaces and hyphens, select Insert|Symbol and click on the Special Characters tab. There, you'll also discover the shortcut keys: Ctrl+Shift+Space and Ctrl+_, respectively.

Page 2

Chapter

50

Academic Papers

Using Word 6's advanced features, creating academic papers is a snap. The template provided on disk, ACADEMIC.DOT, is a collection of styles and macros. ACADEMIC.DOT is designed to eliminate the major stumbling block many writers face when trying to produce an academic paper—formatting. A multipage view of a very short academic article is shown in Figure 50.1.

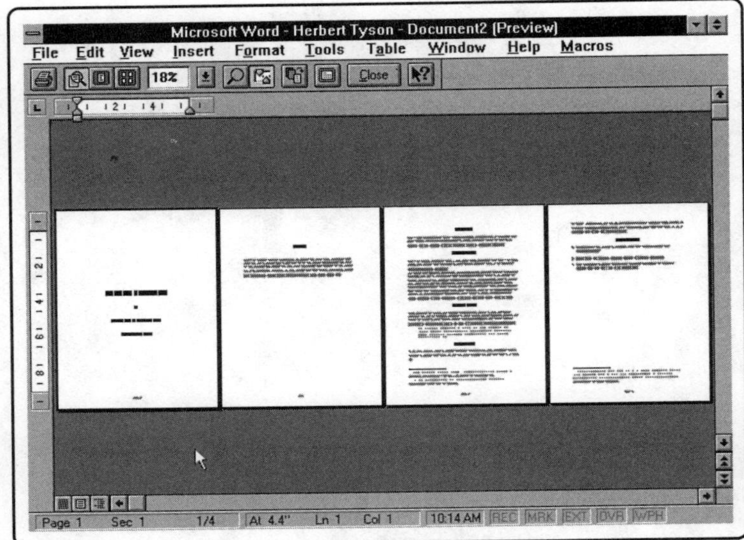

FIGURE 50.1.
From the air, your finished paper might look something like this.

Nothing about the template is carved into stone. Obviously, many different journals have different formats. By concentrating the formatting effort into styles, ACADEMIC.DOT is flexible enough that you can quickly and efficiently transform it into exactly what you need.

SUPER TIP

As you go along, you'll find that different journals, conferences, and symposia have different idiosyncrasies. You can create dedicated templates for each venue. That way, you'll never be in the position of putting your effort into reinventing the wheel instead of writing the actual paper.

Word 6 Features Used

Footnotes
Customized toolbar
Section formatting
Summary Info fields for automating titles and headers
Automatic numbering
Sorting
Styles

Overall Layout

The ACADEMIC.DOT template is a three-section document:

Title Page	Vertically and horizontally centered, unnumbered
Preface	Small roman numerals in a centered footer
Body	Arabic numerals, centered

Toolbar

The academic template has its own special toolbar, called It's Academic, shown in Figure 50.2 and described in Table 50.1. The Academic toolbar contains a number of tools commonly used in academic writing, as well as style buttons for each of the major styles.

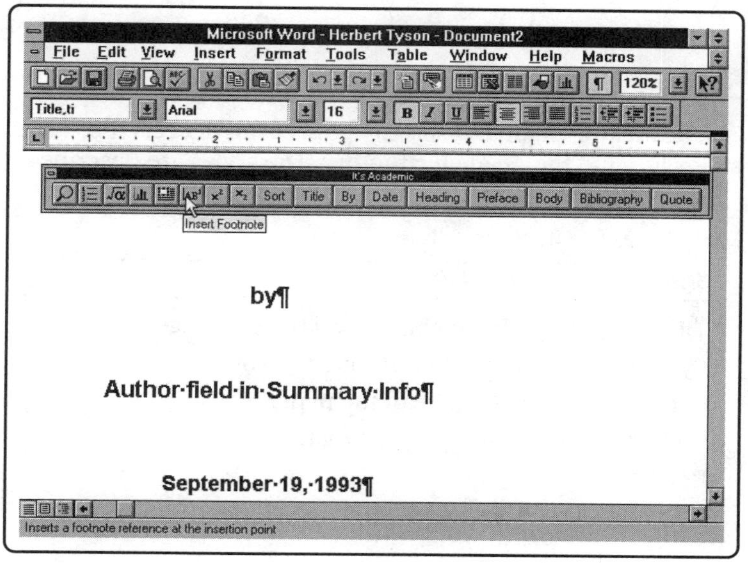

FIGURE 50.2.
The It's Academic toolbar.

Table 50.1. The It's Academic toolbar.

Tool	*Purpose*
Zoom Control	GUI Zoom tool for setting the zoom level
Numbering	Numbers references or other numbered lists
Equation	Inserts Microsoft Equation objects
Insert Chart	Inserts Microsoft Graph objects
Insert Footnote	Inserts footnotes
Insert Frame	Frames equations, graphs, or other objects, if needed
X^2	Superscript
X_2	Subscript
Sort	Sorts references or other lists
Title	Applies the Title style
By	Applies the Byline style
Date	Applies the Date style
Heading	Applies the Heading 2 style
Preface	Applies the Preface style
Body	Applies the Body style
Bibliography	Applies the Bibliography style
Quote	Applies the Quote style

Styles

The academic template uses eight special styles, each of which is available using a style alias and the Academic toolbar. The styles are described in Table 50.2.

Table 50.2. The Academic styles.

Style	*Used For*	*Alias*
Title	The main title, on the title page	ti
Byline	The word *By* and the author name	by
Date	The date of the paper	da
Preface	Used for the Preface title	pr
Body Text	Used for all paragraph text, except for extended quotes	bt

Style	Used For	Alias
Quote	Used for indented quotes	qu
Heading 2	Used for all main headings	h2
Bibliography	Used for bibliographic references	bi

In addition, the Footnote Text style has been modified to provide a slight indentation for footnotes as well as a small break between footnote paragraphs. Ordinarily, you should not need to apply this style, because it is applied automatically each time you insert a footnote. If you need to modify the way footnotes are presented, edit the Footnote Text and Footnote Reference styles. To change the footnote separators or continuation notices, select View | Footnotes and select the item you need to change using the drop-down list. This kind of editing is best performed while editing ACADEMIC.DOT itself, to make sure that the changes are available to subsequent documents you create.

To apply a style using the toolbar, just click the style name. To apply a style using the alias, press Ctrl+Shift+S, type the two-character alias, and press Enter. For example, to apply the indented quote style to this paragraph, you would press Ctrl+Shift+S, then qu, then Enter. To someone not accustomed to using aliases, that might seem like a lot of work. To someone who's been using two-character style codes in Word for the past ten years, however, it's a lot faster than taking your hands off the keyboard, manipulating the mouse, and then returning to the keyboard.

Title Page

The title page is in a separate section. The title, author name, and date are inserted automatically using fields. When you use ACADEMIC to create a document, your name should automatically be used in the author field. Select File | Summary Info to set the document title or to adjust the author name, if needed. The date is inserted as today's date in the form *September 27, 1995*. If necessary, you can press Ctrl+Shift+F9 to unlink the date field, causing it not to change each time the field is updated.

The title page uses large font sizes, which you can adjust for your needs. It's recommended that you make changes to the format by modifying the Title, Byline, and Date styles. That way, you won't have to make special changes each time you write a new paper. The title page is in its own unnumbered section (that is, no page numbers). It is vertically and horizontally centered, as is the usual style for academic papers.

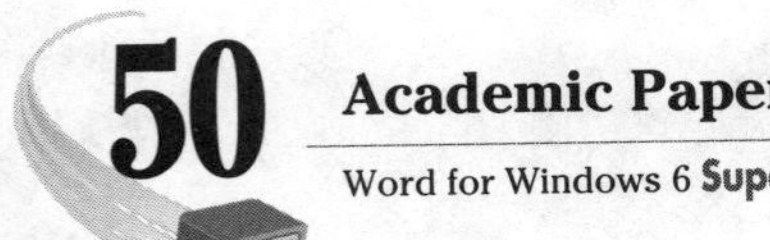

Preface

The Preface is in a separate section. Some academic papers have prefaces, others do not. If you determine that you will not need prefaces, just delete this section. Otherwise, simply replace the dummy preface banter with your own.

Body

The body of this document is divided into three logical parts, but not sections:

Abstract
The Article
Bibliography

The Heading 2 style is used for all section titles. As implemented here, Heading 2 is centered, 14-point, all caps. This is appropriate for many symposium and conference papers. If it's not the correct style for your type of paper, then change it at the style level, and make sure the changes get added to the template.

Body Text

The body of the academic paper is written using the Body Text style. On behalf of the Ad Hoc Committee Against Eyestrain, the Body Text style uses a 12-point font size. As seems to be the current style, it is not indented. If you need Body Text to be formatted differently, then modify the style and make sure that changes get added to the academic template.

Long Quotes

Quotes that go beyond three physical lines generally are presented as indented block, without quotation marks. The Quote style is provided for such quotes. It is set at 10 points (because nobody reads those quotes, anyway). The Quote style is indented by one-half inch on both sides.

Bibliography

Bibliographic entries are inserted by you using the Bibliography style. Adjust the style, if necessary, by modifying the style, and adding the changes to the academic template. As you create the bibliography, don't worry about alphabetical order. After all of the entries are done, select the list of entries, and click the Sort tool in the Academic toolbar. If you need them to be numbered, then click the Numbering tool while you're at it.

Bibliographic entry numbering uses the common style of (x). Because numbering is applied at the style level, it is fully automatic, and numbers are created as you insert text. If you need a different type of numbering, make your changes at the style level.

PROCEDURE 50.1. CHANGING THE NUMBERING STYLE FOR BIBLIOGRAPHIC ENTRIES.

1. Select Format | Style (or press Ctrl+Shift+S, twice).
2. Select the Bibliography style.
3. Click **M**odify, which displays the Modify Style dialog box.
4. Click F**o**rmat, and then click **N**umbering, to display the Bullets and Numbering dialog box, shown in Figure 50.3.
5. Select the basic format you prefer from the palette of options; click **M**odify, if necessary, to further refine your choice, and then click OK.
6. Click OK to close the Modify Style dialog box, and then on **C**lose.

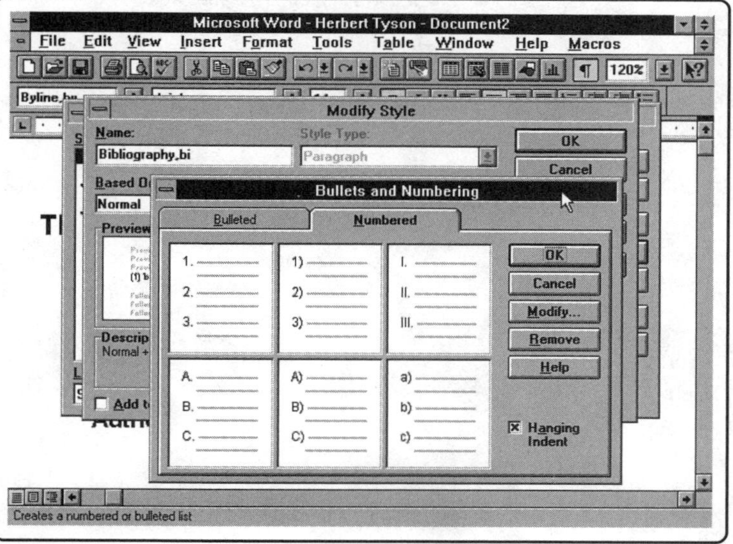

FIGURE 50.3.
The Bullets and Numbering dialog box.

SUPER TIP

If you prefer unnumbered bibliographic entries, then remove numbering from the Bibliography style. To remove numbering from a style, follow Steps 1 through 4 of the preceding procedure. When the Bullets and Numbering dialog box appears in Step 4, however, click **R**emove. Then click OK to close the Modify Styles dialog box.

October 24, 1993

Joe Customer
52 Main Street
USA

Dear Joe:

I'm please to enclose a copy of my latest book, ***The Word for Windows 6 Super Book***. I hope you enjoy it.

The new Word 6 is packed with features to make creating professional-looking documents easier than ever. In addition to covering pretty much how to do anything with the new *Word 6*, my book includes two projects sections--one for macros, and one for documents.

Let me know how you like it, as well as what we can do to improve future editions.

Herb Tyson

Enclosure

Chapter

Business Letter

Using the letter Wizard that comes with Word, you can create a variety of different kinds of letters. For many, the Wizard is just a little *too* much. Also, for all the variety the Wizard provides, it doesn't provide exactly what some users want. In this project, we'll take a look at a somewhat simpler letter Wizard, called BUSINESS.WIZ, which asks you just two questions, and then leaves you to write your letter. Within minutes, you could be the proud owner of the business letter shown in Figure 51.1.

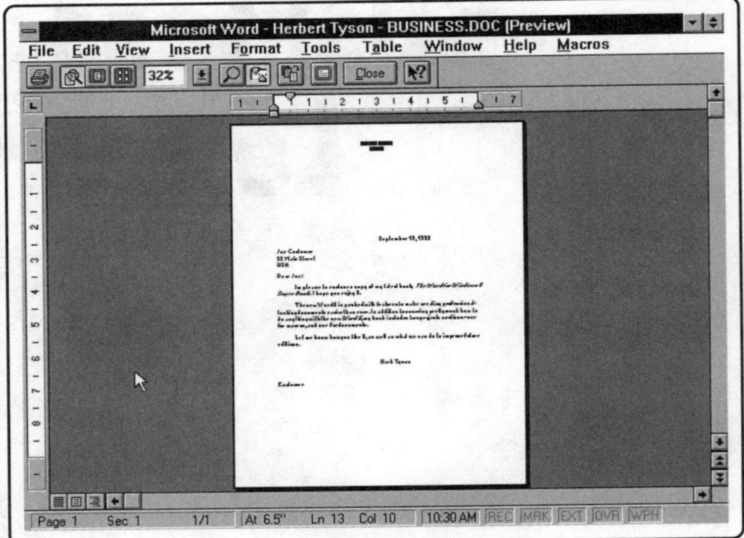

FIGURE 51.1.
A business letter created using BUSINESS.WIZ.

Word 6 Features Used

Automatic macro (AutoNew)
Headers
Envelope address styles for automatic formatting
Bookmarks
Creating your own letterhead
Summary Info fields

Overall Layout

A letter produced using BUSINESS.WIZ starts with a simple first page header for the letterhead, which uses the UserAddress information from the User Info tab of the Tools | Options dialog box. After that, there's a date field. On the inside, there's a post-first page header that uses the document subject field—if present—along with the date and page number.

Toolbar

The Business toolbar, shown in Figure 51.2, contains a few tools commonly needed when composing a business letter, plus buttons for the main styles. The Business toolbar is described in Table 51.1.

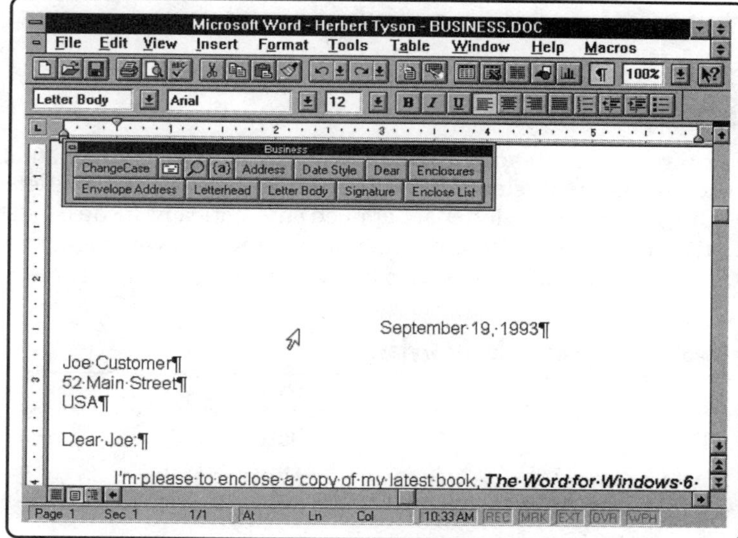

FIGURE 51.2.
The Business toolbar.

Table 51.1. The Business toolbar.

Tool	*Action*
ChangeCase	Toggles the case of selected text
Create Envelope	Creates an envelope
Zoom Control	GUI Zoom tool
View Field Codes	Toggles the display of field codes on and off
Address	Applies the Address style
Date Style	Applies the Date style
Dear	Applies the Dear style
Enclosures	Applies the Enclosures style (for the word Enclosure)
Envelope Address	Applies the Envelope Address style
Letterhead	Applies the Letterhead style
Letter Body	Applies the Letter Body style

continues

Table 51.1. continued

Tool	*Action*
Signature	Applies the Signature style
Enclose List	Applies the Enclosure List style (for the list of enclosure items)

Styles

For the most part, you probably won't have to be concerned about applying styles when using the Business letter template. That's because all of the styles necessary for a simple business letter are applied automatically. If you cancel the AutoNew macro that is run when you create a document, however, you might end up wanting to apply the styles manually. The styles being used are shown in Table 51.2.

Table 51.2. Business letter styles.

Text	*Style*
Date	Date Style
Address	Address style
Salutation	Dear style
Text	Letter Body style
Closing	Signature style (used for *Sincerely* and for your name)
Enclosure	Enclosures style
Enclosure list	Enclosure List style
Letterhead name and address	Letterhead style

Although you don't see it right away, the Envelope Address style plays an important role in this template. When Word creates an envelope, it applies the Envelope Address style to the recipient's address. The first time you create an envelope, you should tell Word to add it to the letter so you can look at it to ensure that it is correct. If the formatting is not to your liking, use the Envelope Address and Envelope Return styles to change the formatting. Make sure you save the changes to the Business template so you don't have to reinvent the wheel later on.

The AutoNew Macro

The Business letter template contains just one macro, called AutoNew. If you interrupt the macro, you're on your own. However, without the macro, this template might not be much use to you. If you like the format but not the process, you could construct your own letter using the styles shown in Table 51.3, and just delete the AutoNew macro.

Each time you create a letter based on this template, the AutoNew macro kicks in. First, it updates all the fields, so information is current. Next, it prompts you to enter the name and address for the Addressee. The same dialog box also asks whether or not you want to include an Enclosure line.

The macro uses the Addressee information to try to guess the Dear *who* of your letter. If you typically address your business correspondents by their first names (assuming you don't adhere to the useless and archaic custom of calling people Mr., Mrs., Ms. or Dr. when composing an address), then the macro guesses correctly. If you do, or if you want the salutation to read *Dear Mr. Smith*, then you'll have to monkey with the macro to get better automation. Open AutoNew and look for the line:

```
Name$ = Mid$(A$, 1, InStr(A$, " ") - 1)
```

The whole addressee text (name, address, city, and so forth) is assigned to the variable `A$`. If you're handy with WordBASIC, you might be able to concoct a statement to a) extract just the last name, and b) deduce the proper title. If not, then perhaps you'll just start addressing people on a more equitable basis (that is, *Dear Bill* instead of *Dear Mr. President*).

After making a stab at who's *dear* to you, the AutoNew macro inserts the Dear line, and then drops to the bottom and inserts Sincerely and a signature line. The signature comes from the UserName field in the UserInfo tab in the Tools | Options dialog box. If you select Enclosure in the first dialog box, the macro deposits the word *Enclosure* at the bottom of the letter, and then moves the insertion point to just after the *Dear* line for you to start writing your letter.

Letterhead

The Business template uses a first page header to create a letterhead. The letterhead format is controlled using the Letterhead style. The letterhead information comes from the UserAddress field, supplied by the UserInfo tab in the Tools | Options dialog box.

Header

If your letter spans multiple pages, the subsequent page header kicks in. It uses four fields to try to create an informative header:

```
Page {page} of {numpages}
{ DATE \@ "MMMM d, yyyy" }
{ subject }
```

The first and second lines are always available. The third line depends on how and whether you use document summary information fields. If you fill out the subject field, then you have a ready-made subject line for your letter headers.

Letter Body

The letter body is composed using the Letter Body style. The style is a simple first-line indent, using 12-point type, and automatic 12-point spacing after each paragraph. If you prefer a different body style, modify the Letter Body style and add the changes to the template.

The Envelope, Please

If you have bookmarks set to display (Tools|Options, View, click Bookmarks), you might notice [brackets] around the letterhead address and the addressee address in the finished letter. The bookmarks used are `envelopereturn` and `envelopeaddress`. When you select the envelope tool button, Word looks to see if these two bookmarks are used in the document. If they are, then Word obtains the return and delivery addresses from those two fields, respectively. This provides additional automation to the process.

John Smith
1 Smithway
Smithfield, VA 23511

TELEPHONE

BUSINESS	{(555) 555-5555}
FAX	{(555) 555-5555}
HOME	{(555) 555-5555}

OBJECTIVE

{e.g., Seeking a position as a product designer, with a career track to senior management. Want to be associated with a growing company that's ecologically responsible.}

SUMMARY OF QUALIFICATIONS

- {Item 1; e.g., Network manager for 16 workstations}
- {Item 2; e.g., Fluent in Latin}
- {Item 3; e.g., Programming in COBOL, BASIC, and FLIMTRAN}
- {Item 4; e.g. Successfully escaped from Alcatraz, twice}

EMPLOYMENT

From {Starting Month, Year} to Present {i.e. Current situation}

{Title} with {Employer} in {Location}

{Description--1-2 sentences}

- {Item 1; Achievements, projects, responsibilities; list five (or so) items most likely to be of interest to the prospective employer}
- {Item 2; e.g., Managed a staff of six wild animal trainers}
- {Item 3; e.g., Solicited 6.17 million dollars in new contracts}
- {Item 4; e.g., Single-handedly talked the IRS out of an audit}
- {Item 5; e.g., Testified in court as an expert witness}

From {Month, Year} to {Month, Year} {i.e., Previous situation}

{Title} with {Employer} in {Location}

{Description--1-2 sentences}

From {Month, Year} to {Month, Year} {Prior relevant situation}

{Title} with {Employer} in {Location}

{Description--1 sentence}

From {Month, Year} to {Month, Year} {Prior relevant situation}

{Title} with {Employer} in {Location}

{Description--1 sentence}

EDUCATION

{Degree}, {Institution}, {Year} {Highest relevant degree, certification, etc.}

Chapter

52

Resumes

Resumes don't have to be flashy to attract attention. The best resumes are the simplest, enabling the reader to quickly determine if the candidate meets the qualifications. Adding irrelevant information that distracts from this basic purpose loses you more points than it gains. The resume template presented in this section is designed to present a clear, clean, and concise picture of your professional and academic credentials, in a way that doesn't waste your time, or that of the person who's searching for qualified job applicants. A two-page view of a resume produced using RESUMESB.DOT is shown in Figure 52.1.

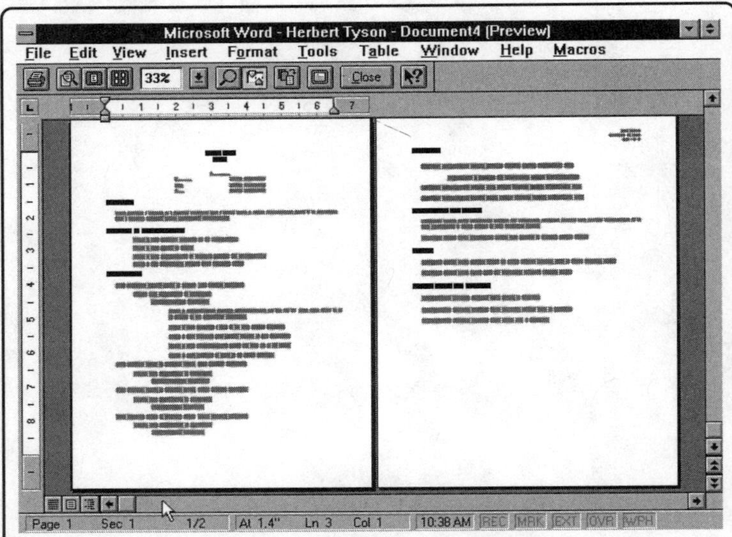

FIGURE 52.1.
A resume created using RESUMESB.DOT.

Word 6 Features Used

Custom toolbar—using styles as tools for quick formatting
Using paragraph text flow settings to keep headings with following text
The UserAddress field
Word Tables
Automatic Bullets

Overall Layout

The ResumeSB template consists of eight major information areas:

- Who you are and how you can be reached
- Your objectives
- A summary of your qualifications

- Employment history
- Education
- Writing credentials
- Recognition of your achievements (awards)
- Other special skills

Not every area is relevant for every job applicant, nor is this list complete for every kind of job. If you add additional areas, try to add them in parallel fashion, using Heading 1 for the major divisions.

Toolbar

The Resume toolbar, shown in Figure 52.2, contains several tools that are commonly needed in working with the ResumeSB template. The tools emphasize that the goal of this project is to produce a resume that is concise, precise, and to the point. Conciseness is a key in presenting your qualifications. Resumes that go on for page after page might be fine when you're trying to impress an academic committee or a judge (when you want to be certified as an expert witness). However, when a busy prospective employer is trying to quickly ascertain whether or not your qualifications and her needs coincide, an otherwise impressive-looking pile of credentials quickly becomes a mound of baloney. Use the tools on the toolbar to check the formatting, to keep it tight. The tools are described in Table 52.1.

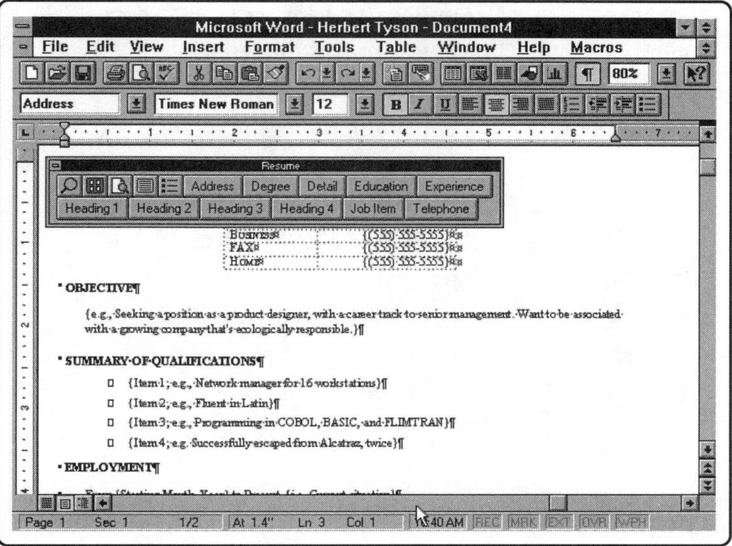

FIGURE 52.2.
The Resume toolbar.

SUPER

If possible, try to get your resume to fit on one sheet of high-quality paper—front and back. A concise, well-organized resume tells a prospective employer that you are confident that your abilities and qualifications speak for themselves, and that you are a get-down-to-business kind of worker. My wife says there are two kinds of employees: employees who *save* you time, and employees who *cost* you time. A concise, well-presented resume can help convince a prospective employer that you're one of the former, not the latter.

Table 52.1. The ResumeSB toolbar.

Tool	*Purpose*
Zoom Control	GUI Zoom control
Multiple Pages	Displays multiple pages in Print Preview or Page Layout view
Print Preview	Switches to Print Preview
Zoom 100%	Switches to Normal view
Bullets	Applies bullet formatting to the selection
Address	Applies the Address style
Degree	Applies the Degree style
Detail	Applies the Detail style
Education	Applies the Education style
Experience	Applies the Experience Bullet style
Heading 1	Applies the Heading 1 style
Heading 2	Applies the Heading 2 style
Heading 3	Applies the Heading 3 style
Heading 4	Applies the Heading 4 style
Job Item	Applies the Job Item style
Telephone	Applies the Telephone style

Styles

The ResumeSB template uses eleven customized styles to create a well-balanced resume design. If you want to change the format of the resume, the best method is to change the styles, rather than applying direct formatting. Make sure you add the changes to the template for future use. The styles are described in Table 52.2.

Table 52.2. The ResumeSB styles.

Style	*Used For*
Address	Name and address information
Degree	Individual degrees or certifications
Detail	Individual items under publications, awards, and special skills
Education	Extra information about your highest degree—that is, dissertation, thesis, areas of concentration, and so on
Experience Bullet	Bulleted list of major qualifications
Heading 1	Main resume divisions, Summary of Qualifications, Education, and so on
Heading 2	Employment dates
Heading 3	Job title, employer, and location of previous job
Heading 4	Description of prior jobs
Job Item	Achievements or responsibilities in jobs
Telephone	Telephone information block

Address

The address section uses the {UserAddress} field, which is set using the UserInfo tab in the **T**ools|**O**ptions dialog box. If your UserAddress setting includes your name, you're all set. Otherwise, you would need to add the {UserName} field just ahead of the address.

Telephone

Telephone numbers are often difficult to present in a clear way. To avoid difficulties, telephone numbers are presented here in a small table. Just fill in the appropriate telephone numbers. If any of the telphone numbers shown don't apply, select the row and use Table|Delete Rows to remove it.

Objective

Use the Objective section to tell what kind of job and responsibilities you're seeking. Many job applicants make the mistake of thinking that being forthright about your goals may rule you out. To the contrary, often an employer advertising for one position has several positions in mind. A clear statement of your employment objectives, in fact, might even result in a new job being created.

Qualifications

The Qualifications block is your chance to summarize your most important assets. Use the Experience Bullet style to list the top five (or so) key points about your qualifications.

Employment (Experience)

Presenting prior employment information is always a pain. Just make sure you're accurate and truthful. When in doubt about the relevancy of a prior job, you're often better off leaving it out, and then mention it in passing in an interview if it seems relevant in context.

Mechanically, adding additional employment blocks is automatic. Use Heading 2 for the date (from/to). When you press Enter, Heading 3 (for the job title, employer, and location) is inserted automatically. When you press Enter at the end of the job specifics, a Heading 4 is created for inserting a description of your job. When you press Enter at the end of a Heading 4, another Heading 2 is created. You can keep on like that forever. But don't—especially if you want your resume read.

Education

Use the Education block, if relevant, to list your degrees and certifications. After the first Degree section, room is provided for listing the details of your highest degree. If you're a Ph.D., you might include the title and subject of your dissertation. If you're an engineer, you might include any special certifications you have. Such details are seldom very important for lesser degrees, so no space was provided. However, you can add items if you want, using the Education Bullet style.

Writings

If relevant, include any books, papers, reports, or other writings you've done that would be of interest to a prospective employer. Use an academic, bibliographic style for listing your writings. However, list from most recent to least recent, rather than in alphabetical order.

Awards

Use this section to list any relevant awards. If you were Phi Betta Kappa, won the Nobel Prize for Physics, or were presented an Employee of the Year award, make sure you include it in your resume.

Special Skills

You never know what might be of interest to a prospective employer. If you possess special skills or licenses that might help paint a larger picture of your qualifications and interests, list them. For example, it might not seem relevant to a particular job that you have an Amateur Radio or Real Estate license, or that you are fluent in Russian. Include them here anyway. They don't take up much space, and, if nothing else, they help provide a prospective employer a picture of a highly-motivated, broadly-based individual with a sense of accomplishment.

CONSULTANT BILLING STATEMENT

Herbert Tyson
SAMS

Tax ID 000-00-0000
Voice (555) 555-5555
FAX (555) 555-5555

This invoice is for consulting services provided to Smith and Jones Shipping for Consulting for the period January 17, 1994 to February 28, 1994. This billing is for a total of $5,850.00. This amount is due and payable upon receipt.

DATE	HOURS	PROJECT	DESCRIPTION
17 Jan 94	6	Projections	1995-2000 Projections
24 Jan 94	8	Projections	Programming 1995-2000 Projections
31 Jan 94	5	Projections	Projection report
11 Feb 94	12	Cost Growth	Calculating 1995-2000 Cost Growth
28 Feb 94	8	Cost Growth	Final Report
TOTAL	**39.0**	$150.00 **PER HOUR**	**$5,850.00**

Date: February 28, 1995 Signature:

Chapter

53

Consulting Invoice

One of the most tedious aspects of consulting is one of the most necessary—preparing invoices. Before they find a good method for preparing invoices, many consultants actually put off sending out invoices, simply because they dread all of the steps to making sure everything was correct. In this workshop, you'll discover a ready-to-use template, and you'll learn a little about putting Word forms to work as well. Using CONSULT.DOT, the invoice shown in Figure 53.1 was cranked out in less than five minutes.

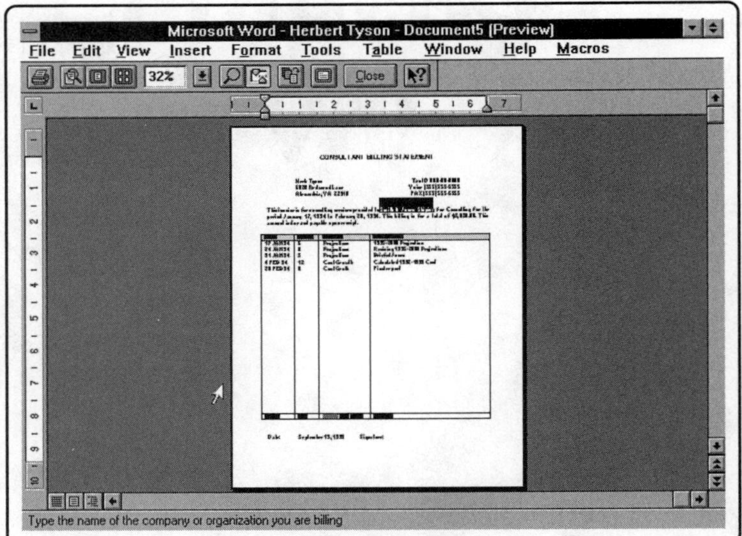

FIGURE 53.1.
An invoice created using CONSULT.DOT.

Word 6 Features Used

- Tables and table math
- Forms and form fields
- UserAddress field
- Document locking
- Macros linked to form fields
- Customized toolbar
- Drop-down form fields

Overall Layout

The consulting invoice, CONSULT.DOT (shown in Figure 53.2), consists of several tables, a number of form fields, and some loose text that holds the pieces together:

- Title
- Consultant information

Billing statement
Detailed record
Date and signature lines

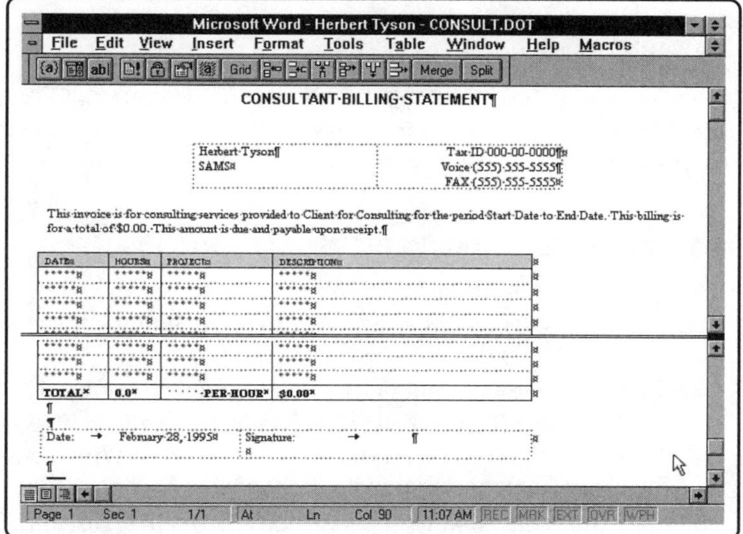

FIGURE 53.2.
An invoice created using CONSULT.DOT.

Before You Use the CONSULT Template...

You will need to make some adjustments to the permanent information. The CONSULT.DOT template uses the {useraddress} field for your name and address. If you prefer, you can replace this field with actual text. You will definitely need to modify the Tax ID and Telephone numbers.

PROCEDURE 53.1. MAKING NECESSARY CHANGES TO CONSULT.DOT.

1. Open CONSULT.DOT for editing.
2. Select **V**iew | **T**oolbars and enable the Consulting Invoice toolbar, if it's not already displayed.
3. Click the Protect Form button to toggle the locked state of the template *off*. This unlocks the forms template so you can make some necessary changes.
4. Find the {useraddress} field (press Alt+F9, if necessary, to display field codes) and verify that it correctly displays your name and address as you want them to appear in the consulting invoices. If not, then either: a) select **T**ools | **O**ptions | **U**ser Info and fill your name and address in the Mailing Address block (yes—your name, too); or b) delete the {useraddress} field and type the information in directly.

5. Change the Tax ID number to match your Social Security or other Tax ID number.
6. Change the telephone numbers to reflect your own.
7. Click the `Protect FormLock` button to toggle the locked state of the template *on*.
8. Press Ctrl+S to save your changes.

Another change you should make is in the hourly rate field. You should change the rate field so that your usual (or only) rate is the built-in default. Unless your rate varies, you aren't stuck having to type it in each time. If it *does* vary, you have the flexibility to change it.

PROCEDURE 53.2. CHANGING THE DEFAULT HOURLY RATE.

1. Open CONSULT.DOT for editing.
2. Select **V**iew | **T**oolbars and enable the Consulting Invoice toolbar, if it's not already displayed.
3. Click the Protect FormLock button to toggle the locked state of the template off. This unlocks the forms template so you can make necessary changes.
4. Select **E**dit | **G**o To, click Bookmark in the Go to **W**hat list, and select Rate in the Enter Bookmark Name field; then click Go **T**o.
5. Click the Form Field Options button, shown in Figure 53.3.
6. In the default number field, shown in Figure 53.4, type your default hourly rate; don't include a $—Word automatically adds the dollar sign for you.

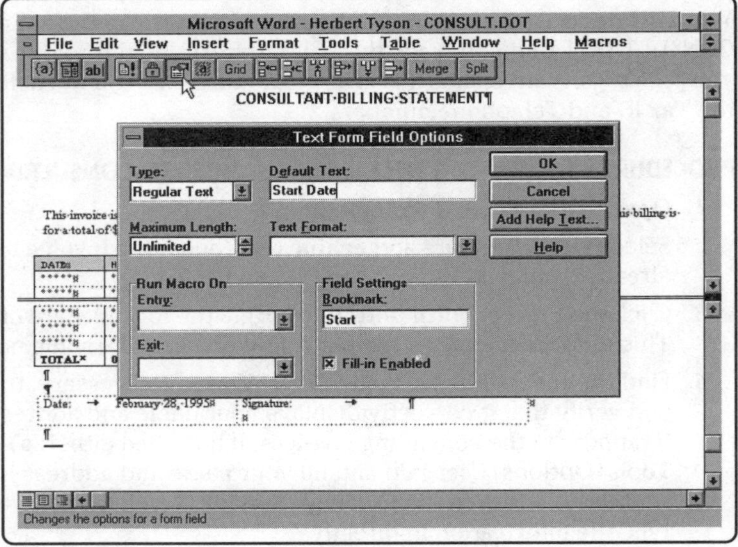

FIGURE 53.3.
Use the Form Field Options button to modify an existing form field.

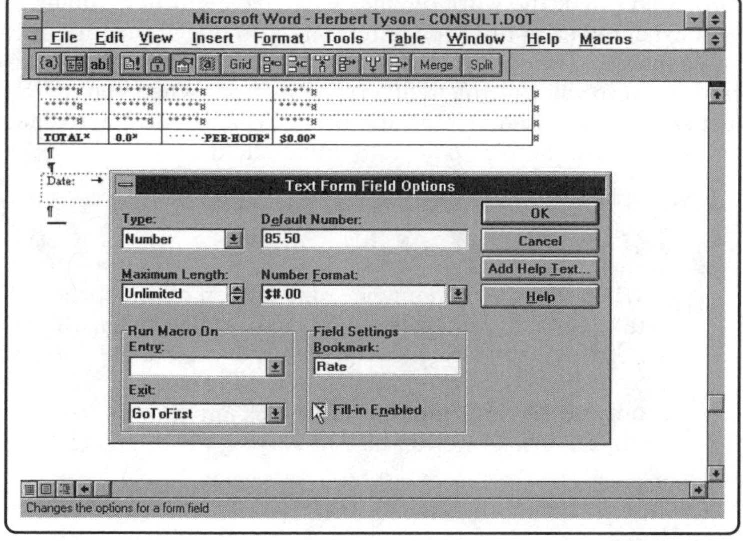

FIGURE 53.4.
Type a number into the Default Number field; Word automatically supplies the $ based on the Number Format setting.

7. Click OK.
8. Click the Protect FormLock button to lock the form from additional editing.
9. Press Ctrl+S to save (or Ctrl+F4 to close).

Important: Always use the Form Field Options dialog box to make changes to a form field. They're different from other fields and cannot be successfully created or edited by modifying the field code directly.

SUPER

Why do you need to lock the file before saving? Good question. When you create a new file using a forms template, Word recognizes whether or not the file was in forms entry mode the last time the file was closed. If it was not, then new documents you create do not open in entry mode. To ensure that you get the benefit of forms mode, the template must be locked when you close it.

Using the CONSULT.DOT Template

To use the Consult template, select File|New and use Consult as the template. It prompts you to type the name of the client, the start and stop dates, and your billing rate. Next, fill in the work details. This invoice form contains an update macro that gets executed each time you enter data into one of the numerical fill-in fields (hours and consulting rate). If you attempt to fill in one of the hours fields before filling in a rate, a macro will nag you to fill in the rate first. When you're finished typing the data, just save the finished invoice and print. Because the macros automatically take care of the updates, there's no need to update fields.

SUPER CAUTION

When filling out an invoice, do *not* turn off the form lock. If you do, and then turn locking back on, all of your data entry will be erased! That's because fields are updated with the original defaults, which is blank. You should not need to unlock the file when you're entering data. The only times you should need to lock and unlock are when you're editing the .DOT file, or otherwise modifying the template.

Toolbar

The Consulting Invoice toolbar, shown in Figure 53.5, contains more tools than you actually need to use the Consult template. Each tool's purpose is described in Table 53.1. When you're actually filling out data, you really would need to use only the display-related tools (Grid, Shading, and field code display), if at all. However, in addition to the mandatory changes described earlier, you might also want to make some adjustments to save yourself from having to enter repetitive text when you use the invoice template.

Table 53.1. The Consulting Invoice toolbar.

Tool	*Purpose*
View Field Codes	Toggles the display of field codes
Drop-Down	Inserts a drop-down form field
Text Form Field	Inserts a text form field
Update Fields	Updates selected fields
Protect Form	Toggles the locked state
Form Options	Displays the options dialog box for the selected form field
Form Field Shading	Toggles the display of shading to make form fields stand out
Grid	Toggles the display of grid lines for working with tables
Insert Cell	Inserts a cell into a table

Tool	Purpose
Insert Rows	Inserts a row into a table
Insert Columns	Inserts a column into a table
Delete Cells	Deletes a cell from a table
Delete Columns	Deletes a column from a table
Delete Rows	Deletes a row from a table
Merge Cells	Merges selected cells into one
Split Cells	Splits selected cells into multiple

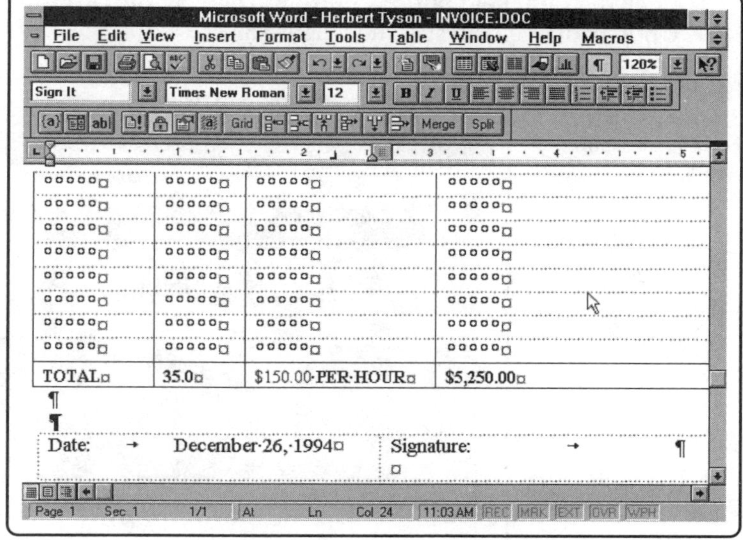

FIGURE 53.5.
The Consulting Invoice toolbar.

For example, straight fill-in text form fields were used for all of the entry points. If you have a stable list of clients, projects, and tasks, however, you might want to consider replacing the Client, Project, and Description text form fields with drop-down form fields. Using drop-down form fields means you won't have to type any of those tedious project numbers.

PROCEDURE 53.3. ADDING A DROP-DOWN FORM FIELD TO THE CONSULT.DOT TEMPLATE.

1. Open CONSULT.DOT for editing.
2. Select **V**iew | **T**oolbars, and enable the Consulting Invoice toolbar, if it's not already displayed.

3. Click the `Protect FormLock` button to toggle the locked state of the template *off*. This unlocks the forms template so you can make some necessary changes.
4. Scroll through the document and locate the field you want to replace with a drop-down form field (Client, Project, Description, and so forth). Important: Do not replace any of the formula fields (Amount, Total, and Invoice) with a drop-down.
5. Double-click the existing field to see its current settings. Note the Exit macro and Bookmark settings, if any (write them *down*).
6. Press Esc to dismiss the options dialog box.
7. Click the drop-down form field in the Consulting toolbar; this replaces the existing field with a blank drop-down form field.
8. Click the form field options button to display the Drop-Down Form Field Options dialog box, shown in Figure 53.6.

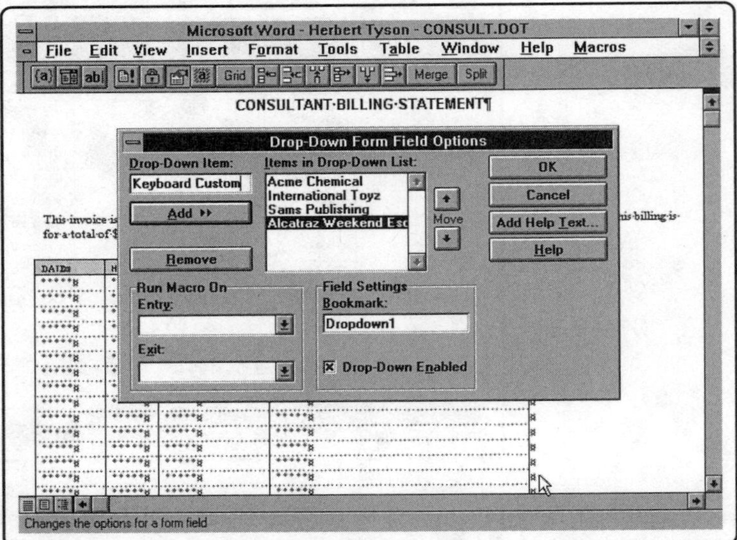

FIGURE 53.6.
The Drop-Down Form Field Options dialog box.

9. In the **D**rop-Down Item box, type the first item (this is the first of the choices you will be given when you are filling in the form), and click Add.
10. Repeat Step 9 for each choice you want to add.
11. Adjust the positions, if desired, by using the Move buttons to the right of the **I**tems in Drop-Down List box.
12. In the E**x**it and **B**ookmark fields, type the information you wrote down in Step 5.

13. If desired, click Add Help Text and compose a help message to display for the field at the status bar or when F1 is pressed; click OK to finish.
14. Click OK to accept the changes.

Styles

Styles are not an issue for using the template, but they may be if you're not satisfied with the fonts, size, or other layout aspects. The Consulting Invoice template uses just a few styles. If you need to reform the template, then modify the styles. The special or modified styles used by the CONSULT.DOT template are shown in Table 53.2.

Table 53.2. Styles used in CONSULT.DOT.

Style	*Used for*
Title	CONSULTANT BILLING STATEMENT
Consultant	User name and telephone numbers
Text	Text statement of what the invoice is for
Column Head	Date, Hours, Project, and Description
Table	Project and hour detail table lines
Total	Last line of the detail table
Sign It	The Date and Signature line

The Consultant Table

Setting up names, addresses, and telephone numbers is a bit of a pain. In this template, they're set up using a simple table format. If you need to adjust the table format, display the table gridlines. Additional table tools are provided in the toolbar for adding, removing, merging, and splitting table elements.

The Details Table

It's possible that your invoices may require additional details. You might even have different billing rates for different projects. If so, then you will need to modify the format of the invoice dramatically. The best approach might be to add two columns between Hours and Project, using the new columns for project-specific rates and the cross-products. This, of course, provides progressively less room for the project and description fields. Another alternative, equally messy, is to use different invoices for projects that have different rates. Yet another alternative would be to change the orientation of the invoice to landscape. This removes the number of possible detail lines, but some compromise clearly would be needed.

Confidential

PROPOSAL

Statement of the Problem

The problem is that the U.S. educational system is decidely out of whack. For years, we've seen an escalating decline is the assumed capabilities of our young. Today, teen suicide, drop out rates, pregnancy, and drug use are on the increase.

History of the Problem

Beginning just after World War II, the whole of American life entered an era of change. The time when a single-earner could adequately provide for a house and a household has slowly but surely faded into history. At the same time, our young have increasingly been isolated and consigned to "care-givers" rather than cared for in a family environment. The result is that children today are being raise largely by people who have neither the incentive nor the training to rear them in the most-needed areas.

Previous Approaches to Solving the Problem

Educational reform, money, larger schools, smaller schools, daycare, and even headstart have failed. Why? Because they tackle the problem as outsiders. For use to succeed, the problem of education must become, once again, a family matter.

Proposed Approach

Turn all of the schools--school by school, district by district, county by county, and state by state--into Montessori learning centers. Montessori educators have demonstrated consistently form most of this century the capability to succeed where modern education has failed.

Confidential

Statement of the Approach

Start with pilot programs and magnet schools. Gradually convert existing teacing facilities to Montessori.

Difference from Prior Approaches

This one will work.

Proposed Schedule

Convert all by 2005.

Date	Deliverable
1995	New York
1996	California
1997	Minnesota
1998	Texas
1999	Alaska

Proposed Costs

Virtually free.

Materials

The human mind.

Labor

Zippo, buddy!

Overhead and Other Indirect Costs

Actually, there will be a tremendous net savings.

Chapter 54

Proposal

Some kinds of proposals—particularly those for government contracts—have a specific and rigid format. The proposal template presented here is not intended to be used for such solicitations. For example, government proposals usually specify separate technical and cost proposals. The proposal template presented here includes the technical and cost proposals in the same document. The proposal template depicted here is intended for more general use, as, say, might be used by a consultant (resumes, invoices, proposals... say, is there a pattern here?) or other small businesses when making general-purpose proposals to other businesses.

Key in any proposal is addressing the issues and laying out your approach and qualifications to do the work, as well as your charges. The proposal used here is relatively simple, but it comprises all of the major elements needed and presents them in a neat, easy-to-assess format. A typical proposal created using PROPOSAL.DOT is shown in Figure 54.1.

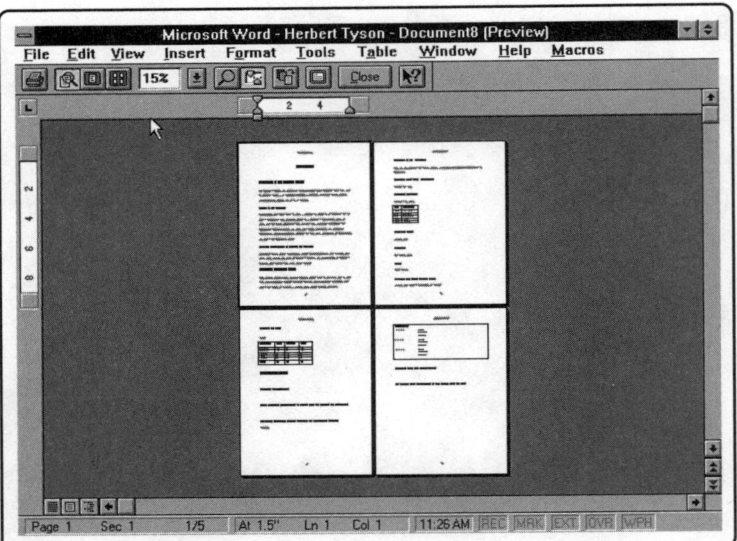

FIGURE 54.1.
A proposal created using PROPOSAL.DOT.

SUPER NOTE

If a solicitation asks for a proposal of no more than ten double-spaced pages, do you then expand your margins, reduce your spacing (slightly), reduce your fonts, and engage in other maneuvers to make your proposal fit within ten pages? If so, it's probably not a good practice. For one thing, it's obvious that you've "cheated." Often, solicitors use the margins for comments. If you've used space-and-a-half, rather than true double-spacing, it leaves less room for comments. This may, in fact, make it more difficult to evaluate your proposal. Small fonts (9 points is clearly not kosher!) also may leave a bad taste in the reviewer's mind. If you have to fax your proposal, small fonts may make an already-marginal reproduction extremely difficult to read. Rather than trying to fit it all in, you'll do yourself a favor if you scan your proposal carefully for excess verbiage and use language as efficiently and concisely as possible. Squeeze it out—not in!

Word 6 Features Used

Styles
Custom toolbar
Tables
The Table Form tool for easy table entry
Margins, headers, and footers

Overall Layout

The proposal template contains all of the major elements usually present in formal proposals. In fact, there may be more structure here than you need for some simpler proposals. Feel free to prune where this structure doesn't suit a particular situation. The general layout is:

- Statement of the problem — Use this section as an opportunity to demonstrate your understanding of why proposals are being solicited. Being able to provide a concise, and often insightful, discussion of the problem is persuasive.
- Your proposed solution— Use this section to discuss how you propose to solve the problem. Include in this section the major steps, what kinds of deliverables you will provide to the clients, when you will provide them, and how much it will cost (and why).
- Your qualifications— Use this section to make a persuasive argument about why you are the most qualified to do the job.
- Appendix— Use this section for resumes and any other supporting materials.

Toolbar

Presenting a concise and direct proposal requires presenting information in a compact but informative style. You often can illustrate more clearly with a single table than by discussing a problem for many pages; to wit, one picture is worth a thousand words. Basic starters for three tables are provided, and tools are provided on the Proposal toolbar to make customizing these, as well as creating others, simple. The Proposal toolbar is shown in Figure 54.2 and described in Table 54.1.

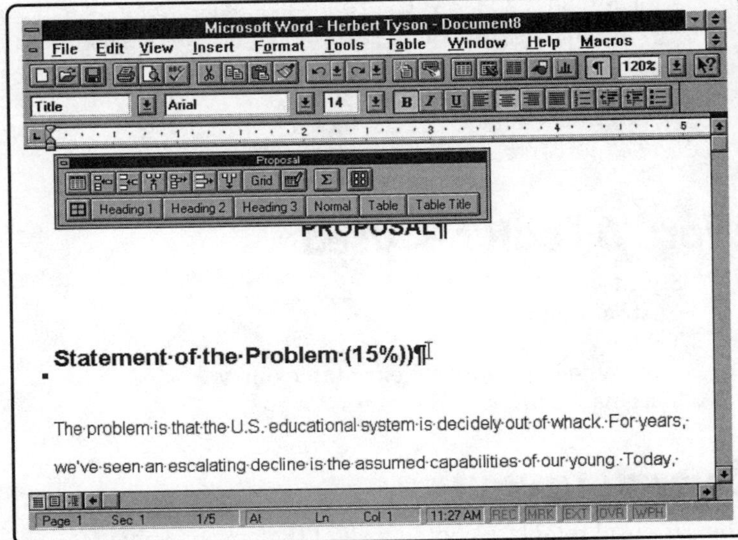

FIGURE 54.2. *The Proposal toolbar.*

Table 54.1. The Proposal toolbar.

Tool	*Purpose*
Insert Table	Creates a table
Insert Cell	Inserts a cell into a table
Insert Rows	Inserts a row into a table
Insert Columns	Inserts a column into a table
Delete Cells	Deletes a cell from a table
Delete Rows	Deletes a row from a table
Delete Columns	Deletes a column from a table
Grid	Toggles the display of grid lines for working with tables
Data Form	Dialog form for entering tabular data
AutoSum	Inserts a sum field in a table
Multiple pages	Shows multiple pages of a document at the same time
Borders	Toggles the Borders toolbar
Heading 1	Applies the Heading 1 style; for major divisions
Heading 2	Applies the Heading 2 style

Tool	Purpose
Heading 3	Applies the Heading 3 style
Normal	Applies the Normal style
Table	Applies the Table style
Table Title	Applies the Table Title style; for the first row in tables

Styles

In writing a proposal, it's generally a good idea not to get too intricate with your formatting. Simple formatting serves you and your reader well. The styles used in PROPOSAL.DOT are shown in Table 54.2.

Table 54.2. Styles for the Proposal.

Style	Used For
Heading 1	Major divisions
Heading 2	Medium divisions
Heading 3	Minor divisions (generally not a good idea to go deeper than three levels in a proposal)
Normal	Paragraph text
Table	All of a table, except for the top row
Table Title	Top and Total rows in tables

Tables

Tables are a key element in presenting information in a concise and compact form. It's also essential to be accurate when presenting data in a table. To facilitate these goals, a number of table tools are provided in the toolbar. One in particular bears mentioning again—the Data Form dialog box.

To use the Data Form dialog box, put the cursor into a table and click the Data Form tool. The dialog box shown in Figure 54.3 is displayed. In effect, Word uses the top row from the table as headers for a minidatabase. This enables you to easily enter data without having to fumble with the mouse and the Tab key. If a table doesn't already have data in it (aside from the first row), Word provides blank spaces for entering the data. Just type and press Enter. When you type the last field, Word advances to the next record (row). When you click OK, Word adds the new rows all at once.

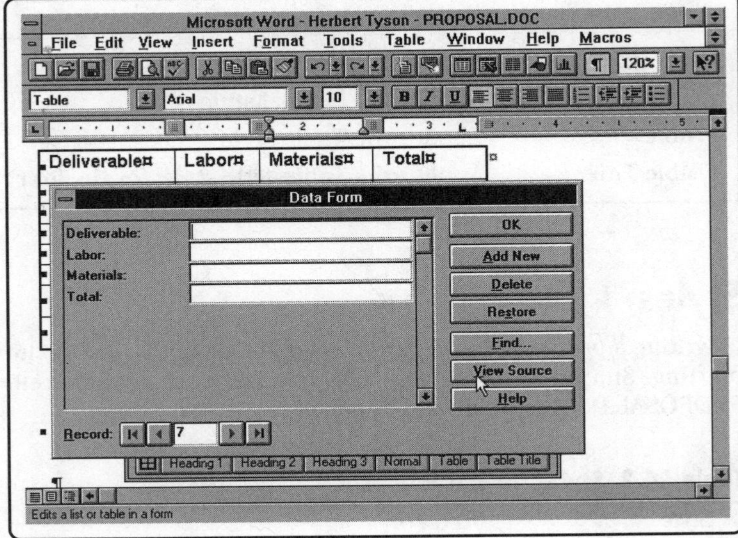

FIGURE 54.3.
The Data Form dialog box.

To add data to the end of an existing table, just click Add New and follow the same procedure, pressing Enter after entering each cell. If you want to supply special formatting, wait until the data are all entered.

How Much?

In each major heading, I've indicated an approximate percentage (spacewise) of the proposal that should be spent in each area. These are rough guidelines, based on having written and reviewed several hundred proposals in some twenty years of consulting. Use these only as approximations. For example, in a ten-page proposal, you might want to spend no more than one to two pages defining the problem, about six to seven pages proposing your approach, and another two pages or so laying out your qualifications.

Margins, Headers, and Footer

Earlier, I noted that you shouldn't try to fudge the margins, line spacing, or fonts, to try to cram a 13-page proposal into 10 pages. Some leeway exists, however, if you're trying to fit a 10.5-page proposal onto 10 pieces of paper (excluding appendices, of course). You could, for example, probably legitimately narrow the left and right margins to one inch left and right. By default, they are set to 1.25 inches on each side in PROPOSAL.DOT. Theoretically, this, and the double-spacing, allows ample room for comments by reviewers. If need be, a 1.2-inch margin might be just what you need to get that last paragraph to fit onto page 10 instead of page 11.

The headers and footers are deliberately spartan. Presumably, your package will arrive as a coherent whole, so you shouldn't need long and redundant headers. In PROPOSAL.DOT, the front section has a simple `Confidential` as the header on each page (front included). The reason is that your pricing and costs may very well be confidential and proprietary. If you work in a competitive market, you probably don't want your competitors to know your costs. The second section—presumably more public than the first—uses a header called `Appendices`, for lack of a better term.

There is a simple -*x*- style page number footer at the bottom of pages in the front section, beginning on page 2. The appendices use small roman numerals, beginning on page ii. If you just have a stack of resumes and reports, however, there's really no reason to incorporate them as actual pages. Just stick a cover sheet between the main proposal and the resumes, and call it `Appendix`.

Research Project Report

by

principal author

other authors

October 29, 1993

Executive Summary

This is all you really need to know about this report. All the rest that follows is pure fluff.

1

Table of Contents

i

Page ii of 17

Chapter

55

Research Project Report

One of the most common uses for word processing programs is writing project reports. As someone who has gone from typewritten to word-processed reports over the past twenty years, I can personally attest to the value of word processing. Ten years ago, as computers began making inroads in offices, it was not unusual for members of a project team to draft reports—using longhand, typewriters, and a mixture of different word processors—and then turn the whole matter over to a production department for actually creating the documents.

Over the past five years, an interesting phenomenon has emerged. First, there was a transition from hand to keyboard, as offices standardized more and more on a single word processor for research and production staff. It was common to see most of a report being done using the same computer software, but with the pieces still being assembled by production staff for final cleanup and tuning. If there were any graphics or tables in the report, however, research staff relied on production to do the "dirty work."

Over the past two or three years, however, researchers have started doing their own equations, their own charts and tables, and their own graphs. And, thanks largely to programs like Word and Excel, they've been turning out some pretty good looking stuff. If this trend continues, it might not be too long before word processing is fully integrated into the complete office fabric and production departments, as we used to know them, cease to exist in the average office. Keep this in mind if you're at all sentimental about the past.

When it comes to writing a research project report, formatting can be one of those little issues that acts as a mental block. Once you have a basic structure, however, the report seems to write itself. Well, almost. Anyway, the goal of this project is to provide a structure and some tools for writing research project reports. The result is shown in Figure 55.1.

Word 6 Features Used

Section formatting
Complex section headers and page numbering
Automatic paragraph numbers (outline style)
Table of contents
List of figures
Index
Automatic captions

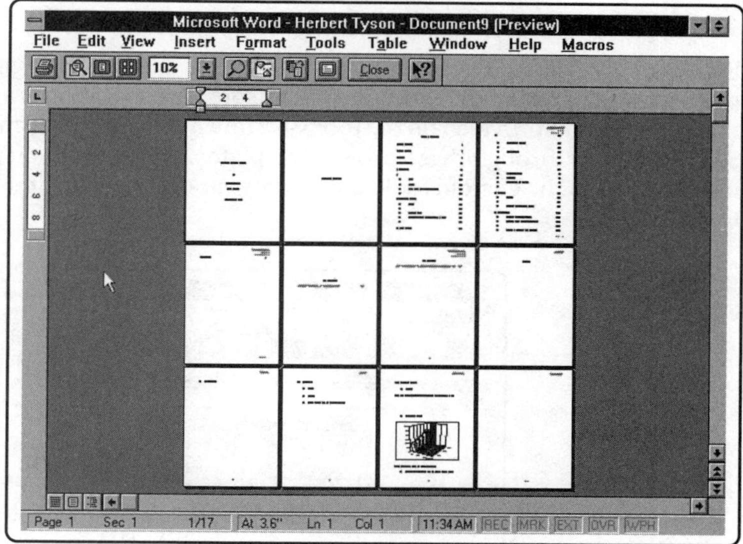

FIGURE 55.1.
A multipage view of a report produced using REPORT.DOT.

Overall Layout

The REPORT.DOT template is in 15 Word sections:

Section 1. Title Page
Section 2. Executive Summary
Section 3. Table of Contents
Section 4. List of Figures
Section 5. List of Tables
Section 6. Preface
Sections 7-13. Report
Section 14. Appendices
Section 15. Index

The report body itself is sectioned to facilitate page numbering (I-*x*, II-*x*, III-*x*, and so on, for the page numbering of each section). Only this level of sectioning is evident to the reader, because the other sections (title, executive summary, and so forth) are actual Word divisions to make document production more straightforward.

Toolbar

Reports vary widely. Because the orientation of this report template is towards the presentation of research results as well as some presentation graphics, tools to aid in their creation are provided on the toolbar (shown in Figure 55.2) and described in Table 55.1. As you go through these project templates, I hope that you feel free to add to or take away from the custom toolbars to suit your own needs. After all, that's what "custom" means.

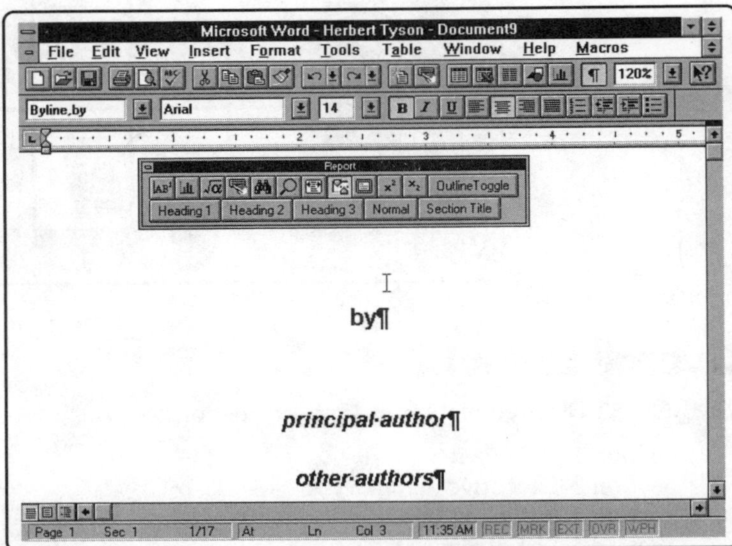

FIGURE 55.2.
The Report toolbar.

Table 55.1. The Report toolbar.

Tool	*Purpose*
Insert Footnote	Inserts a footnote
Insert Chart	Inserts an MS Graph object
Equation Editor	Inserts an MS Equation object
Edit Autotext	Inserts an AutoText entry
Find	Searches for text or formatting
Zoom Control	GUI Zoom control
Zoom Page Width	Scales the view to show the whole width
View/Hide Ruler	Turns off the formatting rulers
Full Screen	Turns off all GUI screen aids

Tool	Purpose
Superscript	Toggles the superscript attribute
Subscript	Toggles the subscript attribute
Outline Toggle	Toggles between current and outline views
Heading 1	Applies Heading 1 style
Heading 2	Applies Heading 2 style
Heading 3	Applies Heading 3 style
Normal	Applies Normal style
Section Title	Applies Section Title style

Styles

I've deliberately kept the number of styles down in the project template. Too much variation in formatting can be a nightmare to manage in a long report. Research reports often run into hundreds of pages. The simpler you can keep it in overall design, the better. Oddly enough, users typically find that large numbers of styles are more manageable in smaller documents, such as brochures, where stylistic formatting and snazzy layout are key elements in presentation. In a research report, on the other hand, the focus is on the results. Snazzy, complicated layouts can tire the reader out—and, frankly, let's face it. Most research reports are so boring going in that the *last* thing you want to do is get your reader *more* tired.

Most research reports benefit greatly from having section numbering. The REPORT.DOT template uses an outline structure for presenting Heading levels 1, 2, 3, and so forth. While only Heading levels 1 through 3 are provided on the toolbar, you can go deeper. Keep in mind, however, that more complexity in your report design makes your method and analysis that much harder to follow. The following outline structure is suggested.

Report

I. Introduction

II. Literature

III. Research Design

IV. Data Design

V. Analysis

VI. Results

VII. Conclusion

However, this outline is provided *only* to get the ball rolling. If *anybody* is able to use this structure without modifying it, nobody would be more suprised than I would. Change it at will. It's only there to suggest a framework, not to lock you into an approach that doesn't suit your needs. For example, if you're writing a research report, this format is appropriate. If you're writing a different kind of report, however, only the skeleton might be useful.

To facilitate consistent numbering, it's important that you use the Heading style levels only in the body of the report and not in the front matter nor in the appendices. If you don't want section numbering, then you can select Format | Heading numbering and click Remove. After that's been taken care of, you no longer get outline-style numbering (and the report interior section numbering is no longer correct), but you are able to use heading level styles in other parts of the document.

Figure and Table Captions

Word can automatically supply a caption number each time you insert a table, figure, or other item you register with the caption command. Note that the sample table and sample figure provided in Section III of the report both have captions:

Figure III-1. *caption text*
Table III-1. *caption text*

In both cases, the Figure and Table (the words) were provided by the caption command—automatically—and the caption text was typed by me.

PROCEDURE 55.1. ENABLING AUTOMATIC CAPTIONING FOR WORD TABLES.

1. Select Insert | Caption to display the dialog box shown in Figure 55.3.
2. Click AutoCaption to display the dialog box shown in Figure 55.4.
3. In the Add Caption When Inserting list, click Microsoft Word 6.0 Table.
4. Verify that the Use Label is set to table (or, if you prefer a different label, then click New Label and type your new label; click OK).
5. To change the numbering, click the Numbering button. For the captions used in REPORT.DOT, I chose to include chapter numbers, with the numbering being supplied by Heading 1 numbers. This gives the I-*x* style of numbering.
6. To change the position for the caption (the default for tables is above the table itself), select a different position using the Position drop-down list (above or below).
7. Click OK to close the AutoCaption dialog box.

Now, each time you insert a Word table, Word automatically adds a Table caption line just ahead of the table (assuming that's what you said in Step 6). To enable automatic captioning for figures, equations, or what-have-you, just repeat the procedure, selecting the appropriate options in Steps 3 through 6.

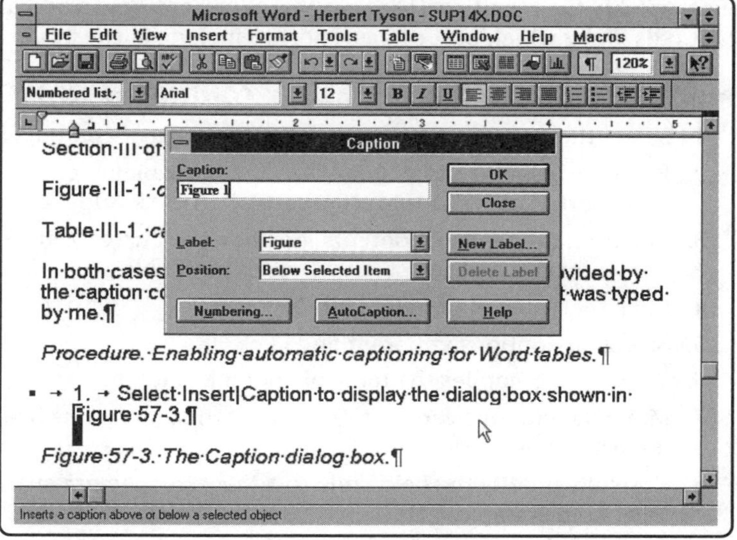

FIGURE 55.3.
The Caption dialog box.

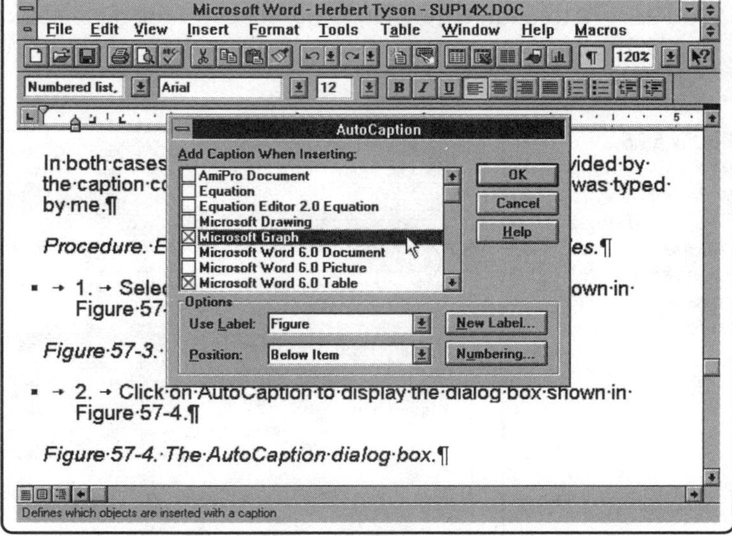

FIGURE 55.4.
The AutoCaption dialog box.

Table of Contents

The table of contents in REPORT.DOT is set up to include all Section Titles after the table of contents itself, as well as all Heading 1-, 2-, and 3-level text. Unfortunately, you cannot use the Insert | Index and Tables command to do the whole job, however. You must modify the resulting TOC field that Word creates to add a bookmark reference that tells Word which part of the report to include in the table.

PROCEDURE 55.2. CREATING THE TABLE OF CONTENTS IN REPORT.DOT.

1. Select the text you want included in the table of contents (see note).
2. Press Ctrl+Shift+F5 to display the Bookmark dialog box, type a name for the bookmark (I called it `TableContents`), and click Add.
3. To insert the table of contents, position the cursor just after the table of contents title, and select Insert | Index and tables.
4. Click the Table of Contents tab.
5. Select any options you want and click OK.
6. Word now compiles the table of contents, and displays it.
7. Move the cursor over the table of contents, and press Shift+F9 to display the underlying field code.
8. Carefully modify the field code to add a `\b` *bookmark* switch just after the TOC—for example, `{ TOC \b "tablecontents" \o "1-3" \t "Section Title,1" }`. The bookmark name should match what you typed in Step 2; case does not matter.
9. Press F9 to update the field; Word displays the dialog box shown in Figure 55.5 and asks what you want to do. Click the second option: Update Entire Table.

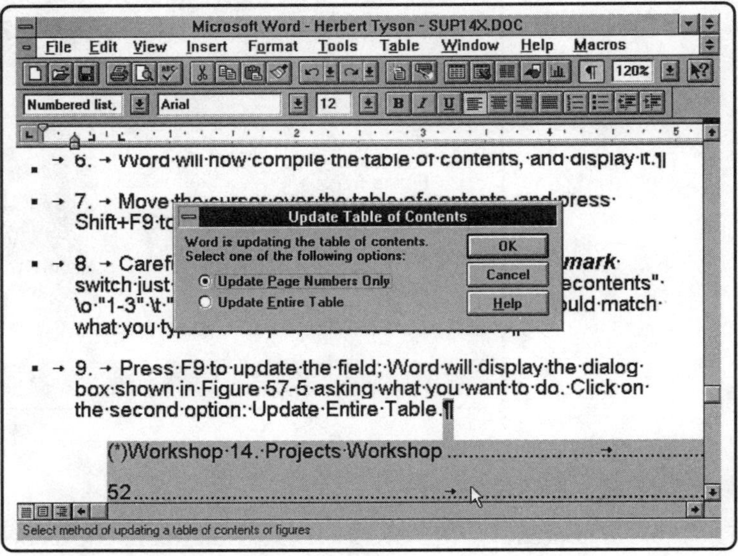

FIGURE 55.5. *When you update a table of contents field, Word gives you the choice of updating just the pages or the whole table.*

SUPER

What to include… For the table of contents in REPORT.DOT, I selected from the list of figures through the end of the Appendices section (presuming that it will eventually be deeper than it is now). Optionally, you could include the index as well. For both the Appendix and Index, the page numbering variations make including the table of contents less useful than if the page numbering is consistent throughout.

Index

Just as the table of contents makes sense only for a certain part of the report, so would an index. For the REPORT.DOT template, the index was limited to just the report and the appendices. There are basically five steps:

1. Use the Mark Index Entry dialog box (Alt+Shift+X) to index the items you want included in the index.
2. Bookmark the area you want to include in the index.
3. Insert the index using **I**nsert | Inde**x** and Tables.
4. Modify the resulting INDEX field to add a `\b` switch. Otherwise, you could end up indexing parts of the table of contents!
5. Press F9 to update the INDEX field, selecting the option to update the entire index.

SUPER TIP

If you use AutoIndex or the Mark All to mark your index entries, you undoubtedly have a number of entries you really do not want included in the index. The XE fields (index entries) are displayed as hidden text. Click the paragraph symbol icon on the standard toolbar to toggle hidden text on, and the XE fields should come into view—along with a lot of other stuff. If you prefer to see less clutter, you can select the Hidden option in **T**ools | **O**ptions | **V**iew.

Das Kapital for Dimwits

A Contemporary Look at Marxism

Groucho Marks

Chapter

56

A Writer's Book Template

Book? I'm writing a template for writing books? What am I, crazy or somthing? Well, perhaps. There are zillions of different kinds of books, different formats, and every publisher has its own idea about what's right and what's wrong. Heck, some publishers can't even seem to agree internally. Two consecutive books from the same publisher might look as different as night and day. So, isn't it just a little weird to imagine that one could actually devise a template for publishing books?

Yes. Quite weird, in fact. So weird, as it happens, that that's not what this session is about. Instead, it's about a *writer's* template. A template designed for writers. Heck, most anyone who writes books these days—okay, so there are some exceptions—knows better than to think that the formatting and layout they choose when writing the book will bear any relationship to the final published form. No matter what you, I, or anyone else does to try to lay out a layout—so to speak—your publisher's going to have a different set of rules for you to follow. So, instead of trying to devise a layout, the purpose of this session is to devise a writing tool (part of which is shown in Figure 56.1)—and how better to do that than to create a writers' toolbar?

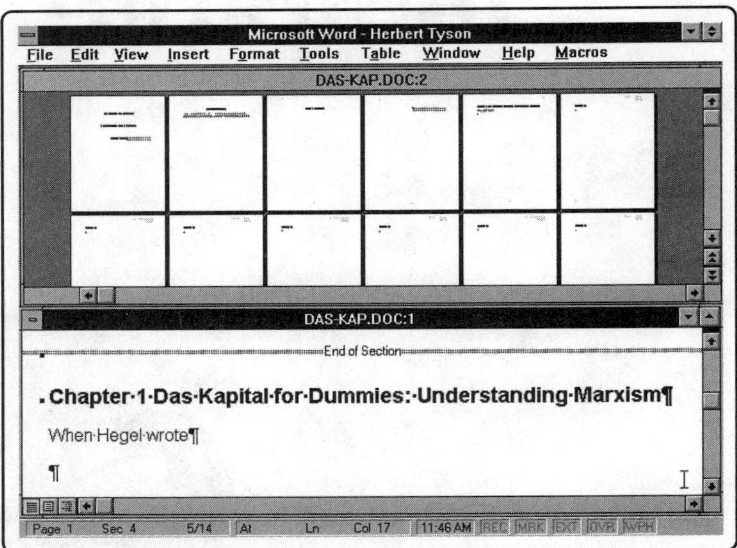

FIGURE 56.1.
A multipage view of a book in progress using the BOOK.DOT template.

Word 6 Features Used

Styles
Master document
Custom toolbar
Autocorrect

Headers
Footers
Varied page numbering
Outlining

Giving the Publishers Something They Can Work with

A good writing tool makes it easy to implement the specific formatting requirements of a publisher. In Word, this usually means creating a handful of styles (or two) that give the editors a way to get a handle on the text you give them. Whether you give them a file in Word for Windows, Word for DOS, WordPerfect, WordStar, or another format, a key element that makes publishing easier for them is a consistent and deliberate use of styles. That enables the publisher to correctly and quickly identify sections of your book that require special attention.

When you write a chapter title, it doesn't matter whether it's 16 points, 24 points, uses drop capitals, or whatever. What matters is that the publisher can identify it as a title. When you create special headings, the format and font aren't important. What's important is that you use a distinct style name so that the publisher can tell that it's a heading, and what kind.

While you're writing the book, therefore, you want to select a font that's comfortable to look at on-screen. Don't worry about the final font. Regardless of what you use to write the book, most publishers will want it in a monospaced font so they can accurately measure the length of the text. So, a well–thought-out book template lets you change all of the fonts to Courier, in one fell swoop.

Things to Remember (and to Forget)

You should remember some things—as well as forget some things—in preparing a manuscript to send to a publisher. Here's my top ten list:

1. Forget those two spaces your typing teacher told you to type after a period. Use only a single space between the punctuation at the end of a sentence and the beginning of the next.
2. Use word wrap. Press Enter only to begin a new paragraph.
3. Don't use the Spacebar to create horizontal spacing. Use Tab instead.
4. Don't hyphenate. Forget that your word processor even has that capability.
5. Do use a spelling checker.

6. Find out if your publisher has a hang-up about passive voice. If so, then use Word's Grammar checker to try to get out of the habit.
7. Use styles for every repetitive change of format. For example, don't use a style to italicize a single word—but if you routinely italicize book titles and think your publisher might want to do something different, then create a character style for those titles.
8. Don't use *its* when you mean *it's*, or vice versa.
9. Publishers like book chapters to be in separate files; if it's easier for you to work with a single file, then use Word's master document feature.
10. If you're going to be late with a deliverable, let your publisher know the week *before*, rather than the week *after*.

Overall Layout

As I said, the layout really isn't the issue. The issue is to provide a good set of writing tools and to make it easy to give your publisher something it can work with. You don't want to have the following conversation:

Editor	Well, it looks fine, really. But, we're going to need a little bit of revising in the first fifteen chapters.
You	Oh, okay. Wait a minute, the book just has eight chapters.
Editor	Yes, well, that's part of the reason why I called. And, you know, this is a little strange, but your document seems to have a lot of formatting in it, but the only style being used is Normal. Did something happen to the file? We really can't use it unless there are style changes. Didn't somebody send you our style guide? And, is your spelling checker working? We'd be happy to send you a dictionary, or a new copy of WordPerfect.

In any event, try to put yourself in the editor's shoes. Editors need something that can be published. Books are more than just words. They're patterns of text that need to be woven into a publishable format.

Toolbar

The Book toolbar (shown in Figure 56.2) is a set of writing tools, for the most part. These tools are designed to help you focus on the task of writing. The toolbar is described in Table 56.1.

FIGURE 56.2.
The Book toolbar.

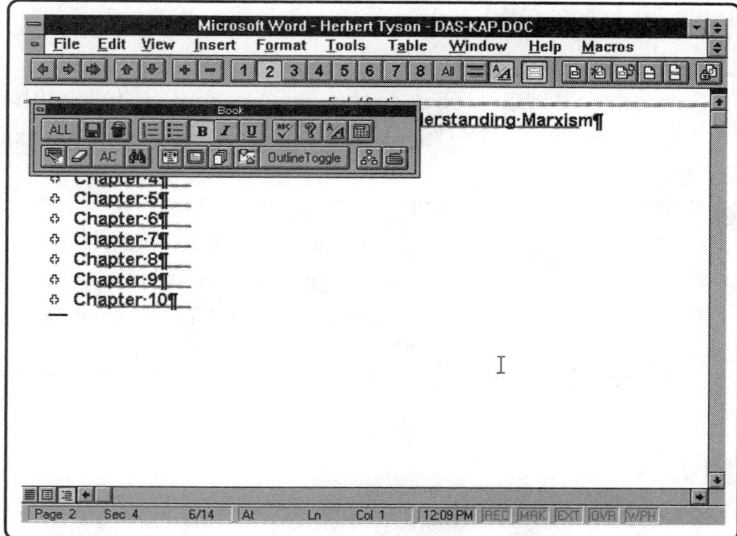

Table 56.1. The Book toolbar.

Tool	*Purpose*
All	Saves all open documents and templates
File Manager	Starts the Windows file manager
Program Manager	Switches to the Windows program manager
Numbering	Applies numbering to a list
Bullets	Applies bullet formatting to a list
Bold	Applies bold formatting to text
Italic	Applies italic formatting to text
Underline	Applies underlining to text
Spell	Spells the word or the selection
Thesaurus	Looks up the word or selection in the thesaurus
Change Case	Displays the Change Case dialog box
Word count	Displays a word count
AutoText	Inserts or defines an autotext entry
AutoCorrect	Defines an AutoCorrect entry
AutoCorrect Toggle	Toggles AutoCorrect on and off
Find	Searches for text or formatting

continues

Table 56.1. continued

Tool	*Purpose*
Zoom Page Width	Scales the view to show the full width of the page
Full Screen	Turns off all screen aids to give a maximum view of the document
Ruler	Toggles rulers on and off
Outline	Toggles Outline view on and off
Macro	Runs, creates, and records macros
Customize	Activates the tabbed Tools I Customize dialog box for toolbars, keys, and menus

Styles

The book styles (shown in Table 56.2) are uncomplicated because of the rationale expressed earlier. The fact that there aren't many styles doesn't mean that you shouldn't use many, if needed. On the contrary, book formats vary widely and often are precisely specified by editors. Use the style guide your editor provides and create special styles that are needed for the book. In using those styles, by the way, you need not conjure up formatting variations for them. In most instances, all your publisher needs are the style names themselves, as tags, so it can see where to apply the *real* formatting. If your publisher uses Word for publishing, then setting up the book is as simple as attaching its own template to your book. If the style names match—presto! Your book is suddenly much closer to finished than you might have imagined.

Table 56.2. The Book Styles.

Style	*Used For*
Author	Author name on title page
Heading 1	Chapter titles
Heading 2	Major heading in chapters
Heading 3	Subheadings in chapters
Normal	All paragraph body text
Publication	Character style used for the names of books and magazines
Section Title	Major sections titles, Table of Contents, and Index
Subtitle	Used for any book subtitle on the title page
Title	Main book title on the title page

Master Document

One way to manage a complicated—and large—document is to use Word 6's Master Document feature. Documents that use the BOOK.DOT template can easily take advantage of this feature. It works by sudividing a single document into several documents, splitting along heading levels. For example, BOOK.DOT *deliberately* uses the heading levels in the text of the book. This enables you to display the book as an outline in Master Document view and split the chapters into separate files. You then can use the Master Document as a handle for the whole documents, managing tasks like cross-references, maintaining consistent page numbering, creating a table of contents, and indexing (if it's that kind of book *and* if you're unlucky enough to have to compile your own index).

PROCEDURE 56.1. CREATING A MASTER DOCUMENT USING BOOK.DOT.

1. Copy BOOK.DOT to your templates directory.
2. Select **F**ile | **O**pen, specify BOOK.DOT as the template, and click OK to create a new document based on BOOK.DOT.
3. Write your book (ha ha!), using the framework provided. Insert or remove chapters, as needed.
4. Select **F**ile | Save **A**s, and give your new document a name.
5. Select **V**iew | **M**aster Document to switch into Master Document view.
6. Click the big **1** to view just level 1 headings.
7. Use the mouse to select all of the headings displayed. Important: Do not use Ctrl+A to select the whole document, as that will select more than just the heading you see. Instead, click the mouse in the first Chapter line, then press Shift and click in the last chapter line. This selects just the contiguous Heading 1 sections.
8. Click the Create Subdocuments button (see Figure 56.3). This creates a separate subdocument (Word file) for each of the Heading 1 levels. Thus, Chapter 1 becomes one file, Chapter 2 another, and so on.
9. Select **F**ile | **S**ave (Ctrl+S). At this point, you'll see Word save the Master Document itself (the file currently loaded) as well as each subdocument. If you keep the same names that are in BOOK.DOT, the resulting files will be named CHAPTER1.DOC through CHAPTER9.DOC and CHAPTE10.DOC. See Chapter 45, "Master Documents," for additional information on renaming the subdocuments if those names don't suit your fancy.

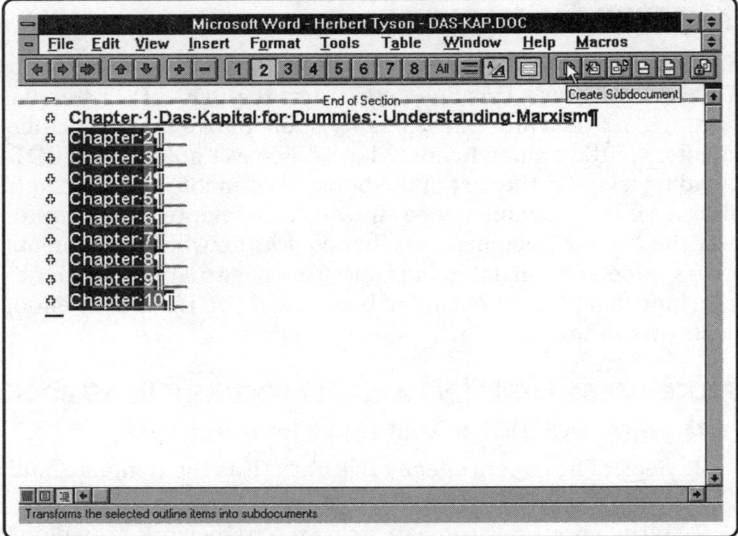

FIGURE 56.3.
The Create Subdocument button.

Headers, Footers, and Page Numbering

Page numbering for this project is done using blank headers for everything prior to the actual chapters. The table of contents has a lowercase, roman numeral, centered footer. For chapter headers, a simple, informative header is used:

`{title}`	From document summary information
`{styleref "header 1" \l }`	Picks up the chapter title from the current chapter
`Page {page}`	The page number, starting at page 2 of the actual chapters.

For publishing a book, you obviously would use a different kind of page numbering. For drafts, however, this style is good. An additional feature is used to force each chapter to begin on a new page. As shown in Figure 56.4, one of the features in the Text Flow tab of the Paragraph dialog box is the Page Break Before setting. By turning this attribute on, you can force each occurrence of a Heading 1 style to begin on a new page.

An additional option you might need to consider is numbering each chapter independently rather than continuously. I've seen publishers—even the same publisher—do it different ways. My sense is that continuous page numbering for the text is the norm. However, you most definitely will find emphatic exceptions. If you don't use the Master Document feature to divide the book into subdocuments, then you would need to insert section breaks between each chapter.

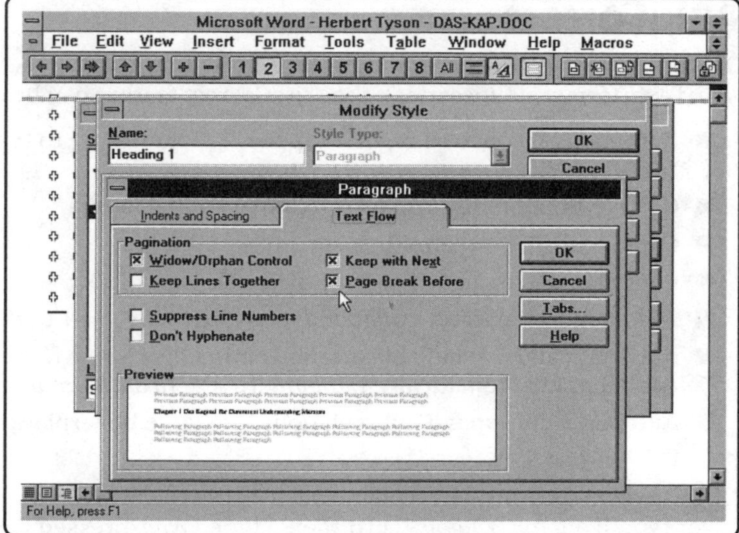

FIGURE 56.4.
Use the Page Break Before setting to make a style start on a new page.

PROCEDURE 56.2. SEPARATING THE CHAPTERS FOR INDEPENDENT NUMBERING.

1. Switch into Outline View (click the outline toggle tool, or select **V**iew | **O**utline).
2. Click the **1** to show just Heading 1-level text.
3. Move the insertion point to the beginning of Chapter 2 (just before the *C* in Chapter).
4. Select **I**nsert | **B**reak.
5. Click **N**ext Page.
6. Click OK.
7. Press the Down key twice to move to the beginning of Chapter 3.
8. Press the F4 (repeat) key to repeat Steps 3 through 5 automatically.
9. Repeat Step 8 until section breaks exist between all of the chapters.

SUPER TIP

Whenever you have to perform a task at the beginning of each heading level, switch into Outline view and set the view at the minimum level you need—level 1, in this instance. That way, you'll be able to move from heading to heading without having to do a lot of scrolling or searching. In this case, there's a double bonus—you get to use the F4 key to repeat the Insert | Break command.

AutoCorrect

One of the neatest new features in Word 6 is the AutoCorrect feature. Similar to AutoText (formerly Glossaries), the AutoCorrect feature can be set up to

- Automatically convert regular typewritten quotes (") to typographic quotes "like 'This'"
- Correct accidentally typing TWo initial capital letters
- Capitalize the first letter in a sentence
- Capitalize the names of days of the week
- Automatically correct common typos (*teh* to *the*, *thier* to *their*, and so forth)
- Automatically expand abbreviations into fuller forms (for example, type *ajp*, and it could automatically expand into *American Journal of Peanuts*)
- Automatically expand abbreviations into large boilerplate sections as well as graphics

As a writer's tool, AutoCorrect is terrific—especially when writing computer books. I never type *Word for Windows*. Just then, I typed *wfw*, pressed Enter, and it automatically expanded into *Word for Windows*. In fact, in order to type the plain *wfw*, I actually had to toggle AutoCorrect off. By the way, I typed just the letters *ac* to get AutoCorrect. Just think of it, *wdc* becomes Washington, DC, *ny* becomes New York, and *tsep* could be *The Saturday Evening Post*, italics and all.

PROCEDURE 56.3. CREATING AN AUTOCORRECT SHORTCUT ENTRY.

1. Type the full form for the text for which you wish to create a shortcut.
2. Select **T**ools | **A**utoCorrect (or, if the Book toolbar is active, just click the AutoCorrect dialog box tool, shown in Figure 56.5).
3. The selected text is shown in the **W**ith field. Type the shortcut in the Replace field.
4. Ensure that the Replace **T**ext as You Type check box is selected.
5. Click OK.

You can use the AutoCorrect dialog box tool at any time to activate the AutoCorrect dialog box. You also can use the AutoCorrect toggle button, immediately to the right of the AutoCorrect dialog box button, to toggle AutoCorrect on and off. You might need to turn it off for a moment if you encounter an odd acronym that unexpectedly expands into somthing in your AutoCorrect list.

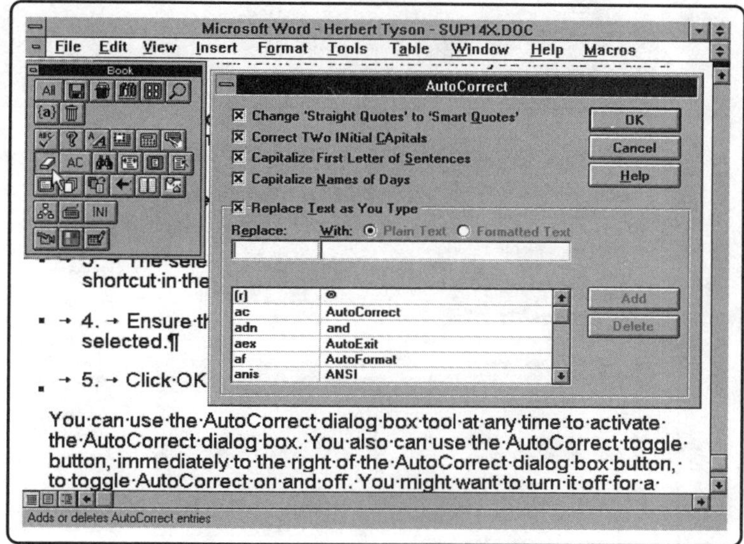

FIGURE 56.5.
The AutoCorrect tool in the Book toolbar looks like a brick.

Why SnapOSwitch™?

SnapOSwitch™ is the computer user's "dream come true. From the makers of ClapOSwitch, this amazing new breakthrough device saves you the time, trouble, and expense of turning your computers on and off by hand. Just listen to what these SnapOSwitch™ users have to say:

SnapOSwitch has changed my life—Aline Kawalskiev, San Diego, California.

With SnapOSwitch, my dog doesn't bark at me anymore—Michael Windau, Sandusky, Ohio.

SnapOSwitch keeps my toes from freezing on cold winter nights—Susan Redfield, Twin Peaks, Iowa.

SnapOSwitch™

Do You Want Ease of Use?

Do You Want to Using Computers to be a Snap?

You asked for it-you got it!

Acme TimeFill Announces:

SnapOSwitch™

Acme TimeFill, Ltd.
127 East Main Street
Callicowicka, ME 11111
(555) 555-5432
(555) 555-5533 (Fax)

By Popular Demand

Hey, Computer User!

Yes, you! Do you want the ease of use you've been promised? Again and again, you've been promised "ease of use." So far, however, the only thing easy is they way they use your credit card.

But, that's history. Now, because of this exciting new breakthrough technology, we're able to finally offer you the ease of use you've been longing for. Never again will you have to turn on your computer by hand. Using the amazing new SnapOSwitch, you'll be able to turn your computer off and on just with a quick snap of your fingers.

Can't snap your fingers? That's okay, too. The amazing new SnapOSwitch works with any snapping sound. Don't be surprised when, the next time you break your leg, SnapOSwitch automatically turns on your computer!

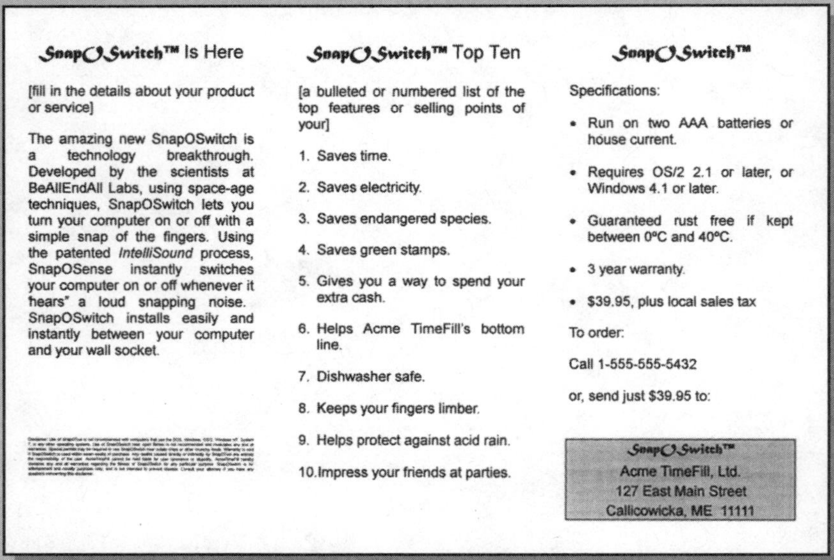

SnapOSwitch™ Is Here

[fill in the details about your product or service]

The amazing new SnapOSwitch is a technology breakthrough. Developed by the scientists at BeAllEndAll Labs, using space-age techniques, SnapOSwitch lets you turn your computer on or off with a simple snap of the fingers. Using the patented *IntelliSound* process, SnapOSense instantly switches your computer on or off whenever it hears" a loud snapping noise. SnapOSwitch installs easily and instantly between your computer and your wall socket.

SnapOSwitch™ Top Ten

[a bulleted or numbered list of the top features or selling points of your]

1. Saves time.
2. Saves electricity.
3. Saves endangered species.
4. Saves green stamps.
5. Gives you a way to spend your extra cash.
6. Helps Acme TimeFill's bottom line.
7. Dishwasher safe.
8. Keeps your fingers limber.
9. Helps protect against acid rain.
10. Impress your friends at parties.

SnapOSwitch™

Specifications:

- Run on two AAA batteries or house current.
- Requires OS/2 2.1 or later, or Windows 4.1 or later.
- Guaranteed rust free if kept between 0°C and 40°C.
- 3 year warranty.
- $39.95, plus local sales tax

To order:

Call 1-555-555-5432

or, send just $39.95 to:

SnapOSwitch™
Acme TimeFill, Ltd.
127 East Main Street
Callicowicka, ME 11111

Chapter

57

Flyers and Newsletters

One of the more difficult documents I ever had to produce was a trifold flyer. At the time, I was using XyWrite III+, which lacked a graphical preview mode, as well as the basics for bordering and shading and other useful desktop publishing features. Thanks to Word's powerful desktop publishing and page layout features, however, producing a trifold flyer like the one shown in Figure 57.1 is now a snap. The trick is in knowing where things will end up once it's folded, and allowing enough room between the various sections so that the folds don't impinge on the text and so that the resulting margins on the folded segments are uniform.

FIGURE 57.1.
Grand layout of a trifold flyer.

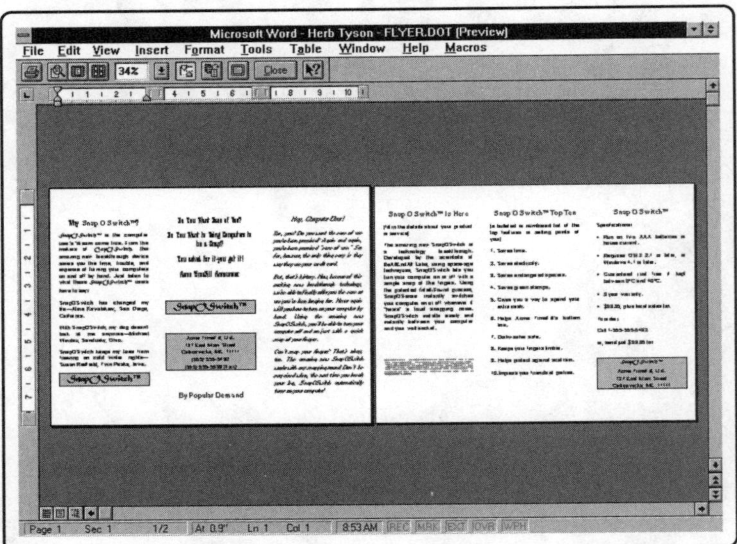

Word 6 Features Used

- Columns
- Centered vertical alignment
- Borders and shading
- Bullets
- Numbering
- AutoCorrect

Overall Layout

The trifold flyer has a landscape orientation and is divided into two physical pages, with three columns (minipages) on each side. Each of the six columns conceptually is a separate minipage, and the trifold forms a "minibook" comprising six minipages.

Optionally, the second physical page (the three inside minipages of the trifold) can have a portrait orientation, but a consistent trifold minibook appearance is generally more convenient and aesthetically more appealing. It also lets you divide your flyer into six distinct topics or presentations.

For this flyer, the middle column of the first physical page is the impact page. This should be the first thing that the recipient sees. Thus, it should use bold and dramatic formatting to catch the reader's eye and attention. Here, I choose simply to hype the product and producer. Alternatively, you might care to replace the bordered, shaded areas with a graphic, either representing the logo of the company or perhaps, if appropriate, even a picture of the product. For example, if you're producing a trifold flyer for a hotel, a picture of the hotel's estate is good impact material, with additional pictures of typical accommodations and facilities on the inside.

The trifold can be folded so that either of the side columns on the first physical page can be on the back. The back often is used for affixing a mailing label (for example, when the flyer is mailed without an envelope) or for additional teasers to tempt the recipient to read the interior.

An additional option you might care to use is to reserve two of the six minipages for an order or response form. For this to work, use WordArt to produce two opposite minipages (the left column of page 1 and the right column of page 2) that form a tear-off response card. On one side, include an ordering form with enough room to indicate quantify, price, tax, and any other ordering information. On the reverse side, include space for a return address and include your own preprinted address, as well as a square for indicating the position of a postage stamp. By using WordArt, you can rotate the orientation of those two minipages to portrait mode.

Page Layout

For the trifold flyer, the general orientation should be landscape, and lateral margins should be kept very small for the best use of space. While margins exceeding one inch are common in full-page documents, the minipages used in a trifold flyer call for much smaller effective margins. For FLYER.DOT, left and right margins were set at .3". Top and bottom margins are usually set economically as well, with settings between .5" and .75" not uncommon. For FLYER.DOT, the top and bottom margins were conservatively set at .5".

PROCEDURE 57.1. SETTING THE PAGE AND MARGIN LAYOUTS.

1. Select File | Page Setup, and click the Margins tab.
2. Ensure that Apply To is set to Whole Document.
3. Set the top and bottom margins to identical values, preferably between .5" and .75" (note that .75" is not displayed when you use the up/down arrows to adjust the margin settings; however, you can type the settings directly and bypass the GUI controls).

4. Set the left and right margins to identical values, preferably no larger than .4".
5. Ensure that the gutter setting remains at 0, and leave the From Edge settings at their built-in defaults (because we don't use headers or footers in a flyer, the From Edge settings are left alone).
6. Click the Paper **S**ize tab.
7. Click to select Landscape orientation (ensuring that Apply To is set at Whole Document).
8. Click the **L**ayout tab.
9. Under Vertical Alignment, select Centered. Note: If you select Justified, any bordered and shaded artwork appears segmented (vertical lines are broken). You can use Justified vertical alignment if you like, but make sure that no lines are messed up because of it.
10. Click OK.

Column Formatting

An important consideration in setting up a trifold is allowing enough room between the columns so that when you fold it, you have equal margins. To to this, the spacing between columns should be double the left and right margins. For FLYER.DOT, the left and right margins are set to .3", and the spacing between columns is set at .6". When you fold between columns, this then allows the .6" to be allocated equally between the two adjacent minipages, with the left and right edges of the physical pages providing the opposite .3" margins for the left and right minipages. For the trifold flyer on the Super Disk, the column formatting has already been done. If you need to set it to something different, use the procedure shown.

PROCEDURE 57.2. SETTING COLUMNS AND BETWEEN-COLUMN SPACING.

1. Select F**o**rmat **C**olumns.
2. Ensure that the number of columns is set to 3.
3. Ensure that Equal Column Widths is checked.
4. Ensure that Apply To is set to Whole Document.
5. In the Spacing control, set the measurement to double the left and right margin values (the left and right margins should be equal and can be set using **F**ile | Page Set**u**p | **M**argins).
6. Optionally, you can turn on the Line Between option. While it makes manual folding easier, it lacks aesthetic appeal under most circumstances.
7. Click OK.

Bordering and Shading

Bordering and shading are easy. Getting distinct borders for vertically adjacent paragraphs, however, can be a little tricky. Notice that on the impact minipage, shown in Figure 57.1, two distinct bordered, shaded boxes are drawn around the product name and the company address block. In order to obtain separate boxes, the two paragraphs must have a paragraph separating them.

PROCEDURE 57.3. SETTING A BOX BORDER WITH SHADING.

1. Select the paragraphs you want to box and shade.
2. Select F**o**rmat | **B**orders and Shading.
3. Click the Borders tab, if necessary.
4. Under Presets, click Box.
5. Click Shading.
6. Under Shading, click 20% for the best effect (more than 20% generally swamps the text too much, and less usually looks too washed out).
7. Click OK.

Creating a Shorthand Using AutoCorrect

You might have noticed that the product title is used multiple times throughout FLYER.DOT. This helps promote product recognition. However, typing it repeatedly gets pretty tiresome. By creating an AutoCorrect or AutoText shorthand, however, you'll only have to type it once.

PROCEDURE 57.4. CREATING AN AUTOCORRECT SHORTHAND.

1. Select an already-typed occurrence of the text (make sure it has whatever formatting you need already applied).
2. Select **T**ools | **A**utoCorrect; note that the selected text is already displayed in the picture window.
3. In the Replace field, type the shorthand you want to use (make sure it's not a word or acronym that you plan to use otherwise).
4. For the best use of this feature, you probably want to use the formatted version, so click to select Formatted Text, after the With field.
5. Ensure that Replace Text as You Type is checked.
6. Click OK.

Now, whenever you type the shorthand version, it is automatically be replaced by the formatted longer version. If the formatted item does not have any point size variations within it, Word also automatically adjusts the point size each time it expands the abbreviation. For example, when you insert the shorthand in a passage that is 18 points high, the long version is inserted in 18 points. If the text passage is 12 points, then so is the long version of the inserted text.

Bullets and Numbering

Bullets and number can be very useful enhancements to advertising flyers. They help draw attention to features in a way that text introductions cannot. Word's bullets and numbers are especially useful because they automatically add bullets and renumber items that are inserted using the same formatting. Thus, if used correctly, you aren't constantly having to reapply the bullets and numbers as you modify text.

SUPER TIP

When using the bullets and numbers tools on the toolbar, they can be used both to apply and to remove bullets and numbers. When bullets or numbers are turned on in a selection, the face of the bullet or number button is whiter than usual. When turned off, the face returns to gray. When you apply bullets, any other numbering formatting is turned off, and bullets are applied. Similarly, when you apply numbering, any existing bullets applied using Word 6 are removed. (Word 6's default bullet and numbering tools can't be used to remove bullets or numbering applied using Word for Windows 2).

Toolbar and Printing

The Flyer toolbar contains tools for printing each side of the flyer as well as formatting borders and shading. Because of the way the flyer is designed to be folded, you must make sure that the front and back sides are aligned properly. For most laser printers, this means printing physical page 1, then removing the paper and manually inserting it so that the unprinted side is face up, and then printing physical page 2. If you're printing multiple copies (rather than having copies made using a copying machine), you would first print physical page 1 on the number of copies you want. Then insert the printed pages, unprinted side up, into the paper tray and repeat the process for physical page 2.

Creating Newsletters using the Newslttr Wizard

Another popular use for Word's desktop publishing capabilities is newsletters. Word 6 comes with a newsletter wizard for creating newsletters. Rather than reinvent the wheel here, we'll just review the steps necessary to produce a newsletter using the wizard.

PROCEDURE 57.5. CREATING A NEWSLETTER USING THE NEWSLETTER WIZARD.

1. Select **File** | **New**, and click the Newslttr Wizard in the Template list.
2. Select Classic or Modern (actually, these terms are arbitrary; just select the one that looks closest to your goal). Note: When you make a choice, Word updates the preview display. This can take quite a long time, especially on slower computers. Click Next when you're satisfied.
3. Select the number of columns for the layout. This and all other choices (except Classic and Modern) can be changed later. Click Next when you've made your selection.
4. Type the title for your newsletter, and click Next.
5. Indicate whether or not the newsletter will be two sided (most newsletters are two-sided, although Word's default choice is single-sided). Click Next to proceed.
6. Indicate the total number of pages you expect. Click Next to continue.
7. Indicate the elements you want to include (table of contents, fancy first letters, date, and volume/issue numbers). Click Next to continue, then click Finish.

Once the base newsletter has been created, you can go in and add the text or otherwise change it as needed. Items you might want to change include the number of columns and the title. One thing to note is that the table of contents Word inserts is not a normal Word table of contents. It is a small Word table for manually inserting your own table of contents. If you want to automate this aspect, see Chapter 42, "Tables of Contents, Figures, and Authorities," for additional information. Note also that the issue number and date are not inserted for you. Instead, you need to replace the inserted dummy numbers with the correct ones for your newsletter.

Macros Workshop

In this workshop, you learn about my favorite Word topic—Macros. Macros give extra dimensions to a word processor, enabling you to add to Word what the designers didn't. Word's macro language, WordBASIC, is a powerful combination of a subset of Microsoft BASIC and Word's built-in commands. While you wouldn't necessarily want to write a full-scale application using WordBASIC, it's flexible enough to solve almost any problem you run up against while using Word, and it will let you automate almost any tiresome task.

Chapter

58

User Macros

One of the most underutilized aspects of Word is its powerful macro facilities. Word provides a way to automate or modify just about any feature it has. If something doesn't quite work the way you want it to—you can change it. If you have a series of procedures that are tedious to execute—record them and turn them into a macro. If you want to invent a new feature—write your own macro.

What Is a Macro, Anyway?

A macro is an action shorthand. It is a single simple action you can take that causes one or more complex actions to occur. Actually, Word has five kinds of macros, only one of which is actually called *macro*:

- Macros—New "commands" invented by the user
- Commands—Built-in Word commands
- AutoText—User-expandable shorthands for text, tables, and graphics
- AutoCorrect—Automatic shorthands for text, tables, and graphics
- Styles—Formatting shorthands

AutoText and AutoCorrect commands are ways that you can use an abbreviation to cause a larger section of text, tables, or graphics to be inserted into your document. Thus, in a very real sense, they are macros. If you didn't have AutoText and AutoCorrect, in fact, you probably could write macros to do the same thing. You might have a macro that examines the text just typed and then compares it to a list of abbreviations, and, if the text is in the list, supplies a substitute for the abbreviation. HomeMadeAutoText is one of several ways you could do it:

```
'HomeMadeAutoText
Sub MAIN
WordLeft 1, 1
Shorthand$ = LCase$(Selection$())
Select Case Shorthand$
     Case "wfw" : Insert "Word for Windows"
     Case "wdc" : Insert "Washington, DC"
     Case "alx" : Insert "Alexandria, Egypt"
End Select
End Sub
```

You might then assign this macro to a key (for example, Alt+X for eXpand). However, you don't have to do that, because Word already has an AutoText command. And, as you've just seen, that command is really a macro.

Styles are formatting macros. If you want to make a paragraph bold, double-spaced, bulleted, and bordered, you could apply all that formatting directly, one at a time. Or, if it's a format you'll want to use again, you could give all that formatting a name—a Style—and then use the Style to apply all of the formatting at once. While you probably won't see the Word reference manual saying so, this effectively makes a style a kind of formatting macro. In fact, before they had styles (using some of those primitive word processing programs that nonetheless had macros, or using a generalizable keystroke macro tool like SuperKey), users used to record macros to apply several formats with one command. Incorporating the notion of applying several formats at once as a style was a logical step forward.

Also, while it might not be obvious, Word's own commands are all macros. This gives you a library of (gulp!) over 817 commands with which to work. A complete list is provided in Appendix C, "Reserved Keywords and Word Commands." Consider, for example, the ToolEnvelopesAndLabels command. It's really a macro. It reads the current document looking for bookmarked text that contains addresses, then opens a new window in which to present an envelope, and can even add that envelope to a new section of your document, or print it.

"So," you say, "if it's a macro, how come I can't edit it the way I can edit macros I create?"

Well, you can. You just have to know how to do it. See the section "Modifying Built-in Word Commands" later in this session. Hint: The built-in ToolEnvelopesAndLabels macro looks like this:

```
Sub MAIN
Dim dlg As ToolsEnvelopesAndLabels
GetCurValues dlg
Dialog dlg
ToolsEnvelopesAndLabels dlg
End Sub
```

Creating Macros

There are three ways to create a Word macro:

- Recording
- Writing from scratch
- Modifying a built-in Word command

Recording

By far the simplest and most educational way is to record your actions, and then open the resulting macro for editing to see what it all looks like. Let's look at what's necessary to record a fairly simple macro. A common macro task is to perform peculiar, nonstyleable edits to a list of items. Consider the following list, which you are perhaps using to describe a cast of characters:

Karen	Bob
Katie	Carol
Jan	Ted
Greg	Alice
Mike	

Perhaps you'd like to apply a hanging-indent style called Cast, then underline the name, then insert a tab with underlining turned off for the descriptive text that follows. To do this manually, you could perform the following steps for each name on the list:

1. Put the cursor in the name.
2. Press Ctrl+Shift+S.
3. Type `Cast`.
4. Press Enter.
5. Select the name.
6. Press Ctrl+U (underlining).
7. Tap the End key to go to the end of the name.
8. Press Ctrl+Spacebar to turn off underlining.
9. Press the Tab key.
10. Press the Down arrow key to move to the next line.

To give you an extra incentive to write the macro, let's also assume that you're a screenwriter and have to do this sort of thing all the time, and that this macro is going to get more use than your coffee cup.

SUPER TIP

This is just an example, by the way, and not necessarily the best Word way to handle this kind of formatting. From a practical standpoint, an easier alternative might be to use a table instead of the hanging-indent Cast style. Just create an empty two-column table set up exactly as you need it: column 1 is always underlined; column 2 is set up to give you the identical effect as hanging indents. Then select the table and give it an AutoText name. The next time you need to insert a Cast list, just type `Cast`, press F3, and you're off and running. You could even then use the Data Form dialog box (available from the Database toolbar) to insert your cast information. Upon reflection, almost any macro I can think of to record could—with a little thinking—be accomplished using formatting. However, let's just assume that the recipients of your script don't want tables. They want a tab and a hanging indent so they can use their existing template more readily.

PROCEDURE 58.1. RECORDING A MACRO TO PERFORM A SERIES OF REPETITIVE EDITS.

1. Position the insertion point where you want it to be when the macro starts, and select Tools | Macro to display the Macro dialog box shown in Figure 58.1.

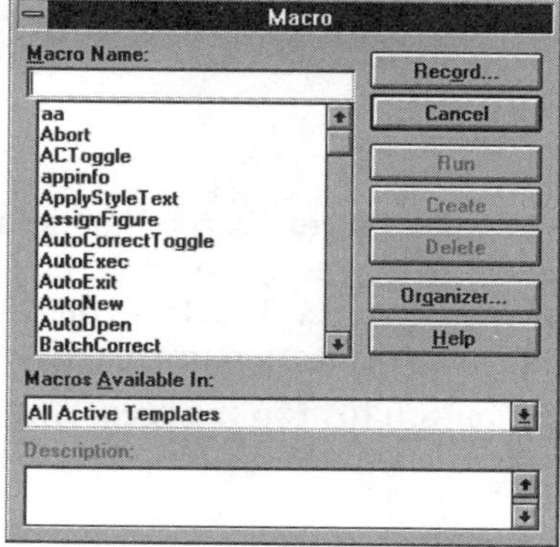

FIGURE 58.1.
The Macro dialog box.

2. Type a name for the macro in the **M**acro Name field (for example, `CastFormat`).
3. In Macros **A**vailable In, select the template where you want to save the macro.
4. Type a description of what the macro is supposed to do in the Descri**p**tion field (this may seem like a lot of bother right now, but two months from now, you may not have any idea what the macro was for—trust me).
5. Click Rec**o**rd. Word now displays the Record Macro dialog box shown in Figure 58.2. You can click Record, or, if desired, you can assign the macro to a key, tool, or menu at this time. Note: It's often useful to assign it to a key for testing purposes, and perhaps even to repeatedly use the identical key each time you write a new macro (see the note following this procedure). To assign a key, click the **K**eyboard tab, press the keystroke (for example, Alt+M, because it's not preassigned by Microsoft), then click Assign and then Close.

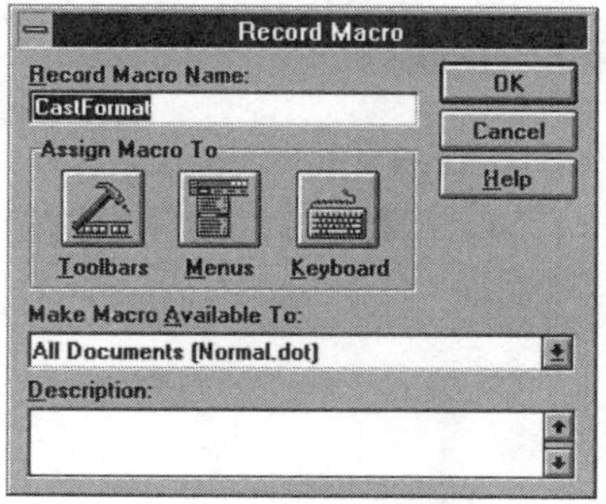

FIGURE 58.2.
The Record Macro dialog box.

6. Word now displays the Macro Record toolbar, as shown in Figure 58.3. Like other toolbars, you can glue the Macro Record toolbar to the top, bottom or sides of the Word window, or just let it float. Use the black button to Stop the recording, and use the red button to Pause.

FIGURE 58.3.
The Record Macro toolbar.

7. Perform your edits; be very careful to include at the end of your macro the steps necessary to correctly position the insertion point where you want it to be when the macro starts. This lets you run your macro successively without having to manually reposition the insertion point between executions.
8. Click the End button to stop the recording (this closes the macro from additional recording at the moment).

SUPER TIP

For easier testing when recording macros, pick a keystroke and use it as a "play last macro recorded" key. It's a big time saver. Alt+M is a good candidate, because it's unassigned by default. After recording a macro, you can immediately play it back by pressing that key.

SUPER TIP

You can jump directly to the Macro Record dialog box by double-clicking the REC button on the status bar, shown in Figure 58.4. The Macro Record dialog box also enables you to select the location for saving the macro. So, if you're going to record a macro, you can save a step by using the REC button. If the Status Bar is turned off, to display it, select Tools | Options, click View, then click Status bar and OK.

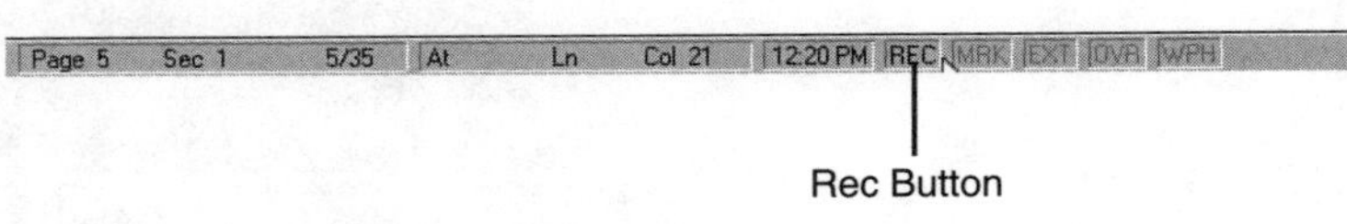

FIGURE 58.4.
Click the REC button to initiate the Record Macro dialog box.

Getting back to the Cast list, the macro I recorded (which applies the Cast style, underlines the name, turns off underlining, inserts a tab, and moves to the next line) produced the commands (Macro Statements) shown in the left column of Table 58.1.

Table 58.1. The CastAssign macro recorded by the macro recorder.

Macro Statement	*Recorded by*
Sub MAIN	Inserted automatically by the recorder
Style "Cast"	Ctrl+Shift+S followed by Enter
StartOfLine	Home key
EndOfLine 1	Shift+End key
Underline	Ctrl+U
EndOfLine	End key
ResetChar	Ctrl+Space
Insert Chr$(9)	Tab key
LineDown 1	Down key
End Sub	Inserted automatically by the recorder

Note that because you moved the cursor into the next line at the end of your macro, you can now immediately rerun the macro to format the next line. If you assigned a key to this macro, you can press it once for each remaining line.

SUPER TIP

When recording a macro, *don't* include the cursor positioning steps before the formatting or editing steps. Include them *after.* The way that macros are run, ideally, you'd like to run a macro, then see if it needs to be run again (that is, if there's another item on the list that needs to be formatted). That means that optimally, you should not have to mentally project where the cursor will be after it gets moved into position by the first few commands in the macro. Sometimes, cursor positioning can be tricky and uncertain. If you include the positioning commands at the end of your macro, you'll be able to see immediately whether or not you've reached the end of the text that needs the formatting or not. Consider, for example, what happens if the cursor-positioning logic uses EditFind instead of the cursor keys. If you have Edit | Find followed by some formatting or editing, then the formatting is applied *even if the Edit | Find was unsuccessful!* You can usually use Alt+Backspace (Undo) to recover, but it's better not to have to. A much better strategy is to make moving the cursor to the next location where the macro is needed *the last step* of the macro. That way, you can tell by looking whether or not rerunning the macro is wise.

Writing a Macro from Scratch

Another approach to writing user-created macros—one that is seldom employed in practice, by the way—is to write a macro from scratch. If there is any editing or cursor movement in the macro at all, you can almost always make it more accurate by recording the part you can, and then editing to add the parts that can't be recorded.

PROCEDURE 58.2. CREATING A MACRO FROM SCRATCH.

1. Select Tools | Macro to display the Macro dialog box.
2. Type a name for the macro in the Macro Name field.
3. Type a description of what the macro is supposed to do in the Description field.
4. Select the template where you want to store the macro using the Macros Available In drop-down list.
5. Click Create.

Word now displays the top and bottom lines of a standard macro (Sub MAIN and End Sub) in a macro window with the Macro toolbar displaying, as shown in Figure 58.5. The Macro toolbar tools and buttons are described in Table 58.2.

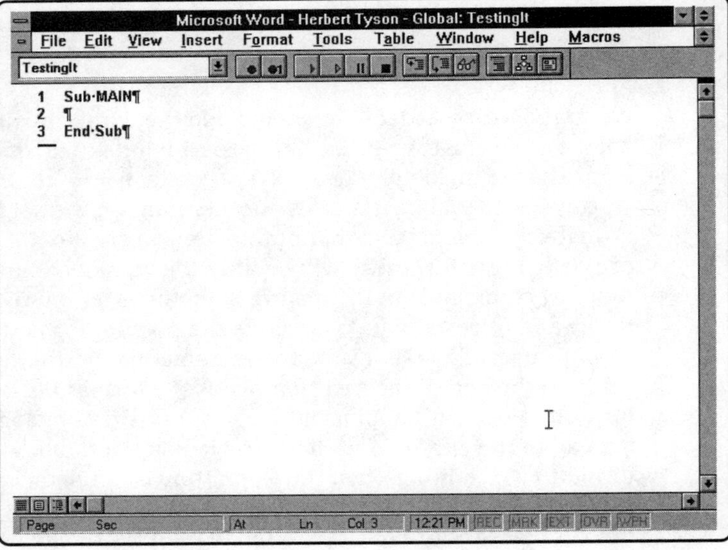

FIGURE 58.5.
When you create a macro, Word automatically supplies the top and bottom lines to get you started.

Table 58.2. The Macro toolbar

Tool	*Used For*
Macro	When multiple macros are being edited in different windows, use this drop-down list to select the macro you want to use
Record	Turns on the recorder. You can record additional commands into an existing macro
Record Next	Records the next command you perform
Start	Starts the macro, when a macro is open (Alt+Shift+S)
Trace	Starts the macro and highlights each command as it is executed (Alt+Shift+R)
Continue	Completes a macro that was paused or single-stepped; when you continue a single-stepped macro, it is run all at once, rather than continued in single-step mode (Alt+Shift+O)
Single Step	Single-steps a macro, running each step of any subroutines one at a time (Alt+Shift+E)
Single SUB	Runs the next step of a macro; subroutines are considered a single step (Alt+Shift+U)
Show Variables	Lists the user-defined variables in the selected macro (Alt+Shift+V)
REM	Adds or removes an REM (remark) at the beginning of the current line
Macro	Activates the Macro dialog box
Dialog Editor	Activates the Dialog Editor for creating user-customized dialog boxes

While a macro is being edited, the Macro toolbar is displayed and is visible in all open documents. This provides the ability to test and observe the macro on actual documents. Some macro commands—notably those that involve formatting—can't be run when a macro-editing window has the focus. Thus, being able to access a macro from nonmacro windows is a key to properly testing and debugging it.

Modifying Built-in Word Commands

A third way to create macros is to modify built-in Word commands. The fact that you can do this seems to elude a number of macro users, perhaps because the method is a little counter-intuitive. Intuitively, you might think that you need to select the Macros Available In source as Word, then choose the command, as shown in Figure 58.6, and then click Edit. As shown here, however, there is no Edit command! In fact, Word seems willing to let you *record* a macro that has the same name as built-in commands, but not to edit one.

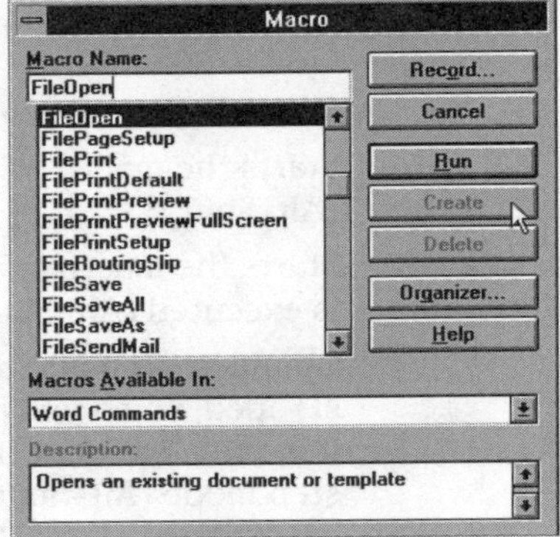

FIGURE 58.6.
At first glance, it looks as if Word won't let you edit built-in command names.

The trick is not to try to edit the built-in command. Instead, you create your own macro with the same name. When you have a macro by the same name, Word gives priority to your macro (except when you run the command from within a macro itself—more on this in a moment).

PROCEDURE 58.3. MODIFYING A BUILT-IN WORD COMMAND.

1. Select Tools | Macro.
2. In the Macros Available In list, select NORMAL.DOT or whatever other template you want to modify.
3. In the Macro Name field, type the name of the command you want to modify.
4. Click Create.

SUPER TIP

If you don't know the exact name of the command you want to edit, or if you prefer not to type it, you can select Word Commands in Step 2, then select the command you want to edit from the list of Word commands. After it's displayed in the Macro Name field, switch the Macros Available In setting back to the template you want to use and click Create. Done this way, you don't have to type the name of the command.

When you follow the procedure shown, Word displays a macro editing window, just as it does when you select Edit or Create for other macros. However, in this instance, Word offers the original built-in macro as the starting point—usually just a single command or the necessary code to initiate the corresponding dialog box. For example, when you try to create a macro called FileOpen, Word offers the following instead of just Sub MAIN and End Sub:

```
Sub MAIN
Dim dlg As EditFind
GetCurValues dlg
Dialog dlg
EditFind dlg
End Sub
```

This is the built-in dialog setup for the EditFind command—the same command that gets run when you press Ctrl+F or select **E**dit | **F**ind from the menu. An explanation of what's going on is shown in Table 58.3.

Table 58.3. Anatomy of the EditFind command.

Sub MAIN	*Beginning of the macro*
Dim dlg As EditFind	Declares dlg as EditFind, a dialog record (a variable used to store the results of a dialog box). The dlg name is completely arbitrary, and one that Word uses by default. If you prefer, you have Dim fred as EditFind, or Dim Search as EditFind
GetCurValues dlg	Gets the current settings for dlg (the Find What field, Match Case setting, search direction, and so forth). At this junction, for example, the current Find What field is now accessible as dlg.Find
Dialog dlg	Displays the dialog box, using the contents of the dlg record. During the dialog box session, the contents of the dlg record are changed by the user
EditFind dlg	Executes the EditFind using the new dlg results
End Sub	End of the macro

So, now's a good time to ask why you might want to do this. Why might you want to edit the EditFind command? Well, there are several reasons. For example, have you ever spent twenty minutes scratching your head because a search wasn't finding something you *knew* was there? And just when you're about to tear your hair out, you realize that you've been searching *up* instead of *down*. If you'd prefer that the search command always default to *down*, you can do it, with the following macro:

```
'EditFindDown: Modified EditFind that defaults to Down for search direction
Sub MAIN
On Error Goto Endit
Dim dlg As EditFind
GetCurValues dlg
dlg.Direction = 0
Dialog dlg
EditFind dlg
EndIt:
Select Case Err
Case 0, 102
Case Else : Error Err
End Select
End Sub
```

Note the addition of the line:

```
dlg.Direction=0
```

This line, which is set just before the dialog gets placed on screen, sets the direction to down. You can still change the direction to All or Up from the dialog box, as needed, but the initial default is always Down.

SUPER TIP

Note also the `On Error` error handling. When you convert a built-in command into a macro, the command no longer takes care of interruptions and errors. Thus, if a "home-made" EditFind macro gets interrupted with an Esc press, you normally would see the message box shown in Figure 58.7. To avoid this untidy message box, you need to tell Word what to do if it encounters an escape interruption (error 102). In this case, we've essentially said "Ignore it." If any other kind of error is encountered, however, Word displays the error message. `Error Err` displays the error message associated with Err, which can be any valid WordBASIC error code number. Error 102 corresponds to "Command Failed," which is the error you get when you press Esc while running a macro.

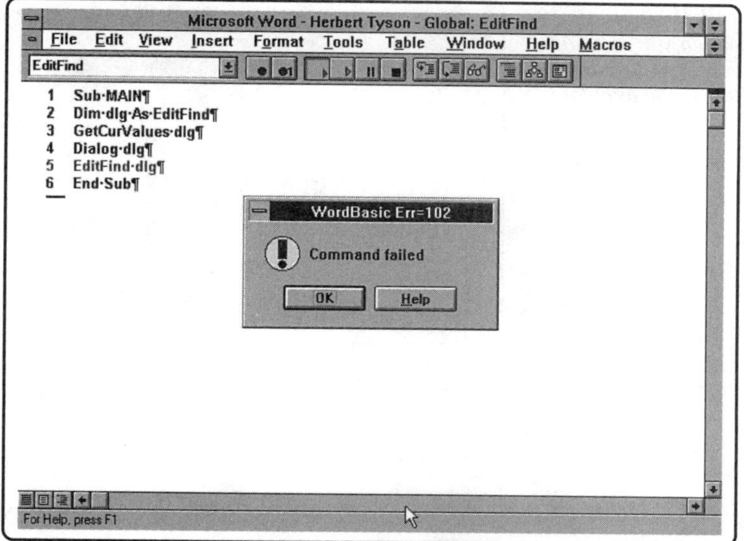

FIGURE 58.7.
To avoid this error message, you need to add error handling to some macros.

Saving

Macros, like AutoText, Menu, Toolbar, and Keyboard customizations, are stored in template files. In order to save macros, you must save the underlying template. In Word 6, the job of saving the template while editing a macro is considerably easier than it was under previous versions of Word. In previous versions, you had to edit your macro, and then say yes to the Save Changes prompt when you closed a macro. Even at that point, however, the actual template wasn't saved. It often wasn't until the last open document based on the template was closed that Word finally saved the template. In the case of NORMAL.DOT, the changes often weren't really secure until you exited from Word completely. This meant that you really had to go out of your way to do a Save All command from the file menu, lest you lose customization changes due to a GPF (general protection fault) or other problem.

In Word 6, however, saving the template when you're editing a macro is as easy as pressing Ctrl+S. Ordinarily, pressing Ctrl+S executes a **F**ile | **S**ave command. When a macro is in the current Word window, however, the file menu changes, and Ctrl+S now runs the Save Template command, as shown in Figure 58.8. So, anytime you're editing a macro and worry about losing your work, just press Ctrl+S.

FIGURE 58.8.
When you're editing a macro, Ctrl+S saves the template.

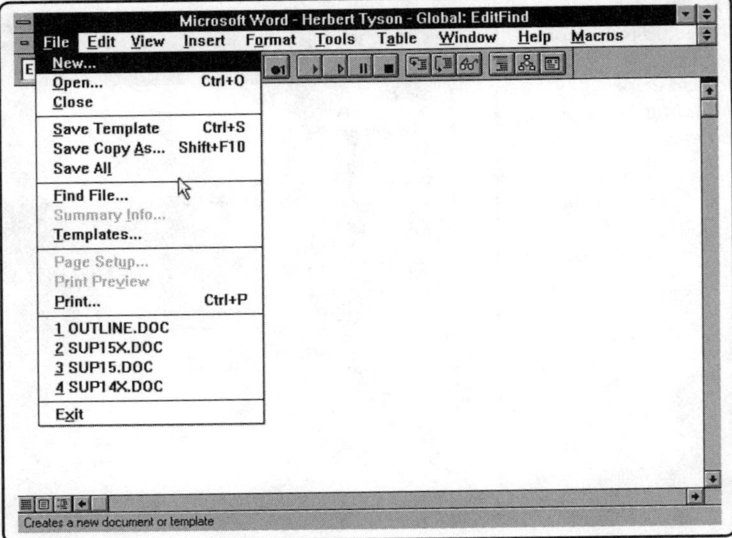

SUPER TIP

In fact, the Save Template command wouldn't be a bad command to have available all the time. It's also useful to be able to quickly save a template after making key, menu, toolbar, or AutoText changes. So, why not add the Save Template command to the menu, or give it a keystroke or a tool, or perhaps do several of these? See the appropriate customization chapter(s) for additional information (in the Customization Workshop).

PROCEDURE 58.4. ASSIGNING SAVE TEMPLATE TO A MENU AND TO A KEY.

1. Select **T**ools | **C**ustomize and click the **M**enus tab.
2. Under Save Changes In, select NORMAL.DOT.
3. Under **C**ategories, click File.
4. Under Change What Men**u**, &File should already be selected, because File is the first item on the main menu bar (unless you've changed it). Select File if it's not already selected.
5. Click in the Co**m**mands list and touch the letter s to move to and select the Save Template command, which is the only item in the list that begins with *s*.

6. Click in the **N**ame on Menu field, and move the `&` from the `s` to a unique letter not already in use on the File menu (m and l are the only two letters in `Save Template` that aren't already in use on the default File menu)—for example, `Save Te&mplate`.
7. Click **A**dd.
8. Click the **K**eyboard tab; note that the Save Template command remains selected.
9. Click in the Press **N**ew Shortcut Key, and press the key combination you want to assign. Note that because Ctrl+S is usually Save, Alt+S might be a logical destination for the Save Template command.
10. Click **A**ssign.
11. Click Close.

Now, if a document based on NORMAL.DOT is open, try your new assignment out. Select the File menu (Alt+F). The Save Template command should now be at the end of the second group, just after Save All, and should have the keystroke you assigned (for example, Alt+S) displayed beside it, as shown in Figure 58.9.

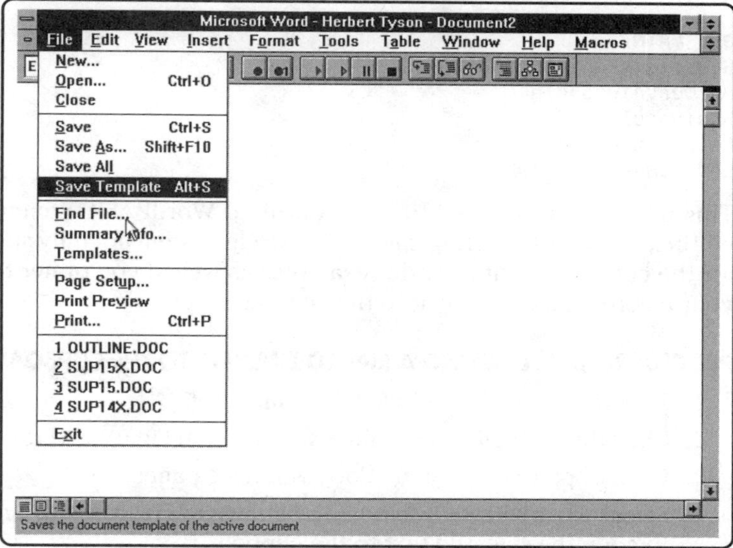

FIGURE 58.9.
When you add a command to a menu, the menu also displays any assigned keystroke.

Getting Help

When a macro is on-screen, you can obtain complete help for the WordBASIC command nearest the cursor by pressing the F1 key. For example, if you display the following macro (actually, the built-in FileOpen command), and press F1 with the cursor on the FileOpen command, Word displays the help panel shown in Figure 58.10:

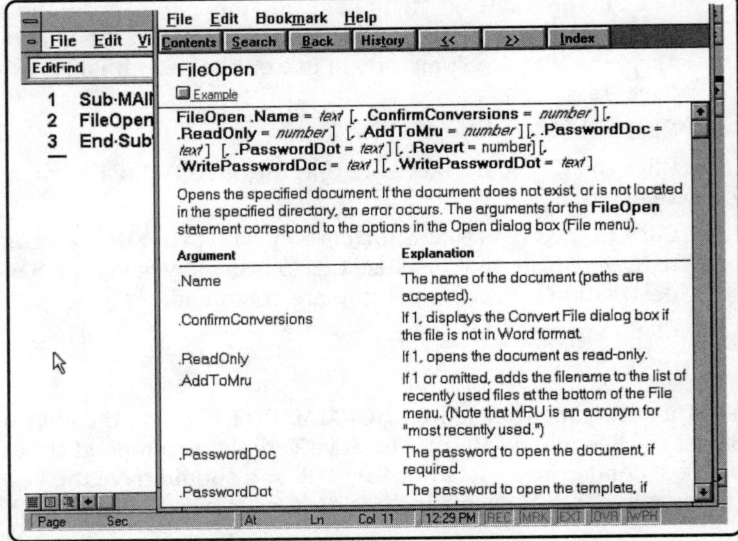

FIGURE 58.10. *Word provides a complete online WordBASIC reference.*

```
Sub MAIN
Dim dlg As FileOpen
GetCurValues dlg
Dialog dlg
FileOpen dlg
End Sub
```

This diminishes the need to have a printed WordBASIC command reference when editing, creating, or testing macros. The Help system not only shows complete syntax for the command, but provides examples as well. If you prefer to use the example in your macro, you can copy it to the clipboard.

PROCEDURE 58.5. COPYING A MACRO EXAMPLE TO THE CLIPBOARD.

1. Press F1 to display help for the command.
2. Click the highlighted Example, as shown in Figure 58.11.
3. Click Copy to display the Copy windows panel.
4. Select what you want to copy, as shown in Figure 58.12, and press Ctrl+Insert to copy the selected text to the clipboard.
5. You can now paste the text wherever you like.

FIGURE 58.11.
Click Example to see how to use a WordBASIC command.

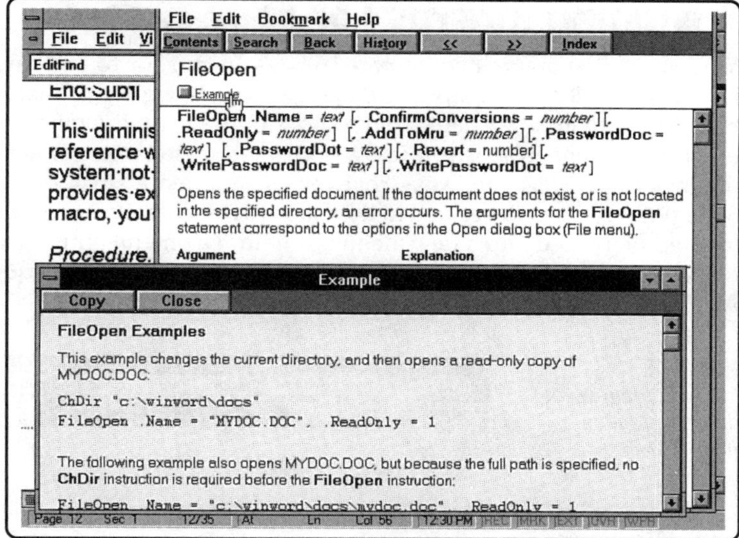

FIGURE 58.12.
You can select as much of the example as you like to use in your own macro.

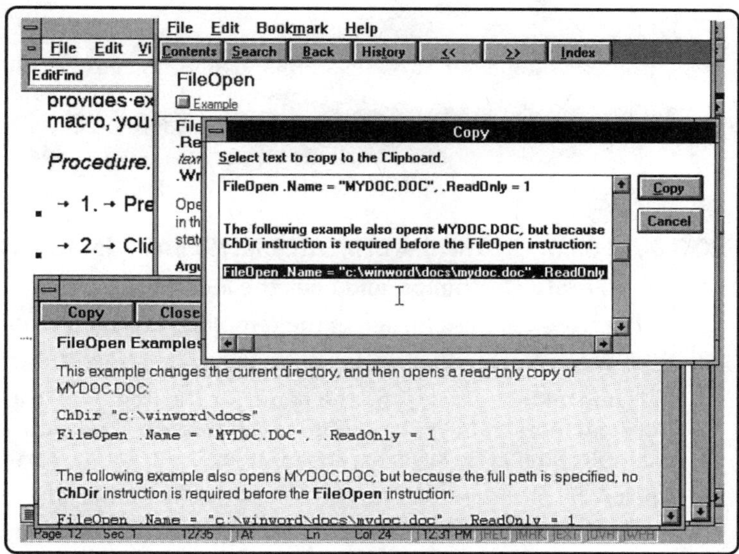

Assigning Macros For Easy Access

You can assign macros you create to keys, menus, or to toolbars, or all three, if you like, using the Tools | Customize dialog box, as shown in the Customization Workshop. One idea is to create a dedicated toolbar or menu on the menu bar, or both, for your most-needed macros. If you use a dedicated menu, you get added benefit in that it documents any assigned keystroke for you automatically. Consider, for example, the StringValue macro described in the Macro Projects session. As shown in Figure 58.13, it could be placed into a new menu bar item. The menu entry also displays the shortcut key. In this case, macros have been assigned a two-key sequence beginning with Alt+M.

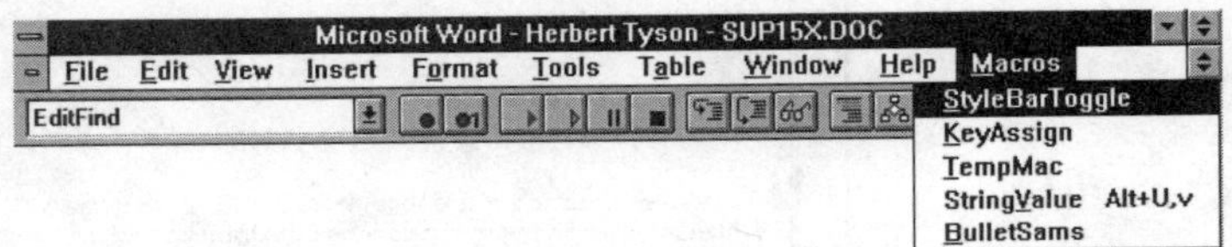

FIGURE 58.13.
You can create a dedicated menu just for your own macros, if you like.

SUPER NOTE

When you make templates global, using the File | Templates dialog box, the macros, AutoText, and customized commands from those templates are available everywhere, but customized menus, toolbars, styles, and keystrokes in global templates are *not* made available everywhere.

PROCEDURE 58.6. CREATING A DEDICATED MENU BAR ITEM FOR YOUR MACROS.

1. Select Tools | Customize, and click the Menus tab.
2. Under Save Changes In, select the template you want to change.
3. Click Menu Bar to display the Menu Bar dialog box, shown in Figure 58.14.
4. In Name on Menu Bar, type the name for the item you want to create, including an ampersand (&) just before the Alt+ access key you want to use—for example, `&Utility`, `&Macros`, `&User`, `&MyMacros`, and so forth.
5. Click Add, and then on Close, to close the Menu Bar dialog box, and to return to the Menus portion of the Customize dialog box, shown in Figure 58.15.
6. Under Change What Menu, select the menu you added in Step 4.
7. Under Categories, select Macros.
8. In the Macros list, select the macro you want to add to the new menu.

FIGURE 58.14.
The Menu Bar dialog box.

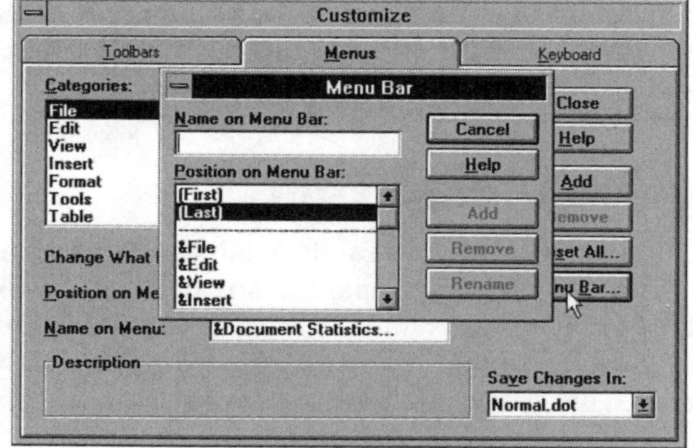

FIGURE 58.15.
The Menus tab in the Customize dialog box.

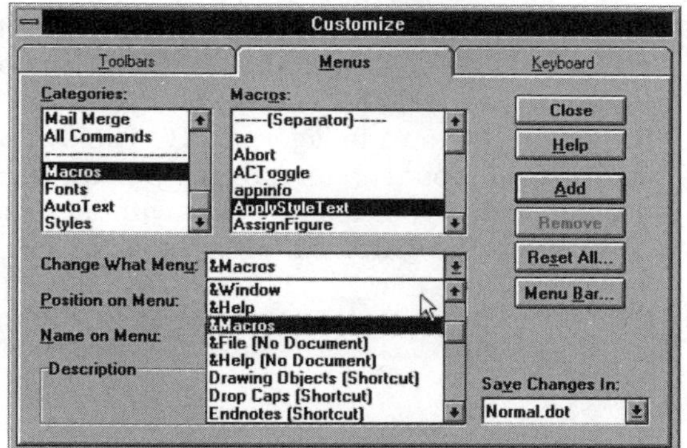

9. Under **P**osition on Menu, you can select (Auto), (At Top), (At Bottom), or a specific item below which to add the new item.
10. Under **N**ame on Menu, adjust the name of the macro, if necessary, placing the & in front of a unique and (hopefully) logical letter in the name.
11. Click **A**dd.
12. Repeat Steps 8 through 10 for any other macros you want to add.
13. Click Close when you're finished.
14. Don't forget to save the changes to the templates you modified!

You also can make this kind of arrangement template-specific. If you create a menu bar item called Macros, and add macros based on different templates, then the Macros menu displays a combination of macros assigned to the menu in NORMAL.DOT and in the active template. So, if your Macros menu gets three macros from NORMAL.DOT and two from LETTER.DOT, then the menu displays three macros when using a document based on NORMAL.DOT, and displays all five (3 + 2) macros when using a document based on LETTER.DOT. In this way, you can make your menus context-sensitive.

Using the Dialog Editor

A dialog box is a GUI (graphical user interface) tool for obtaining information from the users about choices, options, and so on. It's also a useful way to provide information to the user. Word uses hundreds of built-in dialog boxes to make using Word more intuitive. Word also enables you to create your own customized dialog boxes in your own macros. This gives your macros a professional polish and often makes them easier to use, as well.

One of the most important aids in building custom macros is the Dialog Editor. It's possible that you installed it, and never even noticed it. It's called MACROED.EXE (not to be confused with Mister Ed, the horse), and is located on your Word directory. When the Macro toolbar is active, you can use the rightmost button on the toolbar to display the dialog editor, shown in Figure 58.16. The dialog editor is used to construct, piece by piece, the components of a dialog box for use in a Word macro. While it's entirely possible to code your dialog boxes without using the macro editor, you'd be nuts to do it, because the dialog editor makes it so much simpler and so intuitive.

FIGURE 58.16.
Click here to activate the Dialog Editor.

PROCEDURE 58.7. USING THE DIALOG EDITOR TO BUILD A CUSTOM DIALOG BOX.

1. Open the macro to which you wish to add a custom dialog box.
2. Click the rightmost button on the Macro toolbar to display the Dialog Editor, shown in Figure 58.17.
3. Adjust the window size (by dragging the side and/or corners) to ensure that the window is large enough to accommodate the dialog box you want to create. You can adjust the size of the dialog box and the window as you go along.
4. To change the size or shape of the dialog box, move the mouse pointer over any side or corner, and drag it where you want it to go (using the left mouse button), as shown in Figure 58.18.
5. To insert an item into the dialog box, click Item and select the item you want to add; a full slate of items is shown in Figure 58.19.
6. When you add an item using a mouse, you can move it by dragging, or resize it by dragging a corner, as shown in Figure 58.20.

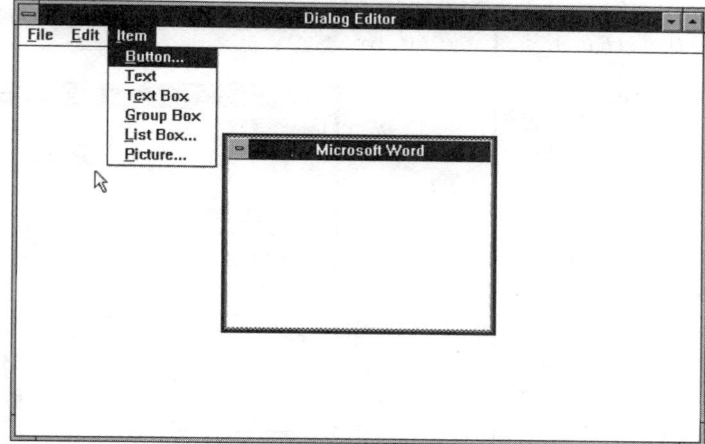

FIGURE 58.17.
The Dialog Editor provides a GUI way to create customized dialog boxes.

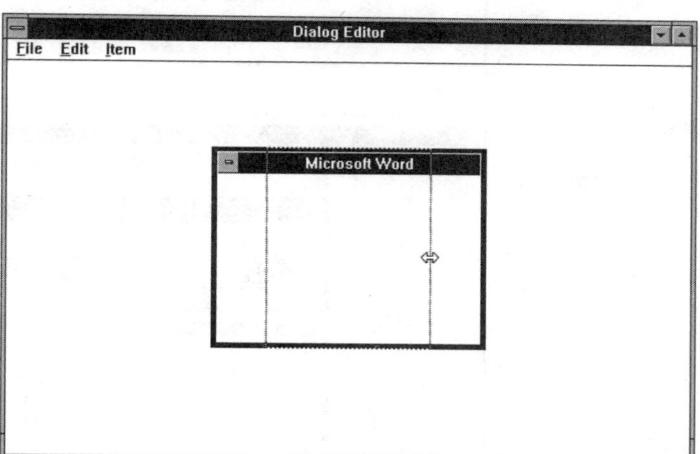

FIGURE 58.18.
Use the mouse to move or resize the dialog box.

7. To further specify an item, double-click it. For example, when you double-click a text item, Word displays the Text Information dialog box, shown in Figure 58.21. Filling in information here saves you a great deal of time later on, because you're able to make the dimensions correct (for example, make the text field wide enough to fit the text you actually want to use, as opposed to the starting dummy value *text*).

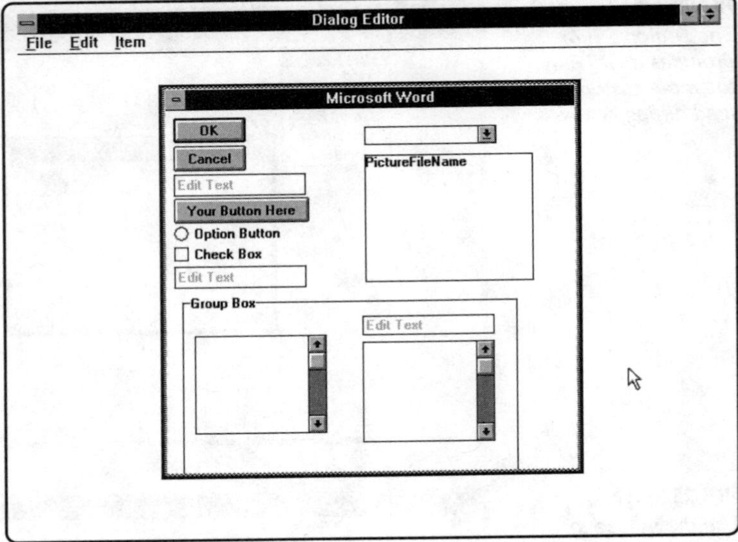

FIGURE 58.19.
The Dialog Editor lets you add a variety of elements.

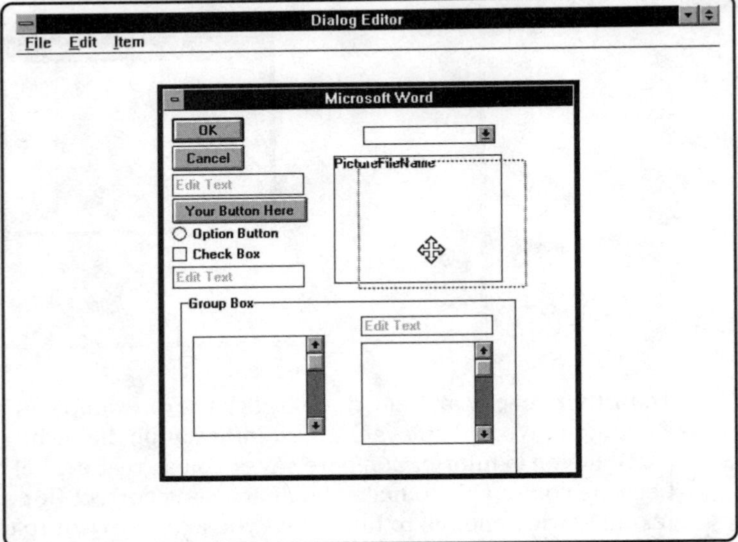

FIGURE 58.20.
Use the mouse to move or resize individual items.

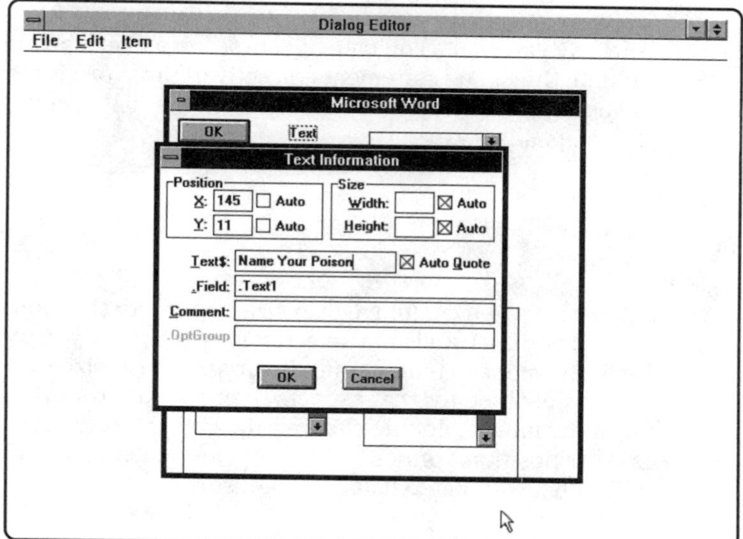

FIGURE 58.21.
Double-click an item to further specify the dialog setup.

8. You can use the dialog editor either to create a whole new dialog box or just to add elements to an existing dialog box. To add selected elements to an existing custom dialog box in a macro, insert the items you want to add, making an effort to position the new items exactly where you'll want them to appear in the existing dialog box, and then select **E**dit | Select **A**ll Items (or, if you've added a group, then select **E**dit | Select **G**roup). To create a whole new dialog box, select **E**dit | **S**elect Dialog.
9. Press Ctrl+Insert to copy the selection to the clipboard. The dialog editor does not copy the graphical image to the clipboard. Rather, it converts the dialog box you designed into the appropriate WordBASIC dialog command specification.
10. Press Ctrl+Esc and switch back to Word.
11. Press Shift+Insert to paste the dialog box specification into place.

SUPER NOTE

In Step 10, I elected to switch back to Word without closing the dialog editor. You could, if memory is in short supply, select **F**ile | **E**xit (no need to confirm copying the items to the clipboard, because you already did that in Step 9) to close the dialog editor and return to Word. The option is yours. If you have sufficient memory, however, it's often a good idea to leave the dialog editor open until you're sure everything is set up just the way you want. You can, of course, also tweak position and size by editing the dialog statements directly in the Word macro. Until you have a good feeling what to tweak, however, the dialog editor can be a good learning aid.

SUPER TIP

Step 6 says you can move or resize items with the mouse. However, that assumes that Auto is not selected for the aspect you want to change with the mouse. Items cannot be dragged or resized with a mouse while Auto is enabled for that aspect. To enable GUI dragging and resizing with the mouse, double-click, as shown in Step 7, and deselect the Auto size or position options. The aspect for which you deselect Auto can then be manipulated using the mouse.

After the dialog box statements are in place, you often still need to add additional supporting statements in the macro. For example, if the dialog box specifies a variable name for a list or other text, you need to make sure that the correct variable is defined earlier so that the dialog box can use it. Also, following the specification for a dialog box, you also need to dimension the dialog box as a UserDialog record so you can exercise the dialog box for collecting information from the user.

Changing the Way Macros Display

You cannot apply formatting in a macro you are editing. This makes many users think that they're stuck with the way macros display in the macro editing window. If so, they're wrong. Perhaps you've never noticed, but there's a special style called Macro Text for every template. This style is used to "format" the way macros display in a macro window. Only, you don't select the text in the macro window and apply the Macro Text style. In fact, you *can't* do that at all. Word just beeps at you. Instead, just change the Macro Text style by editing either the template directly or an ordinary document based on the template you want to change. When performing the following procedure, it helps if you open a macro for editing, and then use Windows | Arrange All to display both the template and a macro based on that template at the same time. Also, make sure the macro window is set to display in Normal view instead of draft.

PROCEDURE 58.8. CHANGING THE WAY MACROS DISPLAY IN A MACRO EDITING WINDOW.

1. Open the template whose macro display you want to change (this is the easiest way, I assure you).

2. Press Ctrl+Shift+S twice to activate the Style dialog box.
3. In the **L**ist section, select All Styles.
4. In the **S**tyles section, select Macro Text.
5. Click **M**odify.
6. Click **F**ormat, then select **F**ont, **P**aragraph, or any other formatting you'd like to be a part of the way your macros display while editing; click OK to close the Font, Paragraph, and so forth, formatting dialog boxes to return to the Modify dialog box.
7. Click OK to close the **M**odify dialog box.
8. Click Close to close the **S**tyle dialog box.

The settings most likely to affect the readability and utility of your Macro Text format are Font and Paragraph. A 10-point Arial and single-spaced lines (no paragraph spacing before or after) generally works well, providing a legible macro that displays an ample number of lines at the same time.

SUPER TIP

Have you ever wanted to be able to refer to parts of your macro by line number? If so, you can use the Macro Text style to display your macros with line numbers that don't affect the macro. In Step 6, above, select the Numbering format option to display the Bullets and Numbering dialog box, and click the Numbered tab. Select the numbering style you prefer (hint: you can use the Modify (Numbering) button to remove the display of the period if you like), and then click OK to return to the previous Modify (Style) dialog box.

SUPER

Sometimes, when editing from a macro window, the Draft and Normal options are dimmed as unavailable or are missing completely from the View menu. If so, you can still toggle between draft and nondraft view by assigning the built-in ViewDraft command to a key or button on a toolbar. I assigned this macro to a keystroke, and it serves me well all the time, not just when editing macros.

PROCEDURE 58.9. ASSIGNING VIEWDRAFT TO A TOOLBAR BUTTON.

1. Select **T**ools | **C**ustomize.
2. Click the **T**oolbars tab.

3. In the Categories list, click All Commands.
4. In the Commands list, select ViewDraft (tap the letter V to accelerate to the V's).
5. In the Save Changes In, select NORMAL.DOT.
6. Drag the ViewDraft command to a toolbar.
7. Click Assign to accept ViewDraft as the name, or if you see a button that you like, choose it and click assign.
8. Click Close.

Alternatively, you can assign it to a keystroke, as described in Chapter 47, "Customizing the Keyboard."

Chapter

59

Automatic Macros

Word reserves several macro names for particular contexts. Called *automatic* macros, these user-definable macros are automatically executed each time Word creates, opens, or closes a document, or each time Word itself starts or exits. These automatic macros are useful for automating documents, as well as making sure that housekeeping and setup tasks are performed the way you like. The AutoNew and AutoOpen macros are also key to the operation of the special Wizard templates that come with Word. You can use automatic macros to create your own Wizards, or just to automate repetitive tasks that you routinely perform by hand.

AutoExec

The AutoExec macro is executed each time you start Word for Windows. You can suppress AutoExec by holding down the Shift key when you start Word, or by including a `/m` switch after Word in the Command Line specification of a Program Properties setting for Word in the Program Manager, as shown in Figure 59.1.

FIGURE 59.1.
Include a `/m` *switch in the Properties setting to prevent AutoExec from running when Word starts.*

Program Item Properties		
Description:	Microsoft Word	OK
Command Line:	:\WORD6\WINWORD.EXE /m	Cancel
Working Directory:	F:\WORD6	Browse...
Shortcut Key:	Ctrl + Shift + Alt + W	Change Icon...
	Run Minimized	Help

SUPER TIP

In addition to specifying `/m` to disable AutoExec, you can use it to specify a different startup macro (or built-in Word command) when Word starts, or even a series of macros. For example, starting Word with `winword.exe /mfile1 /mfile2 /mfile3 /mfile4 /mfile5 /mfile6 /mfile7 /mfile8 /mfile9 /mautoexec` would run the built-in commands `File1` through `File9`—loading the last nine files that Word opened—and then run the AutoExec macro. You can also intersperse filenames and macros on the Word command line if you need to automate tasks, or you can simply have your macros load the necessary files (which probably gives you more leverage, since changing program item properties is a bit of a pain). To intersperse files and macros, just include the filename references (including disk and directory if the file(s) aren't on the default Word directory) wherever you want them opened in the sequence of events. For example, `winword.exe d:\letters\sales.doc \mstartmerge` might initiate a data merge of some kind.

AutoExec macros are blank by default—until you put something in them. They're great for setting Word up just the way you want, including setting the view, opening files, starting Find File, or even using a macro or system profile variable for going to the last-used directory. For example, an AutoExec that automates several actions that many users routinely perform each time they start Word is shown and described in Table 59.1.

Table 59.1. A sample AutoExec Macro, executed each time you open Word.

WordBASIC Command	*Purpose*
`Sub MAIN`	Start of macro
`AppMaximize 1`	Maximize the Word window
`File1`	Open the last file I previously opened
`ViewNormal`	Set the view to Normal
`End Sub`	End of macro

SUPER NOTE

Some automatic macros are template-specific, while two—AutoExec and AutoExit—have an effect only if stored in NORMAL.DOT. When you create an AutoExec macro, make sure you set the Macros Available In line in the Macro dialog box to NORMAL.DOT.

SUPER TIP

Automatic macros invariably exist to replace steps or actions you usually perform one at a time, by hand. The next time you start Word, get ready to exit, open a document, close a document, or create a new document, turn on the macro recorder. In this session, most of the sample automatic macros were created precisely in this way. Just supply the appropriate Auto*name* and record what you do. Nothing could be simpler. Thereafter, each time you work on a specific document, you'll get precisely the kind of setup or close-up you need. If your needs change, then record a new automatic macro and replace the old one.

AutoExit

An AutoExit macro is the flip side of an AutoExec macro. While AutoExec is executed each time Word starts, AutoExit is executed each time Word exits, as the name suggests. Like AutoExec, AutoExit also only has an effect if stored in NORMAL.DOT.

If you have any housekeeping chores that need to be performed each time you close Word, an AutoExit macro might be just the ticket. A rather simple use that I personally use is to set my Word DOC-PATH setting (in WIN.INI) to the last directory I was on when I quit Word. This lets me pick up where I was more easily. That AutoExit macro is shown and explained in Table 59.2.

Table 59.2. A sample AutoExit macro, executed each time you exit from Word.

WordBASIC Command	*Purpose*
`Sub MAIN`	Start of Macro
`CurDir$ = Files$(".")`	Stores the current directory as `CurDir$`
`SetProfileString("Doc-Path", CurDir$)`	Sets the Profile Variable in WIN.INI to `CurDir$`
`End Sub`	End of Macro

AutoOpen

The AutoOpen macro is executed each time that an exiting document based on the host template is opened, or each time the template itself is opened. This is ideal for selectively updating fields and links, as well as turning on-screen aids, such as toolbars, that you need while editing particular documents.

Suppose, for example, that you have a file that contains many graphics, and you get tired of having to turn on the drawing tools each time and switch the document into Page Layout view. You could use an AutoOpen macro to perform those chores for you each time the document is opened, as shown in Table 59.3.

Table 59.3. A sample AutoOpen macro, executed each time you open a file based on the template.

WordBASIC Command	*Purpose*
`Sub MAIN`	Start of Macro
`ViewPage`	Sets the view to Page Layout

WordBASIC Command	*Purpose*
`ViewToolbars .ColorButtons = 1, .LargeButtons = 0, .ToolTips = 1`	Sets buttons to be colored small, and to display name of the button below the button when the mouse is over it. See Figure 59.2. (Note: This option is not available from the menu version of the **View|Toolbars** command.)
`ViewToolbars .Toolbar = "Borders", .Show`	Turns on the Borders toolbar
`ViewToolbars .Toolbar = "Drawing", .Show`	Turns on the Drawing toolbar
`End Sub`	

FIGURE 59.2.
The ToolTips setting lets you display the button name when the mouse is over a button.

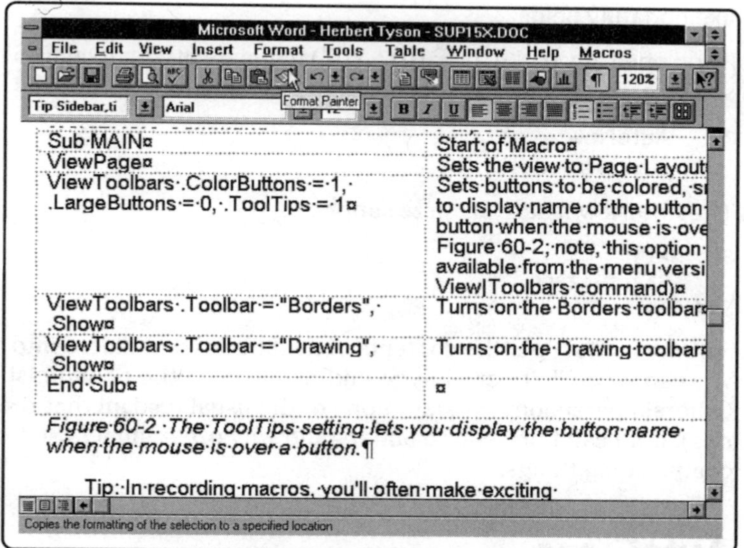

SUPER TIP

In recording macros, you'll often make exciting discoveries about Word's commands. The ViewToolbars command, for example, has a neat option that displays the name of a tool button when you move the mouse over it (except for buttons that use text instead of button images).

AutoNew

The AutoNew automatic macro is the darling of the Wizard. AutoNew macros are executed each time you create a new document based on a specific template. In prior versions of Word for Windows, AutoNew macros were popular ways to set up letters, prompting for addresses, inserting dates, and inserting salutations and signature lines. Use AutoNew macros to perform a one-time setup that doesn't need to be performed again after the document exists. On the other hand, you might use AutoOpen macros to perform maintenance tasks that need to be performed after the document exists, like updating fields.

If you open any of the .Wizard (*.WIZ) template files that come with Word, you'll often see at least two macros specific to that template:

AutoNew
StartWizard

The AutoNew macro is, quite simply:

```
Sub MAIN
    StartWizard
End Sub
```

So, why not just put the contents of the StartWizard macro into the AutoNew macro? Who knows? That certainly would conform to the Economist's Law of Parsimony (wherein parsimony conveys none of the usual disdain that the term ordinarily carries). But I can't pretend to understand why programmers sometimes insist on overcomplicating things.

AutoClose

The AutoClose macro is the flip side of the AutoOpen macro, and gets run each time a document based on the owning template gets closed. AutoClose macros typically are used to perform cleanup operations that are specific to a file. For example, in the discussion of AutoOpen macros, I mentioned that you might want to turn on specific toolbars when opening a particular document. Being the neat and tidy sort, you might also want to turn them off when you close the document. The sample macro shown in Table 59.4 "turns off the lights," so to speak, when leaving a document that contained the AutoOpen macro shown in Table 59.3.

Table 59.4. A sample AutoClose macro that turns off tools that aren't needed anymore.

WordBASIC Command	*Purpose*
`Sub MAIN`	Start of Macro
`ViewNormal`	Sets the view to normal
`ViewToolbars .ToolTips = 0`	Turns off ToolTips because the feature actually slows down using tools, and really isn't need much except when using unfamiliar toolbars
`ViewToolbars .Toolbar = "Borders", .Hide`	Turns off the Borders toolbar
`ViewToolbars .Toolbar = "Drawing", .Hide`	Turns off the Drawing toolbar
`End Sub`	

Chapter

60

Macro Projects

In the Macro Projects session, you'll find a collection of 20 or so macros that I've found useful in writing this book as well as in using Word in general. The purpose for providing them is twofold. First, macro writing is a learn-by-doing and learn-by-watching venture. These macros, along with information about the logic behind some aspects of them, should help you begin to see just how useful and easy writing macros can be.

Second, I hope some of these macros can be not just learning tools, but actual working tools for you. For example, the WindowSplit macro is something I use every day. It lets me instantly divide any two windows horizontally or vertically, without having to do a lot of border dragging. The JustDoIt macros enable me to record one-time macros on the fly, without having to navigate a twisty maze of dialog boxes. And, when you have a growing collection of macros, you'll be happy to know that MultiMacroSearch is there to help you find something you lost.

Why We Sometimes Show the Code, and Other Times Not

Some of the macros presented in this session are very short; others are fairly long. Even though all the macros are available on the Super Book diskette, I'm showing the text of some of the macros in the book as well to better explain the logic and techniques needed to overcome occasional problems with WordBASIC.

Using the Macros on This Super Book Disk

The macros described in this session are on the Super Book disk in the SUPRBOOK.DOT template. In addition, there's SuperBook toolbar with these macros already installed, and ready to go. To try them out, just create a test document based on SUPRBOOK.DOT, and give 'em a whirl.

Copying the SuperBook Macros to Another Template

If you see something you like, Word lets you easily copy it to your own NORMAL.DOT or other template. If you haven't already installed the Super Book diskette to your hard disk, then do so before starting this procedure.

PROCEDURE 60.1. COPYING SUPRBOOK.DOT MACROS TO ANOTHER TEMPLATE.

1. Open the SUPRBOOK.DOT template (**F**ile | **O**pen, set List Files of Type to *.DOT, and navigate to the location of SUPRBOOK.DOT).
2. Select **F**ile | **T**emplates, and click **O**rganizer (or click the Organizer button on the Super Book Toolbar); Word displays the Organizer dialog box with the SUPRBOOK.DOT template in the left-hand list, as shown in Figure 60.1.

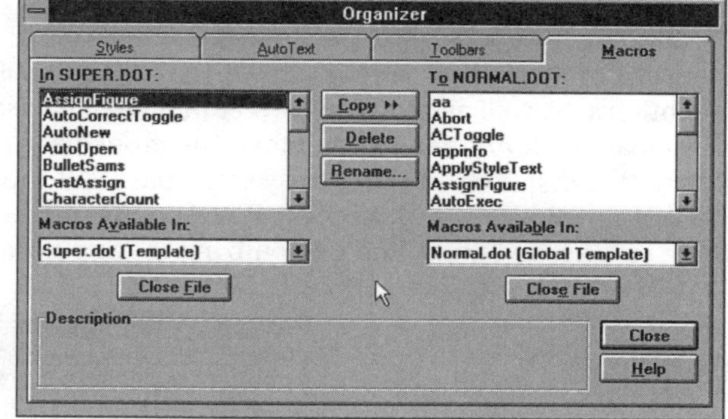

FIGURE 60.1.
Use the Organizer to copy macros from the SUPRBOOK.DOT template to your own templates.

3. Click the **M**acros tab.
4. In the right-hand Macros Availa**b**le In list, select the template to which you want to copy SUPRBOOK.DOT macros; if the template you want to use is not on the list, then click Clo**s**e File (on the right side), and then on the same button when it becomes an Op**e**n File button. Use the dialog box controls to navigate to the template you want, and open it.
5. In the left-hand Macros A**v**ailable In list, use the mouse to select the first macro you want to copy.
6. Press the Ctrl key, and click each additional macro you want to copy.
7. When you've selected all the macros you want to copy, click Copy.
8. If you want to copy the SuperBook toolbar, you can copy it too. Click the **T**oolbars tab, then click the SuperBook toolbar, as shown in Figure 60.2; then click Copy.

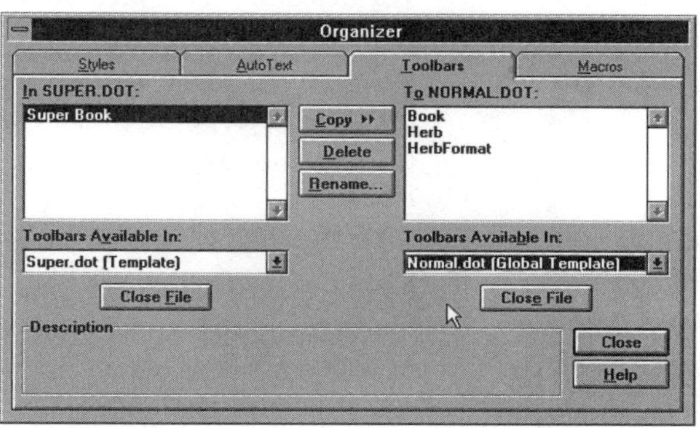

FIGURE 60.2.
You can copy the whole SuperBook toolbar if you like.

9. Click the Close button at the bottom right; if Word prompts to save changes in your template, click Yes to confirm.

The SuperBook Toolbar

The SuperBook toolbar, shown in Figure 60.3, is a collection of macros from this chapter and a few others, as well as built-in Word commands, all assigned to text buttons for easy identification. Note that as you move the mouse across the toolbar, additional explanatory text displays on the Word status bar. The tools are described in Table 60.1. The additional buttons that access Word commands were placed on the toolbar to facilitate testing, installing, and customizing the Super Book macros for your work.

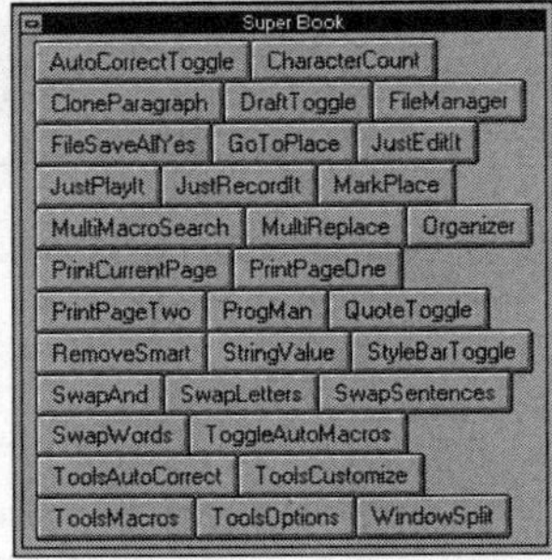

FIGURE 60.3.
The SuperBook toolbar.

Table 60.1. The SuperBook toolbar.

Button	*Purpose*
AutoCorrectToggle	Toggles AutoCorrect's text replace mode on and off
Character Count	Counts the number of characters in a selection
Clone Paragraph	Makes a copy of the current paragraph
DraftToggle	Toggles draft mode on and off
FileManage	Activates the Windows File Manager
FileSaveAllYes	Saves all open files, automatically saying YES to any prompts (except for unnamed files)
GotoPlace	Goes to one of ten bookmarks set by the Mark Place macro
JustEditIt	Edits the JustDoIt macro
JustPlayIt	Runs the JustDoIt macro
JustRecordIt	Starts recording a temporary macro called JustDoIt
MarkPlace	Inserts one of ten temporary bookmarks
MultiMacroSearch	Searches through multiple macros for matching text
MultiReplace	Replaces Find text with a choice of three replacements
Organizer	Activates the Organizer dialog box

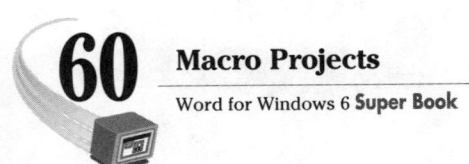

Button	Purpose
PrintCurrentPage	Prints just the current page
PrintPageOne	Prints just page one of the current document
PrintPageTwo	Prints just page two of the current document
ProgMan	Activates the Windows Program Manager
QuoteToggle	Toggles Smart Quotes off and on (for texting the RemoveSmart macro)
Remove Smart	Converts "Smart Quotes" back into dumb quotes
StringValue	Displays the character codes of a selection
StyleBarToggle	Toggles a 1/2" style area width on and off
SwapAnd	Swaps [this] and [that]
SwapLetters	Swaps the two letters on either side of the cursor
SwapWords	Swaps the current and previous word
SwapSentences	Swaps the current and previous sentences
ToggleAutoMacros	Toggles automatic macro execution off and on
ToolsAutoCorrect	Displays the AutoCorrect dialog box
ToolCustomize	Displays the tabbed Customize dialog box for customizing menus, keys, and toolbars
ToolMacros	Displays the Macro dialog box
ToolsOptions	Displays the main Options tabbed dialog
WindowSplit	Enables you to select any two Word windows to be horizontally or vertically split

Three One-Line Macros to Make Macros Made Easier

One thing that frustrates many in using Word's macro recorder is how much setup is involved just to record a simple one-time, *save-a-little-work, just-record-it-and-play-it-back-without-asking-me-a-lot-of-silly-questions* macro. When you have to go through multiple steps to record and play back a macro, it makes doing it so tedious, that you don't bother using the recorder for those on-the-fly formatting tasks.

The solution I use is to create a permanent temporary macro, called JustDoIt. When I press Alt+J,R (Alt+J followed by R), a macro called JustRecordIt, shown in Table 60.2, snaps into action and does the initial setup for recording a JustDoIt macro. This starts the macro recorder for me, saving it into NORMAL.DOT, and I don't have to answer a bunch of stupid questions.

Table 60.2. JustRecordIt.

WordBASIC Command	*Purpose*
`Sub MAIN`	Macro Start
`SendKeys "%rJustDoIt{Enter}%Y"`	Equivalent to pressing Alt+R, typing `JustDoIt`, pressing Enter, and then pressing Alt+Y.
`End Sub`	Macro End

One problem, however, is a quirk in the way that Word 6 records macros. In order to do this trick, you *must* be able to run the built-in ToolsRecordMacroToggle command from a keystroke. Since Alt+R is unassigned by default, I use it. If you choose to use this approach for recording macros, you must either assign ToolsRecordMacroToggle to Alt+R, or assign it to something different and then modify the JustRecordIt macro to reflect the difference. It helps if you speak SendKeys-ese:

`%r`	Alt+R
`%R`	Alt+Shift+R
`^r`	Ctrl+R
`^R`	Ctrl+Shift+R
`%^R`	Ctrl+Alt+Shift+R

Of course, you needn't use `R` at all. However, you must use *some* key for this to work, and you have to replace `%r` in the JustRecordIt macro with your alternative. For additional information on the "wonders" of SendKeys, type `SendKeys` in a macro-editing window and press F1, as shown in Figure 60.4.

When I'm done recording, I just press Alt+R (which I've assigned to ToolsRecordMacroToggle), or click the Stop button (see Figure 60.5) on the Macro Recording toolbar, to stop the recorder. To play it back, I just press Alt+J,P (Alt+J, followed by P). This runs a macro called JustPlayIt, and it runs the JustDoIt macro:

```
Sub MAIN
ToolsMacro .Name = "JustDoIt", .Run, .Show = 1
End Sub
```

By doing it this way, by the way, I don't incur the additional complexity of having to assign a keystroke to the newly-created JustDoIt macro each time I record it. This makes recording and playing back on-the-fly macros a breeze.

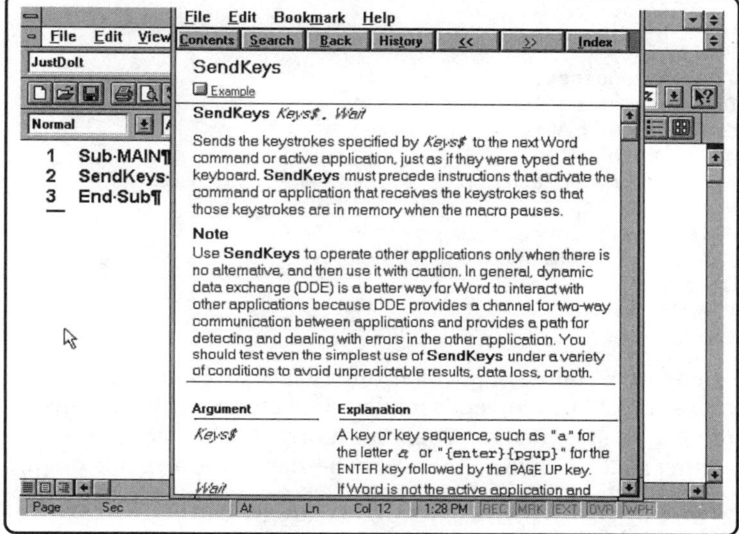

FIGURE 60.4.
SendKeys needs all the help it can get!

FIGURE 60.5.
Click the Stop button to end a recording.

When I want to edit the JustDoIt macro—just in case I want to see what it looks like, or if the whole reason for recording it was to try to learn the syntax for a command—I just press Alt+J,E (Alt+J, followed by E), which runs JustEditIt:

```
Sub MAIN
ToolsMacro .Name = "JustDoIt", .Edit, .Show = 1
End Sub
```

Unfortunately, unlike in previous versions of Word for Windows, Word 6 makes it pretty tedious to rename macros.

AutoCorrectToggle

Have you ever gotten into a situation where you needed to turn AutoCorrect off for a while? I do, on occasion. So, I quickly wrote a macro to toggle AutoCorrect on and off. Some toggles are fairly simple to write—or don't even have to be written as macros—because Word provides a simple two-state toggle (like ViewDraft). AutoCorrect could be equally simple, using just the built-in ToolsAutoCorrectReplaceText command, but I decided to "complicate" it a little in order to demonstrate a problem (as well as a solution) with the Word Print command. Showing the code also provides an opportunity to demonstrate how to obtain information from a dialog box.

AutoCorrectToggle

```
Sub MAIN
ToolsAutoCorrectReplaceText
Dim AutoCor As ToolsAutoCorrect
GetCurValues AutoCor
A$ = "Enabled"
If AutoCor.ReplaceText = 0 Then A$ = "Disabled"
ViewStatusBar 0
Print "Auto Correct is now " + A$
For i = 1 To 1000
Next i
ViewStatusBar 1
End Sub
```

There are a couple of peculiar things about this macro. It begins by toggling the current state of AutoCorrect's Replace text mode, then it dimensions AutoCor as a dialog record, as specified by ToolsAutoCorrect. This lets the macro obtain the resulting setting so it can inform the user whether AutoCorrect is on or off.

Second, notice the `For...Next` loop that goes from 1 to 1000, just after printing the toggle's current state. A peculiarity about Word in this instance is that macros sometimes don't display the result of a Print command long enough on the status bar. In this case, for example, the result is cleared just as soon as it is displayed. By using the `For...Next` loop, we keep the Print result on the status bar for just a few seconds. Without it, the Print result is not visible at all.

SUPER TIP

If you want to suppress just a single automatic replacement (for example, for typing an uncommon abbreviation) when using AutoCorrect's replace-text mode feature, you don't need to toggle AutoCorrect off. Just type the abbreviation and let Word expand it. Immediately press Alt+Backspace or Alt+Z (Undo), and Word will undo the replacement, allowing you to keep on typing without having to toggle automatic replacement off.

CharacterCount

Sometimes you need to know how many characters are in the text of a selection. Perhaps you're preparing a text entry that must not exceed 32, 40, or 255 characters in length. Or, perhaps you're designing a database field entry and need to know how many spaces to allow for a particular phrase. If you select some text and then chose **T**ools | **W**ord Count, Word gladly tells you the number of "characters" in a selection or in the text of a Word document. However, Word omits from the count nonprinting

characters such as spaces, tabs, paragraph marks, and line endings. As shown in Figure 60.6, for example, the Word Count command tells you that the phrase *Cat and Mouse*, which has 11 letters and 2 spaces, is 11 characters. That might be useful in some contexts, but certainly not when you need to know the actual physical monospaced width of text.

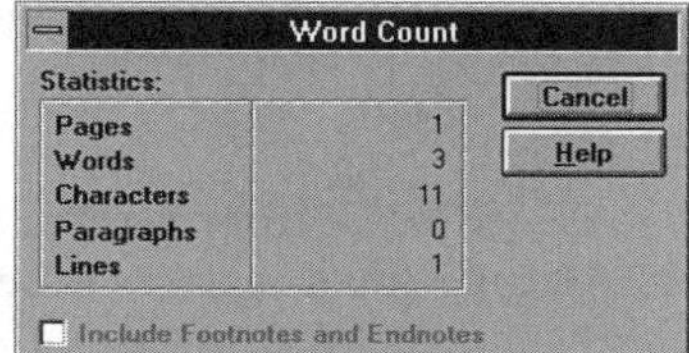

FIGURE 60.6.
Word's own Word Count command doesn't count nonprinting characters.

The CharacterCount macro, as shown in Figure 60.7, correctly reveals that there are 13 characters in the Cat and Mouse phrase. The macro works by using a WordBASIC LEN function to count the number of physical characters in a text string:

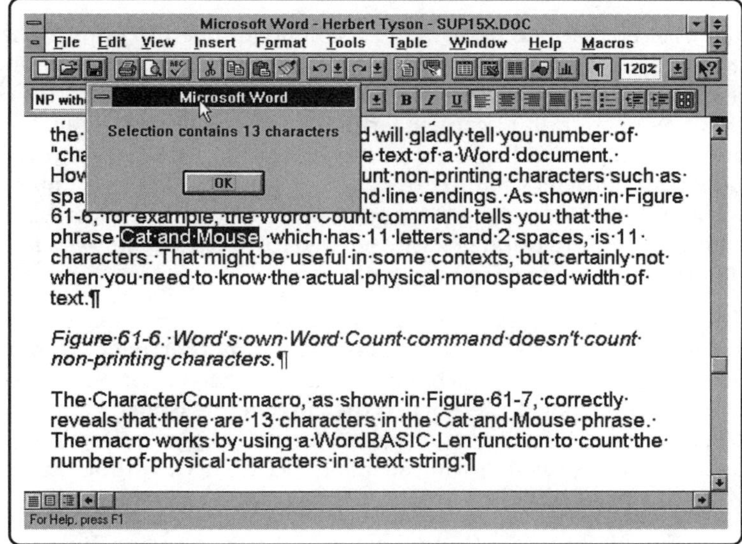

FIGURE 60.7.
Character Count tells you how much space your text actually occupies.

```
Sub MAIN
Length = Len(Selection$())
If Length = 1 Then end$ = "" Else end$ = "s"
MsgBox "Selection contains" + Str$(Length) + " character" + end$
End Sub
```

There are a couple of things you should know about characters in Word. First, while a paragraph mark often is a combination of carriage return (ASCII 13) and line feed (ASCII 10) characters in some applications, in Word it's just a plain 13 characters, so the LEN function counts a paragraph mark produced by Word as only a single character. If you import a file created by a different application, however, you might discover that some of the paragraph marks in the imported text actually contain two characters. For example, when you import a XyWrite document, all of the paragraph marks consume two, instead of one, characters. This isn't necessarily a problem, but rather is something you should be aware of in case the difference matters for your purposes.

Another thing to be aware of is the treatment of Word fields. If a field code is included in the selection, the LEN function's result is different depending on whether the field code or field code result is displayed. For example, CharacterCount counts `{DATE}` as six characters when displayed as a field code, and as 18 characters when displayed as September 17, 1994. Word's Word Count command always counts the displayed length, minus any nonprinting characters (16 characters in this instance).

CloneParagraph

Very often, when composing text, you might need to copy a heading line or a paragraph to use as a starting point for another heading or paragraph. This is particularly useful if an existing line or paragraph contains an unusual pattern of formatting or text that you need to duplicate. In writing this book, for example, I use a lot of Heading 3 and Heading 4 headings, but each must begin with `(c)` or `(d)`, respectively, for my publisher . When I want to create a new one, I could press Enter and style it as Heading 3 or 4, and then add `(c)` or `(4)`. But that's too much work. Early on, I found that a simple CloneParagraph macro, assigned to Alt+C (for me—you might prefer something different), saved me a fair amount of work.

The CloneParagraph macro uses a couple of simple but interesting techniques to ensure the macro works during the creation of another macro (I sometimes need to clone lines there also) as well as to ensure that the current paragraph is cloned, rather than the preceding one. Except when the current line is just a blank paragraph mark (you can duplicate a blank paragraph mark simply by pressing Enter, for which you don't need a macro), the following seems to do the trick without fail:

```
Sub MAIN         Start of Macro
EndOfLine        Go to the end of the current line, but go no further
ParaUp 1         Go to the beginning of the current paragraph
ParaDown 1, 1    Select to the end of the current paragraph
EditCopy         Copy the selection to the clipboard
CharLeft 1       Deselect, putting the cursor at the beginning of the selection
EditPaste        Paste the contents of the clipboard
End Sub          End of Macro
```

There is no single WordBASIC command for selecting a paragraph that works in a macro. In a normal Word document, you could use EditGoto "\Para". However, EditGoto doesn't work in a macro editing window because bookmarks aren't allowed there. So, the next best bet is the ParaUp command, which sends the cursor to the top of the current paragraph. However, if the cursor is already at the beginning of a paragraph, ParaUp goes to the beginning of the *preceding* paragraph. So, something was needed to ensure that the cursor was inside the current paragraph, rather than at the very beginning. The EndOfLine and StartOfLine commands (the Home and End keys, respectively) turn out to be perfect tools for sending the cursor to the end or beginning of a line, but no further. Thus, the combination:

```
EndOfLine
ParaUp 1
```

is a guaranteed way to get to the beginning of the current paragraph *except* when the current paragraph is blank, as noted previously.

FileManager

Some tasks, like copying a file to a floppy disk, take impossibly long using Word's built-in resources. For that reason—among others—it's often useful to be able to quickly access the Windows File Manager. A simple macro provides quick access, which I made even more convenient by using a button on a toolbar. The macro provides an opportunity to demonstrate a simple way that you can access almost any Windows program that's available from the Program Manager (which is itself another easy macro you'll see later). The FileManager macro, quite simply is:

```
Sub MAIN
Shell "WinFile"
End Sub
```

To save you the extensive chore of keying this macro in manually, it's provided for you on the SuperBook diskette.

Notice that the FileManager macro uses the Shell command. The Shell command provides access to both DOS and Windows programs—files that have a registered association in Windows (such as .DOC, .XLS, and .MDB) as well as batch files. If the program is on the default Windows directory, or is in your DOS path, you can access it directly using Shell without having to specify the disk and path. Even if it is in your path, however, when writing macros that will be used only on your own system (that is, if they don't have to be generic enough to run anywhere else), you usually can speed up their execution by including the whole path anyway. That way, Word doesn't have to search through the path levels to find a matching command. Moreover, on those rare occasions when there are two commands by the same name, you don't run the risk of executing the wrong command.

FileSaveAllYes

One annoying thing about Word—at times—is all those darned Yes and No prompts. I sure wish they'd replace all those OK buttons with a simple, ubiquitous **Yes** that could universally be accessed using Alt+Y. However, I digress (as they say). One way to avoid all those prompts—particularly when you're sure you want to save everything in sight— is to do a preemptive save, wherein you tell Word *a priori* that the answer is *Yes, yes, Yes... a thousand times YES!* FileSaveAllYes, or, more simply All, which is what I use on my own toolbar, is a macro that tells Word that the answer is yes. Even so, you can't completely escape those prompts, since if you have any unnamed documents or templates on-screen, Word still needs to know how to handle them. However, if everything is named, and you just want a quick way to say, *"I hear thunder in the distance, save it all quickly"* to your computer, now you can. This macro saves all open files and templates:

```
Sub MAIN
On Error Goto Endit
FileSaveAll 1
EndIt:
Select Case Err
Case 0 : Print "All open files with changes were saved"
Case 102 : MsgBox("File save interrupted—some files were not saved!")
Case Else : Error Err
End Select
End Sub
```

This command could be a lot simpler, but it is important to remember the unnamed document limitation. If, in the course of running the FileSaveAllYes macro, you select Name and save previously unnamed documents, then all files are saved. However, if you ever select the Cancel option in the course of the macro, any files further down the chain of saves are not saved. So, this macro detects a press of the Cancel button and advises you that some of the files you were trying to save were not saved. Often, it's faster to go ahead and say Yes to a default name like DOC2.DOC (assuming you don't really have a document that you're using by that name) than it is to cancel, dispose of the file, and then try the save again. In any event, this macro is just living up to its moral obligation to let you know when it was unable to complete all of the saves.

MarkPlace and GotoPlace

Bookmarks are very useful for a variety of things in Word—like indexing, cross-references, math calculations, and so on. However, what about when you just want to use a bookmark as a, er...well, bookmark. Honestly, if you had to write a name on a piece of paper to use it as a bookmark, how likely would you be to use it as a bookmark? That use of a bookmark should be natural, and shouldn't require a lot of thought to use. That's why I wrote GotoPlace and MarkPlace.

MarkPlace produces the dialog box shown in Figure 60.8, and GoToPlace produces a nearly similar one. MarkPlace gives you a choice of ten temporary bookmarks called Temp1 through Temp10. I assigned keys to MarkPlace and to GotoPlace. Most often, I just press my Mark key and then press Enter to insert a Temp1 bookmark at the current location. Then I move wherever I need to to perform another task. When I'm ready to go back, I just press my Go key (for GotoPlace) and press Enter, and I'm instantly returned to the Temp1 location. On rare occasions, I need to use Temp2 and beyond, so they're there if I need them. Usually, however, Temp1 makes using a bookmark as a placemarker quick, easy, and painless. Also, because of the obvious names of these placemarkers, I don't end up scratching my follically impaired head wondering whether or not the bookmark is something I need.

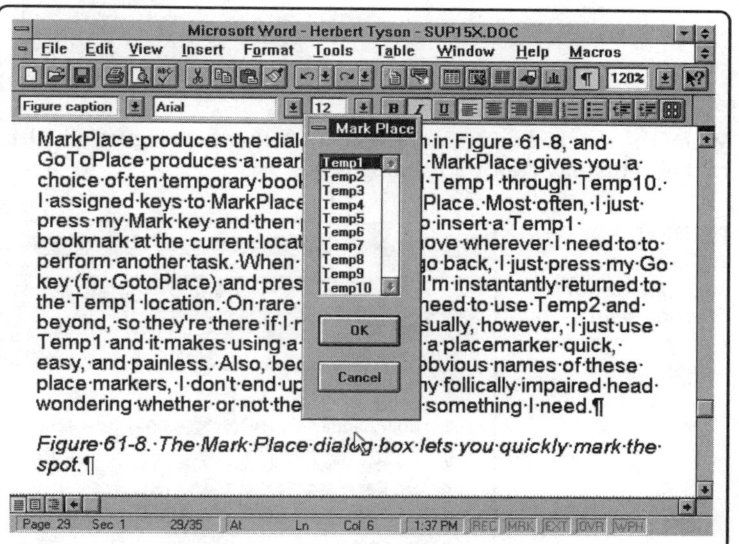

FIGURE 60.8.
The Mark Place dialog box lets you quickly mark the spot.

MultiMacroSearch

One of Word's great needs, for macro writers, is a facility for searching macros for one whose name you've forgotten. If you select **T**ools | **M**acro, and see an empty list, or just two or three macros, you might be wondering, "What's the big deal?" If, however, you have a list of macros that takes five minutes to scroll through, then you might have a sense of what I'm talking about. Unfortunately, Word does not provide any kind of management tools other than descriptions, like dates, times, or the ability to search for text in macros. If you have a macro in which you successfully used a DDEAUTO statement, and now can't get DDEAUTO to work, you really could benefit from a way to see inside a Word template to quickly find any macros that have the text DDEAUTO in them. Or, perhaps another macro reads a data file in a particular way. Or, perhaps something else.

In any event, MultiMacroSearch provides a way to search for matching text in macros residing in NORMAL.DOT or in the current template. When you run the MultiMacroSearch macro (which you can do by clicking the appropriate button on the SuperBook toolbar), it displays the simple dialog box shown in Figure 60.9. Just specify the search text (whether or not you want to match case or look only for whole words, NORMAL.DOT or the current template) and then click OK to start the search.

FIGURE 60.9. *The MultiMacroSearch dialog box.*

When the macro finds matching text, as shown in Figure 60.10, it selects the matching text and displays another dialog box.

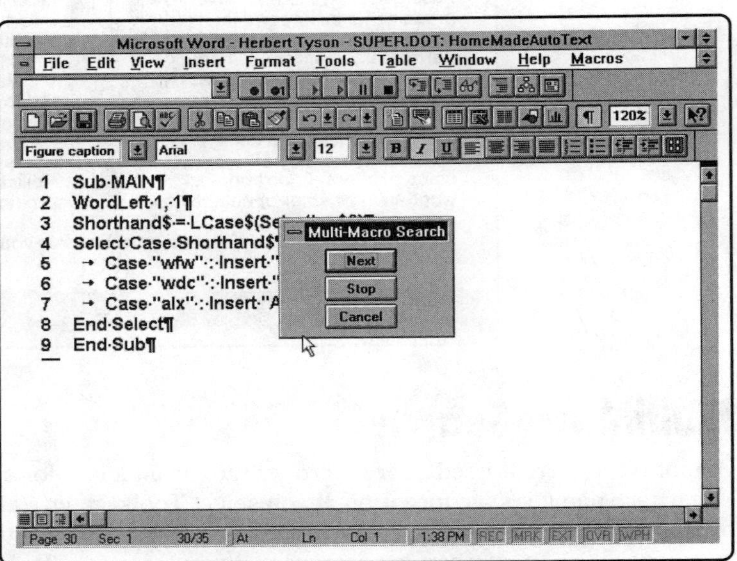

FIGURE 60.10. *When the MultiMacroSearch finds the search text, it prompts for what to do next.*

Here, your choices are the following:

Next	Finds the next match in the current macro
Stop	Stops the search and leaves the current macro open
Cancel	Continues the search with the next macro

MultiReplace

A simple Find and Replace isn't always sufficient. Sometimes, depending on the context of the found text, you want to handle the replace differently. For that reason, when you are doing a Replace operation, Word lets you move freely between the Replace dialog box and the screen, as described in Chapter 28, "Search and Replace." That's the perfect tool for those times when the editing is tedious and unpredictable. Often, however, there are distinct things you want to do, but you simply end up having to perform multiple replace operations.

The MultiReplace macro performs a search, then gives you a choice of up to three replacements. You can try MultiReplace out by clicking the MultiReplace button on the SuperBook toolbar. Shown in Figure 60.11, the MultiReplace dialog box lets you specify the search text, three replacement text strings, and options to match case and search for whole words. Fill in the search and replace strings, and options, and click OK to begin the search. When MultiReplace finds a match, it redisplays the dialog box. Click Replace1, Replace2, or Replace3 to make a replacement. Or, click OK to continue the search at the next match. Click Cancel to discontinue the search.

FIGURE 60.11.
The MultiReplace dialog box.

PrintCurrentPage

Some things are a nuisance to do, in my opinion. Like getting Word to print just the current page. You have to go to all the trouble of clicking that Current page option in the Print dialog box. Okay, so it's not that much of a nuisance. However, it's still more steps than I like to have to perform, and it's something I have to do repeatedly. A very simple macro demonstrates a solution as well as a general concept in Word macros. The macro shown here does a quick print of just the current page, without displaying any dialog boxes:

```
Sub MAIN
FilePrint .Type = 0, .NumCopies = "1", .Range = 2, .From = "", .To = "",
.PrintToFile = 0, \.Collate = 1, .FileName = ""
End Sub
```

It works by specifying a Range of 2, which is the FilePrint command's cute way of saying "the current page."

The other thing this macro demonstrates (as do the next two macros and a variety of others presented in this chapter) is that a macro doesn't have to be elaborate and complicated to be useful. All it has to do is to save you a step or two. And, most such macros can be created just by recording a procedure one time.

PrintPageOne and PrintPageTwo

PrintPageOne was created for those occasions when you find an error on the first page of a letter that you want to send out quickly, and you don't want to reprint the entire letter. Since I have the PrintPageOne macro button right next to my other print button, it's an easy matter to have the laser printer just jet off a fixed copy of the first page. Like PrintCurrentPage, this one's a one-liner, but it saves a little work in that, if you're not already on page one, you either have to scroll there to use the Current Page option, or you have to type the number 1 twice. Actually, that's the part that really annoys many users, and the reason some will find this kind of macro to their liking:

```
Sub MAIN
FilePrint .AppendPrFile = 0, .Range = "4", .PrToFileName = "", .From = "",
.To = "", .Type = 0, .NumCopies = "1", .Pages = "1-1", .Order = 0,
.PrintToFile = 0, .Collate = 1, .FileName = ""
End Sub
```

PrintPageTwo exists for the same reason as PrintPageOne, but cleverly uses a Pages setting of "2-2" instead of "1-1". There is no PrintPageThree for two reasons. First, I seldom write three-page letters. Second, and more importantly, the toolbar was already too crowded.

ProgMan

By now you're perhaps getting the impression that I don't like having to perform two or three steps when one will work. That's why I have a simple macro to access ProgMan. Unlike File Manager, where you must use the Shell command, ProgMan is always running (unless you replaced it with something else, in which case you can substitute the name of its Windows "name" for `Program Manager` in this macro). So, instead of shelling to it, you use the AppActivate command:

```
Sub MAIN
AppActivate "Program Manager"
End Sub
```

When you display the Windows task list (Ctrl+Esc), all of the open windows are listed. Sometimes they are listed with file names. The first part of the name is the name that is registered with Windows, and is the name that the programmers gave it. Even if you change the description of the File Manager in the properties settings to Fred Flintstone, Windows will continue to list it as File Manager. So, to use AppActivate to provide similar shortcuts to other running applications, you need to determine the registered name and use it in place of `Program Manager`.

If more than one copy of the applications is running, you can supply the dash and the name of the file that's loaded to activate the particular instance you want. For example, if there are two Notepad windows open, as shown in Figure 60.12, you can activate the untitled one by using:

```
AppActivate "Notepad - (Untitled)"
```

FIGURE 60.12.
Titles for the AppActivate command must match the title in the Windows task list.

Notepad - (Untitled)

RemoveSmart

Smart quotes are smart until you find applications or publishers with their own way of doing things who don't have any use for writer-supplied embellishments. From time to time, I'll accidentally leave Smart Quotes turned on after writing a brochure or a pamphlet that I'm going to print myself. Then, as I'm writing something for one of those don't-hyphenate-and-don't-try-to-be-a-typesetter publishers, I'll look down and realize that my document is filled with directional quotes. When that happens, I just run my RemoveSmart macro. Thanks to Word's new pattern-matching search feature, this macro just got smaller than it was for previous versions of Word:

```
Sub MAIN
EditReplace .Find = "[" + Chr$(147) + Chr$(148) + "]", .Replace = Chr$(34),
.Direction = 0, .MatchCase = 0, .WholeWord = 0, .PatternMatch = 1,
.SoundsLike = 0, .ReplaceAll, .Format = 0, .Wrap = 1
EditReplace .Find = "[" + Chr$(145) + Chr$(146) + "]", .Replace = Chr$(39),
.Direction = 0, .MatchCase = 0, .WholeWord = 0, .PatternMatch = 1,
.SoundsLike = 0, .ReplaceAll, .Format = 0, .Wrap = 1
End Sub
```

In the first EditReplace command, you can search for the left and right double quote marks (characters 147 and 148) in one command, replacing either with a straight quote mark ("), `Chr$(34)`. In the second, you can search for the single directional quotes, characters 145 and 146, at the same time, replacing either with a straight apostrophe.

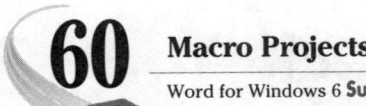

StringValue

From time to time, especially when working with different fonts and imported text, you can get confused about what you're really seeing in your file. The StringValue macro lets you select text and display the character codes of each character in the selection. As shown in Figure 60.13, StringValue, which uses the `ASCII()` function to evaluate each character, shows the characters and their codes in a scrollable list box.

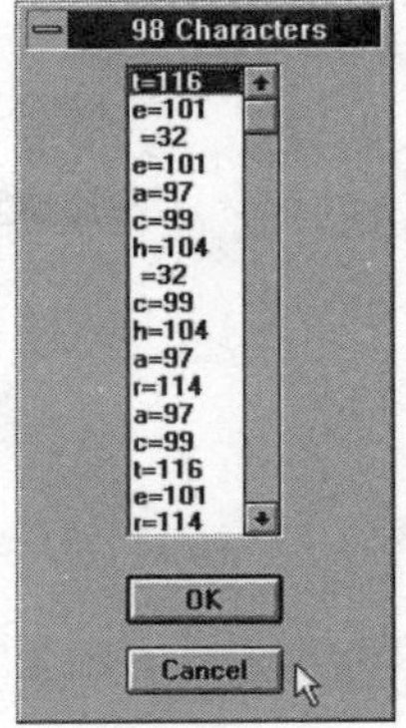

FIGURE 60.13.
StringValue displays the character values of every character in the selection.

One kind of character that StringValue cannot handle is Word 6's new Symbol characters that resist formatting. For example, insert a copyright symbol using the Insert | Symbol command. Now select it (actually, for a single character, just put the insertion point right in front of it) and click the StringValue button on the SuperBook toolbar. Word's `ASCII()` command thinks it's an ASCII 40, which is a left parenthesis. So, don't waste a lot of time trying to figure those out! Another interesting use for the StringValue macro is to try to find new and exciting ways to search for Word features. For example, as shown in Figure 60.14, if you press Ctrl+F9 to insert a pair of field characters, then select them and click StringValue, you'll discover that Word inserted characters 19, 32, 32, and 21. As it turns out, Word uses characters 19 and 21 for the field delimiters, and you can search for fields by specifying `^19` instead of `^d` (isn't that exciting?). More useful, however, is the fact that if you're ever stuck looking at a Word document with a programming editor and are trying to figure out what's what, you'll be able to recognize field codes when you see ASCII 19 and 21 bracketing something else. Keep this in mind if you ever have to write a program to convert Word field codes into something else.

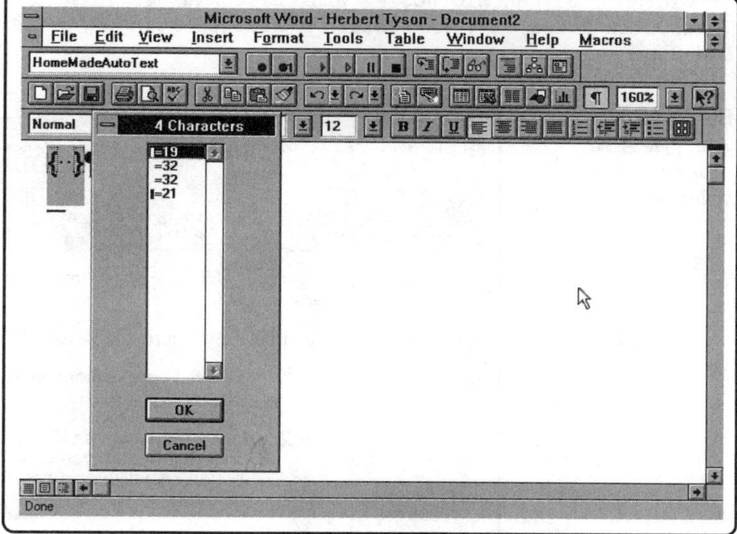

FIGURE 60.14.
StringValue lets you see beneath the surface of Word fields.

StyleBarToggle

Many users don't even know it exists, but it's one of Word's best features. It's the style bar down the left-hand margin of the page. Shown in Figure 60.15, the style area lets you instantly see what styles are where. It's a great tool for working on tightly formatted text. Rather than having to constantly glance away from the text area to the formatting toolbar, you can look directly at the text to see what style is in effect.

So, how do you turn this thing on? Here's how:

1. Select **T**ools | **O**ptions and click the View tab.
2. Find the Style Area Width control at the bottom left and type or spin a setting (in inches, usually) wide enough to display your style names.
3. Click OK.

If it's not big enough, you can drag the style bar to the left or right using the mouse. To turn it off, just drag it completely to the left.

Having to diddle so much with the mouse and the Options dialog box led me to write a simple toggle that toggles a one-half inch style area on and off:

```
Sub MAIN
Dim TOV As ToolsOptionsView
GetCurValues TOV
Widthn = Val(TOV.StyleAreaWidth)
Print Widthn
```

```
If Widthn = 0 Then WidthC$ = "0.5" Else WidthC$ = "0"
ToolsOptionsView .StyleAreaWidth = WidthC$
End Sub
```

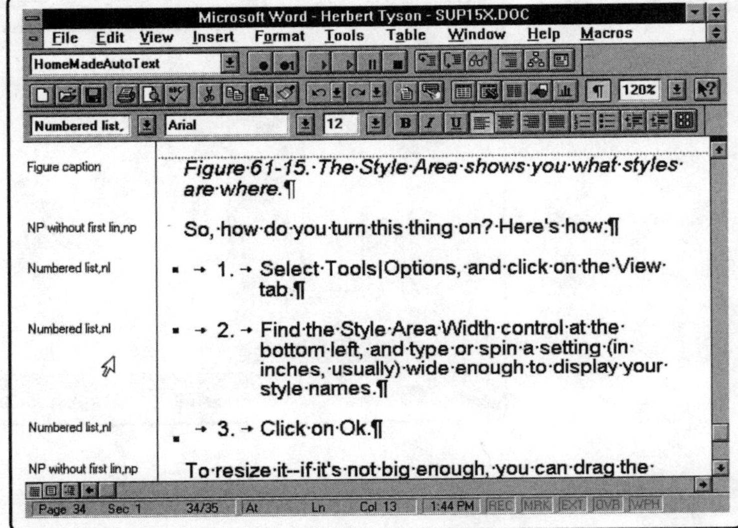

FIGURE 60.15. *The Style Area shows you what styles are where.*

Setting up a toggle turned out not to be straightforward, since there is no "style bar toggle" command. You first have to query the ToolsOptionsView setting to see what the current setting is. Then, if it's 0, you set it to the value you want (.5 works reasonably well for most of the styles I use). If it's not 0, then set it to 0. Then execute the ToolsOptionsView command using the new value. It's just that simple.

ToggleAutoMacros

Have you ever opened a template, or a document based on a template, and been stung by an automatic macro? If so, then you might appreciate ToggleAutoMacros. This macro uses the DisableAutoMacros command to create a toggle. Furthermore, since Word doesn't maintain a user-accessible state (on or off) for whether or not automatic macros are turned on or off, this macro creates one in the Microsoft Word section of WIN.INI using `GetProfileString$`:

```
Sub MAIN
State$ = GetProfileString$("AutoMacros")
If State$ = "1" Then State$ = "0" Else State$ = "1"
SetProfileString "AutoMacros", State$
DisableAutoMacros Val(State$) - 1
If State$ = "0" Then SText$ = "Disabled" Else SText$ = "Enabled"
MsgBox("Automatic Macros are now " + SText$)
End Sub
```

The macro begins by seeing what the last set state was in the AutoMacros profile setting in WIN.INI. If it's 1 (ON) or if there is no current state setting, the macro sets the AutoMacros variable to 0 (OFF) and turns automatic macros off using the DisableAutoMacros command. If the current state is OFF, then the macro sets the AutoMacros variable to ON and uses the DisableAutoMacros command to turn automatic macros ON.

If you're enterprising, you can tap into this further using an AutoExec macro to examine the state of AutoMacros when you first start Word. If it's ON, you continue the AutoExit macro. If it's off, you discontinue. Done this way, the setting for AutoMacros can persist between sessions.

When would you want to use this toggle? Use it when you're just trying to figure out what's what in unfamiliar files. Or, use it when an automatic macro is preventing you from seeing what's happening in a document. Or, use it when an automatic macro is triggering an error condition before you can rush to the rescue.

SUPER

When opening or creating a Word document with an AutoNew or AutoOpen macro, you can suppress it by holding down the Shift key just after giving the command to open the document (usually). If your system is very fast, however, you might still have trouble pressing the shift key in time.

Window Splitting (Arrange Any Two Windows Horizontally or Vertically)

If you have just two Word windows open, Word will gladly arrange them so you can see them both on-screen at the same time, one on top and the other on the bottom. Just select Window | Arrange All. However, if you have more than two windows open, or if you want to arrange them side-by-side instead of top and bottom, Word doesn't provide much help for looking at just two documents. Instead, you pretty much have to drag the borders around—which can take a good minute or so, sometimes (especially if you accidentally click the wrong place)—until they look the way you want.

WindowSplit is a macro that solves this problem. It displays two window lists, as shown in Figure 60.16. In the left list, you select the window you want displayed at the top or left. In the right list, you select the window you want displayed at the bottom or right. When you click the Top/Bottom or Left/Right buttons, the macro then divides the available screen real estate evenly between your two selections.

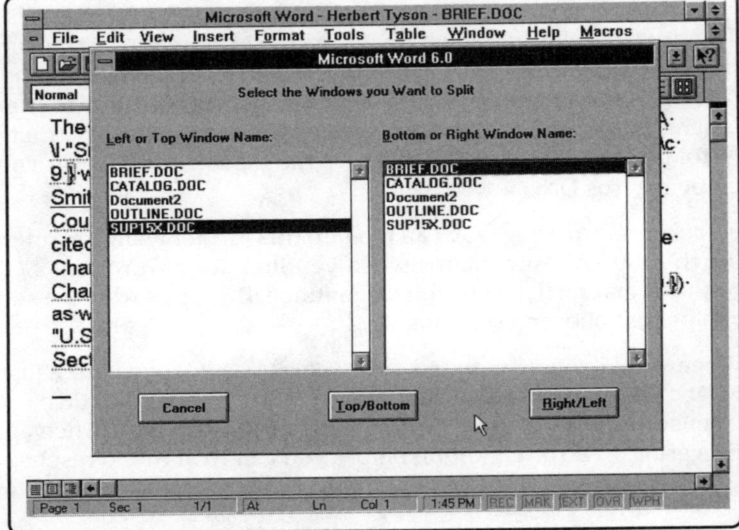

FIGURE 60.16.
Use Window Split to look at any two windows, split horizontally or vertically.

Appendix

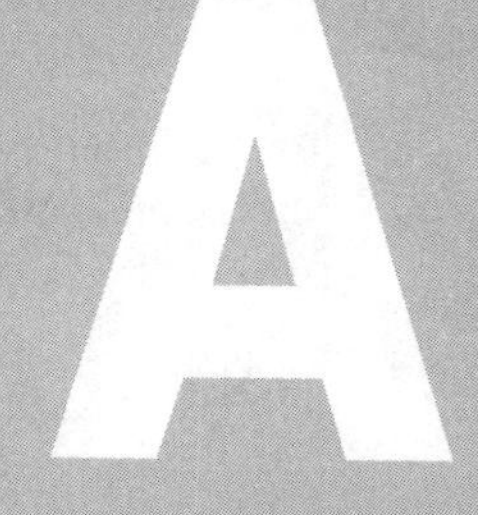

Word Installation and Setup

For the most part, Word setup is very straightforward. To install Word, like most other Microsoft applications, you insert the first diskette into Drive A (or B) and run the Setup program.

PROCEDURE A.1. INSTALLING WORD 6.

1. Make sure no earlier versions of Word are already running.
2. Insert the first or setup diskette into drive A or B.
3. From Program Manager, select **F**ile | **R**un.
4. In the Command Line box, type `A:SETUP` or `B:SETUP`, depending on where the setup diskette is located.
5. Click OK.
6. Follow the instructions displayed by the Word Setup program.

SUPER NOTE

If you previously managed to install MS WordArt, MS Graph, the Equation editor, or other features somewhere other than in the WINDOWS\MSAPPS or WIN\MSAPPS directory, Word 6's installation program *might* install the new versions over the old in your alternative directories, despite the directories indicated during the installation.

SUPER TIP

The ODBC (database) installation option requires over 4M on your Windows directory. Unless you're using MS Access or some other ODBC-aware database application, you might do well to tell Word *not* to install the ODBC option. When and if you acquire an ODBC-aware application, the appropriate ODBC software will be installed at that time. Moreover, it will probably (by then, anyway) be more up to date than the ODBC you install with Word today.

SUPER CAUTION

If you have enough disk space both on the drive where you choose to install Word, as well as on the drive that contains Windows, you will encounter no difficulty in installing and using Word. However, if you have less than 5 megabytes of free space on the Windows directory, you definitely will encounter problems installing the extra applications

(Equation Editor, WordArt, MS Graph, and so forth) and import/export filters that come with Word. Namely, at this writing, Microsoft does not give you a choice. If you run out of space while installing, setup informs you that it could not complete the installation. You're then faced with the double-indignity of having to clean up the botched installation, as well as having to find room for Word and then reinstall. You can save yourself enormous headaches by making sure that you have the disk space called for in the setup program. **Do not proceed with installation until you have enough room for everything you intend to install.**

Relocating MSAPPS

Microsoft makes it extraordinarily difficult to install Word and other Microsoft applications without cluttering up the Windows directory. In particular, the Word setup program not only adds files to the Windows system directory, but it creates or adds to a subdirectory called MSAPPS, which is created off your main Windows directory. Into this directoy, the setup program places the following subdirectories, populated with a variety of files:

```
EQUATION
GRPHFLT
MSGRAPH
MSINFO
PROOF
TEXTCONV
WORDART
```

SUPER CAUTION

Do not attempt to move any of the files or directories created by Word's setup program unless you are emotionally equipped to deal with the inevitable frustration and aggravation. If you find the arrogant intractability of Word's setup program unforgivable, please let Microsoft know about it. Only if sufficient numbers of users complain will they ever come to accept that it might be a problem. Otherwise, it will continue to worsen until you have absolutely no idea what's on your disk or why.

In previous versions of Word, you often could simply relocate any directories after installation, taking care to modify WIN.INI to reflect the changed locations. Not wishing to make life easy for the user, Microsoft, in what has to be a masterstroke of programming arrogance, created something called the Registration Editor. Called REGEDIT.EXE, this monstrous program maintains a file (called REG.DAT) on your

Windows directory. This file is a list of OLE servers—like the Equation Editor, WordArt, and so forth—and their handling instructions *vis-a-vis* different clients. In addition to modifying WIN.INI when you move any of the OLE applications, you also have to use the registration editor.

> **SUPER CAUTION**
>
> When and if you use the registration editor, make a backup copy of REG.DAT before beginning. That way, if you screw anything up, you'll have a fallback position.

> **SUPER CAUTION**
>
> In using the Registration editor, take care to note the differences between any applications that are specific to WinWord 2 versus WinWord 6. Note also, adding to all this merry confusion, that MSWordArt.2 and MSEquation.2, despite what logic might tell you, are in fact the Word 6 versions of those applications. Surprise! The Word 2 versions were called MSGraph and Equation.

In addition, boys and girls, you also will need to take a look at WINWORD6.INI—also on the Windows directory—to make sure that you update any of its references (note: at this writing, it's called WINWORD6.INI—if you don't see it, then look for WINWORD.INI instead). If you make changes in WIN.INI and in the Registration data file but still don't see the expected results, it may very well be that the section you seek is in WINWORD6.INI, instead.

Protecting Word

It makes sense, when making major changes to Word, to protect your customization investments. At a minimum, changes that affect Word are usually found in the following files:

```
WIN.INI        (Windows directory)
WINWORD6.INI   (Windows directory)
REG.DAT        (Windows directory)
WORD6.GRP      (Windows directory; the name might be slightly different
                depending on your setup)
WINWORD.OPT    (WINWORD6 directory)
NORMAL.DOT     (WINWORD\TEMPLATE directory)
```

If you want to ensure that all of your customizations and changes are safe, you need to make backup copies of each of those files. In addition, depending on how you use Word, each of Word's OLE server applications are capable of creating their own entourage of support files on the Windows directory. These include but are not limited to

```
EQNEDIT.INI     Used by the Equation editor
MSTXTCNV.INI    Used by Word's text conversion filters
ODBCINST.INI    Used for database compatibility with ODBC
WORDWIZ.INI     Used by Word's Wizard templates
MSGRAPH.INI     Used by MSGRAPH
WORDART.INI     Used by WordArt
```

Appendix

B

Field Types

Word has 68 distinct field types. In this appendix, you'll see examples of each and suggestions about their use. You also can get complete online help for any field type by pressing the F1 key. For example if the field `{EQ }` is on-screen, pressing the F1 key summons immediate and excellent online help about the EQ field. This help is available both while editing a document as well as when the **Insert|Field** dialog box is active.

Use the = field to evaluate an expression. Expressions can be any supported mathematical expression, cell references within Word tables, and bookmark references to defined expressions, values, or tables within Word. The = field and its operators and functions give you spreadsheet-like capabilities within a Word document. If you have a real spreadsheet program, however, you'll save lots of time by using it, instead of using the = field. While it does work, the syntax is very difficult to master, let alone tolerate.

Still here? Oh, darn. Well, you can't blame a writer for trying. You can use the = field with any of the numeric picture format switches. The = field recognizes the following standard math operators:

```
%
()
^
/ *
+ -

= <> < > <= >=
```

Shown in order of precedence, all higher operations are evaluated first, until all expressions are of equal precedence. Expressions of equal precedence are evaluated from left to right. The `%` operator comes first because it works only with numbers, not expressions. Thus, `15%` is fine; `(20-5)%` generates an error. The expression `15%` is just another way of writing `.15`. After `%`, everything inside `()` is evaluated first.

The = field also supports references to the current table (if the field is contained in a table) as well as bookmark references to other tables. Cell references are the same as those used in standard spreadsheets, with numbered rows and lettered columns.

Bookmarks themselves (without cell, row, or column references) can be used as variables in all calculations. Any cell, column, or row reference, however, can be used only inside one of the reduction functions: Average, Count, Max, Min, Product, and Sum. For example, to multiply A1 by A2, you would need either SUM(A1)*SUM(A2) or PRODUCT(A1,A2). If you want to refer to a specific cell as a variable, you could give it a bookmark name. Otherwise, you must enclose it in one of the noted functions. See the Tables Workshop for a complete description of these and other functions.

SUPER NOTE

The word *reduction* simply means that it's capable of reducing a cell reference to a value.

ADVANCE (New)

You use the ADVANCE function to offset the text following the field up, down, left, right, or to a specific horizontal and vertical position on the page. You can use the following switches with the ADVANCE field:

`\U`*n*	Upward offset by *n* points.
`\D`*n*	Downward offset by *n* points.
`\L`*n*	Left offset by *n* points.
`\R`*n*	Right offset by *n* points.
`\X`*n*	Absolute horizontal distance of *n* points, from the left side of the margin, column, or frame.
`\Y`*n*	Absolute vertical distance of *n* points from the top of the page (`\Y` is ignored in tables, and frames, and margin text (footnotes, annotations, headers, footers, footnotes, and endnotes).

You should be in Page Layout view to see the effects of the ADVANCE field. The field:

```
{ADVANCE \U6}
```

raises whatever follows it. This command usually is used in conjunction with a reciprocal command to bring text back. You might use this type of field if for some reason the built-in superscripting didn't accomplish a specific objective, or if you needed to overprint some characters.

ASK

Use the ASK field to display a dialog box to prompt for text to assign to a bookmark. The ASK field can include the following switches:

`\o`	When doing a mail merge, the ASK field, by default, is triggered once for each record in the data file. The `\o` switch tells Word that this ASK field gets triggered only for the first record. For example, a return address field would likely be the same on all documents printed during the merge. A personalized greeting, on the other hand, might need to be updated for each letter sent (assuming it's a mail merge).
`\d`	Specifies a default value for the response. For example:

```
{ASK sig "How do you want to sign your name?" \d "James Q. Public"}
```

prompts on every record for your signature, and suggests James Q. Public as the default. You might modify it to Jim for some more personal letters, and leave it as is for others. Or, included in a letter template, you might have an UpdateField statement in an AutoNew macro so that the signature prompt gets asked when the document is created, but not thereafter.

There should be a place where the requested information is used. The field:

```
{REF signature}
```

might be inserted where your signature normally appears.

AUTHOR

The AUTHOR field inserts the author's name from the **F**ile | Summary **I**nfo dialog. It is frequently included in headers or footers. Optionally, you can use it to change the author's name on the fly. For example:

```
{AUTHOR "Peter Pan"}
```

instantly changed the author of this section to Peter Pan. I'd better change it back to my name quickly before the editors at Sams call out the folks with the white coats and soothing voices.

AUTONUM

The AUTONUM field inserts an automatic paragraph number field. The resulting numbers are displayed as `1.`, `2.`, `3.`, and so forth. AUTONUM is incremented in each paragraph. If you include multiple AUTONUM fields within the same paragraph, they'll all display the same number. General format switches are ignored by AUTONUM, and updating is performed automatically each time a paragraph is inserted, deleted, or moved. Word doesn't provide a way to suppress the period—see SEQ if you want greater flexibility in numbering.

The AUTONUM field is designed for numbering paragraphs or sections of a document, as, for example, you might need for certain legal or technical formats. You would select *either* AUTONUM, AUTONUMLGL, or AUTONUMOUT, but not all three, for any given document. It's not suitable for numbering lists, tables, or figures. Instead, either use the Numbering tool (on the formatting toolbar) for lists, and SEQ fields for tables.

AUTONUMLGL

AUTONUMLGL inserts an automatic paragraph number field code whose results display in legal style as `1.`, `1.1.`, `1.1.1.`, `1.1.1.1.`. AUTONUMLGL is keyed to heading level styles (Heading 1 is `1.`; Heading 2 is `1.1.`, Heading 3 is `1.1.1.`, and so forth). All general format switches are ignored by AUTONUMLGL, and updating is performed automatically each time a paragraph is inserted, deleted, or moved. AUTONUMLGL displays the same as AUTONUM when used in nonheading style paragraphs.

AUTONUMOUT

AUTONUMOUT inserts an automatic paragraph number field code whose results display using traditional outline numbering (`I.`, `A.`, `1.`, `a`), and so on). Like AUTONUMLGL, AUTONUMOUT works with Heading level styles. All general format switches are ignored by AUTONUMOUT, and updating is performed automatically each time a paragraph is inserted, deleted, or moved.

AUTOTEXT (formerly GLOSSARY)

The AUTOTEXT field has the following syntax:

`AUTOTEXT` *`name`*

and inserts the contents of an autotext item. Unlike normal autotext usage, the AUTOTEXT field results in a dynamic autotext entry. Thus, if the contents of the autotext change, so does the displayed result each time the field is updated. For example:

```
If you need to reach me, I'll be at {AUTOTEXT telephone} until
{AUTOTEXT leavedate}.
```

might be included in messages sent back from someone working at a different location in the field. If this text is included in different messages, the worker needs to specify the telephone number and leave the date only once at each location.

BARCODE (New)

Use the BARCODE field to—you guessed it—create postal bar codes, primarily for envelopes, although it can be used by hobbyists trying to learn to sight-read barcodes. Use the BARCODE field as follows:

`{BARCODE "`*`text`*`" `*`[bookmark] [switches]`*`}`

The BARCODE field can be used with the following switches:

- `\b` Tells Word to obtain the zip code from the address in a bookmark (for example, `{barcode address \b}`).
- `\f`*`x`* Tells Word to insert a Facing Identification Mark (where *x* is A, for courtesy reply, or C, for business reply)—for example, `{ barcode "22310" \fC}`.
- `\u` Identifies the bar code as a US postal address (for example, `{barcode address \b \u}`).

COMMENTS

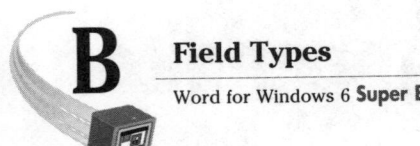

COMMENTS displays or changes the contents of the **F**ile|**S**ummary **I**nfo comments item. Like the AUTHOR field, you can use the Comments field to change the comments field:

```
{comments "these comments will replace any previous comments"}
```

If you use COMMENTS to make nasty remarks about clients, be sure not to insert a COMMENTS field into any document you might be sending out. The term *comments* isn't used by Microsoft Word in quite the same way as it's used in ordinary English. The COMMENTS field is often another way of getting standard but variable information into a document without having to change text everywhere it occurs.

COMPARE (New)

The COMPARE field is used in mail merge operations to test the values of data fields. The format for the compare field is:

```
{COMPARE expression1 operator expression2}
```

Compare returns a logical value of true or false. You might use COMPARE as part of an IF field to determine how to process a given record. You can include ? as a wildcard when comparing zip codes, for example:

```
{COMPARE zip_code = "223??"}
```

CREATEDATE

CREATEDATE is used to insert the document's creation date into a document (for example, in a header or a footer). For example:

```
{FileName} created on { CREATEDATE \@ "MMMM d, yyyy" \* MERGEFORMAT }
```

might display as:

```
SUP9.DOC created on August 27, 1993
```

DATABASE (Formerly DATA)

The Database field usually is inserted by the **I**nsert|**D**atabase command on the menu (see Figure B.1). When you select the **I**nsert Data button, Word creates a table containing the results of a data query. If you select the Insert Data as Field option, Word inserts a Database field that displays as a Word table in the current document. The Database field specifies the database name and can optionally perform an SQL (Structured Query Language) access using the new Open Database Connectivity (ODBC) protocol. The Database field works not only with Word files and text files, but with Microsoft Access as well as all of the different file import types supported by Word.

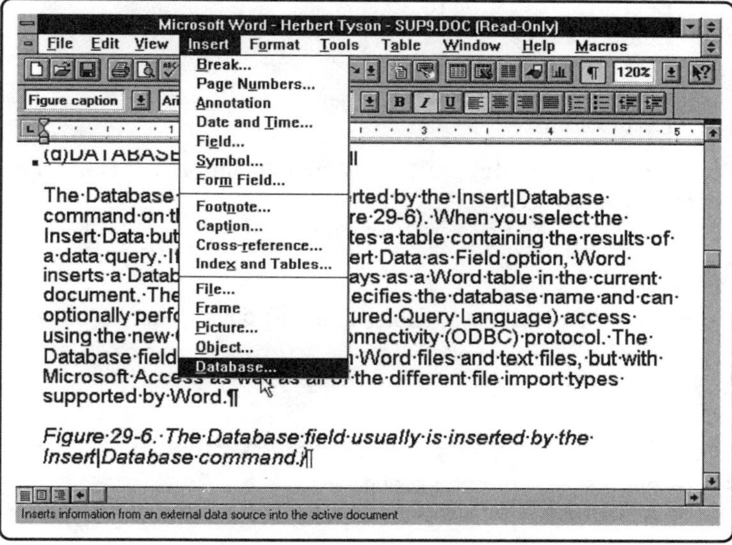

FIGURE B.1.
The Database field usually is inserted by the ***I****nsert* | ***D****atabase command.*

For files not conforming to ODBC, the file must be in a format recognized by Word, preferably:

```
Field1<TAB>Field2<TAB>Field3<TAB>…Fieldn<CARRIAGE RETURN>
```

The first record usually contains the field names, and subsequent records contain data. For example:

```
LAST<tab>FIRST<tab>STREET<tab>CITY<tab>STATE<tab>ZIP
Jones<tab>Davy<tab>1 Locker Circle<tab>New Billings<tab>VA<tab>22333
Gates<tab>William<tab>One Microsoft Way<tab>Redmond<tab>WA<tab>98052
```

Each time you update the field, the data in the query is refreshed. You can use keywords and switches to specify formatting, sorting, as well as the criteria for inclusion in the query. The DATABASE field uses the following switches:

\b

Use the `\b` switch to select an additive combination of formatting attributes from the AutoFormat command, if set with the `\l` switch. Specify `\b` *n* where *n* is the sum of the attributes:

None	0
Borders	1

Shading	2
Font	4
Color	8
Best Fit	16
Heading Rows	32
Last Row	64
First Column	128
Last Column	256

For example, the switches `\l1 \b17` specify Simple 1 (`\l1`), Borders and Best Fit (`\b17`, because 1 + 16 = 17).

\c

ODBC keyword and instructions (such as `QUERY, Sales Data 1993`).

\d

The path and filename of the database. For example:

```
F:\\WORD6\\BOOK\\DATAFILE.DOC
```

\f

Use with `\t` to specify a range by record number. For example, `\f7 \t42` inserts records 7 through 42.

\l

The `\l` switch specifies a numbered format from the Table | AutoFormat dialog box (see Chapter 19, "Tables and AutoTable") for formatting the data. For example, `\l2` applies the Simple 2 format to the Word table. The `\l` numbers are in the same order as the formats in the list box in the AutoFormat dialog box.

\s

Use the `\s` switch to specify the SQL instructions, if needed. When you use the **I**nsert | **D**atabase command, Word often inserts a `\s` switch even when not needed. The SQL instructions to Microsoft Access might be something like `"Select * from Regional Sales"`.

\t

Use the `\t` switch with `\f` to specify the ending record in a range.

Examples

At the simplest, a Database field might just be:

```
{DATABASE \d F:\\WORD6\\BOOK\\DATAFILE.TXT}
```

Alternatively, it might be something more complex, like the following, which (among other things) tells Word to select Zip Codes only in the 20000 series:

```
{DATABASE  \d "F:\\WORD6\\BOOK\\DATAFILE.DOC" \s "SELECT LAST, FIRST,
ADDRESS, CITY, STATE, ZIP FROM F:\\WORD6\\BOOK\\DATAFILE.DOC WHERE ((ZIP >
19999) And (ZIP < 30000))" \l "2" \b "183" }
```

SUPER NOTE

The Database field inserted by Word specified the zips as #19999# and #30000#, which did not work with the DATAFILE.DOC database (a Word file). If you find that a database does not work, then insert it as a field (in the Insert Data dialog box, make sure you click the Insert Data as Field option), and then press F10 to edit the field to remove the # characters, and then press F9 to update the field.

DATE

The Date field has the following syntax:

```
DATE [DatePictureFormat]
```

and, when created, inserts the current date and/or time according to the format specified. Subsequently, the field can be updated either with UpdateFields or when doing a mail merge. The Date field generally is identical to the TIME field inserted using the Insert Date and Time command. For example:

```
August 30, 1993
```

DDE

The DDE field has the following syntax:

```
DDE application file reference
```

The following example:

```
{DDE Excel D:\\QPX\\DATA\\EARN93.WKS Receipts \* charformat}
```

uses a Lotus 123 worksheet that was loaded by Excel. You update DDE fields using the F9 key, when you do a Mail Merge, or when you print with the Update Fields option turned on (Tools | Options | Print). In this example, the reference is a named range called Receipts. This field displays as a two-column table in Word, because the underlying block of data occupied two columns.

The easiest way to use DDE fields is to create them automatically using EditPasteLink. Do this by starting the other application, loading the necessary data, and copying what you need to the Clipboard. Then go back to Word and select EditPasteLink from the menu. If it's a valid option, EditPasteLink will be available on the menu. If the command isn't available, then what you want to do isn't possible. If you specify Auto Update in the EditPasteLink command, it'll be a DDEAUTO field; otherwise, it'll be a DDE field.

DDEAUTO

DDEAUTO uses the same syntax as the DDE command. For example:

```
{DDEAUTO Excel F:\\XL\\AMORTIZ3.XLS R5C2:R11C2 \* mergeformat}
```

This example uses an Excel worksheet and cell references in a DDEAUTO field. The DDEAUTO field is updated instantly, as the underlying source changes. Unlike a DDE field, you can't convert an active DDEAUTO field into nontabular form.

EDITTIME

The EDITTIME field displays the total number of editing minutes for the document, as also displayed in the **File** | Summary Info dialog box. For example, `{EDITTIME}` displays as 1258 in the file I'm editing right now. Good grief! I've been working on the writing tools workshop for over 20 hours already. I'd better hurry!

EQ

The EQ field has the following syntax:

```
EQ specification
```

and is used primarily for instructing Word in the creation of WYSIWYG equations. Please, please, please, save yourself some headaches and use the Equation Editor instead.

Still here? You must be a glutton for punishment. Note that EQ fields are automatically updated when they're displayed, and cannot be unlinked.

The EQ field has 10 modes or types of actions it can perform. They can be used alone or in concert. Each is described in the following sections.

Array

Use the Array switch (\a) to draw arrays. The \a switch works very much like a function. Everything enclosed by parentheses following the \a switch is treated as array elements. Array elements are treated literally, with everything between commas treated literally, including spaces, quotes, or whatever else you type. Array elements can be any valid expression, including subsets of the EQ field itself. Optional switches are:

`\al`	Left-align column element
`\ac`	Center-column elements (the default)
`\ar`	Right-align column elements
`\co`*n*	Number of columns (defaults to 1)
`\vs`*v*	Vertical spacing between lines, measured in points
`\hs`*h*	Horizontal spacing between columns, measured in points

Bracket

Use the Bracket switch (\b) to display bracket character(s) used to enclose all or part of an equation or formula. Parentheses are required after the \b switch to indicate the text that you want bracketed. Given that parentheses themselves (the default bracketing characters) are required to enclose the text or formula you want bracketed, syntax confusion is possible. Optional switches are:

`\lc \`*b*	Selects the left bracket character, where *b* is {, [, or (.
`\rc \`*b*	Selects the right bracket character, where *b* is },], or).
`\Bc \`*b*	Selects a single bracket character for both brackets, *b* might be ¦.

If you specify \lc or \rc alone, then only a single bracketing character is used. You can use this to create grouping effects.

Displace

The Displace switch (\d) is used to precisely control the horizontal location of a character, relative to the one just typed. The displace switch must be used with one of the following options:

`\fo`*f*	Move the next character forward by *f* points.
`\ba`*b*	Move the next character backward by *b* points.
`\li`	Draw an underscore from the displaced character to the end of the preceding character.

The displace switch can be combined with other placement switches (\s, which is vertical placement) to create special effects. The \d switch uses no arguments, and must be followed by empty parentheses. Using the \li switch allows you to draw a line of a precise length.

SUPER NOTE

If you just need displacement, consider using the Advance field, which provides horizontal and vertical displacement as well as exact positioning.

Fraction

The Fraction switch (`\f`) is used to draw a horizontal fraction line between two expressions. The syntax is as follows:

```
EQ \f(x,y)
```

where *x* is the numerator and *y* is the denominator.

Integral

The Integral switch (`\i`) is used to display equations requiring the integral, summation (sigma), multiplication (pi), or any specialized characters your application might require. The syntax for the integral switch is

```
EQ \i\[switch](i,n,x)
```

where *i*, *n*, and *x* are the bottom (from), top (to), and expression components of the equation. In a straight product or summation, *i* is the index start value, *n* is the maximum index value, and *x* is the expression that's being evaluated at each *i*. When evaluating an integral, *i* is the lower limit and *n* is the maximum.

The optional switches really are

`\in`	Puts limits for integral to the right of the integral symbol (in-line) instead of above and below.
`\fc\c`	Substitutes a character you specify *c*, instead of pi, sigma, or the integral sign. The character, *c*, can be any you specify, in any font or point size.
`\vc\c`	Substitutes another character forpi, sigma, or the integral sign. The character, c, can be any you specify, in any font or point size. Unlike `\fc`, the `\vc` character varies in size according to the *x* (expression) parameter, and is approximately twice as tall as *x*.
`\pr`	Selects a capital pi for writing iterative product equations.
`\su`	Selects a capital sigma for writing iterative summation equations.

List

The List switch (\l) lists items separated by commas. The syntax is

```
EQ \l(a,b,c,…,z)
```

where a through z can be any expressions. There's no great advantage to using the \l switch because the identical effects can be created by just listing items with intervening commas—that is, without using a field statement at all.

Overstrike

Overstrike (\o) prints any number of characters in the same position. The syntax is

```
EQ \o\[switch](a,b,c,…,z)
```

where *a* through *z* can be any number of characters. Each character in the list is printed in the same space. The optional switches are:

\ac	Centers each character within its font boundary (default).
\al	Left aligns each character.
\ar	Right aligns each character.

Radical

The Radical switch (\r) is used to form roots. The following:

```
EQ \r(x[,y])
```

draws the *x*th root of *y*. When only a single parameter is used, the square root is drawn. Unfortunately, the *x* and *y* parameters are always printed the same size as each other, regardless of fonts you assign.

Vertical

The Vertical switch (\s) is used for positioning subscripts and superscripts. The syntax is:

```
EQ \s\[switch](x,y])
```

where *x* is a superscript and *y* is a subscript. Switches include:

\up*n*	Raises *x* up by *n* points.
\do*n*	Lowers *x* by *n* points.

When using two parameters (both *x* and *y*), switches are ignored. The *x* and *y* parameters are raised and lowered, respectively, to about the baseline of the host font. This results in considerably better positioning than the default superscript and subscripts achieved through character formatting. Note: Also see the Displace switch.

Box

The Box switch (\x) is used to draw a border around a single expression. This can be useful both in highlighting results as well as achieving special effects. The syntax is

```
EQ \b text
```

where text is the expression you want boxed. Switches can modify the effect of \x:

\to	Draws a top bar only.
\bo	Draws a bottom bar only.
\le	Draws a left bar only.
\ri	Draws a right bar only.

When no switches are specified, a full box is drawn. When switches are specified, only the box components you specify are drawn.

FILENAME

Use the FILENAME field to insert the name of the current file, as obtained from File | Summary Info. It doesn't include the path. If the document is unnamed (new), the temporary reference name is displayed (for example, Document3).

FILESIZE (New)

The FILESIZE field displays the exact size of the file on disk, in bytes. Contrast this with the NUMCHARS field. At the moment, for example, using {FILESIZE} and {NUMCHARS} shows that this file is 184,832 bytes and contains 112,827 characters.

FILLIN

The FILLIN field has the following syntax:

```
FILLIN "instruction" \d "default"] \o]
```

The FILLIN field uses the instruction you type as a prompt and presents you with an input box. The text you type is then associated with the field, which displays as the last text you entered. For example:

```
{FILLIN "Type your signature"}
```

prompts you to fill in your signature. Thereafter, when you update the field, the prompt is reissued and the last-typed text offered as the default. Optionally, you can specify a default to be offered each time, regardless of the current value:

```
{FILLIN "Type your signature" \d "Jacob Sladder"}
```

causes Jacob Sladder to be displayed in the input box before you begin typing. Note that the prompt and the default text are both enclosed in quotes. If you omit the quotes, only the first word of each text item is displayed. If you want the default to be blank each time, use the following:

```
{FILLIN "Type your signature" \d ""}
```

If you include `\d` without `""`, Word generates an error message. Ordinarily, the FILLIN field is updated each time you print, and for each record when you're doing a mail merge. The `\o` switch can be used to force the FILLIN field to prompt only before printing the first record's document, rather than before each record.

GOTOBUTTON

GOTOBUTTON has the following syntax:

```
GOTOBUTTON—where prompt
```

and is typically used in help-type documents. If you double-click the displayed field, Word jumps to the bookmark or other location specified by *where*. The *where* can be a page number or a bookmark name, and *prompt* is the text you see displayed on-screen. For example:

```
{GOTOBUTTON 27 Jump to Page 27}
```

displays as:

```
Jump to Page 27
```

and by double-clicking the field, the insertion point moves to page 27. Or,

```
{GOTOBUTTON HelpData Click for Help}
```

goes to a bookmark called HelpData if the field is double-clicked. Unlike the FILLIN field, GOTOBUTTON doesn't require quotes around the prompt.

IF

The IF field has the following syntax:

```
IF expression "text if true" "text if false"
```

and is used to display different text, depending on the result of an expression. For example:

```
{IF state = VA "VA residents must add 4.5% sales tax" "CA, OK, AK and WA
add appropriate sales tax"}
```

If the state is assigned to a bookmark called *state*, for example, when doing a mail merge, you can test that value to see if a given record's state is VA. Here, if the record is Virginia, the appropriate tax rate is provided. Otherwise, the document tells the reader to add the appropriate tax. (See also NEXTIF.)

You can also use an IF statement to prevent blank lines from occurring in addresses when doing a mail merge. For example, consider the following:

Use a paragraph character in place of `<CR>` if possible.

```
{name}<CR>
{company}<CR>
{address}<CR>
{place}<CR>
{zip}<CR>
```

This produces blanks for data records in which no company name is entered. You can use the IF field to tell Word to print the company field only if it isn't blank.

```
{DATABASE datatest}<CR>
{name}<CR>
{IF {company} <> "" "{company}<CR>
"}{address}<CR>
{place}<CR>
{zip}<CR>
```

The placement of quotes, spaces, and paragraph markers is crucial. Here, if the company field isn't blank (`<> ""`), Word prints the company field followed by a Return. Because the `text if false` field is blank, if `{company}` doesn't contain any data, Word just goes on to the `{address}` field. This procedure can be used anywhere a data file contains blanks.

INCLUDEPICTURE (Replaces IMPORT)

The INCLUDEPICTURE field has the following syntax:

`INCLUDEPICTURE` *`file switches`*

and is used to import a graphic file into Word. The INCLUDEPICTURE field is usually inserted by the **I**nsert | **P**icture command when you select the Link to File option. The file must include an extension if it's something other than .TIF. For example, you might use the following to incorporate a graphic image of your signature:

```
{INCLUDEPICTURE signature.bmp}
```

Optional switches are:

`\c`*converter*	The name of Word's conversion filter (minus the .FLT extension).
`\d`	Tells Word *not* to incorporate the image into the Word document itself. This reduces the required file size at the expense of document speed.

INCLUDETEXT (Formerly INCLUDE)

Use the INCLUDETEXT command to specify a link to a text (nongraphic) file. The INCLUDETEXT field is usually inserted by the **Insert|File** command when you select the Link to File option. The syntax for INCLUDETEXT is

```
INCLUDETEXT filename bookmark/range switches
```

The filename is the name of the file you are including (importing into the current document). The bookmark/range can be a bookmark, a named range (in a spreadsheet), or a range of cell addresses in a spreadsheet. To include a boilerplate no compete clause in a file, you might use:

```
{ INCLUDETEXT D:\\WINWORD\\CONTRACT\\BOOKCONT.DOC no compete}
```

In this example, a file called BOOKCONT.DOC would contain a number of boilerplate clauses, each bookmarked with an identifying name.

Switches for INCLUDETEXT can include:

`\c`*converter*	Converter name (not generally required because Word autodetects file formats).
`\!`	Locks field results; prevents the field from being updated unless the included file has changed. The `\!` switch has no effect, despite documentation to the contrary.

INDEX

The INDEX field has the following syntax:

```
INDEX \ switch switch-instruction
```

and generates an index based on XE (index entry) fields in a document. Unless otherwise limited (see switches), the INDEX field creates an index for all XE fields throughout the entire document. The INDEX field can use the following switches:

\b *bookmark*

Limits the index to the range of pages contained in the specified bookmark. For example, you can tell Word to index just the first ten pages of a document. Mark those pages with a bookmark (select the pages, choose Insert Bookmark, and name the selected range—for example, `FirstTen`). Now the field:

```
{INDEX \b FirstTen}
```

limits the index to just the first ten pages. The field can be placed anywhere, but includes XE fields only in the `FirstTen` bookmark range.

\d *separator*

Used with `\s` switch to select the separator between sequence number (for example, chapter number) and page number. The default separator is the hyphen. For example, if you have an index entry:

```
{XE Bananas}
```

contained within a section that includes:

```
{SEQ Section}
```

Then the INDEX field:

```
{INDEX \s "Section" \d :}
```

creates index items that look like this:

```
Bananas 2:21,3:47,3:49,6:104
```

\e *separator*

Specifies the separator that comes between an index entry (for example, `Bananas`, above) and the listing of page numbers. The default is a single space. For example:

```
{INDEX \e :}
```

would result in index items that look like this:

```
Bananas: 1-3,6,23,101
```

\f *type*

The `\f` switch creates an index using only the specified entry type. For example, the result of the field `{index \f "n"}` includes only entries marked with XE fields that use the same `\f` switch, for example, `{xe "Restaurants" \f "n"}`.

\g *separator*

Specifies a page range separator. For example:

```
{INDEX \g " to "}
```

uses the word *to* instead of a hyphen (-).

\h *break*

Specifies the index break character/separator (that is, the text that comes between alphabetical index groups). For example, any single letter:

```
{INDEX \h A}
```

results in index entries separated by letters of the alphabet:

```
A
Aging 2,5,8,23
Antelopes 5,102
Apples 103,117
B
Biscuits 5,8,11
Bottles 44,88
```

Note that here A was used, but any letter (for example, `\h b`, `\h x`, `\h C`) produces identical results.

\l *separator*

The `\l` switch is used to specify the page number separator. The default is the comma. For example:

```
{field \l \}
```

produces the following:

```
Bananas 1/2/4-5/102
```

\p *range*

The `\p` switch is used to limit the index to a range of letters. For example:

```
{INDEX \p br}
```

limits the index to entries that begin with *br*. The field:

```
{INDEX \p a-m}
```

limits the index to the first half of the alphabet.

\r

The `\r` switch is used to put subcategories of an index entry on the same line. For example, if you have index entries:

```
{XE "Fruit:Apples"}
{XE "Fruit:Oranges"}
{XE "Fruit:Pears"}
```

the default Word index might look like this:

```
Fruit
Apples 1,7,21
Oranges 17
Pears 25,66
```

By specifying:

```
{INDEX \r}
```

you'd get:

```
Fruit: Apples 1,7,21; Oranges 17; Pears 25,66
```

\s *sequence*

The `\s` switch is used to include a sequence number (for example, from chapters, sections, subsections, and so forth) before each page number. For example, if you use `{SEQ chap}` to number each chapter, the following INDEX field:

```
{INDEX \s chap}
```

produces:

```
Apples 1-2,1-5,2-17,3-33
```

with the sequence number (that is, corresponding to subsections of the document) and page number separated by a dash. Use the `\d` switch to specify something other than the dash.

INFO

The INFO field has the following syntax:

```
INFO type new
```

and is used to insert items from the **F**ile|Summary **I**nfo dialog box. The type is the name of the field you want to display, and new is used to change the summary information to something else. For example:

```
{INFO Author}
```

displays the name of the author. The field:

```
{INFO Author "John Q. Public"}
```

changes the name of the author to John Q. Public. Quotes are needed for multiword new settings. Note that the word INFO is optional. For example, `{INFO Author}` is equivalent to `{AUTHOR}` and provides the same options. Info types are:

```
Author new
Comments new
Keywords new
Subject new
Title new
CREATEDATE
EDITTIME
```

```
FILENAME
FILESIZE
LASTSAVEDBY
NUMCHARS
NUMPAGES
NUMWORDS
PRINTDATE
SAVEDATE
REVNUM
TEMPLATE
```

The first five, which correspond to the dialog box you see when you select File|Summary Info from the menu, can be changed as well as displayed. The remaining eleven are read only, and cannot be changed using the Info (or other) field commands.

KEYWORDS

The KEYWORDS field has the following syntax:

```
KEYWORDS new
```

and is used to display and change keywords. For example:

```
{KEYWORDS senate congress house}
```

changes (or creates) the document's keywords to senate, congress, and house. Note that you can't use the KEYWORDS field to add to a list of keywords. KEYWORDS can only create a new list. To add to the existing list, you'd either need to use the dialog box directly or write a macro.

LASTSAVEDBY

The LASTSAVEDBY field displays the name of the last person who issued a save or a close command for the file. For example:

```
{LASTSAVEDBY}
```

usually displays your own name, for most Word users.

LINK (New)

Syntax:

```
LINK Class Filename range switches
```

The LINK field is used to make an OLE link with another program's file. Word inserts this field when you copy part of another application's file using Paste Special from the Edit menu.

Class	The application type of the contents being linked; different types are listed in WIN.INI.
Filename	The complete path specification of the file (including double \\ instead of \ for path references).
Range	Named range or range of cells (for example, in a spreadsheet).

Switches can be:

\a

The \a switch tells Word that the field should be updated automatically, rather than waiting for you to press F9. This is similar to DDEAUTO. \a is the default, and is inserted automatically. To disable automatic updates, you must edit the field and delete the \a switch.

\b

This tells Word to insert the linked object as a bitmap rather than using the native graphic format.

\d

The \d switch tells Word not to store graphics in the Word document file, making the link dependent (and a little slower), but reducing the document file size.

\p

This tells Word to insert the linked object as a Word Picture (the format supported by Word's drawing module).

\r

This tells Word to insert the linked object in rich-text format (RTF). This usually provides the best conversion and compatibility with other word processor formats, including Word for Windows 2.

\t

This tells Word to insert the linked object as a text file, with no further conversion.

MACRO (New)

You use the MACRO field to embed a macro into a document. Unlike the MACROBUTTON field, the MACRO field does not display a result. It often is used within another field to cause a macro to be executed any time the field is updated. The syntax is

```
MACRO macro1 [/s macro2]
```

The *macro1* macro is automatically run any time the field is updated. The optional *macro2* specified after the switch is run any time part of the displayed result of the outer field is selected. You might use the macro field when you need to get more information than you can get from an ASK or FILLIN field.

MACROBUTTON

The MACROBUTTON field has the following syntax:

```
MACROBUTTON macro text
```

and is used to insert a clickable reference in a file that allows the user to execute a macro. The macro is the name of the macro you want to execute, and text is the way the field appears in the file. For example:

```
{MACROBUTTON One Print One Copy}
{MACROBUTTON Two Print Two Copies}
{MACROBUTTON Three Print Three Copies}
```

when included in a file, displays three MACROBUTTONs:

```
Print One Copy
Print Two Copies
Print Three Copies
```

If you have macros called One, Two, and Three that perform the indicated task, then the MACROBUTTONs shown let the user double-click to print the number of copies.

MACROBUTTONs are most useful if they stand out. One way to do this is by formatting them in color and/or by including a border (box) in their paragraph formatting. The text for a MACROBUTTON need not include quotes. But the display text must fit on a single line without wrapping.

MERGEFIELD

Syntax:

```
MERGEFIELD fieldname
```

Use the MERGEFIELD field to merge data from a data source into a main document during a mail merge. The merged item appears in the location of the mergefield command. For example:

```
Dear {mergefield name}:
```

MERGEREC

Syntax:

```
MERGEREC
```

When doing a mail merge, the MERGEREC field inserts the current data file record number. The MERGEREC field serves as a counter of records in the data file, and doesn't count the number of documents actually printed (see MERGESEQ). MERGEREC is incremented by the presence of DATA, NEXT, and NEXTIF fields in a data file. If you skip specific records using SKIPIF, MERGEREC is incremented nonetheless.

One excellent use of MERGEREC is for printing a specific known range of records. For example, if you know you want to print a mailmerge document for the 41st through 80th, include the following at the top of your document file:

```
{SKIPIF {MERGEREC} < 41 }{SKIPIF {MERGEREC} > 80}
```

Here, MERGEREC is used inside fields, and never displays in the document at all. Another use for MERGEREC, if needed, would be to create a displayable serial number, as might be the case in generating invoices. For example:

```
Invoice #{={MERGEREC}+1000}
```

would insert a serialized number beginning at 1001, and would always be linked to your data file.

MERGESEQ

The MERGESEQ field serves as a counter for the number of data records actually merged. If you merge the entire database and do not change the base sorting, MERGESEQ and MERGEREC are identical. Otherwise, MERGESEQ serves as a record number indicator for data records actually used.

NEXT

The NEXT field is used to include more than one record in a given document. Ordinarily, when doing a mail merge, one document is printed for each record. With the NEXT field, however, you can include multiple records in a single document. I find this to be useful when I need to refer to several addresses from a data file. For example:

```
{SKIPIF {MERGEREC} < 92}{SKIPIF {MERGEREC} > 96}
```

and:

```
{name}{address}
{NEXT}
{name}{address}
{NEXT}
{name}{address}
{NEXT}
{name}{address}
{NEXT}
{name}{address}
{NEXT}
```

would include the `{name}` and `{address}` fields from records 92 through 96.

NEXTIF

The NEXTIF statement has the following syntax:

```
NEXTIF expression
```

and works like the NEXT field except that it advances to the next record only if the expression is true. The NEXTIF field doesn't work as documented in the Word reference manual. It can't be used to limit a mail merge to fields matching a specific value. Rather, if the expression is true, the following record is used to complete the current document. If the expression is false, the current document continues uninterrupted.

One use for the NEXTIF field would be to design a slightly more complex record structure. For example, a key field might contain an indicator of whether or not the current record is continued onto the next record. For example, your data file might look like this:

```
name,address,city,state,more
Dave Johns,853 Johns St.,St. John,NE,No
Jan Smith,45 Smith Street,Austin,TX,No
Will Davis,322 Davis Avenue,Butte,MO,Yes
Dentist,37,$95000
Sue West,451 East Drive,Easton,MD,No
Sarah East,851 East Road,Westville,MD,Yes
CEO,48,$182000
```

Here, most records contain name, address, city, state, and a fifth field that's No or Yes. If the fifth field is Yes, then the record that follows contains occupation, age, and salary instead of a new record. You might have the following in your document file:

```
Name:{name}
Address:{address}
City:{city}
State:{state}
```

```
{NEXTIF more = Yes}
Occupation:{name}
Age:{address}
Income:{city}
```

If you were compiling a profile of people in your data file, the presence of a Yes in the fifth field tells you that the record that follows is different. For those records, the name field is used for occupation, address is used for age, and city is used for income. If you leave off the last three lines from the document file, the effect of the NEXTIF statement is to tell Word to skip (different from SKIPIF) the following record if the fifth field in the current record is YES. This effectively tells Word to skip the record because the document doesn't try to use any of the fields in the balance of the document. As shown here, however, the following record is used but is interpreted differently.

NOTEREF

The NOTEREF field has the following syntax:

`NOTEREF` *`bookmark`*

and is used to display the endnote or footnote reference number referred to by the bookmark. This is useful when you're using the same note for more than one reference, as well as in cross-referencing. For example:

```
See Footnote {NOTEREF interactions} for a discussion of the hazards
associated with combining over-the-counter medications.
```

would resolve to the footnote number bookmarked as interactions.

NUMCHARS

The NUMCHARS field displays the number of characters in the current document. It's updated with F9, when you're doing a mail merge, or when the file is printed with the UpdateField option checked. See FILESIZE, also.

NUMPAGES

The NUMPAGES field displays the number of pages in the current document. It's updated with F9, the Update Button in **File** | **Summary Info** | **Statistics**, or each time the file is printed.

NUMWORDS

The NUMWORDS field displays the number of words in the current document. It's updated with F9, the Update Button in **File** | **Summary Info** | **Statistics**, or each time the file is printed.

PAGE

The PAGE field displays the current page. It's used to insert page numbers in a document, usually (but not necessarily) in a footer or a header. For example:

```
Page {PAGE}
```

PAGEREF

PAGEREF has the following syntax:

```
PAGEREF bookmark
```

and is used for creating cross-references to pages. Assuming a bookmark has been defined for text spanning a range of pages, you can refer to that range. For example:

```
See the discussion of contraindications in Appendix 1 (Pages {PAGEREF
contraind}.
```

PRINT

The PRINT field has the following syntax:

```
PRINT data
```

and is used to send codes or data to the printer without interpretation by Word. If you have an HP LaserJet Series II printer, for example, you might sometimes want to send codes directly.

PRINTDATE

The PRINTDATE field displays the last date on which the document was printed. This comes from the **F**ile | **S**ummary **I**nfo dialog box.

QUOTE

QUOTE has the following syntax:

```
QUOTE text
```

and is used to insert literal text into a document. For example:

```
{QUOTE "This is how the QUOTE field works."}
```

RD

The RD (reference document) field has the following syntax:

```
RD document
```

and is used to build a master index or table of contents for a group of related files. The RD field tells Word to include the document you reference in any index or table of contents. Quotes aren't needed around the document string, which can (optionally) include the extension (.DOC) and the path specification. Remember that if you include the path, you must use two \s switches to distinguish the \ character from switches, for example:

```
C:\\WORD\\DOC\\FILETEST.DOC.
```

Unlike the INCLUDETEXT field, the RD field doesn't display the referenced document. Also unlike the INCLUDETEXT field, the RD field works only with Word documents. Furthermore, you can't limit the inclusion to an area covered by a bookmark or range of pages. When using the INCLUDETEXT field, page numbers are taken care of automatically, because included files are displayed in the current document. With the RD field, you must explicitly set the starting page number (in a header or footer) within each included document. This is absolutely crucial.

The RD field can be used exclusively in a document that contains only RD fields. For example:

```
{RD introduce}
{RD ch1}
{RD ch2}
{RD ch3}
{RD ch4}
{RD ch5}
{RD append1}
{RD append2}
{RD append3}
{INDEX}
```

You could list all the components of a book in a compound document whose sole function is to compile an index. Remember, however, that unless you explicitly set pages in each component, the index will find multiple page ones, page twos, and so forth, and will be wrong. See the Long Documents Workshop for more and better options.

The RD field can also be used in a regular document to include additional files for indexing purposes. Just put the RD field(s) where the other text will appear. Done this way, you still have to manually set the page numbers in the RD files.

REF

The REF field has the following syntax:

```
bookmark
```

and is used to display text contained in a bookmark. If you have repetitive text in a document, the REF field can spare you the agony of repeating that text each time. The word REF can be omitted. Used with the SET field, you can create a text variable, every instance of which can be changed with a single command. This is especially useful if the repetitive text is subject to revision.

The REF field is similar to the location component of an INCLUDETEXT field, except that it refers only to a location contained in the current document (rather than an outside document). A primary purpose of the REF field is for use in doing mail-merge operations. See Chapter 37, "Mail Merge," for more on this use.

REVNUM

The REVNUM field is taken from **File** | Summary **Info** | Stat**i**stics. It displays the revision number of the current document. The revision number is incremented each time you save a document. Note that REVNUM can be misleading because it's incremented each time you save at all, not each time you open a document. Thus, if you press the Save key ten times per editing session, and edit the document 10 times, REVNUM will equal 100. This, however, could be a meaningful number for your purposes.

SAVEDATE

The SAVEDATE field displays the last date on which the current document was saved. As with other date fields, the format of SAVEDATE's result can be modified with the date picture switch.

SECTION (New)

The SECTION field inserts the number of the current section. This can be extremely useful in setting up compound numbering that uses pages within section numbers. For example, you might divide your chapters into sections:

```
Page {section}-{page}
```

This assumes, of course, that you've set section numbering to restart with one at the beginning of each section.

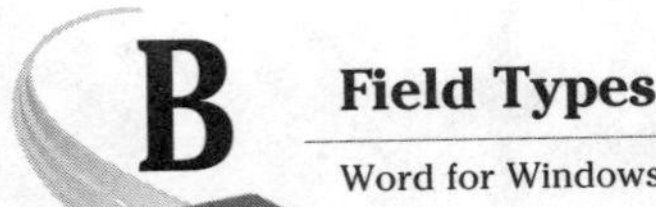

SECTIONPAGES (New!!!)

The SECTIONPAGES field inserts the number of pages in the current section, which solves a very annoying Word for Windows problem. In previous versions of Word for Windows, you had to jump through hoops to get page numbering such as:

```
Page {page} of {numpages}
```

The problem is that `{numpages}` is for the whole document. Thankfully, you can now use `{sectionpages}`:

```
Page {page} of {sectionpages}
```

SEQ

The SEQ field has the following syntax:

`SEQ` *`series-name bookmark switch`*

and is used to insert a sequence number into a document. SEQ is used to number chapters, tables, figures, illustrations, lists, or anything else not already covered by a numbering system (for example, footnotes and outlining, which are controlled by other Word features). The beauty of this system is that you aren't limited in the number of different sequences you can have. Word maintains each one independently.

To use the SEQ field, just substitute it instead of numbers each time you want to number something. For example, use:

```
Table {SEQ table}
```

each time you create a title for a table. It displays as Table 1, Table 2, Table 3, and so forth. If you have a set of figures, use

```
Figure {SEQ fig}
```

The words table and fig inside the SEQ field aren't special keywords. They're names that you create. Thus, `{SEQ table}` could have been `{SEQ tab}` or `{SEQ tabno}`. Just use the same name each time you add another item to the sequence. If you create a series of numbered lists in a document, you could used `{SEQ list1}` to number items in the first list, `{SEQ list2}` for the second, and so forth. Or you could use descriptive names, like `{SEQ shopping}` or `{SEQ todo}`. You can also use the switches `\c`, `\r`, and `\h` with SEQ, as follows:

\c

Use the `\c` switch to repeat the most recently used SEQ from a series. For example, you might have just created a table and included `{SEQ table}` in the title, and now need to refer to it. Obviously, if you just use another `{SEQ table}` field, it produces the next number instead of the same one. But `{SEQ table \c}` tells Word to display the current table number without incrementing it. Thus, use `{SEQ table}` to number tables, and use `{SEQ table \c}` to refer to the table in the text.

\r*n*

The `\r`*n* resets the sequence number to *n*. This is very useful for resetting figure and table numbers at the beginning of specific chapters in a book or report (Figure 1-1, Figure 2-1, and so forth).

\h

The `\h` (high) switch increments the sequence counter without displaying a result. This is very useful when used with the `\r` switch at the beginning of a new chapter or document division. If you use `\r` on a specific figure or table, then the placement becomes too critical. If you put a hidden, reset-to-zero field at the beginning of each section, you don't have to worry about it anymore. For example, I have:

```
{seq figno \r\h}{seq tablenumber \r\h}
```

at the beginning of this and every chapter in this book. Note: When you omit a number, `\r` means *reset to zero.*

The SEQ field can also be used with a bookmark instead of switches. You can't use a bookmark and switches in the same SEQ field statement. While the `\c` switch creates a reference to the previous SEQ field number, you might want to refer to an earlier or later one. To use a bookmark reference, bookmark either the original SEQ field itself or any text between that SEQ field and the next one. When you use:

```
See Table {SEQ table expectancy}
```

Word uses the `{SEQ table}` number that's in effect at the bookmark's location. You need only bookmark any text that has that number in effect. Thus, you can bookmark the `{SEQ table}` field itself, or any text up to the next `{SEQ table}` field.

SET

The SET field has the following syntax:

```
SET bookmark newtext
```

and doesn't display a result. Rather, it's used to change the text referred to by a bookmark. For example:

```
July 4, 1996
```

might be bookmarked as `effectdate` in a document. And you might also be using `{REF effectdate}` to use that date in a number of places. If you want to change the date referred to, you have two options. You can find the original instance and change it. Or you can use the SET field to change it:

```
{SET effectdate "July 25, 1996"}
```

But this changes only the `{REF effectdate}` fields when they're updated, and not the original occurrence. Instead, you might prefer to always use `{REF effectdate}` and to include a single `{SET effectdate newdate}` field before the first reference. (Note: REF can be omitted from bookmark reference fields.)

When no text is already explicitly defined as a bookmark, the SET statement becomes the bookmark's reference point (as used in the GoTo command). If you later select text and give it the same bookmark name, the new text becomes the reference point until the SET statement is updated. If multiple SET fields have the identical bookmark name, the last one updated becomes the reference point for any GoTo bookmark commands.

SKIPIF

The SKIPIF field has the following syntax:

SKIPIF *expression*

and doesn't display a result. The SKIPIF field is used to cancel processing of the current record in a mail merge operation. For example:

```
{SKIPIF zip = 22310}
```

would skip (not print a document for) any records with the zip code 22310.

STYLEREF

The STYLEREF field has the following syntax:

STYLEREF *style name*

and inserts the text of the preceding paragraph having style name. If you continue to think about paragraphs in the conventional sense (that is, a group of sentences), this might not seem all that useful to you. But remember that in Word, any text between two carriage returns is a paragraph. Thus, any heading, which is typically not even a whole sentence, is a paragraph. And in a list, each item is usually a paragraph. Thus, STYLEREF gives you the ability to refer to items or headings—not just a group of sentences (although it can do that, too, depending on what you want). For example, in a style-formatted document, you might need to refer to a heading in the text. Thus:

See the subsection immediately following `{STYLEREF "heading 3"}`

inserts the paragraph associated with the previous use of the heading3 style. Note that quotes are necessary for multiword style names.

The STYLEREF field can be modified by with the `\l` switch in footers and headers. The `\l` switch tells Word to use the last matching paragraph on the current page. This can be useful in creating encyclopedia-type headings. If your individual sections are styled as topic, the following might be useful in a header:

```
{STYLEREF topic} to {STYLEREF topic \l}
```

This prints the beginning and ending topic at the top of each page.

SUBJECT

The SUBJECT field has the following syntax:

```
SUBJECT new
```

and is taken from the **F**ile|Summary **I**nfo dialog box. The SUBJECT field displays the subject in the current document, and is frequently useful in headers for letters and reports. By specifying new, you can change the subject from that point on in the document. Note that only one subject can appear in the **F**ile|Summary **I**nfo box at any given time. But because `{SUBJECT new}` fields are evaluated sequentially in a document, you can use it to cause different subjects to appear within the document in different places. At print time, each occurrence of `{SUBJECT}` is evaluated sequentially. For example:

At the outset, I said that the topic of this report was `{SUBJECT}`. In retrospect, the topic has really been `{SUBJECT "The Urban Experience in the 1960s"}`.

SYMBOL

You can use the SYMBOL field to insert a symbol. The advantage of this (under Word for Windows 2) was that the symbol field is formatting-independent, and wouldn't get zapped if you unthinkingly reformatted your document as arial. The SYMBOL field was formerly inserted using the **I**nsert|**S**ymbol command and now can be created manually or inserted using the **I**nsert|Fi**e**ld command. The SYMBOL field conveys both the symbol and the font. For example:

```
{ SYMBOL 0183 \f Symbol \* MERGEFORMAT }
```

> **SUPER NOTE**
>
> Word 6's new SYMBOL command inserts symbols in a special internal format whose character format cannot be reset by the user.

TA

Use the TA field to define the text and page number for an entry in a table of authorities. A table of authorities is used in legal documents, notably briefs, to cite cases, statutes, and provisions in formal documents (for example, state and federal constitutions). You use the Table of Authorities tab in the Insert | Index and Tables menu to create the TA field. For example:

```
{ TA \s "Robinson v. Polaroid" }
```

The TA field can be used with a variety of switches, described under the following headings.

\b

Makes the entry's page number bold.

\c

Category number for the entry (the default is cases). You can replace the numbered categories with your own—for example, U.S. Court of Appeals, U.S. Supreme Court, and so forth.

\I

Italicizes the entry's page number.

\l

Defines the long citation for the entry in the table of authorities.

\r *bookmark*

Includes a bookmarked range of pages.

\s

Defines the short citation (for quicker reference).

TC

The TC field has the following syntax:

```
TC textswitch
```

and is used to create table of contents entries (similar to XE and TA). The field:

```
{tc "How to Build a Doghouse"}
```

creates a table of contents entry for the page on which the TC field appears, with that title. As a rule (unlike index entries), the text of table of contents items always exactly matches some header or section title in a document. Thus, you might find it beneficial to use headings for automatic creation of a table of contents. If you must create TC entries manually, at the very least you might consider writing a macro to automatically include selected text inside the field so you don't accidentally retype titles incorrectly.

Alternatively, if the text you want to include has a particular style, you can use a STYLEREF field within a TC field. The following TC field, for example:

```
{tc {STYLEREF "figure title"}}
```

produces a table of contents entry that uses the text that most recently (immediately preceding the TC field) used a style called "figure title." The TC field can be used with the following switches.

\f *id*

The `\f` switch is used to create a grouping category (id) for specific tables of contents. For example:

```
{tc "Figure 17" \f A}
```

states that a table of contents entry is generated whenever you specify (with the TOC field) that you're collecting entries for something called A. You could have another series of items called B, C, and so forth. You could then use TOC to collect the items from A into a list of figures, B might be a list of tables, C might be a list of contributors, and so forth.

\l

The `\l` switch is used to assign levels to manually created TC entries. Ordinarily, when you compile a table of contents (from outline levels), Word produces a multilevel table of contents, using toc 1 for level 1, toc 2 for level 2, and so forth. The styles toc # are built-in (up to toc 8) styles that Word uses in formatting a table of contents. By specifying the `\l` switch, you can assign levels (and thereby those styles) to manually inserted TC fields. For example:

```
{TC "Delivery Considerations" \l3}
```

tells Word to use toc 3 for this table of contents item. Presumably, other items have been defined as `\l2` and `\1`, under which this one appears as a subheading of sorts.

\n

Use the `\n` switch to suppress the page number for the entry.

TEMPLATE

The TEMPLATE field displays the name of the template used to create the current file. If no template was specified (that is, if the default Normal was used), this field displays no result.

TIME

The TIME field has the following syntax:

```
TIME switches
```

and displays when the TIME field was last updated. The display can be modified with the time picture switch (see Date-time picture switches, earlier in this chapter). For example:

```
Printed at {TIME} on {DATE}
```

inserts the time and date that a document was printed. Such information is often required in some offices for certain kinds of documents. The TIME field is inserted by the **I**nsert|Date and **T**ime command on the menu.

TITLE

The TITLE field has the following syntax:

```
TITLE new
```

and is used to display the title of the document from the **F**ile|Summary **I**nfo dialog box. If you specify new, the title is changed. For example:

```
{TITLE "Exciting Developments in Ketchup"}
```

creates a fascinating title for the current document. The TITLE field is frequently used in headers, along with other summary information. For example, the following creates an informative header, assuming you don't ignore the summary information screen each time it appears:

```
{TITLE}
{SUBJECT}
{AUTHOR}
{DATE}
Page {PAGE} of {NUMPAGES}
```

TOA

The TOA field is used to generate a table of authorities. You create the TOA field by using the Insert | Index and Tables command in the menu. Or, if you're particularly brave, you can do it manually.

The switches are described in the following headings.

\c *switch*

Specifies the category to compile. This field is required. You need a `\c` switch and specification for each distinct TOA in a document.

\b *bookmark*

Limits the TOA to just the area defined by the bookmark.

\d

The `\d` and `\s` switches are used to define the separator characters used between sequence numbers and page numbers. The `\d` component can be up to four characters. For example:

```
{toa \c2 \s sectionnumber \d "—"}.
```

\e

The `\e` switch specifies the separator characters between a table of authorities entry and page number. This switch has the same rules as `\d`.

\f

Removes the document's formatting of entries.

\g

Use the `\g` switch to set the separator characters used in a page range. It can be up to five characters and must be in quotes.

\h

The `\h` switch is used to includes the category headings for the entries in a table of authorities.

\l

Use the `\l` switch to specify the separator characters used between page numbers for entries with multiple-page references. This has the same rules as the `\h` switch.

\p

Use the `\p` switch to specify passim, which uses the word *passim* when five or more references are made to the same authority.

\s *sequence*

Use the `\s` switch to specify a sequence number for use with page numbers.

TOC

The TOC field has the following syntax:

```
TOC switches
```

and is used to generate tables of contents, figures, tables, illustrations, and so forth. The resulting table is inserted at the cursor's current location. The TOC field can be used with four switches, shown below.

\b

The `\b` switch confines the table to a specific bookmark:

```
{TOC \b "Dental Plan"}
```

This field builds a table of contents only for the text defined by a bookmark called Dental Plan.

\f *id*

The `\f` switch corresponds to the TC `\f` switch, and tells Word to build the table only for entries marked with id. For example, if you have the following TC entries:

```
{tc "Step 1" \f A}
{tc "Step 2" \f A}
{tc "Step 3" \f A}
{tc "Step 4" \f A}
```

then the field:

```
{TOC \f A}
```

collects just these entries for the current table.

\o *levels*

The `\o` switch collects table entries from a specified range of outline levels. For example, the default behavior of Word is to collect entries for all heading levels (1 through 8). For some purposes (for example, a science fiction book) that's way too many, while for a technical reference manual it might be just perfect. The field:

```
{TOC \o 1-3}
```

instructs Word to collect entries for just the first three levels.

\s *text*

The \s switch is used to add a sequence number to the table entries as they're listed. For example:

```
{TOC \s Section}
```

would add a sequence number (identified by Section in connection with `{SEQ Section}` fields) to page references for each item listed in the table. The default separator between this number and the page number is a hyphen. Use the `\d` switch for a different separator.

\d *char*

The `\d` switch modifies the separator used between sequence and age numbers when you're using the `\s` switch. For example:

```
{TOC \s Section \d .}
```

results in entries that look like this:

```
Proceedings.................................2.24
```

USERADDRESS (New)

Use the USERADDRESS to insert the value stored in the USERADDRESS section of WINWORD6.INI. Use Tools | Options | User Info to set the user's address.

USERINITIALS

Use the USERINITIALS to insert the value stored in the USERINITIALS section of WINWORD6.INI. Use Tools | Options | User Info to set the user's initials.

USERNAME

Use the USERNAME to insert the value stored in the USERNAME section of WINWORD6.INI. Use Tools | Options | User Info to set the user's name.

XE

The XE field has the following syntax:

```
XE text switches
```

and is used to insert index entries for inclusion in an index. The XE field doesn't display an immediate result. For example:

```
{xe "Time management"}
```

if inserted on page 27, produces the following index entry:

```
Time management 27
```

in the index. The XE field can be used with these four switches:

\b

The `\b` switch causes the page number for a specific XE to appear in bold. This is typically done for pages containing definitions of a specific term. The entry:

```
{xe "Expanded Memory" \b}
```

might be used for the page on which the term is first defined.

\i

The `\i` switch causes the page number to appear in italics.

\r *bookmark*

The `\r` switch is used to indicate a range of pages, as specified by a bookmark. For example:

```
{xe "Expanded Memory" \r Expanded}
```

tells Word to reference the entire set of pages comprised by the bookmark called Expanded.

\t *text*

The `\t` switch is used to cause text to appear instead of a page reference. For example:

```
{xe "Infancy" \t "See Babies"}
```

SUPER NOTE

Such entries in indexes are infuriating to readers. If possible, use the page number along with the reference.

Appendix

C

Reserved Keywords and Word Commands

One of the most frequent errors you can make when writing a Word macro is inadvertently misusing one of Word 6's reserved words. Word 6 has more than 900 reserved words. Reserved words are the names of commands, functions, and keywords that you use in writing macros and customizing. This appendix contains a list of what is believed to be every reserved Word 6 command, function, and keyword. Functions are indicated by `()` at the end of the command name. Commands are built-in Word procedures that perform some kind of action. Functions are built-in Word procedures that return some kind of result. Keywords are words that are significant when writing macros.

When writing macros, it's expecting a lot for you to know each and every word that's meaningful to Word 6. Often, you'll get an unexpected syntax error message for a command that you think should work. When the syntax looks correct, you should immediately suspect that you've inadvertently used one of Word's reserved keywords or command names as a variable name. You cannot do that. If you get an inexplicable syntax error message, try renaming your variable. Better still, just to be sure, check this list to see if your variable name is on it. If you have a variable named DateSerial, for example, you might be surprised to learn that that's a reserved word. Rename it to DateSerialX and you'll be all set!

In addition to Word 6's commands and functions, there are more than 60 commands and functions from previous versions of Word for Windows that can be accessed by appending `WW2_` and `WW1_` at the front. For example, `WW2_Files$(".")` adds a \ to the end of the path; `Files$(".")` does not. If you use macros from previous versions of Word for Windows, you no doubt will discover a number of such commands and functions that Word inserts automatically the first time you use old macros in the new version.

Complete online information for command syntax, examples, and command use is provided in Word 6's Help system. To obtain help for a specific command or function, select **H**elp | **C**ontents, click Programming, and then click WordBASIC Command and Function Index. Alternatively, if a macro editing window is open, you can obtain complete context-sensitive help for the command or function nearest the cursor simply by pressing the F1 key.

```
Abs()
ActivateObject
AddAddIn
AddButton
AddDropDownItem
AddInState
AllCaps
AnnotationRefFromSel$()
AppActivate
AppClose
AppCount()
AppGetNames
AppHide
AppInfo$()
AppIsRunning()
ApplyHeading1
ApplyHeading2
ApplyHeading3
ApplyListBullet
AppMaximize
AppMinimize
AppMove
AppRestore
AppSendMessage
AppShow
AppSize
```

```
AppWindowHeight
AppWindowPosLeft
AppWindowPosTop
AppWindowWidth
Asc()
AtEndOfDocument()
AtStartOfDocument()
AutoMarkIndexEntries
AutoText
AutoTextName$()
Beep
Begin Dialog...End Dialog
Bold
BookmarkName$()
BorderBottom
BorderInside
BorderLeft
BorderLineStyle
BorderNone
BorderOutside
BorderRight
BorderTop
Call
Cancel
CancelButton
CenterPara
ChangeCase
CharColor
CharLeft
CharLeftExtend
CharRight
CharRightExtend
ChDefaultDir
ChDir
CheckBox
CheckBoxFormField
ChooseButtonImage
Chr$()
CleanString$()
ClearAddIns
Close
ClosePane
ClosePreview
CloseUpPara
CloseViewHeaderFooter
CmpBookmarks()
ColumnSelect
ComboBox
CommandValid()
Connect
ContinueMacro
ControlRun
Converter$()
ConverterLookup
ConvertObject
CopyBookmark
CopyButtonImage
CopyFile
CopyFormat
CopyText
CountAddIns
CountAutoTextEntries()
CountBookmarks()
CountDirectories()
CountFiles()
CountFonts()
CountFoundFiles()
CountKeys()
CountLanguages()
CountMacros()
CountMenuItems()
CountMenus()
CountMergeFields()
CountStyles()
CountToolbarButtons()
CountToolbars()
CountToolsGrammarStatistics()
CountWindows()
CreateSubdocument
Date$()
DateSerial()
DateValue()
Day()
Days360()
DDEExecute
DDEInitiate()
DDEPoke
DDERequest$()
DDETerminate
DDETerminateAll
Declare
DecreaseIndent
DefaultDir$()
DeleteAddIn
DeleteBackWord
DeleteButton
DeleteWord
DemoteList
DemoteToBodyText
Dialog
DialogEditor
Dim
```

DisableAutoMacros
DisableInput
DlgControlId()
DlgEnable
DlgFilePreview
DlgFocus
DlgListBoxArray
DlgSetPicture
DlgText
DlgUpdateFilePreview
DlgValue
DlgVisible
DocClose
DocMaximize
DocMinimize
DocMove
DocRestore
DocSize
DocSplit
DocumentStatistics
DocWindowHeight
DocWindowPosLeft
DocWindowPosTop
DocWindowWidth
DoFieldClick
DOSToWin$()
DottedUnderline
DoubleUnderline
DrawAlign
DrawArc
DrawBringForward
DrawBringInFrontOfText
DrawBringToFront
DrawCallout
DrawClearRange
DrawCount()
DrawCountPolyPoints()
DrawDisassemblePicture
DrawEllipse
DrawExtendSelect
DrawFlipHorizontal
DrawFlipVertical
DrawFreeformPolygon
DrawGetCalloutTextbox
DrawGetPolyPoints
DrawGetType()
DrawGroup
DrawInsertWordPicture
DrawLine
DrawNudgeDown
DrawNudgeDownPixel
DrawNudgeLeft
DrawNudgeLeftPixel
DrawNudgeRight
DrawNudgeRightPixel
DrawNudgeUp
DrawNudgeUpPixel
DrawRectangle
DrawResetWordPicture
DrawReshape
DrawRotateLeft
DrawRotateRight
DrawRoundRectangle
DrawSelect
DrawSelectNext
DrawSelectPrevious
DrawSendBackward
DrawSendBehindText
DrawSendToBack
DrawSetCalloutTextbox
DrawSetInsertToAnchor
DrawSetInsertToTextbox
DrawSetPolyPoints
DrawSetRange
DrawSnapToGrid
DrawTextBox
DrawToggleLayer
DrawUngroup
DrawUnselect
DropDownFormField
DropListBox
EditAutoText
EditBookmark
EditButtonImage
EditClear
EditConvertAllEndnotes
EditConvertAllFootnotes
EditConvertNotes
EditCopy
EditCut
EditFind
EditFindClearFormatting
EditFindFont
EditFindFound()
EditFindLang
EditFindPara
EditFindStyle
EditGoTo
EditLinks
EditObject
EditPaste
EditPasteSpecial

EditPicture
EditRedo
EditRedoOrRepeat
EditRepeat
EditReplace
EditReplaceClearFormatting
EditReplaceFont
EditReplaceLang
EditReplacePara
EditReplaceStyle
EditSelectAll
EditSwapAllNotes
EditTOACategory
EditUndo
EmptyBookmark()
EnableFormField
EndOfColumn
EndOfDocExtend
EndOfDocument
EndOfLine
EndOfLineExtend
EndOfRow
EndOfWindow
EndOfWindowExtend
Environ$()
Eof()
Err
Error
ExistingBookmark()
ExitWindows
ExtendMode()
ExtendSelection
File1
File2
File3
File4
File5
File6
File7
File8
File9
FileClose
FileCloseAll
FileCloseOrCloseAll
FileConfirmConversions
FileExit
FileFind
FileList
FileMacPageSetup
FileName$()
FileNameFromWindow$()
FileNameInfo$()
FileNew
FileNewDefault
FileNumber
FileOpen
FilePageSetup
FilePreview
FilePrint
FilePrintDefault
FilePrintPreview
FilePrintPreviewFullScreen
FilePrintSetup
FileRoutingSlip
Files$()
FileSave
FileSaveAll
FileSaveAs
FileSendMail
FileSummaryInfo
FileTemplates
FileTemplates (Not found)
Font
FontSize
FontSizeSelect
FontSubstitution
For...Next
FormatAddrFonts
FormatAutoFormat
FormatAutoFormatBegin
FormatAutoFormatEnd
FormatAutoFormatNow
FormatBordersAndShading
FormatBulletDefault
FormatBulletsAndNumbering
FormatCallout
FormatChangeCase
FormatColumns
FormatDefineStyleBorders
FormatDefineStyleFont
FormatDefineStyleFrame
FormatDefineStyleLang
FormatDefineStyleNumbers
FormatDefineStylePara
FormatDefineStyleTabs
FormatDrawingObject
FormatDropCap
FormatFillColor
FormatFont
FormatFrame
FormatFrameOrFramePicture
FormatHeaderFooterLink

FormatHeadingNumbering
FormatLineColor
FormatLineStyle
FormatNumberDefault
FormatPageNumber
FormatParagraph
FormatPicture
FormatRetAddrFonts
FormatSectionLayout
FormatStyle
FormatStyleGallery
FormatTabs
FormFieldOptions
FormShading
FoundFileName$()
Function...End Function
GetAddInID()
GetAddInName$()
GetAttr()
GetAutoCorrect$()
GetAutoText$()
GetBookmark$()
GetCurValues
GetDirectory$()
GetDocumentVar$()
GetFieldData$()
GetFormResult()
GetMergeField$
GetPrivateProfileString$()
GetProfileString$()
GetSelEndPos()
GetSelStartPos()
GetSystemInfo
GetText$()
GoBack
Goto
GotoAnnotationScope
GoToAnnotationScope
GoToHeaderFooter
GoToNextAnnotation
GoToNextEndnote
GoToNextFootnote
GoToNextItem
GoToNextPage
GoToNextSection
GoToPreviousAnnotation
GoToPreviousEndnote
GoToPreviousFootnote
GoToPreviousItem
GoToPreviousPage
GoToPreviousSection
GroupBox
GrowFont
GrowFontOnePoint
HangingIndent
Help
HelpAbout
HelpActiveWindow
HelpContents
HelpExamplesAndDemos
HelpIndex
HelpKeyboard
HelpPSSHelp
HelpQuickPreview
HelpSearch
HelpTipOfTheDay
HelpTool
HelpUsingHelp
HelpWordPerfectHelp
HelpWordPerfectHelpOptions
HelpWPHelpOpt
Hidden
HLine
Hour()
HPage
HScroll
If...Then...Else
IncreaseIndent
Indent
Input
Input$()
InputBox$()
Insert
InsertAddCaption
InsertAnnotation
InsertAutoCaption
InsertAutoText
InsertBreak
InsertCaption
InsertCaptionNumbering
InsertChart
InsertColumnBreak
InsertCrossReference
InsertDatabase
InsertDateField
InsertDateTime
InsertDrawing
InsertEmSpace
InsertEndnoteNow
InsertEnSpace
InsertEquation
InsertExcelTable

InsertField
InsertFieldChars
InsertFile
InsertFootnote
InsertFootnoteNow
InsertFormField
InsertFrame
InsertIndex
InsertIndexAndTables
InsertMergeField
InsertObject
InsertPageBreak
InsertPageField
InsertPageNumbers
InsertPara
InsertPicture
InsertSectionBreak
InsertSound
InsertSpike
InsertSubdocument
InsertSymbol
InsertTableOfAuthorities
InsertTableOfContents
InsertTableOfFigures
InsertTimeField
InsertWordArt
InStr()
Int()
IsDocumentDirty()
IsExecuteOnly()
IsMacro()
IsTemplateDirty()
Italic
JustifyPara
KeyCode()
KeyMacro$()
Kill
Language
LCase$()
Left$()
LeftPara
Len()
Let
Line Input
LineDown
LineDownExtend
LineUp
LineUpExtend
ListBox
ListMacros
LockDocument
LockFields
Lof()
LTrim$()
MacroCopy
MacroDesc$()
MacroFileName$()
MacroName$()
MacroNameFromWindow$()
MacroREM
Magnifier
MailMerge
MailMergeAskToConvertChevrons
MailMergeCheck
MailMergeConvertChevrons
MailMergeCreateDataSource
MailMergeCreateEnvelopes
MailMergeCreateHeaderSource
MailMergeCreateLabels
MailMergeDataForm
MailMergeDataSource$()
MailMergeEditDataSource
MailMergeEditHeaderSource
MailMergeEditMainDocument
MailMergeFindRecord
MailMergeFirstRecord
MailMergeGoToRecord
MailMergeGotoRecord
MailMergeHelper
MailMergeInsertAsk
MailMergeInsertFillIn
MailMergeInsertIf
MailMergeInsertMergeRec
MailMergeInsertMergeSeq
MailMergeInsertNext
MailMergeInsertNextIf
MailMergeInsertSet
MailMergeInsertSkipIf
MailMergeLastRecord
MailMergeMainDocumentType
MailMergeNextRecord
MailMergeOpenDataSource
MailMergeOpenHeaderSource
MailMergePrevRecord
MailMergeQueryOptions
MailMergeReset
MailMergeState()
MailMergeToDoc
MailMergeToPrinter
MailMergeViewData
MarkCitation
MarkIndexEntry

MarkTableOfContentsEntry
MenuItemMacro$()
MenuItemText$()
MenuMode
MenuText$()
MergeFieldName$()
MergeSubdocument
MicrosoftAccess
MicrosoftExcel
MicrosoftFox
MicrosoftFoxPro
MicrosoftMail
MicrosoftPowerPoint
MicrosoftProject
MicrosoftPublisher
MicrosoftSchedule
MicrosoftSystemInfo
Mid$()
Minute()
MkDir
Month()
MoveButton
MoveText
MoveToolbar
MsgBox
NewToolbar
NextCell
NextField
NextObject
NextPage
NextTab()
NextWindow
NormalFontPosition
NormalFontSpacing
NormalStyle
NormalViewHeaderArea
NoteOptions
Now()
OK
OKButton
On Error
OnTime
Open
OpenOrCloseUpPara
OpenSubdocument
OpenUpPara
OptionButton
OptionGroup
Organizer
OtherPane
OutlineCollapse
OutlineDemote
OutlineExpand
OutlineLevel()
OutlineMoveDown
OutlineMoveUp
OutlinePromote
OutlineShowFirstLine
OutlineShowFormat
Overtype
PageDown
PageDownExtend
PageUp
PageUpExtend
ParaDown
ParaDownExtend
ParaKeepLinesTogether
ParaKeepWithNext
ParaPageBreakBefore
ParaUp
ParaUpExtend
ParaWidowOrphanControl
PasteButtonImage
PasteFormat
PauseRecorder
Picture
PrevCell
PrevField
PrevObject
PrevPage
PrevTab()
PrevWindow
Print
PromoteList
ProtectForm
PushButton
PutFieldData
Read
RecordNextCommand
ReDim
RemoveAllDropDownItems
RemoveBulletsNumbers
RemoveDropDownItem
RemoveFrames
RemoveSubdocument
RenameMenu
RepeatFind
ResetButtonImage
ResetChar
ResetNoteSepOrNotice
ResetPara
ReviewAutoFormatChanges

Right$()
RightPara
RmDir
Rnd()
RTrim$()
RunPrintManager
SaveTemplate
ScreenRefresh
ScreenUpdating
Second()
Seek
Select Case
SelectCurAlignment
SelectCurColor
SelectCurFont
SelectCurIndent
SelectCurSentence
SelectCurSpacing
SelectCurTabs
SelectCurWord
SelectDrawingObjects
SelInfo()
SelType
SendKeys
SentLeft
SentLeftExtend
SentRight
SentRightExtend
SetAttr
SetAutoText
SetDocumentDirty
SetDocumentVar
SetEndOfBookmark
SetFormResult
SetPrivateProfileString
SetProfileString
SetSelRange
SetStartOfBookmark
SetTemplateDirty
Sgn()
ShadingPattern
Shell
ShowAll
ShowAllHeadings
ShowAnnotationBy
ShowHeading1
ShowHeading2
ShowHeading3
ShowHeading4
ShowHeading5
ShowHeading6
ShowHeading7
ShowHeading8
ShowHeading9
ShowHeadingNumber
ShowNextHeaderFooter
ShowPrevHeaderFooter
ShowVars
ShrinkFont
ShrinkFontOnePoint
ShrinkSelection
SizeToolbar
SkipNumbering
SmallCaps
SortArray
SpacePara1
SpacePara15
SpacePara2
Spike
SplitSubdocument
StartMacro
StartOfColumn
StartOfDocExtend
StartOfDocument
StartOfLine
StartOfLineExtend
StartOfRow
StartOfWindow
StartOfWindowExtend
StepIn
StepOver
Stop
StopMacro
StopMacroRunning
Str$()
Strikethrough
String$()
Style
StyleDesc$()
StyleName$()
Sub...End Sub
Subscript
Superscript
SymbolFont
TabLeader$()
TableAutoFormat
TableAutoSum
TableColumnWidth
TableDeleteCells
TableDeleteColumn
TableDeleteGeneral
TableDeleteRow

TableFormatCell
TableFormula
TableGridlines
TableHeadings
TableInsertCells
TableInsertColumn
TableInsertGeneral
TableInsertRow
TableInsertTable
TableMergeCells
TableRowHeight
TableSelectColumn
TableSelectRow
TableSelectTable
TableSort
TableSortAToZ
TableSortZToA
TableSplit
TableSplitCells
TableToOrFromText
TableToText
TableUpdateAutoFormat
TabType()
Text
TextBox
TextFormField
TextToTable
Time$()
TimeSerial()
TimeValue()
Today()
ToggleFieldDisplay
ToggleFull
ToggleHeaderFooterLink
ToggleMacroRun
ToggleMainTextLayer
TogglePortrait
ToggleScribbleMode
ToolbarButtonMacro$()
ToolbarName$()
ToolbarState()
ToolsAddRecordDefault
ToolsAdvancedSettings
ToolsAutoCorrect
ToolsAutoCorrectDays
ToolsAutoCorrectInitialCaps
ToolsAutoCorrectReplaceText
ToolsAutoCorrectSentenceCaps
ToolsAutoCorrectSmartQuotes
ToolsBulletListDefault
ToolsBulletsNumbers
ToolsCalculate
ToolsCompareVersions
ToolsCreateEnvelope
ToolsCreateLabels
ToolsCustomize
ToolsCustomizeAddMenuShortcut
ToolsCustomizeKeyboard
ToolsCustomizeKeyboardShortcut
ToolsCustomizeMenu
ToolsCustomizeMenuBar
ToolsCustomizeMenus
ToolsCustomizeRemoveMenuShortcut
ToolsCustomizeToolbar
ToolsEnvelopesAndLabels
ToolsGetSpelling
ToolsGetSynonyms
ToolsGrammar
ToolsGrammarStatisticsArray
ToolsHyphenation
ToolsHyphenationManual
ToolsLanguage
ToolsMacro
ToolsManageFields
ToolsMergeRevisions
ToolsNumberListDefault
ToolsOptions
ToolsOptionsAutoFormat
ToolsOptionsCompat
ToolsOptionsCompatibility
ToolsOptionsEdit
ToolsOptionsFileLocations
ToolsOptionsGeneral
ToolsOptionsGrammar
ToolsOptionsPrint
ToolsOptionsRevisions
ToolsOptionsSave
ToolsOptionsSpelling
ToolsOptionsUserInfo
ToolsOptionsView
ToolsProtectDocument
ToolsProtectSection
ToolsProtectUnprotectDocument
ToolsRecordMacroStart
ToolsRecordMacroStop
ToolsRecordMacroToggle
ToolsRemoveRecordDefault
ToolsRepaginate
ToolsRepaginateNow
ToolsReviewRevisions
ToolsRevisionAuthor$()
ToolsRevisionDate$()

```
ToolsRevisionDate()
ToolsRevisions
ToolsRevisionType()
ToolsShrinkToFit
ToolsSpelling
ToolsSpellSelection
ToolsThesaurus
ToolsUnprotectDocument
ToolsWordCount
TraceMacro
UCase$()
Underline
UnHang
UnIndent
UnlinkFields
UnlockFields
UpdateFields
UpdateSource
Val()
ViewAnnotations
ViewBorderToolbar
ViewDraft
ViewDrawingToolbar
ViewEndnoteArea
ViewEndnoteContNotice
ViewEndnoteContSeparator
ViewEndnoteSeparator
ViewFieldCodes
ViewFooter
ViewFootnoteArea
ViewFootnoteContNotice
ViewFootnoteContSeparator
ViewFootnotes
ViewFootnoteSeparator
ViewHeader
ViewMasterDocument
ViewMenus()
ViewNormal
ViewOutline
ViewPage
ViewRibbon
ViewRuler
ViewStatusBar
ViewToggleMasterDocument
ViewToolbars
ViewZoom
ViewZoom100
ViewZoom200
ViewZoom75
ViewZoomPageWidth
ViewZoomWholePage
VLine
VPage
VScroll
WaitCursor
Weekday()
While...Wend
Window()
WindowArrangeAll
WindowList
WindowName$()
WindowNewWindow
WindowNumber
WindowPane()
WinToDOS$()
WordLeft
WordLeftExtend
WordRight
WordRightExtend
WordUnderline
Write
Year()
```

The following are provided for compatibility with previous versions of Word for Windows. While they work in Word 6, there is no guarantee that they will be supported in future versions. When you discover a `WW2_` or `WW1_` procedure in your macros, you would be well-advised to try to rework the macro so that it uses the new counterpart instead of the old.

```
WW1_InsertPara
WW2_ChangeCase
WW2_ChangeRulerMode
WW2_CountMenuItems()
WW2_EditFind
WW2_EditFindChar
WW2_EditReplace
WW2_EditReplaceChar
WW2_FileFind
WW2_Files$()
WW2_FileTemplates
WW2_FootnoteOptions
WW2_FormatBordersAndShading
WW2_FormatCharacter
WW2_FormatDefineStyleChar
WW2_GetToolButton
WW2_GetToolMacro$
WW2_Insert
```

WW2_InsertFootnote
WW2_InsertIndex
WW2_InsertSymbol
WW2_InsertTableOfContents
WW2_KeyCode
WW2_MenuMacro$
WW2_MenuText$
WW2_PrintMerge
WW2_PrintMergeCheck
WW2_PrintMergeCreateDataSource
WW2_PrintMergeCreateHeaderSource
WW2_PrintMergeHelper
WW2_PrintMergeSelection
WW2_PrintMergeToDoc
WW2_PrintMergeToPrinter
WW2_RenameMenu
WW2_RulerMode
WW2_TableColumnWidth
WW2_TableRowHeight
WW2_ToolsHyphenation
WW2_ToolsMacro
WW2_ToolsOptionsGeneral
WW2_ToolsOptionsKeyboard
WW2_ToolsOptionsMenus
WW2_ToolsOptionsPrint
WW2_ToolsOptionsToolbar
WW2_ToolsOptionsView
WW2_ToolsRevisionsMark
WW2_ViewZoom

Appendix

D

The Software on the Super Disk

The *Super Disk* included with this book contains more than 2 megabytes of Word for Windows 6 "goodies," including:

- More than 60 pieces of professionally drawn clip art from the *Masterclips™: The Art of Business* collection
- 12 TrueType fonts from *Publisher's Paradise*
- *WinPost*, the award-winning "sticky notes" program (shareware)
- All document templates from the Projects Workshop
- The author's macros described in the Macros Workshop

Masterclips™: The Art of Business

Masterclips, Inc.
5201 Ravenswood Road, Suite 111
Fort Lauderdale, FL 33312
1-800-292-CLIP (orders only)
(305) 983-7440
(305) 967-9452 (fax)
Location: \WFW6SB\MCLIPS

These clip art samples are a taste of what you'll find in *The Art of Business* collection. This collection is available on CD-ROM and diskettes, and it contains more than 6,000 full color images, all drawn by professional artists. More than 100 categories are represented, and the images are available in CGM format.

The complete package also includes an image browser and a color to black-and-white converter. Be sure to see the ad for Masterclips at the back of this book.

Masterclips also offers Custom Clips™, a service for converting your logos or images into electronic clip art images. These images are hand drawn from your original camera-ready art, which guarantees an exact reproduction of the original.

Your Custom Clips can be produced in full color and in black-and-white, in a variety of graphics formats. Contact Masterclips for more information; you can also fax your logo or image for a free estimate.

TrueType Fonts

Publisher's Paradise BBS
(205) 882-6886 (modem)
Location: \WFW6SB\FONTS

These sample fonts were created by the Publisher's Paradise bulletin board system (BBS). This BBS was created for people with interests in desktop publishing and graphics. See the file README.WRI for more information on how to contact this bulletin board.

WinPost

Eastern Mountain Software
P.O. Box 6394
Bellevue, WA 98008-0394
(206) 391-3483
71570,533 (CompuServe)
Documentation: WINPOST.WRI

WinPost acts like yellow sticky notes, providing an easy-to-use facility for annotations and reminder notes in Word for Windows and other Windows applications.

Up to 100 notes can be in use at any given time, and WinPost will save the state of all notes upon program termination. The next time WinPost is started, the notes will look exactly the same as when the program was exited.

WinPost is distributed as shareware, which means that you can try out the software for a reasonable amount of time. Then, if you find WinPost useful and continue to use it, you should register the program with the author. When you register the program, you will be entitled to technical support.

The Super Disk installation program does not install WinPost to your hard drive. You must run the WinPost SETUP program on the Super Disk to install the software.

1. From Windows File Manager or Program Manager, choose **F**ile + **R**un from the menu.
2. Type `<drive>\WINPOST\SETUP` and press Enter. <*drive*> is the letter of the drive that contains the installation disk. For example, if the disk is in drive B:, type `B:\WINPOST\SETUP` and press Enter.
3. Follow the on-screen instructions in the setup program.

The files will be installed to a directory named \WINPOST, unless you change this name at the beginning of the SETUP program.

SUPER **NOTE**

If you decide to move WinPost files to another directory after the initial installation, you must use the WinPost SETUP program on the Super Disk to reinstall the software. Simply moving the files to another directory will not update the necessary information in the OLE registration database.

Projects

Location: \WFW6SB\PROJECTS

The following is a list of project templates and wizards contained on the Super Disk.

Chapter	*Template/Wizard*
Chapter 50, "Academic Papers"	ACADEMIC.DOT
Chapter 51, "Business Letter"	BUSINESS.WIZ
Chapter 52, "Resumes"	RESUMESB.DOT
Chapter 53, "Consulting Invoice"	CONSULT.DOT
Chapter 54, "Proposal"	PROPOSAL.DOT
Chapter 55, "Research Project Report"	REPORT.DOT
Chapter 56, "A Writer's Book Template"	BOOK.DOT
Chapter 57, "Flyers and Newsletters"	FLYER.DOT

Macros

Location: \WFW6SB\MACROS\SPRBOOK.DOT

The SPRBOOK.DOT template contains the following macros:

Macro	*Purpose*
AutoCorrectToggle	Toggles the replace text mode of AutoCorrect On and Off
AutoNew	Turns on the Super Book toolbar and Tooltips
AutoOpen	Turns on the Super Book toolbar and Tooltips

Macro	*Purpose*
CastAssign	Sample recorded macro from the Macros workshop (note: this macro was altered to prevent you from accidentally running it)
CharacterCount	Counts the number of characters in a selection
CloneParagraph	Makes a duplicate copy of the current paragraph (for example, for duplicating a heading level, a line in a macro, and so forth)
FileManager	Activates the Windows File Manager
FileOpenAll	Runs FileOpen with *.*
FileOpenDoc	Runs FileOpen with *.DOC
FileOpenRTF	Runs FileOpen with *.RTF
FileSaveAllYes	Saves all open windows, saying YES wherever possible (except in unnamed windows)
GoToPlace	Goes to one of 10 temporary bookmark placemarkers
HomeMadeAutoText	Demonstrates how you might create a home-made AutoText command
InsertAny	Inserts any file anywhere, without using any kind of text filter
JustDoIt	Temporary macro created using JustRecordIt
JustEditIt	Edits the JustDoIt macro
JustPlayIt	Runs the JustDoIt macro
JustRecordIt	Records a temporary JustDoIt macro
MacroExpand	Lists all macros in the current template and each's descriptive text. This macro was used to produce the macro list in SUPRBOOK.DOT
MacroList	Lists all macros in the current template and each's descriptive text. This macro was used to produce the macro list in SUPRBOOK.DOT
MarkPlace	Marks one of 10 temporary bookmarks for quick return
MultiMacroSearch	Searches through multiple macros for matching text
MultiReplace	Searches for an item and offers a choice of 3 replacements

continues

Macro	*Purpose*
PrintCurrentPage	Prints just the current page using the current defaults
PrintPageOne	Prints just page one using the current defaults
PrintPageTwo	Prints just page two using the current defaults
ProgMan	Activates the Windows Program Manager
RemoveSmart	Converts typographic quotes (“, ‘, ’, and ”) back into typewrite quotes (" and ')
SaveSelectionAsText	Saves selected text to a text file; this is a good way to transfer text to an application that doesn't support the clipboard
ScrollToggle	Toggles Vertical and Horizontal scrollbars on and off, based on the current state of the Vertical scrollbar
StatusBarToggle	Toggles the Status bar on and off
StringValue	Displays the character code values of a selection
StyleBarToggle	Toggles the display of the style area on the left margin
SwapAnd	Swaps [*this*] and [*that*]; puts the cursor inside the middle word to swap [*this*] with [*that*]
SwapLetters	Swaps the current and previous letters
SwapSentences	Swaps the current and previous sentences
SwapWords	Swaps the current and previous words
ToggleAutoMacros	Toggles automatic macros on and off
Width	Calculates the width of the current selection or character
WindowSplit	Splits two windows horizontally or vertically

Index

Symbols

A

C

Index

D

F

G

J

K

L

M

Index

N

O

P

Q

R

S

T

Index

X-Y-Z

Add to Your Sams Library Today with the Best Books for Programming, Operating Systems, and New Technologies

The easiest way to order is to pick up the phone and call

1-800-428-5331

between 9:00 a.m. and 5:00 p.m. EST.

For faster service please have your credit card available.

ISBN	Quantity	Description of Item	Unit Cost	Total Cost
0-672-30388-4		Souping Up Windows	$29.95	
0-672-30345-0		Wasting Time with Windows (Book/Disk)	$19.95	
0-672-30310-8		Windows Graphics FunPack (Book/Disk)	$19.95	
0-672-30318-3		Windows Sound FunPack (Book/Disk)	$19.95	
0-672-30192-X		Windows 3.1 Revealed	$34.95	
0-672-30343-4		Even You Can Soup Up and Fix PCs	$16.95	
0-672-30282-9		Absolute Beginner's Guide to Memory Management	$16.95	
0-672-30269-1		Absolute Beginner's Guide to Programming	$19.95	
0-672-30326-4		Absolute Beginner's Guide to Networking	$19.95	
0-672-30342-6		Absolute Beginner's Guide to QBasic	$16.95	
0-672-30040-0		Teach Yourself C in 21 Days	$24.95	
0-672-30324-8		Teach Yourself QBasic in 21 Days	$24.95	
0-672-30306-X		Memory Management for All of Us, Deluxe Edition	$39.95	
0-672-30385-X		Excel 5.0 Super Book (Book/Disk)	$39.95	
0-672-30288-8		DOS Secrets Unleashed (Book/Disk)	$39.95	
0-672-30317-5		Your OS/2 2.1 Consultant	$24.95	
		Shipping and Handling: See information below.		
		TOTAL		

❑ 3 ½" Disk

❑ 5 ¼" Disk

Shipping and Handling: $4.00 for the first book and $1.75 for each additional book. Floppy disk: add $1.75 for shipping and handling. If you need to have it NOW, we can ship product to you in 24 hours for an additional charge of approximately $18.00, and you will receive your item overnight or in two days. Overseas shipping and handling adds $2.00 per book and $8.00 for up to three disks. Prices subject to change. Call for availability and pricing information on latest editions.

201 W. 103rd Street, Indianapolis, Indiana 46290

1-800-428-5331 — Orders 1-800-835-3202 — FAX 1-800-858-7674 — Customer Service

Book ISBN 0-672-30384-1

What's on the Super Disk

- 45 pieces of color clip art from the *Masterclips™—The Art of Business* collection
- 17 TrueType fonts from *Publisher's Paradise*
- *WinPost*, the award-winning program that replaces yellow sticky notes (shareware)
- Projects, macros, and example documents from the book

Installing the Super Disk

The software on this disk is stored in a compressed format—you need to run the installation program to install it. You'll need at least 2 megabytes of free space on your hard drive.

1. From Windows File Manager or Program Manager, choose File+Run from the menu.
2. Type **<*drive*>INSTALL** and press Enter. <*drive*> is the letter of the drive that contains the installation disk. For example, if the disk is in drive B:, type **B:INSTALL** and press Enter.

Follow the on-screen instructions in the install program. The files will be installed to a directory named \WFW6SB, unless you change this name during the install program.

When the installation is complete, the file FILEINFO.TXT will be displayed for you to read. This file contains information on the software that was installed.

Be sure to read Appendix D, "The Software on the Super Disk."